BUSINESS LAW AND
THE REGULATORY ENVIRONMENT

CONCEPTS AND CASES

BUSINESS LAW AND THE REGULATORY ENVIRONMENT

CONCEPTS AND CASES

The Certified Employee Benefit Specialist Program Edition

Michael B. Metzger, J.D.

Jane P. Mallor, J.D.

A. James Barnes, J.D.

Thomas Bowers, J.D.

Michael J. Phillips, J.D., L.L.M., S.J.D.

all of
Indiana University

BUSINESS ONE IRWIN
Homewood, Illinois 60430

© RICHARD D. IRWIN, INC., 1946, 1951, 1955, 1959, 1963, 1966, 1970, 1974, 1978, 1982, 1986, 1989, and 1992

Printed in the United States of America
1 2 3 4 5 6 7 8 9 0 ML 0 9 8 7 6 5 4 3

PREFACE

This is the fifteenth edition (and the eighth UCC edition) of a text that first appeared in 1935. Throughout its life, this text has been a leader in the fields of business law and the legal environment of business. The reasons for the book's long-standing success, we feel, are twofold. The first is its lucid and comprehensive treatment of the many subjects that concern businesspeople and that form the heart of the traditional business law curriculum. The second is its responsiveness both to changes in the law and to changed views about that curriculum. In each of these ways, the present edition continues the tradition set by its predecessors.

ACKNOWLEDGMENTS

We would like to extend our recognition and thanks to various people who have assisted in preparation of this edition. Most important here are the able and industrious external reviewers who provided innumerable suggestions for improving the previous edition:

Wayne Anderson   *Southwest Missouri State University*
Frank Chong   *Southeast Missouri State University*
William Elliott   *Saginaw Valley State University*
Michael Engber   *Ball State University*
Gene Marsh   *The University of Alabama*
James Morgan   *California State University, Chico*
Gregory Naples   *Marquette University*
Rick Orsinger   *College of DuPage*
Dennis Pappas   *Columbus State Community College*
Robert Peace   *North Carolina State University*
Carol Rasnic   *Virginia Commonwealth University*
Linda Samuels   *George Mason University*
Daphne Sipes   *University of Texas at San Antonio*

We would like to extend a special recognition and thanks to Sarah Jane Hughes, Visiting Professor of Law at Catholic University Law School, for her contributions to the chapter on checks and documents of title, and to Pam Solie for her technical assistance.

Also in line for thanks are Craig Beytien, Karen Eichorst, Susan Trentacosti, and Jerry Saykes of Richard D. Irwin, Inc. Finally, we wish to extend our appreciation to the faculty and students who have made unsolicited suggestions for improving previous editions.

Michael B. Metzger
Jane P. Mallor
A. James Barnes
Thomas Bowers
Michael J. Phillips

CONTENTS IN BRIEF

BUSINESS LAW AND THE REGULATORY ENVIRONMENT

CONCEPTS AND CASES

FOUNDATIONS OF AMERICAN LAW

CHAPTER 1

THE NATURE OF LAW

INTRODUCTION

Today, businesspeople confront the law at every turn. For example, business firms continually utilize the law of property, the law of contract, the law of agency, and many other basic bodies of law. Indeed, business could hardly function without them. In addition to facilitating business activity, the legal system actively restricts it as well. Today, government regulates almost all aspects of a business's operations—for example, advertising, product safety, the treatment of employees, the issuance of securities, and behavior toward competitors.

Thus, businesspeople constantly use, rely on, react to, plan around—and sometimes violate—innumerable legal rules or laws. For this reason, business managers must have a general knowledge of the legal system and the most important legal rules affecting their firms. This text discusses many of these rules, often in some detail. But your ability to use and apply the legal rules affecting business is incomplete without an understanding of law's general nature, its functions, and the techniques judges use when interpreting legal rules. This understanding could go some way toward reducing business complaints about the law and lawyers.

To help provide such an understanding, this chapter examines law's nature from four different angles. First, it lists, describes, and classifies the various kinds of rules that are regarded as law in the United States. This discussion, however, only partly conveys the nature of *law* in general. Thus, the second section of this chapter discusses a subject known as *jurisprudence* or legal philosophy. One traditional concern of jurisprudence has been to establish a general definition of law, and each of the competing definitions we examine highlights an important facet of law's many-sided nature.

In a shift from the theoretical to the pragmatic, the third section of this chapter examines some of the *functions* law serves—what it *does*. After this, the chapter concludes by discussing *legal reasoning,* the set of techniques judges use when interpreting and applying legal rules. This discussion, we hope, will help dispel the common misconception that the law consists of clear and precise commands that judges merely look up and then mechanically apply.

TYPES AND CLASSIFICATIONS OF LAW

This section describes the various kinds of rules that are commonly regarded as law in the American legal system today. As you will see, most of these different types of law are made by different political bodies. The section concludes by briefly examining three ways in which each of the types of law might be classified.

3

The Types of Law

Constitutions   **Constitutions**, which exist at the state and federal levels, have two general functions.[1] First, they establish the structure of government for the political unit they control (a state or the federal government). This involves stating the branches and subdivisions of the government and the powers given and denied to each. Through its **separation of powers**, for example, the U.S. Constitution establishes a Congress and gives it power to legislate or *make* law in certain areas, provides for a chief executive (the president) whose function is to execute or *enforce* the laws, and enables the creation of a federal judiciary to *interpret* the laws. The U.S. Constitution also structures the relationship between the federal government and the states. In the process, it respects the principle of **federalism** by recognizing the states' power to make law in certain areas.

The second function performed by constitutions is to prevent all units of government within their domain from taking certain actions or passing certain laws. They do so mainly by prohibiting governmental action that restricts certain *individual rights*. The Bill of Rights to the U.S. Constitution is an example. In the *Rochin* case presented later in this chapter, the Supreme Court applied one of the U.S. Constitution's individual rights provisions to a state. By doing so, the Court exercised the power of *judicial review:* the courts' ability to declare the actions of other branches of government unconstitutional.

Statutes   **Statutes** are laws created by Congress or a state legislature. They are stated in an authoritative form in statute books or codes. As you will see later in this chapter, however, their interpretation and application are often difficult.

Throughout this text, you will encounter state statutes that originally were drafted as **uniform acts.** Uniform acts are basically model statutes dealing with business, commercial, or other matters. The aim of such acts is to produce uniformity among the states on the subjects they address. Examples include the Uniform Commercial Code (which deals with a wide range of commercial law subjects), the Uniform Partnership Act, the Revised Uniform Limited Partnership Act, and the Revised Model Business Corporation Act. By themselves, uniform acts are not law because they are not drafted by recognized political authorities. They only become law when, or to the extent that, they are enacted by a legislature.

Common Law   The **common law** (also called judge-made law or case law) is that law made and applied by judges as they decide cases not governed by statutes or other types of law. In theory, common law exists at the state level only. The common law originated in medieval England after the Norman conquest in 1066 and has been continually evolving ever since. It developed from the decisions of judges in settling actual disputes. Over time, judges began to follow the decisions of other judges in similar cases. This practice became formalized in the doctrine of *stare decisis* (let the decision stand). As you will see later in the chapter, *stare decisis* has allowed the common law to evolve to meet changing social conditions. For this reason, the common law rules in force today often differ considerably from the common law rules of earlier times.

The common law was brought to America with the first English settlers and was used by courts during the colonial period.[2] It continued to be applied after the Revolution and the adoption of the Constitution, and is still employed in many cases today. For example, the rules of tort, contract, and agency discussed in this text are mainly common law rules. However, the states have codified (enacted into statute) some parts of the common law, particularly in the criminal area. Also, many states have passed statutes superseding judge-made law in certain situations. As discussed in the Introduction to Contracts chapter, for example, the states have established special rules for contract cases involving the sale of goods by enacting Article 2 of the Uniform Commercial Code.

In the torts, contracts, and agency chapters of this text, you often see references to the *Restatement* rule on a particular subject. The *Restatements* are collections of common law (and occasionally statutory) rules covering various areas of the law. Because they are promulgated by the American Law Institute rather than by courts, the *Restatements* are not law by themselves, and do not bind the courts. However, state courts often find *Restatement* rules persuasive and adopt them as common law rules within their states. Usually, these *Restatement* rules are

---

[1] More detail on how the U.S. Constitution performs these functions can be found in the Business and the Constitution chapter.

[2] However, Louisiana adopted the Code Napoléon, which was based on Roman law, and even today the law of Louisiana differs somewhat from the law of other states. For example, Louisiana has not adopted a portion of the Uniform Commercial Code.

the rules actually followed by a majority of the states. Occasionally, however, the *Restatements* stimulate changes in the common law by stating new rules that the courts decide to follow.[3]

Equity   The body of law called **equity** has traditionally tried to do discretionary "rough justice" in situations where common law rules would produce unfair results. American equity law originated in medieval England. At that time, the existing common law rules were quite technical and rigid and the remedies available in common law courts were too few. This meant that some deserving parties could not obtain adequate relief in the common law courts. As a result, the chancellor, the king's most powerful executive officer, began to hear cases that the common law courts could not resolve satisfactorily.

Eventually, separate equity courts emerged to handle the cases heard by the chancellor. These courts assumed control of a case only when there was no adequate remedy in a regular common law court. In equity courts, procedures were more flexible than in the common law courts and rigid rules of law were de-emphasized in favor of general moral maxims. Equity courts also provided several unique remedies not available in the common law courts (which generally awarded only money damages or the recovery of property). Perhaps the most important of these *equitable remedies* is the **injunction,** a court order forbidding a party to do some act or commanding him to perform some act. Others include the contract remedies of **specific performance** (whereby a party is ordered to perform according to the terms of her contract), **reformation** (in which the court rewrites the contract's terms to reflect the parties' real intentions), and **rescission** (a cancellation of a contract in which the parties often are returned to their precontractual position).

Like the common law, equity principles and practices were brought to the American colonies by the English settlers. They continued to be used after the Revolution and the adoption of the Constitution. Over time, however, the once-sharp line between law and equity has become blurred. Most states have abolished separate equity courts, now allowing one court to handle both legal and equitable claims. Also, equitable principles have tended to merge with common law rules, and

some modern common law and statutory doctrines have equitable roots. An example is the doctrine of unconscionability discussed in the chapter on illegality of contracts. Finally, courts now may combine an award of money damages with an equitable remedy in certain cases.

Administrative Regulations and Decisions   Throughout most of the 20th century, the *administrative agencies* established by Congress and the state legislatures and discussed in the Administrative Agencies chapter have grown steadily in number and size. Today, their power, importance, and influence over business activity are considerable. A major reason for the rise of administrative agencies was the myriad of social and economic problems created by the industrialization of the United States beginning late in the 19th century. Because legislatures generally lacked the time and expertise to deal with these problems on a continuing basis, the creation of specialized, expert agencies was almost inevitable.

Administrative agencies can make law because of a *delegation* (or handing over) of power from the legislature. Agencies normally are created by a statute that specifies the areas in which the agency can make law and the scope of its power in each area. Often, this statutory grant of power is worded so broadly that the legislature has, in effect, merely pointed to a problem and given the agency wide-ranging powers to deal with it. For this reason, and because legislative supervision of agencies is sometimes perfunctory, agencies are often relatively immune from popular control.

The two kinds of law made by administrative agencies are **administrative regulations** (or administrative rules) and **agency decisions.** Like statutes, administrative regulations are stated in a precise form in one authoritative source. However, administrative regulations differ from statutes because the body enacting them is an agency, not the legislature. In addition, some agencies have an internal court structure that enables them to hear cases arising under the statutes and regulations they enforce. The resulting agency decisions are another kind of law. As noted in the next chapter, agency decisions may be appealed to regular state or federal courts. Practically speaking, however, the agency's decision is often final.

Treaties   According to the U.S. Constitution, **treaties** made by the president with foreign governments and approved by two thirds of the U.S. Senate are "the supreme

---

[3] An example is section 402A of the *Restatement (Second) of Torts,* which is discussed in the Product Liability chapter.

Law of the Land." As noted later, treaties can cause state (and occasionally federal) laws to become invalid.

Ordinances   State governments have subordinate units that exercise certain functions. Some of these units, such as school districts, have limited powers. Other units, such as counties, municipalities, and townships, exercise a number of governmental functions. The enactments of municipalities are called **ordinances;** zoning ordinances are an example. The enactments of other political subdivisions may also be referred to as ordinances.

Executive Orders   In theory, the president is a chief executive who enforces the laws but has no lawmaking powers. The same is usually true of state governors. However, these officials sometimes have the power to issue laws called **executive orders.** This power usually results from a legislative delegation. Because such delegations of legislative power are often imprecise and general, the executive's power to make law is sometimes quite broad.

Priority Rules   Occasionally, different types of law conflict. Thus, rules for determining which type takes priority are necessary. The most important such rule is the principle of *federal supremacy,* which makes the U.S. Constitution, federal laws enacted pursuant to it, and treaties "the supreme Law of the Land." This means that federal law defeats conflicting state law. Also, a state constitution defeats all other state laws inconsistent with it; the same is true for the U.S. Constitution and inconsistent federal laws. When a treaty conflicts with a federal statute over a purely domestic matter, the measure that is latest in time usually prevails. Also, state statutes and any laws derived from them by delegation defeat inconsistent common law rules. Within either the state or the federal domain, finally, statutes take priority over other laws that depend on a delegation of power from the legislature for their validity. Within a particular state, for example, statutes defeat inconsistent administrative regulations, and both defeat inconsistent common law rules.

CONCEPT REVIEW

THE TYPES OF POSITIVE LAW COMPARED

	Who Enacts?	State and/or Federal?	Stated in One Authoritative Form?	Remarks
Constitutions	U.S. Constitution originally ratified by states; complex amendment process. States may vary.	Both	Yes, but see the Business and the Constitution chapter on constitutional decisionmaking	Defeat other forms of positive law within sphere (federal or state)
Statutes	Legislatures	Both	Yes, but see this chapter's discussion of statutory interpretation	Defeat other forms of positive law within sphere (federal or state) except constitutions
Common Law	Courts	In theory, state only	No. See this chapter's discussion of legal reasoning	Law of tort, contract, and agency mainly common law
Equity	Formerly equity courts; now usually courts in general	In theory, state only. But equitable principles pervade federal law as well.	No	Traditional separation of law and equity now virtually gone
Administrative Regulations	Administrative agencies	Both	Yes	See the Administrative Agencies chapter

	Who Enacts?	State and/or Federal?	Stated in One Authoritative Form?	Remarks
Administrative Decisions	Administrative agencies	Both	No	See the Administrative Agencies chapter
Treaties	President plus two thirds of Senate	Federal	Yes	Defeat inconsistent state law
Ordinances	Usually local government bodies	State (mainly local)	Yes	
Executive Orders	Chief executives	Both	Yes	Usually based on delegation from legislature

Classifications of Law

Cutting across the different *types* of law just described are three common *classifications* of law. These classifications involve distinctions between: (1) criminal law and civil law, (2) substantive law and procedural law, and (3) public law and private law. One type of law might be classified in each of these ways. For example, a state statute might be criminal, substantive, and public; or civil, procedural, and public.

Criminal and Civil Law   **Criminal law** is the law applied when the government acts in a prosecutorial role by proceeding against someone for the commission of a crime. **Civil law** is the law applied when one party sues another party because the other failed to meet some legal duty owed to the first party. Civil lawsuits usually involve private parties, but the government may be a party to a civil suit (as for instance where a city sues, or is sued by, a construction contractor). Criminal penalties (e.g., imprisonment or fines) differ from civil remedies (e.g., money damages or equitable relief). Also, violations of the criminal law often are said to be wrongs against society as a whole, while violations of the civil law frequently are viewed as injuring only specific private parties.

Although most of the legal rules discussed in this text are civil law rules, the Crimes chapter deals specifically with the criminal law and various criminal provisions are discussed in other chapters. When considering such provisions, be aware that the same behavior can violate both the civil law and the criminal law. For instance, a party whose careless driving causes injury to another may face both a criminal prosecution by the state and a civil suit for damages by the injured party.

Substantive Law and Procedural Law   **Substantive law** sets out the rights and duties of people as they act in society. **Procedural law** controls the behavior of governmental bodies (mainly courts) as they establish and enforce rules of substantive law. A statute making murder a crime, for example, is a rule of substantive law. But the rules describing the proper conduct of a criminal trial are procedural in nature. This text is mainly concerned with substantive law. The Resolution of Private Disputes chapter and the Crimes chapter, however, examine some of the procedural rules governing civil and criminal cases, respectively. Various procedural rules also appear in other chapters.

Public and Private Law   **Public law** is concerned with the powers of government, and with the relations between government and private parties. Examples include constitutional law, administrative law, and criminal law. **Private law** establishes a framework of legal rules that enable private parties to set the rights and duties they owe each other. Examples include the rules of contract, property, and agency.

JURISPRUDENCE

Introduction

The various types of law discussed in the previous section are sometimes referred to as **positive law.** Positive law can be defined as the rules that have been laid down (or posited) by a recognized political authority. Knowing the types of positive law is essential to understanding the American legal system and the business law topics discussed in this text. But defining *law* by listing these

FIGURE 1   A Brief Sketch of the Jurisprudential Schools

	Definition of Law	**Relation between Law and Morality**	**Practical Tendency**
Legal Positivism	Command of a recognized political authority	Separate questions: "law is law, just or not"	Valid positive law should be enforced and obeyed, just or not
Natural Law	All commands of recognized political authorities that are not unjust	"Unjust law is not law"	Unjust positive laws should not be enforced and obeyed
American Legal Realism	What public decisionmakers actually do	Unclear	"Law in action" often more important than "law in the books"
Sociological Jurisprudence	Process of social ordering in accordance with dominant social values and interests	Although moral values influence positive law, no way to say whether this is right or wrong	Law inevitably does (and should?) follow dominant social values and interests

different kinds of positive law is much like defining the word *automobile* by describing all the types of vehicles going by that name. To define law properly, we need a general description that captures its essence.

One concern of the field known as **jurisprudence** or legal philosophy is to arrive at an abstract philosophical definition of law. Over time, different schools of jurisprudence have emerged, each with its own distinctive conception of law. The differences among these schools are not merely an academic matter. As Figure 1 shows, their conceptions of law often affect their approach toward real-life political and legal disputes. Whether the participants in these disputes know it or not, their positions often reflect jurisprudential assumptions.

Legal Positivism

One feature common to all types of positive law is their enactment by a recognized political authority—a legislature, a court, an administrative agency, and so forth. This common feature underlies the definition of law adopted by the school of jurisprudence called **legal positivism.** Legal positivists generally define law as the command of a recognized political authority. To the British political philosopher Thomas Hobbes, for instance, "Law properly, is the word of him, that by right hath command over others."

Legal positivism's idea that law is basically a *command* affects its view of the relationship between law and morality. The commands made by recognized political authorities obviously can be good, bad, or indifferent in moral terms. But as Figure 2 indicates, to positivists such commands are valid law irrespective of

their goodness or badness. For positivists, in other words, legal validity and moral validity are different questions. Sometimes this view is expressed by the slogan: "Law is law, just or not." For this reason, some (but not all) positivists say that every validly enacted positive law should be enforced and obeyed, whether just or not. People who argue that you should obey some law you think is unjust simply because "it's the law" are speaking as legal positivists sometimes do.

Natural Law

At first glance, legal positivism's "law is law, just or not" approach may strike you as perfect common sense. But it presents a problem, for it may mean that *any* positive law (no matter how unjust) is valid law and should be enforced and obeyed so long as some recognized political authority (no matter how wicked) enacted it. Here, the school of jurisprudence known as **natural law** takes issue with legal positivism by rejecting the positivist separation of law and morality.

The basic idea behind most systems of natural law is that some higher law or set of absolute moral rules binds all human beings in all times and places. The Roman statesman Marcus Cicero described natural law as "the highest reason, implanted in nature, which commands what ought to be done and forbids the opposite." Because this higher law determines what is ultimately good and ultimately bad, it is a criterion for evaluating positive law. To Saint Thomas Aquinas, for example, "every human law has just so much of the nature of law, as it is derived from the law of nature." As a practical matter, therefore, natural law thinkers tend to define law in the

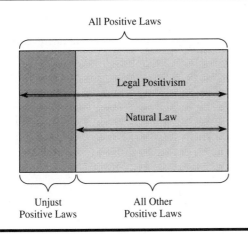

FIGURE 2 The Positivist and Natural Law Definitions of Law

All Positive Laws

Legal Positivism

Natural Law

Unjust
Positive Laws

All Other
Positive Laws

fashion suggested by Figure 2: as those commands of recognized political authorities that do not offend the higher law by being unjust.

Unjust positive laws, on the other hand, simply are not law. As Cicero put it: "What of the many deadly, the many pestilential statutes which are imposed on peoples? These no more deserve to be called laws than the rules a band of robbers might pass in their assembly." This view sometimes is expressed by the slogan: "An unjust law is not law." Because unjust positive laws are not truly law, natural law thinkers conclude that they should not be enforced or obeyed.

Despite a recent revival of interest in ethical matters, relatively few 20th-century British or American legal philosophers have openly advocated natural law. This is partly due to the many skeptical attacks on natural law's central idea: the existence of a higher law binding all people in all times and places. For example, skeptics—some of them legal positivists—note that different people and societies often have conflicting moral views. Moreover, they continue, different *systems of natural law* occasionally emphasize different values. To paper over these problems, the skeptics continue, natural law thinkers often phrase their higher law in broad, empty platitudes that mean what listeners want them to mean and that are consistent with most systems of positive law. In response to all this, natural law thinkers argue that most people and societies actually do agree on many core values, but that these values inevitably find different application in different times and places. No system of natural law, they add, can or should specify every detail of every society's positive law.

If few people openly advocate natural law these days, why should it concern you? For one thing, it is difficult to ignore the perennial moral questions natural law addresses. As the chapter on Business Ethics, Corporate Social Responsibility, and the Control and Governance of Corporations suggests, these are questions *you* may have to confront at some point in your life. In addition, beliefs and positions resembling natural law remain fairly common. The rights-based theories discussed in the business ethics chapter are a possible example. Also, people who criticize certain nations because their legal systems deny human rights are thinking and acting much like advocates of natural law have traditionally thought and acted. Finally, moral ideas resembling natural law influence judges from time to time. Keep this in mind as you read the *Rochin* case at the end of this section.

➢ American Legal Realism

To some people, the preceding debate between natural law and legal positivism seems unreal. Not only is natural law pie-in-the-sky, such people might say, but sometimes positive law does not mean much either. For example, juries sometimes pay little attention to the legal rules that are supposed to guide their decisions, and prosecutors often have discretion whether or not to enforce criminal statutes. In some legal proceedings, moreover, the background, biases, and values of the judge—and not "the law"—strongly influence the result. As the joke goes, justice occasionally is nothing more than what the judge ate for breakfast.

Remarks such as these typify the school of jurisprudence known as **American legal realism.** Legal realists generally regard the positivist "law in the books" as less important than the "law in action"—the conduct of those who enforce and interpret that law. Thus, American legal realism defines law as the behavior of public officials (mainly judges) as they deal with matters before the legal system. Because the actions of such decision-makers—and not the rules in the books—really affect people's lives, the realists say, this behavior is most important and deserves to be called law.

It is doubtful whether the legal realists have ever developed a common position on the relation between law and morality or the duty to obey positive law. But they have been quick to give advice to judges. Many realists feel that the modern judge should be a kind of "social engineer" who weighs all relevant values and considers social science findings before deciding a case. Thus, such a judge would make the positive law only one factor in his or her decision. Because judges inevitably base their decisions on personal factors, the realists seem to say, they should at least do this in an honest and intelligent way. To promote this kind of decisionmaking, the realists have sometimes favored fuzzy, discretionary statutes and regulations that allow judges to decide each case according to its unique facts.[4]

Sociological Jurisprudence

The term **sociological jurisprudence** is a general label uniting a group of diverse jurisprudential approaches whose common aim is to examine law within its social context. Their overall outlook is well captured by the following quotation from Justice Oliver Wendell Holmes:

The life of the law has not been logic: it has been experience. The felt necessities of the time, the prevalent moral and political theories, intuitions of public policy, avowed or unconscious, even the prejudices which judges share with their fellow-men, have had a good deal more to do than the syllogism in determining the rules by which men should be governed. The law embodies the story of a nation's development through many centuries, and it cannot be dealt with as if it contained only the axioms and corollaries of a book of mathematics.[5]

Despite this common outlook, there is no distinctive sociological definition of law. If one were attempted, it might go as follows: "Law is a process of social ordering reflecting society's dominant interests and values."

Different Sociological Approaches   By examining a few well-known examples of sociological legal thinking, we can put some flesh on the definition offered above. The "dominant interests" portion of the definition is exemplified by the writings of Roscoe Pound, an influential 20th-century American legal philosopher. Pound developed a detailed catalog of the social interests that press on government and the legal system and thus shape positive law. During his life, Pound's catalog changed along with changes in American society. An example of the definition's "dominant values" component is the *historical school* of jurisprudence identified with the 19th-century German legal philosopher Friedrich Karl von Savigny. Savigny saw law as an un-

planned, almost unconscious, reflection of the collective spirit (*Volksgeist*) of a particular society. In his view, legal change could only be explained historically, as a slow response to changing social conditions and values.

By describing how dominant social interests and values shape the law, Pound and Savigny undermine the legal positivist view that law is simply the command of some political authority. The early 20th-century Austrian legal philosopher Eugen Ehrlich went even further in rejecting positivism. He did so by distinguishing two different "processes of social ordering" contained within our definition of sociological jurisprudence. The first of these is "state law," or positive law. The second is the "living law," informal social controls such as customs, family ties, and business practices. By regarding both as law, Ehrlich blurred the line between positive law and other kinds of social ordering. In the process, he stimulated people to recognize that positive law is only one element within a spectrum of social controls.

The Implications of Sociological Jurisprudence Because its definition of law includes social values, you might think that sociological jurisprudence resembles natural law. But most sociological thinkers are only concerned with the *fact* that certain moral values influence the law, and not with the goodness or badness of those values. In the Introduction to Contracts chapter, for instance, we note that laissez-faire economic values were widely shared in 19th-century America and strongly influenced the contract law of that period. But we do not discuss whether this was right or wrong. Thus, it might seem that sociological jurisprudence fails to give practical advice to those who must enforce and obey positive law.

However, sociological jurisprudence does have at least one practical implication. This is a general tendency to urge that the law must change to meet changing social conditions and values. This resembles the familiar saying that "the law must keep up with the times." Thus, sociological thinkers sometimes observe that laws that fail to reflect changing social values often become ineffective or irrelevant, and that such laws almost inevitably are eliminated or modified in the long run. Some might hold to this view even when society's values are changing for the worse. To Holmes, for example, "[t]he first requirement of a sound body of law is, that it should correspond with the actual feelings and demands of the community, *whether right or wrong*."[6]

---

[4] Some examples are found in Article 2 of the Uniform Commercial Code, which was principally authored by Karl Llewellyn, a prominent legal realist. See the Introduction to Contracts chapter.

[5] Holmes, *The Common Law* (1881).

[6] The italics have been added.

ROCHIN V. CALIFORNIA[7]

342 U.S. 165 (U.S. Sup. Ct. 1952)

In 1949, three Los Angeles County deputy sheriffs received information that Antonio Rochin was selling narcotics. In search of evidence, they entered Rochin's home one morning and forced open the door to his bedroom. They immediately spotted two capsules on a nightstand beside the bed on which the half-clad Rochin was sitting. After the deputies asked, "Whose stuff is this?" Rochin quickly put the capsules in his mouth. The deputies then jumped Rochin and tried to force the capsules from his mouth. When this proved unsuccessful, they handcuffed Rochin and took him to a hospital. Despite Rochin's opposition, they had a doctor insert a tube into his stomach and force an emetic (vomit-inducing) solution through the tube. This stomach pumping caused Rochin to vomit. Within the material he disgorged were two capsules containing morphine.

Rochin then was tried and convicted for possessing a morphine preparation in violation of California law. The two morphine capsules were the main evidence against him, and the trial court admitted this evidence over Rochin's objection. Even though it found the deputies' behavior illegal, the intermediate appellate court affirmed the conviction. The California Supreme Court also affirmed. Rochin then appealed to the U.S. Supreme Court. The main issue before the Court was whether the methods by which the deputies obtained the capsules violated the Due Process Clause of the U.S. Constitution's Fourteenth Amendment, which states that "No state shall . . . deprive any person of life, liberty, or property, without due process of law." *Note*: At the time this case was decided, evidence obtained through a forced stomach pumping probably was admissible in a majority of the states that had considered the question. Also, the Supreme Court did not then require that state courts exclude evidence obtained through an illegal search or seizure. The Crimes chapter discusses modern search-and-seizure law.

Frankfurter, Justice.   The requirements of the due process clause impose upon this Court an exercise of judgment upon the proceedings resulting in a conviction to ascertain whether they offend those canons of decency and fairness which express the notions of justice of English-speaking peoples even toward those charged with the most heinous offenses. These standards of justice are not authoritatively formulated anywhere as though they were specifics. Due process of law is a summarized guarantee of respect for those personal immunities so rooted in the traditions and conscience of our people as to be fundamental, or implicit in the concept of ordered liberty.

The vague contours of the due process clause do not leave judges at large. We may not draw upon our merely personal and private notions and disregard the limits that bind judges. These limits are derived from considerations that are fused in the whole nature of our judicial process. These are considerations deeply rooted in reason and in the compelling traditions of the legal profession. The due process clause places upon this Court the duty of exercising a judgment upon interests of society pushing in opposite directions. Due process of law thus conceived is not to be derided as a resort to the revival of "natural law."

Applying these general considerations to the present case, we conclude that the proceedings by which this conviction was obtained do more than offend some fastidious squeamishness or private sentimentalism about combatting crime too energetically. This is conduct that shocks the conscience. Illegally breaking into the privacy of Rochin, the struggle to open his mouth and remove what was there, the forcible extraction of his stomach's contents—this course of proceeding is

---

[7] At this point, you may want to examine this chapter's appendix on the reading and briefing of cases.

bound to offend even hardened sensibilities. They are methods too close to the rack and the screw to permit of constitutional differentiation.

Judgment reversed in favor of Rochin.

THE FUNCTIONS OF LAW

In traditional societies, people tended to view law as a body of unchanging rules that deserved obedience because they were part of the natural order of things. By now, however, most lawmakers treat law as a flexible *tool* or *instrument* for the accomplishment of chosen purposes. For example, much of the law of negotiable instruments discussed in this text's section on commercial paper is designed to stimulate commercial activity by promoting the free movement of such money substitutes as promissory notes, checks, and drafts. Throughout this text, moreover, you will see courts manipulating or changing existing legal rules to get the results they desire. One strength of this *instrumentalist* attitude is its willingness to adapt legal rules to further the social good. One weakness is the legal instability and uncertainty those adaptations often produce.

Just as individual legal rules further certain specific purposes, *law as a whole* serves many general social functions. Although many legal rules serve all these functions to some degree, certain areas of the law promote them better than others do. Among the most important of the law's innumerable functions are:

1. *Peacekeeping.* This basic function of any legal system is most clearly furthered by the criminal law rules discussed in the Crimes chapter. Also, as the chapter on The Resolution of Private Disputes suggests, one major function of the civil law rules discussed throughout the text is the resolution of private disputes.

2. *Checking government power and thereby promoting personal freedom.* Obvious examples are the constitutional restrictions on government regulation examined in the Business and the Constitution chapter.

3. *Facilitating planning and the realization of reasonable expectations.* The rules of contract law discussed in the section on Contracts help fulfill this function of law, which is obviously quite important to business.

4. *Promoting economic growth through free competition.* Of the many legal rules that perform this function, those that stand out are the antitrust laws discussed in the two later chapters on the Sherman Act, the Clayton Act, the Robinson–Patman Act, and the antitrust exemptions and immunities.

5. *Promoting social justice.* Throughout this century, government has intervened in private social and economic affairs to correct injustices and give all citizens equal access to life's basic goods. One example is the collection of employer-employee regulations treated in the Employment Law chapter.

6. *Protecting the environment.* The most important federal environmental statutes are discussed in the Environmental Regulation chapter.

Obviously, the law's various functions can conflict with one another. The familiar clash between economic growth and environmental protection is an example. And the *Rochin* case illustrates the equally familiar conflict between effective law enforcement and the preservation of personal rights. Only rarely does the law achieve a particular end without sacrificing other ends to some degree. In law, as in life, there is generally no such thing as a free lunch. Where the law's ends conflict, lawmakers can only try to strike the best possible balance among those ends. How this balance is struck can change over time. As compared with modern American law, for example, 19th-century law gave more weight to economic development and less to protection of the environment.

The preceding discussion suggests that there are limits on the law's usefulness as a device for promoting social goals. The most important reason is that the law's pursuit of one desirable end may force it to sacrifice others. In addition, as our earlier discussion of sociological jurisprudence suggested, it is doubtful whether laws that conflict with dominant social values will ever be enacted, or if enacted, will ever be enforced and obeyed.

As that discussion also revealed, the law is only one form of social ordering. Thus, lawmakers sometimes are reluctant to intrude in areas where other forms of ordering dominate. For example, although laws regulating family matters and the internal affairs of private groups are not uncommon, neither is completely subject to legal controls.

LEGAL REASONING

Introduction

Although it was criticized earlier in the chapter, legal positivism's conception of law as the command of a recognized political authority has at least one big virtue. Such commands usually are laid down in a fairly clear and organized fashion. Unlike the other schools of jurisprudence, therefore, legal positivism enables lawmakers to state legal rules with reasonable precision. For this reason, people and businesses can predict the legal consequences of their actions with some measure of certainty. Thus, although it occasionally examines law from functional and sociological perspectives, this text mainly adopts a positivist approach. It does so by stating the legal rules affecting business as a series of commands issued by recognized political authorities. In addition, it states these rules in what lawyers call "black letter" form, using precise sentences saying that certain legal consequences will occur if certain events happen.

This positivist black letter approach, however, can be misleading. It suggests definiteness, certainty, permanence, and predictability—attributes the law frequently lacks. To illustrate this, and to give you some idea how lawyers think, we now discuss the two most important kinds of legal reasoning: **case law reasoning**[8] and **statutory interpretation.** However, we first must examine legal reasoning in general.

Legal reasoning is basically deductive, or syllogistic. That is, the legal rule is the major premise, the facts are the minor premise, and the result is the product of combining the two. Suppose a state statute says that a driver operating an automobile between 55 and 70 miles per hour must pay a $50 fine (the rule or major premise) and that Jim Smith drives his car at 65 miles per hour (the facts or minor premise). If Jim is arrested, and if the necessary facts can be proved, he will be required to pay the $50 fine. Legal reasoning often is more difficult than this example would suggest. The rules themselves may be inherently imprecise, ambiguities may appear as the rules are applied to new fact situations, and such applications may even cause the rules to change over time.

Case Law Reasoning

In cases governed by the common law, courts find the appropriate legal rules in prior cases or *precedents*. The standard for choosing and applying prior cases to decide present cases is the doctrine of *stare decisis*, which states that like cases should be decided alike.[9] That is, the present case should be decided in the same way as prior cases presenting the same basic facts and legal issues. If a court decides that the alleged precedent is not really "like" the present case and should not control the decision in that case, it *distinguishes* the prior case.[10]

Because every present case differs from the precedents in *some* respect, it is always theoretically possible to distinguish those precedents. For example, one *could* distinguish a prior case because both parties in that case had black hair, while one party in the present case has brown hair. Of course, such distinctions are usually ridiculous, because the differences they identify are insignificant in moral or social policy terms. In other words, a good distinction of a prior case should involve a widely accepted policy reason for treating the present case differently from its predecessor. Because people often disagree about moral ideas, public policies, and the degree to which they are accepted, and because all of these factors change over time, judges sometimes differ on the wisdom of distinguishing a prior case. This is a significant source of uncertainty in the common law. But it also gives the common law the flexibility to adapt to changing social conditions.

The following *MacPherson* case illustrates the common law's ability to change over time. In the series of New York cases it discusses, the **plaintiff** (the party suing) claimed that the **defendant** (the party being sued)

---

[8] The style of legal reasoning used in constitutional cases resembles that used in common law cases, but often is somewhat looser. For the way courts decide constitutional cases, see the chapter on Business and the Constitution.

[9] *Stare decisis* should be distinguished from the doctrine of *res judicata*, which says that a final judicial decision on the merits conclusively settles the rights *of the parties to the case.*

[10] Also, while they exercise the power infrequently, courts sometimes completely *overrule* their prior decisions.

had been negligent in the manufacture or inspection of some product, thus injuring the plaintiff, who later purchased or used the product.[11] In the mid-19th century, such suits often were unsuccessful due to the general rule that a seller or manufacturer could not be liable for negligence unless there was *privity of contract* between the defendant and the plaintiff. Privity of contract is the existence of a direct contractual relationship between two parties. Thus, the no-liability-outside-privity rule prevented the injured plaintiff from recovering against a seller or manufacturer who had sold the product to a dealer who in turn sold it to the plaintiff. Over time,

however, the courts began to allow injured plaintiffs to recover from sellers or manufacturers with whom they had not directly dealt. These courts were creating *exceptions* to the general rule; that is, they were distinguishing prior cases announcing the rule and creating new rules to govern the situations they distinguished. The *MacPherson* case describes the gradual enlargement of such an exception in New York. Eventually, the exception "consumed the rule" by covering so many situations that the original rule became relatively insignificant.[12]

---

[11] Negligence is discussed in the Negligence and Strict Liability chapter.

---

[12] The present status of the old no-liability-outside-privity rule in sale of goods cases is discussed in the Product Liability chapter. Today, it has relatively little impact in negligence cases of this kind. Also, as the introduction to that chapter suggests, sociological jurisprudence helps explain the rule's erosion.

MacPHERSON v. BUICK MOTOR Co.

111 N.E. 1050 (N.Y. Ct. App. 1916)

One wheel of an automobile manufactured by the Buick Motor Company was made of defective wood. Buick could have discovered the wheel's defective condition had it made a reasonable inspection after purchasing the wheel from another manufacturer. Buick sold the car to a retail dealer, who then sold it to MacPherson. While driving the car, MacPherson was injured when the wheel collapsed and he was thrown from the vehicle. He sued Buick in a New York trial court for its negligent failure to inspect the wheel. Buick's main defense was that it had not dealt directly with MacPherson and thus owed no duty to him. Following trial and appellate court judgments in MacPherson's favor, Buick appealed to the New York Court of Appeals, the state's highest court.

Cardozo, Justice.   The foundations of this branch of the law were laid in *Thomas v. Winchester* (1852). A poison was falsely labeled. The sale was made to a druggist, who sold to a customer. The customer recovered damages from the seller who affixed the label. The defendant's negligence, it was said, put human life in imminent danger. A poison, falsely labeled, is likely to injure anyone who gets it. Because the danger is to be foreseen, there is a duty to avoid the injury. *Thomas v. Winchester* became quickly a landmark of the law. In the application of its principle there may, at times, have been uncertainty or even error. There has never been doubt or disavowal of the principle itself.

The chief cases are well known. *Loop v. Litchfield* (1870) was the case of a defect in a small balance wheel used on a circular saw. The manufacturer pointed out the defect to the buyer. The risk can hardly have been an imminent one, for the wheel lasted five years before it broke. In the meanwhile the buyer had made a lease of the machinery. It was held that the manufacturer was not answerable to the lessee. *Loop v. Litchfield* was followed by *Losee v. Clute* (1873), the case of the explosion of a steam boiler. That decision must be confined to its special facts. It was put upon the ground that the risk of injury was too remote. The buyer had not only accepted the boiler, but had tested it. The manufacturer knew that his own test was not the final one. The finality of the test has a bearing on the measure of diligence owing to persons other than the purchaser.

These early cases suggest a narrow construction of the rule. Later cases evince a more liberal spirit. In *Devlin v. Smith* (1882), the defendant contractor built a scaffold for a painter. The painter's workmen were injured. The contractor was held liable. He knew that the scaffold, if improperly constructed, was a most dangerous trap. He knew that it was to be used by the workmen. Building it for their use, he owed them a duty to build it with care. From *Devlin v. Smith* we turn to *Statler v. Ray Manufacturing Co.* (1909). The defendant manufactured a large coffee urn. It was installed in a restaurant. The urn exploded and injured the plaintiff. We held that the manufacturer was liable. We said that the urn was of such a character that it was liable to become a source of great danger if not carefully and properly constructed.

It may be that *Devlin v. Smith* and *Statler v. Ray Manufacturing Co.* have extended the rule of *Thomas v. Winchester*. If so, this court is committed to the extension. The defendant argues that things imminently dangerous to human life are poisons, explosives, deadly weapons—things whose normal function is to injure or destroy. But whatever the rule in *Thomas v. Winchester* may once have been, it no longer has that restricted meaning. A scaffold is not inherently a destructive instrument. No one thinks of [a coffee urn] as an implement whose normal function is destruction.

We hold, then, that the principle of *Thomas v. Winchester* is not limited to things which are implements of destruction. If the nature of a thing is such that it is reasonably certain to place life and limb in peril when negligently made, it is a thing of danger. If to the element of danger there is added knowledge that the thing will be used by persons other than the purchaser, then, irrespective of contract, the manufacturer is under a duty to make it carefully.

The nature of an automobile gives warning of probable danger if its construction is defective. This automobile was designed to go 50 miles an hour. Unless its wheels were sound and strong, injury was almost certain. The defendant knew the danger. It knew that the car would be used by persons other than the buyer, a dealer in cars. The dealer was indeed the one person of whom it might be said with some certainty that by him the car would not be used. Yet the defendant would have us say that he was the one person it was under a legal duty to protect. The law does not lead us to so inconsequent a conclusion. Precedents drawn from the age of travel by stagecoach do not fit the conditions of travel today. The principle that the danger must be imminent does not change, but the things subject to the principle do change. They are whatever the needs of life in a developing civilization require them to be.

Judgment for MacPherson affirmed.

Statutory Interpretation

Because statutes are written in one authoritative form, their interpretation might seem easier than case law reasoning. However, this is not so. One reason for the difficulties courts face when interpreting statutes is the natural ambiguity of language. This is especially true where statutory words that appear to be clear are applied to situations the legislature did not foresee. Also, legislators may deliberately use ambiguous language when they are unwilling or unable to deal specifically with each situation that the statute was enacted to regulate. In such situations, the legislature consciously employs vague language expecting that the courts will fill in the details on a case-by-case basis. Other reasons for deliberate ambiguity include the need for legislative compromise and legislators' desire to avoid taking controversial positions.

Due to problems like these, courts need and use various techniques of statutory interpretation. As you will see shortly, different techniques can dictate different results in a particular case. Moreover, judges sometimes employ the techniques in an instrumentalist or result-oriented fashion, emphasizing the technique that will produce the result they want and downplaying the

FIGURE 3   The Steps in a Statute's Passage and the Techniques of Statutory Interpretation

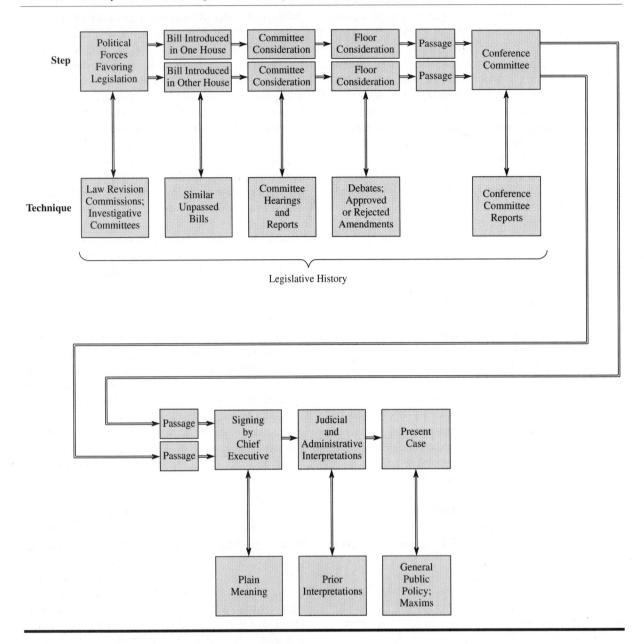

others. For this reason, it is difficult to state which technique should control when different techniques yield different results. Although there are some "rules" on this subject, courts often ignore them.

Figure 3 relates the most common techniques of statutory interpretation to the various steps in the passage of a statute. Of course, some of these techniques may be irrelevant to a particular statute. To further illustrate these techniques, the following discussion occasionally uses a hypothetical air pollution statute requiring emission controls for "automobiles, trucks, buses, and other motorized passenger or cargo vehicles."

Plain Meaning   Courts always begin their interpretation of a statute with its actual language. Where the statute's words have a clear, common, accepted meaning, some courts employ the *plain meaning rule*. This rule states that in such cases the court should simply apply the statute according to the plain, accepted meaning of its words, and should not concern itself with anything else.

Legislative History   Some courts refuse to follow a statute's plain meaning when its *legislative history* suggests a different result. And almost all courts resort to legislative history when the statute's language is ambiguous. A statute's legislative history includes the following sources: the reports of investigative committees or law revision commissions that led to the legislation, the hearings of the legislative committee(s) originally considering the legislation, any reports issued by such a committee, legislative debates, the report of a conference committee reconciling two houses' conflicting versions of the law, amendments or defeated amendments to the legislation, other bills not passed by the legislature but proposing similar legislation, and discrepancies between a bill passed by one house and the final version of the statute.

Sometimes a statute's legislative history provides no information or conflicting information about its meaning, its scope, or its purposes. Also, some sources are more authoritative than others. The worth of debates, for instance, may depend on which legislator (e.g., the sponsor of the bill or an uninformed blowhard) is being quoted. Some sources are useful only in particular situations; prior unpassed bills and amendments or defeated amendments are examples. Suppose that it is unclear whether the "other motorized passenger or cargo vehicles" language in our pollution statute applies to mopeds. If the original version of the statute specifically included mopeds but this reference was removed by amendment, it is unlikely that the legislature wanted mopeds to be covered. The same might be true if six similar unpassed bills had included mopeds but the bill that was eventually passed did not, or if one house had passed a bill including mopeds but mopeds did not appear in the final version of the legislation.

Courts use legislative history in two overlapping but nonetheless distinguishable ways. They may use it to determine *legislative intent*—what the legislature thought about the meaning of specific statutory language. They may also use it to determine *legislative purpose*—the overall aim, end, or goal of the legislation. In the latter case, they then ask whether a particular interpretation of the statute is consistent with this purpose. To illustrate the difference between these two uses of legislative his-

tory, suppose that a court has to consider whether the pollution statute's "other motorized passenger or cargo vehicles" language includes battery-powered vehicles. A court seeking to determine the legislature's intent would scan the legislative history for specific references to battery-powered vehicles or other indications of what the legislature thought about their inclusion. A court making a purpose inquiry, however, would use the same history to determine the overall aims of the statute, and then would ask whether including battery-powered vehicles is consistent with those aims. Because the history probably would reveal that our statute's purpose was to reduce air pollution from internal combustion engines, the court might well conclude that battery-powered vehicles should not be covered. As suggested above, courts sometimes follow the intent or purpose revealed by a statute's legislative history even though the plain meaning is to the contrary. In the following *Weber* case, for example, the Supreme Court evidently thought that the statute's claimed purpose was more important than its apparent plain meaning.

General Public Purpose   Occasionally, courts construe statutory language in the light of various *general public purposes* that they identify. These purposes are *not* the purposes underlying the statute in question; rather, they are widely accepted general notions of public policy. In one case, for example, the U.S. Supreme Court used the general public policy against racial discrimination in education as one argument for denying tax-exempt status to a private university that discriminated on the basis of race.[13]

Prior Interpretations   Courts sometimes follow prior cases (and even administrative decisions) interpreting a statute regardless of the statute's plain meaning or its legislative history. The main argument for following these *prior interpretations* is to promote stability and certainty by preventing each successive court that considers a statute from adopting its own interpretation. Whether courts will follow a prior interpretation depends on such factors as the number of past courts adopting the interpretation, the authoritativeness of those courts, and the number of years that the interpretation has been followed. Note that in *Weber*, the Supreme Court apparently did not follow one of its own prior interpretations.

---

[13] *Bob Jones University v. United States*, 461 U.S. 574 (1983).

UNITED STEELWORKERS v. WEBER

443 U.S. 193 (U.S. Sup. Ct. 1979)

As part of its collective bargaining agreement with the United Steelworkers of America, the Kaiser Aluminum and Chemical Company established a new on-the-job craft training program at its Gramercy, Louisiana, plant. The selection of trainees for the program was based on seniority, but at least 50 percent of the new trainees had to be black until the percentage of black skilled craft workers in the plant approximated the percentage of blacks in the local labor force.

Brian Weber was a rejected white applicant who would have qualified for the program had the racial preference not existed. He sued Kaiser and the union in federal district court, arguing that the racial preference violated Title VII of the 1964 Civil Rights Act. Section 703(a) of the act states that: "It shall be an unlawful employment practice for an employer . . . to discriminate against any individual with respect to his compensation, terms, conditions, or privileges of employment, because of such individual's race, color, religion, sex, or national origin." Section 703(d) of the act had a similar provision specifically forbidding racial discrimination in admission to apprenticeship or other training programs. Weber's suit was successful, and the federal court of appeals affirmed. Kaiser and the union appealed to the U.S. Supreme Court.

Brennan, Justice.   The only question before us is whether Title VII forbids private employers and unions from voluntarily agreeing upon bona fide affirmative action plans that accord racial preferences in the manner and for the purpose provided in the Kaiser-USWA plan. That question was expressly left open in *McDonald v. Santa Fe Trail Transp. Co.* (1976), which held, in a case not involving affirmative action, that Title VII protects whites as well as blacks from racial discrimination.

Weber argues that Congress intended in Title VII to prohibit all race-conscious affirmative action plans. His argument rests upon a literal interpretation of sections 703(a) and (d) of the act. Those sections make it unlawful to discriminate because of race in the selection of apprentices for training programs. Since, the argument runs, *McDonald* settled that Title VII forbids discrimination against whites as well as blacks, and since the Kaiser-USWA plan discriminated against white employees solely because they are white, it follows that the plan violates Title VII.

Weber's argument is not without force. But it overlooks the significance of the fact that the Kaiser-USWA plan is an affirmative action plan voluntarily adopted by private parties to eliminate traditional patterns of racial segregation. It is a familiar rule, that a thing may be within the letter of the statute and yet not within the statute, because not within its spirit. Sections 703(a) and (d) must therefore be read against the background of the legislative history of Title VII and the historical context from which the act arose. Examination of these sources makes clear that an interpretation of the sections that forbade all race-conscious affirmative action would bring about an end completely at variance with the purpose of the statute and must be rejected.

Congress's primary concern in enacting the prohibition against racial discrimination in Title VII was the plight of the Negro in our economy. Before 1964, blacks were largely relegated to unskilled and semi-skilled jobs. Because of automation the number of such jobs was rapidly decreasing. As a consequence the relative position of the Negro worker was steadily worsening. Congress feared that the goal of the Civil Rights Act—the integration of blacks into the mainstream of American society—could not be achieved unless this trend were reversed. Accordingly, it was clear to Congress that the crux of the problem was to open employment opportunities for Negroes in occupations which have traditionally been closed to them, and it was to this problem that Title VII's prohibition against racial discrimination in employment was primarily addressed.

Given this legislative history, we cannot agree with Weber that Congress intended to prohibit the private sector from taking effective steps to accomplish the goal that Congress designed Title VII to achieve. It would be ironic indeed if a law triggered by a nation's concern over centuries of racial injustice and intended to improve the lot of those who had been excluded from the American dream for so long, constituted the first legislative prohibition of all voluntary, private, race-conscious efforts to abolish traditional patterns of racial segregation and hierarchy.

Judgment reversed in favor of Kaiser and the union.

Maxims Maxims are general rules of thumb employed in statutory interpretation. There are many maxims, and courts tend to use them or ignore them at their discretion. One example of a maxim is the *ejusdem generis* rule, which says that when general words follow words of a specific, limited meaning, the general language should be limited to things of the same class as those specifically stated. Suppose that the hypothetical pollution statute quoted earlier listed 32 types of gas-powered vehicles and ended with the words "and other motorized passenger or cargo vehicles." Here, *ejusdem generis* would probably dictate that battery-powered vehicles not be included.

Limits on Courts

From the preceding discussion, you might think that anything goes when courts decide common law cases or interpret statutes. However, many factors discourage courts from adopting a completely freewheeling approach. Due to their legal training and mental makeup, judges tend to respect established precedents and the will of the legislature. Many courts issue written opinions, which expose judges to academic and professional criticism. Trial court judges may be discouraged from innovation by the fear of being overruled by a higher court. Because those higher courts contain several judges, disagreements at this level may cancel each other out, or be moderated in the search for compromise. Finally, certain political factors inhibit judges. For example, some judges are elected, and even judges with lifetime tenure can sometimes be removed.

ETHICAL AND PUBLIC POLICY CONCERNS

1. What might be considered troubling about the result in the *Rochin* case presented in this chapter? (Hint: consult any poll in which Americans identify what they regard as the country's most serious problems.) Modern ethical theory sometimes distinguishes *deontological* ethical theories from *teleological* ethical theories. In their extreme forms, deontological theories say that certain actions are right or wrong and should be pursued or avoided, *no matter what the consequences of doing so.* Teleological theories, on the other hand, generally assess the moral worth of actions *in terms of their consequences.* Which of these approaches best describes the Supreme Court's decision in *Rochin*?

2. Earlier in this chapter, we quoted Justice Holmes's statement that "[t]he first requirement of a sound body of law is, that it should correspond with the actual feelings and demands of the community, whether right or wrong." This statement can be read as asserting that the law should adapt to reflect prevailing moral views, whatever they happen to be. What is good about such an approach to the law and to lawmaking? What is bad about it?

3. Legal positivists often take the position that even morally bad laws are still law and that such laws (or some of them, at least) should still be enforced and obeyed. What *moral* arguments can you make for this position?

SUMMARY

There are at least two ways to answer the question, "What is law?" One is to list and describe all the types of rules typically regarded as law in a particular society. In the United States, these rules are: constitutions, statutes, common law, equity, administrative regulations, administrative decisions, ordinances, treaties, and executive orders. These various types of law also may be classified as: (1) criminal or civil, (2) substantive or procedural, and (3) public or private.

Another way to answer the "What is law?" question is to attempt an abstract definition of law in general. The various efforts to provide such a definition are called *schools of jurisprudence*. The most important jurisprudential schools are *legal positivism* (which defines law as the command of a recognized political authority and excludes morality from its definition), *natural law* (which regards morality as an essential component of law and often claims that bad laws are not law), *American legal realism* (which defines law as what public decisionmakers do), and *sociological jurisprudence* (a term uniting various approaches that view law in a broad social context).

Another way to look at law is to consider the *functions* it performs. Among the law's many functions are peacekeeping, promoting individual freedom by checking government power, facilitating planning, promoting economic growth, furthering social justice, and protecting the environment. These functions can obviously conflict with one another in particular cases.

This text states the most important legal rules affecting business by describing them as a series of black-letter commands. However, this approach sometimes gives the law a false appearance of certainty, precision, stability, and predictability. Examining the reasoning processes that courts use in deciding common law cases and in interpreting statutes helps dispel this misleading impression. The doctrine of *stare decisis* used in deciding common law cases seems to compel the courts to follow the rules announced in similar prior cases. However, because it allows judges to distinguish these cases and effectively create new rules of law to govern the present case, *stare decisis* actually permits flexibility and change.

Even though statutes seem to have the certainty, precision, and stability lacking in judge-made law, legislation is often ambiguous as stated or applied. The different techniques of statutory interpretation help courts to deal with such situations. When the words of the statute have a clear, accepted meaning, some courts simply follow that meaning under the *plain meaning rule*. When the statutory language is ambiguous (or perhaps even when it is plain), courts resort to *legislative history*. They may use the many legislative history sources to determine both the legislative *intent* (some legislative conclusion about the meaning of particular words) or the legislative *purpose* (the aim, end, or object of the statute). Usually, moreover, the courts are bound to follow *prior interpretations* giving statutory language a particular meaning. On occasion, finally, courts may read a statute in light of certain *general public purposes*, or may seek assistance from the many *maxims* of statutory construction.

APPENDIX
Reading and Briefing Cases

In this chapter and most other chapters of the text, you encounter cases—the judicial opinions accompanying actual court decisions. These cases are highly edited versions of their much longer originals. What follows are a few explanations and pointers to assist you in studying these cases.

1. Each case has a *case name* that includes at least some of the parties to the case. Because the order of the parties sometimes changes when a case is appealed, do not assume that the first party listed is the plaintiff (the party suing) and the second the defendant (the party being sued). Also, because some cases have many plaintiffs and/or many defendants, the parties discussed in the court's opinion sometimes differ from those found in the case name. This is true of the *Weber* case, for example.

2. Each case also has a *citation*, which includes the volume and page number of the legal reporter in which the full case can be found, as well as the year the case was decided. The *Weber* case, for instance, begins on page 193 of volume 443 of the United States Reports (the official reporter for U.S. Supreme Court decisions), and was decided in 1979. (Each of the many different legal reporters has its own abbreviation, and they are too numerous for inclusion here.) In the parenthesis accompanying the date, we also give you some information about the court that decided the case. For example: "U.S. Sup. Ct." is the United States Supreme Court, "3d Cir." is the U.S. Court of Appeals for the Third Circuit, "S.D.N.Y." is the U.S. District Court for the Southern District of New York, "Minn. Sup. Ct." is the Minnesota Supreme Court, and "Mich. Ct. App." is the Michigan Court of Appeals (a Michigan intermediate appellate court). The various kinds of courts are described in the chapter on The Resolution of Private Disputes.

3. At the beginning of each case, there is a statement of the most important facts that gave rise to the case. This *statement of facts* is an edited version of the court's original statement, and almost all the facts it contains are important.

4. Immediately after the statement of facts, we give you a summary of the case's *procedural history*. (The chapter on The Resolution of Private Disputes discusses civil procedure and the Crimes chapter discusses criminal procedure.) Basically, this history tells you how the case arrived at the court whose opinion you are reading.

5. After all this, you reach your major concern: the *body of the court's opinion*. Here, the court typically arrives at the applicable rule(s) of law, and applies them to the facts to reach a conclusion. This is where the various examples of legal reasoning discussed in the latter part of the chapter may come into play. In many cases, the court's discussion of the relevant law is elaborate. It may include a description of prior cases, an examination of legislative history, a discussion of applicable policies, and other relevant considerations. The court's application of the law to the facts usually occurs after it has arrived at the applicable legal rule(s), but also may be intertwined with its legal discussion.

6. At the very end of the case, we complete the procedural history by telling you how this court decided the case. For example, "Judgment reversed in favor of Smith" says that a lower court judgment *against* Smith was reversed on appeal, which means that Smith's appeal was successful and Smith wins.

7. Why are the cases important? Their main function is to provide concrete examples of rules stated in the text. (Frequently, in fact, the text tells you what point or points the case illustrates.) In studying law, it is all too easy to conclude that your task is finished once you have memorized a black letter rule. In real life, however, legal problems rarely present themselves as abstract questions of law; instead, they are implicit in particular situations you encounter or particular actions you take. Without some sense of a legal rule's concrete application, therefore, your knowledge of that rule is incomplete. In addition, the cases help you to understand how courts operate and think.

8. In studying this text, you may find it helpful to "brief" the cases it contains. By doing so, you can enhance your understanding of the cases themselves, the legal rules they discuss, the practical application of those rules, and the decisionmaking processes courts use. There is no one correct way to brief a case, but most good briefs contain the following elements: (1) a short, concise statement of the relevant facts, (2) the case's prior history, (3) the question(s) or issue(s) the court had to decide, (4) the answer(s) to those question(s) (how the issue(s) were resolved), (5) the reasoning the court used to justify its decision, and (6) the final result (who won and who lost and, where relevant, whether the lower court's decision was affirmed or reversed). Using the

terms "P" and "D" for the plaintiff and defendant, a brief of the *Weber* case might look like this:

United Steelworkers v. Weber (p. 18)

Facts: The Ds here were a private employer and a union that had voluntarily established a craft training program through a collective bargaining agreement. The procedures for selecting the program's trainees favored black workers over white workers by basing entry on seniority but providing that at least 50 percent of the new trainees had to be black until the black percentage in the program approximated the black percentage of the local labor force. P, a white worker who was denied access to the program, would have qualified had the racial preference not existed.

History: P sued the Ds under Title VII of the 1964 Civil Rights Act, which expressly forbids employment discrimination on the basis of race. He won in federal district court and the court of appeals affirmed. The Ds appealed to the U.S. Supreme Court.

Issue: Does this voluntary racial preference favoring blacks violate Title VII's ban on racial discrimination in employment?

Answer: No.

Reasoning: Even though Title VII's plain meaning favors P and even though there is a prior interpretation holding that Title VII forbids racial discrimination against both whites and blacks, neither point is decisive here. The reason is that holding for P would frustrate Title VII's purpose. Title VII's legislative history and its historical context make clear that its aim was to integrate blacks into the American mainstream. This was especially true in the area of employment, an area in which blacks were falling behind. Here, the Ds' preference for blacks helped further this purpose because it helped blacks get better jobs, and declaring the preference illegal would have frustrated that purpose.

Result: Court of appeals decision reversed; Ds win.

PROBLEM CASES

1. In which way do administrative regulations resemble statutes? In which way do they differ from statutes?

2. Suppose that Congress passes a federal statute that conflicts with a state constitutional provision. The state argues that the constitutional provision should prevail over the statute because constitutions are a higher, more authoritative kind of law than statutes. Is this argument correct? Why or why not?

3. Suppose that someone objects to the president's promulgation of an executive order by claiming that the U.S. Constitution only gives the president the power to *execute* the laws, not the power to make them. What concept explains the president's power to make law through executive orders? Explain its meaning.

4. State A passes a statute declaring that those who sell heroin are to receive a mandatory 30-year prison sentence. Describe this statute in terms of the three classifications of law stated in the text—criminal/civil, substantive/procedural, and public/private.

5. Nation X is a dictatorship in which one ruler has the ultimate lawmaking power. The ruler issues a statute declaring that certain religious minorities are to be exterminated. An international convocation of jurisprudential scholars meets to discuss the question, "Is Nation X's statute truly law?" What would be the typical natural law answer to this question? What would be the typical legal positivist response? Assume that all of those present at the convocation think that Nation X's statute is morally wrong.

6. Nation Y has enacted positive laws forbidding all abnormal sexual relations between consenting adults. However, the police of Nation Y rarely enforce these laws, and even when they do, prosecutors never bring charges against violators. What observation would American legal realists make about this situation? In order to determine what a believer in natural law would think about these laws, what else would you have to know?

7. Some of the states still have so-called Sunday Closing laws—statutes or ordinances forbidding the conduct of certain business on Sunday. Today, these laws often are not obeyed or enforced. What would an extreme legal positivist tend to think about the duty to enforce and obey such laws? What would a natural law exponent who strongly believes in economic freedom tend to think about this question? What about a natural law adherent who is a Christian religious traditionalist? What *observation* would almost any American legal realist make about Sunday Closing laws? Looking at these laws from a sociological perspective, finally, what social factors help explain their original passage, their relative lack of enforcement today, and their continuance "on the books" despite their lack of enforcement?

8. Although you would not know this from reading the *MacPherson* case in this chapter, two of the cases mentioned there distinguished *Thomas v. Winchester* (the case involving the falsely labeled poison) in a certain way. The courts in *Loop v. Litchfield* (the circular saw case) and *Losee v. Clute* (the steam boiler case) both held that *Thomas v. Winchester* should not apply because in *Thomas,* the thing that caused the injury—a poison—was *by its nature intended to cause harm.* In other words, these courts held that a poison should be treated differently from a circular saw that flew apart, or an exploding steam boiler. If the relevant public policy here is to allow recovery for injuries caused by highly dangerous products, does this distinction make any sense?

9. In 1885, Congress passed a statute stating that "it shall be unlawful for any . . . corporation . . . to . . . in any way assist or encourage the importation or migration of any alien or aliens, any foreigner or foreigners, into the United States . . . under contract or agreement . . . to perform labor or service of any kind in the United States." The legislative history of this statute revealed that it was passed because American businesses were contracting with foreigners to prepay their passage to the United States, in return for the immigrant's agreement to work for low wages for a fixed time period. This practice reduced the bargaining power and wages of American laborers.

The Holy Trinity Church, a corporation, contracted with E. Walpole Warren, a U.S. alien residing in England, for Warren to travel to the United States and become Holy Trinity's rector and pastor. Pursuant to the contract, Warren did so. Which technique of statutory interpretation would you use in arguing that this contract is covered by the statute? Which technique would you use if you were arguing the contrary position?

10. In 1910, the White Slave Traffic Act (usually known as the Mann Act) went into effect. The act was passed by Congress in response to an alleged white slave traffic in which gangs of certain nationalities were said to be forcing or luring American women into prostitution. One portion of the act stated that "any person who shall knowingly transport or cause to be transported . . . any woman or girl for the purpose of prostitution or debauchery, or for any other immoral purpose, . . . shall be deemed guilty of a felony." In 1913, F. Drew Caminetti was indicted for transporting a woman from Sacramento, California, to Reno, Nevada, to be his mistress. Which technique of statutory interpretation would you use in arguing that Caminetti *is* guilty under the Mann Act? Which technique would you use to argue that Caminetti should *not* be guilty under the act?

CHAPTER 2

THE RESOLUTION OF PRIVATE DISPUTES

INTRODUCTION

As we noted in the Nature of Law chapter, one way that the law performs its peacekeeping function is by resolving private disputes. The most important example is the courts' application of substantive legal rules to decide civil cases (lawsuits between private parties).[1] Because the courts play such an important role in enforcing and formulating rules of substantive law, your understanding of business law is incomplete without some knowledge about the various kinds of courts, the cases they can decide, and the procedures under which they operate in civil suits.

The United States has 52 separate court systems—a federal system, plus a system for each state and the District of Columbia. After noting some self-imposed limits on the kinds of civil suits courts handle, this chapter describes the various state and federal courts. Included in this discussion is the *jurisdiction* of these courts, their power to decide certain kinds of cases. Then the chapter examines the *procedures* courts follow in civil cases. In-

creasingly, however, private disputes are being resolved outside the formal court system. Thus, the chapter concludes by treating some of the most important methods of *alternative dispute resolution*.

SELF-IMPOSED LIMITS ON COURTS IN CIVIL CASES

At the end of the chapter on the nature of law, we listed some factors that restrict the courts' ability to make law in any fashion they might desire. Here, we consider some doctrines through which the courts *limit themselves* to civil suits involving *real disputes*. Although these doctrines have constitutional dimensions, they mainly have been formulated by the courts and thus are largely self-imposed. They might be summed up by the following proposition: *courts only decide genuine, existing "cases or controversies" between real parties with tangible opposing interests in the lawsuit.*

Thus, courts usually do not issue *advisory opinions* on abstract legal questions presented by the parties if those questions are not part of a real dispute, and do not decide *feigned controversies* concocted by the parties to get answers to such questions. In addition, courts may refuse to rule on disputes that are insufficiently *ripe* because they have not matured into a genuine controversy

---

[1] On the distinctions between civil law and criminal law, and between procedural law and substantive law, see the Nature of Law chapter. Note that the government may sometimes be a party to a civil suit.

in which the parties have real interests at stake. They also refuse to decide disputes that are *moot* because there is no longer a real controversy between the parties and a judicial decision would have no tangible consequences for those parties. Expressing many of these ideas, finally, is the doctrine of *standing to sue*, which generally requires that the party suing have some fairly direct, tangible, and substantial stake in the outcome of the suit.[2]

Despite all these doctrines, however, state and federal *declaratory judgment* statutes enable the courts to determine the parties' rights, legal status, and other legal relations even though their controversy has not advanced to the point where harm has occurred and legal relief may be necessary. These statutes enable parties to determine their legal rights and duties without taking action that could expose them to legal liability. Where one party to a contract thinks that she is not obligated to perform it, for example, she may decide to seek a declaratory judgment on the question rather than break the contract and risk a lawsuit by the other party. For the most part, though, declaratory judgment statutes are applied only when the parties' dispute is sufficiently advanced to constitute an actual case or controversy.

STATE COURTS AND THEIR JURISDICTION

Courts of Limited Jurisdiction

Minor criminal matters and civil controversies involving small amounts of money are frequently decided in *courts of limited jurisdiction* (also known as courts of inferior or special jurisdiction). Common examples include municipal courts, justice of the peace courts, and small claims courts. Courts of limited jurisdiction often handle a large volume of cases. In these courts, the procedures normally are informal, the presiding judicial officer may not be a lawyer, and the parties may argue their own cases. Also, courts of limited jurisdiction usually are not courts of record; that is, they ordinarily do not keep a transcript of the testimony and proceedings. For this reason, appeals from their decisions require a new trial (a trial *de novo*) in a court of record such as a trial court.

Trial Courts

Courts of limited jurisdiction perform the basic tasks involved in the resolution of any legal controversy: finding the relevant facts, identifying the appropriate rule(s) of law, and combining the facts and the law to reach a decision. State trial courts perform the same functions, but differ from inferior courts in at least three ways. First, they are not governed by the limits on civil damages awarded or criminal penalties imposed that govern courts of limited jurisdiction. Thus, cases involving significant dollar amounts or major criminal penalties generally begin at the trial court level. Second, trial courts keep detailed records of their proceedings. Third, the trial court judge almost always is a lawyer. The trial court's fact-finding function may be handled by the judge or by a jury. Determination of the applicable law is always the judge's responsibility.

States usually have one trial court for each county. It may be called a circuit, superior, district, county, or common pleas court. Trial courts often have civil and criminal divisions. They also may contain divisions or special courts set up to hear particular matters—for example, domestic relations courts, probate courts, and juvenile courts.

State Appeals Courts

In general, state appeals (or appellate) courts only decide *legal* questions. Their judges do not make factual findings and they have no juries. Thus, although appellate courts can correct legal errors made by the trial judge, they generally accept the trial court's findings of fact. Appellate courts also may hear appeals from state administrative agency decisions. Some states have only one appeals court (usually called the supreme court), while others also have an intermediate appellate court. As Figure 1 illustrates, this court sits between the trial court and the state's highest court. Appeals from decisions of the state's highest court sometimes are heard by the U.S. Supreme Court.

State Court Jurisdiction and Venue

The party who sues in a civil case (the plaintiff) cannot sue the defendant (the party being sued) in any court he chooses. For the suit to proceed, the chosen court must have **jurisdiction** over the case. Jurisdiction is a court's power to hear a case and to issue a decision binding on the parties. In order to render a binding decision in a civil case, a state court must have *both*: (1) subject-matter jurisdiction and (2) *either* in personam jurisdiction *or*

---

[2] Standing requirements appear in a number of different situations and are formulated in various ways. For an example, see the discussion of standing in the antitrust context in The Sherman Act chapter.

FIGURE 1   An Illustrative State Court System

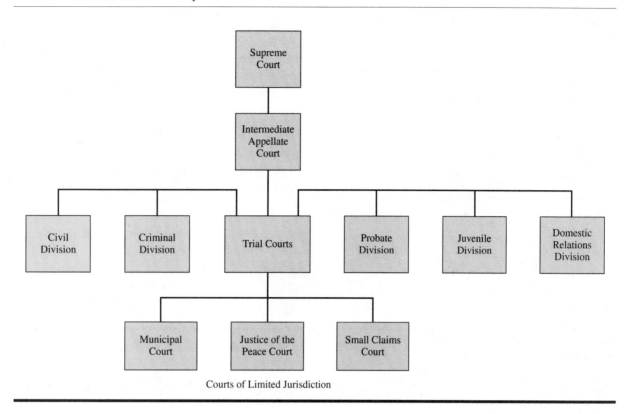

Courts of Limited Jurisdiction

in rem jurisdiction.[3] Even if the court chosen by the plaintiff has the necessary jurisdiction, it also must meet the state's **venue** requirements in order for the suit to proceed there.

Subject-Matter Jurisdiction   **Subject-matter jurisdiction** is the court's power to decide the *type* of controversy involved in the case. Criminal courts, for example, cannot hear civil matters, and a $500,000 suit for breach of contract cannot be pursued in a small claims court.

In Personam Jurisdiction   Even if a court has subject-matter jurisdiction in a civil case, it cannot decide the case if it lacks legal power over either the defendant or the property at issue in the case. The first kind of legal power, called **in personam jurisdiction,** is based on the residence, location, or activities of the defendant. A state court has in personam jurisdiction over defendants who

are citizens or residents of the state (even if situated out-of-state), those who are within the state's borders when the suit is begun by serving process against them (even if nonresidents),[4] and those who consent to the suit (for instance, by entering the state to defend against it).[5]

In addition, many states have enacted "long-arm" statutes giving their courts in personam jurisdiction over certain out-of-state defendants. Under these statutes, nonresident individuals and businesses may become subject to the state's jurisdiction through activities such as doing business within the state, contracting to supply goods or services within the state, and committing a tort (a civil wrong) within the state. As the following *Knowles* case indicates, a state's assertion of in personam jurisdiction over an out-of-state defendant is subject to federal due process standards, and some state long-arm statutes extend the state's in personam jurisdiction as far as federal due process permits.

---

[3] State *criminal* jurisdiction exists when the defendant has allegedly committed acts defined as criminal by state law and has done so within the state.

[4] Service of process is discussed later in this chapter.

[5] In some states, however, out-of-state defendants may make a *special appearance* to challenge the court's jurisdiction without consenting to that jurisdiction.

FIGURE 2   State Court Jurisdiction

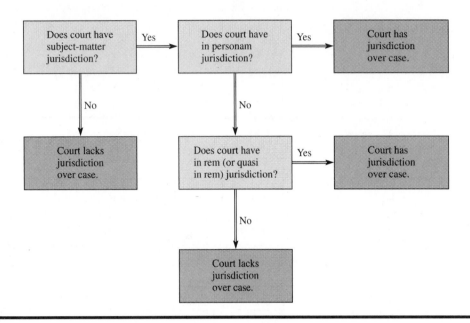

KNOWLES v. MODGLIN

553 So. 2d 563 (Ala. Sup. Ct. 1989)

Albert Knowles, an Alabama truck driver, died of natural causes in California while hauling produce from Alabama to California. After Knowles's body was discovered inside his truck, it was taken to Hems Brothers Mortuaries, where an autopsy was performed by Damon Reference Laboratories at the request of the local coroner. Both Hems and Damon did business in California. After being asked to do so by an Alabama funeral home, Hems prepared Knowles's body for shipment and arranged for it to be flown to his home town. Hems billed the Alabama funeral home for these services and for the price of a casket; it also mailed a statement to Knowles's wife.

Mrs. Knowles did not view her husband's body after its return to Alabama and before its burial, and no one positively identified the body as that of Mr. Knowles during this period. After the burial, Mrs. Knowles received an autopsy report from Damon describing a body that was different from her husband's body. As a result, she had the buried body exhumed and personally viewed it to verify that it actually was her husband's body—which it was. In her examination of the body, Mrs. Knowles found that it had been buried nude, had been packed in cotton in a "disaster pouch," was terribly discolored, and was lying in an awkward position. She described the body as looking like "a monster."

Mrs. Knowles then sued Hems and Damon in an Alabama trial court for the alleged wrongful mishandling of her husband's body. Both Damon and Hems had no contacts with Alabama other than those just described, and each moved to dismiss the claim on the basis that the court lacked in personam jurisdiction. After the court granted Damon's motion but denied Hems's motion, both Mrs. Knowles and Hems appealed to the Alabama Supreme Court.

Houston, Justice.   The issue presented is whether, consistent with the Due Process Clause of the Fourteenth Amendment to the United States Constitution, the defendants have sufficient contacts with this state to make it fair and reasonable to require them to come here to defend against the present action. Due process requires that to subject a defendant to a judgment in personam, he have certain minimum contacts with it such that the maintenance of the suit does not offend traditional notions of fair play and substantive justice. Alabama's long-arm statute has been interpreted to extend the jurisdiction of Alabama courts to the permissible limits of due process.

A relevant factor in a due process analysis is whether the defendant should have reasonably anticipated that he would be sued in the forum state. In determining [this question], it is essential that there be some act by which the defendant purposefully avails itself of the privilege of conducting activities within the forum state, thus invoking the benefits and protections of its laws. Other relevant factors include the burden placed on the defendant, the interest of the forum state in adjudicating the dispute, the plaintiff's interest in obtaining convenient and effective relief, and the interstate judicial system's interest in obtaining the most efficient resolution of the controversy.

The trial court did not err in dismissing Damon for lack of in personam jurisdiction. It does not appear that Damon ever had any contacts with Alabama, with the exception of mailing the autopsy report to Mrs. Knowles. Damon could not have reasonably anticipated that Mr. Knowles's body would make its way to Alabama, that it would not be positively identified by anyone before burial, and that, thereafter, Damon would be haled into an Alabama court to defend against a suit based on a misdescription contained in the autopsy report.

However, Hems established significant contacts with this state by agreeing to prepare and ship Mr. Knowles's body here. In addition, Hems sold Mrs. Knowles a casket, and later solicited payment by mail in Alabama. Hems purposefully availed itself of the privilege of conducting business in Alabama [and] should have reasonably anticipated being summoned to an Alabama court to answer any charges of misconduct in the handling and shipment of Mr. Knowles's body. Furthermore, given the progress in communications and transportation in recent years, we cannot say that it would be unduly burdensome for Hems to defend against the suit in an Alabama court. Considering the nature of Hems's activity, the resultant foreseeability of its being required to defend an action in Alabama, the obvious interest of the plaintiff in obtaining convenient and effective relief, and the relative lack of inconvenience that would be incurred by Hems in appearing and defending, we are convinced that it is fair and reasonable to require Hems to defend against this action in Alabama.

Trial court decision dismissing Mrs. Knowles's suit against Damon for lack of jurisdiction and finding jurisdiction over Hems affirmed.

In Rem Jurisdiction   In rem jurisdiction is based on the fact that *property* is located within the state. It gives state courts the power to determine rights in that property even if the people whose rights are affected are outside the state's in personam jurisdiction. For example, a state court's decision regarding title to land within the state is said to "bind the world."[6]

Venue   Even though a court has jurisdiction over a case, it may lack the power to decide that case because the applicable **venue** requirements have not been met. In general, a court has venue if it is a territorially fair and convenient forum in which to hear the case. Venue requirements are typically set by state statutes, which normally tell the plaintiff the county in which suit must be

---

[6] Another form of jurisdiction, *quasi in rem jurisdiction* or *attachment jurisdiction*, is also based on the location of property within the state. Unlike cases based on in rem jurisdiction, cases based on quasi in rem jurisdiction do not necessarily determine rights in the property itself. Instead, the property is regarded as an extension of the out-of-

state defendant, and this enables the court to decide legal claims unrelated to the property. For example, a plaintiff might attach the defendant's bank account in the state where the bank is located, sue the defendant on a tort or contract claim unrelated to the bank account, and recover the amount of the judgment from the account if the suit is successful.

brought. Such a statute, for instance, might say that a suit concerning land or interests in land must be brought in the county where the land is located, and that other suits must be brought in the county where the defendant resides or is doing business. In certain cases where justice so requires, the defendant may obtain a *change of venue*. This can occur when, for example, a fair trial is impossible within a particular county.

FEDERAL COURTS AND THEIR JURISDICTION

District Courts

In the federal system, lawsuits usually begin in the federal district courts, which are basically federal trial courts. Like state trial courts, the federal district courts have both fact-finding and law-finding functions. As before, fact-finding may be entrusted to either the judge or a jury, and determining the law is the judge's responsibility. Each state has at least one district court, and each district court has at least one judge.

District Court Jurisdiction and Venue   There are many bases of federal district court civil jurisdiction.[7] The two most important are **diversity jurisdiction** and **federal question jurisdiction.** Diversity jurisdiction exists when: (1) the suit is between citizens of different states, and (2) the amount in controversy exceeds $50,000. Diversity jurisdiction also exists in certain suits between citizens of a state and citizens or governments of foreign nations where the amount in controversy exceeds $50,000. Under diversity jurisdiction, a corporation generally is deemed to be a citizen of both the state where it has been incorporated and the state where it has its principal place of business.

Federal question jurisdiction exists when the case arises under the Constitution, laws, or treaties of the United States. Generally, the "arises under" requirement is met when a right created by federal law is a basic part of the plaintiff's case. There is no amount-in-controversy requirement for federal question jurisdiction.

A particular district court's diversity or federal question jurisdiction usually covers only those defendants who would be subject to the in personam jurisdiction of the state where the district court sits. Further limiting the plaintiff's choice of federal district courts are the

federal system's venue requirements. The basic federal venue statute declares that: (1) where jurisdiction is based *solely* on diversity, suit may be brought only in the district where all plaintiffs or all defendants reside, or where the claim arose; and (2) where jurisdiction is not based solely on diversity, suit may be brought only in the district where all defendants reside or where the claim arose. In addition, many special federal venue provisions govern specific cases.

Concurrent Jurisdiction and Removal   The federal district courts have *exclusive jurisdiction* over some matters: for example, patent and copyright cases. This means that such cases must be heard in federal court. Often, however, they have *concurrent jurisdiction* with state courts; here, both state and federal courts have jurisdiction over the case. For example, a plaintiff may be able to assert state court in personam jurisdiction over an out-of-state defendant or may sue in a federal district court under that court's diversity jurisdiction. Also, a state court may decide a case involving a federal question if it has jurisdiction over that case. If concurrent jurisdiction is present and the plaintiff opts for a state court, the defendant may be able to *remove* the case to a federal district court. The case, of course, must be one over which the district court would have had jurisdiction if the plaintiff had sued there.

Specialized Courts

The federal court system also includes certain specialized federal courts, including the Claims Court (which hears claims against the United States), the Court of International Trade (which is concerned with tariff, customs, and other international trade matters), the Bankruptcy Courts (which operate as adjuncts of the district courts), and the Tax Court (which reviews certain IRS determinations). Usually, the decisions of these courts can be appealed to one or more of the federal courts of appeals.

Courts of Appeals

Like state intermediate appellate courts, the U.S. courts of appeals generally do not have a fact-finding function and review only the legal conclusions reached by lower federal courts. As Figure 3 illustrates, there are 13 federal courts of appeals: 11 organized territorially into circuits covering several states each, one for the District of Columbia, and the Court of Appeals for the Federal Circuit.

---

[7] Federal *criminal* jurisdiction is based on the alleged commission of acts defined as criminal by federal law.

FIGURE 3   The Thirteen Federal Judicial Circuits

First Circuit (*Boston, Mass.*) Maine, Massachusetts, New Hampshire, Puerto Rico, Rhode Island	**Second Circuit** (*New York, N.Y.*) Connecticut, New York, Vermont	**Third Circuit** (*Philadelphia, Pa.*) Delaware, New Jersey, Pennsylvania, Virgin Islands	**Fourth Circuit** (*Richmond, Va.*) Maryland, North Carolina, South Carolina, Virginia, West Virginia
Fifth Circuit (*New Orleans, La.*) Louisiana, Mississippi, Texas	**Sixth Circuit** (*Cincinnati, Ohio*) Kentucky, Michigan, Ohio, Tennessee	**Seventh Circuit** (*Chicago, Ill.*) Illinois, Indiana, Wisconsin	**Eighth Circuit** (*St. Louis, Mo.*) Arkansas, Iowa, Minnesota, Missouri, Nebraska, North Dakota, South Dakota
Ninth Circuit (*San Francisco, Calif.*) Alaska, Arizona, California, Guam, Hawaii, Idaho, Montana, Nevada, Northern Mariana Islands, Oregon, Washington	**Tenth Circuit** (*Denver, Colo.*) Colorado, Kansas, New Mexico, Oklahoma, Utah, Wyoming	**Eleventh Circuit** (*Atlanta, Ga.*) Alabama, Florida, Georgia	**District of Columbia Circuit** (*Washington, D.C.*)

Federal Circuit (*Washington, D.C.*)

Except for the Court of Appeals for the Federal Circuit, the most important function of the U.S. courts of appeals is to hear appeals from decisions of the federal district courts. Appeals from a district court ordinarily are taken to the court of appeals for that district court's region. Appeals from the District Court for the Southern District of New York, for example, go to the Second Circuit Court of Appeals. The courts of appeals also hear appeals from the Tax Court and from many administrative agency and Bankruptcy Court decisions. The Court of Appeals for the Federal Circuit hears a wide variety of specialized appeals, including some patent and trademark matters, Claims Court decisions, and decisions by the Court of International Trade.

The U.S. Supreme Court

The U.S. Supreme Court is basically an appellate court, and, like all such courts, is limited to questions of law when it decides appeals. Most of the appeals considered by the Supreme Court come from the federal courts of appeals and the highest state courts.[8] Today, most appealable decisions from these courts fall within the Supreme Court's *certiorari* jurisdiction, under which the Court has discretion whether or not to hear the appeal. In fact, the Court hears only a small percentage of the appeals coming to it through its certiorari jurisdiction. In such cases, the Court is said to "grant certiorari" or "grant cert." When the Court declines to hear the appeal, it "denies certiorari" or "denies cert."

Virtually all cases coming from the federal courts of appeals are within the Court's discretionary certiorari jurisdiction. Cases appealed from the highest state courts are within the certiorari jurisdiction when: (1) the validity of any treaty or federal statute has been questioned; (2) the validity of any state statute is questioned on the basis that it is repugnant to federal law; or (3) any title, right, privilege, or immunity is claimed under federal law. As a general proposition, the Supreme Court

---

[8] There are, however, certain situations in which the Supreme Court will hear appeals directly from the federal district courts.

FIGURE 4   A Simplified Model of the State and Federal Court Systems

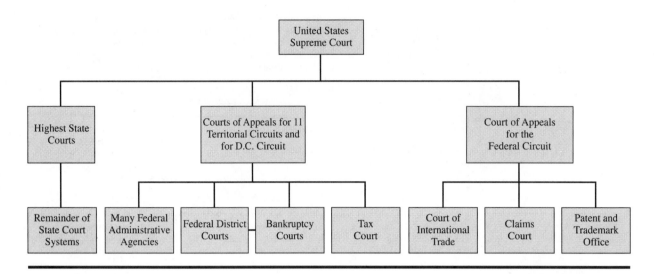

defers to the highest state courts on questions of state law, and does not hear appeals from those courts if the case involves such questions alone.

In certain fairly rare situations, finally, the U.S. Supreme Court possesses *original jurisdiction*, which means that it basically acts as a trial court. The Supreme Court has *original and exclusive* jurisdiction over all controversies between two or more states. It has *original*, but not exclusive, jurisdiction over cases involving foreign ambassadors, ministers, and like parties; controversies between the United States and a state; and cases where a state proceeds against citizens of another state or against aliens.

CIVIL PROCEDURE

Introduction

Civil procedure is the body of legal rules governing the conduct of a trial court case between private parties.[9] Much of this law is complex and technical, and it varies according to the jurisdiction[10] in question. Thus, the fol-

lowing presentation is only a general summary of the most widely accepted rules governing civil cases in state trial courts and the federal district courts. Knowledge of these basic procedural matters is useful if you or your employer become involved in a civil controversy. Such knowledge also helps you to understand the cases that appear throughout this text. Figure 5 presents the major steps through which the normal civil case proceeds and the most significant motions the parties (or *litigants*) can make at each step.

The Adversary System

In many of the stages and motions presented in Figure 5 and described below, the *adversary system* is at work. Through their attorneys, the litigants present contrary positions of fact or law before a theoretically impartial judge and possibly a jury. To win a civil case, the plaintiff must prove each element of his claim by a *preponderance of the evidence*.[11] To do this, the plaintiff must show that the greater weight of the evidence—by *credibility*, not quantity—supports the existence of each element. In other words, the plaintiff must convince the factfinder that the existence of each factual element is more probable than its nonexistence. Thus, the lawyers

---

[9] Criminal procedure is discussed in the Crimes chapter. Also, the procedures used in administrative hearings are discussed in the Administrative Agencies chapter.

[10] In the discussion that follows, the term *jurisdiction* refers to one of the 50 states, the District of Columbia, or the federal government.

[11] However, as discussed in the Crimes chapter, in a criminal case the government must prove the elements of the alleged crime *beyond a reasonable doubt*.

FIGURE 5   The Most Important Stages and Motions in Civil Litigation (Appeals Assumed)

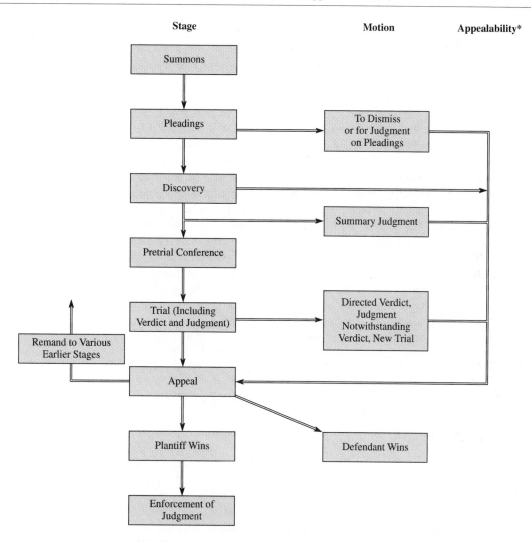

*As discussed later in the chapter, many other trial court rulings also are appealable.

for each party continually present their client's version of the facts, try to convince the judge or jury that this version is true, and attempt to rebut conflicting factual allegations by the other party. Also, the attorneys seek to persuade the judge that their interpretations of the law are correct.

The adversary system reflects the familiar American belief that truth is best discovered through the presentation of competing ideas. Supporters of the adversary system believe that allowing the litigants to make competing arguments of fact and law gives the judge and jury the best chance of making accurate determinations

because it enables both the presentation and the criticism of all relevant arguments. Critics of the adversary system contend that rather than promoting the disinterested search for truth, it encourages the parties to employ incomplete, distorted, and even false arguments if such arguments help them win the case. Defenders of the adversary system reply that it should weed out such arguments because they are attacked by the other party and because an impartial judge is present. This weeding-out process, however, may not work if one or both parties lack competent counsel. Sometimes, for example, the adversary system's competition of ideas is unequal because one litigant has superior resources and thus can obtain better representation.

Service of the Summons

The function of the **summons** is to notify the defendant that she is being sued. The summons typically names the plaintiff and states the time within which the defendant must enter an *appearance* in court (usually through her attorney). In most jurisdictions, it is accompanied by a copy of the plaintiff's complaint (which is described below).

The summons is usually delivered, or served, to the defendant by an appropriate public official after the plaintiff has filed his complaint with the court. To ensure that the defendant is properly notified of the suit, statutes, court rules, and constitutional due process guarantees set standards for proper service of the summons in particular cases. For example, personal delivery of the summons to the defendant almost always meets these standards, and many jurisdictions also permit the summons to be left at the defendant's home or place of business. Service to corporations may often be accomplished by delivery of the summons to the firm's general or managing agent. Many state long-arm statutes permit out-of-state defendants to be served by registered mail. Although inadequate service of process may sometimes defeat the plaintiff's claim, in most jurisdictions the defendant must make her objection early or it will be waived.

The Pleadings

The term **pleadings** refers to the documents that the parties file with the court when they first state their claims and defenses. The pleadings include the complaint, the answer, and (in some jurisdictions) the reply.

The Complaint   The **complaint** fully states the plaintiff's claim in separate, numbered paragraphs. It must contain sufficient facts to show that the plaintiff is entitled to some legal relief and to give the defendant reasonable notice of the nature of the plaintiff's claim. The complaint must also state the remedy requested by the plaintiff.

The Answer   Within a designated time after the complaint has been served, the defendant normally files an **answer** to the complaint. The answer responds to the plaintiff's complaint paragraph by paragraph. Usually, the answer admits the allegations of each paragraph, denies them, or states that the defendant lacks the information to assess the truth or falsity of the allegations (which has much the same effect as a denial).

The answer may also include an **affirmative defense** to the claim asserted in the complaint. An affirmative defense is a rule of law enabling the defendant to win the case even if all the allegations in the plaintiff's complaint are true and, by themselves, would entitle the plaintiff to recover. For example, suppose that the plaintiff bases her suit on a contract that she alleges the defendant has breached (broken). The defendant's answer may admit or deny the existence of the contract or the assertion that the defendant breached it. In addition, the answer may present facts that, if proven, would show that the defendant has an affirmative defense because the plaintiff's fraud induced the defendant to enter the contract.

In certain circumstances, the answer may also contain a **counterclaim.** A counterclaim is a *new* claim by the defendant arising from the matters stated in the complaint. Unlike an affirmative defense, it is not merely an attack on the plaintiff's claim, but is the *defendant's* attempt to obtain legal relief. In addition to using fraud as an affirmative defense to a plaintiff's contract claim, for example, a defendant might counterclaim for damages caused by that fraud.

The Reply   In some jurisdictions, the plaintiff is allowed or required to respond to an affirmative defense or a counterclaim by making a **reply.** The reply is the plaintiff's point-by-point response (a kind of answer) to the new matters raised in the affirmative defense or counterclaim. However, many jurisdictions do not allow a reply to an affirmative defense; instead, the defendant's new allegations are automatically denied. Usually, though, a plaintiff who wishes to contest a counterclaim must reply to it.

The Functions of the Pleadings   Traditionally, the main function of the pleadings has been to define and limit the questions to be decided at later stages of the case. Only those issues raised in the pleadings have been considered part of the case; points omitted from the pleadings have been excluded from further consideration; and few, if any, amendments to the pleadings have been permitted. Also, litigants have usually been bound to allegations admitted in the pleadings; only those allegations that have not been admitted have been regarded as in dispute between them. In addition, there have been many technical pleading rules whose violation could cause a party to lose a case before a decision on the merits.

Many jurisdictions retain some of these rules. Over time, however, the main purpose behind pleading rules has shifted from defining and limiting the questions to be resolved in the case to affording the parties notice of each other's claims. Accompanying this shift have been a greater tendency to decide cases on their merits and a more relaxed attitude toward technical defects in the pleadings. Amendments to the pleadings, for example, are far more available today than they were in the past. Also, courts sometimes grant such amendments to allow issues not raised in the pleadings to be considered at trial.

Motion to Dismiss

Sometimes, it is evident from the complaint or the pleadings that the plaintiff has no case. In such situations, it is wasteful for the suit to proceed further and it is useful to have a procedural device for disposing of it. This device has various names, but it is commonly called the **motion to dismiss.** This motion is often made after the plaintiff has filed his complaint. A similar motion allowed by some jurisdictions, the **motion for judgment on the pleadings,** normally occurs after the pleadings have been completed.

The motion to dismiss may be used for several purposes—for example, attacking inadequate service of process; or, as in the earlier *Knowles* case, attacking the court's jurisdiction. The most important type of motion to dismiss, however, is the motion to dismiss for failure to state a claim upon which relief can be granted, sometimes called the **demurrer.** This motion basically says "So what?" to the factual allegations in the complaint. It asserts that the plaintiff cannot recover even if all of these allegations are true, because there is no rule of law entitling him to win on those facts. Suppose that Potter sues Davis on the theory that Davis's bad breath is a form of "olfactory pollution" entitling Potter to recover damages. Potter's complaint describes Davis's breath and the distress it causes Potter in great detail. Even if all of Potter's factual allegations are true, Davis's motion to dismiss almost certainly will succeed. Thus, Davis will win the case, for there is no rule of law allowing a civil recovery for bad breath. If the defendant's motion to dismiss fails, however, the case proceeds to the steps that follow.

Discovery

Litigants sometimes lack the factual information to prove their cases when the suit begins. To assist them in preparing their arguments and to narrow and clarify the issues to be resolved at trial, all jurisdictions permit the parties to undertake extensive **discovery** of relevant information. The most common types of discovery are **depositions** (oral examinations of a party or a party's witness by the other party's attorney), **interrogatories** (written questions directed to a party, answered in writing, and signed under oath), **requests for documents and other evidence** (including examinations of the other party's files or records), **physical and mental examinations** (which are important in personal injury cases), and **requests for admissions** (one party's written demand that the other party agree to certain statements of fact or law). The permissible limits of discovery are set by the trial judge, whose rulings are controlled by the procedural law of the jurisdiction. In an effort to make civil litigation less of a battle of wits or a sporting event and more of a disinterested search for the truth, many jurisdictions have liberalized their discovery rules to give parties freer access to all relevant facts.

The applicable state or federal law of evidence determines whether or when discovery findings are admissible trial evidence. However, almost all jurisdictions allow some discovery findings to be employed at trial for certain purposes. Depositions, for instance, may sometimes be used as "paper testimony" from dead or distant witnesses, or to attack the credibility of a witness whose trial testimony differs from statements she made at the deposition.

Summary Judgment

The court's consideration of a motion for **summary judgment** might be described as a minitrial or a trial by affidavit. The summary judgment is a device for disposing of relatively clear cases without a trial. To prevail, the party moving for a summary judgment must show that: (1) there is no genuine issue of material (legally significant) fact, and (2) he is entitled to judgment as a matter of law. A summary judgment hearing differs from the judge's decision on a demurrer because it involves factual determinations. The evidence for such determinations includes the pleadings, discovery information, and affidavits (signed and sworn statements regarding matters of fact). The moving party tries to satisfy the first element of the test by using such evidence to convince the judge that there is no genuine question about any significant fact. If the moving party's arguments are persuasive, he must still meet the second element of the test by convincing the judge that, given the established facts, the applicable law directs that he win.

Either or both parties may move for a summary judgment. If the court rules in favor of either party, that party wins the case. If no party's motion for summary judgment is granted, the case proceeds to trial. The judge may also grant a partial summary judgment, which settles some issues in the case but leaves the others to be decided at trial.

The Pretrial Conference

Depending on the jurisdiction, a **pretrial conference** may be either mandatory or called at the discretion of the trial judge. At this conference, the judge meets informally with the attorneys for both litigants. The judge may attempt to get the attorneys to *stipulate*, or agree to, the resolution of certain issues to simplify the trial. He may also encourage them to get their clients to *settle* the case by coming to an agreement that eliminates the need for a trial. Both efforts are intended to help clear the increasingly congested calendars of most civil courts. If the case is not settled, the judge enters a pretrial order including all the attorneys' stipulations and other agreements. Ordinarily, the terms of this order bind the parties throughout the remainder of the case.

The Trial

Once the case has been through discovery and has survived any pretrial motions, it is set for trial. The trial may be before a judge alone, in which case the judge makes separate findings of fact and law before issuing the court's judgment. But if the right to a jury trial exists and either party demands one, the jury handles the fact-finding function, with the resolution of legal questions still entrusted to the judge.[12] At a pretrial jury screening process known as *voir dire*, most jurisdictions: (1) allow biased potential jurors to be removed *for cause*, and (2) give the attorney for each party a certain number of *peremptory challenges* that allow him to remove potential jurors without *any* cause.

The Basic Scenario   The usual trial scenario is much the same whether the trial is before a judge alone or before both a judge and a jury. The attorneys for the plaintiff and the defendant typically make opening statements explaining what they intend to prove. After this, the plaintiff's witnesses and other evidence are introduced and these witnesses are cross-examined by the defendant's attorney. This may be followed by the plaintiff's re-direct examination of his witnesses, and perhaps by the defendant's re-cross-examination of those same witnesses. Then, using the same procedures, the defendant's evidence is presented. Throughout each side's presentation, the opposing attorney may object to the admission of certain evidence. Using the law of evidence, the judge then decides whether the challenged proof is admissible. After the plaintiff and defendant have completed their initial presentations of evidence, each is allowed to offer evidence rebutting the other's evidence. Once all of the evidence has been presented, each attorney makes a closing argument summarizing her position. In nonjury trials, the judge then makes findings of fact and law, renders judgment, and states the relief to which the plaintiff is entitled if the plaintiff is victorious.

Jury Trials   Jury trials differ in some respects from trials before the judge alone. At the end of a jury trial, the judge issues a *charge* or *instruction* to the jury. The charge sets out the rules of law applicable to the case. The judge may also summarize the evidence for the jury. Then, the jury is supposed to make the necessary factual determinations, apply the law to these, and arrive at a **verdict** on which the court's **judgment** is based.

The most common verdict is the **general verdict,** which only requires that the jury declare which party wins and the relief (if any) to be awarded. The general verdict gives the jury freedom to ignore the judge's charge and follow its own inclinations, for the jury need not state its factual findings or its application of the law to those findings. Defenders of the general verdict argue that it allows the jury to soften the law's rigors by bringing common sense and community values to bear on the case. But it also weakens the rule of law and allows juries to commit injustices. The **special verdict** is one response to this problem. Here, the jury only makes specific findings of fact, and the judge then applies the law to these findings. The decision whether to utilize a special verdict usually is within the trial judge's discretion.

Directed Verdict   The freedom that the general verdict gives the jury is a two-edged sword, and the American legal system is ambivalent about the jury. While

---

[12] The rules governing availability of a jury trial are largely beyond the scope of this text. The U.S. Constitution guarantees a jury trial in federal court suits "at common law" whose amount exceeds $20, and most of the states have similar constitutional provisions. Also, Congress and the state legislatures may allow jury trials in a variety of other cases.

granting the jury great power, the system also establishes devices for limiting that power. One of these devices, the motion for a **directed verdict,** basically takes the case away from the jury and gives a judgment to one party before the jury gets a chance to decide. The motion can be made by either party, and it usually occurs after the other (nonmoving) party has presented his evidence. The moving party basically asserts that, even when read most favorably to the other party, the evidence leads to only one result and need not be considered by the jury. Courts differ on the test governing a motion for a directed verdict: some deny the motion if there is *any* evidence favoring the nonmoving party, while others deny the motion only if there is *substantial* evidence favoring the nonmoving party. Under the former test, at least, it is difficult for the moving party to succeed.

Judgment Notwithstanding the Verdict   On occasion, the case is taken away from the jury and judgment is entered for a party even *after* the jury has reached a verdict *against* that party. The device for doing so is the motion for **judgment notwithstanding the verdict** (also known as the judgment *non obstante veredicto* or the judgment n.o.v.). Some jurisdictions require that, in order to make a motion for judgment n.o.v., the moving party have earlier made a motion for a directed verdict. In any event, the standard used to decide the motion for judgment n.o.v. usually is the same standard that the jurisdiction uses to decide the motion for a directed verdict. For this reason, and because the moving party essentially is asking the court to overturn a jury verdict, litigants may face difficulties when they move for judgment notwithstanding the verdict.

Motion for New Trial   In a wide range of situations that vary among jurisdictions, the losing party can successfully move for a new trial. Acceptable reasons for granting a new trial include errors by the judge during the trial, jury or attorney misconduct, new evidence, or an award of excessive damages to the plaintiff.

CONCEPT REVIEW

THE MAJOR CIVIL MOTIONS COMPARED

Motion	When Typically Made	By Whom Typically Made	Typical Test	Typical Effect if Successful
To Dismiss or for Judgment on the Pleadings	After complaint or pleadings	Defendant	Assuming the facts in the complaint are true, can plaintiff win as a matter of law?	Defendant wins case
For Summary Judgment	Varies; often after discovery	Either party	No genuine issue of material fact and moving party entitled to judgment as a matter of law	Moving party wins case; partial summary judgment also possible
For Directed Verdict	After other party has presented evidence at trial	Either party	Two versions. Moving party loses if: (1) *any* evidence favoring nonmoving party; or (2) *substantial* evidence favoring nonmoving party	Moving party wins case
For Judgment Notwithstanding Verdict	After adverse jury verdict	Losing party	Same test jurisdiction uses for directed verdict	Moving party wins case
For New Trial	After adverse judgment or jury verdict	Losing party	Wide range of possible grounds	New trial ordered

Appeal

As you have seen, appellate courts generally consider only alleged errors of law made by the trial court. As Figure 5 indicated earlier in the chapter, among the matters ordinarily considered "legal" and thus appealable are the trial judge's decisions on a motion to dismiss or a motion for judgment on the pleadings, the scope of discovery, a motion for summary judgment, a motion for a directed verdict, a motion for judgment notwithstanding the verdict, and a motion for a new trial. Other matters typically considered appealable include any trial court rulings on service of process, its rulings on the admission of evidence at trial, its legal findings in a nonjury trial, its instruction to the jury in a jury trial, and the damages or other relief awarded. Of course, appellate court decisions on all these matters may be considered by a higher appellate court, if one exists.

Appellate courts may, among other things, *affirm* the trial court's decision, *reverse* it, or affirm one part of the decision and reverse another part. As Figure 5 also suggested, one of three things ordinarily results from the appellate courts' disposition of the appeal: (1) the plaintiff wins the case, (2) the defendant wins the case, or (3) if the case is reversed in whole or in part, it is *remanded* (returned) to the trial court for proceedings not inconsistent with the appellate decision. Which of these results occurs generally depends on the trial court's decision, the party who appealed it, and the way the appellate courts resolved it. For example, if the plaintiff appeals a trial court decision granting the defendant's motion to dismiss and the appellate court(s) affirm that decision, the plaintiff loses. Where an appellate court reverses a trial court verdict and judgment in the defendant's favor, the plaintiff might win outright, or the case might be returned to the trial court for further proceedings not inconsistent with the appellate decision.

Enforcing a Judgment

In this text, you occasionally will see cases where someone was not sued even though he appeared to be liable to the plaintiff, and where another party was sued instead. One possible explanation is that the first party was "judgment-proof": so lacking in assets as to make a civil suit for damages impractical. In other words, a potential defendant's financial condition is an important factor affecting the plaintiff's decision whether or not to sue him. And it also affects a winning plaintiff's ability to actually recover whatever damages she has been awarded.

When the defendant fails to pay as required after losing a civil suit, the winning plaintiff must take steps to enforce the judgment. Ordinarily, the plaintiff obtains a *writ of execution* enabling the sheriff to seize designated property of the defendant and sell it at a judicial sale to satisfy the judgment. A judgment winner may also use a procedure known as *garnishment* to seize property, money, or wages of the defendant that are in the hands of a third party. If the property needed to satisfy the judgment is located in another state, the plaintiff must use the execution or garnishment procedures established by that state. Under the U.S. Constitution, the second state is required to give "full faith and credit" to the judgment of the state where the plaintiff originally sued. Where the court has awarded an equitable remedy such as an injunction, on the other hand, the defendant may be found in contempt of court and subjected to a fine or imprisonment if he fails to obey the court's order.

Class Actions

The preceding review of the stages of a civil case has proceeded as if the plaintiff and the defendant each were a single party. Actually, several plaintiffs and/or defendants can be parties to one lawsuit. Also, each jurisdiction has procedural rules stating when other parties can be *joined* to a suit that begins without them.

One special type of multiparty suit, the **class action,** allows one or more persons to sue on behalf of themselves and all others who have suffered similar harm from substantially the same wrong. Class action suits by, for example, consumers, environmentalists, women, and minorities are now common events. The usual justifications for the class action are that: (1) it allows legal wrongs causing losses to a large number of widely dispersed parties to be fully compensated, and (2) it promotes economy of judicial effort by combining many similar claims into one suit.

The requirements for a class action vary among jurisdictions. The issues addressed by class action statutes include the following: whether there are questions of law and fact common to all members of the alleged class, whether the class is small enough to allow all of its members to join the case as parties rather than use a class action, and whether the plaintiff(s) and their attorney(s) can competently represent the class without conflicts of interest or other forms of unfairness. To protect the individual class member's right to be heard, some jurisdictions have required that unnamed or absent class members be given notice of the suit if this is reasonably possible. The damages awarded in a successful class action are usually apportioned among the entire class. Establishing the total recovery and distributing it to the class, however, pose problems when the class is large, the class members' injuries are indefinite, or some members cannot be identified.

ALTERNATIVE DISPUTE RESOLUTION

Courts are not the only mechanisms for settling civil disputes. Nor are they always the best means of doing so. As the preceding discussion of civil procedure suggests, resolving private disputes through the courts can be a cumbersome, lengthy, and expensive process for litigants. With the advent of a litigious society and the increasing caseloads and delays it has produced, resolving disputes in this fashion also imposes ever-greater *social* costs. For these reasons and others to be discussed later, the various forms of **alternative dispute resolution** (ADR) have assumed increasing importance in recent years.

Some Common Forms of ADR

Not everyone agrees on how to define the term alternative dispute resolution, and new ADR devices are continually emerging. Still, the following methods of dispute resolution can be regarded as forms of ADR.

Settlement   While the settlement of a civil suit is not everyone's idea of an alternative dispute resolution mechanism, it is a very important means of avoiding protracted litigation, one that often represents a sensible compromise for the parties. Many cases settle at some stage in the civil proceedings described previously. The typical settlement agreement is a contract whereby the defendant agrees to pay the plaintiff a certain sum of money, in exchange for the plaintiff's promise to release the defendant from future liability on the claims alleged in his suit.

Arbitration   Arbitration is the submission of a dispute to a nonjudicial third party (the *arbitrator*) who is normally empowered to issue a binding decision on that dispute. Arbitration typically results from the parties' agreement to arbitrate their disputes, but sometimes it is compelled by statute. Such an agreement is usually made before the dispute arises (most often through an *arbitration clause* in a contract), but it can occur after the dispute begins. Today, arbitration is used in a wide variety of situations, including disputes arising under commercial contracts and labor contracts. The arbitrator need not be a lawyer; often, she is a professional who may be expert in the subject matter of the dispute.

Arbitration proceedings normally are less formal than court proceedings, and the arbitrator ordinarily is not required to follow the rules of evidence and procedure governing courts. Also, arbitrators have some freedom to ignore rules of substantive law that would bind a court. The arbitrator's decision, called an *award*, is filed with a court, which will enforce it if necessary. The losing party may object to the arbitrator's award, but the grounds for getting a court to overturn such an award are limited. One example is fraud or other misconduct by the arbitrator.

Court-Annexed Arbitration   This specific form of arbitration does not result from a private agreement. Rather, it is ordered by a judge after a lawsuit has been filed. In jurisdictions that allow court-annexed arbitration, the judge's decision to order it often depends on the subject matter of the dispute and the amount of money at issue. The losing party in a court-annexed arbitration still has the right to a regular trial.

Mediation   In mediation, a neutral third party called the *mediator* helps the parties reach an agreeable, cooperative resolution of their dispute by facilitating communication between them, clarifying their areas of agreement and disagreement, helping them to see each other's viewpoints, suggesting settlement options, and so forth. Unlike arbitrators, mediators cannot make a decision that binds the parties. Mediation most often occurs by agreement of the parties after a dispute has arisen. It is used in a wide variety of situations.

Med/Arb   In this hybrid of mediation and arbitration, the third party first acts as a mediator, and all issues not resolved through mediation are then subjected to binding arbitration. Here, the mediator and the arbitrator may or may not be the same person.

Other ADR Devices   Other ADR methods include: (1) the *minitrial* (an informal, abbreviated, private "trial" before a panel of independent experts and/or an executive from each party, which usually is employed after the initiation of a lawsuit and whose aim is to promote a settlement); (2) the *summary jury trial* (an abbreviated, nonpublic mock jury trial that does not bind the parties unless they so stipulate, and that aims to promote settlement by giving them an idea how they would fare before a real jury); and (3) *private panels* instituted by an industry or an organization to handle claims of certain kinds (e.g., the Better Business Bureau). Also, some formally legal processes are sometimes referred to as ADR devices; examples include small claims courts and the administrative procedures for handling matters such as claims for veterans' benefits or social security benefits.

The Pros and Cons of ADR

Taken collectively, the various forms of ADR have many advantages over litigation before a court. These advantages include:

1. *Quicker resolution of disputes.* This is due mainly to the relative informality of many ADR proceedings.

2. *Lower costs in time, money, and aggravation for the parties.* Again, these benefits flow mainly from the relative informality and speed of many ADR procedures.

3. *Reduced strains on an overloaded court system.*

4. *The possible availability of expert decision makers.* As noted earlier, for example, arbitrators may possess special expertise in the subject matter of the disputes they handle.

5. *Flexibility and consensus-building.* Some ADR methods (e.g., mediation) may help avoid the excessively adversarial climate and tendency toward either-or decisions that characterize formal litigation. Thus, they can promote consensus, compromise solutions by the parties themselves.

6. *Relative privacy.* In general, firms that settle their disputes through ADR rather than litigating them have less need to "air their dirty linen" in public.

As you might suspect, however, ADR also has a number of possible disadvantages. They include:

1. *A tendency to undermine the rule of law.* At its best, the civil law states general norms that are good in themselves, are backed by a wide social consensus, and apply to all the private disputes they cover. ADR decisions, on the other hand, are sometimes ad hoc affairs in which rules of substantive law play little role and precedent even less. Thus, the widespread use of ADR tends to undermine the *generality* and *uniformity* associated with the rule of law.

2. *A diminished role for courts in stating the norms that govern private disputes.* Arbitrators, for example, are often free to downplay the applicable rules of substantive law in making their decisions, which means that court-imposed norms may not govern such decisions. In the American system, however, courts generally are regarded as more legitimate, authoritative, and capable standard setters than private actors like arbitrators.

3. *Inaccurate or biased decisionmaking processes.* One reason for the complexity of the rules of civil procedure and evidence is that they try to give each party the utmost in procedural protection and to ensure that factual determinations are as accurate as possible. The relatively relaxed procedures and evidentiary rules—not to mention the occasional absence of lawyers—in some ADR proceedings may mean that these ends are less likely to be served under ADR.

4. *Second-class justice for the relatively powerless in their disputes with the powerful.* Sometimes, agreements to submit disputes to alternative dispute resolution are buried in complex standard-form contracts drafted by a party with superior size, knowledge, and business sophistication, and are unknowingly agreed to by less knowledgeable parties. Sometimes, too, such clauses compel ADR proceedings before decisionmakers who may be biased in favor of the stronger party.

ETHICAL AND PUBLIC POLICY CONCERNS

1. As you might expect, the preceding arguments against ADR have often come from the legal profession. Are these self-serving arguments? Who stands to lose money and influence if ADR becomes more popular? Assuming that these arguments are self-serving, is this fact alone enough to rebut them?

2. The *Knowles* case presented earlier in this chapter used a style of legal reasoning different from the simple deductive model presented in the Nature of Law chapter. This style might be called *factor-based balancing*, and you will see it again from time to time in this text. Courts using this style of reasoning typically consider several factors when deciding. They assess a particular result in light of each factor, trying to determine whether that result advances or frustrates the values embodied in each factor. Then, they try to assess the overall desirability of that result by weighing its positive and negative effects against each other and determining whether the result has a positive or negative effect on balance. Such determinations naturally vary depending on the facts of the case. In *Knowles*, the decision was easy, because almost all the factors the court considered pulled in the same direction.

What is good about this kind of legal decisionmaking? What is bad about it?

3. Recent debates in the business ethics literature have sometimes stressed the difference between *utilitarian* ethical theories and *deontological rights-based* ethical theories. Utilitarian theories generally argue that we should strive to maximize aggregate satisfaction, and they tend to approve measures that disadvantage particular individuals so long as those measures actually produce maximum *total* satisfaction. Such theories occasionally use social wealth maximization as a rough measure of satisfaction. Deontological rights-based theories generally urge that some rights are so important that they can only be overridden by certain other rights, and *not* by maximum aggregate utility.

Speaking very generally, into which category would many foes of ADR fit? Assume that these people oppose ADR because they feel that due to the looseness and sloppiness of its procedures, it inevitably causes injustices to individuals—injustices that could be avoided were normal court procedures used. Although the widespread use of such procedures costs more money than ADR, they assert, this is of no consequence because basic issues of *justice* are involved.

Speaking very generally, into which category would many proponents of ADR fit? Assume that these people stress the social and economic costs created by the court system and argue that the widespread use of ADR would free money and resources for other purposes, thus making society wealthier. This increase in wealth, they would further contend, easily outweighs the personal suffering caused by whatever injustices ADR permits.

SUMMARY

One of the most important functions performed by the American legal system is the resolution of private disputes. Courts perform this function by deciding civil lawsuits. However, certain judicially created doctrines limit the courts to the resolution of genuine controversies between real parties with tangible opposing interests.

The typical state court system contains the following courts: (1) courts of limited jurisdiction such as justice of the peace courts and municipal courts, (2) trial courts (which resolve questions of law and fact), (3) intermediate appellate courts (which handle appeals from the trial courts' rulings on questions of law), and (4) the supreme court (which handles appeals from lower courts and is the state's highest appellate court). For a state trial court to decide a case, it must have: (1) subject-matter jurisdiction (competence to handle the type of case before it), and (2) *either* in personam jurisdiction (based on the residence, location, or activities of the defendant) *or* some form of in rem jurisdiction (based on the presence of property within the state).

The most important federal courts are: (1) district courts (which resemble state trial courts), (2) courts of appeals (which resemble state intermediate appellate courts), and (3) the U.S. Supreme Court (whose main function is to handle appeals from the lower federal courts and the state supreme courts). The most important bases of district court jurisdiction are *federal question* jurisdiction (requiring an issue of federal law in the plaintiff's case) and *diversity jurisdiction* (requiring that the plaintiff and defendant be citizens of different states and that the amount in controversy exceed $50,000). There are also various specialized federal courts.

The typical procedural steps involved in a civil case before a trial court or a federal district court are: (1) the summons (whose function is to notify the defendant of the suit), (2) the complaint (which states the plaintiff's case), (3) the answer (which responds point-by-point to the complaint), (4) the reply (which "answers" an affirmative defense or a counterclaim in the answer), (5) the motions to dismiss or for judgment on the pleadings (devices for disposing of the case on the basis of the complaint or the pleadings), (6) discovery (a process of pretrial information-gathering), (7) the summary judgment (another device for disposing of the case prior to trial), (8) the pretrial conference, (9) the trial itself, (10) the directed verdict (a device for taking the case away from the jury before it decides), (11) the judgment notwithstanding the verdict (similar to a directed verdict but used after the jury has decided), (12) the motion for a new trial, (13) the trial court's verdict and judgment, (14) the possible appeal of decisions made by the trial court, and (15) the processes by which a winning plaintiff enforces his judgment. The class action, a procedural device of some importance in recent years, permits the consolidation of many similar claims into one suit, thus enabling a plaintiff to represent a larger group.

The courts are not the only means for resolving civil matters, and in recent years the various forms of alternative dispute resolution have become an increasingly important complement to the court system. These include settlement of a court case, arbitration, court-annexed arbitration, mediation, med/arb, and others. ADR processes often offer parties quicker, cheaper, and more flexible resolution of their disputes than normal judicial procedures. But they also suffer from a number of disadvantages.

PROBLEM CASES

✓ **1.** Marco DeFunis was denied admission to the University of Washington Law School. He sued the law school under the Equal Protection Clause of the U.S. Constitution, alleging that the school preferred minority applicants over better qualified white applicants. While DeFunis's suit was making its way through the Washington state courts, he enrolled at another law school. By the time the case reached the U.S. Supreme Court, DeFunis was about to graduate. The Supreme Court dismissed DeFunis's appeal without deciding his equal protection claims. Why did it decide against DeFunis? Assume that DeFunis's claim included a request that he be admitted to the University of Washington Law School.

2. Peters sues Davis. At trial, Peters's lawyer attempts to introduce certain evidence to help make his case. Davis's attorney objects, and the trial judge refuses to allow the evidence to be admitted. Peters eventually loses the case at the trial court level. He appeals, his attorney arguing that the trial judge's decision not to admit the evidence was erroneous. Davis's attorney argues that the appellate court cannot consider this question, because appellate courts only review errors of *law* (not fact) at the trial court level. Is Davis's attorney correct? Why or why not?

3. Phillips sues Dilks for $500,000 in a state small claims court set up to handle cases where the amount in controversy does not exceed $5,000. The court clearly does not have jurisdiction over the case. What *kind* of jurisdiction is absent here?

✓ **4.** Dial, a resident of Indiana, vandalizes a parked car in Columbus, Ohio. This action results in harm to the car, and also prevents its owner from using the car for a period of time. In the meantime, Dial has fled to Indiana and remains there. The owner, an Ohio resident, plans to sue Dial for trespass to personal property, a tort described in the Intentional Torts chapter. He claims $5,000 in damages, and wants to sue either in an Ohio trial court or in a federal district court. Do each of these courts have jurisdiction over the case? Why or why not? Assume for purposes of this problem that: (a) subject-matter jurisdiction is present, (b) Dial has had no other contacts with the state of Ohio, and (c) Ohio has a long-arm statute with all the features described in this chapter.

5. State *two* differences between the motion to dismiss for failure to state a claim upon which relief can be granted (or demurrer) and the motion for summary judgment.

6. In a suit by Pierce against Dodge, the jury has rendered a verdict in favor of Dodge. Pierce and her attorney think that the evidence was overwhelmingly in Pierce's favor. They also have some reason to believe that the jury was bribed by someone connected with Dodge. What *two* motions can Pierce's attorney make at this point in an attempt to overturn the jury's verdict?

7. While driving to work one day, Dember runs over Pearson, causing him severe injuries. Pearson sues Dember in a state trial court. His complaint alleges that Dember's negligent driving caused his injuries. The law of the state declares that if the plaintiff's own negligence contributed to his injury, the defendant has a complete defense and the plaintiff cannot recover. Dember wants to argue that whether he was negligent or not, Pearson's own negligence helped cause his injuries and that Pearson therefore has no case. In order to be *sure* of his ability to raise this argument at trial, what should Dember's attorney do in response to Pearson's complaint?

8. What is the main difference between a motion for a directed verdict and a motion for judgment notwithstanding the verdict?

9. The state of Mississippi is planning to sue the state of Massachusetts. Mississippi's attorney general wants to sue in an appropriate federal district court. Do the federal district courts have jurisdiction over this case? If not, which federal court does have jurisdiction? You can assume that Mississippi's suit involves issues of federal law, and that the amount in controversy exceeds $50,000.

10. Jackson was born in Texas but has had absolutely no contact with that state for 20 years. Jackson's father dies, and a Texas court interprets his will so that Jackson receives none of his father's property, which is located in Texas. Assume that the court had jurisdiction to make this decision. What *kinds* of jurisdiction did it have?

11. Pike sues Dillon, alleging that his parked car was destroyed due to Dillon's negligent driving. After the pleadings and discovery have been completed, Pike's attorney concludes that the case is an obvious winner on both the facts and the law. What motion should the attorney make in an attempt to win the case without having to go to trial?

12. Does ADR really resolve disputes without any help from the courts? Give two examples of ADR processes that depend on courts for their operation or their effectiveness and state *how* they depend on the courts.

CHAPTER 3

BUSINESS AND THE CONSTITUTION

INTRODUCTION

As discussed in The Nature of Law chapter, constitutions serve two general functions. They set up the structure of government, allocating power among its various branches and subdivisions. Constitutions also prevent government from taking certain actions—in particular, actions that restrict individual rights. As the following overview of its provisions suggests, the U.S. Constitution performs both these functions.[1] *How* it performs these functions has definite political implications.

A Brief Overview of the U.S. Constitution

The U.S. Constitution embodies the principle of **separation of powers** by giving distinct powers to Congress, the president, and the federal courts.[2] Thus, Article I of the Constitution establishes a Congress composed of a Senate and a House of Representatives, gives Congress sole power to legislate at the federal level, and sets out rules for the passage of legislation. Also, Article I, section 8 states most of the specific ways Congress can

make law—its *legislative powers*. Three of these powers—Congress's commerce, tax, and spending powers—are discussed later in this chapter.

Article II of the Constitution places the *executive power* (the power to execute or enforce the laws passed by Congress) in the president. Section 2 of that article lists some other powers possessed by the president, including the powers to command the nation's armed forces and to make treaties. Article III gives the *judicial power* of the United States to the Supreme Court and the other federal courts later established by Congress. Article III also defines the scope of the federal judicial power—the kinds of cases the federal courts can decide.

In addition to establishing a separation of powers, Articles I, II, and III of the Constitution also create a system of **checks and balances** among Congress, the president, and the courts. For example, Article I, section 7 gives the president the power to veto legislation passed by Congress, and also allows Congress to override a veto by a two-thirds vote of each House. Article I, section 3 and Article II, section 4 provide that the president, the vice president, and other federal officials may be impeached by a two-thirds vote of the Senate. Article II, section 2 says that treaties made by the president must be approved by a two-thirds vote of the Senate. Article III, section 2 gives Congress some control over the Supreme Court's appellate jurisdiction.

---

[1] The full text of the U.S. Constitution is contained in Appendix A at the end of this book.

[2] The Administrative Agencies chapter discusses some separation of powers issues that pertain to administrative agencies.

The U.S. Constitution also recognizes the principle of **federalism** in the way it structures power relations between the federal government and the states. Article I, section 9 lists certain powers that Congress is not allowed to exercise. And the Tenth Amendment provides that those powers the Constitution neither gives to the federal government nor denies to the states are reserved to the states or the people.

Article VI, however, makes the Constitution, laws, and treaties of the United States supreme over state law. As you will see later in the chapter, this means that where the Constitution gives Congress the power to legislate, Article VI's principle of **federal supremacy** allows federal statutes to *preempt* inconsistent state laws. As also discussed later in this chapter, the U.S. Constitution puts specific limits on the states' law-making powers. One example is Article I, section 10's command that no state shall pass any law impairing the obligation of contracts. As noted immediately below, finally, most Bill of Rights provisions now apply to the states.

Article V sets out the procedures for amending the Constitution, procedures whose details are beyond the scope of this text. By now, the Constitution has been amended 26 times. The first 10 of these amendments comprise the Bill of Rights. Two of these rights, the First Amendment's guarantee of free speech and the Fifth Amendment's due process guarantee, receive some attention later in this chapter. Also discussed later is the Fifth Amendment's command that the government must provide just compensation when it takes private property for public use.

Although the individual rights contained in the first 10 amendments once applied to the federal government alone, most of them now apply to the states as well. As you will learn, this is due to their incorporation within the Due Process Clause of the Fourteenth Amendment, which applies to the states. Another important Fourteenth Amendment provision, its statement that the states cannot deny any person the equal protection of the laws, receives detailed attention later in this chapter.

The Evolution of the Constitution and the Role of the Supreme Court

According to the legal realists discussed in the chapter on the nature of law, understanding the law requires that one examine what public decisionmakers *actually do*. Using this approach, we discover a Constitution that differs from the written Constitution just described. For example, the actual powers of the president today far exceed anything you would imagine merely from reading Article II. As you will see shortly, moreover, Congress's authority under the commerce, tax, and spending powers now has few internal limits. As a result, the Tenth Amendment's reservation of certain powers to the states means little today.

Many of these changes were caused by the way one public decisionmaker—the U.S. Supreme Court—has interpreted the Constitution over time. Although some people apparently regard the Constitution as an unchanging Fundamental Law, many of its provisions have a different practical meaning than they had when first enacted. Thus, constitutional law is much more *evolving* than static.

There are many reasons for the Constitution's flexibility. For one thing, it is a relatively short document some of whose key provisions are vague. Open-ended phrases like "due process of law" and "equal protection of the laws," for instance, invite diverse interpretations. Also, the history surrounding the enactment of constitutional provisions sometimes is sketchy, confused, or contradictory. Perhaps the most important reason for the Constitution's flexibility, however, is the perceived need to adapt it to changing social conditions. According to an old saying, Supreme Court decisions follow the election returns. Thus, the Court's decisions sometimes reflect the social conditions in which it operates. This may well be what the general public really wants; many of the people who believe in an unchanging Constitution, for instance, might be unhappy if they had to live under one.

In theory, constitutional change can be accomplished through the formal amendment process, but the Founders made this process fairly difficult to use and amendments to the Constitution have been relatively infrequent. For better or worse, therefore, the Supreme Court has been the Constitution's main amender. The Court has been able to assume this role because it has the final authority to determine the Constitution's meaning. Under the power of **judicial review**, the Supreme Court (and other courts) can declare the actions of other governmental bodies unconstitutional. How the Supreme Court exercises this power depends on how it chooses to read the Constitution.

Because they can declare the actions of the other branches unconstitutional under standards that are partly of their own making, the Supreme Court and other courts have political power. This is particularly true of the Supreme Court, whose nine justices often are public policymakers. For this reason, the beliefs of the justices are quite important in determining how America

FIGURE 1   Enumerated Powers and Independent Checks

	Law Does Not Conflict with Any Independent Check	Law Conflicts with an Independent Check
Law Is within Congress's Enumerated Powers	Law is constitutional	Law is unconstitutional
Law Is Not within Congress's Enumerated Powers	Law is unconstitutional	Law is unconstitutional

is governed. This is why their nomination and confirmation often involve so much political controversy.

But even though the Constitution is sometimes what the Supreme Court says it is, the Court's power to shape the Constitution has limits. For one thing, the Constitution's language is not completely open-ended; indeed, some of its provisions are quite clear. Also, past constitutional decisions do bind courts to some degree. Moreover, the Supreme Court is dependent on the other branches of government—and ultimately on public belief in the justices' fidelity to the rule of law—to make its decisions effective. Thus, the justices may be wary of power struggles with other, more representative, government bodies like Congress. By freely declaring the actions of these bodies unconstitutional, they run the risk of eventually provoking such conflicts.

The Structure of This Chapter

This chapter examines certain constitutional provisions that are important to business; it does not discuss constitutional law in its entirety. These provisions all help define federal and state power to regulate the economy. One of the U.S. Constitution's major concerns is to limit government power, and it does so in two general ways. First, it restricts *federal* legislative power by listing the powers that Congress can exercise and limiting Congress to these **enumerated powers.** To be constitutional, in other words, federal legislation must be based on a power specifically stated in the Constitution. Second, the U.S. Constitution limits both *state and federal* power by placing certain **independent checks** in the path of each. In effect, the independent checks declare that even if Congress has an enumerated power to act in a particular area or a state constitution authorizes a state to act in a certain way, there still are certain protected spheres into which neither can reach.

At the federal level, therefore, a law must meet two general tests in order to be constitutional. It must be based on an enumerated power of Congress, and it must

not collide with any of the independent checks. As you will see, for example, Congress has the power to regulate commerce among the states. By itself, this power might allow Congress to pass legislation declaring that certain racial minorities cannot cross state lines to buy or sell goods. But such a law, although arguably based on an enumerated power, surely would be unconstitutional. The reason is that it conflicts with an independent check: the equal protection guarantee discussed later in this chapter.

Figure 1 shows how the enumerated powers doctrine and the independent checks limit Congress's regulatory authority. By now, however, the enumerated powers doctrine has lost most of its significance and the independent checks are the main limitations on congressional power. The main reason for the decline of the enumerated powers limitation is the perceived need for greater federal regulation of the economy that began late in the 19th century.

This chapter next discusses the most important state and federal powers to regulate economic matters. Next, the chapter examines certain independent checks that apply to both the federal government and the states. After this, it considers some independent checks affecting the states alone. The chapter concludes by treating a provision—the Takings Clause of the Fifth Amendment—that both recognizes a governmental power and limits its exercise.

STATE AND FEDERAL POWER TO REGULATE

State Regulatory Power

Although state constitutions may do so, the U.S. Constitution does not specifically list the powers state legislatures can exercise. As noted above, however, the U.S. Constitution does place certain independent checks in the path of state lawmaking. It also declares that certain powers (e.g., creating currency and taxing imports) can only be exercised by Congress. In many other areas, though, Congress and the state legislatures have *concurrent powers.* Within those areas, both can make law unless Congress preempts state regulation under the Supremacy Clause. A very important state legislative power that operates concurrently with many congressional powers is called the **police power.** The police power is a broad state power to regulate for the public health, safety, morals, and welfare.

Federal Regulatory Power

Article I, section 8 of the U.S. Constitution states a number of business-related areas in which Congress can legislate. For example, it empowers Congress to coin and borrow money, regulate commerce with foreign nations, establish uniform laws regarding bankruptcies, create post offices, and regulate copyrights and patents. For our purposes, however, the most important congressional powers contained in Article I, section 8 are the powers to regulate commerce among the states, to lay and collect taxes, and to spend for the general welfare. Because they are now read so broadly, these three powers are the main constitutional bases for the extensive federal regulation of business that exists today.

The Commerce Power Article I, section 8 states that "The Congress shall have Power . . . To regulate Commerce . . . among the several States." The original reason for giving Congress this power to regulate *interstate commerce* was to block the protectionist state restrictions on interstate trade that were common after the Revolution, and thus to nationalize economic life. This *Commerce Clause* has two major thrusts. First, as discussed later in this chapter, it is an independent check on state regulation that unduly restricts interstate commerce. Our present concern is the second aspect of the Commerce Clause: its role as a source of congressional regulatory power.

Congress's power under the Commerce Clause was of little concern for most of the 19th century. By today's standards, federal regulation of the economy was fairly infrequent and unintrusive during this period. With the wave of federal regulation that began late in the century, however, the Supreme Court became increasingly concerned with defining the limits of the commerce power. Since the late 1930s, it has abandoned almost all such limits while upholding quite extensive and intrusive federal laws regulating the economy. Today, the Commerce

Clause effectively is an all-purpose federal police power enabling Congress to regulate most activities within a state's borders (*intrastate* matters).

The literal language of the Commerce Clause simply gives Congress power to regulate *commerce* that occurs *among the states.* How, then, has the clause evolved into a broad federal power to regulate for the public health, safety, morals, and welfare, and to reach most intrastate matters while doing so? First, the Supreme Court has allowed Congress to control activities within the states by concluding that the power to regulate *interstate* commerce includes the power to reach *intrastate* activities that have some impact on commerce among the states. In the *Shreveport Rate Cases* (1914), for example, the Supreme Court upheld the Interstate Commerce Commission's regulation of railroad rates within Texas (an *intrastate* matter outside the literal language of the Commerce Clause) because these rates affected rail traffic between Texas and Louisiana (an *interstate* matter with in the clause's language). Originally, the Court limited Congress's regulatory power to intrastate activities that had a *direct* impact on interstate commerce, but this limitation has been abandoned.

The second way the Supreme Court expanded the reach of the Commerce Clause was to allow Congress to use it for noncommercial *police power* ends. In the late 19th and early 20th centuries, the Court did so by upholding federal legislation that restricted the interstate movement of disfavored people or commodities. For instance, Congress was allowed to attack sexual immorality, gambling, and food poisoning by limiting the interstate movement of prostitutes, lottery tickets, and impure food, respectively. Here, Congress was acting within the literal language of the Commerce Clause, but was using it for purposes different from its original purposes.

Eventually, these two expansions of the Commerce Clause—its extension to police matters and the affecting-commerce rationale—merged into one general doctrine. Now, Congress can regulate *intrastate police* matters that have some effect on interstate commerce. In 1964, for example, the Supreme Court upheld the application of the 1964 Civil Rights Act's "public accommodations" section to a family-owned restaurant in Birmingham, Alabama. It did so because the restaurant's racial discrimination affected interstate commerce by: (1) reducing the restaurant's business and limiting its purchases of out-of-state meat, and (2) restricting the ability of blacks to travel among the states.

As this example suggests, by now Congress can regulate intrastate activities even though they have relatively little impact on commerce among the states. In our highly interdependent society, almost all intrastate activities have *some* effect on interstate commerce. Thus, as the following *Wickard* case illustrates, few intrastate matters are outside the reach of the commerce power today.

WICKARD v. FILBURN

317 U.S. 111 (U.S. Sup. Ct. 1942)

Congress enacted the Agricultural Adjustment Act of 1938 to stabilize agricultural production and thus to give farmers reasonable minimum prices. The act empowered the secretary of agriculture to proclaim a yearly national acreage allotment for the coming wheat crop. This was apportioned among the states and their counties, and then among individual farms. Filburn was an Ohio farmer who raised a small acreage of winter wheat, some of which was sold but much of which was used on his farm. Filburn's permitted allotment for 1941 was 11.1 acres. However, he sowed and harvested 23 acres. For this, he was assessed a penalty of $117.11.

Filburn sued the secretary of agriculture (Wickard) for an injunction against enforcement of the penalty. A three-judge district court found in Filburn's favor, and the government appealed to the U.S. Supreme Court.

Jackson, Justice.   It is urged that under the Commerce Clause Congress does not possess the power it has in this instance sought to exercise. The question would merit little consideration, except that this Act extends federal regulation to production not intended in any part for commerce but wholly for consumption on the farm. Such activities are, Filburn urges, beyond the reach of congressional power under the Commerce Clause, since they are local in character, and their effects upon interstate commerce are at most "indirect."

For nearly a century, decisions of this Court dealt rarely with questions of what Congress might do under the Clause, and almost entirely with the permissibility of state activity which discriminated against or burdened interstate commerce. During this period there was perhaps little occasion for the affirmative exercise of the commerce power, and the influence of the clause on American life and law was a negative one, resulting almost wholly from its restraint upon the powers of the states. It was not until 1887, with the enactment of the Interstate Commerce Act, that the commerce power began to exert positive influence in American law and life. This was followed in 1890 by the Sherman Anti-Trust Act and, thereafter, by many others.

When it first dealt with this new legislation, the Court allowed but little scope to the power of Congress. However, other cases called forth broader interpretations of the Commerce Clause destined to supersede the earlier ones. It was soon demonstrated that the effects of many kinds of intrastate activity upon interstate commerce were such as to make them a proper subject of federal regulation. [Thus,] even if Filburn's activity be local, it may still be reached by Congress if it exerts a substantial economic effect on interstate commerce, and this irrespective of whether such effect is what might at some earlier time have been defined as "direct" or "indirect."

The effect of consumption of home-grown wheat on interstate commerce is due to the fact that it constitutes the most variable factor in the disappearance of the wheat crop. Consumption on the farm where grown appears to vary in an amount greater than 20 percent of average production. That Filburn's own contribution to the demand for wheat may be trivial by itself is not enough to remove him from the scope of federal regulation where, as here, his contribution, taken together with that of many others similarly situated, is far from trivial.

The power to regulate commerce includes the power to regulate the prices at which commodities in that commerce are dealt and practices affecting such prices. One of the primary purposes of the Act was to increase the market price of wheat, and to that end to limit the volume thereof that could affect the market. It can hardly be denied that a factor of such volume and variability as home-consumed wheat would have a substantial influence on price and market conditions. This may arise because such wheat overhangs the market and, if induced by rising prices, tends to flow into the market and check price increases. But if we assume that it is never marketed, it supplies a need of the man who grew it which would otherwise be reflected by purchases in the open market. Congress may properly have considered that wheat consumed on the farm where grown, if wholly outside the scheme of regulation, would have a substantial effect in defeating its purpose to stimulate trade therein at increased prices.

Judgment reversed in favor of Wickard.

The Taxing Power　Article I, section 8 of the Constitution also states that "The Congress shall have Power To lay and collect Taxes, Duties, Imposts and Excises." The main purpose behind this *taxing power* is to raise revenue for the federal government.[3] But the taxing power also can serve as a regulatory device. Because "the power to tax is the power to destroy," Congress can regulate by imposing a heavy tax on a disfavored activity. Although some regulatory taxes have been struck down, this has not occurred recently. Today, the reach of the taxing power, while poorly defined, is nonetheless very broad. Sometimes it is said that a regulatory tax is constitutional if its purpose could be furthered by one of Congress's *other* powers. Due to the broad scope of the commerce power, this may mean that the taxing power has few limits.

The Spending Power　If taxing power regulation uses a federal club, congressional *spending power* regulation employs a federal carrot. After stating the taxing power, Article I, section 8 gives Congress a broad ability to spend for the general welfare. By basing the receipt of federal money on the performance of certain conditions, Congress can use its spending power to advance specific regulatory ends. Conditional federal grants to the states, for instance, are common.

Over the past 50 years, congressional spending power regulation invariably has been upheld. Still, as the Supreme Court has recently announced, there are limits on

its use. First, an exercise of the spending power must serve *general* public purposes, and not particular interests. Second, when Congress conditions the receipt of federal money on certain conditions, it must do so unambiguously. Third, the condition must be reasonably related to the purpose behind the federal expenditure. For example, Congress probably cannot condition a state's receipt of federal highway money on the state's adoption of a one-house legislature. Finally, note that federal spending power regulation arguably is less intrusive than other forms of federal regulation because a state theoretically can avoid the condition by refusing federal money.

INDEPENDENT CHECKS ON THE FEDERAL GOVERNMENT AND THE STATES

Even if a regulation is within Congress's enumerated powers or a state's police power, it still is unconstitutional if it collides with one of the Constitution's *independent checks*. In examining the major independent checks affecting government regulation of the economy, we first discuss those checks that limit both the federal government and the states. The three most important such checks are familiar individual rights guarantees: freedom of speech, due process, and equal protection. Before discussing each of these guarantees, however, it is necessary to consider some preliminary matters.

Incorporation

The Fifth Amendment prevents the federal government from depriving any person "of life, liberty, or property,

---

[3] The Constitution imposes some restrictions on the types of taxes that may be used to raise revenue, but these restrictions are beyond the scope of this text.

FIGURE 2   Why Certain Individual Rights Guarantees Apply to Both the Federal Government and the States

Guarantee	Why Applicable to States	Why Applicable to Federal Government
Due Process	Text of Fourteenth Amendment	Text of Fifth Amendment
First Amendment	Incorporation within Fourteenth Amendment	Text of First Amendment
Equal Protection	Text of Fourteenth Amendment	Incorporation within Fifth Amendment

without due process of law," and the Fourteenth Amendment does the same to the states. The First Amendment, however, applies only to the federal government. And the Fourteenth Amendment merely says that no *state* shall "deny to any person . . . the equal protection of the laws." Thus, while due process clearly applies to both the federal government and the states, the First Amendment and the Equal Protection Clause seem to have a more limited reach. But the First Amendment's free speech guarantee has been included within the "liberty" protected by Fourteenth Amendment due process, and thus made applicable to the states. This is part of the process of *incorporation* by which almost all Bill of Rights provisions now apply to the states. The Fourteenth Amendment's Equal Protection Clause, on the other hand, has been made applicable to the federal government by incorporating it within the Fifth Amendment's due process guarantee. Figure 2 summarizes all these points.

Government Action

People often talk as if the Constitution protects them against all individuals or groups who try to restrict personal rights. However, most of the Constitution's individual rights provisions only protect people against the actions of *governmental* bodies, state and federal.[4] *Private* behavior that denies individual rights, while perhaps forbidden by statute, is not supposed to be a constitutional matter. This **government action** or **state action** requirement forces courts to distinguish between governmental behavior and private behavior. Making this distinction has presented immense problems.

---

[4] However, the Thirteenth Amendment, which bans slavery and involuntary servitude throughout the United States, does not have a state action requirement. Also, some *state* constitutions have individual rights provisions that lack a state action requirement.

Before World War II, state action determinations usually were easy because only formal organs of government such as legislatures, administrative agencies, municipalities, courts, prosecutors, and state universities were deemed state actors. But after World War II, the range of activities considered to be government action increased considerably, and all sorts of traditionally private behavior was subjected to individual rights limitations. In *Marsh v. Alabama* (1946), for example, the Supreme Court treated a privately owned company town's restriction of free expression as government action under the *public function* theory because the town was like a normal municipality in most respects. Also, in *Shelley v. Kraemer* (1948), the Supreme Court held that state court enforcement of a private agreement among white homeowners not to sell their homes to blacks was unconstitutional state action under the Equal Protection Clause. Later, in *Burton v. Wilmington Parking Authority* (1961), the Court concluded that racial discrimination by a privately owned restaurant located in a state-owned and state-operated parking garage was unconstitutional state action, in part because the garage and the restaurant were intertwined in a mutually beneficial "symbiotic" relationship. Among the other factors leading courts to find state action during the 1960s and 1970s were extensive government regulation of private activity and government financial aid to a private actor.

Due mainly to the changed composition of the Supreme Court, however, the reach of state action was limited considerably in the 1970s and 1980s. Now, the Court usually treats private behavior as state action only when a regular unit of government is directly *responsible* for the challenged private behavior because it has coerced or encouraged such behavior. Also, the public function doctrine has been limited to situations where a private entity exercises powers that have *traditionally* been *exclusively* reserved to the state; private police protection is a possible example. In addition, government regulation and government funding now are relatively unimportant factors in state action determinations. The following *SFAA* case illustrates the restricted view of state action that prevails today. Despite the Supreme Court's state action cutback, however, the doctrine probably has not returned to its narrow pre–World War II definition, and much uncertainty remains in this area.

SAN FRANCISCO ARTS & ATHLETICS, INC. v. UNITED STATES OLYMPIC COMMITTEE

483 U.S. 522 (U.S. Sup. Ct. 1987)

San Francisco Arts & Athletics, Inc. (SFAA) actively promoted the "Gay Olympic Games" to be held in San Francisco during the latter part of 1982. As part of its promotional efforts, SFAA sought to sell T-shirts, buttons, bumper stickers, and other items bearing the title "Gay Olympic Games."

The United States Olympic Committee (USOC) is a federally chartered corporation. Under the Amateur Sports Act, it has broad powers to handle U.S. participation in international athletic competition and to promote amateur athletics within this country. In August of 1982, the USOC sued SFAA for its promotional activities on behalf of the Gay Olympic Games. It did so under a federal statute giving the USOC near-exclusive rights in the commercial and promotional use of the term "Olympic." A federal district court granted the USOC summary judgment and a permanent injunction against SFAA's use of the term "Olympic," and the court of appeals affirmed. One issue in the case was the SFAA's claim that the USOC had violated the equal protection component of Fifth Amendment due process because it discriminated in its enforcement of the statute. The court of appeals, however, ruled that no government action was present. SFAA appealed to the U.S. Supreme Court.

Powell, Justice.   The fundamental inquiry is whether the USOC is a governmental actor to whom the prohibitions of the Constitution apply. The USOC is a private corporation established under federal law. Congress granted the USOC a corporate charter, imposed certain requirements on the USOC, and provided for some USOC funding through exclusive use of USOC words and symbols and through direct grants.

The fact that Congress granted it a corporate charter does not render the USOC a government agent. All corporations act under charters granted by a government. They do not thereby lose their essentially private character. Even extensive regulation by the government does not transform the actions of the regulated entity into those of the government. Moreover, the intent on the part of Congress to help the USOC obtain funding does not change the analysis. The government may subsidize private entities without assuming constitutional responsibility for their actions.

The Court also has found action to be governmental action when the challenged entity performs functions that have been traditionally the exclusive prerogative of the government. Certainly the activities performed by the USOC serve a national interest. [But] the fact that a private entity serves the public does not make its acts governmental action. The Amateur Sports Act merely authorized the USOC to coordinate activities that always have been performed by private entities. Neither the conduct nor the coordination of amateur sports has been a traditional government function.

Most fundamentally, this Court has held that a government normally can be held responsible for a private decision only when it has exercised coercive power or has provided such significant encouragement, either overt or covert, that the choice must be deemed to be that of the government. The USOC's choice of how to enforce its exclusive right to use the word "Olympic" simply is not a governmental decision. There is no evidence that the federal government coerced or encouraged the USOC in the exercise of its right. At most, the federal government, by failing to supervise the USOC's use of its rights, exercised mere approval or acquiesence in the initiatives of the USOC. This is not enough to make the USOC's actions those of the government.

Because the USOC is not a governmental actor, SFAA's claim that the USOC has enforced its rights in a discriminatory manner must fail.

Court of appeals decision in favor of the USOC affirmed.

Means-Ends Tests

Throughout the remainder of this chapter, you will see tests of constitutionality that are confusing at first glance. One example is the well-established test for determining whether laws that discriminate on the basis of sex violate the Equal Protection Clause. This test says that to be constitutional, such laws must be substantially related to the achievement of an important governmental purpose. What does this language mean, and what are courts doing when they use it? The Equal Protection Clause does not contain such language. Instead, it simply states that "No State shall . . . deny to any person . . . the equal protection of the laws."

The sex discrimination test just stated is a *means-ends* test. Courts create such tests because no constitutional right is absolute; therefore, judges must weigh individual rights against the social purposes served by laws that restrict those rights. In other words, means-ends tests determine how courts strike the *balance* between individual rights and the social needs that may justify their suppression. The "ends" component of a means-ends test specifies how *significant* a social purpose must be in order to justify the restriction of a right. The "means" component states how *effectively* the challenged law must promote that purpose in order to be constitutional. In our sex discrimination test, for example, the challenged law must serve an "important" government purpose (the significance of the end) and must be "substantially" related to the achievement of that purpose (the effectiveness of the means).

Because some constitutional rights are deemed more important than others, courts use tougher tests of constitutionality in such cases and more lenient tests in other situations. Sometimes these tests are wordy, complex, and difficult. Throughout the remainder of this chapter, therefore, we sometimes simplify by employing three general kinds of means-ends tests:

1. *The rational basis test.* This is a very relaxed test of constitutionality that challenged laws usually pass with ease. A typical formulation of the rational basis test might say that government action need only have a *reasonable* relation to the achievement of a *legitimate* government purpose in order to be constitutional.

2. *Intermediate scrutiny.* This comes in many forms; the sex discrimination test we have been discussing is an example. To repeat, this test says that the challenged law must be *substantially* related to the achievement of an *important* government purpose.

3. *Full strict scrutiny.* Here, the court might say that the challenged law must be *necessary* to the fulfillment of a *compelling* government purpose. This is a rigorous test of constitutionality, and government action subjected to full strict scrutiny is almost always struck down.

Business and the First Amendment

Introduction The First Amendment says that "Congress shall make no law . . . abridging the freedom of speech." Despite its language ("*no* law"), the First Amendment has not been read as prohibiting every law that restricts speech. As Justice Oliver Wendell Holmes once remarked, the First Amendment does not protect someone who falsely shouts "Fire!" in a crowded theater. But while the First Amendment's guarantee of free speech is not absolute, government action restricting speech usually receives very strict judicial scrutiny. The justifications for this high level of protection vary, but perhaps the most important is the "marketplace" rationale. In this view, the free competition of ideas is the surest means of attaining truth and the marketplace of ideas best serves this end when restrictions on speech are kept to a minimum and all viewpoints can be considered.

This chapter does not consider most of the situations in which the First Amendment's free speech guarantee has been applied during the 20th century. Nor does it examine *corporate political speech*, which generally receives full First Amendment protection. Instead, we discuss one First Amendment issue of considerable concern to business—the government's power to regulate so-called *commercial speech*. In this area, the marketplace rationale for free speech figures prominently.

Commercial Speech   As the following *Bolger* case illustrates, the line between political speech and commercial speech is unclear. In general, though, commercial speech is expression proposing a commercial transaction; commercial advertising is the most common example. In 1942, the Supreme Court ruled that commercial speech is outside the First Amendment's protection, but the Court reversed its position during the 1970s. Now, restrictions on commercial speech receive an *intermediate* level of means-ends scrutiny that is less rigorous than the *full* strict scrutiny given laws that restrict corporate *political* speech. *Bolger* states the actual test, which is fairly complicated. However, some recent cases suggest that the Supreme Court is applying that test in a lenient fashion and is becoming more tolerant of laws restricting

commercial speech. In any event, the intermediate test stated in *Bolger* does not apply to commercial speech that is false, deceptive, or misleading, or that is related to illegal behavior. These forms of expression can be freely regulated.

The usual justification for protecting commercial speech is to promote informed consumer choice by removing barriers to the flow of commercial information. The Supreme Court's decisions striking down state restrictions on advertising by groups such as pharmacists and lawyers, restrictions that arguably promoted price-fixing within these professions, seem consistent with this marketplace rationale. However, the commercial speech doctrine could also benefit business interests if, for instance, government regulators ever decide to mount a serious attack on advertising that is not false or misleading but that attempts to manipulate consumers by appealing to irrational drives of all sorts.[5] In general, your opinion about protecting commercial speech may depend on your views about the impact of modern mass advertising and how rationally consumers respond to it.

---

[5] For a brief discussion of commercial speech challenges to the FTC's regulation of advertising, see The Federal Trade Commission Act and Consumer Protection Laws chapter. Such challenges generally have been unsuccessful.

BOLGER v. YOUNGS DRUG PRODUCTS CORPORATION

463 U.S. 60 (U.S. Sup. Ct. 1983)

Youngs Drug Products Corporation manufactured, sold, and distributed contraceptive devices (including prophylactics). It planned a marketing campaign involving the unsolicited mass mailing of advertising fliers and related materials to the general public. The mailings were to include: (1) fliers promoting a range of products obtainable in drugstores (including prophylactics); (2) fliers specifically promoting prophylactics; and (3) informational pamphlets discussing the usefulness of prophylactics in preventing venereal disease and aiding family planning. After learning of Youngs's plans, the Postal Service warned Youngs that the mailings would violate a federal statute prohibiting the mailing of unsolicited advertisements for contraceptive devices.

Youngs sued in federal district court for an injunction barring enforcement of the statute against its mailings, arguing that such enforcement would violate the First Amendment. The district court decided in Youngs's favor, and the Postal Service appealed to the U.S. Supreme Court.

Marshall, Justice.   Our decisions have recognized the commonsense distinction between speech proposing a commercial transaction and other varieties of speech. Thus, we have held that the Constitution accords less protection to commercial speech than to other constitutionally safeguarded forms of expression. With respect to noncommercial speech, this Court has sustained content-based restrictions only in the most extraordinary circumstances. By contrast, in light of the greater potential for deception or confusion in the context of certain advertising messages, content-based restrictions on commercial speech may be permissible.

[Thus,] we must first determine the proper classification of the mailings at issue here. Most of Youngs's mailings fall within the core notion of commercial speech—speech which does no more than propose a commercial transaction. Youngs's informational pamphlets, however, cannot be characterized merely as proposals to engage in commercial transactions. The mere fact that these pamphlets are advertisements does not compel the conclusion that they are commercial speech. Similarly, the reference to a specific product does not by itself render the pamphlets commercial speech. Finally, the fact that Youngs has an economic motivation for mailing the pamphlets would clearly be insufficient by itself to turn the materials into commercial speech. The combination of all these characteristics, however, provides strong support for the conclusion that the informational pamphlets are properly characterized as commercial speech. The mailings constitute commercial speech notwithstanding the fact that they contain discussions of important public issues such as venereal disease and family planning.

We have adopted [the following] analysis for assessing the validity of restrictions on commercial speech. First, we determine whether the expression is constitutionally protected. For commercial speech to receive such protection, it at least must concern lawful activity and not be misleading. Second, we ask whether the governmental interest is substantial. If so, we must then determine whether the regulation directly advances the government interest asserted, and whether it is not more extensive than necessary to serve that interest.[6]

The State may deal effectively with false, deceptive, or misleading sales techniques. In this case, however, the government has never claimed that Youngs's mailings fall into any of these categories. Youngs's commercial speech is therefore clearly protected by the First Amendment.

We must next determine whether the government's interest in prohibiting the mailing of unsolicited contraceptive advertisements is a substantial one. The government asserts that the statute: (1) shields recipients of mail from materials that they are likely to find offensive, and (2) aids parents' efforts to control the manner in which their children become informed about sensitive and important subjects such as birth control. The first of these interests carries little weight. At least where obscenity is not involved, we have never held that the government can shut off the flow of mailings to protect those recipients who might potentially be offended. Recipients of objectionable mailings may effectively avoid bombardment of their sensibilities simply by averting their eyes.

The second interest asserted by the government—aiding parents' efforts to discuss birth control with their children—is undoubtedly substantial. As a means of effectuating this interest, however, this statute fails to withstand scrutiny. To begin, it provides only the most limited incremental support for the interest asserted. We can reasonably assume that parents already exercise substantial control over the disposition of mail once it enters their mailboxes. And parents must already cope with the multitude of external stimuli that color their children's perception of sensitive subjects. Under these circumstances, a ban on unsolicited advertisements serves only to assist those parents who desire to keep their children from confronting such mailings, who are otherwise

---

[6] In *Board of Trustees of the State University of New York v. Fox*, 492 U.S. 469 (1989), the Supreme Court clarified the last part of this "means" test by holding that the challenged regulation need not be the least restrictive means of promoting the substantial government purpose. In other words, the regulation might still stand even if another regulation could advance the state's ends with less effect on free commercial speech. Under this standard, however, the result in *Bolger* would not change.

unable to do so, and whose children have remained relatively free from such stimuli. This marginal degree of protection is achieved by purging all mailboxes of unsolicited material that is entirely suitable for adults. A restriction of this scope is more extensive than the Constitution permits, for the government may not reduce the adult population to reading only what is fit for children. The level of discourse reaching a mailbox simply cannot be limited to that which would be suitable for a sandbox.

The justifications offered by the government are insufficient to warrant the sweeping prohibition on the mailing of unsolicited contraceptive advertisements. As applied to Youngs's mailings, the statute is unconstitutional.

Judgment for Youngs affirmed.

Due Process

Procedural Due Process The Fifth and Fourteenth Amendments require that the federal government and the states observe **due process** when they deprive a person of life, liberty, or property. The traditional conception of due process, called **procedural due process,** establishes the procedures that government must follow when it takes life, liberty, or property. Although the requirements of procedural due process vary from situation to situation, their core idea is that people are entitled to adequate *notice* of the government action to be taken against them and to some sort of *fair trial or hearing* before that action can occur.

In order to trigger due process protections, the government must deprive a person of life, liberty, or property. Due process *liberty* includes a very broad and poorly defined range of freedoms. It even includes certain interests in personal reputation. For example, the firing of a government employee might require some kind of due process hearing if it is publicized, the fired employee's reputation is sufficiently damaged, and her future employment opportunities are restricted. The Supreme Court has said that due process *property* is not created by the Constitution, but by existing rules and understandings that stem from an independent source such as state law. These rules and understandings must give a person a *legitimate claim of entitlement* to a benefit, not merely some need, desire, or expectation for it. This definition includes almost all of the usual forms of property. It also includes the job rights of tenured public employees who can be discharged only for cause, but not the rights of untenured or probationary employees.

The following *Adams* case discusses the sort of notice required by procedural due process when government deprives a person of property.

MENNONITE BOARD OF MISSIONS v. ADAMS
462 U.S. 791 (U.S. Sup. Ct. 1983)

Alfred Jean Moore purchased some real property located in Elkhart, Indiana, from the Mennonite Board of Missions (MBM). The sale was on credit, and MBM took a mortgage on the property to secure payment of the $14,000 purchase price. Under the sales agreement, Moore was responsible for paying all property taxes. Unknown to MBM, however, she failed to do so. This eventually led Elkhart County to initiate proceedings for the sale of Moore's property in order to satisfy the tax debt.

Under Indiana law at the time in question, the only forms of notice required to be given to holders of mortgage interests (mortgagees) in property destined for a tax sale were: (1) posted notice in the county courthouse and (2) published notice once each week for three consecutive weeks. The owner of the property, on the other hand, was entitled to notice by certified mail. Elkhart County complied with all of these requirements and eventually sold Moore's property to Richard Adams. Through no fault of its own, MBM did not learn of the tax deficiency or the sale until two years after the sale occurred. By then, the statutory period within which MBM could have redeemed the property had passed and Moore still owed MBM over $8,000.

Adams later sued in an Indiana trial court to quiet title to the property that he had purchased. In opposition to Adams's motion for summary judgment, MBM argued that it had not received constitutionally adequate notice of the tax sale and of its opportunity to redeem the property following the sale. The trial court found for Adams, and a state appellate court affirmed the judgment. MBM appealed to the U.S. Supreme Court.

Marshall, Justice. In *Mullane v. Central Hanover Bank & Trust Co.* (1950), this Court recognized that prior to an action which will affect an interest in life, liberty, or property protected by the Due Process Clause of the Fourteenth Amendment, a State must provide "notice reasonably calculated, under all circumstances, to apprise interested parties of the pendency of the action and afford them an opportunity to present their objections." Invoking this elementary and fundamental requirement of due process, the Court held that published notice of an action to settle the accounts of a common trust fund was not sufficient to inform beneficiaries of the trust whose names and addresses were known. The Court explained that notice by publication was not reasonably calculated to provide actual notice of the pending proceeding and was therefore inadequate to inform those who could be notified by more effective means such as personal service or mailed notice.

This case is controlled by the analysis in *Mullane*. A mortgagee (e.g., MBM) possesses a substantial property interest that is significantly affected by a tax sale. Ultimately, the tax sale may result in the complete nullification of the mortgagee's interest, since the purchaser acquires title free of all liens and other encumbrances at the conclusion of the redemption period.

Since a mortgagee clearly has a legally protected property interest, he is entitled to notice reasonably calculated to apprise him of a pending tax sale. Unless the mortgagee is not reasonably identifiable, constructive notice alone does not satisfy the mandate of *Mullane*.

Neither notice by publication and posting, nor mailed notice to the property owner, are means such as one desirous of actually informing the mortgagee might reasonably adopt to accomplish it. Because they are designed primarily to attract prospective purchasers to the tax sale, publication and posting are unlikely to reach those who, although they have an interest in the property, do not make special efforts to keep abreast of such notices. Notice to the property owner also cannot be expected to lead to actual notice to the mortgagee. The County's use of these less reliable forms of notice is not reasonable where, as here, an inexpensive and efficient mechanism such as mail service is available.

Personal service or mailed notice is required even though sophisticated creditors have means at their disposal to discover whether property taxes have not been paid and whether tax sale proceedings are therefore likely to be initiated. A mortgage need not involve a complex commercial transaction among knowledgeable parties, and it may well be the least sophisticated creditor whose security interest is threatened by a tax sale. More importantly, a party's ability to safeguard its interests does not relieve the state of its constitutional obligation. Notice by mail or other means as certain to ensure actual notice is a minimum constitutional precondition to a proceeding which will adversely affect the liberty or property interests of *any* party, whether unlettered or well versed in commercial practice, if its name and address are reasonably ascertainable.

Judgment reversed in favor of MBM.

Substantive Due Process   A procedural due process claim does not challenge rules of *substantive law*—the rules that set standards of behavior for organized social life. Instead, it attacks the *procedures* used by government actors when they enforce substantive rules. For example, imagine that State X makes adultery a crime and allows people to be convicted of adultery without a trial. Arguments that adultery should not be a crime go to the substance of the statute, while objections to the lack of a trial are procedural in nature.

Sometimes, the Due Process Clauses have been used to attack the substance of government action. For our purposes, the most important example of this **substantive due process** occurred in the late 19th and early 20th centuries, when probusiness courts influenced by laissez-faire economic ideas struck down various kinds of social legislation as denials of due process. They did so mainly by reading freedom of contract and other economic rights into the liberty protected by the Fifth and Fourteenth Amendments and interpreting "due process of law" to require that laws denying such rights be subjected to some kind of means-ends scrutiny. The most famous example is the Supreme Court's 1905 decision in *Lochner v. New York*, where it struck down a state law setting maximum hours of work for bakery employees because the statute limited freedom of contract and did not directly advance the legitimate state goal of promoting worker health.

This "economic" form of substantive due process has been criticized as giving probusiness courts a powerful tool for striking down social and economic regulations designed to protect the powerless. After 1937, the doctrine ceased to be a significant check on government regulation of social and economic matters. Today, substantive due process attacks on such regulations trigger only the most lenient kind of rational basis review and have virtually no chance of success. In the 1970s and 1980s, however, substantive due process became increasingly important as a device for protecting *noneconomic* rights—most importantly, the ambiguously defined constitutional right of privacy. But in 1989 and 1990, the Supreme Court issued several decisions that restricted these modern applications of substantive due process.

Equal Protection

The Fourteenth Amendment and its Equal Protection Clause were added to the Constitution after the Civil War. Some scholars argue that the equal protection guarantee originally was aimed only at racial discrimination, but by the beginning of the 20th century courts applied it to governmental classifications of all sorts. The law inevitably classifies or discriminates in various ways, benefiting or burdening some groups but not others. The equal protection guarantee sets the standards such classifications must meet to be constitutional.

The Rational Basis Test   The basic equal protection standard is the *rational basis* test described earlier. This is the standard usually applied to social and economic regulations that are challenged as denying equal protection. Although formulations of the rational basis test vary, here it generally means that the government's classification must be reasonably related to the accomplishment of a legitimate public purpose. As the following *Stanglin* case indicates, this lenient test usually does not impede state and federal regulation of social and economic matters.

CITY OF DALLAS v. STANGLIN

490 U.S. 19 (U.S. Sup. Ct. 1989)

The city of Dallas, Texas, adopted an ordinance restricting admission to so-called Class E dance halls to persons between the ages of 14 and 18. However, it did not impose similar age limitations on most other establishments where teenagers might congregate—for example, skating rinks. Charles Stanglin, who in one building operated both a Class E dance hall and a roller-skating rink, sued for an injunction against enforcement of the ordinance in a Texas trial court. One of his arguments was that the ordinance denied the equal protection of the laws because its distinction between Class E dance halls and other establishments for teenagers was irrational. The Texas trial court upheld the ordinance, but a higher Texas court struck down its age restriction. The city appealed to the U.S. Supreme Court.

Rehnquist, Chief Justice.   The Dallas ordinance implicates no suspect class. The question remaining is whether the classification survives rational basis scrutiny under the Equal Protection Clause. The city has chosen to impose a rule that separates 14- to 18-year-olds from what may be the corrupting influences of older teenagers and young adults. An urban planner for the city testified: "Older kids can access drugs and alcohol, and they have more mature sexual attitudes, more liberal sexual attitudes in general. . . . And we're concerned about mixing up these individuals with youngsters [who] have not fully matured."

Stanglin claims that this restriction has no real connection with the city's stated objectives. Except for saloons and teenage dance halls, he argues, teenagers and adults in Dallas may associate with each other, including at the skating area of his rink. We think Stanglin's arguments misapprehend the nature of rational basis scrutiny, which is the most relaxed and tolerant form of judicial scrutiny under the Equal Protection Clause. If the classification has some reasonable basis, it does not offend the Constitution simply because the classification is not made with mathematical nicety or because in practice it results in some inequality. The rational basis standard is true to the principle that the Fourteenth Amendment gives the federal courts no power to impose upon the states their views of what constitutes wise economic or social policy.

In the local economic sphere, it is only the invidious discrimination, the wholly arbitrary act, which cannot stand consistently with the Fourteenth Amendment. The city could reasonably conclude that teenagers might be susceptible to corrupting influences if permitted to frequent a dance hall with older persons [and that] limiting dance hall contacts between juveniles and adults would make less likely illicit or undesirable juvenile involvement with alcohol, illegal drugs, and promiscuous sex. It is true that the city allows teenagers and adults to roller-skate together, but skating involves less physical contact than dancing. The differences between the two activities may not be striking, but differentiations need not be striking in order to survive rational basis scrutiny.

Texas court decision reversed in favor of the city.

The rational basis test is the basic equal protection standard. Some classifications, however, get tougher means-ends scrutiny. Specifically, laws that discriminate with respect to *fundamental rights* or involve *suspect classifications* now receive more rigorous review. This is a development that mainly began after World War II and greatly accelerated during the 1960s and 1970s.

Fundamental Rights   The list of rights regarded as "fundamental" for equal protection purposes is not completely clear, but it includes voting, interstate travel, and certain criminal procedure protections. Laws creating unequal enjoyment of these rights receive something resembling *full strict scrutiny*. In 1969, for instance, the Supreme Court struck down the District of Columbia's one-year residency requirement for receiving welfare benefits because that requirement unequally and impermissibly restricted the right of interstate travel.

Suspect Classifications   For various reasons, the Supreme Court has concluded that certain "suspect" bases of classification also trigger more rigorous equal protection review. As of mid-1991, these *suspect classifications* and the level of scrutiny they attract are as follows:

1. *Race and national origin.* Classifications disadvantaging racial or national minorities receive the strictest kind of strict scrutiny and are almost never constitutional. Still, the Supreme Court often has upheld so-called reverse racial discrimination—government

---

CONCEPT REVIEW

THE LEVELS OF EQUAL PROTECTION REVIEW: A ROUGH SUMMARY

Rational Basis Review	Most general social and economic regulations
	Laws discriminating against aliens under the political function exception
Intermediate Scrutiny	Sex discrimination against both men and women
	Discrimination against illegitimates
	Minority preferences enacted by Congress
Full or Nearly Full Strict Scrutiny	Discrimination regarding fundamental rights
	Most discrimination against aliens
	Most race and national origin discrimination

---

action that benefits racial minorities and disadvantages whites. In 1989, however, a majority of the Court concluded that discrimination of this kind should receive the same full strict scrutiny as discrimination *against* racial or national minorities. But in 1990, the Court held that minority preferences enacted *by Congress* should be reviewed under the *sex discrimination* test described below, which is generally regarded as a form of *intermediate scrutiny.*

2. *Alienage.* The Supreme Court has stated that classifications based on one's status as an alien also receive strict scrutiny of some kind, but it is doubtful whether this standard is as tough as the full strict scrutiny normally used in race discrimination cases. Under the "political function" exception, moreover, laws restricting aliens from employment in positions that are intimately related to democratic self-government only receive *rational basis* review. This exception has been read broadly to uphold laws excluding aliens from being state troopers, public school teachers, and probation officers.

3. *Sex.* Although sex has never formally been declared a suspect classification, for about 15 years laws discriminating on the basis of gender have been subjected to *intermediate scrutiny.* Specifically, such laws must be substantially related to the furtherance of an important governmental purpose. Under this test, measures discriminating against women have almost always been struck down. The Supreme Court has stated that classifications disadvantaging men get the same scrutiny as those disadvantaging women, but this has not pre-

vented the Court from upholding men-only draft registration and a law making statutory rape a crime for men alone.

4. *Illegitimacy.* Classifications based on one's illegitimate birth receive a form of *intermediate scrutiny* that is probably less strict than the scrutiny given gender-based classifications. Under this vague standard, the Court has struck down state laws discriminating against illegitimates in areas like recovery for wrongful death, workers' compensation benefits, social security payments, inheritance, and child support.

INDEPENDENT CHECKS APPLYING ONLY TO THE STATES

The Contract Clause

Article I, section 10 of the Constitution says: "No State shall . . . pass any . . . Law impairing the Obligation of Contracts." This *Contract Clause* applies to state laws that change the parties' performance obligations under an *existing* contract *after* that contract has been made.[7] The original purpose behind the Contract Clause was to strike down the many debtor relief statutes passed by the states after the Revolution. These statutes impaired the obligations of existing private contracts by relieving

---

[7]Also, standards similar to the Contract Clause standards described in this section apply to the federal government under the Fifth Amendment's Due Process Clause.

debtors of the obligations they owed to contract creditors. In the famous cases of *Fletcher v. Peck* (1810) and *Dartmouth College v. Woodward* (1819), however, the Contract Clause also was held to protect the obligations of *governmental* contracts and grants.

The Contract Clause probably was the most important constitutional check on state regulation of the economy in the 19th century. Beginning in the latter part of that century, though, the clause gradually became subordinate to legislation based on the states' police powers. By the mid-20th century, most observers treated the clause as a constitutional dead letter. In 1977, however, the Supreme Court gave the Contract Clause new life by announcing a fairly strict constitutional test governing situations where a state impairs *its own* contracts. Such impairments, it said, must be "reasonable and necessary to serve an important public purpose." A year later, without stating a clear constitutional standard, the Court struck down a state's alteration of *private* pension contracts.

During the 1980s, the Court seemingly returned to its earlier pattern of deference toward state regulations that impair the obligations of *private* contracts. The following *Exxon* case is an example. Where a state attempts to impair *its own* contracts, however, the fairly strict test quoted above presumably still applies.

EXXON CORPORATION v. EAGERTON

462 U.S. 176 (U.S. Sup. Ct. 1983)

For years, the Exxon Corporation paid a severance tax on the oil and gas it drilled in Alabama. Under the sales contracts that Exxon made with purchasers of its oil and gas, it was able to pass on any tax increase to the purchasers. In 1979, Alabama raised the severance tax from 4 percent to 6 percent, and forbade producers of oil and gas from passing on the increase to purchasers.

Exxon sued the Alabama commissioner of revenue in an Alabama trial court, seeking a ruling that the pass-on restriction was unconstitutional under the Contract Clause. The trial court found for Exxon, but the Alabama Supreme Court reversed. Exxon appealed to the U.S. Supreme Court.

Marshall, Justice.   By barring Exxon from passing the tax increase through to its purchasers, the pass-through prohibition nullified the purchasers' contractual obligations to reimburse Exxon for any severance taxes. While the prohibition thus affects contractual obligations, it does not follow that the prohibition constituted a "Law impairing the Obligation of Contracts" within the meaning of the Contract Clause. Although the language of the Clause is facially absolute, its prohibition must be accommodated to the inherent police power of the state to safeguard the vital interests of its people. If the law were otherwise, one would be able to obtain immunity from state regulation by making private contractual arrangements.

The Contract Clause does not deprive the states of their broad power to adopt general regulatory measures without being concerned that private contracts will be impaired, or even destroyed, as a result. Thus, a state prohibition law may be applied to contracts for the sale of beer that were valid when entered into, a law barring lotteries may be applied to lottery tickets that were valid when issued, and a workmen's compensation law may be applied to employers and employees operating under preexisting contracts of employment that made no provision for work-related injuries.

Like the laws upheld in these cases, the pass-through prohibition did not prescribe a rule limited in effect to contractual obligations or remedies, but instead imposed a generally applicable rule of conduct designed to advance a broad societal interest, protecting consumers from excessive prices. The prohibition applied to all oil and gas producers, regardless of whether they happened to be parties to sale contracts permitting them to pass tax increases through to their purchasers. The effect of the pass-through prohibition on existing contracts that did contain such a provision was incidental to its main effect of shielding consumers from the burden of the tax increase.

Judgment for the commissioner affirmed on the Contract Clause issue. Case returned to the Alabama Supreme Court for consideration of other questions.

Burden on Interstate Commerce

In addition to empowering Congress to regulate interstate commerce, the Commerce Clause also limits the states' ability to *burden* such commerce. This limitation is not expressly stated in the Constitution. Rather, it arises by implication from the Commerce Clause and reflects that clause's original purpose of blocking state protectionism and assuring free interstate trade. This *burden-on-commerce* limitation operates independently of congressional legislation under the commerce power or other federal powers. If relevant federal regulation is present, the preemption questions discussed in the next section also may arise.

Many different state laws can raise burden-on-commerce problems. For example, state regulation of transportation (e.g., limits on train or truck lengths) have been a prolific source of litigation. The same is true of state restrictions on the importation of goods or resources—for example, laws forbidding the sale of out-of-state food products unless they meet certain standards. Such restrictions sometimes benefit local economic interests. Burden-on-commerce issues also arise when states try to aid their own residents by blocking the exportation of scarce or valuable products, thus denying out-of-state buyers access to those products.

Due in part to the wide range of regulations it has had to confront, the Supreme Court has not adhered to one consistent test for determining when such regulations impermissibly burden interstate commerce. According to a recent case,[8] however, state laws are *almost always unconstitutional* under the Commerce Clause when they do one of the following:

1. *Directly regulate interstate commerce.* This can occur, for example, when state price regulations require firms to post the prices at which they will sell within the state, and to promise that they will not sell below these

prices in other states. Because they affect prices in other states, such regulations directly regulate interstate commerce and usually are unconstitutional.

2. *Discriminate against interstate commerce.* This generally occurs when state laws treat local and interstate commerce unequally on their face. The following *Limbach* case below provides an example.

3. *Favor in-state economic interests over out-of-state interests.* State laws can have this effect even though they do not discriminate against interstate commerce on their face. In one case, for example, the Supreme Court considered a North Carolina statute requiring all closed containers of apples sold within the state to bear only the applicable U.S. grade or standard. Washington State, the nation's largest apple producer, had its own inspection and grading system for Washington apples, a system that generally was regarded as superior to the federal system. The Court struck down the North Carolina statute because it benefited local apple producers by forcing Washington sellers to regrade apples sold in North Carolina (thus raising their costs of doing business), and by undermining the competitive advantage provided by Washington's superior grading system.

Finally, state laws that *regulate evenhandedly and have only incidental effects on interstate commerce* are *constitutional* if they serve legitimate state interests and their local benefits exceed the burden they place on interstate commerce. There is no sharp line between such regulations and those that are almost always unconstitutional under the tests discussed above. In a 1981 Supreme Court case, a state truck-length limitation that differed from the limitations imposed by neighboring states failed to satisfy these tests. First, the Court concluded that the measure did not further the state's legitimate interest in highway safety because the trucks the state banned generally were as safe as those it allowed. Second, whatever marginal safety advantage the law provided was outweighed by the numerous problems it posed for interstate trucking companies.

---

[8] *Brown-Forman Distillers Corp. v. New York State Liquor Authority,* 476 U.S. 573 (1986).

NEW ENERGY COMPANY OF INDIANA v. LIMBACH
486 U.S. 269 (U.S. Sup. Ct. 1988)

Ethanol (ethyl alcohol) is mixed with gasoline in a 1:9 ratio to produce gasohol. Gasohol originally was conceived as a means of promoting energy independence, but lately its use has been justified on environmental grounds because ethanol substitutes for lead in enhancing fuel octane. In 1984, Ohio enacted a gasoline tax credit for each gallon of ethanol sold as a gasohol component by Ohio fuel dealers. This tax credit, however, was denied to ethanol coming from states that did not grant a similar tax credit to ethanol made in Ohio.

The New Energy Company of Indiana is an Indiana ethanol manufacturer. After Indiana repealed its tax subsidy for ethanol in 1985, New Energy's ethanol became ineligible for the Ohio tax credit. Thus, New Energy sued Joanne Limbach, Ohio's Tax Commissioner, for declaratory and injunctive relief in an Ohio trial court, arguing that the Ohio statute violated the Commerce Clause. After the Ohio trial and appellate courts upheld the measure, New Energy appealed to the U.S. Supreme Court.

Scalia, Justice.   The Commerce Clause not only grants Congress the authority to regulate commerce among the states, but also limits the power of the states to discriminate against interstate commerce. This "negative" aspect of the Commerce Clause prohibits economic protectionism—regulatory measures designed to benefit in-state economic interests by burdening out-of-state competitors. Thus, state statutes that discriminate against interstate commerce are routinely struck down, unless the discrimination is demonstrably justified by a valid factor unrelated to economic protectionism.

The Ohio provision explicitly deprives certain products of generally available beneficial tax treatment because they are made in certain other states, and thus on its face appears to violate the cardinal requirement of nondiscrimination. New Energy, in order to sell its product in Ohio, has to cut its profits by reducing its sales price sufficiently to compensate the Ohio purchaser-retailer for the foregone tax credit. The law imposes an economic disadvantage upon out-of-state sellers, and the promise to remove that [disadvantage] if reciprocity is accepted [does not] justify disparity of treatment. The threat used to induce Indiana's acceptance is, in effect, taxing a product made by its manufacturers at a rate higher than the same product made by Ohio manufacturers.

A state may validate a statute that discriminates against interstate commerce by showing that it advances a legitimate local purpose that cannot be adequately served by reasonable nondiscriminatory alternatives. Ohio advances two justifications for the clear discrimination in the present case: health and commerce. It argues that the provision encourages use of ethanol to reduce harmful exhaust emissions. But there is no reason to suppose that ethanol produced in a state that does not offer tax advantages to ethanol produced in Ohio is less healthy, and thus should have its importation into Ohio suppressed by denial of the otherwise standard tax credit. Health is not the purpose of the provision, but is merely an occasional and accidental effect of achieving what *is* its purpose, favorable tax treatment for Ohio-produced ethanol. Essentially the same reasoning also responds to Ohio's second (and related) justification for the discrimination: that the reciprocity requirement is designed to increase commerce in ethanol by encouraging other states to enact ethanol subsidies. What is encouraged is not ethanol subsidies in general, but only favorable treatment for Ohio-produced ethanol. Ohio's health and commerce justifications amount to no more than implausible speculation, which does not suffice to validate this plain discrimination against products of out-of-state manufacture.

Ohio Supreme Court decision against New Energy reversed.

Federal Preemption

The constitutional principle of **federal supremacy** dictates that where state law conflicts with valid federal law, the federal law is supreme. Where a state law conflicts with a federal statute, the state law is said to be *preempted* by the federal regulation. The central question in most federal preemption cases is Congress's intent. Thus, such cases often present questions of statutory interpretation that can be quite complex and that are decided on a case-by-case basis.[9]

Federal preemption of state law generally occurs for one or more of four reasons.

1. There is a direct conflict between the state and federal measures, so that it is impossible to follow

---

[9] See the Nature of Law chapter for a discussion of statutory interpretation.

both simultaneously. The following *McClendon* case involves such a situation.

2. The federal law specifically states that it will preempt state regulation in certain areas. Similar statements may also appear in the federal statute's legislative history, and courts may find such statements persuasive. *McClendon* involves an express statutory preemption clause.

3. The federal regulation is pervasive. The fact that Congress has "occupied the field" by regulating a subject in great breadth and/or in considerable detail suggests its intent to displace state regulation of that subject. This may be especially true where Congress has given an administrative agency broad regulatory power in a particular area.

4. The state regulation is an obstacle to fulfilling the purposes of the federal law.

INGERSOLL-RAND COMPANY v. MCCLENDON

111 S. Ct. 478 (U.S. Sup. Ct. 1990)

Perry McClendon worked as a salesman and distributor for the Ingersoll-Rand Company. In 1981, he was fired after nine years and eight months of service. The discharge supposedly was caused by a companywide reduction in force. However, McClendon believed that he was let go because Ingersoll-Rand wanted to avoid its pension fund responsibilities to him. His rights under the firm's pension plan would have vested after 10 years of service.

McClendon then sued Ingersoll-Rand in a Texas trial court. One of his claims was a common law claim for wrongful discharge. The trial court granted Ingersoll-Rand's motion for summary judgment, and an intermediate appellate court affirmed that ruling. Among each court's reasons was the doctrine of employment at will, which says that employees who are not hired for a definite time period can be terminated at any time for any reason. However, the Texas Supreme Court reversed the lower court's decision and returned the case to the trial court. It held that McClendon's claim fit within the "public policy" exception to the employment-at-will doctrine, which allows discharged employees to recover damages for certain terminations that violate public policy. Ingersoll-Rand then appealed to the U.S. Supreme Court; its argument was that McClendon's common law wrongful discharge claim had been preempted by the federal Employee Retirement Income Security Act (ERISA). McClendon did not sue under this statute.

O'Connor, Justice.   ERISA is a comprehensive statute designed to promote the interests of employees and their beneficiaries in employee benefit plans. The statute imposes participation, funding, and vesting requirements on pension plans. It also sets various uniform standards, including rules concerning reporting, disclosure, and fiduciary responsibility. As part of this regulatory system, Congress [also] included various safeguards to preclude abuse and to completely secure the rights and expectations brought into being by this landmark reform legislation. Prominent among these safeguards are [two] provisions of particular relevance to this case: ERISA's broad preemption provision, and a carefully integrated civil enforcement scheme.

We must decide whether these provisions, singly or in combination, preempt the cause of action at issue in this case. The question whether a certain state action is preempted by federal law is one of congressional intent. To discern Congress's intent, we examine the explicit statutory language and the structure and purpose of the statute. Regardless of the avenue we follow, this state law cause of action cannot be sustained.

Where, as here, Congress has expressly included a broadly worded preemption provision in a comprehensive statute, our task of discerning Congressional intent is considerably simplified. In section 514 of ERISA, Congress provided: "[T]he provisions of this subchapter and subchapter III of this chapter shall supersede any and all State laws insofar as they may now or hereafter relate to any employee benefit plan [covered by relevant ERISA provisions]." [This] preemption clause is conspicuous for its breadth. Its deliberately expansive language was designed to establish pension plan regulation as exclusively a federal concern.

Congress [also] used broad language in defining the "State law" that would be preempted. Such laws include all laws, decisions, rules, regulations, or other state action having the effect of law. [Moreover,] a law "relates to" an employee benefit plan if it has a connection with or reference to such a plan. Under this broad, common sense meaning, a state law may "relate to" a benefit plan, and thereby be preempted, even if the law is not specifically designed to affect such plans, or the effect is only indirect. Preemption is also not precluded simply because a state law is consistent with ERISA's substantive requirements.

The cause of action which the Texas Supreme Court recognized here—a claim that Ingersoll-Rand wrongfully terminated McClendon because of its desire to avoid contributing to or paying benefits under the pension fund—"relates to" an ERISA-covered plan within the meaning of section 514(a), and is therefore preempted. The Texas cause of action makes specific reference to, and indeed is premised on, the existence of a pension plan. To prevail, the plaintiff must plead, and the court must find, that an ERISA plan exists and the employer had a pension-defeating motive in terminating the employment. Because the court's inquiry must be directed to the plan, this judicially created cause of action "relates to" an ERISA plan.

[Our] conclusion is supported by our understanding of the purposes of [section 514(a)]. Section 514(a) was intended to ensure that plans and plan sponsors would be subject to a uniform body of benefit law. It is foreseeable that state courts, exercising their common law powers, might develop different standards applicable to the same employer conduct, requiring the tailoring of plans and employer conduct to the peculiarities of the law of each jurisdiction. Such an outcome is fundamentally at odds with the uniformity Congress sought to implement.

Even if there were no express preemption in this case, the Texas cause of action would be preempted because it conflicts directly with an ERISA cause of action. McClendon's claim falls within ERISA section 510, which protects plan participants from terminations motivated by an employer's desire to prevent a pension plan from vesting. Congress viewed this section as a crucial part of ERISA because without it employers would be able to circumvent the provision of promised benefits. McClendon's claim is prototypical of the kind Congress intended to cover under section 510.

The mere existence of a federal regulatory scheme, however, does not by itself imply preemption of state remedies. Accordingly, we must look for special features warranting preemption. Of particular relevance here is section 502(a)—ERISA's civil enforcement mechanism. Congress intended section 502(a) to be the exclusive remedy for rights guaranteed under ERISA, including those provided by section 510. The exclusive remedy provided by section 502(a) is precisely the kind of feature that warrants preemption in this case. The Texas cause of action purports to provide a remedy for the violation of a right expressly guaranteed by section 510 and exclusively enforced by section 502(a). When it is clear or may fairly be assumed that the activities a State purports to regulate are protected by section 510 of ERISA, state jurisdiction must yield.

Texas Supreme Court decision reversed in favor of Ingersoll-Rand, because McClendon's common law wrongful discharge claim was preempted by ERISA.

THE TAKINGS CLAUSE

The Fifth Amendment provides that "private property [shall not] be taken for public use, without just compensation." This Takings Clause has been incorporated within Fourteenth Amendment due process and thus applies to the states. Traditionally, it has most often come into play when the government formally condemns land through its power of **eminent domain,**[10] but it has many other applications as well.

The Takings Clause recognizes government's power to take private property and also limits the exercise of that power. It does so by requiring that when *property* is subjected to a governmental *taking*, that taking must be for a *public purpose* and the property owner must receive *just compensation.* We now consider these four aspects of the Takings Clause in turn. Figure 3 describes how they interact.

1. *Property.* The Takings Clause protects other property interests besides land and interests in land. Although its full scope is unclear, the clause has been held to cover takings of personal property, liens, trade secrets, and contract rights.

2. *Taking.* Due to the range of property interests it may cover, the Takings Clause potentially has a broad scope. Another reason for the clause's wide possible application is the range of government activities that may be considered takings. Of course, the government's use of formal *condemnation procedures* to acquire private property almost always is a taking. Also, as the following *Seawall* case declares, there is a taking where the government *physically occupies* private property or allows someone else to do so.

In addition, it has long been recognized that government *regulation* may so diminish the value of property or the owner's enjoyment of it as to constitute a taking. Land use regulation such as zoning is an example. Among the factors courts consider in such *regulatory taking* cases are the degree to which government deprives the owner of free possession, use, and disposition of his property; the overall economic impact of the regulation on the owner; and how much the regulation interferes with the owner's reasonable investment-backed expectations regarding the future use of the property. As the *Seawall* case demonstrates, moreover, courts sometimes apply some form of means-ends scrutiny in determining whether a taking has occurred. Although *Seawall* is an exception, this scrutiny often has been fairly relaxed.

3. *Public use.* Once a taking of property has occurred, it is unconstitutional unless it is for a public use. Here, courts now apply a relaxed version of the rational basis test, and the public use requirement is very easy to meet.

4. *Just compensation.* Even if a taking of property is for a public use, it still is unconstitutional if the property owner does not receive just compensation. Although the standards for determining just compensation vary with the circumstances, the basic test is the fair market value of the property at the time of the taking.

In the past, Takings Clause challenges to general regulatory measures usually have not succeeded. The reason is that the just compensation requirement would severely limit government's ability to regulate if many forms of regulation were considered takings. In recent years, however, there have been signs that this attitude is changing. The following *Seawall* case is an example.

---

[10] Eminent domain and the Takings Clause's application to land use problems are discussed in the Real Property and Insurance chapter.

FIGURE 3   Analyzing a Takings Clause Case

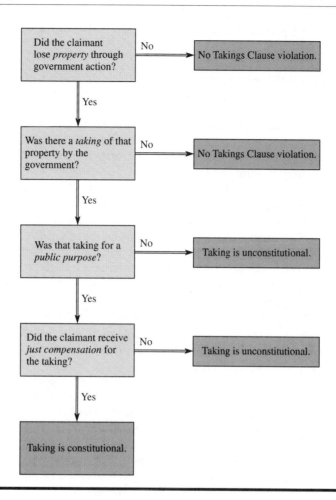

SEAWALL ASSOCIATES v. CITY OF NEW YORK

542 N.E.2d 1059 (N.Y. Ct. App. 1989)

For years, New York City had encouraged the demolition and redevelopment of single-room occupancy (SRO) housing, which it considered substandard. By the mid-1980s, however, this attitude changed because the supply of low-cost rental housing was swiftly declining and home-lessness was increasingly becoming a problem. Thus, the city enacted a number of measures to increase the supply of SRO housing, culminating with the passage of Local Law No. 9 in 1987. Among that law's provisions were: (1) a five-year moratorium on the conversion, alteration, and demolition of buildings containing SRO units; (2) a requirement that property owners with SRO units in their buildings make every such unit habitable; and (3) a requirement that SRO property owners lease every such unit to a bona fide tenant at controlled rents.

A group of real estate developers owning SRO properties challenged Local Law No. 9 as an unconstitutional taking of property without just compensation in a New York trial court. The trial court found the law unconstitutional, but an intermediate appellate court reversed that judgment. The plaintiffs appealed to New York's highest court, the New York Court of Appeals.

Hancock, Judge.   Plaintiffs contend that Local Law No. 9 has resulted in a physical occupation of their properties and is therefore a per se compensable taking. Local Law No. 9 requires the owners to rent their rooms or be subject to severe penalties; to admit persons as tenants with all the possessory and other rights that status entails; and to surrender the most basic attributes of private property, the rights of possession and exclusion. Local Law No. 9 has effected a per se physical taking because it interferes so drastically with the SRO property owners' fundamental rights to possess and to exclude. The law requires nothing less of the owners than to suffer the physical occupation of their building by third parties.

Even if Local Law No. 9 were not a physical taking, it would still be invalid as a regulatory taking. Government regulation involves the adjustment of rights for the public good. Often this adjustment curtails some potential for the use or economic exploitation of private property. There is no set formula for determining when an adjustment of rights has reached the point when justice and fairness require that compensation be paid. However, such a burden-shifting regulation will constitute a taking if: (1) it denies an owner economically viable use of his property, or (2) it does not substantially advance legitimate state interests.

As previously discussed, the coerced rental provisions deprive owners of the fundamental *right to possess* their properties. Moreover, these mandatory rental provisions—along with the prohibition against demolition, alteration, and conversion of the properties to other uses, and the requirement that uninhabitable units be refurbished—deny owners any *right to use* their properties as they see fit. The effect of the law is to strip owners—who may have purchased their properties solely to turn them into profitable investments by tearing down and replacing the existing structures with new ones—of the very right to use their properties for any such purpose. Owners are forced to devote their properties to another use which bears no relation to any economic purpose which could be reasonably contemplated by a private investor. Finally, Local Law No. 9, particularly in those provisions prohibiting redevelopment and mandating rental, impairs the ability of owners to sell their properties for any sums approaching their investments. Thus, the law must also negatively affect the owners' *right to dispose* of their properties. By any test, these restrictions deny the owners economically viable use of their properties.

Moreover, Local Law No. 9 does not substantially advance legitimate state interests. Of course, the end sought by Local Law No. 9 is of the greatest societal importance—alleviating the critical problems of homelessness. However, can it be said that imposing the [law's] burdens on the owners of SRO properties *substantially* advances the aim of alleviating the homelessness problem? The city contends that by increasing the availability of SRO units, [the law] will provide more available low-cost housing and thereby further the aim of alleviating homelessness. The city's own study, however, acknowledges that a ban on converting and destroying SRO units would do little to resolve the crisis. Indeed, the SRO units are not earmarked for the homeless or for potentially homeless low-income families, and there is no assurance that the units will be rented to members of either group. Such a tenuous connection between means and ends cannot justify singling out this group of property owners to bear the costs required by the law.

Local Law No. 9 forces property owners alone to bear public burdens which, in all fairness and justice, should be borne by the public as a whole. Because the owners are afforded no compensation, Local Law No. 9 is invalid under the Takings Clause.

Bellacosa, J., Dissenting.   In 1904, Justice Holmes wrote the quintessential dissenting opinion in *Lochner v. New York*, which presciently warned against his own court's declaring unconstitutional an act of the New York legislature attempting to limit the working hours of [bakery employees]. Eighty-five years after *Lochner*, we observe property rights, like the contract rights of that bygone era, being exalted over the legislature's assessment of social policy. We, as judges, should not inquire into the wisdom of SROs as shelter for potentially 52,000 new, displaced homeless persons—that policy choice belongs to the elected officials who enacted the law.

Appellate court decision reversed in favor of the developers.

ETHICAL AND PUBLIC POLICY CONCERNS

1. Throughout history, the main threat to individual rights of all kinds arguably has come from kings, oligarchs, dictators, and other unrepresentative rulers. Is this true of the rights discussed in this chapter? In the American system of government, who is the main threat to these rights?

2. Courts sometimes state that certain rights are fundamental and then protect those rights by imposing tough means-ends scrutiny on laws that restrict them. What fundamental ethical objection almost always applies to such actions by the courts? *Hint*: Look at the dissenting opinion in the *Seawall* case.

3. Discussions of ethical theory often distinguish between *teleological* ethical theories (which tend to judge the morality of actions by their consequences) and *deontological* theories (which say that some actions are morally obligatory regardless of their consequences). Suppose someone declares that some of the means-ends tests described in this chapter are morally wrong because certain rights are absolute and should *never* be restricted. Means-ends tests, of course, allow rights to be balanced against various social purposes, and in some cases the balancing process may require restriction of the right. Which ethical approach (teleological or deontological) does this declaration most resemble?

4. Although this chapter is mainly concerned with economic rights, one of the great generalizations about American constitutional law is that since 1937, the Supreme Court has shifted from protecting economic rights to protecting personal rights. One example of the Court's former solicitude for economic rights is the doctrine of economic substantive due process mentioned earlier in this chapter. The most important aspect of modern substantive due process, on the other hand, is the constitutional right of privacy. Today, social and economic regulations that are challenged on substantive due process grounds usually get very light means-ends review, while strict scrutiny still applies to some laws that violate privacy rights. Until recently, at least, the most important example of this strict scrutiny was the high degree of constitutional protection given the right to an abortion.

With all of the above in mind, consider the following groups of questions. Throughout, we assume for the sake of argument that it is desirable for courts to give great protection to personal rights.

a. First, consider some familiar attacks on the practice of giving personal rights greater protection than economic rights. Why are personal rights intrinsically more important than economic rights? Why, for example, is the right to an abortion more important than freedom of contract? Or consider the distinction between a right protected by the old-time substantive due process—the right to pursue a trade, occupation, or profession—and freedom of speech. To people in general, which right really matters the most in their daily lives? Finally, does the whole distinction between personal rights and economic rights make any sense? Aren't freedom of contract and the right to pursue a chosen occupation "personal" too?

b. Next, consider the possible consequences of giving greater protection to economic rights. Would this imperil social and economic regulations intended to protect the poor and the powerless? In considering this question, examine the text's discussion of the Supreme Court's 1905 *Lochner* decision and also look at the *Seawall* case. Even if such regulations would be jeopardized, is this a decisive objection to giving greater protection to economic rights?

Also, consider the following possible *positive* consequence of protecting economic rights: that it would increase economic productivity and thereby benefit both rich and poor. Many free-market economists believe that this would happen. On the other hand, even though economic rights have received little constitutional protection over the past 50 years, the U.S. economy still has grown spectacularly during that period.

c. Third, consider a common objection to giving greater protection to economic rights: that the courts are incapable of making intelligent decisions on the questions this would force them to consider. If courts ever do decide to protect economic rights more vigorously, they will have to apply tougher means-ends scrutiny to social and economic regulations. This, in turn, probably means that they will be required to make judgments on a wide range of social and economic questions. Are courts likely to do a good job if they try this? How much do most lawyers know about these matters?

On the other hand, don't courts sometimes have to consider complex questions of social policy when they apply tough scrutiny to laws that restrict *personal* rights? If so, does this mean that courts can also handle issues related to economic rights?

SUMMARY

As written, the U.S. Constitution embodies certain political principles—for example, separation of powers, checks and balances, and federalism. The Constitution as interpreted and applied by the Supreme Court, however, differs from the written Constitution.

The Constitution restricts congressional power to regulate the economy in two ways: by limiting Congress to the exercise of certain *enumerated powers* and by placing certain *independent checks* in the path of Congress when it exercises these enumerated powers. However, the U.S. Constitution does not impose an enumerated powers limitation on the state legislatures. In fact, the most important state regulatory power, the *police power*, is a broad ability to regulate for the public welfare that has few inherent limits. But the U.S. Constitution does place many independent checks on the states.

The most important business-related congressional regulatory powers are its powers to control interstate commerce, to tax, and to spend for the general welfare. By now, there are few inherent limits on the exercise of these powers when they are used to regulate social and economic matters. Today, the *commerce power* is an all-purpose federal police power with a great intrastate reach. By taxing behavior that it deems undesirable, Congress can use the *taxing power* as a regulatory tool. By conditioning the receipt of federal money on the performance of chosen conditions, it does the same with the *spending power.*

The most important business-related independent constitutional checks applying to both the federal government and the states are the *free speech, due process,* and *equal protection* guarantees. The First Amendment's free speech guarantee applies to the states through its incorporation within Fourteenth Amendment due process, and Fourteenth Amendment equal protection applies to the federal government through its incorporation within Fifth Amendment due process. These independent checks operate only where there has been *government action*.

When the government regulates *commercial speech*, the regulation is subjected to an intermediate level of review that is less rigorous than the very strict standards used in most First Amendment cases. Corporate *political* speech, however, receives full First Amendment protection.

Due process can be *procedural* (setting standards of fairness that the government must follow as it enforces its laws) or *substantive* (assessing the policy merits of laws governing social behavior). Today, however, substantive due process is of little or no consequence where government regulates economic activity.

The basic equal protection standard, and the test applied to government regulation of economic matters, is the lenient *rational basis* requirement. However, discrimination with respect to certain *fundamental rights* attracts a high level of *strict scrutiny.* The same is often, but not always, true for discrimination on the bases of race (or national origin) and alienage. Governmental classifications based on gender and illegitimacy receive some *intermediate* degree of scrutiny.

There are three important business-related independent checks that apply only to the states. The *Contract Clause* puts some limits on the states' ability to impair the obligations of existing contracts by measures passed after these contracts have come into existence. Included within the Contract Clause's definition of the term *contracts* are *governmental* contracts and grants.

In addition to serving as a source of congressional power to regulate, the Commerce Clause places an implied check on state laws that unduly *burden interstate commerce.* Over the years, the Supreme Court has not consistently followed any one set of standards when determining whether state laws are unconstitutional under the Commerce Clause.

State measures may be *preempted* by federal regulation. Determining when this occurs is basically a matter of statutory interpretation.

Finally, the Fifth Amendment's *Takings Clause* recognizes government's power to take private property and also limits that power by stating that takings of such property require just compensation and must be for a public purpose. Many forms of *property* are protected by the clause. In addition to formal condemnation procedures and physical occupations of the owners' property, various kinds of government regulation can constitute *takings*. Today, the *public purpose* test is very easy to meet. The usual *just compensation* standard is the fair market value of the property at the time of the taking.

PROBLEM CASES

1. The Kraynak brothers owned a small coal mine in Pennsylvania. They did all of the work in the mine themselves and sold all of the coal they produced, about 10,000 tons annually, to Penntech Papers Company. Penntech was located in Pennsylvania, but its products were distributed nationwide. The Kraynaks claimed that they were exempt from the provisions of the Federal Coal Mine Health and Safety Act (which was based on the Commerce Clause) because of the intrastate nature of their operation. Can the act constitutionally apply to the Kraynaks' mine?

2. In 1984, Congress passed a highway funding bill directing the secretary of transportation to withhold a percentage of the federal highway funds otherwise due to a state, if the state allowed the purchase or possession of alcoholic beverages by those less than 21 years of age. South Dakota, which by statute permitted those 19 or older to buy 3.2 beer, sued to have the statute declared unconstitutional. On what enumerated power is this federal law based? Is it a constitutional exercise of that power? If the statute is constitutional, does this mean that South Dakota cannot permit the purchase or consumption of alcoholic beverages by those under 21?

3. The Metropolitan Edison Company, a privately owned but state-regulated electrical utility, terminated Catherine Jackson's electrical service without notice or a hearing when she became delinquent in paying her electric bills. Jackson sued Metropolitan, arguing that its action violated due process. What *kind* of due process claim is Jackson making here? Assuming that Metropolitan is heavily regulated by the state, is this fact sufficient by itself to make Metropolitan's conduct state action? Can Metropolitan's conduct be state action under the "public function" theory? In answering these last two questions, you might use the *San Francisco Arts & Athletics* case as a reference.

4. The Consolidated Edison Company (Con Ed), a privately owned corporation that is a regulated public utility, placed written inserts touting nuclear power in the bills it sent to its customers. Then, the New York Public Service Commission prohibited state utilities from using bill inserts to discuss controversial public policy issues such as the desirability of nuclear power. Con Ed challenged this regulation as an unconstitutional restriction of freedom of speech under the First Amendment. Are corporations like Con Ed entitled to assert First Amendment claims? What kind of speech is at issue here? What level of scrutiny does such speech receive when laws restricting it are examined by the courts?

5. Virginia had a statute prohibiting licensed pharmacists from advertising the price of prescription drugs. The alleged purpose behind the statute was to protect the public by preventing price competition in the sale of prescription drugs, thus ensuring that the need to meet a competitor's price would not force pharmacists to dispense with full professional services in the compounding, handling, and dispensing of prescription drugs. What type of First Amendment speech is restricted by this statute? Is this speech entitled to full First Amendment protection? Did the statute survive a First Amendment challenge?

6. One provision of the federal Deficit Reduction Act of 1984 established a 15-month freeze on the fees certain physicians could charge medicare patients. A group of physicians challenged the constitutionality of this provision, alleging that it restricted freedom of contract in violation of the Fifth Amendment's Due Process Clause. What *kind* of due process attack is this? Did it succeed?

7. The Minnesota legislature passed a statute banning the sale of milk in plastic nonrefillable, nonreusable containers. However, it allowed sales of milk in other nonrefillable, nonreusable containers such as paperboard cartons. One of the justifications for this ban on plastic jugs was that it would ease the state's solid waste disposal problems because plastic jugs occupy more space in landfills than other nonreturnable milk containers. A group of dairy businesses challenged the statute, arguing that its distinction between plastic containers and other containers was unconstitutional under the Equal Protection Clause. What means-ends test or level of scrutiny applies in this case? Under that test, is easing the state's solid waste disposal problems a sufficiently important *end*? Under that test, is there a sufficiently close "fit" between the classification and that end to make the statutory *means* constitutional? In answering the last question, assume for the sake of argument that in fact there were better ways of alleviating the solid waste disposal problem than banning plastic jugs while allowing paperboard cartons.

8. Oklahoma statutes set the age for drinking 3.2 beer at 21 for men and 18 for women. The asserted purpose behind the statutes (and the sex-based classification that they established) was traffic safety. The statutes were challenged as a denial of equal protection by male residents of Oklahoma. What level of scrutiny would this measure receive if *women* had been denied the right to drink 3.2 beer until they were 21 but men had been allowed to consume it at age 18? Should this standard change because the measure discriminates against *men*? Is the male challenge to the statute likely to be successful?

9. Under a New York law, all distillers of alcoholic beverages had to file a monthly price schedule with the state's liquor authority in order to sell to wholesalers within the state, and had to adhere to the schedule for that month. Also, any distiller filing a price schedule effectively had to promise that it would not make any out-of-state sale at a price lower than the New York price for the month in question. Violations of this promise could lead to the loss of a distiller's New York license to manufacture and sell liquor. As applied to distillers doing business outside New York, did this regulation violate the Commerce Clause?

10. The Federal Insecticide, Fungicide, and Rodenticide Act (FIFRA) requires that all covered pesticides be registered with the Environmental Protection Agency (EPA) before their sale. From 1972 through 1978, registrants under the act had broad powers to block the EPA's disclosure of their trade secrets when such secrets had to be disclosed as part of the registration process. After 1978, FIFRA was amended to give the EPA some ability to disclose such trade secrets to the public and to use trade secret data submitted by one applicant when considering later applications.

The Monsanto Company, a manufacturer of pesticides, sued to have these post-1978 FIFRA provisions declared unconstitutional under the Takings Clause. Monsanto argued that these provisions "took" its property by permitting its trade secrets to be known to competitors and by giving later registrants a free ride through the registration process when the EPA used Monsanto's data in subsequent applications. Are Monsanto's trade secrets property for Takings Clause purposes? On the taking issue, did the post-1978 provisions interfere with Monsanto's earlier reasonable expectations regarding the government's use of its trade secrets? Assuming that there was a taking of property here and that it was for a public purpose, what would the government have to do to make the taking constitutional?

CHAPTER 4

ADMINISTRATIVE AGENCIES

INTRODUCTION

One of the basic themes of this part of this textbook is that businesses today operate in a highly regulated environment. The fundamental vehicle for the creation and enforcement of modern regulation has been the **administrative agency.** Administrative agencies are governmental bodies other than courts or legislatures that have the legal power to take actions affecting the rights of private individuals and organizations. In *FTC v. Ruberoid Co.,*[1] Supreme Court Justice Robert H. Jackson said:

> The rise of administrative bodies probably has been the most significant legal trend of the last century and perhaps more values today are affected by their decisions than by those of all of the courts, review of administrative decisions apart. They also have begun to have important consequences on personal rights. . . . They have become a veritable fourth branch of the Government, which has deranged our three-branch legal theories as much as the concept of a fourth dimension unsettles our three-dimensional thinking.

Although this chapter focuses on federal administrative agencies, you should understand that the great growth

in *federal* regulation we have experienced in this century has been accompanied by a comparable growth in *state and local* regulation and state and local regulatory agencies.

It is difficult to think of an area of modern individual life that is not somehow touched by the action of administrative agencies. The energy that heats and lights your home and workplace, the clothes you wear, the food you eat, the medicines you take, the design of the car you drive, the programs you watch on television, and the contents of (and label on) the pillow on which you lay your head at night are all shaped in some way by regulation.

If anything, this observation is even more appropriate to corporations than to individuals. Virtually every significant aspect of contemporary corporate operations is regulated to the point that the *legal* consequences of a corporation's actions are nearly as important to its future success as the *business* consequences of its decisions.

Because administrative agencies have enormous power and some novel characteristics, they have always been objects of controversy. Are they protectors of the public or impediments to business efficiency? Are they guardians of competitive market structures or a shield behind which noncompetitive firms have sought refuge

---

[1]343 U.S. 470 (U.S. Sup. Ct. 1952).

from more vigorous competitors? Have they been impartial, efficient agents of the public interest or are they more often overzealous, or inept, or "captives" of the industries they supposedly regulate? At various times, and where various agencies are concerned, each of the above allegations has probably been true. Why, then, did we resort to such controversial entities to perform the regulatory function?

The Origins of Administrative Agencies

In the latter decades of the 19th century, the United States was in the midst of a dramatic transformation from an agrarian nation to a major industrial power. Improved means of transportation and communication facilitated a dramatic market expansion. Large business organizations acquired unheard of economic power, and new technologies promised additional social transformations.

The tremendous growth that resulted from these developments, however, was not attained without some cost. Large organizations sometimes abused their power at the expense of their customers, distributors, and competitors. New technologies often posed risks of harm to large numbers of citizens. Yet traditional institutions of legal control, such as courts and legislatures, were not particularly well suited to the regulatory needs of an increasingly complex, interdependent society in the throes of rapid change.

Courts, after all, are passive institutions that must await a genuine "case or controversy" before they can act.[2] Courts also may lack the technical expertise necessary to address many regulatory issues intelligently. In addition, they are constrained by the formalistic rules of procedure and evidence that make litigation a time-consuming and expensive process.

Legislatures, on the other hand, are theoretically able to anticipate social problems and to act in a comprehensive fashion to minimize or avoid social harm. In reality, however, legislatures rarely act until a problem has become severe enough to generate strong political support for a regulatory solution. And like courts, legislatures may lack the expertise necessary to make rational policy regarding highly technical activities.

What was needed, therefore, appeared to be a new type of governmental entity: one exclusively devoted to monitoring a particular area of activity; one that could,

by its exclusive focus and specialized hiring practices, develop a reservoir of expertise about the object of its efforts; and one that could provide the continuous attention and constant policy development demanded by a rapidly changing environment. Such new entities, it was thought, could best perform their regulatory tasks if they were given considerable latitude in the procedures they followed and the approaches they took to achieve regulatory goals.

In 1887, the modern regulatory era was born when Congress, in response to complaints about discriminatory ratemaking practices by railroads, passed the Interstate Commerce Act. This statute created the Interstate Commerce Commission and gave it the power to regulate transportation industry ratemaking practices. Thereafter, new administrative agencies have been added whenever pressing social problems (such as the threat to competition that led to the creation of the Federal Trade Commission) or new technologies, such as aviation (Federal Aviation Administration), communications (Federal Communications Commission), and nuclear power (Nuclear Regulatory Commission), have generated a political consensus in favor of regulation. More recently, developing scientific knowledge about the dangers that modern technologies and industrial processes pose to the environment and to industrial workers has led to the creation of new federal agencies empowered to regulate environmental pollution (Environmental Protection Agency) and to promote workplace safety (Occupational Safety and Health Administration). The following sections examine the legal dimensions of the process by which such administrative agencies are created.

AGENCY CREATION

Enabling Legislation

Administrative agencies are statutorily created when Congress passes **enabling legislation** specifying the name, composition, and powers of the agency. For example, consider the following language from section 1 of the Federal Trade Commission Act:

A commission is created and established, to be known as the Federal Trade Commission, which shall be composed of five commissioners, who shall be appointed by the President, by and with the advice and consent of the Senate.

This section creates the Federal Trade Commission (FTC). Section 5 of the FTC Act prohibits "unfair

---

[2]The "case or controversy" requirement is discussed in the Resolution of Private Disputes chapter.

methods of competition" and "unfair or deceptive acts or practices in commerce" and empowers the FTC to prevent such practices.[3] Section 5 also describes the procedures the Commission must follow to charge persons or organizations with violations of the act and provides for judicial review of agency orders. Subsequent portions of the statute give the FTC the power "to make rules and regulations for the purpose of carrying out the provisions of the Act," to conduct investigations of business practices, to require reports from interstate corporations concerning their practices and operations, to investigate possible violations of the antitrust laws,[4] to publish reports concerning its findings and activities, and to recommend new legislation to Congress.

Thus, Congress has given the FTC powers typically associated with the three traditional branches of government. Like the courts, it can *adjudicate* disputes concerning alleged violations of the statute; like the executive branch, it can *investigate* and *prosecute* alleged violations; and like the legislative branch, it can *promulgate rules* that have binding legal effect on future behavior. The broad mix of governmental powers typically possessed by modern administrative agencies such as the FTC makes these agencies potentially powerful agents of social control.

But great power to do good can also be great power to do evil. Regulatory bias, zeal, insensitivity, or corruption, if left unchecked, can infringe on the basic freedoms that are the essence of our system of government. Accordingly, the fundamental problem in administrative law, a problem that will surface repeatedly throughout the remainder of this chapter, is how to design a system of control over agency action that minimizes the potential for arbitrariness and harm yet preserves the power and flexibility that make administrative agencies uniquely valuable instruments of public policy.

Administrative Agencies and the Constitution

Because administrative agencies are governmental bodies, administrative action is *governmental action* and, as such, is subject to the basic constitutional checks discussed in the Business and the Constitution Chapter. As the *Mallen* case, which follows, demonstrates, this "fourth branch of government" is bound by basic con-

stitutional guarantees such as *due process, equal protection*, and *freedom of speech*, just like the three traditional branches. However, one basic constitutional principle is uniquely important when the creation of administrative agencies is at issue: the principle of **separation of powers.**

One of the fundamental attributes of our Constitution is its dispersion of governmental power among the three branches of government. Lawmaking power is given to the legislative branch, law-enforcing power to the executive branch, and law-interpreting power to the judicial branch. By limiting the powers of each branch, and by giving each branch some checks on the exercise of power by the other branches, the Constitution seeks to assure that governmental power remains accountable to the public will. In reality, of course, this separation is never perfectly complete. As you learned in the chapter The Nature of Law, courts often "make" law when developing common law doctrines or interpreting broadly worded statutes. Likewise, the Merger Guidelines[5] of the Department of Justice (part of the executive branch) do not technically have the force of law, but nonetheless may play a major role in shaping behavior.

Administrative agencies, exercising powers resembling those of each of the three branches of government, create obvious concerns about separation of powers. In particular, the congressional delegation of legislative power to an agency in its enabling legislation may be challenged as violating the separation of powers principle if such legislation is so broadly worded as to indicate that Congress has abdicated its lawmaking responsibilities. Early judicial decisions exploring the manner in which Congress could delegate its power tended to require enabling legislation to contain fairly specific guidelines and standards limiting the exercise of agency discretion.

More recently, the courts have tended to sustain quite broad delegations of power to administrative agencies. For example, section 5 of the FTC Act is a broad delegation of power. A great range of unspecified behavior falls within the statute's prohibition of "unfair methods of competition" and "unfair or deceptive acts or practices." Modern courts tend to approve broad delegations of power when Congress has expressed an "intelligible principle" to guide the agency's actions.[6]

---

[3]Section 5 of the FTC Act is discussed in detail in the Federal Trade Commission Act and Consumer Protection Laws chapter.

[4]The antitrust laws are discussed in detail in the Sherman Act chapter and the Clayton Act chapter.

---

[5] The Justice Department's Merger Guidelines are discussed in the Clayton Act chapter.

[6]*J. W. Hampton, Jr. & Co. v. United States*, 276 U.S. 394 (U.S. Sup. Ct. 1928).

FEDERAL DEPOSIT INSURANCE CORP. v. MALLEN

486 U.S. 230 (U.S. Sup. Ct. 1988)

On December 10, 1986, James Mallen was indicted by a federal grand jury in Iowa for making false statements to the Federal Deposit Insurance Corporation (FDIC) and for making false statements to Farmers State Bank for the purpose of influencing the actions of the FDIC. At the time of the indictment, Mallen was the president and a director of a federally insured bank. On January 20, 1987, the FDIC issued an *ex parte* order finding that Mallen's continued service might "pose a threat to the interests of the bank's depositors or threaten to impair public confidence in the bank," suspending him as president and as a director of the bank, and prohibiting him "from further participation in any manner in the conduct of the affairs of the Bank, or any other bank insured by the FDIC."

In issuing the suspension order without first holding a hearing on the matter, the FDIC was acting pursuant to a section of the Financial Institutions Supervisory Act of 1966 [12 U.S.C. section 1818(g)]. A copy of the order was served on Mallen on January 26, 1987, and four days later Mallen's attorney filed a written request for an "immediate administrative hearing" to commence no later than February 9, 1987. The FDIC set a hearing date for February 18, 1987, but on February 6, 1987, Mallen filed suit against the FDIC in the Federal District Court for the Northern District of Iowa. When the District Court ruled in Mallen's favor, entering a preliminary injunction against the suspension order, the FDIC appealed.

Stevens, Justice.   The District Court expressed no opinion on the merits of the suspension; its decision rested entirely on the perceived procedural shortcomings in the post-suspension process. It is undisputed that Mallen's interest in the right to continue to serve as president of the bank and to participate in the conduct of its affairs is a property right protected by the Fifth Amendment Due Process Clause. The FDIC cannot arbitrarily interfere with Mallen's employment relationship with the bank, nor with his interest as a substantial stockholder in the bank's holding company. It is also undisputed that the FDIC's order affected a deprivation of this property interest.

Once it is determined that due process applies, the question remains what process is due. Mallen does not contend that he was entitled to an opportunity to be heard prior to the order of suspension. An important governmental interest, accompanied by a substantial assurance that the deprivation is not baseless or unwarranted, may in limited cases demanding prompt action justify postponing the opportunity to be heard until after the initial deprivation. In this case, the postponement of the hearing is supported by such an interest. The legislation under scrutiny is premised on the congressional finding that prompt suspension of indicted bank officers may be necessary to protect the interests of depositors and to maintain public confidence in our banking institutions.

Moreover, Mallen's suspension was supported by findings that assure that the suspension was not baseless. A grand jury had determined that there was probable cause to believe that he had committed a felony. Such an *ex parte* finding of probable cause provides sufficient basis for an arrest, which of course consitutes a temporary deprivation of liberty. It should certainly be sufficient to support the order entered in this case even though the FDIC did not provide Mallen with a separate pre-suspension hearing.

We cannot agree with the District Court that Mallen was denied a sufficiently prompt post-deprivation hearing. The District Court was properly concerned about the importance of providing prompt post-deprivation procedures in situations in which an agency's discretionary impairment of an individual's property is not preceded by an opportunity for a pre-deprivation hearing. However, the District Court seems to have been improperly concerned with the danger of an interminable delay by the agency, rather than by what would have happened in this case if the proceedings had not been interrupted, or indeed, if the FDIC had been as dilatory as the statute permits. For even though there is a point at which an unjustified delay in completing a post-deprivation proceeding would become a constitutional violation, the significance of such a delay cannot be evaluated in a vacuum.

Section 1818(g)(3) requires the FDIC to hold a hearing within 30 days of a written request for an opportunity to appear before the agency to contest a suspension and requires that it notify the suspended officer of its decision within 60 days of the hearing. Thus, at a maximum, the suspended officer receives a decision with 90 days of his or her request for a hearing. In this case, the agency reported that it would have been able to issue a written decision within 30 days after the hearing. In addition, the initial hearing was scheduled to take place 19 days after it was formally requested.

Mallen's interest in continued employment is without doubt an important interest that ought not be interrupted without substantial justification. Yet, even assuming that the FDIC required the complete 90 days to hear the case and reach its decision, we are not persuaded that this exceeds permissible limits. In fact, a suspended bank officer has an interest in seeing that a decision concerning his or her continued suspension is not made with excessive haste. The statute imposes a permissive standard for continuing a suspension, and presumably, when in doubt, the agency may give greater weight to the public interest and leave the suspension in place, particularly when the suspension does not impose the additional harm of a significant, incremental injury to reputation. Through the return of an indictment, the Government has already accused Mallen of serious wrongdoing. The incidental suspension is not likely to augment this injury to his reputation. We thus conclude that the 90 day period is not so long that it will always violate due process.

In many cases, perhaps most, it will be justified by an important government interest coupled with factors minimizing the risk of an erroneous deprivation. The magnitude of the public interest in a correct decision counsels strongly against any constitutional imperative that might require overly hasty decisionmaking. Congress has determined that the integrity of the banking industry requires that indicted bank officers be suspended until it is determined that they do not pose a threat to the interests of the bank's depositors or threaten to undermine public confidence in the bank. To return these officers to a position of influence in the conduct of the bank's affairs prior to an opportunity to weigh the evidence carefully would threaten these interests in the same way as allowing them to remain in office from the start.

Moreover, there is little likelihood that the deprivation is without basis. The returning of the indictment establishes that an independent body has determined that there is probable cause to believe that the officer has committed a crime. This finding is relevant in at least two important ways. First, the finding of probable cause by an independent body demonstrates that the suspension is not arbitrary. Second, the indictment itself is an objective fact that will in most cases raise serious public concern that the bank is not being managed in a responsible manner.

The post-suspension procedure authorized by section 1818(g)(3) is not unconstitutional on its face; nor do we find any unfairness in the FDIC's use of that procedure in this case.

District Court preliminary injunction reversed.

AGENCY TYPES AND ORGANIZATION

Agency Types

Administrative agencies may be found under a variety of labels. They may be called "administration," "agency," "authority," "board," "bureau," "commission," "department," "division," or "service." They sometimes have a governing body, which may be appointed or elected. They almost inevitably have an administrative head (variously called "Chairman," "Commissioner," "Director," etc.), and a staff. Since our focus is on federal administrative agencies, it is important for us to distinguish between the two basic types of federal administrative agencies: executive agencies and "independent" agencies.

Executive Agencies   Administrative agencies that reside within the Executive Office of the President or within the executive departments of the president's cabinet are called **executive agencies.** Examples of such executive agencies and their cabinet homes are: the Food and Drug Administration (Department of Health and Human Services); the Nuclear Regulatory Agency and the Federal Energy Regulatory Agency (Department of Energy); the Occupational Safety and Health Administration (Department of Labor); and the Internal Revenue Service (Treasury Department). In addition to their executive home, such agencies share one other important attribute: Their administrative heads serve "at the pleasure of the President"—they are appointed and removable at his will.

Independent Agencies   The Interstate Commerce Commission was the first independent administrative agency created by Congress. Much of the most significant regulation businesses face emanates from independent agencies such as the FTC, the National Labor Relations Board, the Consumer Product Safety Commission, the Equal Employment Opportunity Commission, the Environmental Protection Agency, and the Securities and Exchange Commission. Independent agencies are usually headed by a board or a commission (e.g., the FTC has five commissioners) whose members are appointed by the president "with the advice and consent of the Senate." Commissioners or board members are usually appointed for fixed terms (e.g., FTC commissioners serve seven-year, staggered terms) and are removable only for cause (e.g., FTC commissioners may be removed only for "inefficiency, neglect of duty, or

malfeasance in office"). Finally, it is quite common for enabling legislation to require political balance in agency appointments (e.g., the FTC Act provides that "Not more than three of the commissioners shall be members of the same political party").

Agency Organization

As the organizational chart of the FTC reproduced in Figure 1 indicates, an agency's organizational structure is largely a function of its regulatory mission. Thus, the operational side of the FTC is divided into three bureaus: the Bureau of Competition, which enforces the antitrust laws and unfair competitive practices; the Bureau of Consumer Protection, which focuses on unfair or deceptive trade practices; and the Bureau of Economics, which gathers data, compiles statistics, and furnishes technical assistance to the other bureaus. The Commission is headquartered in Washington, D.C., but it also maintains regional offices in Atlanta, Boston, Chicago, Cleveland, Dallas, Denver, Los Angeles, New York, San Francisco, and Seattle. This regional office system enhances the Commission's enforcement, investigative, and educational missions by locating Commission staff closer to the public it serves.

AGENCY POWERS AND PROCEDURES

Introduction

The powers administrative agencies possess may be classified in a variety of ways. Some agencies' powers are largely *ministerial* in nature, concerned primarily with the routine performance of duties imposed by law. The most important administrative agencies, however, have broad *discretionary* powers that necessitate the exercise of significant discretion and judgment when they are employed. The most important formal discretionary powers agencies can possess are **investigative power, rulemaking power,** and **adjudicatory power.**

The formal powers an agency possesses are those granted by its enabling legislation. Important federal agencies like the FTC normally enjoy significant levels of each of the formal discretionary powers. But, as the following sections illustrate, even such powerful agencies face significant limitations on the exercise of their powers. In addition to explicit limits on agency proceedings contained in enabling legislation, basic constitutional provisions restrict agency action.

FIGURE 1   Federal Trade Commission

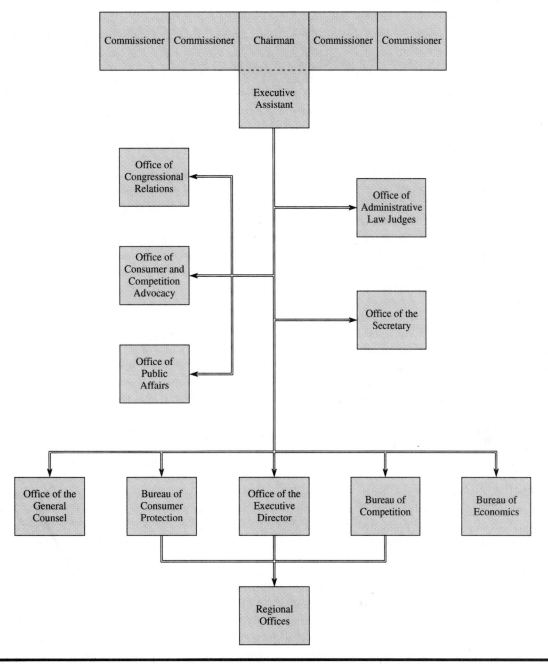

Source: *U.S. Government Manual 1989–90* (Washington, D.C.: U.S. Government Printing Office, 1989), p. 603.

A federal agency's exercise of its rulemaking and adjudicatory powers is also constrained by the **Administrative Procedure Act** (APA). The APA was enacted by Congress in 1946 in an attempt to standardize federal agency procedures and to respond to critics who said that administrative power was out of control. The APA applies to all federal agencies, although it will not displace stricter procedural requirements contained in a particular agency's enabling legislation. In addition to specifying agency procedures, the APA plays a major role in shaping the conditions under which courts will review agency actions and the standards courts will use when conducting such a review. Most states have adopted "baby APAs" to govern the activities of state administrative agencies.

Finally, as later parts of this chapter will confirm, each of the three traditional branches of government possesses substantial powers to mold and constrain the powers of the "fourth branch." That being said, one final point needs to be made before we turn to a detailed examination of formal agency powers and procedures. An agency's formal powers also confer on it significant *informal* power. Agency "advice," "suggestions," or "guidelines," which technically lack the legal force of formal agency regulations or rulings, may nonetheless play a major role in shaping the behavior of regulated industries because they carry with them the implicit or explicit threat of formal agency action in the event that they are ignored. Such gentle persuasion can be a highly effective regulatory tool, and one that is subject to far fewer constraints than formal agency action.

Investigative Power

Effective regulation is impossible without accurate information. Administrative agencies need information about business practices and activities not only so that they can detect and prosecute regulatory violations, but also to enable them to identify areas in which new rules are needed or existing rules are in need of modification. Much of the information agencies require to do their jobs is readily available. "Public interest" groups, complaints from customers or competitors, and other regulatory agencies are all important sources of information.

However, much of the information necessary to effective agency enforcement can come only from sources that may be strongly disinclined to provide it: the individuals and business organizations who are subject to regulation. This reluctance may be due to the desire to avoid or delay the regulation or regulatory action that

disclosure would generate. It might also, however, be the product of more legitimate concerns, such as a desire to protect personal privacy, a desire to prevent competitors from acquiring trade secrets and other sensitive information from agency files, or a reluctance to incur the costs that sometimes can accompany compliance with substantial information demands. Agencies, therefore, need the means to compel unwilling possessors of information to comply with legitimate demands for information. The two most important (and most intrusive) investigative tools employed by administrative agencies are *subpoenas* and *searches and seizures*.

Subpoenas   There are two basic types of subpoena: the subpoena *ad testificandum* and the subpoena *duces tecum*. Subpoenas *ad testificandum* can be used by an agency to compel unwilling witnesses to appear and testify at agency hearings. Subpoenas *duces tecum* can be used by an agency to compel the production of most types of documentary evidence, such as accounting records and office memoranda.

It should be obvious that unlimited agency subpoena power would sacrifice individual liberty and privacy in the name of regulatory efficiency. Accordingly, the courts have formulated a number of limitations that seek to balance an agency's legitimate need to know against an investigated target's legitimate privacy interests.

Agency investigations must be *authorized by law* and *conducted for a legitimate purpose*. The former requirement means that the agency's enabling legislation must have granted the agency the investigative power that it is seeking to assert. The latter requirement prohibits bad faith investigations pursued for improper motives (e.g., Internal Revenue Service investigations undertaken solely to harass political opponents of an incumbent administration).

Even when the investigation is legally authorized and is undertaken for a legitimate purpose, the information sought must be *relevant to that lawful purpose*, as is illustrated in the *Larouche* case, which follows. The Fourth Amendment to the Constitution is the source of this limitation on agency powers. However, an agency seeking the issuance of an administrative subpoena need not demonstrate the "probable cause" that the Fourth Amendment requires for the issuance of regular search warrants.[7] In the words of the Supreme Court, an

---

[7]The Fourth Amendment "warrant clause" is discussed in detail in the Crimes chapter.

agency "can investigate merely on the suspicion that the law is being violated, or even just because it wants assurance that it is not."[8] This lesser standard makes sense in the agency context, since the only evidence of many regulatory violations is documentary and, therefore, "probable cause" might be demonstrable only after inspection of the target's records. In such cases, a probable cause requirement would effectively negate agency enforcement power.

Similarly, agency information demands must be *sufficiently specific* and *not unreasonably burdensome*. This requirement also derives from the Fourth Amendment's prohibition against "unreasonable searches and seizures,"[9] and it means that agency subpoenas must describe adequately the information the agency seeks. It also means that the cost to the target of complying with the agency's demand (e.g., the cost of assembling and

reproducing the data, of disruption of business operations, or the risk that proprietary information will be indirectly disclosed to competitors) must not be unreasonably disproportionate to the agency's interest in obtaining the information.

Finally, the information sought *must not be privileged*. Various statutory and common law privileges can, at times, limit an agency's power to compel the production of information. However, by far the most important privilege in this respect is the Fifth Amendment *privilege against compulsory testimonial self-incrimination*, or "the right to silence." As you learned in the Crimes chapter, however, this privilege is subject to serious limitations in the business context. The "right to silence" in the administrative context is further limited by the fact that it is only available in *criminal* proceedings. In some regulatory contexts, the potential sanctions for violation may be labeled "civil penalties" or "forfeitures." Only when such sanctions are essentially punitive in their intent or effect will they be considered "criminal" for the purpose of allowing the invocation of the privilege.

---

[8]*United States v. Morton Salt*, 338 U.S. 632 (U.S. Sup. Ct. 1950).

[9]The Fourth Amendment guarantee against unreasonable searches and seizures is discussed in detail in the Crimes chapter.

FEDERAL ELECTION COMMISSION v. LAROUCHE CAMPAIGN, INC.
817 F.2d 233 (2d Cir. 1987)

In November 1984, the Federal Election Commission (FEC) began an investigation of the activities of the Lyndon Larouche Campaign for the Democratic Party's presidential nomination. The investigation centered on allegations that the campaign had falsified its records and obtained federal election matching funds by claiming that donations via credit cards had been made by individuals who denied making the donations. In December 1984, the FEC issued a subpoena requiring the campaign to produce records regarding the solicitation of contributions (including the names of solicitors and those solicited), contributions actually received, and all telephone records regarding the solicitation of funds. When the Larouche campaign failed to comply with the subpoena, the FEC brought an action in a federal district court to obtain enforcement. The district court ordered the campaign to comply with the subpoena. The Larouche campaign appealed.

Per Curiam.   In ordinary circumstances, the district court's analysis of this case would be entirely unobjectionable. As is nearly always appropriate, the court accorded substantial deference to the administrative subpoena and applied the familiar test that enforces such a subpoena so long as it is for a proper purpose, the information sought is relevant to that purpose, and the statutory procedures are observed. However, different considerations come into play when a case implicates First Amendment concerns. In that circumstance, the usual deference to the administrative agency is not appropriate, and the protection of the constitutional liberties of the target of the subpoena calls for a more exacting scrutiny of the justification offered by the agency.

The district court erred in holding essentially that because the campaign had not made a showing that disclosure of those associated with it was likely to result in reprisals, harrassment, or threats, the FEC needed only to show the information sought was relevant to the FEC's investigation. In an area rife with First Amendment associational concerns, an admininstrative agency is not automatically entitled to obtain all material that may in some way be relevant to a proper investigation. Rather, when the disclosure sought will compromise the privacy of individual political associations, and hence risks a chilling of unencumbered associational choices, the agency must make some showing of need for the material sought beyond its mere relevance to a proper investigation.

Here, the FEC has failed to make such a showing with regard to the identities of the campaign's solicitors. The focus of the instant investigation is the campaign's suspected use of credit card fraud to obtain contributions that may not have been authorized at all. Investigating such charges surely requires access to the list of contributors, who presumably can tell the FEC whether they did or did not make the claimed donations. But the FEC has not established that once it has access to the list of contributors, it also would have a need to identify the campaign's solicitors that would outweigh the solicitors' First Amendment interests. Absent such a showing, the FEC has failed to demonstrate that there are governmental interests sufficiently important to outweigh the possibility of infringement of the exercise of First Amendment rights.

Thus, the order enforcing compliance with the FEC's subpoena is modified by striking from the subpoena the requirement for disclosure of the names of the campaign's solicitors.

Judgment in favor of the Federal Election Commission affirmed as modified.

Searches and Seizures   Sometimes the evidence necessary to prove a regulatory violation can be obtained only by entering private property such as a home, an office, or a factory. When administrative agencies seek to gather information by such an entry, the Fourth Amendment's prohibition against unreasonable searches and seizures and its warrant requirement come into play. As the *Dow Chemical* case in the Crimes chapter indicates, the owners of commercial property, although afforded less Fourth Amendment protection than the owners of private dwellings, do have some legitimate expectations of privacy in their business premises.

Dow also illustrates, however, that not all agency information-gathering efforts will be considered so intrusive as to amount to a prohibited "search and seizure." In *Dow*, the Environmental Protection Agency's warrantless aerial photography of one of Dow's plants was upheld. Finally, in its most definitive statement on the subject to date, in *State of New York v. Burger*, the Supreme Court upheld the constitutionality of warrantless administrative inspections of the premises of "closely regulated" businesses so long as three criteria are satisfied.[10] There must be a substantial government interest in the regulatory scheme in question, the warrantless inspections must be necessary to further the scheme, and the inspection program must provide a constitutionally adequate substitute for a warrant by giving owners of commercial property adequate notice that their property is subject to inspection and by limiting the discretion of inspecting officers.

Rulemaking Power

An agency's rulemaking power derives from its enabling legislation. For example, the FTC Act gives the FTC the power "to make rules and regulations for the purpose of carrying out the provisions of this Act." The Administrative Procedure Act (APA) defines a rule as "an agency statement of general or particular applicability and future effect designed to complement, interpret or prescribe law or policy." All agency rules are compiled and published in the *Code of Federal Regulations*.

---

[10]482 U.S. 691 (U.S. Sup. Ct. 1987).

FIGURE 2 FTC Procedural Rule

§ 1.10 Advance notice of proposed rulemaking.

(a) Prior to the commencement of any trade regulation rule proceeding, the Commission shall publish in the FEDERAL REGISTER an advance notice of such proposed proceeding.

(b) The advance notice shall: (1) Contain a brief description of the area of inquiry under consideration, the objectives which the Commission seeks to achieve, and possible regulatory alternatives under consideration by the Commission; and (2) invite the response of interested persons with respect to such proposed rulemaking, including any suggestions or alternative methods for achieving such objectives.

(c) The advance notice shall be submitted to the Committee on Commerce, Science, and Transportation of the Senate and to the Committee on Interstate and Foreign Commerce of the House of Representatives.

(d) The Commission may, in addition to the publication of the advance notice, use such additional mechanisms as it considers useful to obtain suggestions regarding the content of the area of inquiry before publication of an initial notice of proposed rulemaking pursuant to § 1.11.

Source: 16 Code of Federal Regulations § 1.10 (1990).

Types of Rules   Administrative agencies create three types of rules: procedural rules, interpretive rules, and legislative rules. *Procedural rules* specify how the agency will conduct itself. Figure 2 provides an example of such a rule, which the FTC adopted to determine the manner in which notice of Commission rulemaking proceedings will be disseminated.

Interpretive rules are designed to advise regulated individuals and entities of the manner in which an agency interprets the statutes it enforces. Interpretive rules technically do not have the force of law and, therefore, are not binding on businesses or on the courts. However, courts engaged in interpreting regulatory statutes often give agency interpretations substantial weight in deference to the agency's familiarity with the statutes it administers and its presumed expertise in the general area being regulated. Business is also likely to pay attention to agency interpretive rules because such rules indicate the circumstances in which an agency is likely to take formal enforcement action. Figure 3 provides an example of an interpretive rule; in this case, an FTC rule interpreting the meaning of the term *consumer product* as used in the Magnuson-Moss Consumer Warranty Act.

Legislative rules, if they are consistent with an agency's enabling legislation and the Constitution, and if they are created in accordance with the procedures dictated by the APA, have the full force and effect of law and are binding on the courts, the public, and the agency. Figure 4 provides an example of an FTC legislative rule.

Given their greater relative importance, you should not be surprised to learn that the process by which legislative rules are promulgated, unlike the process by which procedural and interpretive rules are created, is highly regulated by the APA and closely scrutinized by the courts. At present, there are three basic types of agency rulemaking: informal rulemaking, formal rulemaking, and hybrid rulemaking.

Informal Rulemaking   Informal, or "notice and comment," rulemaking is the rulemaking method most commonly employed by administrative agencies that are not forced by their enabling legislation to follow the more stringent procedures of formal rulemaking. The informal rulemaking process commences with the publication in the *Federal Register* of a "*Notice of Proposed Rulemaking.*" The APA requires that such notices contain: a statement of the time and place at which the proceedings will be held; a statement of the nature of the proceedings; a statement of the legal authority for the proceedings (usually the agency's enabling legislation); and either a statement of the terms of the proposed rule or a description of the subjects or issues to be addressed by the rule.

Publication of notice must then be followed by a *comment period* during which interested parties can submit to the agency written comments detailing their views about the proposed rule. After comments have been received and considered, the agency must publish the regulation in its final form in the *Federal Register.* As a general rule, the rule cannot become effective until at least 30 days after its final publication in the *Federal Register.* The APA, however, recognizes a "good cause" exception to the 30-day-waiting-period requirement, and to the notice-of-rulemaking requirement as well, when notice would be impractical, unnecessary, or contrary to the public interest.

From the above discussion, it should be apparent why agencies tend to favor the informal rulemaking process—it allows quick and efficient regulatory action. Such quickness and efficiency, however, are purchased at

---

FIGURE 3   FTC Interpretive Rule

§ 700.1 Products covered.

(a) The Act applies to written warranties on tangible personal property which is normally used for personal, family, or household purposes. This definition includes property which is intended to be attached to or installed in any real property without regard to whether it is so attached or installed. This means that a product is a "consumer product" if the use of that type of product is not uncommon. The percentage of sales or the use to which a product is put by any individual buyer is not determinative. For example, products such as automobiles and typewriters which are used for both personal and commercial purposes come within the definition of consumer product. Where it is unclear whether a particular product is covered under the definition of consumer product, any ambiguity will be resolved in favor of coverage.

Source: 16 Code of Federal Regulations § 700.1 (1990).

FIGURE 4   FTC Legislative Rule

§ 417.6 The rule.

The Commission hereby promulgates, as a Trade Regulation Rule, its conclusion and determination that in connection with the sale or offering for sale in commerce, as "commerce" is defined in the Federal Trade Commission Act, of quick-freeze aerosol spray products containing Fluorocarbon 12 (Dichlorodifluoromethane) designed for the frosting of beverage glasses it is an unfair or deceptive act or practice to fail to provide a clear and conspicuous warning on the labels of such products, that the contents thereof should not be inhaled in concentrated form and that injury or death may result from such inhalation. Examples of proper warning statements include:

(1) "WARNING: Use only as directed—inhalation of the concentrated vapors of this product is harmful and may cause death."

(2) "WARNING: Use only as directed—misuse of this product by inhaling its concentrated vapors is harmful and may cause death."

Source: 16 Code of Federal Regulations § 417.6 (1990).

---

a significant cost: a relatively minimal opportunity for interested parties to participate in the rule-formation process. Giving interested parties the opportunity to be heard may, in some cases, ultimately further regulatory goals. For example, the vigorous debate about a proposed rule that a public hearing can provide may contribute to the creation of more effective rules. Also, providing interested parties with what they perceive to be an adequate opportunity to participate in the rule-making process helps to legitimatize that process and the rules it produces, thereby enhancing the chances of voluntary compliance by the regulated industry.

Formal Rulemaking   Formal, or "on the record," rulemaking is designed to afford interested parties with a far greater opportunity to make their views heard than that afforded by informal rulemaking. Formal rule-making, like informal rulemaking, begins with publication in the *Federal Register* of a "Notice of Proposed Rulemaking." Unlike the notice employed to announce informal rulemaking procedures, however, this notice must include notice of a time and place at which a public hearing concerning the proposed rule will be held.

Such hearings resemble trials in that the agency must produce evidence justifying the proposed regulation, and interested parties are likewise allowed to present evidence in opposition to it. Both sides are entitled to examine each other's exhibits and to cross-examine each other's witnesses. At the conclusion of the proceedings, the agency must prepare a formal, written document detailing its findings based on the evidence presented in the hearing.

While the formal rulemaking process affords interested parties greatly enhanced opportunities to be heard, this greater access is purchased at significant expense and at the risk that some parties will abuse their access rights to impede the regulatory process. By tireless cross-examination of government witnesses and lengthy presentations of their own, opponents seeking to derail or delay regulation may consume months, or even years, of agency time. The classic example of such behavior is the Food and Drug Administration's hearings on a proposed rule requiring that the minimum peanut content of peanut butter be set at 90 percent. Industry forces favored an 87 percent minimum and were able to delay regulation almost 10 years.

Hybrid Rulemaking Frustration over the lack of access afforded by informal rulemaking and the potential for paralyzing the regulatory process that is inherent in formal rulemaking have led some courts and legislators to attempt the creation of a rulemaking process embodying some of the elements of informal and formal procedures. Although hybrid rulemaking procedures are insufficiently established and standardized at this point to permit a detailed discussion of them, some general tendencies are evident. Hybrid procedures, like formal rulemaking, involve some sort of hearing, but, unlike formal rulemaking procedures, hybrid procedures tend to limit the right of interested parties to cross-examine agency witnesses.

Adjudicatory Power

Most major federal agencies possess substantial adjudicatory powers. They not only have the power to investigate alleged violations and to produce regulations that have legal effect, they can also instigate and hold proceedings to determine whether regulatory or statutory violations have occurred. The administrative adjudication process is at once similar to, but substantially different from, the judicial process you studied in the Resolution of Private Disputes chapter.

The administrative adjudication process normally begins with a complaint filed by the agency. The party charged in the complaint (called the *respondent*) files an answer. Respondents are normally entitled to a hearing before the agency, at which they may be represented by legal counsel, confront and cross-examine agency witnesses, and present evidence of their own. No juries are present in administrative adjudications, however, and the cases are heard by an agency employee usually called an **administrative law judge** (ALJ). Also, unlike normal criminal prosecutions, the burden of proof in administrative proceedings is normally the civil *preponderance of the evidence* standard, and constitutional procedural safeguards such as the exclusionary rule do not protect the respondent.[11]

The agency, in effect, functions as police officer, prosecutor, judge, and jury. The APA attempts to deal with the obvious potential for abuse inherent in this combination in a number of ways. First, the APA attempts to assure that ALJs are as independent as possible by requiring internal separation between an agency's judges and its investigative and prosecutorial functions. Note, for example, the organizational separation of the FTC's Office of Administrative Law Judges illustrated in Figure 1. The APA also prohibits ALJs from having private (*ex parte*) consultations with anyone who is a party to an agency proceeding and shields them from agency disciplinary action other than for "good cause." Finally, insufficient separation between an agency's adjudication function and its other functions can be contrary to basic due process requirements.

After each party to the proceeding has been heard, the ALJ renders a decision stating her findings of fact and conclusions of law and imposing whatever penalty she deems appropriate within the parameters established by the agency's enabling legislation (e.g., a fine or a cease and desist order). If neither party challenges the ALJ's decision, it becomes final.

The losing party, however, may appeal an ALJ's decision, in which case it will be subjected to a **de novo review** by the governing body of the agency (e.g., appeals from FTC ALJ decisions are heard by the five FTC commissioners).[12] *De novo* review means that the agency can treat the proceedings as if they were occurring for the first time and may totally ignore the ALJ's findings. Often, however, an agency will adopt the ALJ's findings, and, in any event, such findings will be part of the record if a disappointed respondent seeks judicial review of an agency's decision.

Finally, when considering agency adjudicatory powers, it is important to note that many agency proceedings are settled by a **consent order** before completion of the adjudication process. Consent orders are similar to the nolo contendere pleas discussed in the Crimes chapter. Respondents who sign consent orders do not admit guilt, but they waive all rights to judicial review, agree to accept a specific sanction imposed by the agency, and commonly agree to discontinue the business practice that triggered the agency action. Figure 5 graphically depicts the major powers of the "fourth branch" of government.

---

[11]*INS v. Lopez-Mendoza*, 468 U.S. 1032 (U.S. Sup. Ct. 1984). The exclusionary rule and the "beyond a reasonable doubt" standard employed in criminal cases are discussed in the Crimes chapter. The "preponderance of the evidence" standard is discussed in the Intentional Torts chapter.

---

[12]For an example of a decision by the full Federal Trade Commission, see the *International Harvester* case in the Federal Trade Commission Act and Consumer Protection Laws chapter.

FIGURE 5   Administrative Agencies and Separation of Powers

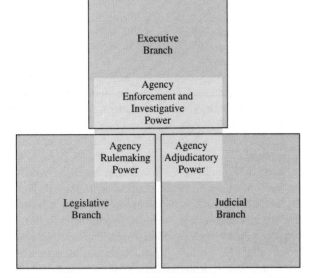

CONTROLLING ADMINISTRATIVE AGENCIES

Introduction

At this point in our discussion of administrative agencies, we have already encountered several legal controls on agency action, such as the terms of an agency's enabling legislation, the procedural requirements imposed by the APA, and the basic constraints that the Constitution places on all governmental action. The following sections continue to focus on the important theme of agency control by examining the various devices, both formal and informal, by which the three traditional branches of government influence and control the actions of the "fourth branch."

Presidential Controls

The executive branch has at its disposal a number of tools that can be employed to shape agency action. The most obvious among them is the president's power to appoint and remove agency administrators. For example you will learn in later chapters that President Reagan's appointees to the Department of Justice and the FTC made major changes in governmental antitrust enforcement policies because of their commitment to "Chicago School" antitrust ideas. This presidential power is obviously more limited in the case of "independent" agencies than it is where executive agencies are concerned, but the president generally has the power to appoint the chairmen of independent agencies, demoting the prior chairman without cause. Skillful use of the new chair's managerial powers, the most important of which is probably the power to influence agency hiring policies, can eventually effect substantial changes in agency policy. Also, significant and sustained policy differences between an independent agency and the executive branch often eventually trigger resignations by agency commissioners, thus providing the president with the opportunity to appoint new members whose philosophies are more congruent with his own.

The executive branch also exercises significant control over agency action through the Office of Management and Budget (OMB). The OMB plays a major role in the creation of the annual executive budget the president presents to Congress. In the process, the OMB reviews, and sometimes modifies, the budgetary requests of executive agencies. In addition, by Executive Order 12291,[13] President Reagan directed all executive agencies to prepare cost-benefit and least-cost analyses for all major proposed rules and to submit such proposals to the OMB for review prior to seeking public comments. This and a subsequent executive order requiring agencies to give the OMB "early warning" as soon as the agency begins to contemplate a possible rule change have made the OMB a powerful player in the rulemaking process.

Finally, the president's power to *veto* legislation concerning administrative agencies represents another point of executive influence over agency operations.

Congressional Controls

Like the executive branch, the legislative branch possesses a number of devices, both formal and informal, by which it can influence agency action. Obvious avenues of congressional control include the Senate's "advice and consent" role in agency appointments, the power to amend an agency's enabling legislation (what Congress has given, Congress can take away), and the power to pass legislation that mandates changes in agency practices or procedures. Examples of the latter include the National Environmental Policy Act (NEPA), which dictated that administrative agencies file *environmental*

---

[13]46 *Federal Register* 13193 (1981).

impact statements for every agency action that might significantly affect the quality of the environment,[14] and the Regulatory Flexibility Act of 1980, which ordered changes in agency rulemaking procedures designed to give small businesses improved notice of agency rulemaking activities that may have a substantial impact on them. Congress can also pass *sunset legislation* providing for the automatic expiration of an agency's authority unless Congress expressly extends it by a specified date. Such legislation ensures periodic congressional review of the initial decision to delegate legislative authority to an administrative agency.

Congress also enjoys several other less obvious, but no less important, points of influence over agency action. For example, Congress must authorize agency budgetary appropriations. Thus, Congress may limit or deny funding for agency programs with which it disagrees. Also, the Governmental Operations Committees of both houses of Congress exercise significant oversight over agency activities, reviewing agency programs, and conducting hearings concerning proposed agency appointments and appropriations. Finally, individual members of Congress may seek to influence agency action through "casework"—informal contacts with an agency on behalf of constituents who are involved with the agency.

Judicial Review

As important as the roles of the executive and legislative branches are in controlling agency action, the courts exercise the greatest amount of control over agency behavior. This may be due, in part, to the fact that they are the branch of government most accessible to members of the public aggrieved by agency action. The APA provides for judicial review of most agency action, which takes place either in one of the U.S. courts of appeals or a U.S. district court, depending on the nature of the agency action at issue. The Supreme Court, if it chooses to grant certiorari, is the court of last resort for review of agency action.[15]

The Right to Judicial Review   Not all agency actions are subject to judicial review and only certain individuals may challenge those that are reviewable. Individuals or organizations seeking judicial review must satisfy a

number of threshold requirements. First, plaintiffs must demonstrate the **reviewability** of the challenged action. Ordinarily, this is not very difficult because the APA creates a strong presumption in favor of reviewability. As indicated by the *Webster* case, which follows, this presumption may be overcome only by a showing that "statutes preclude review" or that the decision in question is "committed to agency discretion by law." These limitations on reviewability come from Congress's power to dictate the jurisdiction of the federal courts and from judicial deference to the proper functions of the other branches of government (e.g., a decision relating to matters of foreign policy is likely to be seen as outside the proper province of the judiciary).

Once reviewability has been established, plaintiffs need to demonstrate that they have **standing to sue,** that is, that they are "an aggrieved party" whose interests have been substantially affected by the challenged action. Initially, the courts took a relatively restrictive view of this basic requirement, requiring plaintiffs to show harm to a legally protected interest. More recently, however, the courts have liberalized the standing requirement somewhat, requiring plaintiffs to demonstrate that they have suffered an "injury" to an interest that lies within the "zone of interests" protected by the statute or constitutional provision that serves as the basis of their challenge. Demonstrating an economic loss remains the surest way to satisfy the "injury" requirement, but emotional, aesthetic, and environmental injuries have been found sufficient on occasion.

Once standing has been established, two further obstacles confront the aspiring plaintiff: **exhaustion** and **ripeness.** Courts do not want to allow regulated parties to short-circuit the regulatory process. They also want to give agencies the chance to correct their own mistakes and to develop fully their positions in disputed matters. Accordingly, they normally insist that aggrieved parties *exhaust available administrative remedies* before they will grant judicial review. The requirement that a dispute be *ripe* for judicial review is a general requirement emanating from the Constitution's insistence that only "cases or controversies" are judicially resolvable.[16] In determining ripeness, the courts weigh the hardship to the parties of withholding judicial review against the degree of refinement of the issues still possible (e.g., might further administrative action alter the nature of the issues or eliminate the need for judicial review?).

---

[14]NEPA and environmental impact statements are discussed in detail in the Environmental Regulation chapter.

[15]The Supreme Court's certiorari jurisdiction is discussed in the Resolution of Private Disputes chapter.

---

[16]Ripeness and the "case or controversy" requirement are discussed in the Resolution of Private Disputes chapter.

WEBSTER v. DOE

486 U.S. 592 (U.S. Sup. Ct. 1988)

John Doe began work at the Central Intelligence Agency (CIA or Agency) in 1973 as a clerk-typist. Periodic fitness reports consistently rated him as an excellent or outstanding employee, and by 1977 he had been promoted to covert electronics technician. In January 1982, Doe voluntarily told a CIA security officer that he was a homosexual. Almost immediately, the Agency placed Doe on paid administrative leave and began an investigation of his sexual orientation and conduct. Doe submitted to an extensive polygraph examination during which he denied having sexual relations with foreign nationals and maintained that he had not disclosed classified information to any of his sexual partners. The polygraph officer told Doe that the test results indicated that his responses had been truthful.

Nonetheless, a month later Doe was told that the Agency's Office of Security had determined that his homosexuality posed a threat to security, but declined to explain the nature of the danger. Doe was asked to resign, and when he refused to do so he was dismissed by CIA Director William Webster, who "deemed it necessary and advisable in the interests of the United States to terminate [Doe's] employment with this Agency pursuant to section 102(c) of the National Security Act." Doe filed suit against the CIA, arguing that his discharge was unconstitutional and violated the Administrative Procedure Act. The CIA moved to dismiss Doe's complaint, arguing that the director's decision was not subject to judicial review. After a federal district court and the Court of Appeals for the District of Columbia held that the decision was judicially reviewable, the Supreme Court granted certiorari.

Rehnquist, Chief Justice.   The APA's provisions allow any person "adversely affected or aggrieved" by an agency action to obtain judicial review, so long as the decision challenged represents a "final agency action for which there is no other adequate remedy in a court." Typically, a litigant will contest an action (or failure to act) by an agency on the ground that the agency has neglected to follow the statutory directives of Congress. Section 701(a), however, limits the application of the entire APA to situations in which judicial review is not precluded by statute [701(a)(1)], and the agency action is not committed to agency discretion by law [701(a)(2)].

In *Citizens to Preserve Overton Park v. Volpe* (1971), we explained the distinction between subsections 701(a)(1) and 701(a)(2). Subsection (a)(1) is concerned with whether Congress expressed an intent to prohibit judicial review; subsection (a)(2) applies in those rare instances where statutes are drawn in such broad terms that in a given case there is no law to apply. Under subsection 701(a)(2), even when Congress has not affirmatively precluded judicial oversight, review is not to be had if the statute is drawn so that a court would have no meaningful standard against which to judge the agency's exercise of discretion.

Subsection 701(a)(2) requires careful examination of the statute on which the claim of agency illegality is based. In the present case, Doe's claims against the CIA arise from the Director's asserted violation of section 102(c) of the National Security Act, which allows termination of an Agency employee whenever the Director "shall *deem* such termination necessary or advisable in the interests of the United States" (emphasis added), not simply when the dismissal *is* necessary or advisable to those interests. This standard fairly exudes deference to the Director, and appears to us to foreclose the application of any meaningful judicial standard of review. Short of permitting cross-examination of the Director concerning his views of the Nation's security and whether the discharged employee was inimical to those interests, we see no basis on which a reviewing court could properly assess an Agency termination decision. The language of section 102(c) thus strongly suggests that its implementation was "committed to agency discretion by law."

So too does the overall structure of the National Security Act. Passed shortly after the close of the Second World War, the NSA created the CIA and gave its Director the responsibility "for protecting intelligence sources and methods from unauthorized disclosure." Section 102(c) is an integral part of that statute, because the Agency's efficacy, and the Nation's security, depend in large measure on the reliability and trustworthiness of the Agency's employees. Employment with the CIA entails a high degree of trust that is perhaps unmatched in government service. We thus find that the language and structure of section 102(c) indicate that Congress meant to commit individual employee discharges to the Director's discretion, and that section 701(a)(2) accordingly precluded judicial review of these decisions under the APA.

In addition to his claim that the Director failed to abide by the statutory dictates of section 102(c), Doe also alleged that the Director's termination of his employment deprived him of property and liberty interests under the Due Process Clause, denied him equal protection of the laws, and unjustifiably burdened his right to privacy. We share the confusion of the Court of Appeals as to the precise nature of Doe's constitutional claims. It is difficult, if not impossible, to ascertain from the complaint whether Doe contends that his termination, based on *his* homosexuality, is constitutionally impermissible, or whether he asserts that a more pervasive discrimination policy exists in the CIA's employment practices regarding *all* homosexuals.

Webster maintains that, no matter what the nature of Doe's constitutional claim, judicial review is precluded by the language and intent of section 102(c). We do not think section 102(c) may be read to exclude review of constitutional claims. Where Congress intends to preclude judicial review of constitutional claims its intent to do so must be clear. Nothing in the language of section 102(c) persuades us that Congress meant to preclude consideration of colorable constitutional claims arising out of the actions of the Director pursuant to that section; we believe that a constitutional claim based on an individual discharge may be reviewed by the District Court.

Judgment of the Court of Appeals affirmed in part and reversed in part; case remanded for further proceedings.

The Bases for Judicial Review There are several legal theories on which agency action may be attacked. It may be alleged that the agency's action was *ultra vires* (exceeded its authority as granted by its enabling legislation) or that the agency substantially *deviated from procedural requirements* contained in the APA or in its enabling legislation. Agency action may also be challengeable as *unconstitutional* or, as illustrated by the following *Bowen* case, it may be attacked as the product of an *erroneous interpretation of statutes*. Finally, agency action may be reversible because it is *unsubstantiated by the facts* before the agency when it acted.

The Standards for Review The degree of scrutiny that courts will apply to agency action depends on the nature of issues under dispute and the type of agency proceedings that produced the challenged action. Courts are least likely to defer to agency action when *questions of law* are at issue. Although courts afford substantial consideration to an agency's interpretations of the statutes it enforces, the courts are still the ultimate arbiters of the meaning of statutes and constitutional provisions.

When *questions of fact* or *policy* are at issue, however, courts are more likely to defer to the agency because presumably it has superior expertise and because the agency fact finders who heard and viewed the evidence were better situated to judge its merit. When agency factual judgments are at stake, the APA provides for three standards of review, the most rigorous of which is *de novo* review.

When conducting a *de novo* review, courts make an independent finding of the facts after conducting a new hearing. Efficiency considerations plainly favor limited judicial review of the facts. Accordingly, *de novo* review is employed only when required by statute, when inadequate fact-finding proceedings were used in an agency adjudicatory proceeding, or when new factual issues that were not before the agency are raised in a proceeding to enforce a nonadjudicatory agency action.

When courts are reviewing formal agency adjudications or formal rulemaking, the APA calls for the application of a *substantial evidence* test. Only agency findings that are "unsupported by substantial evidence" will be overturned. In conducting "substantial evidence" reviews, courts look at the reasonableness of an agency's actions in relation to the facts before it rather than conducting an independent fact-finding hearing, such as that which is done in *de novo* reviews. For an example of an agency order that was set aside for failure to meet the "substantial evidence" test, see the *Tenneco* case in the Clayton Act chapter. The substantial evidence test also tends to be employed in hybrid rulemaking cases.

The judicial standard of review used in cases involving informal agency adjudications or rulemaking is the *arbitrary and capricious* test. This is the least rigorous standard of judicial review, due to the great degree of deference it accords agency decisions. In deciding whether an agency's action was "arbitrary and capricious," a reviewing court theoretically should not substitute its judgment for that of the agency. Instead, it should ask whether there was an adequate factual basis for the agency's action, and should sustain actions that do not amount to a "clear error of judgment." While, in theory, the substantial evidence and arbitrary and capricious tests are separate and distinct, in practice, such distinctions often tend to blur.

BOWEN v. AMERICAN HOSPITAL ASSOCIATION

476 U.S. 610 (U.S. Sup. Ct. 1986)

In April 1982, the parents of an infant with Down's syndrome and other handicaps refused consent to surgery to remove an obstruction in the infant's esophagus that prevented oral feeding. In May 1982, after the child's death, the Secretary of Health and Human Services promulgated rules that, among other things, required hospitals and other health care providers to post notices that health care should not be withheld from infants on the basis of mental or physical handicap. The rules were adopted pursuant to section 504 of the Rehabilitation Act of 1973, which permits the head of any executive branch agency to promulgate rules prohibiting discrimination against an "otherwise qualified handicapped individual . . . solely by reason of his handicap." The American Hospital Association challenged the validity of the rules. The District Court found the rules invalid, and the Second Circuit Court of Appeals affirmed. The secretary appealed to the Supreme Court of the United States.

Stevens, Justice. It is an axiom of administrative law that an agency's explanation of the basis for its decision must include a rational connection between the facts found and the choice made. Agency deference has not come so far that we will uphold regulations whenever it is possible to conceive a basis for administrative action. The mere fact that there is some rational basis within the knowledge and experience of the agency under which it might have concluded that the regulation was necessary to discharge its statutorily authorized mission will not suffice to validate agency decisionmaking. Our recognition of Congress's need to vest administrative agencies with ample power to assist in the difficult task of governing a vast and complex Nation carries with it the correlative responsibility of the agency to explain the rationale and factual basis for its decision, even though we show respect for the agency's judgment in both.

Before examining the Secretary's reasons for issuing the Rules, it is essential to understand the pre-existing state-law framework governing the provision of medical care to handicapped infants. In broad outline, state law vests decisional responsibility in the parents, subject to review in exceptional cases by the State acting as *parens patriae*. Prior to the regulatory activity culminating in the Rules, the federal government was not a participant in the process of making treatment decisions for newborn infants. We presume that this general framework was familiar to Congress when it enacted section 504 of the Rehabilitation Act.

The Secretary contends that a hospital's refusal to furnish a handicapped infant with medically beneficial treatment solely by reason of its handicap constitutes unlawful discrimination. Yet the preamble to the Rules correctly states that when "a non-treatment decision, no matter how discriminatory, is made by parents, rather than by the hospital," section 504 does not mandate that the hospital unilaterally overrule the parental decision and provide treatment notwithstanding the lack of consent by the parents. A hospital's withholding of treatment when no parental consent has been given cannot violate section 504, for without the consent of the parents or a surrogate decisionmaker, the infant is neither "otherwise qualified" for treatment nor has he been denied care "solely by reason of his handicap." Indeed, it would almost certainly be a tort as a matter of state law to operate on an infant without parental consent. This analysis makes clear that the Secretary's heavy reliance on the analogy to race-based refusals is misplaced. If a hospital refused to operate on a black child whose parents had withheld their consent to treatment, the hospital's refusal would not be based on the race of the child even if it were assumed that the parents based *their decision* entirely on a mistaken assumption that the race of the child made the operation inappropriate.

The Rules are not needed to prevent hospitals from denying treatment to handicapped infants. The record contains no evidence that hospitals have ever refused treatment authorized either by the infant's parents or by a court order. In promulgating the Rules, the Secretary relied upon 49 cases that the Department of Health and Human Services had processed prior to December 1, 1983. Curiously, however, *none* of the 49 cases resulted in a finding of discriminatory withholding of medical care. In fact, in the entire list of 49 cases, there is no finding that a hospital failed or refused to provide treatment to a handicapped infant for which parental consent had been given.

The Secretary has substantial leeway to explore areas in which discrimination against the handicapped poses particularly significant problems and to devise regulations to prohibit such discrimination. Even according the greatest respect to the Secretary's action, however, deference cannot fill the lack of an evidentiary foundation on which the Rules must rest. The history of these Rules exposes the inappropriateness of the extraordinary deference—virtually a *carte blanche*—requested by the Secretary. The Secretary regards the mission of the Department of Health and Human Services as one principally concerned with the quality of medical care for handicapped infants rather than with the implementation of section 504. But nothing in the Rehabilitation Act authorizes the Secretary to dispense with the law's focus on discrimination and instead to employ federal resources to save the lives of handicapped newborns, without regard to whether they are victims of discrimination. Section 504 does not authorize the Secretary to give unsolicited advice either to parents or to hospitals who are faced with difficult treatment decisions concerning handicapped children.

Judgment for the American Hospital Association affirmed.

Information Controls

Over the last two decades, Congress has enacted three major statutes aimed at controlling administrative agencies through the regulation of information. Each of these statutes represents a compromise between competing social interests of significant importance. On one hand, we have a strong democratic preference for public disclosure of governmental operations, believing that "government in the dark" is less likely to be consistent with the public interest than is "government in the sunshine."

On the other hand, we also recognize that some sensitive governmental activities must be shielded from the scrutiny of unfriendly parties, and also that disclosure of some information can unjustifiably invade personal privacy, hinder government law enforcement efforts, and provide the competitors of a company about which information is being disclosed with proprietary information that could be used unfairly to the competitors' advantage.

The Freedom of Information Act   Congress passed the **Freedom of Information Act** (FOIA) in 1966 and later amended it in 1974. The FOIA was designed to enable private citizens to have access to documents in the government's possession. Agencies must respond to public requests for documents within 10 days after such a request has been received. An agency bears the burden of justifying any denial of any FOIA request, and denials are appealable to an appropriate federal district court. Successful plaintiffs may recover their costs and attorney's fees.

Not all government-held documents are obtainable under the FOIA, however. The FOIA exempts from disclosure documents that:

1. Must be kept secret in the interest of national security.
2. Concern an agency's internal personnel practices.
3. Are specifically exempted from disclosures by statute.
4. Contain trade secrets or other confidential or privileged commercial or financial information.
5. Reflect internal agency deliberations on matters of policy or proceedings.
6. Contain individual personnel or medical information if disclosure would constitute an invasion of privacy.
7. Would threaten the integrity of a law enforcement agency's investigations or jeopardize an individual's right to a fair trial.
8. Relate to the supervision or regulation of financial institutions.
9. Contain geological or geophysical data.

Frequent users of the FOIA include the media, industry trade associations, "public interest" groups, and companies seeking to obtain useful information about their competitors. It is important to note that although the FOIA allows agencies to refuse to disclose exempted documents, it does not impose on them the affirmative duty to do so. The Supreme Court has held that individuals cannot compel an agency to deny an FOIA request for allegedly exempt documents that contain sensitive information about them.[17]

The FOIA recently has been the focus of considerable controversy on two points. First, governmental budgetary cutbacks have combined with growing numbers of requests for information to produce agency delays as long as two years in responding to information requests. Courts tend to tolerate agency delays if the agency can show that it is making a "due-diligence" effort to respond. Second, the dramatic increase in computerized information storage that has occurred since the passage of the FOIA has created problems unanticipated by the statute, which focuses on information stored in documentary form. Do interested parties have the same rights of access to data stored in agency computers that they have to government documents? May the government destroy electronic mail messages, or must it save them? Future legislative or judicial action will be necessary to resolve such questions.

The Privacy Act of 1974   This federal statute allows individuals to inspect files that agencies maintain on them and to request that erroneous or incomplete records be corrected. It also attempts to prevent agencies from gathering unnecessary information about individuals and forbids the disclosure of an individual's records without his written permission, except in certain specifically exempted circumstances. For example, records may be disclosed to employees of the collecting agency who need them to perform their duties (the "need to know" exception), to law enforcement agencies, to other agencies' personnel for "routine use" (uses for purposes compatible with the purpose for which the record was collected), to persons filing legitimate FOIA requests, and pursuant to court order.

The Government in the Sunshine Act   The Government in the Sunshine Act of 1976 was designed to insure that "Every portion of every meeting of an agency shall be open to public observation." However, complete public access to all agency meetings could have the same negative consequences that unrestrained public access to agency records can sometimes produce. Accordingly, the Sunshine Act exempts certain agency meetings from public scrutiny under circumstances similar to those

---

[17]*Chrysler Corp. v. Brown*, 441 U.S. 281 (U.S. Sup. Ct. 1980).

under which documents are exempt from disclosure under the FOIA.

ISSUES IN REGULATION

"Old" Regulation versus "New" Regulation

Some interested observers of regulatory developments over the last 25 years have noted significant differences between the regulations that originated during the Progressive (1902 to 1914) and New Deal (1933 to 1938) eras and many more recent regulations.[18] They argue not only that the number and scope of regulatory controls have increased substantially in recent years, but also that the focus and the impact of regulation have changed significantly.

Whereas earlier regulation often focused on business practices that harmed the economic interests of specific segments of society (e.g., workers, small-business people, investors), many modern regulations focus on the health and safety of all citizens. Similarly, whereas earlier regulations often focused on a particular industry or group of industries (e.g., the railroads or the securities industry), many modern regulations affect large segments of industry (e.g., Title VII of the Civil Rights Act of 1964 and regulations governing environmental pollution and workplace safety). Finally, whereas earlier congressional delegations of regulatory power tended to be quite broad (e.g., the FTC Act's prohibition of "unfair methods of competition" and "unfair or deceptive acts or practices"), many more recent regulatory statutes (e.g., the Clean Air Acts of 1970 and 1977) have been extremely detailed.

What are the consequences of these changes in the nature of regulation? Far more businesses than ever before feel the impact of federal regulation, and far more areas of internal corporate decision making are affected by regulation. These changes tend to erode the historic distinction between "regulated" and other industries, and to heighten the importance of business-government relations. Detailed regulatory statutes also increase Congress's role in shaping regulatory policy at the expense of administrative discretion, making regulatory policy arguably more vulnerable to legislative lobbying efforts.

---

[18]See, for example, David Vogel, "The 'New' Social Regulation in Historical and Comparative Perspective," in *Regulation in Perspective,* ed. T. McGraw (Cambridge, Mass.: Harvard University Press, 1981), p. 155.

Agency "Capture" versus Agency "Shadows"

Proponents of regulation have traditionally feared that regulatory agencies would become "captives" of the industries they were charged with regulating. Through "revolving door" appointments by which key figures moved back and forth between government and the private sector, and by excessive reliance on "experts" beholden to industry, the independence of administrative agencies may be compromised and their effectiveness as regulators may be destroyed.

More recently, commentators sympathetic to business have argued that similar dangers to agency independence exist in the form of the nonindustry "shadow" groups that "public interest" organizations maintain to monitor agency actions (e.g., the Center for Auto Safety, which monitors the work of the Highway Transportation Safety Administration). Agencies may develop dependency relationships with their "shadows" or at least make decisions based in part on their "shadows'" anticipated reactions. Such informal means of shaping regulatory policy, when combined with the ability to challenge agency actions in court due to liberalized standing rules, have made "public interest" organizations important players in the contemporary regulatory process.

Deregulation versus Reregulation

A useful axiom for understanding the process of social and legal evolution is that *the cost of the status quo is easier to perceive than the cost of change.* Few things are more illustrative of the operation of this axiom than the history of regulation in the United States.

In the latter years of the 19th century, the social costs of living in an unregulated environment were readily apparent. Large business organizations often abused their power at the expense of their customers, suppliers, employees, and distributors, and sought to increase their power by acquiring their competitors or driving them out of business. Market forces, standing alone, were apparently unable to protect the public from defective, and in some cases dangerous, products. As a result of these and numerous other social and historical factors, this century has witnessed a tremendous growth in government and in government regulation of business.

But regulation, too, has its costs. Regulatory bureaucracies generate their own internal momentum and have their own interests to protect. They may become insensitive to the legitimate concerns of the industries they regulate and the public they supposedly serve. They may continue to seek higher and higher levels of safety, heedless of the fact that life necessarily involves some elements of risk and that the total elimination of risk in a modern technological society may be impossible, or, if possible, obtainable at a cost that we cannot afford to pay. At a time when many Americans are legitimately concerned about economic efficiency, as well as the ability of U.S. companies to compete effectively in world markets against competitors who operate in less-regulated environments, these and other costs of regulation are readily apparent.

As a result, in the last decade, we witnessed substantial "deregulation" in a number of industries such as the airline, banking, railroad, and trucking industries. The results of these efforts are, at best, mixed. The case of airline regulation should suffice to make the point. Proponents of deregulation cite the generally lower fares that deregulation has produced. Opponents tend to point to increased airline "overbooking" practices, reduced or eliminated services to smaller communities, and increased safety problems, all of which, they argue, are products of deregulation. The costs of deregulation have generated predictable calls for reregulating the airline industry. The ultimate outcome of the deregulation versus reregulation debate will depend upon which costs we as a society decide we would prefer to pay.

ETHICAL AND PUBLIC POLICY CONCERNS

1. Earlier in the chapter you learned that agency formal rulemaking procedures are vulnerable to industry tactics aimed at delaying regulation (e.g., the example concerning the minimum peanut content of peanut butter). Are such industry tactics ethically justifiable?

2. In our discussion of the Freedom of Information Act you learned that companies seeking to obtain useful information about their competitors frequently seek access to documents covered by the Act. Is this an ethical way to gain access to information?

3. Although the first question above focuses on delaying tactics practiced by industry, it is important to note that agencies also have been known to engage in delay and other tactics designed to frustrate citizens and organizations with whom they interact. For example, an agency may delay its response to an FOIA request, untruthfully arguing that staff shortages prevent a timely response, or it may refuse to turn over documents that it knows are not exempt from disclosure, forcing those seeking disclosure to engage in expensive and time-consuming litigation to attain their ends. Are such agency tactics ethically justifiable?

SUMMARY

Administrative agencies arose because courts and legislatures were incapable of handling all of the regulatory tasks that were necessary in a high-speed, interdependent, technological society. Agencies have a pervasive influence on modern individual and business life, and are sometimes called the *fourth branch of government*.

An agency is created by a statute called *enabling legislation*, which dictates its structure, powers, and procedures. Agencies perform investigative, legislative, and judicial functions normally reserved to the three traditional branches of government. The fundamental problem of administrative law is how to limit agencies' ability to abuse their powers while preserving their ability to achieve regulatory goals.

One of the major checks on agency power is the Constitution. In addition to the basic constitutional safeguards that limit all governmental action, the constitutional principle of separation of powers serves as an important limit on the power that can be delegated to administrative agencies. Enabling legislation that is so broad that it fails to provide an "intelligible principle" to guide agency action is an unconstitutional violation of separation of powers.

There are two basic federal agency types: executive agencies and "independent" agencies. Executive agencies are housed in the executive branch of government, and their heads serve at the will of the president. "Independent" agencies are headed by boards or commissions whose members are presidentially appointed with the "advice and consent" of the Senate for fixed terms and are removable only for cause.

Most major agencies possess both *ministerial* and *discretionary* powers. Ministerial powers involve the routine performance of duties imposed by law. Discretionary powers, such as investigation, rulemaking, and adjudicatory power, involve the exercise of significant discretion and judgment by an agency. The Administrative Procedure Act (APA) places procedural limits on an agency's exercise of rulemaking power and also shapes the standards courts will use to review agency actions. Also, agencies possess important informal powers to influence the behavior of regulated entities.

Major agencies possess substantial investigative powers, the most important of which are the power to subpoena documents and testimony and the power to conduct searches to seize evidence of regulatory violations. The Fourth and Fifth Amendments to the Constitution place important limits on these investigative powers.

Agencies create *procedural* rules to govern their internal operations, *interpretive* rules to inform interested parties of the agencies' interpretation of the statutes they administer, and *legislative* rules that have binding legal effect on regulated entities. The APA dictates the procedures agencies must follow to exercise their rulemaking power.

There are three basic types of agency rulemaking: formal rulemaking, informal rulemaking, and hybrid rulemaking. With formal rulemaking, interested parties appear at a trial-like hearing to examine the agency's evidence, cross-examine its witnesses, and present evidence of their own. With informal rulemaking, interested parties submit written comments about a proposed rule, but they are not entitled to a hearing. Hybrid rulemaking provides a hearing, but limits interested parties' ability to cross-examine agency witnesses.

Agency adjudicatory hearings differ from judicial trials in a number of ways. They are instigated by a complaint filed by the agency and heard by an agency employee called an administrative law judge (ALJ). The APA attempts to insure that ALJs are independent from intra-agency or outside influences, and ALJ decisions are appealable to the governing body of the agency.

Each of the three traditional branches of government enjoys significant control over agency action. The president, through his appointment power, his power to issue executive orders, his veto power, and his ability, through the Office of Management and Budget, to affect executive agency budget requests, has a variety of tools at his disposal to shape agency policy.

Congress also can influence agency action in a variety of ways. It can amend enabling legislation, pass statutes that order changes in agency practice or procedures, deny or limit agency budgetary appropriations, and exercise less-formal influence through congressional "oversight" committees and "casework" on behalf of individual constituents.

The power of the courts to review agency adjudications and rulemaking is probably the most important check on agency action. Not all agency actions are judicially reviewable, however, and plaintiffs who can prove reviewability also must demonstrate that they have standing to sue and that the issues are ripe for judicial review. There are three standards of review of agency factual judgments under the APA: *de novo* review, the "substantial evidence" test, and the "arbitrary and capricious" test.

Finally, Congress has passed several statutes designed to control the information agencies collect and the uses to which that information is put. The Freedom of Information Act requires government agencies to allow interested parties access to documents in their possession. The Privacy Act of 1974 limits the data agencies can collect on individuals and the entities to whom collected data may be disseminated without individual permission. It also allows individuals to obtain access to their records. The Government in the Sunshine Act of 1976 requires that agency meetings be open to public observation.

PROBLEM CASES

1. In 1985, without recourse to notice-and-comment procedures, the Department of Transportation (DOT) issued an "Order Granting Exemption" from an earlier regulation dealing with deceptive practices in airfare advertising. The exemption allowed advertisers to separate a $3 international departure tax adopted by Congress in 1978 from the total advertised price. In 1988, the DOT issued an "Order Amending Exemption," which included all government-imposed surcharges within the exemption. The effect of this order was to allow foreign departure taxes, immigration fees, customs fees, security fees, and any other charges that might be imposed by various governments to be excluded from the total advertised ticket price so long as such charges were clearly identified and stated somewhere else in the ad. The attorneys general of 25 states filed a petition seeking review of the order, arguing that it was contrary to their interpretations of their own states' consumer protection statutes and that the DOT's failure to employ notice-and-comment rulemaking rendered the order invalid. The DOT argued that the states lacked standing to challenge the order and that the order was merely a rule interpreting the 1985 exemption order and therefore was not subject to APA notice-and-comment requirements. Should the order stand?

2. In the late 1960s, the Federal Aviation Administration (FAA), in an attempt to reduce takeoff and landing delays at five major airports, adopted a regulation limiting the number of takeoff and landing slots at those airports. At Washington National Airport, 40 slots per hour were assigned to commercial aircraft. Prior to 1980, the airlines voluntarily allocated these slots among themselves. In 1980, however, a new airline wanted some of the National Airport slots, but none of the existing airlines would voluntarily give up any slots. The airlines' existing slot allocation agreement was due to expire on November 30, 1980. If the slot allocations changed, some lead time was necessary to enable the airlines to make schedule adjustments, notify passengers, and rearrange ticket reservations taken under the existing schedules. To avoid chaos in the skies during the 1980 Thanksgiving–Christmas holiday season, the Secretary of Transportation proposed a regulation allocating the National Airport slots. Notice of the proposed regulation was published in the *Federal Register* on October 20, 1980. The comment period was set for a seven-day period starting on October 16, 1980, the date the proposed regulation was issued by the Secretary. Thirty-seven comments were received from airlines and others. Northwest Airlines, however, filed suit, arguing that the Administrative Procedure Act required at least a 30-day comment period for proposed regulations. Should Northwest win?

3. The Occupational Safety and Health Act was passed "to assure so far as possible every working man and woman in the Nation safe and healthful working conditions." The Act authorized the secretary of labor to promulgate regulatory standards governing workplace health and safety. The Act also provided that the secretary should set standards that, "to the extent possible," assure that no employee will suffer material health consequences even from a lifetime of exposure to an occupational hazard. In 1978, the secretary, acting through the Occupational Safety and Health Administration (OSHA), promulgated a strict standard limiting occupational exposure to cotton dust. The American Textile Manufacturers Institute, an organization representing the cotton industry, challenged the validity of the cotton dust standard, arguing that the Act required the secretary to demonstrate a reasonable relationship between the costs and the benefits associated with the standard. Should the standard be overturned?

4. Fenster, president and part owner of Utica Packing Company, was convicted of bribing a federal meat inspector, an employee of the United States Department of Agriculture (USDA). In a hearing before an administrative law judge (ALJ), the USDA sought a withdrawal of meat inspection services from Utica unless Fenster sold his ownership of Utica and withdrew from its management. The ALJ ruled in the USDA's favor, effectively eliminating Utica's ability to conduct its business. Utica appealed the decision to the USDA judicial officer, Donald Campbell, who had the power to make final adjudicative orders for the USDA. Campbell affirmed the ALJ's decision, and so did a federal district court. The Sixth Circuit Court of Appeals, however, held that Campbell erred by not considering mitigating circumstances in the case. Upon reconsideration, Campbell reluctantly held that the mitigating circumstances prevented him from finding that Utica was unfit to receive inspection services. USDA executive officials strongly disagreed with Campbell's decision. They got the secretary of agriculture to replace Campbell with Deputy Assistant Secretary John Franke, who was not a lawyer and had no adjudicatory experience. Franke then reconsidered Campbell's decision at the USDA's request, finding that the mitigating circumstances were insufficient to justify Fenster's bribing the meat inspector. Utica appealed, arguing that its due process rights had been violated. Is Utica right?

5. The Medicare Act established a health insurance program to be administered by the secretary of health and human services. Judicial review of a denial of a medicare claim is available only after the secretary renders a final decision. A final decision is made only after a medicare claimant has had four opportunities to have his claim considered, including consideration by an administrative law judge (ALJ) and the Appeals Council of the Department of Health and Human Services. In January 1979, the secretary issued an administrative instruction that no medicare payments should be made for a surgical procedure known as bilateral carotid body resection (BCBR) when performed to relieve respiratory distress, on the grounds that BCBR surgery was not reasonable or necessary, the standard required by the Medicare Act. Many claimants whose BCBR claims were initially denied sought review before ALJs, who consistently ruled in favor of BCBR claimants, as did the Appeals Council. In response to these rulings, the secretary issued a formal administrative ruling prohibiting ALJs and the Appeals Council in all cases from ordering medicare payments for BCBR operations performed after October 28, 1980. Sanford Holmes had BCBR surgery before October 28, 1980. His claim for medicare benefits was rejected. Holmes did not seek a hearing on his claim before an ALJ or a review in the Appeals Council. Instead, he sued the secretary in a federal district court, challenging her decision that BCBR surgery was not necessary or reasonable. Will the district court review the secretary's decision?

6. Chaney and other prison inmates were sentenced to death under the laws of Oklahoma and Texas. They were to be executed by lethal injection of drugs. The drugs were approved by the Food and Drug Administration for medical purposes stated on their labels. The FDA had not, however, approved their use for human executions. Chaney claimed that use of the drugs for human executions violated the Food, Drug, and Cosmetic Act (FDCA) as an unapproved use of an approved drug. He argued that, under the FDCA, the FDA was required to approve the drugs as "safe and effective" for human execution before they could be distributed. Chaney asked the FDA to investigate these perceived violations of the FDCA and to take enforcement actions, including seizing the drugs from state prisons and recommending the prosecution of those who knowingly distribute or purchase the drugs with the intent to use them for human executions. The FDA refused to take any action on the grounds that it had no power to interfere with the use of lethal injections in a state criminal justice system. Chaney sought judicial review of the FDA's refusal to act, and the district court held that the FDA's refusal to take enforcement action was not subject to judicial review. Was the district court's decision correct?

7. On August 1, 1982, Larry Morrison, a pilot for Northwest Airlines, piloted a passenger airliner while he was intoxicated. Four days later, Northwest Airlines discharged him as an employee. The next day, Morrison began four weeks of voluntary alcoholism treatment. He attended weekly counseling sessions thereafter. On January 20, 1983, the Federal Aviation Administration (FAA) temporarily suspended his pilot certificate. Without a pilot certificate, Morrison could not pilot airplanes within the United States. On September 2, 1983, Morrison requested recertification, which the FAA granted subject to a few restrictions. Northwest Airlines sought judicial review of the FAA's recertification on the grounds that (1) recertifying Morrison would make the skies unsafe for Northwest airplanes, its crews, and its passengers and (2) the FAA's lenient recertification policy would make it more difficult for Northwest to deter drinking among its pilots and other employees. Are these injuries sufficient to give Northwest standing to seek judicial review of the FAA's decision to recertify Morrison?

8. The Federal Land Policy and Management Act (FLPMA) empowers the secretary of the interior to "dispose of a tract of public land by exchange when the public interest is well served." In 1982, the secretary approved a three-way exchange of land by which the National Park Service received previously privately owned land within the boundaries of Grand Teton National Park and the federal government gave up federal coal lands in the Corral Canyon, Wyoming, area. The Corral Canyon lands were alternate sections of a checkerboard. The recipient of the Corral Canyon lands was Rocky Mountain Energy Company, a coal mining company that already owned land in the Corral Canyon area. The exchange yielded Rocky Mountain a contiguous tract of land more suitable to coal mining. In addition, the lands were close to lines of the Union Pacific Railroad, a company owned by the same corporation that owned Rocky Mountain. The exchange was overwhelmingly supported by all groups, including environmental groups, except the National Coal Association (NCA) and the Mining and Reclamation Council of America (MRCA), trade associations whose members produced most of the nation's coal. The NCA and MRCA claimed that the secretary erred in approving the land exchange, since the Mineral Leasing Act (MLA) prohibited the secretary from leasing federal coal lands to a railroad that is in the business of mining coal. The MLA was enacted out of the fear "that if railroads were allowed to own coal mines they would discriminate in transportation against competing coal mines that depended on rail transportation." The NCA and the MRCA contended that the exchange, by allowing Rocky Mountain Energy to mine a large tract of previously unminable land, threatened their members with more rigorous competition. Is this threat of injury sufficient to give the NCA and the MRCA standing to challenge the secretary's approval of the exchange?

9. An agent of the Pennsylvania Department of Environmental Resources saw Disposal Service's loaded trash truck backing into a building that was used to compact waste to be loaded onto tractor-trailers for transportation and final disposal. Knowing the building's purpose and that Disposal Service did not have the permit to operate it as a transfer station required by the state Solid Waste Management Act (SWMA), the agent entered the property, went into the building, and observed the operation. Disposal Service was later prosecuted for operating a transfer station without a permit. Disposal Service moved to suppress the agent's evidence, arguing that his warrantless entry onto the property violated the Fourth Amendment. The state argued that the SWMA's provisions allowing such warrantless inspections were constitutional. Should the evidence be suppressed?

10. *The New York Times* (the *Times*) filed a Freedom of Information Act (FOIA) request with the National Aeronautics and Space Administration (NASA) asking for "transcripts of all voice and data communications recorded aboard the space shuttle Challenger" on the day when the shuttle self-destructed, killing all seven astronauts on board. The *Times* also requested copies of voice communication tapes. NASA provided a written transcript of the only voice recording made, but refused to turn over a copy of the tape itself, arguing that to do so would violate the privacy of the astronauts' families by exposing them to replays of their loved ones' voices. NASA argued that the tape was exempt from disclosure under Exemption 6 to the FOIA because the human voice, being unique to each individual, "clearly is infor-mation about the individual and identifiable as such." Should NASA turn over the tape?

11. Britt, a major in the Marine Corps Reserve, was investigated by the Naval Investigative Service (NIS) in connection with allegations that one of his Reserve sub-ordinates had improperly stored ordnance in his home. While the investigation was in progress, the NIS con-tacted Britt's regular employer, the Immigration and Naturalization Service (INS), and provided his INS su-pervisor with reports and other material from the inves-tigation. After Britt was later cleared of all charges by the Marines, he filed suit against the NIS arguing that it had violated the Privacy Act by releasing information about the investigation to the INS. Were the NIS's ac-tions proper?

CHAPTER 5

EMPLOYMENT LAW

INTRODUCTION

Years ago, it was unusual to see a separate employment law chapter in a business law text. Traditionally, the rights, duties, and liabilities accompanying employment mainly have been governed by such basic legal institutions as contract, tort, and agency. These common law principles continue to control relations between employers and their employees unless displaced by state or federal regulation, or by new judge-made rules applying specifically to employment. By now, however, such rules and regulations have become so numerous that they touch almost every facet of the employment relationship. This chapter discusses the most important of these legal controls on employment. To see how and why these regulations emerged, and to get some perspective on them, the chapter opens with an historical overview of American employment law.

THE EVOLUTION OF AMERICAN EMPLOYMENT LAW

Early American Employment Law

From colonial times through the mid-19th century, much of the American population was self-employed. For many Americans, therefore, the problems created by the employment relation did not exist. For those who *were* employed during this period, the relation sometimes was authoritarian and paternalistic.

In the apprenticeship relations that were common in early America, for example, a master's duties were frequently compared to those of a parent and an apprentice's to those of a son. Among other things, a master often was obligated to train his apprentices and to see to their religious and secular education. Moreover, many states limited a master's power to discharge his apprentices without good cause. Also common during this period were indentured servants, who basically sold themselves to a master for a period of time and thus resembled temporary slaves. Although the law imposed certain duties of fair and humane treatment on a master, often an indentured servant could not marry without his master's consent and was denied the rights to vote and to engage in trade. In the southern states, moreover, the law regulated and enforced the oppressive system of black slavery. Further reinforcing the employer's power during this period was the courts' tendency to declare that labor unions were illegal criminal conspiracies.

The Period of Industrialization and Laissez-Faire

By the end of the Civil War, self-employment was less prevalent than formerly. In addition, the employment relation had lost much of its earlier authoritarian and paternalistic character. Increasingly, employer and employee came to be regarded as free and equal parties whose relations were governed by the highly individualistic principles of 19th-century contract law,[1] and whose other duties to each other were few.

This change, however, did not markedly improve the employee's position, and may have worsened it in some respects. For one thing, employees frequently bargained from a position of inferior power. Among the reasons were the existence of a large labor pool increasingly composed of immigrants, and the eventual emergence of large corporate employers. For another thing, this changed view of the employment relation helped insulate employers from liability to employees who were injured on the job. This was consistent with one of 19th-century America's main public policy goals: promoting the nation's industrialization by protecting infant industries against potentially crippling damage recoveries. Two important 19th-century legal developments—the employment-at-will rule and the rules governing negligence suits by injured employees—illustrate the individualism and prodevelopment thrust of 19th-century employment law.

Employment at Will   Employment at will first clearly appeared after 1870. The rule states that either party can terminate an employment contract that is not for a definite time period, and can do so for any reason. This includes contracts for "steady," "regular," or "permanent" employment. The termination can occur at any time and can be for good, bad, or no cause. However, employees may recover for work actually done.

The rise of employment at will illustrates how the employment relation was influenced by 19th-century contract law and the economic laissez-faire on which it was based. The rule expresses the 19th-century view that parties should be bound only to contract terms on which they have clearly agreed, and that courts should not imply contract terms. Thus, where a contract left the employment's duration uncertain, courts usually would not impose a definite time term. Without such a term, either party could terminate at any time and for any reason. Employment at will also reflects laissez-faire values in a more general way, because it maximizes the freedom of both employer and employee.

In addition, employment at will has given employers the flexibility to meet changing business conditions by discharging employees whose services are no longer needed. As a result, it has promoted economic efficiency and the development of the American economy. Where labor was mobile and job opportunities were abundant, employment at will probably worked to the employee's advantage as well. In other situations, however, the doctrine's benefits were obtained at the cost of exposing discharged employees to the mercies of an uncertain economy.

Because it lets employers fire employees for any reason, employment at will contrasts with the earlier tendency to permit masters to discharge their apprentices only for good cause. As you will see at the end of this chapter, however, modern courts have moved back toward this earlier view. They have done so by creating exceptions to the employment-at-will rule. These exceptions effectively make employers liable for **unjust dismissal** or **wrongful discharge.**

On-the-Job Injuries   As noted, one of 19th-century America's main public policy goals was to promote industrialization by protecting infant industries from potentially crippling lawsuits. In part for this reason, 19th-century law made it difficult for employees to recover when they sued their employers in negligence[2] for injuries suffered in on-the-job accidents. At that time, employers had an *implied assumption of risk* defense under which an employee was regarded as having assumed all the normal and customary risks of his employment simply by taking the job. Because these risks included the possibility of being injured by a co-employee's negligence, employers had another defense called the *fellow servant rule*, which stated that where an employee's injury resulted from the negligence of a coemployee (or fellow servant), his employer would not be liable. If an employee's own carelessness played some role in his injury, finally, employers often could avoid liability under the traditional rule that even a slight degree of *contributory negligence* is a complete defense to a negligence suit.

The Rise of Organized Labor

By the 1860s, most courts had removed one obstacle to unionization by abandoning the old doctrine that trade

---

[1] See the Introduction to Contracts chapter for a discussion of 19th-century contract law.

[2] See the Negligence and Strict Liability chapter for a discussion of negligence law and the defenses of assumption of risk and contributory negligence.

unions are criminal conspiracies. But the main forces behind organized labor's rise in the late 19th century were the increasing size and power of corporate employers and the workplace hazards accompanying industrialization. Underlying the trade union movement was the belief that the power of corporate groups could only be countered by creating new groups representing the interests of workers. The rise of these new groups triggered various legal responses.

Over time, organized labor's increasing political power and the growing numbers of wage earners in the electorate influenced the state legislatures. As a result, many laws protecting workers were passed in the late 19th and early 20th centuries. These included statutes outlawing "yellow dog" contracts (under which an employee would agree not to join or remain a member of a union), minimum wage and maximum hours legislation, laws regulating the employment of women and children, all sorts of factory safety measures, and the workers' compensation systems to be discussed shortly.

The courts, however, tended to represent business interests during this period. Thus, some of the measures just mentioned were struck down on constitutional grounds. Also, some courts were quick to issue temporary and permanent injunctions to restrain union picketing and boycotts and to help quell strikes. As the remainder of this chapter demonstrates, however, business's efforts to stem the rising tide of legislation protecting workers obviously were unsuccessful in the long run.

Employment Law Today

Throughout the 20th century, both employers and (until recently) unions have grown in size and social power. Today, relatively few people are self-employed, and many work for large public and private organizations with which they cannot deal on an equal footing. Although labor market conditions influence the terms and conditions employers offer, individual job applicants usually have little power to bargain over those terms and conditions. Once employed, they occupy positions and perform functions whose nature is largely determined by the institution for which they work. A person's employer and his position within that organization also affect his nonworking life in various ways. Much sociological writing testifies to the way organizational affiliations determine a person's economic prospects, social position, lifestyle, and even values. For union members, however, employer power is somewhat blunted by the union's

own power. But here, employees gain protection from their employers only by submitting to another organized group.

The importance of the employment relation to most people, their dependence on their employers, and employer power over them have inspired numerous efforts to protect employees against abuses of that power during the 20th century. Thus, despite becoming increasingly subservient to organized groups, the tangible position of employees has improved for most of this century. Employers themselves have come to assume paternalistic duties toward their employees—for example, by providing fringe benefits such as pensions, health insurance, and life insurance. More importantly, legislatures, administrative agencies, and courts have attempted to protect employees by regulating more and more aspects of the employment relation. As Figure 1 illustrates, they have pursued certain general goals in the process. The many employment regulations listed in Figure 1 and discussed in this chapter are basically a series of exceptions to the 19th-century's contract-based model of the employment relation. That is, they are yet another example of government intervention prompted by perceived disparities in power between contracting parties.

SOME BASIC EMPLOYMENT STATUTES

Modern American employment law is so vast and complex a subject that texts designed for lawyers seldom address it in its entirety. Indeed, specialized subjects like labor law and employment discrimination often get book-length treatment in their own right. This chapter's overview of employment law focuses most heavily on three topics that have attracted much attention in recent years—employment discrimination, employee privacy, and the demise of employment at will. But no discussion of employment law is complete without outlining certain basic regulations that significantly affect the conditions of employment for many Americans.

Workers' Compensation

Despite safety advances within most industries, employees continue to face dangerous workplace conditions. As you have seen, 19th-century law made it difficult for workers to sue their employers for on-the-job injuries. Making an injured employee's suit even more difficult was the need to *prove* negligent behavior

FIGURE 1   The Ends and Means of Modern Employment Law

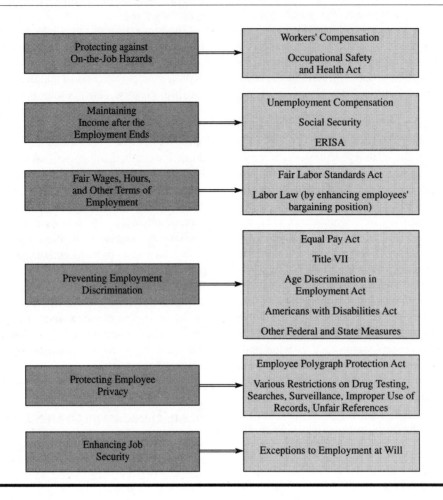

on the employer's part. State workers' compensation statutes, which first began to appear at the beginning of the 20th century, were a response to this situation. Today, all 50 states have such systems.[3]

Basic Features   The coverage of workers' compensation statutes varies from state to state. States usually exempt certain *employers* from the system. One common exemption is for firms employing fewer than a stated number of employees (often three). Also, workers' compensation only protects *employees* and not independent contractors.[4] In addition, many states specifically exempt casual, agricultural, and domestic employees, among others. State and local government employees may be covered by the state's workers' compensation system, or by some alternative state system.

---

[3] In addition, various federal statutes regulate on-the-job injuries suffered by employees of the federal government and other employees such as railroad workers, seamen, longshoremen, and harbor workers.

[4] The chapter entitled The Agency Relationship discusses the employee-independent contractor distinction.

Where they apply, however, all workers' compensation systems share certain basic features. They allow injured employees to recover on the basis of *strict liability*,[5] thus removing any need to prove employer negligence. They also *eliminate the employer's traditional defenses* of contributory negligence, assumption of risk, and the fellow-servant rule. In addition, they make workers' compensation an employee's *exclusive remedy* against her employer for covered injuries. Usually, however, employees who are injured by their employer's *intentional torts* may sue the employer outside workers' compensation.

Workers' compensation is basically a social compromise. Because it is based on strict liability and eliminates the three traditional employer defenses, workers' compensation greatly increases the *probability* that an injured employee will recover. Such recoveries may usually include: (1) hospital and medical expenses (including vocational rehabilitation), (2) disability benefits, (3) specified recoveries for the loss of certain body parts, and (4) death benefits to survivors and/or dependents. But each category of damages usually is limited in various ways, so that the *amount* recoverable under workers' compensation often is lower than the amount obtainable in a successful tort suit. Thus, as the following *Tolbert* case illustrates, injured employees sometimes deny that they are covered by workers' compensation so that they can pursue a tort suit against their employer instead.

Even though workers'-compensation is an injured employee's sole remedy against her *employer*, she may be able to sue *other parties* whose behavior helped cause her injury. One example is a product liability suit against a third-party manufacturer who supplies an employer with defective machinery or raw materials that cause an on-the-job injury. However, a majority of the states give co-employees whose tortious behavior harmed the plaintiff much the same immunity they give an employer. Complicated questions of contribution, indemnity, and subrogation can arise where an injured employee is able to recover, or actually recovers, against both an employer and a third party.

The Work-Related Injury Requirement Another basic feature of workers' compensation is that an employee can recover only for *work-related* injuries. The general test for work-relatedness is that the injury must (1) arise out of the employment and (2) happen in the course of the employment. These tests have been variously interpreted, and they have generated much case law.

The arising-out-of-the-employment test usually requires a sufficiently close relationship between the injury and the *nature* of the employment. As the *Tolbert* case illustrates, there is considerable disagreement about the standards to be used in applying this test. A factory worker assaulted by a trespasser, for example, probably would be denied a workers' compensation recovery under the "increased risk" analysis discussed in *Tolbert*, but probably would recover under the "positional risk" doctrine also described there. If the same trespasser assaulted an on-duty security guard, however, the guard should recover under either approach.

The in-the-course-of-the-employment test requires courts to determine whether the injury occurred within the *time, place, and circumstances* of the employment. Employees injured off the employer's premises generally are outside the course of the employment. For example, injuries suffered while traveling to or from work usually are not compensable under workers' compensation. But an employee may be covered where the off-the-premises injury occurred while she was performing employment-related duties. Injuries suffered during business trips or while running employment-related errands are examples.

Other work-related injury problems on which the courts have disagreed include mental injuries allegedly arising from the employment and injuries resulting from employee horseplay. Virtually all the states, however, regard intentionally self-inflicted injuries as outside the scope of workers' compensation. Recovery for occupational diseases, on the other hand, is usually allowed today. And employees who can prove that a preexisting disease has been aggravated by their employment sometimes recover workers' compensation benefits.

Administration and Funding Workers' compensation systems usually are administered by a state agency that adjudicates workers' claims and administers the system's overall operation. Its decisions on such claims can generally be appealed to the state courts.

---

[5] Strict liability is discussed in the Negligence and Strict Liability chapter.

The states assure funding for workers' compensation recoveries by compelling covered employers to: (1) purchase private insurance, (2) self-insure (e.g., by maintaining a contingency fund), or (3) make payments into a state insurance fund. Because employers generally pass on the costs of insurance to their customers, workers' compensation systems tend to spread the economic risk of workplace injuries throughout society.

TOLBERT v. MARTIN MARIETTA CORPORATION

621 F. Supp. 1099 (D. Colo. 1985)

Deborah Tolbert, a secretary employed by the Martin Marietta Corporation, was raped by a Martin Marietta janitor while on her way to lunch within the secured defense facility where she worked. She sued Martin Marietta, alleging that it had negligently hired the janitor and had negligently failed to make its premises safe for employees. Martin Marietta moved for summary judgment, alleging that Tolbert could not sue in negligence because workers' compensation was her sole remedy.

Carrigan, District Judge.   The sole issue is whether the Colorado Workmen's Compensation Act covers Tolbert's injury. If it does, workers' compensation is her exclusive remedy and this tort action is barred. Tolbert asserts that her injury is not covered by workers' compensation, presumably because she expects that a tort action would yield a larger recovery. Martin Marietta, on the other hand, apparently is willing to pay the workers' compensation award to avoid risking a large tort verdict.

Workers' compensation applies where the injury or death is proximately caused by an injury or occupational disease arising out of and in the course of the employee's employment and is not intentionally self-inflicted. Although her injury did arise in the course of her employment, Tolbert contends that it did not "arise out of" the employment. The "arising out of" condition creates a prerequisite that there be some causal relationship between the employment and the injury. Courts have interpreted the "arising out of" language in a number of different ways. Unfortunately, Colorado courts have not consistently applied any single test. Martin Marietta argues that positional-risk analysis applies to categorize the case as one covered by compensation. The positional-risk doctrine has been defined thus by a leading authority:

An injury arises out of the employment if it would not have occurred but for the fact that the conditions and obligations of the employment placed claimant in the position where he was injured. . . . This theory supports compensation in cases of stray bullets, roving lunatics and other situations in which the only connection of the employment with the injury is that its obligations placed the employee in the particular place at the particular time when he was injured by some neutral force, meaning by "neutral" neither personal to the claimant nor distinctly associated with the employment.

Invoking this rule, Martin Marietta asserts that Tolbert's injury is covered by workers' compensation because: (1) her employment placed her within the building where she was injured, and (2) the assault was a neutral force.

[However,] *Industrial Commission v. Ernest Irvine, Inc.* (1923) . . . applied the "increased-risk" test of causality. Under the increased-risk test, compensation is awarded only if the employment increases the worker's risk of injury above that to which the general public is exposed. If Colorado presently applies the increased-risk analysis, Tolbert would not be covered by workers' compensation. Certainly her employment as a secretary within a secured defense facility would not be expected to increase her risk of sexual assault above that to which women in the general public are exposed.

Colorado first applied positional risk analysis four years after *Ernest Irvine, Inc.* was decided. [In this later case,] the court upheld an award to a farmhand who was struck by lightning. It can readily been seen that the positional-risk test provides substantially broader coverage than does the increased-risk test. Unfortunately, the Colorado courts on several more recent occasions have departed from the positional-risk test to impose a higher standard of causal relationship to the employment.

It is clear that the rape was a nonemployment-motivated act directed at the plaintiff because she was a woman. There is nothing to indicate that any other woman—whether or not a Martin employee—who happened to be in the same area at the time of the attack would not have become the victim. It is clear that Tolbert was not raped because of the nature of her duties or the nature of her workplace environment, or because of any incident or quarrel growing out of the work.

Both applicable Colorado precedent and sound rationale support holding that the workers' compensation statute has not abolished Tolbert's tort claim. Adopting this position has the additional advantage of providing employers an incentive to make reasonable efforts to screen prospective employees so as to avoid hiring rapists or those having the identifiable characteristics of potential rapists. Tort law does not impose strict liability; Tolbert still has the burden of showing negligence, causation, and damages.

Martin Marietta's motion for summary judgment denied; case proceeds to trial on Tolbert's negligence theories.

The Occupational Safety and Health Act

Although it may stimulate employers to remedy hazardous working conditions, workers' compensation does not directly forbid such conditions. However, some states have created various workplace safety regulations, and Congress has enacted health and safety legislation for certain hazardous industries. The most important measure for promoting workplace safety, however, is the federal Occupational Safety and Health Act of 1970.

The Occupational Safety and Health Act generally applies to all employers engaged in a business affecting interstate commerce. Exempted, however, are the U.S. government, the states and their political subdivisions, and certain industries regulated by other federal safety legislation. The Occupational Safety and Health Act is mainly administered by the Occupational Safety and Health Administration (OSHA) of the Department of Labor. It is not intended to preempt state regulation of workplace safety, and the states can regulate areas subject to federal standards, albeit under federal supervision and control.

General Standards The act requires that employers provide their employees with employment and a place of employment free from recognized hazards that are likely to cause death or serious physical harm. It also requires employers to comply with specific regulations promulgated by OSHA. These regulations are voluminous and often quite detailed.

Enforcement and Penalties OSHA can inspect places of employment for violations of the act and its regulations, although employers can require the agency to obtain a search warrant before doing so. (Workers who notify OSHA of possible violations are protected against employer retaliation.) If an employer is found to violate the act's general duty provision or any specific standard, OSHA issues a written citation. It must do so with reasonable promptness, and in no event more than six months after the violation. The citation becomes final after 15 workdays following its service on the employer, unless it is contested. Contested citations are reviewed by the Occupational Safety and Health Review Commission, a three-member body composed of presidential appointees. Further review by the federal courts of appeals is possible.

The main sanctions for violations of the act and the regulations are civil penalties imposed by OSHA. Such penalties are mandatory when an employer receives a citation for a serious violation of the act or its regulations, and discretionary when the violation is nonserious. Other civil penalties are possible for willful or repeated violations and for the failure to correct a violation after a citation. In addition, any employer who commits a willful violation resulting in death to an employee may suffer a fine, imprisonment, or both. Finally, the secretary of labor may seek injunctive relief when an employment hazard presents an imminent danger of death or physical harm that cannot be promptly eliminated by normal citation procedures.

Recordkeeping, Reporting, and Notice Under the act, employers must maintain accurate records of, and make periodic reports on, work-related deaths, illnesses, and injuries other than minor injuries. Employers also must maintain accurate records of employee exposures to certain toxic and harmful materials. Employees exposed to specified concentrations of such materials must receive prompt notification from their employer.

Social Security

Under a system of complete laissez-faire, an employer's financial obligations to its employees would cease once the employment ends, unless the parties had contracted otherwise. Today, however, the law requires employers to assist in ensuring that their employees receive financial protection after termination of the employment. One example is the federal social security system, which began in 1935. Social security is mainly financed by the Federal Insurance Contributions Act (FICA), which applies to a wide range of employers. FICA operates by imposing a flat percentage tax on all employee income below a certain base figure and by requiring employers to pay a similar tax.

Today, FICA revenues finance various forms of financial assistance in addition to the old-age benefits that people usually call social security. These include survi-

vors' benefits to family members of deceased workers, disability benefits, and medical and hospitalization benefits for the elderly (the medicare system).

Unemployment Compensation

Another way that the law protects employees after their employment ends is by providing unemployment compensation for discharged workers. Since 1935, various federal statutes have authorized joint federal-state efforts in this area. Today, each of the states administers its own unemployment compensation system under general federal guidelines; the costs of the system are met by subjecting employers to federal and state unemployment compensation taxes.

Unemployment insurance plans vary somewhat from state to state, but usually are similar in certain general respects. To prevent payments to those who have not recently been employed, states often condition the receipt of benefits on the recipient's having earned a certain minimum income during a specified prior time period. Generally, those who have voluntarily quit work without good cause, have been fired for bad conduct, fail to actively seek suitable new work, or refuse such work are ineligible for benefits. Benefit levels vary from state to state, as does the length of time that benefits can be received. Under federal law and the laws of a few states, the benefit period may be extended under certain circumstances.

ERISA

In addition to making compulsory payments to unemployment compensation systems and to the social security system, many employers voluntarily contribute to their employees' postemployment income by maintaining pension plans. For years, the main federal law regulating private pension plans was the Internal Revenue Code, which did not concern itself with the details of pension plan operation. Partly for this reason, abuses and injustices such as arbitrary plan terminations, arbitrary benefit reductions, and mismanagement of fund assets were not uncommon.

The Employee Retirement Income Security Act of 1974 (ERISA) was a response to these problems. In many ways, ERISA is a cautious regulatory response to the problems it addresses, for Congress did not wish to discourage the creation of pension plans by enacting overly strict controls. Thus, the act does not require employers to establish or fund benefit plans and does not set benefit levels. Instead, it attempts to prevent abuses in the operation of private pension plans and to protect an employee's expectation that promised pension benefits will be paid.

ERISA is a very long, complex, and detailed statute whose main concern is to set certain standards that pension plans must meet. Thus, the act imposes various *fiduciary duties* on pension fund managers. To take just one example, it requires that managers diversify the plan's investments to minimize the risk of large losses, unless this is clearly imprudent under the circumstances. ERISA also imposes *recordkeeping, reporting, and disclosure* requirements. For instance, it requires that covered plans provide annual reports to their participants, and specifies the contents of those reports. In addition, the act has a provision restricting an employer's ability to *delay an employee's participation* in the plan. In some situations, for example, an employee who completes one year of service with an employer cannot be denied participation in a plan. Furthermore, ERISA contains *funding* and *plan termination insurance* requirements designed to help protect plan participants against loss of pension income. The Labor Department's Pension Benefit Guaranty Corporation is the insurance agency established by the act. Finally, ERISA contains complex *vesting* requirements that determine when an employee's right to receive particular pension benefits becomes nonforfeitable. These requirements are important because they help prevent employers from using a late vesting date to avoid pension obligations to employees who change jobs or are fired before that date.

ERISA allows plan participants and beneficiaries to enforce their benefit rights and other rights under the plan. Along with the secretary of labor, they also may obtain equitable relief against violations of the act, and both legal and equitable relief against plan managers who breach their fiduciary duties. In addition, those who willfully violate the act's provisions can suffer criminal penalties.

Labor Law

American labor law is a complex topic whose many details are beyond the scope of this text. However, no discussion of employment law is complete without outlining federal regulation of labor-management relations in the 20th century. The following brief survey of labor law illustrates many of the general themes discussed at the beginning of this chapter.

Introduction During the late 19th and early 20th centuries, the legal system often helped employers check the growing power of organized labor. Employment at will enabled them to fire prounion employees, and employers sometimes blacklisted such employees. Judicial injunctions and restraining orders, and the contempt citations that courts would issue upon their violation, continued to be useful in suppressing strikes and other union activities. Some union tactics were held to violate the antitrust laws. Yellow-dog contracts continued to be used, and state legislation forbidding such contracts sometimes was declared unconstitutional. Despite all these measures, however, the power of organized labor continued to grow. That power was cemented in the 1930s, when Congress explicitly recognized labor's rights to organize and to bargain collectively by passing the National Labor Relations Act. Later federal regulation of labor-management relations mainly has addressed certain perceived abuses by unions. Although such regulations may have limited organized labor's power somewhat, they have not seriously disturbed the position that it achieved in the 1930s.

The rise of organized labor is a clear example of what has been called *countervailing power:* the checking of organized group power by the creation of competing groups. By organizing to counter the influence of corporate groups over their working lives, workers have been able to achieve wages and working conditions that they probably would have been unable to obtain otherwise. In the process, however, they have become subordinate to another organized group—the union.

This section also illustrates a theme that pervades this text: the activist role played by government in the 20th century. In particular, the section emphasizes government's contemporary role as mediator between competing group interests.

The National Labor Relations Act In 1926, Congress passed the Railway Labor Act, which regulates labor relations in the railroad industry, and which later was amended to include airlines. This was followed by the Norris-LaGuardia Act of 1932, which limited the circumstances in which federal courts could enjoin strikes and picketing in labor disputes. The act also prohibited federal court enforcement of yellow-dog contracts.

These two statutes, however, were only a prelude to the most important 20th-century American labor statute, the National Labor Relations Act of 1935 (the NLRA or Wagner Act). The act gave employees the *right to organize* by enabling them to form, join, and assist labor organizations. It also allowed them to *bargain collectively* through representatives of their own choosing and to engage in other activities that would promote collective bargaining. In addition, the Wagner Act prohibited certain employer practices that were believed to discourage collective bargaining, and declared these to be *unfair labor practices*. Included in its list of unfair labor practices are:

1. Interfering with employees in the exercise of their rights to form, join, and assist labor unions.

2. Dominating or interfering with the formation or administration of any labor union, or giving financial or other support to a union.

3. Discriminating against employees in hiring, tenure, or any term of employment because of their union membership.

4. Discriminating against employees because they have filed charges or given testimony under the act.

5. Refusing to bargain collectively with any duly designated representative of the employees.

The NLRA also established the National Labor Relations Board (NLRB). The NLRB's main functions are: (1) to handle representation cases (which involve the process by which a union becomes the certified representative of the employees within a particular bargaining unit), and (2) to decide whether challenged employer or union activity constitutes an unfair labor practice.

The Labor Management Relations Act   In 1947, Congress amended the NLRA by passing the Labor Management Relations Act (LMRA or Taft-Hartley Act). In part, the changes made by the Taft-Hartley Act reflected the more conservative political climate and the revival of business power that emerged after World War II. Perhaps more importantly, they reflected public concern over frequent strikes, the perceived excessive power of union bosses, and various unfair practices by unions. Thus, the Taft-Hartley Act declared that certain acts by *unions* were unfair labor practices. These include:

1. Restraining or coercing employees in the exercise of their guaranteed bargaining rights—in particular, their rights to refrain from joining a union or to engage in collective bargaining.

2. Causing an employer to discriminate against an employee who is not a union member, unless the employee is not a member because of a failure to pay union dues.

3. Refusing to bargain collectively with an employer.

4. Conducting a secondary strike or a secondary boycott for a specified illegal purpose. These are strikes or boycotts aimed at a third party with which the union has no real dispute. Their purpose is to coerce that party not to deal with an employer with which the union does have a dispute, and thus to gain some leverage over the employer.

5. Requiring employees covered by union-shop contracts to pay excessive or discriminatory initiation fees or dues.

6. Featherbedding—forcing an employer to pay for work not actually performed.

The LMRA also established an 80-day cooling off period for strikes that the president finds likely to endanger national safety or health. In addition, it created a Federal Mediation and Conciliation Service to assist employers and unions in settling labor disputes.

The Labor Management Reporting and Disclosure Act   Congressional investigations during the 1950s uncovered much corruption in internal union affairs, and also revealed that the internal procedures of many unions were undemocratic. In response to these findings, Congress enacted the Labor Management Reporting and Disclosure Act (or Landrum-Griffin Act) in 1959. The act established a "bill of rights" for union members and attempted to make internal union affairs more democratic. It also amended the NLRA by adding to the LMRA's list of unfair labor practices by unions.

The Fair Labor Standards Act

Federal labor law is a significant departure from the individualistic model of the employment relation that prevailed during the 19th century. Still, it does permit many terms of employment to be determined by private bargaining. Since the 1930s, however, the law sometimes has directly regulated such key terms of employment as wages and hours worked. The most important example is the Fair Labor Standards Act (FLSA) of 1938.

The FLSA's most important provisions concern the regulation of *wages and hours*. Employees covered by the act are entitled to: (1) a specified minimum wage whose amount has changed over time, and (2) a time-

and-a-half rate for work in excess of 40 hours per week. The FLSA's wages and hours provisions basically apply to employees who are engaged in interstate commerce or the production of goods for such commerce, or who are employed by an enterprise that does the same and that has annual gross sales of sufficient size. State and local employees are also covered. Among the classes of employees exempted from the FLSA's wages-and-hours provisions are executive, administrative, professional, and outside sales personnel.

The FLSA also prohibits certain kinds of *child labor*. It forbids the use of "oppressive child labor" by any employer engaged in interstate commerce or in the production of goods for such commerce, and also forbids the interstate shipment of goods produced in an establishment where oppressive child labor takes place. Oppressive child labor includes: (1) most employment of children below the age of 14; (2) employment of children aged 14–15, unless they work in one of a list of approved occupations set out by the Department of Labor; and (3) employment of children aged 16–17 who work in occupations such as mining that have been declared particularly hazardous by the Labor Department. Subject to conditions that vary with the age of the child, these provisions do not apply to agricultural employment. Also exempt from these provisions are children who work as actors or performers in radio, television, movie, and theatrical productions.

Both injured employees and the Labor Department can sue for violations of the FLSA's wages and hours provisions. They can recover the amount of the unpaid minimum wages or overtime, plus an additional equal amount as liquidated damages. A suit by the Labor Department terminates an employee's right to sue, but the department pays the amounts it recovers to the injured party. In addition, violations of both the act's wages and hours provisions and its child labor provisions may result in civil penalties. Finally, the Labor Department may sue for injunctive relief to enforce the FLSA's various provisions, and willful violations of those provisions subject employers to criminal liability.

The Equal Pay Act

The Equal Pay Act (EPA), which forbids *sex* discrimination regarding *pay*, was passed as an amendment to the FLSA in 1963. Its coverage is very similar to the coverage of the FLSA's minimum wage provisions. Unlike the FLSA, however, the EPA covers executive, administrative, and professional employees.

The Equal Pay Act forbids gender-based pay discrimination against men. But the typical EPA case involves an aggrieved woman who claims that she has received lower pay than a male employee performing substantially equal work for the same employer. The substantially-equal-work requirement is met if the plaintiff's job and the higher-paid male employee's job involve *each* of the following: (1) equal effort, (2) equal skill, (3) equal responsibility, and (4) similar working conditions.

Effort basically means physical or mental exertion. *Skill* refers to the experience, training, education, and ability required for the positions being compared. Here, the question is not whether the two employees actually possess equal skills, but whether the *jobs require or utilize* substantially the same skills. *Responsibility* (or accountability) involves such factors as the degree of supervision each job requires and the importance of each job to the employer. For instance, a retail sales position in which an employee is allowed to approve customer checks without higher-level review probably is not equal to a sales position in which an employee lacks this authority. *Working conditions* refers to such factors as temperature, weather, fumes, ventilation, toxic conditions, and risk of injury. Note that these need only be *similar*, not equal.

Once it has been shown that the two jobs are substantially equal and that they are compensated unequally, an employer must prove one of the EPA's four defenses or it will lose the case. That is, the employer must show that the pay disparity is based on: (1) seniority, (2) merit, (3) quality or quantity of production (e.g., a piecework system), or (4) any factor other than sex. As the following *Grove* case emphasizes in the case of merit, the first three defenses usually require an employer to show some organized, systematic, communicated rating system with predetermined criteria that apply equally to employees of each sex. Highly discretionary, subjective systems capable of serving as a cover for gender discrimination ordinarily do not suffice. The any-factor-other-than-sex defense is a catchall category that may include shift differentials, bonuses paid because the job is part of a training program, and differences in the profitability of the products or services on which the employees work.

The EPA's remedial scheme is very similar to the FLSA scheme described earlier. Under the EPA, however, employee suits are for the amount of *back pay* lost because of an employer's discrimination, not for unpaid minimum wages or overtime. As before, an employee also may recover an equal sum as liquidated damages. In addition, the EPA is enforced by the Equal Employment Opportunity Commission (EEOC), not the Labor Department.[6] Unlike some of the employment discrimina-

tion statutes described later, however, the EPA does not require that private plaintiffs submit their complaints to the EEOC or a state agency for evaluation and attempted conciliation before mounting suit.

The following case, *Grove v. Frostburg National Bank,* considers both the EPA's equal work requirement and some of its defenses. Like many other cases, it does not examine effort, skill, and responsibility individually. Instead, it discusses how they are affected by the male employee's extra tasks.

---

[6] The EEOC, established by the Civil Rights Act of 1964, is an independent federal agency with a sizable staff and many regional offices. The EEOC's functions include: (1) enforcement of most of the employment discrimination laws discussed in this chapter through lawsuits that it initiates or in which it intervenes, (2) conciliation of employment discrimination charges (e.g., by encouraging their negotiated settlement), (3) investigation of a wide range of discrimination-related matters, and (4) interpretation of the statutes it enforces through regulations and guidelines.

GROVE v. FROSTBURG NATIONAL BANK

549 F. Supp. 922 (D. Md. 1982)

Sheila Grove and David Klink were hired as loan tellers by the Frostburg National Bank in 1967. Both were high school graduates at the time, and neither had prior work experience. Each was paid the same yearly starting salary in 1967. Klink was drafted into the army late in 1967, and he returned to the bank in 1969. From that time until 1976, he basically performed a loan teller's duties, although he also took on a variety of miscellaneous tasks. Grove also basically performed loan teller duties during the period 1969–76. Throughout that period, Klink's yearly salary exceeded Grove's. Salary and raise determinations were made by David P. Willetts, the bank's vice president, who based these determinations primarily on his own observations of employees. Grove sued the bank in federal district court under the Equal Pay Act.

Jones, District Judge. The burden is on the plaintiff to make a prima facie showing that the employer pays different wages to males and females for equal work requiring equal skill, effort, and responsibility under similar working conditions. Once that showing is made, the employer has the burden of showing that the pay differential is justified under one of the four statutory exceptions. Only substantial equality of work need be proved; the jobs need not be identical. A wage differential is justified by extra tasks only if they create significant variations in skill, effort, and responsibility. If the purported extra tasks are not done; if females also have extra tasks of equal skill, effort, and responsibility; if females are not given the opportunity to do the extra tasks; or if the extra tasks only involve minimal time and are of peripheral importance, they do not justify a wage differential.

Sheila Grove performed work substantially equal to that of David Klink from 1969 through September, 1976. As loan tellers, [each] had basically the same duties. Klink had some extra tasks from time to time. He set up the drive-in branch in 1970. He reviewed the safe deposit box rent records and noted some delinquencies and increases in 1971. After 1971, he arranged for drilling the boxes. Some time in the 1970s, he began shredding paper.

Setting up the drive-in branch was a one-time task, involving taking supplies and equipment to the drive-in installation. To the extent that it involved any different skills or effort than the normal work of the loan tellers, they were largely physical. Moreover, no female loan teller had an opportunity to perform this task, because it was done at the request of Willetts. Although Klink's initiative in bringing the box rents up to date is commendable, the work did not consume a significant amount of time, as compared with his other duties. It was a one-time project. To the extent that he performed extra tasks thereafter in arranging for the drilling, no significant amount of time was involved. Shredding paper is a task involving less skill, effort, and responsibility than the regular work of loan tellers. It did not involve a significant amount of time, only occasional afternoons or Saturdays.

Grove has sustained her burden of demonstrating that her work as loan teller was substantially equal to that of Klink. The bank tried to justify Klink's higher salary on two grounds. It stated that Klink was paid a higher salary when he returned to the bank in 1969, which was perpetuated through yearly increases, as a reward for his patriotism in serving in the Army. The bank also claimed that Klink received higher pay because he was more responsible, conscientious, and harder-working: that is, on merit.

The bank has failed to show that Klink's 1969 salary was based on a factor other than sex. Even assuming that military service could be a proper reason for a wage differential, Klink was drafted into the service. No female worker could have been.

The bank has also failed to show that the wage differential was based on a legitimate merit system. A merit system need not be in writing to be recognized; it must, however, be an organized and structured procedure with systematic evaluations under predetermined criteria. If it is not in writing, employees must be aware of it. The system used by Willetts does not meet this test. It was not organized or structured; Willetts did not recall, for example, whether he had consulted with department supervisors at the end of each year concerning individual employees. A systematic evaluation, using predetermined criteria, was not made. Although Willetts cited a number of factors that influenced his pay decisions, these were not applied uniformly, and he eventually admitted that the primary criterion was his "gut feeling" about the employee. Finally, employees were not aware of the existence of any merit system.

Judgment for Grove.

Title VII

Introduction

As you may have noticed, there is a significant difference between the Equal Pay Act and the other laws discussed in the previous section. Because it forbids unequal pay on the basis of gender, the EPA is an *employment discrimination* provision. Employment discrimination might be defined as employer behavior that penalizes certain individuals because of personal traits that they cannot control and that bear no relation to effective job performance. Such discrimination was common before the 1960s. In part, this was because traditional social values differed from those that prevail today. The view that women belong in the home and not in the workplace, for example, was much more prevalent

50 or 100 years ago than it is now. But the highly individualistic 19th-century model of the employment relation also helps explain why employment discrimination was so common for so long. To the maximum extent possible, it was felt, no party to an employment contract should be bound to terms not of his choosing. Therefore, employers generally could hire, fire, promote, and compensate on any basis they desired, no matter how arbitrary.

As our earlier discussion has suggested, this traditional thinking has become progressively less influential over the course of the 20th century. But it was not until the 1960s and 1970s that the law began to attack employment discrimination. When the tide finally turned, though, it did so with a vengeance. Today, employers are confronted with a maze of legal rules forbidding employment discrimination on the basis of certain personal traits. Changed social values—mainly, America's greater commitment to equal opportunity and its decreased reverence for freedom of contract—are the most important explanation for this new legal picture.

Of the many employment discrimination laws in force today, the most important is Title VII of the 1964 Civil Rights Act. Unlike the Equal Pay Act, Title VII is a comprehensive employment discrimination provision. It prohibits discrimination based on *race, color, religion, sex, and national origin*. It forbids such discrimination not just when it affects an employee's pay,[7] but also when it occurs in hiring, firing, job assignments, access to training and apprenticeship programs, and most other employment decisions.

Basic Features of Title VII

In discussing Title VII, we first examine some general rules that apply to all the kinds of discrimination it forbids.[8] Then we examine each forbidden basis of discrimination in detail.

Covered Entities   Title VII covers all employers employing 15 or more employees and engaging in an industry affecting interstate commerce. The term *employer* includes individuals, partnerships, corporations, colleges and universities, labor unions (with respect to their own employees), and state and local governments.[9] Also, *referrals* by employment agencies are covered no matter what the size of the agency, if an *employer serviced by the agency* has 15 or more employees. In addition, Title VII covers certain unions—mainly those with 15 or more members—in their capacity as *employee representative*. Among those specifically exempted from Title VII's coverage are religious educational institutions and religious organizations (but only for discrimination based on religion), bona fide tax-exempt private clubs, and Indian tribes.

Procedures   Although the EEOC can sue to enforce Title VII in certain circumstances, the usual Title VII suit is a private action. The complicated procedures that must be followed in private Title VII suits are beyond the scope of this text, but a few points should be kept in mind. Private parties with a Title VII claim have no automatic right to sue. Instead, they first must file a *charge* with the EEOC, or with a state agency in states having suitable fair employment laws and enforcement schemes. The point of this requirement is to allow the EEOC or the state agency to investigate the claim, attempt conciliation if the claim has substance, or sue the employer itself. If a plaintiff files with a state agency and the state fails to act, the plaintiff can still file a charge with the EEOC. Even if the EEOC fails to act on the claim, a plaintiff may still mount his or her own suit. In such situations, the EEOC issues a "right to sue letter" enabling the plaintiff to file suit.

Proving Discrimination   The permissible methods for *proving* a Title VII violation are critical to its effectiveness against employment discrimination. Proof of discrimination is easy in cases such as the *Johnson Controls* case later in this chapter, where the employer had an *express policy* disfavoring one of Title VII's protected classes. *Direct evidence* of a discriminatory motive such as testimony or written evidence obviously is useful to plaintiffs as well. As the following discussion should indicate, however, employers can discriminate without leaving such obvious tracks. If Title VII were unable to prohibit such behavior, it would be a toothless tiger in the fight against employment discrimination.

The methods for proving a Title VII claim mainly have been devised by the courts, and have undergone some change over time. At this chapter's completion in mid-1991, two methods predominated.

The Disparate Treatment Method   Title VII disparate treatment suits usually involve an individual plaintiff who alleges some specific instance or instances of discriminatory treatment. Such cases generally follow a three-step sequence.

1. First, a plaintiff must show a **prima facie case:** a case strong enough to require a counterargument from the defendant. The proof needed for a prima facie case varies with the type of employment decision at issue. In many *hiring* cases, for instance, it must be shown that: (a) the plaintiff is within one of Title VII's five protected classes; (b) she applied for, and was qualified to perform, a job for which the employer was seeking applicants; (c) she was denied the job; and (d) the employer continued to seek applications from people with the plaintiff's qualifications after the rejection.

---

[7] Thus, suits attacking sex-based pay discrimination can proceed under both the EPA and Title VII. As discussed later in this chapter, the EPA's defenses—but not its equal work requirement—apply in Title VII suits of this kind.

[8] This discussion reflects the state of the law as of mid-1991.

[9] Employment discrimination within the federal government is beyond the scope of this text.

2. Once the plaintiff establishes a prima facie case, the defendant must allege *legitimate, nondiscriminatory reasons* for its treatment of the plaintiff or it will lose the lawsuit. In a hiring case, for example, an employer might allege that it refused to hire the plaintiff because she did not meet its criteria for the position in question.

3. If the defendant alleges satisfactory reasons, it will win unless the plaintiff shows that the reasons are merely a *pretext* for a decision made with a discriminatory purpose. For example, a rejected female job applicant might try to show that the employer's allegedly legitimate, nondiscriminatory criteria were not applied to similarly situated men.

The Adverse Impact Method   Title VII's adverse impact (or disparate impact) method of proof most often is used when a group of plaintiffs mount a class action. Its details have been controversial, and some of those details may have changed by the time you read this text. For this reason, we merely outline the method in general terms.

1. First, the plaintiffs must identify the *specific employment practice* of which they complain. Often, this is an employer rule that is neutral on its face but has a disproportionate adverse effect on one of Title VII's protected groups—for example, a height, weight, or high school diploma requirement for hiring, or a written test for hiring or promotion. But other practices qualify as well, including such subjective practices as interviews and qualitative promotion evaluations.

2. The plaintiffs must then show that the practice in question had a *substantial adverse impact* on a group protected by Title VII. For example, blacks alleging racial discrimination might show that a high school diploma requirement for a manufacturing job caused substantially fewer blacks than whites to be hired for that job.

3. If the plaintiffs make the showing just described, the employer must produce evidence that the practice is justified by *business necessity* because it is sufficiently *job-related*. If the employer fails to do so, it will lose the case. In our previous example, this should require the employer to show some significant relationship between its high school diploma requirement and effective job performance.

4. Even if the employer provides satisfactory evidence that the practice is job-related, the plaintiffs still can win if they show that the employer's legitimate business needs can be advanced by *other, less discriminatory* practices. For example, our black plaintiffs might show that the employer's legitimate needs can be met by a test that directly measures the skills needed for the manufacturing job.

Other Methods of Proof   In some Title VII cases (usually suits by the government), it is alleged that the employer has engaged in a pervasive *pattern or practice* of discrimination. Here, the plaintiff's proof is usually statistical, but the statistics can be supplemented with specific evidence of discrimination. Of course, a defendant may be able to rebut the plaintiff's evidence in various ways.

Finally, plaintiffs may argue that the employer has adopted a *neutral rule that perpetuates the effects of past discrimination*. For example, suppose a labor union that has long excluded blacks finally abandons this discrimination, but retains a rule that new members must be related to, or recommended by, current members. In such cases, a defendant may try to justify its rule by business necessity and a plaintiff may allege a less discriminatory alternative means in much the fashion described above.

Defenses   Even if a plaintiff proves a violation of Title VII, the employer still prevails if it can establish one of Title VII's various defenses. The most important such defenses are:

1. *Seniority.* Title VII is not violated if the employer treats different employees differently pursuant to a *bona fide seniority system*. To be bona fide, such a system at least must treat all employees equally on its face, not have been created for discriminatory reasons, and not operate in a discriminatory fashion.

2. *The various "merit" defenses.* An employer also escapes Title VII liability if it acts pursuant to a *bona fide merit system*, a system basing earnings on *quantity or quality of production*, or the results of a *professionally developed ability test*. Presumably, such systems and tests at least must meet the general standards for seniority systems stated above. Also, the EEOC has promulgated lengthy *Uniform Guidelines on Employee Selection Procedures* that speak to these and other matters.

3. *The BFOQ defense.* Finally, Title VII allows employers to discriminate on the bases of sex, religion, or national origin where one of those traits is a *bona fide occupational qualification* (BFOQ) that is reasonably necessary to the business in question. Note that this BFOQ defense does not protect *race or color* discrimination. As the following *Johnson Controls* case makes clear, moreover, the defense is a narrow one even where it does apply. Generally, it is available only where a certain gender, religion, or national origin is necessary for effective job performance. For example, a BFOQ probably would exist where a female is employed to model women's clothing or to fit women's undergarments, or a French restaurant hires a French chef. But the BFOQ defense usually is unavailable where the discrimination is based on stereotypes (e.g., that women are less aggressive than men) or on the preferences of co-workers or customers (e.g., the preference of airline travelers for female rather than male flight attendants). As *Johnson Controls* also suggests, the defense apparently is unavailable where the employer's discriminatory practice promotes goals, such as fetal protection, that do not concern effective job performance.

AUTO WORKERS v. JOHNSON CONTROLS, INC.

111 S. Ct. 1196 (U.S. Sup. Ct. 1991)

Johnson Controls, Inc. manufactures batteries. Lead is a primary ingredient in that manufacturing process. A female employee's occupational exposure to lead involves a risk of harm to any fetus she carries. For this reason, Johnson Controls excluded women who are pregnant or who are capable of bearing children from jobs that involve exposure to lead. Numerous plaintiffs, including a woman who had chosen to be sterilized to avoid losing her job, entered a federal district court class action alleging that Johnson Controls' policy constituted illegal sex discrimination under Title VII. The district court entered a summary judgment for Johnson Controls and the court of appeals affirmed. The plaintiffs appealed to the U.S. Supreme Court.

Blackmun, Justice.   Johnson Controls' fetal-protection policy explicitly discriminates against women on the basis of their sex. The policy excludes women with childbearing capacity from lead-exposed jobs and so creates a facial classification based on gender. [But] an employer may discriminate on the basis of "religion, sex, or national origin in those certain instances where religion, sex, or national origin is a bona fide occupational qualification reasonably necessary to the normal operation of that particular business or enterprise." The BFOQ defense is written narrowly, and this Court has read it narrowly.

Johnson Controls argues that its fetal-protection policy falls within the so-called safety exception [of] the BFOQ. Discrimination on the basis of sex because of safety concerns is allowed only in narrow circumstances. In *Dothard v. Rawlinson* (1977), we allowed the employer to hire only male guards in contact areas of maximum-security male penitentiaries only because more was at stake than the individual woman's decision to weigh and accept the risks of employment. We found sex to be a BFOQ inasmuch as the employment of a female guard would create real risks of safety to others if [rape-related] violence broke out because the guard was a woman. Sex discrimination was tolerated because sex was related to the guard's ability to do the job—maintaining prison security. Similarly, some courts have approved airlines' layoffs of pregnant flight attendants on the ground that the employer's policy was necessary to ensure the safety of passengers. In two of these cases, the courts pointedly indicated that fetal, as opposed to passenger, safety was best left to the mother.

Therefore, the safety exception is limited to instances in which sex or pregnancy actually interferes with the employee's ability to perform the job. . . . [Thus,] Johnson Controls cannot establish a BFOQ. Fertile women, as far as appears in the record, manufacture batteries as efficiently as anyone else. Johnson Controls' professed moral and ethical concerns about the next generation do not suffice to establish a BFOQ of female sterility. Decisions about the welfare of future children must be left to the parents who conceive, bear, support, and raise them rather than to the employers who hire those parents.

Judgment in favor of Johnson Controls reversed; case returned to the lower courts for further proceedings consistent with the Supreme Court's opinion.

White, Justice, Concurring in Part.   For the fetal protection policy in this case to be a BFOQ, the policy must be "reasonably necessary" to the "normal operation" of making batteries, which is Johnson Controls' "particular business." Although that is a difficult standard to satisfy, nothing in the statute's language indicates that it could *never* support a sex-specific fetal protection policy.

A fetal protection policy would be justified if, for example, an employer could show that exclusion of women from certain jobs was reasonably necessary to avoid substantial tort liability. It is part of the normal operation of business to avoid causing injury to third parties, if for no other reason than to avoid tort liability. Every state currently allows children born alive to recover in tort for prenatal injuries caused by third parties, and an increasing number of courts have recognized a right to recover even for prenatal injuries caused by torts committed prior to conception.

The Court dismisses the possibility of tort liability by speculating that if Title VII bans sex-specific fetal protection policies, the employer fully informs the woman of the risk, and the employer has not acted negligently, the basis for holding an employer liable seems remote. Such speculation will be small comfort to employers. First, it is far from clear that compliance with Title VII will preempt state tort liability. Second, although warnings may preclude claims by injured *employees*, they will not preclude claims by injured children. Finally, although state tort liability for prenatal injuries generally requires negligence, it will be difficult for employers to determine in advance what will constitute negligence. Compliance with OSHA standards, for example, has been held not to be a defense to state tort liability. Moreover, it is possible that employers will be held strictly liable if, for example, their manufacturing process is considered "abnormally dangerous."

Remedies   Various remedies are possible once private plaintiffs or the EEOC win a Title VII suit. If the discrimination has caused lost wages, employees can obtain back pay accruing from a date two years before the filing of the charge. A successful private plaintiff is also likely to recover attorney's fees. However, consequential damage recoveries for such things as emotional distress or loss of credit are unlikely, and punitive damage recoveries are very unlikely. As this text was completed in mid-1991, however, Congress was considering legislation that would allow some consequential and punitive damage recoveries.

Title VII also gives courts broad powers to fashion equitable remedies tailored to the case. These can include awards of retroactive seniority and orders compelling a plaintiff's hiring or reinstatement. Various affirmative action orders—for example, injunctions compelling the active recruitment of minorities—are also possible. On occasion, moreover, the courts have ordered quotalike minority preferences in Title VII cases.[10] After determining that an employer has engaged in a pattern or practice of hiring discrimination against racial minorities, for example, a court might order that whites and minorities be hired on a 50-50 basis until minority representation in the employer's work force reaches some specified percentage. Generally speaking, such orders are permissible if: (1) an employer has engaged in severe, widespread, or long-standing discrimination; (2) the order does not unduly restrict the employment interests of white people; and (3) it does not force an employer to hire unqualified workers. This is true even where the beneficiaries of the order did not

---

[10] Occasionally, such preferential relief may be ordered in *sex* discrimination cases as well.

themselves suffer discrimination. Minority preferences may also appear in the *consent decrees* courts issue when approving the terms on which the parties have settled a Title VII case. Such decrees sometimes may provide minorities with broader relief than a court could order on its own after finding the defendant liable under Title VII.

Race or Color Discrimination

At this point in our discussion of Title VII, we consider each of its prohibited bases of discrimination in more detail. *Race or color* discrimination includes discrimination against blacks, other racial minorities, and American Indians.

Title VII also prohibits racial discrimination against whites. In *United Steelworkers v. Weber*,[11] however, the Supreme Court upheld a voluntary employment preference that favored minorities. To survive a Title VII attack under *Weber*, such preferences must: (1) be intended to correct a "manifest imbalance" reflecting underrepresentation of minorities in "traditionally segregated job categories," (2) not "unnecessarily trammel" the rights of white employees or create an absolute bar to their advancement, and (3) be only temporary. Unlike the other examples of reverse discrimination discussed previously, *Weber* does not involve the use of minority preferences as a *remedy* for a Title VII violation. Instead, it considers whether such preferences *themselves violate* Title VII when established by an employer on a voluntary basis.

National Origin Discrimination

National origin discrimination is discrimination based on: (1) the country of one's or one's ancestors' origin; or (2) one's possession of physical, cultural, or linguistic characteristics identified with people of a particular nation. Thus, plaintiffs in national origin discrimination cases need not have been born in the country at issue. In fact, if the discrimination is based on physical, cultural, or linguistic traits identified with a particular nation, even the plaintiff's ancestors need not have been born there. Thus, a person of pure French ancestry may have a Title VII case if she suffers discrimination because she looks like, acts like, or talks like a German.

Certain formally neutral employment practices can also constitute national origin discrimination. Employers who hire only U.S. citizens may violate Title VII if their policy has the purpose or effect of discriminating against one or more national origin groups. This could happen where the employer is located in an area where aliens of a particular nationality are heavily concentrated. Also, employment criteria such as height, weight, and fluency in English may violate Title VII if they have an adverse impact on a national origin group and are not job-related.

Religious Discrimination

For Title VII purposes, the term *religion* is broadly defined. Although not all courts agree, the EEOC's position is that it includes almost any set of moral beliefs that are sincerely held with the same strength as traditional religious views. In fact, Title VII forbids religious discrimination against atheists. It also forbids discrimination based on religious *observances or practices*—for example, grooming, clothing, or the refusal to work on the Sabbath. But such discrimination is permissible if an employer cannot reasonably accommodate the religious practice without undue hardship. Undue hardship exists when the accommodation imposes more than a minimal cost on an employer.

Sex Discrimination

Title VII's ban on sex discrimination was added as a late amendment to the 1964 Civil Rights Act. As a result, there is little legislative history on this provision of Title VII and some disagreement about its scope. Clearly, though, the provision is aimed at *gender* discrimination and does not forbid discrimination on the basis of homosexuality or transsexuality. Just as clearly, Title VII's prohibition of sex discrimination applies to gender-based discrimination against both men and women. Still, certain voluntary employer programs favoring women in hiring or promotion may survive a Title VII attack. To do so, such programs must meet the *Weber* tests for voluntary *racial* preferences that were discussed above. Here, of course, these tests are reformulated to reflect gender rather than race. Finally, a 1978 amendment to Title VII forbids discrimination on the basis of pregnancy or childbirth. This amendment generally requires employers to treat pregnancy like any other condition similarly affecting working ability in their sick leave programs,

---

[11] *Weber* appears in the chapter entitled the Nature of Law. The version of the case excerpted there, however, does not include the language quoted here.

medical benefit and disability plans, and other fringe benefits.

Although the following *Price Waterhouse* case does not fit neatly within the Title VII proof rules discussed earlier, it demonstrates how another kind of sex discrimination—sexual stereotyping—violates Title VII. The decision also demonstrates the problems created by so-called mixed motive cases. By the time you read the case, however, the causation rules set out below may have been changed by Congress.

PRICE WATERHOUSE v. HOPKINS

490 U.S. 228 (1989)

Ann Hopkins was a senior manager at Price Waterhouse, a major national accounting partnership. During Hopkins's five years with Price Waterhouse, her intelligence, competence, integrity, and money-making ability were almost universally praised. Nevertheless, when Hopkins was proposed for admission to the partnership in 1982, she was neither granted nor denied admission to the firm. Later, the firm refused to repropose her for partnership, and eventually she resigned.

At the time in question, Price Waterhouse's system for selecting new partners relied heavily on written comments by the firm's existing partners. From the written comments on Hopkins and other evidence, it was clear that two general factors underlay her failure to make partner. The first was her excessive abrasiveness, especially in her relations with the firm's staff. The second was the apparent feeling among some partners that Hopkins behaved in ways that were inappropriate for a woman. For example, one partner described her as "macho," another wrote that she "overcompensated for being a woman," yet another advised that she take "a course at charm school," and still others objected to her use of profanity. Also, a partner who explained to Hopkins why her partnership application was being placed on hold told her that to improve her chances of making partner, she should walk more femininely, dress more femininely, wear makeup, have her hair styled, and wear jewelry.

Hopkins sued Price Waterhouse in federal district court for sex discrimination under Title VII. The district court held for Hopkins, and the court of appeals affirmed. Price Waterhouse appealed to the U.S. Supreme Court.

Brennan, Justice.   In passing Title VII, Congress made the simple yet momentous announcement that sex, race, religion, and national origin are not relevant to the selection, evaluation, or compensation of employees. Yet the statute does not limit the other qualities and characteristics that employers *may* take into account in making employment decisions. Therefore, Title VII eliminates certain bases for distinguishing among employees while otherwise preserving employers' freedom of choice.

The statute forbids an employer to [discriminate in certain ways against an individual] "*because of* such individual's sex." These words mean that gender must be irrelevant to employment decisions. When, therefore, an employer considers both gender and legitimate factors at the time of making a decision, that decision was "because of" sex and the other, legitimate considerations. [In such cases,] an employer shall not be liable if it can prove that, even if it had not taken gender into account, it would have come to the same decision.

An employer who acts on the basis of a belief that a woman cannot be aggressive, or that she must not be, has acted on the basis of gender. A number of the partners' comments showed sex stereotyping at work. We are beyond the day when an employer could evaluate employees by assuming or insisting that they match the stereotype associated with their group. An employer who objects to aggression in women but whose positions require this trait places women in an intolerable and impermissible Catch-22: out of a job if they behave aggressively and out of a job if they don't.

The courts below held that an employer who has allowed a discriminatory impulse to play a motivating part in an employment decision must prove by clear and convincing evidence that it would have made the same decision in the absence of discrimination. The better rule is that the employer must make this showing by a preponderance of the evidence. The lower courts did not determine whether Price Waterhouse had proved by a preponderance of the evidence that it would have placed Hopkins's candidacy on hold even if it had not permitted sex-linked evaluations to play a part in the decision making process. Thus, we remand the case so that determination can be made.

Court of appeals decision for Hopkins reversed and case remanded to that court for further proceedings consistent with the Supreme Court's opinion.

Comparable Worth   The sex discrimination theory known as *comparable worth* asserts that certain jobs largely held by women, such as secretarial and nursing positions, are systematically underpaid relative to their true worth, and should get the same compensation as jobs of comparable real worth. The usual criterion for determining worth is the job's value to the organization or to society, and *not* the value set by labor markets. This value often is determined by studies that give different jobs point ratings under factors resembling the Equal Pay Act criteria, add the ratings together, and compare the totals. Various jobs, for example, might be given a numerical score reflecting the skill, responsibility, effort, and working conditions they involve. The total number of points received would indicate the worth of the position, thus providing a basis for determining which positions are underpaid.

For reasons too numerous to discuss here, comparable worth is a very controversial sex discrimination theory. Thus, it has not made significant inroads under federal employment discrimination law. Comparable worth suits cannot be brought under the Equal Pay Act because of the EPA's *equal* work requirement. In 1981, however, the Supreme Court opened the door to possible comparable worth suits under Title VII by holding that only the EPA's *defenses*, and not its equal work limitation, apply to Title VII cases alleging sex discrimination regarding pay. However, the Court emphasized that it was not deciding whether Title VII embraces comparable worth claims. Since then, it is probably safe to say that comparable worth has not been received with great enthusiasm by the few courts considering its status under Title VII. As noted later in this chapter, however, some states and localities have adopted loosely worded "pay equity" laws that could be regarded as comparable worth provisions.

Sexual Harassment   Unwelcome sexual advances, requests for sexual favors, and other verbal or physical conduct of a sexual nature can violate Title VII under two different theories.[12] The first, called **quid pro quo** sexual harassment, involves some express or implied linkage between an employee's submission to sexually oriented behavior and tangible job consequences. Such cases usually arise when an employee who refuses to submit suffers a tangible job detriment as a result. An easy example is the situation where a male supervisor fires a female secretary because of her refusal to have sexual relations with him or her refusal to submit to other sex-related behavior. Such conduct by a supervisor would violate Title VII whether or not he expressly told the secretary that she would be fired for refusing to submit. Title VII also is violated if a supervisor denies a female subordinate a deserved promotion or other job benefit for refusing to submit. Most courts require that the plaintiff show some *tangible job detriment* of an economic nature in order to recover for quid pro quo sexual harassment. Thus, an employee who rejects a supervisor's advances but suffers no unfavorable job consequences may not have a case.

---

[12] Where they are relevant, the principles stated here also apply to race, color, religious, and national origin harassment. In addition, men can sue for sexual harassment by women. A few courts have allowed recoveries for homosexually oriented sexual harassment. Suits by employees who were denied deserved job benefits because another employee benefited by submitting to sex-related behavior may also be possible.

But no quid pro quo and no tangible job detriment are required when an employee is subjected to **work environment** sexual harassment. This is unwelcome sexual behavior that has the purpose or effect of unreasonably interfering with an individual's work performance or of creating an intimidating, hostile, or offensive work environment. Work environment sexual harassment can be inflicted by both supervisors and co-workers; the following *Gus* case is an example of the latter. Because such behavior must be *unwelcome*, however, an employee may have trouble recovering if she instigated or contributed to the sex-related behavior. Also, the offending behavior must be *severe or pervasive* before an employee can recover under Title VII.

When is an *employer* liable for sexual harassment committed by its employees? In *Meritor Savings Bank v. Vinson* (1986), the Supreme Court said that courts should consult the common law of agency when determining an employer's liability. After *Meritor*, the courts have settled into the following pattern on the question: (1) employers are strictly liable for quid pro quo harassment, and (2) employers are liable for work environment harassment if they knew or should have known of the harassment and failed to take appropriate corrective action. In *Gus*, the court used agency principles of *direct liability* to justify the second standard and to find the employer liable for its employees' work environment sexual harassment.[13]

---

[13] Direct liability and various other agency principles employed by the courts in sexual harassment cases are discussed in the chapter entitled Third Party Relations of the Principal and the Agent. But while *Gus* is an exception, it is doubtful whether many of the courts' employer liability decisions really can be justified under agency law.

HALL v. GUS CONSTRUCTION COMPANY

842 F.2d 1010 (8th Cir. 1988)

Three women were hired as "flag persons" (traffic controllers) by the Gus Construction Company, an Iowa firm engaged in road construction. No other women worked on the construction crew to which they were assigned. Immediately after the women began work, male members of the crew began to inflict various kinds of sex-related abuse on them. For example, male crew members repeatedly asked one of the women if she wanted to have sexual intercourse and oral sex with them. Male crew members also frequently mooned the women. In addition, male crew members sometimes rubbed their hands down the women's thighs and also grabbed one woman's breasts. Furthermore, the men also used surveying equipment to observe the women urinating into a ditch after refusing to give them a truck to take to town for a bathroom break.

Male crew members also subjected the three women to abuse that was not so obviously of a sexual nature. For example, the men named one of the women "Herpes" after she developed a skin reaction from an allergy to the sun. In addition, several men urinated into the gas tank of another woman's car, causing it to malfunction.

One of Gus's foremen observed all or most of these incidents—and many others—but did little to stop their occurrence. The women eventually quit their jobs about seven months after their hiring. Then they sued Gus for sexual harassment under Title VII. A trial before a federal district court magistrate resulted in a judgment for the women, and Gus appealed.

Wollman, Circuit Judge. Sexual discrimination that creates a hostile or abusive work environment is a violation of Title VII. Unlike quid pro quo sexual harassment, which occurs when submission to sexual conduct is made a condition of concrete employment benefits, hostile work environment harassment arises when sexual conduct has the purpose or effect of unreasonably interfering with an individual's work performance or creating an intimidating, hostile, or offensive working environment.

Gus contends that the district court erred in not distinguishing between conduct of a sexual nature and other forms of harassment. It points to various incidents that it contends were not sexual and should not have been considered. For example, Gus argues that calling one of the women "Herpes" might have been cruel, but was not conduct of a sexual nature. The incident in which the male crew members urinated in the car's gas tank was a practical joke, Gus argues, not conduct of a sexual nature. [But] the acts underlying a sexual harassment claim need not be clearly sexual in nature. Intimidation and hostility toward women because they are women can obviously result from conduct other than explicit sexual advances.

We are convinced that the harassment directed toward each woman was sufficiently severe or pervasive to alter the conditions of her employment and create an abusive working environment. Gus's final challenge to the district court's finding of sexual harassment is that it erred in imposing employer liability. A company will be liable if management-level employees knew or should have known about a barrage of offensive conduct. This principle is sometimes incorrectly described as an application of *respondeat superior*, [which] makes an employer liable only for wrongs of its employees that are committed in furtherance of the employment. The tortfeasing employee must think (however misguidedly) that he is doing the employer's business in committing the wrong. It would be the rare case where harassment against a co-worker could be thought by the author of the harassment to help the employer's business.

But an employer is *directly* liable independently of *respondeat superior* for torts committed against one employee by another that the employer could have prevented by reasonable care in hiring, supervising, or (if necessary) firing the tortfeasor. Consistent with this principle, an employer who has reason to know that one of his employees is being harassed, and does nothing about it, is blameworthy. He is unlikely to know or have reason to know of casual, isolated, and infrequent slurs; it is only when they are egregious, numerous, and concentrated that the employer will be culpable for failing to discover what is going on and to take remedial steps. In this case, the foreman, as the agent of Gus, had actual and constructive notice of the harassment. Even if he did not know everything that went on, the incidents were so numerous that Gus is liable for failing to discover what was going on and to take steps to end it.

District court judgment in favor of the three women affirmed.

OTHER IMPORTANT EMPLOYMENT DISCRIMINATION PROVISIONS

Section 1981

In cases where it applies, a post–Civil War civil rights statute called section 1981 sets employment discrimination standards resembling those of Title VII. Section 1981 has been applied to public and private employment discrimination against blacks, people of certain racially characterized national origins such as Hispanics, and occasionally aliens. In such cases, courts have applied Title VII's methods of proof and its defenses.

Section 1981's coverage currently is unclear. In a controversial 1989 decision denying a racial harassment claim, the Supreme Court limited section 1981 to discrimination regarding the making and enforcement of private contracts—mainly, to discrimination surrounding the hiring process. Some lower courts, however, have tried to circumvent this limitation on the section's scope. This question is important because section 1981 gives plaintiffs certain advantages that Title VII does not provide them. For example, Title VII's limitations on covered employers and its complex procedural requirements do not apply in section 1981 cases, and recoverable damages are apt to be greater under section 1981. For these reasons, Congressional foes of the Supreme Court decision have attempted to pass legislation that effectively would overrule the Court's limitation on section 1981's scope. As of mid-1991, however, such efforts had not succeeded.

The Age Discrimination in Employment Act

The 1967 Age Discrimination in Employment Act (ADEA) prohibits employment-related age discrimination against employees who are *at least 40 years of age*. People within this age group are protected against age discrimination in favor of both younger and older individuals, including favored individuals inside the protected age group.

Coverage The entities covered by the ADEA include individuals, partnerships, labor organizations (as to their employees), and corporations. Each of these entities must: (1) be engaged in an industry affecting interstate commerce and (2) employ at least 20 persons. In addition, the act applies to state and local governments.[14] Referrals by an employment agency to a covered employer are within the ADEA's scope regardless of the agency's size. Moreover, the ADEA covers labor union practices affecting *union members*; usually, unions with 25 or more members are subject to the act. Like Title VII, the ADEA protects covered individuals against discrimination in a wide range of employment contexts, including hiring, firing, pay, job assignment, and fringe benefits.

In 1986, the ADEA was amended to include certain exemptions from coverage that apply through 1993. The amendment allows state and local governments to discharge or refuse to hire *firefighters* and *law enforcement officers* (including prison guards) due to their age. Also, institutions of higher education may retire *tenured instructors* who have reached the age of 70. In the interim, the EEOC must propose guidelines on the use of physical and mental fitness tests for police officers and firefighters, and must study the consequences of eliminating mandatory retirement in higher education.

Procedural Requirements The complex procedural requirements for an ADEA suit are beyond the scope of this text. Like Title VII, the ADEA requires that a private plaintiff file a charge with the EEOC or an appropriate state agency (if one exists) before she can sue in her own right. The EEOC also may sue to enforce the ADEA; such a suit precludes private suits arising from the same alleged violation. For both government and private suits, the statute of limitations is three years

---

[14]Age discrimination in the federal government is beyond the scope of this text.

from the date of an alleged *willful* violation and two years from the date of an alleged *nonwillful* violation.

Proving Age Discrimination Proof of age discrimination is no problem where an employer uses an explicit age classification, and may be easy where there is direct evidence of discrimination such as testimony or incriminating documents. Most ADEA cases, however, are brought under the Title VII disparate treatment theory discussed earlier. In addition, a few courts have used Title VII's adverse impact theory in ADEA cases.

Defenses The ADEA allows employers to discharge or otherwise penalize an employee for *good cause*, and to use *reasonable factors other than age* in their employment decisions. It also allows employers to observe the terms of a *bona fide seniority system*, except where such a system is used to require or permit the involuntary retirement of anyone 40 or over.

In addition, the ADEA has a *bona fide occupational qualification* defense. In general, an employer seeking to use this defense must show that its age classification is reasonably necessary to the proper performance of the job in question. In most cases raising this defense, the employer argues that age is reasonably necessary to safe performance of the job. To succeed, the employer must show *either:* (1) that it had reasonable grounds for believing that all or substantially all employees of a certain age cannot perform the job safely, or (2) that it is impossible or highly impractical to test employees on an individualized basis. For example, an employer that refuses to hire anyone over 60 as a helicopter pilot should have a BFOQ defense if it somehow shows a reasonable basis for concluding that 60-and-over helicopter pilots pose significant safety risks, or that it is not feasible to test older pilots individually. Usually, however, courts construe the ADEA's BFOQ defense narrowly.

Remedies Remedies available after a successful ADEA suit include unpaid back wages and other benefits resulting from the discrimination; an additional equal award of liquidated damages where the employer acted willfully; attorney's fees; and equitable relief, including hiring, reinstatement, and promotion. Most courts do not allow punitive damages and recoveries for pain, suffering, mental distress, and so forth.

The following *Guthrie* case shows the disparate impact theory at work in a suit involving an age-based firing.

GUTHRIE v. J. C. PENNEY CO.

803 F.2d 202 (5th Cir. 1986)

William Guthrie began managing a J. C. Penney Company store in Meridian, Mississippi in 1973. At that time, J. C. Penney had a written policy that all store managers retire at age 60, but Penney later sent its employees a letter announcing a change in this policy to comply with the ADEA. In the spring of 1979, just before Guthrie's 60th birthday, various Penney employees made a series of inquiries about his retirement plans—some of which amounted to not-so-subtle hints that he ought to resign. From 1979 through 1981, however, Guthrie remained as manager of the Meridian store. During this period, he received satisfactory performance ratings and annual merit pay increases, and the store did well in sales and profits. Early in 1982, though, a Penney reorganization placed Guthrie under a new district manager, James Moore. In February of that year, Moore visited the store and reprimanded Guthrie before store employees over a relatively minor matter. During a June 1982 visit to the store, Moore again criticized Guthrie before store employees, and overrode Guthrie's decisions on a number of matters normally reserved to the store manager. After the visit, Moore lowered Guthrie's performance rating and assigned him a number of difficult future performance objectives.

Feeling that his discharge was inevitable, Guthrie resigned in August of 1982. Even though the store's sales and profits declined under the younger manager who succeeded him, this manager received satisfactory performance ratings and was allowed to run the store without interference. Later, Guthrie sued J. C. Penney in federal district court under the ADEA. After a jury found that Penney had constructively discharged Guthrie in violation of the act, Penney appealed.

Johnson, Circuit Judge.   When a plaintiff in an ADEA case cannot present direct evidence of discrimination, the courts have developed a three-part test modeled on the one used by Title VII plaintiffs. First, the plaintiff must make a prima facie case by proving that he was in the age group protected by the act, he was qualified for the position, he was discharged, and he was replaced by a younger employee. In the second stage, the burden shifts to the employer to produce evidence that dismissal was due to a business reason other than age. At the third stage, the plaintiff can prevail by showing that the articulated reason was a pretext. Penney attacks the sufficiency of the evidence supporting the jury's verdict at two points: constructive discharge and the pretextual nature of Penney's business reasons. The court will not overturn the jury verdict unless it is not supported by substantial evidence.

An employee can prove constructive discharge by showing that his employer created conditions so intolerable that a reasonable person in the employee's shoes would have felt compelled to resign. The jury had substantial evidence to find [Guthrie's decision] reasonable.

Secondly, Penney asserts that it acted as it did for business reasons, and that Guthrie did not prove these reasons to be pretextual. Specifically, Penney says that its repeated inquiries about Guthrie's retirement plans were due to the need to anticipate staff vacancies; that Moore's decision to criticize and downgrade Guthrie formed part of a general "get tough" attitude on his part; and that it had the right to assign little weight to the sales and profit performance of Guthrie's store. Penney is correct that the ADEA is not a license to second-guess legitimate business judgments. Thus, the courts would not interfere if Penney in fact decided to ignore sales and profit performance in evaluating store managers. However, the question is what Penney's motive actually was, not what it could have been. In reaching this determination, the jury is entitled to weigh the credibility of witnesses and to disbelieve self-serving testimony.

In this case, the jury could have believed that Penney's repeated inquiries [about Guthrie's retirement plans] constituted intentional harassment. Moreover, the jury heard considerable evidence tending to show that Moore singled out Guthrie for criticism and applied tougher standards to him than to his younger colleagues. For example, Guthrie's younger successor experienced the same problems and received a [higher] rating. While Penney may choose to downplay sales and profit performance in evaluating a manager, its own company manual lists them as key factors.

In sum, the jury heard substantial evidence from which to conclude that Guthrie met his burden of showing that he was constructively discharged and that Penney's stated reasons for doing so were pretextual.

Judgment for Guthrie affirmed so far as ADEA liability is concerned.

The Americans with Disabilities Act

Until recently, federal regulation of employment discrimination against handicapped people mainly was limited to certain federal contractors and recipients of federal financial assistance. By passing Title I of the Americans with Disabilities Act of 1990 (ADA), however, Congress addressed this problem comprehensively. This portion of the ADA becomes effective during the summer of 1992. It is primarily enforced by the EEOC, and its procedures and remedies are the same as for Title VII.

Covered Entities   For two years following its effective date, Title I of the ADA covers employers who have 25 or more employees and who are engaged in an industry affecting interstate commerce. After that, the limit is 15 or more employees. The term *employer* includes individuals, partnerships, corporations, colleges and universities, labor unions (regarding their own employees), and state and local governments. Not included, however, are the U.S. government and its wholly owned corporations, Indian tribes, and certain tax-exempt private clubs. The act also covers certain labor unions in their capacity as employee representative, as well as employment agencies' treatment of their clients.

Substantive Protections   The ADA forbids covered entities from discriminating against *qualified individuals with a disability* because of that disability. It covers discrimination regarding hiring, firing, promotion, pay, and innumerable other employment decisions. The act defines a *disability* as: (1) a physical or mental impairment that substantially limits one or more of an individual's major life activities, (2) a record of such an impairment, or (3) one's being regarded as having such an impairment. (The last two categories protect, among others, those who have previously been misdiagnosed or who have recovered from earlier impairments.) Not protected, however, are those who are discriminated against for currently engaging in the illegal use of drugs. Also, employers may prohibit workplace alcohol use, require that employees not be under the influence of alcohol at the workplace, and hold alcoholics to the same standards as other employees. Furthermore, homosexuality, bisexuality, transvestism, and various other sex-related traits or conditions are not considered disabilities.

A *qualified individual* with a disability is a person who can perform the essential functions of the relevant job either *without or without reasonable accommodation*. Thus, the ADA protects both individuals who can perform their jobs despite their handicap, and handicapped individuals who could perform their jobs if reasonable accommodation is provided. *Reasonable accommodation* includes acts such as making existing facilities readily accessible and usable, acquiring new equipment, restructuring jobs, modifying work schedules, and making reassignments to vacant positions, among others. But employers need not make reasonable accommodation—and thus can discriminate against people whose impairments prevent them from properly performing their jobs—where doing so would cause them to suffer *undue hardship*. The act defines undue hardship as significant difficulty or expense, and lists various factors by which it should be determined. These factors include the cost of the accommodation, the covered entity's overall financial resources, and the accommodation's effect on the covered entity's activities.

Defenses The ADA protects employers whose allegedly discriminatory decisions are based on *job-related criteria and business necessity*, so long as proper job performance cannot be accomplished by reasonable accommodation. This includes situations where the affected individual poses a direct threat to the health or safety of other workers that cannot be eliminated through a reasonable accommodation. Also, employers can refuse to employ as food handlers those with diseases that have been determined by the secretary of health and human services to be transmitted by the handling of food, unless reasonable accommodation can be made.

Executive Order 11246

Executive Order 11246, issued in 1965 and later amended, forbids race, color, national origin, religion, and sex discrimination by certain federal contractors. The order is enforced by the Office of Federal Contract Compliance Programs (OFCCP) of the Labor Department. Under the order and its accompanying OFCCP regulations, each federal agency must insert an "equal opportunity clause" in most of its private-sector contracts for $10,000 or more. Among other things, this clause requires that the contractor not discriminate on the grounds mentioned above and that it undertake affirmative action to prevent such discrimination.

State Antidiscrimination Laws

Most of the states have statutes that parallel Title VII and the ADEA. Many have laws protecting the handicapped. Some of these statutes provide more extensive protection than their federal counterparts. In addition, some states prohibit forms of discrimination not barred by federal law. Examples include discrimination on the bases of marital status, physical appearance, sexual orientation, and political affiliation. Also, many states prohibit discrimination against AIDS victims or people who carry the AIDS virus. Finally, some states and localities have adopted "pay equity" laws that could be read as comparable worth provisions. Many of these laws apply only to public employment.

CONCEPT REVIEW

THE EMPLOYMENT DISCRIMINATION LAWS COMPARED

	Protected Traits	Covered Employer Decisions	Need to File Charge in Private Suit?
Equal Pay Act	Sex only	Pay only	No
Title VII	Race, color, national origin, religion, sex	Wide range	Yes
Section 1981	Race, racially characterized national origin, perhaps alienage	Currently unclear	No
Age Discrimination in Employment Act	Age, if victim 40 or over	Wide range	Yes
Americans with Disabilities Act	Existence of disability, if person qualified to perform job with or without reasonable accommodation	Wide range	Yes
Executive Order 11246	Race, color, religion, national origin, sex	Wide range	Not applicable; enforced by OFCCP

EMPLOYEE PRIVACY

Modern technology has given employers various means for monitoring their employees' reliability and work performance. While doing so, however, employers may violate those employees' sense of selfhood or their personal dignity. Also, an employer's compilation of information regarding an employee may be used in ways that harm her. The term *employee privacy* is often used to describe both this group of personal interests and the legal issues their violation can present. Here, we outline the most important problems that have arisen in this recently emergent and swiftly developing area.

Polygraph Testing

During the 1970s and 1980s, employers made increasing use of polygraph and other lie detector tests—most often, to screen job applicants and to investigate employee thefts. This led to greater concern about the accuracy of such tests; the personal questions sometimes asked by examiners; and the tests' resulting impact on job prospects, job security, and personal privacy. Such worries have led many states to require that people administrating lie detector tests be licensed, to wholly or partially ban those tests in employment, or to restrict the dissemination of their results. In 1988, Congress significantly limited employers' use of lie detector tests by passing the Employee Polygraph Protection Act.

The Employee Polygraph Protection Act mainly regulates lie detector tests, which include polygraph tests and certain other specific mechanical and electrical devices for assessing a person's honesty. Most of its prohibitions apply to employers engaged in, producing goods for, or affecting interstate commerce. Such employers may not: (1) require, suggest, request, or cause employees or prospective employees to take any lie detector test; (2) use, accept, refer to, or inquire about the results of any lie detector test administered to employees or prospective employees; and (3) take or threaten to take almost any unfavorable employment-related action against employees or prospective employees because of the results of any lie detector test, or because such parties failed or refused to take such a test.

However, certain employers and tests are exempt from these provisions. They include: (1) federal, state, and local government employers; (2) certain national defense and security-related tests by the federal government; (3) certain tests by security service firms whose business involves the public health and safety; and (4) certain tests by firms manufacturing and distributing controlled substances. The act also contains a limited exemption for private employers that use polygraph tests when investigating economic losses caused by theft, embezzlement, industrial espionage, and so forth. Finally, the act restricts the disclosure of test results by examiners and by most employers.

The Polygraph Protection Act is enforced by the Labor Department, which has issued regulations in furtherance of that mission. It does not preempt state laws that prohibit lie detector tests or that set standards stricter than those imposed by federal law. Violations of the act or its regulations can result in civil penalties, suits for equitable relief by the Labor Department, and private suits for damages and equitable relief. Under these provisions, workers and job applicants can obtain employment, reinstatement, promotion, and payment of lost wages and benefits.

Drug and Alcohol Testing

Due to their impact on employees' safe and effective job performance, employers have become increasingly concerned about both on-the-job and off-the-job drug and alcohol use. Thus, employers increasingly require employees and job applicants to undergo urine tests for drugs and/or alcohol. Because those who test positive may be either disciplined or induced to undergo treatment, and because the tests themselves can raise privacy concerns, some legal checks on their use have emerged.

Drug and alcohol testing by *public* employers can be attacked under the Fourth Amendment's search-and-seizure provisions. However, such tests generally are constitutional where there is a reasonable basis for suspecting that an employee is illegally using drugs or alcohol, or such use in a particular job could threaten the public interest or public safety. In 1989, for example, the Supreme Court upheld an internal Customs Service drug-testing program requiring urinalysis before employees can be transferred or promoted to jobs involving matters such as drug interdiction and the carrying of firearms.

Due to the government action requirement discussed in the Business and the Constitution chapter, employees generally have no federal constitutional protection against drug and alcohol testing by *private* employers. Some *state* constitutions, however, lack a government action requirement. In addition, a number of states now regulate private drug and/or alcohol testing by statute. Moreover, such testing sometimes is challenged by unionized employees under their collective bargaining agreements. Finally, tort suits for invasion of privacy or infliction of emotional distress may be possible in some cases.[15]

Despite these protections, however, federal law *requires* private-sector drug testing in certain situations. Under a 1988 Defense Department rule, for example, employers who contract with the department must agree to establish a drug-testing program under which employees who work in sensitive positions sometimes may be tested. Also, 1988 Transportation Department regulations require random testing of public and private employees occupying safety-sensitive or security-related positions in industries such as aviation, trucking, railroads, mass transit, and others. Other regulations of this kind may follow.[16] Such rules could be challenged on constitutional grounds. In 1989, however, the Supreme Court upheld a Federal Railroad Administration program mandating drug and urine tests for railroad employees involved in major train accidents.

Employer Searches

Employers concerned about thefts, drug use, and other misbehavior by their employees sometimes conduct searches of those employees' offices, desks, lockers, files, briefcases, packages, vehicles, and even bodies in an effort to confirm their suspicions. In 1987, the Supreme Court held that public employees sometimes may have a reasonable expectation of privacy in areas such as their offices, desks, or files. But it also held that searches of those areas are constitutional under the Fourth Amendment when they are reasonable under the circumstances. In the process, the Court said that neither probable cause nor a warrant is necessary for such searches to proceed.

As noted above, the U.S. Constitution ordinarily does not apply to private employment. Nonetheless, both private and public employees can mount common law invasion of privacy suits against employers who conduct searches. In such cases, courts usually weigh the intrusiveness of the search against the purposes justifying it, and consider the availability of less intrusive alternatives that still would satisfy the employer's legitimate needs. Such suits tend not to succeed where there is some reasonable justification for the search and it was no more intrusive than necessary under the circumstances.

Employer Monitoring

Although employers always have monitored their employees' work, recent technological advances enable such monitoring to occur without those employees' knowledge. Examples include closed-circuit television, telephone monitoring, the monitoring of computer workstations (e.g., by counting keystrokes), and metal detectors at plant entrances. Such monitoring has encountered objections because employees are often unaware that it exists, or may suffer stress when they do know or suspect its existence. Employers counter these objections by stressing that monitoring is highly useful in evaluating employee performance, improving efficiency, and reducing theft.

Telephone monitoring may be illegal under federal wiretapping law, but the relevant provision has many exceptions. Although such claims have been uncommon, invasion of privacy suits may succeed in situations where an employer's need for surveillance is slight and it is conducted in areas such as restrooms and lounges in which employees have a reasonable expectation of privacy. Despite various state and federal bills proposing legislation regulating various forms of monitoring, very few such laws had been passed as of mid-1991.

Records and References

Many states allow both public and private employees access to personnel files maintained by their employers, although some limit the types of documents that can be examined. Also, some states limit third-party access to such records. In addition, employers who transmit such data to third parties may be civilly liable for defamation or invasion of privacy.[17] However, truth is a defense in defamation cases, and in both defamation and invasion of privacy suits the employer's actions may be privileged. These defenses often protect employers who are sued for truthful, good faith statements made in references for former employees.

---

[15]Invasion of privacy and intentional infliction of emotional distress are discussed in the Intentional Torts chapter, and negligent infliction of emotional distress is discussed in the Negligence and Strict Liability chapter.

[16]However, one recent antidrug measure, the Drug-Free Workplace Act of 1988, does not require testing.

---

[17]Defamation and invasion of privacy are discussed in the Intentional Torts chapter, which examines defamation suits against employers by their ex-employees in greater detail than does this chapter.

THE EROSION OF EMPLOYMENT AT WILL

As discussed earlier in this chapter, the traditional employment-at-will doctrine allows either party to an employment contract for an indefinite term to terminate the contract at any time and for any reason. Helping to explain the doctrine's emergence were the individualism of 19th-century society and 19th-century contract law and its tendency to promote economic efficiency by allowing employers to terminate unneeded employees. Although employment at will remains important, it has been eroded by many of the developments described in this chapter. For example, the NLRA forbids dismissal for union affiliation, and labor contracts frequently bar termination without just cause. Also, Title VII prohibits terminations based on certain personal traits, the ADEA blocks firings on the basis of age, and the ADA forbids discharges for covered personal disabilities.

The Common Law Exceptions

In recent years, courts have been carving out further exceptions to employment at will. The three most important such exceptions are discussed immediately below. Although a few courts have flatly refused to do so, most states recognize one or more of these exceptions. In such states, a terminated employee can sue her employer for **unjust dismissal** or **wrongful discharge.** The remedies in successful unjust dismissal cases vary, and depend heavily on whether the plaintiff's claim is regarded as sounding in contract or in tort. Tort remedies, of course, usually are more advantageous for plaintiffs.

The Public Policy Exception   The *public policy* exception to the employment-at-will doctrine, which has been recognized by over three-fourths of the states, is the most common basis for a wrongful discharge suit. It is usually regarded as a tort claim. In such cases, the terminated employee argues that his discharge was unlawful because it violated public policy. Many courts limit "public policy" to the policies furthered by *existing laws* such as constitutional provisions and statutes—and perhaps administrative regulations and common law rules as well. In such states, the ex-employee must show that his termination violated public policy because he was fired for acts, or refusals to act, which were in harmony with the policies expressed in existing legal rules. For example, an employee who is fired for filing a workers' compensation claim normally recovers against her employer, because the act that provoked the firing (filing

the claim) obviously is consistent with the policies furthered by the state's workers' compensation statute.

Other examples of successful public policy exception claims include firings based on employees' performing jury duty, refusing to participate in illegal price-fixing, refusing to commit perjury at a state hearing, whistle-blowing,[18] refusing to date a foreman, insisting that the employer comply with state law, and refusing to take a polygraph test where such tests were forbidden by state law. Situations where the exception was *not* recognized include discharges caused by an employee's objection to the marketing of an allegedly defective product, and by an employee's refusal to work on drug research that she felt to be medically unethical. In the following *Foley* case, the court refused to decide whether public policy should be based only on constitutional or statutory provisions, and decided for the employer because the policy it allegedly violated was not *public.*

The Implied Covenant of Good Faith and Fair Dealing   A wrongful discharge suit based on the *implied covenant of good faith and fair dealing* usually is a contract claim. Here, the employee argues that her discharge was unlawful because it was not made in good faith or did not amount to fair dealing, thus violating the implied contract term. Only about 20 percent of the states have recognized this exception to employment at will, and some of these give it a narrow scope. The apparent reasons are this theory's open-ended nature and its resulting potential for restricting business freedom.

The Implied-in-Fact Contract Exception   Courts sometimes imply additional terms in contracts. One example involves *implied-in-fact* contract terms, which often arise from statements or conduct by the parties at or after the formation of their contract. As *Foley* relates, implied-in-fact contract terms giving employees additional job security come from many sources. By far the most common of these, however, are oral statements made by employers during hiring or employee orientation, or written statements in company employee manuals and handbooks. If such sources expressly state the reasons for which employees will be fired or the procedures accompanying employee terminations and if an employer fails to follow those express promises, it may be liable for breach of contract. As *Foley* suggests, such liability also may stem from other employer behavior in

---

[18] Whistle blowers are employees who publicly disclose dangerous, illegal, or improper employer behavior. A few states have passed statutes protecting the employment rights of certain whistle blowers.

addition to its express promises. At least two-thirds of the states recognize the implied-in-fact contract exception to employment at will.

Recent Developments

Due to the increasing number and size of plaintiffs' recoveries, courts and other lawmakers apparently are having second thoughts about employer liability for wrongful discharge. The *Foley* case is a possible example. In addition, a few courts have enforced express disclaimers of wrongful discharge liability in employment contracts. Others have held that where the cause of the unjust dismissal is employment discrimination or some other wrong dealt with by existing regulations, the case should be decided under those regulations and not under the law of wrongful discharge. Still other emergent or proposed moves to reduce employers' legal exposure include arbitration and limitations on damages. As of mid-1991, work on a uniform employment termination act was underway, and at least one state already had comprehensively regulated and limited unjust dismissal claims by statute.

As our previous discussion suggests, the following *Foley* case involves all three exceptions to the employment-at-will doctrine.

FOLEY v. INTERACTIVE DATA CORPORATION

254 Cal. Rptr. 211 (Cal. Sup. Ct. 1988)

Daniel Foley was hired by the Interactive Data Corporation in 1976. His employment contract did not expressly state the time period of his employment, and also did not expressly limit Interactive Data's ability to fire him. Over the next six years and nine months, Foley received a steady series of salary increases, promotions, bonuses, awards, and superior performance evaluations. During this period, Foley claimed, Interactive Data's officers gave him repeated assurances of job security so long as his work performance remained adequate. Over this time, moreover, the firm maintained written "Termination Guidelines" that set forth express grounds for discharge and a mandatory seven-step pretermination procedure.

In 1982, Interactive Data hired Robert Kuhne, who was ultimately intended to replace Richard Earnest as Foley's immediate supervisor. After learning that Kuhne was under FBI investigation for embezzling funds from his former employer, Foley reported this to Earnest early in 1983, while Earnest was still his supervisor. Approximately two months later, Foley was fired.

Alleging that the firing was due to his statements about Kuhne (who eventually pleaded guilty to embezzlement), Foley sued Interactive Data for wrongful discharge in a California trial court. He had three claims: (1) a tort claim alleging a discharge in violation of public policy, (2) a contract claim for breach of an implied-in-fact promise to discharge only for good cause, and (3) a claim for tortious breach of the implied covenant of good faith and fair dealing. The trial court granted Interactive Data's motion to dismiss each claim, and an intermediate appellate court affirmed. Foley appealed to the California Supreme Court.

Lucas, Chief Justice. *Public Policy.* The employer's right to discharge an at-will employee is subject to limits imposed by public policy. We do not decide in this case whether a tort action alleging a breach of public policy may be based only on policies derived from a statute or constitutional provision, or whether nonlegislative sources may provide the basis for such a claim. Even where a statutory touchstone has been asserted, we must still inquire whether the discharge is against public policy and affects a duty which inures to the benefit of the *public at large* rather than to a particular employer or employee.

Foley alleges that Interactive Data discharged him in derogation of a public policy that imposes a legal duty on employees to report relevant business information to management. An employee is an agent, and [under common law agency rules] is required to disclose to his principal all information relevant to the subject matter of the agency. It is unclear whether the alleged duty [also] is one founded in statute. Whether or not there is a statutory duty, we do not find a substantial public policy prohibiting an employer from discharging an employee for performing that duty. Past decisions recognizing a tort action for discharge in violation of public policy seek to protect the public—by protecting the employee who refuses to commit a crime; who reports criminal activity to proper authorities; or who discloses other illegal, unethical, or unsafe practices. No equivalent *public* interest bars the discharge of Foley.

Breach of Employment Contract. Foley's second cause of action alleged that over the course of his employment, the company's own conduct and personnel policies gave rise to [a contract] not to fire him without good cause. He alleges that a course of conduct, including various oral representations, created a reasonable expectation to that effect. His cause of action is properly described as one for breach of an implied-in-fact contract. [The presumption of at-will employment] may be overcome by evidence that the parties agreed that the employer's power to terminate would be limited in some way. Courts seek to enforce the actual understanding of the parties to a contract, and in so doing may inquire into the parties' conduct to determine if it demonstrates an implied contract.

In the employment context, factors used to ascertain the existence and content of an [implied] agreement include the personnel policies or practices of the employer, the employee's longevity of service, [and] actions or communications by the employer reflecting assurances of continued employment. Six years and nine months is sufficient time for an implied contract. Foley alleged repeated assurances of job security and consistent promotions, salary increases, and bonuses— contributing to his reasonable expectation that he would not be discharged except for good cause. Breach of the written "Termination Guidelines" [also] may be sufficient for breach of an employment contract. The trier of fact can infer an agreement to limit the grounds for termination based on the employee's reasonable reliance on the company's personnel manual or policies. In sum, Foley has pleaded facts which, if proved, may be sufficient for a jury to find an implied-in-fact contract limiting Interactive Data's right to discharge him arbitrarily.

Implied Covenant of Good Faith and Fair Dealing. Foley asserts that we should recognize *tort* remedies for breach [of the implied covenant of good faith and fair dealing] in the employment context. Every contract imposes upon each party a duty of good faith and fair dealing in its performance and its enforcement. The courts employ the good faith doctrine to effectuate the intentions of parties, or to protect their reasonable expectations. The covenant is read into contracts in order to protect the express promises of the contract, not to protect some general public policy not directly tied to the contract's purposes.

Several factors combine to persuade us that contractual remedies should remain the sole available relief for breaches of the implied covenant of good faith and fair dealing in the employment context. It is important that employers not be unduly deprived of discretion to dismiss an employee by the fear that doing so will give rise to potential tort liability in every case. Moreover, it would be difficult to formulate a rule that would assure that only "deserving" cases give rise to tort relief. In a tort action based on an employee's discharge, it is likely that each case would involve a dispute as to the subjective intentions of the employer [his bad faith]. Finally, the expansion of tort remedies in the employment context has potentially enormous consequences for the stability of the business community.

Dismissal of Foley's public policy claim and his claim for tortious breach of the implied covenant of good faith and fair dealing affirmed; dismissal of Foley's implied-in-fact contract claim reversed. Case returned to the lower courts for action consistent with the Supreme Court's opinion.

ETHICAL AND PUBLIC POLICY CONCERNS

1. Over the past 150 years, a moral theory known as *utilitarianism* has been very influential. Although it comes in many forms, utilitarianism basically asserts that the test for determining the rightness or wrongness of actions (including laws) is their ability to produce the greatest net balance of satisfactions over dissatisfactions throughout society as a whole. Give a utilitarian justification for the *traditional* employment-at-will rule described at the beginning of this chapter. You can assume that economic well-being counts as a "satisfaction" for utilitarian purposes. You can also assume that the people fired under the traditional employment-at-will rule suffer from their firing.

2. Suppose someone argues that almost all the 20th-century employment law rules discussed in this chapter demonstrate how this country has abandoned the traditional principles that made it great. In particular, this person asserts, these rules show that America has abandoned the idea that people are—and should be—rugged, self-reliant *individuals* who are capable of making their own contracts in free and equal labor markets. Instead, he continues, Americans have become pathetic weaklings who need government protection throughout the employment relationship. Based on the materials presented in this chapter, what is wrong with this argument? In answering, assume that ruggedness, self-reliance, and so forth are morally desirable traits.

3. The *comparable worth* theory discussed in the chapter is very controversial. Consider the following questions about, and criticisms of, comparable worth.

   a. What are the most likely causes of the wage disparities that comparable worth plans would rectify? Do these disparities really result from *discrimination* in any meaningful sense of the word?

   b. Are the methods for determining the inherent worth of jobs really "objective" and "scientific," or do they necessarily depend on subjective factors?

   c. What would be the likely economic consequences if comparable worth were widely adopted throughout American society?

   d. Which women would and would not benefit if comparable worth were widely adopted?

SUMMARY

Nineteenth-century employment law was heavily influenced by the individualistic principles of that century's contract law, and it usually favored the stronger party—the employer—as a result. In the 20th century, employer power probably has increased, and the employment relationship is even more important to employees. Perhaps for these reasons, employment law has become far more protective of employees. In fact, modern employment law can be seen as a series of exceptions to the contract-based 19th-century model of the employment relation.

Legal protection against on-the-job injuries is a major concern of modern employment law. Thus, state *workers' compensation* systems provide injured employees with a strict liability recovery for work-related injuries. In such cases, the employer's traditional defenses of assumption of risk, contributory negligence, and the fellow-servant rule do not apply; but an injured employee's recovery often is less than would have been obtained in a successful negligence suit. The law also seeks to protect workers through direct regulation of workplace safety. The most important example is the federal *Occupational Safety and Health Act*.

Modern employment law also seeks to maintain the income of those who involuntarily lose their jobs through no fault of their own or who retire. State *unemployment compensation* systems protect the former group for limited time periods. The *Federal Insurance Contributions Act* finances a system of old-age, survivors, disability, and medical and hospital insurance. The *Employee Retirement Income Security Act* protects individuals from abuses in the operation of private pension plans.

Today, the law also protects employees by regulating the terms and conditions of their employment. By recognizing the right of employees to bargain collectively through unions, *federal labor law* has powerfully (if indirectly) affected the terms and conditions of employment. Federal labor law also protects employees by prohibiting certain unfair labor practices by both employers and unions. The *Fair Labor Standards Act* regulates wages and hours worked, and also forbids certain kinds of child labor.

Perhaps the best-known and most discussed aspect of employment law today is its protection against employment discrimination. The *Equal Pay Act* prohibits sex discrimination with respect to pay. *Title VII* of the 1964 Civil Rights Act, the single most important employment discrimination provision, forbids such discrimination on the bases of race, color, national origin, sex, and religion. *Section 1981*, a post–Civil War antidiscrimination measure, affords some protection against discrimination based on an employee's ancestry or ethnic characteristics. The *Age Discrimination in Employment Act* protects those aged 40 or over against employer age discrimination. The new *Americans with Disabilities Act* protects qualified individuals with a disability against discrimination based on their disability. Under *Executive Order 11246*, certain federal contractors are forbidden from discriminating on the bases of race, national origin, religion, and sex; and may be required to undertake affirmative action to prevent such discrimination. Finally, the states usually prohibit these and other forms of employment discrimination.

In recent years, the law has begun to protect *employee privacy* in a variety of different contexts. These include lie detector tests, drug and alcohol testing, searches of the employee's work area, electronic surveillance of employees, and misuse of information about employees and ex-employees. In this emerging and rapidly changing area of legal concern, employees may be able to utilize constitutional search-and-seizure protections, state statutes, and civil suits for defamation or invasion of privacy, depending on the circumstances.

For about a century, the doctrine of *employment at will* has been a centerpiece of American employment law. The doctrine states that either party to an employment contract for an indefinite term can terminate the contract at any time for any reason. The doctrine has been eroded by many of the legal rules described in this chapter. In recent years, courts have further eroded the doctrine by recognizing employee suits for *unjust dismissal* or *wrongful discharge*. They have done so under three theories: (1) that the dismissal is wrongful because it violates public policy (usually, a policy expressed in existing law), (2) that the dismissal is wrongful because it violates an implied term of good faith and fair dealing that courts read into the employment contract, or (3) that the dismissal violates implied-in-fact terms of the employment contract.

Problem Cases

1. Beverly Waters worked as a customer service representative for an insurance agency. Although she occasionally filled in for one of the agency's sales agents, her duties were not the same as those of the firm's male agents. She also was paid less than those male agents. For this reason, she sued her employer under the Equal Pay Act. The employer argued that Waters had no EPA claim because her job was different from the male agents' jobs. However, Waters asserted that the reason for this unequal work was that her employer had discriminated against her on the basis of her gender by not allowing her to work as an agent even though she was qualified for the job. Thus, she argued, her Equal Pay Act claim should succeed. Does the *Grove* case in the text contain any language supporting Waters's argument? If Waters's argument fails under the Equal Pay Act, under what other law could she pursue such a claim, and why?

2. For a long time, T.I.M.E.–D.C., a nationwide trucking concern, and the International Brotherhood of Teamsters had discriminated against blacks and other racial minorities regarding access to the firm's intercity, over-the-road driver positions. Such positions were in a different union bargaining unit than the city driver and service jobs in which blacks and minorities had been concentrated. After the passage of Title VII in 1964, the company significantly reduced this sort of discrimination, but it retained a seniority system that based the ability to get choice jobs and to avoid layoffs on length of service in a particular bargaining unit. This meant that minorities who now could move up to intercity driver positions would have to forfeit all the seniority that they had earned in their previous bargaining unit. This tended to deter minorities from taking such positions. What method of proving a Title VII violation could black or minority plaintiffs use in this case? What defense might the company and the union have?

3. Dianne Rawlinson, a rejected female applicant for employment as a prison guard in the Alabama prison system, challenged certain state rules restricting her employment prospects under Title VII. They were: (1) requirements that all prison employees be at least 5 feet 2 inches tall and weigh at least 120 pounds, and (2) a rule expressly prohibiting women from assuming close-contact prison guard positions in maximum-security prisons (most of which were all male). What method of proving a Title VII case should Rawlinson use in attacking the height and weight requirements? Does she need to use one of these methods to attack the second rule? What argument should the state use if Rawlinson establishes a prima facie case against the height and weight requirements? What Title VII defense might the state have for the second rule? With regard to the second rule, assume that at this time Alabama's maximum security prisons housed their male prisoners dormitory-style rather than putting them in cells, and that they did not separate sex offenders from other prisoners.

4. Farah Manufacturing Company had a long-standing policy against employing aliens. Cecilia Espinoza, a lawfully admitted alien married to an American citizen, applied for employment as a seamstress at Farah. She was rejected, and sued Farah for discrimination on the basis of national origin in violation of Title VII. Did Farah's decision violate Title VII? Assume that Espinoza's suit is based on the policy just described and that she is not making either a disparate treatment or an adverse impact argument.

5. Manjit Bhatia, a machinist for Chevron U.S.A., Inc., was a devout Sikh whose religion forbade the cutting or shaving of any body hair. In compliance with standards promulgated by California's Occupational Safety and Health Administration, Chevron required all machinists whose duties involved potential exposure to toxic gases to shave any facial hair that prevented them from achieving a gas-tight face seal when wearing a respirator. Bhatia was one of these machinists, and he told Chevron that his religious beliefs made it impossible for him to comply with the new policy. Chevron then suspended Bhatia from his machinist position, unsuccessfully tried to find him an equal-paying position that did not require a respirator, and finally offered him various lower-paying jobs. Bhatia accepted one of these jobs, but then sued Chevron under Title VII, arguing that his discharge from the machinist position was due to religious discrimination. Will Chevron succeed if it simply argues that it is not discriminating on the basis of religion, but instead merely is penalizing Bhatia for his refusal to shave his facial hair? Will Chevron have a defense if it claims that it could not retain Bhatia in a machinist position without incurring undue hardship?

6. When the Westinghouse Corporation established a formal wage structure late in the 1930s, all job classifications were segregated by sex. At that time, the "female" jobs were generally lower paid than the "male" jobs. Later, men were employed in what had been women's jobs, and vice versa. In such cases, the pay scales for each job were the same no matter what the gender of the jobholder. In 1965, Westinghouse consolidated all of its job classifications, eliminating the former sex segregation. But the formerly female jobs still generally were lower paid than the formerly male jobs. Moreover, the

vast majority of women were still employed in the formerly female jobs.

The International Union of Electrical Workers sued Westinghouse for sex discrimination under Title VII, arguing that Westinghouse's new system did not provide comparable pay for jobs of comparable worth. Westinghouse defended by arguing that the reach of Title VII is no greater than the reach of the Equal Pay Act. As a result, Westinghouse claimed, Title VII only forbade unequal pay for *equal* work. Will Westinghouse's argument succeed?

7. Mechelle Vinson alleged that during her four years with the Meritor Savings Bank, her supervisor Sidney Taylor repeatedly demanded sexual favors from her, and that she had sexual intercourse with him on 40 to 50 separate occasions. She also contended that Taylor fondled her in front of other employees, followed her into the women's restroom, exposed himself to her, and forcibly raped her on several occasions. Despite these allegations, however, Vinson apparently was well treated by her employer in other respects. In fact, she received three promotions during her time with the bank, and it was undisputed that her advancement was based solely on merit. Assuming that Vinson's allegations are true and that Taylor's behavior was unwelcome to her, can she recover against the bank for quid pro quo sexual harassment? Can she recover for work environment sexual harassment? Assume that the bank would be liable for Taylor's behavior.

8. William Massarsky was hired by General Motors in 1963 at the age of 40. Due to a divisionwide force reduction caused by economic conditions, he was laid off in 1971. The layoff was pursuant to a company policy stating that, where ability, merit, and capacity are equal, those with the least time of service in a particular job classification would be the first to be released. When GM released Massarsky, it retained Joseph Biondo, age 25, an employee with over two years less service than Massarsky. Biondo was a student in the General Motors Institute (GMI), a five-year work-study program allowing its 2,350 tuition-paying students to earn a college degree in engineering or management while working for GM. Because GM felt that it had a considerable investment in GMI students, it had an unpublicized company policy exempting GMI students from layoffs.

Can Massarsky successfully argue that the layoff violated the Age Discrimination in Employment Act because the policy exempting GMI students *expressly* discriminated on the basis of age? If Massarsky mounts a *disparate treatment* suit against GM, what would you argue on GM's behalf to show that it had a legitimate nondiscriminatory reason for favoring Biondo? Finally, if Massarsky sued under a *disparate impact* theory, what would he have to show?

9. At the age of 66, Fleming Tullis was discharged from his job as a school bus driver with a private school. He sued the school under the Age Discrimination in Employment Act. Did the school have a BFOQ defense here? Assume for purposes of this question that tests for determining the driving ability of individual people are available and reliable. Also, assume that the school failed to produce any evidence showing that people in their 60s cannot safely operate school buses.

10. Paul Luedtke was an at-will "driller" with Nabors Alaska Drilling, Inc. His job was to oversee a drilling crew on an oil rig on Alaska's North Slope. After a urinalysis suggested that Luedtke was using marijuana, he was suspended from his job. Then, he was told that he would have to pass two new, scheduled urinalysis tests before he would be allowed to return to work. Luedtke refused to take the first test, claiming that it violated his privacy, and was fired as a result. Can he recover for wrongful discharge under the implied covenant of good faith and fair dealing on the theory that the test violated his privacy rights? Assume that Alaska has adopted this exception to the employment-at-will doctrine, that violation of a public policy can constitute a breach of the covenant, and that the public policy need not be expressed in existing law.

11. Catherine Sue Wagenseller was fired from her job as paramedic coordinator in the Scottsdale Memorial Hospital's emergency department. She sued the hospital for wrongful discharge under the public policy exception to the employment-at-will doctrine, alleging that she was fired because of animosity resulting from her refusal to participate in an off-the-job group parody of the song *Moon River* in which group members mooned the audience. A state statute provided that: "A person commits indecent exposure if he or she exposes his or her genitals or anus . . . and another person is present, and the defendant is reckless about whether such other person, as a reasonable person, would be offended or alarmed by the act." Assuming that the audience to the parody enjoyed watching the mooning, would Wagenseller have been criminally liable if she had participated? Does this necessarily defeat her civil claim for wrongful discharge under the public policy exception?

PART II

CRIMES AND TORTS

CHAPTER 6

CRIMES

INTRODUCTION

At first glance, a chapter on criminal law might seem out of place in a text devoted to the legal environment of business. Contracts, torts, agency, corporations, and the host of other legal topics covered in this text tend to come more readily to mind than crime. These legal subjects are traditionally viewed as being important to people in business. However, a thorough understanding of the nature of the criminal law is also an essential part of a manager's education today because people in business and their corporate employers are more likely than ever before to have some unpleasant contact with the criminal justice system.

This century has witnessed a growing tendency on the part of our legal system to use the criminal law as a major device for controlling corporate behavior. Many modern regulatory statutes provide criminal as well as civil penalties in the event of a statutory violation. Frequently, those criminal penalties apply both to individual employees and to their employers.

Those who advocate using the criminal law in this way commonly argue that the criminal law affords a level of deterrence superior to that produced by purely civil remedies such as damage awards. Corporations may be inclined to treat civil damage awards as a cost of doing business, and therefore may violate regulatory provisions when it is profitable to do so. Criminal prosecutions, on the other hand, threaten corporations with the stigma of a criminal conviction. In some cases, society may impose penalties on individual corporate employees who would not be directly affected by a civil judgment against their employer. Moreover, by alerting private individuals to the existence of a violation that can serve as the basis for a civil damage suit, criminal prosecutions may also increase the likelihood that a corporation will be forced to bear the full costs of its actions.

Whatever the merit of these arguments, the threat of criminal prosecution is an inescapable part of the legal environment of business today. Accordingly, the remainder of this chapter focuses on the nature of the criminal law in general. Then it proceeds with a discussion of many complex problems associated with the operation of the criminal law in the corporate context.

THE CRIMINAL LAW

Nature of Crime

Crimes are *public wrongs*—acts prohibited by the *state*. Criminal prosecutions are initiated by an agent of the state (the prosecutor) in the name of the state. Persons convicted of committing criminal acts are exposed to the uniquely coercive force of *criminal sanctions*—the punishment society has provided for those who violate its most important rules. This punishment may take the form of a fine, imprisonment, or, in extreme cases, execution. In addition to formal punishment, convicted criminals must bear the *stigma* associated with a criminal conviction—the social condemnation that results from being labeled a criminal offender.

Our legal system also contains a wide variety of noncriminal forms of punishment. For example, the next two chapters deal with *torts*, private wrongs punished by awards of money damages. In some cases, this punishment consists of forcing a person who commits a tort to compensate his victim for the damages resulting from the tort. In others, a court may also award punitive damages for the express purpose of punishing the wrongdoer. However, only the criminal sanction combines the threat to life or liberty with the stigma of conviction. This potent combination caused one authority to describe the criminal sanction as "the law's ultimate threat."[1]

Crimes are usually classified as felonies or misdemeanors, depending on the seriousness of the offense. A **felony** is a serious offense, such as murder, rape, or arson. Felonies generally involve serious moral culpability on the part of the offender. They are punishable by confinement to a penitentiary for a substantial period of time. A person convicted of a felony may also suffer other serious consequences, such as *disenfranchisement* (loss of voting rights) and being barred from the practice of certain professions, such as law or medicine. A **misdemeanor** is a lesser offense, such as a minor traffic violation or disorderly conduct. Misdemeanors, which often do not involve significant moral culpability, are punishable by fines or limited confinement in a city or county jail.

Whether a given act is classed as criminal is a social question. As our social values have changed over time, so have our definitions of criminal conduct. Many observers argue that criminal sanctions should be reserved for behavior involving serious moral culpability. As the rest of this chapter indicates, however, we have criminalized a wide variety of behavior that has very little moral content.

---

[1] H. Packer, *The Limits of the Criminal Sanction*, 250 (Stanford, Calif.: Stanford University Press, 1968).

Purpose of the Criminal Sanction

Much of the disagreement about the circumstances in which the criminal sanction should be employed stems from a basic disagreement about the purpose of the criminal sanction. Persons who take a *utilitarian* view of the criminal sanction believe that the *prevention* of socially undesirable behavior is the only proper purpose for applying criminal penalties. The goal of prevention includes three major components: deterrence, rehabilitation, and incapacitation.

Deterrence theory holds that the threat or imposition of punishment deters crime. Deterrence theorists focus on two types: special deterrence and general deterrence. *Special deterrence* occurs when the punishment of a convicted offender deters him from committing further criminal offenses. *General deterrence* results when the punishment of a convicted wrongdoer deters others who might otherwise have been inclined to commit a similar offense. Several factors are generally influential in determining the effectiveness of deterrence. Among these are the likelihood that the crime will be detected, that detection will be followed by prosecution, that prosecution will result in a conviction, and the severity of the punishment likely to be imposed in the event of a conviction. Put in economic terms, effective deterrence requires that the penalty imposed for an offense, discounted by the likelihood of apprehension and conviction, must equal or exceed the gains to the offender from committing the offense.

The fundamental problem with deterrence theories is that we can never say with certainty whether deterrence works because we can never know what the crime rate would be in the absence of punishment. For example, unacceptably high levels of crime and *recidivism* (repeat offenses by previously punished offenders) may be the result of the failure to impose criminal sanctions of sufficient severity and certainty, rather than evidence that criminal sanctions cannot produce deterrence. Deterrence theory has one other fundamental problem—it tends to assume that potential offenders are rational beings who consciously weigh the threat of punishment against the benefits derived from an offense. The threat of punishment, however, may not deter the commission of criminal offenses produced by irrational or unconscious drives.

Another way to prevent undesirable behavior is to *rehabilitate* convicted offenders by changing their attitudes or values so that they are not inclined to commit future offenses. Critics of rehabilitation commonly point to high rates of recidivism as evidence of the general failure of our rehabilitation efforts to date. Even if rehabilitative strategies fail, however, the incarceration of convicted offenders contributes to the goal of prevention by *incapacitating* them. While they are imprisoned, their ability to commit other criminal offenses is drastically reduced.

Prevention is not the only goal advanced for the criminal sanction. Some persons see the central focus of criminal punishment as *retribution*; that is, the infliction of deserved suffering on those who violate society's most fundamental rules. To a retributionist, punishment satisfies community and individual desires for revenge, and it vindicates and reinforces important social values. So, a retributionist is unlikely to see prevention as a sufficient reason for criminalizing behavior that is socially undesirable but morally neutral. On the other hand, when serious moral culpability is present, a retributionist would likely favor punishment even if convinced that it will not prevent future offenses.

Essentials of Crime

Before a person can be convicted of a crime, the state ordinarily must: (1) demonstrate that his alleged actions violated an existing criminal statute; (2) prove beyond a reasonable doubt that he did in fact commit the actions charged against him; and (3) prove that he had the legal capacity to form a criminal intent.

Prior Statutory Prohibition   Criminal offenses are *statutory* offenses. Only the legislature has the power to criminalize behavior. The U.S. Constitution prohibits *ex post facto* criminal laws. This means that a defendant's act must have been prohibited by statute at the time she committed it and the penalty must be the one provided for at the time of her offense.

The Constitution also limits the power of Congress and state legislatures to criminalize behavior in several other ways. They cannot criminalize behavior that is constitutionally protected. For example, as the *Johnson* case, which follows, indicates, the First Amendment to the Constitution prohibits laws that unreasonably restrict freedom of speech and expression. Similarly, in *Griswold v. Connecticut,* the Supreme Court struck down state statutes prohibiting the use of contraceptive devices and the counseling or assisting of others in the use of such devices on the ground that the statutes violated a constitutionally protected *right of privacy* implicit in the Bill of Rights.[2] This decision provided the constitutional basis for the Court's historic decision in *Roe v. Wade* that limited the states' power to criminalize abortions.[3]

---

[2] 381 U.S. 479 (U.S. Sup. Ct. 1965).
[3] 410 U.S. 113 (U.S. Sup. Ct. 1973).

TEXAS v. JOHNSON

109 S. Ct. 2533 (U.S. Sup. Ct. 1989)

Gregory Johnson was arrested and convicted for violating a Texas statute prohibiting the "desecration of a venerated object" after he burned an American flag during a protest demonstration at the Republican National Convention in Dallas in 1984. He was sentenced to a year in prison and fined $2,000. The Texas Court of Criminal Appeals reversed his conviction on First Amendment grounds, and the state appealed.

Brennan, Justice.   The First Amendment literally forbids the abridgement only of "speech," but we have long recognized that its protection does not end at the spoken or written word. While we have rejected the view that an apparently limitless variety of conduct can be labeled "speech" whenever the person engaging in the conduct intends thereby to express an idea, we have acknowledged that conduct may be sufficiently imbued with elements of communication to fall within the scope of the First and Fourteenth Amendments. The expressive, overtly political nature of Johnson's conduct was both intentional and overwhelmingly apparent.

The Government generally has a freer hand in restricting expressive conduct than it has in restricting the written or spoken word. It may not, however, proscribe particular conduct *because* it has expressive elements. Thus, although we have recognized that where "speech" and "non-speech" elements are combined in the same course of conduct, a sufficiently important governmental interest in regulating the nonspeech element can justify incidental limitations on First Amendment freedoms, we have limited the applicability of this standard to those cases in which the governmental interest is unrelated to the suppression of free expression.

Texas claims that its interest in preventing breaches of the peace justifies Johnson's conviction. However, no disturbance of the peace actually occurred or threatened to occur because of Johnson's burning of the flag. The State's position amounts to a claim that an audience that takes serious offense at particular expression is necessarily likely to disturb the peace and that the expression may be prohibited on that basis. Our precedents do not countenance such a presumption. On the contrary, they recognize that a principal function of free speech is to invite dispute. Thus, we have not permitted the Government to assume that every expression of a provocative idea will incite a riot, but have instead required careful consideration of the factual circumstances surrounding such expression, asking whether the expression is directed to inciting or producing imminent lawless action and is likely to incite or produce such action. We conclude that the State's interest in maintaining order is not implicated on these facts.

The State also asserts an interest in preserving the flag as a symbol of nationhood and national unity. It is not the State's ends, but its means, to which we object. It cannot be gainsaid that there is a special place reserved for the flag in this Nation, and thus we do not doubt that the Government has a legitimate interest in making efforts to preserve the flag as an unalloyed symbol of our country. Forbidding criminal punishment for conduct such as Johnson's will not endanger the special role played by our flag or the feelings it inspires. Nobody can suppose that this one gesture of an unknown man will change our Nation's attitude towards its flag.

We are tempted to say, in fact, that the flag's cherished place in our community will be strengthened, not weakened, by our holding today. Our decision is a reaffirmation of the principles of freedom and inclusiveness that the flag best reflects, and of the conviction that our toleration of criticism such as Johnson's is a sign and source of our strength. The way to preserve the flag's special role is not to punish those who feel differently about these matters. It is to persuade them that they are wrong. We can imagine no more appropriate response to burning a flag than waving one's own, no better way to counter a flag-burner's message than by saluting the flag that burns, no surer means of preserving the dignity even of a flag that burned than by—as one witness here did—according its remains a respectful burial. We do not consecrate the flag by punishing its desecration, for in doing so we dilute the freedom that this cherished emblem represents.

Reversal of Johnson's conviction affirmed.

In addition to limiting the *kinds* of behavior that can be made criminal, the Constitution also limits the *manner* in which behavior may be criminalized. The Due Process Clauses of the Fifth and Fourteenth Amendments require that a criminal statute must clearly define the behavior prohibited so that an ordinary person can understand which behavior violates the statute.[4] Statutes that fail to provide such fair notice are stricken down as "void for vagueness." In addition, the Equal Protection

---

[4] The Business and the Constitution chapter discusses due process in greater detail.

Clause of the Fourteenth Amendment[5] prohibits criminal statutes that treat persons of the same class in a discriminatory fashion or that *arbitrarily* discriminate among different classes of persons.[6] As a general rule, legislatures have considerable latitude in making statutory classifications, so long as the classifications have some rational basis. "Suspect" classifications, such as those based on race, however, are subjected to much closer judicial scrutiny.

Finally, the Constitution also limits the *type of punishment* imposed on convicted offenders. The Eighth Amendment forbids the imposition of "cruel and unusual punishments" for criminal offenses. This has been interpreted as barring sentences *disproportionate* to the defendant's offense. In making a disproportionality analysis, courts consider the harshness of the penalty imposed, other sentences imposed in the same jurisdiction for similar offenses, and the sentences imposed in other jurisdictions for the same offense. The Eighth Amendment provides the constitutional basis for those cases establishing constitutional limits on the circumstances in which the death penalty may be imposed.[7]

Proof beyond a Reasonable Doubt   Our legal system has long placed significant limits on the state's power to convict a person of a crime. These limits are thought to be essential due to the serious matters at stake in a criminal case—the life and liberty of the accused. One of the most fundamental safeguards that characterize the criminal justice system is the *presumption of innocence*: defendants in criminal cases are presumed to be innocent until proven guilty. The Due Process Clause requires the state to overcome this presumption by proving every element of the offense charged against the defendant *beyond a reasonable doubt*. Requiring the state to meet that severe burden of proof is the primary way to minimize the risk of erroneous criminal convictions. It also reflects a strong belief shared by all common law juris-

dictions about the proper way laws should be enforced and justice administered.

The Defendant's Capacity   *Mens rea*, or criminal intent, is an element of most serious crimes. The *level* of fault required for a criminal violation depends on the wording of the statute in question. Some criminal statutes require proof of intentional wrongdoing, while others impose liability for *reckless* or *negligent* conduct. In the criminal context, recklessness generally means that the accused consciously disregarded a substantial risk that the harm prohibited by the statute would result from her actions. Negligence, in criminal cases, means that the accused failed to perceive a substantial risk of harm that a reasonable person would have perceived. Criminal intent may be *inferred* from the nature of an accused's behavior, because a person is normally held to have intended the natural and probable consequences of her acts. The basic idea behind requiring intent for criminal responsibility is that the criminal law generally seeks to punish *conscious* wrongdoers. Accordingly, proof that the defendant had the *capacity* to form the required criminal intent is a traditional prerequisite of criminal responsibility. The criminal law recognizes three general types of incapacity: *intoxication*, *infancy*, and *insanity*.

Voluntary intoxication, although not a complete defense to criminal liability, can sometimes diminish the degree of a defendant's liability. This is so because a highly intoxicated person may be incapable of forming the *specific* criminal intent that is an element of some crimes. For example, many first degree murder statutes require proof of *premeditation*, a conscious decision to kill. A person who kills while highly intoxicated may not be capable of premeditation and may, therefore, be convicted of only second degree murder, which generally does not require proof of premeditation. Involuntary intoxication may be a complete defense to criminal liability.

At common law, a child under the age of seven was conclusively presumed to be incapable of forming a criminal intent. Children between the ages of 7 and 14 were presumed to be incapable of doing so, and those between the ages of 14 and 21 were presumed to be capable of doing so. These presumptions about a child's capacity, however, were rebuttable by specific evidence concerning the accused's moral and intellectual development. Most states currently treat juvenile offenders below a certain statutory age (usually 16 or 17) differently from adult offenders, with special juvenile court systems and separate detention facilities. Juvenile law today

---

[5] The Business and the Constitution chapter discusses equal protection in greater detail.

[6] For an example, see *McLaughlin v. Florida*, 379 U.S. 1984 (U.S. Sup. Ct. 1964), where the Court struck down a Florida statute forbidding cohabitation between black males and white females on the ground that no valid statutory purpose justified prohibiting only interracial cohabitation.

[7] See, for example, *Thompson v. Oklahoma*, 487 U.S. 815 (U.S. Sup. Ct. 1988), where the Court held that the Eighth Amendment bars the execution of a defendant who was under 16 at the time of his offense.

tends to emphasize rehabilitation rather than capacity. Repeat offenders or offenders charged with very serious offenses may sometimes be treated as adults.

Insanity on a criminal defendant's part can affect a criminal prosecution in a number of ways. Insanity rendering a defendant incapable of assisting in the defense of his case can delay his trial until he regains his sanity. Insanity that becomes manifest after conviction, but before sentencing, can delay sentencing until sanity is regained. The Supreme Court has recently recognized that the Eighth Amendment's prohibition of cruel and unusual punishment bars the execution of a condemned prisoner who becomes insane while awaiting execution.[8] Finally, insanity at the time a criminal act was committed can serve as a complete defense to liability. This type of insanity has generated much controversy in recent years.

This controversy stems from two major sources: significant disagreement concerning the proper test for insanity in criminal cases and public dissatisfaction with the insanity defense in general. The courts have adopted a variety of tests for criminal responsibility, all of which are designed to punish conscious wrongdoers. These tests are *legal* tests, not medical tests. A defendant who was medically insane at the time of the criminal act may still be legally responsible.

The primary common law test for insanity is the *M'Naghten* rule: a criminal defendant is not responsible if, at the time of the offense, he did not know the nature and quality of his act, or, if he did know it, he did not know that his act was wrong.[9] Some states have replaced or supplemented this rule with the *irresistible impulse* rule. This rule absolves a defendant of responsibility if mental disease rendered her incapable of controlling her behavior and resisting the impulse to commit a crime. One modern insanity test adopted by a large number of jurisdictions is that proposed by the American Law Institute. This test provides that a defendant is not criminally responsible if at the time the act was committed, due to mental disease or defect, he lacked the substantial capacity to appreciate the wrongfulness of his act or to conform his conduct to the law's requirements. Public reaction to certain highly publicized cases in which insanity defenses were raised, however, has produced a noticeable tendency to return to the narrower *M'Naghten* standard. For example, the Comprehensive

---

[8] *Ford v. Wainwright*, 477 U.S. 399 (U.S. Sup. Ct. 1986).

[9] This rule is derived from *Daniel M'Naghten's Case*, 8 Eng. Reprint 718 (House of Lords 1843).

FIGURE 1   Essentials of Crime Checklist

☐ Did the accused violate an existing statute?
☐ Is the statute constitutionally valid?
    Does it prohibit constitutionally protected behavior?
    Does it clearly define the prohibited behavior?
☐ Did the accused have the required criminal intent?
    Did he have the capacity to form the required intent?
    Can the necessary level of intent be inferred from his actions?
☐ Did the state prove each element of the crime beyond a reasonable doubt?

Crime Control Act of 1984 governs the insanity standard applicable in federal criminal cases. It provides that only defendants who are incapable of understanding the nature and wrongfulness of their acts are absolved from responsibility.

Public dissatisfaction with the insanity defense has produced another noticeable trend in recent years: the creation of procedural rules that make it more difficult for defendants to successfully raise an insanity defense. Criminal defendants are presumed to be sane. Traditionally, once an accused had introduced evidence tending to prove insanity, the state had the burden of proving his sanity beyond a reasonable doubt. Today, however, many states treat insanity as an *affirmative defense* and require the defendant to bear the burden of proving insanity. The Comprehensive Crime Control Act of 1984 adopts this approach. In addition, some states have instituted a "guilty, but mentally ill" verdict as an alternative to the traditional "not guilty by reason of insanity" verdict. This new alternative verdict allows jurors to convict rather than acquit mentally ill defendants, with the assurance that they will be given treatment after conviction.

Figure 1 summarizes the essential components of criminal liability under our legal system.

CRIMINAL PROCEDURE

Criminal Prosecutions

Persons who have been arrested for allegedly committing a crime are taken to the police station and booked. *Booking* is an administrative procedure for recording the suspect's arrest and the offenses involved. In some states, temporary release on bail may be available at this stage. After booking, the police file an arrest report with the prosecutor, who decides whether to charge the suspect with an offense. After deciding to prosecute, the prosecutor has a complaint prepared identifying the accused and detailing the charges.

Most states require that arrested suspects be promptly taken before a public official (a magistrate, commissioner, or justice of the peace) for an *initial appearance*. During this appearance the magistrate informs the accused of the charges against him and the nature of his constitutional rights. In misdemeanor cases, when the accused pleads guilty at this point, the sentence may be imposed without further proceedings. If the accused pleads not guilty, the case is set for trial. In felony cases, or misdemeanor cases in which the accused pleads not guilty, the magistrate sets the amount of bail.

In many states, defendants in felony cases are protected against unjustified prosecutions by an additional procedural step, the *preliminary hearing*. The prosecutor must introduce enough evidence at this hearing to convince a magistrate that there is *probable cause* to believe that the accused committed a felony. When the magistrate is so convinced, he binds over the defendant for trial in a criminal court.

After a bindover, the formal charge against the defendant is filed with a criminal court. This is accomplished by either an *information* filed by the prosecutor or an *indictment* returned by a *grand jury*. About half of the states require that a grand jury approve the decision to prosecute a person accused of a felony. Grand juries are bodies of citizens selected in the same manner as the members of a trial (petit) jury; often they are chosen through random drawings from a list of registered voters. Grand juries were originally composed of 23 members, a majority of whose votes were necessary to sustain an indictment. Today, many states have reduced the size of the grand jury; there is significant variation in the number of votes required for an indictment. Indictment of an accused prior to a preliminary hearing normally disposes of the need for a preliminary hearing. This is because the grand jury indictment serves essentially the same function as a magistrate's probable cause determination.

The remainder of the states allow felony defendants to be charged by either indictment or information, at the prosecutor's discretion. An *information* is a formal charge signed by the prosecutor outlining the facts supporting the charges against the defendant. In states that allow felony prosecution by information, the vast majority of felony cases are prosecuted in this way. Misdemeanor cases are almost exclusively prosecuted by information in virtually all jurisdictions.

Once an information or indictment has been filed with a trial court, the defendant is *arraigned* by being brought before the court, informed of the charges, and asked to enter a plea. The defendant may plead guilty, not guilty, or nolo contendere to the charges. Although technically not an admission of guilt, nolo contendere pleas are an indication that the defendant does not contest the charges. Nolo pleas are frequently attractive to corporate defendants who believe that their chances of mounting a successful defense are poor. This is because nolo pleas would be inadmissible as evidence of guilt in later civil suits against them based on the same statutory violations.

At the arraignment, the defendant also elects whether to be tried by a judge or a jury. Persons accused of serious crimes for which incarceration for more than six months is possible have a constitutional right to be tried by a jury of their peers. The accused, however, generally has the power to waive this right.

Procedural Safeguards

In the preceding pages, you have encountered several procedural devices designed to protect persons accused of crime. The Bill of Rights, the first 10 amendments to the U.S. Constitution, contains additional provisions to safeguard the rights of criminal defendants. These procedural safeguards reflect two basic public policies. First, they are designed to protect against unjustified or erroneous criminal convictions. Second, and perhaps equally important, they reflect a conclusion about government's proper role in the administration of justice in a democratic society. Justice Oliver Wendell Holmes aptly addressed this latter point when he said, "I think it less evil that some criminals should escape than that the government should play an ignoble part." Although the specific language of the Bill of Rights applies only to the federal government, the U.S. Supreme Court has applied the most important Bill of Rights guarantees to the states by "selectively incorporating" them into the Fourteenth Amendment's Due Process Clause. Once a particular safeguard has been found to be "implicit in the concept of ordered liberty" or "fundamental to the American scheme of justice," it has been applied equally in state and federal criminal trials.

The Fourth Amendment The Fourth Amendment provides:

The right of the people to be secure in their persons, houses, papers, and effects, against unreasonable searches and seizures, shall not be violated, and no Warrants shall issue, but upon probable cause, supported by Oath or affirmation, and particularly describing the place to be searched, and the persons or things to be seized.

The basic purpose of the Fourth Amendment is to protect individuals from arbitrary and unreasonable governmental violations of their privacy rights. Both the language of the amendment and the case law it has generated reflect the difficulties inherent in finding a proper balance between government's legitimate interest in securing evidence of wrongdoing and its citizens' legitimate expectations of privacy. Citizens are not protected against all searches and seizures—only against unreasonable ones. Because the Fourth Amendment only protects reasonable individual privacy expectations, the Supreme Court has extended its protection to private dwellings and those areas immediately surrounding them (often called the *curtilage*), telephone booths, sealed containers, and first class mail. The Court has denied protection to areas or items in which it found no reasonable expectations of privacy, such as open fields, personal bank records, and voluntary conversations between criminal defendants and government informants. Even where plainly protected items or areas are concerned, not every governmental intrusion is deemed sufficiently intrusive to constitute a search or seizure within the meaning of the Fourth Amendment. Thus, the Court held that exposing an airline traveler's luggage to a narcotics detection dog in a public place was not a search in view of the minimally intrusive nature of the intrusion and the narrow scope of information revealed by such tests.[10] In the *Dow Chemical* case, which follows, the Court refused to hold that aerial photographs of an industrial complex violated the Fourth Amendment.

A similar balancing of individual and governmental interests is evident in the Court's handling of the Fourth Amendment's Warrant Clause. The idea behind the warrant requirement is to further protect individual rights by having a neutral party (a judge or a magistrate) authorize and define the scope of intrusive governmental action. Thus, as a general rule, the Court has held that searches carried out without a proper warrant are, by definition, unreasonable. Nonetheless, the Court has authorized

warrantless searches of the area within the immediate control of an arrestee, of automobiles (due to their highly mobile nature), of premises police enter in hot pursuit of an armed suspect, and of contraband items in the plain view of officers who are otherwise acting lawfully. Customs searches, stop and frisk searches, inventory searches of property in an arrestee's possession, and consensual searches also have been upheld, despite the absence of a warrant. Finally, the Court has upheld warrantless administrative inspections of closely regulated businesses.[11]

The basic device employed by the Court to enforce the Fourth Amendment is the **exclusionary rule:** Evidence seized in illegal searches cannot be used in a subsequent trial against an accused whose constitutional rights have been violated.[12] Because the exclusionary rule often operates to exclude convincing evidence of crime, it has generated enormous controversy. Supporters of the rule argued that it is necessary to deter police from violating citizens' constitutional rights. Opponents of the rule argued that it would not deter police who believed they were acting lawfully. Because the exclusion of illegally seized evidence imposed no direct penalties on police officers who acted unlawfully, opponents believed the rule was a poor device for achieving deterrence. A common complaint was that "because of a policeman's error, a criminal goes free." In recent years, the Court has responded to such criticism by restricting the operation of the rule. For example, in *Nix v. Williams*, the Court held that illegally obtained evidence can be introduced at a trial if the prosecution can convince the trial court that it would inevitably have been obtained by lawful means.[13] More importantly, in *United States v. Leon*, the Court created a "good faith" exception to the exclusionary rule to allow the use of evidence seized by police officers who reasonably believed they were acting under a lawful search warrant.[14] Although the Court has not extended this exception to warrantless searches, it did expand the exception's scope to include searches made in reliance on a statute which is later declared invalid.[15]

---

[10]*United States v. Place*, 426 U.S. 696 (U.S. Sup. Ct. 1983). In this case, however, the Court also held that the warrantless detention of the defendant's luggage for 90 minutes was unlawful, given the fact that the agents in question had several hours' advance notice of the defendant's arrival.

[11] See, e.g., *New York v. Burger*, 482 U.S. 691 (U.S. Sup. Ct. 1987).
[12] The exclusionary rule was first applied to the states in *Mapp v. Ohio*, 367 U.S. 643 (U.S. Sup. Ct. 1961).
[13]467 U.S. 431 (U.S. Sup. Ct. 1984).
[14] 468 U.S. 897 (U.S. Sup. Ct. 1984).
[15]*Illinois v. Krull*, 480 U.S. 340 (U.S. Sup. Ct. 1987).

DOW CHEMICAL CO. v. UNITED STATES

476 U.S. 227 (U.S. Sup. Ct. 1986)

Dow Chemical Company operates a 2,000-acre chemical manufacturing facility at Midland, Michigan. The facility consists of numerous covered buildings, with manufacturing equipment and piping conduits between various buildings plainly visible from the air. At all times, Dow maintained elaborate security around the perimeter of the complex barring ground-level public views of these areas. It also investigated any low-level flights by aircraft over the facility. Dow did not, however, attempt to conceal all manufacturing equipment within the complex from aerial views because the cost was prohibitive.

In early 1978, enforcement officials of the Environmental Protection Agency (EPA) made an on-site inspection of two power plants in this complex with Dow's consent. When a subsequent request for a second inspection was denied, EPA did not thereafter seek an administrative search warrant. Instead, EPA employed a commercial aerial photographer, using a standard floor-mounted, precision aerial mapping camera, to take photographs of the facility from altitudes of 12,000, 3,000, and 1,200 feet. At all times the aircraft was lawfully within navigable airspace.

EPA did not inform Dow of this aerial photography. When Dow became aware of it, the company brought suit in the District Court alleging that EPA's action violated the Fourth Amendment. The District Court granted Dow's motion for summary judgment. EPA was permanently enjoined from taking aerial photographs of Dow's premises and from disseminating, releasing, or copying the photographs already taken. When the Sixth Circuit Court of Appeals reversed, Dow appealed.

Burger, Chief Justice.   Dow claims that the EPA's use of aerial photography was a "search" of an area that was within an "industrial curtilage" rather than an "open field," and that it had a reasonable expectation of privacy from such photography protected by the Fourth Amendment. In making this contention, however, Dow concedes that a simple flyover with naked-eye observation, or the taking of a photograph from a nearby hillside overlooking such a facility, would give rise to no Fourth Amendment problem.

In *California v. Ciraolo*, decided today, we hold that naked-eye aerial observation from an altitude of 1,000 feet of a backyard within the curtilage of a home does not constitute a search under the Fourth Amendment. The curtilage area immediately surrounding a private house has long been given protection as a place where the occupants have a reasonable and legitimate expectation of privacy that society is prepared to accept.

As the curtilage doctrine evolved to protect much the same kind of privacy as that covering the interior of a structure, the contrasting "open fields" doctrine evolved as well. From *Hester v. United States* (1924) to *Oliver v. United States* (1984), the Court has drawn a line as to what expectations are reasonable in the open areas beyond the curtilage of a dwelling; open fields do not provide the setting for those intimate activities that the Fourth Amendment is intended to shelter from governmental interference or surveillance. In *Oliver*, we held that "an individual may not legitimately demand privacy for activities out of doors in fields, except in the area immediately surrounding the home." To fall within the open fields doctrine the area need be neither "open" nor a "field" as those terms are used in common speech.

Dow plainly has a reasonable, legitimate, and objective expectation of privacy within the interior of its covered buildings. Moreover, it could hardly be expected that Dow would erect a huge cover over a 2,000-acre tract. Dow argues that its exposed manufacturing facilities are analogous to the curtilage surrounding a home because it has taken every possible step to bar access from ground level. In *Oliver*, the Court described the curtilage of a dwelling as "the area to which extends the intimate activity associated with the sanctity of a man's home and the privacies of life." The intimate activities associated with family privacy and the home and its curtilage simply do not reach the outdoor areas of spaces between structures and buildings of a manufacturing plant.

Admittedly, Dow's enclosed plant complex does not fall precisely within the "open fields" doctrine. The area at issue here can perhaps be seen as falling somewhere between "open fields" and curtilage, but lacking some of the critical characteristics of both. Dow's inner manufacturing areas are elaborately secured to ensure they are not open or exposed to the public from the ground. Any actual physical entry by EPA into any enclosed area would raise significantly different questions, because the businessman, like the occupant of a residence, has a constitutional right to go about his business free from unreasonable official entries upon his private commercial property. The narrow issue raised by Dow's claim of search and seizure, however, concerns aerial observation of a 2,000-acre outdoor manufacturing facility *without* physical entry. The Government has greater latitude to conduct warrantless inspections of commercial property because the expectation of privacy that the owner of commercial property enjoys in such property differs significantly from the sanctity accorded an individual's home. Unlike a homeowner's interest in his dwelling, the interest of the owner of commercial property is not one in being free from any inspections. With regard to regulatory inspections, we have held that what is observable by the public is observable without a warrant, by the Government inspector as well.

Oliver recognized that in the open field context, "the public and police lawfully may survey lands from the air." Here, the EPA was not employing some unique sensory device that, for example, could penetrate the walls of buildings and record conversations in Dow's plants, offices, or laboratories, but rather a conventional, albeit precise, commercial camera commonly used in mapmaking. The Government asserts it has not yet enlarged the photographs to any significant degree, but Dow points out that simple magnification permits identification of objects such as wires as small as one-half inch diameter.

It may well be that surveillance of private property by using highly sophisticated surveillance equipment not generally available to the public, such as satellite technology, might be constitutionally proscribed absent a warrant. But the photographs here are not so revealing of intimate details as to raise constitutional concerns. The mere fact that human vision is enhanced somewhat, at least to the degree here, does not give rise to constitutional problems.

We conclude that the open areas of an industrial plant complex with numerous plant structures spread over an area of 2,000 acres are not analogous to the curtilage of a dwelling for purposes of aerial surveillance; such an industrial complex is more comparable to an open field and as such it is open to the view and observation of persons in aircraft lawfully in the public airspace immediately above or sufficiently near the area for the reach of cameras.

We hold that the taking of aerial photographs of an industrial plant complex from navigable airspace is not a search prohibited by the Fourth Amendment.

Judgment for the EPA affirmed.

The Fifth Amendment   In addition to the Due Process Clause with its guarantee of basic procedural and substantive fairness, the Fifth Amendment contains two other provisions that safeguard criminal defendants' rights. The Fifth Amendment protects against *compulsory testimonial self-incrimination* by providing that no "person . . . shall be compelled in any criminal case to be a witness against himself." This provision prevents the state from forcing a defendant to assist in his own prosecution by compelling him to make incriminating testimonial admissions. In *Miranda v. Arizona*, the Supreme Court held that the Fifth Amendment required police to warn criminal suspects of their right to remain silent before commencing any custodial interrogation of them.[16] The Court also required police to inform suspects that any statements they make may be used as evidence against them and that they have the right to the presence of an attorney, either retained or appointed. Any incriminating statements that the accused makes in the absence of a *Miranda* warning, or other evidence resulting from such statements, is inadmissible in a subsequent trial.

This right to silence has always been limited in a variety of ways. For example, the traditional limitation of the Fifth Amendment's scope to *testimonial* admissions has long been held to allow the police to compel an accused to furnish nontestimonial evidence such as fingerprints, samples of bodily fluids, and hair. In recent years, however, Supreme Court decisions have recognized further significant limitations on the right to silence. For example, for a long time an implicit part of the right to silence was a corresponding limitation on any prosecutorial trial comments about the accused's failure to speak in her own defense. The Court's recent decisions still support this limitation when an accused's silence after arrest or after receiving a *Miranda* warning is at issue.

However, the Court has allowed prosecutors to use a defendant's pretrial silence to impeach his trial testimony in some circumstances. For example, the Court has held that the Fifth Amendment is not violated when a defendant's silence (either prearrest or postarrest, but in advance of any *Miranda* warning) is used to discredit his trial testimony that he had killed his victim in self-defense.[17]

A similar tendency to narrow *Miranda's* scope is evident in *Moran v. Burbine*, one of the Court's recent controversial Fifth Amendment decisions.[18] In *Moran*, the Court disagreed with the majority of lower federal courts and state courts that had considered the issue and upheld a suspect's waiver of his *Miranda* rights despite the failure of the police to notify him that a lawyer retained for him by a third party was seeking to contact him.

While the preceding discussion of the privilege against self-incrimination has focused on the rights of criminal defendants in general, the Fifth Amendment has long had particular relevance to persons in business who are charged with crimes. Documentary evidence can be of critical importance to the government's case in many white-collar crime prosecutions. To what extent does the Fifth Amendment protect business records? In *Boyd v. United States*, the first case to consider the question, the Supreme Court held that the Fifth Amendment protected individuals against being compelled to produce their private papers.[19] In subsequent decisions, however, the Court has drastically limited the scope of this private papers protection. A number of the Court's decisions have held that the private papers privilege is a *personal* privilege that cannot be asserted by a corporation, partnership, or other "collective entity." Because such entities have no Fifth Amendment rights, the Court has held that an individual officer or member of an organization who has custody of organizational records cannot assert any personal privilege to prevent their disclosure, even if the contents of such records incriminate her personally. Finally, it has long been held that the government has the power to require business proprietors to keep certain records relevant to transactions that are appropriate subjects for government regulation. Such "required records" are not entitled to private papers protection; therefore, they may be subpoenaed and used against the recordkeeper in prosecutions for regulatory violations.

The Court's most recent business records decisions cast further doubt on the future of the private papers doctrine. Instead of focusing on whether the subpoenaed records are private in nature, the Court now focuses on whether the *act of producing* the records in response to a subpoena is sufficiently testimonial to violate the privilege against self-incrimination. In *Fisher v. United States*, the Court held that an individual subpoenaed to produce personal documents may only assert his privilege against compelled self-incrimination if the act of producing such documents would involve incriminating testimonial admissions.[20] This is likely where the individual producing the records is in effect admitting the existence of records previously unknown to the government (demonstrating that he had access to the records and, therefore, possible knowledge of any incriminating contents) or certifying the records' authenticity.

---

[16] 384 U.S. 436 (U.S. Sup. Ct. 1966).

[17] *Fletcher v. Weir*, 455 U.S. 603 (U.S. Sup. Ct. 1982); *Jenkins v. Anderson*, 447 U.S. 231 (U.S. Sup. Ct. 1980).

[18] 475 U.S. 412 (U.S. Sup. Ct. 1986).

[19] 116 U.S. 616 (U.S. Sup. Ct. 1886).

[20] 425 U.S. 391 (U.S. Sup. Ct. 1976).

More recently, in *United States v. Doe*, the Court extended the act-of-production privilege to a sole proprietor whose proprietorship records had been subpoenaed.[21] The Court, however, held that normal business records were not themselves protected by the Fifth Amendment because they were voluntarily prepared, and therefore not the product of compulsion. Some interested observers thought that this new emphasis on the testimonial and potentially incriminatory aspects of the act of producing business records meant that officers of collective entities that are targets of a government investigation might be able to assert their personal privilege against self-incrimination to avoid producing potentially incriminatory business records. Such hopes were dashed when the Court, in *Braswell v. United States*, refused to extend its holding in *Doe* to cover the sole shareholder of a corporation acting in his capacity as custodian of corporate records.[22] Because he operated his business as a corporation, the Court held that Braswell was bound by the collective-entity rule, which says that such entities have no Fifth Amendment privilege. Because he acted in a representative capacity in turning over the requested records, the government could make no evidentiary use of his act of producing the records, but could use the contents of the record against him and his corporation.

One other Fifth Amendment provision worthy of note is the **Double Jeopardy Clause.** This provision protects criminal defendants from multiple prosecutions for the same offense. It prevents an accused from being charged with more than one count of the same statutory violation for one offense, for example, being charged with two robbery violations for a one-time robbery of one individual. This clause also prevents a second prosecution for the same offense after the defendant has been acquitted or convicted of that offense, and it bars the imposition of multiple punishments for the same offense.

The Double Jeopardy Clause does not, however, preclude the possibility that a single criminal act may result in several criminal prosecutions. For example, one criminal act may produce several statutory violations, all of which may be proper subjects for prosecution. A defendant who commits a rape may also be prosecuted for battery, assault with a deadly weapon, and kidnapping if the facts of the case indicate that several statutes were violated. In addition, the Supreme Court has long used a same evidence test to determine what constitutes the same offense.[23] This means that a single criminal act with multiple victims (e.g., a robbery of a restaurant where several patrons are robbed) could result in several prosecutions because the identity of each victim would be an additional fact of proof in each case. Finally, the Double Jeopardy Clause does not protect against multiple prosecutions by *different sovereigns*. A conviction or acquittal in a federal court does not prevent a subsequent prosecution in a state court for a state offense arising out of the same event, or vice versa.

The Sixth Amendment   The Sixth Amendment contains several provisions that safeguard criminal defendants' rights. It entitles defendants in criminal cases to a speedy trial by an impartial jury, at which they may confront and cross-examine the witnesses against them. It also gives the accused in a criminal case the right "to have the assistance of counsel" in her defense. This provision has been interpreted to mean not only that the defendant has the right to employ his own attorney to represent him, but that indigent defendants charged with a crime are entitled to court-appointed counsel.[24] An accused must be informed of his *right to counsel* once he has been taken into custody.[25] Once the accused has requested the assistance of counsel, he may not be interrogated further unless he voluntarily initiates further conversations with the authorities.[26] Finally, an accused is entitled to *effective* assistance by his counsel. This means that the accused is entitled to counsel at a point in the proceedings when counsel can effectively assist him.[27] Inadequate assistance by counsel can be a proper basis for setting aside a conviction and ordering a new trial.[28]

---

[23]*Blockburger v. United States*, 284 U.S. 299 (U.S. Sup. Ct. 1932). The Court has recently qualified *Blockburger* by saying that the Double Jeopardy Clause bars any subsequent prosecution "in which the government, to establish an essential element of an offense charged in that prosecution, will prove conduct that constitutes an offense for which the defendant has already been prosecuted." *Grady v. Corbin*, 110 S. Ct. 2084 (U.S. Sup. Ct. 1990).

[24] *Gideon v. Wainwright*, 372 U.S. 335 (U.S. Sup. Ct. 1963).

[25] *Miranda v. Arizona*, 384 U.S. 436 (U.S. Sup. Ct. 1966).

[26] *Edwards v. Arizona*, 451 U.S. 477 (U.S. Sup. Ct. 1981).

[27] *Powell v. Alabama*, 287 U.S. 45 (U.S. Sup. Ct. 1932).

[28] In *Strickland v. Washington*, 446 U.S. 668 (U.S. Sup. Ct. 1984), the Court held that a defendant's conviction would not be set aside unless his attorney's performance fell below an objective standard of reasonableness and so prejudiced him as to result in the denial of a fair trial.

---

[21] 463 U.S. 605 (U.S. Sup. Ct. 1984).

[22] 487 U.S. 99 (U.S. Sup. Ct. 1988).

FIGURE 2   Major Procedural Safeguards

Fourth Amendment
   Prohibits unreasonable searches and seizures
Fifth Amendment
   Due Process Clause (federal)
      Presumption of innocence
      Prohibits vague criminal statutes
      Requires basic procedural and substantive fairness
   Right to silence
   Double Jeopardy Clause
Sixth Amendment
   Speedy trial
   Impartial jury
   Confront and cross-examine prosecution's witnesses
   Right to counsel
Eighth Amendment
   Forbids cruel and unusual punishments

Figure 2 summarizes the major procedural safeguards enjoyed by defendants under our criminal justice system.

WHITE-COLLAR CRIMES AND THE DILEMMAS OF CORPORATE CONTROL

Introduction

White-collar crime is the term broadly used to describe a wide variety of nonviolent criminal offenses committed by businesspersons and by business organizations. Although this term often includes offenses committed by corporate employees against their corporate employers, such as theft, embezzlement, or accepting a bribe, our discussions in this part of the text focus on criminal offenses committed by corporate employers and their employees against society as a whole. Each year, corporate crime costs consumers billions of dollars. It may take a variety of forms, from consumer fraud, securities fraud, and tax evasion to price-fixing, environmental pollution, and other regulatory violations. Corporate crime confronts our legal system with a variety of problems—problems we have failed to resolve satisfactorily.

Corporations form the backbone of the most successful economic system in history. They dominate the international economic scene, and they have provided us with incalculable benefits in efficiently produced goods and services. Yet these same corporations may pollute the environment, swindle their customers, produce dangerously defective products, and conspire with others to injure or destroy competition. How are we to effectively control these large organizations so important to our existence? Increasingly, we have come to rely on the criminal law as a major instrument of corporate control.

The criminal law, however, was developed with individual wrongdoers in mind. Who is at fault when a large organization causes some social harm? Corporate crime is *organizational* crime: Any given corporate action may be the product of the combined actions of many individuals acting within the corporate hierarchy. None of them may have had sufficient knowledge to possess individually the *mens rea* necessary for criminal responsibility under traditional criminal law principles. How are we to apply such criminal sanctions as imprisonment or death to a legal person like a corporation?

Evolution of Corporate Criminal Liability

The common law initially rejected the idea that corporations could be criminally responsible for the actions of their employees. Early corporations were small in size and number; they had little impact on public life. Their small size meant that it was relatively easy to pinpoint individual wrongdoers within the corporation and thereby avoid the difficult conceptual problems associated with corporate criminal liability. After all, corporations were legal entities; they lacked a "mind," and it was hard to conceive of them as having the criminal intent necessary for common law crimes. Lacking physical bodies, they were immune to imprisonment, the basic common law criminal sanction.

As corporations grew in size and power, however, and the social need to control their activities grew accordingly, the common law rules on corporate criminal liability began to change. The first cases in which criminal liability was imposed on corporations involved suits against public corporations such as municipalities—then the most common corporation—for the failure to perform such public duties as road and bridge repair. As commercial corporations grew in size and number, similar liability was imposed on them by statutes creating *public welfare offenses*, regulatory offenses requiring no proof of *mens rea*.

By the turn of this century, American courts had begun to impose criminal liability on corporations for general criminal offenses that required proof of *mens rea*. This expansion of corporate criminal liability *imputed* the criminal intent of its employees to the corporation in a fashion similar to the imposition of tort or contract liability on corporations under the doctrine of *respondeat superior.*[29]

Today, it is generally thought that a corporation can be criminally liable for almost any criminal offense if the statute in question indicates a legislative intent to hold corporations liable. This legislative intent requirement can sometimes be problematic, because many state criminal statutes are derived from common law crimes and may contain language that suggests an intent to hold only humans liable. For example, many state manslaughter statutes define the offense as "the killing of one human being by the act of another." However, where statutes are framed in more general terms, referring to "persons" for example, the courts are generally willing to apply them to corporate defendants.

Corporate Criminal Liability Today

The modern rule on corporate criminal liability is that a corporation can be held liable for criminal offenses committed by its employees *acting within the scope of their employment* and *for the benefit of the corporation.* A major current issue in corporate criminal liability concerns the classes of corporate employees whose intent can be imputed to the corporation. Some commentators have argued that a corporation should be criminally responsible only for offenses committed by high corporate officials or those linked to them by authorization or acquiescence. (Virtually all courts impose criminal liability on a corporation under such circumstances.) Such arguments are based on notions of fairness: If any group of corporate employees can fairly be said to constitute a corporation's mind, that group is its top officers and directors.

The problem with imposing corporate liability only on the basis of the actions or knowledge of top corporate officers is that such a policy often insulates the corporation from liability. Many corporate offenses may be directly traceable only to middle managers or more subordinate corporate employees. It may be impossible to demonstrate that any higher-level corporate official had sufficient knowledge to constitute *mens rea.* Recognizing this fact, the federal courts have adopted a general rule that a corporation can be criminally liable for the actions of any of its agents, whether or not any link between such agents and higher-level corporate officials can be demonstrated.

Another significant current controversy regarding the nature of corporate criminal responsibility concerns whether courts should recognize a *due diligence* defense to corporate criminal liability. Advocates of such a defense say it is unfair to impute the intent of some employees to their corporate employer without also considering good faith corporate efforts to prevent statutory violations. They also point out that the major justification advanced for corporate criminal liability is deterrence: The hope that the threat or imposition of criminal penalties will encourage corporate efforts to comply with legal rules. Thus, they argue that recognizing a due diligence defense would encourage corporate compliance efforts, whereas imposing liability regardless of such efforts undermines deterrence by discouraging them. Most courts, however, have found these arguments unconvincing and have generally rejected the idea of a due diligence defense.

Problems with Corporate Criminal Liability   Despite the legal theories that justify corporate criminal liability, the punishment of corporations still remains a highly problematic subject. Does a corporate criminal conviction stigmatize a corporation in the same way that being branded a criminal stigmatizes an individual? The idea of viewing a corporation as a criminal may be difficult for most people to embrace. Perhaps the only stigma resulting from a corporate criminal conviction is felt by corporate employees, many of whom are entirely innocent of any wrongdoing. Is it just to punish the innocent in an attempt to punish the guilty?

And what of the cash fine, the primary punishment imposed on convicted corporations? Most critics of contemporary corporate control strategies argue that the fines imposed on convicted corporations tend to be too small to provide effective deterrence. What is needed, they argue, are fines keyed in some fashion to the corporate defendant's wealth, such as a percentage of the defendant's income or total capital. Such large fines present a variety of practical and conceptual difficulties. Where market conditions permit, criminal fines are likely to be passed on to consumers as higher prices; where a pass-on is impossible, corporate shareholders are likely to absorb the loss. Fines large enough to threaten corporate solvency may cause injury to corporate employees and those economically dependent on the corporation's financial well-being. Yet most of these individuals have neither had the power to prevent the violation nor derived any benefit from it. On the other

---

[29] The Third-Party Relations of the Principal and the Agent chapter discusses *respondeat superior in* detail. For an early landmark case on this subject, see *New York Central & Hudson River R.R. v. United States,* 212 U.S. 481 (U.S. Sup. Ct. 1909).

hand, fines imposed on a corporation may place no direct burden on the managers responsible for a violation. Given the element of randomness inherent in criminal fines, legislatures may be unwilling to authorize, and courts reluctant to impose, fines that are large enough to produce deterrence.

Aside from such problems of practicality and fairness, other deficiencies make fines less-than-adequate corporate control devices. Fine strategies tend to assume that all corporations are rationally acting profit-maximizers. Fines of sufficient size, it is argued, will erode the profit drive that underlies most corporate violations. Numerous studies of actual corporate behavior, however, suggest that many corporations are neither profit-maximizers nor rational actors. Mature firms with well-established market shares may embrace goals other than profit maximization, such as technological prominence, increased market share, or higher employee salaries. In addition, the interests of the managers who make corporate decisions and establish corporate policies may not be synonymous with the long-range economic interests of their corporate employers. The fact that their employers may at some future point have to pay a sizable fine may not make much of an impression on top managers, who tend to have relatively short terms in office and are often compensated in part by large bonuses keyed to year-end profitability.

Even if corporate managers were otherwise motivated to avoid corporate violations, there are reasons to doubt whether they would always be capable of doing so. Most organization theorists acknowledge that large organizations suffer from problems of control. Many corporate wrongs result from internal bureaucratic malfunctions rather than the conscious actions of any intracorporate individual or group. Fines are as unlikely to deter such structural violations as they are to encourage internal reform efforts in response to a fine imposed after a violation has occurred.

Individual Liability for Corporate Crime

Individuals committing criminal offenses while acting in their corporate capacities have always been personally exposed to criminal liability. In fact, most European nations reject corporate criminal liability in favor of exclusive reliance on individual criminal responsibility. Certainly, individual liability has many attractive features, particularly in view of the problems connected with imposing criminal liability on corporations. Individual liability is more consistent with traditional criminal law notions about the personal nature of guilt.

Individual liability may provide better deterrence than corporate liability if it enables society to bring the threat of criminal punishment to bear against the individual corporate officers who make important corporate decisions. The possibility of personal liability may induce individuals to resist corporate pressures to violate the law and may prevent corporations from treating financial penalties merely as a cost of doing business. And to the extent that guilty individuals can be identified and punished, the ends of the criminal law may be achieved without unfairly stigmatizing innocent corporate employees or punishing innocent shareholders or consumers.

Problems with Individual Liability   Attractive as individual liability may sound, it too poses some significant problems when applied in the corporate context. Identifying responsible individuals within the corporate hierarchy is a difficult and often impossible task if we adhere to traditional notions of criminal responsibility and insist on proof of some criminal intent as a precondition of liability. The division of authority that typifies large corporations produces a diffusion of responsibility often making it difficult to assign individual responsibility. Corporate decisions are often *collective* decisions, the products of the combined actions of numerous individuals within the corporate hierarchy, none of whom may have had complete knowledge or any specific intent.

It may be particularly difficult to prove knowledge on the part of high-level executives, because bad news may not reach them or because they may consciously avoid such knowledge. It may, therefore, only be possible to demonstrate culpability on the part of middle-level managers. But juries may be unwilling to convict such individuals if they seem to be scapegoats for their unindicted superiors. Finally, some corporate crimes may be structural in the sense that they are the products of internal bureaucratic failures rather than the conscious actions of any individual or group. Even when a culpable individual can be identified, significant problems can prevent effectively applying the criminal sanction to him. The individual in question may have died, retired, or been transferred to another post outside the jurisdiction where the offense occurred. White-collar defendants are rarely imprisoned after conviction; when imprisonment does result, it is commonly in the form of a short sentence to a "country club" institution, where early parole is a high possibility. The reluctance to imprison white-collar offenders is generally attributed to the positive image that such offenders normally possess—they tend to be well-educated, well-spoken community leaders. Also, there are public doubts about the moral culpability involved in most white-collar offenses. Thus, most convicted white-collar offenders merely receive fines that are often small in comparison to their wealth and are frequently indemnified by their corporate employers.[30]

These difficulties in imposing criminal penalties on individual corporate employees have led to the creation of regulatory offenses imposing *strict* or *vicarious* liability on corporate officers. **Strict liability offenses** dispense with the requirement of proof of any criminal

intent on the part of the defendant, but ordinarily require proof that the defendant committed some wrongful act. **Vicarious liability offenses** impose criminal liability on a defendant for the acts of third parties (normally employees under the defendant's personal supervision), but may require proof of some form of *mens rea*, such as a negligent or reckless failure to supervise on the defendant's part. Frequently, a statute embodies elements of both approaches by imposing liability on a corporate executive for the acts or omissions of other corporate employees without requiring proof of criminal intent on the part of any corporate employee. The following *Park* case is probably the most famous recent example of such a prosecution.

---

[30] The Management of Corporations chapter discusses indemnification in detail.

UNITED STATES v. PARK

421 U.S. 658 (U.S. Sup. Ct. 1975)

John R. Park was the chief executive officer of Acme Markets, Inc., a national retail food chain with approximately 36,000 employees, 874 retail outlets, and 16 warehouses. Acme and Park were charged with five counts of violating the Federal Food, Drug, and Cosmetic Act by storing food shipped in interstate commerce in warehouses where it was exposed to rodent contamination.

The violations were detected during Food and Drug Administration (FDA) inspections of Acme's Baltimore warehouse. A 12-day inspection during November and December 1971 disclosed evidence of rodent infestation and unsanitary conditions at the warehouse. Among other things, mouse droppings were found on the floor of the hanging meat room and beside bales of lime Jell-O, and one bale of Jell-O contained a hole chewed by a rodent. The FDA notified Park by letter of these findings. After receiving the letter, Park conferred with Acme's vice president for legal affairs, who told him that the Baltimore division vice president "was investigating the situation immediately and would be taking corrective action." When a subsequent FDA investigation, in March 1972, disclosed continued rodent contamination at the Baltimore warehouse despite improved sanitation there, the charges were filed against Acme and Park. Acme pleaded guilty to the charges, but Park refused to do so. Park was convicted on each count and fined $50 per count.

Park appealed his conviction, arguing that the trial court's instructions to the jury were defective because they could have been interpreted as justifying a conviction based solely on his corporate position. He also argued that the trial court erred in allowing the government to introduce evidence of a 1970 FDA letter that informed him of similar problems at Acme's Philadelphia warehouse. The Fourth Circuit Court of Appeals agreed, reversing Park's conviction. The government appealed.

Burger, Chief Justice. In *United States v. Dotterweich* (1943), this Court looked to the purposes of the Act and noted that they "touch phases of the lives and health of people which, in the circumstances of modern industrialism, are largely beyond self-protection." It observed that the Act is of "a now familiar type" which "dispenses with the conventional requirement for criminal conduct—awareness of some wrongdoing. In the interest of the larger good it puts the burden of acting at hazard upon a person otherwise innocent but standing in responsible relation to a public danger."

The Court was aware of the concern that literal enforcement "might operate too harshly by sweeping within its condemnation any person however remotely entangled in the proscribed shipment." In this context, the Court concluded, the offense was committed "by all who have a responsible share in the furtherance of the transaction which the statute outlaws."

The interpretation given the Act in *Dotterweich*, as holding criminally accountable persons whose failure to exercise authority and supervisory responsibility resulted in the violation, has been confirmed in our subsequent cases. The Court has reaffirmed the proposition that the public interest in the purity of its food is so great as to warrant the imposition of the highest standard of care on distributors.

Thus *Dotterweich* and the cases which have followed reveal that in providing sanctions which reach and touch the individuals who execute the corporate mission—and this is by no means necessarily confined to a single corporate agent or employee—the Act imposes not only a positive duty to seek out and remedy violations when they occur but also, and primarily, a duty to implement measures that will insure that violations will not occur. The duty imposed by Congress on responsible corporate agents is, we emphasize, one that requires the highest standard of foresight and vigilance, but the Act, in its criminal aspect, does not require that which is objectively impossible. The theory upon which responsible corporate agents are held criminally accountable for "causing" violations of the Act permits a claim that a defendant was "powerless" to prevent or correct the violation to be raised defensively at a trial on the merits. If such a claim is made, the defendant has the burden of coming forward with evidence, but this does not alter the Government's ultimate burden of proving beyond a reasonable doubt the defendant's guilt, including his power, in light of the duty imposed by the Act, to prevent or correct the prohibited condition.

Turning to the jury charge in this case, it is arguable that isolated parts can be read as intimating that a finding of guilt could be predicated solely on Park's corporate position. Viewed as a whole, the charge did not permit the jury to find guilt solely on the basis of Park's position; rather, it fairly advised the jury that to find guilt it must find Park "had a responsible relation to the situation," and "by virtue of his position . . . had authority and responsibility" to deal with the situation.

Our conclusion that the Court of Appeals erred in its reading of the jury charge suggests as well our disagreement concerning the admissibility of evidence that Park was advised by FDA in 1970 of unsanitary conditions in Acme's Philadelphia warehouse. Park testified that he had employed a system in which he relied upon his subordinates, and that he was ultimately responsible for this system. He testified further that he had found these subordinates to be "dependable" and had "great confidence" in them. By this and other testimony Park evidently sought to persuade the jury that, as the president of a large corporation, he had no choice but to delegate duties to those in whom he reposed confidence, that he had no reason to suspect his subordinates were failing to insure compliance with the Act, and that, once violations were unearthed, acting through those subordinates he did everything possible to correct them.

This testimony clearly created the need for rebuttal evidence. That evidence was not offered to show that Park had a propensity to commit criminal acts, that the crime charged had been committed; its purpose was to demonstrate that Park was on notice that he could not rely on his system of delegation to subordinates to prevent or correct unsanitary conditions at Acme's warehouses, and that he must have been aware of the deficiencies of this system before the Baltimore violations were discovered. The evidence was therefore relevant since it served to rebut Park's defense that he had justifiably relied upon subordinates to handle sanitation matters.

Judgment of the Court of Appeals reversed; Park's conviction sustained.

Strict liability offenses have been widely criticized on a variety of grounds. First, it is often argued that *mens rea* is a basic principle in our legal system and that it is unjust to stigmatize with a criminal conviction persons who are not morally culpable. Second, the critics commonly express doubts about whether strict liability offenses produce the deterrence that their proponents seek. They may reduce the moral impact of the criminal sanction by applying it to relatively trivial offenses. And they may not result in enough convictions or severe enough penalties to produce deterrence because juries and judges are unwilling to convict or punish defendants who may not be morally culpable. Although the courts have generally upheld the constitutionality of strict liability offenses, they are generally disfavored. Most courts require a clear indication of a legislative intent to dispense with the element of *mens rea*.[31]

Third, even if prosecutors could identify and convict responsible individuals within the corporation and judges and juries imposed significant penalties on such individuals, individual liability in the absence of corporate liability would probably fail to achieve effective corporate control. If corporations were immune from criminal liability, they could benefit financially from employee law violations. Individual liability, unlike corporate fines, does not force a corporation to give up the profits flowing from a violation. Thus, corporations would have no incentive to avoid future violations and incarcerated offenders would merely be replaced by others who might eventually yield to the pressures that produced the violations in the first place. Also, corporate liability may, in some cases, encourage corporate efforts to prevent future violations. Corporate liability is uniquely appropriate when an offense has occurred but no identifiable individual is sufficiently culpable to justify an individual prosecution.

New Directions

The preceding discussion suggests that future efforts at corporate control are likely to include both corporate and individual criminal liability. It also suggests, however, that new approaches are necessary if society is to gain more effective control over corporate activities. We need new remedies reflecting both our historical experience with attempts to apply the criminal sanction in the corporate context and our knowledge of the nature of corporate behavior.

In the area of individual liability, a variety of novel criminal penalties have been suggested. For example, white-collar offenders could be deprived of their leisure time or sentenced to render public service rather than being incarcerated or fined. Some have even suggested the licensing of managers and license suspensions as a penalty for offenders. The common thread in all these approaches is an attempt to create penalties meaningful to the defendant, yet not so severe that judges and juries are unwilling to impose them with sufficient certainty to produce deterrence.

In the area of corporate liability, one of the most novel and promising recent suggestions involves more imaginative judicial use of corporate probation for convicted corporate offenders.[32] Courts could require convicted corporations to do, or hire independent consultants to do, self-studies identifying the source of a violation and proposing appropriate steps to prevent future violations. If bureaucratic failures caused the violation, the court could order a limited restructuring of the corporation's internal decision-making processes as a condition of obtaining probation or avoiding a penalty. Possible orders might include requiring the collection and monitoring of the data necessary to discover or prevent future violations and the creation of new executive positions to monitor such data. Restructuring would minimize the harm to innocent persons inherent in corporate financial penalties. It might also be a more effective way of achieving corporate rehabilitation than relying exclusively on a corporation's desire to avoid future fines as an incentive to police itself. Because restructuring would represent a new form of governmental intrusion into the private sector, it should be applied sparingly and with discretion.

Important White-Collar Crimes

Regulatory Offenses

A wide range of federal and state regulatory statutes prescribe criminal as well as civil liability for violations. Several major federal regulatory offenses are discussed in detail in later chapters, including violations of the Sherman Antitrust Act, the Securities Act of 1933, the

[31] See, for example, *United States v. U.S. Gypsum Co.*, 425 U.S. 422 (U.S. Sup. Ct. 1978).

[32] See Note, "Structural Crime and Institutional Rehabilitation: A New Approach to Corporate Sentencing," 89 *Yale L. J.* 353 (1979).

Securities Exchange Act of 1934, the Clean Waters Act of 1972, the Resource Conservation and Recovery Act, and the Electronic Funds Transfer Act. The Food, Drug, and Cosmetic Act, at issue in the *Park* case, makes it a federal offense to mislabel or adulterate food, drugs, or cosmetic products in interstate commerce.

Fraudulent Acts

Many business crimes involve some form of *fraudulent* conduct. In most states, it is a crime to obtain money or property by fraudulent pretenses, to issue fraudulent checks, to make false credit or advertising statements, or to give short weights or measures. Various forms of fraud in bankruptcy proceedings, such as fraudulent concealment or transfer of a debtor's assets or false claims by creditors, are federal criminal offenses.[33] In addition, federal Mail Fraud and Wire Fraud acts make it a federal offense to use the mail or telephone or telegrams to accomplish a fraudulent scheme. The Travel Act of 1961 makes it a federal offense to travel or use facilities in interstate commerce to commit criminal acts.

Bribery

Offering gifts, favors, or anything of value to *public officials* to influence their official decisions to benefit private interests has long been a criminal offense under state and federal law. In 1977 Congress passed the Foreign Corrupt Practices Act, making it a federal offense to give anything of value to officials of foreign governments in an attempt to influence their official actions.[34] In addition, most states have enacted *commercial bribery* statutes making it illegal to offer kickbacks and payoffs to private individuals to secure some commercial advantage.

RICO

When Congress passed the Racketeer Influenced and Corrupt Organizations Act (RICO)[35] as part of the Organized Crime Control Act of 1970, lawmakers were primarily concerned about organized crime's increasing

---

[33] The Bankruptcy chapter discusses bankruptcy in detail.

[34] The Securities Regulation chapter discusses the Foreign Corrupt Practices Act in detail.

[35] 18 U.S.C. §§ 1961-1968 (1976).

entry into legitimate business enterprises. The broad language of the RICO statute, however, has resulted in its application in a wide variety of cases having nothing to do with organized crime. This development has made RICO one of the most controversial pieces of legislation affecting business in our legal history. Supporters of RICO argue that it has become an effective and much-needed tool for attacking a wide range of unethical business practices. Its critics assert, however, that RICO is an overbroad statute that needlessly taints business reputations. They also argue that it has operated unduly to favor plaintiffs in commercial litigation rather than serving as an aid to law enforcement. The lower federal courts have disagreed on many important points about the meaning of this controversial statute. As a result, some significant issues concerning RICO's scope await ultimate judicial or legislative resolution.

Criminal RICO The criminal sections of the RICO statute make it a federal crime to: (1) use income derived from a "pattern of racketeering activity" to acquire an interest in an enterprise, (2) acquire or maintain an interest in an enterprise through a pattern of racketeering activity, (3) conduct or participate in the affairs of an enterprise through a pattern of racketeering activity, or (4) conspire to do any of the preceding acts. RICO is a *compound* criminal statute because it requires both the proof of a "predicate" criminal offense and a pattern of racketeering activity. *Racketeering activity* includes the commission of 1 of over 30 state or federal criminal offenses. Although most of the offenses that qualify (e.g., arson, gambling, extortion) have no relation to normal business transactions, mail and wire fraud, securities fraud, and bribery are also included. Thus, almost any business fraud may be alleged to be a racketeering activity. To show a *pattern* of such activity, the prosecution must prove the commission of two predicate offenses within a 10-year period. Most courts have interpreted the statutory term *enterprise* broadly to include partnerships and unincorporated associations as well as corporations.

Individuals found guilty of RICO violations are subject to a fine of up to $25,000 per violation and imprisonment for up to 20 years. In addition, they risk the forfeiture of any interest gained in any enterprise as a result of a violation. To prevent defendants from hiding assets that may be forfeitable upon conviction, federal prosecutors may seek pretrial orders freezing a defendant's assets. Some critics of RICO have argued that the harm that such a freeze may work on a defendant's ability to conduct its business, coupled with the threat of forfeiture of most or all of the business upon conviction, has led some business defendants to make plea bargains rather than risk all by fighting prosecutions they believe to be unjustified.

Civil RICO The RICO statute also allows the government to seek numerous civil penalties for violations. These include *divestiture* of a defendant's interest in an enterprise, the *dissolution* or *reorganization* of the enterprise, and *injunctions* against future racketeering activities by the defendant.

The most controversial sections of RICO, however, are those allowing private individuals to recover *treble damages* (three times their actual loss) plus attorney's fees for injuries caused by a statutory violation. This highly attractive remedy has led in recent years to the frequent use of RICO by plaintiffs in commercial fraud cases. Stockbrokers, banks, insurance companies, and accounting firms have been typical targets of recent civil RICO suits. To qualify for recovery under RICO, a plaintiff must allege that the defendant has violated RICO's provisions and that, as a result, the plaintiff was "injured in his business or property."

In its decision in *Sedima, S.P.R.L. v. Imrex Co., Inc.*, the Supreme Court resolved two major issues concerning RICO's scope in an expansive fashion.[36] First, the Court rejected the requirement imposed by some lower federal courts that civil RICO plaintiffs must prove that the defendant had been convicted of a predicate offense. Second, the Court also rejected the idea that civil RICO plaintiffs must prove a "distinct racketeering injury" as a precondition of recovery. The Court also recognized the lower courts' concern with the breadth of the RICO statute and the fact that the majority of civil RICO suits are filed against legitimate businesses, rather than against "the archetypal, intimidating mobster." However, the Court noted that: "This defect—if defect it is— is inherent in the statute as written, and its correction must lie with Congress."

Since *Sedima*, several RICO reform proposals have been unsuccessfully introduced in Congress. As the following *Northwestern Bell* case illustrates, in the absence of Congressional action, the Court has continued to interpret RICO expansively. Most recently, in *Tafflin v. Levitt*, the Court unanimously resolved a split among the lower federal courts by ruling that civil RICO suits may be brought in state courts as well as in federal courts.[37]

---

[36] 473 U.S. 479 (U.S. Sup. Ct. 1985).
[37] 110 S. Ct. 792 (U.S. Sup. Ct. 1990).

H. J. Inc. v. Northwestern Bell Telephone Co.
109 S. Ct. 2893 (U.S. Sup. Ct. 1989)

Customers of Northwestern Bell Telephone Company filed a class action suit alleging violations of RICO based on allegations that between 1980 and 1986 Northwestern Bell sought to influence members of the Minnesota Public Utilities Commission (MPUC) to approve rates for Northwestern in excess of a fair and reasonable amount. They alleged that Northwestern made cash payments to commissioners, negotiated with them regarding future employment, and paid for parties and meals, for tickets to sporting events, and for airline tickets. These acts, they alleged, were in violation of the state bribery statute and state common law prohibiting bribery. The district court dismissed their civil RICO claims because the complaint failed to allege the "multiple illegal schemes" which the Eighth Circuit Court of Appeals had previously held were necessary to establish a "pattern of racketeering activity" under RICO.

Brennan, Justice. In *Sedima, S.P.R.L. v. Imrex Co.*, we acknowledged concern in some quarters over civil RICO's use against "legitimate" businesses, as well as "mobsters and organized criminals." But we suggested that RICO's expansive uses "appear to be primarily the result of the breadth of the predicate offenses, and the failure of Congress and the courts to develop a meaningful concept of 'pattern.'" Congress has done nothing in the interim to illuminate RICO's key requirement of a pattern of racketeering activity, and developing a meaningful concept of "pattern" within the existing statutory framework has proved to be no easy task.

It is, nevertheless, a task we must undertake in order to decide this case. Our guides must be the text of the statute and its legislative history. We find no support in those sources for the proposition that predicate acts of racketeering may form a pattern only when they are a part of separate illegal schemes. Nor can we agree with those courts that have suggested that a pattern is established by proving two predicate acts, or with *amici* in this case who argue that the word "pattern" refers only to predicates that are indicative of a perpetrator involved in organized crime.

As we remarked in *Sedima*, the section of the statute headed "definitions," section 1961, does not so much define a pattern of racketeering activity as state a minimum necessary condition for the existence of such a pattern. Unlike other provisions in section 1961 that tell us what various concepts used in the Act "mean," section 1961(5) says of the phrase "pattern of racketeering activity" only that it "requires at least two acts of racketeering activity, one of which occurred after October 15, 1970 and the last of which occurred within ten years after the commission of a prior act of racketeering activity."

Section 1961(5) does indicate that Congress envisioned circumstances in which no more than two predicates would be necessary to establish a pattern. But the statement that a pattern "requires at least" two predicates implies that while two acts are necessary, they may not be sufficient. Section 1961(5) concerns only the minimum *number* of predicates necessary to establish a pattern; and it assumes that there is something to a RICO pattern *beyond* simply the number of predicate acts involved. The legislative history bears out this interpretation, for the principal sponsor of the Senate bill expressly indicated that "proof of two acts of racketeering activity, without more, does not establish a pattern." Section 1961(5) does not identify, though, these additional prerequisites for establishing the existence of a RICO pattern.

In normal usage, the word "pattern" here would be taken to require more than just a multiplicity of racketeering predicates. A "pattern" is an "arrangement or order of things or activity," 11 Oxford English Dictionary 357 (2d ed. 1989). It is not the number of predicates but the relationship that they bear to each other or to some external organizing principle that renders them "ordered" or "arranged."

RICO's legislative history reveals Congress' intent that to prove a pattern of racketeering activity a plaintiff or prosecutor must show that the racketeering predicates are related, *and* that they amount to or pose a threat of continued criminal activity. In the Organized Crime Control Act of 1970, Congress defined a pattern requirement solely in terms of the *relationship* of the defendant's criminal acts one to another: "criminal conduct forms a pattern if it embraces criminal acts that have the same or similar purposes, results, participants, victims, or methods of commission, or otherwise are interrelated by distinguishing characteristics and are not isolated events." We have no reason to suppose that Congress had in mind for RICO's pattern component any more constrained a notion of the relationships between predicates that would suffice.

RICO's legislative history tells us, however, that the relatedness of racketeering activities is not alone enough to satisfy the pattern element. It must also be shown that the predicates themselves amount to, or that they otherwise constitute a threat of, *continuing* racketeering activity. It is this aspect of RICO's pattern element that has spawned the "multiple scheme" test adopted by the Court of Appeals in this case. But although proof that a defendant has been involved in multiple criminal schemes would certainly be highly relevant to the inquiry into the continuity of the defendant's racketeering activity, it is implausible to suppose that Congress thought continuity might be shown *only* by proof of multiple schemes. We adopt a less inflexible approach that seems to us to derive from a common-sense, everyday understanding of RICO's language and Congress' gloss on it. What a plaintiff or prosecutor must prove is continuity of racketeering activity, or its threat.

A party alleging a RICO violation may demonstrate continuity over a closed period by proving a series of related predicates extending over a substantial period of time. Predicate acts extending over a few weeks or months and threatening no future criminal conduct do not satisfy this requirement: Congress was concerned in RICO with long-term criminal conduct. Often a RICO action will be brought before continuity can be established in this way. In such cases, liability depends on whether the *threat* of continuity is demonstrated.

The threat of continuity is sufficiently established where the predicates can be attributed to a defendant operating as part of a long-term association that exists for criminal purposes. Such associations include, but extend well beyond, those traditionally grouped under the phrase "organized crime." The continuity requirement is likewise satisfied where it is shown that the predicates are a regular way of conducting defendant's ongoing legitimate business, or of conducting or participating in an ongoing ligitimate RICO "enterprise."

Plaintiffs' complaint alleges that at different times over the course of at least a 6-year period the defendants gave five members of the MPUC numerous bribes, in several different forms, with the objective—in which they were allegedly successful—of causing these Commissioners to approve unfair and unreasonable rates. RICO defines bribery as a "racketeering activity," so plaintiffs have alleged multiple predicate acts. They may be able to prove that the multiple predicates alleged constitute a "pattern of racketeering activity," in that they satisfy the requirements of relationship and continuity. The acts of bribery alleged are said to be related to a common purpose, to influence Commissioners to win approval of unfairly high rates for Northwestern Bell. Furthermore, the racketeering predicates allegedly occurred over at least a 6-year period, which may be sufficient to satisfy the continuity requirement. Alternatively, a threat of continuity might be established at trial by showing that the alleged bribes were a regular way of conducting or participating in the conduct of the alleged and ongoing RICO enterprise, the MPUC. The Court of Appeals thus erred in affirming the District Court's dismissal of plaintiff's complaint for failure to plead "a pattern of racketeering activity."

Judgment reversed in favor of plaintiffs; case remanded for trial.

ETHICAL AND PUBLIC POLICY CONCERNS

1. Few issues have managed to provoke more prolonged, heated controversy than the death penalty. Many of the arguments both for and against the death penalty are, at base, ethical arguments. Identify and briefly discuss some fundamental arguments on both sides of the issue.

2. Are strict and vicarious liability ethically defensible? Who would be more likely to support such liability, a utilitarian or a rights theorist? Which form of liability would a rights theorist find more palatable?

3. Business opponents of RICO have argued that federal prosecutors have used the threat of asset forfeitures under the RICO statute to coerce business defendants to enter settlement agreements that they would not

otherwise enter. Assuming these allegations are sometimes true, are such prosecutorial practices defensible?

SUMMARY

A thorough knowledge of the criminal law is an important component of a contemporary businessperson's education because in recent years the criminal sanction has been increasingly used as a major device for controlling business behavior. In major part, this trend reflects the belief that the criminal law provides a greater degree of deterrence than civil remedies.

Crimes are public wrongs, offenses against the state prosecuted by the state. The criminal sanction is the law's ultimate threat because it combines a threat to life or liberty with the stigma of a criminal conviction.

Crimes are classified as felonies or misdemeanors, depending on the seriousness of the offense involved. Conviction of a felony, a serious criminal offense, entails far more serious consequences than does conviction of a misdemeanor.

Significant social disagreement concerns the definition of criminal behavior and the underlying purpose of the criminal sanction. Utilitarians view the prevention of socially undesirable behavior as the only proper justification of criminal penalties. Retributionists see criminal punishment as the infliction of deserved suffering on those who violate fundamental social rules.

Given the powerful nature of the criminal sanction, several important restrictions operate to limit the state's power to convict a person of a crime. All crimes are statutory in the United States. Criminal responsibility requires the violation of an existing statute that does not criminalize constitutionally protected behavior and that is worded clearly enough to give an ordinary person notice of the conduct prohibited. The state must prove each element of a criminal offense beyond a reasonable doubt and within an extensive framework of procedural restraints to safeguard the rights of the accused.

The state must also prove that the defendant had the capacity to entertain the criminal intent required for all serious criminal offenses. Traditionally, the courts have recognized three kinds of incapacity: infancy, insanity, and intoxication. The common law initially refused to hold corporations responsible for criminal offenses. Over time, however, this rule changed to the point where today a corporation can be found to have committed almost any criminal offense that has been given proper statutory wording. Corporate criminal intent is normally derived by imputing the intent of corporate agents to the corporation. Significant disagreement exists, however, about whether a corporation should be criminally responsible for the actions of any of its employees or only for the actions of its higher officials. Disagreement also exists concerning whether good faith corporate efforts to avoid violations should be a defense to liability.

Individual corporate employees who commit crimes in the course of their employment are personally criminally responsible. Due to the nature of corporate decision making, however, it is often difficult to pinpoint the individuals responsible for corporate crimes. This has led to regulatory statutes imposing strict or vicarious criminal responsibility on corporate officers.

For a variety of reasons, neither corporate nor individual liability has been a very effective means of controlling corporate crime. We need to find new approaches that seek to learn from this lack of success and to employ our knowledge about the true nature of corporate behavior if society is to achieve a greater level of control.

PROBLEM CASES

1. In August of 1984, James Miller was convicted by a Florida court of sexual battery with slight force. When the offense in question was committed on April 25, 1984, the sentencing guidelines in effect in Florida would have resulted in a 3 1/2- to 4 1/2-year sentence. On May 8, 1984, the Florida Supreme Court proposed revisions to the guidelines, which were adopted by the Florida legislature and became effective July 1, 1984. When Miller was sentenced on October 2, 1984, the judge applied the revised guidelines to impose a 7-year sentence. Miller appealed on the ground that his sentence was unconstitutional. Was he correct?

2. A jury convicted Liberta of raping and sodomizing his estranged wife in violation of a New York statute. Liberta challenged his conviction on the ground that the statute was unconstitutional because it provided that only men could be guilty of rape. Upon what constitutional provision should Liberta have based his claim? Should his claim succeed?

3. Johnny Paul Penry was convicted of murder and sentenced to death after a jury rejected his insanity defense. His defense had presented evidence that due to organic brain damage he had the intelligence of a six-year-old child. Penry challenged his conviction on a number of grounds, including the argument that the Eighth Amendment forbids execution of the retarded. Was he correct?

4. Police officers who suspected Billy Greenwood of dealing drugs asked trash collectors to pick up and turn over plastic garbage bags that Greenwood left at the curb. The officers found drug-related items in the bags and used them to secure a search warrant for Greenwood's home. The search revealed narcotics and Greenwood was arrested on felony narcotics charges. A California Superior Court dismissed the charges against Greenwood on the ground that the warrantless search of his trash was in violation of the Fourth Amendment. Was the dismissal proper?

5. Doe, the target of a federal grand jury investigation, was subpoenaed to produce records of his accounts in banks in the Cayman Islands and Bermuda. He produced some records, testified that he had no other records in his possession or control, and invoked the Fifth Amendment when asked to reveal the existence or location of other records. After the U.S. branches of Doe's banks cited their nations' bank secrecy laws and refused to comply with subpoenas ordering them to produce records of his accounts, the district court, at the government's request, ordered Doe, without identifying or acknowledging the existence of any such accounts, to sign a consent directive authorizing the banks to turn over records of any and all accounts over which he had a right of withdrawal. When he refused, the court found him in contempt. Would being forced to sign the consent directive violate Doe's Fifth Amendment rights?

6. Reckmeyer was charged with running a massive drug importation and distribution scheme alleged to be a continuing criminal enterprise (CCE) in violation of the federal CCE statute. Relying on a portion of the CCE statute authorizing forfeiture to the government of property acquired as a result of drug violations, the indictment sought forfeiture of specified assets in Reckmeyer's possession. The district court entered a restraining order forbidding Reckmeyer from transferring any of the potentially forfeitable assets, but Reckmeyer nonetheless transferred $25,000 to Caplin & Drysdale, a law firm, for preindictment legal services. The firm placed the money in escrow and continued to represent Reckmeyer after he was indicted. Reckmeyer subsequently entered a plea agreement with the government in which he pled guilty to the CCE charge and agreed to forfeit all the assets listed in the indictment. A forfeiture order was entered by the district court when Reckmeyer was sentenced. Caplin & Drysdale filed a petition challenging the order, claiming an interest in $170,000 of Reckmeyer's assets for expenses incurred in conducting his defense, seeking the $25,000 held in escrow, and arguing that forfeiture of attorney's fees under the CCE statute would violate Reckmeyer's Sixth Amendment right to counsel. Was their argument correct?

7. On November 23, 1976, Warner-Lambert Company retained the investment banking firm of Morgan Stanley & Co. to assess the desirability of acquiring Deseret Pharmaceutical Company, to evaluate Deseret's stock, and to recommend an appropriate price per share for a tender offer for Deseret. On November 30, 1976, E. Jacques Courtois, Jr., an employee of Morgan Stanley's mergers and acquisitions department who had learned of Warner's plans to acquire Deseret, told Adrian Antoniu, an employee of Kuhn Loeb & Co.,

about the impending acquisition and urged him to buy Deseret stock. Antoniu in turn informed James Newman, a stockbroker, who bought 11,700 shares of Deseret for his and their accounts. Newman also advised certain of his customers to buy Deseret. All told, 143,000 shares of Deseret changed hands that day, among them 5,000 shares sold by Michael Moss for $28 per share. On the following day, December 1, 1976, the New York Stock Exchange suspended trading in Deseret pending announcement of a tender offer, which Warner publicly announced (at $38 per share) on December 7, 1976. Moss filed damage claims under the securities laws and RICO against Morgan Stanley and Newman. The federal district court dismissed his RICO claims, in part because Moss had failed to show any tie between the defendants and organized crime. Was this a proper basis for dismissal?

8. Under authority granted by Congress in the Motor Vehicle Information and Cost Savings Act, the Secretary of Transportation mandated that motor vehicle dealers give all buyers a written odometer statement disclosing the mileage registered on the odometer of the vehicle they bought and a notice if the odometer reading was known to be inadequate. The secretary also mandated that dealers retain for four years copies of all odometer statements they issue or receive and keep such records at the dealer's place of business in a systematically retrievable order. In late 1984, the Department of Justice investigated possible violations of the act by some Kentucky automobile dealers. During these investigations, a grand jury issued a subpoena to Randall Underhill, a sole proprietor automobile dealer, calling for him to appear and testify before the grand jury and to bring with him all odometer statements for motor vehicles he bought and sold between June 1, 1981, and June 1, 1982. Underhill moved to quash the subpoena insofar as it required production of the odometer statements on the ground that forcing him to produce them would violate his Fifth Amendment rights. Should he be compelled to produce the records?

9. Several individuals were charged with violating section 647(d) of the California Penal Code, which provides that any person "who loiters in or about any toilet open to the public for the purpose of engaging in or soliciting any lewd or lascivious or any unlawful act" is guilty of a misdemeanor. They argued that the statute was unconstitutionally vague. Was it?

10. In August 1981, Larry Heath hired two men to kill his wife Rebecca, who was then nine-months pregnant, for $2,000. The men kidnapped Rebecca from her home in Alabama, took her across the nearby state line into Georgia, and shot her in the head. On February 10, 1982, Heath pleaded guilty to a murder charge in Georgia in exchange for a sentence of life imprisonment, which he understood could involve his serving as few as seven years in prison. However, on May 5, 1982, an Alabama grand jury indicted Heath for the capital offense of murder during a kidnapping. He was tried, convicted, and sentenced to death. The Alabama Supreme Court rejected his appeal based on the argument that his Alabama conviction violated the Double Jeopardy Clause of the Fifth Amendment. Was the Alabama Court's decision correct?

11. In December of 1983, a grand jury indicted Automated Medical Laboratories, Inc. (AML), Richmond Plasma Corporation (RPC) (a wholly owned AML subsidiary), and three former RPC managers for engaging in a conspiracy that included falsification of logbooks and records required to be maintained by businesses producing blood plasma. The falsification was designed to conceal from the Food and Drug Administration (FDA) various violations of federal regulations governing the plasmapheresis process and facilities. The evidence introduced at trial indicated that the managers and several other members of the team charged with assuring compliance with FDA regulations had actively participated in record falsification. AML was convicted and appealed on the ground that there was no evidence that any officer or director of AML knowingly or willfully participated in or authorized the unlawful practices at RPC. Was AML's conviction in the absence of such proof proper?

CHAPTER 7

INTENTIONAL TORTS

NATURE AND FUNCTION OF TORT LAW

Torts are *private (civil) wrongs* against persons or their property. The basis of tort liability is a breach of a legal duty owed to another person resulting in some legally recognizable harm to that person. The primary aim of tort law is to compensate injured persons for such harms. Thus, persons injured by the tortious act of another may file a civil suit for the *actual (compensatory) damages* that they have suffered as a result of a tort. Depending on the facts of the particular case, these damages may be for direct and immediate harms, such as physical injuries, medical expenses, and lost pay and benefits, or for harms as intangible as loss of privacy, injury to reputation, or emotional distress.

In cases where the behavior of the person committing a tort is particularly reprehensible, injured victims may also be able to recover an award of *punitive damages*. Punitive damages are not intended to compensate tort victims for their losses. Instead, they are designed to punish flagrant wrongdoers and to deter them and others from engaging in similar conduct in the future. Accordingly, they are theoretically reserved for only the most egregious forms of wrongdoing. Punitive damages have always been controversial, but they have grown more so in recent years because of the size of some punitive dam-

age awards and the perception that juries are awarding them in cases where they are not justified.

The punishment function of punitive damage awards is obviously similar to the deterrent function in criminal law. Some kinds of behavior can give rise to both criminal and tort liability. For example, a rapist may be criminally liable for rape and also liable for the torts of assault, battery, false imprisonment, and intentional infliction of mental distress. However, since tort suits are civil rather than criminal, the plaintiff's burden of proof in a tort case is the *preponderance of the evidence*, rather than the more stringent beyond-a-reasonable-doubt standard that applies to criminal cases. This means that the greater weight of the evidence introduced at the trial must support the plaintiff's position on every element of the case. Figure 1 summarizes the important differences between criminal and tort liability.

In tort law, society is engaged in a constant balancing of competing social interests. Excessive protection of some people's physical integrity, for example, may unduly impair other people's freedom of movement. Likewise, undue protection of peace of mind, privacy, and personal reputation may inordinately restrict constitutionally protected freedoms of speech and of the press. Over time, our tort law has demonstrated a tendency to protect an increasingly broad range of personal interests.

FIGURE 1   Crimes and Intentional Torts

	Crimes	Intentional Torts
Nature	Criminal	Civil
Elements	(1) Violation of a statute (2) Intent	(1) Harm to another person or property (2) Intent
Actors	Prosecutor versus defendant	Plaintiff (victim) versus defendant (tortfeasor)
Burden	Prosecutor must establish the defendant's guilt beyond a reasonable doubt	Plaintiff must establish the defendant's liability by a preponderance of the evidence
Punishment	Fines, imprisonment, execution	Defendant may have to pay the plaintiff compensatory and punitive damages

Some commentators have explained this tendency by saying it demonstrates the courts' growing sensitivity to the nature of life in an increasingly interdependent urban industrialized society. Whatever its origins, this and the next chapter demonstrate that, although the range of the human interests that tort law protects is expanding, the courts have remained mindful of the fact that the protection of any given interest necessarily involves a trade-off in the form of limitations placed on other competing social interests.

Torts are generally classified according to the level of fault exhibited by the wrongdoer's behavior. This chapter deals with **intentional torts:** behavior that indicates either the wrongdoer's conscious desire to cause harm to a legally protected interest or the wrongdoer's knowledge that such harm is substantially certain to result from his actions. The following chapter discusses tort liability founded on principles of *negligence* and *strict liability*, neither of which require proof of any intentional wrongdoing by a defendant.

INTERFERENCE WITH PERSONAL RIGHTS

Battery

The tort of **battery** protects a fundamental personal interest—the right to be free from harmful or offensive bodily contacts. Battery is the *intentional, harmful* or *offensive touching of another without* his *consent.* A contact is *harmful* if it produces any bodily injury. As the following *England* case illustrates, even nonharmful contacts may be considered battery if they are *offensive*, that is, calculated to offend a reasonable sense of personal dignity. Direct contact between a wrongdoer's body and the body of another is not necessary for a battery to result. For example, if Delano throws a rock at Stevens or places a harmful or offensive substance in her food, Delano has committed a battery if Stevens is hit by the rock or if she eats the food. Nor is it necessary that the wrongdoer actually intend to produce the contact if contact in fact results and the wrongdoer's intent was merely to threaten the victim with contact. So, if Delano threatens to shoot Stevens with a gun he mistakenly believes is unloaded and ends up shooting Stevens, Delano would be liable for battery.

Also, the person who suffers the harmful or offensive touching does not have to be the person whom the wrongdoer intended to injure for liability for battery to occur. Under a general intentional tort concept called the doctrine of *transferred intent*, a wrongdoer who intends to injure one person, but injures another, is nonetheless liable to the person injured, despite the absence of any specific intent to injure him. So, if Walters is hit by the rock thrown at Stevens, or if he eats Stevens's food, Delano would be liable to Walters for battery. Finally, touching anything connected with a person's body in a harmful or offensive manner can also create liability for battery. So, if Johnson snatches Martin's purse, or kicks her dog while she is walking her dog on a leash, he may be liable for battery even though he has not touched her body.

Some of the most interesting battery cases involve the nature of the *consent* that is necessary to avoid liability for battery. As a general rule, consent must be *freely* and *intelligently* given to be a defense to battery. In some cases, consent may be inferred from a person's voluntary participation in an activity. Such consent is ordinarily limited, however, to contacts that are considered a normal consequence of the activity in question. For example, Joe Frazier would be unable to win a battery suit against Muhammad Ali for injuries he suffered during their famous "Thrilla in Manila" title fight. However, the quarterback who is knifed on the 50-yard line during a game has a valid battery claim.

Assault

The tort of **assault** protects the personal interest in freedom from the *apprehension* of battery. Any *attempt* to cause a harmful or offensive contact with another, or any *offer* to cause such a contact, is an assault if it causes a *well-grounded apprehension of imminent (immediate) battery* in the mind of the person threatened with contact. Whether the threatened contact actually occurs is irrelevant.

Because assault is limited to threats of *imminent* battery, threats of *future* battery do not create liability for assault. Likewise, because assault focuses on the apprehension in the mind of the victim, the threats in question must create a reasonable apprehension of battery in the victim's mind. Therefore, threatening words, unaccompanied by any other acts or circumstances indicating an intent to carry out the threat, do not amount to an assault. Finally, the elements of assault require that the victim must actually experience an apprehension of imminent battery before liability results. Therefore, if Markham fires a rifle at Thomas from a great distance and misses him, and Thomas learns of the attempt on his life only at a later date, Markham is not liable to Thomas for the tort of assault.

ENGLAND v. S & M FOODS, INC.

511 So.2d 1313 (La. Ct. App. 1987)

Betty England worked at a Dairy Queen restaurant owned by S & M Foods in Tallulah, Louisiana. One day while she was at work, her manager, Larry Garley, became upset when several incorrectly prepared hamburgers were returned by a customer. Garley allegedly expressed his dissatisfaction by using profane language and throwing a hamburger, which hit England on the leg. England filed a battery suit against Garley and S & M and won a $1,000 judgment. Garley and S & M appealed.

Jones, Judge. Defendants contend no battery was committed because Garley did not intend to inflict bodily harm upon England. They argue Garley was disgusted about the returned hamburgers and threw one toward the trash can and it inadvertantly splattered on her and Alcie Rash, another employee. They contend that England's embarrassment was caused as much by her overreaction to the situation as by Garley's conduct.

England said that Garley used profane language when he told her to prepare the hamburgers correctly. She said Garley, while looking straight at her, then threw the hamburger which hit her on the leg. She testified that she argued with Garley about the matter and that several patrons observed the incident, which caused her to cry and become emotionally upset.

Rash said that she did not see Garley throw the hamburger, but observed it hit the floor and splatter mayonnaise and mustard on her and England.

A battery is any intentional and unpermitted contact with the plaintiff's person or anything attached to it. In the area of intentional torts, intent means the defendant either desired to bring about the physical results of his act or believed they were substantially certain to follow from what he did. Mental distress and humiliation in connection with a battery are compensable items of damage.

The totality of the evidence provided a substantial basis for the trial judge to conclude Garley must have been substantially certain the hamburger would hit England or splatter on her when he threw it toward her. His contact with her was, therefore, intentional and unpermitted and constituted a battery.

Judgment for England affirmed.

False Imprisonment

The tort of **false imprisonment** protects the personal interest in freedom from *confinement*. False imprisonment is the intentional *confinement of another* for an *appreciable time* (a few minutes is enough) *without his consent*. Confinement may result from physical barriers to the plaintiff's freedom of movement, such as locking a person in a room with no other doors or windows, or the use of physical force or the threat to use physical force against the plaintiff. Confinement also results from the assertion of legal authority to detain the plaintiff, or the detention of the plaintiff's property, for example, a purse containing a large sum of money. Likewise, a threat to harm another, such as the plaintiff's spouse or child, can also be confinement if it prevents the plaintiff from moving.

The confinement required for false imprisonment must be *complete*. Partial confinement of another by blocking her path or by depriving her of one means of escape where several exist, such as locking one door of a building having other, unlocked doors, does not amount to false imprisonment. The fact that a means of escape exists, however, does not render a confinement partial if the plaintiff cannot reasonably be expected to know of its existence. The same is true if it involves some unreasonable risk of harm to the plaintiff, such as walking a tightrope or climbing out of a second-story window, or some affront to his sense of personal dignity (e.g., Jones steals Smith's clothes while Smith is swimming in the nude).

The personal interest in freedom from confinement protected by false imprisonment involves a mental element, knowledge of confinement, as well as a physical element, freedom of movement. Therefore, courts generally hold that the plaintiff must have *knowledge* of his confinement before liability for false imprisonment arises. Similarly, liability for false imprisonment does not arise in cases where the person has *consented* to his confinement. Such consent, however, must be freely given; consent in the face of an implied or actual threat of force or an assertion of legal authority by the confiner is not freely given. As the following *Speight* case indicates, many contemporary false imprisonment cases involve shoplifting. The common law held store owners liable for any torts committed while detaining a suspected shoplifter if subsequent investigation revealed that the detainee was innocent of any wrongdoing. In an attempt to accommodate the legitimate interests of store owners in preventing theft of their property, most states have passed statutes giving store owners a *conditional privilege* to stop persons who they reasonably believe are shoplifting. However, the owner must act in a reasonable manner and only detain the suspect for a reasonable length of time. Store owners who act within the scope of such a statute are not liable for any torts committed in the process of detaining a suspected shoplifter.

J. H. HARVEY CO. v. SPEIGHT

344 S.E.2d 701 (Ga. Ct. App. 1986)

Acting upon information that someone had just stolen several cartons of cigarettes from the store, the manager of Harvey's Supermarket stepped outside and approached Speight, who had himself walked out of the store only moments earlier. Upon being asked by the manager if he had anything that did not belong to him, Speight answered, "No, do you want to see?" He then briefly held the sides of his jacket open and let them close, at which point the manager parted the jacket with his hands to see if anything was concealed there. Simultaneously, Speight pointed to another person in the immediate vicinity and said, "I think that is the man you are looking for." The manager then left Speight to pursue this other person. Speight subsequently filed suit against Harvey's for false imprisonment and assault and battery. When a jury awarded him $2,500 in compensatory damages and $30,000 in punitive damages, Harvey's appealed.

Banke, Chief Judge. Speight testified that the store manager had not been rude to him but stated that he did not consider the manager's conduct in looking inside his jacket as courteous. He admitted that he had invited this search and that the manager had not cursed him nor spoken loudly to him; however, he testified that he felt the manager was angry because of the look in his eyes and the fact that several people had followed the manager out of the store. At trial, Speight testified that the entire encounter had lasted about 45 seconds, whereas during an earlier deposition he had testified that the encounter lasted between 15 and 30 seconds.

According to *Prosser, Law of Torts* (4th ed.), in false imprisonment:

"[T]he imprisonment need not be for more than an appreciable length of time, and . . . it is not necessary that any damage result from it other than the confinement itself, since the tort is complete with even a brief restraint of the plaintiff's freedom. . . . It is essential, however, that the restraint be against the plaintiff's will, and if he agrees of his own free choice to surrender his freedom of motion, as by remaining in a room or accompanying the defendant voluntarily, to clear himself of suspicion or to accommodate the desires of another, rather than yielding to the constraint of a threat, then there is no imprisonment."

Speight's testimony in this case fails to establish any involuntary restraint by Harvey's store manager or employees. Although a person need not make an effort to escape or await application of open force before he can recover, there must be restraint whether by force or fear. With regard to the second count of the complaint, Speight admitted that any touching of his person had been invited by him; and such invitation is inconsistent with the torts of assault and battery. The evidence was consequently insufficient to support any recovery.

Judgment reversed in favor of Harvey's.

Defamation

The tort of *defamation* protects the individual's interest in his *reputation*. It recognizes the value that society places on reputation, not only the individual's personal dignity, but also the value that a good reputation has in the individual's business dealings with others. Defamation is ordinarily defined as the unprivileged *publication of false and defamatory statements* concerning another. A defamatory statement is one that harms the reputation of another by injuring his community's estimation of him or by deterring others from associating or dealing with him. Whether an ambiguous statement is defamatory is ordinarily decided by a jury.

Because the primary focus of defamation is to protect the *individual's* right to reputation, an essential element of defamation is that the alleged defamatory statement must be "of and concerning" the plaintiff. That is, the statement must harm the particular plaintiff's reputation. This causes several problems. First, can allegedly fictional accounts such as those found in novels and short stories amount to defamation if the fictional characters bear a substantial resemblance to real persons? Most courts that have dealt with the issue say they can, if a reasonable reader would identify the plaintiff as the subject of the story. Similarly, humorous or satirical accounts ordinarily do not amount to defamation unless a reasonable reader would believe that they purport to describe real events. Likewise, statements of personal opinion are ordinarily not the proper subjects of defamation because they are not statements of fact concerning the plaintiff, unless such statements imply the existence of undisclosed facts that are false and defamatory. Thus, the statement that "Smedley is a lousy governor" would probably not be actionable. However, the statement "I think Irving must be a thief" may be defamatory, because a jury may believe that the statement implies that its maker knows facts that justify this opinion.

What about defamatory statements concerning particular groups of persons? The courts generally hold that an individual member of a defamed group cannot recover for damage to her personal reputation unless the group is so small that the statement can reasonably be understood as referring to specific members. This is also true when the circumstances in which the statement is made are such that it is reasonable to conclude that a particular group member is being referred to. So, the statement that "all Germans are thieves," standing alone, would not provide the basis for a defamation suit by any person of German descent. However, if Schmidt, a person of German origin, is being considered for a controller's position in her employer's company and a fellow employee makes the same statement in response to a question concerning Schmidt's qualifications for the job, the statement would probably be a proper basis for a defamation suit.

Finally, the courts have placed some limits on the persons or entities that can suffer injury to reputation. For example, it is generally held that no liability attaches to defamatory statements concerning the dead. Corporations and other business entities have a limited right to reputation and can file suit for defamatory statements that harm them in conducting their business or deter others from dealing with them. As a general rule, statements about a corporation's officers, employees, or shareholders do not amount to defamation of the corporation unless such statements also reflect on the manner in which the corporation conducts its business. Statements concerning the quality of a corporation's products or the quality of its title to land or other property may be the basis of an *injurious falsehood* suit.[1]

Publication   The elements of the tort of defamation require *publication* of a defamatory statement before liability for defamation arises. This requirement can be misleading because, as a general rule, no widespread communication of a defamatory statement is required for publication. Communication of the defamatory statement to *one person* other than the person defamed is ordinarily sufficient for publication. Making a defamatory statement about a person in a personal conversation with him or in a private letter sent to him does not, therefore, satisfy the publication requirement. In addition, the courts generally hold that one who repeats or republishes a defamatory statement is liable for defamation, regardless of whether he identifies the source of the statement.

Libel and Slander   The courts have divided the tort of defamation into two categories, libel and slander, depending on the medium used to communicate the defamatory statement. **Libel** refers to written or printed defamations, or to those that have a physical form, such as a defamatory picture or statue. **Slander** refers to oral defamation. The advent of radio and television initially resulted in some judicial confusion concerning the proper classification of defamatory statements communicated by these new media. Today, the great majority of courts treat broadcast defamations as libel. The distinction between libel and slander is important because the courts have traditionally held that libel, due to its more permanent nature and the seriousness that we tend to attach to the written word, is actionable without any proof of special damage (the loss of anything of monetary value) to the plaintiff. Slander, however, is generally not actionable without proof of special damage, unless the nature of the slanderous statement is so serious that it can be classified as *slander per se*. In slander per se, injury to the plaintiff's reputation is presumed. Four defamatory statements ordinarily qualify for per se treatment: allegations that the plaintiff has committed a crime involving moral turpitude or potential imprisonment, that he has a loathsome disease (usually a venereal disease or leprosy), that he is professionally incompetent or guilty of professional misconduct, or that he is guilty of serious sexual misconduct.

Defamation and the Constitution   Nowhere is the social balancing task of tort law more obvious than in cases of defamation. Overzealous protection of individual reputation could result in an infringement of our constitutionally protected freedoms of speech and of the press, and thereby inhibit the free flow of information necessary to a free society. In recent years, the Supreme Court has balanced these conflicting social interests in a series of important cases that define the amount of protection the Constitution affords to otherwise defamatory statements. Under the common law, defendants were

---

[1] The Intellectual Property, Competitive Torts, and Unfair Competition chapter discusses injurious falsehood in detail.

strictly liable (liable without fault) for defamatory statements. In *New York Times v. Sullivan*, however, the Court held that *public officials* seeking to recover for defamatory statements relating to performance of their official duties must prove *actual malice* (knowledge of falsity or reckless disregard for the truth) on the part of a media defendant to recover any damages.[2] This significant limitation on public officials' right to reputation was justified largely by the public interest in "free and unfettered debate" on important social issues.

For similar reasons, the Court subsequently extended the actual malice test to *public figures*, that is, persons in the public eye because of their celebrity status or because they have voluntarily involved themselves in matters of public controversy.[3] Then, in *Gertz v. Robert Welch, Inc.*, the Court refused to extend the actual malice test to media defamation of private citizens who involuntarily become involved in matters of public concern.[4] Instead, the Court held that to recover compensatory damages such persons must prove some degree of fault at least amounting to negligence on the part of the defendant and that to recover punitive damages they must prove actual malice. Most recent was *Dun & Bradstreet, Inc. v. Greenmoss Builders, Inc.*, a case involving a private figure plaintiff—a construction contractor—and defamatory speech about a matter of purely private concern—a false credit report.[5] The Court refused to apply the *Gertz* standard and upheld a recovery based on the common law strict liability standard.

The amount of protection the Constitution affords to otherwise defamatory statements appears to depend on two factors: whether the plaintiff is a public figure/official or private person and whether the subject matter of the speech at issue is a matter of public concern or private concern. The Court has yet to speak definitively on the standard that it will apply to cases involving defamatory statements about private matters concerning public figures and officials. Its decisions to date, however, suggest that the *Gertz* test is likely to be applied to such cases.

Defenses to Defamation   *Truth* is an absolute defense to defamation. The tort of defamation requires that a statement serving as the basis of a defamation suit be *false* as well as defamatory.

Even where defamatory statements are false, a defense of *privilege* may serve to prevent liability in some cases. The idea of privilege recognizes the fact that, in some circumstances, other social interests may be more important than an individual's right to reputation. Privileges are either *absolute* or *conditional*. Absolute privileges shield the author of a defamatory statement regardless of her knowledge, motive, or intent. Absolutely privileged statements include those made by participants in judicial proceedings, by legislators or witnesses in the course of legislative proceedings, by certain executive officials in the course of their official duties, and by spouses in private. Conditional privileges are conditioned on their proper use. One who *abuses* a conditional privilege by making a defamatory statement with the knowledge that it is false, or in reckless disregard of the truth, loses the protection afforded by the privilege. Conditional privileges are abused when the author of a defamatory statement acts with an improper motive, such as a purpose other than protecting the interests justifying the privilege. The author can also exceed the scope of the privilege by communicating the defamation unnecessarily to third persons who do not share his interests. Conditional privileges are often recognized when the author of a defamatory statement acts to protect her own legitimate interests or those of a third person with whom she shares some interest or to whom she owes some duty.

In recent years, the courts have also begun to recognize a conditional privilege of "fair comment." This privilege protects fair and accurate media reports of defamatory matter in reports or proceedings of official action or originating from public meetings. The privilege is justified by the public's right to know what occurs in such proceedings and meetings. The conditional privilege most important to business, however, is the traditional privilege enjoyed by employers who provide prospective employers with reference letters about former employees. Despite this privilege, employers in recent years have faced a growing number of defamation claims from disgruntled former employees. As a result, many companies as a matter of policy refuse to divulge any information about former employees other than to confirm that they did work for the company at one time and the duration of their employment. However, as the following *Lewis* case indicates, even such a policy does not always shield employers from liability.

---

[2] 376 U.S. 254 (U.S. Sup. Ct. 1964).

[3] *Curtis Publishing Co. v. Butts*, 388 U.S. 130 (U.S. Sup. Ct. 1967).

[4] 418 U.S. 323 (U.S. Sup. Ct. 1974).

[5] 472 U.S. 749 (U.S. Sup. Ct. 1985).

LEWIS v. EQUITABLE LIFE ASSURANCE SOCIETY

389 N.W. 2d 876 (Minn. Sup. Ct. 1986)

Carole Lewis, Mary Smith, Michelle Rafferty, and Suzanne Loizeaux were employed as dental claim approvers in the St. Paul, Minnesota, office of the Equitable Life Assurance Society of the United States. In October of 1980 they were sent to assist in Equitable's Pittsburgh office. None of the women had ever traveled on company business before, and they departed for Pittsburgh without being given copies of Equitable's travel expense policies or being told that expense reports would have to be filed. Instead, they were verbally given information on Equitable's daily meal and maid tip allowances and told to keep receipts for hotel bills and airfare. In addition, each was given a $1,400 travel allowance which, having no instruction to the contrary, they spent in full.

When they returned to St. Paul, each of the women received a personal letter from management commending her on her job performance in Pittsburgh. Each was also told for the first time that she would have to submit expense reports detailing her daily expenses in Pittsburgh. This they did, but a dispute subsequently arose over the amount of allowable expenses because Equitable's written guidelines differed from the instructions they had received prior to departure. After first changing their reports with respect to maid tips, they were asked to change their reports again, the net effect of which would have been to obligate each employee to return approximately $200 to Equitable. They refused to do this, arguing that the expenses shown on their reports were honestly incurred, a claim that Equitable never disputed. Subsequently, the women were fired for "gross insubordination."

In seeking new jobs, each woman was asked by prospective employers why she had left Equitable, and each said she had been terminated. When asked in interviews to explain their terminations, each stated that she had been terminated for gross insubordination and attempted to explain the situation. Only one of the women found a new job by being forthright with a prospective employer about her termination from Equitable. The others had various difficulties finding new jobs. They filed a defamation suit against Equitable, and when a jury ruled in their favor, Equitable appealed.

Amdahl, Chief Justice.   In order for a statement to be considered defamatory, it must be communicated to someone other than the plaintiff, it must be false, and it must tend to harm the plaintiff's reputation. Generally, there is no publication where a defendant communicates a statement directly to a plaintiff, who then communicates it to a third person. Plaintiffs themselves informed prospective employers that they had been terminated for gross insubordination. They did so because prospective employers inquired why they had left their previous employment. The question raised is whether a defendant can ever be held liable for defamation when the statement in question was published to a third person only by the plaintiff.

We have not previously been presented with the question of defamation by means of "self-publication." Courts that have considered the question, however, have recognized a narrow exception to the general rule that communication of a defamatory statement to a third person by the person defamed is not actionable. These courts have recognized that if a defamed person was in some way compelled to communicate the defamatory statement to a third person, and if it was foreseeable to the defendant that the defamed person would be so compelled, then the defendant could be held liable for the defamation.

Several courts have specifically recognized this exception for compelled self-publication in the context of employment discharges. The trend of modern authority persuades us that Minnesota law should recognize the doctrine. Compelled self-publication does no more than hold the originator of the defamatory statement liable for damages caused by the statement where the originator knows, or should know, of circumstances whereby the defamed person has no reasonable means of avoiding publication of the statement or avoiding the resulting damages. In such circumstances, the damages are fairly viewed as the direct result of the originator's actions.

The St. Paul office manager admitted that it was foreseeable that plaintiffs would be asked by prospective employers to identify the reason that they were discharged. Their only choice would be to tell them "gross insubordination" or to lie. Fabrication, however, is an unacceptable alternative.

Finding that there was a publication, we next turn to the issue of truth. True statements, however disparaging, are not actionable. The company contends the relevant statement to consider when analyzing the defense of truth is the one that plaintiffs made to their prospective employers, that is, that they had been fired for gross insubordination. Plaintiffs counter that it is the truth or falsity of the underlying statement—that they engaged in gross insubordination—that is relevant.

Requiring that truth as a defense go to the underlying implication of the statement, at least where the statement involves more than a simple allegation, appears to be the better view. Here, the company's charges against plaintiffs went beyond accusations and were conclusory statements that plaintiffs had engaged in gross insubordination. The record amply supports the jury verdict that the charge of gross insubordination was false. Even though an untrue defamatory statement has been published, the originator of the statement will not be held liable if the statement is published under circumstances that make it conditionally privileged and if privilege is not abused. The doctrine of privileged communication rests upon public policy considerations. The existence of a privilege results from the court's determination that statements made in particular contexts or on certain occasions should be encouraged despite the risk that the statements might be defamatory.

In the context of employment recommendations, the law generally recognizes a qualified privilege between former and prospective employers as long as the statements are made in good faith and for a legitimate purpose. Plaintiffs argue that a self-publication case does not properly fit within the qualified privilege doctrine, but the logic of imposing liability upon a former employer in a self-publication case appears to compel recognition of a qualified privilege. A former employer in a compelled self-publication case may be held liable as if it had actually published the defamatory statement directly to prospective employers. Where an employer would be entitled to a privilege if it had actually published the statement, it makes little sense to deny the privilege where the identical communication is made to identical third parties with the only difference being the mode of publication. Finally, recognition of a qualified privilege seems to be the only effective means of addressing the concern that every time an employer states the reason for discharging an employee it will subject itself to potential liability for defamation. It is in the public interest that information regarding an employee's discharge be readily available to the discharged employee and to prospective employers, and we are concerned that, unless a significant privilege is recognized by the courts, employers will decline to inform employees of reasons for discharges.

This conclusion does not necessarily determine that the company's statements were privileged. A qualified privilege is abused and therefore lost if the plaintiff demonstrates that the defendant acted with actual malice. The jury found that the company's statements were "actuated by actual malice."

Judgment for the plaintiffs affirmed.

Invasion of Privacy

The recognition of a personal *right of privacy* is a relatively recent development in tort law. At present, four distinct behaviors provide a proper basis for an invasion of privacy suit: (1) intrusion on a person's solitude or seclusion, (2) public disclosure of private facts concerning a person, (3) publicity placing a person in a false light in the public eye, and (4) appropriation of a person's name or likeness for commercial purposes. The thread tying these different behaviors together is that they all infringe on a person's "right to be let alone."

Intrusion on Solitude   Any intentional intrusion on the solitude or seclusion of another constitutes an invasion of privacy if that intrusion would be highly offensive to a reasonable individual. The intrusion in question may be physical, such as illegal searches of a person's home or body or the opening of his mail. It may also be a nonphysical intrusion such as tapping his telephone, examining his bank account, or subjecting him to harassing telephone calls. As a general rule, no liability attaches to examining public records concerning a person, or observing or photographing him in a public place, because a person does not have a reasonable expectation of privacy in these instances.

Publicity Concerning Private Facts   Publicizing facts concerning a person's private life can be an invasion of privacy if their publicity would be highly offensive to a reasonable person. The idea is that the public has no legitimate right to know certain aspects of a person's private life. Thus, publicity concerning a person's failure to pay his debts, humiliating illnesses that he has suffered, and details concerning his sex life constitute an invasion of privacy. Truth is *not* a defense to this type of invasion of privacy, because the essence of the tort is giving unjustified publicity to purely private matters. Publicity in this context means a widespread dissemination of private details.

This variant of invasion of privacy, similiar to the tort of defamation, represents a potential source of conflict with the constitutionally protected freedoms of the press and of speech. The courts have attempted to accommodate these conflicting social interests in several ways. First, no liability ordinarily attaches to publicity concerning matters of public record or of legitimate public interest. Second, public figures and public officials have no right of privacy concerning information that is reasonably related to their public lives.

False Light   Publicity that places a person in a *false light* in the public eye can be an invasion of privacy if that false light would be highly offensive to a reasonable person. This variant of invasion of privacy may in some cases also involve defamation. As in defamation cases, truth is an absolute defense to liability. For liability for invasion of privacy to arise, however, it is not necessary that a person be defamed by the false light in which he is placed. All that is required is unreasonable and highly objectionable publicity attributing to a person characteristics that he does not possess or beliefs that he does not hold. Signing a person's name to a public telegram or letter without her consent or attributing authorship of an inferior scholarly or artistic work to her are examples of this form of invasion of privacy. Because of the overlap between this form of invasion of privacy and defamation, and the obvious First Amendment issues at stake, defendants in false light cases enjoy constitutional protection similar to that enjoyed by defamation defendants.

Appropriation of Name or Likeness   Some of the earliest invasion of privacy cases involved the appropriation of a person's name or likeness for commercial purposes without his consent. Liability for invasion of privacy can be created by using a person's name or image in an advertisement to imply his endorsement of a product or service or a nonexistent connection with the person or business placing the ad. This variant of invasion of privacy differs markedly from those previously discussed in that it recognizes the personal property right connected with a person's identity and that he has the exclusive right to its control.

The potential for conflict between this property right and the freedoms of speech and of the press has been illustrated in recent years by cases involving public figures' *right of publicity*, such as the following *Midler* case. To what extent do public persons have the right to control the use of their names, likenesses, or other matters associated with their identities? For example, should a well-known movie star have the right to prevent the writing of a book about her life or the televising of a docudrama about her? At this point, the scope of a public person's right of publicity varies greatly from state to state; considerable disagreement exists concerning such issues as its duration and inheritability.

Other Limitations   In addition to the various limitations on the right of privacy discussed earlier, two further limits are applicable to invasion of privacy actions. First, with the exception in some states of cases involving the appropriation of a person's name or likeness, the right of privacy is a purely *personal* right. This means that only living individuals whose personal privacy has been invaded can bring suit for invasion of privacy. Therefore, family members of a person exposed to publicity ordinarily cannot maintain an invasion of privacy action unless their personal privacy has also been violated. Second, corporations and other business organiza- tions generally have no personal right of privacy. They do, however, have limited rights associated with the use of their names and identities. These rights are protected by the law of unfair competition.[6]

---

[6] The Intellectual Property, Competitive Torts, and Unfair Competition chapter discusses this subject in detail.

MIDLER v. FORD MOTOR CO.
849 F.2d 460 (9th Cir. 1988)

In 1985, Ford Motor Company and its advertising agency, Young & Rubicam, Inc., ran a series of 19 television commercials in what the agency called "The Yuppie Campaign." The aim was to make an emotional connection with Yuppies, bringing back memories of their college days. Different pop songs of the 70s were sung on each commercial, and the agency tried to get the original artists to sing the songs. One of the songs selected was "Do You Want to Dance," a song from Bette Midler's 1973 album, "The Divine Miss M." The agency acquired a license from the copyright holder to use the song, but Midler refused to do the commercial.

The agency then hired a former backup singer for Midler to record the commercial, instructing her to "sound as much as possible like the Bette Midler record." After the commercial was aired, a number of people told Midler that it "sounded exactly" like her recording. Midler filed suit against Ford and Young & Rubicam. The trial judge described the defendants' conduct as that "of the average thief" who decided, "If we can't buy it, we'll take it." Nonetheless, he granted summary judgment for the defendants because he believed no legal principle prevented the imitation of Midler's voice. Midler appealed.

Noonan, Circuit Judge.   The First Amendment protects much of what the media do in the reproduction of likenesses or sounds. A primary value is freedom of speech and press. The purpose of the media's use of a person's identity is central. If the purpose is informative and cultural, the use is immune; if it serves no such function but merely exploits the individual portrayed, immunity will not be granted.

Moreover, federal copyright law preempts much of the area. Mere imitation of a recorded performance would not constitute a copyright infringement even where one performer deliber- ately sets out to simulate another's performance as exactly as possible. Midler does not seek damages for Ford's use of "Do You Want to Dance," and thus her claim is not preempted by copyright law. Copyright protects "original works of authorship fixed in any tangible medium of expression." A voice is not copyrightable. What is put forward as protectible here is more personal than any work of authorship.

In *Motschenbacher v. R.J. Reynolds Tobacco Co.* (1974) the defendants used in the television commercial for Winston cigarettes a photograph of a famous racing driver's car. The number of the car was changed and a "spoiler" was attached to the car; the car's features of white pinpoint- ing, an oval medallion, and solid red coloring were retained. The driver, Lothar Motschenbacher, was in the car but his features were not visible. Some persons, viewing the commercial, correctly inferred that the car was his and that he was in the car and was therefore endorsing the product. The defendants were held to have invaded a proprietary interest of Motschenbacher in his own identity.

Midler's case is different from Motschenbacher's. He and his car were physically used by the tobacco company's ad; he made part of his living out of giving commercial endorsements. But, as Judge Koelsch expressed it in *Motschenbacher*, California will recognize an injury from "an appropriation of the attributes of one's identity." It was irrelevant that Motschenbacher could not be identified in the ad. The ad suggested that it was he. The ad did so by emphasizing signs or symbols associated with him. In the same way the defendants here used an imitation to convey the impression that Midler was singing for them.

Why did they ask Midler to sing if her voice was not of value to them? Why did they studiously acquire the services of a sound-alike and instruct her to imitate Midler if Midler's voice was not of value to them? What they sought was an attribute of Midler's identity. Its value was what the market would have paid for Midler to have sung the commercial in person.

A voice is more distinctive and more personal than the automobile protected in *Motschenbacher*. A voice is as distinctive and personal as a face. The human voice is one of the most palpable ways identity is manifested. We are all aware that a friend is at once known by a few words on the phone. These observations hold true of singing, especially singing by a singer of renown. The singer manifests herself in the song. To impersonate her voice is to pirate her identity.

We need not and do not go so far as to hold that every imitation of a voice to advertise merchandise is actionable. We hold only that when a distinctive voice of a professional singer is widely known and is deliberately imitated in order to sell a product, the sellers have appropriated what is not theirs and have committed a tort in California.

Summary judgment against Midler reversed; case remanded for trial.

Infliction of Emotional Distress

For many years, the courts refused to allow recovery for purely emotional injuries in the absence of some other tort. Thus, victims of such torts as assault, battery, and false imprisonment could recover for the emotional injuries resulting from these torts, but the courts were unwilling to recognize an independent tort of infliction of emotional distress. The reasons for this judicial reluctance included a fear of spurious or trivial claims, concerns about the difficulty in proving purely emotional harms, and uncertainty concerning the proper boundaries of an independent tort of intentional infliction of emotional distress. Recent advances in medical knowledge concerning emotional injuries, however, have helped to overcome some of these judicial impediments. Today, most courts allow recovery for *severe* emotional distress regardless of whether the elements of any other tort are proven.

The courts are not, however, in complete agreement on the elements of this new tort. All courts require that a wrongdoer's conduct must be *outrageous* before liability for emotional distress arises. The *Restatement (Second) of Torts* speaks of conduct "so outrageous in character, and so extreme in degree as to go beyond all possible bounds of decency, and to be regarded as atrocious and utterly intolerable in a civilized community."[7] Some courts, however, still fear fictitious claims and require proof of some bodily harm resulting from the victim's emotional distress. The courts also differ in the extent to which they allow recovery for emotional distress suffered as a result of witnessing outrageous conduct directed at persons other than the plaintiff. The *Restatement (Second) of Torts* suggests that persons be allowed to recover for severe emotional distress resulting from witnessing outrageous behavior toward a member of their immediate family.[8] Where the third person is not a member of the plaintiff's immediate family, the *Restatement (Second)* restricts liability to severe emotional distress that results in some bodily harm.[9]

The tendency to expand the circumstances in which recovery for intentional infliction of emotional distress

---

[7]*Restatement (Second) of Torts* § 46, comment *d* (1965).

[8]*Restatement (Second) of Torts* § 46(2)(a) (1965).

[9]*Restatement (Second) of Torts* § 46(2)(b) (1965).

will be allowed is a matter of growing concern for business because in recent years a number of emotional distress claims have been filed by employees who have been discharged or required to take drug tests. As the *Ford* case that follows indicates, sexual harassment cases can also give rise to emotional distress claims.

FORD v. REVLON, INC.
734 P.2d 580 (Ariz. Sup. Ct. 1987)

Leta Fay Ford's supervisor in the purchasing department of Revlon, Inc., Karl Braun, made numerous sexual advances toward her. At Revlon's annual service awards picnic on May 3, 1980, Braun grabbed Ford, restrained her in a chokehold with his right arm, and ran his hand over her breasts, stomach, and crotch. Later in May, Ford began a series of meetings with various members of Revlon management to report her complaints about Braun, who continued to verbally harass her. Despite the fact that Ford spoke with numerous persons at Revlon, no action was taken until nine months after her first complaint, when a meeting was held in the personnel office. Ford submitted a handwritten complaint about Braun's actions, asked for protection from him, and said she was collapsing emotionally and physically due to Braun's actions. Braun was called in and confronted, and Ford was told that he would be closely monitored.

Three months later, Revlon's personnel director submitted a report confirming Ford's charges and recommending that Braun be censured. One month later, Revlon gave Braun a letter of censure. During the time of the harassment, Ford developed high blood pressure, a nervous tic in her left eye, chest pains, rapid breathing, and other symptoms of emotional stress. Four months after Braun's censure, Ford attempted suicide. Later, Ford filed suit against Revlon for intentional infliction of emotional distress. When a jury ruled in her favor, Revlon appealed.

Cameron, Justice.   The *Restatement* states that the tort of emotional distress inflicted intentionally or recklessly is recognized as a separate and distinct basis of tort liability. There is no need to show elements of other torts such as assault and battery. A comment to section 46 states that there is liability:

where the conduct has been so outrageous in character, and so extreme in degree, as to go beyond all possible bounds of decency, and to be regarded as atrocious, and utterly intolerable in a civilized community . . . in which . . . an average member of the community would . . . exclaim, "Outrageous!"

Intentional infliction of emotional distress is often based upon claims of sexual harassment. The failure of an employer to promptly investigate complaints of sexual harassment is significant in making a determination to impose liability on an employer for its supervisors' acts of sexual harassment.

The three required elements of intentional infliction of emotional distress are: *first*, the conduct by the defendant must be "extreme" and "outrageous"; *second*, the defendant must either intend to cause emotional distress or recklessly disregard the near certainty that such distress will result from his conduct; and *third*, severe emotional distress must indeed occur as a result of defendant's conduct.

We believe that the conduct of Revlon met these requirements. First, Revlon's conduct can be classified as extreme or outrageous. Ford did everything that could be done, both within the announced policies of Revlon and without, to bring this matter to Revlon's attention. Revlon ignored her and the situation she faced, dragging the matter out for months and leaving Ford without redress.

Second, even if Revlon did not intend to cause emotional distress, Revlon's reckless disregard of Braun's conduct made it nearly certain that such emotional distress would in fact occur. Revlon knew that Braun had subjected Ford to physical assaults, vulgar remarks, that Ford continued to feel threatened by Braun, and that Ford was emotionally distraught, all of which led to a manifestation of physical problems. Despite Ford's complaints, Braun was not confronted for nine months, and then only upon *Ford's* demand for a group meeting. Another three months elapsed before Braun was censured. Revlon not only had actual knowledge of the situation but it also failed to conduct promptly any investigation of Ford's complaint.

Third, it is obvious that emotional distress did occur. Ample evidence, both medical and otherwise, was presented describing Ford's emotional distress.

We also note that Revlon had a specific policy and several guidelines for the handling of sexual harassment claims and other employee complaints, yet Revlon recklessly disregarded these policies and guidelines. Ford was entitled to rely on the policy statements made by Revlon. Once an employer proclaims a policy, the employer may not treat the policy as illusory.

Judgment for Ford affirmed.

Misuse of Legal Proceedings

Three intentional tort theories protect persons against the harm that can result from wrongfully instituted legal proceedings. **Malicious prosecution** affords a remedy for the financial and emotional harm, and the injury to reputation, that can result when *criminal* proceedings are wrongfully brought against a person. This tort balances society's interest in efficient enforcement of the criminal law against the individual's interest in freedom from unjustified criminal prosecutions. A plaintiff seeking to recover for malicious prosecution must prove *both* that the defendant *acted maliciously*, that is, without probable cause to believe that an offense had been committed and for an improper purpose, and that the criminal proceedings were *terminated in the plaintiff's favor*. As a general rule, proof that the defendant acted in good faith on the advice of legal counsel, after fully disclosing the relevant facts, conclusively establishes probable cause. Also, proof of the plaintiff's guilt is generally held to be a complete defense to liability, and the issue of his guilt can be retried in the malicious prosecution suit, despite his acquittal in the criminal proceedings. Proof of the plaintiff's innocence, however, cannot support a malicious prosecution action if the criminal proceedings were not terminated in his favor.

The tort of **wrongful use of civil proceedings** is similar to malicious prosecution, but is designed to protect persons from wrongfully instituted *civil* suits. Its elements are very similar to those of malicious prosecution: It requires proof that the civil proceedings were initiated without probable cause and for an improper purpose and proof that the suit was terminated in favor of the person sued.

The tort of **abuse of process** imposes liability on those who initiate legal proceedings for a primary purpose other than the one for which such proceedings are designed. Abuse of process cases normally involve situations in which the legal proceedings compel the other person to take some action unrelated to the subject of the suit. For example, Rogers wishes to buy Herbert's property, but Herbert refuses to sell. To pressure him into selling, Rogers files a nuisance suit against Herbert contending that Herbert's activities on his land interfere with Rogers' use and enjoyment of his adjoining property. Rogers may be liable to Herbert for abuse of process despite the fact that he had probable cause to file the suit and regardless of whether he wins the suit.

Deceit (Fraud)

Deceit is the formal name of the tort action for damages that is available to victims of knowing misrepresentation, often called *fraud*. The elements of deceit are a false statement of material fact, knowingly made by the defendant, with the intent to induce reliance by the plaintiff, justifiable reliance by the plaintiff, and harm to the plaintiff due to his reliance. The second element, technically called *scienter*, separates deceit from other forms of misrepresentation. Scienter is present only when the maker of a statement believes it is untrue, doesn't believe it is the truth, or recklessly disregards its truth. So, neither negligent nor innocent misrepresentations can serve as the basis for a deceit action.[10] Because most deceit actions arise in a contractual setting, and because a tort action for deceit is only one of the remedies available to a victim of fraud, a fuller discussion of this topic is deferred until the Reality of Consent chapter.

INTERFERENCE WITH PROPERTY RIGHTS

Nature of Property Rights

The rights associated with the acquisition and use of property have traditionally occupied an important position in our legal system. Tortious interference with property rights is generally treated as an offense against the right to *possession*. Therefore, where the party entitled to possession is not the same as the owner of the property in question (e.g., a tenant leasing property from its owner), the party entitled to possession is ordinarily the proper person to file suit for interference with his possessory rights. If the interference also results in lasting damage to the property, however, its owner may also have a right to recover for such damage.

Trespass to Land

A person is liable for **trespass** if he (1) intentionally and unlawfully enters land in the possession of another, (2) unlawfully remains on such land after entering lawfully, such as a tenant who refuses to move at the end of a lease,

---

[10] The Legal Responsibilities of Accountants chapter discusses negligent misrepresentation as an important basis of professional liability for accountants. Innocent misrepresentations can sometimes serve as a defense to the enforcement of a contract. The Reality of Consent chapter discusses this aspect of misrepresentation in detail.

(3) unlawfully causes anything to enter such land, or (4) fails to remove anything that he has a duty to remove from such land. No actual harm to the land is required for liability for intentional trespasses, but actual harm is required for liability for reckless or negligent trespasses. In addition, a person can be liable for trespass even though the trespass resulted from his mistaken belief that his entry was legally justified. This could arise from a belief that he had a right to possess the land, had the consent of the party entitled to possession, or had some other legal right or privilege entitling him to enter.

Nuisance

Unlawful and unreasonable interferences with another person's right to the use or enjoyment of his land are called **nuisances.** Nuisance suits, unlike trespass actions, do not necessarily involve any physical invasion of a person's property. Noise, vibration, and unpleasant odors are all examples of things that could be nuisances but would not justify a trespass action. In nuisance suits, the courts attempt to balance the competing interests of landowners to use their land as they see fit. Nuisance law recognizes an unfortunate fact of life: To preserve freedom, it must be limited. Put another way, my free use of my property may destroy your enjoyment of yours. For example, should I be able to open a solid waste disposal plant next to your restaurant? The law of nuisance attempts to resolve such perplexing issues.[11] As the following *Borland* case illustrates, it is sometimes very difficult to distinguish between nuisance and trespass.

---

[11] The Real Property and Insurance chapter discusses nuisances in detail.

BORLAND v. SANDERS LEAD CO.

369 So. 2d 523 (Ala. Sup. Ct. 1979)

In 1968, Sanders Lead Company started an operation for recovering lead from used automobile batteries on property near 159 acres of farmland owned by J. H. and Sarah Borland. Sanders's smelter, which reduced plates from batteries, was located on the part of Sanders's land that was closest to the Borlands' property. The Borlands argued that, despite the fact that the smelter was equipped with a filter system designed to reduce lead particulate emissions, their property had been damaged by a dangerous accumulation of lead particulates and sulfoxide deposits from the smelter. They filed a trespass suit against Sanders. When the trial judge ruled in Sanders's favor, the Borlands appealed.

Jones, Justice.   In *Rushing v. Hooper-McDonald, Inc.* (1974), this Court held that a trespass need not be inflicted directly on another's realty, but may be committed by discharging foreign polluting matter at a point beyond the boundary of such realty. *Rushing* specifically held that a trespass is committed by one who knowingly discharges asphalt in such a manner that it will in due course invade a neighbor's realty and cause harm. *Rushing* further cited with approval the case of *Martin v. Reynolds Metals Co.* (Or. 1959). In *Martin*, a case remarkably similar to the present case, the plaintiffs alleged that the operation by defendants of an aluminum reduction plant caused certain fluoride compounds in the form of gases and particulates, invisible to the naked eye, to become airborne and settle on plaintiffs' property, rendering it unfit for raising livestock.

The defendants in *Martin* contended that there had not been a sufficient invasion of plaintiffs' property to constitute trespass, but at most, defendants' acts constituted a nuisance. This would have allowed the defendants to set up Oregon's two-year statute of limitations applicable to non-possessory injuries to land rather than Oregon's six-year statute for trespass to land. The *Martin* Court pointed out that trespass and nuisance are separate torts for the protection of different interests invaded—trespass protecting the possessor's interest in exclusive possession of property and nuisance protecting the interest in use and enjoyment. The Court noted, and we agree, that the same conduct on the part of a defendant may, and often does, result in the actionable invasion of both interests.

In the traditional sense, the law of nuisance applies where the invasion results in no substantial damage to the land, but where there is interference with the use and enjoyment of one's property. The classic cases of the barking dog, the neighboring bawdy house, noise, smoke, fumes, or obnoxious odors generally invoke the law of nuisance. These intrusions are not relegated to the nuisance remedy simply because of their indirect nature; rather, they do not constitute a trespass because all of the requisite elements of trespass to land are not present.

For an indirect invasion to amount to an actionable trespass, there must be an interference with plaintiff's exclusive possessory interest; that is, through the defendant's intentional conduct, and with reasonable foreseeability, some substance has entered upon the land itself, affecting its nature and character, and causing substantial actual damage to it. For example, if the smoke or polluting substance emitting from a defendant's operation causes discomfort and annoyance to the plaintiff in his use and employment of the property, then the plaintiff's remedy is for nuisance; but if, as a result of the defendant's operation, the polluting substance is deposited upon the plaintiff's property, thus interfering with his exclusive possessory interest by causing substantial damage to the property, then the plaintiff may seek his remedy in trespass.

It might appear from our holding today that every property owner in this State would have a cause of action against any neighboring industry which emitted particulate matter into the atmosphere, or even a passing motorist, whose exhaust emissions come to rest upon another's property. But we hasten to point out that there is a point where the entry is so lacking in substance that the law will refuse to recognize it, applying the maxim *de minimis non curat lex*—the law does not concern itself with trifles. In the present case, however, we are not faced with a trifling complaint. The Borlands have suffered a real and substantial invasion of a protected interest.

Judgment reversed in favor of the Borlands.

Trespass to Personal Property

Any intentional intermeddling with personal property in the possession of another is a trespass if it (1) results in harm to that property (e.g., Franks strikes Goode's dog or throws paint on his car), or (2) deprives the party entitled to possession of its use for an appreciable time (e.g., Franks hides Goode's car and Goode cannot find it for several hours).

Conversion

Conversion is the intentional exercise of dominion or control over another's property. To amount to conversion, the defendant's actions must be such a serious interference with another's right to control the property that they justify requiring the defendant to pay damages for the full value of the property. The difference between conversion and trespass to personal property is based on the *degree* of interference with another's property rights. In considering whether an interference with another's property amounts to its conversion, the courts consider such factors as the extent of the harm done to the property, the extent and duration of the interference with the other's right to control the property, and whether the defendant acted in good faith. For example, Sharp goes to Friendly Motors and asks to test-drive a new Ford Thunderbird. If Sharp either wrecks the car, causing major damage, or drives it across the United States, he is probably liable for conversion and obligated to pay Friendly Motors the reasonable value of the car. On the other hand, if Sharp is merely involved in a fender bender, or keeps the car for eight hours, he is probably only liable for trespass. Therefore, he is only obligated to pay damages to compensate Friendly for the loss in value of the car or for its loss of use of the car.

Evolving Concepts of Tort Liability

Recent developments indicate a continuing tendency to expand the scope of tort law as society recognizes an increasing range of personal interests that deserve legal protection. For example, recent cases have recognized the right of fired employees to recover against their employers for a new tort of *wrongful* or *abusive discharge*.[12] Also, some courts have allowed plaintiffs to recover punitive damages in tort suits arising out of a defendant's bad faith breach of contract,[13] and employee drug testing programs have spawned a number of claims against employers on intentional tort theories such as defamation, intentional infliction of emotional distress, and invasion of privacy.

Finally, plaintiffs in so-called toxic tort suits, mass actions seeking to recover for a variety of injuries resulting from exposure to toxic substances, are currently attempting to employ novel tort theories to support their claims. Should persons exposed to carcinogenic substances be able to recover for the emotional distress caused by the fear that they may contract cancer in the future? Should employees whose employers knowingly expose them to such substances in the workplace be allowed to sue their employers for damages in tort that would not be recoverable under their state's workers' compensation statute? All of these examples illustrate the dynamic nature of our legal system in general and of tort law in particular. Given the historical development of tort law, one can reasonably expect that as growing technical knowledge or changing social circumstances create the need to protect new personal interests, tort law will evolve to satisfy that need.

Business Torts

Figure 2 summarizes the many and varied interests protected by the intentional tort theories we have discussed in this chapter. Today, courts also recognize a variety of tort actions designed to protect various economic interests. The Intellectual Property, and Competitive Torts, and Unfair Competition chapter discusses these torts in detail.

---

[12] The Employment Law chapter discusses this subject in detail.

[13] The Performance and Remedies chapter discusses this subject in detail.

FIGURE 2   Interests Protected by Tort Law

Interest	Tort Theory
Freedom from harmful/offensive contacts	Battery
Freedom from apprehension of battery	Assault
Freedom from confinement	False imprisonment
Right to reputation	Defamation
Right of privacy	Invasion of privacy
Freedom from disagreeable emotions	Intentional infliction of emotional distress
Freedom from improper criminal proceedings	Malicious prosecution
Freedom from improper civil proceedings	Wrongful use of civil proceedings and abuse of process
Possession and enjoyment of personal property	Trespass and conversion
Possession and enjoyment of real property	Trespass and nuisance
Freedom from knowing misstatements	Deceit

ETHICAL AND PUBLIC POLICY CONCERNS

1. Tort law attempts to protect various individual interests by giving persons whose rights are violated by others the right to sue for money damages. Can monetary awards, however, ever truly compensate persons who have suffered harms such as an invasion of privacy or emotional distress? If not, how do we justify such awards?

2. Safeco Plastics Corporation owns a plant upstream from Morrison's farm. Safeco periodically discharges large amounts of water into the stream, a practice that occasionally results in the flooding of Morrison's property. Assuming that it is cheaper for Safeco to pay damages to Morrison for trespass than it is to take corrective steps to prevent the flooding, is it ethically proper for Safeco to continue to flood Morrison's land?

3. Maxwell is defamed by an article in a local newspaper as a result of careless reporting. When confronted with its error, the paper promptly apologizes and runs an article retracting the defamatory statement. Maxwell has noticed no negative effects from the article, but his lawyer advises him that he would have no trouble proving defamation by the paper and that, as a result, the paper's liability insurance company would probably be eager to settle in the event that Maxwell files suit. Should Maxwell sue?

SUMMARY

The basis of tort liability is a breach of a legal duty owed to another person resulting in a legally recognizable harm to that person. Tort law seeks to compensate injured persons by allowing them to recover money damages for any harm they have suffered. In some cases, tort law also allows injured persons to recover punitive damages in excess of their actual losses. Punitive damages are designed to punish flagrant wrongdoers and to deter them and others from engaging in similar conduct in the future. Tort law involves a constant attempt to balance conflicting social rights and duties. Over time, the law of torts has recognized an expanding number of personal interests deserving of protection. At present, tort law protects a wide variety of personal interests: the right to be free from harmful or offensive bodily contacts (battery), the right to be free from the apprehension of such contacts (assault), the right to reputation (defamation), the right to privacy (invasion of privacy), the right to be free from disagreeable emotions (intentional infliction of emotional distress), and the right to be free from improperly instituted criminal or civil proceedings (malicious prosecution, wrongful use of civil proceedings, and abuse of process).

Intentionally causing a harmful or offensive contact with another can give rise to liability for battery. Causing another to have a reasonable apprehension of an imminent battery constitutes assault. Confining another against his will for an appreciable time can create liability for false imprisonment. The publication of false and defamatory statements about another can result in liability for defamation. Defamation is divided into slander (verbal defamation) and libel (written defamation). Broadcast defamations, whether by radio or television, are normally treated as libels. To balance the individual's right to reputation against the constitutionally protected rights of freedom of speech and of the press, public officials and public figures face higher burdens of proof in defamation suits than do private persons. Also, the law recognizes several other defenses to defamation. Truth is an absolute defense to defamation, and some defamatory statements, though untrue, may be privileged.

The tort of invasion of privacy protects the individual's right to be let alone by imposing liability for four behaviors: intruding on a person's physical solitude or seclusion, publicizing private facts about a person, casting a person in a false light in the public eye, and appropriating a person's name or likeness for commercial purposes. As in the case of defamation, public officials and public figures enjoy narrower privacy rights than do private persons.

Although the courts disagree on the elements of the tort, most courts now recognize an independent tort of intentional infliction of emotional distress. The courts do agree, however, that only outrageous conduct creates liability and that the resulting emotional distress must be severe. Some courts also require some significant bodily harm to the plaintiff as a result of the emotional distress she suffered, but there is a discernible trend in favor of allowing recovery for severe emotional distress standing alone.

The tort of malicious prosecution protects against wrongful initiation of criminal proceedings. Both it and the tort of wrongful use of civil proceedings require that the proceedings in question be initiated without probable cause and that they be terminated in favor of the person wrongfully subjected to them. The tort of abuse of process imposes liability on those who employ legal proceedings for wrongful purposes. Unlike liability for either malicious prosecution or wrongful use of civil proceedings, liability for abuse of process is possible even if the defendant had probable cause to initiate legal proceedings and in spite of the fact that the proceedings were ultimately resolved against the person wrongfully subjected to them.

Tort law also protects personal rights in property. The torts of trespass and nuisance protect an individual's right to possess and enjoy the use of his land. The torts of trespass and conversion protect the individual's rights in the possession and enjoyment of her personal property. The basic distinction between trespass and conversion is that conversion deals with interferences that are serious enough to justify forcing the defendant to pay the full value of the property in question, rather than requiring him merely to pay for the loss of value or use of the property.

PROBLEM CASES

1. Barbara A. hired John G., an attorney, to represent her in a legal proceeding. When he subsequently filed suit against her for legal fees, she filed a cross-complaint against him for battery and deceit. She alleged that she had twice had sex with him and, as a result, had suffered a tubal pregnancy which necessitated surgery that rendered her sterile. She also alleged that she had sex with him despite the fact that neither party used any means of contraception because he had assured her: "I can't possibly get anyone pregnant." The trial court dismissed her claim for failure to state a cause of action. Was the dismissal proper?

2. On September 16, 1975, David Manning, Jr., was a spectator at Fenway Park in Boston for a baseball game between the Baltimore Orioles and the Boston Red Sox. Ross Grimsley was a pitcher for Baltimore. During the first three innings, Grimsley was warming up by throwing a ball from a pitcher's mound to a plate in the bull pen located near the right-field bleachers. The spectators in the bleachers continuously heckled Grimsley. On several occasions immediately following the heckling, Grimsley looked directly at the hecklers, not just into the stands. At the end of the third inning, after his catcher had left his position and was walking over to the bench, Grimsley faced the bleachers and wound up or stretched as though to pitch in the direction of the plate. Instead, the ball traveled from Grimsley's hand at more than 80 miles per hour at an angle of 90 degrees to the path from the pitcher's mound to the plate and directly toward the hecklers in the bleachers. The ball passed through the wire mesh fence in front of the bleachers and struck Manning. Manning filed a battery action against Grimsley. The trial judge directed a verdict for Grimsley. Should Manning win his appeal?

3. On April 14, 1984, during the "Saturday Night News" segment of NBC's "Saturday Night Live" program, a skit was presented as the "Fast Frank Feature." A performer was introduced to the audience as Maurice Frank, a tax consultant. The performer bore a noticeable physical resemblance to Maurice Frank, a resident of Westchester County, New York, who was engaged in business as an accountant, tax consultant, and financial planner. The performer proceeded to give "ludicrously inappropriate" tax advice, suggesting, among other things, that viewers claim houseplants as dependents and write off acne medicine under an oil depletion allowance, and guaranteeing that taxpayers who used his service would receive refunds in excess of their earnings. The real Maurice Frank filed a defamation suit against the network. Was he defamed by the skit?

4. In February of 1986, Lois Grimsley, a 46-year-old security inspector, unexpectedly gave birth in her home less than two days after doctors had told her that her stomach pains were nothing more than a urinary tract infection and a case of hemorrhoids. A reporter from a local newspaper interviewed Grimsley about the birth, and Grimsley provided details about it and posed for a picture with the child. The story appeared in the local paper the following day, was subsequently picked up by the Associated Press, and also appeared in several other newspapers. In July 1986, a synopsis of the article (including a photo of Grimsley and her son) appeared in the "Hard Times" section of *Penthouse* magazine (a section that the magazine describes as "a compendium of bizarre, idiotic, lurid, and ofttimes witless driblets of information culled from the nation's press") under the heading "Birth of a Hemorrhoid." Grimsley filed suit against *Penthouse* for defamation, invasion of privacy, and intentional infliction of mental distress. Should her suit succeed?

5. In September 1987, *The National Enquirer* ran an article reporting Henry Dempsey's harrowing escape from injury or death when he fell out of a small airplane while in flight but clung to the open boarding ladder of the plane, surviving his copilot's landing with only a few scratches. Dempsey had refused to be interviewed for the article, despite repeated attempts by an *Enquirer* reporter to gain an interview. The reporter allegedly came to his home twice, repeatedly drove past his home for three quarters of an hour after the first refusal, and followed him to a restaurant where she attempted to photograph him and again requested an interview. After the article appeared, Dempsey filed suit against the *Enquirer* for invasion of privacy and intentional infliction of emotional distress. Should Dempsey's suit succeed?

6. On February 25 and 26, 1987, ABC broadcast an investigative new report entitled "South Africa Connection" which purported to describe efforts by the Reagan administration to enlist the assistance of South Africa in aiding the Nicaraguan Contras by supplying aircraft and flight crews. In an attempt to flesh out the alleged connection, the program highlighted the participation of Southern Air Transport in the venture, and stated at one point that Southern Air was "known for its past relationship with the Central Intelligence Agency." Southern Air filed suit against the network for libel and invasion of privacy, arguing that its business had suffered as a result of the program. The network moved to dismiss the suit on the ground that a corporation cannot be defamed and possesses no right of privacy. Should the network's motion be granted?

7. Susan B. went to the Crisis Pregnancy Center for a "free pregnancy test." During an interview with a counselor she disclosed the fact that she had had an abortion at age 15 and had found it to be a traumatic experience. She told the counselor that if she were pregnant she would not consider aborting the child. She also said that she had been hospitalized for depression and that she was taking antidepressant and antianxiety medications prescribed by a psychiatrist. Susan's pregnancy test was negative, but the Center withheld this information from her. Instead, she said that they showed her a film "featuring mutilated advanced fetuses" and containing "purported personal and medical" comments on "the evil of abortion and the ineradicable harm" it does to pregnant women. After the film was shown, the counselor and another employee of the Center told Susan their personal moral views on sex and abortion, and told her that religion was the "sole means of expiation" for a woman who had undergone an abortion. They then told her she was not pregnant. Susan filed suit against the Center for intentional infliction of emotional distress, arguing that she became highly distressed as a result of the experience, necessitating emergency psychiatric care and increased dosages of her medication. Was the trial court order dismissing her suit proper?

8. The Blanks purchased a lot in the Indian Fork subdivision next to a lot owned by Gary Rawson. When Rawson built his home, he located a basketball goal and dog pen immediately next to the property separating the two lots. The Blanks complained to the subdivision developer that Rawson was violating the minimum setback restrictions applicable to the subdivision and were told that Rawson had received permission from the developer to do so. They then filed a nuisance suit against Rawson. At the trial, they alleged that the sound of the basketball hitting the backboard when Rawson's son played was offensive and that, when he missed, the ball could come into their yard. They also stated that the dog was a large one and that the pen was not cleaned regularly, with the result that offensive odors continued to reach their property despite the 10-foot privacy fence Rawson had erected between their properties shortly after their complaint against him was filed. Was the trial judge's order forcing Rawson to remove or relocate the goal and the dog pen proper?

9. Moore was receiving treatment for hairy-cell leukemia at a university hospital. After his spleen was removed as part of that treatment, the treating physician and another university employee determined that his cells were unique. Without Moore's knowledge or consent, they applied genetic engineering techniques to his cells, producing a cell line that they patented and marketed very successfully through agreements with a pharmaceutical company and a biotechnology firm. To further their research, they continued to monitor him and take tissue samples from him for almost seven years after his spleen was removed. When Moore discovered the truth, he filed a conversion suit against the university, which moved to dismiss his claim, arguing that he had no property right in his spleen and that, in any event, his cells were worthless without their subsequent modifications to them. Should Moore's suit survive their motion to dismiss?

10. Gilbert Smith owned land in Alviso, California, that he leased by oral agreement to George Interiano. Without Smith's knowledge, Interiano subleased the property to Carson Grimes, who was in the used lumber business. Grimes arranged for Cap Concrete to deliver between 60 to 70 loads of broken concrete material to the property to use as fill. When Smith learned of the presence of the concrete on his property a month later, he filed a trespass suit against Cap Concrete. The evidence at trial indicated that it would cost $6,000 to remove the concrete and that the presence of the concrete on the land seriously reduced the land's utility for other purposes. Cap argued that Grimes was the only party who could properly file a trespass suit over the concrete and that, in any event, Grimes's consent to the deliveries barred any suit by Smith. The trial court ruled in Cap's favor and Smith appealed. Should his appeal succeed?

CHAPTER 8

NEGLIGENCE AND STRICT LIABILITY

NEGLIGENCE

Origins and Elements

The Industrial Revolution that changed the face of 19th-century America created serious problems for the law of torts. Railroads, machinery, and other newly developing technologies contributed to a growing number of injuries to persons and their property. These injuries did not fit within the intentional torts framework, however, because most of them were unintended. Some injuries were simply the unavoidable consequences of life in a high-speed, technologically advanced, modern society. Holding infant industries totally responsible for all of the harms they caused could have seriously impeded the process of industrial development. To avoid such a result, new tort rules were needed. In response to these growing social pressures, the courts created the law of negligence.

Negligence focuses on conduct that falls below the legal standards that the law has established to protect members of society against unreasonable risks of harm. Negligence essentially involves an unintentional breach of a legal duty owed to another that results in some legally recognizable injury to the other's person or property. A plaintiff in a negligence suit must prove several things to recover: (1) that the defendant had a *duty* not to

injure him, (2) that the defendant *breached* that duty, and (3) that the defendant's breach of duty was the *actual* and *legal (proximate) cause* of his *injury*. To be successful, a plaintiff must also overcome any *defenses* to negligence liability that are raised by the defendant. Most of these defenses involve behavior by the plaintiff that may have originally contributed to his injury. (These elements are summarized graphically in Figure 2, which appears later in the chapter.)

Duty

The basic idea of negligence is that each member of society has a duty to conduct her affairs in a way that avoids an unreasonable risk of harm to others. The law of negligence holds each of us up to an *objective*, yet *flexible* standard of conduct: that of a "reasonable person of ordinary prudence in similar circumstances." This standard is objective because the reasonable person is a hypothetical person who is always thoughtful and cautious and never unreasonably endangers others. It is flexible because it allows consideration of all the circumstances surrounding a particular injury. For example, the law does not require the same level of caution and deliberation of a person confronted with an emergency requiring rapid decisions and action as it does of a person in circumstances allowing for calm reflection and deliberate action. Likewise, to a limited extent, the law considers the personal characteristics of the particular defendant whose conduct is being judged. For example, children are generally required to act as a reasonable person of similar age, intelligence, and experience would act under similar circumstances. Persons with physical disabilities are required to act as would a reasonable person with the same disability. Mental deficiencies, however, ordinarily do not relieve a person from the duty to conform to the reasonable person standard.

Special Duties   The question of whether a particular duty exists is entirely a question of law. Does the law recognize a duty of the defendant to protect the interests of this particular plaintiff from harm? Legal duties can originate from several sources. A *contractual relationship* between the plaintiff and the defendant can give rise to a variety of duties that might not exist otherwise. For example, most professional malpractice cases are based on claims that professionals negligently breached professional duties owed to their clients or to third persons who rely on their competent performance of professional tasks.[1]

Other *special relationships* between the parties have long been recognized as the source of special legal duties. For example, common carriers and innkeepers have long been held virtually strictly liable for damaging or losing the property of their customers. In recent years, many courts have extended this duty to include an affirmative duty to protect passengers or guests against the foreseeable wrongful acts of third persons. This has happened despite the fact that the law has long refused to recognize any general duty to aid and protect others from third-party wrongdoing unless a defendant's actions foreseeably increased the risk of such wrongdoing. Some recent decisions have imposed a similar duty on landlords to protect their tenants against the foreseeable criminal acts of others.

The relationship between the parties can also affect the *level* of duty that one person owes to another. For example, the common law has long held that the level of duty that a person in possession of land owes to other persons who enter on the land depends on whether such persons were invitees, licensees, or trespassers. **Invitees** are members of the public who are lawfully on public land, such as a park, swimming pool, or government

office; they are also customers, delivery persons, or paying boarders, who are on private premises for a purpose connected with the business interests of the possessor of the land. **Licensees** are those whose privilege to enter on the land depends entirely on the possessor's consent. Licensees include persons who are on the land solely for their own purposes such as someone soliciting money for charity, members of the possessor's household, and social guests. **Trespassers** are persons who enter or remain on another's land without any legal right or privilege to do so.

At common law, a possessor of land owed invitees a duty to exercise reasonable care to keep the premises in reasonably safe condition for their use. He also had a duty to protect invitees against dangerous conditions on the premises that he knew about, or reasonably should have discovered, and that they were unlikely to discover. He only owed licensees a duty to warn them of known dangerous conditions that they were unlikely to discover. The possessor of land owed no duty to trespassers to maintain his premises in a safe condition, and only a duty not to willfully and wantonly injure them once their presence was known. Recent years have seen a marked tendency to erode these common law distinctions. Many courts today, for example, no longer distinguish between licensees and invitees, holding that the possessor of land owes the same duties to licensees that he owes to invitees. Also, the courts have made numerous exceptions to the minimal duties that possessors of land owe to trespassers. For example, a higher level of duty is ordinarily owed to trespassers who the possessor of land knows are constantly entering the land (e.g., using a well-worn path across the land) and greater duties are ordinarily owed to protect children if the possessor of land knows that they are likely to trespass.

Finally, *statutes* can create legal duties that can be the source of a negligence action. The doctrine of **negligence per se** provides that one who violates a statute is guilty of negligent conduct if a harm that the statute was designed to prevent results to a person whom the statute was intended to protect. The defendant who has violated a statute may still seek to avoid liability by arguing that his violation was not the legal cause of the plaintiff's injury or by asserting some other general defense to liability, but the statutory violation is generally held to be conclusive evidence of breach of duty. The *Nixon* case later in this chapter is a good example of a court imposing a duty on the basis of a statute where other courts, such as the court in the following *Waters* case, have been unwilling to do so in the absence of a statute.

---

[1] The Legal Responsibilities of Accountants chapter discusses this subject in detail.

WATERS v. NEW YORK CITY HOUSING AUTHORITY

505 N.E.2d 922 (N.Y. Ct. App. 1987)

At 6:45 A.M. on July 25, 1982, Simone Waters, 16 years of age, was walking on a public street where she was accosted by a knife-wielding man who forced her to walk with him to a building around the corner. Once inside the building, which was unlocked, the man forced her to the roof and, after taking her money, sodomized her. The building was owned by the New York Housing Authority.

The evidence at the trial indicated that the front door locks on the building had been either broken or missing for at least two years before Simone was attacked, that several tenants had complained about the condition over that two-year period, and that there had been at least five criminal incidents in the building involving outsiders. The evidence also included an affidavit from an investigator employed by Waters stating that "had the door locks on this building been in proper working order, this sexual attack would in all probability not have occurred." When the trial court granted a summary judgment in favor of the Housing Authority, Waters appealed.

Titone, Judge.   It is now beyond dispute that a landlord, private or public, may have a duty to take reasonable precautionary measures to secure the premises if it has notice of a likelihood of criminal intrusions posing a threat to safety. A building owner who breaches such a duty may be held liable to an individual who is injured in a reasonably foreseeable criminal encounter that was proximately caused by the absence of adequate security. These basic principles, however, do not resolve the unusual problem presented here. Although Waters has made the necessary allegations of negligent security maintenance, notice of prior criminal intrusion, and proximately caused injury, her case differs significantly from those in which the landowner's liability for inadequate security has previously been upheld. Unlike the tenant in *Miller v. State of New York* and the business guest in *Nallan v. Helmsley-Spear, Inc.*, Waters had no connection whatsoever to the building in which her injuries ultimately occurred. Accordingly, we must look beyond *Nallan* and *Miller* to determine whether a landlord's duty should be extended to a person in Waters's position.

The question of the scope of an alleged tort-feasor's duty is, in the first instance, a legal issue for the court to resolve. In this analysis, not only logic and science, but policy play an important role. The common law of torts is, at its foundation, a means of apportioning risks and allocating the burden of loss. While moral and logical judgments are significant components of the analysis, we are also bound to consider the larger social consequences of our decisions and to tailor our notion of duty so that the legal consequences of wrongs are limited to a controllable degree.

With these principles in mind, we turn now to the question whether Waters was within the orbit of duty imposed on the owner of the building in which her injuries occurred. Initially, we note that the duty that was allegedly breached——to maintain the front door locks in working condition—exists principally to protect the safety and possessions of the tenants and visitors inside the premises. The risk to be reasonably apprehended in this instance is that of intrusion by outsiders with criminal motive who might do harm to those who have a right to feel at least minimally secure inside a dwelling place. In this case both logic and public policy weigh heavily in favor of confining the scope of defendant landowner's duty to protect against criminal acts to tenants and others who might reasonably be expected to be on the premises. An important consideration in this context is the fact that the landowner has no control over either the acts of the primary wrongdoer or the conditions on the public byways that make such acts all too commonplace. Another significant factor is the virtually limitless liability to which defendant and other landowners would be exposed if their legal obligations were extended to Waters and to all others in her position.

Finally, we note that the important public goals of minimizing crime and encouraging the maintenance of urban property would not materially be advanced by expanding the scope of landowners' duties in the manner Waters suggests. The possibility of tort liability arising from injury to tenants or others on the premises provides a strong incentive to landlords to keep locks and other security systems in good repair. Moreover, it is unlikely that the incidence of street crime would be meaningfully affected, since the urban environment includes many nooks and crannies, other than unsecured dwellings, which afford malefactors the privacy they need to commit their misdeeds. Thus, the social benefits to be gained do not warrant the extension of the landowner's duty to maintain secure premises to the millions of individuals who use the sidewalks of New York City each day and are thereby exposed to the dangers of street crime.

Judgment for the Housing Authority affirmed.

Breach

A person is guilty of breach of duty if she exposes another to an *unreasonable, foreseeable* risk of harm. Negligence consists of doing something that a reasonable person would not have done under the circumstances, or failing to do something that a reasonable person would have done under the same circumstances. If a person guards against all foreseeable risks and exercises reasonable care, but harm to others nonetheless occurs, no liability for negligence ordinarily results. For example, if Wilson is carefully driving his car within the speed limit and has a heart attack that causes him to lose control and crash into a car driven by Thomas, Wilson would ordinarily not be liable to Thomas for his injuries. As another member of the public using the highways, Wilson owed Thomas a duty to exercise reasonable care while driving. However, the accident was not the result of any breach of that duty because it was unforeseeable. If, on the other hand, Wilson's doctor had advised him that he had a heart condition that made driving dangerous, his failure to heed his doctor's warning would probably amount to a breach of duty because he was plainly exposing others to a foreseeable risk of harm by driving.

Of course, many behaviors involve some risk of harm to others, but the risk must be an *unreasonable* one before that behavior amounts to a breach of duty. In deciding the reasonableness of the risk, the courts balance the social utility of a person's conduct and the ease of avoiding or minimizing the risk against the likelihood that harm will result and the probable seriousness of that harm. As the risk of serious harm to others increases, so does the duty to take steps to avoid that harm. The following *Culli* case illustrates the steps a court follows in deciding whether a business has breached its duty to an invitee.

CULLI v. MARATHON PETROLEUM CO.

862 F. 2d 119 (7th Cir. 1988)

On Saturday, August 4, 1984, Elizabeth Culli stopped at a 24-hour self-service gas station operated by Marathon Petroleum in Mt. Vernon, Illinois. She filled her gas tank and then picked up five eight-pack cartons of soda that were featured as part of a special soda sale the station was running that day. After paying for the gas, she headed back toward her car. Before she reached her car, however, she slipped and fell on what an ambulance attendant who was called to the scene later described as a "clearish" slippery substance in a pool approximately 8 to 10 inches in width and length. Culli suffered a compound fracture of her ankle and had to use a wheelchair and walker for several months thereafter.

At the trial of her suit against Marathon, the evidence indicated that the station was typically staffed by one person, who would primarily stay inside and run the cash register, and who was also responsible for replenishing supplies of the other items sold at the station, such as milk, candy, hot food, and sandwiches. The station lot was normally swept once a day during the night shift, but the attendant on duty the evening prior to the accident could not recall whether or not he had swept that night. There was also testimony that spills in general occurred once or twice each day and that one employee had asked the station manager to hire more help because the station was understaffed, a request which he relayed to his superiors, but which went unheeded. When a jury awarded Culli $87,500, Marathon appealed.

Will, Senior District Judge.   The defendant owed the plaintiff invitee the duty of maintaining its property in a reasonably safe condition. This includes a duty to inspect and repair dangerous conditions on the property or give adequate warnings to prevent injury. To be liable, Marathon must have had actual or constructive notice of the dangerous condition. Both parties agree that Marathon did not have actual notice.

Constructive notice can be established under Illinois law under two alternative theories: (1) the dangerous condition existed for a sufficient amount of time so that it would have been discovered by the exercise of ordinary care, or (2) the dangerous condition was part of a pattern of conduct or a recurring incident.

In *Hresil v. Sears, Roebuck & Co.* (1980), plaintiff sought damages for injuries she suffered when she slipped on a "gob" of phlegm in the defendant's self-service store. At the time of her accident, there were few customers in the store and, due to the inactivity in the store at the place where she fell, the foreign substance could have been on the floor for at least 10 minutes. The court found that, as a matter of law, 10 minutes was not long enough to give Sears constructive notice of the gob, and "to charge the store with constuctive notice would place upon the store the unfair requirement of the constant patrolling of its aisles."

Because of the lack of testimony establishing how long the substance in this case was present, we do not know if it was present for a period of time which would have placed Marathon on constructive notice of it. It could have been present for a few minutes or several hours. Under the first constructive notice theory evidence establishing how long the particular substance was present is necessary.

Under the second constructive notice theory what is needed is a pattern of dangerous conditions which were not attended to within a reasonable time. There was substantial evidence presented at trial establishing that there were spills on a daily basis in the pump area and that the volume of sales on the day in question made it unreasonable for Marathon to sweep the lot only at night and operate for most of the day with only one attendant who was primarily confined to the cash register. The evidence is sufficient to support the jury's verdict that Marathon's maintenance of its property was unreasonable and proximately caused Culli's injury.

Judgment for Culli affirmed.

Causation

Even if a person breaches a duty that he owes to another person, no liability for negligence results unless the breach of duty was the *actual cause*, or the cause in fact, of injury to the other person. To determine the existence of actual cause, many courts employ a *but for* test: A defendant's conduct is the actual cause of a plaintiff's injury if that injury would not have occurred *but for* the defendant's breach of duty. In some cases, however, a person's negligent conduct may combine with the negligent conduct of another to cause a plaintiff's injury. For example, on a windy day Allen negligently starts a fire by using gasoline to start his charcoal grill. The fire started by Allen spreads and joins forces with another fire started by Baker, who was burning brush on his property but who failed to take any precautions to prevent the fire from spreading. The combined fires burn Clark's home to the ground. Clark sues both Allen and Baker for negligence. In such a case, the court would ask whether each defendant's conduct was a *substantial factor* in bringing about Clark's loss. If the evidence indicates that Clark's house would have been destroyed by either fire in the absence of the other, both Allen and Baker are liable for Clark's loss.

Proximate Cause   Holding persons guilty of negligent conduct responsible for all of the harms that actually result from their negligence could, in some cases, expose them to potentially catastrophic liability. Although the law has long said that those who are guilty of intentional wrongdoing are liable for all of the direct consequences of their acts, however bizarre or unforeseeable, the courts have also recognized that a person who was merely negligent should not necessarily be responsible for every injury actually caused by her negligence. This idea of placing some legal limit on a negligent defendant's liability for the consequences of her actions is called **proximate cause.** Courts often say that a negligent defendant is liable only for the *proximate* results of her conduct. Thus, although a defendant's conduct may have been the *actual cause* of a particular plaintiff's injury, she is liable only if her conduct was also the *proximate (legal) cause* of that injury.

The courts have not, however, reached any substantial agreement on the test that should be employed for proximate cause. In reality, the proximate cause question is one of social policy. In deciding which test to adopt, a court must weigh the possibility that negligent persons

can be exposed to catastrophic liability by a lenient test for proximate cause against the fact that a restrictive test inevitably prevents some innocent victims from recovering any compensation for their losses. Courts have responded in a variety of ways to this difficult choice.

Some courts have said that a negligent person is liable only for the "natural and probable consequences" of his actions. Others have limited a negligent person's liability for unforeseeable injuries by saying that he is liable only to plaintiffs who are within the "scope of the foreseeable risk." Thus, such courts hold that if the defendant could not have reasonably foreseen *some* injury to the plaintiff as a result of his actions, he is not liable to the plaintiff for any injury that in fact results from his negligence. Although this rule is often characterized as a rule of causation, in reality it is a rule limiting the defendant's *duty*, because courts adopting the rule hold that a defendant owes *no duty* to those to whom he cannot foresee any injury. On the other hand, such courts commonly hold that a defendant may be liable even for unforeseeable injuries to persons whom he has exposed to a foreseeable risk of harm.[2] The *Restatement (Second) of Torts* suggests that a defendant's negligence is not the legal cause of a plaintiff's injury if, looking back after the harm, it appears "highly extraordinary" to the court that the defendant's negligence should have brought about the plaintiff's injury.[3] In the following *Republic of France* case the defendant is able to avoid tremendous liability because the court refuses to hold the defendant responsible for unforeseeable consequences of its negligence.

[2] The most famous case adopting this approach is *Palsgraf v. Long Island Railroad Co.*, 12 N.E. 99 (N.Y. Ct. App. 1928).

[3] *Restatement (Second) of Torts* § 435(2) (1965).

REPUBLIC OF FRANCE v. UNITED STATES

290 F. 2d 395 (5th Cir. 1961)

On April 16, 1947, the SS *Grandchamp*, a cargo ship owned by the Republic of France and operated by the French Line, which was also 80 percent owned by the Republic of France, was loading a cargo of Fertilizer Grade Ammonium Nitrate (FGAN) at Texas City, Texas. A fire began on board the ship, apparently as a result of a cigarette or match carelessly discarded by a longshoreman in one of the ship's holds. Despite attempts to put it out, the fire spread quickly. A little over an hour after the fire was first discovered, the *Grandchamp* exploded with tremendous force.

Fire and burning debris spread throughout the waterfront, touching off accompanying fires and explosions in other ships, refineries, gasoline storage tanks, and chemical plants which were not brought under complete control for days. When the conflagration was over, 500 people had been killed and more than 3,000 had been injured.

The evidence indicated that despite the fact that ammonium nitrate was known throughout the transportation industry as an oxidizing agent and as a fire hazard, no one aboard the *Grandchamp* made any attempt to prevent smoking in the ship's holds. Numerous lawsuits were filed after the incident, many of them against the United States because the FGAN had been manufactured in army ordinance plants. After the United States was found not liable, Congress passed the Texas City Relief Act in 1955. The act left insurance underwriters to bear their own losses, but allowed those with uninsured claims to recover up to $25,000 per claim. The government paid out approximately $16 million to victims of the disaster, obtaining in return assignments of their claims for death, personal injuries, and property damage totalling approximately $70 million. The government sought to recover the full $70 million. The Republic of France and the French Line argued that they should not be liable for claims arising out of the explosion because FGAN was not known to be capable of exploding under such circumstances. When the trial court rejected their petition for limitation of liability, they appealed.

Rives, Circuit Judge.   In Texas, as elsewhere, not only proximate causal connection but also the very existence of a duty depends upon reasonable foreseeability of consequences. The test of whether a negligent act or omission is a proximate cause of an injury is whether the wrongdoer might by the exercise of ordinary care have foreseen that *some similar injury* might result from the negligence.

The United States argues with much force that the district court found that fault or negligence of the owners caused the fire and permitted it to increase in intensity, and that the fire caused the disastrous explosion. It insists that that causal connection is sufficient. The fallacy in that chain of argument is that it is only the operation of natural forces theretofore recognized as normal which one is charged with foreseeing.

The district court found it "undoubtedly true that the force and devastating effects of this explosion shocked and surprised the scientific field as well as the transportation industry." The court further found as to ammonium nitrate, which constituted approximately 95 percent of the FGAN, and which, with the benefit of hindsight, we now know to be the explosive part of the mixture:

Despite its use as a principal ingredient of high explosives, at the time of the disaster ammonium nitrate was not, and is not now, classified as an "explosive" for transportation purposes by the Interstate Commerce Commission or the Coast Guard. This is true because it was considered that to cause the detonation of ammonium nitrate, an initial shock or "booster" of considerable magnitude was required. The chances of such an initial or booster detonation being encountered in normal conditions of transportation has always been considered so remote as to be negligible.

Substantially all of the evidence is to the effect that the explosion, as distinguished from the fire, could not reasonably have been foreseen.

It would be ironic indeed if the United States were permitted to impose liability for these claims on the Republic of France and the French Line by claiming now that, unlike the officials and employees of the United States, the officials and employees of the French Government and the master of the *Grandchamp* should have known that FGAN was a dangerous explosive and that an explosion from fire should reasonably have been anticipated.

Judgment reversed in favor of the Republic of France.

Superseding Causes   In some cases, an *intervening force* occurring after a defendant's negligence may play a significant role in bringing about a particular plaintiff's injury. For example, a high wind may spring up that causes a fire set by Davis to spread and damage Parker's property, or, after Davis negligently runs Parker down with his car, a thief may steal Parker's wallet while he is lying unconscious in the street. Such cases present difficult problems for the courts, which must decide when an intervening force should relieve a negligent defendant from liability. As the following *Nixon* case indicates, if the intervening force is a *foreseeable* one, either because it frequently occurs in the ordinary course of human events or because the defendant's negligence substantially increases the risk of its occurrence, it will *not* relieve the defendant from liability. So, in the first example given above, if high winds are a reasonably common occurrence in the locality in question, Davis may be liable for the damage to Parker's property even though his fire would not have spread that far under the wind conditions that existed when he started it. Likewise, in our second example, Davis may be responsible for the theft of Parker's wallet if the theft is foreseeable, given the time and location of the accident.

On the other hand, if the intervening force that contributes to the plaintiff's injury is unforeseeable, most courts hold that it is a **superseding** or **intervening cause** that absolves the defendant of any liability for negligence. For example, Dalton negligently starts a fire that causes injury to several persons. The driver of an ambulance summoned to the scene to aid the injured has been drinking on duty and, as a result, loses control of his ambulance and runs up onto a sidewalk, injuring several pedestrians. Most courts would not hold Dalton responsible for the pedestrians' injuries. One important exception to this general rule, however, concerns intervening forces that produce a harm identical to the harm risked by the defendant's negligence. For example, the owners of a concert hall fail to install the number of emergency exits required by law for the protection of patrons. A negligently operated aircraft crashes into the hall during a concert, and many patrons are burned to death in the ensuing fire because the few available exits are jammed by panicked patrons trying to escape. Most courts would probably find that the owners of the hall were liable for the patrons' deaths.

NIXON v. MR. PROPERTY MANAGEMENT

690 S.W. 2d 546 (Tex. Sup. Ct. 1985)

At about 7:00 P.M. on August 7, 1981, a young man abducted R.M.V., age 10, from the sidewalk in front of her home and dragged her across the street to a vacant apartment at the Chalmette Apartments. He raped her, put her in the closet, told her not to leave, and disappeared. The apartment in question was described by the police officer called to the scene as "empty, filthy, dirty, and full of debris." Glass was broken from its windows and the front door was off its hinges.

In the two years prior to the attack on R.M.V., Dallas police had investigated numerous crimes committed at the Chalmette Apartments complex, including 1 attempted murder, 2 robberies, 2 aggravated assaults, 16 apartment burglaries, 4 vehicle burglaries, 4 cases of theft, and 5 cases of criminal mischief. A Dallas City Ordinance established minimum standards for property owners, requiring them, among other things, to "keep the doors and windows of a vacant structure or vacant portion of a structure securely closed to prevent unauthorized entry." Gaile Nixon, R.M.V.'s mother, filed a negligence suit against Brett Davis, Chalmette's owner, and Mr. Property Management Company, Inc., the manager of the complex. When the trial court granted a summary judgment in favor of Davis and Mr. Property, Nixon appealed.

Hill, Chief Justice.   In affirming the trial court's judgment, the court of appeals held that, since R.M.V. was on Mr. Property's property without its knowledge and consent, R.M.V. was a trespasser and Mr. Property's duty toward her was no greater than not to injure her willfully, wantonly, or through gross negligence. The court also held that the condition of the apartment complex was not a proximate cause of the rape because R.M.V.'s abduction and rape were not a reasonably foreseeable consequence thereof.

In this case, the question of what duty Mr. Property owed to R.M.V. is answered by the ordinance. This ordinance legislatively imposes a standard of conduct which we adopt to define the conduct of a reasonably prudent person. The unexcused violation of a statute or ordinance constitutes negligence as a matter of law if such statute or ordinance was designed to prevent injury to the class of persons to which the injured party belongs. A reasonable interpretation of this ordinance is that it was designed to deter criminal activity by reducing the conspicuous opportunities for criminal conduct. An ordinance requiring apartment owners to do their part in deterring crime is designed to prevent injury to the general public. R.M.V. falls within this class. Since the ordinance was meant to protect a larger class than invitees and licensees, and since R.M.V. committed no wrong in coming onto the property, these premise liability distinctions are irrelevant to our analysis.

Using the mandated standard for reviewing summary judgment, we conclude that a genuine issue of material fact exists as to Mr. Property's breach of duty. If the trier of fact concludes that Mr. Property violated the ordinance without a valid excuse, Mr. Property is negligent per se. This does not end our inquiry; we must still determine if there is a material fact issue on the question of proximate cause.

The two elements of proximate cause are cause in fact and foreseeability. Cause in fact denotes that the negligent act or omission was a substantial factor in bringing about the injury and without it no harm would have been incurred. Viewing the summary judgment as we must, drawing all reasonable inferences in favor of R.M.V., we conclude that a reasonable inference exists that, but for Mr. Property's failure to comply with the ordinance regarding maintenance of its apartment complex, this crime would have never taken place. There is evidence that the assailant took R.M.V. "directly to a vacant apartment," the inference being that the assailant was acutely aware of the vacant unit's existence and embarked upon his course of criminal conduct at this particular time and place knowing that this unit was an easily accessible place in which to perpetrate this assault in isolation.

Finally, we turn to the question of foreseeability. Foreseeability means that the actor, as a person of ordinary intelligence, should have anticipated the dangers that his negligent act created for others. Usually, the criminal conduct of a third party is a superseding cause relieving the negligent actor from liability. However, the tortfeasor's negligence will not be excused where the criminal conduct is a foreseeable result of such negligence. The evidence is replete with instances of prior violent crimes occurring at Chalmette Apartments. This record certainly provides evidence that further acts of violence were reasonably foreseeable. Evidence of specific previous crimes on or near the premises raises a fact issue on the foreseeability of criminal activity.

Judgment reversed in favor of Nixon; case remanded for trial.

Generally Accepted Causation Rules Whatever test for proximate cause a court says it adopts, most courts generally agree on certain basic principles of causation. One such basic principle is that persons guilty of negligence "take their victims as they find them." This means that a negligent defendant is liable for the full extent of his victim's injuries even if those injuries are aggravated by some preexisting physical characteristic of the victim. Similarly, negligent defendants are normally held liable for diseases contracted by their victims while in a weakened state caused by their injuries. They are *jointly* liable—along with the attending physician—

for negligent medical care that their victims receive for their injuries.

Negligent defendants also are commonly held responsible for injuries sustained by persons seeking to avoid being injured by the defendant's negligence. For example, Peters swerves to avoid being hit by Denning's negligently driven car and in the process loses control of her own car and is injured. Denning is liable for Peters's injuries. Finally, it is commonly said that "danger invites rescue." This means that negligent persons are liable to those injured in attempting to rescue the victims of their negligence. One corollary of this rescue rule is that the claim of a would-be rescuer ordinarily is not defeated by contributory fault on the part of the rescuer so long as he is not reckless in making the rescue attempt.

Res Ipsa Loquitur

In some cases, negligence may be difficult to prove because the defendant has superior knowledge of the circumstances surrounding the plaintiff's injury. Thus, it may not be in the defendant's best interests to disclose those circumstances if they point to liability on his part. Consider, for example, the position of a person who goes into the hospital for an appendectomy and awakens after the operation to find that both of his legs have been amputated. Since he was anesthetized during the operation, he has no way of knowing what caused his loss. The only persons who do know are the hospital personnel who performed the operation, but the odds are that they are the ones responsible for the tragedy. The doctrine of *res ipsa loquitur* ("the thing speaks for itself") can aid such a plaintiff in proving his case. *Res ipsa* applies when (1) the defendant has *exclusive control* of the instrumentality of harm (and therefore probable knowledge of, and responsibility for, the cause of the harm), (2) the harm that occurred *would not ordinarily occur* in the absence of negligence, and (3) the plaintiff was in no way responsible for his own injury. When these elements are present, most states hold that an *inference* may arise that the defendant was negligent and that her negligence was the cause of the plaintiff's injury. Practically speaking, this may force the defendant to come forward with evidence to rebut the inference that she is responsible. If she fails to do so, a court or jury *may* choose to impose liability on her. Some courts, however, give *res ipsa* much greater effect, holding that it creates a *presumption* of negligence that requires a directed verdict for the plaintiff in the absence of proof by the defendant rebutting the presumption.

Injury

The plaintiff in a negligence case must prove not only that the defendant breached a duty owed to the plaintiff and that the breach of duty was the legal cause of her injury, but also that the resulting injury was to an interest that the law seeks to protect. Ordinarily, purely physical injuries to a person or her property present no problem in this respect, because the law has long protected such interests. Serious problems arise, however, when injuries are purely *emotional* in nature. As you learned in the Intentional Torts chapter, the law has long demonstrated a considerable reluctance to afford recovery for purely emotional harms. The courts' reluctance is due, among other things, to the danger of spurious claims and the difficulty inherent in placing a monetary value on emotional injuries. Given our great reluctance to impose liability for purely emotional harms caused by intentional wrongs, one might correctly assume that an even greater reluctance would exist when the conduct producing an emotional injury was merely negligent.

Negligent Infliction of Emotional Distress   Until fairly recently, most courts would not allow a plaintiff to recover for emotional injuries resulting from a defendant's negligent behavior in the absence of some impact or contact with the plaintiff's person. Today, many courts have abandoned the impact rule and allow recovery for foreseeable emotional injuries standing alone. A large number of such courts, however, still require, as a precondition of recovery, proof that some serious physical injury or symptoms resulted from the plaintiff's emotional distress. Nonetheless, a growing number of courts have dispensed with the injury requirement where the plaintiff has suffered serious emotional distress as a foreseeable consequence of the defendant's negligent conduct.

Third-Party Emotional Distress   In recent years, more and more negligence cases have involved claims by third persons for emotional injuries that they suffered by witnessing a negligently caused harm to another person, usually a spouse or child. For example, Mr. Porter has a heart attack after seeing Mrs. Porter run down by a car negligently driven by Denton. Is Denton liable for Mr. Porter's injury? Until fairly recently, most courts would have denied Mr. Porter any recovery on the ground that he had suffered no impact as a result of Denton's negligence. In recent years, however, many courts have abandoned the impact rule in third-party cases in favor of the "zone of danger" test. This test allows third parties who are themselves in the zone of danger created by a defendant's negligence to recover for emotional injuries resulting from the threat of harm to them, regardless of whether any impact ever occurred. Courts following this rule would, therefore, allow Mr. Porter to recover if he was close enough to his wife to be in danger of being hit by Denton's car. Some courts would insist, in addition, that Mr. Porter prove that he suffered some physical injury as a result of his emotional distress.

Today, some courts have abandoned the zone of danger requirement entirely and allow recovery for emotional injuries suffered by third parties, regardless of whether there was any threat of injury to them. However, as the following *Mazzagatti* case indicates, most courts that have taken this step still attempt to limit recovery in a variety of ways. For example, such courts commonly require that a close personal relationship exist between the third-party plaintiff and the direct victim of the defendant's negligence and that the third party's emotional distress result from actually witnessing the injury to the direct victim. Also, they impose a requirement that the third party demonstrate some physical "injury" resulting from his emotional distress. This area of the law is undergoing rapid development, however, and some recent cases may be found dispensing with the injury requirement or allowing recovery for emotional distress suffered as a result of seeing the direct victim in an injured state shortly after the injury occurred.

MAZZAGATTI v. EVERINGHAM

516 A.2d 672 (Pa. Sup. Ct. 1986)

On August 12, 1980, 14-year-old Mumtaz Mazzagatti was struck and fatally injured by a car driven by Ricky Allen Everingham. Mazzagatti had been riding her bike in the residential area near her home. At the time of the accident her mother, Jane Mazzagatti, was at work, approximately one mile away. She received a telephone call immediately after the collision informing her that her daughter had been involved in an automobile accident. She arrived on the scene a few minutes later and saw her daughter lying in the road. She filed a negligent infliction of emotional distress suit against Everingham. In her complaint she alleged that she "became hysterical, unnerved, and emotionally shattered" at the sight of her injured daughter and that as a result of the observation, she suffered shock to her nervous system and grievous mental pain and suffering, resulting in severe depression and an acute nervous condition. She also alleged that she was tortured by flashbacks and nightmares in which she saw Mumtaz lying in the road. When the trial court granted a summary judgment in favor of Everingham, Mazzagatti appealed.

Nix, Chief Justice. In *Sinn v. Burd*, we were confronted with the issue whether a close relative who witnessed the accident, albeit outside of the zone of danger, could recover for the negligent infliction of emotional distress. We concluded that in such instances the defendant did owe a duty of care to the bystander, noting that "the scope of potential liability commonly finds theoretical expression in such concepts as duty and proximate cause." We held that the resultant harm was foreseeable and stated:

We are confident that the application of the traditional tort concept of foreseeability will reasonably circumscribe the tortfeasor's liability in such cases. Foreseeability enters into the determination of liability in determining whether the emotional injuries sustained by the plaintiff were reasonably foreseeable to the defendant.

We adopted the *Dillon v. Legg* (Cal. Sup. Ct. 1968), parameters for determining whether the infliction of emotional distress was reasonably foreseeable. We held that a cause of action is stated when the following criteria are met:

(1) Whether plaintiff was located near the scene of the accident as contrasted with one who was a distance away from it;
(2) Whether the shock resulted from a direct emotional impact upon plaintiff from the sensory and contemporaneous observance of the accident, as contrasted with learning of the accident from others after its occurrence;
(3) Whether plaintiff and the victim were closely related as contrasted with an absence of any relationship or the presence of only a distant relationship.

In *Sinn* the plaintiff-mother was present at the time of the accident and actually witnessed the injury to her child. We thus found a contemporaneous observation of the accident which proximately caused emotional distress to the mother. We limited our holding solely to those cases in which the plaintiff alleges psychic injury as a result of actually witnessing the defendant's negligent act.

When a plaintiff is a distance away from the scene of the accident and learns of the accident from others after its occurrence rather than from a contemporaneous observance, the sum total of policy considerations weigh against the conclusion that that particular plaintiff is legally entitled to protection from the harm suffered. We believe that where the close relative is not present at the scene of the accident, but instead learns of the accident from a third party, the close relative's prior knowledge of the injury to the victim serves as a buffer against the full impact of observing the accident scene. By contrast, the relative who contemporaneously observes the tortious conduct has no time span in which to brace his or her emotional system. The negligent tortfeasor inflicts upon this bystander an injury separate and apart from the injury to the victim. Hence, the critical element for establishing such liability is the contemporaneous observance of the injury to the close relative. Where, as here, the plaintiff has no contemporaneous sensory perception of the injury, the emotional distress results more from the particular emotional makeup of the plaintiff rather than from the nature of defendant's actions.

In reality this is a claim for affectional loss or solatium to recompense a surviving relative for her feelings of anguish, bereavement and grief caused by the fact of the injury to and death of the decedent. In *Sinn* we noted that the common law has traditionally denied a damage award for solatium. The feelings of anguish and bereavement suffered by Mazzagatti are not substantially different from those suffered by any parent who sees his or her dying injured child, whether it be at the scene of the accident or in the hospital room afterwards.

Judgment for Everingham affirmed.

Defenses to Negligence

The common law traditionally recognized two defenses to negligence: **contributory negligence** and **assumption of risk.** Both of these defenses are based on the idea of *contributory fault*: If a plaintiff's own behavior contributed in some way to his injury, this fact should relieve the defendant from liability. As the following paragraphs indicate, however, the contributory fault idea often produced harsh results, and recent years have witnessed a significant erosion of its impact in negligence cases.

Contributory Negligence   The doctrine of *contributory negligence* provides that plaintiffs who *fail to exercise reasonable care for their own safety* are totally

FIGURE 1   Plaintiff's Recovery under Contributory and Comparative Negligence Systems

Plaintiff's Relative Fault	Contributory Negligence	Comparative Negligence (Pure)	Comparative Negligence (Mixed)
0%	100%	100%	100%
10	0	90	90
60	0	40	0
90	0	10	0

barred from any recovery if their contributory negligence is a *substantial factor* in producing their injury. So, if Parker steps into the path of Dworkin's speeding car without first checking to see whether any cars are coming, Parker would be denied any recovery against Dworkin because of the clear causal relationship between his injury and his failure to exercise reasonable care for his own safety. On the other hand, if Parker is injured one night when his speeding car crashes into a large, unmarked hole in the street caused by a city street repair project, and the facts indicate that the accident would have occurred even if Parker had been driving at a legal speed, he is not barred from recovering damages from the city for its negligence.

In some cases, a contributorily negligent plaintiff may be able to overcome an otherwise valid contributory negligence defense by arguing that the defendant had the **last clear chance** to avoid harm. The doctrine of last clear chance focuses on who was *last* at fault *in time*. Therefore, if despite the plaintiff's contributory negligence, the harm could have been avoided if the defendant had exercised reasonable care, the defendant's *superior opportunity* to avoid the accident makes him more at fault. For example, Durban pulls into the path of Preston's speeding car without looking, causing an accident. When Preston files suit to recover for the damage, Durban argues that the fact that Preston was speeding amounts to contributory negligence. If Preston can convince the court that the accident could have been avoided if Durban had looked before pulling onto the highway, she has a good chance of overcoming Durban's contributory negligence defense.

Comparative Negligence   Contributory negligence can sometimes produce harsh results because it may operate to prevent slightly negligent persons from recovering any compensation for their losses. In reaction to this potential unfairness, a growing majority of the states have adopted **comparative negligence** systems either by statute or by judicial decision. The details of these systems vary by state, but the principle underlying them is essentially the same: Courts seek to determine the *relative fault* of the parties to a negligence action and award damages in proportion to the degree of fault determined. For a simple example, assume that Dunne negligently injures Porter and Porter suffers $10,000 in damages. A jury, however, determines that Porter was 20 percent at fault. Under a comparative negligence system, Porter could recover only $8,000 from Dunne. But what if Porter is determined to be 60 percent at fault? Here, the results vary depending on whether the state in question has adopted a *pure* or a *mixed* comparative fault system. Under a pure comparative fault system, plaintiffs are allowed to recover a portion of their damages even if they are more at fault than the defendant, so Porter could recover $4,000. Under a mixed system, plaintiffs who are as much at fault as, or, in some states, more at fault than, the defendant are denied any recovery. Such a state refuses Porter any recovery, just as though contributory negligence principles still applied. Figure 1 graphically illustrates the effects of the various ways of handling plaintiffs' contributory fault.

The full extent of the impact that comparative fault systems will have on tort law is as yet undetermined. What is clear, however, is that comparative fault is affecting other tort doctrines besides contributory negligence. For example, as the following *Roggow* case indicates, many comparative negligence states have discarded the doctrine of last clear chance. In addition, some states now apply comparative fault principles to recklessness and strict liability cases, as well as to negligence cases.

ROGGOW v. MINERAL PROCESSING CORP.

698 F. Supp. 1441 (S.D. Ind. 1988)

Charles Roggow, a long-distance truck driver out of Buffalo, New York, made a delivery of scrap aluminum to a processing plant located in Needmore, Indiana, and owned by Mineral Processing Corporation—Needmore Division (Needmore). After making delivery, Roggow was to pick up an unloaded trailer. Because Needmore's employees had failed to secure the header bar of the trailer (the part that secures the sides of the trailer to prevent damaging vibration), Roggow had to fasten the bar before leaving Needmore's plant. The bar had to be set in place at the very top of the trailer, but Needmore had no ladder available for Roggow's use. Consequently, Tracy Phillips, a Needmore employee, offered to assist Roggow by placing him in the bucket of a highloader and raising him high enough to set the bar in place.

Roggow accepted the offer and succeeded in fastening the header bar, but as Phillips was lowering him to the ground, Phillips's sleeve caught the highloader's dump lever, causing the bucket to overturn and dump Roggow approximately 9 feet onto a concrete floor. Roggow filed suit against Needmore. The jury found Roggow's damages to be $80,000, but reduced his award to $48,000 because they found him to be 40 percent at fault. Roggow filed a motion for a new trial, arguing, among other things, that the trial court erred in refusing to instruct the jury on the doctrine of last clear chance.

Endsley, U.S. Magistrate.   This matter was tried under Indiana's Comparative Fault Act (the Act). Prior to the enactment of comparative fault, Indiana followed the common law rule of contributory negligence. This antiquated "all-or-nothing" rule totally bars a plaintiff from recovering damages for injuries if he is guilty of negligence, albeit slight. During the twentieth century, common law doctrines were developed to alleviate the harsh results of contributory negligence. Last clear chance was one of those doctrines. Roggow now invites the Court to determine the applicability of this exception to contributory negligence under the Act even though the statute is silent and no Indiana court of review has yet passed on these issues.

Because no Indiana court has addressed this issue, this federal court must determine how the highest court in Indiana would decide this issue if it were presented with the question. Under the Act, assumption of risk is not available as an absolute defense for the defendant. Specifically, "assumption of risk not constituting an enforceable express consent" is a factor to be considered by the fact finder when weighing the fault attibutable to the individual actors. Similarly, by its definition in the Act, "fault" necessarily includes the factors which make up last clear chance. The Indiana legislature defined fault as "any act or omission that is negligent, willful, wanton, or reckless toward the person or property of the actor or others." Consequently, just as assumed risk is no longer available to completely excuse the negligence of the defendant, so too, this Court believes, is the doctrine of last clear chance no longer available to completely excuse the negligence of the plaintiff. This conclusion is in accord with the holdings and statutes of a majority of states which have addressed the issue. Consequently, failure to give Roggow's tendered instruction was not error in this case.

Motion for new trial denied.

FIGURE 2   Elements of Negligence

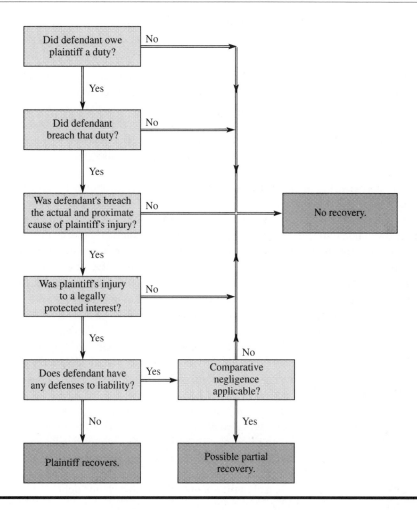

Assumption of Risk   In some cases, a plaintiff has *voluntarily* exposed herself to a *known danger* created by the defendant's negligence. Such plaintiffs are said to have *assumed the risk* of their injury and ordinarily are denied any recovery for it. The idea here is that the plaintiff *impliedly* consented to accept the risk, thereby relieving the defendant of the duty to protect her against it. For example, Stevens voluntarily goes for a ride in Markley's car, even though Markley has told her that his brakes are not working properly. Stevens has assumed the risk of injury as a result of the car's defective brakes. A person must fully understand the nature and extent of the risk, however, to be held to have assumed it. A plaintiff can also assume the risk of injury *expressly* by enter-

ing a contract containing a provision purporting to relieve the defendant of a duty of care that he would otherwise owe to the plaintiff. Such contract provisions are called *exculpatory clauses*. The Illegality chapter discusses in detail exculpatory clauses and the numerous limitations that courts have imposed on their enforceability. As the *Roggow* case indicated, some states that have adopted comparative negligence systems have done away with the assumption of risk defense in negligence cases and treat all forms of contributory fault under their comparative negligence scheme. The following *Hull* case, however, proves that assumption of risk remains a viable defense in some jurisdictions. Figure 2 graphically illustrates all of the elements of a negligence case.

HULL v. MERCK & CO., INC.

758 F. 2d 1474 (11th Cir. 1985)

On September 4, 1980, Augusta Fiberglass Coatings (AFC) began work replacing fiberglass sewer lines at three adjacent Albany, Georgia, chemical plants operated by Merck & Co., Inc. The lines delivered waste chemicals into a 1-million-gallon neutralizing pool. Merck warned AFC that it intended to continue in operation throughout the replacement activity, and that bypass pipes and various safety equipment would be necessary to the work. AFC relayed Merck's warnings to its employees and provided them with rubber boots, pants, coats, and gloves, as well as goggles and masks.

Jim Dale Hull was AFC's supervisor on the job at Merck. Although Hull had substantial experience working with chemicals, he quit wearing any of the safety gear after a few days on the job. Hull spent four hours each day in the trench dug to expose the pipelines. He regularly breathed gases and allowed liquid to spill on his clothing and body. He noted at the time that the chemical fumes in and around the pipes were a health hazard. On September 22, 1980, Hull stuck his head inside a 20-inch connecting pipe that, due to an accidental spill in the factories, contained an 80 to 85 percent solution of toluene, rather than the 2 percent solution the pipes were supposed to carry. He became dizzy and nauseous and was given oxygen at the plant infirmary.

Within a year after completion of the Merck contract, Hull suffered bone marrow depression, followed by leukemia. Hull sued Merck for $2.5 million plus punitive damages, alleging that (1) Merck had negligently failed to disclose the nature and health dangers of the waste chemicals carried by the pipelines, (2) Merck had negligently failed to inform him adequately of the necessity for wearing protective gear during construction, (3) the intermittent discharge without warning of high-concentration spills into the pipelines resulted from the negligent operation of the factories, and (4) Merck's decision to continue plant operations and consequently the flow of waste chemicals during the pipeline replacement project amounted to negligence. After being charged by the trial judge that assumption of risk on Hull's part would bar his recovery under Georgia's comparative fault law, the jury ruled in favor of Merck. Hull appealed.

Per Curiam.   Under Georgia law, a plaintiff assumes the risk when he "deliberately chooses an obviously perilous course of conduct and fully appreciates the danger involved." The plaintiff must do so voluntarily, "without restriction from his freedom of choice either by the circumstances or by coercion." Georgia typically applies assumption of risk to situations where the plaintiff races to beat a train at a crossing, drag races, or walks onto a pond covered with thin ice. Although assumption of the risk presupposes awareness of the nature and extent of the threat posed, perfect knowledge is not necessary. But Georgia law offers little guidance as to the depth of knowledge a plaintiff must possess to assume the sometimes very subtle risks posed by chemical exposure.

There was ample evidence to justify the charge in this case, especially as it pertained to Hull's allegation that Merck negligently decided to operate the factories during the replacement of the pipelines. Hull knew before he ever entered the plant grounds that Merck and AFC planned for operations to continue, with waste chemicals to be expelled via a bypass system of hoses assembled by AFC workers. Although Hull might or might not have had knowledge of any specific carcinogenic risk posed by toluene, he knew from long experience that the handling of waste chemicals warranted protective measures, and that coping with a continued flow of waste warranted an even greater degree of caution.

He also knew Merck and AFC were supplying adequate safety gear, which he used only for the first few days, but which many of his coworkers wore throughout the project without hampering their work. The gear remained available for his use at all times. He testified that while he was working he concluded the fumes were dangerous to good health. Finally, his severe exposure on September 22, 1980 forcefully brought home the risk posed by Merck's operations, yet he voluntarily remained, exposing himself for another month or more. The evidence at the trial left the jury free to conclude that Hull's leukemia was caused by post-September 22nd exposure, and Hull's remaining after that date might be construed as a knowing assumption of all four of the risks arising from Merck's alleged negligence. In any case, there was more than enough evidence to warrant the jury finding that Hull assumed the risk posed by working around a continuing flow of waste chemicals during the replacement of the pipes.

Judgment for Merck affirmed.

RECKLESSNESS

Behavior that indicates a conscious disregard for a known high risk of probable harm to others amounts to **recklessness.** In terms of the moral culpability of the defendant, recklessness lies midway between intentional wrongdoing and negligence. Recklessness involves conduct posing a foreseeable risk of harm to others, but that risk of harm must be significantly greater than the degree of risk necessary to make conduct negligent. In recklessness, as in negligence, the objective reasonable person test is applied to the defendant. Would a reasonable person, knowing all the facts at the defendant's disposal, have perceived the aggravated risk of harm to others that resulted from her conduct?

Proof of reckless behavior offers a plaintiff several significant advantages over proof of mere negligence. First, as a general rule, mere contributory negligence on the part of the plaintiff does *not* prevent recovery for recklessly caused injuries. Only proof that the plaintiff acted in reckless disregard for his own safety or assumed the risk of injury created by the defendant's recklessness operates as a defense to recklessness. For example, Roberts bets his friends that he can drive down a busy street blindfolded. In doing so, he runs down Mann. Because Roberts's conduct amounted to recklessness, the fact that Mann stepped into the path of Roberts's car without looking would *not* bar Mann's recovery. However, if Mann saw Roberts's car weaving down the road and still attempted to cross the street in front of it, or if Mann had bet Roberts's friends that he could run in front of the car without being hit, Mann *would* be denied any recovery. Also, as a general rule, courts are more willing to find that a reckless defendant's conduct was the legal cause of a plaintiff's injuries than they would be if the defendant's conduct was merely negligent. Finally, because reckless-

ness involves a higher degree of fault than negligence, a plaintiff who can prove recklessness on the defendant's part stands a good chance of recovering punitive as well as compensatory damages. Ordinarily, compensatory damages are the only damages recoverable for mere negligence.

STRICT LIABILITY

Introduction

In addition to intentional wrongdoing and negligence, the third fundamental basis of tort liability is **strict liability.** Strict liability means that defendants who participate in certain harm-producing activities may be held *strictly liable* for any harm that results to others, even though they did not intend to cause the harm and did everything in their power to prevent it. Also, defendants in strict liability cases traditionally have fewer defenses to liability than do defendants in negligence cases. This is because most courts hold that contributory negligence is *not* a defense to strict liability, although assumption of risk is a good defense. The imposition of strict liability represents a social policy decision that the risk associated with an activity should be borne by those who pursue it, rather than by wholly innocent persons who are exposed to that risk.

Such liability has been justified either by the defendant's voluntary decision to engage in a particularly risky activity or, more recently, by the defendant's superior ability to bear losses. Thus, corporations are often said to be superior to individuals as risk-bearers due to their ability to pass the costs of liability on to consumers in the form of higher prices for goods or services. The owners of trespassing livestock and the keepers of naturally dangerous wild animals were among the first classes of defendants on whom the courts imposed strict liability. Today, the two most important activities subject to judicially imposed strict liability are *abnormally dangerous (or ultrahazardous) activities* and the *manufacture or sale of defective and unreasonably dangerous products*. The Product Liability chapter discusses the product liability dimension of strict liability in detail.

Abnormally Dangerous Activities

Abnormally dangerous activities are those that *necessarily involve a risk of harm to others that cannot be eliminated by the exercise of reasonable care*. Activities that have been classed as abnormally dangerous include blasting, crop dusting, stunt flying, and, in one case, the transportation of large quantities of gasoline by truck. The following *American Cyanamid* case discusses the numerous factors that courts must consider before deciding whether a particular activity should be classified as abnormally dangerous. It also illustrates the fact that the greater the social utility attached to an activity and the greater the costs of minimizing the risk associated with that activity, the less likely a court is to label the activity as an abnormally dangerous one.

INDIANA HARBOR BELT RAILROAD CO. v. AMERICAN CYANAMID CO.

916 F. 2d 1174 (7th Cir. 1990)

On January 9, 1979, a railroad car leased by American Cyanamid Co. (American) and containing 20,000 gallons of acrylonitrile manufactured by American began leaking. At the time, the car was sitting just south of Chicago in the Blue Island yard of the Indiana Harbor Belt Railroad Co. (Indiana) awaiting switching to Conrail for delivery to its final destination. Indiana's employees were able to stop the leak, but were uncertain about how much of the car's contents had escaped. Because acrylonitrile (a chemical used in the manufacture of plastics, dyes, acrylic fibers, and pharmaceutical chemicals) is flammable, highly toxic, and possibly carcinogenic, Illinois authorities ordered homes near the yard temporarily evacuated.

Later, it was discovered that only about one quarter of the car's contents had leaked, but the Illinois Department of Environmental Protection, fearing that the soil and water had been contaminated, ordered Indiana to take decontamination measures costing $981,000. Indiana filed suit against American on negligence and strict liability theories seeking to recover its expenses. When the trial court dismissed Indiana's negligence claim but entered summary judgment for Indiana on the strict liability claim, both parties appealed.

Posner, Circuit Judge.   The question whether the shipper of a hazardous chemical by rail should be strictly liable for the consequences of a spill or other accident to the shipment en route is a novel one in Illinois. The parties agree that the question is a question of law, so we owe no particular deference to the conclusion of the district court. They also agree that the Supreme Court of Illinois would treat as authoritative the provisions of the *Restatement (Second) of Torts* governing abnormally dangerous activities. The key provision is section 520, which sets forth six factors to be considered in deciding whether an activity is abnormally dangerous.

The roots of section 520 are in nineteenth-century cases. The most famous one is *Rylands v. Fletcher* (1868), but a more illuminating one in the present context is *Guille v. Swan*, 19 Johns. (N.Y.) 381 (1822). A man took off in a hot-air balloon and landed, without intending to, in a vegetable garden in New York City. A crowd that had been anxiously watching his involuntary descent trampled the vegetables in their endeavor to rescue him when he landed. The owner of the garden sued the balloonist for the resulting damage, and won. Yet the balloonist had not been careless. In the then state of ballooning it was impossible to make a pinpoint landing.

Guille was a paradigmatic case for strict liability. (a) The risk (probability) of harm was great, and (b) the harm that would ensue if the risk materialized could be, although luckily was not, great (the balloonist could have crashed into the crowd). The confluence of these two factors established the urgency of seeking to prevent such accidents. (c) Yet such accidents could not be prevented by the exercise of due care; the technology of ballooning was insufficiently developed. (d) The activity was not a matter of common usage, so there was no presumption that it was a highly valuable activity despite its unavoidable riskiness. (e) The activity was inappropriate to the place in which it took place—densely populated New York City. (f) Reinforcing (d), the value to the community of the activity of recreational ballooning did not appear to be great enough to offset its unavoidable risks.

These are, of course, the six factors in section 520. Each is a different facet of a common quest for a proper legal regime to govern accidents that negligence liability cannot adequately control. The interrelations might be more perspicuous if the six factors were reordered. One might for example start with (c), inability to eliminate the risk of an accident by the exercise of due care. The baseline common law regime of tort liability is negligence. When it is a workable regime, because the hazards of an activity can be avoided by being careful, there is no need to switch to strict liability. Sometimes, however, a particular type of accident cannot be prevented by taking care but can be avoided, or its consequences minimized, by shifting the activity to another locale, where the risk or harm of an accident will be less [(e)]. By making the actor strictly liable—by denying him in other words an excuse based on his inability to avoid accidents by being more careful—we give him an incentive, missing in negligence, to experiment with methods of preventing accidents that involve not greater exertions of care, assumed to be futile, but instead relocating, changing or reducing (perhaps to the vanishing point) the activity giving rise to the accident.

The greater the risk of an accident [(a)] and the costs of an accident if one occurs [(b)], the more we want the actor to consider the possibility of making accident-reducing activity changes; the stronger, therefore, is the case for strict liability. Finally, if an activity is extremely common [(d)], like driving an automobile, it is unlikely either that its hazards are perceived as great or that there is no technology of care available to minimize them; so the case for strict liability is weakened.

Against this background we turn to the particulars of acrylonitrile, one of a large number of chemicals that are hazardous in the sense of being flammable, toxic, or both. A table in the record contains a list of 125 hazardous materials that are shipped in highest volume on the nation's railroads. Acrylonitrile is the 53rd most hazardous on the list. Among the other materials that rank higher on the hazard scale are phosphorous (number 1), anhydrous ammonia, liquified petroleum gas, vinyl chloride, gasoline, crude petroleum, motor fuel antiknock compound, methyl and ethyl chloride, sulphuric acid, and chloroform. The plaintiff's lawyer acknowledged at argument that the logic of the district court's opinion dictated strict liability for all 52 materials that rank higher than acrylonitrile on the list, and quite possibly for the 72 that rank lower as well, since all are hazardous if spilled in quantity while being shipped by rail. Every shipper of any of the materials would therefore be strictly liable for the consequences of a spill or other accident that occurred while the material was being shipped through a metropolitan area.

No cases recognize so sweeping a liability. Several reject it, though none has facts much like those of the present case. Cases that impose strict liability for the storage of a dangerous chemical provide a potentially helpful analogy to our case, but they can be distinguished on the ground that the storer (like the transporter) has more control than the shipper. So we can get little help from precedent, and might as well apply section 520 to the acrylonitrile problem from the ground up. To begin with, we have been given no reason for believing that negligence is not perfectly adequate to remedy and deter, at reasonable cost, the accidental spillage of acrylonitrile from rail cars. Although acrylonitrile is flammable and toxic, it is not so corrosive or otherwise destructive that it will eat through or otherwise damage or weaken a tank car's valves although they are maintained with due care. No one suggests that the leak in this case was caused by the inherent properties of acrylonitrile. It was caused by carelessness—whether that of the lessor in failing to maintain or inspect the car properly, or of American in failing to maintain or inspect it, or of the railroad which had custody of the car prior to Indiana, or of Indiana itself in failing to notice the ruptured lid which caused the leak, or some combination of these possible failures of care. Accidents due to a lack of care can be prevented by taking care; and when a lack of care can be shown in court, such accidents are adequately deterred by the threat of liability for negligence.

The district judge and the plaintiff's lawyer make much of the fact that the spill occurred in a densely populated metropolitan area. But this argument overlooks the fact that the railroad network is a hub-and-spoke system and the hubs are in metropolitan areas. With most hazardous chemicals (by volume of shipment) being at least as hazardous as acrylonitrile, it is unlikely that they can be rerouted around all metropolitan areas in the country, except at prohibitive cost. Even if it were feasible to reroute them one would hardly expect shippers, as distinct from carriers, to be the firms best situated to do the rerouting. The difference between shipper and carrier points to a deep flaw in the plaintiff's case. Unlike *Guille*, here it is not the actor—that is, the transporters of acrylonitrile and other chemicals—but the manufacturers, who are sought to be held strictly liable. Is it realistic to suppose that shippers will become students of railroading in order to lay out the safest route by which to ship their goods? Anyway, rerouting is no panacea. Often it will increase the length of the journey, or compel the use of poorer track, or both. When this happens, the probability of an accident is increased, even if the consequences of an accident if one occurs are reduced; so the expected accident cost, being the product of the probability of an accident and the harm if the accident occurs, may rise. It is easy to see how the accident in this case might have been prevented at reasonable cost by greater care on the part of those who handled the tank car of acrylonitrile. It is difficult to see how it might have been prevented at reasonable cost by a change in the activity of transporting the chemical. This is therefore not an apt case for strict liability.

Judgment of trial court reversed; case remanded for trial on the issue of negligence.

Statutory Strict Liability

Strict liability is not an exclusive creation of the courts. Strict liability principles are also embodied in modern legislation. The most important examples of this phenomenon are the *Workers' Compensation Acts* passed by most states in the early decades of this century. Such statutes allow employees to recover statutorily limited amounts from their employers despite the absence of any fault on the part of the employer or the presence of contributory fault on the part of the employee. Employers participate in a compulsory liability insurance system and are expected to pass the costs of the system on to consumers, who then become the ultimate bearers of the human costs of industrial production. Other examples of statutory strict liability include the Dram Shop statutes of some states; such laws impose liability on sellers of alcoholic beverages without proof of any negligence when third parties are harmed due to a buyer's intoxication. Also included is the statutory liability without proof of fault that some states impose on the operators of aircraft for ground damage resulting from aviation accidents.

TORT REFORM

By 1990, most states had enacted some form of tort reform legislation. The primary beneficiaries of such legislation were physicians, local governments, and manufacturers. The main driving force behind the tort reform movement is the "crisis" in the liability insurance system. In recent years, the insurance system has been characterized by outright refusals of coverage, reductions in coverage, and dramatically escalating premiums when coverage remains available. The supporters of tort reform argue that the main factors underlying the insurance crisis are the trend toward strict liability for various harms and escalating damage awards. Observers often attribute this latter factor to the increased frequency with which punitive damages are awarded and to a tendency toward more frequent damage awards for noneconomic harms, such as pain and suffering, in tort cases.

Tort reform advocates also argue that large jury awards contribute to inflation because, where market conditions permit, those who initially bear the cost of liability insurance will pass such costs on to their customers in the form of higher prices. Supporters of tort reform also argue that the threat of huge jury awards impedes the development of new products and technologies.

States have enacted a variety of devices in the name of tort reform. Statutes that limit the amounts recoverable for noneconomic harms are now fairly common, as are statutes that limit the liability of social hosts or businesses for the damage caused by intoxicated persons to whom they serve alcohol. Local governments in many states now enjoy statutory limits on their liability for negligence, affording them partial relief from the negligence claims for improper maintenance of streets and traffic signals; such claims now routinely accompany many automobile accident cases. Likewise, physicians in a number of states have received some relief from spiraling liability costs by reform devices such as caps on the amount recoverable in liability suits and mandatory pretrial mediation of all claims over a prescribed threshold. Finally, statutory ceilings on punitive damage awards or rules making such damages more difficult to recover are also common reform measures.

Critics of the tort reform movement argue that the liability insurance crisis is largely the fault of the insurance industry. Some have argued that insurers have manufactured the crisis to get unjustified premium increases and to divert attention from insurer mismanagement of invested premium income. Others argue that insurers are raising premiums to offset income losses resulting from the drop in interest rates in recent years. Whatever the truth of such allegations, it is becoming increasingly common for state legislatures to couple tort reform legislation with increased regulation of insurers, something that is understandably dulling the insurance industry's enthusiasm for tort reform. For example, Florida forced a rate rollback as a price of tort reform. Other common reform devices include requiring prior approval of rate increases and placing closer restraints on insurer policy cancellation and nonrenewal practices.

The battle for tort reform is far from over, however. Tort reform opponents who lost the fight against tort reform in the legislature have continued it in the courts. Thus, tort reform statutes have been challenged by arguments that statutes capping damage awards violate state constitutional provisions guaranteeing jury trials because they limit jury discretion in setting damages, and by arguments that reform measures targeted at certain types of cases (e.g., medical malpractice cases) violate equal protection guarantees by unjustifiably discriminating against plaintiffs in such cases. Such challenges have succeeded in some states and have been rebuffed in others. Whatever the outcome of the current struggle, the tort reform debate highlights the perennial dilemma facing tort law: how to fashion a system adequately compensating the victims of civil wrongs in an economically efficient manner that does not impose undue burdens on business or society as a whole.

ETHICAL AND PUBLIC POLICY CONCERNS

1. In the *Waters* case earlier in this chapter, the New York City Housing Authority escapes liability to Simone Waters because the court found they had no duty to her. Yet the investigator who testified at the trial said that Waters would probably not have been attacked if the Housing Authority properly maintained the locks on its building. If this testimony is true and the Housing Authority contributed in this way to the attack, does it have any ethical duty to Waters even if it has no legal duty?

2. Implicit in the idea of proximate cause is the fact that a negligent defendant can be the actual cause of some plaintiffs' injuries but avoid any liability for those injuries because his negligence was not the proximate cause of such injuries. Is the doctrine of proximate cause ethically justifiable?

3. While the doctrine of proximate cause allows defendants to avoid responsibility for some consequences of their negligence, the doctrine of strict liability imposes liability on persons who participate in abnormally dangerous activities even though they exercised all possible care to avoid injuring anyone. Can such liability be ethically justified?

SUMMARY

Negligence is the unintentional breach of a duty owed to another person that results in some legally recognizable injury to that person or her property. Each member of society has a general duty to conduct himself as would a reasonable person of ordinary prudence in similar circumstances. Other sources of duty include statutes and contractual or other special relationships between the parties. Statutory violations amount to negligence per se (a presumption of negligence) if they result in the suffering of a harm that the statute was designed to prevent by a person whom the statute was designed to protect.

Breach of duty results when a defendant exposes a person to whom the duty is owed to an unreasonable, foreseeable risk of harm. To determine whether a particular risk of harm is an unreasonable one, the courts balance the social utility of the defendant's conduct and the ease of reducing or eliminating the risk against the likelihood that harm will occur and the seriousness of the probable harm.

Breach of duty standing alone, however, does not produce negligence liability. The plaintiff in a negligence suit must also prove that the defendant's breach of duty was the actual and proximate (legal) cause of his injury. To determine the existence of actual cause, courts employ a "but for" or a "substantial factor" test. The courts have employed a variety of tests for proximate cause. The *Restatement (Second) of Torts* suggests that negligent defendants should not be held responsible for highly extraordinary consequences of their negligence. In some cases, intervening forces may combine with a negligent defendant's conduct to produce a particular plaintiff's injury. Whether such intervening forces amount to an intervening or superseding cause that absolves the defendant of liability depends on several factors. The most prominent factors are the foreseeability of the intervening force, whether the defendant's act increased the risk that the intervening force would come into play, and whether the resulting harm is similar in nature to the harm risked by the defendant's conduct.

In some cases, negligence may be difficult to prove because the person or persons who are most likely to be responsible for the plaintiff's injury have superior knowledge about the causes of the injury and a strong disincentive to share that knowledge with the plaintiff if it points to their liability. The doctrine of *res ipsa loquitur* aids plaintiffs in such cases by creating an inference of negligence when the harm that occurred would not ordinarily occur in the absence of negligence and the defendant had exclusive control of the instrumentality of harm. Where *res ipsa* applies, a defendant must come forward with evidence to rebut the inference that he was negligent and that his negligence caused the plaintiff's injury, or risk being found liable by a court or jury.

In recent years, there has been a trend toward increasing the kinds of injuries for which negligent defendants may be held responsible. Fearing spurious claims and concerned about the difficulties in evaluating purely emotional injuries, the courts long refused to allow persons who had suffered negligently inflicted emotional distress to recover for their injuries in the absence of some impact or physical contact with the victim. Recently, many courts have dispensed with the impact requirement, but many still require some physical injury or symptoms as a result of the victim's emotional distress before they allow recovery. Similarly, the courts traditionally refused to allow recovery for emotional distress caused by witnessing negligently inflicted harms to third persons in the absence of some impact with the person suffering the emotional injury. Today, many courts allow third parties who were themselves within the zone of danger created by the defendant's negligence to recover for their emotional injuries. Some courts have gone even farther and dispensed with the zone of danger requirement where the person injured was a close relative of the third party suffering emotional distress and the distress was the product of the third party's witnessing of the harm to the person injured. However, many courts taking this more liberal position still insist on proof of some physical injury or symptoms resulting from the third party's emotional distress.

Even if a defendant's breach of duty was the actual and proximate cause of a plaintiff's injury, contributory fault on the plaintiff's part can operate to bar or diminish the plaintiff's right to recover. The doctrine of contributory negligence bars any recovery by plaintiffs whose failure to exercise reasonable care for their own safety was a substantial factor in producing their injury. In some cases, however, contributorily negligent plaintiffs can still recover if they can prove that the defendant had the last clear chance to avoid the harm. A growing majority of the states have reacted to the potential harshness of contributory negligence by adopting comparative negligence systems. The details of these systems vary by state, but the essential idea of comparative negligence involves weighing the relative fault of the parties and diminishing a plaintiff's recovery in proportion to his fault.

Plaintiffs who voluntarily expose themselves to a known risk of harm created by a defendant's negligence are held to have assumed the risk of injury and are barred from any recovery. After adopting comparative negligence systems, some states have dispensed with both assumption of risk and contributory negligence, treating all issues of contributory fault in negligence cases under their comparative negligence system. Some states also apply comparative fault principles in recklessness and strict liability cases.

Conduct that demonstrates a conscious disregard for a known high degree of probable harm to others constitutes recklessness. In terms of moral culpability, recklessness lies midway between negligence and intentional wrongdoing. Mere contributory negligence by the plaintiff is not a good defense to recklessness. Reckless defendants are more likely to be found legally responsible for the consequences of their actions and to be subjected to punitive damages than are defendants who were merely negligent.

In some instances, the law imposes strict liability on defendants for injuries produced by their activities, even though the defendants did not intend any harm and may have done everything possible to avoid harm. Strict liability represents a social policy decision that those who participate in certain activities must shoulder all of the risks associated with them. The two most important types of conduct that are subjected to strict liability are the manufacture or sale of defective and unreasonably dangerous products and participation in ultrahazardous or abnormally dangerous activities. We discuss the product liability dimension of strict liability later in the text. Abnormally dangerous activities are those necessarily involving a significant risk of harm to others; this risk cannot be eliminated by the exercise of reasonable care. The decision to classify a particular activity as abnormally dangerous involves judicial consideration of a wide variety of factors in addition to the risk associated with the activity. These include the social utility of the activity, the costs associated with minimizing or eliminating the risk, and whether the activity is one commonly pursued in the area in which the injury occurred. Finally, as a general rule, mere contributory negligence by a plaintiff does not prevent her recovery on a strict liability theory, but assumption of risk by the plaintiff bars recovery.

PROBLEM CASES

1. On September 5, 1984, the Citizens for Bob Olexo Campaign Committee rented three tanks of helium from James Dawes Company. The helium was to be used to fill balloons that were to be handed out to the public during the Belmont County Fair. Although the agreement with Dawes called for the Committee to return the used cylinders, they were left at the fairgrounds leaning up against a commercial building. On September 28, Philip C. Jeffers III, age 14, attended a football game at the fairgrounds, where he and some friends discovered the tanks. Despite the warning on the tanks that said "CAUTION! HIGH PRESSURE GAS. CAN CAUSE RAPID SUFFOCATION," Jeffers inhaled some helium from one of the tanks, collapsed, and died. Jeffers's father sued the Dawes Company, which moved for a summary judgment on a number of grounds, among which was the argument that it owed no duty to Jeffers. Should Dawes's motion be granted?

2. At 1:45 A.M. on September 26, 1982, Gary Knapstad seriously injured his knee when he tripped over a tipped-over "no parking" sign lying in Smith's Management Corporation's parking lot while jogging across the lot to Smith's store. The sign was normally placed in front of the store, along with several barrels, to prevent customers from parking in the fire lane. At the time of his fall, the store was open and the lot was well lit. Knapstad sued Smith's for negligence and won a $22,855 verdict. Smith's appealed, arguing that the trial court's instructions improperly suggested that Smith's would be negligent if, as an expert witness hired by Knapstad testified, the sign failed to comply with federal and state occupational safety and health statutes aimed at providing a safer work environment for employees. Was the trial court's instruction proper?

3. On September 3, 1984, Valerie Jones, a lab technician at Kelco's chemical plant in Okmulgee, Oklahoma, stole a cupful of sulphuric acid from the plant. After work, she drove to the home of her sister-in-law, Gwendolyn Henry. After a brief verbal altercation with Henry over the fact that Henry, who had been babysitting Jones's two-year-old son, had trimmed the child's hair, she threw the acid in Henry's face. Henry suffered severe and permanent injuries, and Jones was ultimately sentenced to seven years in prison for the attack. Henry filed a negligence suit against Kelco, and a jury awarded her $450,000. Kelco appealed, arguing that it owed no duty to Henry and that, in any event, Jones's act was an intervening cause that relieved it of liability. The evidence at trial indicated that Jones had been a model employee who had to have access to the chemical storage area to perform her duties. Should the jury's verdict be reversed?

4. On July 9, 1980, Erroll Dobelle was a passenger on an Amtrak passenger train that left New York City bound for Philadelphia. When the train reached Linden, New Jersey, it passed an Amtrak work train proceeding in the opposite direction on adjoining tracks. As the trains passed, a 15-foot section of unsecured steel buffer rail carried on the work train struck the passenger train, which was moving at 60 miles per hour. The 755-pound buffer rail sliced through the passenger car in which Dobelle was riding, dismembering and killing one passenger, and critically injuring 17 others. Dobelle saw the rail come through the car, feared it would strike him, and at first thought it had because he was spattered with blood. The man on his immediate left was hit, but Dobelle emerged unscathed. When he realized he was all right, he began to help rescue workers assisting the injured passengers. Dobelle suffered serious emotional and psychological problems after the accident, was fired from his position as a vice president of a multimillion dollar company, and was hospitalized on three separate occasions seeking treatment for acute depression. He filed suit against Amtrak for negligent infliction of emotional distress. Amtrak admitted negligence, but moved to dismiss Dobelle's claim. It argued that his emotional injuries were caused by witnessing the harm to the other passengers, and that since none of those injured was a close relative of Dobelle's, he was barred from recovering for those injuries. Should the trial court dismiss Dobelle's claim?

5. Higgins and some friends went to a night baseball game at Comiskey Park in Chicago. Near the end of the game, Higgins went to the men's room. On his way back to his seat, he walked down a corridor that ran past a concession stand. As he passed the stand, the door to the front of the stand (a 4-foot by 6-foot sheet of plywood attached to the top of the stand and hooked to an eyelet in the ceiling when opened) fell from its open position and struck him on the head, causing permanent head and neck injuries. None of the eyewitnesses to the incident saw anyone touch either the door or the hook securing it, or do anything that might have caused the door to fall. There was, however, testimony that, just before the door fell, the crowd in the stadium was screaming and stamping, and that one "could feel the place tremble." Higgins filed suit against the Chicago White Sox, owners of the stadium, arguing that *res ipsa loquitur* should be applied to the case. Was he right?

6. Between 1982 and 1983, Long and Adams, then residents of Cobb County, Georgia, were involved in a sexual relationship. In 1984 Long filed suit against Ad-

ams, arguing that she had negligently infected him with genital herpes. Long argued that Adams knew she was infected with the disease, but had failed to inform him of this crucial fact before having sexual relations with him. Adams moved for a summary judgment on the ground that she owed Long no duty of disclosure. The trial court agreed and granted her motion. Should the trial court's decision be reversed on appeal?

7. Jenkins, an employee of Acme Paper Stock Company, was riding on a freight elevator in Acme's plant when the elevator cable broke. As a result, the hoist motor fell on Jenkins, fatally injuring him. The hoist motor and lifting cables had been installed by Edwards Transfer Company. The evidence at trial indicated that Edwards used steel cables to mount the hoist from an I-beam that ran along the ceiling of Acme's plant, but failed to use "softeners" to protect the cables against the sharp edges of the beam. The evidence also indicated that Acme had warned employees that the elevator was only to be used for freight and was not safe for use as a personnel elevator, and that Jenkins himself had told an Edwards employee prior to the accident that the hoist was improperly secured. Jenkins's heirs filed a negligence suit against Edwards. The trial judge refused to instruct the jury on contributory negligence on the ground that Jenkins could not reasonably have foreseen that he could be injured by the falling hoist motor. Was this refusal proper?

8. On April 25, 1984, Allen Beckett, a fourth-year player on his high school baseball team, was injured when he collided with another player during outfielder practice. The accident occurred after the coach conducting the practice hit a fly ball to Beckett. Beckett called for the ball, but the wind was blowing so hard that neither the coach nor the other players heard him. The coach called for another player to catch the ball, and that player and Beckett collided head-on. Beckett's jaw was broken, and he filed suit against the school, arguing that it had failed to warn him of the danger of such collisions, failed to adequately supervise the practice, and had conducted the practice in an unreasonably dangerous manner. At one point in his testimony Beckett denied that he had ever heard of baseball players colliding and said that he had no knowledge of any accidents happening on baseball fields. Under cross-examination, however, he admitted that his coaches had repeatedly stressed communication among players to avoid accidents, that it was possible on such a windy day for his voice to have gotten lost in the wind, and that the same type of thing could have happened in a game. Was the trial court summary judgment in favor of the school proper?

9. Chris Ewing went to the Cloverleaf Bowl on his 21st birthday. In the cocktail lounge of the bowling alley, Ewing was given a free vodka collins when the bartender discovered that it was his birthday. In the next hour and a half, despite the fact that he was obviously becoming intoxicated, Ewing was served 10 straight shots of 151-proof rum and two beer chasers. He died of acute alcohol poisoning the following day. His two small sons filed suit against the Cloverleaf Bowl. The trial court granted Cloverleaf's motion for a nonsuit, finding as a matter of law that Ewing was guilty of contributory negligence and that the bartender was not reckless. Should the trial court have allowed the jury to hear the case?

10. Lee Ann Laird, age 12, was injured when her bicycle was hit by a car driven by Larry Kostman. Lee Ann was in the process of pulling into the street from a driveway, and she emerged from behind a van parked at the curb. At the trial, Kostman testified that he hit his brakes as soon as he saw the bicycle. His passenger testified that Laird "came out of nowhere," and that he didn't see her until the moment of impact. Laird testified that she saw Kostman's car turn onto the street from an intersection more than 200 feet from the point of impact, that no more than two feet of her bicycle extended into the street from behind the parked van, and that, when she tried to move the bike back to avoid the collision, the brakes locked. After the trial judge refused to instruct the jury on the doctrine of last clear chance, the jury ruled in favor of Kostman. Was the trial judge's refusal proper?

11. Kent, a state highway worker, was killed when the aluminum handle of a rake he was using came into contact with a high voltage distribution line belonging to Gulf States Utilities. Kent's father sued Gulf States, and won a $1 million jury award. Gulf States appealed, and the Louisiana Court of Appeals reversed the trial award on the ground that Kent had been contributorily negligent. Kent's father appealed to the Lousiana Supreme Court, arguing that Gulf States should be held strictly liable for his son's death. Should the jury verdict be reinstated?

CHAPTER 9

INTELLECTUAL PROPERTY, COMPETITIVE TORTS, AND UNFAIR COMPETITION

INTRODUCTION

This chapter discusses a number of legal rules that limit free competition by allowing business parties to recover for certain abuses of that freedom. It opens by considering three such abuses—patent, copyright, and trademark infringement—that together involve the law of *intellectual property.* After examining the misappropriation of *trade secrets,* the chapter then describes three *intentional torts* that limit the behavior in which competitors can engage. The chapter concludes by briefly considering an evolving provision that often is regarded as a general federal ban on unfair competition—section 43(a) of the Lanham Act. Indeed, the term *unfair competition* is sometimes used to collectively describe the rules discussed in this chapter.[1]

Most of the rules discussed in this chapter are supported by one or both of two general policies. The first is to stimulate creative and inventive endeavor and thus to benefit society. If competition is so free that individuals cannot protect the results of such endeavor, their incentive to create and innovate may be reduced. Similarly, in a system of utterly free competition where *anything* goes, creative and inventive people might fall prey to ruthless competitors. Thus, society would be denied the fruits of their endeavor. Second, most of the rules described here further ends that have little to do with stimulating creativity and innovation. By establishing certain minimum standards of ethical competitive behavior, such rules make commercial life more humane and civilized than would otherwise be the case.

PATENTS

Introduction

A patent can be regarded as an agreement between its inventor and the federal government. Under the terms of this agreement, the inventor gets an exclusive right to make, use, and sell his invention, in return for making the invention public by submitting information to the government. The temporary monopoly acquired by the patent holder, or **patentee,** encourages the creation and disclosure of inventions, because there is less incentive to create and to disclose one's creations if others can freely appropriate them. Also, the submission of information to the government enables third parties to learn about the patented invention and to develop it in ways that do not infringe the patentee's rights.

---

[1] You should note that the law regulates unfair competition in other ways besides allowing private parties to recover when they are injured by such competition. Perhaps the clearest example is section 5 of the Federal Trade Commission Act, which gives the FTC the power to attack unfair or deceptive acts or practices.

What Is Patentable?

Any of the following may be the subject matter of a patent: (1) a *process* (as described in the following *Diamond* case), (2) a *machine*, (3) a *manufacture* or product, (4) a *composition of matter* (a combination of elements possessing qualities not found in the elements taken individually, such as a new chemical compound), (5) an *improvement* of any of the above, (6) an *ornamental design* for a product, and (7) a *plant* produced by asexual reproduction. Naturally occurring things (e.g., a new wild plant) and new business methods (e.g., an innovative accounting technique) are not patentable. Also, as the *Diamond* case states, abstract ideas, scientific laws, and other mental concepts are not patentable, although their practical applications often are.

Even though an invention fits within one of the above categories, it is not patentable if it lacks novelty, is obvious, or is without utility.[2] One example of the *novelty* requirement is the doctrine of *anticipation*, which states that no patent should be issued where *before the invention's creation* it has been: (1) known or used in the United States, (2) patented in the United States or a foreign country, or (3) described in a printed publication in the United States or a foreign country. Another example is the requirement that no patent should be issued if more than one year before the *patent application* the invention was: (1) patented in the United States or a foreign country, (2) described in a printed publication in the United States or a foreign country, or (3) in public

use or on sale in the United States. In addition, there can be no patent if at the time of its occurrence the invention would have been *obvious* to a person having ordinary skill in the area. Finally, there is a general requirement that the invention possess *utility*, or usefulness, in order to be patentable.

Also, there can be no patent if the party seeking it did not create the invention in question, or if she abandoned the invention. *Creation* problems frequently arise where several people allegedly contributed to the invention. *Abandonment* can be by express statement, such as publicly devoting an invention to mankind, or by implication from conduct, such as delaying for an unreasonable length of time before making a patent application.

Obtaining a Patent

The Patent and Trademark Office of the Department of Commerce handles patent applications. The application must include a *specification* describing the invention with sufficient detail and clarity to enable any person skilled in the area to make and use it. It must also state the inventor's *claims*: the allegedly novel, nonobvious, and useful features of the invention. The Patent Office checks the application for detail and clarity of description, and determines whether the invention meets the various tests for patentability. If the application is rejected, the applicant may amend and resubmit it. Once any of the applicant's claims has been twice rejected, the applicant may appeal to the Office's Board of Patent Appeals and Interferences. Subsequent appeals to the federal courts also are possible. In the *Diamond* case, the government appealed a federal court decision in favor of the patentee.

---

[2] Plant and design patents are subject to slightly different requirements than those stated in this section.

DIAMOND v. DIEHR

450 U.S. 175 (U.S. Sup. Ct. 1981)

Diehr and Lutton attempted to obtain a patent covering a process for molding raw, uncured synthetic rubber into cured precision products. The process used a mold for shaping the uncured rubber under heat and pressure and then curing it in the mold. Previous efforts at curing and molding synthetic rubber had suffered from an inability to measure the temperature inside the molding press, and thus to determine a precise curing time. Diehr and Lutton's invention involved a process for constantly measuring the temperature inside the mold, feeding this information to a computer that constantly recalculated the curing time, and enabling the computer to signal the molding press to open at the correct instant.

The patent examiner rejected Diehr and Lutton's patent application. The Patent and Trademark Office Board of Appeals (now the Board of Patent Appeals and Interferences) agreed with the examiner, but the now-defunct Court of Customs and Patent Appeals reversed. The Patent Office appealed to the U.S. Supreme Court.

Rehnquist, Justice. In defining the nature of a patentable process, this Court has stated:

A process is a mode of treatment of certain materials to produce a given result. It is an act, or a series of acts, performed upon the subject matter to be transformed and reduced to a different state or thing. If new and useful, it is just as patentable as is a piece of machinery. The machinery pointed out as suitable to perform the process may or may not be new or patentable; whilst the process itself may be altogether new and produce an entirely new result.

Recently, we repeated the above definition, adding: "Transformation and reduction of an article to a different state or thing is the clue to the patentability of a process claim that does not include particular machines." That Diehr and Lutton's claims involve the transformation of an article, raw uncured synthetic rubber, into a different state or thing cannot be disputed. Industrial processes such as this have historically been eligible to receive the protection of our patent laws.

Excluded from patent protection are laws of nature, physical phenomena, and abstract ideas. Only last Term, we explained:

A new mineral discovered in the earth or a new plant found in the wild is not patentable subject matter. Likewise, Einstein could not patent his celebrated law that $E = mc^2$; nor could Newton have patented the law of gravity. Such discoveries are manifestations of nature, free to all men and reserved exclusively to none.

Diehr and Lutton do not seek to patent a mathematical formula. Instead, they seek patent protection for a process of curing synthetic rubber. Their process employs a well-known mathematical equation, but they do not seek to preempt the use of that equation. They seek only to foreclose from others the use of that equation in conjunction with all the other steps in their process. It is now a commonplace that an *application* of a law of nature or mathematical formula to a known structure or process may be deserving of patent protection.

It may later be determined that the process is not deserving of patent protection because it fails to satisfy the statutory conditions of novelty or nonobviousness. A rejection on either of these grounds does not affect the determination that Diehr and Lutton's claims recited subject matter which was eligible for patent protection.

Judgment for Diehr and Lutton affirmed.

Ownership and Transfer of Patent Rights

One who obtains a patent generally gets exclusive rights to make, use, and sell the patented invention for a 17-year period. Design patents, however, are effective for only 14 years. The patentee can transfer title to all or part of his patent rights by *assigning* them. He may also retain title and *license* all or some of his rights.

Usually, the party who created the invention is the patent holder. What happens, however, when the creator of the invention is an employee and her employer seeks rights in her invention? If the invention was developed by an employee *hired to do inventive or creative work*, she must use the invention solely for the employer's benefit and must assign any patents she obtains to the employer. But if the employee was hired for purposes *other than invention or creation*, she owns any patent she acquires. Regardless of the purpose for which the employee was hired, finally, the *shop right* doctrine gives the employer a nonexclusive, royalty-free *license* to use the employee's invention if it was created on company time and through company facilities. In such situations, the employee still has normal patent rights against parties other than the employer.

Patent Infringement

A *direct* patent infringement occurs when a third party makes, uses, or sells a patented invention without the patentee's authorization. It is fairly easy to establish a direct infringement where the subject matter made, used, or sold is clearly within the language of a successful patent application. Courts also find direct infringement where this subject matter is substantially equivalent to the protected subject matter. Under this *doctrine of equivalents*, an infringement occurs where the third party's subject matter performs substantially the same function as the protected invention in substantially the same way to produce substantially the same result. The aim of this doctrine is to prevent third parties from capitalizing on the patentee's creativity by slightly altering the patented invention before making, using, or selling it.

Also, one who *actively induced* another's infringement of a patent is liable as an infringer if he knew and intended that the infringement occur. This can happen where, for example, a party sells an instruction manual for using a patented machine to a direct patent infringer. Finally, if one knowingly sells to a direct patent infringer a component of a patented invention or something useful in employing a patented process, the seller may be liable for *contributory infringement*. For such liability to exist, the thing sold must be a material part of the invention and must not be a staple article of commerce with some other significant use. For example, suppose that Davis directly infringes Potter's patent for a radio by selling almost-identical radios. If Thomas sells Davis sophisticated circuitry for the radios with knowledge of Davis's infringement, Thomas may be liable for contributory infringement if the circuitry is an important component of the radios and has no other significant uses. This would be true even where the circuitry itself is not patented or patentable.

Defenses   An obvious defense to a patent infringement suit is that the subject matter of the alleged infringement is neither within the literal scope of the patent nor substantially equivalent to the patented invention. Also, the alleged infringer may defend by attacking the validity of the patent. Despite their approval by the Patent and Trademark Office, many patents are declared invalid when challenged in court.

Further, in certain cases the defendant may be able to assert that the patentee has been guilty of *patent misuse*. This is behavior unjustifiably exploiting the patent monopoly. For example, the patent owner may require the purchaser of a license on his patent to buy his unpatented goods, or may tie the obtaining of a license on one of his patented inventions to the purchase of a license on another.[3] In such cases, one who refuses to accept the patentee's terms and later infringes the patent may be able to escape liability by arguing that the patent holder misused his monopoly position.

Remedies   If successful in an infringement suit, the patentee gets damages adequate to compensate for the infringement, plus court costs and interest. The damages must not be less than a reasonable royalty for the use made of the invention by the infringer. Also, the court may in its discretion award damages of up to three times those actually found to exist. Finally, injunctive relief is available to prevent violation of any right secured by the patent, and attorney's fees may be awarded in exceptional cases.

COPYRIGHTS

Introduction

By giving creative people certain exclusive rights to their intellectual endeavors, copyright law lets them prevent others from using their work in certain ways. This benefits society by giving such individuals an incentive toward innovative activity. But copyright law also attempts to balance this purpose against the equally compelling public interest in the free movement of ideas, information, and commerce. It does so mainly by limiting the intellectual products it protects, and by allowing the fair use defense described later.

Coverage

Federal copyright law protects a wide range of creative works, including books, periodicals, dramatic and musical compositions, works of art, motion pictures, sound recordings, lectures, computer programs, and architectural plans. To merit copyright protection, such works must be *fixed*: set out in any tangible medium of expression from which they can be perceived, reproduced, or communicated. They must also be *original* (the author's own work), but unlike

---

[3] Some forms of patent misuse may be antitrust violations. This text's second antitrust chapter discusses the interaction between patent law and antitrust law.

the inventions protected by patent law, they need not be novel.

Copyright protection does not extend to ideas, concepts, principles, discoveries, procedures, processes, systems, and methods of operation as such. However, it may protect the *form in which they are expressed*. The story line of a play, for instance, probably is protected, but the original idea underlying it or an abstract statement of its theme probably is not. Although there can be no copyright in facts as such, nonfiction works and compilations of fact are protectible if their creation involved originality. The *Narell* case at the end of this section discusses the protection of phrases and expressions within a copyrighted work.

Creation and Notice

A copyright comes into existence upon the creation and fixing of a protected work. For works created in 1978 and thereafter, the copyright usually lasts for *the life of the author plus 50 years*. Although a copyright owner may register the copyright with the Copyright Office of the Library of Congress, registration is not necessary for the copyright to exist. However, registration often *is* necessary before the owner can begin a suit for copyright infringement, which we discuss shortly.[4]

Copyright owners often provide *notice* of the copyright once the work is published. Federal law authorizes various forms of notice for different copyrighted works. A book, for example, might include the term *Copyright*, the year of its first publication, and the name of the copyright owner in a location likely to give reasonable notice to readers. Due to a 1988 amendment to federal copyright law, notice now is only optional, but it can be useful to copyright owners. If proper notice is present, for example, the defendant in an infringement suit usually cannot reduce the actual or statutory damages described at the end of this section by claiming that the infringement was innocent.

Ownership Rights

The owner of a copyright has the exclusive rights to: (1) reproduce the copyrighted work, (2) prepare derivative works based on it (e.g., a movie version of a novel), (3) distribute copies of the work by sale or otherwise, and

(4) perform or display the work publicly. Because these rights are exclusive, a valid copyright blocks their exercise by parties other than the owner.

Ownership of a copyright initially resides in the creator of the copyrighted work, but the copyright may be transferred to another party. Also, the original owner may individually transfer each of the listed rights, or a portion of each, without losing ownership of the remaining rights. Most transfers of copyright ownership require a writing signed by the owner or his agent. The owner also may retain ownership while licensing the copyrighted work or a portion of it.

Infringement

Anyone violating any of the copyright owner's exclusive rights may be liable for *copyright infringement*. Infringement is easily proven where direct evidence of copying exists; verbatim copying of protected material is an example. But as the *Narell* case states, infringement usually is established by showing that the defendant had *access* to the copyrighted work and that there is *substantial similarity* between that work and the allegedly infringing work. Access can be proven circumstantially—for example, by wide circulation of the copyrighted work. Determining substantial similarity necessarily involves discretionary case-by-case judgments; *Narell* provides one example.

Fair Use   The main defense to a copyright infringement suit is the doctrine of **fair use.** This defense involves the weighing of several factors whose application varies from case to case. These factors are: (1) the purpose and character of the use, (2) the nature of the copyrighted work, (3) the amount and substantiality of the portion used in relation to the copyrighted work as a whole, and (4) the effect of the use on the potential market for the copyrighted work or on its value. *Narell* discusses and applies these factors.

Remedies   The basic remedy available in a successful copyright infringement suit is an award of the owner's actual damages plus the profits received by the infringer. However, the plaintiff may elect to receive statutory damages in lieu of the basic remedy. Now, these range from $500 to $20,000 for nonwillful infringements, with a ceiling of $100,000 where the infringement was willful. Injunctive relief and awards of costs and attorney's fees are possible in certain cases. Criminal penalties for willful infringements involving the pursuit of commercial advantage also exist.

---

[4] Due to the Berne Convention Implementation Act of 1988, registration is *not* a prerequisite to suits for the infringement of copyrights in certain works whose country of origin is not the United States.

NARELL v. FREEMAN

872 F.2d 907 (9th Cir. 1989)

Irena Narell wrote a social history of the Bay area Jewish community entitled *Our City: The Jews of San Francisco*. After its publication in 1981, her book sold fewer than 5,000 copies. In 1986, Narell repurchased the copyright and the remaining inventory from the publisher.

Illusions of Love, a novel by Cynthia Freeman, was published in hardcover in 1984 and in paperback in 1986, selling approximately 1 million copies. *Illusions* told a fictional story about the heir of a large, wealthy Jewish family who had to choose between his family and a lover from a vastly different background. Freeman consulted and used *Our City* in writing *Illusions*, and portions of *Illusions* were based on historical events described in *Our City*. Also, *Illusions* contained several instances of verbatim copying from *Our City*; these totaled about 300 words. On several more occasions, Freeman also paraphrased passages from Narell's book.

Narell sued Freeman and her publishers for copyright infringement in federal district court. The court granted the defendants' motion for summary judgment and Narell appealed.

Farris, Circuit Judge.   To establish a successful copyright infringement claim, Narell must show that she owns the copyright and that Freeman copied protected elements of the work. Because in most copyright cases direct evidence of copying is not available, a plaintiff may establish copying by showing that the infringer had access to the work and that the two works are substantially similar. Narell's ownership of the copyright and Freeman's access to Narell's work are not in dispute.

The [first] question is whether Freeman's admitted takings—several instances of identical phrases and the more numerous paraphrases—were of protected material. Copyright law protects only an author's expression. Facts and ideas within a work are not protected. Freeman largely took unprotected factual information from *Our City*.

Freeman did copy a few phrases from Narell. Ordinary phrases [and] phrases and expressions conveying an idea typically expressed in a limited number of stereotyped fashions are not subject to copyright protection. Most of the phrases Freeman copied are commonly used expressions, such as describing a muddy street as a "cow path." The appropriation of expressive elements is minimal. The more numerous paraphrasings cited by Narell [also] cannot be said to take the expressive elements of her work. Instead, unprotected factual details are taken, although in some cases commonly used expressions are echoed, such as "mosquitos ravished his flesh" versus "mosquitos feasted on his flesh." Freeman's borrowings did not take a sequence of creative expression, as opposed to an ordinary phrase, and therefore were not infringing.

The arguments of the parties and the decision of the district court focused on the issues of substantial similarity and fair use. Viewed as a whole, the two works have slight resemblance to each other. *Illusions* is a romantic novel. *Our City* is a historical treatment of the Bay area Jewish community. The similarities between the two works are neither quantitatively nor qualitatively significant. Quantitatively insignificant infringement may be substantial only if the material is qualitatively important to either work. The passages at issue are a small part of Narell's book. The material taken is not qualitatively important to either book. Because of the fundamental differences between the works and the insubstantial nature of the copied passages, no reasonable reader could conclude that the works are substantially similar.

The doctrine of fair use allows [one] to use copyrighted material in a reasonable manner without the consent of the copyright owner. The copyright act sets out four factors for evaluating whether a use is a fair use.

Purpose and Character of the Use—The first factor strongly weighs against Freeman, because commercial use of copyrighted material is presumptively unfair. Freeman's use is admittedly commercial.

Nature of the Copyrighted Work—The scope of permissible fair use is greater with an informational work than a creative work. Although this factor weighs slightly in Freeman's favor, Narell's work contains enough creative expression that any use of it is not presumptively fair.

Amount and Substantiality of Portions Used—This factor essentially repeats the analysis of the substantial similarity test. This factor weighs strongly in Freeman's favor.

Effect on the Market—This is the single most important element of fair use. The publication of *Illusions* has not had, and is not likely to have, any effect on the value or marketability of *Our City.* The works are directed to fundamentally different purposes. Readers interested in Narell's book are highly unlikely to find historical romance novels an acceptable substitute.

In sum, the first factor weighs strongly in Narell's favor and the second factor slightly favors Freeman. However, the third and final factors strongly favor Freeman. Because of the predominant role of the market factor, the district court's grant of summary judgment on the fair use defense should be affirmed.

Summary judgment for Freeman affirmed.

TRADEMARKS

Introduction

The main reason trademark owners enjoy legal protection against users of their marks is to help purchasers identify favored products and services. This end would be defeated if competition were so free that anyone could use another's trademark whenever he desired. Also, sellers and manufacturers would have less incentive to innovate and to strive for quality if consumers could not identify the source of superior products or services because competitors were free to appropriate each other's trademarks. For these reasons, trademarks are protected under the federal Lanham Act.[5]

Protected Marks

The Lanham Act recognizes four kinds of marks. It defines a *trademark* as any word, name, symbol, device, or combination thereof used by a manufacturer or seller to identify its products and to distinguish them from the products of competitors. On occasion, federal trademark protection has been extended to colors, pictures, label and package designs, slogans, sounds, arrangements of numbers and/or letters (e.g., "7-Eleven"), and shapes of goods or their containers (e.g., Coca-Cola bottles). *Service marks* are similar to trademarks, but are used to identify and distinguish services.

Certification marks certify the origin, materials, quality, method of manufacture, or other aspects of goods and services. Here, the user of the mark and its owner are distinct parties. A retailer, for example, may sell products bearing the Good Housekeeping Seal of Approval. *Collective marks* are trademarks or service marks used by organizations to identify themselves as the source of goods or services. Trade union and trade association marks fall into this category. Although all of these different marks receive federal protection, the discussion in this text mainly involves trademarks and service marks, using the terms *mark* or *trademark* to refer to both.

Distinctiveness

Because their aim is to help consumers identify products and services, trademarks must be *distinctive* to merit maximum Lanham Act protection. As stated later in the *Levi Strauss* case, marks fall into four general categories of distinctiveness:

---

[5] In addition, the owner of a trademark may enjoy legal protection under common law trademark doctrines and state trademark statutes.

1. *Arbitrary or fanciful marks.* These marks are the most distinctive—and the most likely to be protected—because they do not describe or suggest the qualities of the product or service they identify. The "Exxon" trademark is an example.

2. *Suggestive marks.* These marks convey the nature of a product or service only through the exercise of imagination, thought, and perception. A "Dietene" trademark for a dietary food supplement is an example. Although not as secure as arbitrary or fanciful marks, suggestive marks still are good candidates for protection.

3. *Descriptive marks.* These marks directly describe the product or service they identify—for example, "Exquisite" wearing apparel. Descriptive marks are usually not protected unless they acquire a *secondary meaning*. This occurs when their identification with particular goods or services has become firmly established in the minds of a substantial number of buyers. Among the factors considered in secondary meaning determinations are the length of time the mark has been used, the volume of sales associated with that use, and the nature of the advertising employing the mark. When applied to a package delivery service, for instance, the term "overnight" is usually just descriptive and thus not protectible. But it may come to deserve trademark protection through long use by a single firm that advertised it extensively and made many sales while doing so.

4. *Generic marks.* Generic marks (e.g., "diamond" or "truck") simply refer to the general class of which the particular product or service is one example. Because any seller has the right to call a product or service by its common name, generic marks are quite unlikely to receive Lanham Act protection.

Federal Registration

Once the seller of a product or service uses a mark in commerce or forms a bona fide intention to do so, she may attempt to register the mark with the U.S. Patent and Trademark Office. The office reviews applications for distinctiveness. Its decision to deny or grant the application can usually be contested either by the applicant or by a party who feels that he would be injured by registration of the mark. Such challenges eventually may find their way to the federal courts.

Trademarks that are sufficiently distinctive are placed on the Principal Register of the Patent and Trademark Office. A mark's inclusion in the Principal Register gives its owner several advantages. For example, it: (1) is prima facie evidence that the registrant owns the mark, which is useful in trademark infringement suits; (2) gives nationwide constructive notice of the owner's exclusive right to use the mark as of the time the application was filed, thus eliminating the need to show that the defendant in an infringement suit had notice of the mark; and (3) makes the mark incontestable after five years, as described later.

Excluded Marks   Regardless of their distinctiveness, however, some kinds of marks are specifically denied placement on the Principal Register. Examples include marks that: (1) consist of the flags or other insignia of governments; (2) consist of the name, portrait, or signature of a living person; (3) are immoral, deceptive, or scandalous; or (4) are likely to cause confusion or deceive because they resemble a mark previously registered or used in the United States. Certain other marks are not placed on the Principal Register unless they have acquired a secondary meaning. Examples include marks that: (1) are deceptively misdescriptive (such as "Dura-Skin" plastic gloves); (2) are geographically descriptive (e.g., "Nationwide" Life Insurance); or (3) are primarily a surname (because everyone should have the right to use his own name in connection with his business).

Transfer of Rights

Due to the purposes underlying trademark law, the transfer of trademark rights is more difficult than the transfer of copyright or patent interests. The owner of a trademark may license the use of the mark, but only if the licensee is a related company through which the owner can control the nature and quality of the goods or services identified by the mark. An uncontrolled "naked license" would allow the sale of goods or services bearing the mark but lacking the qualities formerly associated with it, and could confuse purchasers. Trademark rights also may be assigned or sold, but only along with the sale of the goodwill of the business originally using the mark.

Losing Federal Trademark Protection

Due to a 1988 amendment to the Lanham Act, federal registration of a trademark now lasts for 10 years rather than the previous 20 years. Renewals for additional

10-year periods are possible. However, trademark protection may be lost before the period expires. First, a third party may undertake a successful *cancellation proceeding* before the Patent and Trademark Office. If the mark is on the Principal Register, the proceeding must occur within five years of its issuance or the mark becomes *incontestable*. This means that a challenger's permissible reasons for attacking the mark become quite limited.

A second way in which the owner may lose trademark protection is by *abandonment*. This can occur through an express statement or agreement to abandon, through the mark's losing its significance as an indication of origin, or through the owner's failure to use the mark. Abandonment of the mark is presumed if it is not used for two years. Thirdly, the owner may lose protection if the trademark acquires a *generic meaning* by coming to refer to a class of products or services rather than a particular product or service. This has happened to such once-protected marks as aspirin and cellophane, and may yet happen to Xerox copiers. Finally, *improperly licensing or assigning* trademark rights under the rules described above may also result in their loss.

Trademark Infringement

Under section 32(1) of the Lanham Act, a registered trademark is infringed when, without the registrant's consent, another party uses a substantially similar mark in connection with the advertisement or sale of goods or services, and this is likely to cause confusion, mistake, or deception regarding their origin. The *Levi Strauss* case discusses many of the factors that courts sift and weigh when determining whether the use is likely to cause confusion, mistake, or deception.[6]

Remedies   A trademark owner who wins an infringement suit can obtain an injunction against uses of the mark that are likely to cause confusion. In certain circumstances, the owner can also obtain money damages for provable injury resulting from the infringement and for profits realized by the defendant from the sale of infringing products or services.

---

[6] As the case indicates, Lanham Act section 43(a), which is discussed at the end of the chapter, also provides a remedy for trademark infringement. In fact, section 43(a)'s protection extends to *unregistered* trademarks.

LOIS SPORTSWEAR, INC. v. LEVI STRAUSS & CO.

799 F. 2d 867 (2d Cir. 1986)

Levi Strauss & Co. makes Levi Jeans. Each pair of Levi Jeans has a distinctive back pocket stitching pattern consisting of two intersecting arcs that roughly bisect both pockets. Levi Strauss has continuously used this pattern on all its jeans since 1873, and has an incontestable federal trademark in the pattern. Over the years, the pattern has become strongly identified with Levi Jeans in the minds of consumers.

Lois Sportswear, Inc. imported jeans made by a Spanish manufacturer into the United States. These jeans had a back pocket stitching pattern substantially similar to the Levi Strauss pattern. Levi Strauss sued Lois under the Lanham Act in federal district court. After Levi Strauss successfully moved for a summary judgment, Lois appealed.

Timbers, Circuit Judge.   As a threshold matter, we have found it useful to decide how much protection a trademark is to be given by determining what type of trademark is at issue. Arrayed in an ascending order which roughly reflects their eligibility to trademark status and the degree of protection accorded, the classes are: (1) generic, (2) descriptive, (3) suggestive, and (4) arbitrary or fanciful. Superimposed on this framework is the rule that registered trademarks are presumed to be distinctive and should be afforded the utmost protection. Under this framework, Levi

Strauss's pattern deserves the highest degree of protection. First, the mark is registered and incontestable. Second, the mark, being a fanciful pattern of interconnected arcs, is entitled to the most protection the Lanham Act can provide.

In either a claim of trademark infringement under [Lanham Act] section 32 or a claim of unfair competition under section 43, a prima facie case is made out by showing the use of one's trademark by another in a way that is likely to confuse consumers as to the source of the product. In deciding the issue of likelihood of confusion, [we rely] on a multifactor balancing test. The factors serve as a useful guide through a difficult quagmire.

The first factor—the strength of the mark—weighs heavily in Levi Strauss's favor. The strength of a mark [is] its tendency to identify goods as emanating from a particular source. Levi Strauss's stitching pattern is a fanciful registered trademark with a very strong secondary meaning. Virtually all jeans customers associate the pattern with Levi Strauss's products. This makes it likely that consumers will assume wrongly that Levi Strauss is somehow associated with Lois's jeans or has authorized the use of its mark.

The second factor—the degree of similarity of the marks—also weighs in favor of Levi Strauss. The two stitching patterns are essentially identical. The third factor—the proximity of the products—likewise weighs in favor of Levi Strauss. Both products are jeans. Although Lois argues that its jeans are designer jeans and are sold to a different market segment than Levi Strauss's jeans, there is evidence of an overlap of market segments. Even if the two jeans are in different segments, a consumer observing Levi Strauss's striking pattern on Lois's designer jeans might assume that Levi Strauss had chosen to enter that market segment using a subsidiary corporation.

The fourth factor—bridging the gap—does not aid Lois's case. Under this factor, if the owner of a trademark can show that it intends to enter the market of an alleged infringer, that showing helps establish a future likelihood of confusion. Levi Strauss has an interest in preserving its trademark should it ever wish to produce designer jeans with the stitching pattern.

The fifth factor—actual confusion—while not helping Levi Strauss, does not really hurt its case. Levi Strauss's only evidence of actual confusion was a consumer survey which the district court discounted due to methodological defects. Of course, actual confusion need not be shown to prevail under the Lanham Act, since actual confusion is very difficult to prove and the act only requires a likelihood of confusion. While the complete absence of actual confusion evidence may weigh in a defendant's favor, the survey evidence, even with its defects, is still somewhat probative of actual confusion.

The sixth factor—the junior user's good faith in adopting the mark—weighs in favor of Lois. The evidence indicates that Lois happened on the stitching pattern serendipitously. The seventh factor—the quality of the respective goods—also adds some weight to Lois's position. Lois's jeans are not of an inferior quality, arguably reducing Levi Strauss's interest in protecting its reputation from debasement.

The eighth and final factor—the sophistication of relevant buyers—does not favor Lois. The typical buyer of designer jeans is sophisticated with respect to jeans buying. It is a sophisticated jeans consumer who is most likely to assume that the presence of Levi Strauss's stitching pattern on Lois's jeans indicates some sort of association between the two. Presumably, it is these sophisticated buyers who pay the most attention to back pocket stitching patterns and their "meanings."

Judgment in favor of Levi Strauss affirmed.

CONCEPT REVIEW

THE THREE FORMS OF INTELLECTUAL PROPERTY COMPARED

	Patent	**Copyright**	**Trademark**
What Is Protected?	Process, machine, product, composition of matter, improvement, ornamental design, plant produced by asexual reproduction, if *novel*, *nonobvious*, and *useful*	Wide range of creative works that are *fixed* and *original*	Trademarks, service marks, certification marks, and collective marks of sufficient distinctiveness
Registration Needed?	Yes	Although copyright exists absent registration, registration often necessary for infringement suit	Necessary for infringement suit under section 32(1). Unregistered marks protected under section 43(a).
Duration	17 years (14 years for design patents)	Life of author plus 50 years	10 years, with 10-year renewals possible
Transferability	By assignment or license	By assignment or license	Limited
How Infringed	Making, using, or selling patented invention or its substantial equivalent	Violation of owner's exclusive rights to reproduce, prepare derivative works, distribute copies, perform, or display. But *fair use* defense available.	Use of mark in connection with advertisement or sale that is likely to cause confusion, mistake, or deception regarding origin

TRADE SECRETS

Introduction

By providing a civil remedy for the misappropriation of trade secrets, the law affords an alternative means of protecting creative inventions. Owners of such inventions may go public and obtain monopoly patent rights. Or they may keep the invention secret and rely on trade secrets law to protect it. Figure 1 sketches some of the advantages and disadvantages of each alternative.

However, the policies underlying the granting of patent rights and the protection of trade secrets differ. As you have seen, the general aim of patent law is to encourage the creation and disclosure of inventions by granting the patentee a temporary monopoly in the patented invention in exchange for his making the invention public. Trade secrets, however, are nonpublic by definition. Although protecting valuable trade secret information may stimulate creative activity, it also keeps the information from becoming public knowledge. Thus, the main justification for such protection is simply to preserve certain standards of commercial ethics. In general, parties who acquire another's trade secrets are only liable when they use improper means or breach some duty of confidentiality.

Definition of a Trade Secret

A trade secret can be defined as any secret formula, pattern, process, program, device, method, technique, or compilation of information that is used in its owner's business and that gives the owner an advantage over competitors who do not know it or use it.[7] Examples

---

[7] This definition comes mainly from *Restatement of Torts* section 757, comment b (1939), with some additions from *Uniform Trade Secrets Act* section 1(4) (1985). About half of the states have adopted the Uniform Trade Secrets Act (UTSA) in some form. The discussion in this text is a composite of the *Restatement's* and the UTSA's rules. One difference between the *Restatement's* and the UTSA's definitions of a trade secret is that the UTSA does not require that the secret be used in the owner's business. Thus, the UTSA's broader definition of a trade secret protects owners who have not yet put their secret information to use.

FIGURE 1   Patent and Trade Secrets Protection Compared

Factor	Patent Law	Trade Secrets Law
Range of Protected Matter?	Probably narrower than trade secrets law	Probably broader than patent law
Need to Register?	Yes	No
Burden of Maintaining Secrecy?	No	Yes
Duration	Usually 17 years	So long as secrecy maintained?
Transferability	Fairly easy	Fairly easy
Ability to Keep Knowledge Secret?	No	Yes, if secrecy really maintained
Effective Monopoly over Protected Matter?	Yes	No, because discovery/use by proper means is permissible

include chemical formulas, manufacturing processes, designs for machines, and customer lists. To be protectible, a trade secret usually must have the kind of value or originality that provides an actual or potential competitive advantage. But it need not possess the novelty required for patent protection.

The following *Mason* case lists and applies some factors courts may consider when determining whether a trade secret exists. As several of those factors suggest, a trade secret must actually be *secret*. Absolute secrecy is not required, but a substantial measure of secrecy is necessary. Thus, information that becomes public knowledge or becomes generally known in the industry cannot be a trade secret. Also, information that is reasonably discoverable by proper means may not be protected. Here, *proper means* include independent invention of the secret, observation of a publicly displayed product, the owner's advertising, published literature, product analysis, and reverse engineering (starting with a legitimately acquired product and working backward to discover how it was developed).

In addition, a firm claiming a trade secret must usually show that it took *reasonable measures to assure secrecy*. Examples of such measures include advising employees about the secrecy of the secret, limiting access to the secret on a need-to-know basis, requiring those given access to sign a nondisclosure agreement, disclosing the secret only on a confidential basis, and controlling access to an office or plant. Because the owner is only required to make such efforts as are reasonable under the circumstances, the required measure or measures vary with the facts of the case. As a general

rule, though, owners are not required to adopt extreme measures to block every ingenious form of industrial espionage.

Ownership and Transfer of Trade Secrets

Usually, the owner of a trade secret is the person who developed it or the business under whose auspices it was generated. But establishing the original ownership of a trade secret can be a problem where an employee has developed a secret in the course of her employment. In such cases, courts often find the *employer* to be the owner if: (1) the employee was hired to do creative work related to the secret, (2) the employee agreed not to divulge or use trade secrets, or (3) other employees contributed to the development of the secret. Even where the employee owns the secret, the employer still may obtain a royalty-free license to use it through the shop right doctrine discussed in the section on patents earlier in this chapter.

The actual owner of a trade secret can transfer rights in the secret to third parties. This can occur by assignment (in which case the owner loses title) or by license (in which case the owner retains title but allows the transferee certain uses of the secret).

Misappropriation of Trade Secrets

Misappropriation of a trade secret can occur in various ways, most of which involve *disclosure or use* of the secret. For example, misappropriation liability occurs when the secret is disclosed or used by one who:

1. Acquired it by *improper means*. In general, improper means are means that fall below generally accepted standards of commercial morality and reasonable conduct. These include theft, trespass, wiretapping, spying, bugging, bribery, fraud, impersonation, and eavesdropping.

2. Acquired it from a party who *is known or should be known* to have obtained it by improper means. For example, a free-lance industrial spy might obtain one firm's trade secrets by improper means and sell them to the firm's competitors. If those competitors know or have reason to know that the spy obtained the secrets by improper means, they are liable for misappropriation along with the spy.

3. *Breached a duty of confidentiality* regarding the secret. Where an employer owns a trade secret, for example, an employee generally is bound not to use or disclose it either during her employment or thereafter. The employee may, however, utilize general knowledge and skills acquired during her employment.[8]

Remedies

A plaintiff who is successful in a suit for misappropriation of a trade secret may obtain damages, which might include both the actual loss caused by the misappropriation and the defendant's unjust enrichment (where this is not duplicative). In some states, punitive damages are awarded for willful and malicious misappropriations. Also, an injunction may be issued against actual or threatened misappropriations.

---

[8] This is an application of the agent's duty of loyalty, which is discussed in this text's first agency law chapter.

MASON v. JACK DANIEL DISTILLERY

518 So. 2d 130 (Ala. Civ. App. 1987)

Tony Mason created a mixed drink that he named "Lynchburg Lemonade." The drink consisted of Jack Daniel's whiskey, Triple Sec, sweet and sour mix, and 7-Up. Mason served the drink at his restaurant and lounge, where it became very popular. Later, Winston Randle, a sales representative for Jack Daniel Distillery, drank Lynchburg Lemonade while in Mason's restaurant and lounge. Although the source of his information was not clear, he also learned the recipe for the drink at this time. Randle informed his superiors about Lynchburg Lemonade and its recipe, and about one year later Jack Daniel was developing a national promotion campaign for the drink.

Mason, who never received any compensation for this use of Lynchburg Lemonade, sued Jack Daniel and Winston for misappropriation of a trade secret. Mason won a trial court jury verdict, and the defendants appealed the trial court's refusal to grant their motion for a directed verdict.

Holmes, Judge. The defendants contend that Mason's recipe for Lynchburg Lemonade was not a trade secret. The *Restatement* provides in pertinent part:

A trade secret may consist of any formula, pattern, device, or compilation of information which is used in one's business, and which gives him an opportunity to obtain an advantage over competitors who do not know or use it. . . .

An exact definition of a trade secret is not possible. Some factors to be considered in determining whether given information is one's trade secret are: (1) the extent to which the information is known outside of his business; (2) the extent to which it is known by employees and others involved in his business; (3) the extent of measures taken by him to guard the secrecy of his information; (4) the value of the information to him and to his competitors; (5) the amount of effort or money expended by him in developing the information; (6) the ease or difficulty with which the information could be properly acquired or duplicated by others. *Restatement of Torts* section 757, comment b (1939).

Applying these factors to this case, we find that some support and some negate the conclusion that Lynchburg Lemonade was Mason's trade secret.

Mason apparently spent little time, effort, or money in concocting the recipe for Lynchburg Lemonade. He seems to have created the beverage one evening to ease a sore throat. However, he put much effort into making the beverage an exclusive specialty of his restaurant and lounge. Mason testified that Lynchburg Lemonade comprised about a third of his total sales of alcoholic drinks. Obviously, the exclusive sale of Lynchburg Lemonade was of great value to Mason. The beverage could also have been valuable to his competitors in the area.

Mason [also] testified that he told only a few of his employees the recipe. He stated that each one was specifically instructed not to tell anyone the recipe. To prevent customers from learning the recipe, the beverage was mixed in the back of the restaurant and lounge. Mason's efforts to keep the recipe a secret were apparently successful until Randle learned the recipe. It appears that one could not order a Lynchburg Lemonade in any establishment other than that of the plaintiff. Absolute secrecy is not required for the recipe to constitute a trade secret—a substantial element of secrecy is all that is necessary.

The defendants contend that Mason's recipe was not a trade secret because it could be easily duplicated by others. The defendants' [expert] testimony characterized Lynchburg Lemonade as a member of the Collins family of drinks, of which there are dozens, if not hundreds, with essentially the same elements. At least one witness testified that he could duplicate the recipe after tasting a Lynchburg Lemonade. Certainly, this testimony is a strong factor against the conclusion that Mason's recipe was a trade secret. We do not think, however, that this evidence in and of itself could prevent such a conclusion. Rather, this evidence should be weighed and considered along with the evidence tending to show the existence of a trade secret. Courts have protected information as a trade secret despite evidence that it could easily be duplicated by others competent in the given field.

A motion for directed verdict should not be granted if there is a scintilla of evidence supporting an element essential to the plaintiff's claim. Our review of the record indicates that Mason did present a scintilla of evidence that his recipe, or formula, for Lynchburg Lemonade was a trade secret.

Trial court's refusal to grant the defendants' motion for a directed verdict affirmed.

COMMERCIAL TORTS

In addition to the intentional torts discussed in the Intentional Torts chapter, certain other intentional torts apply mainly to business or commercial activities, especially the activities of competitors. These torts may help promote innovation by protecting creative businesses against certain competitive abuses. But their main aim is simply to uphold certain minimum standards of commercial morality.

Injurious Falsehood

The tort of injurious falsehood also is known by names such as product disparagement, slander of title, and trade libel. It involves the publication of false statements that disparage another's business, property, or title to property and thus harm another's economic interests. The two most common kinds of injurious falsehood are false statements disparaging another's *property rights* in land, things, or intangibles; and false statements disparaging the *quality* of another's land, things, or intangibles. These two types of injurious falsehood cover all of the legally protected property interests that are capable of being sold. Examples include leases, mineral rights, trademarks, copyrights, and corporate stock. As the later *Atlas* case indicates, injurious falsehood also covers false statements that harm another's economic interests and cause loss even though they do not disparage property as such.

Elements and Damages   In injurious falsehood cases, the plaintiff must prove a statement of the sort just described, its falsity, and its communication to a third party. As the *Atlas* case suggests, the degree of fault required for liability is not completely clear. It is often said that the standard is malice, but formulations of this have differed widely. The *Restatement* requires either knowledge that the statement is false, or reckless disregard as to its truth or falsity.[9] There is usually no liability for false statements that are made negligently and in good faith.

A plaintiff seeking to recover for injurious falsehood must also prove that the false statement played a substantial part in causing him to suffer *special damages*, or economic loss. These special damages may include: losses resulting from the diminished value of disparaged property, the expense of measures for counteracting the false statement (e.g., advertising or litigation expenses), losses resulting from the breach of an existing contract by a third party, and the loss of prospective business. In cases involving the loss of prospective business, the plaintiff usually is required to show that some specific person(s) refused to buy because of the disparagement. But as *Atlas* states, this rule is often relaxed where these losses are difficult to prove.

The special damages that the plaintiff is required to prove are his usual remedy in injurious falsehood cases. Damages such as personal injury, emotional distress, and amounts that would have been earned by utilizing or investing the proceeds from lost business generally are not recoverable. Punitive damages and injunctive relief are sometimes obtainable. Because proof of special damages is part of the plaintiff's cause of action, these last two remedies are available only when special damages have been shown.

Injurious Falsehood and Defamation   Injurious falsehood and defamation can overlap in some cases. Statements impugning a businessperson's character or conduct probably are only defamatory. If the false statement is limited to the plaintiff's business, property, or property rights, on the other hand, his normal claim is for injurious falsehood. Both claims may be made where the injurious falsehood implies something about the plaintiff's character and affects his overall reputation. For example, suppose that the defendant falsely alleges that the plaintiff knowingly sells dangerous products to children.

Defamation law's various absolute and conditional privileges generally apply to injurious falsehood.[10] Certain additional privileges are also recognized in injurious falsehood cases. For example, a rival claimant may in good faith disparage another's property rights by asserting his own competing rights. Similarly, one may make a good faith allegation that a competitor is infringing one's patent, copyright, or trademark. Finally, a person may sometimes make unfavorable comparisons between her own property and that of a competitor. This privilege is generally limited to sales talk asserting the superiority of one's own property (e.g., "I sell the best cars in town"). It does not cover specific unfavorable statements about the competitor's property.

---

[9]*Restatement (Second) of Torts* § 623A(b) (1977).

[10]On these privileges, see the Intentional Torts chapter.

CHARLES ATLAS, LTD. v. TIME-LIFE BOOKS, INC.

570 F. Supp. 150 (S.D.N.Y. 1983)

Time-Life Books, Inc. published a book entitled *Exercising for Fitness*. The book contained a reproduction of the famous Charles Atlas advertisement depicting a 97-pound weakling who uses Atlas's Dynamic Tension body-building program to become a real man after a bully kicks sand in his face and the face of his girlfriend. The caption accompanying the reproduction told the book's readers that Atlas's program is a system of isometric exercises. On the same page of the book, the author warned readers about the extreme dangers of isometric exercises.

Charles Atlas, Ltd. sued Time-Life Books in federal district court for product disparagement (injurious falsehood). It basically alleged that the book's caption was false because Atlas's method was not isometric, and that this falsehood, coupled with the text warning about the dangers of isometric exercises, caused it to suffer economic loss. Time-Life moved to dismiss Atlas's complaint. The question before the court was whether the facts in the complaint were sufficient to state a claim upon which relief could be granted.

Goettel, District Judge.   This court cannot say as a matter of law that the alleged misstatements are not reasonably susceptible to a defamatory meaning and that no reasonable reader could conclude that the statements [concern] the plaintiff's product. When the caption is read in conjunction with the text, a reasonable reader could conclude that Atlas markets an isometric exercise program, that isometric exercises are dangerous, and that therefore Atlas's exercise program is dangerous. Whether the trier of fact will conclude that a defamatory connotation was indeed conveyed will have to await trial.

Malice is pleaded adequately. It is extremely questionable whether the plaintiff must show common law malice to state a claim for product disparagement. Rather, it appears that the plaintiff must show knowledge of the alleged false statement or reckless disregard as to the truth of the statement [citing the *Restatement*]. Atlas alleges that the allegedly false statements were known by Time-Life to be false when they were made, or were made with recklessness, malice, and intent to injure Atlas.

Finally, Atlas has pleaded special damages adequately. According to Atlas, the alleged disparagement has caused it to lose $30,323 in sales and revenues and to expend $14,000 in special advertising expenses and $16,687 in legal expenses to counteract the alleged disparagement. Special damage is the pecuniary loss resulting directly from the effect of a defendant's allegedly wrongful conduct. Among the losses deemed to constitute special damages are the expenses necessary to counteract the alleged wrongful conduct. Thus, Atlas can recover at least the special advertising expenses incurred to counteract the alleged product disparagement, and the pleading of these expenses is sufficient to support the claim at this stage of the litigation.

Loss of sales is also a proper item of special damages. However, Time-Life argues that Atlas has failed to plead this adequately because it has failed to identify lost customers. Adopting such a rule would be grossly unfair in this case. Atlas sells only through mail orders. It is, therefore, virtually impossible to identify those who did not order Atlas's product because of *Exercising for Fitness*. As Dean Prosser has noted: "[A] more liberal rule has been applied, requiring the plaintiff to be particular only where it is reasonable to expect him to do so. It is probably still the law everywhere that he must either offer the names of those who have failed to purchase or explain why it is impossible for him to do so; but where he cannot, the matter is dealt with by analogy to the proof of lost profits resulting from breach of contract."

Whether legal fees expended to prosecute a claim for product disparagement can be recovered as an item of special damages is an interesting issue. It can be argued that the expenses incurred in bringing the lawsuit are similar to other expenses necessary to counteract the alleged wrongful conduct. Be that as it may, the court need not resolve the question at this time because it has already determined that Atlas has stated a claim for product disparagement.

Time-Life's motion to dismiss denied.

Interference with Contractual Relations

In cases of intentional interference with contractual relations, one party to a contract sues the defendant because the defendant's interference with the other party's performance of the contract caused the plaintiff to lose the benefit of that performance. A defendant can interfere with the performance of a contract by causing the other party to repudiate it, or by wholly or partly preventing that party's performance. The means of interference can range from threats of violence at one extreme, to mere persuasion at the other.

Liability for interference with contractual relations occurs only where the interference affected performance of an *existing* contract. This includes contracts that are voidable, unenforceable, or subject to contract defenses. However, there is no liability for interference with void bargains, contracts that are illegal on public policy grounds, or contracts to marry. To be liable, the defendant must have *intended* to cause the breach; there usually is no liability for negligent contract interferences.

Improper Interference   Even if the plaintiff proves the threshold requirements just stated, the defendant is liable only if his behavior was *improper*. The following *Bar J Bar* case lists the factors the *Restatement* uses for determining whether performance is improper. Despite the flexible, case-by-case nature of such situations, a few generalizations about improper interference are possible.

1. Where the contract's performance was blocked by such clearly improper means as threats of physical violence, misrepresentations, defamatory statements, bribery, harassment, or bad faith civil or criminal actions, the defendant usually is liable. Liability also is likely where it can be shown that the interference was motivated *solely* by malice, spite, or a simple desire to meddle.

2. Assuming that his means or motives are legitimate, the defendant generally is not liable when he acts in the *public interest*—for example, by informing an airport that an air traffic controller is a habitual user of hallucinogenic drugs. The same is true where the defendant acts to *protect a person for whose welfare she is responsible*—for example, where a mother induces a private school to discharge a diseased student who could infect her children.

3. A contract interference resulting from the defendant's good faith effort to protect her own *existing* legal or economic interests usually does not create liability so long as appropriate means are used. For example, a landowner who leases land to a tenant probably can induce the tenant to breach a sublease to a party whose business detracts from the land's value. However, business parties generally cannot interfere with existing contract rights merely to further some *prospective* competitive advantage. For example, a seller cannot entice its competitors' customers to break existing contracts with those competitors.

4. Finally, competitors are unlikely to incur liability where, as is often still true of employment contracts, the agreement interfered with is *terminable at will*.[11] The reason is that in such cases the plaintiff only has an *expectancy* that the contract will be continued, and not a *right* to have it continued. Thus, a firm that hires away its competitors' at-will employees usually escapes liability. This factor also may help explain the result in *Bar J Bar*.

Damages   The basic measure of damages for intentional interference with contractual relations is the value of the lost contract performance. In addition, some courts award compensatory damages reasonably linked to the interference (including emotional distress and damage to reputation). In certain cases, the plaintiff may obtain an injunction prohibiting further interferences.

---

[11]The Employment Law chapter discusses terminable-at-will employment contracts.

BAR J BAR CATTLE CO. v. PACE

763 P.2d 545 (Ariz. Ct. App. 1988)

The New Mexico and Arizona Land Company (New Mexico) owned a sizable tract of land in Arizona. It leased a valuable portion of this land containing water for grazing to the Bar J Bar Cattle Company. New Mexico had the right to cancel the lease on 30 days' notice once it sold the land.

Malcolm Pace owned a ranch adjoining the Bar J Bar ranch. Even though Pace's ranch had ample water supplies, he had long tried to get Bar J Bar to sublease its leasehold interest to him. However, Bar J Bar repeatedly rebuffed him. Eventually, Pace got control of the land leased to Bar J Bar by purchasing it from New Mexico. Immediately after signing the contract of sale, New Mexico gave Bar J Bar 30 days' notice of termination.

Bar J Bar sued Pace for intentional interference with contractual relations in an Arizona trial court. The court granted Pace's motion for summary judgment, and Bar J Bar appealed.

Ares, Judge.   The elements of intentional interference with contract in Arizona are: (1) a valid contractual relationship, (2) knowledge of the relationship on the part of the interferer, (3) intentional interference inducing or causing a breach, (4) resultant damage to the party whose relationship has been disrupted, and (5) improper action on the part of the defendant. The evidence establishes four of these five elements. Pace, knowing that Bar J Bar was the lessee of the property, successfully negotiated to buy the property and thereby caused New Mexico to exercise its right to cancel the lease. The cancellation clearly damaged Bar J Bar's interests.

The somewhat amorphous [fifth] standard of liability, *improper* action, must be applied with discrimination, particularly in the context of competitive business activities. Caution is doubly required where the effect of the actor's interference is only to cause the cancellation of a terminable contract. In the case before us, two ranchers sought control of grazing land through which life-giving water flows. Under circumstances like these, courts must take care that in their desire to protect the reasonable expectations of parties to contracts, they do not impose undesirable restrictions on competition.

The [Arizona] Supreme Court [has] adopted the seven factors enumerated in *Restatement (Second) of Torts* section 767 in determining whether interfering conduct was improper. Under this standard, the court should consider: (a) the nature of the actor's conduct, (b) the actor's motive, (c) the interests of the other with which the actor's conduct interferes, (d) the interests sought to be advanced by the actor, (e) the social interests in protecting the freedom of action of the actor and the contractual interests of the other, (f) the proximity or remoteness of the actor's conduct to the interference, and (g) the relations between the parties.

Nature of Pace's Conduct. Bar J Bar had to offer evidence that Pace acted illegally or inequitably, as for example, committing fraud [or] duress or abusing economic power. There is no evidence that Pace's conduct in offering to purchase the property was improper.

Pace's Motive. Bar J Bar argues that Pace had an improper motive in that he was acting out of ill will toward Bar J Bar because it had earlier declined to sublease the property to him. We reject the argument for two reasons. First, to attribute a motive of revenge or spite on this slim footing requires utter speculation. The most that one could conclude is that Pace continued to want the property. Second, even if Pace had an improper motive, that would not necessarily make him liable. One who interferes with the contractual rights of another for a legitimate competitive reason does not become a tortfeasor simply because he may also bear ill will toward his competitor.

Interests of the Parties. Bar J Bar argues that its interest in retaining access to [the grazing water] far outweighs Pace's interest in acquiring more water because he already has ample windmills and stock tanks. To make the entire decision turn simply on the weight of one party's interest as compared to the other's would be to ignore all the other elements of the calculus. Moreover, the interests of both parties are legitimate and substantial. Bar J Bar had access to [the water] for years and wanted to keep it. Pace sought to add [the land] to his own ranch as a buffer against unwanted development and as a source of water. To attempt to weigh these interests against each other would involve the court in a risky and perhaps impossible task.

The Social Interests at Stake. The tort of unlawful interference with contract operates as a restraint on competition and freedom of contract. In this case, because it is asserted with respect to a contract to sell land, its effect would be to impose a restraint on New Mexico's right to sell its land as it chose and on Pace's right to pursue his economic interests as he viewed them.

Summary judgment for Pace affirmed.

Interference with Prospective Advantage

The rules and remedies for interference with prospective advantage parallel those for interference with contractual relations. The main difference is that the former tort covers interferences with *prospective* relations rather than existing contracts. The future relations protected against interference are mainly potential contractual relations of a business or commercial sort. Liability for interference with such relations is based on intent, and plaintiffs usually cannot sue for negligent interferences.

The "improper interference" factors weighed in interference with contract cases generally apply to interference with prospective advantage as well. One difference, however, is that interference with prospective advantage can be justified if: (1) the plaintiff and the defendant are in competition for the prospective relation with which the defendant interferes; (2) the defendant's purpose is at least partly competitive; (3) the defendant does not use such improper means as physical threats, misrepresentations, bad faith lawsuits, and so forth; and (4) the defendant's behavior does not create an unlawful restraint of trade under the antitrust laws or other regulations.[12]

Thus, a competitor can ordinarily win customers by offering lower prices, and can attract suppliers by offering higher prices. Unless this is illegal under antitrust law or other regulations, he can also refuse to deal with suppliers or buyers who also deal with his competitors. Remember, however, that such conduct often results in liability for intentional interference with contractual relations if the defendant disrupts an *existing* contract. Here, the social interest in the security of established contract rights outweighs society's interest in free competition.

LANHAM ACT SECTION 43(a)

Section 43(a) of the Lanham Act, which was amended in 1988, has long been regarded as creating a general federal law of unfair competition. Section 43(a) is not a consumer remedy; it is normally available only to commercial parties, who are usually the defendant's competitors. The section creates civil liability for a wide range of false, misleading, confusing, or deceptive descriptions of fact made in connection with goods or services. Among section 43(a)'s many applications are the following:

1. *Common law tort suits for "palming off" or "passing off."* This tort involves false representations that are likely to induce third parties to believe that the defendant's goods or services are those of the plaintiff. Such representations include imitations of the plaintiff's trademarks, trade names, packages, labels, containers, employee uniforms, and place of business.

2. *Trade dress infringement claims.* A product's trade dress is its overall appearance and sales image. Section 43(a) prohibits a party from passing off its goods or services as those of a competitor by employing a substantially similar trade dress that is likely to confuse consumers as to the source of its products or services.

---

[12] *Restatement (Second) of Torts* § 768 (1979).

For example, a competitor that sells antifreeze in jugs that are similar in size, shape, and color to a well-known competitor's jugs may face section 43(a) liability. As this discussion suggests, trade dress cases resemble palming off cases.

3. The infringement of both *registered and unregistered* trademarks.

4. Some cases involving a form of invasion of privacy discussed in the Intentional Torts chapter: *the appropriation of another's name or likeness for commercial purposes.*

5. *Commercial advertising that misrepresents the nature of goods or services.*[13] Before its 1988 amendment, section 43(a) only covered ads involving false statements about the advertiser's *own* products or services. Now, however, it also applies to ads that misrepresent the nature or origin of a *competitor's* products and services.

This application of section 43(a) also covers ads that are likely to deceive buyers even if they are not clearly false on their face. The legislative history to the new section 43(a) suggests that it may apply to advertising containing certain deceptive *omissions* as well. To illustrate these last two points, a seller of artificial fur coats that calls one of its brands "Normink" and does not disclose the coat's true nature may be liable under section 43(a).

ETHICAL AND PUBLIC POLICY CONCERNS

1. An ethical theory known as *utilitarianism* generally urges that the test for assessing the worth of actions is their ability to produce the greatest degree of aggregate net satisfaction throughout society. Some utilitarians say that satisfaction is maximized when people are best able to realize their individual preferences. Some say that one measure of satisfaction is the creation of economic wealth.

Look at the portion of this chapter's introduction that states the two general purposes underlying the legal rules discussed in this chapter. Which of these is most clearly utilitarian? Why? Also, look at the purposes said

---

[13] Deceptive advertising also may be attacked by the Federal Trade Commission under FTC Act section 5. See this text's chapter on the FTC Act and consumer protection laws.

to underlie trademark law. Are these generally utilitarian? Why or why not?

2. Legal reasoning sometimes is deductive or syllogistic. In such cases, the court states a general rule as a major premise, treats the facts as a minor premise, and applies the rule to the facts to generate a result. But another style of legal reasoning called *factor-based balancing* proceeds differently. In cases of this kind, the court states various factors that are relevant to its decision and decides by weighing these factors against one another under the facts before it. Which cases in this chapter use this method in whole or in part? Based on those cases, what is good about this style of legal reasoning? Are sensible decisions possible in any other way? On the other hand, what is bad about this decision-making process? In answering the last question, consider how well this process enables business parties to predict the legal consequences of their behavior.

3. People who defend free competition might do so on either of two grounds. They might justify free competition by its ability to promote economic efficiency and to maximize wealth over time. Or they might assert that free competition involves economic liberties which are so innately valuable that they should be protected regardless of whether they maximize wealth or not. Of course, defenders of free competition might stress both justifications.

With all this in mind, look at the *Bar J Bar* case earlier in the chapter. Which rationale for free economic activity predominates there? Back up your conclusion with specific language from the court's opinion.

SUMMARY

This chapter discusses certain forms of unfair competition whose main objects are to provide incentives for innovation and to preserve certain basic standards of competitive morality. By protecting the works of creative persons against infringement, copyright law motivates such persons to express their ideas in tangible form, and thus gives society the benefit of those ideas. Similarly, patent law promotes the creation and disclosure of new devices, products, processes, and designs by blocking infringing uses of such inventions. By allowing competitors to preserve the secrecy of their innovations, trade secrets law provides an alternative means for realizing these ends. The Lanham Act's prohibitions against trademark infringement also provide incentives for innovation and superior quality by making it easier for consumers to identify products possessing those traits. Perhaps more importantly, they also promote informed consumer choice by helping prevent confusion about the origin of favored products.

Many of the same considerations underlie the various commercial torts discussed in this chapter. An environment where injurious falsehoods, interferences with established contracts, and interferences with prospective business relations run rampant is an environment where creativity, inventiveness, and superior quality probably receive less than their maximum reward. However, the most important justification for these rules is their tendency to uphold certain minimum standards of ethical business behavior.

Finally, section 43(a) of the Lanham Act has created a federal law of unfair competition with a wide potential sweep. Section 43(a)'s most important application, however, is to false or deceptive advertising.

PROBLEM CASES

1. Huey J. Rivet patented an "amphibious marsh craft" for hauling loads and laying pipeline in swamps. Rivet's model could "walk" over stumps for extended periods while carrying heavy loads. Later, Robert Wilson, who had once worked for Rivet as a welder, began marketing a similar craft. The craft sold by Wilson differed from the craft described in the specification accompanying Rivet's patent application in several respects. Overall, though, the Wilson boat performed much the same functions about as effectively as the Rivet craft, and used much the same engineering techniques and concepts to do so. Has Wilson infringed Rivet's patent?

2. Lorna Nelson, half sister of the rock star Prince, sued Prince for copyright infringement. She alleged that Prince's hit "U Got the look" infringed her copyrighted song "What's Cooking in This Book." Lorna's song, to which Prince had access, had six verses totaling 35 lines and 176 words. "U Got the look" had eight verses totaling 47 lines and 242 words. The alleged infringements concerned the following verses and words from the two songs:

a. *Lorna's Verse Two*: "I glanced up and saw you, a smile so pretty." *Prince's Verses Two and Seven*: "I woke up, I've never seen such a pretty girl."

b. *Lorna's Verse Three*: "Makeup was rolling down my face." *Prince's Verse Five*: "A whole hour just to make up your face."

c. *Lorna's Verse Six*: "What's cooking in this book, what's cooking in . . ." *Prince's Verses Four and Six*: "U sho 'nuf do be cooking in my book."

d. *Lorna's Verses One and Six*: "Take a look, Take another look." *Prince's Verses One and Seven*: "U got the look."

The main issue in the case was whether there was substantial similarity between the lyrics just quoted. Do you think that these lyrics are sufficiently similar to justify imposing liability on Prince?

3. In 1970–71, James Doran, a student at Iowa State University, helped produce a 28-minute film biography of Dan Gable, an Iowa State wrestler who eventually won a gold medal at the 1972 Olympics. Iowa State obtained a valid statutory copyright to the film. In 1972, when Doran was employed by the American Broadcasting Company, he helped arrange for ABC to use a $2\frac{1}{2}$-minute segment of the film for the network's broadcasts of the 1972 Olympics. He did so without Iowa State's knowledge or consent. Is the fact that ABC only used about 9 percent of the film sufficient by itself to give ABC a fair use defense in a copyright infringement suit by Iowa State?

4. Accuride, International, Inc. is a wholly owned subsidiary of Standard Precision, Inc., a leading producer of drawer slide mechanisms. Standard Precision and Accuride market drawer slide mechanisms under the "ACCURIDE" trademark. Is this mark arbitrary or fanciful, suggestive, descriptive, or generic?

5. Suppose that Toys "R" Us, Inc., a chain of children's toy and clothing stores, has a registered trademark in the name Toys "R" Us. Is this mark best described as suggestive or descriptive? So far as protection of the mark against use by third parties is concerned, does it matter which characterization is best? In answering the second question, assume that Toys has been doing business under the mark for at least 20 years, and that the association between its products and its mark is well established in the minds of consumers.

6. E. I. du Pont de Nemours & Co., Inc. was building a plant to develop a highly secret unpatented process for producing methanol. During the construction, some of its trade secrets were exposed to view from the air because the plant in which they were contained did not yet have a roof. These secrets were photographed from an airplane by two photographers who were hired by persons unknown to take pictures of the new construction. Did this action amount to a misappropriation of du Pont's trade secrets?

7. Frank and Frances Gardner sued Sailboat Key, Inc. to prevent it from constructing certain improvements pursuant to building permits issued by the city of Miami. Sailboat Key later sued the Gardners for injurious falsehood. It alleged that false statements contained in the Gardners' pleadings in the earlier case caused it to lose its interest in the land where the construction was to occur, because it could not obtain financing. The Gardners claimed that defamation law's absolute privilege for statements made in the course of judicial proceedings also applied to this injurious falsehood action, and thus protected them from liability. Are the Gardners correct?

8. Joanna Wells and Paula Snyder visited the Brownsville Golden Age Nursing Home in connection with their interest in placing a relative in a nursing home. Appalled at the conditions they found there, Wells and Snyder communicated their concerns to a variety of sources, including the governor of Pennsylvania, President Ronald Reagan, CBS News, and the television show "60 Minutes." Their various communications eventually caused Golden Age to lose its state operating license due to various violations of state regulations. Golden Age sued Wells and Snyder for intentional interference with its contractual relations. Did Golden Age win? Why or why not?

9. After retiring from professional football, ex-Notre Dame and Green Bay Packer star Paul Hornung began a career as a television sports announcer. From the mid-1960s until 1980 he worked as a play-by-play announcer and color commentator at both college and professional games. In 1981 or 1982, the Atlanta television station WTBS contracted with the NCAA to telecast 19 college football games during the 1982 and 1983 seasons. The contract gave the NCAA the right to approve or disapprove any announcer or color commentator used on the broadcasts. When WTBS proposed Hornung as a color analyst for the games, the NCAA rejected him. The stated reasons for Hornung's rejection were his close association with professional football, his suspension for gambling while an NFL player, and his participation in Miller Lite beer commercials. The NCAA, however, itself accepted advertising revenue from the Miller Brewing Company.

Hornung sued the NCAA for intentional interference with prospective advantage. Did he win? Why or why not?

10. A television commercial for the "Premium Pack" orange juice manufactured by Tropicana Products, Inc. showed Olympic athlete Bruce Jenner squeezing an orange while saying: "It's pure, pasteurized juice as it comes from the orange." The ad then showed Jenner pouring the fresh-squeezed juice into a Tropicana carton. In fact, pasteurization involves heating the juice to approximately 200 degrees Fahrenheit, and Premium Pack juice is heated and sometimes frozen before packaging. The Coca-Cola Company, which makes Minute Maid orange juice, sued Tropicana for false advertising. Can Coca-Cola recover against Tropicana on the theory that the ad amounts to injurious falsehood? On what other claim discussed in the text might Coca-Cola succeed in recovering against Tropicana?

CONTRACTS

CHAPTER 10

INTRODUCTION TO CONTRACTS

THE NATURE OF CONTRACTS

If a covenant be made, wherein neither of the parties perform presently, but trust one another; in the condition of mere nature, which is a condition of war of every man against every man, upon any reasonable suspicion, it is void: but if there be a common power set over them both, with right and force sufficient to compel performance, it is not void. For he that performeth first, has no assurance the other will perform after; because the bonds of words are too weak to bridle men's ambition, avarice, anger, and other passions, without the fear of some coercive power; which in the condition of mere nature, where all men are equal, and judges of the justness of their own fears, cannot possibly be supposed. And therefore he which performeth first, does but betray himself to his enemy; contrary to the right, he can never abandon, of defending his life, and means of living.

Thomas Hobbes, *Leviathan*

Definition

Scholars and courts have formulated numerous definitions of the term *contract*. The *Restatement (Second) of Contracts* defines a contract as "a promise or set of promises for the breach of which the law gives a remedy, or the performance of which the law in some way recognizes as a duty."[1] The essence of this definition for our

---

[1] *Restatement (Second) of Contracts* § 1 (1981).

purposes is that a contract is a *legally enforceable promise or set of promises*. In other words, parties to contracts are entitled to call upon the state (the "common" or "coercive" power referred to by Hobbes in the quotation above) to force those with whom they have contracted to honor their promises. However, not all of the promises that people make attain the status of contracts. We have all made and broken numerous promises without fear of being sued by those to whom our promises were made. If you promise to take a friend out to dinner, but fail to do so, you do not expect to be sued for breaching your promise. What separates such social promises from legally enforceable contracts?

Elements

Over the years, the common law courts have developed several basic tests that a promise must meet before it is treated as a contract. These tests comprise the basic elements of contract. A contract is an *agreement* (an *offer*, made and *accepted*) that is *voluntarily* created by persons with the *capacity* to contract. The objectives of the agreement must be *legal* and, in most cases, the agreement must be supported by some *consideration* (a bargained-for exchange of legal value). Finally, the law requires *written* evidence of the existence of some agreements before enforcing them. Figure 1 shows how these elements relate to deciding whether a contract

FIGURE 1   Getting to Contract

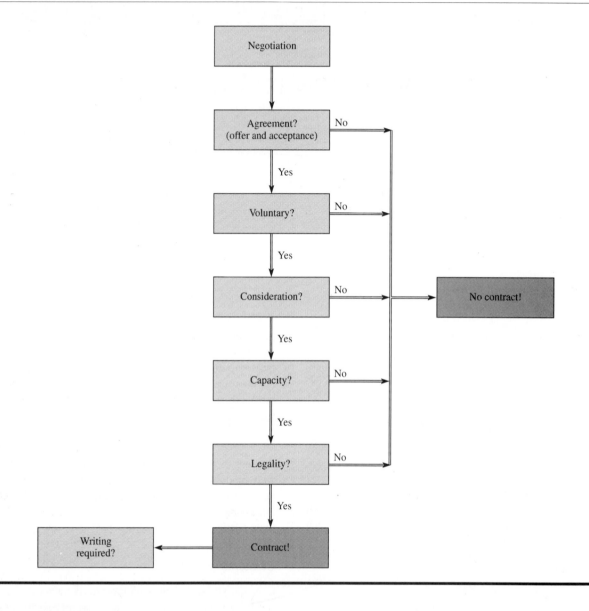

exists. The following chapters discuss each of these elements and other points necessary to enable you to distinguish contracts from unenforceable, social promises.

THE SOCIAL UTILITY OF CONTRACTS

As the introductory quotation indicates, contracts enable persons acting in their own interests to enlist the support of the law in furthering their personal objec-

tives. Contracts enable us to enter into agreements with others with the confidence that we may call on the law, and not merely the good faith of the other party, to ensure that those agreements will be honored. Within broad limits defined by contract doctrine and public policy, the contract device enables us to create the private law that governs our relations with others: the terms of the agreements we make.

Contracts facilitate the private planning that is necessary in a modern, industrialized society. Few people would invest in a business enterprise if they could not rely on the fact that the builders and suppliers of their facilities and equipment, the suppliers of the raw materials necessary to manufacture products, and the customers who agree to purchase those products will all honor their commitments. How could we make loans, sell goods on credit, or rent property unless loan agreements, conditional sales agreements, and leases were backed by the force of the law? Contract, then, is an inescapable and valuable part of the world as we know it. Like that world, its particulars tend to change over time, while its general characteristics remain largely stable.

THE EVOLUTION OF CONTRACT LAW

Classical Contract Law

The contract idea is ancient. Thousands of years ago, Egyptians and Mesopotamians recognized devices like contracts; by the 15th century, the common law courts of England had developed a variety of theories to justify enforcing certain promises. Contract law did not, however, assume major importance in our legal system until the 19th century, when numerous social factors combined to shape the common law of contract. Laissez-faire (free market) economic ideas had a profound influence on public policy thinking during this period, and the Industrial Revolution created a perceived need for private planning and certainty in commercial transactions. The typical contract situation in the early decades of the 19th century involved face-to-face transactions between parties with relatively equal bargaining power who dealt with relatively simple goods.

The contract law that emerged from this period was strongly influenced by these factors. Its central tenet was *freedom of contract*: Contracts should be enforced because they are the products of the free wills of their creators, who should, within broad limits, be free to determine the extent of their obligations. The proper role of the courts in such a system of contract was to enforce these freely made bargains, but otherwise to adopt a hands-off stance. Contractual liability should not be imposed unless the parties clearly agreed to assume it, but once an agreement had been made, liability was near absolute. The fact that the items exchanged were of unequal value was usually legally irrelevant. The freedom to make good deals carried with it the risk of making bad deals. As long as a person voluntarily entered a contract, it would generally be enforced against him, even if the result was grossly unfair. And since equal bargaining power tended to be assumed, the courts were usually unwilling to hear defenses based on unequal bargaining power. This judicial posture allowed the courts to formulate a pure contract law consisting of precise, clear, and technical rules that were capable of general, almost mechanical, application. Such a law of contract met the needs of the marketplace by affording the predictable and consistent results necessary to facilitate private planning.

Modern Contract Law Development

As long as most contracts resembled the typical transaction envisioned by 19th-century contract law, such rules made perfect sense. If the parties dealt face to face, they were likely to know each other personally or at least to know each other's reputation for fair dealing. Face-to-face deals enabled the parties to inspect the goods in advance of the sale, and since the subject matter of most contracts was relatively simple, the odds were great that the parties had relatively equal knowledge about the items they bought and sold. If the parties also had equal bargaining power, it was probably fair to assume that they were capable of protecting themselves and negotiating an agreement that seemed fair at the time. Given the truth of these assumptions, there was arguably no good reason for judicial interference with private contracts.

America's Industrial Revolution, however, undermined many of these assumptions. Regional, and later national, markets produced longer chains of distribution. This fact, combined with more-efficient means of communication, meant that people often contracted with persons whom they did not know for goods that they had never seen. And rapidly developing technology meant that those goods were becoming increasingly complex. Thus, sellers often knew far more about their products than did the buyers with whom they dealt. Finally, the emergence of large business organizations after the Civil War produced obvious disparities of bargaining power in many contract situations. These large organizations found it more efficient to standardize their numerous transactions by employing standard form contracts, which also could be used to exploit disproportionate bargaining power by dictating the terms of their agreements. Figure 2 highlights these factors that shaped modern contract law.

The upshot of all this is that many contracts today no longer resemble the stereotypical agreements envisioned by the common law of contract. It has been estimated that over 90 percent of all contracts today are form

FIGURE 2   Factors that Shaped Modern Contract Law

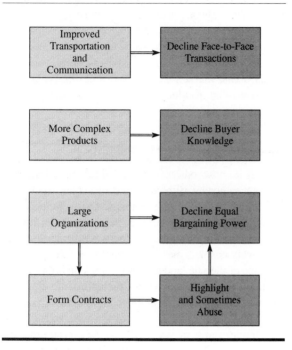

contracts.[2] How should courts respond to contracts where the terms have been dictated by one party to another party who may not have read or understood them, and who, in any event, may have lacked the power to bargain for better terms? Contract law is changing to reflect these changes in social reality. The 20th century has witnessed a dramatic increase in public intervention into private contractual relationships. Think of all the statutes governing the terms of what were once purely private contractual relationships. Legislatures commonly dictate many of the basic terms of insurance contracts. Employment contracts are governed by a host of laws concerning maximum hours worked, minimum wages paid, employer liability for on-the-job injuries, unemployment compensation, and retirement benefits. In some circumstances, product liability statutes impose liability on the manufacturers and sellers of products regardless of the terms of their sales contracts. The avowed purpose of much of this public intervention has been to protect persons who lack sufficient bargaining power to protect themselves.

---

[2] Slawson, "Standard Form Contracts and Democratic Control of Lawmaking Power," 84 *Harv. L. Rev.* 529 (1971).

Nor have the legislatures been the only source of public supervision of private agreements. Twentieth-century courts have been increasingly concerned with creating contract rules that produce just results. The result of this concern has been an increasingly hands-on posture by courts that often feel compelled to intervene in private contractual relationships to protect weaker parties. In the name of avoiding injustice, some modern contract doctrines impose contractual liability, or something quite like it, in situations where traditional contract rules would have denied liability. Similarly, other modern contract doctrines allow parties to avoid contract liability in cases where traditional common law rules would have recognized a binding agreement and imposed liability.

As contract law evolves to accommodate changing social circumstances, the basic nature of contract rules is changing. The precise, technical rules that characterized traditional common law contract are giving way to broader, imprecise standards such as good faith, injustice, reasonableness, and unconscionability. The reason for such standards is clear. If courts are increasingly called on to intervene in private contracts in the name of fairness, it is necessary to fashion rules that afford the degree of judicial discretion required to reach just decisions in the increasingly complex and varied situations where intervention is needed.

This heightened emphasis on fairness, like every other choice made by law, carries with it some cost. Imprecise, discretionary modern contract rules do not produce the same measure of certainty and predictability that their precise and abstract predecessors afforded. And because modern contract rules often impose liability in the absence of the clear consent required by traditional common law contract rules, one price of increased fairness in contract cases has been a diminished ability of private parties to control the nature and extent of their contractual obligations.

This change in the nature of contract law is far from complete, however. The idea that a contract is an agreement freely entered into by the parties still lies at the heart of contract law today, and contract cases may be found that differ very little in their spirit or ultimate resolution from their 19th-century predecessors. It is probably fair to say, however, that these are most likely to be cases where 19th-century assumptions about the nature of contracts are still largely valid. Thus, these cases involve contracts between parties with relatively equal bargaining power and relatively equal knowledge about the subject of the contract. Despite the existence of such cases, it is evident that contract law is in the process of significant change. Subsequent chapters highlighting the differences between modern contract rules and their traditional common law forebears render this conclusion inescapable. Before discussing particular examples of this new thrust in contract law, however, we should familiarize ourselves with the basic contract terminology that is used throughout the text.

Basic Contract Concepts and Types

Bilateral and Unilateral Contracts

Contracts have traditionally been classified as **bilateral** or **unilateral,** depending on whether one or both of the parties have made a promise. In unilateral contracts, only one party makes a promise. For example, if a homeowner says to a painter, "I will pay you $1,000 if you paint my house," the homeowner has made an offer for a unilateral contract, a contract that will be created only if and when the painter paints the house. If the homeowner instead says to the painter, "If you promise to paint my house, I will promise to pay you $1,000," he has asked the painter to commit to painting the house rather than just to perform the act of painting. This offer contemplates the formation of a bilateral contract. If the painter makes the requested promise to paint the house, a bilateral contract is created at that point.

In succeeding chapters, you will learn that unilateral contracts cause some particular problems related to offer and acceptance and to mutuality of obligation. These problems have caused many commentators to argue that the unilateral-bilateral contract distinction should be abandoned. The *Restatement (Second) of Contracts* and the Uniform Commercial Code, both of which are discussed later in this chapter, do not expressly use unilateral-bilateral terminology. However, both of these important sources of modern contract principles contain provisions for dealing with typical unilateral contract problems. Despite this evidence of disfavor, the courts continue to use unilateral contract terminology, in part because it enables them to do justice in some cases by imposing contractual liability on one party without the necessity of finding a return promise of the other party. For example, many recent employment cases have used unilateral contract analyses to hold employers liable for promises relating to pension rights, bonuses or incentive pay, and profit-sharing benefits, though the employees in question did not make any clear return promise to con-

tinue their employment for any specified time or to do anything else in exchange for the employer's promise.[3]

Valid, Unenforceable, Voidable, and Void Contracts

A **valid contract** is one that meets all of the legal requirements for a binding contract. Valid contracts are, therefore, enforceable in court.

An **unenforceable contract** is one that meets the basic legal requirements for a contract but may not be enforceable due to some other legal rule. The Writing chapter discusses the statute of frauds, which requires written evidence of certain contracts. An otherwise valid oral contract that the statute of frauds requires to be in writing, for example, may be unenforceable due to the parties' failure to reduce the contract to written form. Another example of an unenforceable contract is an otherwise valid contract whose enforcement is barred by the applicable contract statute of limitations.

Voidable contracts are those in which one or more of the parties have the legal right to cancel their obligations under the contract. They are enforceable against both parties unless a party with the power to void the contract has exercised that power. The Reality of Consent chapter, for example, states that contracts induced by misrepresentation, fraud, duress, or undue influence are voidable at the election of the injured party.

Void contracts are agreements that create no legal obligations because they fail to contain one or more of the basic elements required for enforceability. A void contract is, in a sense, a contradiction in terms. It would be more accurate to say that no contract was created in such cases. The Illegality chapter, for example, mentions that a contract to commit a crime, such as an agreement for the sale of cocaine, does not create a binding legal obligation. Nonetheless, practical constraints may sometimes encourage a party to such a contract to perform his agreement rather than raise an illegality defense.

Express and Implied Contracts

In an **express contract,** the parties have directly stated the terms of their contract orally or in writing at the time the contract was formed. As the following *Cook v. Cook* case illustrates, however, the mutual agreement

---

[3] See Petit, "Modern Unilateral Contracts," 63 *B.U.L. Rev.* 551 (1983).

necessary to create a contract may also be demonstrated by the conduct of the parties. When the surrounding facts and circumstances indicate that an agreement has in fact been reached, an **implied contract** (also called a *contract implied in fact*) has been created. When you go to a doctor for treatment, for example, you do not ordinarily state the terms of your agreement in advance, although it is clear that you do, in fact, have an agreement. A court would infer a promise by your doctor to use reasonable care and skill in treating you and a return promise on your part to pay a reasonable fee for her services.

Executed and Executory Contracts

A contract is **executed** when all of the parties have fully performed their contractual duties, and it is **executory** until such duties have been fully performed.

Any contract may be described using one or more of the above terms. For example, Eurocars, Inc. orders five new Mercedes-Benz 500 SLs from Mercedes. Mercedes sends Eurocars its standard acknowledgment form accepting the order. The parties have a *valid, express, bilateral* contract that will be *executory* until Mercedes delivers the cars and Eurocars pays for them.

COOK v. COOK
691 P.2d 664 (Ariz. Sup. Ct. 1984)

Intending to marry as soon as Donald's divorce became final, Rose Elsten and Donald Cook moved to Tucson in 1969 and lived there together until 1981. Although they did not marry, Rose used Donald's last name and they represented themselves to the community as husband and wife. Both parties worked throughout most of the relationship, pooling their income in two joint accounts and acquiring a house, two cars, and a number of shares of stock, all owned as joint tenants with right of survivorship. Rose left Donald in 1981. Of their joint assets, she received only one car and a few hundred dollars; Donald retained the balance.

Rose filed suit against Donald, arguing that he had breached their agreement to share their assets equally. In her deposition she said: "[E]verything we did and purchased, whether it be a vacuum cleaner or a car, was together as husband and wife. It was just something *that we agreed on*, that is how we were going to do it." When the trial court ruled against her, she appealed.

Feldman, Justice. The *sine qua non* of any contract is the exchange of promises. From this exchange flows the obligation of one party to another. Although it is most apparent that two parties have exchanged promises when their words express a spoken or written statement of promissory intention, mutual promises need not be express in order to create an enforceable contract. Indeed, a promise "may be inferred wholly or partly from conduct," and "there is no distinction in the effect of the promise whether it is expressed in writing, or orally, or in acts, or partly in one of these ways and partly in others." *Restatement (Second) of Contracts.*

Thus, two parties may by their course of conduct express their agreement, though no words are ever spoken. From their conduct alone the finder of fact can determine the existence of an agreement. Although isolated acts of joint participation such as cohabitation or the opening of a joint account may not suffice to create a contract, the fact finder may infer an exchange of promises, and the existence of the contract, from the entire course of conduct between the parties.

The conduct of the parties certainly demonstrates such an agreement and intent. Rose and Donald maintained two joint accounts, a checking account and a credit union savings account, in the names of "Rose and Don Cook" and held them as joint tenants with right of survivorship. Neither Rose nor Donald maintained a separate account. Both deposited portions of their paychecks into the accounts and used the funds to pay for household expenses and various assets they purchased. In addition, Rose and Donald held jointly a number of shares of Southwest Gas stock purchased with funds from the credit union account. In 1972 they purchased a house, taking the deed as husband and wife in joint tenancy with right of survivorship. Both signed the mortgage, incurring liability for the full purchase price of the house, and payments on the mortgage were made out of the joint checking account. There is ample evidence to support a finding that Rose and Donald agreed to pool their resources and share equally in certain accumulations; their course of conduct may be seen as consistently demonstrating the existence of such an agreement.

Judgment reversed in favor of Rose; case remanded for further proceedings.

QUASI-CONTRACT

The traditional common law insistence on the presence of all the elements required for a binding contract before contractual obligation is imposed can cause injustice in some cases. One person may have provided goods or services to another person who benefited from them but has no contractual obligation to pay for them, because no facts exist that would justify a court in implying a promise to pay for them. Such a situation can also arise in cases where the parties contemplated entering into a binding contract but some legal defense exists that prevents the enforcement of the agreement. Consider the following examples:

1. Jones paints Smith's house by mistake, thinking it belongs to Reed. Smith knows that Jones is painting his house but does not inform him of his error. There are no facts from which a court can infer that Jones and Smith have a contract, because the parties have had no prior discussions or dealings.

2. Thomas Products fraudulently induces Perkins to buy a household products franchise by grossly misstating the average revenues of its franchisees. Perkins discovers the misrepresentation after he has resold some products that he has received but before he has paid

Thomas for them. Perkins elects to rescind (cancel) the franchise contract on the basis of the fraud.

In the preceding examples, both Smith and Perkins have good defenses to contract liability; however, enabling Smith to get a free paint job and Perkins to avoid paying for the goods he resold would *unjustly enrich* them at the expense of Jones and Thomas. To deal with such cases and to prevent such unjust enrichment, the courts imply *as a matter of law* a promise by the benefited party to pay the *reasonable value* of the benefits he received. This idea is called **quasi-contract** (or contract implied in law) because it represents an obligation imposed by law to avoid injustice, not a contractual obligation created by voluntary consent. Quasi-contract liability has been imposed in situations too numerous and varied to detail. In general, however, quasi-contract liability is imposed when one party *confers a benefit* on another who *knowingly accepts it* and *retains it* under circumstances that make it *unjust* to do so without paying for it. So, if Jones painted Smith's house while Smith was away on vacation, Smith would probably not be liable for the reasonable value of the paint job because he did *not* knowingly accept it and because he has no way to return it to Jones. The following *Salamon* case highlights the centrality of the unjust enrichment idea to quasi-contract liability.

SALAMON v. TERRA
477 N.E.2d 1029 (Mass. Sup. Ct. 1985)

In February of 1981, Walter Salamon, a builder, entered into written agreements to buy two lots owned by Albert Terra, Jr., for $9,000 each. The agreement provided that Salamon would take possession of the lots by April 15, 1981, but would not have to pay the bulk of the purchase price ($8,500 per lot) until delivery of the deeds in August 1981. Salamon intended to build a house on each lot and then sell the houses to third parties, paying off Terra with the proceeds of the house sales. Salamon partially completed the two houses, but due to adverse economic conditions was unable either to obtain financing to complete them or to find purchasers for them. Terra extended the date of performance under the purchase agreements by several months, but because Salamon was never able to pay for the lots he retained ownership of them. Salamon filed a quasi-contract suit against Terra seeking to recover the value of the partially completed houses. The trial judge ruled that Terra had been unjustly enriched in the amount of $15,000, but the Appellate Division reversed the trial court's decision. Salamon appealed.

Abrams, Justice. A quasi-contract or a contract implied in law is an obligation created by law "for reasons of justice, without any expressions of assent and sometimes even against a clear expression of dissent . . . [C]onsiderations of equity and morality play a large part in constructing a quasi-contract. . . ." 1 A. Corbin, *Contracts* § 19 (1963). The underlying basis for awarding damages in a quasi-contract case is unjust enrichment of one party and unjust detriment to the other party. The Appellate Division stated the rule as follows: "The injustice of the enrichment or detriment in quasi-contract equates with the defeat of someone's reasonable expectations."

Generally, if a landowner has requested that a person construct a structure on his or her property, it is reasonably expected that the landowner will pay for the services and benefit conferred, even if there was no express contract for the construction or if a contract has been violated. The evidence in this case, however, does not support a conclusion that either party should reasonably have expected that Terra would pay for the value of partially completed houses or expenses incurred by Salamon in the building of partially completed houses on his property. Terra did not request or even desire that houses be built on property which he intended to use or to retain. He intended to convey the lots to Salamon in exchange for cash. The fact that Salamon built two houses on property owned by Terra was merely part of the financing arrangement. Terra had no interest in the value or expense of the houses, but was interested only in receiving the balance of the purchase price of the lots. There was no agreement that Terra would pay for unfinished (or finished) houses on his land in the event that Salamon was unable to fulfill his contractual obligations. Salamon could reasonably have expected that he would be paid for his labor, but both parties understood payment would be made by a third party purchaser of the houses. Terra could not reasonably have been expected to pay for Salamon's efforts in what appears to have been a speculative commercial transaction. Where a builder, with the permission of a seller, undertakes the construction of a house in furtherance of his own objectives (payment for lots from proceeds of sales) and at his own risk, he cannot recover his disbursements.

Judgment for Terra affirmed.

PROMISSORY ESTOPPEL

Another very important idea that 20th-century courts have developed to deal with the unfairness that would sometimes result from the strict application of traditional contract principles is the doctrine of **promissory estoppel.** In numerous situations, one person may *rely* on a promise made by another even though the promise and surrounding circumstances are not sufficient to justify the conclusion that a contract has been created, because one or more of the required elements is missing. To allow the person who made such a promise (the promisor) to argue that no contract was created would sometimes work an injustice on the person who relied on the promise (the promisee). For example, John's parents told him that they would give him the family farm when they died. Relying on this promise, John stayed at home and worked on the farm for several years. However, when John's parents died, they left the farm to his sister Martha. Should Martha and the parents' estate be allowed to defeat John's claim to the farm by arguing that the parents' promise was unenforceable because John gave no consideration for the promise? His parents did not request that John stay home and work on the farm in exchange for their promise.

In the early decades of this century, many courts began to protect the reliance of promisees like John. They said that persons who made promises that produced such reliance were *estopped*, or equitably prevented, from raising any defense they had to the enforcement of their promise. Out of such cases grew the doctrine of promissory estoppel. Section 90 of the *Restatement (Second) of Contracts* states:

A promise which the promisor should reasonably expect to induce action or forbearance on the part of the promisee or a third person and which does induce such action or forbearance is binding if injustice can be avoided only by enforcement of the promise. The remedy granted for breach may be limited as justice requires.

Thus, the elements of promissory estoppel are a *promise* that the *promisor should foresee is likely to induce reliance, reliance* on the promise by the promisee, and *injustice* as a result of that reliance.

When you consider these elements, it is obvious that promissory estoppel is fundamentally different from traditional contract principles. Contract is traditionally thought of as protecting *agreements* or bargains. Promissory estoppel, on the other hand, protects *reliance*. Early promissory estoppel cases applied the doctrine only to donative or gift promises like the one made by John's parents in the previous example. As subsequent chapters demonstrate, however, promissory estoppel is now being used by the courts to prevent offerors from revoking their offers, to enforce indefinite promises, and to enforce oral promises that would ordinarily have to be in writing. Given the basic conceptual differences between estoppel and contract, and the judicial tendency to use promissory estoppel to compensate for the absence of the traditional elements of contract, its growth as a new device for enforcing promises is one of the most important developments in modern contract law.

CONCEPT REVIEW

CONTRACT AND CONTRACTLIKE THEORIES OF RECOVERY

Theory	Key Concept	Remedy
Contract	Voluntary agreement	Enforce promise
Quasi-Contract	Unjust enrichment	Reasonable value of services
Promissory Estoppel	Foreseeable reliance	Enforce promise or recover reliance losses

THE UNIFORM COMMERCIAL CODE

Origins and Purposes of the Code

The Uniform Commercial Code (UCC) was created by the American Law Institute and the National Conference of Commissioners on Uniform State Laws. All of the states have adopted it except Louisiana, which has adopted only part of the Code. The drafters of the Code had several purposes in mind, the most obvious of which was to establish a uniform set of rules to govern commercial transactions, which are often conducted across state lines in today's national markets. Despite the Code's almost national adoption, however, complete uniformity has not been achieved. Many states have varied or amended the Code's language in specific instances, and some Code provisions were drafted in alternative ways, giving the states more than one version of particular Code provisions to choose from. Also, the various state courts have reached different conclusions about the meaning of particular Code sections.

In addition to promoting uniformity, the drafters of the Code sought to create a body of rules that would realistically and fairly solve the common problems occurring in everyday commercial transactions. Finally, the drafters tried to formulate rules that would promote fair dealing and higher standards in the marketplace.

Scope of the Code

The Code contains nine substantive articles, most of which are discussed in detail in Parts IV, VI, and VII of this book. The most important Code article for our present purposes is Article 2, the sales article of the Code.

Nature of Article 2

Many of the provisions of Article 2 exhibit the basic tendencies of modern contract law discussed earlier in this chapter. Accordingly, they differ from traditional contract law rules in a variety of important ways. The Code is more concerned with rewarding people's legitimate expectations than with technical rules, so it is generally more flexible than contract law. A court that applies the Code is more likely to find that the parties had a contract than is a court that applies contract law [2–204] (the numbers in brackets refer to specific Code sections). In some cases, the Code gives less weight than does contract law to technical requirements such as consideration [2–205 and 2–209].

The drafters of the Code sought to create practical rules to deal with what people actually do in today's marketplace. We live in the day of the form contract, so some of the Code's rules try to deal fairly with that fact [2–205, 2–207, 2–209(2), and 2–302]. The words *reasonable, commercially reasonable*, and *seasonably* (within a reasonable time) are found throughout the Code. This reasonableness standard is different from the hypothetical reasonable person standard in tort law. A court that tries to decide what is reasonable under the Code is more likely to be concerned with what people really do in the marketplace than with what a nonexistent reasonable person would do.

The drafters of the Code wanted to promote fair dealing and higher standards in the marketplace, so they imposed a **duty of good faith** [1–203] in the performance and enforcement of every contract under the Code. Good faith means "honesty in fact," which is required of all parties to sales contracts [1–201(19)]. In addition, merchants are required to observe "reasonable commercial standards of fair dealing" [2–103(1)(b)]. The parties cannot alter this duty of good faith by agreement [1–102(3)]. Finally, the Code expressly recognizes the concept of an **unconscionable contract,** one that is grossly unfair or one-sided, and it gives the courts broad discretionary powers to deal fairly with such contracts [2–302].[4]

The Code also recognizes that buyers tend to place more reliance on professional sellers and that professionals are generally more knowledgeable and better able to protect themselves than nonprofessionals. So, the Code distinguishes between **merchants** and nonmerchants by holding merchants to a higher standard in some cases [2–201(2), 2–205, and 2–207(2)]. The Code defines the term *merchant* [2–104(1)] on a case-by-case basis. If a person regularly deals in the kind of goods being sold, or pretends to have some special knowledge about the goods, or employed an agent in the sale who fits either of these two descriptions, that person is a merchant for the purposes of the contract in question. So, if you buy a used car from a used-car dealer, the dealer is a merchant for the purposes of your contract. But, if you buy a refrigerator from a used-car dealer, the dealer is probably not a merchant.

Application of the Code

Article 2 expressly applies only to *contracts for the sale of goods* [2–102]. The Code contains a somewhat complicated definition of *goods* [2–105], but the essence of the definition is that *goods* are tangible, movable, personal property. So, contracts for the sale of such items as motor vehicles, books, appliances, and clothing are covered by Article 2. But Article 2 does *not* apply to contracts for the sale of real estate, stocks and bonds, or other intangibles. Article 2 also does not apply to *service* contracts. This can cause confusion because, although contracts of employment or other personal services are clearly not covered by Article 2, many contracts involve elements of both goods and services. As the following *Neilson* case illustrates, the test that the courts most frequently use to determine whether Article 2 applies to such a contract is to ask which element, goods or services, *predominates* in the contract. Is the major purpose or thrust of the agreement the rendering of a service, or is it the sale of goods, with any services involved being merely incidental to that sale? This means that contracts calling for services that involve significant elements of personal skill or judgment in addition to goods probably are not governed by Article 2. Construction contracts, remodeling contracts, and auto repair contracts are all examples of mixed goods and services contracts that may be considered outside the scope of the Code.

Two other important qualifications must be made concerning the application of Code contract principles. First, the Code does not change *all* of the traditional contract rules. Where no specific Code rule exists, traditional contract law rules apply to contracts for the sale of goods. Second, and ultimately far more important, the courts have demonstrated a significant tendency to apply Code contract concepts by analogy to contracts not specifically covered by Article 2. For example, the Code concepts of good faith dealing and unconscionability have enjoyed wide application in cases that are technically outside the scope of Article 2. Thus, the Code is an

---

[4] The Illegality chapter discusses unconscionability in detail.

FIGURE 3   When the Code Applies

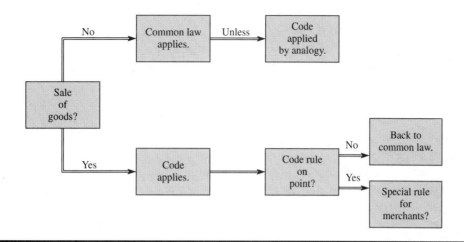

important influence in shaping the evolution of contract law in general, and if this trend toward broader application of Code principles continues, the time may come when the dichotomy between Code principles and traditional contract rules is a thing of the past. Figure 3 illustrates the rules governing the Code's application.

NEILSON BUSINESS EQUIPMENT CENTER v. MONTELEONE

524 A.2d 1172 (Del. Sup. Ct. 1987)

Dr. Italo V. Monteleone, a neurologist, entered into a lease-purchase agreement for a turnkey computer system from Neilson Business Equipment Center, Inc. The system included both hardware and software recommended by Neilson after two Neilson representatives studied Dr. Monteleone's manual billing system. When the computer was delivered in July of 1982, problems immediately developed. The system printed a separate bill for each treatment instead of one bill listing all of the doctor's services to a patient during a billing period. The bills and medical insurance forms were incompatible with Dr. Monteleone's records, and incorrect balances appeared in the accounts receivable register.

Neilson's initial attempts to modify the software, which it had acquired elsewhere and renamed the "Neilson Medical Office Management System," were unsuccessful. In August of 1982, Neilson hired a consultant to solve the problems. However, in February of 1983, before the consultant was able effectively to make the needed modifications, Dr. Monteleone notified Neilson that he was terminating the lease for cause. Dr. Monteleone later filed suit against Neilson, and the trial court awarded him $34,983.42 in damages for breaches of the implied warranties of merchantability and fitness for a particular purpose. Neilson appealed, arguing that the trial court had erred in holding that the case was governed by the UCC.

Moore, Justice.   The central issue before us is whether a contract for a computer system consisting of computer hardware, software, and services constitutes "goods" under the UCC. Article Two of the UCC applies to "transactions in goods." The contract between Dr. Monteleone and

Neilson is a mixed contract for both goods and services. When a mixed contract is presented, it is necessary for a court to review the factual circumstances surrounding the negotiation, formation, and contemplated performance of the contract to determine whether the contract is predominantly or primarily a contract for the sale of goods. If so, the provisions of Article Two apply.

Neilson urges us to separate the contract into three distinct subparts—hardware, software, and services. It contends that only the hardware can be classified as "goods" under the Code, that there was nothing defective about the hardware, and thus Monteleone's claims for breaches of implied warranties fail. Neilson further argues that software is an intangible, and that intangibles do not constitute "goods" subject to the Code.

That argument is innovative, but unpersuasive. Neilson contracted to supply a turn-key computer system; that is, a system sold as a package which is ready to function immediately. The hardware and software elements are combined into a single unit—the computer system—prior to sale. The trial court's factual conclusion that the computer system is predominantly "goods" is supported by substantial evidence. Dr. Monteleone did not intend to contract separately for hardware and software. Rather, he bought a computer system to meet his information processing needs. Any consulting services rendered by Neilson were ancillary to the contract, and cannot reasonably be treated as standing separately to escape the implied warranties of the UCC.

Judgment for Dr. Monteleone affirmed.

RESTATEMENT (SECOND) OF CONTRACTS

Nature and Origins

In 1932, the American Law Institute published the first *Restatement of Contracts*,[5] an attempt to codify and systematize the soundest principles of contract law gleaned from thousands of often conflicting judicial decisions. As the product of a private organization, the *Restatement* did not have the force of law, but as the considered judgment of some of the leading scholars of the legal profession, it was highly influential in shaping the evolution of contract law. The *Restatement (Second) of Contracts,* issued in 1979, is an attempt to reflect the significant changes that have occurred in contract law in the years following the birth of the first *Restatement*. The tone of the *Restatement Second* differs dramatically from that of the *Restatement*, which is often characterized as a positivist attempt to formulate a system of black letter rules of contract law. The *Restatement Second*, in contrast, reflects the "shift from rules to standards" in modern contract law: the shift from precise, technical rules to broader, discretionary principles that

produce just results.[6] The *Restatement Second* plainly bears the mark of the legal realists, discussed in The Nature of Law chapter, and has been heavily influenced by the UCC. In fact, many *Restatement Second* provisions are virtually identical to their Code analogues. For example, the *Restatement Second* has explicitly embraced the Code concepts of *good faith*[7] and *unconscionability*.[8]

Impact

The *Restatement Second*, like its predecessor, does not have the force of law, and its relative newness prevents any accurate assessment of its impact on contemporary contract cases. Nonetheless, given the influential role played by the first *Restatement* and the previously mentioned tendency of the courts to employ Code principles by analogy in contract cases, it seems fair to assume that the *Restatement Second* will serve as a major inspiration for contract developments in the decades to come. For this reason, we give significant attention to the *Restatement Second* in the following chapters.

---

[5] See the Nature of Law chapter for a general discussion of the *Restatement* phenomenon.

[6] Speidel, "*Restatement Second*: Omitted Terms and Contract Method," 67 *Cornell L. Rev.* 785, 786 (1982).

[7] *Restatement (Second) of Contracts* § 205 (1981).

[8] *Restatement (Second) of Contracts* § 208 (1981).

ETHICAL AND PUBLIC POLICY CONCERNS

1. Compare and contrast the ethical values at the heart of classical contract law with those at the heart of modern contract law. If all contracts today fit the typical model assumed by classical contract law, would we necessarily feel ethically compelled to treat them differently than they were treated under classical contract law?

2. Do a brief social cost-benefit analysis of the "shift from rules to standards" that has occurred in modern contract law. Do a contrasting cost-benefit analysis of the rule-oriented approach of classical contract law.

3. The idea that contracts should be enforced because they are voluntary agreements can obviously be justified on ethical grounds. What ethical justifications, if any, can you give for departing from the notion of voluntary agreement in quasi-contract and promissory estoppel cases?

SUMMARY

Contracts are legally enforceable promises or sets of promises. To attain contract status, promises must conform to certain legal requirements prescribed by contract law. Contract law, like other bodies of law, is constantly changing in response to changing social needs and values. Modern contract law, in a quest for just results, is evolving in the direction of increased public supervision of private contracts and broad, discretionary rules. The basic essence of contract law, however, still derives from the idea that contracts are consensual, private agreements.

In their search for justice, the courts have developed doctrines that can operate to impose obligations on people in the absence of the agreement required by traditional contract law. *Quasi-contract* doctrine is used by the courts to prevent persons who have received goods or services from others from being unjustly enriched, by implying a promise to pay for those goods or services as a matter of law. *Promissory estoppel* protects persons who rely on the promises of others by preventing promisors from raising legal defenses to the enforcement of their promises. In recent years, promissory estoppel principles have been applied to an increasing range of contract problems, leading some scholars to conclude that contract is in danger of being eclipsed by promissory estoppel.

Article 2 of the Uniform Commercial Code is an important source of modern contract principles. Technically, it applies only to contracts for the sale of *goods*, and it dramatically changes some of the basic rules governing such contracts. The Code, however, has had significant influence on the rules governing other contracts because the courts often apply Code principles to such contracts by analogy.

The *Restatement (Second) of Contracts* clearly reflects the influence of the Code. Many *Restatement Second* provisions were obviously inspired by their Code counterparts. The *Restatement Second* is also similar to the Code in its tendency to employ broad discretionary standards that facilitate judicial supervision of contracts in the name of fairness. Although the *Restatement Second* does not have the force of law, the influence formerly enjoyed by the first *Restatement* and the existing tendency of many courts to employ Code principles like those adopted by the *Restatement Second* suggest that it will also be a significant source of inspiration for future contract developments.

PROBLEM CASES

1. In 1973, Baker and Ratzlaff entered a contract requiring Ratzlaff to grow 380 acres of popcorn and Baker to buy it at $4.75 per hundredweight. The contract gave Ratzlaff the right to terminate if Baker failed to pay for any of the popcorn on delivery. Early in 1974, Ratzlaff made the first two deliveries under the contract to Baker's plant. Baker's plant manager gave Ratzlaff weight tickets acknowledging receipt of the popcorn. Ratzlaff was not given payment and did not ask for it. Nor did he stop by Baker's business office, which was on a direct route between his farm and Baker's plant, to ask for payment. When Baker called to ask for further deliveries, Ratzlaff offered excuses, but did not mention payment. Ratzlaff later told Baker he was terminating due to Baker's failure to pay upon delivery, selling the remaining 1.6 million pounds of popcorn elsewhere for $8.00 per hundredweight. After hearing evidence that Baker's normal practice was to make payments at its office on the basis of copies of weight tickets sent from the plant, and that Baker would have paid promptly had Ratzlaff requested payment, the trial court ruled that Ratzlaff's termination was a breach of his duty to act in good faith. Was this ruling proper?

2. The Schinmanns had been growing spearmint and peppermint for oil since 1946. In 1981, they wanted to purchase Scotch mint (spearmint) roots and approached the Moores. At first, the Moores said they had none for sale, but later decided to take out and sell one field of roots. Although the Moores had been raising mint for oil since the early 1960s, this was their first sale of roots. Later, a dispute arose among the parties over the quality of the roots. The Schinmanns argued that the Moores were merchants under the UCC and, as such, they had made and breached an implied warranty of merchantability in the sale of the mint roots. Were the Moores merchants?

3. Edgar C. Faris conceived the idea for a sports quiz show. He contacted television sports announcer Dick Enberg to see whether Enberg would be willing to be the show's master of ceremonies. He also offered Enberg the opportunity of becoming a coproducer and part owner of the show. Enberg met with Faris, expressed interest in his proposal, and asked for and was given a copy of the format for the show. Later, the "Sports Challenge" show appeared on television with a different producer and with Enberg as master of ceremonies. There were certain differences and similarities between the show and Faris's idea. Faris filed suit against Enberg for breach of implied contract. Did Enberg have a contract with Faris?

4. First National Bank filed suit against Jessie Ordoyne and Patricia Ordoyne Bordelon for failure to pay sums due on a VISA card account. Ordoyne argued that he did not know that the account existed until the bank called him to inquire about his failure to make payments. He then told the bank that he and Patricia were divorced, and that she must have forged his signature to the account application form. The bank argued that he was nonetheless liable on a quasi-contractual basis, although it failed to prove that he had received any of the merchandise charged to the card. Was the trial court's decision in Jessie's favor correct?

5. On December 13, 1978, Benjamin Ravelo was informed that his application for a job as a police officer with the County of Hawaii had been accepted and that he would be sworn in as a police recruit on January 2, 1979. Ravelo then resigned from his job as a police officer with the Honolulu Police Department, and his wife also gave notice of termination to her employer. On December 20, 1978, Ravelo was informed by the county that he would not be hired after all. He and his wife tried to cancel their resignations, but were told it was too late

to get their old jobs back. When Ravelo filed suit, the county moved to dismiss his complaint on the ground that under the applicable provisions of the civil service law Ravelo was at best a probationary employee who could be dismissed without cause at any time. The trial court agreed and dismissed Ravelo's suit. Should the dismissal be reversed on appeal?

6. Commercial Cornice, a subcontractor, entered a contract with Camel Construction, a general contractor, to furnish labor and materials for a construction project owned by Malarkey's, Inc. Commercial completed its obligations under the contract, but only received $78,000 of the $177,773. When Commercial filed suit against Camel and Malarkey's for the remaining $99,773, Malarkey's moved to dismiss Commercial's claims against it on the ground that Commercial's only contract was with Camel. The trial court granted Malarkey's motion, despite the fact that the evidence indicated that Malarkey's had never payed Camel for the work. Was the dismissal of Commercial's claim against Malarkey's proper?

7. Early in 1986, Gray Communications contacted various television tower builders concerning the manufacture and erection of a television tower. After several discussions with Kline Iron & Steel, Gray received a signed written proposal from Kline to build and install the tower for $1,485,368. The proposal said that it could be revoked or modified by Kline prior to acceptance by Gray, and it required Kline's approval after acceptance by Gray. Gray refused to sign the proposal after Kline would not lower its bid to meet a competitor's lower bid, and Kline filed suit for breach of contract. At trial, Gray argued that no contract existed, and that even if a contract existed it was unenforceable because Gray had never signed the writing the UCC requires for all contracts for $500 or more. Kline argued that the contract was not covered by the UCC because it was a services contract. The evidence at trial indicated that the service component of the agreement amounted at most to 26 percent of the total cost. Should the court apply the UCC?

8. Data Processing Services, Inc. (DPS), a custom computer programmer, entered into an agreement to develop computer software for an accounting system for the L. H. Smith Oil Corporation. Smith refused to pay DPS's final billing on the ground that DPS's work had been unsatisfactory. DPS filed a breach of contract suit against Smith, and Smith counterclaimed for damages resulting from DPS's alleged failure to perform satisfactorily. The trial court ruled that the UCC applied to the parties' dispute. Was the trial court's ruling correct?

9. Stephen Gall and his family became ill after drinking contaminated water supplied to their home by the McKeesport Municipal Water Authority. They filed suit against the utility, arguing, among other things, that the utility had breached the UCC implied warranty of merchantability when it sold them contaminated water. The utility moved to dismiss their complaint, arguing that since water was not "goods" the UCC did not apply. Should the Galls's complaint be dismissed?

10. Tedesco listed his property for sale with Judd Realty, signing a "listing contract" which obligated him to pay Judd an 8% commission if Judd found a "purchaser" for the property. Two days before the listing agreement was due to expire, Judd's president delivered to Tedesco a signed written offer to purchase the property for the stated price, together with a $1,000 deposit check from the buyer. Tedesco then said he had changed his mind and did not want to sell. He refused to sign the agreement or pay Judd's commission. When Judd filed suit, Tedesco argued that there was no contract because the sale was not consummated and therefore the buyer found by Judd never became a "purchaser" within the meaning of the listing agreement. Was Judd entitled to a commission?

CHAPTER 11

THE AGREEMENT: OFFER

INTRODUCTION

The concept of mutual agreement lies at the heart of traditional contract law. Courts faced with deciding whether two or more persons entered into a contract look first for an *agreement* between the parties. Did the parties arrive at an understanding on terms that each party found acceptable, or did their negotiations falter before a true agreement was reached? But should courts seeking to answer such questions concern themselves with the *subjective* (actual) intent of the parties, or with the *objective* intent manifested by their words and deeds? Early American courts took a subjective approach to contract formation, asking whether there truly was a "meeting of the minds" between the parties. This subjective standard, however, threatened the certainty and predictability of contracts because it left every contract vulnerable to disputes about actual intent. The desire to meet the needs of the marketplace by affording predictable and consistent results in contract cases dictated a shift toward an *objective theory of contract*. By the middle of the 19th century, the objective approach to contract formation was firmly established in American law. Judge Learned Hand once described the effect of objective contract theory as follows:

A contract has, strictly speaking, nothing to do with the personal, or individual, intent of the parties. A contract is an obligation attached by the mere force of law to certain acts of the parties, usually words, which ordinarily accompany and represent a known intent. If however, it were proved by twenty bishops that either party when he used the words intended something else than the usual meaning which the law imposes on them, he would still be held, unless there were mutual mistake or something else of that sort.[1]

Keep the objective theory well in mind as you read the following material on the contract formation process. You will see many examples of its operation.

WHAT IS AN OFFER?

Definition

Section 24 of the *Restatement (Second) of Contracts* defines an offer as "the manifestation of willingness to enter into a bargain, so made as to justify another person in understanding that his assent to that bargain is invited and will conclude it." In other words, when we consider all that the parties said and did, did one of the parties ever, in effect, say to the other: "This is it—if you agree to these terms, we have a contract." The question of whether an offer was ever made is a critically important

---

[1]*Hotchkiss v. National City Bank*, 200 F. 287, 293 (S.D.N.Y. 1911).

first step in the contract formation process. A person who makes an offer (the **offeror**) gives the person to whom she makes the offer (the **offeree**) the power to bind her to a contract by accepting the offer. If no offer was ever made, however, there was nothing to accept and no contract results.

Traditional contract law rules on contract formation are designed to assure that persons are never bound to contracts unless they clearly intend to be bound. Therefore, the basic thing that the courts require for the creation of an offer is some objective indication of a *present intent to contract* on the part of the offeror. Two of the most important things from which courts infer an intent to contract are the *definiteness* of the alleged offer and the fact that it has been *communicated to the offeree*.

Definiteness of Terms

If an alleged offer fails to state specifically what the offeror is willing to do and what he asks in return for his performance, there is a good chance that the parties are still in the process of negotiation. If Smith says to Ford, "I'd like to buy your house," and Ford responds, "You've got a deal," do we have a contract? Obviously not. Smith's statement is merely an invitation to offer or an invitation to negotiate. It does not indicate a present intent to contract on Smith's part. It merely indicates a willingness to contract in the future if the parties can reach agreement on mutually acceptable terms. However, if Smith sends Ford a detailed and specific written document stating all of the material terms and conditions on which he is willing to buy the house and Ford writes back agreeing to Smith's terms, a contract has probably been created.

Definiteness and specificity in offers are also important in contract law because the offer often contains all the terms of the parties' contract. This is so because all that offerees are allowed to do in most cases is to accept or reject the terms of the offer. Agreements that are incomplete or indefinite because they omit material terms or imprecisely state such terms pose several problems for courts applying traditional contract principles. The fact that the parties' agreement is indefinite on some important points or lacks certain significant terms that such contracts normally address may, of course, indicate that the parties never, in fact, reached agreement on the omitted or indefinite terms. Even if the parties apparently intended to create a binding contract, how can a court that takes the traditional hands-off approach justify imposing contractual liability when the parties have failed to clearly indicate their intent on a particular issue? Classical contract principles see courts as contract enforcers, not as contract makers. Therefore, as the following *Action Ads* case indicates, agreements that are too indefinite are generally unenforceable at common law.

ACTION ADS, INC. v. JUDES
671 P.2d 309 (Wyo. Sup. Ct. 1983)

On April 23, 1981, Action Ads, Inc., hired Kenneth Judes as a salesman in the Sheridan, Wyoming, area. The employment contract provided that: "Sixty days from your date of hire, Action Ads will provide a medical insurance program for you and your dependents." Judes was not very successful as a salesman for Action, earning only $580.09 in commissions during the entire tenure of his employment with the company. Action never provided the promised medical insurance, a fact Judes learned when he inquired about whether he was covered on August 27, 1981.

Judes did little or no solicitation for Action after August, and the last order he placed with Action was in October of 1981. During the period in which he was purportedly working for Action, Judes held himself out as unemployed, collecting $2,448 in employment benefits. On November 14, 1981, Judes was seriously burned in a gas explosion at a mobile home. He filed suit against Action to recover his medical expenses, arguing that Action had breached the employment contract by failing to provide insurance coverage for him. When a trial court awarded Judes $18,824.86, Action appealed.

Rose, Justice.   The determinative question on appeal is whether the agreement by Action to provide insurance coverage was sufficiently definite and certain to constitute an enforceable contract. In a suit on a contract to procure insurance, the plaintiff has the burden of proving the elements of the insurance policy with sufficient certainty to enable the court to establish damages in the event of a breach. The corollary to that principle is a well-known rule: The measure of damages for breach of a contract to obtain insurance is that amount which would have been recovered had the insurance been furnished as agreed. Judes offered no evidence as to the risks insured against, the amount of coverage, or any other details of the "insurance program" that Action Ads, Inc., was obligated to provide. There was no proof of the insurance carrier contemplated by the parties. Most important, there was no showing that the injury actually sustained by Judes would have been covered by the insurance program had Action Ads fully complied with the employment contract.

It is apparent that the pertinent contract term is not sufficiently definite and certain to permit this court to determine the extent of the promised performance. Without that information, we are unable to measure the damages to which Judes might reasonably be entitled in the event of a breach. The indefiniteness of the agreement is due to the absence of any evidence whatsoever concerning the elements of the insurance coverage that Action Ads was obligated to provide. Since Judes failed to show to what extent, if any, the promised insurance program would have compensated him for his injury, we hold that the agreement to provide insurance was too uncertain and indefinite to be enforceable.

Judgment reversed in favor of Action Ads.

Definiteness and Modern Contract Law   The traditional contract law insistence on definiteness can serve useful ends. It can prevent a person from being held to an agreement when none was reached or from being bound by a contract term to which he never assented. Often, however, it can operate to frustrate the expectations of parties who intend to contract but, for whatever reason, fail to procure an agreement that is sufficiently definite. Modern contract principles, with their increased emphasis on furthering people's justifiable expectations and their encouragement of a hands-on approach by the courts, often create contractual liability in situations where no contract would have resulted at common law. Perhaps no part of the Code better illustrates this basic difference between modern contract principles and their classical counterparts than does the basic Code section on contract formation [2–204]. Sales contracts under Article 2 can be created "in any manner sufficient to show agreement, including conduct which recognizes the existence of a contract" [2–204(1)]. So, if the parties are acting as though they have a contract by delivering or accepting goods or payment, for example, this may be enough to create a binding contract, even if it is impossible to point to a particular moment in time when the contract was created [2–204(2)].

As the following *Schmieding* case illustrates, the fact that the parties left open one or more terms of their agreement does not necessarily mean that their agreement is too indefinite to enforce. A sales contract is created if the court finds that the parties *intended* to make a contract and that their agreement is complete enough to allow the court to reach a fair settlement of their dispute ("a reasonably certain basis for giving an appropriate remedy" [2–204(3)]). The Code contains a series of gap-filling rules to enable courts to fill in the blanks on matters of price [2–305], quantity [2–306], delivery [2–307, 2–308, and 2–309(1)], and time for payment [2–310] when such terms have been left open by the parties.[2] Of course, if a term was left out because the parties were *unable* to reach agreement about it, this would indicate that the intent to contract was absent and no contract would result, even under the Code's more liberal rules. Intention is still at the heart of these modern contract rules; the difference is that courts applying Code principles seek to further the parties' *underlying* intent to contract even though the parties have failed to express their intention about specific aspects of their agreement.

---

[2] The Formation and Terms of Sales Contracts chapter discusses these Code provisions in detail.

H. C. SCHMIEDING PRODUCE CO. v. CAGLE

529 So.2d 243 (Ala. Sup. Ct. 1988)

On March 6, 1985, Alvin Cagle, a potato farmer, entered into a written agreement to buy seed potatoes from H. C. Schmieding Produce Company. The terms of the contract obligated Cagle to pay a portion of the purchase price immediately, with the balance to be paid when the crop to be raised from the seed potatoes was harvested. Cagle paid the preharvest portion of the price and proceeded to cultivate the potatoes. He failed to harvest most of the resulting crop, however, or to pay Schmieding the postharvest portion of the purchase price.

When Schmieding sued him for breach of contract, Cagle filed a counterclaim arguing that Schmieding had breached a second contract, which obligated him to purchase Cagle's crop. According to Cagle, this second contract resulted from two telephone conversations with Schmieding's employees, occurring in late February of 1985 and in May of 1985. Cagle introduced evidence to show that Schmieding had agreed in those conversations to pay him $5.50 per bag for approximately 10,000 bags of white potatoes and to pay him market price at harvest time for all of his red potatoes grown on 30 acres of land. Cagle also introduced a letter from Schmieding, dated May 26, 1985, which said: "We are looking forward to working with you on the shipment of your crop," and asked him to "give us a week notice before you are ready to ship, in order for us to prepare our sales orders." When the trial court directed a verdict for Schmieding against Cagle on the contract for seed potatoes and the jury found in favor of Cagle on the contract for the purchase of Cagle's crop, Schmieding appealed.

Houston, Justice. A contract for the sale of potatoes to be harvested is manifestly a "transaction in goods," and we will therefore apply the UCC to this case. Schmieding argues that the alleged contract fails for indefiniteness due to its numerous "open terms," such as time and place of delivery and various warranties that the potatoes would meet certain specifications. In addition, Schmieding also argues that the price term for the red potatoes, i.e., "market price at time of harvest," is also too indefinite to allow enforcement of the contract.

Although Schmieding's argument might have had some merit under pre-UCC cases, this argument has no chance of success under the UCC. The controlling section is 2–204(3), which provides:

Even though one or more terms are left open a contract for sale does not fail for indefiniteness if the parties have intended to make a contract and there is a reasonably certain basis for giving an appropriate remedy.

Evidence was presented at trial indicating that at least the following terms were agreed upon: 1) the type of potatoes ordered (red and white), 2) the quantity ordered (in terms of bags or acreage), 3) the price to be paid for the quantity ordered ($5.50 per bag for whites, market price at harvest for reds), and 4) the approximate delivery date (at harvest).

This evidence puts to rest any argument as to whether the parties "intended to make a contract"—sufficient evidence was introduced by Cagle to require that this question of fact be submitted to the jury. Similarly, these terms, if in fact entered into, would also provide a "reasonably certain basis for giving an appropriate remedy." The value of this contract to either party is susceptible to reasonably certain measurement by a court and jury, and an appropriate remedy for its breach could be provided.

Accordingly, even though the contract contains several open terms in addition to those expressly noted, the contract does not fail for indefiniteness, because such open terms may be supplemented by the UCC's "gap-filler" provisions. For instance, time, place, and manner of delivery are dealt with in sections 2–307, –308, –309, and similarly, the quality of the potatoes would likely have been guaranteed under one or more of the Code's warranty provisions. Moreover, a market-based open price term (such as that chosen for the red potatoes in the instant contract) is expressly recognized by the Code as an acceptable price term in section 2–305(1)(c). The trial court did not err in submitting this claim to the jury.

Judgment in favor of Cagle affirmed.

The *Restatement (Second) of Contracts* takes an approach to the definiteness question that is quite similar to the Code approach. The terms of an alleged offer must be reasonably certain before they can form the basis of a contract.[3] Reasonable certainty merely means that those terms "provide a basis for determining the existence of a breach and for giving an appropriate remedy."[4] The basic thrust of the *Restatement Second*, however, is still to further the intent of the parties; it expressly recognizes the fact that open or uncertain terms may indicate the absence of an intent to contract.[5] Where an agreement is sufficiently definite to be a contract, but essential terms are left open, the *Restatement Second* provides that "a term which is reasonable in the circumstances is supplied by the court."[6] Similar to the Code, the *Restatement Second* specifically indicates that where the parties' conduct indicates an intent to contract, a contract may result "even though neither offer nor acceptance can be identified and even though the moment of formation cannot be determined."[7] Unlike the Code, the *Restatement Second* also indicates that "action in reliance" on an indefinite agreement may justify its full or partial enforcement.[8] This provision highlights one of the most intriguing recent developments in contract law—the use of **promissory estoppel** to enforce indefinite agreements.[9] It has long been the rule that promissory estoppel could not be used to enforce indefinite agreements because their indefiniteness meant that the court was left with no promise capable of being enforced. Sometimes people do, however, act in reliance on

indefinite agreements, and to protect that reliance a few courts have deviated from the general rule. In such cases, it is common for courts to overcome the indefiniteness problem by awarding damages based on the promisee's losses due to reliance rather than by attempting to enforce the indefinite agreement.

Hoffman v. Red Owl Stores, Inc., is probably the most famous case of this type.[10] Hoffman wanted to acquire a Red Owl franchised convenience store and, in reliance on Red Owl's promises during their negotiations, sold his bakery at a loss, bought a small grocery to gain experience, moved his family, and bought an option on a proposed site for the franchised store. The negotiations fell through, and when Hoffman sued, Red Owl argued that no contract resulted, because the parties had never reached agreement on the essential terms governing their relationship. The Supreme Court of Wisconsin agreed, but nonetheless allowed Hoffman to recover his reliance losses on the basis of promissory estoppel. In doing so, the court noted that nothing in the language of section 90 of the *Restatement* required that a promise serving as the basis of promissory estoppel be "so comprehensive in scope as to meet the requirements of an offer."

Considering cases like *Hoffman* and the way in which the definiteness problem is handled by both the Code and the *Restatement Second*, it is safe to say that indefiniteness is no longer the obstacle to the creation of contractual liability that it once was.

Communication to Offeree

When an offeror communicates the terms of an offer to an offeree, he objectively indicates an intent to be bound by those terms. An uncommunicated offer, on the other hand, may be evidence that the offeror has not yet decided to enter into a binding agreement. For example,

---

[3] *Restatement (Second) of Contracts* § 33(1) (1981).

[4] *Restatement (Second) of Contracts* § 33(2) (1981).

[5] *Restatement (Second) of Contracts* § 33(3) (1981).

[6] *Restatement (Second) of Contracts* § 204 (1981).

[7] *Restatement (Second) of Contracts* § 22(2) (1981).

[8] *Restatement (Second) of Contracts* § 34(3) (1981).

[9] See the general discussion of promissory estoppel in the Introduction to Contracts chapter.

[10] 26 Wis.2d 683, 133 N.W.2d 267 (Wis. Sup. Ct. 1965).

assume that Stevens and Meyer have been negotiating over the sale of Meyer's restaurant. Reilly, Stevens's secretary, tells Meyer that Stevens has decided to offer him $150,000 for the restaurant and has drawn up a written offer to that effect. After learning the details of the offer from Reilly, Meyer telephones Stevens and says, "I accept your offer." Is Stevens now contractually obligated to buy the restaurant? No. Since Stevens did not communicate the proposal to Meyer, there was no offer for Meyer to accept.

SPECIAL OFFER PROBLEM AREAS

Advertisements

The courts have generally held that advertisements for the sale of goods at specified prices are *not* offers; instead, they are treated as invitations to offer or negotiate. The same rule is generally applied to signs, handbills, displayed goods, catalogs, price lists, and price quotations. This rule probably fairly reflects the intentions of the sellers involved, who probably only have a limited number of items to sell, and do not intend to give every person who sees their ad, sign, or catalog the power to bind them to contract. Thus, would-be buyers are, in legal effect, making *offers* to purchase the goods, which the seller is free to accept or reject. This is so because the buyer is manifesting a present intent to contract on the definite terms of the ad, sign, or catalog and there is no offer for him to accept.

In some cases, however, particular ads have been held to amount to offers. Such ads are usually highly specific about the nature and number of items offered for sale and what is requested in return. This specificity precludes the possibility that the offeror could become contractually bound to an infinite number of offerees. In addition, many of the ads treated as offers have required special performance by would-be buyers or have in some other way clearly indicated that immediate buyer action creates a binding agreement. The potential for unfairness to those who attempt to accept such ads and their fundamental difference from ordinary ads probably justify treating them as offers. So, if Monarch Motors runs this special 10th anniversary advertisement, "Our 10th customer on Saturday, March 25, 1992, will be entitled to purchase a new Rolls-Royce Silver Shadow with every available option for 10 percent under dealer cost," most courts would probably hold that this ad was an offer and that the 10th customer was entitled to purchase the car as advertised.

Rewards

Advertisements offering rewards for lost property, for information, or for the capture of criminals are generally treated as offers for unilateral contracts. To accept the offer and be entitled to the stated reward, offerees must perform the requested act—return the lost property, supply the requested information, or capture the wanted criminal. Some courts have held that only offerees who started performance with knowledge of the offer are entitled to the reward. Other courts, however, have indicated the only requirement is that the offeree know of the reward before completing performance. In reality, the result in most such cases probably reflects the court's perception of the equities of the particular case at hand.

Auctions

Sellers at auctions are generally treated as making an invitation to offer. Those who bid on offered goods are, therefore, treated as making offers that the owner of the goods may accept or reject. Acceptance occurs only when the auctioneer strikes the goods off to the highest bidder; the auctioneer may withdraw the goods at any time before acceptance. However, when an auction is advertised as being "without reserve," the seller is treated as having made an offer to sell the goods to the highest bidder and the goods cannot be withdrawn after a call for bids has been made unless no bids are made within a reasonable time.[11]

Bids

The bidding process is a fertile source of contract disputes. Advertisements for bids are generally treated as invitations to offer. Those who submit bids are treated as offerors. According to general contract principles, bidders can withdraw their bids at any time prior to acceptance by the offeree inviting the bids and the offeree is free to accept or reject any bid. The previously announced terms of the bidding may alter these rules, however. For example, if the advertisement for bids unconditionally states that the contract will be awarded to the lowest responsible bidder, this will be treated as an offer that is accepted by the lowest bidder. Only proof by the offeror that the lowest bidder is not responsible can prevent the formation of a contract. Also, under some circumstances discussed later in this chapter,

---

[11] These rules and others concerned with the sale of goods by auction are contained in section 2–328 of the UCC.

promissory estoppel may operate to prevent bidders from withdrawing their bids.

Bids for governmental contracts are generally covered by specific statutes rather than by general contract principles. Such statutes ordinarily establish the rules governing the bidding process, often require that the contract be awarded to the lowest bidder, and frequently establish special rules or penalties governing the withdrawal of bids.

WHICH TERMS ARE INCLUDED IN OFFERS?

After making a determination that an offer existed, a court must decide which terms were included in the offer so that it can determine the terms of the parties' contract. Put another way, which terms of the offer are binding on the offeree who accepts it? Should offerees, for example, be bound by fine print clauses or by clauses on the back of the contract? Originally, the courts tended to hold that offerees were bound by all the terms of the offer on the theory that every person had a duty to protect himself by reading agreements carefully before signing them.

In today's world of lengthy, complex form contracts, however, people often sign agreements that they have not fully read or do not fully understand. As the follow-ing *McAdoo* case indicates, modern courts tend to recognize this fact by saying that offerees are bound only by terms of which they had *actual* or *reasonable notice*. If the offeree actually read the term in question, or if a reasonable person should have been aware of it, it will probably become part of the parties' contract. So, a fine-print provision on the back of a theater ticket would probably not be binding on a theater patron, because a reasonable person would not expect such a ticket to contain contractual terms. However, the terms printed on a multipage airline or steamship ticket might well be considered binding on the purchaser.

This modern approach to deciding the terms of a contract gives courts an indirect, but effective, way of promoting fair dealing by refusing to enforce unfair contract terms on the ground that the offeree lacked reasonable notice of them. Disclaimers and exculpatory clauses (contract provisions that seek to relieve offerors of some legal duty that they would otherwise owe to offerees) are particularly likely to be subjected to close judicial scrutiny. Many courts insist on proof that the offeree had actual notice of such terms before they are considered a part of the contract. Also, as you will learn in greater detail in the Illegality chapter, even terms that would otherwise clearly be part of the parties' contract may be inoperative if they are unconscionable or contrary to public policy.

ST. JOHN'S EPISCOPAL HOSPITAL v. MCADOO

405 N.Y.S.2d 935 (N.Y. City Civ. Ct. 1978)

Less than an hour before his estranged wife underwent emergency surgery for an ectopic pregnancy caused by another man, Charles McAdoo was asked to sign a standard form contract prepared by St. John's Episcopal Hospital. McAdoo testified that at the time he signed the form his wife's physical appearance and declared mental state convinced him that she was near death. Further, he stated that, under such circumstances, it did not occur to him to read carefully or question the implications of the papers he was being asked to sign. The form contained a provision that read as follows:

ASSIGNMENT OF INSURANCE BENEFITS: I hereby authorize payment directly to the above named hospital of the hospital expense benefits otherwise payable to me but not to exceed the hospital's regular charges for this period of hospitalization. *I understand that I am financially responsible to the hospital for the charges not covered by my group insurance plan.*

Mrs. McAdoo survived and was discharged from St. John's eight days later. McAdoo did not visit her after the day of the operation and had not had any further contact with her when the hospital filed suit against him to collect her hospital bill.

Feldman, Judge.   The principle that signed contracts are binding cannot be lightly disregarded. To do so would endanger the orderly functioning of commerce and allow individuals to escape the consequences of their agreements because of a change in circumstance. However, it is also unrealistic to continue insisting that in a society of mass marketing it is reasonable still to expect individuals, unrepresented by counsel, to read each clause of the many standardized contracts used by the various institutions with which we all deal. In certain instances it is certainly appropriate for courts to examine the circumstances under which a contract was signed in order to determine whether 1) there was a genuine opportunity for the signer to have read the clause in dispute; or 2) if he did not read it whether a reasonable person should have expected to find such a clause in the particular instrument he was signing. Where there are negative answers to these questions, a court can then address itself to the fairness of enforcing that clause.

It is reasonable in this situation for McAdoo to have seen himself as powerless to do anything other than sign the form. A hospital emergency room is certainly not a place in which any but the strongest can be expected to exercise calm and dispassionate judgment. The law of contracts is not intended to use "superman" as its model. If the reasonable man standard is applied here, McAdoo's failure to read the document or to give it more than the most cursory attention is understandable.

It thus becomes vital that a document like the form involved here be clearly labeled and organized so that the signer is made aware of what it entails. Here, the paragraph signed by McAdoo bore a heading totally unrelated to the sentence on which St. John's now relies to argue his financial liability. McAdoo would have been entirely justified in concluding from the heading that he was agreeing only to have his union insurance pay for his wife's hospital bills. This is a far cry from agreeing to assume personal liability.

St. John's is surely no stranger to the trauma and anxiety experienced by those confronted with emergency medical crises. Armed with this knowledge it should have prepared the form so that the person being asked to sign it can readily grasp its meaning, even through a quick reading. Moreover, St. John's should not be permitted to enforce a contractual obligation entered into under such tension-laden circumstances as those McAdoo described.

Judgment for McAdoo.

TERMINATION OF OFFERS

After a court has determined the existence and content of an offer, it must determine the *duration* of the offer. Was the offer still in existence when the offeree attempted to accept it? If not, no contract was created and the offeree is treated as having made an offer that the original offeror is free to accept or reject. This is so because, by attempting to accept an offer that has terminated, the offeree has indicated a present intent to contract on the terms of the original offer though he lacks the power to bind the offeror to a contract due to the original offer's termination.

Terms of the Offer

The offeror is often said to be "the master of the offer." This means that offerors have the power to determine the terms and conditions under which they are bound to a contract. As the following *Newman* case indicates, an offeror may include terms in the offer that limit its effective life. These may be specific terms, such as "you must accept by December 5, 1989" or "this offer good for five days," or more general terms, such as "for immediate acceptance," "prompt wire acceptance," or "by return mail." General time limitation language in an offer can raise difficult problems of interpretation for courts trying to decide whether an offeree accepted before the offer terminated. Even more specific language, such as "this offer good for five days," can cause problems if the offer does not specify whether the five-day period be-

gins when the offer is sent or when the offeree receives it. Not all courts agree on such questions, so wise offerors should be as specific as possible in stating when their offers terminate.

NEWMAN v. SCHIFF
778 F.2d 460 (8th Cir. 1985)

Irwin Schiff, a self-styled tax rebel who had made a career out of his tax protest activities, appeared live on the February 7, 1983, CBS News "Nightwatch" program. During the course of the program, which had a viewer participation format, Schiff repeated his longstanding position that "there is nothing in the Internal Revenue Code which says anyone is legally required to pay the tax." Later in the program, Schiff stated: "If anybody calls this show and cites any section of this Code that says an individual is required to file a tax return, I will pay them $100,000."

Attorney John Newman failed to see Schiff live on "Nightwatch," but saw a two-minute taped segment of the original "Nightwatch" interview several hours later on the "CBS Morning News." Certain that Schiff's statements were incorrect, Newman telephoned and wrote "CBS Morning News," attempting to accept Schiff's offer by citing Internal Revenue Code provisions requiring individuals to pay federal income tax. CBS forwarded Newman's letter to Schiff, who refused to pay on the ground that Newman had not properly accepted his offer. Newman sued Schiff for breach of contract. The trial court ruled in Schiff's favor, and Newman appealed.

Bright, Senior Circuit Judge.   It is a basic legal principle that mutual assent is necessary for the formation of a contract. A significant doctrinal struggle in the development of contract law revolved around whether it was a party's actual or apparent assent that was necessary. This was a struggle between subjective and objective theorists. The subjectivists looked to actual assent. Both parties had to actually assent to an agreement for there to be a contract. The objectivists, on the other hand, looked to apparent assent. The expression of mutual assent, and not the assent itself, was the essential element in the formation of a contract. By the end of the nineteenth century the objective approach to the mutual assent requirement had become predominant, and courts continue to use it today.

Courts determine whether the parties expressed their assent to a contract by analyzing their agreement process in terms of offer and acceptance. An offer is the "manifestation of willingness to enter into a bargain, so made as to justify another person in understanding that his assent to that bargain is invited and will conclude it." *Restatement (Second) of Contracts* § 24 (1981). Schiff's statement on "Nightwatch" that he would pay $100,000 to anyone who called the show and cited any section of the Internal Revenue Code "that says an individual is required to file a tax return" constituted a valid offer for a reward. If anyone had called the show and cited the code sections that Newman produced, a contract would have been formed and Schiff would have been obligated to pay the $100,000 reward.

Newman, however, never saw the live CBS "Nightwatch" program on which Schiff appeared and this lawsuit is not predicated on Schiff's "Nightwatch" offer. Newman saw the "CBS Morning News" rebroadcast of Schiff's "Nightwatch" appearance. This rebroadcast served not to renew or extend Schiff's offer, but rather only to inform viewers that Schiff had made an offer on "Nightwatch." An offeror is the master of his offer and it is clear that Schiff by his words, "If anybody calls this show," limited his offer in time to remain open only until the conclusion of the live "Nightwatch" broadcast. A reasonable person listening to the news rebroadcast could not conclude that the above language constituted a new offer rather than what it actually was, a news report of the offer previously made, which had already expired.

Although Newman has not "won" his lawsuit in the traditional sense of recovering a reward that he sought, he has accomplished an important goal in the public interest of unmasking the "blatant nonsense" dispensed by Schiff. For that he deserves great commendation from the public. Perhaps now CBS and other communication media who have given Schiff's mistaken views widespread publicity will give John Newman equal time in the public interest.

Judgment for Schiff affirmed.

Lapse of Time

Offers that fail to provide a specific time for acceptance are valid for a *reasonable time*. What constitutes a reasonable time depends on the circumstances surrounding the offer. How long would a reasonable person in the offeree's position believe she had to accept the offer? Offers involving things subject to rapid fluctuations in value, such as stocks, bonds, or commodities futures, have a very brief duration. The same is true for offers involving goods that may spoil, such as produce.

The nature of the parties' negotiations is another factor relevant to determining the duration of an offer. Most courts hold that when parties bargain face-to-face or over the telephone, the normal time for acceptance does not extend past the conclusion of their conversation unless the offeror indicates a contrary intention. Where negotiations are carried out by mail or telegram, the time for acceptance would ordinarily include at least the normal time for communicating the offer and a prompt response by the offeree. It is often said, for example, that a mailed offer is promptly accepted when an acceptance is mailed at any time on the day the offer was received. However, the absence of any rapid fluctuations in the value of the items offered could extend the time for acceptance. Finally, in cases where the parties have dealt with each other on a regular basis in the past, the timing of their prior transactions would be highly relevant in measuring the reasonable time for acceptance.

Revocation

As the masters of their offers, offerors can give offerees the power to bind them to contracts by making offers. They can also terminate that power by *revoking* their offers. The general common law rule on revocations is that offerors may revoke their offers *at any time prior to acceptance*, even if they have promised to hold the offer open for a stated period of time. However, several exceptions to this general rule can prevent offerors from revoking. Figure 1 summarizes the situations when offerors cannot revoke their offers.

Options   An **option** is a separate contract in which an offeror agrees not to revoke her offer for a stated time in exchange for some valuable consideration.[12] The offeree who enters an option contract has no obligation to accept the offeror's offer; in effect, she has merely purchased the right to consider the offer for the stated time without fear that the offeror will revoke it. The traditional common law rule on options requires the actual payment of the agreed-on consideration before an option contract becomes enforceable. Therefore, if, in exchange for $100, Martin gave Berry a 30-day option to purchase his house for $150,000 and Berry never, in fact, paid the $100, no option was created and Martin could revoke his offer at any time prior to its acceptance by Berry.

Firm Offers   The Code makes a major change in the common law rules governing the revocability of offers by recognizing the concept of a **firm offer** [2–205]. A firm offer is irrevocable for the *time stated in the offer*. If no time is stated, it is irrevocable for a *reasonable time*. Regardless of the terms of the offer, the outer limit on a firm offer's irrevocability is three months. Not all offers

---

[12] The Consideration chapter discusses consideration in detail.

FIGURE 1	When Offerors Cannot Revoke
Options	Offeror has promised to hold offer open and has received consideration for that promise
Firm Offers	Merchant offeror makes written offer to sell goods, giving assurances offer will be held open
Unilateral Contract Offers	Offeree has started to perform requested act before offeror revokes
Promissory Estoppel	Offeree foreseeably and reasonably relies on offer being held open, and will suffer injustice if it is revoked

for the sale of goods qualify as firm offers, however. To be a firm offer, an offer must be made by a *merchant* in a *signed writing* that contains *assurances* that the offer will be held open and not revoked. An offer for the sale of goods that fails to satisfy these three requirements is governed by the general common law rule and revocable at any time prior to acceptance.

Indicating that an offer will be held open for a particular time can sometimes serve an offeror's interests because it may increase the likelihood of ultimate acceptance by an offeree who is given assurance that sufficient time will be available to investigate the merits of the offer. The receipt of such an offer creates obvious expectations about the duration of the offer in the minds of offerees; the Code's firm offer provision is designed to protect these expectations. In some cases, however, *offerees* are the true originators of an assurance term in an offer. When offerees have effective control of the terms of the offer by providing their customers with preprinted purchase order forms or order blanks, they may be tempted to take advantage of their merchant customers by placing an assurance term in their order forms. This would allow offerees to await market developments before deciding whether to fill the order, while their merchant customers, who may have signed the order without reading all of its terms, would be powerless to revoke. To prevent such unfairness, the Code requires that assurance terms on forms provided by offerees be *separately signed* by the offeror to effect a firm offer.

Offers for Unilateral Contracts The general rule that an offeror can revoke at any time prior to acceptance

causes special problems when applied to offers for unilateral contracts. Because the offeree in a unilateral contract must fully perform the requested act to accept, the application of the general rule would allow an offeror to revoke after the offeree has begun performance but before he has had a chance to complete it. To prevent injustice to offerees who rely on such offers by beginning performance, two basic approaches are available to modern courts. Some courts have held that once the offeree has begun to perform, the offeror's power to revoke is suspended for the amount of time reasonably necessary for the offeree to complete performance. Section 45 of the *Restatement Second* takes a similar approach for offers that unequivocally require acceptance by performance by stating that once the offeree begins performance, an option contract is created. The offeror's duty to perform his side of the bargain is conditional on full performance by the offeree. This approach clearly protects the offeree, but from an offeror's standpoint it is less than desirable because the offeree has no duty to complete the requested performance.

Another approach to the unilateral contract dilemma is to hold that a bilateral contract is created once the offeree begins performance. This is essentially the position taken by section 62 of the *Restatement Second*, which states that when the offer invites acceptance either by a return promise or performance, the beginning of performance operates as an acceptance and a promise by the offeree to render complete performance. This approach protects both the offeror and the offeree, but may be contrary to the actual intent of the parties, neither of whom may wish to be bound to a contract until achieving complete performance.

Promissory Estoppel In some cases, the doctrine of promissory estoppel can operate to prevent offerors from revoking their offers prior to acceptance. Section 87(2) of the *Restatement Second* says:

An offer which the offeror should reasonably expect to induce action or forbearance of a substantial character on the part of the offeree before acceptance and which does induce such action or forbearance is binding as an option contract to the extent necessary to avoid injustice.

As the following *Warner Electric* case illustrates, promissory estoppel has often been used to prevent revocation in the bidding context.

JOHN PRICE ASSOCIATES, INC. v. WARNER ELECTRIC, INC.

723 F.2d 755 (10th Cir. 1983)

Warner Electric, an electrical subcontractor, submitted a bid to the Utah Subcontractors Bid Depository Service for the electrical subcontract on the construction of the General Services Administration (GSA) Metallurgy Research Center in Salt Lake City, Utah. Warner based its bid on specifications and bid forms supplied by the GSA. John Price Associates, a general contractor, used Warner's subcontract bid, which was the lowest submitted, in preparing its bid for the general contract.

Price was the lowest bidder and was awarded the contract for the project. A few days after Price had signed a contract with the GSA, Warner told Price that it had a problem with its subcontract bid because the bid did not include certain laboratory work described in section 11600 of the GSA plans, work which Warner had thought would be performed by the general contractor. Warner refused to sign the subcontract without a promise of additional payment for the section 11600 work. Price notified Warner by mailgram that it was accepting Warner's bid. Later that day, Warner's attorney delivered a letter to Price withdrawing Warner's bid.

Price then contacted the other subcontractors who had submitted bids asking for new bids. It ultimately hired the lowest bidder in the second round of bidding, the Foley Company, for $94,845 more than Warner's bid price. Foley, like Warner, had not initially included the section 11600 work in its original bid, but its revised bid included the increased costs attributable to that work. Price later filed a claim against the GSA for its losses due to Warner's withdrawal, arguing, as Warner had, that the specifications for the project were ambiguous. After the GSA Board of Contract Appeals denied his claim he filed suit against Warner. When the trial court ruled in Price's favor, Warner appealed.

Logan, Circuit Judge.   We agree with the trial court that the doctrine of promissory estoppel barred Warner from withdrawing its bid. That doctrine provides that a promise that the promisor should reasonably expect to induce action by the promisee and that does induce such action is binding if injustice can be avoided only by enforcement of the promise. Warner submitted a bid through the Subcontractors Bid Service with the expectation that companies bidding on the general contract would rely on its bid in making their bids. Price relied on Warner's bid, and when Price found out that it would probably get the general contract, Price notified Warner of its reliance. Price had entered into a binding contract before Warner notified it of any problems with the bid. In this situation promissory estoppel should prevent Warner from withdrawing its bid.

Ambiguity in the GSA plans and specifications should not constitute a legal defense in the instant case. The government, not Price, provided the plans and specifications. The accompanying materials directed that inquiries about them be directed to government officials. Nothing put Price on notice that something was wrong with Warner's bid. The difference between Warner's bid and those of other electrical subcontractors was insufficient to raise Price's suspicion that Warner had made a mistake in computing its bid. Before Warner discovered its error Price was bound as general contractor on the project. Under these circumstances, the trial court correctly required Warner rather than Price to bear any loss caused by the alleged ambiguity.

When Warner withdrew its bid, Price acted reasonably. Price contacted the four next lowest bidders, who were no longer bound by their original bids, and accepted the lowest bid on resubmittal. At this point the only other step Price could take to mitigate damages was to seek additional payments from the GSA because of the alleged ambiguities in the plans.

Price pursued this remedy at its own expense. The trial court properly awarded Price damages and interest.

Judgment for Price affirmed.

Effectiveness of Revocations   The question of when a revocation is effective to terminate an offer is often a critical issue in the contract formation process. For example, Davis offers to landscape Winter's property for $1,500. Two days after making the offer, Davis changes his mind and mails Winter a letter revoking the offer. The next day, Winter, who has not received Davis's letter, telephones Davis and attempts to accept. Contract? Yes. As the following *Lyon* case indicates, the general rule on this point is that revocations are effective only when they are *actually received* by the offeree. The basic idea behind this rule is that the offeree is justified in relying on the intent to contract manifested by the offeror's offer until she actually knows that the offeror has changed his mind.

This explains why many courts have also held that if the offeree receives reliable information indicating that the offeror has taken action inconsistent with an intent to enter the contract proposed by the offer, such as selling the property that was the subject of the offer to someone else, this terminates the offer. In such circumstances, the offeree would be unjustified in believing that the offer could still be accepted.

The only major exception to the general rule on effectiveness of revocations concerns offers to the general public. Because it would be impossible in most cases to reach every offeree with a revocation, it is generally held that a revocation made in the same manner as the offer is effective when published, without proof of communication to the offeree.

LYON v. ADGRAPHICS
540 A.2d 398 (Conn. Ct. App. 1988)

Edward Sherman engaged V. R. Brokers as listing agent for the sale of Adgraphics, his business. On December 5, 1985, William Lyon made a written offer to purchase the business for $75,000 and attached certain conditions to the offer. Later the same day, Sherman signed a written counteroffer offering to sell for $80,000 and rejecting two of the conditions contained in Lyon's offer. On December 7, at 11:35 A.M., Lyon signed the counteroffer before a notary public and then brought it to the office of V. R. Brokers around noon on that day. Before Lyon could hand the signed counteroffer to Robert Renault, the principal of V. R. Brokers, Renault told him that Sherman wanted to cancel his counteroffer. Lyon filed a breach of contract suit, and, when the trial court ruled in his favor, Sherman appealed.

Borden, Judge.   It is a basic principle of contract law that in order to form a binding contract there must be an offer and acceptance based on a mutual understanding of the parties. The counter offer by Sherman created a power of acceptance in Lyon. That counteroffer, however, was revocable by Sherman at any time prior to acceptance by Lyon.

The trial court's conclusion that Lyon's acceptance of the counteroffer was effective when he signed it was contrary to our law. Revocation of an offer in order to be effectual must be received by the offeree before he has exercised his power of creating a contract by acceptance of the offer. Acceptance is operative, if transmitted by means which the offeror has authorized, as soon as its transmission begins and it is put out of the offeree's possession. Lyon's act of signing the written counteroffer failed to communicate the acceptance to Sherman or his agent and failed to put the acceptance out of Lyon's possession. It was, therefore, ineffective to create a contract.

When Sherman, through his agent, informed Lyon that the counteroffer was withdrawn, Lyon's power to accept the counteroffer no longer existed. This was done before Lyon had properly accepted the counteroffer by transmitting the signed counteroffer to Renault. Accordingly, no enforceable contract between the parties was ever created.

Judgment reversed in favor of Sherman.

Rejection

An offeree may *expressly reject* an offer by indicating that he is unwilling to accept it. He may also *impliedly reject* it by making a **counteroffer,** an offer to contract on terms materially different from the terms of the offer.[13] As a general rule, either form of rejection by the offeree terminates his power to accept the offer. This is so because an offeror who receives a rejection may rely on the offeree's expressed desire not to accept the offer by making another offer to a different offeree. Therefore, if either party manifests an intent to keep the offer open despite a rejection, many courts hold that no termination has occurred. If the offeror indicates in the offer that it will continue in effect despite a rejection, there is no need to fear that he will rely on rejection terminating the offer. Likewise, if the offeree indicates that she rejects the offer at the present time but will take it under advisement in the future, there is no basis for reliance by the offeror. One further exception to the general rule that rejections terminate offers concerns offers that are the subject of an option contract. Some courts hold that a rejection does not terminate an option contract and that the offeree who rejects still has the power to accept the offer later, so long as the acceptance is effective within the option period.[14]

Effectiveness of Rejections   As a general rule, rejections, like revocations, are effective only when *actually received* by the offeror. This is because there is no possibility that the offeror can rely on a rejection by making another offer to a different offeree until she actually has notice of the rejection. Therefore, an offeree who has mailed a rejection could still change her mind and accept

if she communicates the acceptance before the offeror receives the rejection.[15]

Death or Insanity of Either Party

The death or insanity of either party to an offer automatically terminates the offer without notice. A meeting of the minds is obviously impossible when one of the parties has died or become insane.

Destruction of Subject Matter

If, prior to an acceptance of an offer, the subject matter of a proposed contract is destroyed without the knowledge or fault of either party, the offer is terminated.[16] So, if Marks offers to sell Wiggins his lakeside cottage and the cottage is destroyed by fire before Wiggins accepts, the offer was terminated on the destruction of the cottage. Subsequent acceptance by Wiggins would not create a contract.

Intervening Illegality

An offer is terminated if the performance of the contract it proposes becomes illegal before the offer is accepted. So, if a computer manufacturer has offered to sell sophisticated computer equipment to the Republic of South Africa, but two days later, before the offer has been accepted, Congress places an embargo on all sales to South Africa to protest apartheid, the offer is terminated by the embargo.[17]

---

[13] The Acceptance chapter discusses counteroffers in detail.

[14] Section 37 of the *Restatement Second* adopts this rule.

[15] The Acceptance chapter discusses this subject in detail.

[16] In some circumstances, destruction of subject matter can also serve as a legal excuse for a party's failure to perform his obligations under an existing contract. The Performance and Remedies chapter discusses this subject.

[17] In some circumstances, intervening illegality can also serve as a legal excuse for a party's failure to perform his obligations under an existing contract. The Performance and Remedies chapter discusses this subject.

CONCEPT REVIEW

WHAT TERMINATES OFFERS?

- ☐ Their own terms
- ☐ Lapse of time
- ☐ Revocation
- ☐ Rejection
- ☐ Death or insanity of offeror or offeree
- ☐ Destruction of subject matter
- ☐ Intervening illegality

ETHICAL AND PUBLIC POLICY CONCERNS

1. Classical contract theory has traditionally found strong ethical justification in the notion of voluntary consent. To parties who want out of their contracts and ask why they should be held to them, the law has often responded: "Because you agreed to them." How does this ethical justification square with the objective theory of contract, which can in some cases result in holding people to agreements that are inconsistent with their subjective intent? Is there some other ethical justification for holding people to the objective manifestations of consent, regardless of their actual or subjective intent?

2. Compare and contrast the underlying ethical justifications of the classical and modern contract positions on what terms are included in offers. Is it ethical for businesses who deal with consumers or other unsophisticated parties to "hide" contract terms under misleading headings, in small print, or on the reverse side of contracts? What about putting form contracts in complex, technical language that consumers are unlikely to understand?

3. As you learned earlier in this chapter, there are now a number of exceptions to the traditional rule that offerors can revoke at any time prior to acceptance, even if they have promised not to. Is there an ethical basis for each of these exceptions? If so, what is it?

SUMMARY

Courts seeking to determine the existence of a contract look for evidence of an agreement between the parties. The first step in this process is to determine whether an offer existed that, when accepted by the offeree, resulted in the formation of a contract. An offer is a combination of facts and circumstances that objectively indicate a present intent to contract on the part of the offeror. Traditional contract law principles require not only that an alleged offer be definite and specific but also that it be communicated to the offeree by the offeror. Modern contract principles embodied in the UCC and the *Restatement (Second) of Contracts*, however, require a significantly lesser degree of definiteness in offers, with the result that courts applying these principles are more likely to recognize the existence of a contract and, in some cases, to supply contract terms omitted or left indefinite by the parties.

Several common business situations involve questions concerning the existence of offers. Advertisements, price quotes, catalogs, signs, and so forth are generally treated as invitations to offer. As a result, in such cases, would-be buyers are normally treated as offerors, not offerees. Under some extraordinary circumstances, however, an advertisement or a price quote can amount to an offer. Offers of rewards are generally treated as offers for unilateral contracts that can only be accepted by performance of the act that the reward requests. Bids are generally treated as offers that the bidder may revoke at any time prior to acceptance and that the offeree is free to accept or reject. In some circumstances, an offeree's reliance on a bid may operate to estop the offeror from revoking it. Bidders at auctions are normally treated as making offers unless the auction is "without reserve," in which case the seller is treated as having made an offer to sell to the highest bidder; that offer cannot be revoked once bidding starts.

Modern courts hold that offerees are bound by all the terms in the offer of which they have reasonable notice. In some cases, this means that fine print terms or terms on the back of the contract are not part of the parties' contract. Disclaimers and exculpatory clauses are particularly likely to be excluded from a contract on this basis.

The duration of offers is limited. Offerees who attempt to accept terminated offers are treated as having made an offer that the original offeror is free to accept or reject. An offer may expire by its own terms or, if no terms are stated, after the passage of a reasonable time. As a general rule, offerors can revoke their offers at any time prior to acceptance. There are several limitations on this rule, however. Offerors who enter option contracts, agreeing not to revoke in exchange for some valuable consideration, cannot revoke for the option period. The Code recognizes the concept of an irrevocable firm offer, which applies to offers for the sale of goods that meet certain other qualifications. Promissory estoppel may also operate to prevent revocation in some circumstances. Finally, once an offeree attempts to accept an offer for a unilateral contract by beginning performance of the acts requested by the offer, modern courts employ a variety of theories to prevent the offeror from revoking prior to the offeree's completion of performance.

Rejection of an offer by the offeree, whether express or implied, also terminates the offer. Both revocations and rejections are effective only when actually communicated to the other party. The death or insanity of either party automatically terminates an offer. Likewise, destruction of the subject matter of an offer or the subsequent illegality of the performance called for by an offer also cause termination.

PROBLEM CASES

1. After some negotiations, Empro Manufacturing sent Ball-Co a three-page "letter of intent" to purchase Ball-Co's assets. Empro proposed a price of $2.4 million, with $650,000 to be paid on closing and a 10-year promissory note for the remainder, secured by Ball-Co's inventory and equipment. The letter provided that it was "subject to . . . a definitive Asset Purchase Agreement signed by both parties" and that the purchase was also "subject to" the satisfaction of certain other conditions, including the approval of Empro's shareholders and board. Ball-Co signed the letter of intent, but later broke off discussions after Empro refused to secure the promissory note with a security interest in the land under Ball-Co's plant. Empro filed suit against Ball-Co, arguing that by signing the letter of intent Ball-Co had contracted to sell to Empro. Was the trial court justified in dismissing Empro's suit?

2. Rhen Marshall (RM) received a mailed "Christmas Comes Early at Purolator" advertising circular describing premiums available with orders for Purolator products. Premiums varied with order size. Deal 5A stated that an order for 100,000 pounds of Purolator products entitled customers to a premium of a new 1978 Buick Electra automobile and 100 EK-6 Kodak Instant cameras. The ad said: "You will be billed $500 for the package, which has a retail value of $17,450." RM ordered over 100,000 pounds of Purolator oil filters and also ordered "Deal 5A as outlined in your brochure." The circular contained no billing or discount provisions. RM's order requested a 5 percent truckload discount and "30–60–90 day billing." (In previous dealings between these parties, a "30–60–90 day billing" meant a

2 percent discount if paid within 30 days, a 1 percent discount if paid within 60 days, or payment in full at the end of 90 days.) Purolator rejected RM's order, and RM filed suit for breach of contract. Should RM have recovered?

3. On August 4, 1980, Normile made a written offer to buy property owned by Miller. Miller signed and returned the offer after making several substantial changes in its terms and initialing those changes. The executed form was delivered to Normile by Byer, the real estate agent who had shown him the property. In the early afternoon of August 5, 1980, Miller accepted an offer by Segal to buy her property on terms similar to those in the modified offer she had returned to Normile. At 2:00 P.M. that day, Byer told Normile: "You snooze, you lose; the property has been sold." Shortly thereafter, Normile attempted to accept Miller's proposal. Was the trial court correct in ruling that Normile and Miller had no contract?

4. In November of 1977, Cagle went to Buckner Chevrolet to discuss the purchase of a 1978 Limited Edition Corvette (referred to as an "Indy Vette" because one or more of them was used as a pace car at Indianapolis). Cagle talked to Buckner's used car manager, who partially filled out a buyer's order form, which was then presented to Kelly, Buckner's new car sales manager. After discussing the matter, Kelly agreed to sell Cagle an Indy Vette at list price. He wrote "list price" and signed his name on the partially completed form, signing in the middle of the page, rather than in the space provided for the signature of an officer of Buckner. Cagle also signed the form and made a $500 deposit. At the time, Buckner did not have any Indy Vettes. Two were later received, but, in the interim, market demand for the cars had driven their value far above list price. Buckner refused to deliver either car to Cagle and attempted to return his deposit, arguing that the order form was too indefinite to amount to a contract. Did the parties have a contract?

5. Hulsey enrolled in a First Jump Course at the Elsinore Parachute Center (EPC). He signed an "Agreement and Release of Liability," which, in bold-faced capital letters, warned of the risk of injury and death associated with sport parachuting and purported to release EPC of any liability for injury to him. During classroom instruction at EPC, the instructor advised students that students occasionally break their legs when jumping. On Hulsey's first jump, he was unable to reach the target landing area, colliding instead with electric power lines as he tried to land in a vacant lot. He broke his wrist in the accident and later filed suit against EPC. At trial, Hulsey said that he did not remember reading or signing the release. Was the trial court justified in granting EPC's motion for summary judgment?

6. Phyllis Chaplin filed a class action suit against Consolidated Edison (Con Ed) for allegedly discriminating against epileptics in violation of the Rehabilitation Act of 1973. In August 1981, Con Ed's lawyer sent Chaplin's lawyer a settlement offer. Chaplin's lawyer replied by saying that Chaplin had "objections" to the proposed settlement. On September 16, 1981, Con Ed's lawyer replied, saying: "Any further negotiation is an impossibility; if this agreement is not satisfactory to your client in its present form, I must withdraw all offers of settlement." In a letter dated September 17, 1981 Chaplin's lawyer answered that "after careful consideration" Chaplin still had "objections" to Con Ed's offer. Later, on September 17, a federal appellate court ruled that private suits such as Chaplin's were not allowed under the Rehabilitation Act. On September 30, 1981, Chaplin's lawyer told Con Ed's lawyer Chaplin had had "a change of heart" and was accepting the settlement offer. Con Ed's lawyer replied that the settlement was no longer acceptable. Was Con Ed bound by the settlement offer?

7. In October of 1981, Christy and Andrus were involved in an automobile accident. On November 8, 1982, Aetna Casualty and Surety Company, Andrus's insurer, sent a letter to Christy and his insurer, Travelers Insurance Company, offering to settle Christy's claim against Andrus for $8,507. Neither Christy nor Travelers responded to this letter until February 4, 1984, when an attorney for Travelers sent Aetna a letter attempting to accept the settlement offer. Aetna then responded that any claim Christy had against Andrus was barred by the state's two-year statute of limitations and that Travelers' attempt to accept was not timely. Christy filed suit against Andrus and Aetna, arguing that they were bound by the settlement. At trial, Aetna introduced uncontradicted testimony that customary practice in the insurance industry was to respond to settlement offers within a few weeks. Was the trial court decision in Aetna's favor correct?

8. City University of New York (CUNY) solicited "firm" bids for the sale of a used IBM computer system. The highest bid was submitted by Finalco, Inc. Finalco, however, attempted to withdraw its bid because the customer to whom it intended to lease the computer had backed out of the lease deal. CUNY accepted Finalco's bid, and after Finalco refused to take delivery of the computer CUNY sued Finalco for breach of contract. At trial, Finalco argued that it had revoked its bid prior to acceptance by CUNY and that even if it lacked the power to revoke, its bid, which contained price, packaging, and delivery terms, was too indefinite to amount to an offer because it failed to include certain other terms. Was the trial court's decision in favor of CUNY correct?

9. On June 19, 1973, Berryman signed an agreement giving Kmoch, a real estate broker, a 120-day option to purchase 960 acres of Berryman's land in exchange for "$10.00 and other valuable consideration," which was never paid. Kmoch hired two agricultural consultants to produce a report that he intended to use in order to interest other investors in joining him to exercise the option. In late July 1973, Berryman telephoned Kmoch and asked to be released from the option agreement. Nothing definite was agreed to, and Berryman later sold the land to another person. In August, Kmoch decided to exercise the option and contacted the local Federal Land Bank representative to make arrangements to buy the land. After being told by the representative that Berryman had sold the property, Kmoch sent Berryman a letter attempting to exercise the option. Kmoch argued that the option was still in effect and that, in any event, Berryman was estopped from revoking it. Was Kmoch right?

10. Thomson was a tenant in a building owned by Coronet properties that Coronet decided to convert into a cooperative. The applicable state law required Coronet to offer existing tenants the right to purchase cooperative shares at a less-than-market insider price. Coronet made the required offer to Thomson, but she died before accepting. When De Kovessey, the executrix of Thomson's estate, attempted to accept Coronet's offer on behalf of the estate, Coronet refused to go through with the deal. Did De Kovessey have the power to accept?

CHAPTER 12

THE AGREEMENT: ACCEPTANCE

WHAT IS AN ACCEPTANCE?

The idea of *mutual agreement* lies at the heart of traditional contract law. Thus, after determining that one of the parties to a dispute made an *offer*, the court next seeks to determine whether the offeree *accepted* that offer. In this inquiry, the court is looking for the same *present intent to contract* on the part of the offeree that it found on the part of the offeror. The difference is that the offeree must objectively indicate a present intent to contract *on the terms of the offer* before a contract results. As the master of the offer, the offeror may specify in detail what behavior is required of the offeree to bind him to a contract. If the offeror does so, the offeree must ordinarily comply with all the terms of the offer before a contract results. These requirements for acceptance are evident in the *Restatement (Second) of Contracts* definition of an **acceptance** as "a manifestation of assent to the terms [of the offer] made by the offeree in the manner invited or required by the offer."[1]

---

[1] *Restatement (Second) of Contracts* § 50(1) (1981).

Intention to Accept: Counteroffers

The traditional contract law rule is that an acceptance must be the mirror image of the offer. As the following *Benya* case indicates, attempts by offerees to change the terms of the offer or to add new terms to it are treated as **counteroffers** because they impliedly indicate an intent by the offeree to reject the offer instead of being bound by its terms. However, if an offeree merely asks about the terms of the offer without indicating its rejection (an *inquiry regarding terms*), or accepts the offer's terms while complaining about them (a *grumbling acceptance*), no rejection is implied. Also, recent years have witnessed a judicial tendency to apply the mirror image rule in a more liberal fashion by holding that only material variances between an offer and a purported acceptance result in an implied rejection of the offer. Distinguishing among a counteroffer, an inquiry regarding terms, and a grumbling acceptance is often a difficult task. The fundamental issue, however, remains the same: Did the offeree objectively indicate a present intent to be bound by the terms of the offer?

BENYA v. STEVENS AND THOMPSON PAPER CO.

468 A.2d 929 (Vt. Sup. Ct. 1983)

On September 24, 1979, Vincent Benya's agent presented Stevens and Thompson Paper Company (S&T) with a sales agreement to purchase 5,243 acres of timber land owned by S&T for $605,366.50. S&T's lawyer made several modifications to the agreement, raising the cash to be paid at closing from $5,000 to $10,000, raising the interest rate on the mortgage S&T would hold on the property until it was fully paid for from 9 percent to 10 percent, providing for quarterly rather than annual payments on the mortgage, and changing the deed S&T was to provide from a warranty to a special warranty deed. S&T's vice president then initialed each change and signed the document, which was mailed back to Benya's agent. In early November, S&T received a new sales agreement from Benya, which differed from the two previous versions in a number of ways. S&T neither signed this agreement nor responded to it in any way. On November 7, S&T sold the property to someone else. Benya filed suit for breach of contract, and, when the trial court ruled in his favor, S&T appealed.

Billings, Chief Justice.   The trial court found that the September 24th sales agreement constituted a binding contract as both parties had signed it. The court concluded that the changes made by S&T to Benya's sales agreement were minor since the purchase price, closing date and deposit were substantially the same, and therefore did not constitute a counteroffer.

The law relative to contract formation has long been well settled in Vermont and elsewhere. For an acceptance of an offer to be valid, it must substantially comply with the terms of the offer. An acceptance that modifies or includes new terms is not an acceptance of the original offer; it is a counteroffer by the offeree that must be accepted or rejected by the original offeror. The offeror's acceptance of the offeree's counteroffer may be accomplished either expressly or by conduct.

On the record before us it is clear that the September 24th purchase and sales agreement was an offer from Benya to S&T that S&T never accepted. Instead, S&T significantly altered the terms of Benya's offer. These changes were not, as characterized by the trial court, minor and therefore of no effect on Benya's offer. Taken together, they constitute S&T's proposal for a new deal, or, more precisely, a counteroffer. Also clear from the record is that Benya never accepted, either expressly or otherwise, S&T's counteroffer. After Benya and his agent discussed S&T's counteroffer, the decision was made to draft a third proposal, which in turn altered the deposit and time of payment terms of S&T's counteroffer. S&T never signed or in any other way expressed its assent to this proposal. Additionally, the conduct of the parties demonstrates their understanding that agreement had not yet been reached.

Judgment reversed in favor of S&T.

The "Battle of the Forms"   Strictly applying the mirror image rule to modern commercial transactions, most of which are carried out by using preprinted form contracts, would often result in frustrating the parties' true intent. Offerors use standard order forms prepared by their lawyers, and offerees use standard acceptance or acknowledgment forms drafted by their counsel. The odds that these forms will agree in every detail are slight, as are the odds that the parties will read each other's forms in their entirety. Instead, the parties to such transactions are likely to read only crucial provisions concerning the goods ordered, the price, and the delivery

FIGURE 1 The "Battle of the Forms"—A Section 2–207 Flow Chart

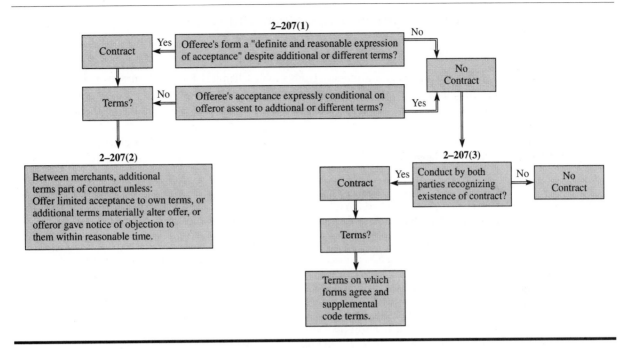

date called for, and if these terms are agreeable, believe that they have a contract. If a dispute arose before the parties started to perform, however, a court strictly applying the mirror image rule would hold that no contract resulted, due to the variance in their forms. If a dispute arose after performance had commenced, the court would probably hold that the offeror had impliedly accepted the offeree's counteroffer and was bound by its terms.

Because neither of these results is very satisfactory, the Code, in a very controversial provision often called the "Battle of the Forms" section [2–207] (see Figure 1), has changed the common law mirror image rule for contracts involving the sale of goods. As the following *Egan Machinery* case indicates, the Code provides that a definite and timely *expression of acceptance* creates a contract, even if it includes terms that are *different* from those stated in the offer or even if it states *additional* terms on points that the offer did not address [2–207(1)]. The only exception to this rule occurs when the attempted acceptance is *expressly conditional* on the offeror's agreement to the terms of the acceptance [2–207(1)].

What are the terms of a contract created in this fashion? The *additional* terms are treated as "proposals for

addition to the contract." If the parties are both *merchants*, the *additional* terms become part of the contract unless: (1) the offer *expressly* limited acceptance to its own terms; (2) the new terms would *materially alter* the offer; or (3) the offeror gives *notice of objection* to the new terms within a reasonable time after receiving the acceptance [2–207(2)].

When the offeree has made his acceptance expressly conditional on the offeror's agreement to the new terms or when the offeree's response to the offer is clearly not "an expression of acceptance" (e.g., an express rejection), no contract is created under section 2–207(1). A contract will only result in such cases if the parties engage in conduct that "recognizes the existence of a contract," such as an exchange of performance. Unlike his counterpart under traditional contract principles, however, the offeror who accepts performance in the face of an express rejection or expressly conditional acceptance is not thereby bound to all of the terms contained in the offeree's response. Instead, the Code provides that the terms of a contract created by such performance are those on which the parties' writings *agree*, supplemented by appropriate gap-filling provisions from the Code [2–207(3)].

EGAN MACHINERY CO. v. MOBIL CHEMICAL CO.

660 F. Supp. 35 (D. Conn. 1986)

On April 27, 1973, in response to a request from Mobil Chemical for a bid on a two-sided precoater, Egan Machinery submitted a "quotation" describing the components of the precoater and the details of its operation. The quotation stated a price for the precoater, but did not contain conditions of sale.

On May 2, 1973, Mobil sent Egan a purchase order for the precoater. The purchase order contained the following language:

Important—this order expressly limits acceptance to terms stated herein, and any additional or different terms proposed by the seller are rejected unless expressly agreed to in writing.

Egan responded with an order acknowledgment on May 8, 1973, which provided that:

This order is accepted on the condition that our Standard Conditions of Sale, which are attached hereto and made a part hereof, are accepted by you, notwithstanding any modifying or additive conditions contained on your purchase order. Receipt of this acknowledgment by you without prompt written objection thereto shall constitute an acceptance of these terms and conditions.

One of the terms included in Egan's Standard Conditions required Mobil to indemnify Egan against any liability Egan might incur to persons injured by the precoater if the injury resulted from Mobil's failure to require its employees to follow safety procedures and/or use safety devices while operating it. When a Mobil employee who was injured while operating the precoater later won a $75,000 judgment against Egan, Egan filed suit against Mobil seeking indemnity. Mobil moved for a summary judgment on the ground that the indemnity clause was not part of its contract with Egan.

Eginton, District Judge.   In a classic UCC section 2–207 battle of the forms the warring parties use their boilerplate armies in an attempt to control the high ground by making their assent conditional on their right to set the conditions of the contract. In fashioning a peace between the combatants the court first looks to whether the exchanged forms created a contract. If a contract has been formed, the court next determines which additional or different terms control by reference to section 2–207(2).

The clause in Egan's Acknowledgment conditioning acceptance on Egan's Standard Conditions of Sale is not sufficiently explicit to declare Egan's intention to abort the contract unless it were sure of Mobil's assent to additional or different terms. Courts have required that clauses such as the one here be strictly construed. The conditional acceptance clause will convert an acceptance into a counteroffer only where the offeree clearly reveals its unwillingness to proceed with the transaction unless it is assured of the offeror's assent to additional or different terms. This Egan's clause did not do. The focus of 2–207(1) is on explicit, not implicit, statements of intent.

Egan's failure to explicitly declare its unwillingness to proceed with the contract unless its conditions were accepted compels the conclusion that a contract was formed by the exchanged forms on the consistent terms but leaves unresolved the issue of whether the indemnity provision became a term of the contract. With this established, the question narrows to whether Mobil's offer, under 2–207(2)(a), expressly limits acceptance to the terms of the offer. This it clearly did with the language "this order expressly limits acceptance to terms stated herein." As a result, the indemnity provision did not become part of the contract.

Mobil's motion for summary judgment granted.

Acceptance in Unilateral Contracts

A unilateral contract involves the exchange of a promise for an act. To accept an offer to enter such a contract, the offeree must *perform the requested act*. As you learned in the last chapter, however, courts applying modern contract rules may prevent an offeror from revoking such an offer once the offeree has begun performance. This is achieved by holding either that a bilateral contract is created by the beginning of performance or that the offeror's power to revoke is suspended for the period of time reasonably necessary for the offeree to complete performance.

Acceptance in Bilateral Contracts

A bilateral contract involves the exchange of a promise for a promise. As a general rule, to accept an offer to enter such a contract, an offeree must *make the promise requested by the offer*. This may be done in a variety of ways. For example, Wallace sends Stevens a detailed offer for the purchase of Stevens's business. Within the time period prescribed by the offer, Stevens sends Wallace a letter that says, "I accept your offer." Stevens has *expressly* accepted Wallace's offer, creating a contract on the terms of the offer. Acceptance, however, can be *implied* as well as *express*. Offerees who take action that objectively indicates agreement risk the formation of a contract. For example, offerees who act in a manner that is inconsistent with an offeror's ownership of offered property are commonly held to have accepted the offeror's terms. So, if Arnold, a farmer, leaves 10 bushels of corn with Porter, the owner of a grocery store, saying, "Look this corn over. If you want it, it's $5 a bushel," and Porter sells the corn, he has impliedly accepted Arnold's offer. But what if Porter just let the corn sit and, when Arnold returned a week later, Porter told Arnold that he did not want it? Could Porter's failure to act ever amount to an acceptance?

Silence as Acceptance   Since contract law generally requires some objective indication that an offeree intends to contract, the general rule is that an offeree's silence, without more, is *not* an acceptance. In addition, it is generally held that an offeror cannot impose on the offeree a duty to respond to the offer. So, even if Arnold had said to Porter, "If I don't hear from you in three days, I'll assume you're buying the corn," Porter's silence would still not amount to acceptance.

On the other hand, the circumstances of a case sometimes impose a duty on the offeree to reject the offer affirmatively or be bound by its terms. These are cases in which the offeree's silence objectively indicates an intent to accept. Customary trade practice or prior dealings between the parties may indicate that silence signals acceptance. So, if Arnold and Porter had dealt with each other on numerous occasions and Porter had always promptly returned items that he did not want, Porter's silent retention of the goods for a week would probably constitute an acceptance. Likewise, an offeree's silence can also operate as an acceptance if the offeree has indicated that it will. For example, Porter tells Arnold, "If you don't hear from me in three days, I accept."

Finally, it is generally held that offerees who accept an offeror's performance knowing what the offeror expects in return for his performance have impliedly accepted the offeror's terms. So, if Apex Paving Corporation offers to do the paving work on a new subdivision being developed by Majestic Homes Corporation, and Majestic fails to respond to Apex's offer but allows Apex to do the work, most courts would hold that Majestic is bound by the terms of Apex's offer.

Acceptance when a Writing Is Anticipated   Frequently, the parties to a contract intend to prepare a written draft of their agreement for both parties to sign. This is a good idea not only because the law requires written evidence of some contracts,[2] but also because it provides

---

[2] The Writing chapter discusses this subject in detail.

written evidence of the terms of the agreement if a dispute arises at a later date. If a dispute arises before such a writing has been prepared or signed, however, a question may arise concerning whether the signing of the agreement was a necessary condition to the creation of a contract. A party to the agreement who now wants out of the deal may argue that the parties did not intend to be bound until both parties signed the writing. As the following *Texaco* case indicates, a clear expression of such an intent by the parties during the negotiation process prevents the formation of a contract until both parties

have signed. However, in the absence of such a clear expression of intent, the courts ask whether a reasonable person familiar with all the circumstances of the parties' negotiations would conclude that the parties intended to be bound only when a formal agreement was signed. If it appears that the parties had concluded their negotiations and reached agreement on all the essential aspects of the transaction, most courts would probably find a contract at the time agreement was reached, even though no formal agreement had been signed.

TEXACO, INC. v. PENNZOIL, CO.

729 S.W.2d 768 (Tex. Ct. App. 1987)

On December 28, 1983, in the wake of well-publicized dissension between the board of directors of Getty Oil Company and Gordon Getty, Pennzoil announced an unsolicited, public tender offer for 16 million shares of Getty Oil at $100 each. Gordon Getty was a director of Getty Oil and the owner, as trustee of the Sarah C. Getty Trust, of 40.2 percent of the 79.1 million outstanding shares of Getty Oil. Shortly thereafter, Pennzoil contacted both Gordon Getty and a representative of the J. Paul Getty Museum, which held 11.8 percent of the shares of Getty Oil, to discuss the tender offer and the possible purchase of Getty Oil.

The parties drafted and signed a Memorandum of Agreement providing that Pennzoil and the Trust (with Gordon Getty as trustee) were to become partners on a $3/7$ths to $4/7$ths basis, respectively, in owning and operating Getty Oil. The museum was to receive $110 per share for its 11.8 percent ownership, and all other outstanding public shares were to be cashed in by the company at $110 per share. The memorandum provided that it was subject to the approval of Getty Oil's board. On January 2, 1984, the board voted to reject the memorandum price as too low and made a counterproposal to Pennzoil of $110 per share plus a $10 debenture. On January 3, the board received a revised Pennzoil proposal of $110 per share plus a $3 "stub" that was to be paid after the sale of a Getty Oil subsidiary. After discussion, the board voted 15 to 1 to accept Pennzoil's proposal if the stub price was raised to $5. This counteroffer was accepted by Pennzoil later the same day. On January 4, Getty Oil and Pennzoil issued identical press releases announcing an agreement in principle on the terms of the Memorandum of Agreement. Pennzoil's lawyers began working on a formal transaction agreement describing the deal in more detail than the outline of terms contained in the Memorandum of Agreement and press release.

On January 5, the board of Texaco, which had been in contact with Getty Oil's investment banker, authorized its officers to make an offer for 100 percent of Getty Oil's stock. Texaco first contacted the Getty Museum, which, after discussion, agreed to sell its shares to Texaco. Later that evening, Gordon Getty accepted Texaco's offer of $125 per share. On January 6, the Getty Board voted to withdraw its previous counteroffer to Pennzoil and to accept Texaco's offer. Pennzoil later filed suit against Texaco for tortious interference with its contract with the Getty entities. At trial, Texaco argued, among other things, that no contract had existed between Pennzoil and the Getty entities. The jury disagreed, awarding Pennzoil $7.53 billion in actual damages and $3 billion in punitive damages. Texaco appealed.

Warren, Justice.   Texaco contends that there was insufficient evidence to support the jury's finding that at the end of the Getty Oil board meeting on January 3, the Getty entities intended to bind themselves to an agreement with Pennzoil. Pennzoil contends that the evidence showed that the parties intended to be bound to the terms in the Memorandum of Agreement plus a price term of $110 plus a $5 stub, even though the parties may have contemplated a later, more formal document to memorialize the agreement already reached.

If parties do not intend to be bound to an agreement until it is reduced to writing and signed by both parties, then there is no contract until that event occurs. If there is no understanding that a signed writing is necessary before the parties will be bound, and the parties have agreed upon all substantial terms, then an informal agreement can be binding, even though the parties contemplated evidencing their agreement in a formal document later. It is the parties' expressed intent that controls which rule of contract formation applies. Only the outward expressions of intent are considered—secret or subjective intent is immaterial to the question of whether the parties were bound.

Several factors have been articulated to help determine whether the parties intended to be bound only by a formal, signed writing: (1) whether a party expressly reserved the right to be bound only when a written agreement is signed; (2) whether there was any partial performance by one party that the party disclaiming the contract accepted; (3) whether all essential terms of the alleged contract had been agreed upon; and (4) whether the complexity or magnitude of the transaction was such that a formal, executed writing would normally be expected.

Any intent of the parties not to be bound before signing a formal document is not so clearly expressed in the press release to establish, as a matter of law, that there was no contract at that time. The press release does refer to an agreement "in principle" and states that the "transaction" is subject to execution of a definitive merger agreement. But the release as a whole is worded in indicative terms, not in subjunctive or hypothetical ones. The press release describes what shareholders *will* receive, what Pennzoil *will* contribute, that Pennzoil *will* be granted an option, etc.

We find little relevant partial performance in this case that might show that the parties believed that they were bound by a contract. However, the absence of relevant part performance in this short period of time does not compel the conclusion that no contract existed.

There was sufficient evidence for the jury to conclude that the parties had reached agreement on all essential terms of the transaction with only the mechanics and details left to be supplied by the parties' attorneys. Although there may have been many specific items relating to the transaction agreement draft that had yet to be put in final form, there is sufficient evidence to support a conclusion by the jury that the parties did not consider any of Texaco's asserted "open items" significant obstacles precluding an intent to be bound.

Although the magnitude of the transaction here was such that normally a signed writing would be expected, there was sufficient evidence to support an inference by the jury that that expectation was satisfied here initially by the Memorandum of Agreement, signed by a majority of shareholders of Getty Oil and approved by the board with a higher price, and by the transaction agreement in progress that had been intended to memorialize the agreement previously reached.

Judgment for Pennzoil affirmed.

[Note: The court's decision was contingent on a reduction in the punitive damages awarded by the jury from $3 billion to $1 billion. Texaco ultimately sought reorganization under the protection of the Bankruptcy Court and the parties finally settled the case for $3 billion.]

Acceptance of Ambiguous Offers

Although offerors have the power to specify the manner in which their offers can be accepted by requiring that the offeree make a return promise (a bilateral contract) or perform a specific act (a unilateral contract), often an offer is unclear about which form of acceptance is necessary to create a contract. In such a case, both the Code [2–206(1)(a)] and the *Restatement Second*[3] suggest that the offer may be accepted in any manner that is *reasonable* in light of the circumstances surrounding the offer. Thus, either a promise to perform or performance, if reasonable, creates a contract.

Acceptance by Shipment   The Code specifically elaborates on the rule stated in the preceding section by stating that an order requesting prompt or current shipment of goods may be accepted either by a *prompt promise to ship* or by a *prompt* or *current shipment* of the goods [2–206(1)(b)]. So, if Ampex Corporation orders 500 IBM personal computers from Marks Office Supply, to be shipped immediately, Marks could accept either by promptly promising to ship the goods or by promptly shipping them. If Marks accepts by shipping, any subsequent attempt by Ampex to revoke the order will be ineffective.

But what if Marks did not have 500 IBMs in stock and Marks knew that Ampex desperately needed the goods? Marks might be tempted to ship another brand of computers, hoping that Ampex would be forced by its circumstances to accept them because by the time they arrived it would be too late to get the correct goods elsewhere. Marks would argue that by shipping the wrong goods it had made a counteroffer because it had not performed the act requested by Ampex's order. If Ampex accepts the goods, Marks could argue that Ampex has impliedly accepted the counteroffer. If Ampex rejects the goods, Marks would arguably have no liability since it did not accept the order. The Code prevents such a result by providing that prompt shipment of either *conforming goods* (what the order asked for) or *nonconforming goods* (something else) operates as an acceptance of the order [2–206(1)(b)]. This protects buyers such as Ampex because sellers who ship the wrong goods have simultaneously *accepted* their offers and *breached* the contract by sending the wrong merchandise.

---

[3] *Restatement (Second) of Contracts* § 30(2) (1981).

But what if Marks is an honest seller merely trying to help out a customer that has placed a rush order? Must Marks expose itself to liability for breach of contract in the process? The Code prevents such a result by providing that no contract is created if the seller notifies the buyer within a reasonable time that the shipment of nonconforming goods is intended as an accommodation [2–206(1)(b)]. In this case, the shipment is merely a counteroffer that the buyer is free to accept or reject and the seller's notification gives the buyer the opportunity to seek the goods he needs elsewhere.

Who Can Accept an Offer?

As the masters of their offers, offerees have the right to determine who can bind them to a contract. So, the only person with the legal power to accept an offer and create a contract is the *original offeree*. An attempt to accept by anyone other than the offeree is treated as an offer, because the party attempting to accept is indicating a present intent to contract on the original offer's terms. For example, Price offers to sell his car to Waterhouse for $5,000. Anderson learns of the offer, calls Price, and attempts to accept. Anderson has made an offer that Price is free to accept or reject.

COMMUNICATION OF ACCEPTANCE

Necessity of Communication

To accept an offer for a *bilateral* contract, the offeree must make the *promise* requested by the offer. In the Offer chapter, you learned that an offeror must communicate the terms of his proposal to the offeree before an offer results. This is so because communication is a necessary component of the present intent to contract required for the creation of an offer. For similar reasons, it is generally held that an offeree must communicate his intent to be bound by the offer before a contract can be created. To accept an offer for a *unilateral contract*, however, the offeree must *perform the requested act*. The traditional contract law rule on this point assumes that the offeror will learn of the offeree's performance and holds that no further notice from the offeree is necessary to create a contract unless the offeror specifically requests notice.

Because this rule can sometimes cause hardship to offerors who may not, in fact, know that the offeree has commenced performance, the Code and the *Restatement*

Second have modified the traditional rule. If the offeree has reason to know that the offeror has no way of learning of his performance with reasonable promptness and certainty, the *Restatement Second* provides that the offeror may be discharged from any contractual obligation.[4] This is so unless the offeree takes reasonable steps to notify him of performance, the offeror learns of performance within a reasonable time, or the offer indicates that notification of acceptance is not required.

The Code takes a different approach by saying that, in cases where the *beginning of performance* operates as an acceptance, an offeror who is not notified of acceptance within a reasonable time may treat the offer as having lapsed before acceptance [2–206(2)]. The full meaning of this provision is unclear. It apparently does not require notice when the offeree accepts by *performing*, for example, by shipping the goods. In such a case, it is apparently assumed that the offeror will learn of performance within a reasonable time. It expressly applies only when acceptance is accomplished by *beginning performance*. Whether loading goods on a truck for shipment is enough to constitute beginning performance, or whether the statute is intended to apply only to more specific offeree behavior, such as beginning to manufacture specially ordered goods, is not apparent from the language of the statute.

Manner of Communication

As the following *Great Western Sugar* case indicates, the offeror, as the master of the offer, has the power to specify the precise time, place, and manner in which acceptance must be communicated. If the offeror does so, and the offeree deviates from the offer's instructions in any significant way, no contract results unless the offeror indicates a willingness to be bound by the deviating acceptance. If the offer merely suggests a method or place of communication, or is silent on such matters, the offeree may accept within a reasonable time by any reasonable means of communication.

---

[4] *Restatement (Second) of Contracts* § 54 (2) (1981).

GREAT WESTERN SUGAR CO. v. LONE STAR DONUT CO.
567 F. Supp. 340 (N.D. Texas 1983)

Since 1974, Lone Star Donut Company had placed orders for its sugar requirements with Great Western Sugar Co. (GWS) through a sugar broker. In October of 1980, GWS adopted a new policy of requiring a letter agreement for each order. The first such letter was forwarded from GWS to Lone Star by the broker on October 9, 1980. It concluded with the following language:

> This letter is a written confirmation of our agreement, and unless it is signed by the buyer and returned to Great Western within 15 days of the date hereof, the agreement shall be deemed breached by Buyer and automatically terminated. Please sign and return to me the enclosed counterpart of this letter signalling your acceptance of the above agreement.

Lone Star signed and returned this letter. On December 2, Lone Star again ordered sugar. GWS initially neglected to send a letter agreement, finally doing so in late January of 1981, in response to prodding by the broker. This letter concluded as follows:

> This letter is a written confirmation of our agreement. Please sign and return to me the enclosed counterpart of this letter signalling your acceptance of the above agreement.

Lone Star, angered over the delay, refused to sign and subsequently refused to purchase sugar. When GWS filed suit for breach of contract, Lone Star moved for summary judgment arguing that no contract was ever created.

Fish, District Judge.   In *Southwestern Stationery & Bank Supply, Inc. v. Harris Corp.* (10th Cir. 1980), the court had before it a purchase order signed by buyer and returned to seller, specifying that the order was subject to acceptance by the seller, who was to indicate acceptance by mailing the purchaser a signed duplicate copy. Seller did not sign the purchase order. The court denied the buyer recovery against the seller. The court noted that under the Uniform Commercial Code parties retain their power to require specific methods of acceptance.

Dealing with a dispute over a tender offer, the court in *Kroeze v. Chloride Group* (1978) relied both on the common law and, by analogy, the UCC. The court emphasized a cardinal rule of contracts, that the offeror is the master of his offer. He may prescribe as many conditions, terms, or the like as he may wish, including but not limited to, the time, place and method of acceptance. The drafters of the UCC explicitly recognized this principle in section 2–206(1)(a). In *Kroeze*, the court reasoned that because the offeror had expressly and unambiguously required signing of the transmittal letter to effect acceptance of the offer, the offerees who had not signed the transmittal letters could not recover.

In the case before this court, GWS has unambiguously indicated, by the language concluding the letter agreement, the manner and medium of acceptance: the buyer was to sign and return a copy. While the 1981 letter agreement, in contrast to the 1980 letter agreement, no longer specified that the agreement would be terminated if the buyer did not sign and return the copy, the only reasonable construction of GWS's requirement that the buyer signal acceptance is that if he failed to do so, he would not be bound.

Summary judgment granted for Lone Star.

When Is Acceptance Communicated?

The question of when an acceptance has been effectively communicated is often a critically important issue in contract cases. The offeror may be trying to revoke an offer that the offeree is desperately trying to accept. A mailed or telegraphed acceptance may get lost and never be received by the offeror. The time limit for accepting the offer may be rapidly approaching. Was the offer accepted before a revocation was received or before the offer expired? Does a lost acceptance create a contract when it is dispatched, or is it totally ineffective?

When the parties are dealing face-to-face or the offeree is accepting by telephone, these problems are minimized. As soon as the offeree says, "I accept," or words to that effect, a contract is created as long as the offer is still in existence. Problems with the timing of acceptances multiply, however, when the offeree is using a means of communication that creates a time lag between the dispatching of the acceptance and its actual receipt by the offeror. Offerors have the power to minimize these problems by requiring in their offer that they must *actually receive* the acceptance for it to be effective. Offerors who do this maximize the time that they have to revoke their offers and ensure that they will never be bound by an acceptance that they have not received.

Offerors who fail to require actual receipt of an acceptance may find to their dismay that the law has developed rules that make some acceptances effective the moment they are dispatched, regardless of whether the offeror ever receives them. These rules generally apply when the offeror has made the offer under circumstances that might reasonably lead the offeree to believe that acceptance by some means other than telephone or face-to-face communication is acceptable. They protect the offeree's reasonable belief that a binding contract was created when the acceptance was dispatched.

Authorized Means of Communication   As the following *Soldau* case illustrates, an acceptance is generally effective *when dispatched*, or delivered to the agency of communication, if the offeree accepts by the **authorized means** of communication. This is so even if the acceptance is never received by the offeror. An offeror may *expressly* authorize acceptance by a particular means of communication by saying, in effect: "You *may* accept by mail." If the offeror does so, the offeree's acceptance is effective when mailed. Any attempt by the offeror to revoke thereafter, such as by a letter of revocation mailed before the acceptance was mailed but received after it was mailed, would be ineffective.

A means of communication may also be *impliedly* authorized by the offeror. Under traditional contract principles, if the offer or circumstances do not indicate otherwise, the offeror impliedly authorizes the offeree to accept by the *same means* that the offeror used to communicate the offer. So, mailed offers impliedly invite mailed acceptances, telegraphed offers impliedly invite acceptance by telegram, and so forth. In addition, *trade usage* can impliedly authorize a given means of acceptance. Thus, if the parties are both members of a particular trade and the trade custom is to offer by mail and accept by telegram, a telegram would be the impliedly authorized means of accepting such an offer unless the offer indicates to the contrary.

In recent years, the authorized means concept has been broadened considerably by numerous cases holding that offerors who remain silent impliedly authorize acceptance by *any reasonable means*. What is reasonable depends on the circumstances in which the offer was made. These include the speed and reliability of the means used by the offeree, the nature of the transaction (e.g., does the agreement involve goods subject to rapid price fluctuations?), the existence of any trade usage governing the transaction, and the existence of prior dealings between the parties (e.g., has the offeree previously used the mail to accept telegraphed offers from the offeror?). So, under proper circumstances, a mailed response to a telegraphed offer or a telegraphed response to a mailed offer might be considered reasonable, and therefore effective on dispatch. The Code expressly adopts the reasonable means test for offers involving the sale of goods [2–206(1)(a)], and the *Restatement Second* suggests that it be used in all contract cases.[5]

---

[5] *Restatement (Second) of Contracts* §§ 30(2), 63, 65 (1981).

SOLDAU v. ORGANON, INC.
860 F.2d 355 (9th Cir. 1988)

John Soldau was fired by Organon, Inc. He received a letter from Organon offering to pay him double the normal severance pay if he would sign a release giving up all claims against the company. The letter incorporated the proposed release, which Soldau signed, dated, and deposited in a mailbox outside a post office. When he returned home, Soldau found that he had received a check from Organon in the amount of the increased severance pay. He returned to the post office and persuaded a postal employee to open the mailbox and retrieve the release. Soldau cashed Organon's check and subsequently filed an age discrimination suit against Organon. When the trial court granted a summary judgment in Organon's favor, Soldau appealed.

Per Curiam.   The district court held that "the release was deemed fully communicated to Organon, and a binding contract was formed, at the time Soldau deposited the executed release in the mailbox. The fact that he retrieved the release from the mailbox is of no consequence under California law." Soldau contends that the formation and validity of the release are governed by federal law, and would not have been effective unless and until it had been received by Organon.

We need not decide which body of law controls. Under federal as well as California law, Soldau's acceptance was effective when it was mailed. The so-called "mailbox" or "effective when mailed" rule was adopted and followed as federal common law by the Supreme Court prior to *Erie R.R. Co. v. Thompkins* (1938). We could not change the rule, and there is no reason to believe the Supreme Court would be inclined to do so. It is almost universally accepted in the common law world.

Soldau rests his case upon decisions of the Court of Claims, beginning with *Dick v. United States* (1949), rejecting mailing of the acceptance as the crucial event resulting in a contract, in favor of the receipt of the acceptance by the offeror. No other federal court has agreed. Commentators are also virtually unanimous in rejecting the Court of Claims' repudiation of the "effective when mailed" rule, pointing to the long history of the rule; its importance in creating certainty for the contracting parties; and its essential soundness, on balance, as a means of allocating the risk during the period between the making of the offer and the communication of the acceptance to the offeror.

Since Soldau's contractual obligation to release Organon in return for Organon's payment arose when Soldau deposited his acceptance in the mailbox, his subsequent withdrawal of the acceptance was ineffectual.

Judgment for Organon affirmed.

Acceptance by Nonauthorized Means   What if an offeree attempts to accept the offer by mail when the authorized means for acceptance was clearly by telegram? The traditional rule in such cases is that an acceptance by a nonauthorized means is effective only when it is *actually received* by the offeror, provided that it is received within the time that an acceptance by the authorized means would have been received. This rule seems somewhat artificial, however, because once an acceptance reaches the offeror, she has actual notice that a contract has been created and is not in any danger of acting in reliance on the impression that she is not bound by a contract by selling offered goods to a third party. At this point, the means that the offeree used to communicate acceptance would logically seem to be irrelevant because the end result from the offeror's standpoint is the same, regardless of the means used by the offeree. Why, then, should we allow the offeror to revoke prior to timely receipt of an acceptance by a nonauthorized means but deny her the power to revoke after the dispatch of an acceptance by the authorized means? The Code has accepted this reasoning by providing that in all contracts for the sale of goods an acceptance by a nonauthorized means is effective *on dispatch* if it is received within the time that an acceptance by the authorized means would normally have arrived [1–201(38)]. Section 67 of the *Restatement Second* adopts the Code rule for all contracts.

Contradictory Offeree Responses   Consider this example: White mails Case an offer to sell his house for $75,000. Case mails White a counteroffer, offering to pay $70,000 for the house. In the last chapter, you learned that Case's counteroffer would be effective to terminate White's offer only when White actually receives it. Therefore, if Case changed his mind and communicated an acceptance of the offer to White before White received his counteroffer, a contract would result. But what if Case mails an acceptance to White four hours after mailing the counteroffer? If we applied the normal rules of offer and acceptance to these facts, we might conclude that the parties had a contract because Case's acceptance by mail—the authorized means—was effective on dispatch, and was probably dispatched before White received Case's counteroffer. White, however, may receive Case's counteroffer and sell the house to a third party before he receives Case's acceptance. To prevent such an unfair result, most courts hold that when an offeree dispatches an acceptance after first dispatching a rejection, the acceptance does not create a contract unless it is received before the rejection. Therefore, if White receives the counteroffer before he receives the acceptance, no contract results. If, on the other hand, he receives the acceptance before receiving the counteroffer, a contract results.

However, what if Case mailed White an acceptance, changed his mind, and shortly thereafter mailed White a rejection? Applying normal offer and acceptance rules to these facts, we would conclude that Case's acceptance was effective on dispatch and that Case no longer had the power to reject the offer. But what if White received Case's rejection first and relied on it by selling to someone else? In such a situation, Case would be *estopped* from enforcing the contract due to White's reliance.

Stipulated Means of Communication   An offer may *stipulate* the means of communication that the offeree must use to accept by saying, in effect: "You *must* accept by mail." An acceptance by the **stipulated means** of communication is effective on dispatch, just like an acceptance by an authorized means of communi-

cation. The difference is that an acceptance by other than the stipulated means does not create a contract because it is an acceptance at variance with the terms of the offer.

CONCEPT REVIEW

WHEN ACCEPTANCE IS EFFECTIVE

Means of Communication	Traditional Contract Law	UCC and *Restatement Second*
Authorized	Dispatch (even if never received)	Dispatch (even if never received)
Nonauthorized	Receipt (if received when authorized acceptance would have been received)	Dispatch (if received when authorized acceptance would have been received)

ETHICAL AND PUBLIC POLICY CONCERNS

1. It should be apparent to you from the discussion of section 2–207 of the Code, the "Battle of the Forms" section, that the application of that section can sometimes result in a party being held to a contract term that she has not actually consented to. How can this be justified?

2. Compare the ethical standards underlying the traditional contract law approach to the seller who ships nonconforming goods with the ethical standards reflected by section 2–206(1)(b) of the Code.

3. Compare the public policy stances implicit in the different ways in which classical contract law and the UCC treat offeree attempts to accept by a nonauthorized means of communication.

SUMMARY

In determining whether an offer was accepted to create a binding contract, the courts look for behavior by an offeree that objectively indicates a present intent to contract on the terms of the offer. This behavior may be in the form of words or action by the offeree. Also, in some limited cases, silence or inaction by the offeree may signal his assent to the terms of the offer. Acceptance of offers for unilateral contracts requires that the offeree

perform the act requested by the offer. In bilateral contract cases, the offeree must make the promise requested by the offer. In some cases, the offer is unclear about whether acceptance may be accomplished by performing an act or making a promise. In such cases, both the Code and the *Restatement Second* provide that an offeree can accept either by performing or promising to perform.

Traditional contract principles require the offeree's acceptance to be the mirror image of the offer and treat acceptances that attempt to vary the terms of an offer as counteroffers. Recent years, however, have witnessed a judicial tendency to relax the strict application of this rule by treating only acceptances containing material variances as counteroffers. The Code, in its controversial "Battle of the Forms" section [2–207], expressly changes the mirror image rule by allowing acceptances stating additional or different terms to operate as acceptances. Between merchants, these new terms become part of the contract unless the offer limits acceptance to its own terms, the new terms would materially alter the offer, or the offeror objects to the new terms within a reasonable time after he has notice of them.

As a general rule, acceptances, like offers, must be communicated to the other party to the agreement before they become effective. In the case of offers for unilateral contracts, however, the traditional rule is that the offeree's performance of the act requested by the offer is all that is required for acceptance. To prevent unfairness to offerors who may assume that no acceptance has occurred because they have not, in fact, learned of the offeree's performance, the Code and the *Restatement Second* require in some cases that the offeree give notice of performance to the offeror.

As the master of the offer, the offeror can specify the exact means that the offeree must use to accept the offer. Attempts by offerees to accept in any other way do not create a contract. When the offeror fails to specify the exact means of acceptance, the offeree may accept by any reasonable means.

When the parties are dealing face-to-face or over the telephone, an acceptance is effective the instant that it is communicated to the other party. When the offeree uses some delayed means of communication, such as mail or telegram, critical timing questions can arise about when an acceptance is effective. An offeror can specify that she will be bound to a contract only after she actually receives an acceptance. In the absence of such a statement by the offeror, an acceptance is effective when dispatched by the offeree if the offeree uses the *authorized means* of communication. A means of communication may be expressly or impliedly authorized. Traditional contract law rules provide that the offeror who does not indicate a contrary intent impliedly authorizes the offeree to accept by the same means of communication used to communicate the offer. Trade usage can also operate to authorize a particular means of communication. Many contemporary courts have broadened these rules by holding that the offeror who remains silent impliedly authorizes acceptance by any reasonable means. The Code and the *Restatement Second* adopt this position.

Under traditional contract principles, an acceptance by a nonauthorized means is effective only when it is received by the offeror, and then only if it is received within the time in which a properly dispatched acceptance would have been received. The Code and the *Restatement Second* change this rule by providing that an acceptance by a nonauthorized means is effective on dispatch if it reaches the offeror within the same time in which a properly dispatched acceptance would have been received.

An offeror may also *stipulate* that the offeree must accept by a particular means of communication. Acceptances by a stipulated means, like those by an authorized means, are effective on dispatch, even if never received by the offeror. Acceptances by a nonstipulated means, however, are never effective to create a contract.

PROBLEM CASES

1. In April of 1975, Bio-Zyme Enterprises, a livestock feed manufacturer, began selling feed to Vanderhoof, a feed dealer, on open account. The monthly statements Vanderhoof received from Bio-Zyme contained the following sentence at the bottom of each statement: "Accounts not paid within 30 days will on our billing date (the 26th day of each month) be charged 1 percent each month." Whenever a finance charge was imposed, this was conspicuously noted on the statement. By April of 1976, Vanderhoof, owed Bio-Zyme over $45,000. When Bio-Zyme filed suit on the account, Vanderhoof argued that he had not agreed to pay the 1 percent finance charge. Was he right?

2. First Texas Savings Association promoted a "$5,000 Scoreboard Challenge" contest. Contestants who completed an entry form and deposited it with First Texas were eligible for a random drawing. The winner was to receive an $80 savings account with First Texas, plus four tickets to a Dallas Mavericks home basketball game chosen by First Texas. If the Mavericks held their opponent in the chosen game to 89 or fewer points, the winner was to receive an additional $5,000 money market certificate. In October of 1982, Jergins deposited a completed entry form with First Texas. On November 1, 1982, First tried to amend the contest rules by posting notice at its branches that the Mavericks would have to hold their opponent to 85 or fewer points before the contest winner would receive the $5,000. In late December, Jergins was notified that she had won the $80 savings account and tickets to the January 22, 1983, game against the Utah Jazz. The notice contained the revised contest terms. The Mavericks held the Jazz to 88 points. Was Jergins entitled to the $5,000?

3. The Stortroens, through Panio, a realtor who showed them property owned by Beneficial Finance under a multiple-listing agreement, submitted an offer of $105,000 for the property. Beneficial responded with a counteroffer delivered to the Stortroens by Panio and offering to sell for $110,000. While its counteroffer was still in effect, Beneficial received an offer through another broker for $112,000. Wishing to accept this higher offer, Beneficial had the listing broker call Panio's office at 4:30 P.M. and leave a phone message withdrawing its counteroffer. Beneficial then accepted the higher offer. Unbeknownst to Beneficial, Panio had taken the counteroffer to the Stortroens' home and they had signed it at 4:10 P.M. that same day. Beneficial refused to convey the property to the Stortroens. Assuming Panio was legally Beneficial's agent, was it contractually bound to convey to the Stortroens?

4. Atwood bought a new pickup truck from Best Buick. When he took it home, his wife objected to the purchase. Atwood returned the car to Best, which agreed to take the truck back as a trade-in on another vehicle. Atwood traded for a new station wagon, which he registered and insured and sought to title in his name. When he took the car home, however, his wife objected to the color of its interior. Atwood returned the car to Best, but refused to accept any of the numerous other vehicles Best made available to him. He also refused to sign an application that would allow Best to retrieve the title to the car so it could sell it to someone else. Best then told him that unless he removed the car from its premises it would charge him a $5 per day storage fee. The Atwoods later sued Best for the return of the purchase price. Best counterclaimed for the storage fee. Should the Atwoods prevail?

5. Western Tire, Inc., had a lease on a building owned by the Skredes that was due to expire on April 30, 1978. The lease gave Western the right to renew the lease for an additional five-year term if the Skredes were given written notice of Western's intent to renew at least 30 days prior to the expiration date. It also specifically provided that notice would only be effective when it was deposited in a U.S. Post Office by registered or certified mail. On February 27, Western's attorney sent the Skredes a notice of Western's intent to renew by ordinary mail, which the Skredes did not receive until after April 1, 1978. On April 5, 1978, Western's lawyer, discovering his mistake, sent a second notice by certified mail. On April 14, 1978, the Skredes told Western the lease was cancelled. Did they have the right to cancel?

6. In September of 1969, Roberts, an insurance agent, sent Buske a policy that was a renewal of one Buske's father had previously held. Buske had not ordered or requested issuance of this policy, but he accepted it and paid the premium. In September of 1970, just prior to the expiration date of the policy, Roberts sent a second unsolicited renewal to Buske and attached to it a printed notice stating that if Buske did not wish to accept it he must return it or be liable for the premium. Buske did not respond either to this notice or to two subsequent bills mailed to him. When Roberts telephoned Buske in December to ask about the premium, Buske said he had purchased a policy from another company in August and would not pay for the renewal since

he had not ordered it. The policy was then returned to the insurer and canceled, resulting in a loss to Roberts for the prorated portion of the premium that he had advanced. Should the trial court's ruling for Roberts be reversed on appeal?

7. Foremost, a photofinisher, submitted two orders to Kodak for photofinishing equipment. The order forms were supplied by Kodak's sales representatives, specified no delivery date, and specifically stated that all orders were "subject to acceptance" by Kodak. Kodak had no further communications with Foremost, but ultimately shipped the goods Foremost had ordered. Foremost later filed a breach of contract suit against Kodak, arguing that Kodak's delivery of the goods had been untimely. Should Kodak be liable for breach of contract?

8. On March 30, Cushing, a member of an antinuclear protest group, applied to the New Hampshire adjutant general's office for permission to hold a dance in the Portsmouth armory. On March 31, the adjutant general mailed a signed contract offer agreeing to rent the armory to the group. The agreement required Cushing to accept by signing a copy of the agreement and returning it to the adjutant general within five days after its receipt. On April 3, Cushing received the offer and signed it. At 6:30 P.M. on April 4, Cushing received a call from the adjutant general attempting to revoke the offer. Cushing told the adjutant general that he had signed the contract and placed it in the office outbox on April 3, customary office practice being to collect all mail from outboxes at the end of the day and deposit it in the U.S. mail. On April 6, the adjutant general's office received the signed contract in the mail, dated April 3 and postmarked April 5. Assuming Cushing was telling the truth, did the parties have a contract?

9. Krack Corporation bought steel tubing from Metal-Matic for 10 years. The parties' usual practice was for Krack to send Metal-Matic purchase orders to which Metal-Matic would respond by sending an acknowledgment form and shipping the requested tubing. Metal-Matic's form provided that its acceptance was "expressly made conditional" on Krack's assent to the acknowledgment's terms, which included a clause limiting Metal-Matic's liability for consequential damages due to breach of warranty. Krack sold a cooling unit it had made with Metal-Matic's tubing to Diamond Fruit. The tubing was defective, causing losses to Diamond's fruit. When Diamond sued Krack, Krack sought indemnity from Metal-Matic. Metal-Matic argued that it was not responsible, citing the consequential damages clause in its acknowledgment. Was that clause part of the contract between Krack and Metal-Matic?

10. H&W Industries, a Mississippi pipe manufacturer, mailed a purchase order for resin (which is manufactured in Louisiana) to Occidental Chemical's office in Pottstown, Pennsylvania. Occidental replied with an acceptance form that said H&W's order was accepted subject to the terms and conditions appearing on the face and reverse side of the acceptance. Later, a dispute arose between the parties and Occidental filed a breach of contract suit against H&W in a U.S. district court in Pennsylvania. H&W moved to dismiss Occidental's complaint on the ground that the court lacked jurisdiction over the case. Occidental admitted that this would normally be true, but pointed to a forum selection clause on the back of its acceptance form stating: "The parties agree that any litigation arising out of this agreement shall be brought only in the federal or state courts in the State of Pennsylvania." Is H&W bound by this clause?

CHAPTER 13

CONSIDERATION

THE IDEA OF CONSIDERATION

One of the things that separates a contract from an unenforceable social promise is that a contract requires *voluntary agreement* by two or more parties. Not all agreements, however, are enforceable contracts. At a fairly early point in the development of classical contract law, the common law courts decided not to enforce gratuitous (free) promises. Instead, only promises *supported by consideration* were enforceable in a court of law. This was consistent with the notion that the purpose of contract law was to enforce freely made *bargains*. As one 19th-century work on contract put it: "The common law . . . gives effect only to contracts that are founded on the mutual exigencies of men, and does not compel the performance of any merely gratuitous agreements."[1] A common definition of **consideration** is *legal value, bargained for and given in exchange for an act or a promise*. Thus, a promise generally cannot be enforced against the person who made it (the *promisor*) unless the person to whom the promise was made (the *promisee*) has given up something of legal value in exchange for the promise. In effect, the requirement of consideration means that a promisee must pay the price that the promisor asked to gain the right to enforce the promisor's promise. So, if the promisor did not ask for anything in exchange for making her promise or if what the promisor asked for did not have legal value (e.g., because it was something to which she was already entitled), her promise is not enforceable against her because it is not supported by consideration. Figure 1 graphically illustrates the elements of consideration.

Consider the early case of *Thorne v. Deas*, in which the part owner of a sailing ship named the *Sea Nymph* promised his co-owners that he would insure the ship for an upcoming voyage.[2] He failed to do so, and when the ship was lost at sea, the court found that he was not liable to his co-owners for breaching his promise to insure the ship. Why? Because his promise was purely gratuitous; he had neither asked for nor received anything in exchange for making it. Therefore, it was unenforceable because it was not supported by consideration.

This early example illustrates two important aspects of the consideration requirement. First, the requirement *tended to limit the scope of a promisor's liability for his promises* by insulating him from liability for gratuitous

---

[1] T. Metcalf, *Principles of the Law of Contracts*, p. 161 (1874).

[2] 4 Johns. 84 (N.Y. 1809).

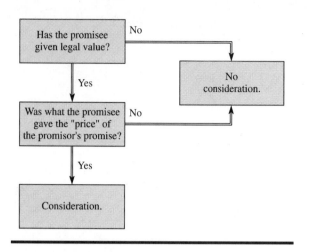

promises and by protecting him against liability for reliance on such promises. Second, the mechanical application of the requirement *often produced unfair results*. This potential for unfairness has produced considerable dissatisfaction with the consideration concept. As the rest of this chapter indicates, the relative importance of consideration in modern contract law has been somewhat eroded by numerous exceptions to the consideration requirement and by judicial applications of consideration principles designed to produce fair results.

LEGAL VALUE

Consideration can be an *act* in the case of a unilateral contract or a *promise* in the case of a bilateral contract. An act or a promise can have *legal value* in one of two ways. If, in exchange for the promisor's promise, the promisee does, or agrees to do, something he had no prior legal duty to do, that provides legal value. If, in exchange for the promisor's promise, the promisee refrains from doing, or agrees not to do, something she has a legal right to do, that also provides legal value. Note that this definition does not require that an act or a promise have *monetary* (economic) value to amount to consideration. Thus, in a famous 19th-century case, *Hamer v. Sidway,*[3] an uncle's promise to pay his nephew $5,000

---

[3] 27 N.E. 256 (N.Y. Ct. App. 1891).

if he refrained from using tobacco, drinking, swearing, and playing cards or billiards for money until his 21st birthday was held to be supported by consideration. Indeed, the nephew had refrained from doing any of these acts, even though he may have benefited from so refraining. He had a legal right to indulge in such activities, yet he had refrained from doing so at his uncle's request and in exchange for his uncle's promise. This was all that was required for consideration.

Adequacy of Consideration

The point that the legal value requirement is not concerned with actual value is further borne out by the fact that the courts generally will not concern themselves with questions regarding the *adequacy* of the consideration that the promisee gave. As the *Harrington* case on the opposite page plainly demonstrates, this means that as long as the promisee's act or promise satisfies the legal value test, the courts do not ask whether that act or promise was worth what the promisor gave, or promised to give, in return for it. This rule on adequacy of consideration reflects the laissez-faire assumptions underlying classical contract law. Freedom of contract includes the freedom to make bad bargains as well as good ones, so promisors' promises are enforceable if they got what they asked for in exchange for making their promises, even if what they asked for was not nearly so valuable in worldly terms as what they promised in return. Also, a court taking a hands-off stance concerning private contracts would be reluctant to step in and second-guess the parties by setting aside a transaction that both parties at one time considered satisfactory. Finally, the rule against considering the adequacy of consideration can promote certainty and predictability in commercial transactions by denying legal effect to what would otherwise be a possible basis for challenging the enforceability of a contract: the inequality of the exchange.

Several qualifications must be made concerning the general rule on adequacy of consideration. First, if the inadequacy of consideration is apparent *on the face of the agreement*, most courts conclude that the agreement was a disguised gift rather than an enforceable bargain. Thus, an agreement calling for an unequal exchange of money (e.g., $500 for $1,000) or identical goods (20 business law textbooks for 40 identical business law textbooks) and containing no other terms would probably be unenforceable.

Gross inadequacy of consideration may also give rise to an inference of fraud, duress, lack of capacity, or some other independent basis for setting aside a contract. However, inadequacy of consideration, standing alone, is never sufficient to prove lack of true consent or contractual capacity.

Although gross inadequacy of consideration is not, by itself, ordinarily a sufficient reason to set aside a contract, the courts may refuse to grant specific performance or other equitable remedies to persons seeking to enforce unfair bargains. Finally, some agreements recite "$1," or "$1 and other valuable consideration," or some other small amount as consideration for a promise. If no other consideration is actually exchanged, this is called *nominal consideration*. Often, such agreements are attempts to make gratuitous promises look like true bargains by reciting a nonexistent consideration. Most courts refuse to enforce such agreements unless they find that the stated consideration was truly bargained for. Similar reasoning (holding that an agreement is not a true bargain) has been employed by a few courts to strike down agreements where the alleged consideration was so inadequate that it "shocks the conscience of the court."

Adequacy and Unconscionability   The advent of the Uniform Commercial Code has given modern courts a potentially powerful tool for policing unfair agreements: the Code's broad section on unconscionable contracts [2–302].[4] In recent years, a few courts have used this section to strike down contracts involving grossly unfair

---

[4] The Illegality chapter discusses unconscionability in detail.

price provisions. These cases normally involve situations where a consumer has agreed to pay a merchant two or three times the market price for the goods. They also commonly involve other factors frequently encountered in unconscionability cases, such as complex, well-hidden, or deceptive contract terms and high-pressure sales tactics. Although such cases are still fairly rare, they may represent the seeds of a significant new direction in the evolution of contract law.

Illusory Promises

For a promise to serve as consideration in a bilateral contract, the promisee must have promised to do, or to refrain from doing, something at the promisor's request. It seems obvious, therefore, that if the promisee's promise is *illusory* because it really does not bind the promisee to do or refrain from doing anything, such a promise could not serve as consideration. Such agreements are often said to lack the *mutuality of obligation* required for an agreement to be enforceable. So, a promisee's promise to "buy all the sugar that I want" or to "paint your house if I feel like it" would not be sufficient consideration for a promisor's return promise to sell sugar or hire a painter. In neither case has the promisee given the promisor anything of legal value in exchange for the promisor's promise. The following *Harrington* case reminds us, however, that so long as the promisee has given legal value the agreement will be enforceable even though what the promisee gave is worth substantially less than what the promisor promised in return.

HARRINGTON v. HARRINGTON

365 N.W.2d 552 (N.D. Sup. Ct. 1985)

When Nancy and Gerald Harrington were divorced in 1981, they executed a property settlement agreement giving him ownership of their farm. In return, he agreed to pay her $150,000; a $10,000 down payment and 15 annual payments. He gave her two mortgages on the farm to secure the debt. Gerald paid Nancy the initial $10,000, but was able to pay her only $3,000 in subsequent payments due to financial difficulties.

Late in 1981, Gerald asked Nancy to execute satisfactions of the two mortgages so he could obtain refinancing of previous bank loans, which lenders were unwilling to provide as long as the farm was encumbered by the mortgages she held. At that time Nancy and Gerald's son, Ronn, was farming the land with Gerald. Nancy was afraid that Ronn would not inherit the farm because Gerald had remarried and his wife had become pregnant. In exchange for Gerald's promise to will the farm to Ronn, Nancy promised on December 30, 1981, to execute satisfactions of the mortgages and to release Gerald from liability on his debt to her under their original agreement.

Gerald subsequently made a will leaving his land to Ronn, but Nancy did not execute satisfactions of the mortgages. Instead, on October 3, 1983, she filed a foreclosure suit against Gerald. When the trial court found that she was bound by her December 30, 1981, promise to satisfy the mortgages and release Gerald from liability for the debt, she appealed.

Gierke, Justice.   If consideration exists, courts will generally not inquire into the adequacy of the consideration. However, it is important to distinguish the adequacy of consideration from its existence. One instance where the lack of consideration invalidates a contract is when the contract is illusory. An illusory contract may be defined as an expression cloaked in promissory terms, but which, upon closer examination, reveals that the promisor has not committed himself in any manner. In other words, an illusory promise is a promise that is not a promise.

Nancy argues that Gerald's promises contained in the December 30, 1981, agreement were illusory. The agreement subjected the devise to Ronn to the following conditions: Ronn would inherit the land subject to all its encumbrances; Ronn would be obligated to make annual payments of 25 percent of all the crops raised on the land to Gerald's widow as long as she had any farm-related debt; Gerald is permitted to convey a portion of the land for purposes of continuing the farming operation in the event "future economic exigencies" so require; and finally, Ronn was granted the first option to purchase any of the farm land sold by Gerald.

Although the agreement may not be entirely equitable for Nancy, it is not illusory and is supported by consideration—in return for Nancy's satisfaction of the mortgages and underlying debt Gerald gave up something which he was privileged to retain: the legal right to devise his farm land to one of his own choosing. The fairness of the agreement is irrelevant. Gerald's relinquishment of a legal right constituted consideration for the agreement regardless of the value of that right to Nancy.

The possibility that Ronn may inherit only a reduced and encumbered portion of the farm land does not alter the fact that Gerald relinquished a legal right which constitutes consideration. Merely because future events may affect the nature and extent of Ronn's devise does not invalidate the legal detriment suffered by Gerald.

Judgment for Gerald affirmed.

Cancellation or Termination Clauses   The fact that an agreement allows one or both of the parties to cancel or terminate their contractual obligations does not necessarily mean that the party or parties with the power to cancel have given an illusory promise. Such provisions are a common and necessary part of many business relationships. The central issue in such cases concerns whether a promise subject to cancellation or termination actually represents a binding obligation. A right to cancel or terminate at any time, for any reason, and without any notice would clearly render illusory any other promise by the party possessing such a right. However, limits on the circumstances under which cancellation may occur, such as a dealer's failure to live up to dealership obligations; or the time in which cancellation may occur, such as no cancellations for the first 90 days; or a requirement of advance notice of cancellation, such as a 30-day notice requirement, would all effectively remove a promise from the illusory category. This is so because in each case the party making such a promise has bound himself to do *something* in exchange for the other party's promise.

Of course, some parties to agreements may not want their agreements to amount to binding contracts. For example, a manufacturer selling through a system of independent retail dealers may want to retain maximum flexibility by giving itself a unilateral right to terminate a dealer at any time, for any reason, without notice. Such an "intentional no contract" strategy relies on the fact that the manufacturer's greater bargaining power may allow it to impose such terms on its dealers. This kind of business strategy is very difficult, if not impossible, to pursue today, however, given the numerous "dealer day in court" statutes that past abuses have produced and the fact that many courts have stricken down unilateral cancellation clauses as unconscionable.

Output and Requirements Contracts Contracts in which one party to the agreement agrees to buy all of the other party's production of a particular commodity (*output* contracts) or to supply all of another party's needs for a particular commodity (*requirements* contracts) are common business transactions that serve legitimate business purposes. They can reduce a seller's selling costs and provide buyers with a secure source of supply. Nonetheless, many common law courts refused to enforce such agreements on the ground that their failure to specify the quantity of goods to be produced or purchased rendered them illusory. The courts also feared that a party to such an agreement might be tempted to exploit the other party. For example, subsequent market conditions could make it profitable for the seller in an output contract or the buyer in a requirements contract to demand that the other party buy or provide more of the particular commodity than the other party had actually intended to buy or sell. The Code legitimizes such contracts by limiting a party's demands to those quantity needs that occur in good faith and are not unreasonably disproportionate to any quantity estimate contained in the contract, or to any normal prior output or requirements if no estimate is stated [2–306(1)]. The Formation and Terms of Sales Contracts chapter discusses this subject in greater detail.

Exclusive Dealing Contracts When a manufacturer of goods enters an agreement giving a distributor the exclusive right to sell the manufacturer's products in a particular territory, does such an agreement impose sufficient obligations on both parties to meet the legal value test? Put another way, does the distributor have any duty to sell the manufacturer's products and does the manufacturer have any duty to supply any particular number of products? Such agreements are commonly encountered in today's business world, and they can serve the legitimate interests of both parties. The Code recognizes

this fact by providing that, unless the parties agree to the contrary, an exclusive dealing contract imposes a duty on the distributor to use her best efforts to sell the goods and imposes a reciprocal duty on the manufacturer to use his best efforts to supply the goods [2–306(2)].

Preexisting Duties

The legal value component of our consideration definition requires that promisees do, or promise to do, something in exchange for a promisor's promise that they had *no prior legal duty* to do. Thus, as a general rule, performing or agreeing to perform a preexisting duty is *not* consideration. This seems fair because the promisor in such a case has effectively made a gratuitous promise, since she was already entitled to the promisee's performance.

Preexisting Public Duties Every member of society has a duty to obey the law and refrain from committing crimes or torts. Therefore, a promisee's promise not to commit such an act can never be consideration. So, Thomas's promise to pay Brown $100 a year in exchange for Brown's promise not to burn Thomas's barn would not be enforceable against Thomas. Since Brown has a preexisting duty not to burn Thomas's barn, his promise lacks legal value.

Similarly, public officials, by virtue of their offices, have a preexisting legal duty to perform their public responsibilities. For example, Smith, the owner of a liquor store, promises to pay Fawcett, a police officer whose beat includes Smith's store, $50 a week to keep an eye on the store while walking her beat. Smith's promise is unenforceable because Fawcett has agreed to do something that she already has a duty to do.

Preexisting Contractual Duties The most important preexisting duty cases are those involving preexisting *contractual* duties. These cases generally occur when the parties to an existing contract agree to *modify* that contract. As the *Gross* case which follows indicates, the general common law rule on contract modification holds that an agreement to modify an existing contract requires some *new consideration* to be binding.

For example, Turner enters into a contract with Acme Construction Company for the construction of a new office building for $350,000. When the construction is partially completed, Acme tells Turner that due to rising labor and materials costs it will stop construction unless Turner agrees to pay an extra $50,000. Turner, having already entered into contracts to lease office space in the new building, promises to pay the extra amount. When the construction is finished, Turner refuses to pay more than $350,000. Is Turner's promise to pay the extra $50,000 enforceable against him? No. All Acme has done in exchange for Turner's promise to pay more is build the building, something that Acme had a preexisting contractual duty to do. Therefore, Acme's performance is not consideration for Turner's promise to pay more.

Although the result in the preceding example seems fair (why should Turner have to pay $400,000 for something he had a right to receive for $350,000?) and is consistent with consideration theory, the application of the preexisting duty rule to contract modifications has generated a great deal of criticism. Plainly, the rule can protect a party to a contract such as Turner from being pressured into paying more because the other party to the contract is trying to take advantage of his situation by demanding an additional amount for performance. However, mechanical application of the rule could also produce unfair results when the parties have freely agreed to a fair modification of their contract. Some critics argue that the purpose of contract modification law should be to enforce freely made modifications of existing contracts and to deny enforcement to coerced modifications. Such critics commonly suggest that general principles such as good faith and unconscionability, rather than technical consideration rules, should be used to police contract modifications.

Other observers argue that most courts in fact apply the preexisting duty rule in a manner calculated to reach fair results, because several exceptions to the rule can be used to enforce a fair modification agreement. For example, any new consideration furnished by the promisee provides sufficient consideration to support a promise to modify an existing contract. So, if Acme had promised to finish construction a week before the completion date called for in the original contract, or had promised to make some change in the original contract specifications such as to install a better grade of carpet, Acme would have done something that it had no legal duty to do in exchange for Turner's new promise. Turner's promise to pay more would then be enforceable because it would be supported by new consideration.

Many courts also enforce an agreement to modify an existing contract if the modification resulted from *unforeseen circumstances* that a party could not reasonably be expected to have foreseen, and which made that party's performance far more difficult than the parties originally anticipated. For example, if Acme had requested the extra payment because abnormal subsurface rock formations made excavation on the construction site far more costly and time consuming than could have been reasonably expected, many courts would enforce Turner's promise to pay more.

Courts can also enforce fair modification agreements by holding that the parties mutually agreed to terminate their original contract and then entered a new one. Because contracts are created by the will of the parties, they can be terminated in the same fashion. Each party agrees to release the other party from his contractual obligations in exchange for the other party's promise to do the same. Because such a mutual agreement terminates all duties owed under the original agreement, any subsequent agreement by the parties would not be subject to the preexisting duty rule. A court is likely to take this approach, however, only when it is convinced that the modification agreement was fair and free from coercion.

GROSS v. DIEHL SPECIALTIES INTERNATIONAL

776 S.W.2d 879 (Mo. Ct. App. 1989)

In 1977, Dairy Specialties, Inc. (Dairy), hired George Gross to develop nondairy products for customers allergic to milk and to serve as general manager. The employment contract was for a term of 15 years and provided for annual wages of $14,400 plus cost of living increases. It also provided that when 10 percent of Dairy's gross profits exceeded Gross's annual salary he would receive the difference between the two figures, and gave Gross a royalty of 1 percent of the selling price of all products Dairy produced using one or more of Gross's inventions or formulae. This royalty increased to 2 percent after the expiration of the agreement, at which time ownership of the inventions and formulae (which was jointly held during the term of the agreement) would revert to Gross.

In 1982, Dairy was bought from its original owner by the Diehl family. The Diehls insisted on renegotiation of Gross's contract with Dairy as a condition of the purchase. Although he was not a party to the sale and received nothing tangible from it, Gross agreed to a new contract that had the same expiration date as the first one, but that eliminated his cost of living increases, gave Dairy exclusive ownership of his inventions and formulae during and after the term of the agreement, and eliminated his right to royalties after the agreement expired. After the sale, Gross was given additional duties but no additional compensation. In 1984, after a business downturn, Gross was fired. He filed suit, arguing that his termination benefits should be calculated under his original contract. When the trial court ruled in the company's favor, he appealed.

Smith, Presiding Judge.   A modification of a contract constitutes the making of a new contract and such new contract must be supported by consideration. Where a contract has not been fully performed at the time of the new agreement, the substitution of a new provision, resulting in a modification of the obligation of *both* sides, for a provision in the old contract still unperformed is sufficient consideration for the new contract. A promise to carry out an existing contractual duty does not constitute consideration.

Under the 1982 agreement the company undertook no greater obligations than it already had. Gross on the other hand received less than he had under the original contract. His base pay was reduced back to its 1977 amount despite the provision in the 1977 contract calling for cost of living adjustments. He lost his equal ownership in his formulae during the term of the agreement and his exclusive ownership after the termination of the agreement. He lost all royalties after termination of the agreement. In exchange for nothing, the company acquired exclusive ownership of the formulae during and after the agreement, eliminated royalties after the agreement terminated, and achieved a reduction in Gross's base salary. The company did no more than promise to carry out an already existing contractual duty. There was no consideration for the 1982 agreement.

Judgment reversed in favor of Gross; case remanded for recalculation of damages.

Code Contract Modification   The drafters of the Code sought to avoid many of the problems caused by the consideration requirement by dispensing with it in two important situations: As discussed in the Offer chapter, the Code does not require consideration for firm offers [2–205]. The Code also provides that an agreement to modify a contract for the sale of goods needs *no consideration* to be binding [2–209(1)]. For example, Video World orders 500 RCA videodisc players at $150 per unit in response to an RCA promotional campaign heralding the introduction of this new home entertainment device. Initial sales figures indicate, however, that the consuming public is unimpressed with videodisc technology. Video World seeks to cancel its order, but RCA refuses to agree to cancellation. Instead, RCA seeks to mollify a valued customer by offering to reduce the price to $100 per unit. Video World agrees, but when the players arrive, RCA bills Video World for $150 per unit. Under classical contract principles, RCA's promise to reduce the price of the goods would not be enforceable because Video World has furnished no new consideration in exchange for RCA's promise. Under the Code, no new consideration is necessary and the agreement to modify the contract is enforceable.

Several things should be made clear about the operation of this Code rule. First, RCA had no duty to agree to a modification and could have insisted on payment of $150 per unit. Second, as the following *Roth Steel Products* case illustrates, modification agreements under the Code are still subject to scrutiny under the general Code principles of good faith and unconscionability, so unfair agreements or agreements that are the product of coercion are unlikely to be enforced. Finally, the Code contains two provisions to protect people from fictitious claims that an agreement has been modified. If the original agreement requires any modification to be in writing, an oral modification is unenforceable [2–209(2)]. Regardless of what the original agreement says, if the price of the goods in the modified contract is $500 or more, the modification is unenforceable unless the requirements of the Code's statute of frauds section [2–201] are satisfied [2–209(3)].[5]

---

[5] The Writing chapter discusses section 2–201 of the Code in detail.

ROTH STEEL PRODUCTS v. SHARON STEEL CORPORATION

705 F.2d 134 (6th Cir. 1983)

In November 1972, when conditions in the steel industry were highly competitive and the industry was operating at about 70 percent of its capacity, Sharon Steel Corporation agreed to sell Roth Steel Products several types of steel at prices well below Sharon's published book prices for such steel. These prices were to be effective from January 1 until December 31, 1973.

In early 1973, however, several factors changed the market for steel. Federal price controls simultaneously discouraged foreign steel imports and encouraged domestic steel producers to export a substantial portion of their production to avoid domestic price controls, sharply reducing the domestic steel supply. In addition, the steel industry experienced substantial increases in labor, raw material, and energy costs, compelling steel producers to increase prices. The increased domestic demand for steel and the attractive export market caused the entire industry to operate at full capacity; as a consequence, nearly every domestic steel producer experienced substantial delays in delivery.

On March 23, 1973, Sharon notified Roth that it was discontinuing all price discounts. Roth protested, and Sharon agreed to continue to sell at the discount price until June 30, 1973, but refused to sell thereafter unless Roth agreed to pay a modified price that was higher than that agreed to the previous November, but still lower than the book prices Sharon was charging other customers. Because Roth was unable to purchase enough steel elsewhere to meet its production requirements, it agreed to pay the increased prices. When a subsequent dispute arose between the parties over late deliveries and unfilled orders by Sharon in 1974, Roth filed a breach of contract suit against Sharon, arguing, among other things, that the 1973 modification agreement was unenforceable. When the trial court ruled in favor of Roth, Sharon appealed.

Celebrezze, Senior Circuit Judge. The ability of a party to modify a contract which is subject to Article Two of the UCC is broader than common law, primarily because the modification needs no consideration to be binding. [UCC Sec. 2–209(1)]. A party's ability to modify an agreement is limited only by Article Two's general obligation of good faith. In determining whether a particular modification was obtained in good faith, a court must make two distinct inquiries: whether the party's conduct is consistent with "reasonable commercial standards of fair dealing in the trade," and whether the parties were in fact motivated to seek modification by an honest desire to compensate for commercial exigencies.

The first inquiry is relatively straightforward; the party asserting the modification must demonstrate that his decision to seek modification was the result of a factor, such as increased costs, which would cause an ordinary merchant to seek a modification of the contract. The second inquiry, regarding the subjective honesty of the parties, is less clearly defined. Essentially, this requires the party asserting the modification to demonstrate that he was, in fact, motivated by a legitimate commercial reason and that such a reason is not offered merely as a pretext. Moreover, the trier of fact must determine whether the means used to obtain the modification are an impermissible attempt to obtain a modification by extortion or overreaching.

The single most important consideration in determining whether the decision to seek a modification is justified is whether, because of changes in the market or other unforeseeable conditions, performance of the contract has come to involve a loss. In this case, the district court found that Sharon suffered substantial losses by performing the contract as modified. We are convinced that unforeseen economic exigencies existed which would prompt an ordinary merchant to seek a modification to avoid a loss on the contract.

The second part of the analysis, honesty in fact, is pivotal. The district court found that Sharon "threatened not to sell Roth any steel if Roth refused to pay increased prices after July 1, 1973" and, consequently, that Sharon acted wrongfully. We believe that the district court's conclusion that Sharon acted in bad faith by using coercive conduct to extract the price modification is not clearly erroneous. Therefore, we hold that Sharon's attempt to modify the November 1972 contract, in order to compensate for increased costs which made performance come to involve a loss, is ineffective because Sharon did not act in a manner consistent with Article Two's requirement of honesty in fact when it refused to perform its remaining obligations under the contract at 1972 prices.

Judgment for Roth affirmed.

Debt Settlement Agreements

One special variant of the preexisting duty rule that causes considerable confusion occurs when a debtor offers to pay a creditor a sum less than the creditor is demanding, in exchange for the creditor's promise to accept the part payment as full payment of the debt. If the creditor later sues for the balance of the debt, is the creditor's promise to take less enforceable? The answer depends on the nature of the debt and on the circumstances of the debtor's payment.

Liquidated Debts A promise to discharge a **liquidated debt** for part payment of the debt *at or after* its due date is *unenforceable* for lack of consideration. Liquidated debts are both *due* and *certain*; that is, there is no bona fide dispute about either the *existence* or the *amount* of the debt. If a debtor does nothing more than pay less than an amount he clearly owes, how could that be consideration for a creditor's promise to take less? Such a debtor has actually done less than he had a preexisting legal duty to do, namely, to pay the full amount of the debt.

For example, Connor borrows $10,000 from Friendly Finance Company, payable in one year. On the day payment is due, Connor sends Friendly a check for $9,000 marked: "Payment in full for all claims Friendly Finance has against me." Friendly cashes Connor's check, thus impliedly promising to accept it as full payment by cashing it, and later sues Connor for $1,000. Friendly is entitled to the $1,000 because Connor has given no consideration to support Friendly's implied promise to accept $9,000 as full payment.

However, had Connor done something he had no preexisting duty to do in exchange for Friendly's promise to settle for part payment, he could enforce Friendly's promise and avoid paying the $1,000. For example, if Connor had paid early, before the loan contract called for payment, or in a different medium of exchange than that called for in the loan contract (such as $4,000 in cash and a car worth $5,000), he would have given consideration for Friendly's promise to accept early or different payment as full payment.

Unliquidated Debts A bona fide (good faith) dispute about either the existence or the amount of a debt makes the debt an **unliquidated debt.** For example, Computer Corner, a retailer, orders 50 personal computers and associated software packages from Computech for $75,000. After receiving the goods, Computer Corner refuses to pay Computech the full $75,000, arguing that some of the computers were defective and that some of the software it received did not conform to its order. Computer Corner sends Computech a check for $60,000 marked: "Payment in full for all goods received from Computech." A creditor in Computech's position obviously faces a real dilemma. If Computech cashes Computer Corner's check, it will be held to have impliedly promised to accept $60,000 as full payment. This promise would be enforceable against Computech if it later sought to collect the remaining $15,000, because by agreeing to settle a disputed claim, Computech has entered a binding **accord and satisfaction.** Computech's promise to accept part payment as full payment would be enforceable because Computer Corner has given consideration to support it: Computer Corner has given up its right to have a court determine the amount it owes Computech. This is something that Computer Corner had no duty to do; by giving up this right and the $60,000 in exchange for Computech's implied promise, the consideration requirement is satisfied. The result in this case is supported not only by consideration theory but also by a strong public policy in favor of encouraging parties to settle their disputes out of court. Who would bother to settle disputed claims out of court if settlement agreements were unenforceable?

Computech could refuse to accept Computer Corner's settlement offer and sue for the full $75,000, but doing so involves several risks. A court may decide that Computer Corner's arguments are valid and award Computech less than $60,000. Even if Computech is successful, it may take years to resolve the case in the courts through the expensive and time-consuming litigation process. And, there is always the chance that Computer Corner may file for bankruptcy before any judgment can be collected. Faced with such risks, Computech may feel that it has no practical alternative other than to cash Computer Corner's check.

In some states, a creditor such as Computech has a third, and much more desirable, alternative course of action to either returning the debtor's full-payment check or cashing it and entering an accord and satisfaction. Some state courts have held that the Code has changed the common law accord and satisfaction rule by allowing a creditor to accept a full-payment check "under protest" or "without prejudice" without giving up any rights to sue for the balance due under the contract [1–207]. As the following *County Fire Door* case indicates, whether section 1–207 was ever intended to have this effect is a matter of controversy, and many courts have rejected such an interpretation of the Code. However, in states where the courts have applied section 1–207 to accord and satisfaction cases, a creditor can now accept part payment under protest and still seek to collect the remainder of the debt.

County Fire Door Corp. v. C. F. Wooding Co.

520 A.2d 1028 (Conn. Sup. Ct. 1987)

On November 17, 1981, C. F. Wooding Company (Wooding) ordered a number of metal doors and door frames from County Fire Door Corporation (County) for a construction project Wooding was working on. After County was allegedly late in delivering the goods to the work site, Wooding told County that it would only pay $416.88 of the $2,618.88 that County claimed was the balance due because the delays in delivery caused Wooding additional installation expenses. County denied the validity of Wooding's claim and insisted that the full amount was due.

Wooding then sent County a check for $416.88. On its face was a notation stating that it was final payment for the project, and on its reverse side the check stated: "By its endorsement, the payee accepts this check in full satisfaction of all claims against the C. F. Wooding Co. arising out of or relating to Purchase Order #3302, dated 11/17/81." County cashed the check, but only after crossing out the conditional language on the reverse side and adding the following language: "This check is accepted under protest and with full reservation of rights to collect the unpaid balance for which this check is offered in settlement."

County filed suit against Wooding for the unpaid balance, arguing that section 1–207 of the UCC prevented its cashing of Wooding's check from amounting to an accord and satisfaction. The trial court ruled in County's favor, and Wooding appealed.

Peters, Chief Justice. When there is a good faith dispute about the existence of a debt or about the amount that is owed, the common law authorizes the debtor and the creditor to negotiate a contract of accord to settle the outstanding claim. Such a contract is often initiated by the debtor, who offers an accord by tendering a check as "payment in full" or "in full satisfaction." If the creditor knowingly cashes such a check, or otherwise exercises full dominion over it, the creditor is deemed to have assented to the offer of accord. Upon acceptance of the offer of accord, the creditor's receipt of the promised payment discharges the underlying debt and bars any further claim relating thereto.

Application of these settled principles to this case establishes that the parties entered into a valid accord and satisfaction. Wooding offered in good faith to settle an unliquidated debt by tendering, in full satisfaction, the payment of an amount less than that demanded by County. Under the common law, County could not simultaneously cash such a check and disown the condition on which it had been tendered.

The principal dispute between the parties is what meaning to ascribe to section 1–207 when it states that: "A party who with explicit reservation of rights assents to performance in a manner offered by the other party does not thereby prejudice the rights reserved. Such words as 'without prejudice,' 'under protest' or the like are sufficient." County contends that this section gave it the authority to cash Wooding's check "under protest" while reserving the right to pursue the remainder of its underlying claim against Wooding at a later time. We noted in *Kelly v. Kowalsky* (1982) that there was considerable disagreement in the cases and the scholarly commentaries about the scope of the transactions governed by section 1–207, but did not then undertake to resolve this disagreement.

It is apparent that section 1–207 contemplates a reservation of rights about some aspect of a possibly nonconforming tender of goods or services or payment in a situation where the aggrieved party may prefer not to terminate the underlying contract as a whole. Indeed, the Official Comment to section 1–207 itself explains that the section supports ongoing contractual relations by providing "machinery for the continuation of performance along the lines contemplated by the contract despite a pending dispute." It is significant, furthermore, that the text of section 1–207 recurrently refers to "performance," for "performance" is a central aspect of the sales transactions governed by article 2.

By contrast, article 3 instruments, which promise or order the payment of money, are not characteristically described as being performed by anyone. The contracts encapsulated in various forms of negotiable instruments instead envisage conduct of negotiation or transfer, indorsement or guaranty, payment or acceptance, and honor or dishonor. We conclude, therefore, that in circumstances like the present, when performance of a sales contract has come to an end, section 1–207 was not intended to empower a seller, as payee of a negotiable instrument, to alter that instrument by adding words of protest to a check tendered by a buyer on condition that it be accepted in full satisfaction of an unliquidated debt.

Our conclusion is supported by the emerging majority of cases in other jurisdictions. It is now the view of the substantial majority of courts that have addressed the issue that section 1–207 does not overrule the common law of accord and satisfaction. The majority finds support as well in much of the recent scholarly commentary. Both under prevailing common law principles, and under the Uniform Commercial Code, the parties in this case negotiated a contract of accord whose satisfaction discharged Wooding from any further monetary obligation to County. County might have avoided this result by returning Wooding's check uncashed, but could not simultaneously disregard the condition on which the check was tendered and deposit its proceeds in County's bank account.

Judgment reversed in favor of Wooding.

Composition Agreements   Composition agreements are agreements between a debtor and two or more creditors who agree to accept as full payment a stated percentage of their liquidated claims against the debtor at or after the date on which those claims are payable. Composition agreements are generally enforced by the courts despite the fact that enforcement appears to be contrary to the general rule on part payment of liquidated debts. Many courts have justified enforcing composition agreements on the ground that the creditors' mutual agreement to accept less than the amount due them provides the necessary consideration. The main reason why creditors agree to compositions is that they fear that their failure to do so may force the debtor into bankruptcy proceedings, in which case they might ultimately recover a smaller percentage of their claims than that agreed to in the composition.

Forbearance to Sue

An agreement by a promisee to refrain, or forbear, from pursuing a legal claim against a promisor can be valid consideration to support a return promise—usually to pay a sum of money—by a promisor. The promisee has agreed not to file suit, something that she has a legal right to do, in exchange for the promisor's promise. The courts do not wish to sanction extortion by allowing people to threaten to file spurious claims against others in the hope that those threatened will agree to some payment to avoid the expense or embarrassment associated with defending a lawsuit. On the other hand, we have a strong public policy favoring private settlement of disputes and we do not want to require people to second-guess the courts. Therefore, it is generally said that the promisee must have a *good faith* belief in the validity of his or her claim before forbearance amounts to consideration.

BARGAINED FOR EXCHANGE

Up to this point, we have focused on the legal value component of our consideration definition. But the fact

that a promisee's act or promise provides legal value is not, in itself, a sufficient basis for finding that it amounted to consideration. In addition, the promisee's act or promise must have been *bargained for* and *given in exchange* for the promisor's promise. In effect, it must be the price that the promisor asked for in exchange for making his promise. Over a hundred years ago, Oliver Wendell Holmes, one of our most renowned jurists, expressed this idea when he said, "It is the essence of a consideration that, by the terms of the agreement, it is given and accepted as the motive or inducement of the promise."[6]

Past Consideration

It is generally said that *past consideration is no consideration.* To understand the meaning of this statement, consider once again the famous case of *Hamer v. Sidway*, discussed earlier in this chapter. There, an uncle's promise to pay his nephew $5,000 for refraining from smoking, drinking, swearing, and other delightful pastimes until his 21st birthday was supported by consideration because the nephew had given legal value by refraining from participating in the prohibited activities. However, what if the uncle had said to his nephew on the eve of his 21st birthday: "Your mother tells me you've been a good lad and abstained from tobacco, hard drink, foul language, and gambling. Such goodness should be rewarded. Tomorrow, I'll give you a check for $5,000." Should the uncle's promise be enforceable against him? Clearly not, because although his nephew's behavior still passes the legal value test, in this case it was not bargained for and given in exchange for the uncle's promise. The following *Spickelmier* case is a contemporary illustration of the operation of the past consideration rule.

Moral Obligation

As a general rule, promises made to satisfy a preexisting moral obligation are unenforceable for lack of

---

[6] O. W. Holmes, *The Common Law*, p. 230 (1881).

SPICKELMIER INDUSTRIES, INC. v. PASSANDER

359 N.E.2d 563 (Ind. Ct. App. 1977)

Robert Passander was executive vice president of Spickelmier Industries. Because Spickelmier was facing financial difficulties, a committee of creditors had been formed to oversee its operations. In November of 1971, the committee projected a small profit for the year and recommended that bonuses be given to certain key employees if the profit materialized. This recommendation was adopted by Spickelmier's board of directors in late December, and Passander was promised a $1,500 bonus.

In January of 1972, however, the board's executive committee discovered that the earlier profit estimates had been overly optimistic and that insufficient funds were available to pay the bonuses. Instead of taking the board's recommendation that the bonuses not be paid, the chairman of the board negotiated a compromise whereby one half of the originally specified bonus would be paid as planned, with the balance to be paid when funds were available. Passander accepted the half bonus, and later in the month his contract with Spickelmier was renegotiated to provide for a 25 percent salary increase and guaranteed quarterly bonuses of $500.

In June of 1972, Passander quit his job, later filing suit against Spickelmier for the remaining half of his 1971 bonus. When the trial court ruled in his favor, Spickelmier appealed.

Buchanan, Presiding Judge.   Not every promise creates a legal obligation which the law will enforce. A promise must be predicated upon adequate consideration before it can command performance. The record is barren of any evidence indicating Passander furnished consideration for Spickelmier's promise. The promise of a year-end bonus was made after Passander had already performed the terms of his 1971 employment contract. It was a promise of more compensation to an employee who had already performed the agreed services.

"[A] new promise of additional compensation should not be enforceable if it is made after the first party has already rendered his promised performance. In such a case the promisor bargains for nothing and receives nothing in exchange for his promise. He has already received everything before he makes the new promise. The element of agreed exchange, or bargain, is lacking. In addition, the promisee has done nothing in reliance on the new promise, so that the action in reliance doctrine is also inapplicable."

Corbin on Contracts, section 235 (1952). So, Passander's prior service in 1971 was not in reliance on payment of a year-end bonus, and no consideration therefore existed for Spickelmier's promise. Nor did Passander make a reciprocal promise or perform any act concomitant with Spickelmier's promise. The bonus was merely a means by which Spickelmier could reward Passander's diligence during 1971. There was no evidence the bonus was intended to elicit any present response from Passander other than ordinary gratitude.

Judgment reversed in favor of Spickelmier.

consideration. The fact that a promisor or some member of the promisor's family, for example, has received some benefit from the promisee in the past (e.g., food and lodging, or emergency care) would not constitute consideration for a promisor's promise to pay for that benefit, due to the absence of the bargain element. Some courts find this result distressing and enforce such promises despite the absence of consideration. In addition, a few states have passed statutes making promises to pay for past benefits enforceable if such a promise is contained

---

CONCEPT REVIEW

CONSIDERATION

Consideration*	Not Consideration
Doing something you had no preexisting duty to do	Doing something you had a preexisting duty to do
Promising to do something you had no preexisting duty to do	Promising to do something you had a preexisting duty to do
Paying part of a liquidated debt prior to the date the debt is due	Nominal consideration (unless actually bargained for)
Paying a liquidated debt in a different medium of exchange than originally agreed to	Paying part of a liquidated debt at or after the date the debt is due
Agreeing to settle an unliquidated debt	Making an illusory promise
Agreeing not to file suit when you have a good faith belief in your claim's validity	Past consideration
*Assuming bargained for	Preexisting moral obligation

---

in a writing that clearly expresses the promisor's intent to be bound.

EXCEPTIONS TO THE CONSIDERATION REQUIREMENT

The consideration requirement is a classic example of a traditional contract law rule. It is precise, abstract, and capable of almost mechanical application. It can also, in some instances, result in significant injustice. Modern courts and legislatures have responded to this potential for injustice by carving out numerous exceptions to the requirement of consideration. Some of these exceptions (for example, the Code firm offer and contract modification rules) have already been discussed in this and preceding chapters. In the remaining portion of this chapter, we focus on several other important exceptions to the consideration requirement.

Promissory Estoppel

As discussed in the Introduction to Contracts chapter, the doctrine of **promissory estoppel** first emerged from attempts by courts around the turn of this century to reach just results in donative (gift) promise cases. Classical contract consideration principles did not recognize a promisee's reliance on a donative promise as a sufficient basis for enforcing the promise against the promisor. Instead, donative promises were unenforceable because they were not supported by consideration. In fact, the essence of a donative promise is that it does not seek or require any bargained-for exchange. Yet people continued to act in reliance on donative promises, often to their considerable disadvantage.

Refer to the facts of *Thorne v. Deas*, discussed earlier in this chapter. The co-owners of the *Sea Nymph* clearly relied to their injury on their fellow co-owner's promise to get insurance for the ship. Some courts in the early years of this century began to protect such relying promisees by *estopping* promisors from raising the defense that their promises were not supported by consideration. In a wide variety of cases involving gratuitous agency promises (like *Thorne v. Deas*), promises of bonuses or pensions made to employees, and promises of gifts of land, courts began to use a promisee's detrimental (harmful) reliance on a donative promise as, in effect, a *substitute for* consideration.

In 1932 the first *Restatement of Contracts* legitimized these cases by expressly recognizing promissory estoppel in section 90. The elements of promissory estoppel were then essentially the same as they are today: a *promise* that the promisor should reasonably expect to induce reliance, *reliance* on the promise by the promisee, and *injustice* to the promisee as a result of that reliance. As the following *Grouse* case illustrates, promissory estoppel is now widely used as a consideration substitute, not only in donative promise cases, but also in cases involving commercial promises, those contemplating a bargained-for exchange. The construction contract bid cases discussed in the Offer chapter are another example of this expansion of promissory estoppel's reach. In fact, although promissory estoppel has expanded far beyond its initial role as a consideration substitute into other areas of contract law, it is probably fair to say that it is still most widely accepted in the consideration context.

GROUSE v. GROUP HEALTH PLAN, INC.

306 N.W.2d 114 (Minn. Sup. Ct. 1980)

John Grouse, a recently graduated pharmacist who was working as a retail pharmacist for Richter Drug, applied for a job with Group Health Plan, Inc. Grouse was interviewed at Group Health by Cyrus Elliott, Chief Pharmacist, and Donald Shoberg, General Manager. On December 4, 1975, Elliott telephoned Grouse at work and offered him a job as a pharmacist at Group Health's St. Louis Park Clinic. Grouse accepted, informing Elliott that he would give Richter two weeks' notice. That afternoon Grouse received an offer from a Veterans Administration Hospital in Virginia which he declined because of Group Health's offer. Elliott called back to confirm that Grouse had resigned.

Sometime in the next few days, Elliott mentioned to Shoberg that he had hired, or was thinking of hiring, Grouse. Shoberg told him that company hiring requirements included a favorable written reference, a background check, and approval of the general manager. Elliott contacted two faculty members at the University of Minnesota School of Pharmacy who declined to give references. He also contacted an internship employer and several pharmacies where Grouse had done relief work. Their responses were that they had not had enough exposure to Grouse's work to form a judgment about his capabilities.

Because Elliott was unable to supply a favorable reference for Grouse, Shoberg hired another person to fill the position. On December 15, 1975, Grouse called Group Health and reported that he was free to begin work. Elliott informed Grouse that someone else had been hired. Grouse had difficulty regaining full-time employment and suffered wage loss as a result. He filed suit against Group Health, and when the trial court ruled in Group Health's favor, he appealed.

Otis, Justice.   The parties focus their arguments on whether an employment contract which is terminable at will can give rise to an action for damages if anticipatorily repudiated. Group Health contends that recognition of a cause of action on these facts would result in the anomalous rule that an employee who is told not to report to work the day before he is scheduled to begin has a remedy while an employee who is discharged after the first day does not. We cannot agree since under appropriate circumstances we believe section 90 would apply even after employment has begun.

In our view the principle of contract law applicable here is promissory estoppel. On these facts no contract exists because due to the bilateral power of termination neither party is committed to performance and the promises are, therefore, illusory. The elements of promissory estoppel are stated in Restatement of Contracts section 90 (1932):

A promise which the promisor should reasonably expect to induce action or forbear . . . on the part of the promisee and which does induce such action or forbearance is binding if injustice can be avoided only by enforcement of the promise.

Group Health knew that to accept its offer Grouse would have to resign his employment at Richter. Grouse promptly gave notice to Richter and informed Group Health that he had done so when specifically asked by Elliott. Under these circumstances it would be unjust not to hold Group Health to its promise.

The conclusion we reach does not imply that an employer will be liable whenever he discharges an employee whose term of employment is at will. What we do hold is that under the facts of this case Grouse had a right to assume he would be given a good faith opportunity to perform his duties to the satisfaction of Group Health once he was on the job. He was not only denied that opportunity but resigned the position he already held in reliance on the offer which Group Health tendered him. Since, as Group Health points out, the prospective employment might have been terminated at any time, the measure of damages is not so much what he would have earned from Group Health as what he lost in quitting the job he held and in declining at least one other offer of employment elsewhere.

Judgment reversed in favor of Grouse and remanded for a new trial on the issue of damages.

Debts Barred by Statutes of Limitations

Statutes of limitations set an express statutory time limit on a person's ability to pursue any legal claim. A creditor who fails to file suit to collect a debt within the time prescribed by the appropriate statute of limitations loses the right to collect it. Many states, however, enforce a *new promise* by a debtor to pay such a debt, even though technically such promises are not supported by consideration because the creditor has given nothing in exchange for the new promise. Most states afford debtors some protection in such cases, however, by requiring that the new promise be in writing to be enforceable.

Debts Barred by Bankruptcy Discharge

Once a bankrupt debtor is granted a discharge,[7] creditors no longer have the legal right to collect discharged debts. Most states enforce a new promise by the debtor to pay (reaffirm) the debt regardless of whether the creditor has given any consideration to support it. To reduce creditor attempts to pressure debtors to reaffirm, the Bankruptcy Reform Act of 1978 made it much more difficult for debtors to reaffirm debts discharged in bankruptcy proceedings. The act requires that a reaffirmation promise be made prior to the date of the discharge, and gives the debtor the right to revoke his promise within 30 days after it becomes enforceable. This act also requires the Bankruptcy Court to counsel individual (as opposed to corporate) debtors about the legal effects of reaffirmation, and requires Bankruptcy Court approval of reaffirmations by individual debtors. In addition, a few states require reaffirmation promises to be in writing to be enforceable.

Charitable Subscriptions

Promises to make gifts for charitable or educational purposes are often enforced, despite the absence of consideration, when the institution or organization to which the promise was made has acted in reliance on the promised gift. This result is usually justified on the basis of either promissory estoppel or public policy.

ETHICAL AND PUBLIC POLICY CONCERNS

1. In this chapter you learned the general rule that the law does not enforce promises that are not supported by consideration. Are there ethical arguments that one could make to support the proposition that people should generally honor their promises to others regardless of whether they are legally required to do so? What might those arguments be? Do any of them help to explain the doctrine of promissory estoppel as an exception to the consideration requirement?

---

[7] The Bankruptcy chapter discusses bankruptcy in detail.

2. Discuss the public policy behind the rule that courts will not inquire into the adequacy of consideration. What social benefits are purchased by such a rule and at what price? Refer to the *Harrington* case earlier in the chapter: What ethical arguments can you make for and against holding Mrs. Harrington to her promise to execute satisfactions of the mortgages?

3. Discuss the ethical dimensions of offers by debtors to satisfy a liquidated debt by part payment before the due date. Are such offers ever ethical? What factors would be relevant in determining whether such an offer was ethical?

SUMMARY

As a general rule, only promises supported by consideration are enforceable as contracts. Consideration is defined as legal value, bargained for and given in exchange for an act or a promise. Legal value means that, in exchange for the promisor's promise, a promisee must have done, or agreed to do, something that he had no duty to do, or that a promisee refrained from doing, or agreed not to do, something that he had a right to do. Illusory promises—those that do not really obligate a promisee to do anything—cannot serve as consideration.

Likewise, performing or agreeing to perform an act that the promisee had a preexisting duty to perform does not amount to consideration. This is true whether the preexisting duty is public or contractual in nature. At common law, an agreement to modify an existing contract must be supported by new consideration to be enforceable. Some commentators have argued that this rule, while it properly prevents the enforcement of coerced modifications, can also prevent the enforcement of voluntary and equitable modification agreements. There are many ways, however, in which a court can enforce a fair modification agreement. Any new consideration furnished by the promisee, however slight, can support a modification agreement. Modification agreements made in the face of unforeseeable circumstances that make performance of the contract unduly burdensome are also commonly enforced by the courts. Also, a court may find that the parties mutually agreed to terminate their original agreement and their duties to each other under that agreement. In such circumstances, a subsequent agreement entered into by the parties would be supported by consideration even though one of the parties has not agreed to do anything more than he was obli-

gated to do under the original contract, because the termination of the original contract relieved him of any duty to perform.

The Code simplifies the contract modification process by providing that agreements to modify contracts for the sale of goods do not need to be supported by consideration [2–209(1)]. Such agreements must meet the Code good faith requirements, however, and unconscionable modification agreements are not enforced. In some circumstances, oral modification agreements may be unenforceable under the Code [2–209(2) and (3)].

Agreements to settle debts for part payment may or may not be enforceable, depending on the nature of the debt and on the circumstances of the part payment. An agreement to settle a liquidated debt for part payment received at or after the due date of the debt is unenforceable for lack of consideration. An agreement to settle an unliquidated debt, however, creates a binding accord and satisfaction. Some state courts have interpreted section 1–207 of the Code in a way that would allow a creditor to accept a partial payment of an unliquidated debt without entering an accord and satisfaction, even though the debtor clearly intends the part payment to fully satisfy the debt. Other courts have rejected this interpretation of the Code. Also, composition agreements are ordinarily enforced on public policy grounds despite the fact that they involve the settlement of liquidated claims by part payment.

Forbearing or agreeing to forbear from asserting a legal right can amount to consideration. As a general rule, the courts do not require that a forbearing promisee have a legally valid claim, but do require that the promisee have a good faith belief in the validity of her claim.

To say that a promisee's act or promise must have legal value, however, does not mean that it must have any actual value or that its value must in any way equal the value of the promisor's promise. As a general rule, the courts do not inquire into the adequacy of consideration. However, grossly inadequate consideration may be evidence of fraud, duress, or contractual incapacity; many courts refuse to grant equitable remedies such as specific performance to promisees who have driven too hard a bargain. Grossly inadequate consideration may also support the conclusion that the agreement in question is a disguised gift rather than an enforceable bargain. Finally, a few courts have refused to enforce contracts for the sale of goods at prices far in excess of their value on the ground that such contracts are unconscionable.

In addition to having legal value, a promisee's act or promise must be bargained for if it is to serve as consideration. This means that it must be the price that the promisor asked for in exchange for making his promise. Thus, past performances by a promisee cannot serve as consideration for a present promise by a promisor, because performance rendered in advance of a promise is, by definition, unbargained for. The common law courts adhered to the rule that "past consideration is no consideration" even in cases where the promisee's prior performance could be viewed as creating a moral duty on the part of the promisor to pay for that performance. Some modern courts, however, enforce promises based on moral obligations; a few states have passed statutes making such promises enforceable if they are made in writing.

In recent years, the courts have made a number of exceptions to the requirement of consideration. The most important of these is the doctrine of promissory estoppel, which originated in cases where courts sought to protect reliance on gratuitous promises. Promises to pay debts barred by bankruptcy discharge or by the applicable statute of limitations are enforced by many courts despite the absence of consideration. Promises of charitable subscriptions are also commonly enforced when the institution or organization to which the promise was made has acted in reliance on the promised gift.

PROBLEM CASES

1. Dr. Browning entered into a contract to sell his osteopathy practice to Dr. Johnson. Browning later changed his mind, however, and asked to be released from the contract. Johnson initially refused to do so, but after Browning offered to pay him $40,000 at a specified future date in exchange for the release, Johnson released him from the sale contract. Later, Browning filed suit for a declaratory judgment that he was not bound by his promise to pay Johnson the $40,000 on the ground that his promise was not supported by consideration. Was Johnson's cancellation of the contract consideration?

2. Omni Group, Inc., signed an earnest money agreement offering Mr. and Mrs. John Clark $2,000 per acre for a piece of property the Clarks owned, which was thought to contain about 59 acres. The agreement provided that Omni's obligation was subject to receipt of a satisfactory engineer's and architect's feasibility report assessing the property's development potential. The Clarks signed the earnest money agreement, but later refused to proceed with the sale. When Omni filed suit

for breach of contract, the Clarks argued that their promise to sell was unenforceable because Omni's promise to buy was illusory due to the fact that it was conditioned on a satisfactory feasibility report. Was Omni's promise illusory?

3. In 1971, the Sederlunds signed a "royalty pool" agreement covering land they owned in Brookfield Township, Michigan. The royalty pool was a device to spread among participants the benefits of discovery of oil or gas and the risk that no oil or gas would be discovered. Under the pool agreement, landowners agreed to contribute one half of all royalties they received from oil and gas production on their property to a common pool. Later, after oil was discovered on their land, the Sederlunds moved to have the agreement set aside, arguing that they had to contribute far more to the pool than their common share of the pool allowed them to withdraw from it. Are they bound by the terms of the agreement?

4. When Mademoiselle Fashions received clothing it had ordered from Buccaneer Sportswear, it was dissatisfied with the quality and condition of several items. In response to Mademoiselle's complaint, Buccaneer gave Mademoiselle a credit for several of the items. Buccaneer later sent Mademoiselle a bill for the amount owed for the shipment, less the agreed-on credit. Mademoiselle sent back a check for $11,520, the full face amount of invoice no. 6832, one of the three it had received with the goods. The check contained the following language: "Invoices 6832–6833 and 6508, this represents any and all debt paid in full." Buccaneer cashed the check, and when Mademoiselle refused to make any further payments, Buccaneer filed suit to recover the $3,633.29 due on the remaining invoices. Mademoiselle raised the defense of accord and satisfaction. Was the trial court's decision in Buccaneer's favor correct?

5. Roland and Leslie lived together for four years and had a child together. In June of 1983, Roland filed suit to evict Leslie from his house in Duxbury, Massachusetts and to obtain custody of their child. Leslie then filed a breach of contract action against Roland arguing that she had a right to a share of the property. In September of 1983, Leslie and Roland agreed to settle both actions. She and his child were to return to live with him and he was to support them. Roland also promised to pay her legal fees from both actions. Roland and Leslie later separated again, and he refused to pay her legal fees, arguing that his promise was not supported by consideration because Massachusetts does not recognize "palimony" actions by unmarried cohabitants. Is Roland right?

6. Marna Balin, who had suffered two automobile accidents in 1972, hired Norman Kallen, an attorney, to represent her. Kallen did not do much work on the cases and urged Balin to settle for $25,000. She became dissatisfied with his representation, and in 1974 she asked Samuel Delug, another attorney, to take over the cases and get her files from Kallen. Delug wrote and called Kallen several times, but Kallen refused to forward the files or sign a Substitution of Attorney form (things he was obligated to do by the California rules of professional conduct) because he was afraid Balin would not pay him for the work he had done. Only when Delug promised to give him 40 percent of his attorney's fee did Kallen forward the files and sign the form. Delug negotiated a settlement of $810,000, and the attorney's fees amounted to $324,000. When he refused to pay Kallen 40 percent, Kallen filed suit. Is Delug's promise enforceable?

7. The Larabees owned a farm in Dearborn County, Indiana, subject to a life estate held by Mrs. Larabee's mother. In the autumn of 1971, the Larabees gave their friends, the Booths, permission to build a summer cottage on the farm. Construction began in the spring of 1972. Shortly thereafter, the Booths asked if they could build a permanent home there, and Mrs. Larabee agreed. In September of 1972, she and her husband signed an agreement promising to convey a piece of the farm to the Booths on the expiration of Mrs. Larabee's mother's life estate. The agreement specifically provided that the land was to be conveyed for "no consideration." When the house was completed and Mrs. Larabee's mother had died, however, the Larabees refused to convey the land as promised. Is their promise to convey enforceable?

8. Moyer, a subcontractor, entered into a contract with Crookham, a general contractor, to do excavation and dirt work on a project to build a railroad extension for the Little Rock Port Authority. The Port Authority's Invitation to Bid required each bidder to inspect the job site and provided that bidders whose bids were accepted would not be relieved of any contract duties due to their failure to inspect. Moyer inspected the site and then submitted a bid, which was later accepted. Shortly after he commenced work, Moyer discovered that water would not drain from the ditches he dug due to clogged culverts. This caused his ditches to collapse, necessitating extra digging. He told Crookham that he would not continue work unless he received extra pay for redigging the ditches. Crookham later refused to pay the extra amount. Crookham argued its promise to pay extra was not supported by consideration. Was Crookham right?

9. T & S Brass, a plumbing fixture manufacturer, contracted with Pic-Air, Inc., for the purchase of 52,500 faucet handles to be used by T & S in its own production. The contract provided that time was of the essence and provided that Pic-Air would bear the expense of delivery. As the time for delivery approached, Pic-Air told T & S that it would not be able to deliver on time unless T & S agreed to pay to have the handles shipped by air freight. T & S agreed to pay the air freight, but in a later lawsuit argued that it was not bound by its promise. Was T & S right?

10. Sigler lived in Mariotte's home and paid rent to her from 1949 until 1977. During this period, Sigler and Mariotte were close companions and shared food expenses. In 1976, Mariotte was hospitalized and later entered a nursing home. Anxious for Mariotte to return home, Sigler told Mariotte's son that if Mariotte were released from the nursing home, she would take care of her at no charge. Because he felt that more than one person was needed to care for Mariotte, the son hired another woman to care for her full-time after she came home for $85 a week plus room and board. Sigler assisted the woman in taking care of Mariotte, and on December 21, 1977, she demanded compensation for taking care of Mariotte. Mariotte's son then agreed to pay for her room and board. On June 15, 1979, Mariotte signed a document prepared by Sigler directing the administrator of her estate to pay Sigler $85 per week, plus room and board, from August 1, 1976, for as long as Sigler continued to live with her and care for her. The payment was to be deferred until after Mariotte's death. Was the 1979 agreement enforceable?

CHAPTER 14

REALITY OF CONSENT

INTRODUCTION

In a complex economy that depends on planning for the future, it is crucial that the law can be counted on to enforce contracts. In some situations, however, there are compelling reasons for permitting people to escape or *avoid* their contracts. An agreement obtained by force, trickery, unfair persuasion, or error is not the product of mutual and voluntary consent. A person who has made an agreement under these circumstances will be able to avoid it, because his consent was not *real*.

Five doctrines that permit people to avoid their contracts because of the absence of real consent are discussed: misrepresentation, fraud, mistake, duress, and undue influence. Two doctrines that involve similar considerations, capacity and unconscionability, will be discussed in the Capacity to Contract chapter and the Illegality chapter.

Effect of Doctrines Discussed in This Chapter

Contracts that involve the circumstances discussed in this chapter are generally considered to be **voidable.** This means that the person whose consent was not real has the power to **rescind** (cancel) the contract. Upon rescission, the person who rescinds is entitled to the return of anything he gave the other party. By the same token, he must return anything that he has received from the other party.

Necessity for Prompt and Unequivocal Rescission

A person who wants to rescind a contract on one of the grounds discussed in this chapter must act promptly and unequivocally. He must avoid any behavior that would suggest that he affirms or **ratifies** the contract. Ratification of a voidable contract means that a person who had the right to rescind has elected not to do so. The effect of ratification is that he loses the right to rescind.

A person who has grounds to rescind a contract must object promptly upon learning the facts that give him the right to rescind and must clearly express his intent to cancel the contract. He should avoid unreasonable delay in notifying the other party of his rescission, because unreasonable delay communicates that he has ratified the contract. He should also avoid any conduct that would send a "mixed message," such as continuing to accept benefits from the other party or behaving in any other way that is inconsistent with his expressed intent to rescind.

Misrepresentation and Fraud

Nature of Misrepresentation

A *misrepresentation* is an assertion that is not in accord with the truth. When a person enters a contract because of his justifiable reliance on a misrepresentation about some important fact, the contract is voidable.

It is not necessary that the misrepresentation be intentionally deceptive. Misrepresentations can be either "innocent" (not intentionally deceptive) or "fraudulent" (made with knowledge of falsity and intent to deceive). A contract may be voidable even if the person making the misrepresentation believes in good faith that what he says is true. Either innocent misrepresentation or fraud gives the complaining party the right to rescind a contract.

Nature of Fraud

Fraud is the type of misrepresentation that is committed knowingly, with the intent to deceive. The legal term for this knowledge of falsity, which distinguishes fraud from innocent misrepresentation, is **scienter.** A misrepresentation is "knowingly" made if the defendant knew that his statement was false, if he knew that he did not have a basis for making the statement, or even if he made the statement without being confident that it was true. The intent to deceive can be inferred from the fact that the defendant knowingly made a misstatement of fact to a person who was likely to rely on it.

As is true for innocent misrepresentation, the contract remedy for fraudulent misrepresentation is rescission. The tort liability of a person who commits fraud is different from that of a person who commits innocent misrepresentation, however. A person who commits fraud may be liable for damages, possibly including punitive damages, for the tort of **deceit.**[1] As you will learn in following sections, innocent misrepresentation and fraud share a common core of elements.

Election of Remedies In some states, a person injured by fraud cannot rescind the contract *and* sue for damages for deceit; he must elect (choose) between these remedies. In other states, however, an injured party may

pursue both rescission and damage remedies, and does not have to elect between them. Under every state's law, however, a person injured by fraud in a contract for the *sale of goods* can both rescind the contract and sue for damages. This is made clear by section 2–721 of the Uniform Commercial Code, which specifically states that no election of remedies is required in contracts for the sale of goods.

Requirements for Rescission on the Ground of Misrepresentation

The fact that one of the parties has made an untrue assertion does not in itself make the contract voidable. Courts do not want to permit people who have exercised poor business judgment or poor common sense to avoid their contractual obligations, nor do they want to grant rescission of a contract when there have been only minor and unintentional misstatements of relatively unimportant details. A drastic remedy such as rescission should be used only when a person has been seriously misled about a fact important to the contract by someone he had the right to rely on. A person seeking to rescind a contract on the ground of innocent or fraudulent misrepresentation must be able to establish each of the following elements:

1. An untrue assertion of fact was made.
2. The fact asserted was material *or* the assertion was fraudulent.
3. The complaining party entered the contract because of his reliance on the assertion.
4. The reliance of the complaining party was reasonable.

In tort actions in which the plaintiff is seeking to recover damages for deceit, the plaintiff would have to establish a *fifth* element: injury. He would have to prove that he had suffered actual economic injury because of his reliance on the fraudulent assertion. In cases in which the injured person seeks only rescission of the contract, however, proof of economic injury usually is not required.

Untrue Assertion of Fact

To have misrepresentation, one of the parties must have made an untrue assertion of fact or engaged in some conduct that is the equivalent of an untrue assertion of

---

[1] The tort of deceit is discussed in the Intentional Torts chapter.

fact. The fact asserted must be a *past or existing fact*, as distinguished from a promise or prediction about some future happening.

The **concealment** of a fact through some active conduct intended to prevent the other party from discovering the fact is considered to be the equivalent of an assertion. Like a false statement of fact, concealment can be the basis for a claim of misrepresentation or fraud. For example, if Summers is offering his house for sale and paints the ceilings to conceal the fact that the roof leaks, his active concealment constitutes an assertion of fact. Under some circumstances, **nondisclosure** also can be the equivalent of an assertion of fact. Nondisclosure differs from concealment in that concealment involves the active hiding of a fact, while nondisclosure is the failure to offer information.

Problem Area: Nondisclosure Suppose you are a prospective home buyer who inspects a house for possible purchase. The seller of the house knows that there is a hidden but serious structural defect in the house that will cost approximately $30,000 to correct, but does not mention this to you. Neither you nor the professional inspector you hire to examine the house for defects observes any evidence of structural defects, and you contract to purchase the house based on your assumption that it is in good condition. You later learn about the existence of this defect. Do you have the right to rescind the contract? The issue raised by this problem is whether the seller's silence about the defect was misrepresentation. In other words, was his nondisclosure the equivalent of an assertion that the structural defect did not exist?

Under traditional contract law, the answer to this question probably would have been "no." Under the traditional view of nondisclosure, the circumstances under which the law required disclosure were very limited. (These are the first three circumstances described in the next section.) Mere silence on the part of a contracting party generally did not amount to misrepresentation. One reason for this treatment of nondisclosure was that, unlike concealment and outright statements of fact, which are active forms of misconduct, nondisclosure is passive. Fundamentally, though, the traditional view of nondisclosure expressed the highly individualistic philosophy that each contracting party is responsible for taking care of himself and is not his "brother's keeper."

In recent years, however, courts and legislatures have expanded the circumstances under which a person has

the duty to take affirmative steps to disclose relevant information. This is consistent with modern contract law's emphasis on influencing ethical standards of conduct and achieving fair results. Some duties of disclosure have been created by statutes, such as the Truth in Lending Act[2] and the federal securities laws,[3] but courts also have been increasingly active in expanding the duty to disclose. In addition to the circumstances in which federal or state statutes would require a contracting party to disclose facts, there are four circumstances in which most courts today require disclosure.

When Nondisclosure Is the Equivalent of an Assertion of Fact Under the circumstances listed below, the law requires individuals to disclose information material to a contract. In these situations, the person's failure to disclose a fact would be the equivalent of an assertion that the fact did not exist.

1. *Fiduciary relationship.* If a fiduciary relationship (a relationship of trust and confidence) exists between the parties to the contract, a party who knows of an important fact that the other person does not know about would have the duty to disclose it. This makes sense, because a person who has good reason to believe that the other party is looking out for his welfare will not approach the contract with the same degree of vigilance as the person who is dealing at arm's length with a stranger. This sort of duty to disclose would not apply to ordinary contracting parties who are bargaining at arm's length.

2. *Correcting "half-truths."* The saying that "a half-truth is a whole lie" recognizes that it is possible to create a very distorted impression in the mind of another person by revealing only part of the truth. The law has long held that when a person makes a statement about a situation, he has the duty to disclose any facts that would be necessary to correct a half-truth. For example, Carlson, a car salesman who is trying to sell a used car, knows that the previous owner of the car used it exclusively for drag racing on Sundays. If Carlson tells a customer that the previous owner of the car "drove it only on Sundays," he would have the legal duty to disclose the additional material fact that the car had been used exclusively for drag racing.

---

[2] See the Introduction to Credit and Secured Transactions chapter for a discussion of the Truth in Lending Act.

[3] These laws are discussed in the Securities Regulation chapter.

3. *Correcting statements made false by supervening events.* A person has the duty to disclose information that will be necessary to correct a previous statement that may have been true when made, but that has become false because of supervening events. For example, White, who wants to sell her house, tells a prospective purchaser truthfully that the roof of the house does not leak. Several days later, the roof leaks after a heavy storm. White has the legal duty to make the disclosure that is necessary to correct her previous statement.

4. *Good faith and fair dealing require correcting the other party's mistake about a basic assumption.* In the hypothetical case with which we began this discussion of nondisclosure—the case of the seller who failed to disclose the existence of a hidden structural defect in the house he was selling—the home buyer entered into the contract under the mistaken assumption that the house was free of structural defects. The *Restatement (Second) of Contracts* provides for a duty to disclose that would be applicable in this situation. Under section 161 of the *Restatement*, a person must disclose facts necessary to correct the other party's mistake about a basic assumption of the contract when nondisclosure amounts to a failure to act in good faith and in accordance with reasonable standards of fair dealing. Most states today apply a duty to disclose along these lines.

Note that this sort of duty to disclose has broader application than the first three circumstances described above, because it can apply even when the parties are dealing at arm's length and no partial disclosures have been made. Note also that this duty to disclose is intertwined with concepts of good faith and fair dealing. The *Restatement* does *not* say that a person who possesses information always has the obligation to educate the other party. Rather, the duty to speak arises only when failing to do so would constitute a failure to behave in a way that is in accord with prevailing concepts of good faith and reasonable standards of dealing. Nondisclosure is most likely to constitute a failure to act reasonably and in good faith when a party has access to information that is not readily available to the other party. In addition, sellers are more likely to be required to disclose information than are buyers.

Transactions involving the sale of real estate are among the most common situations in which this duty to disclose arises. Most states now hold that a seller who knows about a latent (hidden) defect that materially affects the value of the property he is selling has the obligation to speak up about this defect. *Reed v. King*, which follows, involves an interesting application of the duty to disclose in the context of a sale of real estate.

REED v. KING

193 Cal. Rptr. 130 (Cal. Ct. App. 1983)

Dorris Reed purchased a house from Robert King. Neither King nor his real estate agents told Reed that a woman and her four children had been murdered there 10 years earlier. Reed learned of the gruesome episode from a neighbor after the sale. She sued King and his real estate agents, seeking rescission of the contract and damages. The trial court dismissed Reed's complaint on the ground that it failed to state a claim. Reed appealed the dismissal.

Blease, Associate Justice. The critical question is: does the seller have the duty to disclose here? Resolution of this question depends on the materiality of the fact of the murders.

In general, a seller of real property has a duty to disclose where the seller knows of facts *materially* affecting the value or desirability of the property which are known or accessible only to him and also knows that such facts are not known to, or within the reach of the diligent attention and observation of the buyer.

Numerous cases have found nondisclosure of physical defects and legal impediments to the use of real property are material. However, to our knowledge, no prior real estate sale case has faced an issue of nondisclosure of the kind presented here. Should this variety of ill-repute be required to be disclosed? Is this a circumstance where nondisclosure of the fact amounts to a failure to act in good faith and in accordance with reasonable standards of fair dealing?

The paramount argument against an affirmative conclusion is if such an "irrational" consideration is permitted as a basis of rescission, the stability of all conveyances will be seriously undermined. Any fact that might disquiet the enjoyment of some segment of the buying public may be seized upon by a disgruntled purchaser to void a bargain. In our view, keeping this genie in the bottle is not as difficult a task as these arguments assume.

Reed alleges the fact of the murders has a quantifiable effect on the market value of the premises. If information known or accessible only to the seller has a significant and measurable effect on market value, and the seller is aware of this effect, we see no principled basis for making the duty to disclose turn upon the character of the information. Reputation and history can have a significant effect on the value of realty. "George Washington slept here" is worth something, however physically inconsequential that consideration may be. Ill-repute or "bad will" conversely may depress the value of property.

Whether Reed will be able to prove her allegation that the decade-old multiple murder has a significant effect on market value we cannot determine. If she is able to do so by competent evidence she is entitled to a favorable ruling on the issues of materiality and duty to disclose. Her demonstration of objective tangible harm would still the concern that permitting her to go forward will open the floodgates to rescission on subjective and idiosyncratic grounds.

Judgment reversed in favor of Reed, reinstating her action.

Problem Area: Statements of Opinion Although contract law traditionally has distinguished between assertions of *fact* and assertions of *opinion*, such a distinction is hard to maintain because an assertion of opinion *is* an assertion of fact—it is an assertion of fact about one's state of mind. Thus, if Johnson, a seller of an apartment building, tells Rice, a prospective buyer, that the electrical system is "good," Rice is entitled to conclude that Johnson is being truthful about his state of mind and that he knows no facts that are inconsistent with his statement.

There is an important distinction between a statement that communicates a person's knowledge and a statement that communicates only his uncertain belief about a fact or his personal judgment about such matters as quality or value, however. The latter sort of statement usually cannot be the basis of a misrepresentation claim because the person to whom such a statement of opinion is made is not justified in relying on it. This is especially true when the statement relates to something about which the parties have relatively equal knowledge and people's points of view are likely to differ. In such a case, each party is expected to form his own opinion. A classic

example of this sort of statement of opinion is a seller's "puff" (sales talk or general praise of an item being sold), such as "This suit will look terrific on you."

Even when the statement is clearly one of opinion, there are three situations in which the statement of opinion can be the basis of a misrepresentation claim because reliance is justifiable under the circumstances.[4] These include:

1. *Relationship of trust and confidence.* A person can be justified in relying on a statement of opinion if it is reasonable to do so because of a relationship of trust and confidence between him and the speaker. For example, if Madison, the longtime financial adviser of the elderly Holden, persuades Holden to invest her money in Madison's failing business by telling her that it is a wise investment, Holden would be justified in relying on Holden's statement of opinion.

2. *Relying party is unusually susceptible.* Reliance on a statement of opinion can be justifiable when the relying party is someone who is particularly susceptible

---

[4] *Restatement (Second) of Contracts* § 169.

to the particular type of misrepresentation involved. This sort of case would be likely to involve relying parties who are vulnerable to being misled because of some obvious disadvantage such as illiteracy or lack of intelligence or experience.

3. *Reliance on person who has superior skill or judgment.* Reliance on an assertion of opinion also can be justifiable when the relying party reasonably believes that the person on whose opinion he is relying has superior skill or judgment about the subject matter of the contract. This would apply when the opinion relates to some matter about which superior training or experience is necessary to form the opinion. For example, Buyer, who knows that Salesman is an experienced auto mechanic, would be justified in relying on Salesman's statement that a particular used car is "in A-1 condition."

Materiality

If the misrepresentation was innocent, the person seeking to rescind the contract must establish that the fact asserted was **material.** A fact will be considered to be material if it is likely to play a significant role in inducing a reasonable person to enter the contract or if the person asserting the fact knows that the other person is likely to rely on the fact. For example, Rogers, who is trying to sell his car to Ferguson and knows that Ferguson idolizes professional bowlers, tells Ferguson that a professional bowler once rode in the car. Relying on that representation, Ferguson buys the car. Although the fact Rogers asserted might not be important to most people, it would be material here because Rogers knew that his representation would be likely to induce Ferguson to enter the contract.

Even if the fact asserted was not material, the contract may be rescinded if the misrepresentation was *fraudulent.* The rationale for this rule is that a person who fraudulently misrepresents a fact, even one that is not material under the standards previously discussed, should not be able to profit from his intentionally deceptive conduct.

Actual Reliance

Reliance means that a person pursues some course of action because of his faith in an assertion made to him.

For misrepresentation to exist, there must have been a causal connection between the assertion and the complaining party's decision to enter the contract. If the complaining party knew that the assertion was false or was not aware that an assertion had been made, there has been no reliance.

Justifiable Reliance

Courts also scrutinize the reasonableness of the behavior of the complaining party by requiring that his reliance be *justifiable.* A person does not act justifiably if he relies on an assertion that is obviously false or not to be taken seriously.

Problem Area: The Relying Party's Failure to Investigate the Accuracy of an Assertion One problem involving the justifiable reliance element is determining the extent to which the relying party is responsible for investigating the accuracy of the statement on which he relies. Classical contract law held that a person who did not attempt to discover readily discoverable facts generally was not justified in relying on the other party's statements about them. For example, under traditional law, a person would not be entitled to rely on the other party's assertions about facts that are a matter of public record or that could be discovered through a reasonable inspection of available documents or records.

The extent of the responsibility placed on a relying party to conduct an independent investigation has declined in modern contract law, however. For example, section 172 of the *Restatement* states that the complaining party's fault in not knowing or discovering facts before entering the contract does not make his reliance unjustifiable unless the degree of his fault was so extreme as to amount to a failure to act in good faith and in accordance with reasonable standards of fair dealing. Recognizing that the traditional rule operated to encourage misrepresentation, courts in recent years have tended to decrease the responsibility of the relying party and to place a greater degree of accountability on the person who makes the assertion. The case of *Cousineau v. Walker*, which follows, is an excellent example of this trend.

COUSINEAU v. WALKER

613 P.2d 608 (Alaska Sup. Ct. 1980)

Devin and Joan Walker owned property in Eagle River, Alaska. In 1976, they listed the property for sale with a real estate broker. They signed a multiple listing agreement, which described the property as having 580 feet of highway frontage and stated, "ENGINEER REPORT SAYS OVER 1 MILLION IN GRAVEL ON PROP." A later listing contract signed with the same broker described the property as having 580 feet of highway frontage, but listed the gravel content as "minimum 80,000 cubic yds of gravel." An appraisal prepared to determine the property's value stated that it did not take any gravel into account, but described the ground as "all good gravel base."

Wayne Cousineau, a contractor who was also in the gravel extraction business, became aware of the property when he saw the multiple listing. After visiting the property with his real estate broker and discussing gravel extraction with Mr. Walker, Cousineau offered to purchase the property. He then attempted to determine the lot's road frontage, but was unsuccessful because the property was covered with snow. He was also unsuccessful in obtaining the engineer's report allegedly showing "over 1 million in gravel." Walker admitted at trial that he had never seen a copy of the report either. Nevertheless, the parties signed and consummated a contract of sale for the purchase price of $385,000. There was no reference to the amount of highway frontage in the purchase agreement.

After the sale was completed, Cousineau began developing the property and removing gravel. Cousineau learned that the description of highway frontage contained in the real estate listing was incorrect when a neighbor threatened to sue him for removing gravel from the neighbor's adjacent lot. A subsequent survey revealed that the highway frontage was 410 feet—not 580 feet, as advertised. At about the same time, the gravel ran out after Cousineau had removed only 6,000 cubic yards.

Cousineau stopped making payments and informed the Walkers of his intention to rescind the contract. Cousineau brought an action against the Walkers, seeking the return of his money. The trial court found for the Walkers, and Cousineau appealed.

Boochever, Justice.   An innocent misrepresentation may be the basis for rescinding a contract. There is no question that the statements made by Walker and his real estate agent in the multiple listing were false.

The bulk of the Walkers' brief is devoted to the argument that Cousineau's unquestioning reliance on Walker and his real estate agent was imprudent and unreasonable. Cousineau failed to obtain and review the engineer's report. He failed to obtain a survey or examine the plat available at the recorder's office. He failed to make calculations that would have revealed the true frontage of the lot. Although the property was covered with snow, the buyer, according to Walker, had ample time to inspect it. The buyer was an experienced businessman who frequently bought and sold real estate. Discrepancies existed in the various property descriptions which should have alerted Cousineau to potential problems. In short, the Walkers urge that the doctrine of *caveat emptor* precludes recovery.

There is a split of authority regarding a buyer's duty to investigate a vendor's fraudulent statements, but the prevailing trend is toward placing a minimal duty on a buyer. The recent draft of the *Restatement of Contracts* allows rescission for an innocent material misrepresentation unless a buyer's fault was so negligent as to amount to "a failure to act in good faith and in accordance with reasonable standards of fair dealing." We conclude that a purchaser of land may rely on material representations made by the seller and is not obligated to ascertain whether such representations are truthful. A buyer of land, relying on an innocent misrepresentation, is barred from recovery only if the buyer's acts in failing to discover defects were wholly irrational, preposterous, or in bad faith.

Although Cousineau's actions may well have exhibited poor judgment for an experienced businessman, they were not so unreasonable or preposterous in view of Walker's description of the property that recovery should be denied.

Judgment reversed in favor of Cousineau.

CONCEPT REVIEW

MISREPRESENTATION AND FRAUD

	Innocent Misrepresentation	Fraud
Remedy	Rescission	Rescission *or* action for damages

Elements	1. Untrue assertion of fact
	Includes:
	a. Statement of past or existing fact
	b. Concealment
	c. Nondisclosure if:
	  (1) Relationship of trust and confidence,
	  (2) Half-truth,
	  (3) Statement made false by supervening event, or
	  (4) Good faith and fair dealing require correcting party's mistake about basic assumption
	d. Statement of opinion if:
	  (1) Relationship of trust and confidence,
	  (2) Unusually susceptible party, or
	  (3) Person stating opinion has superior skill or judgment	

	2. Assertion relates to material fact	2. Assertion made with knowledge of falsity (*scienter*) and intent to deceive
	3. Actual reliance 4. Justifiable reliance	
		5. Economic loss (in action for damages)

MISTAKE

Nature of Mistake

Anyone who enters a contract does so on the basis of his understanding of the facts that are relevant to the contract. His decision about what he is willing to exchange with the other party is based on this understanding. If the parties are wrong about an important fact, the exchange that they make is likely to be quite different than what they contemplated when they entered the contract, and this difference will be due to simple error rather than to any external events such as an increase in market price. For example, Fox contracts to sell to Ward a half-carat stone, which both believe to be a tourmaline, at a price of $65. If they are wrong and the stone is actually a diamond worth at least $2,500, Fox will have suffered an unexpected loss and Ward will have reaped an unexpected gain. The contract would not have been made at a price of $65 if the parties' belief about the nature of the stone had been in accord with the facts. In such cases, the person adversely affected by the mistake can avoid the contract under the doctrine of mistake. The purpose of the doctrine of mistake is to prevent unexpected and unbargained-for losses that result when the parties are mistaken about a fact central to their contract.

What Is a Mistake? In ordinary conversation, we may use the term "mistake" to mean an error in judgment or an unfortunate act. In contract law, however, a mistake is a *belief about a fact* that is *not in accord with the truth.*[5] The erroneous belief forming the basis of a mistake case must relate to facts as they exist at the time the contract is created. An erroneous belief or prediction about facts that might occur in the future would not qualify as a mistake.

As in misrepresentation cases, the complaining party in a mistake case enters a contract because of a belief that is at variance with the actual facts. Mistake is unlike misrepresentation, however, in that the erroneous belief is not the result of the other party's untrue statements.

The *Wilkin v. 1st Source Bank* case illustrates the concept and effect of mistake in contract law.

---

[5] *Restatement (Second) of Contracts* § 151.

WILKIN v. 1ST SOURCE BANK

548 N.E.2d 170 (Ind. Ct. App. 1990)

Olga Mestrovic, the widow of internationally known sculptor and artist, Ivan Mestrovic, owned a large number of works of art created by her late husband. Mrs. Mestrovic died, leaving a will in which she directed that all the works of art created by her husband were to be sold and the proceeds distributed to surviving members of the Mestrovic family. Mrs. Mestrovic also owned real estate at the time of her death. 1st Source Bank, as the personal representative of Mrs. Mestrovic's estate, entered into a contract to sell this real estate to Terrence and Antoinette Wilkin. The purchase agreement provided that certain personal property on the premises would be sold to the Wilkins, too: specifically, the stove, refrigerator, dishwasher, drapes, curtains, sconces, and French doors in the attic.

After taking possession of the property, the Wilkins complained to the bank that the property was left in a cluttered condition and would require substantial cleaning effort. The trust officer of the bank offered the Wilkins two options: Either the bank would obtain a rubbish removal service to clean the property or the Wilkins could clean the property and keep any items of personal property they wanted. The Wilkins opted to clean the property themselves. At the time these arrangements were made, neither the bank nor the Wilkins suspected that any works of art remained on the premises.

During the clean-up efforts, the Wilkins found eight drawings apparently created by Ivan Mestrovic. They also found a plaster sculpture of the figure of Christ with three small children. The Wilkins claimed ownership of these works of art by virtue of their agreement with the bank. The probate court ruled that there was no agreement for the purchase of the artwork, and the Wilkins appealed.

Hoffman, Judge. Mutual assent is a prerequisite to the creation of a contract. Where both parties share a common assumption about a vital fact upon which they based their bargain, and that assumption is false, the transaction may be avoided if because of the mistake a quite different exchange of values occurs from the exchange of values contemplated by the parties. *J. Calamari & J. Perillo, The Law of Contracts* section 9–26 (1987).

The necessity of mutual assent is illustrated in the classic case of *Sherwood v. Walker* (1887). The owners of a blooded cow indicated to the purchaser that the cow was barren. The purchaser appeared to believe that the cow was barren. Consequently, a bargain was made to sell at a price per pound at which the cow would have brought approximately $80.00. Before delivery, it was discovered that the cow was with calf and that she was, therefore, worth from $750.00 to $1,000.00. The court ruled that the transaction was voidable: "[T]he mistake . . . went to the very nature of the thing. A barren cow is substantially a different creature than a breeding one."

Like the parties in *Sherwood*, the parties in the instant case shared a common presupposition as to the existence of certain facts which proved false. The bank and the Wilkins considered the real estate which the Wilkins had purchased to be cluttered with items of personal property variously characterized as "junk," "stuff," or "trash." Neither party suspected that works of art created by Ivan Mestrovic remained on the premises.

As in *Sherwood*, one party experienced an unexpected, unbargained-for gain while the other experienced an unexpected, unbargained-for loss. Because the bank and the Wilkins did not know that the eight drawings and the plaster sculpture were included in the items of personalty that cluttered the real property, the discovery of those works of art by the Wilkins was unexpected. The resultant gain to the Wilkins and loss to the Bank were not contemplated by the parties when the bank agreed that the Wilkins could clean the premises and keep such personal property as they wished.

The following commentary on *Sherwood* is equally applicable to the case at bar:

"Here the buyer sought to retain a gain that was produced, not by a subsequent change in circumstances, nor by the favorable resolution of known uncertainties when the contract was made, but by the presence of facts quite different from those on which the parties based their bargain." *Palmer, Mistake and Unjust Enrichment* 16–17 (1962).

The probate court properly concluded that there was no agreement for the purchase, sale, or other disposition of the eight drawings and plaster sculpture.

Judgment for 1st Source Bank affirmed.

Mistakes of Law

A number of the older mistake cases state that mistake about a principle of law will not justify rescission. The rationale for this view was that everyone was presumed to know the law. More modern cases, however, have granted relief even when the mistake is an erroneous belief about some aspect of law.

Negligence and the Right to Avoid on the Ground of Mistake

Courts sometimes state that relief will not be granted when a person's mistake was caused by his own negligence. However, a review of mistake cases reveals that courts have often granted rescission even when the mistaken party was somewhat negligent. Section 157 of the *Restatement (Second) of Contracts* focuses on the *degree* of a party's negligence in making the mistake. It states that a person's fault in failing to know or discover facts before entering the contract will not bar relief unless his fault amounted to a failure to act in good faith.

Effect of Mistake

The mere fact that the contracting parties have made a mistake is not, standing alone, a sufficient ground for avoidance of the contract. The right to avoid a contract because of mistake depends on several factors that are discussed in following sections. One important factor that affects the right to avoid is whether the mistake was made by just one of the parties (**unilateral mistake**) or by both parties (**mutual mistake**).

Mutual Mistake

A mutual mistake exists when both parties to the contract have erroneous assumptions about the same fact. A contract can be avoided on the ground of mutual mistake if the three following elements are present:

1. Both parties made a mistake as to a basic assumption on which the contract was made.
2. The mistake has a material effect on the agreed-upon exchange.
3. The party adversely affected by the mistake does not bear the risk of the mistake.[6]

Mistake about a Basic Assumption Even if the mistake is mutual, the adversely affected party will not have the right to avoid the contract unless the mistake concerns a *basic assumption* on which the contract was based. Assumptions about the identity, existence, quality, or quantity of the subject matter of the contract are among the basic assumptions on which contracts typically are founded. It is not necessary that the parties be consciously aware of the assumption; an assumption may be so basic that they take it for granted. For example, if Peterson contracts to buy a house from Tharp, it is likely that both of them assume at the time of contracting that the house is in existence and that it is legally permissible for the house to be used as a residence.

An assumption, even if shared by both parties, would not be considered a basic assumption if it concerns a matter that bears an indirect or collateral relationship to the subject matter of the contract. For example, mistakes about matters such as a party's financial ability or market conditions usually would not give rise to avoidance of the contract.

Material Effect on Agreed-Upon Exchange A person adversely affected by a mistake will be able to avoid a contract only if the mistake has a *material effect on the agreed-upon exchange*. It is not enough for the adversely affected person to show that the exchange is something different from what he expected. He must show that the imbalance caused by the mistake is so severe that it would be unfair for the law to require him to perform the contract. He will have a better chance of establishing this element if he can show not only that the contract is *less* desirable for him because of the mistake, but also that the other party has received an unbargained for advantage.

Adversely Affected Party Does Not Bear the Risk of Mistake Even if the first two elements are present, a party adversely affected by a mistake cannot avoid the contract if he is considered to bear the risk of mistake.[7] Courts have the power to allocate the risk of a mistake to the adversely affected person whenever it is reasonable under the circumstances to do so.

One situation in which an adversely affected person would bear the risk of mistake is when he has expressly contracted to do so. For example, if Buyer contracted to accept property "as is," he may be considered to have accepted the risk that his assumption about the quality of the property may be erroneous.

The adversely affected party also bears the risk of mistake when he contracts with *conscious awareness* that he is ignorant or has limited information about a fact—in other words, he *knows that he does not know* the true state of affairs about a particular fact, but he binds himself to perform anyway. Suppose someone gives you an old, locked safe. Without trying to open it, you sell it and "all of its contents" to one of your friends for $25. When your friend succeeds in opening the safe, he finds $10,000 in cash. In this case, you would not be able to rescind the contract because, in essence, you gambled on your limited knowledge . . . and lost.

Mutual Mistakes in Drafting Writings

Sometimes, mutual mistake takes the form of erroneous *expression* of an agreement, frequently caused by a clerical error in drafting or typing a contract, deed, or other

---

[6] *Restatement (Second) of Contracts* § 152.

[7] *Restatement (Second) of Contracts* § 154.

document. In such cases, the remedy is *reformation* of the writing rather than avoidance of the contract. Reformation means modification of the written instrument to express the agreement that the parties made but failed to express correctly. Suppose Arnold agrees to sell Barber a vacant lot next to Arnold's home. The vacant lot is "Lot 3, block 1"; Arnold's home is on "Lot 2, block 1." The person typing the contract strikes the wrong key, and the contract reads, "Lot 2, block 1." Neither Arnold nor Barber notices this error when they read and sign the contract, yet clearly they did not intend to have Arnold sell the lot on which his house stands. In such a case, a court will reform the contract to conform to Arnold and Baker's true agreement.

Unilateral Mistake

A unilateral mistake exists when only one of the parties makes a mistake about a basic assumption on which he made the contract. For example, Plummer contracts to buy from Taylor 25 shares of Worthright Enterprises, Inc., believing that he is buying 25 shares of the much more valuable Worthwrite Industries. Taylor is correct in his belief about the identity of the stock he is selling; only Plummer is mistaken in his assumption about the identity of the stock.

Courts are more likely to allow avoidance of a contract when both parties are mistaken than when only one is mistaken. The reason it is more difficult to avoid a contract in cases of unilateral mistake is that, in such cases, at least one party's assumption about the facts was correct, and allowing avoidance disappoints the reasonable expectations of that nonmistaken party.

A person who wants to avoid a contract because of unilateral mistake must establish the same elements discussed earlier that a person who wants to avoid for mutual mistake must establish. That is, he must show (1) that he made a mistake as to a basic assumption on which he entered the contract, (2) that the mistake had a material effect on the agreed exchange of performance, and (3) that he does not bear the risk of mistake. *In addition* to these elements, he must prove *either one* of the following elements to be able to avoid the contract:

1. The effect of the mistake was such that it would be unconscionable to enforce the contract, or

2. The other party caused the mistake or had reason to know of the mistake.[8]

Unconscionable to Enforce the Contract To meet this element, the mistaken party would have to show that the consequences of the mistake were such that it would be unreasonably harsh or oppressive to enforce the contract.[9] For example, Ace Electrical Company makes an error when preparing a bid that it submits to Gorge General Contracting. Without any reason to realize that a mistake has been made, Gorge accepts the bid. Ace might show that it would be unconscionable to enforce the contract by showing that not only will its profit margin not be what Ace contemplated when it made its offer, but also that it would suffer a grave loss by having to perform at the mistaken price. As you will read in the Illegality chapter, however, unconscionability is a flexible concept that depends heavily on the circumstances of an individual case. In the foregoing hypothetical, for example, it is less likely that enforcing the contract between Ace and Gorge would be unconscionable if Gorge had relied on Ace's bid, say, by preparing and submitting a bid of its own that incorporated Ace's bid.

Other Party Caused or Had Reason to Know of Mistake Courts permit avoidance in cases of unilateral mistake if the nonmistaken party caused the mistake, knew of the mistake, or even if the mistake was so obvious that the nonmistaken party had reason to realize that a mistake had been made. This is true even if enforcing the contract would not be so harsh as to be unconscionable. For example, if the mistake in Ace's bid was so obvious that Gorge knew about it when it accepted Ace's offer, Ace could avoid the contract.

The reasoning behind this rule is that the nonmistaken person could have prevented the loss by acting in good faith and informing the person in error that he had made a mistake. It also reflects the judgment that people should not take advantage of the mistakes of others.

---

[8] *Restatement (Second) of Contracts* § 153.

[9] The concept of unconscionability is developed more fully in the Illegality chapter.

CONCEPT REVIEW

AVOIDANCE ON THE GROUND OF MISTAKE

	Mutual Mistake	Unilateral Mistake
Description	Both parties mistaken about same fact	One party mistaken about fact
Elements	1. Mistake about basic assumption on which contract was made. 2. Material effect on agreed exchange. 3. Person adversely affected by mistake does not bear the risk of the mistake.	
		4. Effect of mistake is such that it would be unconscionable to enforce the contract or Nonmistaken party caused mistake or had reason to know of mistake

---

DURESS

Nature of Duress

Duress is wrongful coercion that induces a person to enter or modify a contract. One kind of duress is physical compulsion to enter a contract. For example, Thorp overpowers Grimes, grasps his hand, and forces him to sign a contract. This kind of duress is rare, but when it occurs, a court would find that the contract was **void**. A far more common type of duress occurs when a person is induced to enter a contract by a *threat* of physical, emotional, or economic harm. In these cases, the contract is considered **voidable** at the option of the victimized person. This is the form of duress addressed in this chapter.

The elements of duress have undergone dramatic changes. Classical contract law took a very narrow view of the type of coercion that constituted duress, limiting duress to threats of imprisonment or serious physical harm. Today, however, courts take a much broader view of the types of coercion that will constitute duress. For example, modern courts recognize that threats to a person's economic interests can be duress.

Elements of Duress

To rescind a contract because of duress, one must be able to establish the following elements:

1. The contract was induced by an improper threat and

2. The victim had no reasonable alternative but to enter the contract.[10]

Improper Threat   Every contract negotiation involves the implied threat that a person will not enter the contract unless his demands are met. This is not the type of threat that is considered to be duress. The threat must be one that the law would consider *improper*. A threat to commit a crime or a tort would clearly be improper, but many actions that are not torts or crimes can be considered to be an improper way of inducing a contract.

Under some circumstances, threats to institute legal actions can be considered improper threats that will constitute duress. A threat to file either a civil or a criminal suit without a legal basis for doing so would clearly be improper. What of a threat to file a well-founded lawsuit or prosecution? Generally, if there is a good faith dispute over a matter, a person's threat to file a lawsuit to resolve that dispute is *not* considered to be improper. Otherwise, every person who settled a suit out of court could later claim duress. However, if the threat to sue is made in bad faith and for a purpose unrelated to the issues in the lawsuit, the threat can be considered improper. In one case, for example, duress was found when a husband who was in the process of divorcing his wife threatened to sue for custody of their children—something he had

---

[10] *Restatement (Second) of Contracts* § 175.

the right to do—unless the wife transferred to him stock that she owned in his company.[11] Section 176 of the *Restatement (Second) of Contracts* takes the position that a threat to institute a criminal prosecution is always impermissible pressure to enter a contract, even if the person making the threat has good reason to believe that the other person has committed a crime.

The *Restatement* also provides that it is improper for a contracting party to make a threat that would constitute a breach of the duty of good faith and fair dealing under his contract with the person who is the recipient of the threat.[12] This provision is relevant to the many duress cases that arise in the context of coerced modifications of existing contracts or settlements of existing debts.

Victim Had No Reasonable Alternative   The person complaining of duress must be able to prove that the coercive nature of the improper threat was such that he had no reasonable alternative but to enter or modify the contract. Classical contract law applied an objective standard of coercion, which required that the degree of coercion exercised had to be sufficient to overcome the will of a person of ordinary courage. The more modern standard for coercion focuses on the alternatives open to the complaining party. For example, Barry, a traveling salesman, takes his car to Cheatum Motors for repair. Barry pays Cheatum the full amount previously agreed upon for the repair, but Cheatum refuses to return Barry's car to him unless Barry agrees to pay substantially more than the contract price for the repairs. Because of his urgent need for the return of his car, Barry agrees to do this. In this case, Barry technically had the alternative of filing a legal action to recover his car. However, this would not be a *reasonable alternative* for someone who needs the car urgently because of the time, expense, and uncertainty involved in pursuing a lawsuit. Thus, Barry could avoid his agreement to pay more money under a theory of duress.

Problem Area: Economic Duress   Today, the doctrine of duress is often applied in a business context. **Economic duress,** or **business compulsion,** are terms commonly used to describe situations in which one person induces the formation or modification of a contract by threatening another person's economic interests. A common coercive strategy is to threaten to breach the contract unless the other party agrees to modify its terms. For example, Moore, who has contracted to sell goods to Stephens, knows that Stephens needs timely delivery of the goods. Moore threatens to withhold delivery unless Stephens agrees to pay a higher price. Another common situation involving economic duress occurs when one of the parties offers a disproportionately small amount of money in settlement of a debt and refuses to pay more. Such a strategy exerts great economic pressure on a creditor who is in a desperate financial situation to accept the settlement because he cannot afford the time and expense of bringing a lawsuit.

Classical contract law did not recognize economic duress because this type of hard bargaining was considered neither improper nor coercive. After all, the victim of the sorts of economic pressure described above had at least the theoretical right to file a lawsuit to enforce his rights under the contract. Modern courts recognize that improper economic pressure can prevent a resulting contract or contract modification from being truly voluntary, and the concept of economic duress is well accepted today. Even in recent cases, however, it is not always clear how much hard bargaining is tolerated. *Rich & Whillock, Inc. v. Ashton Development, Inc.,* is a good example of hard bargaining that went too far.

---

[11] *Link v. Link,* 179 S.E.2d 697 (1971).

[12] *Restatement (Second) of Contracts* § 176.

RICH & WHILLOCK, INC. v. ASHTON DEVELOPMENT, INC.

204 Cal. Rptr. 86 (Cal. Ct. App. 1984)

Ashton Development, acting through its general contractor, Bob Britton, hired Jim Rich and Greg Whillock, subcontractors doing business as Rich & Whillock, Inc., to do grading and excavating work for $112,990 on one of Ashton's construction projects. After a month's work, Rich & Whillock encountered rock on the project site. Britton and Ashton's president agreed that the rock would have to be blasted and that this would involve extra costs since the original contract between Ashton and Rich & Whillock specified that any rock encountered would be considered an extra. Britton directed Rich & Whillock to go ahead with the blasting and bill for the extra cost. Rich & Whillock did so, submitting separate invoices for the regular contract work and the extra blasting work and receiving payment every two weeks.

After completing the work and receiving payments totalling over $190,000, Rich & Whillock submitted a final billing for an additional $72,286.45. This time Britton refused to pay, stating that he and Ashton's president had no money left to pay the final billing. Whillock told Britton that Rich & Whillock would "go broke" without this final payment because it was a new business with rented equipment and numerous subcontractors waiting to be paid. In response, Britton replied that he and Ashton would pay $50,000 or nothing, and Rich & Whillock could sue for the full amount if unsatisfied with the compromise.

The next month, Britton presented Rich with an agreement for a final compromise payment of $50,000, stating, "I have a check for you, and just take it or leave it, this is all you get. If you don't want this, you have got to sue me." Rich then signed the settlement agreement and received a $25,000 check after telling Britton the agreement was "blackmail" and he was signing it only because he had to in order to survive. Rich & Whillock later signed a release form and received a second check for $25,000. Several months afterward, however, they filed this action for breach of contract against Ashton and Bob Britton. The trial court found that the settlement agreement and release were unenforceable due to economic duress and entered judgment in favor of Rich & Whillock for the $22,286.45 balance due under the contract. Ashton and Britton appealed this judgment.

Wiener, Associate Judge. Economic duress may come into play upon the doing of a wrongful act which is sufficiently coercive to cause a reasonably prudent person faced with no reasonable alternative to succumb to the perpetrator's pressure. The assertion of a claim known to be false or a bad faith threat to breach a contract or to withhold a payment may constitute a wrongful act for purposes of the economic duress doctrine.

The underlying concern of the economic duress doctrine is the enforcement in the marketplace of certain minimal standards of business ethics. Hard bargaining, "efficient" breaches, and reasonable settlements of good faith disputes are all acceptable, even desirable, in our economic system. That system can be viewed as a game in which everybody wins, to one degree or another, so long as everyone plays by the common rules. Those rules are not limited to precepts of rationality and self-interest. They include equitable notions of fairness and propriety which preclude the wrongful exploitation of business exigencies to obtain disproportionate exchanges of value. Such exchanges make a mockery of freedom of contract and undermine the proper functioning of our economic system. The economic duress doctrine serves as a last resort to correct these aberrations when conventional alternatives and remedies are unavailing.

Here, Britton and Ashton acted in bad faith when they refused to pay Rich & Whillock's final billing and offered instead to pay a compromise amount. At the time of their bad faith breach and settlement offer, Britton, and through him, Ashton, knew Rich & Whillock was a new company overextended to creditors and subcontractors and faced with imminent bankruptcy if not paid its final billing. Whillock and Rich strenuously protested these coercive tactics, and succumbed to them only to avoid economic disaster to themselves and the adverse ripple effects of their bankruptcy on those to whom they were indebted. Under these circumstances, the trial court's finding that the agreement and release were the product of economic duress is consistent with legal principles and supported by substantial evidence.

Judgment for Rich & Whillock affirmed.

UNDUE INFLUENCE

Nature of Undue Influence

Undue influence is unfair persuasion. Like duress, undue influence involves wrongful pressure exerted on a person during the bargaining process. In undue influence, however, the pressure is exerted through *persuasion* rather than through coercion. The doctrine of undue influence was developed to give relief to persons who are unfairly persuaded to enter a contract while in a position of weakness that makes them particularly vulnerable to being preyed upon by those they trust or fear. Undue influence is not a tort, so the only remedy is rescission of the contract. A large proportion of undue influence cases arise after the death of the person who has been the subject of undue influence, when his relatives seek to set aside that person's contracts or wills.

Determining Undue Influence   All contracts are based on persuasion. There is no precise dividing line between permissible persuasion and impermissible persuasion. Nevertheless, several hallmarks of undue influence cases can be identified. Undue influence cases normally involve the following elements:

1. The relationship between the parties is either one of trust and confidence or one in which the person exercising the persuasion dominates the person being persuaded, and
2. The persuasion is unfair. [13]

Relation between the Parties   In normal bargaining situations, individuals who have capacity to contract are expected to be able to fend for themselves, resist the persuasion of others, and make their own choices about whether to enter a contract. In undue influence cases,

however, this normal expectation is not realistic. Undue influence cases involve people who, though they have capacity to enter a contract, are in a position of particular vulnerability in relationship to the other party to the contract. This relationship can be one of trust and confidence, in which the person being influenced justifiably believes that the other party is looking out for his interests, or at least that he would not do anything contrary to his welfare. Examples of such relationships would include parent and child, husband and wife, or lawyer and client.

The relationship also can be one in which one of the parties holds dominant psychological power that is not derived from a confidential relationship. For example, Royce, an elderly man, is dependent on his housekeeper, Smith, to care for him. Smith persuades Royce to withdraw most of his life savings from the bank and make an interest-free loan to her. If the persuasion Smith used was unfair, the transaction could be avoided because of undue influence.

Unfair Persuasion   The mere existence of a close or dependent relationship between the parties that results in economic advantage to one of them is not sufficient for undue influence. It must also appear that the weaker person entered the contract because he was subjected to unfair methods of persuasion. In determining this, a court will look at all of the surrounding facts and circumstances. Was the person isolated and hurried into the contract, or did he have access to outsiders for advice and time to consider his alternatives? Was the contract he entered a reasonably fair one that he might have entered voluntarily, or was it so lopsided and unfair that one could infer that the person probably would not have entered it unless he had been unduly influenced by the other party? In *Odorizzi v. Bloomfield School District*, which follows, the court discusses the factors to be considered in determining whether the line between permissible and impermissible persuasion has been crossed.

---

[13] *Restatement (Second) of Contracts* § 177.

ODORIZZI v. BLOOMFIELD SCHOOL DISTRICT

54 Cal. Rptr. 533 (Cal. Dist. Ct. 1966)

Donald Odorizzi was an elementary school teacher employed by the Bloomfield School District. He was arrested on criminal charges of homosexual activity. After having been arrested, questioned by police, booked, and released on bail, and going 40 hours without sleep, he was visited in his home by the superintendent of the school district and the principal of his school. They told him that they were trying to help him and that they had his best interests at heart. They advised him to resign immediately, stating that there was no time to consult an attorney. They said that if he did not resign immediately, the district would dismiss him and publicize the proceedings, but that, if he resigned at once, the incident would not be publicized and would not jeopardize his chances of securing employment as a teacher elsewhere. Odorizzi gave them a written letter of resignation, which they accepted.

The criminal charges against Odorizzi were later dismissed, and he sought to resume his employment with the district. When the district refused to reinstate him, he attempted to rescind his letter of resignation on several grounds, including undue influence. (He also alleged duress, but the facts of his case did not constitute duress under California law.) His complaint was dismissed, and he appealed.

Fleming, Justice.   In essence, undue influence involves the use of excessive pressure applied by a dominant subject to a servient object. In combination, the elements of undue susceptibility in the servient person and excessive pressure by the dominating person make the latter's influence undue. Undue susceptibility may consist of weakness which need not be longlasting nor wholly incapacitating, but may be merely a lack of full vigor due to age, physical condition, emotional anguish, or a combination of such factors. In the present case, Odorizzi has pleaded that such weakness at the time he signed his resignation prevented him from freely and competently applying his judgment to the problem before him. He declares he was under severe mental and emotional strain at the time. It is possible that exhaustion and emotional turmoil may incapacitate a person from exercising his judgment.

Overpersuasion is generally accompanied by certain characteristics which tend to create a pattern. The pattern usually involves several of the following elements: (1) discussion of the transaction at an unusual or inappropriate time, (2) consummation of the transaction in an unusual place, (3) insistent demand that the business be finished at once, (4) extreme emphasis on untoward consequences of delay, (5) the use of multiple persuaders by the dominant side against a single servient party, (6) absence of third-party advisers to the servient party, (7) statements that there is no time to consult financial advisers or attorneys.

The difference between legitimate persuasion and excessive pressure rests to a considerable extent in the manner in which the parties go about their business. For example, if a day or two after Odorizzi's release on bail the superintendent of the school district had called him into his office during business hours and directed his attention to those provisions of the Education Code compelling his leave of absence and authorizing his suspension on the filing of written charges, had told him that the district contemplated filing written charges against him, had pointed out the alternative of resignation available to him, had informed him he was free to consult counsel or any adviser he wished and to consider the matter overnight and return with his decision the next day, it is extremely unlikely that any complaint about the use of excessive pressure could ever have been made against the school district. Rather, the representatives of the school board undertook to achieve their objective by overpersuasion and imposition to secure Odorizzi's signature but not his consent to his resignation through a high-pressure carrot-and-stick technique. Odorizzi has stated sufficient facts to put in issue the question whether his free will had been overborne by the district at a time when he was unable to function in a normal manner.

Judgment reversed in favor of Odorizzi.

CONCEPT REVIEW

WRONGFUL PRESSURE IN THE BARGAINING PROCESS

	Duress	Undue Influence
Nature of Pressure	Coercion	Unfair persuasion of susceptible individual
Elements	1. Contract induced by improper threat 2. Threat leaves party no reasonable alternative but to enter or modify contract	1. Relationship of trust and confidence or dominance 2. Unfair persuasion

ETHICAL AND PUBLIC POLICY CONCERNS

1. You read that modern contract law has expanded the circumstances under which a contracting party has the duty to disclose facts material to the contract. Keep in mind that the facts that he is required to disclose would almost always harm his bargaining position—otherwise he would have been only too happy to have volunteered the information. What are some ethical and public policy justifications for requiring an individual to volunteer information that is contrary to his interests?

2. Do you think the legal rules applied today regarding misrepresentation and duress encourage a higher standard of ethical dealing than did the legal rules applicable under classical contract law? Why or why not?

3. In this chapter you learned a few of the circumstances under which a contracting party owes a higher duty of conduct to someone with whom he is in a relationship of trust and confidence than he would owe to individuals with whom he stood in an arm's-length relationship. What is the justification for requiring a higher standard of ethical dealing in such relationships? Would you favor the law's imposing the same high standards of conduct in relation to the rest of the world? Why or why not?

SUMMARY

The doctrines discussed in this chapter involve situations in which people have the ability to avoid contractual obligations because their consent was either based on a distorted impression of important facts or extorted through unscrupulous means. Generally, contracts induced by misrepresentation, fraud, mistake, duress, or undue influence are voidable. To take advantage of this right to avoid a contract, the complaining party must disaffirm the contract promptly and unequivocally. If he does not, he will be deemed to have ratified the contract, the effect of that is to surrender his right to avoid the contract.

Misrepresentation is an assertion about a fact material to a contract that is not in accordance with the truth and upon which the other party justifiably relies. Misrepresentation can be either innocent or fraudulent, depending on the knowledge and intent of the person making the misrepresentation. Fraud is misrepresentation knowingly made (*scienter*) with intent to deceive. Fraud may lead to either rescission or liability for the tort of deceit. The remedy for innocent misrepresentation is rescission.

A person seeking to prove misrepresentation must prove that there had been an untrue assertion of past or existing fact. Concealment of a material fact is the equivalent of an assertion of fact. Although traditional law normally held that a person's mere silence was not misrepresentation, modern law has created duties of disclosure in a broadening range of situations. In such a situation, nondisclosure can be the equivalent of an assertion of fact. Although statements of opinion, especially those classified as "sales talk" or "puffing," may not be considered an assertion of fact on which a person is justified in relying, modern contract law has developed a variety of situations in which reliance on a statement of opinion could permit a party to avoid a contract.

The untrue assertion must be either fraudulent or material. The person seeking a remedy for fraud or misrepresentation must have relied on the assertion, and his reliance must have been reasonable. Modern contract law has reduced the responsibility of the relying party to investigate the truth of assertions made to him. Under modern law, his fault in failing to discover the truth will not prevent rescission unless he failed to comply with the duty of good faith and with reasonable standards of commercial dealing. To recover damages for fraud, the plaintiff must be able to prove economic loss resulting from the fraud.

Mistake is an erroneous belief about some fact that exists at the time of formation of the contract. Mistake must be distinguished from ignorance, limited knowledge, or poor judgment. One who enters a contract knowing that he is ignorant or has limited knowledge about a material fact relating to the contract cannot later escape the contract by claiming mistake. However, there are circumstances under which the courts will relieve a party of a contractual obligation on the ground of mistake. In determining whether to grant relief in the form of rescission or reformation, courts distinguish between mutual mistakes and unilateral mistakes. If both parties are mistaken about a material fact (mutual mistake), courts will allow avoidance of the contract if the mistake relates to a fact that was a basic assumption on which the contract was made, the fact was material, and the person adversely affected by the mistake does not bear the risk of the mistake. If only one of the parties is mistaken (unilateral mistake), the person seeking avoidance must prove, *in addition to* the elements of mutual mistake, that the consequences of the mistake are such that it would be unconscionable to enforce the contract *or* that the other party caused or had reason to know about his mistake.

Though courts have often said that no relief will be granted where the mistake flows from a party's own negligence, in practice, they have granted rescission or reformation in cases involving some negligence on the part of mistaken parties. Mistakes in drafting documents will be corrected through the remedy of reformation.

Duress is the exertion of wrongful coercion that induces another person to enter a contract. To constitute duress, the threat must be one that the law considers improper. Threats to commit a tort or a crime, file an unfounded criminal or civil lawsuit, or breach a contract without justification are all considered to be improper and can be the basis for a claim of duress. Sometimes, threatening to do an act that one has the right to do can be considered improper if the threat is made in bad faith, for an ulterior motive. The degree of coercion must have been such that it left the wronged party no reasonable alternative but to consent to the contract. In recent decades, courts have been much more willing to recognize threats to economic interests as coercive.

Undue influence is unfair persuasion of a person by one who stands in a relationship of trust and confidence or domination with that person. If such a relationship exists between the parties and the stronger one has used his position to effect a transaction by which he benefits at the expense of the weaker one, the courts will hold the transaction voidable on the ground of undue influence.

PROBLEM CASES

1. King Chevrolet provided a 1982 Chevrolet Cavalier to one of its salesmen, Stein. During the eight months Stein drove the car, it was repaired or adjusted 10 times. There were repairs to the carburetor, choke, speedometer, door moldings, seat belt buzzer alarm, and spark plugs as well as a complete paint job. Of the 36 demonstrators Stein had driven over the years as a car salesman, this was the worst. Stein finally complained to the service department about the car and asked Lewis, King Chevrolet's sales manager, if he could have another demonstrator because his car was so unreliable. Not long afterward, Muzelak, who had purchased her previous car from Lewis, contacted Lewis about buying a new car. Lewis told her that the "right car for her" was the 1982 Chevrolet Cavalier demonstrator that Stein had used. Lewis did tell Muzelak that the car was a demonstrator, but he did not mention any of the previous repair problems with the car. (Stein later testified that Lewis told him it took someone with his sales ability to "get rid of" that car.) Muzelak bought the car. Over the course of the next eight months, Muzelak's car was in King Chevrolet's service department for repairs 13 times. Some of the problems were never corrected. The car was so unreliable that Muzelak did not drive it after the first eight months of use. Does Muzelak have grounds for an action for fraud?

2. On May 17, Cobaugh was playing in the East End Open Golf Tournament. When he arrived at the ninth tee, he found a new Chevrolet Beretta, together with signs which proclaimed: "HOLE-IN-ONE Wins this 1988 Chevrolet Beretta GT Courtesy of KLICK-LEWIS Buick Chevy Pontiac $49.00 OVER FACTORY INVOICE in Palmyra." Cobaugh aced the ninth hole and attempted to claim his prize. Klick-Lewis refused to deliver the car, however. Klick-Lewis had offered the car as a prize for a charity golf tournament sponsored by the Hershey-Palmyra Sertoma Club two days earlier and had neglected to remove the car and signs prior to Cobaugh's hole-in-one. Cobaugh sued to compel delivery of the car. Would the doctrine of mistake provide a ground for Klick-Lewis to avoid the contract?

3. West Branch Land Co. owned a tract of land, which it listed for sale. The listing that was published in the local multiple-listing service listing sheet and distributed to all subscribing real estate agencies described the property as being "zoned multi for 35 townhouses" when in fact it was really zoned for only 30. Acleson, a licensed real estate broker, received a copy of the listing and, after calculating the costs per unit on the basis of 35 units, submitted an offer to purchase the property. The parties ultimately contracted for the sale of the property for $65,000. The final contract made no mention of the acreage of the land or of its zoning status. Acleson could have determined the true acreage and zoning status by checking the plat map that was available at the local city planner's office. Almost two years after the sale, Acleson learned that the property was really zoned for only 30 units. Will Acleson's failure to investigate the zoning of the land prevent him from obtaining a remedy for misrepresentation or fraud?

4. For many years, Briggs had been Smoker's attorney. In 1970, Smoker executed a will that Briggs had prepared. The will named Briggs as attorney for the estate and provided for payment of $1,000 to Briggs as well as payment of all of Briggs's son's college and graduate educational expenses. Six years later, in November of 1976, Smoker signed documents again prepared by Briggs. In these documents, she stated that she wanted Briggs to be appointed as her guardian if she should need one, agreed to pay Briggs $10,000 for legal services and "kindnesses" that he had rendered to her in the past and might render her until her death, and executed a check to pay for those services. At the time, Smoker was a diabetic and suffered periods of blackouts when she did not know what she was doing. Shortly thereafter, she was hospitalized for insulin imbalance and Briggs had himself appointed as Smoker's guardian. When her physical condition improved, she stated that she had no memory of the documents she had signed in November and sought to rescind them on the ground of undue influence. Will she be successful?

5. Mullan had been a teacher at Bishop Moore School for 25 years. He had a written employment contract that covered the academic year 1986–87 and that permitted termination during that time only for good cause as described in the contract. In the fall of 1986, Mullan's principal, Massaro, told Mullan that he was being terminated because of an accusation that he had hit a student while disciplining him. When Mullan protested, Massaro told him that he (Mullan) could resign with compensation or be fired without being paid, but that

either way, Mullan was "gone." Massaro presented Mullan with a typed resignation, which Mullan signed. Mullan denied hitting the student. He filed suit in which he claimed that his resignation was procured by duress. Are the elements of duress present here?

6. Boskett, a part-time coin dealer, paid $450 for a dime purportedly minted in 1916 at Denver and two additional coins of relatively small value. After carefully examining the dime, Beachcomber Coins, a retail coin dealer, bought the coin from Boskett for $500. Beachcomber then received an offer from a third party to purchase the dime for $700, subject to certification of its genuineness from the American Numismatic Society. That organization labeled the coin a counterfeit. Can Beachcomber rescind the contract with Boskett on the ground of mistake?

7. Eikill and Schilling owned a tract of land, which they listed for sale. The listing agreement stated that the property was zoned M-1 (industrial). Newspaper advertisements described the property as commercial property. Gartner expressed his interest in buying the land for investment or speculation. He asked Eikill and Schilling's real estate agent how the property was zoned, and the agent responded that it was zoned M-1, industrial, which was commercial, or "better than commercial." Gartner did not ask specifically whether the property was available for development, and the real estate agent made no representation about that. In fact, a rezoning decision by the City Council some years before Eikill and Schilling bought the land had imposed a restriction allowing only one building ever to be built on the land. The one permitted building had been built years before the land in question was sold to Eikill and Schilling. Thus, while it was true that the land was zoned M-1, it could not be used for any commercial or industrial purpose because no additional structure could be built on the property. Eikill, Schilling, and Gartner were all completely unaware of this restriction. Gartner contracted to purchase the land for $40,000. He learned of the one-building restriction a year later. Gartner then sent Eikill and Schilling a letter demanding cancellation of the sale. Does he have the right to avoid the contract on the ground of mutual mistake?

8. Robert and Wendy Pfister asked Foster & Marshall, a stock brokerage firm, to evaluate some stocks that they owned. One of these stocks was 100 shares of Tracor Computing Corporation. The stock was no longer traded on the New York Stock Exchange. The Pfisters did not know the value of the stock, but they believed it to be of little value. They were surprised when Foster & Marshall told them that the stock was trading at $49.50 under its new name, Continuum Co., Inc., so that the value of the Pfisters' stock was $4,950. They asked Foster & Marshall to recheck the figures and brought their stock certificates in for verification. Based on Foster & Marshall's reassurances that they owned 100 shares of Continuum and that these were worth $4,950, the Pfisters sold the stock to Foster & Marshall. As a result of receiving this money for the stock, the Pfisters made a commitment to build a new home, which before the sale had been a "borderline decision." A year after the transaction, Foster & Marshall discovered that the Tracor Computing stock had been exchanged for Continuum stock at a 10-to-1 ratio and that the Pfisters had owned only 10 shares of Continuum. Foster & Marshall claimed relief under the doctrine of mistake and sued the Pfisters to recover the $4,466.25 it had overpaid them. Will Foster & Marshall win?

9. Reilly, who was interested in purchasing purebred Arabian horses of the Egyptian strain, approached Forbis, who owned and operated a breeding farm. Forbis had been in the business of breeding Arabian horses for 25 years and had published several books and numerous magazine articles on Arabian horses. Reilly visited Forbis's farm to examine a broodmare called Il Shirin. Il Shirin had produced one colt previously and was at that time in foal with another. During this visit, Forbis allegedly stated that Il Shirin was very reasonably priced and that she was "a good mare to start a breeding program with." Reilly bought Il Shirin for $30,000. After the sale, Il Shirin lost the foal she was carrying and despite numerous attempts to breed her, she never conceived again. Reilly sues Forbis for rescission and damages on the ground of fraud. What result?

10. Wurtz owned a hotel, which Fleishman wanted to purchase. For tax reasons, Wurtz wanted to exchange the property for real estate rather than cash. After long negotiations, they agreed that Fleishman would buy a McDonald's restaurant in New Mexico and a warehouse in Wisconsin to exchange for Wurtz's hotel. Fleishman made commitments to purchase these properties and spent substantial sums for architectural studies, title investigation, and legal fees related to the hotel. The night before the closing, Wurtz threatened to back out of the deal unless Fleishman agreed to pay him $50,000 extra. Fleishman feared bankruptcy if the deal fell through and offered Wurtz stock worth $47,000. After the closing, Fleishman refused to transfer the promised stock, however, claiming economic duress. Wurtz sued to get the stock. Will Wurtz win?

11. The Mancinis were interested in buying the Morrows' house. The first time they inspected the house, they noticed a musty odor in the basement. However, they could not see any water stains on either the floor or walls of the basement because most of the floor was covered by a large area rug. There also were eight large posters on the basement walls, and numerous large boxes of ceiling tiles were lined along the perimeter of the basement floor. They inspected the garage and found it to be in a cluttered condition. In addition, a paneled wall was obscured by pool equipment hung on the wall and access was blocked by a work bench. The next day, the Mancinis signed a contract to buy the house. They asked several times to inspect it again, but were only permitted one further inspection before the final consummation of the sale. They did not notice anything new at this inspection. After buying the house, however, the Mancinis soon discovered that the basement had had severe water damage, that it became inundated by six inches of water following a normal rainfall, and that the plywood paneling on the wall of the garage concealed a cracked and bulging wall that would have alerted the buyers to a structural defect present there. The Mancinis claim that the Morrows committed fraud. Did they?

CHAPTER 15

CAPACITY TO CONTRACT

INTRODUCTION

One of the major justifications for enforcing a contract is that the parties *voluntarily consented* to be bound by it. It follows, then, that a person must have the *ability* to give consent before he can be legally bound to an agreement. For truly voluntary agreements to exist, this ability to give consent must involve more than the mere physical ability to say yes or shake hands or sign one's name. Rather, the person's maturity and mental ability must be such that it is fair to presume that he is capable of representing his own interests effectively. This concept is embodied in the legal term **capacity.**

Capacity means the ability to incur legal obligations and acquire legal rights. Today, the primary classes of people who are considered to lack capacity are minors (who, in legal terms, are known as *infants*), persons suffering from mental illnesses or defects, and intoxicated persons.[1] Contract law gives them the right to *avoid* (escape) contracts that they enter during incapacity. This rule provides a means of protecting people who, because of mental impairment, intoxication, or youth and inexperience, are disadvantaged in the normal give and take of the bargaining process.

---

[1] In times past, married women, convicts, and aliens were also among the classes of persons who lacked capacity to contract. These limitations on capacity have been removed by statute and court rule, however.

Usually, lack of capacity to contract comes up in court in one of two ways. In some cases, it is asserted by a plaintiff as the basis of a lawsuit for the money or other benefits that he gave the other party under their contract. In others, it arises as a defense to the enforcement of an contract when the defendant is the party who lacked capacity. The responsibility for alleging and proving incapacity is placed on the person who bases his claim or defense on his lack of capacity.

Degrees of Capacity

There are varying degrees of contractual capacity. It might be helpful to visualize capacity on a continuum like the one shown in Figure 1. The validity of a contract will depend on the degree to which the contracting parties have capacity to contract. At one end of the continuum, both parties have full capacity to contract. Provided that the other requirements of a valid contract are met, the contract will be valid. At the other end of the continuum, one or more of the parties completely lacks capacity to contract because at the time the agreement was made either (1) a court had already **adjudicated** (adjudged or decreed) him to be mentally incompetent or (2) he was so impaired that he could not even manifest assent (for example, he was comatose or unconscious). In such a case, the contract is considered to be *void*. In cases in the middle, in which one or more of the parties

FIGURE 1   Capacity to Contract

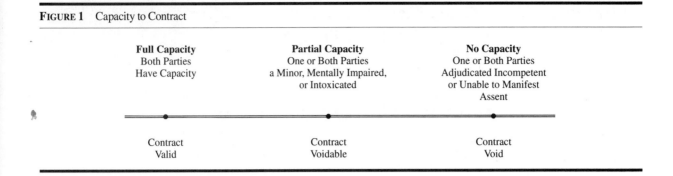

Full Capacity	Partial Capacity	No Capacity
Both Parties Have Capacity	One or Both Parties a Minor, Mentally Impaired, or Intoxicated	One or Both Parties Adjudicated Incompetent or Unable to Manifest Assent
Contract Valid	Contract Voidable	Contract Void

was younger than the age of majority, mentally incapacitated (but had not yet been adjudicated incompetent at the time of contracting), or intoxicated, the parties are considered to have at least partial capacity. In these cases, the contracts are **voidable.** They may enter a contract and enforce it if they wish, but they also have the right to avoid the contract.

Minors' Contracts

Minor's Right to Disaffirm

Courts have long recognized that minors are in a vulnerable position in their dealings with adults. Courts granted minors the right to avoid contracts as a means of protecting against their own improvidence and against overreaching by adults. The exercise of this right to avoid a contract is called **disaffirmance.** The right to disaffirm is personal to the minor. That is, only the minor or a legal representative such as a guardian may disaffirm the contract. No formal act or written statement is required to make a valid disaffirmance. Any words or acts that effectively communicate the minor's desire to cancel the contract can constitute disaffirmance.

If, on the other hand, the minor wishes to enforce the contract instead of disaffirming it, the adult party must perform. You can see that the minor's right to disaffirm puts any adult contracting with a minor in an undesirable position: He is bound on the contract unless it is to the minor's advantage to disaffirm it. The right to disaffirm has the effect of discouraging adults from dealing with minors.

Exceptions to the Minor's Right to Disaffirm   Not every contract involving a minor is voidable, however. State law often creates statutory exceptions to the mi-

nor's right to disaffirm. These statutes prevent minors from disaffirming such transactions as marriage, agreements to support their children, educational loans, life and medical insurance contracts, contracts for transportation by common carriers, and certain types of contracts approved by a court (such as contracts to employ a child actor).

Period of Minority

At common law, the age of majority was 21. However, the ratification in 1971 of the 26th Amendment to the Constitution giving 18-year-olds the right to vote stimulated a trend toward reducing the age of majority. The age of majority has been lowered by 49 states. In almost all of these states, the age of majority for contracting purposes is now 18.

Emancipation

Emancipation is the termination of a parent's right to control a child and receive services and wages from him. There are no formal requirements for emancipation. It can occur by the parent's express or implied consent or by the occurrence of some events such as the marriage of the child. In most states, the mere fact that a minor is emancipated does *not* give him capacity to contract. A person younger than the legal age of majority is generally held to lack capacity to enter a contract, even if he is married and employed full-time.

Time of Disaffirmance

Contracts entered during minority that affect title to *real estate* cannot be disaffirmed until majority. This rule is apparently based on the special importance of real estate and on the need to protect a minor from improvidently

FIGURE 2   Timeline Showing Effect of Ratification

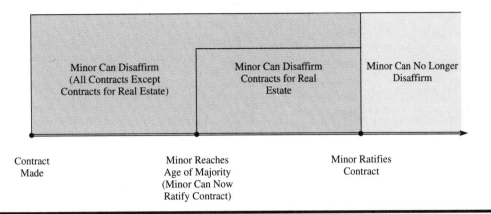

disaffirming a transaction (such as a mortgage or conveyance) involving real estate. All other contracts entered during minority may be disaffirmed as soon as the contract is formed. The minor's power to avoid his contracts does not end on the day he reaches the age of majority. It continues for a period of time after he reaches majority.

How long after reaching majority does a person retain the right to disaffirm the contracts he made while a minor? A few states have statutes that prescribe a definite time limit on the power of avoidance. In Oklahoma, for example, a person who wishes to disaffirm a contract must do so within one year after reaching majority.[2] In most states, however, there is no set limit on the time during which a person may disaffirm after reaching majority. In determining whether a person has the right to disaffirm, a major factor that courts consider is whether the adult has rendered performance under the contract or relied on the contract. If the adult has relied on the contract or has given something of value to the minor, the minor must disaffirm within a reasonable time after reaching majority. If he delays longer than a period of time that is considered to be reasonable under the circumstances, he will run the risk of **ratifying** (affirming) the contract. (The concept and consequences of ratification are discussed in the next section.) If the adult has neither performed nor relied on the contract, however, the former minor is likely to be accorded a longer period of time in which to disaffirm, sometimes even years after he has reached majority.

[2] Okla. Stat. Ann. tit. 15 sec. 18 (1983).

Ratification

Though a person has the right to disaffirm contracts made during minority, this right can be given up after the person reaches the age of majority. When a person who has reached majority indicates that he intends to be bound by a contract that he made while still a minor, he surrenders his right to disaffirm. This act of affirming the contract and surrendering the right to avoid the contract is known as **ratification.** Ratification makes a contract valid from its inception. Because ratification represents the former minor's election to be bound by the contract, he cannot later disaffirm. Ratification can be done effectively only after the minor reaches majority. Otherwise, it would be as voidable as the initial contract. The effect of ratification is illustrated in Figure 2.

There are no formal requirements for ratification. Any of the former minor's words or acts after reaching majority that indicate with reasonable clarity his intent to be bound by the contract are sufficient. Ratification can be *expressed* in an oral or written statement, or, as is more often the case, it can be *implied* by conduct on the part of the former minor. Naturally, ratification is clearest when the former minor has made some express statement of his intent to be bound. Predicting whether a court will determine that a contract has been ratified is a bit more difficult when the only evidence of the alleged ratification is the conduct of the minor. A former minor's acceptance or retention of benefits given by the other party for an unreasonable time after he has reached majority can constitute ratification. Also, a former minor's continued performance of his part of the contract after reaching majority has been held to imply his intent to ratify the contract.

Duty to Return Consideration upon Disaffirmance

If neither party has performed his part of the contract, the parties' relationship will simply be canceled by the disaffirmance. Since neither party has given anything to the other party, no further adjustments are necessary. But what about the situation where, as is often the case, the minor has paid money to the adult and the adult has given property to the minor?

Upon disaffirmance, each party has the duty to return to the other any consideration that the other has given. This means that the minor must return any consideration given to him by the adult that remains in his possession. However, if the minor is unable to return the consideration, most states will still permit him to disaffirm the contract.

The duty to return consideration also means that the minor has the right to recover any consideration he has given to the adult party. He even has the right to recover some property that has been transferred to third parties. One exception to the minor's right to recover property from third parties is found in section 2–403 of the Uniform Commercial Code, however. Under this section, a minor cannot recover *goods* that have been transferred to a good-faith purchaser. For example, Simpson, a minor, sells a 1980 Ford to Mort's Car Lot. Mort's then sells the car to Vane, a good-faith purchaser. If Simpson disaffirmed the contract with Mort's, he would *not* have the right to recover the Ford from Vane.

Must the Disaffirming Minor Make Restitution?: A Split of Authority

If the consideration given by the adult party has been lost, damaged, destroyed, or simply has depreciated in value, is the minor required to make restitution to the adult for the loss? The traditional rule is that the minor who cannot fully return the consideration that was given to him is *not* obligated to pay the adult for the benefits he has received or to compensate the adult for loss or depreciation of the consideration. Most states still follow this traditional rule. (As you will read in the next section, however, a minor's misrepresentation of age can, in some states, make him responsible for reimbursing the other party upon disaffirmance.) The rule that restitution is not required is designed to protect minors by discouraging adults from dealing with them. After all, if an adult knew that he might be able to demand the return of anything that he transferred to a minor, he would have little incentive to refrain from entering into contracts with minors.

The traditional rule can work harsh results for innocent adults who have dealt fairly with minors, however. It strikes many people as unprincipled that a doctrine intended to protect against unfair exploitation of one class of people can be used to unfairly exploit another class of people. As courts sometimes say, the minor's right to disaffirm was designed to be used as a "shield rather than as a sword." For these reasons, a number (although still a minority) of states have rejected the traditional rule. The courts and legislatures of these states have adopted rules that require disaffirming minors to place the adult in *status quo* (the position he was in before the creation of the contract) by reimbursing him for use or depreciation of his property. The following case, *Dodson v. Shrader*, discusses this controversy.

DODSON v. SHRADER

1989 Tenn. App. Lexis 683 (Tenn. Ct. App. 1989)

Joseph Dodson, age 16, bought a 1984 Chevrolet truck from Shrader's Auto Sales for $4,900 cash. At the time, Shrader's did not ask Dodson's age and Dodson did not disclose it. Dodson drove the truck for about eight months when he learned from an auto mechanic that there was a burned valve in the engine. He continued to drive the truck without repair for another month until the engine "blew up" and stopped operating. While parked, the truck was later struck by an unknown automobile and further damaged. Dodson disaffirmed the contract and offered to return the truck and the title to the truck, but Shrader's refused to return Dodson's money. It argued that Dodson should be responsible for paying the difference between the present value of the truck ($500) and the $4,900 purchase price.

Dodson sued to recover his money. The trial court found in his favor and Shrader's appealed.

Todd, Presiding Judge. Shrader's [insists] that the law of Tennessee ought to be revised to require a minor to restore the consideration in full, that is, to tender the depreciated property and the amount of depreciation in order to rescind a contract, or the recovery of Dodson should be reduced by the difference between the value of the truck when delivered to him and its value when delivered to Shrader's.

Tennessee authorities recognize the general rule that the contract of a minor is voidable. But no Tennessee authority is found which would require a disaffirming minor to return more than the consideration remaining in his possession at the time of disaffirmance. The general policy of the law of infancy is stated in 43 C.J.S., Infants, section 166, pp. 448, as follows: "It is the policy of the law to protect infants against their own mistakes or improvidence, and from designs of others, and to discourage adults from contracting with an infant. A person who deals with an infant does so at his peril. . . ."

Seventeen states unequivocally deny depreciation absent misrepresentation or tort. Minnesota denies depreciation unless the contract is fair, reasonable and provident. Idaho denies use, and Utah denies depreciation by statute. Depreciation is allowed by court opinion in four states and by statute in three states. The distinct weight of authority supports the admittedly harsh rule which penalizes the adult who deals with a minor.

Reason and justice also support the view that any change in the traditional harsh rule should be accomplished by statute rather than by court decision. Aside from the traditional reluctance of the judiciary to legislate, there is the difficulty of effective date and age limitations of a change. Legislation would constitute fair notice to all makers of future contracts as to the law applicable thereto.

Admittedly, it "goes against the grain" to permit a minor who is a few days or weeks short of majority to negotiate and subsequently disaffirm a contract to the severe loss of the other contracting party. The correction of this apparent injustice by a ruling affecting all minors regardless of their tender age would countenance a greater injustice. Courts are ill equipped and have doubtful authority to determine an arbitrary age limit within which the harsh rule should be relaxed. The Legislature is far better equipped and has clear authority to make such a determination. Indeed, the Legislature has already acted to reduce the age of majority from 21 to 18. This court has therefore determined that the traditional harsh rule should not be relaxed by the courts, and that the judgment of the trial court should be affirmed.

Judgment for Dodson affirmed.

Effect of Misrepresentation of Age: No Uniform Rule

It is not unheard of for a minor occasionally to pretend to be older than he is. Many of the normal rules dealing with the minor's right to disaffirm and his duties upon disaffirmance can be affected by a minor's misrepresen-

tation of his age.[3] Suppose, for example, that Jones, age 17, wants to lease a car from Acme Auto Rentals, but knows that Acme rents only to people who are at

---

[3] You might want to refer back to the Reality of Consent chapter to review the elements of misrepresentation.

least 18. Jones induces Acme to lease a car to him by showing false identification that represents his age to be 18. Acme relies on the misrepresentation. Jones wrecks the car, attempts to disaffirm the contract, and asks for the return of his money. What is the effect of Jones's misrepresentation?

The answer depends on which state's law applies, because there is no uniform rule regarding misrepresentation of age. The different approaches to the problems fall into four categories:

1. *Traditional rule: Misrepresentation has no effect.* The traditional rule, which is followed in some states, is that a minor's misrepresentation about his age does not affect his right to disaffirm and does not create any obligation to pay for benefits received. The theory behind this rule, which can create severe hardship for innocent adults who rely on minors' misrepresentations of age, is that one who lacks capacity cannot acquire it merely by claiming to be of legal age.

2. *Minor estopped from disaffirming.* Other states take the position that the minor who misrepresents his age will be *estopped* (prevented) from asserting his infancy as a defense. In other words, he will be treated as if he really were of legal age and will be prevented from disaffirming the contract.

3. *Minor liable for tort of deceit.* Some states hold the misrepresenting minor liable for damages for the tort of deceit. The amount of damages in such a case is likely to be the amount of depreciation of the relying party's property.

4. *Disaffirming minor must place adult in status quo.* Still other states condition the minor's right to disaffirm upon his placing the relying party in *status quo.* Even in a state that usually follows the majority rule that disaffirming minors need only return the consideration that remains in their possession, a minor who has misrepresented his age may be required to reimburse the relying adult for use or depreciation of his property. You will see an example of this approach and the estoppel approach in the following case, *Haydocy Pontiac, Inc. v. Lee.*

HAYDOCY PONTIAC, INC. v. LEE

250 N.E.2d 898 (Ohio Ct. App. 1969)

At a time when the age of majority in Ohio was 21, Jennifer Lee, age 20, contracted to buy a 1964 Plymouth Fury for $1,552 from Haydocy Pontiac. Lee represented herself to be 21 when entering the contract. She paid for the car by trading in another car worth $150 and financing the balance. Immediately following delivery of the car to her, Lee permitted one John Roberts to take possession of it. Roberts delivered the car to someone else, and it was never recovered. Lee failed to make payments on the car, and Haydocy Pontiac sued her to recover the car or the amount due on the contract. Lee repudiated the contract on the ground that she was a minor at the time of purchase. The trial court found in favor of Lee, and Haydocy Pontiac appealed.

Strausbaugh, Judge. At a time when we see young persons between 18 and 21 years of age demanding and assuming more responsibilities in their daily lives; when we see such persons emancipated, married, and raising families; when we see such persons charged with the responsibility for committing crimes; when we see such persons being sued in tort claims for acts of negligence; when we see such persons subject to military service; when we see such persons engaged in business and acting in almost all other respects as an adult, it seems timely to reexamine the case law pertaining to contractual rights and responsibilities of infants to see if the law as pronounced and applied by the courts should be redefined.

To allow infants to avoid a transaction without being required to restore the consideration received where the infant has used or otherwise disposed of it causes hardship on the other party. We hold that where the consideration received by the infant cannot be returned upon disaffirmance because it has been disposed of, the infant must account for the value of it, not in excess of the purchase price, where the other party is free from any fraud or bad faith and where the contract has been induced by a false representation of the age of the infant. Under this factual situation, the infant is estopped from pleading infancy as a defense where the contract has been induced by a false representation that the infant was of age.

The necessity of returning the consideration as a prerequisite to obtaining equitable relief is still clearer where the infant misrepresents age and perpetrated an actual fraud on the other party. The common law has bestowed upon the infant the privilege of disaffirming his contracts in conservation of his rights and interests. Where the infant, 20 years of age, through falsehood and deceit enters into a contract with another who enters therein in honesty and good faith and, thereafter the infant seeks to disaffirm the contract without tendering back the consideration, no right or interest of the infant exists which needs protection. The privilege given the infant thereupon becomes a weapon of injustice.

Judgment reversed in favor of Haydocy Pontiac.

Minors' Obligation to Pay Reasonable Value of Necessaries

Though the law regarding minors' contracts is designed to discourage adults from dealing with (and possibly taking advantage of) minors, it would be undesirable for the law to discourage adults from selling minors the items that they need for basic survival. For this reason, disaffirming minors are required to pay the reasonable value of items that have been furnished to them that are classified as "necessaries." A necessary is something that is essential for the minor's continued existence and general welfare that has not been provided by the minor's parents or guardian. Examples of necessaries include food, clothing, shelter, medical care, tools of the minor's trade, and basic educational or vocational training.

A minor's liability for necessaries supplied to him is **quasi-contractual.** That is, the minor is liable for the *reasonable value* of the necessaries that she actually receives. She is not liable for the entire price agreed upon if that price exceeds the actual value of the necessaries, and she is not liable for necessaries that she contracted for but did not receive. For example, Joy Jones, a minor, signs a one-year lease for an apartment in Mountain Park

at a rent of $300 per month. After living in the apartment for three months, Joy breaks her lease and moves out. Because she is a minor, Joy has the right to disaffirm the lease. If shelter is a necessary in this case, however, she must pay the reasonable value of what she has actually received—three months' rent. If she can establish that the actual value of what she has received is less than $300 per month, she will be bound to pay only that lesser amount. Furthermore, she will not be obligated to pay for the remaining nine months' rent, because she has not received any benefits from the remainder of the lease.

Whether a given item is considered a necessary depends on the facts of a particular case. The minor's age, station in life, and personal circumstances are all relevant to this issue. As is emphasized in the *Webster Street Partnership* case, which follows, an item sold to a minor is not considered a necessary if the minor's parent or guardian has already supplied him with similar items. For this reason, the range of items that will be considered necessaries is broader for married minors and other emancipated minors than it is for unemancipated minors.

WEBSTER STREET PARTNERSHIP v. SHERIDAN

368 N.W.2d 439 (S. Ct. Neb. 1985)

Webster Street owns real estate in Omaha, Nebraska. On September 18, 1982, Webster Street entered into a written contract to lease an apartment to Matthew Sheridan and Pat Wilwerding for one year at a rental of $250 per month. Although Webster Street did not know this, both Sheridan and Wilwerding were younger than the age of majority (which was 19) when the lease was signed.

Sheridan and Wilwerding paid $150 as a security deposit and rent for the remainder of September and the month of October, for a total of $500. They failed to pay their November rent on time, however, and Webster Street notified them that they would be required to move out unless they paid immediately. Unable to pay rent, Sheridan and Wilwerding moved out of the apartment on November 12. Webster Street later demanded that they pay the expenses it incurred in attempting to rerent the property, rent for the months of November and December (apparently the two months it took to find a new tenant), and assorted damages and fees, amounting to $630.94. Sheridan and Wilwerding refused to pay any of the amount demanded on the ground of minority and demanded the return of their security deposit. Webster Street then filed this lawsuit. The district court found that the apartment was a necessary and that Sheridan and Wilwerding were liable for the 12 days in November in which they had actually possessed the apartment without paying rent, but that they were entitled to the return of their security deposit. Webster Street appealed from this ruling.

Krivosha, Chief Justice.   The privilege of infancy will not enable an infant to escape liability under all circumstances. For example, it is well established that an infant is liable for the value of necessaries furnished him. Just what are necessaries, however, has no exact definition. The term is flexible and varies according to the facts of each individual case. A number of factors must be considered before a court can conclude whether a particular product or service is a necessary. The articles must be useful and suitable. To be necessaries the articles must supply the infant's personal needs, either those of his body or those of his mind. However, the term "necessaries" is not confined to merely such things as are required for bare subsistence. What may be considered necessary for one infant may not be necessaries for another infant whose state is different as to rank, social position, fortune, health, or other circumstances. To enable an infant to contract for articles as necessaries, he must have been in actual need of them, and obliged to procure them for himself. They are not necessaries as to him, however necessary they may be in their nature, if he was already supplied with sufficient articles of the kind, or if he had a parent or guardian who was able and willing to supply them. The burden of proof is on the plaintiff to show that the infant was destitute of the articles and had no way of procuring them except by his own contract.

The undisputed testimony is that both tenants were living away from home, apparently with the understanding that they could return home at any time. It would appear that neither Sheridan nor Wilwerding was in need of shelter but, rather, had chosen to voluntarily leave home, with the understanding that they could return whenever they desired. One may at first blush believe that such a rule is unfair. Yet, on further consideration, the wisdom of such a rule is apparent. If landlords may not contract with minors, except at their peril, they may refuse to do so. In that event, minors who voluntarily leave home but who are free to return will be compelled to return to their parents' home—a result which is desirable. We therefore hold that the district court erred in finding that the apartment was a necessary.

Because the rental of the apartment was not a necessary, the minors had the right to avoid the contract, either during their minority or within a reasonable time after reaching their majority. Disaffirmance by an infant completely puts an end to the contract's existence both as to him and as to the adult with whom he contracted. Because the parties then stand as if no contract had ever existed, the infant can recover payments made to the adult, and the adult is entitled to the return of whatever was received by the infant.

The record shows that Wilwerding clearly disaffirmed the contract during his minority. Moreover, when Webster Street ordered the minors out for failure to pay rent and they vacated the premises, Sheridan likewise disaffirmed the contract. The record indicates that Sheridan reached majority on November 5. To suggest that a lapse of 7 days was not disaffirmance within a reasonable time would be foolish. Once disaffirmed, no contract existed between the parties and the minors were entitled to recover all of the moneys which they paid and to be relieved of any further obligation under the contract. The judgment of the district court is therefore reversed and the cause remanded with directions to vacate the judgment in favor of Webster Street and to enter a judgment in favor of Matthew Sheridan and Pat Wilwerding in the amount of $500, representing September rent in the amount of $100, October rent in the amount of $250, and the security deposit in the amount of $150.

Judgment reversed in favor of Sheridan and Wilwerding.

CAPACITY OF MENTALLY IMPAIRED PERSONS

Theory of Incapacity

Like minors, people who suffer from a mental illness or defect are at a disadvantage in their ability to protect their own interests in the bargaining process. Contract law makes their contracts either void or voidable to protect them from the results of their own impaired perceptions and judgment and from others who might take advantage of them.

Test for Mental Incapacity

Incapacity on grounds of mental illness or defect, often referred to in cases and texts as "insanity," encompasses a broad range of causes of impaired mental functioning, such as mental illness, brain damage, mental retardation, or senility. The mere fact that a person suffers from some mental illness or defect does not necessarily mean that he lacks capacity to contract, however. He could still have full capacity unless the defect or illness affects the particular transaction in question. For example, a person could have periodic psychotic episodes, yet enter a binding contract during a lucid period.

The usual test for mental incapacity is a *cognitive* one; that is, courts ask whether the person had sufficient mental capacity to understand the nature and effect of the contract. Some courts have criticized the traditional test as unscientific because it does not take into account the fact that a person suffering from a mental illness or defect might be unable to *control* his conduct. The *Restatement (Second) of Contracts* provides that a person's contracts are voidable if he is unable to *act* in a reasonable manner in relation to the transaction and the other party has reason to know of his condition.[4] Where the

other party has reason to know of the condition of the mentally impaired person, the *Restatement* standard would provide protection to people who understood the transaction but, because of some mental defect or illness, were unable to exercise appropriate judgment or to control their conduct effectively.

The Effect of Incapacity Caused by Mental Impairment

The contracts of people who are suffering from a mental defect at the time of contracting are usually considered to be *voidable*. In some situations, however, severe mental or physical impairment may prevent a person from even being able to manifest consent. In such a case, no contract could be formed.

As mentioned at the beginning of this chapter, contract law makes a distinction between a contract involving a person who has been **adjudicated** (judged by a court) incompetent at the time the contract was made and a contract involving a person who was suffering from some mental impairment at the time the contract was entered but whose incompetency was not established until *after* the contract was formed. If a person is under guardianship at the time the contract is formed—that is, if a court has found a person mentally incompetent after holding a hearing on his mental competency and has appointed a guardian for him—the contract is considered **void.** On the other hand, if, *after* a contract has been formed, a court finds that the person who manifested consent lacked capacity on grounds of mental illness or defect, the contract is usually considered **voidable** at the election of the party who lacked capacity (or his guardian or personal representative).

The Right to Disaffirm

If a contract is found to be voidable on the ground of mental impairment, the person who lacked capacity at

---

[4] *Restatement (Second) of Contracts* § 15.

the time the contract was made has the right to disaffirm the contract. A person formerly incapacitated by mental impairment can ratify a contract if he regains his capacity. Thus, if he regains capacity, he must disaffirm the contract unequivocally within a reasonable time, or he will be deemed to have ratified it.

As is true of a disaffirming minor, a person disaffirming on the ground of mental impairment must return any consideration given by the other party that remains in his possession. A person under this type of mental incapacity is liable for the reasonable value of **necessaries** in the same manner as are minors. Must the incapacitated party reimburse the other party for loss, damage, or depreciation of nonnecessaries given to him? This is generally said to depend on whether the contract was basically fair and on whether the other party had reason to be aware of his impairment. If the contract is fair, bargained for in good faith, and the other party had no reasonable cause to know of the incapacity, the contract cannot be disaffirmed unless the other party is placed in *status quo*. However, if the other party had reason to know of the incapacity, the incapacitated party is allowed to disaffirm without placing the other party in *status quo*. This distinction discourages people from attempting to take advantage of mentally impaired people, but it spares those who are dealing in good faith and have no such intent.

CONTRACTS OF INTOXICATED PERSONS

Intoxication and Capacity

Intoxication (either from alcohol or the use of drugs) can deprive a person of capacity to contract. The mere fact that a party to a contract had been drinking when the contract was formed would *not* normally affect his capacity to contract, however. Intoxication is a ground for lack of capacity only when it is so extreme that the person is unable to understand the nature of the business at hand. The *Restatement (Second) of Contracts* further provides that intoxication is a ground for lack of capacity only if *the other party has reason to know* that the affected person is so intoxicated that he cannot understand or act reasonably in relation to the transaction.[5]

The rules governing the capacity of intoxicated persons are very similar to those applied to the capacity of people who are mentally impaired. The basic right to disaffirm contracts made during incapacity, the duties upon disaffirmance, and the possibility of ratification upon regaining capacity are the same for an intoxicated person as for a person under a mental impairment. In practice, however, courts traditionally have been less sympathetic with a person who was intoxicated at the time of contracting than with minors or those suffering from a mental impairment. It is rare for a person to actually escape his contractual obligations on the ground of intoxication. As the following case, *First Bank of Sinai v. Hyland*, demonstrates, a person incapacitated by intoxication at the time of contracting might nevertheless be bound to his contract if he fails to disaffirm in a timely manner.

---

[5] *Restatement (Second) of Contracts* § 16.

FIRST BANK OF SINAI v. HYLAND

399 N.W.2d 894 (S.D. S. Ct. 1987)

Randy Hyland owed money to the First State Bank of Sinai on two promissory notes that had already become due. On October 20, 1981, William Buck, acting for the bank, agreed to extend the time of payment if Randy's father, Mervin, acted as a cosigner. Mervin had executed approximately 60 promissory notes with the bank and was a good customer. A new note was prepared for Mervin's signature. Buck knew that Mervin drank, but later testified that he was unaware of any alcohol-related problems.

Mervin had been drinking heavily from late summer through the early winter of 1981. During this period, his wife and son managed the farm, and Mervin was weak, unconcerned with family and business matters, uncooperative, and uncommunicative. When he was drinking, he spent most of his time at home, in bed. He was involuntarily committed to hospitals twice during this period. He was released from his first commitment on September 19 and again committed on November 20. Between the periods of his commitments, he did transact some business himself, such as paying for farm goods and services, hauling his grain to storage elevators, and making decisions concerning when grain was to be sold.

When Randy brought this note home, Mervin was drunk and in bed. On October 20 or 21, he rose from the bed, walked into the kitchen and signed the note. Later, Randy returned to the bank with the note, which Mervin had properly signed, and added his own signature. The due date on this note was April 20, 1982.

On April 20, the note was unpaid. Buck notified Randy of the overdue note, and on May 5, Randy brought to the bank a blank check signed by Mervin with which the interest on the note was to be paid. Randy filled in the check for the amount of interest owing. No further payments were made on the note, and Randy filed for bankruptcy in June of 1982. After unsuccessfully demanding the note's payment from Mervin, the bank ultimately filed this suit against Mervin. Mervin asserted incapacity on the ground of intoxication, claiming that he had no recollection of seeing the note, discussing it with his son, or signing it. The trial court rendered judgment for Mervin, and the bank appealed.

Henderson, Justice.   Contractual obligations incurred by intoxicated persons may be voidable. Voidable contracts (contracts other than those entered into following a judicial determination of incapacity) may be rescinded by the previously disabled party. However, disaffirmance must be prompt, upon the recovery of the intoxicated party's mental abilities, and upon his notice of the agreement, if he had forgotten it. A delay in rescission which causes prejudice to the other party will extinguish the first party's right to disaffirm.

A voidable contract may also be ratified by the party who had contracted while disabled. Upon ratification, the contract becomes a fully valid legal obligation. Ratification can either be express or implied by conduct. In addition, a failure of a party to disaffirm a contract over a period of time may, by itself, ripen into a ratification, especially if rescission will result in prejudice to the other party.

Mervin received both verbal notice from Randy and written notice from the bank on or about April 27, 1982, that the note was overdue. On May 5, Mervin paid the interest owing with a check which Randy delivered to the bank. This by itself could amount to ratification through conduct. If Mervin wished to avoid the contract, he should have then exercised his right of rescission.

Mervin's failure to rescind, coupled with his apparent ratification, could have jeopardized the bank's chances of ever receiving payment on the note. As we know, Mervin unquestionably was aware of his obligation in late April 1982. If he had disaffirmed then, the bank could have actively pursued Randy and possibly collected part of the debt. By delaying his rescission and by paying the note's back interest, Mervin lulled the bank into a false sense of security that may have hurt it when on June 22, 1982, Randy filed for bankruptcy and was later fully discharged of his obligation on the note.

We conclude that Mervin's obligation on the note was voidable and his subsequent failure to disaffirm and his payment of interest then transformed the voidable contract into one that is fully binding upon him.

Judgment reversed in favor of the bank.

ETHICAL AND PUBLIC POLICY CONCERNS

1. You read that the age of majority for contracting purposes is 18 in almost all states today. We all know that maturity at a given age varies greatly from individual to individual. Does it make sense for the law to *presume* that a person is sufficiently mature to be responsible for his agreements merely because he has reached the age of 18? Would public policy be better served if the maturity of contracting parties were determined on a case-by-case basis in the same way that we now determine the capacity of those who are mentally impaired or intoxicated? Why or why not?

2. In *Dodson v. Shrader*, the court held that a minor who disaffirmed a contract was not required to make restitution to the adult party for damage to the adult's property. The court stated that this rule "goes against the grain," but it opined that it is the role of the legislature rather than the court to change the rule. It stated that "[t]he correction of this apparent injustice by a ruling affecting all minors regardless of their tender age would countenance a greater injustice." Should the rule permitting minors to disaffirm without paying for use, damage, or depreciation be changed? Why or why not? Do you agree that it is not the proper role of a court to change this rule? Discuss.

3. In recent years, there has been growing public concern over alcohol and drug abuse. Through legal developments such as vigorous enforcement of drunken driving laws and the imposition of tort liability on the part of alcohol suppliers, the law encourages moderation in the use of alcohol. Yet, the law also makes it possible for a person who is so intoxicated that he does not appreciate the business at hand to escape his contractual obligations. Is this rule about the capacity of intoxicated persons out of step with sound public policy?

SUMMARY

Minors, people suffering from mental illnesses or defects, and intoxicated persons are considered to lack capacity to enter a contract because they are at an inherent disadvantage in their dealings with others. When a contracting party is so impaired that he is unable to manifest assent or where he has been adjudicated (judged by a court to be) incompetent before the time of contracting, the contract is void. Other contracts in which one or more of the parties lacks capacity because of age, mental impairment, or intoxication are considered voidable.

The age of majority in almost all states is 18. A contract formed when a party is younger than the age of majority is voidable at the option of the minor. The minor has the right to avoid his obligations under a contract by disaffirming the contract. In most states, this is true for emancipated minors, too. Contracts for the sale of real estate cannot be disaffirmed until after the former minor reaches majority. A minor may disaffirm all other types of contracts as soon as they are formed. Contracts made during minority can be disaffirmed for a period of time after the former minor has reached majority. Some states specify this period of time in statutes. Generally, however, courts distinguish between contracts in which the adult has performed or relied on the contract and those that are completely executory. In executory contracts, the former minor will be allowed a considerable period of time—possibly years—after reaching majority in which to disaffirm. When the adult has given performance or relied on the contract, however, the minor must disaffirm within a reasonable time after reaching majority. His failure to do so can be considered ratification of the contract.

Once a minor reaches majority, he can ratify a contract in any way that shows his intent to be bound by the contract. Ratification operates as a surrender of the right to avoid the contract. It can be made expressly, in specific words, or impliedly, through conduct of the former minor. When a contract has been ratified, it is treated as valid from its inception and cannot later be disaffirmed.

If the minor disaffirms, however, he must return any consideration given him by the other party that remains in his possession. The majority rule is that the disaffirming minor is entitled to the return of anything he has given the other party and that he does not have to pay the other party for loss or depreciation in value of the consideration given to him by that party. Some states have declined to follow this rule, however, and have designed other rules to promote the fair treatment of innocent adults who have dealt fairly with minors. If the disaffirming minor has purchased something from the other party that is considered to be a *necessary*, the minor must pay the reasonable value of what he has actually received.

A minor's misrepresentation of his age has different results in different states. In some states, misrepresentation of age makes no difference in the minor's rights and obligations. In others, it places an obligation on the minor to put the adult in *status quo* (the position he was in before the contract was formed), makes him liable in tort for deceit, or precludes him from asserting his minority as a claim or defense.

A contract entered into by a person who lacks capacity because of a mental illness or defect is voidable, unless the person was under guardianship at the time the contract was formed. In that case, the contract would be considered void. In determining mental capacity, courts generally ask whether the person was capable of understanding the nature and consequences of the contract. The *Restatement* and some courts permit disaffirmance if a person is unable to act reasonably because of a mental defect or illness and the other party has reason to know of his impairment. Upon disaffirmance, the incapacitated person must return any consideration that remains in his possession. He may be obligated to place the other party in *status quo* if the contract was fair and the other party had no reason to know of his mental impairment. Like the minor, the mentally incapacitated person must pay the reasonable value of necessaries that he has actually received and can, upon obtaining full mental capacity, bind himself to a contract made during incapacity by ratifying it.

Persons who are so intoxicated at the time they enter a contract that they do not understand the nature and consequences of a contract are often treated as lacking capacity to contract. The *Restatement* provides that a contract formed at a time when one of the parties was intoxicated to this extent would be voidable if the other person had reason to know that he was unable to understand the contract or act in a reasonable way in relation to it because of his intoxication. If he wants to avoid the contract, he must disaffirm it within a reasonable time after regaining sobriety, or he may be deemed to have ratified it.

PROBLEM CASES

1. Smith, age 17, purchased a car from Bobby Floars Toyota, signing an agreement to pay the balance of the purchase price in 30 monthly installments. Ten months after he reached majority (which was 18 in that state), Smith voluntarily returned the car to Floars and stopped making payments. At this point, he had made 11 monthly payments, 10 of which were made after his 18th birthday. Floars sold the car at public auction and sued Smith for the remaining debt. Will Smith be required to pay?

2. Robertson, while a minor, contracted to borrow money from his father for a college education. His father mortgaged his home and took out loans against his life insurance policies to get some of the money he lent to Robertson, who ultimately graduated from dental school. Two years after Robertson's graduation, his father asked him to begin paying back the amount of $30,000 at $400 per month. Robertson agreed to pay $24,000 at $100 per month. He did this for three years before stopping the payments. His father sued for the balance of the debt. Could Robertson disaffirm the contract?

3. Green, age 16, contracted to buy a Camaro from Star Chevrolet. Green lived about six miles from school and one mile from his job and used the Camaro to go back and forth to school and work. When he did not have the car, he used a car pool to get to school and work. Several months later, the car became inoperable due to a blown head gasket, and Green gave notice of disaffirmance to Star Chevrolet. Star Chevrolet refused to refund the purchase price, claiming in part that the car was a necessary. Was it?

4. In 1983, George Lloyd purchased an annuity and named his daughters by a previous marriage, Jordan and Pitts, as co-beneficiaries. In June of 1985, he executed a will in which he devised property to his daughters but made no provision for his current wife, Olivia Lloyd. Mr. and Mrs. Lloyd were divorced after the execution of the will. In April of 1987, Mr. Lloyd's physician noticed that Lloyd was showing signs of mental instability and chronic dementia. In August of 1987, Mr. and Mrs. Lloyd remarried. That same month, Mrs. Lloyd obtained a change of beneficiary form and Mr. Lloyd executed the form to change the beneficiary of the annuity to Mrs. Lloyd. Mrs. Lloyd later testified that she "couldn't say" that Mr. Lloyd "knew what he was doing on the day he signed the form." His mental condition deteriorated to the point that he was adjudicated mentally incompetent in September of 1987 and a guardian was appointed for him. Is the change of beneficiary form that he executed in August of 1987 valid?

5. Odem, a minor, contracted for medical services to be provided by Children's Hospital to her infant son. The hospital treated Odem's son, and Odem later disaffirmed the contract. The hospital sued Odem to collect the hospital bill plus the legal fees incurred by the hospital in collecting the bill. Must Odem pay for the medical services? What about the hospital's legal fees?

6. Ortolere had been a teacher for 40 years when she suffered a nervous breakdown at the age of 60 and went on a leave of absence. She was under the care of a psychiatrist, who diagnosed her illness as involutional psychosis and cerebral arteriosclerosis. Ortolere belonged to a retirement system that gave her the right to certain retirement and death benefits. While still under the care of her psychiatrist, Ortolere wrote a letter to the retirement board stating that she intended to retire and listing eight detailed questions that reflected great understanding of the retirement system and the various alternatives available. Within a few days, she changed her election of retirement benefits, selecting an option that did not make much sense in her situation. She died several months later. Her husband filed suit to disaffirm her second selection of retirement benefits on the ground of mental incapacity. Did Ortolere lack capacity because of mental impairment?

7. Howard and Carol Scherer, a married couple, had decided to get a divorce. In December of 1976, they met with a lawyer and both signed a separation agreement that contained a property settlement and a power of attorney that was to be used to obtain a divorce in the Dominican Republic. Mr. Scherer later claimed that he had had a "considerable amount" to drink the night before signing, that the parties were drinking when the documents were signed, and that he had been taking Valium as a tranquilizer and did not realize that mixing it with alcohol caused him to feel "high and uncaring" as to his actions. In January of 1977, the divorce was obtained in the Dominican Republic. Mr. Scherer later told people that he was divorced and that he had plans to remarry. In July of 1977, however, he filed a divorce action in Indiana against Mrs. Scherer and requested an equitable division of property. This suit claimed that the power of attorney that had enabled his wife to get the Dominican divorce was invalid because of his intoxication at the time of signing the documents. Will Mr. Scherer be bound by the documents he signed?

8. Halbman, a minor employed at a gas station managed by Lemke, agreed to buy a 1968 Oldsmobile from Lemke for $1,250. Halbman paid $1,000 in cash and took possession of the car. He agreed to pay $25 per week until the balance was paid. About five weeks later, after Halbman had paid $1,100 of the purchase price, a connecting rod in the car's engine broke. Halbman took the car to a garage to be repaired. He disaffirmed the contract and demanded the return of his money, but Lemke refused to return it. When the repair bill remained unpaid for several months, the garage removed the car's engine and transmission in satisfaction of the debt and had the rest of the car towed to the house of Halbman's father. There, the car was vandalized, making it unsalvageable. Halbman brought suit, seeking the return of the $1,110 he had paid toward the contract. Lemke argues that he should be compensated for the value of the car up to the time of disaffirmance. What will the result be under the majority rule regarding minors' duties after disaffirmance?

CHAPTER 16

ILLEGALITY

INTRODUCTION

The public interest normally favors the enforcement of contracts. Sometimes, however, the interests that usually favor the enforcement of an agreement are subordinated to conflicting social concerns. As you read in the Reality of Consent chapter and Capacity to Contract chapter, for example, people who did not truly consent to a contract or who lacked the capacity to contract have the power to cancel their contracts. In these situations, concerns about protecting disadvantaged persons and preserving the integrity of the bargaining process outweigh the usual public interest in enforcing private agreements. Similarly, when an agreement involves an act or promise that violates some legislative or court-made rule, the public interests threatened by the agreement outweigh the interests that favor its enforcement. Such an agreement will be denied enforcement on grounds of **illegality,** even if there is voluntary consent between two parties who have capacity to contract.

Meaning of Illegality

When a court says that an agreement is illegal, it does not necessarily mean that the agreement violates a criminal law—although an agreement to commit a crime is one type of illegal agreement. Rather, an agreement is illegal either because the legislature has declared that particular type of contract to be unenforceable or void or because the agreement violates a **public policy** that has been developed by courts or that has been manifested in constitutions, statutes, administrative regulations, or other sources of law.

The term **public policy** is impossible to define precisely; generally, it is taken to mean a widely shared view about what ideas, interests, institutions, or freedoms promote public welfare. For example, in our society there are strong public policies favoring the protection of human life and health, free competition, and private property. Judges' and legislators' perceptions of desirable public policy influence the decisions they make about the resolution of cases or the enactment of statutes. Public policy may be based on a prevailing moral code, on an economic philosophy, or on the need to protect a valued social institution such as the family or the judicial system. If the enforcement of an agreement would create a threat to a public policy, a court may determine that it is illegal.

Determining whether an Agreement Is Illegal

If a statute states that a particular type of agreement is unenforceable or void, courts will apply the statute and refuse to enforce the agreement. Relatively few such statutes exist, however. More frequently, a legislature will forbid certain conduct but will not address the enforceability of contracts that involve the forbidden conduct. In such cases, courts must determine whether the importance of the public policy that underlies the statute in question and the degree of interference with that policy are sufficiently great to outweigh any interests that favor enforcement of the agreement.

In some cases, it is relatively easy to predict that an agreement will be held to be illegal. For example, an agreement to commit a serious crime is certain to be illegal. However, the many laws enacted by legislatures are of differing degrees of importance to the public welfare. The determination of illegality would not be so clear if the agreement violated a statute that was of relatively small importance to the public welfare. For example, in one Illinois case,[1] a seller of fertilizer failed to comply with an Illinois statute that required that a descriptive statement accompany the delivery of the fertilizer. The sellers prepared the statements and offered them to the buyers, but did not give them to the buyers at the time of delivery. The court enforced the contract despite the sellers' technical violation of the law because the contract was not seriously injurious to public welfare.

Similarly, the public policies developed by courts are rarely absolute; they, too, depend on a balancing of several factors. In determining whether to hold an agreement illegal, a court will consider the importance of the public policy involved and the extent to which enforcement of the agreement would interfere with that policy. They will also consider the seriousness of any wrongdoing involved in the agreement and how directly that wrongdoing was connected with the agreement.

For purposes of our discussion, illegal agreements will be classified into three main categories: (1) agreements that violate statutes, (2) agreements that violate public policy developed by courts, and (3) unconscionable agreements, which violate both statutory and judicial bans on unconscionability.

AGREEMENTS IN VIOLATION OF STATUTE

Agreements Declared Illegal by Statute

State legislatures occasionally enact statutes that declare certain types of agreements unenforceable, void, or voidable. In a case in which a legislature has specifically stated that a particular type of contract is void, a court need only interpret and apply the statute. These statutes differ from state to state. Some are relatively uncommon. For example, Indiana's legislature recently enacted a statute declaring surrogate birth contracts to be void.[2] Others are relatively common. Three of the most frequently encountered statutes invalidating certain types of contracts are *usury statutes, Sunday laws*, and *wagering statutes*.

Usury Statutes   Federal law and the law of most states set limits on the amount of interest that can be charged for a loan or forbearance (refraining from making a demand for money that is already due). **Usury** means obtaining interest beyond the amount that is authorized by law for these transactions. A contract that requires payment of a usurious interest rate would be illegal under such laws.

The statutes that define usury and set the maximum permissible limit for interest are not uniform in their prohibitions or their penalties. Some states have tended to deregulate usury. States frequently make distinctions among different types of debtors, setting limits on interest as to some debtors and providing higher limits or no limits as to others. For example, usury statutes often make distinctions between loans to individuals and loans to corporations.

When a transaction is covered by usury laws and the rate of interest charged for the use of money exceeds the statutory limit, the contract to pay that interest rate is unenforceable. The precise effect of usury differs from state to state, however. Some jurisdictions employ the traditional remedy for usury, in which the lender forfeits both principal and interest. The usual penalty for usury is forfeiture of interest earned on the transaction, either the entire interest or the excessive interest. In some states, there are also criminal penalties for usury.

Sunday Laws   *Sunday laws* are statutes that prohibit the transaction of certain business and the performance of certain types of work on Sunday. Like usury laws, Sunday laws vary substantially from state to state. Under some Sunday laws, contracts and sales made on Sunday are invalidated if they are not the result of necessity or charity. Although Sunday laws used to be prevalent, many states today have either repealed their Sunday laws or no longer vigorously enforce them.

---

[1] *Amoco Oil Co. v. Toppert*, 56 Ill. App. 3d 1294 (Ill. Ct. App. 1978).

[2] Ind. Code 31-8-2-2 (1988).

Wagering Statutes All states either prohibit or regulate wagering, or gambling. There is a thin line separating wagering, which is illegal, from well-accepted, lawful transactions in which a person will profit from the happening of an uncertain event. How is illegal wagering distinguished from insurance contracts and stock and commodity transactions, for example? The hallmark of a wager is that neither party has any financial stake or interest in the uncertain event except for the stake that he has created by making the bet. The person making a wager *creates* the risk that he may lose the money or property wagered upon the happening of an uncertain event. Suppose Ames bets Baker $20 that the Cubs will win the pennant this year. Ames has no financial interest in a Cubs victory other than that which he has created through his bet. Rather, he has created the risk of losing $20 for the sole purpose of bearing that risk. If, however, people make an agreement about who shall bear an existing risk in which one of them has an actual stake or interest, that is a legal risk-shifting agreement. Property insurance contracts are classic examples of risk-shifting agreements. The owner of the property pays the insurance company a fee (premium) in return for the company's agreement to bear the risk of the uncertain event that the property will be damaged or destroyed. If, however, the person who takes out the policy had no legitimate economic interest in the insured property (called an **insurable interest** in insurance law), the agreement is an illegal wager.

Stock and commodity market transactions are good examples of speculative bargains that are legal. In both cases, the purchasers are obviously hoping that their purchases will increase in value and the sellers believe that they will not. The difference between these transactions and wagers lies in the fact that the parties to stock and commodities transactions are legally bound to the purchase agreement, even though the purchaser may never intend to take delivery of the stock or commodity. In an illegal wager—such as a bet on the performance of certain stock—no purchase or ownership is involved. Nothing is at stake except the risk that the parties have created by their bet.

Agreements that Violate the Public Policy of a Statute

As stated earlier, an agreement can be illegal even if no statute specifically states that that particular sort of agreement is illegal. Legislatures enact statutes in an effort to resolve some particular problem. If courts enforced agreements that involve the violation of a statute, they would frustrate the purpose for which the legislature passed the statute. They would also promote disobedience of the law and disrespect for the courts.

Agreements to Commit a Crime For the reasons stated above, contracts that require the violation of a criminal statute are illegal. If Grimes promises to pay Judge John Doe a bribe of $5,000 to dismiss a criminal case against Grimes, for example, the agreement is illegal. Sometimes the very formation of a certain type of contract is a crime, even if the acts agreed upon are never carried out. An example of this is an agreement to murder another person. Naturally, such agreements are considered illegal under contract law as well as under criminal law. Contracts in which a party agrees to obstruct justice by refraining from disclosing a crime or prosecuting a crime are also illegal.

Agreements that Promote Violations of Statutes Sometimes a contract of a type that is usually perfectly legal—say, a contract to sell goods—is deemed to be illegal under the circumstances of the case because it promotes or facilitates the violation of a statute. Suppose Davis sells Sims goods on credit. Sims uses the goods in some illegal manner and then refuses to pay Davis for the goods. Can Davis recover the price of the goods from Sims? The answer depends on whether Davis knew of the illegal purpose and whether she intended the sale to further that illegal purpose. Generally speaking, such agreements will be legal unless there is a direct connection between the illegal conduct and the agreement in the form of active, intentional participation in or facilitation of the illegal act. Knowledge of the other party's illegal purpose, standing alone, generally is not sufficient to render an agreement illegal. When a person is aware of the other's illegal purpose *and* actively helps to accomplish that purpose, an otherwise legal agreement—such as a sale of goods—might be labeled illegal.

The *Blossom Farm Products* case, which follows, is an example of a case in which the court found the connection between the agreement and a violation of statute sufficiently close for the public interest to be harmed by enforcement of the agreement.

BLOSSOM FARM PRODUCTS CO. v. KASSON CHEESE CO.
395 N.W.2d 619 (Wis. Ct. App. 1986)

PTX Corp. manufactured a product known as Isokappacase, which is used in the production of cheese. The label on Isokappacase says that it is "a starter medium, a bacteriophage preventative medium." Because of its high protein content, Isokappacase can also be used as a yield enhancer by adding it directly into cheese milk. When the product is used in this way, however, federal law requires that the resulting product be labeled as an imitation cheese and that it list the ingredients in the end product to reflect the characteristics of imitation cheese. Julian Podell, a salesman for Blossom, was the sole U.S. distributor for PTX's sale of Isokappacase. Over the course of three years, Blossom sold a large volume of Isokappacase to Kasson Cheese.

Kasson used Isokappacase as a yield enhancer, introducing it directly into cheese milk to enhance cheese yields from the milk, but did not label its final product as imitation cheese as required by federal standards. Had Kasson labeled its end product as an imitation cheese, it would have been able to sell the end product for only $.70 per pound rather than the $1.40 per pound it received for selling it as real cheese. Blossom was aware of the fact that Kasson's extremely large volume purchases of the product could only be accounted for by Kasson's use of Isokappacase as a yield enhancer. Podell acknowledged that once he recognized that Kasson was ordering about one hundred times more Isokappacase than would be needed if it were using the products as a starter medium, he realized that such large volume orders could only mean that Kasson was using the product as a yield enhancer. Blossom also tacitly knew that Kasson was mislabeling its product. Both Kasson and Blossom benefited economically from this volume purchase and use.

This case arose when Kasson failed to pay $138,306 for its last order of Isokappacase, and Blossom brought suit to collect the money. Kasson defended on the ground that the contract was illegal. The trial court agreed and dismissed Blossom's action. Blossom then brought this appeal.

Scott, Chief Justice. Generally, if a promisee has substantially performed its part of the contract, enforcement of a promise is not precluded on grounds of public policy because of some improper use that the promisor intends to make of what he obtains; however, if the promisee acts for the purpose of furthering the promisor's improper use, the promisee is barred from recovering. Whether the promisee has acted for such purpose is a question of fact which may be evidenced by the promisee's doing of specific acts to facilitate the promisor's improper use and/or a course of dealing with persons engaged in improper conduct.

Even with Kasson's intended purpose of improperly labeling its end product, enforcement of Kasson's promise to pay Blossom for sale and delivery of the Isokappacase would not be precluded on grounds of public policy without knowledgeable involvement by Blossom. Testimony from several parties provides sufficient evidence of Blossom's knowledgeable involvement in Kasson's improper conduct. Based on this evidence, the trial court had sufficient evidence on which to base its finding that Blossom, aware of Kasson's use of Isokappacase and subsequent mislabeling of its end product, nonetheless continued to sell Isokappacase to Kasson in large quantities, thereby facilitating Kasson's improper conduct.

State legislation which adopted federal standards of identity enforces the public policy of accurately distinguishing imitation or analog cheese from real cheese and labeling it accordingly. Because mislabeling cheese involves conduct offensive to public policy, the trial court correctly concluded that the transaction which anticipated such improper conduct is unenforceable.

Judgment for Kasson affirmed.

Licensing Laws: Agreement to Perform an Act for which a Party Is Not Properly Licensed Congress and the state legislatures have enacted a variety of statutes that regulate professions and businesses. A common type of regulatory statute is one that requires a person to obtain a license, permit, or registration before engaging in a certain business or profession. For example, state statutes require lawyers, physicians, dentists, teachers, and other professionals to be licensed to practice their professions. In order to obtain the required license, they must meet specified requirements such as attaining a certain educational degree and passing an examination. Real estate brokers, stockbrokers, insurance agents, sellers of liquor and tobacco, pawnbrokers, electricians, barbers, and others too numerous to mention are also often required by state statute to meet licensing requirements to perform services or sell regulated commodities to members of the public.

What is the status of an agreement in which one of the parties agrees to perform an act regulated by state law for which she is not properly licensed? Once again, the answer to this question depends on a balancing of the public interest that would be harmed by enforcement against the public and individual interests that favor enforcement. In determining whether to enforce the agreement, a court will consider the importance of the public policy that has been offended by the agreement. This will often be determined by looking at the purpose of the legislation that the unlicensed party has violated. If the statute is **regulatory**—that is, the purpose of the legislation is to protect the public against dishonest or incompetent practitioners—an agreement by an unlicensed person is generally held to be unenforceable. For example, if Spencer, a first-year law student, agrees to draft a will for Rowen for a fee of $150, Spencer could not enforce the agreement and collect a fee from Rowen for drafting the will, because she is not licensed to practice law. This result makes sense, even though it imposes a hardship on Spencer. The public interest in assuring that people on whose legal advice others rely have an appropriate educational background and proficiency in the subject matter outweighs any interest in seeing that Spencer receives what she bargained for.

On the other hand, where the licensing statute was intended primarily as a **revenue-raising measure**— as a means of collecting money rather than as a means of protecting the public—an agreement to pay a person for performing an act for which she is not licensed will generally be enforced. For example, suppose that in the above example, Spencer is a lawyer who is licensed to practice law in her state and who met all of her state's educational, testing, and character requirements but neglected to pay her annual registration fee. In this situation, there is no compelling public interest that would justify the harsh measure of refusing enforcement and possibly inflicting forfeiture on the unlicensed person.

Whether a statute is a regulatory statute or a revenue-raising statute depends on the intent of the legislature, which may not always be expressed clearly. Generally, statutes that require proof of character and skill and impose penalties for violation are considered to be regulatory in nature. Their requirements indicate that they were intended for the protection of the public. Those that impose a significant license fee and allow anyone who pays the fee to obtain a license are usually classified as revenue raising. The fact that no requirement other than the payment of the fee is imposed indicates that the purpose of the law is to raise money rather than to protect the public. Because such a statute is not designed for the protection of the public, a violation of the statute is not as threatening to the public interest as is a violation of a regulatory statute.

CONCEPT REVIEW

CONTRACTS THAT VIOLATE A LICENSING STATUTE

Type of Licensing Statute	Regulatory	Revenue Raising
Purpose of Statute	Protect the public welfare	Provide source of revenue
Typical Characteristics of Statute	Require proof of character, training, or character and impose penalties for violation	Impose fee with no or few other requirements
Status of Contracts that Violate Statute	Contracts violating statute usually illegal	Contracts violating statute still legal (validity of contract not affected by statute)

It would be misleading to imply that cases involving unlicensed parties always follow such a mechanical test. In some cases, courts may grant recovery to an unlicensed party even where a regulatory statute is violated. If the public policy promoted by the statute is relatively trivial in relation to the amount that would be forfeited by the unlicensed person and the unlicensed person is neither dishonest nor incompetent, a court may conclude that the statutory penalty for violation of the regulatory statute is sufficient to protect the public interest and that enforcement of the agreement is appropriate. Under section 181 of the *Restatement (Second) of Contracts*, an agreement to pay an unlicensed person for doing an act for which a license is required is unenforceable only if the licensing statute has a regulatory purpose *and* if the interest in enforcement of the promise is clearly outweighed by the public policy behind the statute. The *Noble* case, which follows, is a good example of the method by which courts analyze cases involving unlicensed parties.

NOBLE v. ALIS

474 N.E.2d 109 (Ind. Ct. App. 1985)

Andrew Noble and Stuart Odle signed a lease to rent an apartment in Bloomington, Indiana, from Linda Alis for one year, to begin on August 16, 1983. In August, prior to their arrival in Bloomington, Noble and Odle decided not to take possession of the apartment and attempted to find a sublessee. On August 29, they showed the apartment to prospective sublessees and noticed several defects. They contacted the City of Bloomington's Housing Code Enforcement Officer and requested that he inspect the premises for housing code violations. After the inspection, the enforcement officer informed Noble and Odle that the landlord was in violation of Bloomington Municipal Code Sec. 16.12.080(e), which states that "[i]t shall be a violation of this chapter for any owner to maintain a rental unit without an occupancy permit." The landlord had also failed to register it as a residential unit, as required by the Housing Code. Further, the enforcement officer advised Noble and Odle that, even if the house were registered, it would not pass a housing inspection. Believing that they could not legally find a sublessee and that their lease was void, Noble and Odle informed Alis on September 1 that they would no longer assume responsibility for locating a sublessee. The property was later rented to other tenants. Alis brought suit against Noble and Odle in small claims court for rent and damages she alleged that they owed. The court awarded her $1,266, and Noble and Odle appealed. Although the Housing Code does not address the enforceability of lease agreements for unregistered and permit-less property, Noble and Odle based their appeal on the argument that the lease was illegal because it violated the Housing Code.

Neal, Judge.   Broadly speaking, a contract made in violation of a statute is void. Courts hesitate to brand an "illegal" bargain necessarily void; they engage in a balancing test and evaluate circumstances such as the nature of the subject matter of the contract, the strength of the public policy underlying the statute, the likelihood that a refusal to enforce the bargain or term will further the policy, and how serious or deserved would be the forfeiture suffered by the party attempting to enforce the bargain. Judicial decisions emphasize a distinction between statutes for revenue and statutes for protection of the public health, safety, and welfare. In the case of an agreement made in contravention of a statute designed for the protection of the public, it is more likely that the statute breaker will be denied the enforcement of his bargain.

In our opinion, the lease in the instant case is unenforceable. We agree with Noble and Odle's contention that the policies of protection of public health, safety, and welfare and encouragement of compliance with the housing code are advanced by the registration and occupancy permit provisions of the Municipal Code. The procedure to receive such a permit necessitates compliance with minimum housing standards: Once the unit is registered residential, a temporary occupancy permit is issued. The issuance of the temporary permit triggers an inspection by the Housing Department. After the inspection, an occupancy permit is issued; or, if the unit did not "pass" inspection, additional time is granted to make the repairs necessary to bring the unit into compliance with the code. Clearly, the policy of protecting the public from substandard housing is served by the registration-inspection-permit process: until the unit is registered, the Housing Code Enforcement Office is not aware of its existence and thus is unable to check its compliance with the housing standards set down in the code. Another important factor in our determination turns on the specific factual pattern of this case. Here, Noble and Odle never moved into the apartment and thus never benefited in any way from the lease agreement.

In conclusion, the clear purpose of the Bloomington Housing Code is to provide minimum standards for rental units to protect the health, safety, and welfare of the public. To that end, Bloomington clearly forbids landlords to rent property for the human habitation without complying with the ordinance. Any contrary decision by us would render the ordinance a nullity and permit landlords to ignore it and continue to rent substandard housing as before, taking a chance that the renters, ignorant of the ordinance, would not complain.

The decision of the trial court as to damages for rental payments is reversed, and Alis is ordered to return the $330 security deposit plus interest accrued at the statutory rate.

Judgment reversed in favor of Noble and Odle.

Agreements in Violation of Public Policy Articulated by Courts

Legislative bodies manifest public policy by the laws they enact, which contain rules that lawmakers consider necessary for the public welfare. Courts, too, have broad discretion to articulate public policy and to decline to lend their powers of enforcement to an agreement that would contravene what they deem to be in the best interests of society. There is no simple rule for determining when a particular agreement is contrary to public policy. Public policy may change with the times; changing social and economic conditions may make behavior that was acceptable in an earlier time unacceptable today, or vice versa. The following are examples of agreements that are frequently considered vulnerable to attack on public policy grounds.

Agreements in Restraint of Competition

The policy against restrictions on competition is one of the oldest public policies declared by the common law. This same policy is also the basis of the federal and state antitrust statutes. The policy against restraints on competition is based on the economic judgment that the public interest is best served by free competition. Nevertheless, courts have long recognized that some contractual restrictions on competition serve legitimate business interests and should be enforced. Therefore, agreements that limit competition are scrutinized very closely by the courts to determine whether the restraint imposed is in violation of public policy.

If the *sole* purpose of an agreement is to restrain competition, it violates the public policy and is illegal. For example, if Martin and Bloom, who own competing businesses, enter an agreement whereby each agrees not to solicit or sell to the other's customers, such an agreement would be unenforceable. Where the restriction on competition was part of (*ancillary to*) an otherwise legal contract, the result may be different because the parties may have a legitimate interest to be protected by the restriction on competition.

For example, if Martin had *purchased* Bloom's business, the goodwill of the business was part of what she paid for. She has a legitimate interest in making sure that Bloom does not open a competing business soon after the sale and attract away the very customers whose goodwill she paid for. Or suppose that Martin hired Walker to work as a salesperson in her business. She wants to assure herself that she does not disclose trade secrets, confidential information, or lists of regular customers to Walker only to have Walker quit and enter a competing business.

To protect herself, the buyer or the employer in the above examples might bargain for a contractual clause that would provide that the seller or employee agrees not to engage in a particular competing activity in a specified *geographic area* for a specified *time* after the sale of the business or the termination of employment. This type of clause is called an **ancillary covenant not to compete,** or as it is more commonly known, a **non-competition clause.** They most frequently appear in *employment contracts, contracts for the sale of a business, partnership agreements*, and *small business buy-sell agreements*. In an employment contract, the non-competition clause might be the only part of the contract that the parties put in writing.

Enforceability of Non-Competition Clause
Although non-competition clauses restrict competition and thereby affect the public policy favoring free competition, courts enforce them if they meet the following three criteria.

1. *Clause must serve a legitimate business purpose.* This means that the person protected by the clause must have some justifiable interest—such as an interest in protecting goodwill or trade secrets—that is to be protected by the non-competition clause. It also means that the clause must be *ancillary* to (part of) an otherwise valid contract. For example, a non-competition clause that is one term of an existing employment contract would be ancillary to that contract. By contrast, a promise not to compete would not be enforced if the employee made the promise *after* he had already resigned his job, because the promise not to compete was not ancillary to any existing contract.

2. *The restriction on competition must be reasonable in time, geographic area, and scope.* Another way of stating this is that the restrictions must not be any greater than necessary to protect a legitimate interest. It would be unreasonable for an employer or buyer of a business to restrain the other party from engaging in some activity that is not a competing activity or from doing business in a territory in which the employer or buyer does not do business, because this would not threaten his legitimate interests. Of course, what is reasonable depends on the facts of the case. In the sale of a business conducted throughout a three-state area, a restriction on the seller's engaging in the same business in those three states would probably be reasonable. If the company sold engages in business only within a 30-mile radius of the capital city of one of those states, however, the three-state restriction would be unreasonable.

3. *The non-competition clause should not impose an undue hardship.* A court will not enforce a non-competition clause if its restraints are unduly burdensome either on the public or on the party whose ability to compete would be restrained. In one recent case, for example, the court refused to enforce a non-competition clause against a gastroenterologist because of evidence that the restriction would have imposed a hardship on patients and other physicians requiring his services.[3]

Non-competition clauses in employment contracts that have the practical effect of preventing the restrained person from earning a livelihood are unlikely to be enforced as well. This is discussed further in the next section.

Non-Competition Clauses in Employment Contracts
Restrictions on competition work a greater hardship on an employee than on a person who has sold a business. For this reason, courts tend to judge non-competition clauses contained in employment contracts by a stricter standard than they judge similar clauses contained in contracts for the sale of a business. In fact, there is a trend toward refusing enforcement of these clauses in employment contracts unless the employer can bring forth very good evidence that he has a protectible interest that justifies enforcement of the clause. The employer can do this by showing that he has entrusted the employee with trade secrets or confidential information, or that his goodwill with "near-permanent" customers is threatened. Absent this kind of proof, a court might conclude that the employer is just trying to avoid competition with a more efficient competitor and refuse enforcement because there is no legitimate business interest that requires protection. You will see this approach in the case of *Steamatic of Kansas City, Inc. v. Rhea*, which follows.

Furthermore, many courts refuse to enforce non-competition clauses if they restrict employees from engaging in a "common calling." A *common calling* is an occupation that does not require extensive or highly sophisticated training and which involves relatively simple, repetitive tasks. Under this common calling restriction, various courts have refused to enforce non-competition clauses against salespersons, a barber, and an auto-trim repairperson. In some states, statutes prohibit or limit the use of non-competition clauses in employment contracts.

---

[3] *Iredell Digestive Disease Clinic, P.A. v. Petrozza*, 373 S.E.2d 449 (N.C. Ct. App. 1988).

STEAMATIC OF KANSAS CITY, INC. v. RHEA

763 S.W.2d 190 (Mo. Ct. App. 1988)

Steamatic of Kansas City, Inc., specialized in cleaning and restoring property damaged by fire, smoke, water, or other elements. It employed Samuel Rhea as a marketing representative. His duties included soliciting customers, preparing cost estimates, supervising restoration work, and conducting seminars. At the time of his employment, Rhea signed a non-competition agreement prohibiting him from entering into a business in competition with Steamatic within six counties of the Kansas City area for a period of two years after the termination of his employment with Steamatic.

Late in 1987, Rhea decided to leave Steamatic. In contemplation of the move, he secretly extracted the agreement restricting his postemployment activity from the company's files and destroyed it. Steamatic learned of this and discharged Rhea. Steamatic filed suit against Rhea to enforce the non-competition agreement when it learned that he was entering a competing business. The trial court enforced the non-competition agreement and granted an injunction against Rhea. Rhea appealed.

Clark, Presiding Judge.   Covenants not to compete restrain commerce and limit the freedom of an employee to pursue his trade. Enforcement of such agreements is, therefore, carefully restricted. An employer cannot extract a restrictive covenant from an employee merely to protect himself from competition but a limited time and geographical restraint may be deemed reasonable and enforceable if a legitimate protectible interest of the employer is served. An employer has a protectible and proprietary right in his "stock of customers" and their good will.

In the present case, before Steamatic may claim to enforce the agreement prohibiting Rhea from engaging in a competing business, it must appear that Steamatic has a stock of customers who regularly deal with Steamatic. A customer in this sense is one who repeatedly has business dealings with a particular tradesman or business. Unless the proponent of the restrictive covenant has a trade following, that is, a group of customers who regularly patronize the business of the particular employer, there can be no stock of customers and no protectible interest.

In this case the facts showed that disaster victims engaged Steamatic to provide restoration services only on a single occasion after the event of a fire or other casualty. The only possible repeat business which Steamatic could anticipate would be in those rare instances when a second casualty befell the same victim. No evidence was adduced to show that such had occurred in the past, or, indeed, that Steamatic enjoyed any repeat business at all. Steamatic was not shown to have had any contact with the customer before the casualty gave rise to a need for restoration services. After the services were performed, there was no repeat business. Prospects for restoration services were not contacted and solicited through any confidential or privileged source, but merely upon knowledge generally available to the public at large that a casualty had occurred. There was, therefore, no ongoing customer relationship between Steamatic and any identifiable persons or companies.

Steamatic cites *Osage Glass, Inc. v. Donovan* to support enjoining Rhea from engaging in a business in competition with Steamatic. The case is distinguishable. Osage was in the business of installing automobile windshields. Its dealings were with insurance companies, fleet operators, body shops and automobile dealerships. Donovan was the manager of the Kansas City office and, as such, he had developed substantial customer contacts. After leaving Osage and taking employment with a competitor, he was in a position, if not enjoined, to divert that business from Osage to his new employer. It was on this ground that the court decided in favor of enforcing the restrictive covenant. There were no comparable facts in the present case because Rhea was not shown to have any customer following nor, indeed, were there any identifiable customer contacts by reason of the nature of the business.

The evidence did show that Rhea was careful to maintain a good reputation for Steamatic with the [insurance] adjustors as a company which "got the job done" and satisfied the insured. The purpose was to procure a favorable recommendation for Steamatic by the adjustor if the latter's advice were sought by a disaster victim. The evidence was that the owner of the damaged property decided whether to employ Steamatic, or some other company, and it was the owner's responsibility to pay the charges even though the proceeds of an insurance claim would defray the expense in whole or in part. The insurance companies were not Steamatic customers and therefore Steamatic had no protectible interest in the good will of the adjustors.

It is apparent Rhea set about to enter employment competitive with Steamatic under the impression that he would be in violation of his agreement. His conduct in surreptitiously removing and destroying the agreements leads to this conclusion. Guilty conduct, however, is not the test by which the availability of injunctive relief is measured. The question is whether Steamatic had a protectible interest in a stock of customers. It did not and therefore Rhea's conduct in removing his papers from Steamatic's files is not relevant. The trial court erred when it enjoined Rhea from engaging in the damage restoration business.

Judgment reversed in favor of Rhea.

The Effect of Overly Broad Non-Competition Clauses   The courts of different states treat unreasonably broad non-competition clauses in different ways. Some courts will strike the entire restriction if they find it to be unreasonable, and will refuse to grant the buyer or employer any protection. Others will refuse to enforce the restraint as written, but will adjust the clause and impose such restraints as would be reasonable. In case of breach of an enforceable non-competition clause, the person benefited by the clause may seek damages or an injunction (a court order preventing the promisor from violating the covenant).

Exculpatory Clauses

An **exculpatory clause** is a provision in a contract that purports to relieve one of the parties from tort liability. Exculpatory clauses are suspect on public policy grounds for two reasons. First, courts are concerned that a party who can contract away his liability for negligence will not have the incentive to use care to avoid hurting others. Second, courts are concerned that an agreement that accords one party such a powerful advantage might have been the result of the abuse of superior bargaining power rather than truly voluntary choice. Although exculpatory agreements are often said to be "disfavored" in the law, courts do not want to prevent parties who are dealing on a fair and voluntary basis from determining how the risks of their transaction shall be borne if their agreement does not threaten public health or safety.

Courts enforce exculpatory clauses in some cases and refuse to enforce them in others, depending on the circumstances of the case, the characteristics and relationship of the parties, and the language of the agreement. A few ground rules can be stated. First, an exculpatory clause cannot protect a party from liability for any wrongdoing greater than negligence. One that purports to relieve a person from liability for fraud or some other willful tort will be considered to be against public policy. In some cases, in fact, exculpatory clauses have been invalidated on this ground because of broad language stating that one of the parties was relieved of "all liability." Second, exculpatory clauses will not be effective to exclude tort liability on the part of a party who owes a duty to the public (such as an airline), because this would present an obvious threat to the public health and safety.

A third possible limitation on the enforceability of exculpatory clauses arises from the increasing array of statutes and common law rules that impose certain obligations on one party to a contract for the benefit of the other party to the contract. Workers' compensation statutes and laws requiring landlords to maintain leased property in a habitable condition are examples of such laws. Sometimes the person on whom such an obligation is placed will attempt to escape it by inserting an exculpatory or waiver provision in a contract. Such clauses are often—though not always—found to be against public policy because, if enforced, they would frustrate the very purpose of imposing the duty in question. For example, an employee's agreement to relieve her employer from workers' compensation liability is likely to be held illegal as a violation of public policy.

Even if a clause is not against public policy on any of the above three grounds, a court may still refuse to enforce it if a court finds that the clause was **unconscionable** or the product of abuse of superior bargaining power. (Unconscionability is discussed later in this chapter.) This determination depends on all of the facts of the case. Facts that tend to show that the exculpatory clause was the product of *knowing* consent will increase the likelihood that it will be enforced. For example, a clause that is written in clear language and conspicuous print is more likely to be enforced than one written in "legalese" and presented in fine print. Facts that tend to show that the exculpatory clause was the product of *voluntary* consent increase the likelihood of enforcement of the clause. For example, a clause contained in a contract for a frivolous or unnecessary activity, such as the Ironman Decathlon in *Milligan v. Big Valley Corporation*, is more likely to be enforced than is an exculpatory clause contained in a contract for a necessary activity such as medical care.

MILLIGAN v. BIG VALLEY CORPORATION

754 P.2d 1063 (Sup. Ct. Wyo. 1988)

Dean Griffin, an expert skier and certified ski instructor, entered the Ironman Decathlon held at the Grand Targhee ski resort, which was owned and operated by Big Valley Corporation. The decathlon was held for fun rather than profit. It consisted of several events, including swimming five pool laps, bowling one line, drinking a quart of beer, throwing darts, and skiing in both downhill and cross-country races. The downhill ski race was the first event in the decathlon. It was held early in the morning before the resort was opened to the public. Prior to the race, Griffin and all of the other downhill contestants were required to sign a document entitled "General Release of Claim." This provided in part:

In consideration of my being allowed to participate in IRONMAN DECATHLON at Targhee Resort, Alta, Wyoming, I irrevocably and forever hereby release and discharge any and all of the employees, agents, or servants and owners of Targhee Resort and the other sponsors of IRONMAN DECATHLON officially connected with this event of and from any and all legal claims or legal liability of any kind involving bodily injury or death sustained by me during my stay at Targhee Resort. I hereby personally assume all risks in connection with said event and I further release the aforementioned resort, its agents, and operators, for any harm which might befall me as a participant in this event, whether foreseen or unforeseen and further save and hold harmless said resort and persons from any claim by me or my family, estate, heirs or assigns.

/s/ Dean Griffin 4/13/84

About ten minutes after the race began, Griffin was found unconscious approximately three quarters of the way down the mountain. He died a few hours later. No one witnessed the incident that caused his death, but it was speculated that he lost control of his skis and hit a tree.

Elizabeth Milligan, as personal representative for Griffin's estate, filed a wrongful death action against Big Valley on behalf of Griffin's son. The trial court granted a summary judgment in favor of Big Valley on the ground that the exculpatory agreement signed by Griffin released Big Valley from all liability. Milligan appealed.

Cardine, Justice. Exculpatory agreements releasing parties from negligence liability for damages or injury are valid and enforceable in Wyoming if they do not violate public policy. Generally, agreements absolving participants and proprietors from negligence liability during hazardous recreational activities are enforceable, subject to willful misconduct limitations.

To determine whether this type of release is valid and enforceable, we consider:

(1) Whether there exists a duty to the public;

(2) The nature of the service performed;

(3) Whether the contract was fairly entered into;

(4) Whether the intention of the parties is expressed in clear and unambiguous language.

A duty to the public exists if the nature of the business or service affects the public interest and the service performed is considered an essential service. Types of services thought to be subject to public regulation and therefore demanding a public duty or considered essential have included common carriers, hospitals and doctors, public utilities, innkeepers, public warehousemen, employers, and services involving extra-hazardous activities. Generally, a private recreational business does not qualify as a service demanding a special duty to the public, nor are its services of a special, highly necessary or essential nature. The Ironman Decathlon can best be labeled a recreational type of activity of no great public import.

The agreement in question does not involve severe disparity of bargaining power. A disparity of bargaining power will be found when a contracting party with little or no bargaining strength has no reasonable alternative to entering the contract at the mercy of the other's negligence. For example, a member of the public contracting with a public utility, common carrier, hospital, or employer often has no real choice or alternative and is, therefore, at the mercy of the other. Such is not the case here. Grand Targhee did not force Griffin to ski in the race. Skiing in the race was not a matter of practical necessity for the public, and putting on the race was not an essential service. Thus, no decisive bargaining advantage existed. No evidence suggests that Griffin was unfairly pressured into signing the agreement or that he was deprived of an opportunity to understand its implications.

Milligan argues that the release was entered into unfairly because it contained boilerplate language prepared solely by the resort and was an adhesive contract. The argument is without merit. The mere fact that a contract is on a printed form prepared by one party and offered on a "take it or leave it" basis does not automatically establish it as an adhesive contract. There must be a showing that the parties were greatly disparate in bargaining power and that there was no opportunity for negotiation for services which could not be obtained elsewhere. Here no such showing was made. Indeed, the evidence is to the contrary. The release was fairly executed and satisfies the first three criteria.

The final factor requires us to determine whether the release agreement evidences the parties' intent to release Big Valley from liability for negligent acts in clear and unambiguous language. The language could not be clearer. Examining the release in light of the purpose of the contract, it is clear that the parties intended to release the ski resort and all those involved in the Ironman Decathlon from liability. It is clear that the intent was to release Big Valley from negligence liability. The absence of the word "negligence" is not fatal to an exculpatory clause if the terms of the contract clearly show intent to extinguish liability.

We conclude that the release is not void as a matter of public policy and that Big Valley was entitled to judgment as a matter of law.

Judgment for Big Valley affirmed.

Family Relationships and Public Policy   In view of the central position of the family as a valued social institution, it is not surprising that an agreement that unreasonably tends to interfere with family relationships will be considered illegal. Examples of this type of contract include agreements whereby one of the parties agrees to divorce a spouse or agrees not to marry.

In recent years, courts have been presented with an increasing number of agreements between unmarried cohabitants that purport to agree upon the manner in which the parties' property will be shared or divided upon separation. It used to be widely held that contracts between unmarried cohabitants were against public policy because they were based on an immoral relationship. As unmarried cohabitation has become more widespread, however, the law concerning the enforceability of agreements between unmarried couples has changed. For example, in the 1976 case of *Marvin v. Marvin*, the California Supreme Court held that an agreement between an unmarried couple to pool income and share property could be enforceable.[4] Today, most courts hold that agreements between unmarried couples are not against public policy unless they are explicitly based on illegal sexual relations as the consideration for the contract or unless one or more of the parties is married to someone else.

UNCONSCIONABILITY

Development of the Doctrine of Unconscionability

Under classical contract law, courts were reluctant to inquire into the fairness of an agreement. Because the prevailing social attitudes and economic philosophy strongly favored freedom of contract, American courts took the position that so long as there had been no fraud, duress, misrepresentation, mistake, or undue influence in the bargaining process, unfairness in an agreement entered into by competent adults did not render the agreement unenforceable.

As the changing nature of our society produced many contract situations in which the bargaining positions of the parties were grossly unequal, the classical contract assumption that each party was capable of protecting himself was no longer persuasive. Legislatures responded to this problem by enacting a variety of statutory measures to protect individuals against the abuse of superior bargaining power in specific situations. Examples of such legislation include minimum wage laws and rent control ordinances. Courts became more sensitive to the fact that superior bargaining power often led to **contracts of adhesion** (contracts in which a stronger party is able to dictate unfair terms to a weaker party, leaving the weaker party no practical choice but to "adhere" to the terms). Some courts responded by borrowing a doctrine that had been developed and used for a long time in courts of equity,[5] the doctrine of **unconscionability.** Under this doctrine, courts would refuse to grant the equitable remedy of specific performance for breach of a contract if they found the contract to be oppressively unfair, or unconscionable.

One of the most far-reaching efforts to correct abuses of superior bargaining power was the enactment of section 2–302 of the Uniform Commercial Code, which gives courts the power to refuse to enforce all or part of a contract for the sale of goods or to modify such a contract if it is found to be unconscionable. By virtue of its inclusion in Article 2 of the Uniform Commercial Code, the prohibition against unconscionable terms applies to every contract for the sale of goods. The concept of unconscionability is not confined to contracts for the sale of goods, however. Section 208 of the *Restatement (Second) of Contracts*, which closely resembles the unconscionability section of the UCC, provides that courts may decline to enforce unconscionable terms or contracts. The prohibition of unconscionability has been adopted as part of the public policy of many states by courts in cases that did not involve the sale of goods, such as banking transactions and contracts for the sale or rental of real estate. It is therefore fair to state that the concept of unconscionability has become part of the general body of contract law.

Meaning of Unconscionability

Neither the UCC nor the *Restatement (Second) of Contracts* attempts to define the term unconscionability. Though the concept is impossible to define with precision, unconscionability is generally taken to mean the *absence of meaningful choice* together with *terms unreasonably advantageous* to one of the parties.

---

[4] 134 Cal. Rptr. 815 (1976).

[5] The Nature of Law chapter discusses courts of equity.

The facts of each individual case are crucial to determining whether a contract term is unconscionable. Courts will scrutinize the process by which the contract was reached to see if the agreement was reached by fair methods and whether it can fairly be said to be the product of knowing and voluntary consent.

Procedural Unconscionability   Courts and writers often refer to unfairness in the bargaining process as *procedural unconscionability*. Some facts that may point to procedural unconscionability include the use of fine print or inconspicuously placed terms; complex, legalistic language; and high-pressure sales tactics. One of the most significant facts pointing to procedural unconscionability is the lack of voluntariness as shown by a marked imbalance in the parties' bargaining positions, particularly where the weaker party is unable to negotiate more favorable terms because of economic need, lack of time, or market factors. In fact, in most contracts that have been found to be unconscionable, there has been a serious inequality of bargaining power between the parties. It is important to note, however, that the mere existence of unequal bargaining power does not make a contract unconscionable. If it did, every consumer's contract with the telephone company or the electric company would be unenforceable. Rather, in an unconscionable contract, the party with the stronger bargaining power *exploits* that power by driving a bargain containing a term or terms that are so unfair that they "shock the conscience of the court." You will see several examples of procedural unconscionability in *John Deere Leasing Company v. Blubaugh*.

JOHN DEERE LEASING COMPANY v. BLUBAUGH

636 F. Supp. 1569 (U.S. Dist. Ct., D. Kan. 1986)

Reuben Blubaugh, a farmer, leased a Model 6620 combine from John Deere Leasing (JDL). The lease, which was printed on very lightweight paper, provided that Blubaugh would pay four annual rentals of $15,991.37, beginning July 1983, and at the end of the lease term would have the option to purchase the equipment for $27,191.25. On the reverse side of the lease, printed in light colored fine print, were several terms that spelled out what JDL's remedies would be if Blubaugh failed to make a rental payment. These provisions gave JDL the right to repossess the combine, sell it, and keep the proceeds of such a sale. Even though Blubaugh was only agreeing to rent the combine rather than to buy it, these default provisions also made Blubaugh responsible for an additional amount of money that represented the difference between the "termination value" of the combine (as defined in a complicated formula on the reverse side of the lease) and any money received by JDL if it repossessed and sold the combine.

Blubaugh read and signed the front of the contract but did not read the back. His understanding was that he had entered a basic lease with an option to purchase arrangement. His potential liability under the lease was not explained to him by anyone from JDL. Blubaugh paid $30,939.16 toward the first two rental payments, then made no further payments. JDL repossessed the combine and sold it for $42,000. JDL then sued Blubaugh for an additional $12,054.63, which was the amount due under the default clauses on the reverse side of the lease. Blubaugh defended on the ground that the default clauses were unconscionable.

Kelly, District Judge.   Before turning to the discussion of the legal principles which are controlling in this case, the court makes the following observations. The terms in question herein are on the back of the lease, and are written in such fine, light print as to be nearly illegible. In fact, the print is so light that neither party was able to obtain a satisfactory photocopy. The court was required to use a magnifying glass to read the reverse side. The court found the wording to be unreasonably complex. It is as if the scrivener intended to conceal the thrust of the agreement in the convoluted language and fine print. The term which provides for the addition of the option price to the lessee's liability on default is a term quite outside the norm. JDL's contention that Blubaugh had a duty to ascertain the meaning of all terms, in the face of the near concealment of this unusually harsh remedy, is inexcusably inadequate and need not be tolerated by any court. This court is surprised that a reputable company such as Deere would stoop to this.

The contract in the case at bar is a lease agreement. The UCC's application is primarily limited to contracts for the sale of goods. However, the unconscionability doctrine of the UCC has often been extended by analogy to other areas of the law. Similarly, it may be extended to a case involving a lease of farm equipment.

The term "unconscionability" is not defined in the UCC. Courts, in attempting to define "unconscionability" under UCC 2–302, have distinguished between "procedural" and "substantive" unconscionability. An illustrative case is *Bank of Indiana, N.A. v. Holyfield*, wherein the court stated:

The indicators of procedural unconscionability generally fall into two areas: (1) lack of knowledge, and (2) lack of voluntariness. A lack of knowledge is demonstrated by a lack of understanding of the contract terms arising from inconspicuous print or the use of complex, legalistic language, disparity in sophistication of parties, and lack of opportunity to study the contract and inquire about contract terms. A lack of voluntariness is demonstrated in contracts of adhesion when there is a great imbalance in the parties' relative bargaining power, the stronger party's terms are unnegotiable, and the weaker party is prevented by market factors, timing or other pressures from being able to contract with another party on more favorable terms or to refrain from contracting at all.

Substantive unconscionability is found when the terms of the contract are of such an oppressive character as to be unconscionable. It is present when there is a one-sided agreement whereby one party is deprived of all the benefits of the agreement or left without a remedy for another party's nonperformance or breach, a large disparity between the cost and price or a price far in excess of that prevailing in the market price, or terms which bear no reasonable relationship to business risks assumed by the parties.

In the case at bar, *both* procedural and substantive unconscionability are present. First, the lease was procedurally unconscionable because Blubaugh agreed to terms of which he had no knowledge, and his agreement was not "voluntary." While it is true that Blubaugh failed to read the back of the lease, he probably did not read it because he did not see it. On the first try here the court did not! Moreover, the court is convinced that even if he had read it, he would not have understood it. The lease was preprinted and so complex by virtue of its legalistic language that a party with no training in law or finance could not possibly decipher the potential for disadvantage. As previously noted, the term in question was in minute print on the back of the lease, and was in such light grey type as to be illegible. The definition of "termination value" was *not* next to the section on "lessor's remedies" but was hidden behind a mass of additional terms. Further, there was clearly a disparity in sophistication between JDL and Blubaugh, a farmer. Undoubtedly Blubaugh relied on JDL's superior knowledge. Therefore, Blubaugh lacked knowledge of his risk of liability when he signed the lease.

Additionally, the surrounding circumstances indicate Blubaugh's agreement to the detrimental term was not voluntary. The lease was an "adhesion" contract that was obviously drafted by JDL for its benefit and presented to Blubaugh in a manner that did not leave room for negotiations. The court is convinced that a farmer is more akin to a consumer than to a commercial party. JDL was clearly in superior bargaining position. Because Blubaugh lacked knowledge and voluntariness, the contract was procedurally unconscionable.

The clause was also substantively unconscionable in that it exacted a penalty on Blubaugh for terminating the lease. In this case, the lessor's remedies allowed JDL to add the "purchase option" amount to the rental deficiency, and then to set this amount off against the sale proceeds. Here, however, no binding contract of sale existed. Allowing JDL to recoup the option to purchase price from Blubaugh is a penalty and would allow JDL to reap a windfall. Accordingly, the court finds the provision to be substantively unconscionable.

For the foregoing reasons the court finds the lease provision which allows lessor to recover the option price upon the lessee's breach to be unconscionable as a matter of law. Therefore, the court in its discretion will not enforce the lease provision.

Judgment entered in favor of Blubaugh.

Substantive Unconscionability   In addition to looking at facts that might indicate procedural unconscionability, courts will scrutinize the contract terms themselves to determine whether they are oppressive, unreasonably one-sided, or unjustifiably harsh. This aspect of unconscionability is often referred to as *substantive unconscionability*. Examples include situations in which a party to the contract bears a disproportionate amount of the risk or other negative aspects of the transaction and situations in which a party is deprived of a remedy for the other party's breach. In some cases, unconscionability has been found in situations in which the contract provides for a price that is greatly in excess of the usual market price.

There is no mechanical test for determining whether a clause is unconscionable. Generally, in cases in which courts have found a contract term to be unconscionable, there are elements of *both* procedural and substantive unconscionability. Though courts have broad discretion to determine what contracts will be deemed to be unconscionable, it must be remembered that the doctrine of unconscionability is designed to prevent oppression and unfair surprise—not to relieve people of the effects of unwise bargains.

The cases concerning unconscionability are quite diverse. Some courts, such as the court in the following case, *Murphy v. McNamara*, have found unconscionability in contracts involving grossly unfair sales prices. Although the doctrine of unconscionability has been raised primarily by victimized consumers, there have been cases in which businesspeople in an inherently weak bargaining position have been successful in asserting unconscionability.

MURPHY v. MCNAMARA

416 A.2d 170 (Conn. Super. Ct. 1979)

Carolyn Murphy, a welfare recipient with four minor children, saw an advertisement in the local newspaper that had been placed by Brian McNamara, a television and stereo dealer. It stated the following:

Why buy when you can rent? Color TV and stereos. *Rent to own!* Use our Rent-to-own plan and let TV Rentals deliver either of these models to your home. *We feature*—Never a repair bill—No deposit—No credit needed—No long-term obligation—Weekly or monthly rates available—Order by phone—Call today—Watch color TV tonight.

As a result of this advertisement, Murphy leased a 25-inch Philco color console television set from McNamara under the "Rent-to-own" plan. The lease agreement provided that Murphy would pay a $20 delivery charge and 78 weekly payments of $16. At the end of this period, Murphy would own the set. The agreement also provided that the customer could return the set at any time and terminate the lease as long as all rental payments had been made up to the return date. Murphy entered the lease because she believed that she could acquire ownership of a television set without first establishing credit, as was stressed in McNamara's ads. At no time did McNamara inform Murphy that the terms of the lease required her to pay a total of $1,268 for the set. The retail sales price for the same set was $499.

After making $436 in payments over a period of about six months, Murphy read a newspaper article criticizing the lease plan and realized the amount that the agreement required her to pay. She stopped making payments, and McNamara sought to repossess the set, threatening to file a criminal complaint against her if she failed to return it. Murphy, claiming that the agreement was unconscionable, filed suit for an injunction barring McNamara from repossessing the TV set or filing charges against her.

Berdon, Judge. An excessive price charged a consumer with unequal bargaining power can constitute a violation of 2–302 of the Uniform Commercial Code. In the case of *Jones v. Star Credit Corp.*, the plaintiffs, welfare recipients, purchased a home freezer unit for $900.00. The freezer had a retail value of approximately $300.00. The court held the contract was unconscionable under 2–302 of the Uniform Commercial Code and reformed the contract by excusing further payments over the $600.00 already paid by the plaintiffs. There have been similar holdings by other courts. The failure on the part of McNamara to advise Murphy of the total price she would be required to pay under the terms of the contract further compounded the unfairness of his trade practices.

In sum, an agreement for the sale of consumer goods entered into with a consumer having unequal bargaining power and which calls for an unconscionable purchase price, constitutes an unfair trade practice. By unequal bargaining power, the court means that at the time the contract was made there was such an inequality of bargaining power (for example, because of the consumer's need for credit) that the merchant could insist on the inclusion of unconscionable terms in the contract which were not justifiable on the grounds of commercial necessity. The intent of this rule is not to erase the doctrine of freedom of contract, but to make realistic the assumption of the law that the agreement has resulted from real bargaining between parties who had freedom of choice and understanding and ability to negotiate in a meaningful fashion. Viewed in that sense, freedom to contract survives but the marketers of consumer goods are brought to an awareness that the restraint of unconscionability is always hovering over their operations and that courts will employ it to balance the interests of the consumer public and those of the seller.

Injunction granted, prohibiting McNamara from repossessing the TV set, using harassing collection techniques, or filing criminal charges against Murphy, but permitting McNamara to file suit for the difference between the amount Murphy paid and the value of the set.

Procedure for Determining Unconscionability

Section 2–302 states that when a claim of unconscionability is asserted or when it appears to the court that a term may be unconscionable, the court must afford the parties the opportunity to present evidence about the setting, purpose, and effect of the contract. This apparently means that the court must hold a hearing on the issue of unconscionability. The purpose of such a hearing is to enable the court to make a determination of whether the term is unconscionable. Section 2–302 specifically states that unconscionability is a *matter of law.* That is, only the judge can decide whether a clause is unconscionable; it is not a matter for consideration by the jury.

Consequences of Unconscionability

The UCC and the *Restatement* sections on unconscionability give courts the power to manipulate a contract containing an unconscionable provision so as to reach a just result. If a court finds that a contract or a term in a contract is unconscionable, it can do one of three things: it can refuse to enforce the entire agreement; it can refuse to enforce the unconscionable provision but enforce the rest of the contract; or it can "limit the application of the unconscionable clause so as to avoid any unconscionable result." This last alternative has been taken by courts to mean that they can make adjustments in the terms of the contract.

EFFECT OF ILLEGALITY

General Rule

As a general rule, courts will refuse to give any remedy for the breach of an illegal agreement. A court will refuse to enforce an illegal agreement and will also refuse to permit a party who has fully or partially performed her part of the agreement to recover what she has parted with. This "hands-off illegal agreements" approach is reflected in the *Blossom Farm Products* case, which appeared earlier in this chapter. The reason for this rule is to serve the public interest, not to punish the parties.

In some cases, the public interest is best served by allowing some recovery to one or both of the parties. Such cases constitute exceptions to the "hands off" rule. The following discussion concerns the most common situations in which courts will grant some remedy even though they find the agreement to be illegal.

Excusable Ignorance of Facts or Legislation

Though it is often said that ignorance of the law is no excuse, courts will, under certain circumstances, permit a party to an illegal agreement who was excusably ignorant of facts or legislation that rendered the agreement illegal to recover damages for breach of the agreement. This exception is used where only *one* of the parties acted in ignorance of the illegality of the agreement and the other party was aware that the agreement was illegal. For this exception to apply, the facts or legislation of which the person claiming damages was ignorant must be of a relatively minor character—that is, it must not involve an immoral act or a serious threat to the public welfare. Finally, the person who is claiming damages cannot recover damages for anything that he does after learning of the illegality. For example, Warren enters a contract to perform in a play at Craig's theater. Warren does not know that Craig does not have the license to operate a theater as required by statute. Warren can recover the wages agreed upon in the parties' contract for work that he performed before learning of the illegality.

When *both* of the parties are ignorant of facts or legislation of a relatively minor character, courts will not permit them to enforce the agreement and receive what they had bargained for, but they will permit the parties to recover what they have parted with.

Rights of Parties Not Equally in the Wrong

The courts will often permit a party who is not equally in the wrong (in technical legal terms, not *in pari delicto*) to recover what she has parted with under an illegal agreement. One of the most common situations in which this exception is used involves the rights of "protected parties"—people who were intended to be protected by a regulatory statute—who contract with parties who are not properly licensed under that statute. Most regulatory statutes are intended to protect the public. As a general rule, if a person guilty of violating a regulatory statute enters into an agreement with another person for whose protection the statute was adopted, the agreement will be enforceable by the party whom the legislature intended to protect. For example, most states require foreign corporations—those incorporated outside the state—to get a license before doing business in the state. These statutes often specifically provide that an unlicensed corporation cannot enforce contracts that it enters into with citizens of the state. Citizens of the licensing state, however, are generally allowed to enforce their contracts with the foreign corporation.

Another common situation in which courts will grant a remedy to a party who is not equally in the wrong is one in which the less guilty party has been induced to enter the agreement by misrepresentation, fraud, duress, or undue influence.

Rescission before Performance of Illegal Act

Obviously, public policy is best served by any rule that encourages people not to commit illegal acts. People who have fully or partially performed their part of an illegal contract have little incentive to raise the question

FIGURE 1   Effect of Illegality

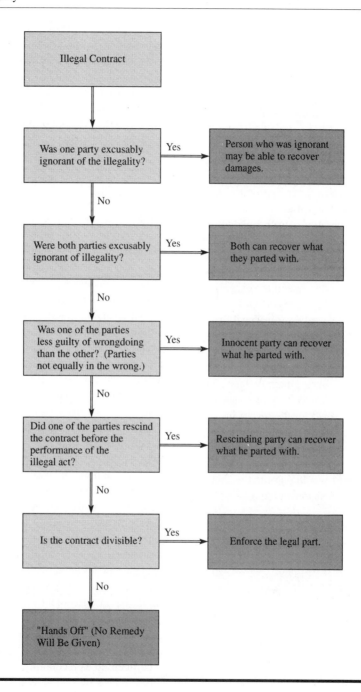

of illegality if they know that they will be unable to recover what they have given because of the courts' hands-off approach to illegal agreements. To encourage people to cancel illegal contracts, courts will allow a person who rescinds such a contract before any illegal act has

been performed to recover any consideration that he has given. For example, Dixon, the owner of a restaurant, pays O'Leary, an employee of a competitor's restaurant, $1,000 to obtain some of the competitor's recipes. If Dixon has second thoughts and tells O'Leary the deal is off before receiving any recipes, he can recover the $1,000 he paid O'Leary.

Divisible Contracts

If part of an agreement is legal and part is illegal, the courts will enforce the legal part so long as it is possible to separate the two parts. A contract is said to be *divisible*—that is, the legal part can be separated from the illegal part—if the contract consists of several promises or acts by one party, each of which corresponds with an act or a promise by the other party. In other words, there must be a separate consideration for each promise or act for a contract to be considered divisible.

Where no separate consideration is exchanged for the legal and illegal parts of an agreement, the agreement is said to be *indivisible*. As a general rule, an indivisible contract that contains an illegal part will be entirely unenforceable unless it comes within one of the exceptions discussed above. However, if the major portion of a contract is legal, but the contract contains an illegal provision that does not affect the primary, legal portion, courts will often enforce the legal part of the agreement and simply decline to enforce the illegal part. For example, suppose Alberts sells his barbershop to Bates. The contract of sale provides that Alberts will not engage in barbering anywhere in the world for the rest of his life. The major portion of the contract—the sale of the business—is perfectly legal. A provision of the contract—the ancillary covenant not to compete—is overly restrictive, and thus illegal. A court would enforce the sale of the business but modify or refuse to enforce the restraint provision.

Figure 1 illustrates the effect of illegality.

ETHICAL AND PUBLIC POLICY CONCERNS

1. Was it right that the defendant in the *Blossom Farm Products* case did not have to pay its debt to the plaintiff, when the defendant was the one who used the product for an illegal purpose? What is the justification for giving a windfall to the primary wrongdoer?

2. You read that the law makes a distinction between contracts that violate regulatory statutes and contracts that violate revenue-raising statutes. What is the rationale for this distinction? Would it be better for the law simply to hold that *any* contract that violates *any* statute would be illegal? Why or why not?

3. What are some ethical justifications for the decisions that the courts reached in the *Murphy* and *Blubaugh* cases? In both cases, the contracts in question were held to be unconscionable even though the individuals who signed the contracts *could have* read them and figured out their obligations. Who should have the responsibility to make sure that the person signing a contract understands his obligations, the person who drafts and offers the contract or the person who signs it?

SUMMARY

An illegal agreement is one that involves a violation of some *public policy* (public interest recognized by a court, legislature, or other lawmaker) and threatens the public welfare to the extent that the normal interests favoring enforcement of contracts are outweighed by the need to avoid the danger to the public. Deciding whether to hold an agreement illegal requires courts to balance a number of factors. They must consider how important the public policy is and how much the agreement in question would interfere with that policy. They must also consider whether any serious wrongdoing was involved in the agreement and how directly the agreement was connected with any wrongdoing.

Sometimes, a legislature, in a statute prohibiting a certain act, will expressly provide that a contract that involves the performance of that act is void. Examples of such statutes include statutes prohibiting usury, wagering, and certain transactions on Sundays. Agreements that involve violations of statutes can also be illegal, even if the statute in question does not specifically address the enforceability of contracts that involve a violation of the statute. If the formation or performance of an agreement requires the commission of a serious crime, the agreement will be considered illegal. Similarly, an agreement that promotes the commission of a crime can be illegal.

State and local legislation also require persons who practice a variety of trades, businesses, and professions to be licensed as a condition of doing business. When a person enters into an agreement to perform a regulated act for which she is not properly licensed, the agreement would be considered illegal if the violated licensing statute was *regulatory*, that is, designed for the protection of the public. If the purpose of the licensing statute was *revenue raising*, or if the purpose of the statute is relatively unimportant compared to the forfeiture that would result from a denial of enforcement, the agreement is not illegal.

Courts have broad discretion to articulate public policies and to refuse to enforce agreements that present a serious threat to those policies. One such policy is the public policy against restrictions on competition. If the sole purpose of an agreement is to restrain competition, it is illegal. If an agreement that restrains competition is part of an otherwise legal contract, the agreement is called an *ancillary covenant not to compete* or *noncompetition clause*. Such clauses are legal so long as they serve a legitimate business purpose, the restriction is no greater than is needed to protect a valid business interest, and they present no undue hardship to the public or to the person whose freedom is restricted. Non-competition clauses in employment contracts are usually subjected to a stricter standard of scrutiny than are such clauses in contracts for the sale of a business. The employer must be able to satisfy the court that it had some protectible interest such as trade secrets, confidential information, or the goodwill of a stock of regular customers. The non-competition clause will be scrutinized to determine whether the nature of the restriction and the time and geographic area of the restriction are reasonable. If a court finds that the restriction is too broad, it may refuse to enforce it completely or it may enforce the restriction to the extent that is reasonable under the circumstances.

Exculpatory agreements (agreements to relieve a party of tort liability) are held to be illegal if the exculpated party owes a duty to the public or if such an agreement purports to excuse a person from liability for fraud or other willful torts. Such agreements are often held to be ineffective in relieving a party to a contract from a statutory or common law duty to act for the benefit of the other party to the contract. An exculpatory clause relieving a person who owes no duty to the public from negligence liability might still be found to be against public policy if the parties to the agreement were not dealing on a fair and equal bargaining basis or other facts tended to show the lack of voluntary, knowing consent. In such a situation, the exculpatory agreement might be found to be unconscionable. A variety of other public policies have been recognized by courts, such as the public policy favoring the protection of the family.

A very important development in contract law regarding the protection of public policy is the enactment of section 2–302 of the Uniform Commercial Code, which gives courts the power to refuse to enforce *uncon-scionable* provisions in contracts. An unconscionable provision is a term that is unreasonably favorable to one of the parties and about which the other party had no meaningful choice. If a court finds, after holding a hearing at which evidence about unconscionability is presented, that a provision in a contract is unconscionable, the court can refuse to enforce the entire contract, refuse to enforce the unconscionable provision, or make adjustments in the contract so as to avoid the unconscionable result. The doctrine of unconscionability has been adopted widely as part of the common law of many states, so that it is frequently applied even in cases that do not involve the sale of goods.

When an agreement is held to be illegal, it is generally unenforceable. Furthermore, a party who has partially or fully performed his part of an illegal agreement generally will not be able to recover what he has parted with. Courts make exceptions to this rule when it is in the public interest to do so. When one of the parties to an illegal agreement was excusably ignorant of the facts or laws that made the agreement illegal, courts will permit him to enforce the agreement as to any performance rendered before he learned of the illegality, provided that the law involved is of a relatively minor character. If both parties are ignorant of a fact or law under conditions similar to those stated above, either will be able to recover for consideration given.

Another exception is that a party who is not equally in the wrong with the other party to an illegal agreement may have a remedy. A party protected by a regulatory statute may recover for breach of an agreement entered into with a person who has not complied with the provisions of the statute. A person who has been induced to enter an illegal agreement by fraud, misrepresentation, duress, or undue influence may recover any consideration he has parted with.

Another exception to the rule that courts will give no remedy to parties to an illegal agreement is that a person who withdraws from an illegal agreement by rescinding it before the illegal act has been committed will be permitted to recover any consideration given. An additional exception is that if an agreement is *divisible*, courts will enforce the legal portion and refuse enforcement to the illegal portion. If an agreement that contains an illegal portion is indivisible, courts will normally refuse enforcement to the entire agreement unless the illegal part is a relatively minor provision of the agreement that does not affect the major, legal portion.

PROBLEM CASES

1. Zientara and Kaszuba, both citizens of Indiana, were friends and coworkers. Kaszuba's wife worked in an Illinois tavern that sold Illinois Lotto tickets. Zientara requested that Kaszuba obtain an Illinois Lotto ticket for him, as he had done in the past. Kaszuba agreed and Zientara gave him an envelope containing the purchase price and the number selections for the ticket. Zientara's was a winning number combination worth $1,696,800, but Kaszuba refused to give Zientara the ticket and made an effort to collect the winnings. At the time of this case, Indiana law prohibited lotteries, the sale of lottery tickets in Indiana, and gambling. Zientara filed suit in Indiana against Kaszuba, claiming the proceeds of the ticket. Kaszuba filed a motion to dismiss on the basis that the parties had entered an illegal, and therefore unenforceable, transaction. Was the transaction illegal?

2. Discount Fabric House, Inc., had placed an ad in the Yellow Pages every year since 1975. Each year, it signed an advertising contract with Wisconsin Telephone Company for the Yellow Pages ad. The contract was a printed form used by all subscribers who desired to place such an ad. No subscriber could bargain for or change any terms. One of the terms of the contract was that the subscriber agreed to relieve the telephone company of liability for any negligent act. In 1978, the telephone company omitted important trade identification from Discount Fabric House's ad. Discount Fabric House sued the telephone company for business losses resulting from this omission. As a defense, the telephone company set up the exculpatory clause contained in the advertising contract. Will the exculpatory clause be enforced?

3. Stern and Whitehead entered into a surrogacy contract in New Jersey. The contract provided that in exchange for $10,000, Whitehead would become pregnant through artificial insemination using Stern's sperm, carry the child to term, bear it, and surrender her parental rights to the child so that the child could be adopted by Stern's wife. A New Jersey criminal statute prohibits paying or accepting money in connection with any placement of a child for adoption. New Jersey also has a comprehensive statutory scheme regulating the termination of parental rights. This law provides that parental rights can be terminated only in cases of voluntary, written surrender of a child to an approved agency or where there has been a showing of parental abandonment or unfitness.

Whitehead did become pregnant with Stern's child and carried it to term. After the child's birth, however, she resisted surrendering the child. Stern sued to enforce the surrogacy contract, but Whitehead asserted that it was illegal. Should the surrogacy contract be enforced?

4. James Strickland attempted to bribe Judge Sylvania Woods to show leniency toward one of Strickland's friends who had a case pending before the judge. Judge Woods immediately reported this to the state's attorney and was asked to play along with Strickland until the actual payment of money occurred. Strickland gave $2,500 to the judge, who promptly turned it over to the state's attorney's office. Strickland was indicted for bribery, pled guilty, and was sentenced to a four-year prison term. Three months after the criminal trial, Strickland filed a motion for the return of his $2,500. Will the court order the return of his money?

5. Baker Pacific Corp., a licensed asbestos abatement and remediation contractor, contracted with Metropolitan Life to remove asbestos from one of Metropolitan's buildings. As was required by its contract with Metropolitan, Baker Pacific made it a condition of employment for workers on this project to sign an exculpatory agreement that released Baker Pacific and Metropolitan from "any and all claims whatsoever, at common law or otherwise" with the exception of liability under worker's compensation laws and in which the workers relinquished "any and all claims of every nature" that are related to exposure to asbestos. Is this exculpatory agreement enforceable?

6. Ben Lee Wilson had been licensed to practice architecture in the state of Hawaii, but his license lapsed in 1971 because he failed to pay a required $15 renewal fee. A Hawaii statute provides that any person who practices architecture without having been registered and "without having a valid unexpired certificate of registration . . . shall be fined not more than $500 or imprisoned not more than one year, or both." In 1972, Wilson performed architectural and engineering services for Kealakekua Ranch, for which he billed the Ranch $33,994.36. When the Ranch failed to pay Wilson's fee, he brought this action for breach of contract. What will the result be?

7. Ralph contracted to purchase a business, American Horse Enterprises, from Bovard. He executed promissory notes to Bovard in connection with this purchase. American Horse Enterprises was primarily in the business of manufacturing drug paraphernalia such as "roach clips" and "bongs" used to smoke marijuana. At the time of the sale of American Horse Enterprises, the manufacture of drug paraphernalia was not itself illegal, but state criminal statutes made it illegal to possess, use, and transfer marijuana. Both Ralph and Bovard knew that the products produced by American Horse Enterprises were used for illegal purposes. Ralph defaulted on the promissory notes and Bovard sued to recover on them. Ralph defends on the ground that the sale of the business was illegal. Was it?

8. Dr. Ellis, an orthopedic surgeon, entered into a contract of employment with the Elko Clinic. Among other provisions, the contract of employment contained a non-competition clause in which Dr. Ellis agreed not to practice medicine within a distance of five miles from the city limits of Elko, Nevada, for a period of two years from the termination date of his employment. During Dr. Ellis's employment, he treated patients who would otherwise have had to travel to Reno, Salt Lake City, or elsewhere to seek the services of an orthopedic surgeon. At the expiration of his employment contract, Dr. Ellis gave notice to the Clinic that he intended to establish his own office in Elko for the practice of his specialty. The Clinic sued Dr. Ellis to enforce the non-competition clause. Should the non-competition clause be enforced as written?

9. Hiram Ricker & Sons contracted with the Students International Meditation Society (SIDS) to furnish lodging and food to approximately 1,000 SIDS students at a one-month teacher training course to be held on Ricker's property in Poland Springs, Maine. At the end of the month, SIDS paid $185,000 to Ricker. Alleging that SIDS owed an additional $65,780, Ricker filed suit against SIDS for breach of contract. SIDS defended on the ground that the contract was illegal because Ricker's victualer's license, which was required by state law, had expired and because Ricker did not have sanitation permits for all of its premises during the entire period of the contract. SIDS demands the return of the $185,000 it paid. What should the result be?

10. Gianni Sport was a New York manufacturer and distributor of women's clothing. Gantos was a clothing retailer headquartered in Grand Rapids, Michigan. In 1980, Gantos's sales total was 20 times greater than Gianni Sport's, and in this industry, buyers were "in the driver's seat." In June of 1980, Gantos submitted to Gianni Sport a purchase order for women's holiday clothing to be delivered on October 10, 1980. The purchase order contained the following clause:

Buyer reserves the right to terminate by notice to Seller all or any part of this Purchase Order with respect to Goods that have not actually been shipped by Seller or as to Goods which are not timely delivered for any reason whatsoever.

Gianni Sport made the goods in question especially for Gantos. This holiday order comprised 20 to 22 percent of Gianni Sport's business. In late September of 1980, before the goods were shipped, Gantos canceled the order. It later agreed to accept the shipment in exchange for a 50 percent price reduction. Was the cancellation clause unconscionable?

11. Jones signed a contract with Free Flight Sport Aviation that gave him the right to use Free Flight's recreational skydiving facilities, including an airplane that ferried skydivers to the parachute jumping site. An exculpatory clause exempting Free Flight from liability for negligence was included in the contract. About one year later, Jones was injured while riding in a Free Flight airplane that crashed shortly after takeoff. He sued Free Flight for negligence, and Free Flight asserted the exculpatory clause as a defense. Will the exculpatory clause be enforced?

12. Triangle Leasing, which was in the business of leasing vans, trucks, and cars in Alabama, Georgia, and North Carolina, hired McMahon as the manager of its Wilmington, North Carolina, office. As part of his employment contract, McMahon signed a non-competition agreement. The non-competition agreement restricted McMahon from soliciting or attempting to procure Triangle Leasing's customers and from attempting to make car or truck-van rentals to any Triangle Leasing customers. According to the agreement, these activities were restricted within the state of North Carolina and any other state in which Triangle Leasing did business. The agreed-upon duration of the restriction was two years after the termination of McMahon's employment. Triangle Leasing trained McMahon and gave him access to its list of regular customers in Wilmington and other confidential information relating to the Wilmington market. Although McMahon's only contact with Triangle Leasing's customers was with Wilmington customers, Triangle Leasing also maintained offices in Greensboro-High Point and Raleigh-Durham, North Carolina. McMahon decided to terminate his employment and start his own rental business in North Carolina. Is the non-competition agreement likely to be enforced as written?

CHAPTER 17

WRITING

INTRODUCTION

Your study of contract law so far has focused on the requirements for the formation of a valid contract. You should be aware, however, that even when all the elements of a valid contract exist, the enforceability of the contract and the nature of the parties' obligations can be greatly affected by the *form* in which the contract is set out and by the *language* that is used to express the agreement. An otherwise valid contract can become unenforceable if it does not comply with the formalities required by state law. A person may be unable to offer evidence about promises and agreements made in preliminary negotiations, because the parties later adopted a written contract that did not contain those terms. And, of course, the legal effect of any contract is determined in large part by the way in which a court interprets the language it contains. This chapter discusses the ways in which the enforceability of a contract and the scope of contractual obligations can be affected by the manner in which people express their agreements.

THE STATUTE OF FRAUDS

Despite what many people believe, there is no general requirement that contracts be in writing. In most situations, oral contracts are legally enforceable, assuming that they can be proven. Still, oral contracts are less desirable than written contracts in many ways. They are more easily misunderstood or forgotten than written contracts. They are also more subject to the danger that a person might fabricate terms or fraudulently claim to have made an oral contract where none exists.

In 17th-century England, the dangers inherent in oral contracts were exacerbated by a legal rule that prohibited parties to a lawsuit from testifying in their own cases. Since the parties to an oral contract could not give testimony, the only way they could prove the existence of the contract was through the testimony of third parties. As you might expect, third parties were sometimes persuaded to offer false testimony about the existence of contracts. In an attempt to stop the widespread fraud and perjury that resulted, Parliament enacted the Statute of Frauds in 1677. It required written evidence before certain classes of contracts would be enforced. Although the possibility of fraud exists in every contract, the statute focused on contracts in which the potential for fraud was great or the consequences of fraud were especially serious.

The legislatures of American states adopted very similar statutes, also known as statutes of frauds. These statutes, which require certain kinds of contracts to be evidenced by a signed writing, are exceptions to the general rule that oral contracts are enforceable.

Statutes of frauds have produced a great deal of litigation, due in part to the public's ignorance of their provisions. It is difficult to imagine an aspect of contract law that is more practical for businesspeople to know about than the circumstances under which an oral contract will not suffice.

EFFECT OF FAILURE TO COMPLY WITH THE STATUTE OF FRAUDS

The statute of frauds applies only to executory contracts. If an oral contract has been completely performed by both parties, the fact that it did not comply with the statute of frauds would *not* be a ground for rescission of the contract.

What happens if an executory contract is within the statute of frauds but has not been evidenced by the type of writing required by the statute? It is not treated as an illegal contract because the statute of frauds is more of a formal rule than a rule of substantive law. Rather, the contract that fails to comply with the statute of frauds is *unenforceable*. Although the contract will not be enforced, a person who has conferred some benefit on the other party pursuant to the contract can recover the reasonable value of his performance in an action based on *quasi-contract*.

CONTRACTS WITHIN THE STATUTE OF FRAUDS

A contract is said to be "within" the statute of frauds if the statute requires that sort of contract to be evidenced by a writing. In almost all states, the following types of contracts are within the statute of frauds:

1. Collateral contracts in which a person promises to perform the obligation of another person.
2. Contracts for the sale of an interest in real estate.
3. Bilateral contracts that cannot be performed within a year from the date of their formation.
4. Contracts for the sale of goods for a price of $500 or more.
5. Contracts in which an executor or administrator promises to be personally liable for the debt of an estate.
6. Contracts in which marriage is the consideration.

Of this list, the first four sorts of contracts have the most significance today, and our discussion will focus primarily on them.

The statutes of frauds of the various states are not uniform. Some states require written evidence of other contracts in addition to those listed above. For example, a number of states require written evidence of contracts to pay a commission for the sale of real estate. Others require written evidence of ratifications of infants' promises or promises to pay debts that have been barred by the statute of limitations or discharged by bankruptcy.

The following discussion examines in greater detail the sorts of contracts that are within most states' statute of frauds.

Collateral Contracts

A *collateral contract* is one in which one person (the *guarantor*) agrees to pay the debt or obligation that a second person (the *principal debtor*) owes to a third person (the *obligee*) if the principal debtor fails to perform. For example, Cohn, who wants to help Davis establish a business, promises First Bank that he will repay the loan that First Bank makes to Davis if Davis fails to pay it. Here, Cohn is the guarantor, Davis is the principal debtor, and First Bank is the obligee. Cohn's promise to First Bank must be in writing to be enforceable.

As you can see in Figure 1, a collateral contract involves at least three parties and at least *two* promises to perform (a promise by the principal debtor to pay the obligee and a promise by the guarantor to pay the obligee). In a collateral contract, the guarantor promises to pay *only if the principal debtor fails to do so.* The essence of the collateral contract is that the debt or obligation is owed primarily by the principal debtor and the guarantor's debt is *secondary*. Thus, not all three party transactions are collateral contracts. The contracts described below are common three-party situations that are *not* within the statute of frauds.

Not within Statute of Frauds: Three-Party Contracts that Are Original Rather than Collateral   When a person undertakes an obligation that is not conditioned on the default of another person, and the debt is his own rather than that of another person, his obligation is said to be *original* or *direct*, not collateral. For example, when Timmons calls Johnson Florist Company and says, "Send flowers to Elrod," Timmons is undertaking

FIGURE 1 Collateral Contract

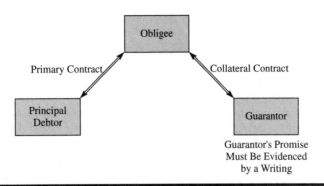

Guarantor's Promise
Must Be Evidenced
by a Writing

an obligation to pay his *own*—not someone else's—debt. This is not changed by the fact that Elrod is benefited by the contract between Timmons and Johnson Florist. The contract between Timmons and Johnson Florist is an original contract and would not have to be in writing.

The same result is reached when a creditor agrees to accept a contract with a new debtor in satisfaction of a debt previously owed by another debtor. Such transactions are called **novations.** In a novation, a creditor releases the original debtor and permits a new debtor to take his place. For example, Barnes owes $300 to First Bank. First Bank accepts Williamson's promise to pay Barnes's debt as satisfaction of that debt. This is a type of original contract, because Barnes has been released from liability for the debt and Williamson is now the only debtor.

Another common three-party transaction that is outside the statute of frauds occurs when two people are *jointly liable* on a debt to a third person. For example, if Brice and Evans together borrow money from First Bank to buy inventory for their joint business, they are *both* personally liable for the loan. Both of their promises are original, and no writing is required.

Exception: Main Purpose or Leading Object Rule
There are some situations in which a contract that is technically collateral is treated like an original contract because the person promising to pay the debt of another does so for the primary purpose of securing some personal benefit. Under the **main purpose** or **leading object** rule, no writing is required where the guarantor makes a collateral promise for the main purpose of obtaining some personal economic advantage. When the consideration given in exchange for the collateral promise is something the guarantor seeks primarily for his own benefit rather than for the benefit of the primary debtor, the contract is outside the statute of frauds and does not have to be in writing. *Al Booth's, Inc. v. Boyd-Scarp Enterprises, Inc.,* which follows, is a good example of the operation of this exception.

AL BOOTH'S, INC. v. BOYD-SCARP ENTERPRISES, INC.

518 So. 2d 422 (Fla. Ct. App. 1988)

Boyd-Scarp Enterprises, a building contractor, was building a new home for James Rathmann. Rathmann paid Boyd-Scarp for appliances for the new home and Boyd-Scarp contracted with Al Booth's, an appliance supplier, for the purchase of the appliances. Al Booth's had heard that Boyd-Scarp was having financial problems. Before delivering the appliances to the Rathmann's new home, it contacted Rathmann and asked him to guarantee payment. Al Booth's alleges that Rathmann orally promised to pay for the appliances if Boyd-Scarp failed to pay. Al Booth's then delivered the appliances. Boyd-Scarp became insolvent and did not pay Al Booth's for the appliances. Al Booth's turned to Rathmann for payment. It later brought this action when Rathmann refused to pay for the appliances. Rathmann asserted the statute of frauds as a defense, and the trial court granted a summary judgment in favor of Rathmann on the ground that the action was barred by the statute of frauds.

Upchurch, Chief Judge. Our statute of frauds, section 725.01, Florida Statutes, provides that "no action shall be brought to charge the defendant upon any special promise to answer for the debt of another person unless the agreement or promise upon which such action shall be brought or some note or memorandum thereof shall be in writing and signed by the party to be charged." This statutory language creates a distinction between direct promises and collateral promises to pay debts. Where the alleged oral promise is a direct promise to be obligated in the first instance, it is outside the statute of frauds and enforceable.

In the present case, the evidence reflects that if in fact Rathmann made a promise, it was a promise to pay in the event Boyd-Scarp did not. Such a promise would be a promise to answer for the debt of another. However, this does not necessarily mean that the statute of frauds bars Al Booth's action. Florida case law on the point is in accord with the weight of authority in following the "leading object" rule.

The "leading object" rule recognizes that an important difference exists between cases where the promisor makes his promise for the benefit of another and where the promisor makes it for his own pecuniary benefit. One court has explained the rule as providing that a promise, though collateral, is deemed enforceable because the promisor does not need the protection against his own generous impulses afforded by the statute of frauds. If the promisor's main purpose was to advance his own interests and he received a substantial, immediate and pecuniary benefit, the promise is outside the statute of frauds.

Since there is evidence here indicating that Rathmann agreed to guarantee payment and that the promise was for his own economic benefit, the "leading object" rule applies to take the promise out of the statute of frauds. This being so, summary judgment was improperly entered for Rathmann.

Reversed and remanded in favor of Al Booth's.

Interest in Land

Any contract that creates or transfers an interest in land is within the statute of frauds. The inclusion of real estate contracts in the statute of frauds reflects the values of an earlier, agrarian society in which land was the primary basis of wealth. Our legal system historically has treated land as being more important than other forms of property. Courts have interpreted the land provision of the statute of frauds broadly to require written evidence of any transaction that will affect the ownership of an interest in land. Thus, a contract to sell or mortgage real estate must be evidenced by a writing, as must an option to purchase real estate or a contract to grant an easement or permit the mining and removal of minerals on land. A lease is also a transfer of an interest in land, but most states' statutes of frauds do not require leases to be in writing unless they are long-term leases, usually those for one year or more. On the other hand, a contract to erect a building or to insure a building would not be within the real estate provision of the statute of frauds, because such contracts do not involve the transfer of interests in land.[1]

---

[1] Note, however, that a writing might be required under state insurance statutes.

Exception: Full Performance by the Vendor An oral contract for the sale of land that has been completely performed by the vendor (seller) is "taken out of the statute of frauds," that is, is enforceable without a writing. For example, Peterson and Lincoln enter into an oral contract for the sale of Peterson's farm at an agreed-upon price and Peterson, the vendor, delivers a deed to the farm to Lincoln. In this situation, the vendor has completely performed and most states would treat the oral contract as being enforceable.

Exception: Part Performance (Action in Reliance) by the Vendee When the vendee (purchaser of land) does an act in clear reliance on an oral contract for the sale of land, an equitable doctrine commonly known as the "part performance doctrine" permits the vendee to enforce the contract notwithstanding the fact that it was oral. The part performance doctrine is based on both evidentiary and reliance considerations. The doctrine recognizes that a person's conduct can "speak louder than words" and can indicate the existence of a contract almost as well as a writing can. The part performance doctrine is also based on the desire to avoid the injustice that would otherwise result if the contract were repudiated after the vendee's reliance.

Under section 129 of the *Restatement (Second) of Contracts*, a contract for the transfer of an interest in land can be enforced even without a writing if the person seeking enforcement:

1. Has *reasonably relied* on the contract and on the other party's assent.

2. Has changed his position to such an extent that *enforcement of the contract is the only way to prevent injustice.*

In other words, the vendee must have done some act in reliance on the contract and the nature of the act must be such that restitution (returning his money) would not be an adequate remedy. The part performance doctrine will not permit the vendee to collect damages for breach of contract, but it will permit him to obtain the equitable remedy of **specific performance,** a remedy whereby the court orders the breaching party to perform his contract.[2]

A vendee's reliance on an oral contract could be shown in many ways. Traditionally, many states have required that the vendee pay part or all of the purchase price and either make substantial improvements on the property or take possession of it. For example, Contreras and Miller orally enter into a contract for the sale of Contreras's land. If Miller pays Contreras a substantial part of the purchase price and either takes possession of the land or begins to make improvements on it, the contract would be enforceable without a writing under the part performance doctrine. These are not the only sorts of acts in reliance that would make an oral contract enforceable, however. Under the *Restatement* approach, if the promise to transfer land is clearly proven or is admitted by the breaching party, it is not necessary that the act of reliance include making payment, taking possession, or making improvements.[3] It still is necessary, however, that the reliance be such that restitution would not be an adequate remedy. For this reason, a vendee's payment of the purchase price, standing alone, usually is *not* sufficient for the part performance doctrine. The following *Hickey v. Green* case provides a good example of the use of the part performance doctrine.

---

[2] Specific performance is discussed in more detail in the Performance and Remedies chapter.

[3] *Restatement (Second) of Contracts* § 129, comment d.

HICKEY v. GREEN

442 N.E.2d 37 (Mass. Ct. App. 1982)

Gladys Green owns a lot (Lot S) in the Manomet section of Plymouth, Massachusetts. In July 1980, she advertised it for sale. On July 11 and 12, Thomas and Patricia Hickey discussed with Green purchasing Lot S and orally agreed to a sale for $15,000. On July 12, Green accepted the Hickeys's check for $500. Hickey had left the payee line of the deposit check blank, because of uncertainty whether Green or her brother was to receive the check. Hickey asked Green to fill in the appropriate name. Green, however, held the check, did not fill in the payee's name, and neither cashed nor endorsed it. Hickey told Green that his intention was to sell his home and build on the lot he was buying from Green. Relying on the arrangements with Green, the Hickeys advertised their house in newspapers for three days in July. They found a purchaser quickly. Within a short time, they contracted with a purchaser for the sale of their house and accepted the purchaser's deposit check. On the back of this check, above the Hickeys's signatures endorsing the check, was noted: "Deposit on purchase of property at Sachem Rd. and First St., Manomet, Ma. Sale price, $44,000."

On July 24, Green told Hickey that she no longer intended to sell her property to him and instead had decided to sell it to someone else for $16,000. Hickey offered to pay Green $16,000 for the lot, but she refused this offer. The Hickeys then filed a complaint against Green seeking specific performance. Green asserted that relief was barred by the Statute of Frauds, but the trial court granted specific performance. Green appealed.

Cutter, J. The present rule applicable in most jurisdictions in the United States is succinctly set forth in *Restatement (Second) of Contracts* section 129 (1981). The section reads: "A contract for the transfer of an interest in land may be specifically enforced notwithstanding failure to comply with the Statute of Frauds if it is established that the party seeking enforcement, in reasonable reliance on the contract and on the continuing assent of the party against whom enforcement is sought, has so changed his position that injustice can be avoided only by specific enforcement." Two distinct elements enter into the application of the rule of this Section: first, the extent to which the evidentiary function of the statutory formalities is fulfilled by the conduct of the parties; second, the reliance of the promisee, providing a compelling basis for relief in addition to the expectations created by the promise.

The present facts reveal a simple case of a proposed purchase of a residential vacant lot, where the vendor, Green, knew that the Hickeys were planning to sell their former home (possibly to obtain funds to pay her) and build on Lot S. The Hickeys, relying on Green's oral promise, moved rapidly to make their sale without obtaining any adequate memorandum of the terms of what appears to have been intended to be a quick cash sale of Lot S. So rapid was action by the Hickeys that, by July 21, less than ten days after giving their deposit to Green, they had accepted a deposit check for the sale of their house, endorsed the check, and placed it in their bank account. Above their signatures endorsing the check was a memorandum probably sufficient to satisfy the Statute of Frauds. At the very least, the Hickeys had bound themselves in a manner which, to avoid a transfer of their own house, they might have had to engage in expensive litigation. No attorney has been shown to have been used either in the transaction between Green and the Hickeys or in that between the Hickeys and their purchaser.

There is no denial by Green of the oral contract between her and the Hickeys. This, under section 129 of the *Restatement*, is of some significance. There can be no doubt that Green made the promise on which the Hickeys so promptly relied, and also that she, nearly as promptly, but not promptly enough, repudiated it because she had a better opportunity. In equity, Green's conduct cannot be condoned. This is not a case where either party is shown to have contemplated the negotiation of a purchase and sale agreement. If a written agreement had been expected, even by only one party, or would have been natural, a different situation might have existed. It is a permissible inference from the facts that the rapid sale of the Hickeys' house was both appropriate and expected.

[At the time of the trial court's decision in this case], the principal facts bearing on the extent of the injury to the Hickeys were those based on the Hickeys's obligation to convey their house to a purchaser. Performance of that agreement had been extended. If enforcement of that agreement still will be sought, or if that agreement has been carried out, the conveyance of Lot S by Green should be required now.

Remanded to trial court for action consistent with this opinion. If the Hickeys's contract to sell their house has been performed or will be performed, the trial court is to order Green to convey Lot S. If the Hickeys will not be required to sell their house, however, Green will be ordered to reimburse the Hickeys for any deposits or expenses of advertising and litigation rather than being ordered to convey the lot.

Contracts that Cannot Be Performed within One Year

A bilateral, executory contract that cannot be performed within one year from the day on which it comes into existence is within the statute of frauds and must be evidenced by a writing. The apparent purpose of this provision is to guard against the risk of faulty or willfully inaccurate recollection of long-term contracts. Courts have tended to construe it very narrowly.

One aspect of this narrow construction is that most states hold that a contract that has been fully performed by *one* of the parties is "taken out of the statute of frauds" and is enforceable without a writing. For example, Nash enters into an oral contract to perform services for Thomas for thirteen months. If Nash has already fully performed his part of the contract, Thomas will be required to pay him the contract price.

In addition, this provision of the statute has been held to apply only when the *terms* of the contract make it impossible for the contract to be completed within one year. If the contract is for an indefinite period of time, it is not within the statute of frauds. This is true even if, in retrospect, the contract was *not* completed within a year. Thus, Weinberg's agreement to work for Wolf for an indefinite period of time would not have to be evidenced by a writing, even if Weinberg eventually works for Wolf for many years. As demonstrated by *Hodge v. Evans Financial Corporation*, which follows, the mere fact that performance is unlikely to be completed in one year does not bring the contract within the statute of frauds. In most states, a contract "for life" is not within the statute of frauds, because it is possible—since death is an uncertain event—for the contract to be performed within a year. In a few states, such as New York, contracts for life are within the statute of frauds.

HODGE v. EVANS FINANCIAL CORPORATION
823 F.2d 559 (D.C. Cir. 1987)

On two occasions in 1980, Albert Hodge met with John Tilley, president and chief operating officer of Evans Financial Corporation, to discuss Hodge's possible employment by Evans. Hodge was 54 years old at that time and was assistant counsel and assistant secretary of Mellon National Corporation and Mellon Bank of Pittsburgh. During these discussions, Tilley asked Hodge what his conditions were for accepting employment with Evans, and Hodge replied, "No. 1, the job must be permanent. Because of my age, I have a great fear about going back into the marketplace again. I want to be here until I retire." Tilley allegedly responded, "I accept that condition." Regarding his retirement plans, Hodge later testifed, "I really questioned whether I was going to go much beyond 65." Hodge subsequently accepted Evans's offer of employment as vice president and general counsel. He moved from Pittsburgh to Washington, D.C., in September 1980 and worked for Evans from that time until he was fired by Tilley on May 7, 1981.

Hodge brought a breach of contract suit against Evans. The case was tried before a jury, which rendered a verdict in favor of Hodge for $175,000. Evans appeals.

Wald, Chief Justice. Evans argues that the oral employment agreement between Evans and Hodge is unenforceable under the statute of frauds. Because the agreement here contemplated long-term employment for a number of years, Evans argues that the statute requires it to have been in writing in order to be enforceable.

Despite its sweeping terms, the one-year provision of the statute has long been construed narrowly and literally. Under prevailing interpretation, the enforceability of a contract under the statute does not depend on the actual course of subsequent events or on the expectations of the parties. Instead, the statute applies only to those contracts whose performance could not possibly or conceivably be completed within one year. The statute of frauds is thus inapplicable if, at the time the contract is formed, any contingent event could complete the terms of the contract within one year.

Hodge argues that, under this interpretation of the statute of frauds, a permanent or lifetime employment contract does not fall within the statute because it is capable of full performance within one year if the employee were to die within the period. Hodge's view of the statute's application to lifetime or permanent employment contracts has, in fact, been accepted by an overwhelming majority of courts and commentators.

The employment contract in this case cannot reasonably be interpreted as a contract for a specified period of time. Hodge unequivocally alleged a contract for permanent employment, not a contract until he reached age sixty-five or for any other stated period of time. The fact that Hodge expected to retire at some point does not mean that his contract could not possibly be performed within one year. All employment contracts of permanent, lifetime, or indefinite duration undoubtedly contemplate retirement; such contracts certainly do not mean that employees are bound to work until the moment they drop dead. Hodge's permanent employment contract with Evans could therefore be fully performed, according to its terms, upon Hodge's retirement or upon his death. Under the conventional view the latter possibility is sufficient to take the contract out of the statute. That Hodge expected to retire before he died is completely irrelevant to this case so long as the contract was legally susceptible of performance within one year. The applicability of the statute of frauds does not depend on the expectations of the parties.

We recognize that the conventional view of the statute is somewhat "legalistic." Yet the statute of frauds itself is widely understood as a formal device that shields promise breakers from the consequences of otherwise enforceable agreements. The conventional, narrowing interpretation overwhelmingly adopted by courts and commentators is designed to mollify the often harsh and unintended consequences of the statute. Here the jury concluded, despite Evans's vigorous defense, that Hodge was promised permanent employment and that he was nonetheless fired without cause. Under the traditional, narrow view of the statute, the statute of frauds does not bar the enforcement of such jury verdicts.

Judgment for Hodge affirmed.

Computing Time In determining whether a contract is within the one-year provision, courts begin counting time on the date on which the contract comes into existence. If, under the terms of the contract, it is possible to perform it within one year from this date, the contract does not fall within the statute of frauds and does not have to be in writing. If, however, the terms of the contract make it impossible to complete performance of the contract (without breaching it) within one year from the date on which the contract came into existence, the contract falls within the statute and must meet its requirements to be enforceable. Thus, if Hammer Co. and

McCrea agree on August 1, 1986, that McCrea will work for Hammer Co. for one year, beginning October 1, 1986, the terms of the contract dictate that it is not possible to complete performance until October 1, 1987. Because that date is more than one year from the date on which the contract came into existence, the contract falls within the statute of frauds and must be evidenced by a writing to be enforceable.

Sale of Goods for $500 or More

The original English Statute of Frauds required a writing for contracts for the sale of goods for a price of 10 pounds sterling or more. In the United States today, the writing requirement for the sale of goods is governed by section 2–201 of the Uniform Commercial Code. This section provides that contracts for the sale of goods for the price of $500 or more are not enforceable without a writing or other specified evidence that a contract was made. There are a number of alternative ways of satisfying the requirements of section 2–201. These will be explained later in this chapter.

Modifications of Existing Sales Contracts   Just as some contracts to extend the time for performance fall within the one-year provision of the statute of frauds, agreements to modify existing sales contracts can fall within the statute of frauds if the contract as modified is for a price of $500 or more.[4] Section 2–209(3) provides that the requirements of the statute of frauds must be satisfied if the contract as modified is within its provisions. For example, if Carroll and Kestler enter into a contract for the sale of goods at a price of $490, the original contract does *not* fall within the statute of frauds. However, if they later modify the contract by increasing the contract price to $510, the modification falls within the statute of frauds and must meet its requirements to be enforceable.

Promise of Executor or Administrator to Pay a Decedent's Debt Personally

When a person dies, a personal representative is appointed to administer his estate. One of the important tasks of this personal representative, who is called an executor if the person dies leaving a will or an administrator if the person dies without a will, is to pay the debts

owed by the decedent. No writing is required when an executor or administrator—acting in his representative capacity—promises to pay the decedent's debts from the funds of the decedent's estate. The statute of frauds requires a writing, however, if the executor, acting in her capacity as a private individual rather than in her representative capacity, promises to pay one of the *decedent's* debts out of her own (the executor's) funds. For example, Thomas, who has been appointed executor of his Uncle Max's estate, is presented with a bill for $10,500 for medical services rendered to Uncle Max during his last illness by the family doctor, Dr. Barnes. Feeling bad that there are not adequate funds in the estate to compensate Dr. Barnes for his services, Thomas promises to pay Dr. Barnes from his own funds. Thomas's promise would have to be evidenced by a writing to be enforceable.

Contracts in which Marriage Is the Consideration

The statute of frauds also requires a writing when marriage is the consideration to support a contract. The marriage provision has been interpreted to be inapplicable to agreements that involve only mutual promises to marry. It can apply to any other contract in which one party's promise is given in exchange for marriage or the promise to marry on the part of the other party. This is true whether the promisor is one of the parties to the marriage or a third party. For example, if Hicks promises to deed his ranch to Everett in exchange for Everett's agreement to marry Hicks's son, Everett could not enforce Hicks's promise without written evidence of the promise.

Prenuptial (or **antenuptial**) agreements present a common contemporary application of the marriage provision of the statute of frauds. These are agreements between couples who contemplate marriage. They usually involve such matters as transfers of property, division of property upon divorce or death, and various lifestyle issues. Assuming that marriage or the promise to marry is the consideration supporting these agreements, they are within the statute of frauds and must be evidenced by a writing.[5]

---

[4] Modifications of sales contracts are discussed in greater detail in the Consideration chapter.

[5] Note, however, that "nonmarital" agreements between unmarried cohabitants who do not plan marriage are not within the marriage provision of the statute of frauds, even though the agreement may concern the same sorts of matters that are typically covered in a prenuptial agreement. The legality of agreements between unmarried cohabitants is discussed in the Illegality chapter.

CONCEPT REVIEW

CONTRACTS "WITHIN" THE STATUTE OF FRAUDS

Provision	Description	Exceptions (situations in which contract does not require a writing)
Marriage	Contracts, other than mutual promises to marry, where marriage is the consideration	—
Year	Bilateral contracts that, *by their terms*, cannot be performed within one year from the date on which the contract was formed	Full (complete) performance by one of the parties

Land	Contract that creates or transfers an ownership interest in real property	1. Full performance by vendor (vendor deeds property to vendees)
		 or
		 2. "Part performance" doctrine: Vendee relies on oral contract, for example, by:
		   a. Paying substantial part of purchase price and
		   b. Taking possession or making improvements

Executor's Promise	Executor promises to pay estate's debt out of his own funds	—
Sale of Goods at Price of $500 or More (UCC 2–201)	Contracts for the sale of goods for a contract price of $500 or more; also applies to modifications of contracts for goods where price as modified is $500 or more	See alternative ways of satisfying statute of frauds under UCC
Collateral Contracts, Guaranty	Contracts where promisor promises to pay the debt of another if the primary debtor fails to pay	"Main purpose" or "leading object" exception: Guarantor makes promise primarily for her own economic benefit

---

MEETING THE REQUIREMENTS OF THE STATUTE OF FRAUDS

Nature of the Writing Required

The statutes of frauds of the various states are not uniform in their formal requirements. However, most states require only a *memorandum* of the parties' agreement; they do not require that the entire contract be in writing. The memorandum must provide written evidence that a contract was made, but it need not have been created with the intent that the memorandum itself would be binding. In fact, in some cases, written offers that were accepted orally have been held sufficient to satisfy the writing requirement. A memorandum may be in any form, including letters, telegrams, receipts, or any other writing indicating that the parties had a contract. The

memorandum need not be made at the same time the contract comes into being; in fact, the memorandum may be made at any time before suit is filed. If a memorandum of the parties' agreement is lost, its loss and its contents may be proven by oral testimony.

Contents of the Memorandum   Although there is a general trend away from requiring complete writings to satisfy the statute of frauds, an adequate memorandum must still contain several things. Generally, the essential terms of the contract must be indicated in the memorandum, although states differ in their requirements concerning how specifically the terms must be stated. The identity of the parties must be indicated in some way, and the subject matter of the contract must be identified with reasonable certainty. This last requirement causes particular problems in contracts for the sale of land, since many statutes require a detailed description of the property to be sold.

Contents of Memorandum under UCC   The standard for determining the sufficiency of the contents of a memorandum is more flexible in cases concerning contracts for the sale of goods. This looser standard is created by the language of UCC section 2–201, which states that the writing must be sufficient to indicate that a contract for sale has been made between the parties but a writing can be sufficient even if it omits or incorrectly states a term agreed upon. However, the memorandum is not enforceable for more than the *quantity* of goods stated in the memorandum. Thus, a writing that does not indicate the quantity of goods to be sold would not satisfy the Code's writing requirement.

Signature Requirement   The memorandum must be signed by the *party to be charged* or his authorized agent. (The *party to be charged* is the person using the statute of frauds as a defense—generally the *defendant* unless the statute of frauds is asserted as a defense to a counterclaim.) This means that it is not necessary for purposes of meeting the statute of frauds for *both* parties' signatures to appear on the document. It is, however, in the best interests of both parties for both signatures to appear on the writing; otherwise, the contract evidenced by the writing is enforceable only against the signing party. Unless the statute expressly provides that the memorandum or contract must be signed at the end, the signature may appear any place on the memorandum. Any writing, mark, initials, stamp, engraving, or other symbol placed or printed on a memorandum will suffice as a signature, as long as the party to be charged intended it to authenticate (indicate the genuineness of) the writing.

Memorandum Consisting of Several Writings   In many situations, the elements required for a memorandum are divided among several documents. For example, Wayman and Allen enter into a contract for the sale of real estate, intending to memorialize their agreement in a formal written document later. While final drafts of a written contract are being prepared, Wayman repudiates the contract. Allen has a copy of an unsigned preliminary draft of the contract that identifies the parties and contains all of the material terms of the parties' agreement, an unsigned note written by Wayman that contains the legal description of the property, and a letter signed by Wayman that refers to the contract and to the other

two documents. None of these documents, standing alone, would be sufficient to satisfy the statute of frauds. However, Allen can combine them to meet the requirements of the statute, provided that they all relate to the same agreement. This can be shown by physical attachment, as where the documents are stapled or bound together, or by references in the documents themselves that indicate that they all apply to the same transaction. In some cases, it has also been shown by the fact that the various documents were executed at the same time.

ALTERNATIVE MEANS OF SATISFYING THE STATUTE OF FRAUDS IN SALE OF GOODS CONTRACTS

As you have learned, the basic requirement of the UCC statute of frauds [2–201] is that a contract for the sale of goods for the purchase price of $500 or more must be evidenced by a written memorandum that indicates the existence of the contract, states the quantity of goods to be sold, and is signed by the party to be charged. Recognizing that the underlying purpose of the statute of frauds is to provide more evidence of the existence of a contract than the mere oral testimony of one of the parties, however, the Code also permits the statute of frauds to be satisfied by any of four other types of evidence. Under the UCC, then, a contract for the sale of goods for a purchase price of $500 or more for which there is no written memorandum signed by the party to be charged can meet the requirements of the statute of frauds in any of the ways discussed below. These different methods of satisfying the UCC statute of frauds are depicted in Figure 2.

Confirmatory Memo between Merchants

Suppose Gardner and Roth enter into a contract over the telephone for the sale of goods at a price of $5,000. Gardner then sends a memorandum to Roth confirming the deal they made orally. If Roth receives the memo and does not object to it, it would be fair to say that the parties' conduct provides some evidence that a contract exists. Under some circumstances, the UCC permits such confirmatory memoranda to satisfy the statute of frauds even though the writing is signed by the party who is seeking to enforce the contract rather than the party against whom enforcement is sought [2–201(2)]. This exception applies only when *both* of the parties to a contract are *merchants*. (As you will see in the following case, *Goldkist, Inc. v. Brownlee*, it is sometimes difficult to determine whether a seller will be deemed to be a merchant.) Furthermore, the memo must be sent within a reasonable time after the contract is made and must be sufficient to bind the person who sent it if enforcement were sought against him (that is, it must indicate that a contract was made, state a quantity, and be signed by the sender). If the party against whom enforcement is sought receives the memo, has reason to know its contents, and yet fails to give written notice of objection to the contents of the memo within 10 days after receiving it, the memo can be introduced to meet the requirements of the statute of frauds. The *Goldkist* case illustrates the satisfaction of the statute of frauds by a confirmatory memorandum.

GOLDKIST, INC. v. BROWNLEE
355 S.E.2d 773 (Ga. Ct. App. 1987)

Mark and Barney Brownlee were farmers who, as a partnership doing business as Brownlee Brothers, grew and sold crops. In addition to farming, Barney Brownlee owned a gas station. On July 22, 1983, Barney Brownlee allegedly telephoned Goldkist and, after checking on the current price of soybeans, allegedly agreed to deliver 5,000 bushels of soybeans to Goldkist between August 22 and September 22, at $6.88 per pound. Although no written agreement signed by either of the Brownlees was created, Goldkist did send the Brownlees a written memorandum dated July 22, which confirmed the agreement to sell 5,000 bushels of soybeans on the terms described above. The Brownlees received the memorandum but did not respond to it. They also did not deliver the soybeans, and Goldkist was forced to "cover" the contract (buy soybeans from another source). Goldkist then brought this action to recover its losses arising out of the necessity to cover.

The Brownlees asserted as a defense the fact that there was no writing signed by either of them as required by UCC section 2–201. The trial court agreed with the Brownlees and granted summary judgment in their favor. Goldkist appealed.

Beasley, Judge.   The [trial] court agreed with the Brownlees that the circumstances did not fit any of the exceptions provided for in UCC section 2–201. On appeal, Goldkist asserts that the Brownlees came within subsection (2), relating to dealings "between merchants." The Brownlees admit that their crops are "goods." The partnership had been operating the row crop farming business for 14 years, producing peanuts, soybeans, corn, milo, and wheat on 1,350 acres, and selling the crops.

It is also established that Barney Brownlee was familiar with the marketing procedure of "booking" crops, which sometimes occurred over the telephone between the farmer and the buyer, rather than in person, and a written contract would be signed later. He periodically called Goldkist's agent to check the price, which fluctuated. If the price met his approval, he sold soybeans. At this time the partnership still had some of its 1982 crop in storage, and the price was rising slowly. Mr. Brownlee received a written confirmation in the mail concerning a sale of soybeans and did not contact Goldkist to contest it but simply did nothing.

To allow a farmer who deals in crops of the kind at issue, or who otherwise comes within the definition of "merchant" to renege on a confirmed oral booking for the sale of crops would result in a fraud on the buyer. The farmer could abide by the booking if the price thereafter declined but reject it if the price rose; the buyer, on the other hand, would be forced to sell the crop following the booking at its peril, or wait until the farmer decides whether to honor the booking or not.

The Brownlees' narrow construction of "merchant" would, given the booking procedure used for the sale of farm products, thus guarantee to the farmers the best of both possible worlds (fulfill booking if price goes down after booking and reject it if price improves) and to the buyers the worst of both possible worlds. On the other hand, construing "merchants" as not excluding as a matter of law farmers such as the ones in this case protects them equally as well as the buyer. If the market price declines after the booking, they are assured of the higher booking price; the buyer cannot renege, as UCC section 2–201(2) would apply.

We believe this is the proper construction to give the two statutes, UCC section 2–104 [which defines "merchant"] and 2–201, as taken together they are thus further branches stemming from the centuries-old simple legal idea *pacta servanda sunt*—agreements are to be kept. So construed, they evince the legislative intent to enforce the accepted practices of the marketplace among those who frequent it.

Judgment reversed in favor of Goldkist.

Part Payment or Part Delivery

Suppose Rice and Cooper enter a contract for the sale of 1,000 units of goods at $1 each. After Rice has paid $600, Cooper refuses to deliver the goods and asserts the statute of frauds as a defense to enforcement of the contract. The Code permits part payment or part delivery to satisfy the statute of frauds, but *only for the quantity of goods that have been delivered or paid for* [2–201(3)(c)]. Thus, Cooper would be required to deliver only 600 units rather than the 1,000 units Rice alleges that he agreed to sell.

Admission in Pleadings or Court

Another situation in which the UCC statute of frauds can be satisfied without a writing occurs when the party being sued admits the existence of the oral contract in his trial testimony or in any document that he files with the court. For example, Nelson refuses to perform an oral contract he made with Smith for the sale of $2,000 worth of goods, and Smith sues him. If Nelson admits the existence of the oral contract in pleadings or in court proceedings, his admission is sufficient to meet the statute of frauds. This exception is justified by the strong evidence that such an admission provides. After all, what better evidence of a contract can there be than is provided when the party being sued admits under penalty of perjury that a contract exists? When such an admission is made, the statute of frauds is satisfied as to *the quantity of goods admitted* [2–201(3)(b)]. For example, if Nelson only admits contracting for $1,000 worth of goods, the contract is enforceable only to that extent.

Specially Manufactured Goods

Finally, an oral contract within the UCC statute of frauds can be enforced without a writing in some situations involving the sale of *specially manufactured goods*. This exception to the writing requirement will apply only if the nature of the specially manufactured goods is such that they are not suitable for sale in the ordinary course of the seller's business. Completely executory oral contracts are not enforceable under this exception. The seller must have made a substantial beginning in manufacturing the goods for the buyer, or must have made commitments for their procurement, before receiving notice that the buyer was repudiating the sale [2–201(3)(a)]. For example, Bennett Co. has an oral contract with Stevenson for the sale of $2,500 worth of calendars imprinted with Bennett Co.'s name and address. If Bennett Co. repudiates the contract *before* Stevenson has made a substantial beginning in manufacturing the calendars, the contract will be unenforceable under the statute of frauds. If, however, Bennett Co. repudiated the contract *after* Stevenson had made a substantial beginning, the oral contract would be enforceable.

The specially manufactured goods provision is based both on the evidentiary value of the seller's conduct and on the need to avoid the injustice that would otherwise result from the seller's reliance.

FIGURE 2 Satisfying the Statute of Frauds for a Contract for the Sale of Goods for a Price of $500 or More

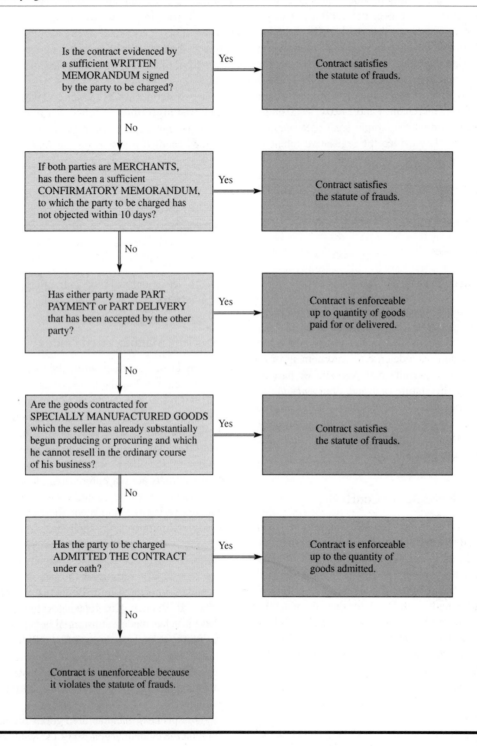

PROMISSORY ESTOPPEL AND THE STATUTE OF FRAUDS

The statute of frauds, which was created to prevent fraud and perjury, has often been criticized because it can create unjust results. One of the troubling features of the statute is that it can as easily be used to defeat a contract that was actually made as it can to defeat a fictitious agreement. As you have seen, courts and legislatures have created several exceptions to the statute of frauds that reduce the statute's potential for creating unfair results. In recent years, courts in some states have begun to use the doctrine of **promissory estoppel**[6] to allow some parties to recover under oral contracts that the statute of frauds would ordinarily render unenforceable.

Courts in these states hold that, when one of the parties would suffer serious losses because of her reliance on an oral contract, the other party is estopped from raising the statute of frauds as a defense. This position has been approved in the *Restatement (Second) of Contracts*. Section 139 of the *Restatement* provides that a promise that induces action or forbearance can be enforceable notwithstanding the statute of frauds if the reliance was foreseeable to the person making the promise and if injustice can be avoided only by enforcing the promise. The idea behind this section and the cases employing promissory estoppel is that the statute of frauds, which is designed to prevent injustice, should not be allowed to work an injustice. Section 139 and these cases also impliedly recognize the fact that the reliance required by promissory estoppel to some extent provides evidence of the existence of a contract between the parties, since it is unlikely that a person would materially rely on a nonexistent promise.

The use of promissory estoppel as a means of circumventing the statute of frauds is still controversial, however. Many courts fear that enforcing oral contracts on the basis of a party's reliance will essentially negate the statute. In cases involving the UCC statute of frauds, an additional source of concern involves the interpretation of section 2–201. Some courts have construed the provisions listing specific alternative methods of satisfying 2–201's formal requirements to be *exclusive*, precluding the creation of any further exceptions by courts.

---

[6] The doctrine of promissory estoppel is discussed in the Introduction to Contracts chapter and the Consideration chapter.

THE PAROL EVIDENCE RULE

Explanation of the Rule

In many situations, contracting parties prefer to express their agreements in writing even when they are not required to do so by the statute of frauds. Written contracts rarely come into being without some prior discussions or negotiations between the parties, however. Various promises, proposals, or representations are usually made by one or both of the parties before the execution of a written contract. What happens when one of those prior promises, proposals, or representations is not included in the terms of the written contract? For example, suppose that Jackson wants to buy Stone's house. During the course of negotiations, Stone states that he will pay for any major repairs that the house needs for the first year that Jackson owns it. The written contract that the parties ultimately sign, however, does not say anything about Stone paying for repairs, and, in fact, states that Jackson will take the house "as is." The furnace breaks down three months after the sale, and Stone refuses to pay for its repair. What is the status of Stone's promise to pay for repairs? The basic problem is one of defining the boundaries of the parties' agreement. Are all the promises made in the process of negotiation part of the contract, or do the terms of the written document that the parties signed supersede any preliminary agreements?

The **parol evidence rule** provides the answer to this question. The term *parol evidence* means written or spoken statements that are *not contained in the written contract*. The parol evidence rule provides that, when parties enter a *written contract* that they intend as a complete **integration** (a complete and final statement of their agreement), a court will not permit the use of evidence of *prior* or *contemporaneous* statements to add to, alter, or contradict the terms of the written contract. This rule is based on the presumption that when people enter into a written contract, the best evidence of their agreement is the written contract itself. It also reflects the idea that later expressions of intent are presumed to prevail over earlier expressions of intent. In the hypothetical case involving Stone and Jackson, assuming that they intended the written contract to be the final integration of their agreement, Jackson would not be able to introduce evidence of Stone's promise to pay for repairs. The effect of excluding preliminary promises or statements from consideration is, of course, to confine the parties' contract to the terms of the written agreement. The lesson to be learned from this example is that people who put their agreements in writing should make sure that all the terms of their agreement are included in the writing. The following case, *Slivinsky v. Watkins-Johnson Company*, illustrates the application of the parol evidence rule.

SLIVINSKY v. WATKINS-JOHNSON COMPANY

270 Cal. Rptr. 585 (Cal Ct. App. 1990)

In July of 1984, Sandra Slivinsky applied for a job as a materials scientist with Watkins-Johnson Company, a large aerospace manufacturer. Directly above the signature line on the application she signed was the statement: "I understand that employment by WATKINS-JOHNSON COMPANY is conditional upon . . . execution of an Employment Agreement. . . . I further understand that if I become employed by Watkins-Johnson Company, there will be no agreement, expressed or implied, between the company and me for any specific period of employment, nor for continuing or long-term employment." Over the next several months, Watkins-Johnson contacted Slivinsky's references, requested her transcripts, and set up a series of interviews. Slivinsky claims that at these interviews she was promised "long-term," "indefinite," and "permanent" employment, not dependent on business cycles, and subject to termination only for cause. Finally, Watkins-Johnson made a verbal offer of employment to Slivinsky and she accepted. On January 7, 1985, which was Slivinksky's first day at work, Slivinsky signed the employee agreement that had been referred to in her employment application. Set apart in bold type, the last paragraph of this agreement provided that there was no express or implied agreement between the parties regarding the duration of her employment and that the employment could be terminated at any time with or without cause.

As a result of the space shuttle Challenger disaster in January 1986, Watkins-Johnson experienced significant business losses and government contract cancellations. The management decided that employee cutbacks were essential to cope with the loss of business. Ultimately, 24 employees, including Slivinsky, were selected for the Reduction in Force program. Watkins-Johnson terminated her employment in June of 1986.

Slivinsky brought suit against Watkins-Johnson for breach of the employment contract, asserting that she had been terminated without cause in violation of the parties' express and implied agreement. She also claimed that the reasons given for her termination were pretextual and that she was really fired for other reasons such as her supervisor disliking her. The trial court granted Watkins-Johnson's motion for summary judgment, and Slivinsky appealed.

Cottle, Associate Justice.　Slivinsky claims that the parties' employment agreement includes factors such as oral assurances of job security and Watkins-Johnson's personnel policies and practices not to terminate employees except for good cause. Watkins-Johnson [argues] that it is limited to the parties' express written contract defining the employment as at-will.

The dispositive issue, therefore, is whether we can look beyond the four corners of the parties' written agreements to ascertain the complete agreement of the parties. The answer to that question involves application of the parol evidence rule, a rule of substantive law precluding the introduction of evidence which varies or contradicts the terms of an integrated written instrument. If the parties intended that the Application and Employment Agreement constituted an integration, *i.e.*, the final expression of their agreement with respect to grounds for termination, then those agreements may not be contradicted by evidence of any prior agreement or of a contemporaneous oral agreement. No particular form is required for an integrated agreement. When only part of the agreement is integrated, the parol evidence rule applies to that part.

Applying these standards, we conclude that the contract was integrated with respect to the grounds for termination. Slivinsky's employment application specifically conditioned employment upon execution of an employment agreement. It further provided that if Slivinsky were to become employed by Watkins-Johnson, there "will be no agreement, expressed or implied, . . . for any specific period of employment, nor for continuing or long term employment." When Slivinsky executed the Employee Agreement, she acknowledged "that there is no agreement, express or implied, between employee and the Company for any specific period of employment, nor for continuing or long-term employment. Employee and the Company each have a right to terminate employment, with or without cause." Reading these documents together, the only reasonable conclusion that can be drawn is that the parties intended that there would be no other agreement regarding termination other than that set forth in the Employee Agreement. Consequently, evidence of an implied agreement which contradicts the terms of the written agreement is not admissible. There cannot be a valid express contract and an implied contract, each embracing the same subject, but requiring different results.

Because we hold that the contract is a contract for employment terminable at will, we do not reach the issues regarding whether good cause existed for Slivinsky's termination based on Watkins-Johnson's decision to reduce its work force. Even if the reduction in force were a pretextual ground for terminating Slivinsky's employment, it would not be actionable with an at-will employment contract unless the employer's motivation for a discharge contravenes some significant public policy principle. No such public policy violation is alleged here.

Judgment for Watkins-Johnson affirmed.

Scope of the Parol Evidence Rule ✴

The parol evidence rule is relevant only in cases in which the parties have expressed their agreement in a *written* contract. Thus, it would *not* apply to a case involving an oral contract or to a case in which writings existed that were not intended to embody the final statement of at least part of the parties' contract. The parol evidence rule has been made a part of the law of sales in the Uniform Commercial Code [2–202], so it is applicable to contracts for the sale of goods as well as to contracts governed by the common law of contracts. Furthermore, the rule excludes only evidence of statements made *prior to* or *during* the signing of the written contract. It does not apply to statements made *after* the signing of the contract. Thus, evidence of *subsequent statements* is freely admissible.

Admissible Parol Evidence

In some situations, evidence of statements made outside the written contract is admissible notwithstanding the parol evidence rule. Parol evidence is permitted in the situations discussed below either because the writing is not the best evidence of the contract or because the evidence is offered, not to contradict the terms of the writing, but to explain the writing or to challenge the underlying contractual obligation that the writing represents.

Additional Terms in Partially Integrated Contracts In many instances, parties will desire to introduce evidence of statements or agreements that would *supplement* rather than contradict the written contract. Whether they can do this depends on whether the written contract is characterized as **completely integrated** or **partially integrated.** A completely integrated contract is one that the parties intend as a *complete and exclusive* statement of their entire agreement. A partially integrated contract is one that expresses the parties' final agreement as to some but not all of the terms of their contract. When a contract is only partially integrated, the parties are permitted to use parol evidence to prove the *additional* terms of their agreement. Such evidence cannot, however, be used to contradict the written terms of the contract.

To determine whether a contract is completely or partially integrated, a court must determine the parties' intent. A court judges intent by looking at the language of the contract, the apparent completeness of the writing, and all the surrounding circumstances. It will also consider whether the contract contains a **merger clause** (also known as an **integration clause).** These clauses, which are very common in form contracts and commercial contracts, provide that the written contract is the complete integration of the parties' agreement. They are designed to prevent a party from giving testimony about prior statements or agreements and are generally effective in indicating that the writing was a complete integration. Even though a contract contains a merger clause, parol evidence could be admissible under one of the following exceptions.

Explaining Ambiguities   Parol evidence can be offered to *explain an ambiguity* in the written contract. Suppose a written contract between Lowen and Matthews provides that Lowen will buy "Matthews's truck," but Matthews has two trucks. The parties could offer evidence of negotiations, statements, and other circumstances preceding the creation of the written contract to identify the truck to which the writing refers. Used in this way, parol evidence helps the court interpret the contract. It does not contradict the written contract.

Circumstances Invalidating Contract   Any circumstances that would be relevant to show that a contract is not valid can be proven by parol evidence. For example, evidence that Holden pointed a gun at Dickson and said, "Sign this contract, or I'll kill you," would be admissible to show that the contract was voidable because of duress. Likewise, parol evidence would be admissible to show that a contract was illegal or was induced by fraud, misrepresentation, undue influence, or mistake.

Existence of Condition   It is also permissible to use parol evidence to show that a writing was executed with the understanding that it was *not to take effect until the occurrence of a condition* (a future, uncertain event that creates a duty to perform).[7] Suppose Farnsworth signs a contract to purchase a car with the agreement that the contract is not to be effective unless and until Farnsworth gets a new job. If the written contract is silent about any conditions that must occur before it becomes effective, Farnsworth could introduce parol evidence to prove the existence of the condition. Such proof merely elaborates on, but does not contradict, the terms of the writing.

Subsequent Agreements   As you read earlier, the parol evidence rule does not forbid parties to introduce proof of *subsequent agreements.* This is true even if the terms of the later agreement cancel, subtract from, or add to the obligations stated in the written contract. The idea here is that when a writing is followed by a later statement or agreement, the writing is no longer the best evidence of the agreement. You should be aware, however, that subsequent modifications of contracts may sometimes be unenforceable due to lack of consideration or failure to comply with the statute of frauds. In addition, contracts sometimes expressly provide that modifications must be written. In this situation, an oral modification would be unenforceable.

---

[7] Conditions are discussed in greater detail in the Performance and Remedies chapter.

CONCEPT REVIEW

PAROL EVIDENCE RULE

The Parol Evidence Rule	*Applies when . . .* parties create a writing intended as a final and complete integration of at least part of the parties' contract.	*Provides that . . .* evidence of statements or promises made before or during the creation of the writing cannot be used to supplement, change, or contradict the terms of the written contract.
But Parol Evidence *Can* Be Used to	1. Prove consistent, additional terms when the contract is *partially integrated.* 2. Explain an ambiguity in the written contract. 3. Prove that the contract is void, voidable, or unenforceable. 4. Prove that the contract was subject to a condition. 5. Prove that the parties subsequently modified the contract or made a new agreement.	

INTERPRETATION OF CONTRACTS

Once a court has decided what promises are included in a contract, it is faced with *interpreting* the contract to determine the *meaning* and *legal effect* of the terms used by the parties. Courts have adopted broad, basic standards of interpretation that guide them in the interpretation process.

The court will first attempt to determine the parties' *principal objective*. Every clause will then be determined in the light of this principal objective. Ordinary words will be given their usual meaning and technical words (such as those that have a special meaning in the parties' trade or business) will be given their technical meaning, unless a different meaning was clearly intended.

Guidelines grounded in common sense are also used to determine the relationship of the various terms of the contract. Specific terms that follow general terms are presumed to qualify those general terms. Suppose that a provision that states that the subject of the contract is "guaranteed for one year" is followed by a provision describing the "one-year guarantee against defects in workmanship." Here, it is fair to conclude that the more specific term qualifies the more general term and that the guarantee described in the contract is a guarantee of workmanship only, and not of parts and materials.

Sometimes, there is internal conflict in the terms of an agreement and courts must determine which term should prevail. When the parties use a form contract or some other type of contract that is partially printed and partially handwritten, the handwritten provisions will prevail. If the contract was drafted by one of the parties, any ambiguities will be resolved *against* the party who drafted the contract.

If both parties to the contract are members of a trade, profession, or community in which certain words are commonly given a particular meaning (this is called a *usage*), the courts will presume that the parties intended the meaning that the usage gives to the terms they use. For example, if the word *dozen* in the bakery business means 13 rather than 12, a contract between two bakers for the purchase of 10 dozen loaves of bread will be presumed to mean 130 loaves of bread rather than 120. Usages can also add provisions to the parties' agreement. If the court finds that a certain practice is a matter of common usage in the parties' trade, it will assume that the parties intended to include that practice in their agreement. If contracting parties are members of the same trade, business, or community but do not intend to

be bound by usage, they should specifically say so in their agreement.

ETHICAL AND PUBLIC POLICY CONCERNS

1. The statute of frauds requires written evidence of *some*, but not all, contracts. Is this defensible from a public policy standpoint? Would it be preferable for the law to simply require that *all* contracts be evidenced by a writing?

2. What ethical problem was the statute of frauds designed to prevent, and what ethical problem does the statute of frauds create? Is the "cure worse than the disease"?

3. Under the law of some states, the doctrine of promissory estoppel permits the enforcement of promises that induce reliance, even when those promises do not comply with the statute of frauds. Should all states adopt this position? What effect would this have on the statute of frauds?

4. For those parties who draft and proffer standardized form contracts, the parol evidence rule can be a powerful ally because it has the effect of limiting the scope of an integrated, written contract to the terms of the writing. Although statements and promises made to a person before he signs a contract might be highly influential in persuading him to enter the contract, the parol evidence rule effectively prevents these precontract communications from being legally enforceable. Consider also that standardized form contracts are usually drafted for the benefit of and proffered by the more sophisticated and powerful party in a contract (e.g., the insurance company rather than the insured, the automobile dealer rather than the customer, the landlord rather than the tenant). Considering all of this, do you believe that the parol evidence rule promotes ethical behavior?

SUMMARY

All states have enacted statutes patterned after the English Statute of Frauds. These statutes state that certain types of contracts must be evidenced by a writing to be enforceable. Although the statutes are not uniform, generally included in the class of contracts for which a writing is required are collateral contracts; contracts for the sale of an interest in land; bilateral, executory contracts that cannot be performed within a year from the date on which the contract came into existence; and contracts for the sale of goods for a price of $500 or more. The statute of frauds applies only to executory contracts. A contract that fails to comply with the requirements of the statute of frauds is unenforceable, not void or voidable. Violation of the statute of frauds will not be a ground for invalidating a contract that has already been performed. A person who has conferred benefits pursuant to a contract that is unenforceable because of the statute of frauds can recover what he has parted with under the doctrine of *quasi-contract*.

A collateral contract is a contract in which one person promises to pay the debt or obligation of another person. A collateral contract must be distinguished from an original contract (in which a person obligates herself to perform an obligation in all events rather than merely to pay if another person fails to do so). No writing is required for an original contract unless it falls within some other provision of the statute of frauds. If a person's primary purpose in promising to pay the debt of another is to benefit himself, the *leading object* or *main purpose* exception to the statute of frauds provides that the promise does not have to be evidenced by a writing.

A contract involving the creation or transfer of ownership of any interest in land is within the statute of frauds. This includes ownership interests less than full ownership, such as easements, long-term leases, options, and mortgages. If a person has done acts in reliance on an oral contract for the sale of land, he may be able to obtain specific performance of the contract (but not damages) if the nature of his reliance is such that restitution (the return of what he parted with) would not be an adequate remedy.

Bilateral contracts that cannot be performed within a year from the date on which the contract came into existence are also within the statute of frauds. To determine whether a contract comes within the one-year provision, the amount of time between the date on which the contract came into being and the date on which the terms provide that performance will be completed must be calculated. Contracts for an indefinite period of time, even those "for life," are not within the statute of frauds of most states, because they *can* be performed within a year. In most states, complete performance by one of the parties will take the contract out of the statute of frauds and an oral contract will be enforceable.

Under UCC section 2–201, contracts for the sale of goods for a price of $500 or more are within the statute of frauds and must be evidenced by a writing or come within an exception to the writing requirement specified in the UCC. Modifications of sale of goods contracts are within the statute of frauds if the sales price of the contract as modified exceeds $500.

If a contract is within the statute of frauds and none of the exceptions to the statute of frauds is applicable, the contract must be evidenced by a memorandum indicating the existence of the contract. The memorandum does not have to *be* the contract, or even be intended by the parties as binding, but it must provide written evidence tending to prove that a contract exists. The memorandum must be signed by the party who is using the statute of frauds as a defense ("the party to be charged"). It must identify the parties and the subject matter and, to varying degrees controlled by state law, describe the important terms of the agreement. In sale of goods contracts, the UCC states that it does not matter whether the memorandum states all of the important terms, or even states some of them incorrectly, but the contract cannot be enforced for more than the quantity indicated in the memorandum.

The UCC provides for four additional ways of satisfying the statute of frauds in sale of goods contracts for $500 or more. Parties can use these ways to satisfy the statute when they do not have a writing or when they have a writing, but it is not signed by the party to be charged. First, if both parties are merchants and one of them sends a *confirmatory memorandum* signed by him, stating a quantity and indicating that a contract has been made, the memo will be sufficient to meet the statute of frauds if the other party receives it, has reason to know of its contents, and does not object in writing within 10 days. Second, an oral contract for the sale of $500 or more worth of *specially manufactured goods* is enforceable if the specially manufactured goods are of a type that cannot be resold in the ordinary course of the seller's business and if the seller has already made a substantial beginning in manufacturing the goods or has made commitments to procure the goods. Third, an oral contract for the sale of goods for a price of $500 or more can be enforced up to the quantity paid for or delivered if there has been *part payment or part delivery*. Fourth, an oral sale of goods contract for a price of $500 or more can be enforced up to the quantity admitted if the party against whom enforcement is sought *admits the existence of the contract* in court proceedings or pleadings.

In some states, the doctrine of promissory estoppel has been applied to estop a party from asserting the statute of frauds when the other party has been induced to rely materially on an oral contract and would suffer serious losses if the contract were not enforced.

The parol evidence rule provides that evidence of statements made prior to or during the signing of a written contract cannot be admitted to add to, alter, or vary the terms of the written contract. The parol evidence rule is part of the UCC as well as the common law of contracts. There are a variety of purposes for which parol evidence (evidence of statements not contained in the written contract) can be used, however. First, the parol evidence rule applies to prevent the use of evidence of prior or contemporaneous statements only. Evidence of *subsequent agreements* is admissible. Second, parol evidence can be used to add to or supplement a written contract if the contract is only *partially integrated.* Courts will look at the language and completeness of the contract and all the surrounding circumstances to tell whether the contract is completely or partially integrated. Contracts often contain *merger clauses* (also known as *integration clauses*), which specifically state that the writing is the complete statement of the parties' agreement. Third, parol evidence can be used to demonstrate *circumstances invalidating the contract,* for example, to show that the contract was unenforceable due to illegality or voidable due to duress, undue influence, mistake, fraud, or misrepresentation. Fourth, parol evidence can be used to *explain ambiguous terms* in the contract. Fifth, parol evidence is admissible to show that *the contract was not to be effective until the occurrence of a condition.*

Courts have developed guidelines to help them interpret the meaning and legal effect of language in a contract. They attempt to understand the parties' principal objective and to interpret the individual provisions of the contract so as to further that objective. Courts use specific rules to resolve situations in which ambiguity exists or there is an internal inconsistency in the terms used in the contract. Usages of a trade or industry are also helpful in determining the meaning and effect of contract terms.

PROBLEM CASES

1. Golomb allegedly orally agreed to sell to Lee for $275,000 the Ferrari once owned by King Leopold of Belgium. Golomb ultimately refused to sell the car and Lee sued him. At trial, Golomb denied ever promising to sell the car to Lee. Can Lee enforce this alleged promise?

2. Gross was the primary creditor of Wind Surfing, a manufacturer of ski apparel. Gross, who had loaned $47,000 to Wind Surfing, also had hopes of acquiring a one-third interest in the company. Wind Surfing also owed money to White Stag, and White Stag was unwilling to fill any new orders until Wind Surfing's past due balance was paid. Gross persuaded White Stag to extend credit to Wind Surfing for the upcoming ski season by assuring it that he would give White Stag a letter of credit or his personal guaranty to secure payment of Wind Surfing's past due balance. White Stag agreed to give Wind Surfing an open line of credit for $25,000 if Gross would give his guaranty or provide a bank letter of credit. White Stag sent Gross a confirmatory letter, with which it enclosed a personal guaranty form for Gross to sign. The personal guaranty form was never signed and returned. White Stag nevertheless released Wind Surfing's order and made shipments of goods over the next months until Wind Surfing's outstanding balance was $49,637.87. Wind Surfing never paid its accounts. White Stag sued Gross to collect the debt. Is Gross's oral promise to guarantee the debt enforceable?

3. In 1977, Barrett and her husband moved to San Antonio to live in a house that stood on property owned by her father, Field. The parties agreed that the Barretts would live in it and pay rent for at least six months before deciding whether to buy it. The Barretts spent two or three months fixing up the house before they moved in. When they moved in, they began paying Field $100 per month rent. After several years, the Barretts orally agreed to buy the property from Field. Under the terms of this agreement, the purchase price was to be the appraised value of the property, payments were to be $100 per month, and the money that they had paid Field for rent was to be applied to the purchase price. Field and Mr. Barrett "paced off" the land that was to be sold. A survey performed later indicated that this was 2.981 acres. All of the monthly checks for $100 that the Barretts wrote to Field were labeled "rent." Field died as a result of an unsolved homicide. His residence was largely destroyed by arson. No records were found pertaining to the sale of the property to the Barretts. Is the oral contract enforceable?

4. The Palermos orally ordered carpeting, padding, and tile for a sales price of more than $4,000 from Colorado Carpet, a retailer and installer of such goods. All of these items were stock items with no special dying, cutting, or other special features. Colorado Carpet ordered the carpeting from manufacturers, who filled the orders and delivered the carpeting to a Denver warehouse. Colorado Carpet also purchased and delivered tile to the Palermos, but, after a disagreement with the Palermos, Colorado Carpet removed the tile, returned half of it to the supplier for a refund, and sold the other half. It also shipped part of the carpeting back to its manufacturer for some credit and sold the rest to a local purchaser. Colorado Carpet then sued the Palermos for its lost profits, labor, and storage and shipping costs. Is its contract with the Palermos enforceable?

5. In June 1976, Moore went to First National Bank and requested the president of the bank to allow his sons, Rocky and Mike, to open an account in the name of Texas Continental Express, Inc. Moore promised to bring his own business to the bank and orally agreed to make good any losses that the bank might incur from receiving dishonored checks from Texas Continental. The bank then furnished regular checking account and bank draft services to Texas Continental. Several years later, Texas Continental wrote checks totaling $448,942.05 that were returned for insufficient funds. Texas Continental did not cover the checks, and the bank turned to Moore for payment. When Moore refused to pay, the bank sued him. Does Moore have a good statute of frauds defense?

6. In January 1980, Mayer entered into an oral contract of employment with King Cola for a three-year term. Mayer moved from Chattanooga to St. Louis and began working. King Cola paid his moving expenses. In accordance with the parties' negotiations, Mayer awaited a written contract, but none was ever executed. The employment relationship soon began to deteriorate, and after several months King Cola's president told Mayer that he was not going to be given a contract. In May 1980, King Cola discharged Mayer. In a state that does not recognize the doctrine of promissory estoppel as an exception to the statute of frauds, will Mayer be able to enforce the contract?

7. Everlener Dyer purchased a used Ford from Walt Bennett Ford for $5,895. She signed a written contract, which showed that no taxes were included in the sales price. Dyer contended, however, that the salesman who negotiated the purchase with her told her both before and after her signing of the contract that the sales tax on the automobile had been paid. The contract Dyer signed contained the following language:

The above comprises the entire agreement pertaining to this purchase and no other agreement of any kind, verbal understanding, representation, or promise whatsoever will be recognized.

It also stated:

This contract constitutes the entire agreement between the parties and no modification hereof shall be valid in any event and Buyer expressly waives the right to rely thereon, unless made in writing, signed by Seller.

Later, when Dyer attempted to license the automobile, she discovered that the Arkansas sales tax had not been paid on it. She paid the sales tax and sued Bennett for breach of contract. What result?

8. On Labor Day weekend, Grove participated in the Dickinson Elks Club's annual Labor Day Golf Tournament, which he had learned about from a poster that was placed at a golf course. Included in the poster was an offer by Charbonneau Buick-Pontiac of a 1974 automobile "to the first entry who shoots a hole-in-one on Hole No. 8." This offer was also placed on a sign on the automobile at the tournament. The Dickinson golf course at which the tournament was played had only 9 holes, but there were 18 separately located and marked tee areas, so that the course could be played as an 18-hole course by going around the 9-hole course twice. The first nine tees were marked with blue markers and tee numbers. The second nine tees were marked with red markers and tee numbers. Because of this layout of the course, the tee area marked "8" and the tee area marked "17" were both played to the eighth hole. The tee area marked "17" lay to one side of the tee area marked "8" and was approximately 60 yards farther from the hole. Grove scored a hole-in-one on hole No. 8 on the first day of the tournament while playing from the 17th tee in an 18-hole match. Grove claimed the prize, but Charbonneau refused to award it, insisting that Grove had not scored his hole-in-one on the 8th hole, as required, but had scored it on the 17th hole. Grove brought suit against Charbonneau for breach of contract. Will he win?

9. Wilson entered into an oral contract over the telephone to sell Cargill 28,000 bushels of ordinary winter wheat at $1.48 per bushel and 6,000 bushels of higher-protein wheat at $1.63 per bushel. Both parties were merchants. Following the telephone call, Cargill's manager completed two standard grain purchase contracts, signed them as Cargill's agent, signed Wilson's name to them, and sent them to Wilson. Wilson received the contracts and made no objection to their contents or to the fact that Cargill's manager had signed Wilson's name to them. Wilson began delivering wheat, but several months later Cargill discovered that Wilson did not intend to deliver the rest of the wheat. It sued Wilson for breach of contract. Wilson asserted the statute of frauds as a defense. Will Cargill prevail?

10. Katz, by his agent, made a written offer to buy real estate from the Joiners. On October 13, Katz called Mr. Joiner to ask his intentions. Mr. Joiner replied that everything was agreeable, that they had a deal, and that he was going to execute the contract and mail it back. The Joiners signed the contract and deposited it in the mail on October 20 to be delivered to Katz. Also on October 20, however, Mr. Joiner sent a telegram to arrive before the arrival of the contract. It stated, "In reference to Earnest Money Contract for Lot 4, Block 19, CB 9919 Unit 3, Rollingwood Estates, Bexar County, Texas. I have signed and returned contract but have changed my mind. Do not wish to sell property." Does this contract satisfy the requirements of the statute of frauds?

11. Lovely was living in Ann Arbor, Michigan, and working at two jobs there when Dierkes offered Lovely employment with the Real Food Company in Jackson, Michigan. Dierkes promised Lovely a three-year employment contract, a salary of $400 per week, and a percentage interest in Real Food. He also promised that Lovely would not be discharged without good cause. Lovely relocated his family to Jackson in reliance on Dierkes's promise. He began performing under the agreement and requested several times that Dierkes reduce the contract to writing. Dierkes allegedly assured Lovely that a writing was forthcoming. After two months of employment, Dierkes discharged Lovely. Lovely sued Dierkes and Real Food for breach of contract. Dierkes claims that the contract is unenforceable because of the statute of frauds. Can Lovely enforce this contract?

CHAPTER 18

RIGHTS OF THIRD PARTIES

INTRODUCTION

In preceding chapters, we have emphasized the way in which an agreement between two or more people creates legal rights and duties *on the part of the contracting parties*. Since a contract is founded upon the consent of the contracting parties, it might seem to follow that they are the only ones who have rights and duties under the contract. Although this is generally true, there are two situations in which people who were not parties to a contract have legally enforceable rights under it: when a contract has been **assigned** (transferred) to a third party and when a contract is intended to benefit a third person **(third party beneficiary).** This chapter discusses the circumstances in which third parties have rights under a contract.

ASSIGNMENTS OF CONTRACTS

Contracts give people both rights and duties. If Murphy buys Wagner's motorcycle and promises to pay him $1,000 for it, Wagner has the *right* to receive Murphy's promised performance (the payment of the $1,000) and Murphy has the *duty* to perform the promise by paying $1,000. In most situations, contract rights can be transferred to a third person and contract duties can be dele-

gated to a third person. The transfer of a *right* under a contract is called an **assignment.** The appointment of another person *to perform a duty* under a contract is called a **delegation.**

Nature of Assignment of Rights

A person who owes a duty to perform under a contract is called an **obligor.** The person to whom he owes the duty is called the **obligee.** For example, Samson borrows $500 from Jordan, promising to repay Jordan in six months. Samson, who owes the duty to pay the money, is the obligor, and Jordan, who has the right to receive the money, is the obligee. An assignment occurs when the obligee transfers his right to receive the obligor's performance to a third person. When there has been an assignment, the person making the assignment—the original obligee—is then called the **assignor.** The person to whom the right has been transferred is called the **assignee.**

Suppose that Jordan, the obligee in the example above, assigns his right to receive Samson's payment to Kane. Here, Jordan is the assignor and Kane is the assignee. The relationship between the three parties is represented in Figure 1. Notice that the assignment is a separate transaction; it occurs *after* the formation of the original contract.

Figure 1   Assignment of Rights

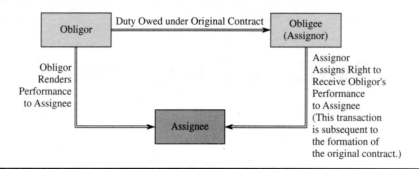

The effect of the assignment is to extinguish the assignor's right to receive performance and to transfer that right to the assignee. In the above example, Kane now owns the right to collect payment from Samson. If Samson fails to pay, Kane, as an assignee, now has the right to file suit against Samson to collect the debt.

People assign rights for a variety of reasons. A person might assign a right to a third party to satisfy a debt that he owes. For example, Jordan, the assignor in the above example, owes money to Kane, so he assigns to Kelly the right to receive the $500 that Samson owes him. A person might also sell or pledge the rights owed to him to obtain financing. In the case of a business, the money owed to a business by customers and clients is called *accounts receivable.* A business's accounts receivable are an asset to the business that can be used to raise money in several ways. For example, the business may pledge its accounts receivable as collateral for a loan. Suppose Ace Tree Trimming Co. wants to borrow money from First Bank and gives First Bank a security interest (an interest in the debtor's property that secures the debtor's performance of an obligation) in its accounts receivable.[1] If Ace defaults in its payments to First Bank, First Bank will acquire Ace's rights to collect the accounts receivable. A person might also make an assignment of a contract right as a gift. For example, Lansing owes $2,000 to Father. Father assigns the right to receive Lansing's performance to Son as a graduation gift.

Evolution of the Law Regarding Assignments   Contract rights have not always been transferable. Early common law refused to permit assignment or delegation

because debts were considered to be too personal to transfer. A debtor who failed to pay an honest debt was subject to severe penalties, including imprisonment, because such a failure to pay was viewed as the equivalent of theft. The identity of the creditor was of great importance to the debtor, since one creditor might be more lenient than another. Courts also feared that the assignment of debts would stir up unwanted litigation. In an economy that was primarily land-based, the extension of credit was of relatively small importance. As trade increased and became more complex, however, the practice of extending credit became more common. The needs of an increasingly commercial society demanded that people be able to trade freely in intangible assets such as debts. Consequently, the rules of law regarding the assignment of contracts gradually became more liberal. Today, public policy favors free assignability of contracts.

Sources of Assignment Law Today   Legal principles regarding assignment are found not only in the common law of contracts, but also in Articles 2 and 9 of the Uniform Commercial Code. Section 2–210 of Article 2 contains principles applicable to assignments of rights under a *contract for the sale of goods.* Article 9 governs security interests in accounts and other contract rights as well as the outright sale of accounts. Article 9's treatment of assignments will be discussed in more detail in the Security Interests in Personal Property chapter but some provisions of Article 9 relating to assignments will be discussed in this chapter.

Creating an Assignment

An assignment can be made in any way that is sufficient to show the assignor's intent to assign. No formal

---

[1] Security interests in accounts and other property are discussed in the Security Interests in Personal Property chapter.

language is required, and a writing is not necessary unless required by a provision of the statute of frauds or some other statute. Many states do have statutes requiring certain types of assignments to be evidenced by a writing, however. Additionally, an assignment for the purposes of security must meet Article 9's formal requirements for security interests.[2]

It is not necessary that the assignee give any consideration to the assignor in exchange for the assignment. Gratuitous assignments (those for which the assignee gives no value) are generally revocable until such time as the obligor satisfies the obligation, however. They can be revoked by the assignor's death or incapacity or by notification of revocation given by the assignor to the assignee.

Assignability of Rights

Most, but not all, contract rights are assignable. Although the free assignability of contract rights performs a valuable function in our modern credit-based economy, assignment is undesirable if it would adversely affect some important public policy or if it would materially vary the bargained-for expectations of the parties. There are several basic limitations on the assignability of contract rights.

First, an assignment will not be effective if it is *contrary to public policy*. For example, most states have enacted statutes that prohibit or regulate a wage earner's assignment of future wages. These statutes are designed to protect people against unwisely impoverishing themselves by signing away their future incomes.

Second, an assignment will not be effective if it *adversely affects the obligor in some significant way*. An assignment is ineffective if it materially changes the obligor's duty or increases the burden or risk on the obligor. Naturally, any assignment will change an obligor's duty

to some extent. The obligor will have to pay money or deliver goods or render some other performance to X instead of to Y. These changes are not considered to be sufficiently material to render an assignment ineffective. Thus, a right to receive money or goods or land is generally assignable. In addition, covenants not to compete are generally considered to be assignable to buyers of businesses. For example, Jefferson sells RX Drugstore to Waldman, including in the contract of sale a covenant whereby Jefferson promises not to operate a competing drugstore within a 30-mile radius of RX for 10 years after the sale. Waldman later sells RX to Tharp. Here, Tharp could enforce the covenant not to compete against Jefferson. The reason for permitting assignment of covenants not to compete is that the purpose of such covenants is to protect an asset of the business—goodwill—for which the buyer has paid.

An assignment could be ineffective because of its variation of the obligor's duty, however, if the contract right involved a *personal relationship* or an element of *personal skill, judgment, or character*. For this reason, contracts of employment in which an employee works under the direct and personal supervision of an employer cannot be assigned to a new employer. An employer could assign a contract of employment, however, if the assignee-employer could perform the contract without adversely affecting the interests of the employee, such as would be the case when an employment relationship does not involve personal supervision by an individual employer. This point is illustrated by the following case, *Special Products Manufacturing, Inc. v. Douglass*.

A purported assignment is ineffective if it significantly increases the burden of the obligor's performance. For example, if Walker contracts to sell Dwyer all of its requirements of wheat, a purported assignment of Dwyer's rights to a corporation that has much greater requirements of wheat would probably be ineffective because it would significantly increase the burden on Walker.

---

[2] These requirements are discussed in the Security Interests in Personal Property chapter.

SPECIAL PRODUCTS MANUFACTURING, INC. v. DOUGLASS

553 N.Y.S.2d 506 (N.Y. S. Ct., App. Div. 1990)

Thaddeus Douglass was a highly trained servicer of hardness-testing machinery who was employed by Page-Wilson Corporation. In August and April of 1983, Douglass signed two employment agreements governing the terms and conditions of his employment with Page-Wilson. The first agreement prohibited Douglass, while he was working for Page-Wilson and for one year after the termination of his employment, from using, to Page-Wilson's detriment, any of its customer lists or other intellectual property acquired from his job there. The second agreement, which applied to the same time period, prohibited Douglass from accepting employment from or serving as a consultant to any business that was in competition with Page-Wilson. In April of 1987, Canrad Corporation purchased all assets and contractual rights of Page-Wilson, including Douglass's two employment contracts. Special Products Manufacturing (Special Products), a wholly owned subsidiary of Canrad, assumed plant operations. Douglass worked for Special Products until his resignation in February of 1988.

Shortly after that, Special Products filed this lawsuit against Douglass, alleging that Douglass had affixed his name and home telephone number to the machines he serviced, so that the ensuing maintenance calls would reach him personally. It also alleged that, following his resignation, Douglass established a competing business and actively solicited Special Products's clientele. Douglass did not answer the complaint in a timely manner, and, after a long delay, the trial judge entered a default judgment in favor of Special Products. Douglass appealed this order, arguing in part that Special Products did not have the right to enforce the agreements not to compete.

Yesawich, Justice.   We perceive no merit in the contention that because Douglass entered into the agreements with Page-Wilson, they are unenforceable by Special Products. In an uncontroverted affidavit based upon personal knowledge, Special Products's vice-president of sales avows that Special Products acquired all of Page-Wilson's contract rights, including Douglass's. Douglass's consent was not required to effectuate this transfer. When the original parties to an agreement so intend, a covenant not to compete is freely assignable. Here, such intent is unmistakably evident in the first employment agreement which expressly "inure[s] to the benefit of the successors and assigns of Page-Wilson." And, while the second document contains no similar provision, neither does it specifically forbid assignment. Because executory contracts, which do not involve exceptional personal skills on the part of the assignor and which the assignee can perform without adversely affecting the rights and interests of the adverse party, are freely assignable absent a contractual, statutory or public policy prohibition, a clear and unambiguous prohibition is essential to effectively prevent assignment. Accordingly, the assignment to Special Products perpetuated the restrictive covenant provision, the very terms of which Douglass violated without justification.

Order in favor of Special Products affirmed.

Contract Clauses Prohibiting Assignment   A contract right may also be nonassignable because *the original contract expressly forbids assignment*. For example, leases often contain provisions forbidding assignment or requiring the tenant to obtain the landlord's permission for assignment.[3]

Antiassignment clauses in contracts generally are enforceable. Because of the strong public policy favoring assignability, however, such clauses are often interpreted narrowly. For example, a court might view an assignment made in violation of an antiassignment clause as a breach of contract for which damages may be recovered, but not as an invalidation of the assignment. Another tactic is to interpret a contractual ban on assignment as prohibiting only the delegation of duties.

The UCC takes this latter position. Under section 2–210(2), a contract term that forbids assignment is interpreted as forbidding only the delegation of duties. Section 2–210 also states that a right to damages for breach of a whole sales contract or a right arising out of the assignor's performance of his entire obligation may be assigned even if a provision of the original sales contract prohibited assignment. In addition, UCC section 9–318(4) invalidates contract terms that prohibit (or re-

---

[3] The assignment of leases is discussed further in the Landlord and Tenant chapter.

quire the debtor's consent to) an assignment of an account or creation of a security interest in a right to receive money that is now due or that will become due.

Nature of Assignee's Rights

When an assignment occurs, the assignee is said to "step into the shoes of his assignor." This means that the assignee acquires all of the rights that his assignor had under the contract. The assignee has the right to receive the obligor's performance, and if performance is not forthcoming, the assignee has the right to sue in his own name for breach of the obligation. By the same token, the assignee acquires no greater rights than those possessed by the assignor.

Because the assignee has no greater rights than did the assignor, the obligor may assert any defense or claim against the assignee that he could have asserted against the assignor, subject to certain time limitations discussed below. A contract that is void, voidable, or unenforceable as between the original parties does not become enforceable just because it has been assigned to a third party. For example, if Richards induces Dillman's consent to a contract by duress and subsequently assigns his rights under the contract to Keith, Dillman can assert the doctrine of duress against Keith as a ground for avoiding the contract.

Importance of Notifying the Obligor   An assignee should promptly notify the obligor of the assignment. Although notification of the obligor is not necessary for the assignment to be valid, such notice is of great practical importance. One reason notice is important is that an obligor who does not have reason to know of the assignment could render performance to the assignor and claim that his obligation had been discharged by performance. An obligor who renders performance to the assignor without notice of the assignment has no further liability under the contract. For example, McKay borrows $500 from Goodheart, promising to repay the debt by June 1. Goodheart assigns the debt to Rogers, but no one informs McKay of the assignment, and McKay pays the $500 to Goodheart, the assignor. In this case, McKay is not liable for any further payment. But if Rogers had immediately notified McKay of the assignment and, after receiving notice, McKay had mistakenly paid the debt to Goodheart, McKay would still have the legal obligation to pay $500 to Rogers. Having been given adequate notice of the assignment, he may remain liable to the assignee even if he later renders performance to the assignor.

An assignor who accepts performance from the obligor after the assignment holds any benefits that he receives as a trustee for the assignee. If the assignor fails to pay those benefits to the assignee, however, an obligor who has been notified of the assignment and renders performance to the wrong person may have to pay the same debt twice.

An obligor who receives notice of an assignment from the assignee will want to assure himself that the assignment has in fact occurred. He may ask for written evidence of the assignment or contact the assignee and ask for verification of the assignment. Under UCC section 9–318(3), a notification of assignment is ineffective unless it reasonably identifies the rights assigned. If requested by the account debtor (an obligor who owes money for goods sold or leased or services rendered), the assignee must furnish reasonable proof that the assignment has been made, and, unless he does so, the account debtor may disregard the notice and pay the assignor.

Defenses against the Assignee   An assignee's rights in an assignment are subject to the defenses that the obligor could have asserted against the assignor. Keep in mind that the assignee's rights are limited by the terms of the underlying contract between the assignor and the obligor. When defenses arise from the terms or performance of that contract, they can be asserted against the assignee even if they arise after the obligor receives notice of the assignment. For example, on June 1, Worldwide Widgets assigns to First Bank its rights under a contract with Widgetech, Inc. This contract obligates Worldwide Widgets to deliver a quantity of widgets to Widgetech by September 1, in return for which Widgetech is obligated to pay a stated purchase price. First Bank gives prompt notice of the assignment to Widgetech. Worldwide Widget fails to deliver the widgets and Widgetech refuses to pay. If First Bank brought an action against Widgetech to recover the purchase price of the widgets, Widgetech could assert Worldwide Widget's breach as a defense, even though the breach occurred after Widgetech received notice of the assignment.[4]

---

[4] Similarly, if the assignor's rights were subject to discharge because of other factors such as the nonoccurrence of a condition, impossibility, impracticability, or public policy, this can be asserted as a defense against the assignee even if the event occurs after the obligor receives notice of assignment. See *Restatement (Second) of Contracts* § 336(3). The doctrines relating to discharge from performance are explained in the Performance of Remedies chapter.

In determining what other defenses can be asserted against the assignee, the time of notification plays an important role. After notification, as we discussed earlier, payment by the obligor to the assignor will not discharge the obligor.

Counterclaims against the Assignee The obligor may also assert against the assignee certain counterclaims (claims entitling the obligor to some relief or remedy) that he could have asserted against the assignor. Unless the assignee has contracted for greater liability, he is liable on a counterclaim only to the extent of his claim against the obligor. In other words, a counterclaim by the obligor will only operate to subtract from the amount of the money to which the assignee is entitled.

A claim asserted by the obligor that arises from the original contract between assignor and obligor is known as **recoupment.** Such claims can be asserted even if they arise after notice of assignment. In the hypothetical case described earlier concerning the delivery of widgets, suppose that Worldwide Widgets had delivered widgets by September 1, but it breached a warranty by delivering widgets that were defective. When First Bank attempts to recover the purchase price of the widgets from Widgetech, Widgetech can assert Worldwide Widget's breach of warranty as a recoupment. The effect will be to reduce or negate its debt to First Bank.

An obligor is also permitted to assert against the assignee certain claims against the assignor that arose independently of the assigned contract. When an obligor asserts a counterclaim based on some obligation that arose independent of the assigned contract, this is called **set off.** An important limitation on the right of set off is that the claim must have accrued *before the obligor receives notification of the assignment.* For example, Doaks, the owner of an office building, leases space to Margolis. On April 1, Doaks makes an interest-free loan of $5,000 to Margolis, which Margolis agrees to repay in full on July 1. In an unrelated transaction on April 2, Doaks agrees to reimburse Margolis for the $200 that Margolis has spent to have a plumber repair some leaky pipes in the leased space. On June 1, Doaks assigns to Ruiz the right to receive the $5,000 from Margolis. Ruiz gives prompt notice of the assignment. If Margolis fails to pay his debt on time and Ruiz sues him to collect the $5,000, Margolis would be entitled to set off (subtract from that debt) the $200 that Doaks had agreed to pay for the plumber's bill.

Subsequent Assignments

An assignee may "reassign" a right to a third party, who would be called a **subassignee.** The subassignee then acquires the rights held by the prior assignee. He should give the obligor prompt notice of the subsequent assignment, because he takes his interest subject to the same principles discussed above regarding the claims and defenses that can be asserted against him.

Successive Assignments

Notice to the obligor may be important in one other situation. If an assignor assigns the same right to two assignees in succession, both of whom pay for the assignment, a question of priority results. An assignor who assigns the same right to different people will be held liable to the assignee who acquires no rights against the obligor, but which assignee is entitled to the obligor's performance? Which assignee will have recourse only against the assignor? There are several views on this point.

In states that follow the "American rule," the first assignee has the better right. This view is based on the rule of property law that a person cannot transfer greater rights in property that he owns. In states that follow the "English rule," however, the assignee who first gives notice of the assignment to the obligor, without knowledge of the other assignee's claim, has the better right. The *Restatement (Second) of Contracts* takes a third position. Section 342 of the *Restatement* provides that the first assignee has priority unless the subsequent assignee gives value (pays for the assignment) and, without having reason to know of the other assignee's claim, does one of the following: obtains payment of the obligation, gets a judgment against the obligor, obtains a new contract with the obligor by novation, or possesses a writing of a type customarily accepted as a symbol or evidence of the right assigned (such as a passbook for a savings account).

Assignor's Warranty Liability to Assignee

Suppose that Ross, a 16-year-old boy, contracts to buy a used car for $2,000 from Donaldson. Ross pays Donaldson $500 as a down payment and agrees to pay the balance in equal monthly installments. Donaldson assigns his right to receive the balance of the purchase price to Beckman, who pays $1,000 in cash for the assignment. When Beckman later attempts to enforce the contract, however, Ross disaffirms the contract on grounds of lack of capacity. Thus, Beckman has paid $1,000 for a worthless claim. Does Beckman have any recourse against Donaldson? When an assignor is *paid* for making an assignment, the assignor is held to have made certain *implied warranties* about the claim assigned.

The assignor impliedly warrants that the claim assigned is *valid*. This means that the obligor has capacity to contract, the contract is not illegal, the contract is not voidable for any other reason known to the assignor (such as fraud or duress), and the contract has not been discharged prior to assignment. The assignor also warrants that he has *good title* to the rights assigned and that any written instrument representing the assigned claim is *genuine*. In addition, the assignor impliedly agrees that he *will not do anything to impair the value of the assignment*. These guarantees are imposed by law unless the assignment agreement clearly indicates to the contrary. One important aspect of the assigned right that the assignor does *not* impliedly warrant, however, is that the obligor is *solvent*.

DELEGATION OF DUTIES

Nature of Delegation

A delegation of duties occurs when an obligor indicates his intent to appoint another person to perform his duties under a contract. For example, White owns a furniture store. He has numerous existing contracts to deliver furniture to customers, including a contract to deliver a sofa to Coombs. White is the *obligor* of the duty to deliver the sofa and Coombs is the *obligee*. White decides to sell his business to Rosen. As a part of the sale of the business, White assigns the rights in the existing contracts to Rosen and delegates to him the performance of those contracts, including the duty to deliver the sofa to Coombs. Here White is the *delegator*, Rosen is the *delegatee*. White is appointing Rosen to carry out his duties to the obligee, Coombs. A diagram of the delegation of a duty appears in Figure 2.

In contrast to an assignment of a *right*, which extinguishes the assignor's right and transfers it to the assignee, the delegation of a *duty* does *not* extinguish the duty owed by the delegator. This point is made clearly in *Brooks v. Hayes*. The delegator remains liable to the obligee unless the obligee agrees to substitute the delegatee's promise for that of the delegator (this is called a **novation,** and will be discussed in greater detail below). This makes sense, because, if it were possible for a person to escape his duties under a contract by merely delegating them to another, any party to a contract could avoid liability by delegating duties to an insolvent acquaintance. The significance of an effective delegation is that *performance* by the delegatee will discharge the delegating party. In addition, if the duty is a delegable one, the obligee cannot insist on performance by the delegator; he must accept the performance of the delegatee.

FIGURE 2   Delegation of Duties

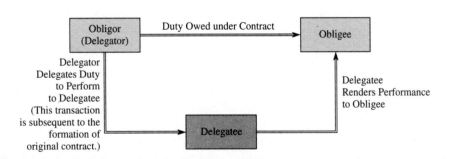

BROOKS v. HAYES

395 N.W.2d 167 (Wis. S. Ct. 1986)

In May of 1978, John and Judith Brooks contracted with Wayne Hayes, doing business as Wayne Hayes Real Estate, to construct a Windsor Home (a packaged, predesigned, and precut home) on a lot that they owned. Hayes was primarily a real estate broker, but also sold Windsor Homes. The construction contract required Hayes to "provide all necessary labor and materials and perform all work of every nature whatsoever to be done in the erection of a residence for" the Brookses. The Brookses and Hayes contemplated that Hayes would hire subcontractors to perform much of the home construction work and Hayes, who had no personal experience in construction, would not control the method of construction. During the construction, the Brookses requested that a "heatilator" be installed as an extra to increase the efficiency of the fireplace. Claude Marr, the mason hired by Hayes to do the fireplace and other masonry work, installed the heatilator.

The Brookses moved into the house in the winter of 1978. When they used the fireplace, they smelled smoke in areas of the house remote from the fireplace. Both the Brookses and Hayes hired several masons to inspect the fireplace system, but none of the masons was able to discover the cause of the problem. The Brookses used the fireplace with some frequency until November 1980, when a fire in the home caused structural damage around the fireplace and smoke damage to the house and the couple's personal property. It was discovered that Marr's negligence in installing the heatilator had caused the fire. The Brookses sued both Marr and Hayes. The case against Marr was dismissed because Marr went bankrupt. The trial court also dismissed the complaint against Hayes on the ground that Hayes was neither personally negligent nor legally responsible for the negligence of an independent contractor. Mr. and Mrs. Brooks appealed.

Abrahamson, Justice.   The Brookses contend that the contract implicitly imposed on Hayes the duty to perform with due care. Their interpretation is supported by *Colton v. Foulkes*, in which the court adopted the rule that "accompanying every contract is a common law duty to perform with care, skill, reasonable expediency, and faithfulness the thing they agreed to be done, and a negligent failure to observe any of these conditions is a tort, as well as a breach of contract."

Although Hayes assumed a contractual duty to the Brookses to perform the construction contract with skill and due care, Hayes delegated the performance of the contract to others. The question then is whether the delegation of performance of the masonry work relieved Hayes of liability for breach of contract when the mason, an independent contractor, negligently performed that part of Hayes' contractual obligation.

The Brookses assert that Hayes may not avoid responsibility to them for his failure to perform his contractual duty of due care merely by hiring an independent contractor. We agree with this assertion. The hornbook principle of contract law is that the delegation of the performance of a contract does not, unless the obligee agrees otherwise, discharge the liability of the delegating obligor to the obligee for breach of contract.

Hayes argues he is not liable for breach of contract for the mason's negligence because the Brookses knew about and acquiesced in his hiring the independent contractor. We are not persuaded by Hayes' argument. Hayes has confused delegation of the performance of an obligation with delegation of responsibility for the performance of an obligation. The rule for delegation of the performance of a contractual obligation is that the obligor may delegate a contractual duty without the obligee's consent unless the duty is "personal." The rule for delegation of responsibility is that if the obligor delegates the performance of an obligation, the obligor is not relieved of responsibility for fulfilling that obligation.

Where the obligee consents to the delegation, the consent itself does not release the obligor from liability for breach of contract. More than the obligee's consent to a delegation of performance is needed to release the obligor from liability for breach of contract. For the obligor to be released from liability, the obligee must agree to the release. If there is an agreement between the obligor, obligee, and a third party by which the third party agrees to be substituted for the obligor and the obligee assents thereto, the obligor is released from liability and the third person takes the place of the obligor. Such an agreement is known as a novation. This court cannot make such findings on the record.

We hold that Hayes could hire subcontractors to perform the construction contract but that Hayes' delegation of the performance part of the contract to an independent contractor did not itself relieve Hayes of liability to the Brookses. Although we conclude that the Brookses have a good cause of action against Hayes, this court cannot make a final determination of Hayes' liability on the record before it. There are several issues that the circuit court did not consider. For example, Hayes argues that the heatilator was not part of the construction contract and that he had no responsibility for it. We cannot decide these issues. For the reasons set forth, we hold that Hayes may be liable for the mason's negligence and that the cause must be remanded to the circuit court for a new trial.

Judgment reversed in favor of the Brookses and remanded for a new trial.

Delegable Duties

A duty that can be performed fully by a number of different persons is delegable. Not all duties are delegable, however. The grounds for finding a duty to be nondelegable resemble closely the grounds for finding a right to be nonassignable. A duty is nondelegable if delegation would violate public policy or if the original contract between the parties forbids delegation. In addition, both section 2–210(1) of the UCC and section 318(2) of the *Restatement (Second) of Contracts* take the position that a party to a contract may delegate his duty to perform to another person unless the parties have agreed to the contrary or unless the other party has a "substantial interest" in having the original obligor perform the acts required by the contract. The key factor used in determining whether the obligee has such a substantial interest is the degree to which performance is dependent on the individual traits, skill, or judgment of the person who owes the duty to perform. For example, if Jansen hires Skelton, an artist, to paint her portrait, Skelton could not effectively delegate the duty to paint the portrait to another artist. Similarly, an employee could not normally delegate her duties under an employment contract to some third person, because employment contracts are made with the understanding that the person the employer hires will perform the work. The situation in which a person hires a general contractor to perform specific work is distinguishable, however. In that situation (typified by *Brooks v. Hayes*), the person hiring the general contractor would normally understand that at least part of the work would be delegated to subcontractors.

Language Creating a Delegation

No special, formal language is necessary to create an effective delegation of duties. In fact, since parties frequently confuse the terms *assignment* and *delegation*, one of the problems frequently presented to courts is determining whether the parties intended an assignment only or both an assignment and a delegation. Unless the agreement indicates a contrary intent, courts tend to interpret assignments as *including* a delegation of the assignor's duties. Both the UCC 2–210(4) and section 328 of the *Restatement (Second) of Contracts* provide that, unless the language or the circumstances indicate to the contrary, general language of assignment such as an assignment of "the contract" or of "all my rights under the contract" is to be interpreted as creating *both* an assignment and a delegation.

Assumption of Duties by Delegatee

A delegation gives the delegatee the right to perform the duties of the delegator. The mere fact that duties have been delegated does not always place legal responsibility on the delegatee to perform. The delegatee who fails to perform will not be liable to either the delegator or the obligee unless the delegatee has *assumed* the duty by expressly or impliedly undertaking the obligation to perform. However, both section 2–210(4) of the UCC and section 328 of the *Restatement* provide that an assignee's acceptance of an assignment is to be construed as a promise by him to perform the duties under the contract, unless the language of the assignment or the circumstances indicate to the contrary. Frequently, a term of the contract between the delegator and the delegatee provides that the delegatee assumes responsibility for performance. A common example of this is the *assumption* of an existing mortgage debt by a purchaser of real estate. Suppose Morgan buys a house from Friedman, agreeing to assume the outstanding mortgage on the property held by First Bank. By this assumption, Morgan undertakes personal liability to both Friedman and First Bank. If Morgan fails to make the mortgage payments, First Bank has a cause of action against Morgan personally. An assumption does *not* release the delegator from liability, however. Rather, it creates a situation in which both the delegator and the assuming delegatee owe duties to the obligee. If the assuming delegatee fails to pay, the delegator can be held liable. Thus, in the example described above, if Morgan fails to make mortgage payments and First Bank is unable to collect the debt from Morgan, Friedman would have secondary liability. Friedman, of course, would have an action against Morgan for breach of their contract.

Discharge of Delegator by Novation

As you have seen, the mere delegation of duties—even when the delegatee assumes those duties—does not release the delegator from his legal obligation to the obligee. A delegator can, however, be discharged from performance by **novation.**

A *novation* is a particular type of substituted contract in which the obligee agrees to discharge the original obligor and to substitute a new obligor in his place. The effects of a novation are that the original obligor has no further obligation under the contract and the obligee has the right to look to the new obligor for fulfillment of the contract. A novation requires more than the obligee's consent to having the delegatee perform the duties. In the example used above, the mere fact that First Bank accepted mortgage payments from Morgan would not create a novation. Rather, there must be some evidence that the obligee agrees to *discharge* the old obligor and substitute a new obligor. This can be inferred from language of a contract or such other factors as the obligee's conduct or the surrounding circumstances.

THIRD PARTY BENEFICIARIES

There are many situations in which the performance of a contract would constitute some benefit to a person who was not a party to the contract. Despite the fact that a nonparty may expect to derive advantage from the performance of a contract, the general rule is that no one but the parties to a contract or their assignees can enforce it. In some situations, however, parties contract for the purpose of benefiting some third person. In such cases, the benefit to the third person is an essential part of the contract, not just an incidental result of a contract that was really designed to benefit the parties. Where the parties to a contract *intended* to benefit a third party, courts will give effect to their intent and permit the third party to enforce the contract. Such third parties are called **third party beneficiaries.** Figure 3 illustrates the relationship of third party beneficiaries to the contracting parties.

Intended Beneficiaries versus Incidental Beneficiaries

For a third person (other than an assignee) to have the right to enforce a contract, she must be able to establish that the contract was made with the *intent* to benefit her. A few courts have required that *both* parties must have intended to benefit the third party. Most courts, however, have found it to be sufficient if the person to whom the promise to perform was made (the *promisee*) intended to benefit the third party. In ascertaining intent to benefit the third party, a court will look at the language used by the parties and all the surrounding circumstances. One factor that is frequently important in determining intent to benefit is whether the party making the promise to perform (the *promisor*) was to render performance directly to the third party. For example, if Allison contracts with Jones Florist to deliver flowers to Kirsch, the fact that performance was to be rendered to Kirsch would be good evidence that the parties intended to benefit

FIGURE 3 Third Party Beneficiaries

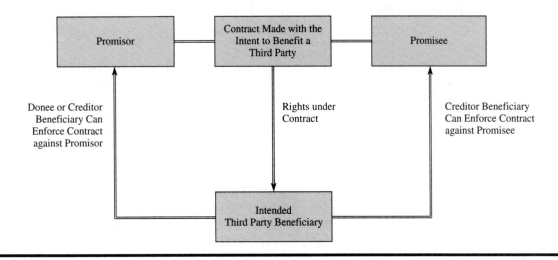

Kirsch. This factor is not conclusive, however. There are some cases in which intent to benefit a third party has been found even though performance was to be rendered to the promisee rather than to the third party. Intended beneficiaries are often classified as either *donee* or *creditor* beneficiaries. These classifications are discussed in greater detail below.

A third party who is unable to establish that the contract was made with the intent to benefit her is called an *incidental beneficiary.* A third party is classified as an incidental beneficiary when the benefit derived by that third party was merely an unintended by-product of a contract that was created for the benefit of those who were parties to it. Incidental beneficiaries acquire no rights under a contract. For example, Hutton contracts with Long Construction Company to build a valuable structure on his land. The performance of the contract would constitute a benefit to Keller, Hutton's next-door neighbor, by increasing the value of Keller's land. The contract between Hutton and Long was made for the purpose of benefiting themselves, however. Any advantage derived by Keller is purely incidental to their primary purpose. Thus, Keller could not sue and recover damages if either Hutton or Long breaches the contract.

As a general rule, members of the public are held to be incidental beneficiaries of contracts entered into by their municipalities or other governmental units in the regular course of carrying on governmental functions. A member of the public cannot recover a judgment in a suit against a promisor of such a contract, even though all taxpayers will suffer some injury from nonperformance. A different result may be reached, however, if a party contracting with a governmental unit agrees to reimburse members of the public for damages or if the party undertakes to perform some duty for individual members of the public.

Donee Beneficiaries If the promisee's primary purpose in contracting is to make a *gift* of the agreed-upon performance to a third party, that third party is classified as a *donee beneficiary.* If the contract is breached, the donee beneficiary will have a cause of action against the promisor, but not against the promisee (donor). For example, Miller contracts with Perpetual Life Insurance Company, agreeing to pay premiums in return for which Perpetual agrees to pay $100,000 to Miller's husband when Miller dies. Miller's husband is a donee beneficiary and can bring suit and recover judgment against Perpetual if Miller dies and Perpetual does not pay. The following case, *Warren v. Monahan Beaches Jewelry Center, Inc.*, provides another example of a donee beneficiary. It also demonstrates the implications of a person's status as an intended beneficiary.

WARREN v. MONAHAN BEACHES JEWELRY CENTER, INC.

548 So. 2d 870 (Fla. Ct. App. 1989)

Jay Andreson went to Monahan Beaches Jewelry Center (Monahan) to shop for a diamond engagement ring for his fiancée, Laneya Warren. Andreson told Monahan that the ring was to be given to Warren. Andreson and a salesman discussed several aspects of the size, type, and style of the ring, and the salesman made suggestions about what would be likely to be pleasing to Warren. Shortly before Christmas, Monahan sold Andreson a ring, which Monahan represented as being a diamond ring, for $3,974.25. Andreson gave the ring to Warren for Christmas as a symbol of their engagement. Warren soon noticed a small chip in the stone under the setting. She returned the ring to Monahan shortly after the Christmas holidays, and Monahan agreed to replace the stone with one of equal or greater value at no charge to Warren. After making this agreement, Warren took the ring to another jeweler to have it appraised. There she learned for the first time that the alleged diamond that Monahan sold to Andreson was in fact nothing more than cut glass or cubic zirconia.

Warren filed suit against Monahan on several counts, including breach of contract and violation of the Florida Deceptive and Unfair Trade Practices Act. The trial court dismissed her complaint and Warren appealed.

Booth, Judge. The law is that a person not party to a contract may sue for breach of contract where the parties' dealings clearly express the parties' intent to create a right primarily and directly benefiting a third party. In the present case, the precontract dealings between Andreson and Monahan, and the subsequent dealings between Warren and Monahan, clearly establish Warren as an intended third party beneficiary of the contract at issue. The complaint properly alleges that Monahan breached the contract when he failed to deliver a diamond ring to Andreson. The alleged breach of contract deprived Warren of the benefit of owning a diamond ring, which was the purpose of the sale. Warren has a valid cause of action for breach of contract as an intended third party beneficiary.

The trial court also erred in dismissing Warren's claim brought pursuant to [the Florida Deceptive and Unfair Trade Practices Act]. One of the purposes of Florida's Deceptive and Unfair Trade Practices Act is to protect consumers from suppliers who commit deceptive and unfair trade practices. Nothing in the statute or case law limits causes of action to the immediate purchaser. The issue of whether the intended beneficiary of a gift may be classified as a "consumer" appears to be an issue of first impression in this state. We hold that [the Act] applies and that Warren, as the beneficiary of the consumer transaction is a "consumer" in her own right and entitled to the remedies afforded.

Judgment reversed in favor of Warren and case remanded for further proceedings.

Creditor Beneficiaries If the promisor's performance is intended to *satisfy a legal duty* that the promisee owes to a third party, the third party is a *creditor benefi-* *ciary.* The creditor beneficiary has rights against *both* the promisee (because of the original obligation) and the promisor. For example, Smith buys a car on credit from

Jones Auto Sales. Smith later sells the car to Carmichael, who agrees to pay the balance due on the car to Jones Auto Sales. (Note that Smith is *delegating* his duty to pay to Carmichael, and Carmichael is *assuming* the personal obligation to do so). In this case, Jones Auto Sales is a creditor beneficiary of the contract between Smith and Carmichael. It has rights against both Carmichael and Smith if Carmichael does not perform. *Spiklevitz v. Markmil Corporation*, which follows, presents an example of a creditor beneficiary.

SPIKLEVITZ v. MARKMIL CORPORATION
357 N.W.2d 721 (Mich. Ct. App. 1984)

In 1974, Stuart Spiklevitz loaned money to Vincent and Geraldine Heron. The Herons signed a promissory note agreeing to repay the debt by January 15, 1975. On April 1, 1980, the Herons sold their business to Markmil Corp. At that time, $3,510 of their debt to Spiklevitz remained unpaid. Markmil executed an "Assumption of Obligation," which stated that as part of the purchase price of the Herons' business, Markmil agreed to pay the list of debts written on an attached sheet of paper labeled "Exhibit A." Spiklevitz was listed as a creditor in Exhibit A for the balance owed to him.

In June of 1981, Spiklevitz sued Markmil to recover the amount remaining due on the note. Markmil moved for judgment in its favor, claiming that Spiklevitz could no longer enforce Herons' debt because the statute of limitations had elapsed on the promissory note executed by the Herons back in 1974. Markmil further denied that Spiklevitz was a third party beneficiary of the "Assumption of Obligation" contract between Markmil and the Herons. The trial court held for Markmil, and Spiklevitz appealed.

Per Curiam. Where a person makes an agreement to pay off another's obligation, it creates a new and separate obligation; a right of action on this obligation accrues only from the date on which the new obligation becomes overdue. Markmil can prevail only if Spiklevitz was not an intended beneficiary of the contract embodied in the "Assumption of Obligation" entered into between it and the Herons.

Any person for whose benefit a promise is made by way of contract has the same right to enforce the promise that he would have had if the promise had been made directly to him as the promisee. A promise is construed to have been made for the benefit of a person whenever the promisor has undertaken to give or to do or refrain from doing something directly to or for said person.

Spiklevitz is not an atypical third party beneficiary. Instead, this is the normal creditor beneficiary type of case where the promise is to pay the promisee's own debt to his creditor, the beneficiary. Where one sells his business or other property and the buyer undertakes to pay the seller's debts, those to be paid are creditor beneficiaries and actions by them lie against the buyer on his promise. Under Michigan law, Spiklevitz was a third party beneficiary of the contract between Markmil and the Herons.

Judgment reversed in favor of Spiklevitz.

Defenses against Beneficiary

The promisor who breaches a contract that was intended to benefit a third party is subject to suit by both the promisee and the third party beneficiary. Since the rights of the third party beneficiary derive from the original contract between the promisor and the promisee, any circumstances that make that contract unenforceable or voidable can defeat the claim of the third party beneficiary. In a suit brought by the third party beneficiary against the promisor, the promisor can assert any defenses against the third party beneficiary that he could assert against the promisee (such as fraud and lack of consideration).

Vesting of Beneficiary's Rights

Another possible threat to the interests of the third party beneficiary is that the promisor and the promisee might modify or discharge their contract so as to extinguish or alter the beneficiary's rights. For example, Gates, who owes $500 to Sorenson, enters into a contract with Connor whereby Connor agrees to pay the $500 to Sorenson. What happens if, before Sorenson is paid, Connor pays the money to Gates and Gates accepts it or Connor and Gates otherwise modify the contract? Courts have held that there is a point at which the rights of the beneficiary *vest*, that is, the beneficiary's rights cannot be lost by modification or discharge. A modification or discharge that occurs after the beneficiary's rights have vested cannot be asserted as a defense to a suit brought by the beneficiary. The exact time at which the beneficiary's rights vest differs from jurisdiction to jurisdiction. Some courts have held that vesting occurs when the contract is formed, while others hold that vesting does not occur until the beneficiary learns of the contract and consents to it or does some act in reliance on the promise.

The contracting parties' ability to vary the rights of the third party beneficiary can also be affected by the terms of their agreement. A provision of the contract between the promisor and the promisee stating that the duty to the beneficiary cannot be modified would be effective to prevent modification. Likewise, a contract provision in which the parties specifically reserved the right to change beneficiaries or modify the duty to the beneficiary would be enforced. For example, provisions reserving the right to change beneficiaries are very common in insurance contracts.

ETHICAL AND PUBLIC POLICY CONCERNS

1. You learned that an assignor's rights are extinguished as soon as he assigns them. Should a delegator's duties be extinguished by his delegation of them?

2. Why does public policy favor allowing third parties to enforce contracts made for their benefit? Should incidental beneficiaries have a right to enforce contracts? Why or why not?

SUMMARY

There are two situations in which people who were not parties to a contract can claim rights under the contract. The first is where there has been an assignment of a contract right. An assignment occurs when a person (the assignor) who has a right to receive the performance of an obligor transfers that right to a third person (the assignee). An assignment extinguishes the rights of the assignor and gives the assignee the right to enforce the contract. Most contract rights can be assigned. There are, however, three limitations on assignability. First, an assignment that would materially change the obligor's duty or increase the risk or burden on the obligor will be held ineffective. Second, an assignment that would violate public policy will be held ineffective. Third, an agreement between the assignor and the obligor specifically prohibiting assignment of rights will prevent effective assignment if the agreement is held to be enforceable. Courts tend to interpret such agreements narrowly, however.

The assignee is subject to any claims or defenses arising from the assigned contract that the obligor could have asserted against the assignor. The obligor should be notified of the assignment promptly, or his rendering of performance to the assignor will be a discharge of the claim. Once the obligor has received notice of the assignment, however, the assignee's rights will not be defeated by the obligor's performance to the assignor. The assignee's rights are also subject to any claims against the assignor that arose independent of the assigned contract and that have accrued before the time of notification. This is called *set off.*

In making an assignment, the assignor impliedly warrants that he has title to the claim, that any writings on which the claim is based are genuine, that the claim is valid, and that he will not do anything to defeat or impair the value of the claim. Thus, the assignee will be able to recover damages from the assignor if the assignee's rights are defeated by a defense asserted by the obligor. The assignor is also subject to liability to the assignee if he collects the assigned claim or if he causes the assignee to lose his right to the performance by making successive assignments of the same claim. The assignor does not, however, impliedly warrant the obligor's solvency.

The appointment of another person (the delegatee) to perform the duties of the obligor (the delegator) under a contract is called a *delegation*. Duties are delegable unless the obligee has a substantial interest in having the delegator perform or supervise the performance of the contract (as where performance depends on the personal skill, discretion, or character of the delegator), or public policy would be violated by a delegation, or the parties have agreed in their contract that delegation will not be permitted. Unless the language of the contract or the surrounding circumstances indicate to the contrary, general language of assignment is held to constitute a delegation of duties as well as an assignment of rights. An effective delegation only means that performance by the delegatee will discharge the duty. It does *not* release the delegator from his duty to the obligee.

The delegatee is not under a legal duty to perform unless he has expressly or impliedly *assumed* the duty of performance. The UCC and the *Restatement* presume that a delegatee's acceptance of an assignment is to be construed as a promise by him to carry out the duties owed under the contract. If a delegatee assumes a duty, he undertakes a legal duty to both the delegator and the obligee. Assumption does not discharge the delegator. When assumption occurs, both the delegator and the delegatee are under a duty to the obligee. The delegator remains liable for the performance of the duty unless the obligee has released him by novation. A novation occurs when the obligee agrees to release the delegator in return for the delegatee's promise to perform. The obligee's mere acceptance of performance from the delegatee— even when there has been an assumption—is not sufficient to constitute a novation. Some further evidence of the obligee's intent to substitute the delegatee's duty to perform for that of the delegator is necessary for a novation.

A second situation in which a third party can claim rights under a contract occurs when the contracting parties made the contract with the intent to benefit a third person. Such third persons are called third party benefi-

ciaries. In order to claim rights as a third party beneficiary, the third party must prove that she was an *intended beneficiary*. This means that she must prove that the promisee intended to benefit her. Intended beneficiaries are generally classified as either *donee beneficiaries* or *creditor beneficiaries*. When the promisee intended to bestow the promised performance as a gift, the beneficiary is called a *donee beneficiary*. When the promisee intended the performance to satisfy a legal duty to the third party, the beneficiary is called a *creditor beneficiary*. If a person can prove that she was an intended beneficiary, either donee or creditor, she can bring suit to enforce the contract. The creditor beneficiary will also have rights against the *promisee* under the original obligation. When the benefit to a third person is merely incidental and the contracting parties formed the contract primarily for their own benefit, the third person is classified as an *incidental beneficiary*. An incidental beneficiary has no rights under a contract, and cannot sue for its nonperformance.

Although intended beneficiaries can sue to enforce a contract, they are subject to any defenses that the promisor could assert against the *promisee*. Unless the contracting parties have agreed not to modify the rights of the third party beneficiary, those rights are subject to modification or discharge by the original contracting parties if the modification or discharge occurs before the rights of the third party beneficiary have *vested*. There are several views about the time at which the rights of a third party beneficiary vest (become invulnerable to modification or discharge). The variation of the rights of a third party beneficiary can be affected by an agreement between the contracting parties forbidding modification or reserving the right to modify.

PROBLEM CASES

1. In 1976, C. W. and C. T. White executed a lease with Lewis Grocery Co. whereby the Whites agreed to build a convenience food store and parking lot and lease it to Lewis for 10 years with an option to renew. One of provisions of the lease stated that if the leased property were to be destroyed by fire, the elements, or other casualty, the Whites would repair the damages or rebuild within a reasonable time after such an occurrence. The lease was later assigned to John Ford. Only three days after the assignment to Ford, a series of tornadoes struck the area, and the building was destroyed. Ford called the Whites requesting that they fulfill their contractual duty to rebuild, but they did not act upon these calls. Ford brought suit against the Whites because of their refusal to reconstruct the store and parking lot, and the Whites filed a motion to dismiss Ford's complaint on the ground that no contractual relationship existed between the Whites and Ford. Should the court dismiss Ford's complaint?

2. Peterson was employed by Post–Newsweek as a newscaster-anchorman on station WTOP–TV (Channel 9) under a three-year employment contract that was to end June 30, 1980, and could be extended for two additional one-year terms at the option of Post–Newsweek. In June 1978, Post–Newsweek sold its operating license to the Evening News Association (Evening News), and Channel 9 was then designated as WDVM-TV. The contract of sale between Post–Newsweek and Evening News provided for the assignment of all contracts, including Peterson's employment contract. Peterson continued working for the station for more than a year after the change of ownership and received all of the compensation and benefits provided by his contract with Post–Newsweek. In early August 1979, he negotiated a new contract with a competing television station and tendered his resignation to Evening News. Evening News sued Peterson. Peterson defended on the ground that his employment contract was not assignable. Is he correct?

3. Milford sold a registered quarter horse, Hired Chico, to Stewart. The parties signed a written contract in which Milford reserved the right to two breedings each year on Hired Chico, "regardless to whom the horse may be sold to." Stewart later sold the horse to McKinnie, who knew of and had read the contract between Milford and Stewart. After McKinnie purchased the horse, he refused to permit Milford any of the breedings provided for in the original agreement. Was McKinnie obligated by the terms of the contract?

4. On April 20, Chapman-Harkey Company ordered a quantity of toys known as "hang-ups" from A. G. Bond Company, at a total cost of $13,378.56. Under the agreement between Chapman-Harkey and A. G. Bond, the hang-ups were sold on a "guaranteed-sale" basis; that is, Chapman-Harkey could return to A. G. Bond any hang-ups that it could not sell and receive a credit. On May 17, Chapman-Harkey received notice that A. G. Bond had assigned the account for this sale to Equitable Factors. In a letter dated May 19, Chapman-Harkey received written confirmation from

A. G. Bond's agent that the goods were being sold on a guaranteed-sale basis. Chapman-Harkey failed to pay for the hang-ups, and Equitable Factors brought suit against it to recover the purchase price of the goods sold. At this point, Chapman-Harkey still had in its possession $5,753.78 worth of hang-ups, which it had been unable to sell. Can the guaranteed-sale term be raised as a defense against Equitable Factors, even though the defense did not become available until after notification of the assignment?

5. Jones paid Sullivan, the chief of the Addison Police Department, $6,400 in exchange for Sullivan's cooperation in allowing Jones and others to bring marijuana by airplane into the Addison airport without police intervention. Instead of performing the requested service, Sullivan arrested Jones. The $6,400 was turned over to the district attorney's office and was introduced into evidence in the subsequent trial in which Jones was tried for and convicted of bribery. After his conviction, Jones assigned his alleged claim to the $6,400 to Melvyn Bruder. Based on the assignment, Bruder brought suit against the state of Texas to obtain possession of the money. Will he be successful?

6. Friendly Mobile Manor, Inc. owned and operated a mobile home park, in which it sold mobile homes and rented mobile home sites. Friendly also had agreed to be legally responsible for indebtedness to certain banks that had financed the original purchase of several of the mobile homes on its property. In 1986, Friendly sold its real property and 30 mobile homes situated on the property to Homa. Homa assumed the debt on those homes. Later in 1986, Homa assigned all of his rights and interests in the sales contract with Friendly to P/T Ltd. During the negotiations leading up to that assignment, P/T made it perfectly clear to Homa that under no circumstances would P/T assume any liability for the debts on the mobile homes. P/T refused to sign a first draft of a contract that contained language providing that P/T would assume the mobile home debt. Finally, Homa and P/T reached and signed an agreement that did not contain any assumption language. P/T did agree to forward monthly installment checks to the banks that had financed these mobile homes from rents that came in from the tenants of those homes. In early 1987, some of the tenants who were occupying some of the financed mobile homes were evicted for nonpayment of rent. Since no rent money was coming in, P/T did not forward installment payments to the banks involved. The banks foreclosed on the mobile homes and sought payment of the remaining debt from P/T. Is P/T legally responsible for the debts?

7. Jay Beard Trucks entered into a franchise Dealer Sales and Service Agreement with General Motors (GMC). The agreement contained a provision limiting the possible future transfer of ownership of the dealership. These provisions required Beard to give notice to GMC of any proposed sale of the dealership and gave GMC the right to select each successor and replacement dealer. The contract also provided that GMC "shall not arbitrarily refuse to agree to such proposed change or sale" and that, in determining whether the proposal is acceptable to it, "GMC will take into account the qualifications, personal and business reputation, and financial standing of the proposed dealer operator and owners." Noller, the owner-operator of a Ford dealership and a Toyota dealership and one of the top 100 Ford dealers in the country, entered into negotiations to purchase Beard's dealership. The parties worked out a proposed buy-sell agreement and submitted it to GMC. GMC never contacted Noller, sent dealership transfer applications to him, obtained any documentation or additional information from him, nor made inquiries to Beard about Noller's qualifications. Without doing an investigation about these matters, GMC refused to grant the franchise to Noller, apparently because he was also a Ford dealer. As a result, the contract between Noller and Beard fell through and Beard sold the dealership to a third party. Noller brought suit against GMC, asserting that he was an intended beneficiary of the Dealer Sales and Service Agreement between GMC and Beard, wherein GMC had agreed to specifically consider the proposed dealer's qualifications, personal and business reputation, and financial standing. Was he an intended beneficiary?

8. Spartan, a general contractor, hired Sunbelt to perform the electrical work on a project known as the "Logo Shops" for the 1984 World's Fair. The World's Fair filed for bankruptcy without having fully paid its general contractors, and Spartan did not pay Sunbelt. On October 22, Sunbelt assigned its right to payment to Powerhouse. Powerhouse gave notification of the assignment on October 24. Powerhouse eventually sued Spartan to collect the debt. Spartan asserted that it was entitled to set off the damages that Sunbelt had caused Spartan by abandoning an unrelated project involving the electrical work that Sunbelt had been obligated to perform on the Sea King Restaurant. These damages were caused when Spartan had had to pay another electrical subcontractor to complete the job that Sunbelt had abandoned. The first of these payments was made on October 8, the second on October 23, and the third on October 31. Can Spartan set these payments off against the amount it owes Powerhouse?

9. Mercantile-Safe Deposit & Trust Company frequently advised its long-time customer, Chaplin, about the planning of her estate. Merrick, Chaplin's former son-in-law, maintained a close relationship with Chaplin, and this relationship was reflected in the wills that Chaplin executed. At Chaplin's request, one of Mercantile's trust officers visited her at her home to discuss making certain changes in her will. Without first consulting with Mercantile's attorneys or other estate planning personnel about the appropriateness of these changes, the trust officer instructed Chaplin's attorney to draft a new will reflecting the changes that Chaplin requested. Merrick would have benefited under this will. The will was executed and Chaplin died in 1981. Because of a technical problem overlooked by Mercantile's trust officer, the will provision benefiting Merrick and his children was held to be ineffective and Merrick lost the bequest that he would have had otherwise. Merrick brought suit against Mercantile because of its failure to advise Chaplin properly. Does Merrick have any rights under the contract between Chaplin and Mercantile?

10. In June of 1979, Ruwet-Sibley Equipment Corporation leased a 1979 International Harvester truck to Stebbins, a proprietor of a refuse collection business. The lease was for 60 months and required Stebbins to pay $1,186.87 per month. In August of 1981, Stebbins and Greenbaum, the proprietor of another refuse collection business, met in Ruwet-Sibley's office and signed an agreement whereby Stebbins agreed to turn over the truck to Greenbaum and Greenbaum would thereafter make the payments due under the lease. Shortly after this agreement was made, however, Greenbaum defaulted and made no further payments under the lease. Greenbaum later filed for bankruptcy. In June of 1983, the truck was returned to Ruwet-Sibley in inoperable condition. Ruwet-Sibley sued Stebbins to collect the outstanding lease payments plus the cost of repairs. Stebbins asserted that his contract with Greenbaum excused him from all liability under the lease and established Greenbaum as the sole debtor. Is he correct?

CHAPTER 19

PERFORMANCE AND REMEDIES

INTRODUCTION

Contracts generally are formed before either of the parties renders any actual performance to the other. A person may be content to bargain for and receive the other person's promise at the formation stage of a contract because this permits him to plan for the future. Ultimately, however, all parties bargain for the *performance* of the promises that have been made to them.

In most contracts, each party carries out his promise and is **discharged** (released from all of his obligations under the contract) when his performance is complete. Sometimes, however, a party fails to perform or performs in an unsatisfactory manner. In such cases, courts are often called upon to determine the respective rights and duties of the parties. This frequently involves deciding such questions as whether performance was due, whether the contract was breached, to what extent it was breached, and whether performance was excused. This task is made more difficult by the fact that contracts often fail to specify the consequences of nonperformance or defective performance. In deciding questions involving the performance of contracts and remedies for breach of contract, courts draw upon a variety of legal principles that attempt to do justice, prevent forfeiture and unjust enrichment, and effectuate the parties' presumed intent.

This chapter presents an overview of the legal concepts that are used to resolve disputes arising in the performance stage of contracting. It describes how courts determine whether performance is due and what kind of performance is due, the consequences of contract breach, and the excuses for a party's failure to perform. It also includes a discussion of the remedies that are used when a court determines that a contract has been breached.

CONDITIONS

Nature of Conditions

One issue that frequently arises in the performance stage of a contract is whether a party has the duty to perform. Some duties are *unconditional* or *absolute*—that is, the duty to perform does not depend on the occurrence of any further event other than the passage of time. For example, if Root promises to pay Downing $100, Root's duty is unconditional. When a party's duty is unconditional, he has the duty to perform unless his performance is *excused*. (The various excuses for nonperformance will be discussed later in this chapter.) When a duty is unconditional, the promisor's failure to perform constitutes a *breach of contract*.

405

In many situations, however, a promisor's duty to perform depends on the occurrence of some event that is called a **condition.** A condition is an uncertain, future event that affects a party's duty to perform. For example, if Melman contracts to buy Lance's house on condition that First Bank approve Melman's application for a mortgage loan by January 10, Melman's duty to buy Lance's house is *conditioned* on the bank's approving his loan application by January 10. When a promisor's duty is conditional, his duty to perform is affected by the occurrence of the condition. In this case, if the condition does not occur, Melman has no duty to buy the house.

His failure to buy it because of the nonoccurrence of the condition will *not* constitute a breach of contract. Rather, he is discharged from further obligation under the contract. The case of *Gildea v. Kapenis* provides an example of the effect of nonoccurrence of a condition.

Almost any event can be a condition. Some conditions are beyond the control of either party, such as when Morehead promises to buy Pratt's business if the prime rate drops by a specified amount. Others are within the control of a party, such as when one party's performance of a duty under the contract is a condition of the other party's duty to perform.

GILDEA v. KAPENIS

402 N.W.2d 457 (Iowa Ct. App. 1987)

In October of 1984, David and Penny Gildea put their house on the market and held an open house to attract potential buyers. James Kapenis went to the open house. That evening, Kapenis met with the Gildeas' realtor, Susan Murphy, to talk about making a bid on the Gildea home. Murphy told Kapenis that First Federal Savings & Loan offered a 25-year adjustable rate mortgage with monthly payments of $343 and that the interest rate under this type of mortgage could be adjusted only once a year. Murphy prepared several purchase offers and, after some negotiation, both Kapenis and the Gildeas agreed to a contract that contained a clause stating that the contract was "subject to buyer obtaining suitable financing interest rate no greater than $12\frac{3}{4}\%$." Kapenis and Murphy then began a search for financing.

When Kapenis talked with an officer of First Federal Savings & Loan, he learned that under this mortgage his interest rate could be adjusted *twice* a year and that 2 percentage points could be added to the adjusted rate after the two-year fixed period. He was dissatisfied with this and asked that Murphy find additional forms of financing. Murphy continued to inform Kapenis about various loan programs, but Kapenis rejected them because the monthly payments were too high. Another broker located a loan program of a 15-year term at $12\frac{1}{2}\%$ interest with monthly payments of $419, but Kapenis stated that the monthly payments would be too high and not assumable and that these terms were unsatisfactory. Kapenis then informed the Gildeas that he could not find suitable financing and that he was withdrawing his offer. The Gildeas then filed a lawsuit against Kapenis. The trial court found in favor of the Gildeas, and Kapenis appealed.

Donielson, Presiding Judge. The "subject to financing" clause, such as the one which is the subject of this appeal, has been held to constitute a condition precedent. Conditions precedent are those facts and events occurring subsequently to the making of a valid contract that must occur before there is a right to immediate performance, before there is a breach of contract duty, before the usual judicial remedies are available. A determination that a condition precedent exists does not, however, depend on the particular form of the words used, but rather depends upon the intention of the parties gathered from the language of the entire instrument. The document must be read in light of the surrounding circumstances and will be given such a practical meaning as the parties themselves have placed upon it. Doubtful language will be construed against the party which selected it.

We believe that the term "suitable financing" as used by the parties in the present case means suitable according to the ability of Kapenis to repay. The financing clause contains only a general provision that the interest rate be no greater than $12\frac{3}{4}\%$ and is silent as to the amount, the term of the note, and points. We recognize that in today's financial lending market, there are a wide variety of financial packages available. The length of the mortgage, the monthly repayments, discount points, and amortization provisions contained in a mortgage are all important factors to be considered by a buyer when applying for financing. A mortgage taken on an interest rate of 12% may not be as favorable in its terms as a mortgage taken on $12\frac{3}{4}\%$ interest. All the above noted factors are interdependent, and a provision for a ceiling cap of $12\frac{3}{4}\%$ does little to aid in a determination as to what constitutes suitable financing.

The actions of the parties and the circumstances surrounding the present agreement indicate that the sale of the Gildea property was conditioned upon Kapenis obtaining financing terms compatible with his ability to repay. At the time Kapenis made his purchase offer, he did not consider what interest rate to specify, nor was he familiar with what financing was available. Murphy, the Gildeas' realtor, suggested that he put in an interest rate in the financing clause and also suggested that the term "suitable financing" be included in the clause. At trial, Murphy testified that she had included the term "suitable financing" to enable Kapenis the opportunity to determine what he could afford. Mr. Gildea additionally admitted that the term "suitable financing" meant financing that would be acceptable to the buyer.

We therefore conclude, based upon the circumstances and events surrounding the contract between the parties, that the term "suitable financing" meant financing terms that were acceptable to Kapenis. Kapenis entered the offer to purchase with the expectation that he would be able to obtain favorable financing. It is apparent from the conduct of the parties that the condition precedent, stating that the purchase was contingent upon Kapenis's obtaining financing at an interest rate of no greater than $12\frac{3}{4}\%$, was intended to benefit Kapenis. When Kapenis was unable to obtain favorable financing, the condition precedent did not occur, and the contract therefore was no longer valid.

Reversed in favor of Kapenis.

Types of Conditions

There are two ways of classifying conditions. One way of classifying conditions focuses on the effect of the condition on the duty to perform. The other way focuses on the way in which the condition is created.

Classifications of Conditions Based on Their Effect on the Duty to Perform   As Figure 1 illustrates, conditions vary in their effects on the duty to perform.

1. *Condition precedent.* A **condition precedent** is a future, uncertain event that *creates* the duty to perform. If the condition does not occur, performance becomes due. If the condition does occur, the duty to perform

arises. In *Gildea v. Kapenis*, Kapenis's duty to purchase the house was subject to a condition precedent.

2. *Concurrent condition.* When the contract calls for the parties to perform at the same time, each person's performance is conditioned on the performance or **tender** of performance (offer of performance) by the other. Such conditions are called **concurrent conditions.** For example, if Martin promises to buy Johnson's car for $5,000, the parties' respective duties to perform are subject to a concurrent condition. Martin does not have the duty to perform unless Johnson tenders his performance, and vice versa.

3. *Condition subsequent.* A **condition subsequent** is a future, uncertain event that *discharges* the duty to

– AFTER has become Absolute

FIGURE 1   Effect of Conditions

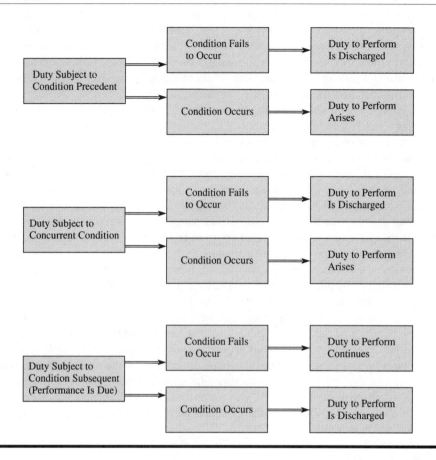

perform. When a duty is subject to a condition subsequent, the duty to perform arises, but is discharged if the future, uncertain event occurs. For example, Wilkinson and Jones agree that Wilkinson will begin paying Jones $2,000 per month but that, if XYZ Corporation dissolves, Wilkinson's obligation to pay will cease. In this case, Wilkinson's duty to pay is subject to being discharged by a condition subsequent. The major significance of the distinction between conditions precedent and conditions subsequent is that the plaintiff bears the burden of proving the occurrence of a condition precedent, while the defendant bears the burden of proving the occurrence of a condition subsequent.

Classifications of Conditions Based on the Way in which They Were Created   Another way of classifying conditions is to focus on the means by which the condition was created.

1. *Express condition.* An **express condition** is a condition that is specified in the language of the parties' contract. For example, if Grant promises to sell his regular season football tickets to Carson *on condition that* Indiana University wins the Rose Bowl, Indiana's winning the Rose Bowl is an express condition of Grant's duty to sell the tickets. The "subject to suitable financing" condition in *Gildea v. Kapenis* is another example of an express condition.

When the contract expressly provides that a party's duty is subject to a condition, courts take it very seriously. When a duty is subject to an express condition, that condition must be strictly complied with in order to give rise to the duty to perform.

2. *Implied-in-fact condition.* An **implied-in-fact condition** is one that is not specifically stated by the parties but is *implied* by the nature of the parties' promises. For example, if Summers promises to unload cargo

Implied in Law.

from Knight's ship, the ship's arrival in port would be an implied-in-fact condition of Summer's duty to unload the cargo.

3. *Constructive condition.* **Constructive conditions** (also known as *implied-in-law conditions*) are conditions that are imposed by law rather than by the agreement of the parties. The law imposes constructive conditions to do justice between the parties. In contracts in which one of the parties is expected to perform before the other, the law normally infers that that performance is a constructive condition of the other party's duty to perform. For example, if Thomas promises to build a house for King, and the parties' understanding is that King will pay Thomas an agreed-upon price when the house is built, King's duty to pay is subject to the constructive condition that Thomas complete the house. Without such a constructive condition, a person who did not receive the performance promised him would still have to render his own performance.

Creation of Express Conditions

Although no particular language is required to create an express condition, the conditional nature of promises is usually indicated by such words as *provided that, subject to, on condition that, if, when, while, after*, and *as soon as*. The process of determining the meaning of conditions is not a mechanical one. Courts look at the parties' overall intent as indicated in language of the entire contract.

The following discussion explores two common types of express conditions.

Example of Express Condition: Satisfaction of Third Parties   It is common for building and construction contracts to provide that the property owner's duty to pay is conditioned on the builder's production of certificates to be issued by a specific architect or engineer. These certificates indicate the satisfaction of the architect or engineer with the builder's work. They often are issued at each stage of completion, after the architect or engineer has inspected the work done.

The standard usually used to determine whether the condition has occurred is a *good faith* standard. As a general rule, if the architect or engineer is acting honestly and has some good-faith reason for withholding a certificate, the builder cannot recover payments due. In legal terms, the condition that will create the owner's duty to pay has not occurred. The rationale for this is

that the court will not substitute its judgment for that of the architect or engineer for whose expert judgment the parties freely contracted.

If the builder can prove that the withholding of the certificate was fraudulent or done in bad faith (as a result of collusion with the owner, for example), the court may order that payment be made despite the absence of the certificate. In addition, production of the certificate may be excused by the death, insanity, or incapacitating illness of the named architect or engineer.

Example of Express Condition: Personal Satisfaction   Contracts sometimes provide that a promisee's duty to perform is conditioned on his *personal satisfaction* with the promisee's performance. For example, Moore commissions Allen to paint a portrait of Moore's wife, but the contract provides that Moore's duty to pay is conditioned on his personal satisfaction with the portrait. How will a court determine whether the condition of personal satisfaction has occurred? If the court applies a standard of actual, subjective satisfaction and Moore asserts that he is not satisfied, it would be very difficult for Allen to prove that the condition has occurred. If, on the other hand, the court applies an objective, "reasonable man" standard of satisfaction Allen stands a better chance of proving that the condition has occurred.

In determining which standard of satisfaction to apply, courts distinguish between cases in which the performance bargained for involves personal taste and comfort and cases that involve mechanical fitness or suitability for a particular purpose. If personal taste and comfort are involved, as they would be in the hypothetical case described above, a promisor who is honestly dissatisfied with the promisee's performance has the right to reject the performance without being liable to the promisee. If, however, the performance involves mechanical fitness or suitability, the court will apply a reasonable man test. If the court finds that a reasonable man would be satisfied with the performance, the condition of personal satisfaction has been met and the promisor must accept the performance and pay the contract price. For example, Kitt Manufacturing Company hires Pace to design a conveyor belt system for use in its factory, conditioning its duty to pay on its personal satisfaction with the system. A court would be likely to find that this is a contract involving mechanical fitness and suitability for which an objective test of satisfaction could be used. These standards are illustrated in Figure 2. Because the "honest satisfaction" standard involves a danger of

FIGURE 2 Duty to Perform Conditioned on "Personal Satisfaction" (A Form of Express Condition Precedent)

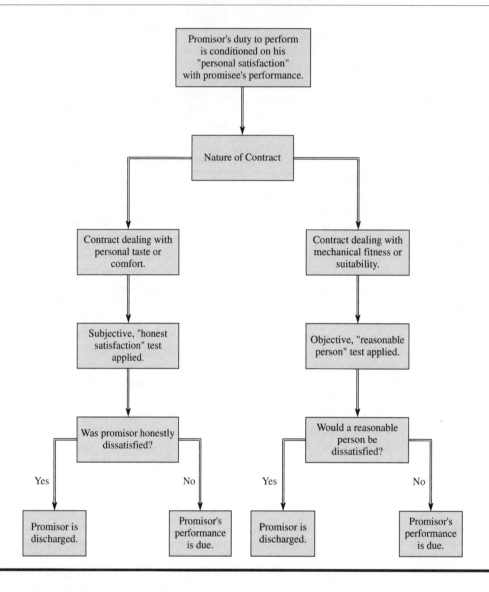

forfeiture by the performing party, courts prefer the objective test of satisfaction when objective evaluation is feasible.

Excuse of Conditions

In most situations involving conditional duties, the promisor does not have the duty to perform unless and until the condition occurs. There are, however, a variety of situations in which the occurrence of a condition will be *excused*. In such a case, the person whose duty is conditional will have to perform even though the condition has not occurred.

One ground for excusing a condition is that the occurrence of the condition has been *prevented* or *hindered* by the party who is benefited by the condition. For example, Connor hires Ingle to construct a garage on Connor's land, but when Ingle attempts to begin construction, Connor refuses to allow Ingle access to the land. In this case, Connor's duty to pay would normally be subject to a constructive condition that Ingle build the garage. However, since Connor prevented the occurence of the condition, the condition will be excused, and Ingle can sue Connor for damages for breach of contract even though the condition has not occurred.

Other grounds for excuse of a condition include **waiver** and **estoppel.** When a person whose duty is conditional voluntarily gives up his right to the occurrence of the condition (waiver), the condition will be excused. Suppose that Buchman contracts to sell his car to Fox on condition that Fox pay him $2,000 by June 14. Fox fails to pay on June 14, but, when he tenders payment on June 20, Buchman accepts and cashes the check without reservation. Buchman has thereby *waived* the condition of payment by June 14.

When a person whose duty is conditional leads the other party to rely on his noninsistence on the condition, the condition will be excused because of estoppel. For example, McDonald agrees to sell his business to Brown on condition that Brown provide a credit report and personal financial statement by July 17. On July 5, McDonald tells Brown that he can have until the end of the month to provide the necessary documents. Relying on McDonald's assurances, Brown does not provide the credit report and financial statement until July 29. In this case, McDonald would be *estopped* (precluded) from claiming that the condition did not occur.

A condition may also be excused when performance of the act that constitutes the condition becomes *impossible*. For example, if a building contract provides that the owner's duty to pay is conditioned on the production of a certificate from a named architect, the condition would be excused if the named architect died or became incapacitated before issuing the certificate.

In all of these situations, the significance of excuse of a condition is that the person whose duty otherwise would not arise until the occurrence of the condition will have the duty to perform even though the condition has not occurred.

PERFORMANCE OF CONTRACTS

When a promisor has performed his duties under a contract, he is discharged. Because his performance constitutes the occurrence of a constructive condition, the other party's duty to perform is also triggered, and the person who has performed has the right to receive the other party's performance. In determining whether a promisor is discharged by performance and whether the constructive condition of his performance has been fulfilled, courts must consider the standard of performance expected of him.

Level of Performance Expected of the Promisor

In some situations, no deviation from the promisor's promised performance is tolerated; in others, less-than-perfect performance will be sufficient to discharge the promisor and give him the right to recover under the contract.

1. *Strict performance.* A **strict performance** standard is a standard of performance that requires virtually perfect compliance with the contract terms. Remember that, when a party's duty is subject to an express condition, that condition must be strictly and completely complied with in order to give rise to a duty of performance. Thus, when a promisor's performance is an express condition of the promisee's duty to perform, that performance must *strictly* and *completely* comply with the contract in order to give rise to the other promisee's duty to perform. For example, if McMillan agrees to pay Jester $500 for painting his house "on condition that" Jester finish the job no later than June 1, 1992, a standard of strict or complete performance would be applied to Jester's performance. If Jester does not finish the job by June 1, his breach will have several consequences. First, since the condition precedent to McMillan's duty to pay has not occurred, McMillan does not have a duty to pay the contract price. Second, since it is now too late for the condition to occur, McMillan is discharged. Third, McMillan can sue Jester for breach of contract. The law's commitment to freedom of contract justifies such results in cases in which the parties have expressly bargained for strict compliance with the terms of the contract.

The strict performance standard is also applied to contractual obligations that can be performed either exactly or to a high degree of perfection. Examples of this type of obligation include promises to pay money, deliver deeds, and, generally, promises to deliver goods. A promisor who performs such promises completely and in strict compliance with the contract is entitled to receive the entire contract price. The promisor whose performance deviates from perfection is not entitled to receive the other party's performance if he does not render perfect performance within an appropriate time. He may, however, be able to recover the value of any benefits that he has conferred on the other party under a theory of quasi-contract.

2. *Substantial performance.* A **substantial performance** standard is a somewhat lower standard of performance that is applied to duties that are difficult to perform without some deviation from perfection *if* performance of those duties is *not* an express condition.

A common example of this type of obligation is a promise to erect a building. Other examples include promises to construct roads, to cultivate crops, and to render some types of personal or professional services. Substantial performance is performance that falls short of complete performance in minor respects. As you will see in *Reale v. Linder*, it does not apply when a contracting party has been deprived of a material part of the consideration he bargained for. When a substantial performance standard is applied, the promisor who has substantially performed is discharged. His substantial performance triggers the other party's duty to pay the contract price less any damages resulting from the defects in his performance. The obvious purpose behind the doctrine of substantial performance is to prevent forfeiture by a promisor who has given the injured party most of what he bargained for. Substantial performance is generally held to be inapplicable to a situation in which the breach of contract has been *willful*, however.

REALE v. LINDER

514 N.Y.S.2d 1004 (N.Y. Dist. Ct. 1987)

Thomas Linder hired Orlando Reale to build a 12 foot by 12 foot extension on his house with a raised wooden deck, sliding glass doors, and a gas-fired barbeque. Their written contract made no provision regarding obtaining a building permit or compliance with building codes, although it did contain a notation stating "plairs (sic) and permit $500 Dep." The agreed price for these improvements was $22,560.

It became evident that several features of the finished addition deviated from the state building code and the building plans that had been approved by the town. Reale had built the crawl space beneath the addition some 4 to 7 inches less than the 18 inches mandated by the state building code, which prevented inspection underneath the addition for structural defects. In addition, Reale sealed the framing of the addition, where substantial problems existed, without a prior inspection by the city building department or his own architect. Serious defects existed in the roof, and the plumbing work was not done by a licensed plumber, although it was later corrected. Improper or incomplete materials were used for the gas line for the barbeque, which caused a gas leak that had to be corrected. The steps leading down from the main dwelling to the addition are each 4 inches high rather than the 6 and 8 inches each that appear in the plan. In addition, Reale did no grade survey of the property before building, although expert witnesses testified that a grade survey was necessary to build the addition properly. The city building department initially denied a certificate of occupancy because the construction had been "closed up" and could not be inspected. It was issued only after Reale procured an architect's affadavit stating that he had inspected the location and that the work had been done in conformity with the approved plans and the state fire and building code, but this was apparently based on false information that Reale gave to the architect.

Linder made partial payment under the contract but withheld $5,855. Reale sued Linder to collect the unpaid balance. A trial was held before a judge and this is the trial court's opinion.

Mogil, Judge. The crux of Reale's argument in support of his complaint is that he substantially performed the contract. In order for a building contractor to be able to take advantage of the doctrine of substantial performance, he must not be guilty of a willful or intentional departure from the terms of his contract. This doctrine, however, permits compensation for all defects caused by the contractor's performance. Under this rule the party sued is protected as to any damages he may suffer due to the contractor's failure to strictly perform. The contractor must prove that the defects or omissions were insubstantial. This he has not done.

Although the written agreement does not expressly provide that the contract be performed in conformance with state and local fire prevention and building code regulations, it must be presumed that the parties intended that the contract be performed in accordance with state and local laws. In every home improvement contract, the contractor has an implied duty to perform the contract in accordance with fire prevention and building code requirements. The consumer homeowner relies upon the contractor's skill and expertise to perform the improvements. Reale's failure to construct the extension to code requirements renders the alterations illegal and frustrates the purpose of the contract.

The doctrine of substantial performance is an equitable one intended to prevent injustice where a contractor inadvertently caused trivial, minor, non-essential deficiencies which may be easily and inexpensively remedied. Where the defect cannot be corrected without partially reconstructing the building, the doctrine of substantial performance does not apply. It has been shown that any request for a new or currently revised certificate of occupancy will be denied unless the defect of an improper crawl space is corrected. To correct the defect, the floor of the extension must be removed, the walls braced, excavations undertaken to remove additional earth, and the concrete and floor rebuilt. These corrections are tantamount to reconstructing the addition. Reale has not therefore shown either complete or substantial performance.

Judgment entered in favor of Linder.

CONCEPT REVIEW

SUBSTANTIAL PERFORMANCE

Definition	Application	Effects	Limitation
Performance that falls short of complete performance in some minor respect, but which does not deprive the other party of a material part of the consideration for which he bargained	Applies to performance that (1) is *not* an express condition of the other party's duty to perform and (2) is difficult to do perfectly	Triggers other party's duty to perform. Requires other party to pay the contract price minus any damages caused by defects in performance	Breach cannot have been willful

Good Faith Performance

One of the most significant trends in modern contract law is that courts and legislatures have created a duty to perform in good faith in an expanding range of contracts.[1] The Uniform Commercial Code specifically imposes a duty of good faith in every contract within the scope of any of the articles of the Code [1–203]. A growing number of courts have applied the duty to use good faith in transactions between lenders and their customers as well as insurance contracts, employment contracts, and contracts for the sale of real property.

This obligation to carry out a contract in good faith is usually called the **implied covenant of good faith and fair dealing.** It is a broad and flexible duty that is imposed by law rather than by the agreement of the parties. It is generally taken to mean that neither party to a contract will do anything to prevent the other from obtaining the benefits that he has the right to expect from the

[1] This trend is discussed in the Introduction to Contracts chapter.

parties' agreement or their contractual relationship. The law's purpose in imposing such a term in contracts is to prevent abuses of power and encourage ethical behavior.

Breach of the implied covenant of good faith gives rise to a contract remedy. In some states, it can also constitute a tort, depending on the severity of the breach. A tort action for breach of the implied covenant of good faith is more likely to be recognized in situations in which a contract involves a special relationship of dependency and trust between the parties or where the public interest is adversely affected by a contracting party's practices. Numerous cases exist, for example, in which insurance companies' bad faith refusal to settle claims or perform duties to their insured has led to large damage verdicts against the insurers. Likewise, in states in which the implied duty of good faith has been held applicable to contracts of employment, employers who discharge employees in bad faith have been held liable for damages.[2] In the emerging area of professional liability known as *lender liability*, lenders who have failed to exercise good faith in their dealings with customers have recently been subjected to tort liability for breach of the duty of good faith.

BREACH OF CONTRACT

When a person's performance is due, any failure to perform that is not excused is a breach of contract. Not all breaches of contract are of equal seriousness, however. Some are relatively minor deviations, whereas others are so extreme that they deprive the promisee of the essence of what he bargained for. The legal consequences of a given breach depend on the extent of the breach.

At a minimum, a party's breach of contract gives the nonbreaching party the right to sue and recover for any damages caused by that breach. When the breach is serious enough to be called a **material breach,** further legal consequences ensue.

Effect of Material Breach

A *material breach* occurs when the promisor's performance fails to reach the level of performance that the promisee is justified in expecting under the circumstances. In a situation in which the promisor's performance is judged by a *substantial performance* standard,

saying that he failed to give substantial performance is the same thing as saying that he materially breached the contract.

The party who is injured by a material breach has the right to withhold his own performance. He is discharged from further obligations under the contract and may cancel it. He also has the right to sue for damages for total breach of contract.

Effect of Nonmaterial Breach   By contrast, when the breach is *not* serious enough to be material, the nonbreaching party may sue for only those damages caused by the particular breach. In addition, he does not have the right to cancel the contract, although a nonmaterial breach can give him the right to suspend his performance until the breach is remedied. Once the breach is remedied, however, the nonbreaching party must go ahead and render his performance, minus any damages caused by the breach.

Determining the Materiality of the Breach   The standard for determining materiality is a flexible one that takes into account the facts of each individual case. The key question is whether the breach deprives the injured party of the benefits that he reasonably expected. For example, Norman, who is running for mayor, orders campaign literature from Prompt Press, to be delivered in September. Prompt Press's failure to deliver the literature until after the election in November deprives Norman of the essence of what he bargained for and would be considered a material breach.

In determining materiality, courts take into account the extent to which the breaching party will suffer forfeiture if the breach is held to be material. They also consider the magnitude (amount) of the breach and the willfulness or good faith exercised by the breaching party. The timing of the breach can also be important. A breach that occurs early on in the parties' relationship is more likely to be viewed as material than is one that occurs after an extended period of performance. Courts also consider the extent to which the injured party can be adequately compensated by the payment of damages.

Time for Performance   A party's failure to perform on time is a breach of contract that may be serious enough to constitute a material breach, or it may be relatively trivial under the circumstances.

At the outset, it is necessary to determine when performance is due. Some contracts specifically

---

[2] This is discussed in the Employment Law chapter.

state the time for performance, which makes it easy to determine the time for performance. In some contracts that do not specifically state the time for performance, such a time can be inferred from the circumstances surrounding the contract. In the Norman and Prompt Press hypothetical example, the circumstances surrounding the contract probably would have implied that the time for performance was some time before the election, even if the parties had not specified the time for performance. In still other contracts, no time for performance is either stated or implied. When no time for performance is stated or implied, performance must be completed within a "reasonable time," as judged by the circumstances of each case.

Consequences of Late Performance   After a court determines when performance was due, it must determine the *consequences* of late performance. In some contracts, the parties expressly state that "time is of the essence" or that timely performance is "vital." This means that each party's timely performance by a specific date is an *express condition* of the other party's duty to perform. Thus, in a contract that contains a time is of the essence provision, any delay by either party constitutes a *material* breach. You will see an example of this in *F. J. Miceli and Slonim Development Corporation v. Dierberg*, which follows. Sometimes, courts will imply such a term even when the language of the contract does not state that time is of the essence. A court would be likely to do this if late performance is of little or no value to the promisee. For example, Schrader contracts with the local newspaper to run an advertisement for Christmas trees from December 15, 1991, to December 24, 1991, but the newspaper does not run the ad until December 26, 1991. In this case, the time for performance is an essential part of the contract and the newspaper has committed a material breach.

When a contract does not contain language indicating that time is of the essence and a court determines that the time for performance is not a particularly important part of the contract, the promisee must accept late performance rendered within a reasonable time after performance was due. The promisee is then entitled to deduct or set off from the contract price any losses caused by the delay. Late performance is not a material breach in such cases unless it is *unreasonably* late.

F. J. MICELI AND SLONIM DEVELOPMENT CORPORATION v. DIERBERG

773 S.W.2d 154 (Mo. Ct. App. 1989)

Joanne and Louis Basso contracted with Mary Dierberg to purchase her property for $1,310,000. One term of the contract stated "The sale under this contract shall be closed . . . at the office of Community Title Company . . . on May 16, 1988 at 10:00 A.M. . . . . Time is of the essence of this contract." After forming this contract, the Bassos assigned their right to purchase Dierberg's property to F. J. Miceli and Slonim Development Corporation.

At 10:00 A.M. on May 16, 1988, Dierberg appeared at Community Title Company for closing. No representative of Miceli and Slonim was there, nor did anyone from Miceli and Slonim inform Dierberg that there would be any delay in the closing. At 10:20 A.M., Dierberg declared the contract null and void because the closing did not take place as agreed, and she left the title company office shortly thereafter. Dierberg had intended to use the purchase money to close another contract to purchase real estate later in the day. At about 10:30 A.M., a representantive of Miceli and Slonim appeared at Community Title Company to begin the closing procedures, but the representative did not have the funds for payment until 1:30 P.M. Dierberg refused to return to the title company to close, stating that Miceli and Slonim had breached the contract by failing to tender payment on time. She had already made alternative arrangements to finance her purchase of other real estate to meet her obligation under that contract.

Miceli and Slonim sued Dierberg for specific performance of the contract, claiming that the contract did not require closing exactly at 10:00 A.M., but rather sometime on the day of May 16. Dierberg filed a motion for summary judgment, and the trial court granted it. Miceli and Slonim appealed.

Karohl, Judge. Parties to a contract may provide that time is of the essence. A clause specifying time is of the essence ordinarily means a specific contractual provision fixing the time of performance is to be regarded as a vital element of the contract. If a contract specifies a certain time for performance, the contract must be performed at that time, even if time is specified by the hour. Custom will not alter express agreement of the parties.

Here, the contract clearly and precisely stated closing was to occur at 10:00 A.M. on May 16, 1988. Time and date were specifically referred to in three separate sections of the contract. It was agreed time was of the essence of the contract. This provision would relate to all three times and dates. Dierberg was obligated to close under another contract to purchase real estate later the same day. She relied on receiving the proceeds of her sale at 10:00 A.M. Because closing did not occur as agreed, Dierberg was required to make other arrangements to meet her obligation. These facts lend meaning to the judgment of the trial court that "10:00 A.M." was the agreement of Bassos and Dierberg, not a mere guideline.

When there is no ambiguity in a contract, it is the duty of the court to state its clear meaning. Here, the court found there was no ambiguity in the contract and that the contract required closing at or reasonably near 10:00 A.M. We find no error in the judgment. Miceli and Slonim's failure to tender payment until 1:30 P.M. combined with its failure to inform Dierberg of the delay in closing, was a breach of contract. On undisputed facts, summary judgment was proper.

Summary judgment for Dierberg affirmed.

CONCEPT REVIEW

TIME FOR PERFORMANCE

Contract Language	Time for Performance	Consequences of Late Performance
"Time is of the essence" or similar language	The time stated in the contract	Material breach
Specific time is stated in or implied by the contract and late performance would have little or no value	The time stated in or implied by the contract	Material breach
Specific time is stated in or implied by the contract, but the time for performance is a relatively unimportant part of the contract	The time stated in or implied by the contract	Not a material breach unless performance is unreasonably late
No time for performance is stated in or implied by the contract	Within a reasonable time	Not a material breach unless performance is unreasonably late

*10

CHAPTER 19 PERFORMANCE AND REMEDIES   **417**

Anticipatory Repudiation One type of breach of contract occurs when the promisor indicates *before the time for his performance* that he is unwilling or unable to carry out the contract. This is called **anticipatory repudiation** or **anticipatory breach.** Anticipatory breach generally constitutes a material breach of contract that discharges the promisee from all further obligation under the contract.

In determining what constitutes anticipatory repudiation, courts look for some unequivocal statement or voluntary act that clearly indicates that the promisor cannot or will not perform his duties under the contract. This may take the form of an express statement by the promisor. The promisor's intent not to perform could also be implied from actions of the promisor such as selling to a third party the property that the promisor was obligated to sell to the promisee. For example, if Ross, who is obligated to convey real estate to Davis, conveys the property to some third person instead, Ross has repudiated the contract.

When anticipatory repudiation occurs, the promisee is faced with several choices. For example, Marsh and Davis enter a contract in which Davis agrees to deliver a quantity of bricks to Marsh on September 1, 1992, and Marsh agrees to pay Davis a sum of money in two installments. The agreement specifies that Marsh will pay 50 percent of the purchase price on July 15, 1992, and 50 percent of the purchase price within 30 days after delivery. On July 1, 1992, Davis writes Marsh and unequivocally states that he will not deliver the bricks. Must Marsh go ahead and send the payment that is due on July 15? Must he wait until September 1 to bring suit for total breach of contract? The answer to both questions is no.

When anticipatory repudiation occurs, the nonbreaching party is justified in withholding his own performance and suing for damages right away, without waiting for the time for performance to arrive.[3] If he can show that he was ready, willing, and able to perform his part of the contract, he can recover damages for total breach of the contract. The nonbreaching party is not obligated to do this, however. If he chooses, he may wait until the time for performance in case the other party changes his mind and decides to perform.

Recovery by a Party Who Has Committed Material Breach

A party who has materially breached the contract (that is, has not substantially performed) does not have the right to recover the contract price. If a promisor who has given some performance to the promisee cannot recover under the contract, however, the promisor will face forfeiture and the promisee will have obtained an unearned gain. There are two possible avenues for a party who has committed material breach to obtain some compensation for the performance he has conferred on the nonbreaching party.

1. *Quasi-contract.* A party who has materially breached a contract might recover the reasonable value of any benefits he has conferred on the promisee by bringing an action under quasi-contract.[4] This would enable him to obtain compensation for the value of any performance he has given that has benefited the nonbreaching party. Some courts take the position that a person in material breach should not be able to recover for benefits he has conferred, however.

2. *Partial performance of a divisible contract.* Some contracts are **divisible.** That is, each party's performance can be divided in two or more parts and each part is exchanged for some corresponding consideration from the other party. For example, if Johnson agrees to mow Peterson's lawn for $20 and clean Peterson's gutters for $50, the contract is divisible. When a promisor performs one part of the contract, but materially breaches another part, he can recover at the contract price for the part that he did perform. For example, if Johnson breached his duty to clean the gutters but fully performed his obligation to mow the lawn, he could recover at the contract price for the lawn-mowing part of the contract.

EXCUSES FOR NONPERFORMANCE

Although nonperformance of a duty that has become due will ordinarily constitute a breach of contract, there are some situations in which nonperformance is excused because of factors that arise after the formation of the contract. When this occurs, the person whose performance

---

[3] Uniform Commercial Code rules regarding anticipatory repudiation in contracts for the sale of goods are discussed in the Performance of Sales Contracts chapter.

[4] Quasi-contract is discussed in the Introduction to Contracts chapter. It involves the use of the remedy of restitution, which is discussed later in this chapter.

is made impossible or impracticable by these factors is discharged from further obligation under the contract. The following discussion concerns the most common grounds for excuse of nonperformance.

Impossibility

When performance of a contractual duty becomes impossible after the formation of the contract, the duty will be discharged on grounds of **impossibility.** This does not mean that a person can be discharged merely because he has contracted to do something that he is simply unable to do or that causes him hardship or difficulty. Impossibility in the legal sense of the word means "it cannot be done by anyone" rather than "I cannot do it." Thus, promisors who find that they have agreed to perform duties that are beyond their capabilities or that turn out to be unprofitable or burdensome generally are not excused from performance of their duties. Impossibility will provide an excuse for nonperformance, however, when some unexpected event arises *after* the formation of the contract and renders performance objectively impossible. The event that causes the impossibility need not have been entirely unforeseeable. It must, however, have been one that the parties would not have reasonably thought of as a real possibility that would affect performance.

There are a variety of situations in which a person's duty to perform may be discharged on grounds of impossibility. The three most common situations involve illness or death of the promisor, supervening illegality, and destruction of the subject matter of the contract.

Illness or Death of Promisor   Incapacitating illness or death of the promisor excuses nonperformance when the promisor has contracted to perform personal services. For example, if Pauling, a college professor who has a contract with State University to teach for an academic year, dies before the completion of the contract, her estate will not be liable for breach of contract. The promisor's death or illness does *not*, however, excuse the nonperformance of duties that can be delegated to another, such as the duty to deliver goods, pay money, or convey real estate. For example, if Odell had contracted to convey real estate to Ruskin and died before the closing date, Ruskin could enforce the contract against Odell's estate.

Supervening Illegality   If a statute or governmental regulation enacted after the creation of a contract makes performance of a party's duties illegal, the promisor is excused from performing. Statutes or regulations that merely make performance more difficult or less profitable do not, however, excuse nonperformance.

Destruction of the Subject Matter of the Contract
If something that is essential to the promisor's performance is destroyed after the formation of the contract through no fault of the promisor, the promisor is excused from performing. For example, Woolridge contracts to sell his car to Rivkin. If an explosion destroys the car after the contract has been formed but before Woolridge has made delivery, Woolridge's nonperformance will be excused. The destruction of nonessential items that the promisor intended to use in performing does not excuse nonperformance if substitutes are available, even though securing them makes performance more difficult or less profitable. Suppose that Ace Construction Company had planned to use a particular piece of machinery in fulfilling a contract to build a building for Worldwide Widgets Company. If the piece of machinery is destroyed but substitutes are available, destruction of the machinery before the contract is performed would *not* give Ace an excuse for failing to perform.

Frustration of Venture

Closely associated with impossibility is the doctrine of **frustration of venture** (also known as **commercial frustration** or **frustration of purpose**). This doctrine provides an excuse for nonperformance when events that occur after the formation of the contract would deprive the promisor of the benefit of return performance. Although courts often include frustration cases within the general terminology of impossibility, frustration can be distinguished from impossibility and impracticability by the fact that the promisor in a frustration case is not necessarily prevented from performing. Rather, in frustration cases, the promisor is excused because the return performance by the other party has become worthless to him. For example, Boyd signs a contract for a one-year membership in an Eden Exercise Salon, for which he agrees to pay $50 per month. One week after signing the contract, Boyd is involved in a serious automobile accident and suffers injuries that cause him to be bedridden for a year. In such a case, the automobile accident and Boyd's resulting injuries did not prevent him from performing his duties under the contract (paying money each month), but this unexpected event does deprive Boyd of the benefit of receiving Eden's return perfomance. In such a case, a court might excuse Boyd's performance on the ground of frustration of venture.

Commercial Impracticability

Section 2–615 of the Uniform Commercial Code has extended the scope of the common law doctrine of impossibility to cases in which unforeseen developments make performance by the promisor highly impracticable, unreasonably expensive, or of little value to the promisee. Rather than using a standard of impossibility, then, the Code uses the more relaxed standard of **impracticability.** Despite the less stringent standard applied, cases actually excusing nonperformance on grounds of impracticability are relatively rare. To be successful in claiming excuse based on impracticability, a promisor must be able to establish that the event that makes performance impracticable occurred without his fault and that the contract was made with the basic assumption that this event would not occur. This basically means that the event was beyond the scope of the risks that the parties contemplated at the time of contracting and that the promisor did not expressly or impliedly assume the risk that the event would occur.

Case law and official comments to section 2–615 indicate that neither increased cost nor collapse of a market for particular goods is sufficient to excuse nonperformance, because those are the types of business risks that every promisor assumes. However, drastic price increases or severe shortages of goods resulting from unforeseen circumstances such as wars and crop failures can give rise to impracticability.

If the event causing impracticability affects only a part of the seller's capacity to perform, the seller must allocate production and deliveries among customers in a "fair and reasonable" manner and must notify them of any delay or any limited allocation of the goods. You can read more about commercial impracticability in the Performance of Sales Contracts chapter.

The impracticability standard has been adopted in section 261 of the *Restatement (Second) of Contracts,* which closely resembles the provisions of section 2–615 of the UCC. States that follow the *Restatement* approach apply the impracticability standard to all types of contracts, not just those for the sale of goods. You will see an example of the use of the *Restatement* standard in the following case, *The Opera Company of Boston, Inc. v. The Wolf Trap Foundation for the Performing Arts.*

THE OPERA COMPANY OF BOSTON, INC. v. THE WOLF TRAP FOUNDATION FOR THE PERFORMING ARTS

817 F.2d 1094 (4th Cir. 1987)

Wolf Trap, an organization for the advancement of the performing arts, sponsors operas and other artistic programs at the Filene Center. The Filene Center is located in the Wolf Trap National Park, a national park owned by the United States government and operated by the National Park Service. The Center, which consists of a main stage tower, an auditorium, and an open lawn, provides both covered and uncovered seating for approximately 6,500 people. The park provides the parking space, which is separated from the Center and accessible by a number of pathways. Wolf Trap entered into a contract with the Opera Company of Boston whereby it agreed to pay the Opera Company $272,000 to perform four operas at the Filene Center on the nights of June 12, 13, 14, and 15, 1980. Among Wolf Trap's duties under the contract was the duty "to provide lighting equipment as shall be specified by the Opera Company of Boston's lighting designer."

All four performances were sold out. Both parties performed their obligations for the first three performances. On June 15, the day of the last performance, however, the weather was hot, humid, and rainy. In the early evening, there was a severe thunderstorm, which caused an electrical power outage that blacked out all electrical service in the park, its roadways, parking area, pathways, and auditorium. Representatives of the National Park Service and Wolf Trap held several conferences to decide what to do about the performance. The public utility advised that electrical service would not be resumed in the park until 11:00 P.M. or perhaps not even until the next morning. Various alternatives for supplying power were considered but none was regarded as being sufficient to resolve the problem. The Park Service was concerned about the safety of the 3,000 people who were already in the park; 3,500 more were expected before 8:00 P.M. The Park Service recommended the immediate cancellation of the performance and advised Wolf Trap that it disclaimed responsibility for the safety of the people who were to attend the performance. Wolf Trap agreed and the performance was canceled. A representative of the Opera Company was present at this meeting, but she neither took part in the decision nor voiced objection to the decision.

Since the performance was canceled, Wolf Trap did not make the final payment called for in the contract to the Opera Company. The Opera Company sued Wolf Trap to recover the balance due under the contract, and Wolf Trap defended on the ground of impossibility. The trial court rejected this defense on the ground that Wolf Trap was obligated to provide sufficient lighting and power outages were reasonably foreseeable. It entered judgment in favor of the Opera Company, and Wolf Trap appealed.

Russell, Circuit Judge.   The modern doctrine of impossibility or impracticability has been formulated in section 265 of the *Restatement (Second) of Contracts* in these words:

Where, after a contract is made, a party's principal purpose is substantially frustrated without his fault by the occurrence of an event the non-occurrence of which was a basic assumption on which the contract was made, his remaining duties to render performance are discharged, unless the language or the circumstances indicate the contrary.

Impossibility arises as a defense to breach of contract when the circumstances causing the breach have made performance so vitally different from what was anticipated that the contract cannot reasonably be thought to govern. It is implicit in the doctrine of impossibility (and the companion rule of frustration of purpose) that certain risks are so unusual and have such severe consequences that they must have been beyond the scope of the assignment of risks inherent in the contract, that is, beyond the agreement made by the parties.

Manifestly the first fact to be established in making out this defense of impossibility or impracticability of performance is the existence of an "occurrence of an event, the non-occurrence of which was a basic assumption on which the contract was made." The occurrence must be unexpected but it does not necessarily have to have been unforeseeable. A requirement of absolute nonforeseeability as a condition to the application of the doctrine would in effect nullify the doctrine. Practically any event can be foreseen but whether the foreseeability is sufficient to render unacceptable the defense of impossibility is one of degree of the foreseeability.

The second fact to be determined in the application of the doctrine is that the frustration of performance was substantial. To satisfy this requirement the frustration must be so severe that it is not fairly to be regarded as within the risks the obligor assumed under the contract. And, finally, the defendant asserting the defense must establish that performance was impossible as that term has been defined in the refinements of the doctrine.

Applying the law to the facts of this case, we conclude that the existence of electric power was necessary for the satisfactory performance by the Opera Company on the night of June 15. The district judge, however, refused to sustain the defense because he held that if the contingency that occurred was one that could have been foreseen, reliance on the doctrine of impossibility as a defense to a breach of contract suit is absolutely barred. As we have said, this is not the modern rule. Foreseeability, as we have said, is at best one fact to be considered in resolving whether its occurrence, based on past experience, was of such reasonable likelihood that the obligor should not merely foresee the risk but, because of the degree of its likelihood, the obligor should have guarded against it or provided for non-liability against the risk.

The judgment must be vacated and the action remanded to the district court to make findings whether the possible foreseeability of the power failure in this case was of that degree of reasonable likelihood as to make improper the assertion by Wolf Trap of the defense of impossiblity of performance.

Judgment vacated and remanded in favor of Wolf Trap.

OTHER GROUNDS FOR DISCHARGE

Additional Grounds for Discharge

Earlier in this chapter, you learned about several situations in which a party's duty to perform could be discharged even though that party had not himself performed. These include the nonoccurrence of a condition precedent or concurrent condition, the occurrence of a condition subsequent, performance, material breach by the other party, and excuse from performance by impossibility, impracticability, or frustration. The following discussion deals with additional ways in which a discharge can occur.

Discharge by Mutual Agreement

Just as contracts are created by mutual agreement, they can also be discharged by *mutual agreement*. An agreement to discharge a contract must be supported by consideration to be enforceable.

Discharge by Accord and Satisfaction

An **accord** is an agreement whereby a promisee who has an existing claim agrees with the promisor that he will accept some performance different from that which was originally agreed upon. When the promisor performs the accord, that is called a **satisfaction.**[5] When accord and satisfaction occurs, the parties are discharged. For example, Root contracts with May to build a garage on May's property for $30,000. After Root has performed his part of the bargain, the parties then agree that instead of paying money, May will transfer a one-year-old

Porsche to Root instead. When this is done, both parties are discharged.

Discharge by Waiver

A party to a contract may voluntarily relinquish any right he has under a contract, including the right to receive return performance. Such a relinquishment of rights is known as a **waiver.** If one party tenders an incomplete or defective performance and the other party accepts that performance without objection, knowing that the defects will not be remedied, the party to whom performance was due will have discharged the other party from his duty of performance. For example, a real estate lease requires Long, the tenant, to pay a $5 late charge for late payments of rent. Long pays his rent late each month for five months but the landlord accepts it without objection and without assessing the late charge. In this situation, the landlord has probably waived his right to collect the late charge. The Uniform Commercial Code provides in section 1–107 that "any claim or right arising out of an alleged breach can be discharged in whole or in part without consideration by a written waiver or renunciation signed and delivered by the aggrieved party."

To avoid waiving rights, a person who has received defective performance should give the other party prompt notice that she expects complete performance and will seek damages if the defects are not corrected.

Discharge by Alteration

If the contract is represented by a *written* instrument, and one of the parties intentionally makes a material alteration in the instrument without the other's consent, the alteration acts as a discharge of the other party. If the other party consents to the alteration or does not object

---

[5] Accord and satisfaction is also discussed in the Consideration chapter.

to it when he learns of it, he is not discharged. Alteration by a third party without the knowledge or consent of the contracting parties does not affect the parties' rights.

Discharge by Statute of Limitations

Courts have long refused to grant a remedy to a person who delays bringing a lawsuit for an unreasonable time. All of the states have enacted statutes known as **statutes of limitation,** which specify the period of time in which a person can bring a lawsuit.

The time period for bringing a contract action varies from state to state, and many states prescribe time periods for cases concerning oral contracts that are different from those for cases concerning written contracts. Section 2–725 of the Uniform Commercial Code provides for a four-year statute of limitations for contracts involving the sale of goods.

The statutory period ordinarily begins to run from the date of the breach. It may be delayed if the party who has the right to sue is under some incapacity at that time (such as minority or insanity) or is beyond the jurisdiction of the state. A person who has breached a contractual duty is discharged from liability for breach if no lawsuit is brought before the statutory period elapses.

Discharge by Decree of Bankruptcy

The contractual obligations of a debtor are generally discharged by a decree of bankruptcy. Bankruptcy is discussed in a later chapter.

REMEDIES FOR BREACH OF CONTRACT

Our discussion of the performance stage of contracts so far has focused on the circumstances under which a party has the duty to perform or is excused from performing. In situations in which a person is injured by a breach of contract and is unable to obtain compensation by a settlement out of court, a further important issue remains: What remedy will a court fashion to compensate for breach of contract?

Contract law seeks to encourage people to rely on the promises made to them by others. The objective of granting a remedy in a case of breach of contract is not to punish the breaching party. Contract remedies focus on the economic loss caused by breach of contract, not on the moral obligation to perform a promise. The objective of contract remedies is simply to compensate the injured party.

Types of Contract Remedies

There are a variety of ways in which this can be done. The basic categories of contract remedies include:

1. Legal remedies (money damages).
2. Equitable remedies.
3. Restitution.

The usual remedy is an award of money damages that will compensate the injured party for his losses. This is called a **legal remedy** or **remedy at law**, because the imposition of money damages in our legal system originated in courts of law. Less frequently used but still important are **equitable remedies**, such as specific performance. Equitable remedies are those remedies that had their origins in courts of equity rather than in courts of law.[6] Today they are available at the discretion of the judge. A final possible remedy is **restitution**, which requires the defendant to pay the value of the benefits that the plaintiff has conferred on him.

Interests Protected by Contract Remedies

Remedies for breach of contract protect one or more of the following interests that a promisee may have:[7]

1. *Expectation interest.* A promisee's **expectation interest** is his interest in obtaining the objective or opportunity for gain that he bargained for and "expected." Courts attempt to protect this interest by formulating a remedy that will place the promisee in the position he would have been in if the contract had been performed as promised.

2. *Reliance interest.* A promisee's **reliance interest** is his interest in being compensated for losses that he has suffered by changing his position in reliance on the other party's promise. In some cases, such as when a promisee is unable to prove his expectation interest with reasonable certainty, the promisee may seek a remedy to compensate for the *loss suffered* as a result of relying on the promisor's promise rather than for the expectation of profit.

3. *Restitution interest.* A **restitution interest** is a party's interest in recovering the amount by which he has enriched or benefited the other. Both the reliance and restitution interests involve promisees who have changed

---

[6] The nature of equitable remedies is also discussed in the Nature of Law chapter.

[7] *Restatement (Second) of Contracts* section 344.

their position. The difference between the two is that the reliance interest involves a loss to the promisee that does not benefit the promisor, whereas the restitution interest involves a loss to the promisee that *does* constitute an unjust enrichment to the promisor. A remedy based on restitution enables a party who has performed or partially performed her contract and has benefited the other party to obtain compensation for the value of the benefits that she has conferred.

LEGAL REMEDIES (DAMAGES)

Limitations on Recovery of Damages in Contract Cases

An injured party's ability to recover damages in a contract action is limited by three principles:

1. *A party can recover damages only for those losses that he can prove with reasonable certainty.* Losses that are purely speculative are not recoverable. Thus, if Jones Publishing Company breaches a contract to publish Powell's memoirs, Powell may not be able to recover damages for lost royalties (her expectation interest), since she may be unable to establish, beyond speculation, how much money she would have earned in royalties if the book had been published. (Note, however, that Powell's reliance interest might be protected here; she could be allowed to recover provable losses incurred in reliance on the contract.)

2. *A breaching party is responsible for paying only those losses that were foreseeable to him at the time of contracting.* A loss is foreseeable if it would ordinarily be expected to result from a breach or if the breaching party had reason to know of particular circumstances that would make the loss likely. For example, if Prince Manufacturing Company renders late performance in a contract to deliver parts to Cheatum Motors without knowing that Cheatum is shut down waiting for the parts, Prince will not have to pay the business losses that result from Cheatum's having to close its operation.

3. *Plaintiffs injured by a breach of contract have the duty to* **mitigate** *(avoid or minimize) damages.* A party cannot recover for losses that he could have avoided without undue risk, burden, or humiliation. For example, an employee who has been wrongfully fired would be entitled to damages equal to his wages for the remainder of the employment period. The employee, however, has the duty to minimize the damages by making reasonable efforts to seek a similar job elsewhere. The *Parker v. Twentieth Century-Fox Film Corporation* case involves the question of whether an injured party carried out her duty to mitigate.

PARKER V. TWENTIETH CENTURY-FOX FILM CORPORATION
474 P.2d 689 (Cal. Sup. Ct. 1970)

Shirley MacLaine Parker entered into a contract with Twentieth Century-Fox to play the female lead in Fox's contemplated production of a movie entitled *Bloomer Girl*. The contract provided that Fox would pay Parker a minimum "guaranteed compensation" of $53,571.42 per week for 14 weeks, beginning May 23, 1966, for a total of $750,000. Fox decided not to produce the movie, and in a letter dated April 4, 1966, it notified Parker that it would not "comply with our obligations to you under" the written contract. In the same letter, with the professed purpose "to avoid any damage to you," Fox instead offered to employ Parker as the leading actress in another movie, tentatively entitled *Big Country, Big Man*. The compensation offered was identical. Unlike *Bloomer Girl*, however, which was to have been a musical production, *Big Country* was to be a dramatic "western type" movie. *Bloomer Girl* was to have been filmed in California; *Big Country* was to be produced in Australia. Certain other terms of the substitute contract varied from those of the original. Parker was given one week within which to accept. She did not, and the offer lapsed. Parker then filed suit against Fox for recovery of the agreed-upon guaranteed compensation. The trial court held for Parker, and Fox appealed.

Burke, Justice.   The general rule is that the measure of recovery by a wrongfully discharged employee is the amount of salary agreed upon for the period of service, less the amount which the employer affirmatively proves the employee has earned or with reasonable effort might have earned from other employment. However, before projected earnings from other employment opportunities not sought or accepted by the discharged employee can be applied in mitigation, the employer must show that the other employment was comparable, or substantially similar, to that of which the employee has been deprived; the employee's rejection of or failure to seek other available employment of a different or inferior kind may not be resorted to in order to mitigate damages.

In the present case, the sole issue is whether Parker's refusal of Fox's substitute offer of "Big Country" may be used in mitigation. Nor, if the "Big Country" offer was of employment different or inferior when compared with the original "Bloomer Girl" employment, is there an issue as to whether Parker acted reasonably in refusing the substitute offer.

It is clear that the trial court correctly ruled that Parker's failure to accept Fox's tendered substitute employment could not be applied in mitigation of damages because the offer of the "Big Country" lead was of employment both different and inferior. The mere circumstance that "Bloomer Girl" was to be a musical review calling upon Parker's talents as a dancer as well as an actress, and was to be produced in the City of Los Angeles, whereas "Big Country" was a straight dramatic role in a "western type" story taking place in an opal mine in Australia, demonstrates the difference in kind between the two employments; the female lead in a western style motion picture can by no stretch of the imagination be considered the equivalent of or substantially similar to the lead in a song-and-dance production.

Judgment for Parker affirmed.

Compensatory Damages

Subject to the limitations discussed above, a person who has been injured by a breach of contract is entitled to recover **compensatory damages.** In calculating the compensatory remedy, a court will attempt to protect the expectation interest of the injured party by giving him the "benefit of his bargain" (placing him in the position he would have been in *had the contract been performed as promised*). To do this, the court must compensate the injured person for the provable losses he has suffered as well as for the provable gains that he has been prevented from realizing by the breach of contract. Normally, compensatory damages include one or more of three possible items: loss in value, any allowable consequential damages, and any allowable incidental damages.

1. *Loss in value.* The starting point in calculating compensatory damages is to determine the **loss in value** of the performance that the plaintiff had the right to expect. This is a way of measuring the expectation interest.

The calculation of the loss in value experienced by an injured party differs according to the sort of contract involved and the circumstances of the breach. In contracts involving nonperformance of the sale of real estate, for example, courts normally measure loss in value by the difference between the contract price and the market price of the property. Thus, if Willis repudiates a contract with Renfrew whereby Renfrew was to purchase land worth $20,000 from Willis for $10,000, Renfrew's loss in value was $10,000. Where a seller has failed to perform a contract for the sale of goods, courts may measure loss in value by the difference between the contract price and the price that the buyer had to pay to procure substitute goods.[8] In cases in which a party breaches by rendering defective performance—say, by

---

[8] Remedies under Article 2 of the Uniform Commercial Code are discussed in detail in the Remedies for Breach of Sales Contracts chapter.

breaching a warranty in the sale of goods—the loss in value would be measured by the difference between the value of the goods if they had been in the condition warranted by the seller and the value of the goods in their defective condition.[9]

2. *Consequential damages.* **Consequential damages** (also called **special damages**) compensate for losses that occur as a consequence of the breach of contract. Consequential losses occur because of some special or unusual circumstances of the particular contractual relationship of the parties. For example, Apex Trucking Company buys a computer system from ABC Computers. The system fails to operate properly, and Apex is forced to pay its employees to perform the tasks manually, spending $10,000 in overtime pay. In this situation, Apex might seek to recover the $10,000 in overtime pay in addition to the loss of value that it has experienced.

Lost profits flowing from a breach of contract can be recovered as consequential damages if they are foreseeable and can be proven with reasonable certainty. It is important to remember, however, that the recovery of consequential damages is subject to the limitations on damage recovery discussed earlier. As *Richmond Medical Supply Co., Inc. v. Clifton* indicates, foreseeability of the damages is of particular concern in cases in which consequential damages are sought.

3. *Incidental damages.* **Incidental damages** compensate for reasonable costs that the injured party incurs after the breach in an effort to avoid further loss. For example, if Smith Construction Company breaches an employment contract with Brice, Brice could recover as incidental damages those reasonable expenses he must incur in attempting to procure substitute employment, such as long-distance telephone tolls or the cost of printing new resumes.

---

[9] See the Product Liability chapter for further discussion of the damages for breach of warranty in the sale of goods.

RICHMOND MEDICAL SUPPLY CO., INC. v. CLIFTON
369 S.E.2d 407 (Va. Sup. Ct. 1988)

Richmond Medical Supply (RMS) occupied commercial space that it leased from Robert Clifton. When the lease was renewed, the parties included an addendum that required Clifton to make certain repairs, including "replacement and make in good working order the rear overhead door on or before the commencement of this lease, August 1, 1983." RMS continued in possession of the property even though Clifton failed to repair or replace the door. On November 8, 1983, thieves broke into the leased property by knocking out a wooden panel in the overhead door and removed cases, equipment, and inventory valued by RMS at $60,000, none of which was ever recovered.

RMS brought this action for breach of contract, alleging that its loss was the direct consequence of Clifton's breach of his express promise to replace the door and that the damages RMS had sustained were within the contemplation of the parties. (Under Virginia law, a tort action against Clifton would not have been successful.) Clifton moved for summary judgment, and the trial court granted summary judgment in his favor. RMS appealed.

Russell, Justice.   There are two broad categories of damages which may arise from a breach of contract. Direct damages are those which naturally or ordinarily flow from the breach; consequential damages arise from the intervention of special circumstances not ordinarily predictable. Consequential damages are compensable only if it is determined *as a matter of fact* that the special circumstances were within the contemplation of the contracting parties at the time of contracting. "Contemplation," in this context, includes both that which was actually foreseen and that which was reasonably foreseeable. Whether special circumstances were within the contemplation of the parties so as to justify the recovery of consequential damages is a question of fact for the jury. Thus, having properly determined that RMS's claimed damages were consequential in nature, the trial court erred in failing to submit the "contemplation" issue to the jury unless the recovery of any damages was barred by the doctrine of *Gulf Reston, Inc. v. Rogers*.

In *Gulf Reston*, we considered a claim that a landlord was liable in tort to a tenant for failure to protect the tenant from the criminal act of a third party. We held that the landlord had no duty to provide such protection. We were faced with the determination whether a duty was imposed by general law upon the defendant somehow to foresee and to take effective measures to guard against the danger of criminal acts by a third person. The defendant [had not] expressly assumed a duty, by contract, to take some specific action to protect the plaintiff from a danger within the contemplation of the parties at the time of contracting.

Contracting parties are entirely capable of assuming duties toward one another beyond those imposed by general law and, in fact, do so in nearly every contractual arrangement. RMS pleaded a contractual duty, a breach thereof, and damages flowing from the breach. Each of these should have been considered by the fact-finder. Accordingly we reverse the order granting summary judgment and remand the case for further proceedings consistent with this opinion.

Summary judgment reversed in favor of RMS.

Alternative Measures of Damages The foregoing discussion has focused on the most common formulation of damage remedies in contracts cases. The normal measure of compensatory damages is not appropriate in every case, however. When it is not appropriate, a court may use an alternative measure of damages. For example, where a party has suffered losses by performing or preparing to perform, he might seek damages based on his *reliance interest* instead of his expectation interest. In such a case, he would be compensated for the provable losses he suffered by relying on the other party's promise. This measure of damages is often used in cases in which a promise is enforceable under promissory estoppel.[10]

Nominal Damages

Nominal damages are very small damage awards that are given when a technical breach of contract has occurred without causing any actual or provable economic loss. The sums awarded as nominal damages typically vary from two cents to a dollar.

Liquidated Damages

The parties to a contract may expressly provide in their contract that a specific sum shall be recoverable if the contract is breached. Such provisions are called **liquidated damages** provisions. For example, Murchison rents space in a shopping mall in which she plans to operate a retail clothing store. She must make improvements in the space before opening the store, and it is very important to her to have the store opened for the Christmas shopping season. She hires Ace Construction Company to construct the improvements. The parties agree to include in the contract a liquidated damages provision stating that, if Ace is late in completing the construction, Murchison will be able to recover a specified sum for each day of delay. Such a provision is highly desirable from Murchison's point of view because, without a liquidated damages provision, she would have a difficult time in establishing the precise losses that would result from delay. Courts scrutinize these agreed-upon damages carefully, however.

If the amount specified in a liquidated damages provision is reasonable and if the nature of the contract is such that actual damages would be difficult to determine, a court will enforce the provision. When liquidated damages provisions are enforced, the amount of damages agreed upon will be the injured party's exclusive damage remedy. If the amount specified is unreasonably great in relation to the probable loss or injury, however, or if the amount of damages could be readily determined in the event of breach, the courts will declare the provision to be a *penalty* and will refuse to enforce it.

---

[10] Promissory estoppel is discussed in the Introduction to Contracts; Offer; Acceptance; and Writing chapters.

Punitive Damages

[IF TORT IS INVOLVED]
Generally NOT Contract situations

(3) **Punitive damages** are damages awarded *in addition to* the compensatory remedy that are designed to punish a defendant for particularly reprehensible behavior and to deter the defendant and others from committing similar behavior in the future. The traditional rule is that punitive damages are *not* recoverable in contracts cases unless a specific statutory provision (such as some consumer protection statutes) allows them or the defendant has committed *fraud* or some other *independent tort*. A few states will permit the use of punitive damages in contracts cases in which the defendant's conduct, though not technically a tort, was malicious, oppressive, or tortious in nature.

Punitive damages have also been awarded in many of the cases involving breach of the implied covenant of good faith. In such cases, courts usually circumvent the traditional rule against awarding punitive damages in contracts cases by holding that breach of the duty of good faith is an independent tort. The availability of punitive damages in such cases operates to deter a contracting party from deliberately disregarding the other party's rights. Insurance companies have been the most frequent target for punitive damages awards in bad-faith cases, but employers and banks have also been subjected to punitive damages verdicts.

EQUITABLE REMEDIES

In exceptional cases in which money damages alone are not adequate to fully compensate for a party's injuries, a court may grant an **equitable remedy** either alone or in combination with a legal remedy. Equitable relief is subject to several limitations, however, and will be granted only when justice is served by doing so. The primary equitable remedies for breach of contract are *specific performance* and *injunction*.[11]

Specific Performance

Specific performance is an equitable remedy whereby the court orders the breaching party to perform his contractual duties as promised. For example, if Barnes breached a contract to sell a tract of land to Metzger and a court granted specific performance of the contract, the court would require Barnes to deed the land to Metzger. (Metzger, of course, must pay the purchase price.) This remedy can be advantageous to the injured party because he is not faced with the complexities of proving damages, he does not have to worry about whether he can actually collect the damages, and he gets exactly what he bargained for. However, the availability of this remedy is subject to the limitations discussed below.

The Availability of Specific Performance   Specific performance, like other equitable remedies, is available only when the injured party has no adequate remedy at law—in other words, when money damages do not adequately compensate the injured party. This generally requires a showing that the subject of the contract is *unique* or at least that no substitutes are available. Even if this requirement is met, a court will withhold specific performance if the injured party has acted in bad faith, if he unreasonably delayed in asserting his rights, or if specific performance would require an excessive amount of supervision by the court.

Contracts for the sale of real estate are the most common subjects of specific performance decrees because every tract of real estate is considered to be unique. Specific performance is rarely granted for breach of a contract for the sale of goods because the injured party can usually procure substitute goods. However, there are situations involving sales of goods contracts in which specific performance is given. These cases involve goods that are unique or goods for which no substitute can be found. Examples include antiques, heirlooms, works of art, and objects of purely sentimental value.[12] Specific performance is not available for the breach of a promise to perform a personal service (such as a contract for employment, artistic performance, or consulting services). A decree requiring a person to specifically perform a personal-services contract would probably be ineffective in giving the injured party what he bargained for. It would also require a great deal of supervision by the court. In addition, an application of specific performance in such cases would amount to a form of involuntary servitude.

---

[11]Another equitable remedy, *reformation*, allows a court to reform or "rewrite" a written contract when the parties have made an error in expressing their agreement. Reformation is discussed along with the doctrine of mistake in the Reality of Consent chapter.

---

[12] Specific performance under section 2–716(1) of the UCC is discussed in the Remedies for Breach of Sales Contracts chapter.

Injunction

Injunction is an equitable remedy that is employed in many different contexts and is sometimes used as a remedy for breach of contract. An **injunction** is a court order requiring a person to do something (**mandatory injunction**) or ordering a person to refrain from doing something (**negative injunction**). Unlike legal remedies that apply only when the breach has already occurred, the equitable remedy of injunction can be invoked when a breach has merely been *threatened*. Injunctions are available only when the breach or threatened breach is likely to cause *irreparable injury.*

In the contract context, specific performance is a form of mandatory injunction. Negative injunctions are appropriately used in several situations, such as contract cases in which a party whose duty under the contract is forbearance threatens to breach the contract. For example, Norris sells his restaurant in Gas City, Indiana, to Ford. A term of the contract of sale provides that Norris agrees not to own, operate, or be employed in any restaurant within 30 miles of Gas City for a period of two years after the sale.[13] If Norris threatens to open a new restaurant in Gas City several months after the sale is consummated, a court could *enjoin* Norris from opening the new restaurant.

RESTITUTION

Restitution is a remedy that can be obtained either at law or in equity. Restitution applies when one party's performance or reliance has conferred a benefit on the other. A party's restitution interest is protected by compensating him for the value of benefits he has conferred on the other person.[14] This can be done through **specific restitution,** in which the defendant is required to return the exact property conferred on him by the plaintiff, or **substitutionary restitution,** in which a court awards the plaintiff a sum of money that reflects the amount by which he benefited the defendant. In an action for damages based on quasi-contract, substitutionary restitution would be the remedy.

Restitution can be used in a number of circumstances. Sometimes, parties injured by breach of contract seek restitution as an alternative remedy instead of damages that focus on their expectation interest. In other situations, a *breaching party* who has partially performed seeks restitution for the value of benefits he conferred in excess of the losses he caused. In addition, restitution often applies in cases in which a person rescinds a contract on the grounds of lack of capacity, misrepresentation, fraud, duress, undue influence, or mistake. Upon rescission, each party who has been benefited by the other's performance must compensate the other for the value of the benefit conferred.[15] Another application of restitution occurs when a party to a contract that violates the statute of frauds confers a benefit on the other party.[16] For example, Boyer gives Blake a $10,000 down payment on an oral contract for the sale of a farm. Although the contract is unenforceable (that is, Boyer could not get compensation for his expectation interest), the court would give Boyer restitution of his down payment.

1. Is it good public policy for a party who has materially breached a contract to be able to obtain restitution for the benefits he has conferred on the nonbreaching party?

2. How does the duty of good faith and fair dealing encourage ethical dealings? Do you see any problems with such a duty?

3. You have seen that contract remedies focus solely on the economic effect of contract breaches rather than on the moral implications of such breaches or the emotional harms that might result from a breach of contract. As a result, contract remedies are much more limited than are remedies in tort cases. Is this sound public policy? Explain.

SUMMARY

A problem arising in the performance stage of contracts that is frequently presented to courts is determining when performance is due. A party's duty to perform is absolute unless it is subject to some condition. A

---

[13] Ancillary covenants not to compete, or noncompetition agreements, are discussed in detail in the Illegality chapter.

[14] Quasi-contract is discussed in detail in the Introduction to Contracts chapter.

[15] These doctrines are discussed in the Reality of Consent chapter and Capacity to Contract chapter.

[16] The statute of frauds is discussed in the Writing chapter.

condition is an uncertain event, other than the passage of time, that affects a party's duty to perform. An event that must occur before performance is due is called a *condition precedent*. An event that discharges a party from his duty to perform is called a *condition subsequent*. A condition that requires simultaneous performance of duties by the parties is called a *concurrent condition*.

Conditions may be created in several ways. They may be created by the express language of a contract (express conditions) or implied by the circumstances surrounding the contract or by the nature of the contract (implied-in-fact conditions). Although no particular language is necessary to create an express condition, such conditions are usually created by such language as "on condition that," "so long as," "subject to," and "provided that."

A type of express condition that is common in building contracts is a contractual provision stating that one party's duty to perform is conditioned on a third party's satisfaction with the promisor's performance. The third person is held to a standard of honest satisfaction. Another type of express condition exists when a contract provides that a party's duty to pay is conditioned on his personal satisfaction with the other party's performance. In such cases, the standard for determining whether the condition has occurred will depend on whether the subject of the contract involves a matter of personal taste or convenience or whether it involves mechanical suitability or use. In the former type of case, a standard of honest or good faith satisfaction is applied. In the latter type of case, an objective, reasonable man standard is used to determine whether the condition has occurred.

Sometimes, conditions are imposed by courts even when the parties' contract does not state or imply a condition. This type of condition is called a constructive condition or an implied-in-law condition. It is imposed to do justice between the parties.

Although a party whose duty is conditional normally has no obligation to perform unless a condition occurs, there are some circumstances under which the occurrence of a condition may be excused. When a condition is excused, a party whose duty is conditional will have the obligation to perform notwithstanding the nonoccurrence of the condition.

When a promisor's performance is an express condition of the promisee's duty to render return performance or when a contract is capable of perfect performance, the promisor will be held to a standard of strict compliance with the contract. However, when performance is only a constructive condition and the nature of the contract is such that the promised performance is very diffi-

cult to render perfectly, the promisor will be held to the lower standard of substantial performance. Substantial performance falls somewhat short of complete performance, but does not deprive the promisee of a material part of the consideration for which he bargained. If the promisor substantially performs his obligations, he will be entitled to receive the other party's promised performance. Any recovery that he might receive is decreased by the amount of damages that his imperfect performance has caused. If the promisor's performance is defective in some major respect, he is guilty of material breach. When material breach occurs, the promisee is entitled to withhold his own performance. If the breach is not cured, he is discharged from further obligations and entitled to sue for damages for total breach of contract.

Modern contract law places the duty on each party to a contract to perform in good faith. The implied covenant of good faith and fair dealing has been imposed in an increasing range of contracts. The UCC places a duty of good faith on each party to a contract covered by any article of the UCC. Courts have also implied the duty of good faith in many contracts outside the scope of the UCC, such as insurance contracts. Breach of the duty of good faith creates contract liability. Depending on state law and the circumstances of the breach, a breach of the duty of good faith may give rise to tort liability.

In some exceptional circumstances in which unforeseen events occur after the formation of a contract, a promisor will be excused from performing. That is, even though the promisor had the legal duty to perform, his nonperformance will not be considered a breach of contract and he will be discharged from his obligations. A major basis for excusing nonperformance is impossibility. When an event occurs after the formation of the contract that renders performance impossible to carry out, the promisor will be excused. Impossibility means that the act cannot be done, not that the promisor is personally unable to do it. The mere fact that the promisor contracted to do something that he was incapable of doing or has suffered insolvency does not render the performance impossible. Impossibility generally arises in one of three situations: incapacitating illness or death of the promisor in contracts that require the promisor to perform personal services, supervening illegality caused by the enactment of statutes or governmental regulations that make performance illegal, and destruction of subject matter essential to the performance of the contract.

The UCC adopted a somewhat lower standard for excuse based on unforeseen events. It provides that performance is excused if performance is made *commercially impracticable* by a contingency occurring after the formation of the contract, the nonoccurrence of which was a basic assumption of the contract. The *Restatement (Second) of Contracts* contains a similar provision. A basis for excuse that is closely related to impossibility and impracticability is the doctrine of commercial frustration or frustration of venture. When a promisor has contracted to obtain a specific objective, his performance can be excused if an event that occurs subsequent to the formation of the contract would cause that objective to be frustrated.

When a party is released from further duties under a contract, it is said that his duties are *discharged*. Contracts are generally discharged by performance. Duties are also discharged by the other party's material breach, nonoccurrence of a condition precedent (unless such a condition has been excused), occurrence of a condition subsequent, and impossibility or the related doctrines of impracticability or frustration. Discharge can also occur by mutual agreement, waiver, or the promisee's failure to comply with the statute of limitations.

A variety of remedies are available for compensating parties who have been injured by a breach of contract. Included among the possibilities are legal remedies (money damages), equitable remedies, and restitution. The remedies available for breach of contract seek to protect one or more distinct interests on the part of a promisee: the expectation interest, the reliance interest, and the restitution interest.

To recover damages in a contract case, the plaintiff must be able to prove his loss with reasonable certainty, and the loss must be one that was foreseeable to the breaching party at the time of contracting. When a contract has been breached, the injured party has the duty to take actions to mitigate, or decrease, the amount of damages that he might suffer. The objective in granting a remedy that protects a party's expectation interest is to place the injured party in the position in which he would have been if the contract had been performed as promised. Compensatory damages for breach of contract consist of the net value of the unfulfilled promise plus allowable consequential and incidental damages. Consequential damages are those that result from special circumstances of the injured party that are a direct result of the breach of contract. Incidental damages compensate for reasonable costs incurred by the plaintiff in attempting to avoid further loss. Courts sometimes use alternative damage remedies, such as permitting an injured party to recover money spent in reliance on the contract, when the normal measure of damages is inappropriate.

Nominal damages are damages in a very small amount that are awarded in cases in which there has been a technical breach of contract that has caused no actual loss. Sometimes, parties will include a term in their contract whereby they agree that damages in a specified sum will be due upon breach of contract. These provisions are called *liquidated damages provisions*. Courts will enforce liquidated damages provisions where the amount of damages specified is reasonable in light of the injured party's probable losses and where it would be difficult to assess the amount of damages. Where the amount of damages specified is unreasonably great in relation to probable losses or where damages would be easy to calculate, courts will refuse to enforce the liquidated damages provision on the ground that it constitutes a penalty. Punitive damages generally are not awarded in contracts cases unless the breaching party is guilty of fraud or some other independent tort (including tortious breach of the implied covenant of good faith and fair dealing). A few states will, however, impose punitive damages in contracts cases in which the breaching party has been guilty of oppressive or malicious conduct.

When damages remedies alone appear to be inadequate to fully compensate the injured party, courts will sometimes grant an equitable remedy. The two most common equitable remedies are specific performance and injunction. When specific performance is decreed, the breaching party is ordered to perform his duties under the contract. One limitation on specific performance is that it is used only when the subject of the contract is unique. Contracts for the sale of real property are the most frequent subjects of specific performance, because each tract of real property is considered to be unique. Specific performance is not given in cases concerning contracts for personal property unless the property is of a special, unique nature, such as antiques or works of art or is the type of property for which substitutes cannot be found. Specific performance is not granted in contracts for the performance of personal services. An injunction is an order to do a certain act (mandatory injunction) or to refrain from doing a certain act (negative injunction). They may be granted only when an act threatens to do irreparable harm to an injured party.

Restitution is a remedy that applies when a plaintiff has conferred a benefit on the defendant. It requires the defendant to return the benefit or to pay the plaintiff the value of the benefit. It is used in a variety of contracting situations involving a contract that has been partially performed but the remedy compensating for the party's expectation interest is either unavailable or undesirable.

PROBLEM CASES

1. Commercial Cotton maintained an essentially dormant non-interest-bearing commercial checking account at the United California Bank, with only two or three checks a month being written. The sole signatory on the account since 1972 had been Calvin, a practicing neurosurgeon who was Commercial Cotton's principal shareholder. In 1972, Calvin's wife reported to the bank the loss of a series of blank checks. She did not report the checks stolen because she thought they had only been inadvertently discarded. Four years later, one of the missing checks in the amount of $4,000 containing two unauthorized signatures was negligently paid by the bank. This showed up on Commercial Cotton's bank statement for September of 1976, but Calvin did not read the statement or discover the loss until March of 1978. He then promptly presented the faulty check to the branch manager of the bank. The bank admitted that it had erred but refused to reimburse Calvin. Even though a California Supreme Court case directly involving the bank as a defendant had held that a three-year statute of limitations applies when a bank has been negligent, the bank persisted in claiming that Calvin's claim was barred by a *one-year* statute of limitations. Commercial Cotton ultimately filed suit against the bank. Does it have a good claim for breach of the implied covenant of good faith and fair dealing?

2. Asphalt International chartered a tanker, the *Oswego Tarmac*, from Enterprise Shipping. The contract provided that Enterprise was obligated to maintain the vessel in good order but that it was absolved of responsibility for any loss or damage resulting from a collision and that, if the vessel should be lost, the contract would cease. While loading cargo alongside a pier, the *Oswego Tarmac* was rammed amidships by the bow of the motor vessel *Elektra* with such heavy impact that four of its tanks ruptured and heated asphalt spewed across the harbor. Expert appraisers estimated the cost of repair at not less than $1.5 million. The fair market value of the *Oswego Tarmac* prior to the collision was $750,000. Enterprise advised Asphalt International that the *Oswego Tarmac* was a complete loss. It refused Asphalt International's request to repair the vehicle. Asphalt International brought suit against Enterprise for breach of contract. Will it be successful?

3. Light contracted to build a house for the Mullers. After the job was completed, the Mullers refused to pay Light the balance they owed him under the contract, claiming that he had done some of the work in an un-

workmanlike manner. When Light sued for the money, the Mullers counterclaimed for $5,700 damages for delay under a liquidated damages clause in the contract. The clause provided that Light must pay $100 per day for every day of delay in completion of the construction. The evidence indicated that the rental value of the home was between $400 and $415 per month. Should the liquidated damages provision be enforced?

4. The Warrens hired Denison, a building contractor, to build a house on their property. They executed a written contract in which the Warrens agreed to pay $73,400 for the construction. Denison's construction deviated somewhat from the specifications for the project. These deviations were presumably unintentional, and the cost of repairing them was $1,961.50. The finished house had a market value somewhat higher than the market value would have been without the deviations. The Warrens failed to pay the $48,400 balance due under the contract, alleging that Denison had used poor workmanship in constructing the house and that they were under no obligation to perform further duties under the contract. Are they correct?

5. Forman made a written offer to buy real estate from Benson under terms whereby Forman would pay the purchase price over a 10-year period. Benson did not know Forman and was concerned about his creditworthiness, so Forman's real estate agent suggested a term stating that the contract was "subject to seller's approving buyer's credit report." This term was agreed to by both parties and was inserted in the contract before it was signed. Forman then gave Benson a credit report and a personal financial statement. Benson said that the report "looks real good" and that he would have his attorney review it and begin the title work on the property. Over the course of the next six weeks, however, Benson met with Forman three times. During these meetings, he attempted to negotiate for a higher purchase price and interest rate. He also requested more financial information. Finally, Benson informed Forman that he rejected Forman's credit rating. Forman brought suit to enforce the contract. Will he prevail?

6. Kim, a homeowner, entered into a contract with Kilianek, an experienced contractor, to add an additional room onto his home. The architectural work in designing the room was to be done by Park & Associates. One provision of the contract between Kim and Kilianek stated that "Final payment . . . shall be paid by the Owner to the Contractor when the work has been completed, the contract fully performed, and a final Certificate for Payment has been issued by the Architect."

Kim made periodic payments for a total of $14,100 toward the costs of construction. Although no final certificate for payment was issued by the architect, Kilianek demanded a final payment of $2,739. Is Kim obligated to make this payment?

7. In March of 1986, Bowling Green State University (BGSU) made a request for bids for carpet installation at Conklin West, a student housing facility at BGSU. This request contained a completion date of August 1, 1986. BGSU canceled this request for bids. On June 2, 1986, BGSU made another request for bids for the Conklin West project. This time, the request did not contain a completion date. Turner Brooks of Ohio, Inc. ("Turner Brooks"), submitted a bid (an offer) to perform the carpet installation on the Conklin West project. BGSU selected Turner Brooks and accepted its offer on June 20. Turner Brooks immediately placed an order for carpet to be installed at Conklin West. Customarily, the receipt of the carpet ordered occurs within six to eight weeks. In this case, Turner Brooks received the carpet five weeks after it ordered it, on July 29. Turner Brooks began the installation the very next day. During the installation, an abnormal floor surface that was not previously known to Turner Brooks caused some unforeseen labor. Turner Brooks completed the Conklin West project on or about August 22, 1986. BGSU claimed that Turner Brooks's performance was not timely and withheld more than $7,000 from the contract price as a setoff for custodial overtime purportedly incurred from Turner Brooks's alleged delay in completion. Did BGSU have the right to withhold this money?

8. Elmore Bean Warehouse contracted to buy pinto beans from a grower, Lawrance, at a fixed price. When the market price of beans dropped dramatically below the contract price, Elmore attempted to avoid paying the agreed price on the ground of commercial impracticability. Is this defense likely to be successful?

PROPERTY

CHAPTER 20

PERSONAL PROPERTY AND BAILMENTS

INTRODUCTION

The concept of property is crucial to the organization of society. The essential nature of a particular society is often reflected in the way it views property, including the degree to which property ownership is concentrated in the state, the extent it permits individual ownership of property, and the rules that govern such ownership. History is replete with wars and revolutions that arose out of conflicting claims to, or views concerning, property. Significant documents in our own Anglo-American legal tradition, such as the Magna Carta and the Constitution, deal explicitly with property rights.

This chapter will discuss the nature and classification of property. It will also examine the various ways that interests in personal property can be obtained and transferred, such as by production, purchase, or gift. The last half of the chapter explores the law of bailments. A bailment is involved, for example, when you check your coat in a coatroom at a restaurant or when you park your car in a public parking garage and leave your keys with the attendant.

NATURE OF PROPERTY

The word *property* is used in several distinct ways. The word sometimes is used to refers to *a thing that is capable of being owned*. It is also used to refer to *a right or interest* associated with a thing that gives the owner the ability to exercise dominion over that thing.

When we talk about ownership of property, we are talking about a *bundle of rights* that are recognized and enforced by the law. For example, ownership of a building includes the exclusive right to use, enjoy, sell, mortgage, or rent the building. If someone else tries to use the property without the owner's consent, the owner can use the courts and legal procedures to eject that person. Ownership of a patent includes the right to sell it, to license others to use it, or to produce the patented article personally.

In the United States, private ownership of property is protected by the Constitution, which provides that the government shall deprive no person of "life, liberty or property without due process of law." We recognize and encourage the rights of individuals to acquire, enjoy, and use property. These rights, however, are not unlimited. For example, a person cannot use property in an unreasonable manner to the injury of others. Also, the state has **police power** through which it can impose reasonable regulations on the use of property, tax it, and take it for public use by paying the owner compensation for it.

Property can be divided into a number of categories based on its characteristics. The same piece of property may fall into more than one class. The following discussion explores the meaning of **personal property** and the numerous ways of classifying property.

CLASSIFICATIONS OF PROPERTY

What Is Personal Property?—
Personal Property versus Real Property

Personal property is defined by process of exclusion. The term *personal property* is used in contrast to *real property*. Real property is the earth's crust and all things firmly attached to it.[1] For example, land, office buildings, and houses are all considered to be real property. All other objects and rights that can be owned are personal property. Clothing, books, bank accounts, and stock in a corporation are all examples of personal property.

Real property can be turned into personal property if it is detached from the earth. Similarly, personal property can be attached to the earth and become real property. For example, marble in the ground is real property. When the marble is quarried, it becomes personal property, but if it is used in constructing a building, it becomes real property again. Perennial vegetation that does not have to be seeded every year, such as trees, shrubs, and grass, is usually treated as part of the real property on which it is growing. When trees and shrubs are severed from the land, they become personal property. Crops that must be planted each year, such as corn, oats, and potatoes, are usually treated as personal property. However, if the real property on which they are growing is sold, the new owner of the real property also becomes the owner of the crops.

When personal property is attached to, or used in conjunction with, real property in such a way as to be treated as part of the real property, it is known as a **fixture.** The law concerning fixtures is discussed in the next chapter.

Tangible versus Intangible Personal Property

Personal property can be either *tangible* or *intangible*. Tangible property has a physical existence. Cars, animals, and computers are examples. Property that has no physical existence is called intangible property. For example, rights under a patent, copyright, or trademark would be intangible property.[2]

The distinction between tangible and intangible property is important primarily for tax and estate planning purposes. Generally, tangible property is subject to tax in the state in which it is located, whereas intangible property is usually taxable in the state where its owner lives.

Public and Private Property

Property is also classified as public or private based on the ownership of the property. If the property is owned by the government or a governmental unit, it is classified as public property. If it is owned by an individual, a group of individuals, a corporation, or some other business organization, it is private property.

ACQUIRING OWNERSHIP OF PERSONAL PROPERTY

Production or Purchase

The most common ways of obtaining ownership of property are by producing it or purchasing it. A person owns the property that he makes unless the person has agreed to do the work for someone else. In that case, the employer is the owner of the product of the work. For example, a person who creates a painting, knits a sweater, or develops a computer program is the owner unless he has been hired by someone to do the painting, knit the sweater, or develop the program. Another major way of acquiring property is by purchase. The law regarding the purchase of tangible personal property (that is, sale of goods) is discussed in the Formation and Terms of Sales Contracts chapter.

---

[1] The law of real property is treated in the Real Property and Insurance chapter.

[2] These important types of intangible property are discussed in the Intellectual Property, Competitive Torts, and Unfair Competition chapter.

Possession of Unowned Property

In very early times, the most common way of obtaining ownership of personal property was simply by *taking possession* of unowned property. For example, the first person to take possession of a wild animal became its owner. Today, one can still acquire ownership of personal property by possessing it *if the property is unowned*. The two major examples of unowned property that can be acquired by possession are *wild animals* and *abandoned property*. Abandoned property will be discussed in the next section, which focuses on the rights of finders.

The first person to take possession of a wild animal property normally becomes the owner.[3] To acquire ownership of a wild animal by taking possession, a person must obtain enough control over it to deprive it of its freedom. If a person fatally wounds a wild animal, the person becomes the owner. Wild animals caught in a trap or fish caught in a net are usually considered to be the property of the person who set the trap or net. If a captured wild animal escapes and is caught by another person, that person generally becomes the owner. However, if that person knows that the animal is an escaped animal and that the prior owner is chasing it to recapture it, then he does not become the owner.

RIGHTS OF FINDERS OF LOST, MISLAID, AND ABANDONED PROPERTY

The old saying "finders keepers, losers weepers" is *not* a reliable way of predicting the legal rights of those who find personal property that originally belonged—or still belongs—to another. The rights of the finder will be determined by whether the property he finds is classified as *abandoned*, *lost*, or *mislaid*.

1. *Abandoned property.* Property is considered to be *abandoned* if the owner intentionally placed the property out of his possession with the intent to relinquish ownership of it. For example, Norris takes his TV set to the city dump and leaves it there. The finder of abandoned property who takes possession of abandoned property with intent to claim ownership becomes the owner of the property. This means he acquires better rights to the property than anyone else in the world,

including the original owner. For example, if Fox finds the TV set, puts it in his car, and takes it home, Fox becomes the owner of the TV set.

2. *Lost property.* Property is considered to be *lost* when the owner did not intend to part with possession of the property. For example, if Barber's camera fell out of her handbag while she was walking down the street, it would be considered lost property. The person who finds lost property does not acquire ownership of it, but he acquires better rights to the lost property than anyone other than the true owner. For example, suppose Lawrence finds Barber's camera in the grass where it fell. Jones then steals the camera from Lawrence's house. Under these facts, Barber is still the owner of the camera. She has the right to have it returned to her if she discovers where it is—or if Lawrence knows that it belongs to Barber. As the finder of lost property, though, Lawrence has a better right to the camera than anyone else except Barber. This means that Lawrence has the right to require Jones to return it to him if he finds out that Jones has it.

If the finder does not know who the true owner is or cannot easily find out, the finder must still return the property if the real owner shows up and asks for the property. If the finder of lost property knows who the owner is and refuses to return it, the finder is guilty of conversion and must pay the owner the fair value of the property.[4]

A finder who sells the property that he has found can only pass to the purchaser those rights that he has; he cannot pass any better title to the property than he himself has. Thus, the true owner could recover the property from the purchaser.

3. *Mislaid property.* Property is considered to be mislaid if the owner intentionally placed the property somewhere and accidentally left it there, not intending to relinquish ownership of the property. For example, Fields places her backpack on a coatrack at Campus Bookstore while shopping for textbooks. Forgetting the backpack, Fields leaves the store and goes home. The backpack would be considered to be mislaid rather than lost because Fields intentionally and voluntarily placed it on the coatrack. The consequences of property being classified as mislaid are that the finder acquires no rights to the property. Rather, the person in possession of the real property on which the personal property was mislaid has the right to hold the property for the true owner

---

[3]As wildlife is increasingly protected by law, however, some wild animals cannot be owned because it is illegal to capture them (e.g., endangered species).

[4]The tort of conversion is discussed in the Intentional Torts chapter.

and has better rights to the property than anyone other than the true owner. For example, if Stevens found Fields's backpack in Campus Bookstore, Campus Bookstore would have the right to hold the mislaid property for Fields. Stevens would acquire neither possession nor ownership of the backpack.

The rationale for this rule is that it increases the chances that the property will be returned to its real owner. A person who knowingly placed the property somewhere but forgot to pick it up might well remember later where she left the property and return for it.

Some states have a statute that allows finders of property to clear their title to the property. The statutes generally provide that the person must give public notice of the fact that the property has been found, perhaps by putting an ad in a local newspaper. All states have **statutes of limitations** that require the true owner of property to claim it or bring a legal action to recover possession of it within a certain number of years. A person who keeps possession of lost or unclaimed property for longer than that period of time will become its owner.

The following case, *Michael v. First Chicago Corporation,* presents an example of a conflict between a finder and an original owner over rights to personal property.

MICHAEL v. FIRST CHICAGO CORPORATION

487 N.E.2d 403 (Ill. Ct. App. 1986)

First National Bank of Chicago (First Chicago) sold a number of used file cabinets on an "as is" basis to Zibton, a new and secondhand office supply and furniture dealer. Zibton had bought used furniture from First Chicago before. On this and previous occasions, Zibton bought the used furniture as a group even if some pieces were damaged or locked.

In the summer of 1983, Zibton sold some of these cabinets to Charles Strayve. Strayve gave one of the cabinets, a locked one with no keys, to his friend, Richard Michael. About six weeks later, Michael was moving the file cabinet in his garage when it fell over and several of the locked drawers opened. Inside were more than 1,600 certificates of deposit (CDs), including seven that had not been canceled or stamped paid and that were worth a total of $6,687,948.85, with maturity dates ranging from October 1982 to January 1983. Six of the CDs were payable to "Bearer."

First Chicago had placed the CDs in the cabinet between March and May of 1983, when the responsibility for storing paid CDs was changed to a different unit of the bank. The CDs were moved from a vault to file cabinets at that time. Each drawer had been labeled with a card stating "Paid Negotiable CDs" and indicating the numbers of the CDs contained in the drawer. The new unit responsible for storing CDs determined that they could not use the file cabinets, so the CDs were transferred to tote boxes. First Chicago employees randomly checked to determine if the contents were gone and then transferred the file cabinets to the warehouse for sale.

Michael called the FBI, which took possession of all of the CDs. Michael and his wife then filed this declaratory judgment to determine who owned the CDs. The trial court ruled in favor of First Chicago, and the Michaels appealed.

Reinhard, Justice. The Michaels' primary argument is that they were entitled to possession of the CDs because the certificates were the subject of a sale from First Chicago. They maintain that First Chicago's actions in the handling and sale of the CDs showed an objective intent to transfer the certificates along with the used file cabinets in which the documents were stored.

Here, First Chicago was selling only used furniture to Zibton. Neither First Chicago nor Zibton suspected that CDs or any other type of valuable had been left in the file cabinet. The evidence clearly shows that the intention of the parties was for First Chicago to sell used furniture only, and Zibton was not speculating that other valuable items might be contained in the used furniture.

Where both buyer and seller were ignorant of the existence or presence of the concealed valuable, and the contract was not broad enough to indicate an intent to convey all the contents, known or unknown, the courts have generally held that as between the owner and purchaser, title to the hidden article did not pass by the sale. The evidence here is that used office furniture was being sold, and the possibility that something valuable might be in any of the used furniture had nothing to do with the sale. The fact that the sale of the used furniture was "as is" indicates the furniture was sold in its present condition, damaged or otherwise, and does not show an intent to sell the contents of the used furniture. Accordingly, the evidence does not support the Michaels' contention that the CDs as contents of the used furniture were intended by either party to the sale to be sold along with the furniture.

The Michaels' alternative contention is that the CDs are abandoned property, rather than lost or mislaid property, which the finder is entitled to keep. Mislaid property is that which is intentionally put in a certain place and later forgotten; property is lost when it is unintentionally separated from the dominion of its owner; and property is abandoned when the owner, intending to relinquish all rights to the property, leaves it free to be appropriated by any other person. A finder of property acquires no rights in mislaid property, is entitled to possession of lost property against everyone except the true owner, and is entitled to keep abandoned property.

For the purposes of this appeal, we need only determine whether the CDs are abandoned property. If otherwise, the owner is entitled to possession. Abandonment is generally defined as an intentional relinquishment of a known right. As a general rule, abandonment is not presumed and the party seeking to declare an abandonment must prove the abandoning party intended to do so.

The Michaels basically argue that the CDs were abandoned as shown by evidence that they were intentionally placed in the cabinets, they were not forgotten, and the cabinets were sold with no reservations. We disagree. It is readily apparent from the evidence that the CDs were to be transferred to other storage and some simply were overlooked and left in the file cabinets. The relinquishment of possession, under the circumstances here, without a showing of an intention to permanently give up all right to the CDs is not enough to show abandonment.

Judgment for First Chicago affirmed.

CONCEPT REVIEW

RIGHTS OF FINDERS OF PERSONAL PROPERTY

Character of Property	Description	Rights of Finder	Rights of Original Owner
Lost	Owner unintentionally parted with possession	Rights superior to everyone except the owner	Retains ownership; has the right to the return of the property
Mislaid	Owner intentionally put property in a place but unintentionally left it there	None; person in possession of real property on which mislaid property was found holds it for the owner, and has rights superior to everyone except owner	Retains ownership; has the right to the return of the property
Abandoned	Owner intentionally placed property out of his possession with intent to relinquish ownership of it	Finder who takes possession with intent to claim ownership acquires ownership of property	None

Leasing

A lease of personal property is a transfer of the right to possess and use personal property belonging to another.[5] Although the rights of one who leases personal property (a **lessee**) do not constitute ownership of personal property, leasing is mentioned here because it is becoming an increasingly important way of acquiring the use of many kinds of personal property, from automobiles to farm equipment.

In most states, Article 2 and Article 9 of the UCC are applied to personal property leases by analogy. However, rules contained in these articles sometimes are inadequate to resolve special problems presented by leasing. For this reason, a new article of the UCC dealing exclusively with leases of goods, Article 2A, was written in 1987. Article 2A has been presented to state legislatures for possible adoption, but only six states have adopted Article 2A as of the time of this writing.

Gifts

Title to personal property can be obtained by gift. A gift is a voluntary transfer of property to the **donee** (the person who receives a gift), for which the **donor** (the person who gives the gift) gets no consideration in return. To have a valid gift, the following elements are necessary:

1. The donor must intend to make a gift,
2. The donor must make delivery of the gift, and
3. The donee must accept the gift.

The most critical requirement is delivery. The person who makes the gift must actually give up possession and control of the property either to the donee or to a third person to hold it for the donee. Delivery is important because it makes clear to the donor that he is voluntarily giving up ownership without getting something in exchange. A promise to make a gift is usually not enforceable;[6] the person must actually part with the property. In some cases, the delivery may be *symbolic* or *constructive*. For example, handing over the key to a strongbox can be symbolic delivery of the property in the strongbox.

There are two kinds of gifts: gifts *inter vivos* and gifts *causa mortis*. A gift *inter vivos* is a gift between two living persons. For example, when Tweedle's parents give her a car for her 21st birthday, that is a gift *inter vivos*. A gift *causa mortis* is a gift made in contemplation of death. For example, Uncle John, who is about to undergo a serious heart operation, gives his watch to his nephew, Sam, and tells Sam that he wants him to have it if he does not survive the operation. A gift *causa mortis* is a *conditional* gift. A gift *causa mortis* is effective *unless any of the following occurs:*

1. The donor recovers from the peril or sickness under fear of which the gift was made, or
2. The donor revokes or withdraws the gift before he dies, or
3. The donee dies before the donor.

If one of these events takes place, ownership of the property goes back to the donor.

The elements of a valid gift, as well as the difference between an *inter vivos* gift and a gift *causa mortis,* are discussed in the *Welton v. Gallagher* case, which follows.

---

[5]A lease of personal property is a form of bailment, a "bailment for hire." Bailments are discussed later in this chapter.

[6]This idea is discussed in the Consideration chapter.

WELTON v. GALLAGHER

630 P.2d 1077 (Hawaii Ct. App. 1981)

In October 1973, Richard Welton, a businessman in his late 60s, met Florence Gallagher, a widow in her late 40s. Welton subsequently underwent several operations for cancer. After he was released from the hospital, Gallagher devoted much time and attention to him. In 1975, she helped him operate an ice cream business that he had purchased. Shortly thereafter, he moved into her house and spent considerable money fixing it up. Welton subsequently moved out to live with Gallagher's niece, Sandra Kwock, a woman in her 20s, who agreed to take care of him for the rest of his life in return for his giving her $25,000 in bearer bonds. Kwock left town with the bonds, much to Welton's dismay. In April 1976, Welton moved back in with Gallagher, gave her $20,000 in bearer bonds, and told her to place them in her safe-deposit box. Gallagher said that he told her he wanted her to have them as a gift because she was much more deserving than her niece. Later in 1976, Welton and Gallagher ended their relationship and he moved out of her house. He also demanded that she return the bonds, but she refused.

Welton filed suit against Gallagher seeking return of the bonds. The trial court held that Welton had made a completed *inter vivos* gift of the bonds. Welton appealed.

Burns, Judge. Mr. Welton asserts that Mrs. Gallagher has failed to prove the elements of gift. For a transaction to amount to a gift, it must appear that there was a sufficient delivery of the property, an acceptance of the property, and an intention to make a gift.

Delivery is not a complex matter. As the Hawaii Supreme Court stated in *Siko v. Sequirant,* "[a] donor must divest himself of control of the gift for delivery to be complete." In other words, the donor must do acts sufficient to strip himself of dominion and control over the property. Here, Mr. Welton gave Mrs. Gallagher bearer bonds, bonds which by definition are redeemable by whosoever holds them. She testified that he told her he was giving her the bonds with no strings attached and that she should place the bonds in her own safe-deposit box, a box to which he had no rights of entry. Clearly he ceased to have any control over the bonds and can be deemed therefore to have delivered them to Mrs. Gallagher.

The matter of acceptance is likewise fairly straightforward. The exercise by the donee of dominion over the subject of the gift or an assertion of a right thereto is generally held to be evidence of acceptance; and where the gift is beneficial to the donee and imposes no burdens upon her, acceptance is presumed. Here, Mrs. Gallagher exercised dominion over the bonds by placing them in her safe-deposit box. She has always maintained they belong to her; certainly they benefit and do not burden her. Therefore, acceptance is presumed.

The final element necessary for a finding of a valid gift is donative intent. The most difficult element to establish a completed gift is the donative intent of the donor. Whether such an intent exists is addressed to the perception of the trial court. The existence or absence of intent to make a gift is an evidentiary issue to be resolved by the finder of fact. His resolution of that issue will not be overturned on appeal if his finding is supported by substantial evidence.

The trial court did base its finding of donative intent on substantial evidence: Mr. Welton was very fond of Mrs. Gallagher; he had made substantial gifts to her in the past. He was particularly grateful to her for taking him back after his misadventure with Sandra Kwock. He was an experienced businessman and was fully aware of the consequences of relinquishing all control over bearer bonds. He did not demand that the bonds be placed in a joint account or depository; he did not convey any written instructions or reservation of authority when he gave the bonds to Mrs. Gallagher. Because all the elements of a valid gift are present, we hold that there was no error in the finding of the lower court that such a gift was made.

Mr. Welton's alternative theory on this appeal is that even though a valid gift was made, it was a gift *causa mortis* and, therefore, revocable. The elements of a gift *causa mortis* are these: (1) The gift must be made in view of approaching death from some existing sickness or peril; (2) the donor must die from such sickness or peril without having revoked the gift; (3) there must be a delivery of the subject of the gift to the donee, subject, however, to revocation in the event of recovery from the pending sickness. The vital, although not the only difference between a gift *causa mortis* and one *inter vivos* is that the former may be revoked by the donor if he survives the pending sickness or peril, and does not pass an irrevocable title until the death of the donor, while a gift *inter vivos* is irrevocable and vests an immediate title. In this case, although Mr. Welton had undergone cancer surgery in 1973, there is no indication in the testimony that in April of 1976 he felt himself to be in immediate peril. Indeed his own statements regarding starting a new business and his active social life strongly indicate that he was not preeminently occupied in contemplating the transience of life and the prospect of his own imminent departure therefrom. The trial court was correct in finding that the gift was *inter vivos*.

Judgment for Gallagher affirmed.

Conditional Gifts   Sometimes, a gift is made on condition that the donee comply with certain restrictions or perform certain actions. A conditional gift is not a completed gift, and it may be revoked by the donor before the donee complies with the conditions. Gifts in contemplation of marriage, such as engagement rings, are the primary example of a conditional gift. Such gifts are generally considered to have been made on an implied condition that marriage between the donor and donee take place. If the donee breaks the engagement without legal justification or if the engagement is broken by mutual consent, the donor will be able to recover the ring or other engagement gift. However, if the engagement is unjustifiably broken by the donor, he or she is generally not entitled to recover gifts made in contemplation of marriage. These rules are not uniformly applied in all states, however. Some states have enacted legislation prescribing the rules applicable to the return of engagement presents.

Uniform Transfers to Minors Act   The Uniform Transfers to Minors Act, which has been adopted in one form or another in every state, provides a fairly simple and flexible method for making gifts and other transfers of property to minors.[7] As defined in this act, a minor is anyone under the age of 21. Under the act, an adult may transfer money, securities, real property, insurance policies, and other property. The specific ways of doing this vary according to the type of property transferred. In general, however, the transferor (the person who gives or otherwise transfers the property) delivers, pays, or assigns the property to, or registers the property with, a custodian who acts for the benefit of the minor "under the Uniform Transfers to Minors Act." The custodian is given fairly broad discretion to use the gift for the mi-

nor's benefit and may not use it for the custodian's personal benefit. The custodian may be the transferor himself, another adult, or a trust company, depending again on the type of property transferred. If the donor or other transferor fully complies with the Uniform Transfers to Minors Act, the transfer is considered to be irrevocable.

Will or Inheritance

Ownership of personal property can also be transferred upon the death of the former owner. The property may pass under the terms of a will if the will was validly executed. If there is no valid will, the property is transferred to the heirs of the owner according to state laws. Transfer of property at the death of the owner will be discussed in the Estates and Trusts chapter.

Confusion

Title to personal property can be obtained by **confusion.** Confusion is the intermixing of goods that belong to different owners in such a way that they cannot later be separated. For example, suppose wheat belonging to several different people is mixed in a grain elevator. If the mixing was by agreement or if it resulted from an accident without negligence on anyone's part, each person owns his proportionate share of the entire quantity of wheat. However, a different result would be reached if the wheat was wrongfully or negligently mixed. Suppose a thief steals a truckload of Grade #1 wheat worth $8.50 a bushel from a farmer. The thief dumps the wheat into his storage bin, which contains a lower-grade wheat worth $4.50 a bushel, with the result that the mixture is worth only $4.50 a bushel. The farmer has first claim against the entire mixture to recover the value of his wheat that was mixed in. The thief, or any other person whose intentional or negligent act results in confusion of goods, must bear any loss caused by the confusion.

---

[7]This statute was formerly called, and is still called in some states, the Uniform Gift to Minors Act.

Accession

Ownership of personal property can also be acquired by **accession.** Accession means increasing the value of property by adding materials or labor, or both. As a general rule, the owner of the original property becomes the owner of the improvements. This is particularly likely to be true if the improvement was done with the permission of the owner. For example, Hudson takes his automobile to a shop that replaces the engine with a larger engine and puts in a new four-speed transmission. Hudson is still the owner of the automobile as well as the owner of the parts added by the auto shop.

Problems can arise if materials are added or work is performed on personal property without the consent of the owner. If property is stolen from one person and improved by the thief, the original owner can get it back and does not have to reimburse the thief for the work done or the materials used in improving it. For example, a thief steals Rourke's used car, puts a new engine in it, replaces the tires, and repairs the muffler. Rourke is entitled to get his car back from the thief and does not have to pay him for the engine, tires, or muffler.

The result is less easy to predict, however, if property is mistakenly improved *in good faith* by someone who believes that he is the owner of the property. In such a case, a court must weigh the respective interests of two *innocent* parties: the original owner and the improver. For example, Johnson, a stonecarver, finds a block of limestone by the side of the road and, assuming that it has been abandoned, takes it home and carves it into a sculpture. In fact, the block was owned by Hayes and, having fallen off a flatbed truck during transportation, is merely lost property, which Hayes ordinarily could recover from the finder. In a case such as this, a court could decide the case in one of two ways. The first alternative would be to give the original owner (Hayes) ownership of the improved property, but to allow the person who has improved the property in good faith (Johnson) to recover the cost of the improvements. The second alternative would be to hold that the improver, Johnson, has acquired ownership of the sculpture, but that he is required to pay the original owner the value of the property as of the time he obtained it. The greater the extent to which the improvements have increased the value of the property, the more likely it is that the court will choose the second alternative and permit the improver to acquire ownership of the improved property.

BAILMENTS

Nature of Bailments

A **bailment** is the delivery of personal property by its owner or one who has the right to possess it (the **bailor**) to another person (the **bailee**) who accepts it and is under an express or implied agreement to return it to the bailor or to someone designated by the bailor. Only personal property can be the subject of bailments.

Although the legal terminology used to describe bailments might be unfamiliar to most people, everyone is familiar with transactions that constitute bailments. For example, Lincoln takes his car to a parking garage where the attendant gives Lincoln a claim check and then drives the car down the ramp to park it. Charles borrows his neighbor's lawn mower to cut his grass. Carne, who lives next door to Axe, agrees to take care of Axe's cat while Axe goes on a vacation. These are just a few of the everyday situations that involve bailments. The case of *York v. Jones,* which follows, involves a bailment that is much more unusual, but nevertheless illustrates the essential characteristics of a bailment.

YORK v. JONES

717 F. Supp. 421 (E.D. Va. 1989)

Steven York and Risa Adler-York contacted the Jones Institute for Reproductive Medicine to determine if they were viable candidates for in vitro fertilization (IVF). This process involves removing one or more oocytes or eggs from the woman's body, fertilizing those eggs in vitro (outside of the womb) with the husband's sperm, and then depositing the developing masses into the woman's uterus. The Yorks were accepted into the Jones Institute's IVF program. In May of 1987, the

Yorks signed a Cryopreservation Agreement outlining the procedure for cryopreservation or freezing of pre-zygotes and detailing the Yorks' rights in the frozen pre-zygote. The agreement explained that the cryopreservation procedure is available if more than five pre-zygotes are retrieved during the IVF treatment, so that the possibility for multiple births could be reduced while maintaining optimal chances for pregnancy. The agreement also provided in part:

We may withdraw our consent and discontinue participation at any time . . . and we understand our pre-zygotes will be stored only as long as we are active IVF patients at . . . Jones Institute. . . . We have the principal responsibility to decide the disposition of our pre-zygotes. Our frozen pre-zygotes will not be released from storage for the purposee of intrauterine transfer without the written consent of us both. In the event of divorce, we understand legal ownership of any stored pre-zygotes must be determined in a property settlement. . . . Should we for any reason no longer wish to attempt to initiate a pregnancy, we understand we may choose one of three fates for our pre-zygotes that remain in frozen storage. *Our pre-zygotes may be: 1) donated to another infertile couple. . . . 2) donated for approved research investigation 3) thawed but not allowed to undergo further development.*

The Yorks underwent IVF treatment on four occasions. Six eggs were removed from Mrs. York and fertilized with her husband's sperm, creating six embryos. Five of these embryos were transferred to Mrs. York's uterus, and the remaining embryo was cryogenically preserved in accordance with the procedures outlined in the Cryopreservation Agreement. None of the in vitro fertilization attempts resulted in pregnancy.

During the course of treatment, the Yorks moved to California. They sought to have the remaining frozen pre-zygote transferred from the Jones Institute in Norfolk, Virginia, to the Institute for Reproductive Research in Los Angeles, where the Yorks planned to attempt in vitro fertilization again. The Yorks arranged for proper transportation and handling of the pre-zygote, but the Jones Institute refused to allow such a transfer.

The Yorks brought suit against the Jones Institute and its physicians, claiming that its continued dominion and control over the pre-zygote was contrary to law and the parties' agreement. The Jones Institute filed a motion to dismiss, alleging that the Yorks' complaint did not state a claim on which relief could be granted. This is the trial court's ruling on that motion.

Clarke, Jr., United States District Judge.

The Yorks' complaint in this case raises an issue of first impression in the rapidly developing field of human reproductive technology. The Jones Institute argues that the Yorks' proprietary rights in the pre-zygote are limited to the "three fates" enumerated in the [Cryopreservation Agreement] because there is no established protocol for the inter-institutional transfer of pre-zygotes.

The court begins its analysis by noting that the Cryopreservation Agreement created a bailor-bailee relationship between the Yorks and Jones Institute. While the parties in this case expressed no intent to create a bailment, under Virginia law, no formal contract or actual meeting of the minds is necessary. Rather, all that is needed is the element of lawful possession however created, and duty to account for the thing as the property of another that creates the bailment. The essential nature of a bailment relationship imposes on the bailee, when the purpose of the bailment has terminated, an absolute obligation to return the subject matter of the bailment to the bailor. The obligation to return the property is implied from the fact of lawful possession of the personal property of another.

In the instant case, the requisite elements of a bailment relationship are present. The Jones Institute consistently refers to the pre-zygote as the "property" of the Yorks. Although the Cryopreservation Agreement constitutes a bailment contract, the Agreement is nevertheless governed by the same principles as apply to other contracts.

The Cryopreservation Agreement should be more strictly construed against the Jones Institute, the parties who drafted the Agreement. The Jones Institute has defined the extent of its possession interest as bailee of the pre-zygote by the following provision of the Agreement: "We may withdraw our consent and discontinue participation at any time . . . and . . . our pre-zygote will be stored only as long as we are active IVF patients at the [Jones Institute.]" The Jones Institute has further defined the limits of its possessory interest by recognizing the Yorks' proprietary rights in the pre-zygote. The Agreement repeatedly refers to "our pre-zygote" and further provides that the Yorks have the "principal responsibility to decide the disposition" of the pre-zygote.

The Jones Institute takes the position that the plain language of the Cryopreservation Agreement limits the Yorks' proprietary right to the pre-zygote to the "three fates" listed in the Agreement. The Court finds, however, that the applicability of the three fates is limited by the following language, "Should we for any reason no longer wish to initiate a pregnancy, we understand we may chose one of three fates for our pre-zygotes. . . ." The allegations of the Yorks' complaint and the entire thrust of this litigation suggest that the Yorks continue to desire to achieve pregnancy. The Agreement does not state that the attempt to initiate a pregnancy is restricted to procedures employed at the Jones Institute. The "three fates" are therefore inapplicable to the case at bar. For the reasons stated, the Court finds that the Yorks' complaint states a claim upon which relief can be granted.

Motion to dismiss denied in favor of the Yorks.

Elements of a Bailment

The essential elements of a bailment are as follows:

1. The bailor must own or have the right to possess the property,
2. The bailor must deliver exclusive possession of and control over the property to the bailee, and
3. The bailee must knowingly accept the property with the understanding that he owes a duty to return the property as directed by the bailor.

Creation of a Bailment

A bailment is created by an express or implied contract. Whether the elements of a bailment have been fulfilled is determined by examining all the facts and circumstances of the particular situation. For example, a patron goes into a restaurant and hangs her hat and coat on an unattended rack. It is unlikely that this created a bailment, because the restaurant owner never assumed exclusive control over the hat and coat. However, if there is a checkroom and the hat and coat are checked with the attendant, a bailment will arise. If a customer parks his car in a parking lot, keeps the keys, and can drive the car out himself whenever he wishes, a bailment has not been created. The courts treat this situation as a lease of space. Suppose he takes his car to a parking garage where an attendant gives him a claim check and then the attendant parks the car. There is a bailment of the car because the parking garage has accepted delivery and possession of the car. However, a distinction is made between the car and some packages locked in the trunk. If the parking garage was not aware of the packages, it would probably not be a bailee of them as it did not knowingly accept possession of them.

The creation of a bailment is illustrated in Figure 1.

Types of Bailments

Bailments are commonly divided into three different categories:

1. Bailments for the sole benefit of the bailor.
2. Bailments for the sole benefit of the bailee.
3. Bailments for mutual benefit.

The type of bailment involved in a case can be important in determining the liability of the bailee for loss of or damages to the property. As will be discussed later, however, some courts no longer rely on these distinctions for this purpose.

Bailments for Benefit of Bailor   A bailment for the sole benefit of the bailor is one in which the bailee renders some service but does not receive a benefit in return. For example, Brown allows his neighbor, Reston, to park her car in Brown's garage while she is on vacation and Brown does not ask for any compensation. Here, Reston, the bailor, has received a benefit from the bailee, Brown, but Brown has not received a benefit in return.

FIGURE 1   Creation of a Bailment

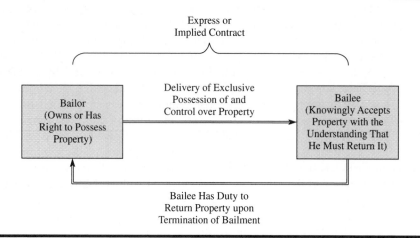

Express or
Implied Contract

Bailor
(Owns or Has
Right to Possess
Property)

Delivery of Exclusive
Possession of and
Control over Property

Bailee
(Knowingly Accepts
Property with the
Understanding That
He Must Return It)

Bailee Has Duty to
Return Property upon
Termination of Bailment

Bailments for Benefit of Bailee   A bailment for the sole benefit of the bailee is one in which the owner of the goods allows someone else to use them free of charge. For example, Anderson lends a lawn mower to her neighbor, Moss, so he can cut his grass.

Bailments for Mutual Benefit   If both the bailee and the bailor receive benefits from the bailment, it is a bailment for mutual benefit. For example, Sutton rents china for his daughter's wedding from E-Z Party Supplies for an agreed-on price. Sutton, the bailee, benefits by being able to use the china, while E-Z benefits from his payment of the rental charge. On some occasions, the benefit to the bailee is less tangible. For example, a customer checks a coat at an attended coatroom at a restaurant. Even if no charge is made for the service, it is likely to be treated as a bailment for mutual benefit because the restaurant is benefiting from the customer's patronage.

Special Bailments

Certain kinds of professional bailees, such as innkeepers and common carriers, are treated somewhat differently by the law and are held to a higher level of responsibility than is the ordinary bailee. The rules applicable to common carriers and innkeepers are detailed later in this chapter.

Duties of the Bailee

The bailee has two basic duties:

1. To take care of the property that has been entrusted to him.

2. To return the property at the termination of the bailment.

The following discussion examines the scope of these duties.

Duty of Bailee to Take Care of Property

The bailee is responsible for taking steps to protect the property during the time he has possession of it. If the bailee does not exercise proper care and the property is lost or damaged, the bailee is liable for negligence. The bailee would then be required to reimburse the bailor for the amount of loss or damage. If the property is lost or damaged without the fault or negligence of the bailee, however, the bailee is not liable to the bailor.

The degree of care required of the bailee traditionally has depended in large part on the type of bailment involved—that is, which party or parties are benefiting from the bailment.

1. *Bailment for the benefit of the bailor.* If the bailment is solely for the benefit of the bailor, the bailee is expected to exercise only a minimal, or slight, degree of care for the protection of the bailed property. He would be liable, then, only if he were grossly negligent in his care of the bailed property. The rationale for this is that if the bailee is doing the bailor a favor, it is not reasonable to expect him to be as careful as when he is deriving some benefit from keeping the goods.

2. *Bailment for mutual benefit.* Where the bailment is a bailment for mutual benefit, the bailee is expected to exercise ordinary or reasonable care. This degree of care requires the bailee to use the same kind of care a reasonable person would use to protect his own property in that situation. If the bailee is a professional that holds itself out as a professional bailee, such as a warehouse, it must use the degree of care that would be used by a person in that profession. This is likely to be more care than the ordinary person would use. In addition, there is usually a duty on a professional bailee to explain any loss or damage to property, that is, to show it was not negligent. If it cannot do so, it will be liable to the bailor.

3. *Bailment for the benefit of the bailee.* If the bailment is solely for the benefit of the bailee, the bailee is expected to exercise a high degree of care. A person who lends a sailboat to a neighbor would probably expect the neighbor to be even more careful with the sailboat than the owner might be, for example. In such a case, the bailee would be liable for damage to the property if he committed a relatively small degree of negligence.

A number of courts today view the type of bailment involved in a case as just one factor to be considered in determining whether the bailee should be liable for loss or damage to bailed goods. The modern trend appears to be moving in the direction of imposing a duty of reasonable care on bailees, regardless of the type of bailment. This flexible standard of care permits courts to take into account a variety of factors such as the nature and value of the property, the provisions of the parties' agreement, the payment of consideration for the bailment, and the experience of the bailee. In addition, the bailee is required to use the property only as was agreed between the parties. For example, Jones borrows Morrow's lawn mower to mow his lawn. If Jones uses the mower to cut the weeds on a trash-filled vacant lot and the mower is damaged, he would be liable because he was exceeding the agreed purpose of the bailment—to cut his lawn.

Bailee's Duty to Return the Property

One of the essential elements of a bailment is the duty of the bailee to return the property at the termination of the bailment. If the bailed property is taken from the bailee by legal process, the bailee should notify the bailor and must take whatever action is necessary to protect the bailor's interest. In most instances, the bailee must return the identical property that was bailed. A person who lends a 1985 Volkswagen Rabbit to a friend expects to have that particular car returned. In some cases, the bailor does not expect the return of the identical goods. For example, a farmer who stores 1,500 bushels of Grade #1 wheat at a local grain elevator expects to get back 1,500 bushels of Grade #1 wheat when the bailment is terminated, but not the identical wheat he deposited.

The bailee must return the goods in an undamaged condition to the bailor or to someone designated by the bailor. If the goods have been damaged, destroyed, or lost, there is a rebuttable presumption of negligence on the part of the bailee. To overcome the presumption, the bailee must come forward with evidence showing that the accident, damage, or loss resulted from some cause consistent with the exercise of the relevant level of due care on his part. The operation of the rebuttable presumption can be seen in the *Magee v. Walbro* case, which follows. If the property is lost or damaged without the fault or negligence of the bailee, however, the bailee is not liable to the bailor.

MAGEE v. WALBRO, INC.

525 N.E.2d 975 (Ill. Ct. App. 1988)

Walbro, Inc., doing business as Mysel Furs, was in the business of storing furs. It had arranged for United Parcel Service (UPS) to pick up furs from its customers and deliver them to Mysel's. In May 1982, Mysel's solicited Crella Magee's business to store her furs for the summer, and Magee agreed. Pursuant to an arrangement with Mysel's to pick up three furs from Magee, UPS delivered three empty boxes labeled with unique call numbers to Magee on May 25. Magee inserted a fur in each of the boxes, and UPS then picked up the three boxes, giving Magee's husband three tickets bearing call numbers identical to those marked on the boxes. UPS delivered the boxes to

Mysel's on May 26. A Mysel's employee signed for the boxes, but did not check to be sure that none of the boxes was empty. In July, Mysel's issued a storage receipt to Magee that showed only two furs. This storage receipt also contained a term that limited Mysel's liability for lost property to $100. Magee called Mysel's immediately and received assurances that the three furs were in storage. When Magee went to pick up her three furs in October of 1982, however, one of them—a blue fox jacket worth $3,400—was missing. Mysel's did not compensate Magee, arguing that its liability for lost articles was limited to $100. Magee then brought suit against Walbro, Mysel's, and UPS for breach of bailment and conversion. The trial court ruled for the defendants, and Magee appealed. (Magee voluntarily dismissed her case against UPS, so its liability is not involved in this appeal.)

O'Connor, Justice.   Establishing a *prima facie* case of bailment raises a presumption of negligence by the defendant, which the defendant must rebut with evidence sufficient to support a finding of the nonexistence of the presumed fact. The trial court ruled that the evidence established a bailment between Magee and Walbro and Mysel's, thus raising the presumption of negligence. Walbro and Mysel produced no evidence, however, to rebut the presumption of negligence.

Based on the evidence presented, the trial court ruled that the lost jacket was delivered to Mysel Furs. Walbro and Mysel's argued that, assuming delivery of the jacket, any presumption of negligence was defeated by the procedures used in storing furs. The furs were placed in a locked, alarmed vault to which several, identifiable Mysel's employees had access. Mysel's then prepared and issued a storage receipt to the customer. Walbro presented no evidence to show that these procedures were followed for Magee's furs, and the storage receipt was not issued until six weeks after the jacket was delivered. It is reasonable to assume that the defendants' procedures and security precautions customarily resulted in the return of the customer's fur. Magee's fur was not returned; therefore, without showing more than the mere existence of safety and security measures, the defendants failed to rebut the presumption of negligence. Magee was therefore entitled to recover her damages.

Finally, the defendants asserted the defense of limitation of liability. Walbro and Mysel's argue that they effectively limited their liability to $100, citing *Schoen v. Wallace,* which upheld an agreement between a fur owner and fur storage company to limit the storage company's liability to $100. *Schoen* and [other cases] indicate, however, that the customer was aware of the limitation of liability *before* the furs were placed in storage. The *Schoen* decision was based in part on the fact that the plaintiff had dealt with the defendant before, knew of its insurance practices, [and] could have chosen another furrier had she found the limitation objectionable.

In the instant case, Magee testified that she was not told of the limitation until after the fur was lost. Defendants rely on the receipt of July 1982, which stated that liability was limited to $100. Magee should have known of the limitation after she received the receipt in July, but by that time her furs had been at Mysel's for six weeks.

The limitation does not apply in the instant case because Magee had no knowledge of the limitation before agreeing to store her furs. In *Schoen*, the court stated that it would be "unjust to permit the plaintiff to repudiate [the agreement to limit liability] because the coat was lost." In the instant case, it would be unjust to permit Mysel and Walbro to assert a limitation that was not made clear at the time that the bailment contract was made because the coat was lost. We therefore hold that the $100 limitation of liability is inapplicable in this case.

For the foregoing reasons, judgment in favor of the defendants is reversed, and this case is remanded to the trial court to enter judgment against Walbro and Mysel's and in favor of Magee in the amount of $3,400.

Reversed and remanded in favor of Magee.

Bailee's Liability for Misdelivery The bailee is also liable to the bailor if he misdelivers the bailed property at the termination of the bailment. The property must be returned to the bailor or to someone specified by the bailor.

If a third person claims to have rights in the bailed property that are superior to the rights of the bailor and demands possession of the bailed property, the bailee is in a dilemma. If the bailee refuses to deliver the bailed property to the third-person claimant and the third-person claimant is entitled to its possession, the bailee is liable to the claimant. If the bailee delivers the bailed property to the third-party claimant and the third-party claimant is not entitled to possession, the bailee is liable to the bailor. The circumstances may be such that the conflicting claims of the bailor and the third-person claimant can be determined only by judicial decision. In some cases, the bailee may protect himself by bringing the third-party claimant into a lawsuit along with the bailor so that all the competing claims can be adjudicated by the court before the bailee releases the property, but this remedy is not always available.

Limits on Liability

Bailees may try to limit or relieve themselves of liability for the bailed property. Some examples include the storage receipt purporting to limit liability to $100 in the *Magee v. Walbro, Inc.* case, signs near checkrooms, such as "Not responsible for loss of or damage to checked property," and disclaimers on claim checks, such as "Goods left at owner's risk." The standards used to determine whether such limitations and disclaimers are enforceable are discussed in detail in the Illegality chapter.

Any attempt by the bailee to be relieved of liability for *intentional wrongful acts* is against public policy and will not be enforced. A bailee's ability to be relieved of liability for *negligence* is also limited. Courts look to see whether the disclaimer or limitation of liability was communicated to the bailor at the time of the bailment. Did the attendant point out the sign near the checkroom to the person when the coat was checked? Did the parking lot attendant call the person's attention to the disclaimer on the back of the claim check? If not, as in the *Magee* case, the court may hold that the disclaimer was not communicated to the bailor and did not become part of the bailment contract. Even if the bailor was aware of the disclaimer, it still may not be enforced on the ground that it is contrary to public policy.

If the disclaimer was offered on a take-it-or-leave-it basis and was not the subject of arm's-length bargaining, it is less likely to be enforced than if it has been negotiated and voluntarily agreed upon. A bailee may be able to limit liability to a certain amount or to relieve himself of liability for certain perils. Ideally, the bailee will give the bailor a chance to declare a higher value and to pay an additional charge to be protected up to the declared value of the goods. Common carriers, such as railroads and trucking companies, often take this approach. Courts do not look with favor on efforts by a person to be relieved of liability for negligence. For this reason, terms limiting the liability of a bailee stand a better chance of being enforced than do terms completely relieving the bailee of liability.

The bailor's knowledge of the bailee's facilities or of his method of doing business or the nature of prior dealings may give rise to an implied agreement as to the bailee's duties. The bailee may, if he wishes, assume all the risks incident to the bailment and contract to return the bailed property undamaged or to pay any damage to or loss of the property.

Right to Compensation

The express or implied contract creating the bailment controls whether the bailee has the right to receive compensation for keeping the property or must pay for having the right to use it. If the bailment is made as a favor, then the bailee is not entitled to compensation even though the bailment is for the sole benefit of the bailor. If the bailment is the rental of property, then the bailee must pay the agreed rental rate. If the bailment is for the storage or repair of property, then the bailee is entitled to the contract price for the storage or repair services. If no specific price was agreed upon, yet compensation was contemplated by the parties, then the bailee gets the reasonable value of the services provided.

In many instances, the bailee will have a **lien** (a charge against property to secure the payment of a debt) on the bailed property for the reasonable value of the services. For example, Silver takes a chair to Ace Upholstery to have it recovered. When the chair has been recovered, Ace has the right to keep it until the agreed price—or, if no price was set, the reasonable value of the work—is paid. This is an example of an **artisan's lien**, which is discussed in greater detail in the Security Interests in Personal Property chapter.

Bailor's Liability for Defects in the Bailed Property

When personal property is rented or loaned, the bailor makes an implied warranty that the property has no hidden defects that make it unsafe for use. If the bailment is for the sole benefit of the bailee, then the bailor is liable for injuries that result from defects in the bailed property only if the bailor knew about the defects and did not tell the bailee. For example, Price lends his car, which he knows has bad brakes, to Sloan. If Price does not tell Sloan about the bad brakes and if Sloan is injured in an accident because the brakes fail, Price is liable for Sloan's injuries.

If the bailment is a bailment for mutual benefit, then the bailor has a larger obligation. The bailor must use reasonable care in inspecting the property and seeing that it is safe for the purpose for which it is intended. The bailor is liable for injuries suffered by the bailee because of defects that the bailor either knew about or should have discovered by reasonable inspection. For example, Friedman's Rent-All, which rents trailers, does not inspect the trailers after they are returned. A wheel has come loose on a trailer that Friedman's rents to Hirsch. If the wheel comes off while Hirsch is using the trailer and the goods Hirsch is carrying in it are damaged, Friedman's is liable to Hirsch.

In addition, product liability doctrines that apply a higher standard of legal responsibility have been applied to bailors who are commercial lessors of personal property.[8] Express or implied warranties of quality under either Article 2 or Article 2A of the UCC may apply. Liability under these warranties does not depend on whether the bailor knew about or should have discovered the defect. The only question is whether the property's condition complied with the warranty. Some courts have also imposed strict liability on lessors-bailors of goods that cause personal injury or property damage to the lessee-bailee because they are defective and unreasonably dangerous. This liability is imposed regardless of whether the lessor was negligent.

---

[8]Product liability doctrines are discussed in the Product Liability chapter.

CONCEPT REVIEW

DUTIES OF BAILEES AND BAILORS

Type of Bailment	Duties of Bailee	Duties of Bailor
Sole Benefit of Bailee	1. Must use great care; liable for even slight negligence. 2. Must return goods to bailor or dispose of them at his direction. 3. May have duty to compensate bailor.	1. Must notify the bailee of any known defects.
Mutual Benefit	1. Must use reasonable care; liable for ordinary negligence. 2. Must return goods to bailor or dispose of them at his direction. 3. May have duty to compensate bailor.	1. Must notify bailee of all known defects and any defects that could be discovered on reasonable inspection. 2. Commercial lessors may be subject to warranties of quality and/or strict liability in tort. 3. May have duty to compensate bailee.
Sole Benefit of Bailor	1. Must use at least slight care; liable for gross negligence. 2. Must return goods to bailor or dispose of them at his direction.	1. Must notify bailee of all known defects and any hidden defects that are known or could be discovered on reasonable inspection. 2. May have duty to compensate bailee.

SPECIAL BAILMENTS

Common Carriers

Bailees that are **common carriers** are held to a higher level of responsibility than that to which bailees that are private carriers are held. Common carriers are licensed by governmental agencies to carry the property of anyone who requests the service. Airlines licensed by the Department of Transportation and trucks and buses licensed by the Interstate Commerce Commission are examples of common carriers. *Private contract carriers* carry goods only for persons selected by the carrier.

Both common carriers and private contract carriers are bailees. However, the law makes the common carrier an absolute insurer of the goods it carries. The common carrier is responsible for any loss of or damage to goods entrusted to it. The common carrier can avoid responsibility only if it can show that the loss or damage was caused by:

1. An act of God,
2. An act of a public enemy,
3. An act or order of the government,
4. An act of the person who shipped the goods, or
5. The nature of the goods themselves.

The common carrier is liable if goods entrusted to it are stolen by some unknown person but not if the goods are destroyed when a tornado hits the warehouse. If goods are damaged because the shipper improperly packages or crates them, then the carrier is not liable. Similarly, if perishable goods are not in suitable condition to be shipped and deteriorate in the course of shipment, the carrier is not liable so long as it used reasonable care in handling them.

Common carriers are usually permitted to limit their liability to a stated value unless the bailor declares a higher value for the property and pays an additional fee.

Hotelkeepers

Hotelkeepers are engaged in the business of offering food and/or lodging to transient persons. They hold themselves out to serve the public and are obligated to do so. Like the common carrier, the hotelkeeper is held to a higher standard of care than that of the ordinary bailee.

The hotelkeeper is not a bailee in the strict sense of the word. The guest does not usually surrender the ex-clusive possession of his property to the hotelkeeper. However, the hotelkeeper is treated as the virtual insurer of the guest's property. The hotelkeeper is not liable for loss of or damage to property if he can show that it was caused by:

1. An act of God,
2. An act of a public enemy,
3. An act of a governmental authority,
4. The fault of a member of the guest's party, or
5. The nature of the goods.

Most states have passed laws that limit the hotelkeeper's liability, however. Commonly, the law requires the hotel owner to post a notice advising guests that any valuables should be checked into the hotel vault. The hotelkeeper's liability is then limited, usually to a fixed amount, for valuables that are not so checked.

Safe-Deposit Boxes

If a person rents a safe-deposit box at a local bank and places some property in the box, the box and the property are in the manual possession of the bank. However, it takes both the renter's key and the key held by the bank to open the box, and in most cases the bank does not know the nature, amount, or value of the goods in the box. Although a few courts have held the rental of a safe-deposit box not to be a bailment, most courts have found that the renter of the box is a bailor and the bank is a bailee. As such, the bank is not an insurer of the contents of the box. However, it is obligated to use due care and to come forward and explain loss of or damage to the property entrusted to it.

Involuntary Bailments

Suppose a person owns a cottage on a beach. After a violent storm, a sailboat washed up on his beach. As the finder of lost or misplaced property, he may be considered the **involuntary bailee** or **constructive bailee** of the sailboat. This relationship may arise when a person finds himself in possession of property that belongs to someone else without having agreed to accept possession.

The duties of the involuntary bailee are not well defined. The bailee does not have the right to destroy the property or to use it. If the true owner shows up, the property must be returned to him. Under some circumstances, the involuntary bailee may be under an obligation to assume control of the property or to take some minimal steps to ascertain who the owner is, or both.

In the case that follows, *Capezzaro v. Winfrey,* a constructive and involuntary bailee was held liable for disposing of the bailed property because it had knowledge of an adverse claim to the property.

CAPEZZARO v. WINFREY

379 A.2d 493 (N.J. Super. Ct. 1977)

Michael Capezzaro reported to the police that he had been robbed of $7,500 at gunpoint by a woman. The following day, Henrietta Winfrey was arrested with a total of $2,480.66 in her possession. Capezzaro positively identified her as the woman who had robbed him and claimed that the money found on her was part of the money that she had taken from him. Winfrey was jailed, and the money was impounded by the police as evidence of the crime. Several months later, Winfrey was indicted for the armed robbery of Capezzaro. Approximately two years afterward, this and other indictments against Winfrey were dismissed by the prosecutor based on medical opinion that she was unable to know right from wrong at the time she allegedly committed the crimes with which she had been charged.

When the warden of the county jail notified the police officers in charge of the police department's property room that the indictment against Winfrey had been dismissed, the police officers released the $2,480.66 claimed by Capezzaro to Winfrey. Eventually, Capezzaro found out about the dismissal of the indictment and the release of the money. He then instituted a lawsuit against Winfrey and the city of Newark, claiming that the released money was his. The trial court held in his favor and the city appealed.

Per Curiam.   A constructive bailment or a bailment by operation of law may be created when a person comes into possession of personal property of another, receives nothing from the owner of the property, and has no right to recover from the owner for what he does in caring for the property. Such person is ordinarily considered to be a gratuitous bailee, liable only to the bailor for bad faith or gross negligence. *Zuppa v. Hertz Corp.* states:

It is the element of lawful possession, however created, and the duty to account for the thing as the property of another, that creates the bailment, regardless of whether such possession is based upon contract in the ordinary sense or not.

Where possession has been acquired accidentally, fortuitously, through mistake or by an agreement for some other purpose since terminated, the possessor, "upon principles of justice," should keep it safely and restore or deliver it to its owner. Under such circumstances, the courts have considered the possession quasi-contracts of bailment or constructive and involuntary bailments.

Here the police seized and obtained custody of the money which was found in Winfrey's girdle during a search in her cell after her arrest on the robbery charge and after Capezzaro claimed Winfrey had stolen it from him. It is undisputed that the money was being kept by the police as evidence for use in Winfrey's prosecution. It follows, then, that the City of Newark, through its police department, was holding the money for its own benefit as well as for the benefit of its rightful owner.

Ordinarily, a person who has possession of property may be presumed by another to be the rightful owner thereof in the absence of any knowledge to the contrary. However, here the police were fully aware of Capezzaro's adverse claim, but notwithstanding such knowledge and without notice to Capezzaro turned the money over to Winfrey.

The city contends that when the indictment was dismissed, any claim by Capezzaro lost its validity and it was obligated to return the monies in question to Winfrey as bailor. We disagree. A bailee with knowledge of an adverse claim makes delivery to the bailor at his peril, and only if he is ignorant of such a claim will he be protected against a subsequent claim by the rightful owner.

The police returned the money to Winfrey after being informed by the warden of the county jail that the indictments had been dismissed. They did not contact Capezzaro before doing so, even though they were on notice of his adverse claim. The dismissal of the indictment for the reasons here present did not vitiate Capezzaro's adverse claim to the money. Inherent in the jury's verdict is a finding that the city was negligent in releasing the money without a determination of the validity of the adverse claim. This finding and the verdict are amply supported by the evidence.

Judgment for Capezzaro affirmed.

ETHICAL AND PUBLIC POLICY CONCERNS

1. Does a finder of lost or mislaid property have an ethical duty to look for the owner of the property? How effective are the legal principles that you learned in encouraging a finder to do so?

2. What part does ethical conduct play in determining whether a person acquires ownership of personal property by confusion? By accession?

3. You learned that, in formulating the degree of care that a bailee must exercise over bailed property, courts traditionally have applied standards based on the amount of relative benefit the parties derive from the bailment. Where both parties benefit, reasonable care is required; where the bailee alone benefits, great care is required; and where the bailor alone benefits, only slight care is required. Modern courts seem to be moving in the direction of applying a standard of *reasonable care* to all bailments, however. Which approach is preferable, and why?

SUMMARY

Ownership of property is the exclusive right to possess, enjoy, and dispose of objects or rights having economic value. In law, property is a bundle of legal rights to things having economic value, which rights are recognized and protected by society. Property is classified according to its various characteristics. The earth's crust and all things firmly attached to it are classified as real property. All other objects and rights subject to ownership are classified as personal property. Property that has a physical existence is classified as tangible property. Rights that have economic value but are not related to things having a physical existence are classified as intangible property. Property owned by the government or a governmental unit is classified as public property. Property owned by any person or association, even though used exclusively for public purposes, is classified as private property.

Ownership of personal property may be acquired by (1) production or purchase, (2) taking possession of unowned property, (3) finding lost property (the finder acquires rights superior to everyone except the owner), (4) gift, (5) will or inheritance, (6) confusion, and (7) accession. In addition, the right to exclusive use and possession of personal property is frequently acquired by leasing.

A person owns property produced by his own labor or by the labor of persons whom he hires to work for him. The owner of personal property may sell or barter his property to another, and the purchaser then becomes the owner of the property. The person who first reduces unowned property—wildlife or abandoned property—to possession with the intent of claiming ownership of the property acquires ownership.

A gift is the transfer of the ownership of property from the donor to the donee without any consideration being given by the donee. To have a valid gift, the donor must deliver the possession of the property to the donee or to some third person with the intent of vesting ownership in the donee.

The finder of lost property acquires ownership of the property against everyone except the original owner. When property is mislaid, however, the owner of the real property on which it is found has the right to possess the property as a bailee until the true owner is found. If a person confuses his property with that of another person, the other person may acquire ownership of the entire mass through the doctrine of confusion. If property is improved by the labor and addition of materials by another without the owner's consent, the owner of the original property becomes the owner of the property in its improved state. This is known as obtaining title by accession.

A bailment is created when an owner of personal property, the bailor, delivers the possession of the property to another, the bailee, who intends to take control of it and who is obligated to return the property to the bailor or to dispose of it as directed by the bailor. A bailment is created by an express or implied agreement.

The bailee owes a duty of due care to prevent loss of or damage to the bailed property. In determining whether or not due care has been exercised by the bailee, the nature of the bailment is of considerable importance, as is the type of property and the bailee's skill. The trend today is to apply a standard of reasonable care to all bailees. Within the limits of the legality of their contract, the parties may, by agreement, increase or decrease the scope of the bailee's liability.

When the bailment terminates, the bailee must return the bailed property to the bailor or dispose of it according to the bailor's direction. If a third person having a right of possession superior to that of the bailor demands the surrender of the property, the bailee is obligated to deliver the property to that person.

The bailee is entitled to any compensation expressly or impliedly agreed upon for services rendered in the care of the property. If the bailor rents property to the bailee, the bailor owes a duty to inspect the property to see that it is free from dangerous defects. Product liability doctrines such as implied warranty and strict liability have been applied to commercial lessors of personal property.

A common carrier is the insurer of the goods it carries against loss or damage, unless such loss or damage is caused by an act of God, an act of a public enemy, an act of the state, an act of the shipper, or the nature of the goods. A hotelkeeper is an insurer of the goods of his guests, subject to certain exceptions. Many states have statutes permitting hotelkeepers to limit their liability.

A person may become an involuntary bailee if the goods of another are placed in his possession, such as where goods are deposited on his land by storm or flood or by the acts of third persons, where he finds lost or mislaid property, or if the domestic animals of another stray onto his land. Such a bailee owes a minimum duty of care. He cannot willfully destroy the property or convert it to his own use.

PROBLEM CASES

1. Charrier was an amateur archeologist. After researching colonial maps and records, he concluded that the Trudeau Plantation near Angola, Louisiana, was the possible site of an ancient village of the Tunica Indians. Charrier obtained the permission of the caretaker of the Trudeau Plantation to survey the property with a metal detector for possible burial locations. At the time, he mistakenly believed that the caretaker was the Plantation's owner. He located and, over the next three years, excavated approximately 150 burial sites containing: beads, European ceramics, stoneware, glass bottles, iron kettles, vessels, skillets, knives, muskets, gunflints, balls, shots, crucifixes, rings, bracelets, and native pottery. Did Charrier acquire ownership of the burial goods?

2. Vallejo, a customer at Martin Chevrolet Sales, requested and received permission to test-drive a 1986 Chevrolet Camaro IROC. Vallejo took the car out for a test-drive alone. While test-driving the car, Vallejo was involved in an accident and "totaled" the car, which was worth more than $13,000. Martin Chevrolet's insurer brought suit against Vallejo on a bailment theory, claiming that the car had been damaged due to Vallejo's "willful and wanton" acts. Vallejo argued that there was no bailment relationship between Martin Chevrolet and himself. Is he correct?

3. Jackson was a maid in a hotel owned by Steinberg. She found eight $100 bills under the paper lining in a dresser in a guest room. She turned the money over to Steinberg. Steinberg tried to locate the true owner by sending a letter to everyone who had occupied the room over the last three months. However, no one claimed it.

Jackson demanded that the money be returned to her, but Steinberg refused. Was Jackson entitled to the money she found in the dresser drawer in Steinberg's hotel?

4. Taylor lived with Hattie Smith. Taylor rented a safe-deposit box at the Crown Center Bank in the name of Hattie Smith and gave her both keys to the box. Smith signed a card that authorized and directed the bank to allow Hunter Taylor to enter "my box" at any time. On several occasions, Taylor borrowed the key to the box without explanation and then returned it to Smith. Smith claimed that Taylor told her he had put money in the box, and none was put in the day the box was rented. Taylor was murdered, and at the time of the murder he had both of the keys to the box in his possession. Smith had the box opened by the bank, and $8,000 was found in it. The administrator of Taylor's estate claimed the money for the estate. Smith claimed that the money was a gift to her. Had Taylor made a valid gift of the money to Smith?

5. The Kahrs put their silver (worth about $3,800), jewelry, and a wallet containing their credit cards in bags and stored them in their attic while they were on vacation. After they returned, they retrieved the bags containing the valuables and placed them on their dining room table along with bags containing some used clothing that they had decided to donate to Goodwill. Mr. Kahr mistakenly picked up the bags containing the silver and wallet and delivered them to Goodwill along with the bags of used clothing. He told Goodwill at that time that he was donating used clothing. A Goodwill employee who was marking the items for resale found the Kahrs's wallet in a bag and, realizing it was a mistake, called the Kahrs's residence about the wallet. She did not mention the silver, though, because she had not yet found it. Even when she did find it, she did not realize that it was sterling silver. The Kahrs realized the mistake about two hours later. They called Goodwill only to find that the silver had been sold for $15 to Markland. Markland refused to return the silver, and the Kahrs brought suit. Can the Kahrs get their silver back?

6. Ochoa's Studebaker automobile was stolen. Eleven months later, the automobile somehow found its way into the hands of the U.S. government, which sold it at a "junk" auction for $85 to Rogers. At the time it was purchased by Rogers, no part of the car was intact. It had no top except a part of the frame; it had no steering wheel, tires, rims, cushions, or battery; the motor, radiator, and gears were out of the car; one wheel was gone,

as was one axle; the fenders were partly gone; and the frame was broken. It was no longer an automobile but a pile of broken and dismantled parts of what was once Ochoa's car. Having purchased these parts, Rogers used them in the construction of a delivery truck at an expense of approximately $800. When the truck was completed, he put it to use in his furniture business. Several months later, Ochoa was passing Rogers' place of business and recognized the vehicle from a mark on the hood and another on the radiator. He discovered that the serial and engine numbers matched those on the car he had owned. Ochoa demanded the vehicle from Rogers, who refused to surrender it. Ochoa brought suit to recover possession of the property. In the alternative, he asked for the value of the vehicle at the time of the suit, which he alleged to be $1,000, and for the value of the use of the car from the time Rogers purchased it from the government. Was Ochoa entitled to recover possession of his property, which Rogers had substantially improved?

7. Pond owned and operated a parking lot. Rehling parked his automobile on Pond's lot, which was near Crosley Field, and proceeded with others to a night baseball game. Rehling paid $1 to the parking lot attendant, for which he received a "claim check." Before leaving his automobile, Rehling rolled up the windows, locked the doors, and took the keys with him. When he returned after the ballgame to get his automobile, it was gone. The parking lot attendants testified that at about the third inning of the ballgame, they saw a person walk directly to Rehling's automobile, get in, back up, and drive away. There was no showing that the claim check was ever used for anything but identification in case a patron was unable to find his automobile on the lot. Is Pond liable as bailee for the loss of the automobile?

8. Dolitsky rented a safe-deposit box from Dollar Savings Bank. The safe-deposit vault of the bank was in the basement, and the vault area was walled off from all other parts of the bank. Only box renters and officers and employees of the bank were admitted to this area. To gain access to the area, a box renter had to obtain an admission slip, fill in the box number and sign the slip, have the box number and signature checked by an employee against the records of the bank, and then present the slip to a guard who admitted the renter to the vault area. On November 7, 1951, Dolitsky requested access to her box. While Dolitsky was in the booth, she was looking through an advertising folder that the bank had placed there and found a $100 bill, which she turned over to the attendant. Dolitsky waited one year, and during that time the rightful owner of the $100 bill made no claim for it. Dolitsky then demanded that the bank surrender the bill to her, claiming that she was entitled to the bill as finder. The bank claimed that the bill was mislaid property and that it owed a duty to keep the bill for the rightful owner. Is this correct?

9. Pringle, the head of the drapery department at Wardrobe Cleaners, went to the Axelrods' home to inspect some dining room draperies for dry-cleaning purposes. He spent about 30 minutes looking at the drapes and inspected both the drapes and the lining. He pointed out some roach spots on the lining that could not be removed by cleaning, but this was not of concern to the Axelrods. He did not indicate to them that the fabric had deteriorated from sunburn, age, dust, or air conditioning so as to make it unsuitable for dry cleaning. He took the drapes and had them dry cleaned. When the drapes were returned, they were unfit for use. The fabric had been a gold floral design on an eggshell-white background. When returned, it was a blotchy gold. Wardrobe Cleaners stated that it was difficult to predict how imported fabrics would respond to the dry-cleaning process and that the company was not equipped to pretest the fabric to see whether it was colorfast. The Axelrods sued Wardrobe Cleaners for $1,000, the replacement value of the drapes. Was Wardrobe Cleaners liable for the damage caused to the drapes during the dry-cleaning process?

10. In the spring of 1973, Carter brought her fur coat to Reichlin Furriers for cleaning, glazing, and storage until the next winter season. She was given a printed form of receipt, upon the front of which an employee of Reichlin had written $100 as the valuation of the coat. There was no discussion of the value of the coat, and Carter did not realize that such a value had been written on the receipt, which she did not read at the time. A space for the customer's signature on the front of the receipt was left blank. Below this space in prominent type appeared a notice to "see reverse side for terms and conditions." The other side of the receipt stated that it was a storage contract and that by its acceptance the customer would be deemed to have agreed to its terms unless notice to the contrary were given within 10 days. Fifteen conditions were listed. One of the conditions was

as follows: "Storage charges are based upon valuation herein declared by the depositor, and amount recoverable for loss or damage to the article shall not exceed its actual value or the cost of repair or replacement with materials of like kind and quality or the depositor's valuation appearing in this receipt, whichever is less." In the fall of 1973, after Carter had paid the bill for storage and other services on the coat, Reichlin informed her that the coat was lost. At that time, the fair market value of the coat was $450. Carter sued Reichlin for loss of the coat and sought $450 damages. Reichlin claimed that its liability was limited to $100. Is this correct?

11. The Satterthwaites operated the Crystal Palace Barber and Beauty Shop. The Crystal Palace consisted of a suite of three rooms, the back room being the barber shop, the middle room being the operating area of the beauty shop, and the room facing the outside—which is visible to outsiders through a glass door—being a reception room. There was a conspicuous sign in the shop that read, "Not responsible for hats, coats, and purses." Theobald had patronized the beauty shop numerous times and knew the arrangement of the rooms. On a previous visit, she had asked Mrs. Satterthwaite if the reception room was a safe place to leave her coat and had been assured that it was safe. Nothing had been stolen from the reception room in 20 years of operation, and the hooks there were the only ones on which customers could hang their coats. There was no bell or warning device on the door that sounded when someone entered the reception room. A thief could well see into the reception room, remove a coat, and leave without being seen from the operating area of the beauty shop. On December 24, 1946, Theobald came into the beauty shop to get a permanent and sat in the reception room wearing a fur coat until it was time for her appointment. She then removed her fur coat, hung it on a hook in the reception area, and went into the operating area of the beauty shop. Neither of the Satterthwaites was aware that Theobald had worn her fur coat that day. While Theobald was getting her permanent, someone stole the coat. Theobald alleges that there was a bailment and the Satterthwaites are therefore responsible for the loss of the coat. Was there a bailment?

12. Andrews delivered his quarter horse mare named "I'll Call Ya" to Oak Hills Ranch and its owner Stone for the purpose of boarding. Stone was in the business of brokering, stabling, and training racehorses for profit. Several months later, Andrews asked Stone if he would arrange for I'll Call Ya to be transported to a trainer in Louisiana. Consequently, when the Allen brothers, who were also in the business of boarding and training horses for profit and had previously done business with Stone, delivered two horses to Oak Hills Ranch, Stone asked them if they would haul I'll Call Ya back to their training stable in east Texas where the Louisiana trainer could pick her up. Andrews agreed to these plans even though he did not know the Allen brothers. On March 16, 1983, the Allens loaded I'll Call Ya into their trailer and began the drive to east Texas. Shortly after leaving Oak Hills Ranch, the trailer became disengaged from the Allens' truck, rolled over, and came to rest on the side of the road. I'll Call Ya was severely cut and bruised as a result of the accident and lingered for several hours by the side of the road before she died without veterinary treatment. The fair market value of the horse before the accident was $150,000. Andrews brought suit against Stone and the Allens to recover the value of I'll Call Ya. Will he prevail?

CHAPTER 21

REAL PROPERTY AND INSURANCE

INTRODUCTION

Land has always occupied a position of special importance in the law. In the agrarian society of previous eras, land was the basic measure and source of wealth. In an industrialized society, land is not only a source of food, clothing, and shelter but also an instrument of commercial and industrial development. It is not surprising, then, that a complex body of law exists regarding the ownership, acquisition, and use of land. This body of law is known as the law of **real property.**

This chapter presents an overview of the law of real property. It will discuss the scope of real property, the various ownership interests in real property, the ways in which real property is transferred, and the controls that society places on an owner's use of real property. It will also present a brief overview of insurance concepts applying to property insurance.

SCOPE OF REAL PROPERTY

Real property includes not only land but also things that are firmly attached to the land or embedded in the land. Thus, buildings and other permanent structures are considered part of real property. The person who owns a tract of real property also owns the air above his property, the minerals below its surface, and any trees or other vegetation growing on the property.[1] Real property is distinguished from personal property by the fact that real property is *immovable* or attached to something immovable, while personal property is not. The distinction is important because the rules of law governing real property transactions such as sale, taxation, and inheritance are frequently different from those applied to personal property transactions.

It is possible for an item of personal property to be attached to or used in conjunction with real property in such a way that it is treated as being part of the real property. This type of personal property is called a **fixture.**

Fixtures

A **fixture** is a type of property that bridges the gap between real and personal property. When an item is found to be a fixture, it ceases to be personal property and becomes part of the real property to which it is attached. A conveyance (transfer of ownership) of the real property will also convey the fixtures on that property, even if the fixtures are not specifically mentioned.

---

[1]Ownership of air above one's property is not an unlimited interest, however. Courts have held that the flight of aircraft above one's property is not a violation of a landowner's rights, so long as it does not unduly interfere with the owner's enjoyment of his land.

It is very common for people to install items of personal property on the real property that they own or rent. A variety of disputes can arise regarding rights to such property. Suppose that Lubarsky buys a chandelier and installs it in his home. When he sells the house to Jarrett, can Lubarsky remove the chandelier, or is it part of the home that Jarrett has bought? Suppose Winston, a commercial tenant, installs showcases and tracklights in the store that he leases from Johnson. When Winston's lease expires, can he remove the showcases and the lights, or do they now belong to Johnson? If the parties' contract is silent on these matters, a court will resolve the case by referring to the law of fixtures.

Factors Determining whether an Item Is a Fixture
There is no mechanical formula for determining whether an item has become a fixture, but courts will consider the following factors:

1. *Attachment.* One of the factors that helps to determine whether an item is a fixture is the degree to which the item is **attached** or **annexed** to the real property. If the item is firmly attached to the real property and cannot be removed without damaging the property, it is likely to be considered a fixture. An item of personal property that can be removed with little or no injury to the property is less likely to be considered a fixture.

Actual physical attachment to real property is not necessary, however. A close physical connection between the item of personal property and the real property may be sufficient for a court to conclude that the item is **constructively annexed.** For example, heavy machinery or automatic garage door openers can be considered fixtures even though they are not physically attached to real property.

2. *Adaptation.* Another factor to be considered is the degree to which the use of the item is necessary or beneficial to the use of the real property. This factor is called *adaptation.* It is particularly relevant in cases in which the item is either not physically attached to the real property at all or the physical attachment is slight. When an item would be of little value except for use with a particular piece of property, it is likely to be considered a fixture even though it is unattached or could easily be removed. For example, keys and custom-sized window screens and storm windows have been held to be fixtures.

3. *Intent.* The third factor to be considered is the *intent* of the person who installed the item. Intent is judged not by what that person subjectively intended, but by what the circumstances indicate that he intended. To a great extent, intent is indicated by the first two factors, annexation and adaptation. There is a presumption that an owner of real property who improves it by attaching items of personal property intended those items to become part of the real estate. Thus, if the owner does *not* want an item to be considered a fixture, he must specifically reserve the right to keep the attached property. A seller of a house who wants to keep an antique chandelier that has been installed in the house should either replace the chandelier before the house is shown to prospective purchasers or make it clear in the contract of sale that the chandelier will be excluded from the sale.

The *Ford v. Venard* case, which follows, presents a typical example of a court's analysis of whether an item of personal property has become a fixture.

FORD v. VENARD
340 N.W.2d 270 (S. Ct. Iowa 1983)

In 1973, Norman Van Sickle moved his double wide mobile home to a plot of land owned by Luelia Jedlicka. Van Sickle had the real estate landscaped, a foundation poured, concrete blocks set, and steel girders aligned on the blocks. After removing the hitches and wheels from the mobile home, he had it set on the foundation by a crane and hooked together. Since that time, Van Sickle substantially modified his residence by welding it into a single unit, placing a roof over the entire building, and joining the exterior with siding to the point that it could not be disassembled without tearing it apart and could not be moved as one unit except by a house mover.

Van Sickle had paid Jedlicka $500 as a down payment for the purchase of the land back in 1973, but had never made any further payments. He had never been asked to pay taxes and was told by Jedlicka that she paid them. Van Sickle had been told by the bank that held a security interest on the mobile home that the house would become part of Jedlicka's real estate after it was set on a foundation. He did not consider himself the owner of the real estate; he believed the land belonged to Jedlicka.

In 1977, Henry Edsel Ford contracted with Jedlicka to buy the land. A clause of the contract between Ford and Jedlicka specified that all "attached fixtures" were included as part of the real estate included in the sale. The ownership of the mobile home was brought to a head in 1982, when William Venard, a creditor of Van Sickle's, attempted to enforce a judgment against Van Sickle by attaching the mobile home and executing against it. Ford brought this action claiming that he owns the mobile home. He requested an injunction to restrain Venard from executing against the mobile home, and the trial court granted the injunction. Venard appeals.

Harris, J. The question is whether the mobile home was a fixture included under the terms of the land contract between Jedlicka and Ford. We think it plainly was. Under our common law rule personal property becomes a fixture when:

(1) it is actually annexed to the realty, or to something appurtenant thereto;
(2) it is put to the same use as the realty with which it is connected; and
(3) the party making the annexation intends to make a permanent accession to the freehold.

The intention of the party annexing the improvement is the "paramount factor" in determining whether the improvement is a fixture. Physical attachment of the structure to the soil or to an appurtenance thereto is not essential to make the structure a part of the realty. On the other hand, a building which cannot be removed without destruction of a substantial part of its value becomes almost unavoidably an integral part of the real estate.

Venard argues that Van Sickle's home was not physically annexed to the realty and that Van Sickle never intended for his home to be permanently attached to the freehold. Ford, on the other hand, relies on the facts that the home's tongues and wheels have been removed; it was set on a foundation and girders; it has been extensively remodeled into a single unit; and its removal would be expensive and damaging. He points out that the home was used as a homestead, which is the use for which the realty had been appropriated. He points to the bank's advice to Van Sickle that his home would become the property of Jedlicka when set on her land.

We have found buildings to be fixtures in a number of cases. We are convinced the home became attached to the land. It could not be removed from its present location except in the sense that any permanent home could be. We hold that it has become an integral part of the real estate. The trial court was right in ordering the issuance of the permanent injunction.

Affirmed in favor of Ford.

Express Agreement If the parties have formed an express agreement that clearly states their intent about whether a particular item is to be considered a fixture, a court will generally enforce that agreement. For example, the buyer and seller of a house might agree to permit the seller to remove a fence or shrubbery that would otherwise be considered a fixture. The parties' right to dictate the classification of property is not unlimited, however. A court would not enforce an agreement that provided that a piece of land was to be treated as personal property, for example.

Tenants' Fixtures An exception to the normal rules about fixtures is made when a *tenant* attaches personal property to leased premises for the purpose of carrying on his trade or business. Such fixtures are called **trade fixtures.** Trade fixtures remain the personal property of the tenant and can be removed at the termination of the lease. The purpose of making an exception for trade fixtures is to encourage trade and industry.

There are two limitations on the tenant's right to remove trade fixtures. First, the tenant cannot remove the fixtures if doing so would cause substantial damage to the landlord's realty. Second, the tenant must remove the fixtures by the end of the lease if the lease is for a definite period; if the lease is for an indefinite period, the tenant may be given a reasonable time after the expiration of the lease to remove the fixtures. If she does not remove the fixtures within the appropriate time, they become the property of the landlord.

Leases may contain terms that expressly address the parties' rights in any fixtures. A lease might give the tenant the right to attach items or make other improvements and to remove them later. The reverse may also be true. The lease might state that any improvements made or fixtures attached will become the property of the landlord at the termination of the lease. Courts will gen-erally enforce the parties' agreement about the ownership of fixtures.

Security Interests in Fixtures   Special rules apply to personal property that is subject to a lien or security interest[2] at the time it is attached to real property. For example, a person buys a dishwasher on a time-payment plan from an appliance store and has it installed in his kitchen. To protect itself, the appliance store must take a security interest in the dishwasher and perfect that interest by filing a financing statement in the local real estate records within a period of time specified by the Uniform Commercial Code. The appliance store would then be able to remove the dishwasher if the buyer defaulted in his payments. It could, however, be liable to third parties, such as prior real estate mortgagees, for any damage to the real estate caused by the removal of the dishwasher. The rules concerning security interests in personal property that will become fixtures are covered in the Security Interests in Personal Property chapter.

---

[2]Liens and security interests are discussed in the Security Interests in Personal Property chapter.

CONCEPT REVIEW

FIXTURES

Concept	A *fixture* is an item of personal property attached to or used in conjunction with real property in such a way that it is treated as being part of the real property.
Significance	A conveyance of the real property will also convey the fixtures on that property.
Factors Considered in Determining whether Property Is a Fixture	1. Attachment: Is the item physically attached or closely connected to the real property? 2. Adaption: How necessary or beneficial is the item to the use of the real property? 3. Intent: Did the person who installed the item manifest intent for the property to become part of the real property?
Express Agreement	Express agreements clearly stating intent about whether property is a fixture are generally enforceable.
Trade Fixtures (Tenants' Fixtures)	Definition of *trade fixture:* personal property attached to leased real property by a tenant for the purpose of carrying on his trade or business. Trade fixtures can be removed and retained by the tenant at the termination of the lease except when one or more of the following apply: 1. Removal would cause substantial damage to the landlord's real property. 2. Tenant fails to remove the fixtures by the end of the lease (or within a reasonable time, if the lease is for an indefinite period of time). 3. An express agreement between the landlord and tenant provides otherwise.

RIGHTS AND INTERESTS IN REAL PROPERTY

When we think of ownership of real property, we normally think of one person owning all of the rights in a particular piece of land. However, real property involves a *bundle of rights* capable of ownership—sometimes by different people. The discussion that follows will examine the most common forms of present, **possessory interests** (rights to exclusive possession of real property): **fee simple absolute** and **life estate.** It will also explore the various ways in which two or more people can share ownership of the same possessory interest in real property. Finally, it will examine the interests and rights that one may have in another person's real property, such as the right to use another's property or restrict the way he uses it. These include **easements, profits, licenses,** and **restrictive covenants.** Each of these rights and interests will be discussed in turn.

Estates in Land

The term **estate** is used to describe the nature of a person's ownership interests in real property. Estates in land can be classified as being either **freehold estates** or **nonfreehold estates.** Nonfreehold (or leasehold) estates are those held by persons who lease real property. They will be discussed in the next chapter, which focuses on landlord-tenant law. Freehold estates are ownership interests in real property that are of uncertain duration. The most common types of freehold estates are fee simple absolute and life estates.

Fee Simple Absolute   The **fee simple absolute** is the highest form of land ownership in the United States. What we normally think of as "full ownership" of land is the fee simple absolute. A person who owns real property in fee simple absolute has the right to possess and use the property for an unlimited period of time, subject only to governmental regulations or private restrictions. He also has the unconditional power to dispose of the property during his lifetime or upon his death. A person who owns land in fee simple absolute may grant many rights to others without giving up the ownership of his fee simple. For example, he may lease the property to a tenant or grant mineral rights, easements, or mortgages to another.

Life Estate   A **life estate** is a property interest that gives a person the right to possess and use property for a time that is measured by his lifetime or that of another person. For example, if Toffler has a life estate in Black-

acre (a hypothetical tract of land) that is measured by his life, he has the right to use Blackacre during his life. At his death, the property will revert to the person who conveyed the estate to him or it will pass to some other designated person. While a life tenant such as Toffler has the right to use the property, he has the obligation not to do acts that will result in permanent injury to the property.

Co-Ownership of Real Property

Co-ownership of real property exists when two or more persons share the same estate (the same type of ownership interest) in the same property. The co-owners do not have separate rights to any portion of the real property; each has a share in the whole property. Seven types of co-ownership are recognized in the United States.

Tenancy in Common   People who own property under a **tenancy in common** have undivided interests in the property and equal rights to possess the property. When property is transferred to two or more people without a specification about their form of co-ownership, there is a presumption that they will take the property as tenants in common. The ownership interests of the tenants in common do not have to be equal. Thus, one tenant could have a two-thirds ownership interest in the property and the other tenant could have a one-third interest.

Each tenant in common has the right to possess and use the property. However, she cannot exclude the other tenants in common from also possessing and using the property. If the property is rented or otherwise produces income, each tenant has the right to share in the income in proportion to her share of ownership. Similarly, each must pay her proportionate share of the cost of taxes and necessary repairs. Where one tenant is in sole possession of the property and receives no rents or profits from the property, she is not required to pay rent to her cotenant unless her possession is adverse to or inconsistent with her cotenant's property interests.

A tenant in common can dispose of her interest in the property during life and at death. Similarly, her interest is subject to the claims of her creditors. When one tenant dies, her share passes to her heirs or, if she has made a will, to the person or persons specified in her will. Suppose Reynolds and MacGuire own Blackacre as tenants in common. Reynolds dies, having executed a valid will in which she leaves her share to a third person, Kelly. In this situation, MacGuire and Kelly become tenants in common.

Figure 1 Tenancy in Common, Joint Tenancy, and Tenancy by the Entirety

	Tenancy in Common	**Joint Tenancy**	**Tenancy by the Entirety**
Equal Possession and Use?	Yes	Yes	Yes
Share Income?	Yes	Yes	Presumably
Contribution Requirement?	Generally	Generally	Generally
Free Conveyance of Interest?	Yes; transferee becomes tenant in common	Yes, but joint tenancy is severed on conveyance and reverts to tenancy in common	Both must agree; divorce severs tenancy
Effect of Death?	Interest transferable at death by will or inheritance	Right of survivorship; surviving joint tenant(s) take decedent's share	Right of survivorship; surviving spouse takes decedent's share

Tenants in common can sever the cotenancy by agreeing to divide up the property or, if they are unable to agree, by petitioning a court for **partition** of the property. The court will physically divide the property if that is feasible, so that each tenant will get her proportionate share. If physical division is not appropriate, the court will order the property sold and divide the proceeds.

Joint Tenancy A **joint tenancy** is created when *equal* interests in real property are conveyed to two or more people by a single document that specifies that they are to own the property as joint tenants. The rights of use, possession, contribution, and partition are the same for a joint tenancy as for a tenancy in common. The distinguishing feature of a joint tenancy is that it gives the owners the **right of survivorship.** This means that upon the death of one of the joint tenants, that person's interest automatically passes to the surviving joint tenant(s). This feature makes it easy for a person to transfer property at death without making a will. For example, Bromwell buys property with his grandson, the two of them taking title to the property as joint tenants. At Bromwell's death, his interest will pass to his grandson without even going through the normal probate process.[3] By the same token, a provision in a joint tenant's will that purports to devise (transfer by will) his interest to someone other than his surviving joint tenants is ineffective.

A joint tenant may mortgage, sell, or give away his interest in the property during his lifetime. For that reason, a joint tenant's interest in property is subject to the claims of his creditors. When a joint tenant transfers his interest, the joint tenancy is *severed* and a tenancy in common is created as to the share affected by the transaction. When a joint tenant sells his interest to a third person, the third person becomes a tenant in common with the remaining joint tenant(s).

Tenancy by the Entirety Approximately half of the states permit married couples to own real property as **tenants by the entirety.** A tenancy by the entirety is basically a type of joint tenancy with the added requirement that the owners be married. Like the joint tenancy, the tenancy by the entirety involves the right of survivorship. Neither spouse can transfer the property by will if the other is still living. Upon the death of the husband or wife, the property passes automatically to the surviving spouse.

This tenancy cannot be severed by the act of only one of the parties. Neither spouse can transfer the property unless the other one also signs the deed. Thus, a creditor of one tenant cannot claim an interest in that person's share of the property held in tenancy by the entirety. Divorce, however, will sever a tenancy by the entirety and transform it into a tenancy in common. Figure 1 compares the features of tenancy in common, joint tenancy, and tenancy by the entirety.

Community Property A number of western and southern states recognize a system of co-ownership of property by married couples that is known as **community property.** This type of co-ownership is based on the theory that marriage is a partnership in which each spouse contributes to the property base of the family.

---

[3]The probate process is discussed in the Estates and Trusts chapter.

Property that is acquired during the marriage through a spouse's industry or efforts is classified as *community* property, in which each spouse has an equal interest. This is true regardless of who produced or earned the property. Since each spouse has an equal share in the community property, neither can convey the property without the other's joining in the transaction. A number of community property states permit the parties to dispose of their interests in community property at death.

Not all property owned by a married person is community property, however. Property that a spouse owned before marriage or acquired during marriage by gift or inheritance is *separate property*. Property exchanged for separate property also remains separately owned. The details of each state's community property system vary, depending on the specific provisions of that state's community property statutes.

Tenancy in Partnership   When a partnership takes title to property in the name of the partnership, its form of co-ownership is called **tenancy in partnership.** The incidents of tenancy in partnership are set out in the Uniform Partnership Act. You can read more about this form of co-ownership in the Introduction to Forms of Business and Formation of Partnerships chapter.

Condominium Ownership   Condominiums are an ancient form of co-ownership that has become very common in the United States in recent years, even in locations outside urban and resort areas. In a condominium, a purchaser takes title to her individual unit and also becomes a tenant in common with other unit owners in facilities that are shared, such as hallways, elevators, swimming pools, and parking areas. The condominium owner pays property taxes on her individual unit. She can generally mortgage or sell her individual unit without the approval of the other unit owners. She also makes a monthly payment for the maintenance of the common areas. For federal income tax purposes, she is treated in the same way as the owner of a single-family home and is allowed to deduct her property taxes and mortgage interest expenses.

Cooperative Ownership   In a cooperative, an entire building is owned by a corporation or by a group of people. A person who wants to buy a unit buys stock in the corporation and holds his apartment under a long-term lease (called a **proprietary lease**), which he can renew. Frequently, the cooperative owner must obtain the approval of the other owners to sell or sublease his unit.

INTERESTS IN REAL PROPERTY OWNED BY OTHERS

In a variety of situations, a person may hold a legally protected interest in real property that is owned by someone else. Such interests are not *possessory,* that is, they do not give their holder the right to complete dominion over the land. Rather, they give him the right to *use* another person's property or to limit the way in which the other person uses his own property. The following discussion explores the nature of these types of interests.

Easements

An **easement** is the right to make certain uses of another person's property (*affirmative easement*) or the right to prevent another person from making certain uses of his own property (*negative easement*). The right to run a sewer line across another person's property is an example of an affirmative easement. An easement that prevents a neighbor from erecting a structure on his land that would block your solar collector is an example of a negative easement.

When an easement is considered to be an **easement appurtenant,** it will pass with the land. This means that if the owner of the land benefited by an easement appurtenant sells or otherwise conveys his tract, the new owner will also get the easement. An easement appurtenant is one that is primarily designed to benefit a certain tract of land, rather than merely giving an individual a personal right. For example, Agnew and Gross are next-door neighbors. They share a common driveway that runs along the borderline of their property. Each has an easement in the part of the driveway that lies on the other's property. If Agnew sells his property to a third person, Donaldson, Donaldson will also get the easement in the part of the driveway that is on Gross's land. By the same token, Gross still has an easement in the part of the driveway that lies on Donaldson's land.

Creation of Easements

Easements can be acquired in a number of different ways:

1. *By grant.* When an owner of property expressly gives an easement in his property to another while retaining his ownership of the property, he is said to **grant** an easement. For example, Long may sell or give Madison, the owner of adjoining property, the right to use his land to reach an alley behind his land.

2. *By reservation.* When a person transfers ownership of his land but retains the right to use the transferred land for some specified purpose, he is said to **reserve** an easement in the land that was once his. For example, Swanson sells land to Jentz, reserving the mineral rights to the property and also reserving an easement to enter the land to remove the minerals.

3. *By prescription.* An **easement by prescription** is created when one person uses another person's land openly, continuously, and in a manner adverse to the owner's rights for a period of time specified by state statute. (This period of time varies from state to state.) The property owner should thus be on notice that someone else is acting as if he has certain rights to use the property. If the property owner does not take action to assert his rights during the statutory period, he may lose his right to stop the other person from making use of his property. Suppose State X provides that easements by prescription can be obtained through 15 years of prescriptive use. Daniels, who lives in State X, uses the driveway of his next-door neighbor, Solt, for 20 years. He does this openly, on a daily basis, and without Solt's permission. If Solt does not take action to stop Daniels within the 15-year period provided by statute, Daniels will have obtained an easement by prescription. This means that Daniels not only has the right to use the driveway while Solt owns the property but also that if Solt sells his property to a third person, Daniels still will

be entitled to use the driveway. This type of easement is similar to the concept of *adverse possession,* which will be discussed later in the chapter.

4. *By implication.* Sometimes, easements are *implied* by the nature of the transaction rather than created by express agreement of the parties. Such easements are called **easements by implication.** There are two types of easements by implication: *easements by prior use* and *easements by necessity.*

An **easement by prior use** is created when land is subdivided and a path, road, or other apparent and beneficial use exists at the time that part of the land is conveyed to another person. In this situation, the new owner will have an easement to continue using the path, road, or other prior use that runs across the other person's land. For example, a private road running through Greenacre from north to south links the house located on the northern portion of Greenacre to the highway that lies beyond Greenacre to the south. Durant, the owner of Greenacre, sells the northern portion of Greenacre to Cohen. Cohen would have an easement by implication to continue making use of the private road running across the portion of the land that has been retained by Durant. To prevent this type of easement from arising, the parties must specify in their contract that such an easement will not exist.

An **easement by necessity** is created when real property once held in common ownership is subdivided in such a way that the only way the new owner can gain access to his land is through passage over the land of another that was once part of the same tract. An easement by necessity is based on the *necessity* of obtaining access to property. *Attaway v. Davis,* which follows, presents a good example of the acquisition of an easement by necessity.

ATTAWAY v. DAVIS

707 S.W.2d 302 (S. Ct. Ark. 1986)

Hester Davis bought a 12-acre tract of land in 1967. The tract was landlocked, although it had some frontage on Beaver Lake, a navigable watercourse. At one time, a single owner, A. O. Clark, had owned all the land now owned by Davis, her neighbors, Albert and Sarah Attaway, and others in the area. At first, Davis got to her property by using an old trail across the Attaways' property and another tract. In 1975, however, the Attaways put in a gate to obstruct that trail. After that, Davis walked to her land. She later filed this action to acquire a right-of-way giving her access from a public road, Walnut Road, to her tract. The trial court awarded Davis a right-of-way running along the east side of the Attaways' property, and the Attaways appealed this order.

Smith, J.   Davis's right to obtain access arises from her status as a landlocked owner. [One of the Attaways'] argument is that Davis already has access to her property, because it has some frontage on Beaver Lake, a navigable watercourse. The statute does refer to access to a public road or a navigable watercourse, but this law was adopted more than a century ago, in 1871. What Davis must show is a reasonable necessity for a road, not an absolute necessity. Now that travel even for short distances is almost always by motor vehicle, it is not reasonable to require Davis and those wishing to visit her to make the trip by boat.

The Attaways insist that they have been willing since 1975 to permit Davis to reach her property by using a second trail that crosses their land. Any such use of neighboring property would be permissive and revocable. Davis is entitled to obtain a permanent right-of-way by proceeding under the statute and paying reasonable compensation.

Order for Davis affirmed.

Easements and the Statute of Frauds   Because an easement is a type of interest in land, it is within the coverage of the statute of frauds.[4] An express agreement granting or reserving an easement must be in writing and signed by the party to be charged to be enforceable. Under the statutes of most states, the grant of an easement must be executed with the same formalities as are observed in executing the grant of a fee simple interest in real property. However, easements not granted expressly, such as easements by prior use, necessity, or prescription, are enforceable even though they are not in writing.

Profits

A **profit** is a right to enter another person's land and remove some product of the land (such as timber) or some part of the land (such as gravel or minerals). For example, Jones is the holder of a profit that allows him to enter Wilson's land to drill for oil and remove such oil as he may find. Generally, profits are governed by the same rules that govern easements. In fact, profits are sometimes called **easements with a profit.**

License

A **license** is a temporary right to enter the land of another for a specific purpose. A license is generally much

more informal than an easement and may be created orally or in any other manner that shows the landowner's permission for the licensee to enter the property. Licenses are considered to be personal rights that are not really interests in land. A license can be revoked at the will of the licensor unless the license is coupled with an interest, such as ownership of personal property that exists on the licensor's property, or unless the licensee has paid money or something else of value for the license or in reliance on the license. For example, Woolridge pays Arbuckle $600 for trees on Arbuckle's land, which are to be cut and hauled away. Woolridge has an irrevocable license to enter Arbuckle's land to cut and haul away the trees.

Restrictive Covenants   Within certain limitations, owners of real estate can create private and enforceable agreements that restrict the use of real property. Such private agreements are called **restrictive covenants.** For example, Daily owns two adjacent lots. He sells one to Grant with the express agreement that Grant promises not to operate on the property any business involving the sale of liquor. This commitment is included in the deed that Daily gives to Grant. Similarly, a developer sells lots in a subdivision, placing a restriction in each deed concerning the minimum size of houses that can be built on the property.

The validity and enforceability of such private restrictions on the use of real property depend on the purpose, nature, and scope of the restriction. A restraint that

---

[4]The land provision of the statute of frauds is discussed in the Writing chapter.

violates a statute or other public policy will not be enforced. For example, under the Fair Housing Act, a federal law that will be discussed later in this chapter, it is illegal for a person covered by the law to enforce a covenant that precludes the sale or rental of a dwelling to any person because of his race, color, religion, sex, handicap, familial status, or national origin.[5]

A restrictive covenant will also be unenforceable if it effectively prevents the sale or transfer of the property. This would constitute a violation of the public policy that favors free alienation (transfer) of land. Since public policy favors the unlimited use and transfer of land, ambiguous language in a restrictive covenant is construed in favor of the less restrictive interpretation. However, a restraint that is clearly expressed and that does not unduly restrict the use and transfer of the property or otherwise violate public policy will be enforced. For example, restrictions that relate to the minimum size of lots, maintenance of the area as a residential community, or the size and design of buildings are usually enforceable.

An important question that frequently arises regarding restrictive covenants is whether subsequent owners of the property are bound by the restriction even though they were not parties to the original agreement. Under certain circumstances, the covenant is said to "run with the land" so as to bind subsequent owners of the restricted land. For a covenant to run with the land, it must have been *binding* on the people who were originally parties to it and must show that the original parties *intended* the covenant to bind their successors. The covenant must also *"touch and concern"* the restricted land. This means that it must involve the use, value, or character of the land in question and not just a personal obligation of one of the original parties. In addition, a covenant will not bind a subsequent purchaser unless he had *notice* of the existence of the covenant at the time he took his interest. This notice would commonly be provided by the recording of the deed or other document containing the covenant.

Restrictive covenants can be enforced by the parties to the agreement, by persons who were intended to benefit from the covenant, and—if the covenant runs with the land—by the successors of the original parties. If the restriction is contained in a subdivision plat (recorded description of a subdivision) in the form of a general

building scheme, other property owners in the subdivision may be able to enforce it.

Termination of Restrictive Covenants Restrictive covenants can be terminated in a variety of ways. They can be voluntarily relinquished, or *waived*. They can also be terminated *by their own terms* (such as when the covenant specifies that it is to endure for a certain length of time) or by *dramatically changed circumstances*. For example, if Brown's property is subject to a restrictive covenant that restricts it to residential use, the covenant may be terminated by the fact that all of the surrounding property has come to be used for industrial purposes. When a restriction has been held invalid or has been terminated, the basic deed remains valid but is treated as if the restriction had been stricken from it.

ACQUISITION OF REAL PROPERTY

Title to real property can be obtained in a number of ways, including purchase, gift, will or inheritance, tax sale, and adverse possession. Original title to land in the United States was acquired either from the federal government or from a country that held the land prior to its acquisition by the United States. The land in the 13 original colonies had been granted by the king of England either to the colonies or to certain individuals. The land in the Northwest Territory was ceded by the states to the federal government, which in turn issued grants or patents of land. Original ownership of much of the land in Florida and the Southwest came by grants from the rulers of Spain.

Acquisition by Purchase

The right to sell real property is a basic ownership right. In fact, unreasonable restrictions on the right of an owner to sell her property are considered to be unenforceable as against public policy. Most people who own real property acquired title by buying it from someone else. Each state sets the requirements for the conveyance of real property located within that state. The various elements of selling and buying real property will be discussed later in this chapter.

Acquisition by Gift

Ownership of real property may be acquired by gift. For such a gift to be valid, the donor must deliver a properly

---

[5]24 C.F.R. section 100.80 (b) (1990).

executed deed to the property to the donee or to some third person who is to hold it for the donee. It is not necessary that the donee or the third person actually take possession of the property. The essential element of the gift is the *delivery* of the deed. Suppose West makes out a deed to the family farm and leaves it in a safe-deposit box for delivery to her son when she dies. The attempted gift will not be valid, because West did not deliver the gift during her lifetime.

Acquisition by Will or Inheritance

The owner of real property generally has the right to dispose of that property by will. The requirements for making a valid will are discussed in the Estates and Trusts chapter. If the owner of real property dies without leaving a valid will, the property will go to his heirs as determined under the laws of the state in which the real property is located.

Acquisition by Tax Sale

If the taxes assessed on real property are not paid, they become a *lien* on the property. This lien has priority over all other claims to the land. If the taxes remain unpaid for a period of time, the government can sell the land at a tax sale, and the purchaser at the tax sale acquires title to the property. However, some states have statutes that give the original owner a limited time (perhaps a year) in which to buy the property back from the tax sale purchaser for his cost plus interest.

Acquisition by Adverse Possession Each state has a statute of limitations that gives an owner of land a specific number of years in which to bring a lawsuit to regain possession of his land from someone who is trespassing on it. This period generally ranges from 5 to 20 years, depending on the state. If someone wrongfully possesses land and acts as if he were the owner, the real owner must take steps to have the person ejected from the land. If this is not done within the statutory period, the right to eject the possessor will be lost. The person who stayed in possession of the property for the statutory period will acquire title to the land by **adverse possession.**

To acquire title to land by adverse possession, a person must possess land in a manner that puts the true owner on notice that he has a cause of action against that person. The adverse possessor's possession must be:

1. Open,
2. Actual,
3. Continuous,
4. Exclusive,
5. Hostile (or adverse) to the owner's rights.

As you will read in *Chaplin v. Sanders,* the hostility element is not a matter of subjective intent. Rather, it means that the adverse possessor's possession must be inconsistent with the owner's rights. If a person is in possession of another's property under a lease, as a cotenant, or with the permission of the owner, his possession is not hostile. In some states, the person in possession of land must also pay the taxes on the land in order to gain title by adverse possession.

It is not necessary that the same person occupy the land for the statutory period. The periods of possession of several adverse possessors can be "tacked" together for purposes of calculating the period of possession if each possessor claims rights from the other. The possession must, however, be continuous for the necessary time.

CHAPLIN v. SANDERS

676 P.2d 431 (Wash. Sup. Ct. 1984) (en banc)

In 1957 or 1958, Mr. and Mrs. Hibbard decided to clear their land of woods and overgrowth and set up a trailer park. There was no obvious boundary between the Hibbards' land and the land of their neighbor to the east, so they cleared the land up to a deep drainage ditch and opened their park. Mr. Hibbard also built a road to be used for entering and leaving the park. In 1960, the Hibbards' neighbor, Mr. McMurray, had a survey conducted and discovered that the Hibbards had encroached on his land ("the eastern parcel") by approximately 20 feet. He informed the Hibbards of this. In 1962, the Hibbards sold their land ("the western parcel") to the Gilberts. The contract between these two parties specifically noted that the Hibbards' road encroached on the eastern parcel. Over the course of ensuing years, the western parcel changed hands several times until Peter and Patricia Sanders bought it in 1976. The Sanders had actual notice of the contract provision referring to McMurray's claim, but purportedly mistook which road the contract referred to. In 1978, Kent and Barbara Chaplin bought the eastern parcel without having a survey conducted.

There was little change in the use of the western parcel since its initial development by Hibbard. The road remained in continuous use in connection with the trailer park. The area between the road and the drainage ditch was also used by trailer park residents for parking, storage, garbage removal, and picnicking. Trailer personnel and tenants moved grass up to the drainage ditch and planted flowers. In the spring of 1978, the Sanders installed underground wiring and surface power poles in the area between the roadway and the drainage ditch.

The eastern parcel remained essentially undeveloped, but soon after the Chaplins bought it, they contacted an architectural consultant for the purpose of designing commercial buildings for their property. A survey conducted for this purpose discovered the Sanders's encroachments. The Chaplins then brought this action to quiet title to the road and its shoulder ("Parcel A") and the area between the road and the drainage ditch ("Parcel B"). The trial court held that the Sanders had acquired Parcel A by adverse possession, but had not acquired Parcel B because their use of it was not open and notorious. The case was appealed and the Court of Appeals found that the Sanders had not acquired *either* parcel because they had had actual notice of McMurray's ownership of the disputed area of land and therefore their possession was not hostile.

Utter, Justice.   To establish a claim of adverse possession, the possession must be (1) exclusive, (2) actual and uninterrupted, (3) open and notorious, and (4) hostile and under a claim of right made in good faith. The period throughout which these elements must concurrently exist is 10 years. Hostility, as defined by this court, does not import enmity or ill-will, but rather imports that the claimant is in possession as owner, in contradistinction to holding in recognition of or subordination to the true owner. We have traditionally treated the hostility and claim of right requirements as one and the same.

The doctrine of adverse possession was formulated at law for the purpose of assuring maximum utilization of land, encouraging the rejection of stale claims and, most important, quieting titles. Because the doctrine was formulated at law and not at equity, it was originally intended to protect both those who knowingly appropriated the land of others and those who honestly entered and held possession in full belief that the land was theirs. Thus, when the original purpose of the adverse possession doctrine is considered, it becomes apparent that the claimant's motive in possessing the land is irrelevant and no inquiry should be made into his guilt or innocence.

For these reasons, we are convinced that the dual requirement that the claimant take possession in "good faith" and not recognize another's superior interest does not serve the purpose of the adverse possession doctrine. The "hostility/claim of right" element of adverse possession requires only that the claimant treat the land as his own as against the world throughout the statutory period. The nature of his possession will be determined solely on the basis of the manner in which he treats the property. His subjective belief regarding his true interest in the land and his intent to dispossess or not dispossess another is irrelevant to this determination. Under this analysis, permission to occupy the land, given by the true title owner to the claimant or his predecessors, will still operate to negate the element of hostility. Under our holding today, what is relevant is the objective character of Hibbard's possession and that of his successors in interest.

The trial court found the character of possession [of Parcel A] to have been hostile for at least a 10-year period. We agree. The Sanders and their predecessors used and maintained the property as though it was their own for over the statutory period. This was sufficient to satisfy the element of hostility.

The Sanders also appeal from the trial court's finding that Parcel B was not possessed in an open and notorious manner. The requirement of open and notorious [use] is satisfied if the title holder has actual notice of the adverse use throughout the statutory period. We are compelled to conclude, from the evidence, that McMurray was aware of the Hibbards' use of the strip abutting the roadway. This conclusion is all the more compelling when the disparate condition of McMurray's undeveloped, overgrown property and the cleared, mowed, and maintained strip of land separating the roadway and McMurray's land is considered. In determining what acts are sufficiently open and notorious to manifest to others a claim to land, the character of the land must be considered. The necessary use and occupancy need only be of the character that a true owner would assert in view of its nature and location. Accordingly, the case is reversed and remanded with directions to quiet title to the disputed property in the Sanders.

Judgment reversed in favor of the Sanders.

TRANSFER BY SALE

Steps in a Sale

The major steps normally involved in the sale of real property are:

1. Contracting with a real estate broker to locate a buyer for the property.

2. Negotiating and signing a contract to sell the property.

3. Arranging for the financing of the purchase and the satisfaction of other requirements, such as arranging for a survey or for the acquisition of title insurance.

4. Closing the sale, at which time the sale is consummated, usually by payment of the purchase price and transfer of the deed.

5. Recording the deed.

Contracting with a Real Estate Broker

Although engaging a real estate broker is not a legal requirement for the sale of real property, it is common for a person who wants to sell his property to "list" the property with a broker. A listing contract empowers the seller's broker to act as his agent in procuring a ready, willing, and able buyer on the seller's terms and managing the details of the transfer of the property. A number of states' statutes of frauds require listing contracts to be evidenced by a writing and signed by the party to be charged.

Real estate brokers are regulated by state and some federal law. As trusted agents, real estate brokers owe **fiduciary duties** (duties of trust and confidence) to their clients. You can read more about the types of duties imposed on such agents in the Agency Relationship chapter.

Types of Listing Contracts   Matters such as the duration of the listing period, the terms on which the seller will sell, and the amount and terms of the broker's commission are specified in the listing contract. There are several different types of listing contracts.

1. *Open listing.* In an open listing contract, the broker is authorized to sell the property, but this right is *not exclusive.* This means that the seller or a third party (for example, another broker) also have the right to find a buyer for the property. Under an open listing, the broker would have the right to a commission only if he were the first one to find a ready, willing, and able buyer.

2. *Exclusive agency listing.* Under an exclusive agency listing, the broker will earn a commission if he *or any other agent* finds a buyer during the period of time specified in the contract. Thus, the broker under an exclusive agency listing would have the right to a commission if the seller had employed another broker who found a ready, willing, and able buyer. Under the exclusive agency listing, however, the seller retains the right to sell the property himself without paying a commission.

3. *Exclusive right to sell.* Under an exclusive right to sell listing, the broker will earn his commission no matter who procures the buyer. As the name suggests, he is given the exclusive right to sell the property for a specified period of time. Under this type of listing, a seller would have to pay the commission even if the seller or some third party found a buyer during the duration of the listing contract.

Contract for Sale

The principles regarding contract formation, performance, assignment, and remedies that you learned in earlier chapters are applicable to contracts for the sale of real estate. The contract provides for such matters as the purchase price, the type of deed the purchaser will get, the items of personal property that are included in the sale, and any other aspect of the transaction that is important to the parties. The contract may make the "closing" of the sale contingent on the buyer's finding financing at a specified rate of interest and the seller's procurement of a survey, title insurance, and termite insurance. Because the contract is within the statute of frauds, it must be evidenced by a writing and signed by the party to be charged to be enforceable.

Fair Housing Act

The Fair Housing Act, first enacted by Congress in 1968 and substantially revised in 1988, is designed to prevent discrimination in the housing market. Its provisions apply to real estate brokers, sellers (other than those selling their own single-family dwellings without the use of a broker), lenders, lessors, and appraisers. Originally, the Act prohibited discrimination on the basis of race, color, religion, sex, and national origin. The 1988 amendments added handicap and "familial status" to this list. The familial status category was intended to prevent discrimination in the housing market against families with children and pregnant women.[6] "Adult" or "senior citizen" communities restricting residents' age are not illegal under the Fair Housing Act—even though they exclude families with children—so long as the housing meets the requirements of the Act's "housing for older persons" exemption.[7]

The Act prohibits discrimination in a wide range of activities relating to the sale or lease of housing, such as refusing to sell or rent, discriminating in the terms, conditions, or privileges of sale or rental, the provision of services and facilities involved in sale or rental, and representing that housing is not available when, in fact, it is.[8] It also prohibits discrimination in appraisals and financing of dwellings and in the provision of brokerage services.

Included in the concept of discrimination on the basis of handicap are the refusal to permit a handicapped person to make (at his own expense) reasonable modifications in the property and the refusal to make reasonable accommodations in rules, policies, practices, or services when such modifications or accommodations are necessary to afford the handicapped person full enjoyment of the property. The Act also makes it unlawful to build multifamily housing that is inaccessible to people with handicaps. The Fair Housing Act invalidates any state or municipal law that requires or permits an action that would be a discriminatory housing practice within the meaning of federal law.

A violation of the Fair Housing Act can result in a civil action brought by either the government or the aggrieved individual. The 1988 amendments give aggrieved persons the right to bring a private civil action. When such a person prevails, a court may award actual and punitive damages, injunctions, attorney's fees and costs, or any other appropriate relief.

Financing the Purchase The various arrangements for financing the purchase of real property, such as mortgages, land contracts, and deeds of trust, are discussed in the Introduction to Credit and Secured Transactions chapter.

---

[6] Familial status is defined as one or more individuals under the age of 18 who are domiciled with a parent, some other person who has custody over them, or the designee of such parent or custodial individual. It also applies to a person who is pregnant or in the process of attempting to secure custody of children under the age of 18.

[7] The Fair Housing Act defines "housing for older persons" as housing provided under any state or federal program that the Secretary of HUD finds is specifically designed and operated to assist elderly persons, housing intended for and solely occupied by persons 62 years old or older, or housing intended and operated for occupancy by at least one person 55 years old or older and that meets the requirements of federal regulations.

[8] The aspects of the Fair Housing Act that apply to rentals are discussed in the Landlord and Tenant chapter.

Deeds

Each state has statutes that set out the formalities necessary to accomplish a valid conveyance of land. As a general rule, a valid conveyance is accomplished by the execution and delivery of a **deed.** A deed is a written instrument that conveys title from one person *(the grantor)* to another person *(the grantee)*. There are three basic types of deeds in general use in the United States: *quitclaim deeds, warranty deeds,* and *deeds of bargain and sale* (also called *grant deeds*). The precise rights conveyed by a deed depend on the type of deed that the parties use.

Quitclaim Deeds A **quitclaim deed** conveys whatever title the grantor has at the time he executes the deed. It does not, however, contain any warranties of title. The grantor who executes a quitclaim deed does not claim to have good title, or in fact, any title at all. The grantee has no action against the grantor under a quitclaim deed if the title proves to be defective. Quitclaim deeds are frequently used to cure a technical defect in the chain of title to property.

Warranty Deeds A **warranty deed,** unlike a quitclaim deed, contains covenants of warranty. In addition to conveying title to the property, the grantor who executes a warranty deed guarantees the title that she has conveyed. There are two types of warranty deeds.

1. *General warranty deed.* In a general warranty deed, the grantor warrants against (and agrees to defend against) all defects in the title and all encumbrances (such as liens and easements), even those that arose before the grantor received her title.

2. *Special warranty deed.* In a special warranty deed, the grantor warrants against (and agrees to defend against) those defects in the title or those encumbrances that arose after she acquired the property. If the property conveyed is subject to some encumbrance such as a mortgage, a long-term lease, or an easement, it is a common practice for the grantor to give a special warranty deed that contains a provision excepting those specific encumbrances from the warranty.

Deed of Bargain and Sale In a **deed of bargain and sale,** also known as a **grant deed,** the grantor does not make covenants. The grantor uses language such as "I grant" or "I bargain and sell" or "I convey" property. In such a deed, it is implied that the grantor is at least making the representation that he owns the land and that he has not previously conveyed the property to someone else or encumbered it.

Form and Execution of Deed

Some states have enacted statutes setting out a suggested form for deeds. The statutory requirements of the different states for the execution of deeds are not uniform, but they do follow a similar pattern. As a general rule, a deed states the *name of the grantee,* contains a *recitation of consideration* and a *description of the property conveyed,* and is *signed by the grantor.* In most states, the deed must be notarized (acknowledged by the grantor before a notary public or other authorized officer) to be eligible for recording in public records.

No technical words of conveyance are necessary for a valid deed. Any language is sufficient if it indicates with reasonable certainty the intent to transfer the ownership of property. The phrases "grant, bargain, and sell" and "convey and warrant" are commonly used. Deeds contain recitations of consideration primarily for historical reasons. The consideration recited is not necessarily the purchase price of the property. Deeds often state that the consideration for the conveyance is "one dollar and other valuable consideration."

The property conveyed must be described in such a manner that it can be identified. Generally, this means that the *legal description* of the property must be used. Several methods of legal description are used in the United States. In urban areas, descriptions are usually by lot, block, and plat. In rural areas in which the land has been surveyed by the government, property is usually described by reference to the government survey. It may also be described by a metes and bounds description that specifies the boundaries of the tract of land.

Recording Deeds

The delivery of a valid deed conveys title from a grantor to a grantee. Nevertheless, in order to prevent his interest from being defeated by third parties who may claim an interest in the same property, the grantee should immediately **record** the deed. The grantee will have to pay a fee for recording the deed. When a deed is recorded, it is deposited and indexed in a systematic way in a public office, where it operates to give notice of the grantee's interest to the rest of the world.

Recording Statutes Each state has a **recording statute** that establishes a system for the recording of all transactions that affect the ownership of real property. The statutes are not uniform in their provisions. In general, they provide for the recording of all deeds, mortgages, land contracts, and similar documents.

Types of Recording Statutes   State recording statutes also provide for priority among competing claimants to rights in real property, in case conflicting rights or interests in property should be deeded to more than one person. (Obviously, a grantor has no right to deed the same property to two different people, but, in case it should occur, these statutes provide rules to decide which of the purchasers has superior title.) These rules apply only to grantees who have given value for their deeds (primarily purchasers and lenders), and not to donees. There are three basic types of priority systems provided by state recording statutes.

1. *Race statute.* Under a "race" statute—so called because the person who wins the race to the courthouse wins the property—the first grantee who records a deed to a tract of land has superior title. For example, if Grantor deeds Blackacre to Jones on March 1 and deeds Blackacre to McBride on April 1, McBride will have superior title to Blackacre *if he records his deed before Jones does.* Race statutes are relatively uncommon today.

2. *Notice statutes.* Under a notice system of priority, a grantee who acquires his interest without notice of an unrecorded deed to any other grantee will have superior title. For example, Grantor deeds Greenacre to Wright on June 1, but Wright does not record his deed. On July 1, Bopp buys Greenacre, not knowing of Wright's competing claim, and Grantor executes and delivers a deed to Bopp. In this situation, Bopp would have superior rights to Greenacre even if Wright ultimately records his deed before Bopp does.

3. *Race-notice statutes.* The race-notice priority system combines elements of both systems discussed previously. Under race-notice statutes, the grantee who has priority is the one who both takes his interest without notice of any prior unrecorded claim *and* records first. For example, Grantor deeds Redacre to Pratt on September 1. On October 1, at which time Pratt has not yet recorded his deed, Grantor deeds Redacre to Allen. If Allen records his deed before Pratt, Allen has superior rights to Redacre.

Methods of Assuring Title

One of the things that a person must be concerned about in buying real property is whether the seller of the property has *good title* to it. In buying property, a buyer is really buying the seller's ownership interests. Because the buyer does not want to pay a large sum of money for something that turns out to be worthless, it is important for him to obtain some assurance that the seller has good title to the property. This is commonly done in one of three ways.

1. *Title opinion.* In some locations, it is customary to have an **abstract of title** examined by an attorney. An abstract of title is a history of the passage of title of a piece of real property according to the public records. It is *not* a guarantee of good title. After examining the abstract, an attorney will render an opinion about whether the grantor has **marketable title** to the property. Marketable title is title that is free from defects or reasonable doubt about its validity. If the title is defective, the nature of the defects will be stated in the title opinion.

2. *Torrens system.* A method of title assurance that is possible in a few states is the **Torrens system** of title registration. Under this system, a person who owns land in fee simple obtains a certificate of title. When the property is sold, the grantor delivers a deed and a certificate of title to the grantee. All liens and encumbrances against the title are noted on the certificate, so that the purchaser is assured that the title is good except as to the liens and encumbrances noted on the certificate. However, some claims or encumbrances, such as adverse possession, do not appear on the records and must be discovered by making an inspection of the property. In some Torrens states, certain encumbrances, such as tax liens, short term leases, and highway rights, are valid against the purchaser even though they do not appear on the certificate.

3. *Title insurance.* The preferred and most common means of protecting title to real property is to purchase a policy of **title insurance.** Title insurance is designed to reimburse the insured for loss if the title turns out to be defective. Title insurance not only compensates for loss of the title; it also pays litigation costs if the insured must go to court to defend the title. Lenders commonly require that a separate policy of title insurance be obtained for the lender's protection. Title insurance may be obtained in combination with the other methods of assuring title that were discussed earlier.

Seller's Responsibilities Regarding the Quality of Residential Property

A major concern of buyers of improved real estate is that the structures on the property be in good condition. This concern is especially acute if the buyer intends to use the property for residential purposes. Traditionally, the rule of *caveat emptor* ("let the buyer beware") applied to the sale of real property unless the seller committed fraud or misrepresentation or made *express warranties* about the condition of the property. In addition, under most situations, sellers had no duty to disclose hidden defects that they knew about. The legal environment for sellers, especially for real estate professionals such as developers and builder-vendors of residential property, has changed substantially, however. The following discussion explores two important sources of liability for sellers of real property.

Implied Warranty of Habitability

Traditionally, sellers made no *implied warranties* that property sold for residential purposes was habitable or suitable for the buyer's use. The law's attitude toward the relationship of buyer and seller in the sale of residential property began to change as a result of the rapid growth of product liability law in the late 1960s. Courts began to see that the same policies that favored the creation of implied warranties in the sale of goods applied with equal force to the sale of residential real estate.[9] Like goods, housing is frequently mass-produced. As in the sale of goods, there is often a disparity of knowledge and bargaining power between the builder-vendor and the buyer of a house. Many defects in houses are of a type that evades discovery during a buyer's inspection. This creates the possibility of serious loss, since the purchase of a home is often the largest single investment that a person ever makes.

For these reasons, courts in the majority of states now hold that builders, builder-vendors (persons who build and sell houses), and developers make an **implied warranty of habitability** when they build or sell real property for residential purposes.

The implied warranty of habitability is basically a guarantee that the house is free of *latent* (that is, hidden) defects that would render it unsafe or unsuitable for human habitation. A breach of warranty will subject the defendant to liability for damages, measured by either the cost of repairs or the loss in value of the house.[10] The application of the warranty has been limited to builders,

builder-vendors, and developers. That is, an ordinary seller of a house who is not the builder or developer does not make a warranty of habitability.

One further issue that has caused a great deal of litigation is whether the warranty extends to subsequent purchasers of the house. For example, ABC Development Co. builds a house and sells it to Sharp. If Sharp later sells the house to Richey, can Richey sue ABC for breach of warranty if a serious defect renders the house uninhabitable? Although some courts have rejected the possibility of implied warranty actions brought by subsequent purchasers, the bulk of opinion today is that an implied warranty of habitability made by a builder-vendor would extend to a subsequent purchaser.

Another issue that has arisen regarding the implied warranty of habitability is whether the warranty can be *disclaimed* or *limited* in the contract of sale. Subject to the doctrine of unconscionability, concerns about public policy,[11] and doctrines of contract interpretation,[12] it appears to be at least possible to disclaim or limit the warranty by a contract provision. Courts construe such clauses very strictly against the builder-vendor, however, and often reject disclaimers that are not specific about the rights that the purchaser waives.

Duty to Disclose Hidden Defects

Under traditional contract law, a seller had no duty to *disclose* to the buyer defects in the property he was selling, even if the seller knew about the defects and there was no reasonable way for the buyer to find out about them on his own. Since the seller had no duty to volunteer information, his failure to do so could not constitute fraud or innocent misrepresentation. This rule was another expression of the prevailing notion of *caveat emptor*.

The traditional rule of nondisclosure was subject to a number of exceptions.[13] For example, a person who stood in a confidential or fiduciary relationship with the other party to the contract would have the duty to make disclosures of material defects. The typical buyer-seller relationship was considered to be an arm's-length transaction, however, and *not* a confidential or fiduciary

---

[9]See the Product Liability chapter for a discussion of the development of similar doctrines in the law of product liability.

[10]Remedies are discussed in the Performance and Remedies chapter.

[11]See the Illegality chapter for further discussion of these doctrines.

[12]The interpretation of contracts is discussed in the Writing chapter.

[13]These traditional exceptions are discussed in detail in the Reality of Consent chapter.

relationship, so there was no duty to disclose in most sales of real property.

Today, courts in many jurisdictions have substantially eroded the traditional rule regarding nondisclosure and have placed a duty on the seller to disclose any known defect that materially affects the property's value and is not reasonably observable by the buyer. His failure to make disclosure under these circumstances is the equiv-alent of an assertion that the defect does not exist, and that assertion may form the basis for a finding of fraud or misrepresentation.[14] *Johnson v. Davis* presents an ex-ample of the trend of expanding the duty to disclose.

---

[14]Fraud and misrepresentation are discussed in the Reality of Consent chapter.

JOHNSON v. DAVIS
480 So. 2d 625 (Fla. Sup. Ct. 1985)

In May of 1982, Morton and Edna Davis entered into a contract to buy a house from Clarence and Dana Johnson for $310,000. The house was three years old at the time. The contract required a $5,000 initial deposit payment and an additional $26,000 deposit payment within five days. After the Davises had paid the initial $5,000 deposit but before they had paid the $26,000 deposit, Mrs. Davis noticed some buckling and peeling plaster around the corner of a window frame and stains on ceilings in several rooms. Mrs. Davis inquired about this, and Mr. Johnson told her that the window had had a minor problem that had been corrected long ago and that the stains were wallpaper glue. The parties disagree about whether Mr. Johnson told Mrs. Davis at this time that there had never been any problems with the roof or ceilings. The Davises then paid the remaining $26,000 deposit and the Johnsons moved out of the house. Several days later, following a heavy rain, Mrs. Davis entered the house and discovered water gushing in from around the window frame, the ceiling of the family room, the light fixtures, the glass doors, and the stove in the kitchen. The Davises hired roofers, who reported that the roof was inherently defective and that any repairs would be temporary because the roof was "slipping." Only a new roof (at a cost of $15,000) could be watertight. The Davises then filed this action alleging breach of contract, fraud, and misrepresentation, and seeking rescission of the contract and return of their deposit payments. The trial court awarded the Davises $26,000 plus interest but permitted the Johnsons to keep the initial $5,000 deposit plus interest. Both parties appealed from this judgment, and the District Court of Appeals held that the entire deposit should have been returned to the Davises. The Johnsons appealed.

Adkins, Justice. We agree with the district court's conclusions under a theory of fraud and find that the Johnsons' statements to the Davises regarding the condition of the roof constituted a fraudulent misrepresentation entitling the Davises to the return of the $26,000 deposit payment. The record reflects that the statement made by the Johnsons was a false representation of material fact, made with knowledge of its falsity, upon which the Davises relied to their detriment as evidenced by the $26,000 paid to the Johnsons. The fact that the false statements as to the quality of the roof were made after the signing of the purchase agreement does not excuse the seller from liability where the misrepresentations were made prior to the conveyance of the property.

In determining whether a seller of a home has a duty to disclose latent material defects to a buyer, the established tort law distinction between misfeasance and nonfeasance, action and inaction, must carefully be analyzed. The highly individualistic philosophy of the earlier common law consistently imposed liability upon the commission of affirmative acts of harm, but shrank from converting the courts into an institution for forcing men to help one another. Liability for nonfeasance has therefore been slow to receive recognition in the evolution of tort law.

In theory, the difference between misfeasance and nonfeasance is quite simple and obvious; however, in practice it is not always easy to draw the line and determine whether conduct is active or passive. That is, where failure to disclose a material fact is calculated to induce a false belief, the distinction between concealment and affirmative representations is tenuous. Both proceed from the same motives and are attended with the same consequences; both are violative of the principles of fair dealing and good faith.

Still there exists in much of our case law the old tort notion that there can be no liability for nonfeasance. The courts in some jurisdictions hold that where the parties are dealing at arm's length and the facts lie equally open to both parties, with equal opportunity of examination, mere nondisclosure does not constitute a fraudulent concealment.

These unappetizing cases are not in tune with the times and do not conform with current notions of justice, equity, and fair dealing. One should not be able to stand behind the impervious shield of caveat emptor and take advantage of another's ignorance. Our courts have taken great strides since the days when the judicial emphasis was on rigid rules and ancient precedents. Modern concepts of justice and fair dealing have given our courts the opportunity and latitude to change legal precepts in order to conform to society's needs. Thus, the tendency of the more recent cases has been to restrict rather than extend the doctrine of caveat emptor. The law appears to be working toward the ultimate conclusion that full disclosure of all material facts must be made whenever elementary fair conduct demands it.

The harness placed on the doctrine of caveat emptor in a number of other jurisdictions has resulted in the seller of a home being liable for failing to disclose material defects of which he was aware. We are of the opinion that the same philosophy regarding the sale of homes should also be the law in the state of Florida. Accordingly we hold that where the seller of a home knows of facts materially affecting the value of the property which are not readily observable and are not known to the buyer, the seller is under a duty to disclose them to the buyer. This duty is equally applicable to all forms of real property, new and used.

In the case at bar, the evidence shows that the Johnsons knew of and failed to disclose that there had been problems with the roof of the house. Mr. Johnson admitted during his testimony that the Johnsons were aware of roof problems prior to entering into the contract of sale and receiving the $5,000 deposit payment. Thus, we find that the Johnsons' fraudulent concealment also entitles the Davises to the return of the $5,000 deposit payment plus interest.

Judgment for the Davises affirmed.

LAND USE CONTROL

Introduction

While an owner of real property generally has the right to make such use of his property as he desires, society has placed a number of limitations on this right. This is one example of the principle that, to protect freedom, it is sometimes necessary to limit it. A property owner's unrestrained use of his property may destroy the value of his neighbor's property. One such limitation on the use of property is found in nuisance law, which permits public and private actions against landowners who use their property in a way that causes injury to others. Other limitations are created by zoning and subdivision ordinances, which contain specific requirements and prohibitions about the use of real property. Finally, the government, through its power of eminent domain, can deprive a person of his ownership of land. The following discussion explores in detail these controls on land use.

Nuisance Law

A person's enjoyment of his own land depends to a great extent on the uses that his neighbors make of their land. When the uses of neighboring landowners conflict, the aggrieved party frequently resorts to a court for resolution of the conflict. A person who unreasonably interferes with another person's interest in the use or enjoyment of his property is subject to an action for **nuisance.**

The term *nuisance* has no set definition. It may be conceived of as any use or activity that unreasonably interferes with the rights of others. Property uses that are inappropriate to the neighborhood (such as operating a funeral parlor in a single-family residential neighborhood), bothersome to neighbors (such as keeping a pack of barking dogs in one's backyard), dangerous to others (such as storing large quantities of gasoline in 50-gallon drums in one's garage), or immoral (such as operating a house of prostitution) can all be held to be nuisances. To amount to a nuisance, a use does not have to be illegal. The mere fact that a use is permitted under relevant zoning laws does not mean that it cannot be a nuisance. Furthermore, the fact that a use was in existence before neighboring landowners acquired their property does not mean that it cannot be a nuisance.

The test for determining whether conduct will be considered a nuisance is necessarily flexible and highly dependent on the facts of the individual case. A court will balance a number of factors, such as the social importance of the parties' respective uses, the extent and duration of the aggrieved party's loss, and the feasibility of abating (stopping) the nuisance. A plaintiff who puts his land to an unusually sensitive or "delicate" use cannot enjoin the activities of others that interfere with the delicate use.

Nuisances may be *private* or *public.* To bring a *private nuisance* action, the plaintiff must be a landowner or occupier whose enjoyment of his own land is substantially lessened because of a nuisance. The remedies for private nuisance include damages and injunctive relief. A *public nuisance* occurs when a nuisance causes harm to members of the public, who need not necessarily be injured in their use of property. For example, if a power plant creates noise and emissions that constitute a health hazard to pedestrians and workers in nearby buildings, a public nuisance may exist even though the nature of the injury is something other than the loss of enjoyment of the injured persons' property. Public nuisances involve a broader class of affected parties than do private nuisances. The action to abate the nuisance must usually be brought by the government in the name of the public. Remedies generally include criminal-type fines and injunctive relief. Private parties can sue for the abatement of a public nuisance or for damages caused by a public nuisance only when they can show that they have suffered a unique harm different from that suffered by the general public.

The following case, *Wood v. Picillo,* concerns the application of nuisance law to a property owner who maintained a hazardous waste dump.[15]

---

[15]For a detailed discussion of liability relating to hazardous waste, see the Environmental Regulation chapter.

WOOD v. PICILLO
443 A.2d 1244 (R.I. Sup. Ct. 1982)

The Picillos maintained a chemical dump site on a clearing on the their land. The site was a huge trench about 200 feet long, 15 to 30 feet wide, and 15 to 20 feet deep. A thick layer of pungent, varicolored liquid covered the trench bottom. Along the periphery of the pit lay more than 100 55-gallon drums and 5-gallon pail containers, some of which were upright and sealed, some tipped, and some partially buried. About 600 feet downhill of this site is a marshy wetland that drains into a river and several ponds. A witness testified that he saw the operator of a truck knock barrels marked "Combustible" off the truck's tailgate directly onto the earth, where the chemicals poured freely from the damaged barrels into the trench. Neighbors smelled "sickening," "heavy," and "terrible" odors that forced them to stay inside their homes. Several neighbors were made ill by the odors.

The attention of state officials was drawn to the site when an enormous explosion erupted into 50-foot flames in a trench on the Picillos' land and the fire could not be extinguished. Investigators from the state environmental management department began an investigation of the site and the state fire marshal ordered the dumping to cease, but dumping operations continued. Edward Wood and other plaintiffs brought a nuisance action against the Picillos. The trial court found that the dumping operation was a nuisance. It entered an injunction against further chemical disposal operations on the Picillo property and ordered them to finance the cleanup and removal of the toxic wastes. The Picillos appealed.

Weisberger, J.   The dump site proper might best be described in the succinct expresssion of the trial justice as "a chemical nightmare." At trial expert witnesses developed a scientific connection between the neighbors' experiences and the Picillos' operations. Laboratory analyses of samples taken from the trench, monitoring wells, and adjacent waters revealed the presence of five chemicals: toluene, xylene, chloroform, III trichloroethane, and trichloroethylene. According to the experts, the chemicals present on the Picillos' property and in the marsh, left unchecked, would eventually threaten wildlife and humans well downstream from the dump site. Expert testimony further revealed that the chemicals had traveled and would continue to travel from the dump site into the marsh at the rate of about one foot per day. From the marsh, predicted the experts, the chemicals would flow [into waters that are] inhabited by fish and used by humans for recreational and agricultural purposes.

The Picillos contend that the evidence adduced at trial was insufficient to support a finding of public and private nuisance. We find [this] to be without merit. The essential element of an actionable nuisance is that persons have suffered harm or are threatened with injuries that they ought not to have to bear. Distinguished from negligence liability, liability in nuisance is predicated upon unreasonable injury rather than upon unreasonable conduct. Thus, plaintiffs may recover in nuisance despite the otherwise nontortious nature of the conduct which creates the injury.

The Picillos have accurately stated that the injury produced by an actionable nuisance "must be real and not fanciful or imaginary." The Picillos next suggest that the injuries in the case at bar are of the insubstantial, unactionable type. It is this statement, however, rather than the purported injuries, that is fanciful. The testimony to which reference is made in this opinion clearly establishes that the Picillos' dumping operations have already caused substantial injury to their neighbors and threaten to cause incalculable damage to the general public. The Picillos' neighbors have displayed physical symptoms of exposure to toxic chemicals and have been restricted in the reasonable use of their property. Moreover, expert testimony showed that the chemical presence on the Picillos' property threatens both aquatic wildlife and human beings with possible death, cancer, and liver disease. Thus, there was ample evidence at trial to support the finding of substantial injury.

For the reasons stated, the Picillos' appeal is denied and dismissed.

Judgment for Wood affirmed.

Eminent Domain

The Fifth Amendment to the Constitution provides that private property shall not be taken for public use without just compensation. Implicit in this provision is the principle that the state has the power to take property for public use by paying "just compensation" to the owner of the property. This power, which is called the power of **eminent domain,** makes it possible for the government to acquire private property for highways, water control projects, municipal and civic centers, public housing, urban renewal, and other public uses. Governmental units can delegate their power of eminent domain to private corporations such as railroads and public utilities.

Although the eminent domain power is probably necessary to efficient government, there are several major problems inherent in its use. One of them is determining when the power can be properly exercised. When the governmental unit itself uses the property taken, as would be the case in property acquired for the use of a municipal building or a public highway, the exercise of the power is proper. The exercise of the power is not so clearly justified, however, when the government acquires the property and resells it to a private developer. Although such acquisitions may be more vulnerable to challenge, recent cases have applied a very lenient standard in determining what constitutes a public use[16]

Another problem with regard to the eminent domain power is determining what is meant by *just compensation.* A property owner is entitled to receive the "fair market value" of his property, but some people believe that this measure of compensation falls short of reimbursing the owner for what he has lost, since it does not cover the lost goodwill of a business or the emotional attachment a person may have to his home.

A third problem is determining when a "taking" has occurred. The answer to this is easy when the government institutes a legal action to condemn property. In some cases, however, the government causes or permits the physical invasion of a landowner's property without having instituted formal condemnation proceedings. For example, a government engaging in building a dam floods Johnson's land. In such cases, courts have recognized the right of property owners to institute an action for compensation against the governmental unit that has taken their land. These cases are called **inverse condemnation** cases. In an inverse condemnation case, the property owner says, in effect, "You have taken my land, now pay for it."

Zoning and Subdivision Laws

State legislatures commonly delegate to cities and other political subdivisions the *police power* to impose reasonable regulations designed to promote the public health, safety, and morals and the general welfare of the community. **Zoning ordinances,** which regulate the use

of real property, are created in the exercise of this police power. Normally, zoning ordinances divide a city or town into a number of districts and specify or limit the use to which property in those districts can be put. They also prescribe and restrict the improvements that are built on the land.

Zoning ordinances restrict the use of property in a number of ways. One common type of restriction is a *control of uses* on the land, such as restriction of an area to single-family or high-density residential uses or commercial, light industry, or heavy industry uses. Another type of restriction is *control of height and bulk,* which prescribe the height of buildings; the setback from front, side, and rear lot lines; and the portion of a lot that can be covered by a building. *Control of population density* is another common type of restriction. Such restrictions specify the amount of living space that must be provided for each person and specify the maximum number of persons who can be housed in a given area. Zoning ordinances also commonly contain *controls of aesthetics,* whereby the use of land is restricted to maintain or create a certain aesthetic character of the community. Restrictions on the architectural style of buildings, the use of billboards and other signs, and the creation of special zones for historical buildings are examples of this type of restriction.

Many local governments also have ordinances dealing with proposed subdivisions. These ordinances often require that the developer meet certain requirements as to lot size, street and sidewalk layout, and sanitary facilities. They also require that the city or town approve the proposed development. The purpose of such ordinances is to protect the prospective purchasers of property in the subdivision and the community as a whole, by ensuring that minimum standards are met by the developer.

Nonconforming Uses　A zoning ordinance has prospective effect. That is, the uses and buildings that already exist at the time the ordinance is passed (*nonconforming uses*) are permitted to continue. However, the ordinance may provide for the gradual phasing out (*amortization*) of nonconforming uses and buildings that do not conform to the general zoning plan.

Relief from Zoning Ordinances　A property owner who wants to initiate some use of his property that is not permitted by the existing zoning ordinance can try several avenues of relief from that ordinance. He can try to have the zoning law **amended** on the ground that the proposed amendments are in accordance with the

---

[16]This and other issues relating to eminent domain are discussed further in the Business and the Constitution chapter.

overall zoning plan. To seek an amendment is to seek a change in the law itself.

A different approach would be to seek permission to deviate from the zoning law. This is called a **variance.** A person seeking a variance would claim that the ordinance works an undue hardship on him by depriving him of opportunity to make reasonable use of his land. For example, a landowner might attempt to obtain a variance to use the property in some way that is not normally allowed or to deviate from normal setback or building size requirements.

Attempts to obtain amendments or variances often produce heated battles before the zoning authorities because they often conflict with the interests of nearby property owners who have a vested interest in maintaining the status quo.

Challenges to the Validity of the Zoning Ordinance

A disgruntled property owner might also attack the validity of the zoning ordinance. Zoning ordinances have produced a great deal of litigation in recent years, as cities and towns have used their zoning power as a means of social control. For example, a city might create special zoning requirements for adult bookstores or other uses that are considered moral threats to the community. This has given rise to challenges that such ordinances unconstitutionally restrict freedom of speech. The Supreme Court has upheld the constitutionality of a zoning ordinance that prohibited the operation of adult bookstores within 1,000 feet of specified uses such as residential areas and schools, even though the ordinance had the effect of restricting adult bookstores to a small area of the community in which no property was currently available.[17]

Another type of litigation has involved ordinances by which some municipalities have attempted to "zone out" residential facilities such as group homes for mentally retarded adults. The Supreme Court held that a zoning ordinance that required a special use permit for a group home for the mentally retarded was an unconstitutional

violation of the Equal Protection Clause of the Constitution.[18] The 1988 amendments to the Fair Housing Act, which forbid discrimination on the basis of handicap and familial status, also have been used as a basis for challenging zoning decisions that operate to zone out group homes. It appears that such a challenge can be successful when the plaintiff can show that the zoning board's actions were a mere pretext for discrimination.[19]

Many cities and towns have attempted to restrict single-family residential zones to living units of traditional families related by blood or marriage and to prevent the presence of other living groups such as groups of unrelated students, communes, or religious cults by specifically defining the term *family* in a way that excludes these groups. In the case of *Belle Terre v. Boraas,*[20] the Supreme Court upheld such an ordinance as applied to a group of unrelated students. It subsequently held, however, that an ordinance that defined "family" in such a way as to prohibit a grandmother from living with her grandsons was an unconstitutional intrusion on personal freedom regarding marriage and family life.[21] In some cases, restrictive definitions of the term *family* have been held unconstitutional under *state constitutions.* In others, such definitions have been narrowly construed by the courts.

Land Use Regulation and "Taking" An additional type of litigation has involved zoning laws and other land use regulations that restrict the use of land in a way that makes it less profitable for development.[22] Affected property owners have challenged the application of such regulations on the ground that they constitute an unconstitutional "taking" of property without just compensation. States have broad discretion to use their police power for the public benefit, even when that means interfering to some extent with an owner's right to develop his property as he desires. While it is possible for a regulation to interfere with an owner's use of his property to such an extent that it constitutes a taking, the mere fact that the regulation deprives the owner of the highest and

---

[17]*City of Renton v. Playtime Theatres, Inc.,* 106 S. Ct. 925 (U.S. Sup. Ct. 1986). In a recent case, however, the Supreme Court held that a licensing scheme in a comprehensive zoning ordinance that required licensing of adult cabarets and other adult entertainment establishments was an unconstitutional violation of the First Amendment, because the ordinance did not have appropriate procedural safeguards against arbitrary denials of the licenses. (The ordinance failed to provide for a time limit within which city authorities were required to act on such a license application.) *FW/PBS, Inc. v. City of Dallas,* 110 S. Ct. 596 (U.S. Sup. Ct. 1990).

[18]*City of Cleburne v. Cleburne Living Centers,* 473 U.S. 432 (U.S. Sup. Ct. 1985).

[19]For example, see *Baxter v. City of Nashville,* 720 F. Supp. 720 (S.D. Ill. 1989), which involves a challenge by a hospice for AIDS patients to a city's denial of a special use permit.

[20]416 U.S. 1 (U.S. Sup Ct. 1974).

[21]*Moore v. City of East Cleveland,* 431 U.S. 494 (U.S. Sup. Ct. 1977).

[22]This issue is also discussed in the Business and the Constitution chapter.

most profitable use of his property does not mean that there has been a taking.

There is no set formula used to determine whether a regulation has gone "too far" and has become a taking. Courts look at all the facts of the case and weigh a variety of factors, such as the economic impact of the regulation, the degree to which the regulation interferes with an investor's reasonable expectations, and the character of the government's invasion. In *Nollan v. California Coastal Commission,* which follows, you will see an example of a case in which the Supreme Court found regulation to constitute a taking.

NOLLAN v. CALIFORNIA COASTAL COMMISSION

107 S. Ct. 3141 (U.S. Sup. Ct. 1987)

James and Marilyn Nollan own a beachfront lot in Ventura County, California. A quarter mile north of their property is Faria County Park, an oceanside public park with a public beach. Another public beach area, known as "the Cove," lies 1,800 feet south of their lot. A concrete seawall separates the beach portion of the Nollans' property from the rest of the lot. The historic mean high-tide line determines the lot's oceanside boundary.

The Nollans wanted to tear down a small bungalow that was on the property and build a three-bedroom house on the lot. California law required that they obtain a coastal development permit from the California Coastal Commission to do this. They submitted the permit application and were later informed that they could have the permit on condition that they allow the public an easement to pass across a portion of their property bounded by the mean high-tide line on one side and their seawall on the other. This would make it easier for the public to get to Faria County Park and the Cove. The Nollans challenged the access condition, but the Commission affirmed it. On appeal, the California Court of Appeals upheld the action of the Coastal Commission. The Nollans appealed to the United States Supreme Court, arguing that the access condition was a taking.

Scalia, Justice.   Had California simply required the Nollans to make an easement across their beachfront available to the public on a permanent basis to increase public access to the beach, rather than conditioning their permit to rebuild their house on their agreeing to do so, we would have no doubt there would have been a taking. Indeed, one of the principal uses of the eminent domain power is to assure that the government be able to require conveyance of just such interests, so long as it pays for them. We have repeatedly held that, as to property reserved by its owner for private use, the right to exclude others is one of the most essential sticks in the bundle of rights that are commonly characterized as property.

Where governmental action results in a permanent physical occupation of the property, by the government itself or by others, our cases uniformly have found a taking to the extent of the occupation, without regard to whether the action achieves an important public benefit or has only minimal economic impact on the owner. We think a "permanent physical occupation" has occurred, for purposes of that rule, where individuals are given a permanent and continuous right to pass to and fro, so that the real property may continuously be traversed.

Given that requiring uncompensated conveyance of the easement outright would violate the Fourteenth Amendment, the question becomes whether requiring it to be conveyed as a condition for issuing a land use permit alters the outcome. We have long recognized that land use regulation does not effect a taking if it substantially advances legitimate state interests and does not deny an owner economically viable use of his land.

The Commission argues that among these permissible purposes are protecting the public's ability to see the beach, assisting the public in overcoming the "psychological barrier" to using the beach created by a developed shorefront, and preventing congestion on the public beaches. We assume that the Commission would be able to deny the Nollans their permit outright if their new house would substantially impede these purposes, unless the denial would interfere so drastically with the Nollans' use of their property as to constitute a taking. If the Commission attached to the permit some condition that would have protected the public's ability to see the beach notwithstanding construction of the new house—for example, a height limitation, a width restriction, or a ban on fences—so long as the Commission could have exercised its police power to forbid construction of the house altogether, imposition of the condition would also be constitutional.

The evident constitutional propriety disappears, however, if the conditional substituted for the prohibition utterly fails to further the end advanced as the justification for the prohibition. The lack of nexus between the condition and the original purpose of the building restriction converts that purpose to something other than what it was. The purpose then becomes, quite simply, the obtaining of an easement to serve some valid governmental purpose, but without payment of compensation. In short, unless the permit condition serves the same governmental purpose as the development ban, the building restriction is not a valid regulation of land use but "an out-and-out plan of extortion."

It is quite impossible to understand how a requirement that people already on the public beaches be able to walk across the Nollans' property reduces any obstacles to viewing the beach created by the new house. It is also impossible to understand how it lowers any "psychological barrier" to using the public beaches, or how it helps to remedy any additional congestion on them caused by construction of the Nollans' new house. We therefore find that the Commission's imposition of the permit condition cannot be treated as an exercise of its land use power for any of these purposes. California is free to advance its "comprehensive program" if it wishes, by using its power of eminent domain for this public purpose, but if it wants an easement across the Nollans' property, it must pay for it.

Reversed in favor of the Nollans.

Another Supreme Court case, *First English Evangelical Lutheran Church of Glendale v. County of Los Angeles,*[23] dealt with the issue of remedies for regulatory taking. In this case, the Court held that when the government takes land by a land use regulation, the landowner may recover damages in an inverse condemnation action, even if the taking was temporary because the regulation was later declared invalid.

INSURANCE

One of the risks faced by a property owner is the possibility that his property might be damaged or destroyed

by any number of perils beyond his control—fire, lightning, or flood, just to name a few. Although the property owner may not be able to prevent harm to his property, he can secure some protection against the resulting financial loss by contracting for insurance. The purpose of insurance contracts is to allow people to shift to another a risk of loss that they would ordinarily have to bear.

There are many different kinds of insurance, each of which protects against different types of risks. For example, you are undoubtedly familiar with life insurance, health insurance, and automobile insurance and the risks they insure against. Earlier in this chapter, we discussed another type of insurance—title insurance—which protects an owner of property against the possibility of loss caused by a faulty title. Our discussion in this part of the chapter will explore some basic concepts in insurance

---

[23]107 S. Ct. 1987 (U.S. Sup. Ct. 1987).

law. It will also present an overview of a form of property insurance that is important to property owners: **fire insurance.**

The Nature of an Insurance Contract

The insurance relationship is a contract that may involve more than two persons. The **insurer** (usually a corporation), in exchange for the payment of consideration (called a **premium**), agrees to pay for losses caused by specific events (**perils**). The **beneficiary** is the person to whom the insurance proceeds are payable. The **insured** is the person who acquires insurance on property in which she possesses an interest or, in the case of life insurance, the person whose life is being insured. In most instances, the insured will also be the *owner* of the policy (the person who can exercise the contractual rights set out in the insurance contract); however, this is not always the case.

A distinction is made between valid insurance contracts and wagering contracts. A wagering contract creates a new risk that did not previously exist and is illegal as contrary to public policy. Insurance contracts, on the other hand, transfer existing risks.

Insurable Interest

In order for an insurance contract not to be considered an illegal wagering contract, the person who purchases the policy (the owner) must have an **insurable interest** in the property being insured. To have an insurable interest, a person must have a legal or equitable interest in the property such that he has some economic interest in the property's continued existence and in the preservation of its condition. Another way of putting this is that a person has an insurable interest if he will suffer a financial loss from the destruction of the insured property. If no insurable interest is present, the policy is void.

Those who have an insurable interest in property must have that interest at the time the loss occurs. This means that in addition to the legal owner of the insured property, any other person who has an interest in the insured property when the loss occurs has the required insurable interest. Thus, both the buyer and the seller of property, lessees, secured creditors (mortgagees or lienholders), and those holding other interests in the insured property all have the required insurable interest.

The extent of a person's insurable interest in property is limited to the value of his or her interest in the property. For example, Fidelity Savings & Loan extends Williams a $65,000 loan on her home and retains a mortgage interest in the house as security. In order to protect this investment, it obtains a $65,000 insurance policy on the property. Several years later, the house is completely destroyed by fire. At the time of the fire, the balance due on the loan is $43,000. Accordingly, $43,000 is all that Fidelity can recover under the insurance policy. That amount is the full extent of its insurable interest.

The concept of insurable interest is illustrated in the *Crowell v. Delafield Farmers Mutual Fire Insurance Company,* which follows.

CROWELL v. DELAFIELD FARMERS MUTUAL FIRE INSURANCE COMPANY

453 N.W.2d 724 (Minn. Ct. App. 1990)

Earl and Vonette Crowell own and operate a farm in Cottonwood County, Minnesota. In 1980, the Crowells took out a mortgage on the property with Farm Credit Services. They also took out a fire insurance policy with Delafield Farmers Mutual Insurance Company, which ran from October 1985 until October 1988. The Crowells failed to make their mortgage payments and Farm Credit began foreclosure proceedings. Upon foreclosure, mortgagors such as the Crowells have a right of redemption for a specified time, during which they have the right to buy back their property *after* it has been sold to another. In November of 1987, the Crowells' right of redemption ended. Under

Minnesota law, however, farmers who lose their farms to corporate lenders are given an additional opportunity to repurchase their farms under a "right of first refusal." Under this law, Farm Credit was forbidden to sell the farm to anyone else before offering it to the Crowells at a price no higher than the highest price offered by a third party. Farm Credit allowed the Crowells to remain on the farm while they tried to secure financing to buy the property under their right of first refusal.

On November 27, 1987, the farmhouse was substantially destroyed by fire. The Crowells filed a claim for the loss with Delafield. Delafield paid the claim on the Crowells' personal effects inside the house, but denied the claim on the structure itself. It claimed that since the Crowells' period of redemption had expired, they no longer had an insurable interest in the farmhouse. The Crowells brought suit. The trial court granted summary judgment for the Crowells and Delafield appealed.

Kalitowski, Judge.   To be entitled to recovery for a loss, an insured must have an insurable interest in the property covered by the policy. To have an insurable interest, the party must suffer a loss of property interest that is substantial and real. A person has an insurable interest in property when the relationship between him and the property is such that he has a reasonable expectation, based upon a real or legal right, of benefit to be derived from the continued existence of the property and of loss or liability from its destruction. The Minnesota Supreme Court has stated that it is not necessary that the insured should have an absolute right of property, and that he has an insurable interest if, by the destruction of the property, he will suffer a loss, whether he has or has not any title to, lien upon, or possession of the property itself.

Farm Credit foreclosed on the Crowells' farm mortgage. The Crowells remained on and continued to operate the farm. After the redemption period, Farm Credit became the absolute owner of the property. The record indicates Farm Credit allowed the Crowells to remain on the farm after the redemption period expired because it was involved in the Crowells' effort to secure financing to enable them to exercise their statutory right of first refusal. In addition, Farm Credit did not purchase and the Crowells did not cancel fire insurance on the property.

By creating a right of first refusal, the legislature gave financially distressed farmers who had lost their farms to corporate lenders an opportunity to repurchase the farms. The legislative purpose of this right of first refusal is to encourage and protect the family farm as a basic economic unit, to insure it as the most socially desirable mode of agricultural production, and to enhance and promote the stability and well-being of rural society in Minnesota and the nuclear family.

This right of first refusal gives family farmers some additional right or interest in the property they lost to corporate lenders. Based on this legal right in the property, the Crowells had a reasonable expectation to derive a benefit from the continued existence of the farmhouse. Although the Crowells no longer had title to the farm, they were allowed to remain on the land with all parties' knowledge and intention that they would exercise their right of first refusal and regain the farm. Therefore, they expected the benefit of living in the farmhouse until they exercised that right.

It is clear the Crowells suffered a loss from the destruction of the farmhouse. Since the fire the Crowells have been unable to live in the farmhouse. This situation forces the Crowells to live several miles from their farm and commute between their home and the farm, causing additional expenses and inconvenience. The advantage of living on the farm is clearly lost.

Under the facts of this case we hold the trial court was correct in holding this right gave the Crowells an insurable interest in the farm and its structures.

Judgment for the Crowells affirmed.

FIGURE 2   Insurance Recovery for a Total Loss

Face Value of Policy	Fair Market Value at Time of Loss	Recovery	
		Valued Policy	Open Policy
$50,000	$42,000	$50,000	$42,000
50,000	65,000	50,000	50,000

FIRE INSURANCE CONTRACTS

Fire insurance, as the name suggests, insures against losses caused by accidental fire. Companies that write fire insurance commonly also insure against loss caused by other perils such as lightning, water, wind, and hail. Fire insurance contracts are **indemnity** contracts. This means that the insurer is obligated to reimburse the insured for any actual losses that the insured suffered due to damage to the insured property. The loss must occur during the period of time that the policy is in force. The amount that the insured may recover is generally limited to the extent of the loss sustained as long as it does not exceed the amount of coverage that the insured purchased.

Types of Losses Covered

Fire insurance contracts distinguish between *friendly fires,* which are those contained in a place intended for a fire, such as fires in a woodstove or fireplace, and *hostile fires,* which burn where no fire is intended to be, such as fires caused by lightning, outside sources, electrical shorts, or those that started out as a friendly fire and escaped their boundaries. Generally, fire insurance policies cover the losses caused by hostile fires and not those caused by friendly fires. The insurer will cover losses caused by negligent acts of the insured's employees, but not those resulting from intentional destruction of the insured's property.

Fire insurance policies generally cover more than direct damage caused by the fire. They also cover indirect damage caused by smoke and heat, and the damage caused by the efforts of firefighters to put out the fire. Generally, however, lost profits are not covered.

Types of Policies

Some fire insurance contracts are called **valued policies.** If property covered by a valued policy is totally

destroyed, the insured can recover the face amount of the policy regardless of the fair market value of the building. For example, Smith bought a home with a fair market value of $50,000 in 1980 and purchased a valued policy with a face value of $50,000 to insure the house against the risk of fire. In the next few years, because of deterioration in the surrounding neighborhood, the home's fair market value decreased. In 1985, when the home had a fair market value of only $42,000, it was totally destroyed by fire. Despite the reduced fair market value, Smith is entitled to $50,000 (the face value of the policy).

Most fire insurance policies are **open policies.** Open policies allow the insured to recover the fair market value of the property at the time it was destroyed, up to the limits stated in the policy. Thus, in the example presented in the previous paragraph, Smith would be entitled to only $42,000 when the home was destroyed in 1985.

Suppose instead that Smith's home had increased in value so that at the time of the fire its fair market value was $65,000. In this case, it does not matter what type of policy Smith had. Under both the valued and open policies, his recovery would be limited to the face value of the policy—$50,000.

Figure 2 illustrates the recovery under both of these types of policies.

Special Terms of a Fire Insurance Contract

The insurance contract may contain special terms relating to the insured's rights upon destruction of the property. It is common for some policies to give the insurer the option of replacing or restoring the damaged property instead of paying its fair market value.

Coinsurance Clause   Some fire insurance policies contain a coinsurance clause that can operate to limit the insured's right to recovery. The coinsurance provision

FIGURE 3   Coinsurance Clause

Fair Market Value at Time of Loss	Face Value of Policy	Amount of Insurance Required	Actual Loss	Recovery
$100,000	$60,000	$80,000	$ 40,000	$30,000
100,000	60,000	80,000	100,000	60,000

requires the insured to insure the property to a specified percentage of its fair market value in order to fully recover the value of partial losses. Generally, most policies require that the insured purchase insurance equal to at least 80 percent of the fair market value.

For example, ABC Manufacturing Company has a fire insurance policy on its warehouse with Friendly Mutual Insurance Group. The policy has an 80 percent coinsurance clause. The warehouse had a fair market value of $100,000. (Therefore ABC was required to carry at least $80,000 of insurance on the building.) However, ABC purchased a policy with a face value of only $60,000. A fire partially destroyed the building, causing $40,000 worth of damage to the structure. Because of the coinsurance clause, ABC will recover only $30,000 from Friendly. (This figure was arrived at by taking the amount of insurance carried ($60,000) divided by the amount of insurance required ($80,000) times the loss ($40,000).)

The coinsurance formula for recovery for partial losses is stated as follows:

$$\frac{\text{Amount of insurance carried}}{\text{Coinsurance percent} \times \text{Fair market value}} \times \text{Loss} = \text{Recovery}$$

Remember that the coinsurance formula only applies to "partial" losses of property. If the warehouse had been totally destroyed by the fire, ABC could have recovered $60,000 (the face value of the policy), and the formula would not have been applicable. If the formula had been used, it would have indicated that Friendly owed ABC $75,000. Yet this would have been more than the face amount of the policy. This is not possible; whether the loss is total or partial, the insured can never recover more than the face value of the policy. This example is depicted in Figure 3.

Pro Rata Clause   With the limited exception of the valued policy discussed above, the insured can never re-

cover more than the amount of the actual loss. To allow otherwise would encourage unscrupulous people to destroy their property intentionally. Accordingly, when the insured has purchased insurance policies from more than one insurer, the loss will be apportioned among the insurance companies. The amount for which any particular insurer is liable is calculated by determining the total amount of the insurer's policy in proportion to the total amount of insurance covering the property. For example, Andrews purchases two insurance policies to cover his home against the risk of fire. His policy from Farmers Mutual has a face value of $50,000 while the coverage by States Insurance is for $100,000. The home is partially destroyed by fire with the losses amounting to $30,000. As you will see in Figure 4, Farmers Mutual is responsible for $10,000, while States Insurance is liable for the remaining $20,000.

The formula for determining each insurer's liability is stated as follows:

$$\frac{\text{Amount of insurer's policy}}{\text{Total coverage by all insurers}} \times \text{Loss} = \text{Liability of insurer}$$

Thus, Farmers' liability was calculated as follows:

$$\frac{\$50,000 \text{ (Farmers' policy)}}{\$150,000 \text{ (Total of both policies)}} \times \$30,000 \text{ (Loss)} = \$10,000$$

The liability of States Insurance could be similarly calculated by substituting $100,000 (States' policy) for the $50,000 (Farmers' policy) in the numerator of the equation. This formula may be used for both partial and total losses. However, each company's liability is limited by the face value of the policy. Thus, Farmers could never be liable for more than $50,000 and States' liability is limited to a maximum of $100,000.

INSURANCE POLICIES AS CONTRACTS

The insurance relationship is basically contractual in nature. As a result, insurance policies must satisfy all of the elements required for a binding contract.

FIGURE 4   Pro Rata Insurance

Policy A	Policy B	Total Insurance (Policy A plus Policy B)	Actual Loss	Liability of Insurer A	Liability of Insurer B
$50,000	$100,000	$150,000	$30,000	$10,000	$20,000

Offer and Acceptance   The standard practice in insurance is to have the potential insured make an offer to enter an insurance contract by completing an application provided by the insurer's agent and submitting it and the premium to the insurer. The insurer may then either accept or reject this offer. What constitutes acceptance depends on the kind of insurance requested and the language of the application. It is very important to know the precise time when an acceptance occurs. Any losses suffered prior to this point must be borne by the insured, not the insurer.

In fire insurance contracts, the application may be worded so that insurance coverage begins when the insured signs the application. This can provide temporary coverage until the insurer either accepts or rejects the policy. The same result may also be achieved by the use of a **binder,** an agreement for temporary insurance pending the insurer's decision to accept or reject the risk. Acceptance in fire insurance contracts generally occurs when the insurer (or agent, if authorized to do so) indicates to the insured an intent to accept the application. Figure 5 depicts the formation of an insurance contract.

A common problem that occurs in insurance law is the effect of the insurer's delay in acting on the application. If the applicant suffers a loss after applying, but before the insured formally accepts, who must bear the loss? As a general rule, the insurer's delay does not constitute acceptance. Some states, however, have held that an insurer's retention of the premium for an unreasonable time constitutes an acceptance. Others have allowed tort suits against insurers for negligent delay in acting on an application. The theory of these cases is that insurance companies have a public duty to insure qualified applicants and that an unreasonable delay prevents applicants from obtaining insurance protection from some other source. A few states have also enacted statutes holding that insurers are bound to the insurance contract unless they have rejected the application within a specified period of time.

Misrepresentation

Applicants for insurance have a duty to reveal to insurers all the material facts about the nature of the risk so that the insurer can make an intelligent decision about whether to accept the risk. When an insured makes a statement about a material fact and that statement is not substantially correct, the insured's misrepresentation, if relied upon, has the same effect that it would in other contracts: It makes the contract voidable at the election of the insurer. This means that the insurer can avoid paying the claim. Similarly, failure to act in good faith to disclose known material facts to the insurer permits the insurer to avoid the policy.

It is important to distinguish between warranties and representations that the insured makes to induce the insurer to enter an insurance contract. Warranties are express terms in an insurance policy that are intended to operate as conditions on which the insurer's liability is based. Breach of such a condition by the insured terminates the insurer's duty to perform under the policy. Traditionally, this has been true whether or not the breach was material to the insurer's risk. In view of the potential harshness of this rule, some states have refused to allow insurers to escape liability on the ground of breach of warranty unless such breach was material.

Capacity

Generally speaking, both parties to a contract must have the capacity to contract for the agreement to be enforceable. Therefore, an insurance policy taken out by a minor would be voidable at the election of the minor. Many states, however, have made the insurance contracts of minors enforceable against them by statute.[24]

---

[24]An insurance contract taken out on the life of a minor (the insured) by an adult (the owner) is not voidable, however. It is only when the minor is the owner of the policy that this rule of capacity comes into effect.

FIGURE 5   Creation of an Insurance Contract

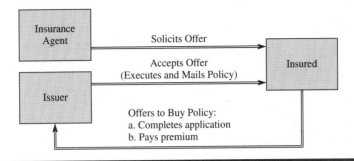

Form and Content

State law governs whether insurance contracts are within the statute of frauds and must be evidenced by a writing. Some states require specific types of insurance contracts to be in writing. Contracts for fire insurance are not usually within the statute of frauds, and thus may be either written or oral unless they come within some provision of the statute of frauds such as the "one-year" provision.[25] Even when a writing is not legally required, however, wisdom dictates that the parties reduce their agreement to written form whenever possible.

The insurance business is highly regulated. This is due partly to the importance of the interests protected by insurance and partly to the states' recognition of the difference in bargaining power that often exists between insurers and their insureds. Many states, in an attempt to remedy this imbalance, require the inclusion of certain standard clauses in insurance policies. Some states also regulate such matters as the size and style of the print used in insurance policies.

Interpreting Insurance Contracts

Modern courts realize that many people who buy insurance do not have the training to fully understand the technical language contained in many policies. As a result, such courts interpret provisions in insurance contracts as they would be understood by an average person. Any ambiguities in insurance contracts are generally interpreted against the insurer that drafted the contract.

---

[25]The usual provisions of the statute of frauds are discussed in detail in the Writing chapter.

Third Parties and Insurance Contracts   As a general rule, contracts are assignable only when the assignment will not materially alter the promisor's burden of performance. An important element of the risk in fire insurance policies is the character of the insured. Therefore, such policies are generally nonassignable. It is also common for the policy's terms to limit assignability. Those who purchase property from the insured get no interest in any policy the insured owned covering the purchased property. After a loss has occurred, however, the insured can assign the right to receive benefits under the policy, since no change in the insurer's risk is involved.

Many policies require notice to the insurer of any assignment. Failure to comply with such requirements renders an attempted assignment void.

NOTICE AND PROOF OF LOSS

A person who seeks to recover benefits under an insurance policy must notify the insurer that a loss covered by the policy has occurred and must furnish proof of loss. Fire insurance policies ordinarily require the insured to furnish a sworn statement of loss.

Time Limits

It is common for insurance policies to specify that notice and proof of loss must be given within a specified time. The policy may state that compliance with these requirements is a condition of the insured's recovery and that failure to comply terminates the insurer's obligation. Some policies, however, merely provide that failure to comply suspends the insurer's duty to pay until proper compliance is made. Some courts require the insurer to prove it has been injured by the insured's failure to give notice before they allow the insurer to avoid liability on the ground of tardy notice.

Right of Subrogation

The insurer may be able to exercise a right of subrogation if it is required to pay for the loss of property under a fire insurance contract. Under the right of subrogation, the insurer obtains all of the insured's rights to pursue legal remedies against anyone who may have negligently or intentionally caused the fire. For example, Ellis purchased a fire insurance policy on her home from Countywide Insurance Company. The house was completely destroyed in a fire that was caused when Davidson threw a firecracker in the garage while Ellis was away at work. After Countywide pays Ellis the face amount of her policy, it may sue Davidson for that amount under its right of subrogation.

A general release of the third party from liability by the insured will release the insurer from liability to the insured. Thus, in the previous example, suppose that Davidson persuaded Ellis to sign an agreement releasing him from any liability for the fire. Because this interferes with Countywide's right of subrogation, it may not have to pay Ellis for the loss. A partial release between David-

son and Ellis will relieve Countywide of liability to Ellis to the extent of her release. (The right of subrogation is not available in life insurance contracts.)

CANCELLATION AND LAPSE

Cancellation of an insurance policy occurs when a party who has the power to terminate the policy (extinguish all rights under the policy) has exercised that power. Lapse occurs when the policy is permitted to expire by failure to renew it after its term has run, or by some default on the part of the insured.

Cancellation

Property insurance policies frequently contain clauses that terminate the insurer's liability if the insured does anything that materially increases the insurer's risk. They may also specifically list certain kinds of behavior that will cause termination. Common examples of such behavior are keeping flammable or explosive material and allowing the premises to remain vacant for a stated period of time. You will see an example of "increase of hazard" in the following case, *Good v. Continental Insurance Company.*

GOOD v. CONTINENTAL INSURANCE COMPANY
291 S.E.2d 198 (Sup. Ct. S.C. 1982)

Sims and Dorothy Good purchased a standard fire insurance policy on their home from Continental Insurance Company. The policy contained an "increased hazard" clause that held that the insurer would not be liable if the risk of fire was increased "by any means within the control or knowledge of the insured." A fire occurring on November 29, 1977, almost completely destroyed the house. While putting out the fire, firefighters discovered an illegal liquor still on the second floor concealed in a false closet under the eaves of the roof. The still, encased by bricks and mortar, consisted of a 90-gallon copper vat over an 8- to 10-inch butane gas burner. Firefighters also discovered 22 half-gallons of "moonshine" and many 55-gallon drums full or partially full of mash. A police department detective who dismantled and examined the still's burner after the fire opined that the still was in operation when the fire occurred. Good denied this, although he admitted installing the still two years earlier, some time after his insurance policy became effective. Continental refused to pay for the destruction on the grounds that the still was an increased hazard.

The Goods brought suit against Continental to recover proceeds under the policy. The trial court awarded damages to the Goods, and Continental appealed.

Harwell, Justice.   In [previous cases], this court held that coverage under an insurance policy was suspended if the increased risk was permanent and continuous even though it did not produce the loss. However, if the increased risk caused the loss, an occasional, temporary increase of risk was sufficient to void a policy.

In addition to these guidelines, to void the policy the increase of hazard must be material and substantial such that the insurer could not reasonably be presumed to have contracted to assume it. Also, according to the policy, increased hazard must be accomplished by means solely within the control and knowledge of Good after the insurance contract was effected.

The evidence leads unmistakably to the following: the distillery was permanently installed; it was regularly used at least during the holiday season; Good installed the still after the insurance policy became effective; and only he operated the still. We conclude that the only reasonable inference from the evidence is that there had been an increase of hazard, thereby voiding the policy.

The use to which the Goods put their dwelling was so foreign to the normal uses of a dwelling as to become beyond the contemplation of the insurer. Surely the insurer did not contemplate providing insurance coverage on a residence which concealed an illegal still and the fruits of its operation.

Reversed in favor of Continental.

Lapse

Insurance policies that are written for a stated period of time lapse at the expiration of the policy term. The insured's failure to pay premiums also causes a policy to lapse.

ETHICAL AND PUBLIC POLICY CONCERNS

1. You read that a person can acquire title to another person's real property by adversely possessing that property for a certain period of time. What are some justifications for this doctrine?

2. In recent years, the law has placed increasing duties on sellers of real property regarding the quality of their property, such as a seller's duty to disclose hidden defects in property and the implied warranty of habitability, which guarantees that a home purchased from a builder-vendor or developer will be fit for human habitation. Do you believe these developments are steps in the right direction? Should the law go further and impose the implied warranty of habitability on *all* sellers, and not just on builder-vendors and developers? Should it require disclosure of all defects, not just hidden ones?

3. The law requires that the person who purchases fire insurance must have an insurable interest in the property being insured. Why? Does this requirement encourage ethical conduct?

SUMMARY

Real property includes not only land but also things that are firmly attached to it or embedded under it. A fixture is an item of personal property which, because of its attachment or association with land, is regarded as real property. In determining whether articles shall be considered fixtures, courts consider the intent of the party who annexed the articles, the manner in which the articles are annexed or attached to the property, and the degree to which the articles are necessary or beneficial to the use of the property. Fixtures become part of real property and are conveyed along with a conveyance of the property to which they are attached. An exception to this rule is made in the case of fixtures attached by a tenant for the purpose of carrying on a trade or business. Trade fixtures can be removed by the tenant, provided that she does so by the time the lease expires and provided that removal does not cause substantial harm to the leased property.

There are a variety of ownership interests in real property. The basic form of ownership is fee simple absolute. Another common form of ownership is the life estate. Seven types of co-ownership of real property are recognized: (1) tenancy in common, (2) joint tenancy, (3) tenancy by the entirety, (4) community property, (5) tenancy in partnership, (6) condominiums, and (7) cooperatives.

A person can also have a right or interest in land owned by another. Such interests include easements, profits, licenses, and restrictive covenants. These interests are not possessory, meaning that they do not give the holder of the interest the right to possess another person's land. Rather, they give him the right to use the land for certain purposes or to limit the way in which the land is used by the owner.

Real property may be acquired in a number of ways. The formal requirements for the transfer of real property are determined by the statutes of the state in which it is located. The most common way of acquiring real property is by purchasing it, whereby the vendor delivers a deed to the purchaser in exchange for some consideration. Real property may also be acquired by gift. To have a valid gift, the donor must deliver to the donee or to some third person for the benefit of the donee, a deed that complies with the statutory requirements of the given state. A person may also acquire real property through adverse possession. Adverse possession requires that a person possess property openly, exclusively, continuously, and adversely for the statutory period. In addition, some states require that the adverse possessor pay taxes on the property. Real property may also be acquired at a tax sale. Under the laws of most states, the government can have property sold to collect unpaid taxes. The purchaser at the tax sale will be given a tax deed that, if valid, cuts off prior claims to the real property.

As noted earlier, the most common means of acquiring ownership of real property is by purchasing it. One of the earliest steps most people take with regard to the sale of real property is to contract with a real estate broker. There are several different types of listing contracts, and the broker's right to a commission will depend in part on which type of listing contract was agreed upon.

Parties arranging the purchase of real property will enter a contract. This contract is governed by the rules of contract law discussed in earlier chapters. Any agreement affecting an interest in land and a conveyance of real property is required to be in writing. The Fair Housing Act is a comprehensive federal law that forbids discrimination on the basis of race, color, sex, religion, national origin, handicap, or familial status in selling, leasing, financing, advertising, and appraising dwellings and in providing brokerage services.

Three forms of deeds are in general use in the United States: the quitclaim deed, the warranty deed, and the deed of bargain and sale (grant deed). In a quitclaim deed, the grantor conveys his interest in the property, whatever that interest may be. The quitclaim deed does not represent that the grantor has good title, or any title at all. In the warranty deed, on the other hand, the grantor conveys his interest and, in addition, warrants the title to be free from all defects except those stated in the deed. In the deed of bargain and sale, the grantor does not make warranties, but he does impliedly represent that he has title to the land and has not encumbered it. To be valid, a deed must comply with certain formal requirements. These requirements are not uniform, but, as a general rule, the deed must name the grantee, contain words of conveyance, describe the property, and be executed by the grantor.

Once the deed is delivered to the grantee, it should be recorded promptly. State recording statutes provide the means by which a person who has an interest in land can put the rest of the world on notice of his interest. These statutes also provide priority systems that are applied in case two or more people have conflicting rights in the same property. There are three types of recording statutes: race statutes, notice statutes, and race-notice statutes.

There are three means by which a buyer of real property can attempt to get assurance of the seller's title: have a lawyer examine an abstract of title and render a title opinion; register the property and obtain a certificate of title through the Torrens system (which is in use in some states); or purchase a title insurance policy.

In recent years, most states have imposed on builder-vendors of residential property an implied warranty of habitability, which is an implied guarantee that the property will be safe and suitable for human habitation. A number of courts have extended this warranty to subsequent purchasers of residential property. In addition, a seller today is required to disclose to a buyer any hidden defects in the property that the buyer would be unlikely to discover.

Society places a number of restraints on the ownership of real property. First, a person may not create or contribute to a nuisance on property that unreasonably interferes with another person's enjoyment of his own land. Second, legislative bodies have the police power to regulate health, safety, and welfare, which they may use to impose reasonable restrictions on the use of real property, as is done in zoning ordinances. Third, the government may acquire ownership of property for public use through the power of eminent domain. This requires that the government pay the owner just compensation for the property.

A property owner will usually purchase insurance to protect his property against a variety of perils. This insurance will permit him to shift to his insurer the risk of loss that the property owner would normally bear. In an insurance contract, the insured is the person who acquires insurance on his property. The insurer is the business that, in exchange for consideration (a premium), agrees to pay for losses caused by specific perils. To have a valid insurance contract, the insured must have an insurable interest in the property that is insured. This means that he must have some legal or equitable interest in the property so that he stands to gain economically by the continued existence and good condition of the property and he stands to lose economically by its destruction.

Fire insurance is a common sort of property insurance. Fire insurance protects losses caused by *hostile fires,* including indirect damage caused by smoke, heat, and the efforts of firefighters to extinguish the fire. Other perils may be covered as well. Fire insurance policies may be either valued, which give the insured the ability to recover the face amount of the policy, or open policies, which permit the insured to recover the fair market value of the property at the time it was destroyed, up to the limits stated in the policy. Some fire insurance policies contain a coinsurance clause, which requires the insured to insure the property to a specified percentage of its fair market value in order to fully recover the value of partial losses. Under pro rata clauses, which apply to situations in which the insured has purchased insurance policies from more than one insurer, the loss will be apportioned among the insurance companies.

Insurance contracts generally are governed by the same rules that apply to other types of contracts. The offer to enter the contract is normally made by the prospective insured, who completes an application and submits it with a premium to the insurer. The time at which the acceptance occurs depends on the language of the application and the type of insurance. As in other contracts, the insured's material misrepresentation or bad-faith failure to disclose material information has the effect of permitting the insurer to avoid the contract. State law controls whether insurance contracts need to be evidenced by a writing, but, generally, fire insurance contracts can be either oral or in writing. In interpreting insurance contracts, courts interpret provisions as they would normally be interpreted by an average person. In case of ambiguity, the court will interpret the contract against the insurer who drafted the contract.

A person who seeks to recover benefits under an insurance policy must notify the insurer that a loss covered by the policy has occurred and must furnish proof of the loss. The policy may provide that such notice and proof of loss must occur within a stated time. The insurer may be able to exercise a right of subrogation if it covers a loss; that is, it obtains all of the insured's rights to pursue legal remedies against anyone who might be responsible for the loss. Insurance contracts can end by either cancellation or lapse.

PROBLEM CASES

1. In 1971, Swafford bought three metal buildings and installed them on his ranch. The buildings included (1) a horse barn with a dirt floor middle; (2) an office, a trophy room, and a tack room; and (3) an open-air hay shed with no siding. The buildings were prefabricated at a factory and were assembled at the ranch by Swafford's agent and bolted to concrete slabs. They were never moved after their assembly and installation. In 1973, Swafford mortgaged the property to Kerman. Swafford later defaulted on the debt, and Kerman instituted foreclosure proceedings. Kerman bought the ranch at the foreclosure sale. Swafford claims that the portable buildings belong to him and that he can remove them. Do they belong to Swafford?

2. The Grant family owned property from 1938 to 1946. The property was separated from neighboring property by a fence attached to a hickory tree. In 1946, the Grants sold the property to Ford. The fence was still standing at this time. Some time prior to 1960, the fence was removed. Ford, however, continued to mow and take care of what she believed to be her property up to where the fence had been located. In 1960, the property on the other side of where the fence had been located was sold to Eckert. A survey disclosed that the true boundary line between Ford's property and Eckert's was not the line assumed by Ford and that the strip she had been mowing was in fact located on Eckert's side of the line. Applying a 20-year statute of limitations for adverse possession, had Ford acquired ownership of the disputed strip by adverse possession by 1960?

3. In 1956, the Wakes owned a tract of land, part of which they used for the operation of a farm and part of which they used as a cattle ranch. As part of the ranching operation, the Wakes drove their cattle from the ranch each spring and autumn over an access road on the farm to Butler Springs, which was also located on the farm. From Butler Springs, they ranged the cattle further eastward onto adjacent government land, where they used their grazing rights. In December 1956, the Wakes sold the farm portion of the land on contract to the Hesses. The contract of sale between the Wakes and the Hesses contained a clause expressly reserving an easement in the Wakes (1) to use the Butler Springs water and (2) to use the right-of-way from Butler Springs across the property to the federal reserve land. The contract described the Butler Springs area, but it did not describe the access road leading to Butler Springs from the county road. In 1963, the Hesses sold the farm to the Johnsons, and the contract between these parties referred to the easement held by the Wakes. The Wakes continued to use the access road and Butler Springs until 1964, when they sold their ranch. The sale of the ranch specifically granted the Butler Springs easement to the purchasers. The ranch then changed hands several times, but all of the owners continued to use the access road and Butler Springs. In 1978, the Nelsons bought the ranch. Shortly after the Nelsons took possession of the ranch, the Johnsons sent a letter to them "revoking permission" for the use of the access road. Later, the Johnsons placed locks on the gates across the access road. The Nelsons alleged that they had easement rights in *both* the Butler Springs area and the access road leading to it. Do they?

4. Major developed a subdivision in which he built a number of houses and offered them for sale. The Rozells bought a house from Major. Upon the first rain, water entered under the crawl space of the house and accumulated to a depth of 17 inches in a room in which the furnace and hot water heater were located, frequently putting out the hot water heater. Major's attempts to keep the water out were unsuccessful. Water continued to accumulate in the room every time there was a rainfall of any consequence. As a result, the house was damp and had a peculiar odor and things mildewed. Do the Rozells have a cause of action against Major?

5. The Pecks owned a lawn and garden supply store. Standard Marine was the insurer of the store and its contents. The Pecks placed a fireworks display in the store, where it was subsequently set off by a young boy. A fire resulted that damaged or destroyed much of the Pecks's merchandise. Standard Marine refused to reimburse the Pecks for their loss, citing a clause in the policy that read: "The Company shall not be liable for loss occurring while the hazard is increased by any means within the control or knowledge of the insured." Is Standard Marine liable for the Pecks's loss?

6. The Parkers use part of their property for the purposes of housing, breeding, raising, and selling German shepherd dogs. As many as 25 dogs have been on the Parkers' property at one time. Many of these dogs are trained as guard dogs, protection dogs, or attack dogs. The dogs' barking and offensive odors annoyed adjacent property owners. The Parkers sometimes let some of their dogs wander around the neighborhood unsupervised, which raised concerns on the part of neighbors for the safety of their children. The defendants' property was subject to a restriction that prohibited any noxious or offensive activity and provided that no animal could be raised, bred, or kept for any purpose except household pets. Three homeowners of adjacent homes brought suit against the Parkers, seeking to enjoin them from keeping a number of dogs. The Parkers argue that the subdivision restriction does not prohibit them from keeping the dogs. Will the neighbors be able to obtain an injunction against the Parkers? If so, on what grounds?

7. In 1972, Betty DeWitt and her husband, Joseph, bought a house, taking title in Betty's name. On March 5, 1979, the DeWitts were divorced. As a part of the divorce settlement, Joseph was given possession of the house and Betty was ordered to sign the deed over to him. On January 29, 1980, Joseph died. Soon thereafter, Betty moved into the house and purchased a fire insurance policy from American Family Mutual Insurance Company with a face value of $38,500. In August of 1980, the house was completely destroyed by fire. At this time, American Family learned of her divorce and the decree ordering her to convey title to Joseph. It refused to pay on the policy, arguing that she did not have an insurable interest. Was it correct?

8. The opening and a considerable portion of the cavity of Marengo Cave were located on land owned by the Marengo Cave Company. From 1883, when the cave was discovered, until 1932, Marengo Cave Company and its predecessors in title exercised complete control over the entire cave, charging a fee for admission to others who wished to view it and making improvements in the cave. In 1908, Ross bought land adjoining the Marengo Cave Company land. In 1932, a survey showed that part of the cave lay under Ross's land. Marengo Cave Company claims adverse possession of the part of the cave that extends under Ross's land. Are the elements of adverse possession met here?

9. Glover and Santangelo are the owners of adjacent parcels of property in Oregon. Both lots are on a hillside with a view of Mt. Shasta and overlooking Lake Ewana and the downtown area of Klamath Falls. Santangelo's lot (Lot 10), which is on the downhill side of Glover's lot (Lot 9), is encumbered by a restrictive covenant that was executed at a time when Glover's house was almost completed and Lot 10 was bare. The covenant prohibits any second story from ever being erected on any building in a specified area of Lot 10. The covenant expressly stated that it was intended to run with the land and that it was executed "so that the value of Lot 9 as a 'view lot' would not be impaired by future erections on Lot 10." Santangelo began construction on his house, a substantial proportion of which lay in the portion of Lot 10 that was covered by the restrictive covenant. The house consisted of a main level and a "daylight basement." On the uphill side of the house, approximately one third of the basement was constructed above what would have been the original grade of the property. This basement had windows on the uphill side and the main floor was raised several feet off the ground. The house substantially impaired Glover's western view, but did not disturb Glover's view to the south, across another neighbor's land. As it became apparent to Glover that the house would impair his western view, he attempted to halt the construction. With full knowledge of Glover's complaint, Santangelo proceeded to complete the house. What are Glover's legal rights in this case?

10. Catherine lived with William for a number of years until his death in 1978, but they were not legally married because William was married to another woman, Arlene. Catherine and William owned their home as tenants in common. Upon William's death, Arlene inherited William's share in the home he had shared with Catherine. Catherine remained in the house, living there alone. Arlene sought possession of the property and claimed that Catherine was required to pay her rent, since Catherine was living in the house. In what form of co-ownership do Arlene and Catherine hold this property? Is Catherine legally required to pay rent to Arlene?

11. Mosher was a member of a food cooperative in which members pooled their grocery money to buy in bulk at lower unit prices. In response to a newspaper advertisement by Hudson Food Warehouse Corporation, displaying lower prices than competitive stores and advising shoppers to "check and compare," Mosher and his family drove to the food warehouse with the intention of purchasing food for the cooperative. Upon entering the store, Mosher began to write down prices, as was his custom, so that he could make comparisons for the most economical purchases. Mosher was then approached by Hudson employees who informed him that it was against store policy to write down prices and that he must either stop doing so or leave the store. Mosher refused either alternative. Did Mosher have the right to remain on Hudson's property after being asked to leave?

12. The Duchaines own real estate that they leased to Southern Massachusetts Broadcasters for the period September 1, 1975, to August 31, 1980. Southern installed a radio tower, which it used to transmit radio broadcasts. The tower is a 390-foot steel-frame structure standing on three legs and attached by iron bolts to five-foot-square cement foundations. Although the tower was capable of being removed from the property, Southern did not attempt to remove the tower or claim the right to remove it until two and one-quarter years after vacating Duchaines's property. Southern then filed suit claiming ownership of the tower. Will it prevail?

CHAPTER 22

BANKRUPTCY

INTRODUCTION

When an individual, a partnership, or a corporation is unable to pay its debts to creditors, problems can arise. Some creditors may demand security for past debts or start court actions on their claims in an effort to protect themselves. Such actions may adversely affect other creditors by depriving them of their fair share of the debtor's assets. Also, quick depletion of the debtor's assets may effectively prevent the debtor who needs additional time to pay off his debts from having an opportunity to do so.

At the same time, creditors need to be protected against the actions a debtor in financial difficulty might be tempted to take to their detriment. For example, the debtor might run off with his remaining assets or might use them to pay certain favored creditors, leaving nothing for the other creditors. Finally, a means is needed by which a debtor can get a fresh start financially and not continue to be saddled with debts beyond his ability to pay. This chapter focuses on the body of law and procedure that has developed to deal with the competing interests when a debtor is unable to pay his debts in a timely manner.

The Bankruptcy Act

The Bankruptcy Act is a federal law that provides an organized procedure under the supervision of a federal court for dealing with insolvent debtors. Debtors are considered insolvent if they are unable or fail to pay their debts as they become due. The power of Congress to enact bankruptcy legislation is provided in the Constitution. Through the years, there have been many amendments to the Bankruptcy Act. Congress completely revised the act in 1978 and then passed significant amendments to it in 1984. In 1986, Congress added provisions dealing with family farms.

The Bankruptcy Act has several major purposes. One is to assure that the debtor's property is fairly distributed to the creditors and that some creditors do not obtain unfair advantage over the others. At the same time, the act protects all of the creditors against actions by the debtor that would unreasonably diminish the debtor's assets to which they are entitled. The act also provides the honest debtor with a measure of protection against the demands for payment by his creditors. Under some circumstances, the debtor is given additional time to pay the creditors, freeing him of those pressures creditors might otherwise exert. If the debtor makes a full and honest accounting of his assets and liabilities and deals fairly with his creditors, the debtor may have most—if not all—of the debts discharged so as to have a fresh start.

At one time, bankruptcy carried a strong stigma for the debtors who became involved in it. Today, this is less true. It is still desirable that a person conduct her financial affairs in a responsible manner. However, there is a greater understanding that such events as accidents, natural disasters, illness, divorce, and severe economic dislocations are often beyond the ability of individuals to control and may lead to financial difficulty and bankruptcy.

Bankruptcy Proceedings

The Bankruptcy Act covers a number of bankruptcy proceedings. In this chapter, our focus will be on:

1. Straight bankruptcy (liquidations).
2. Reorganizations.
3. Family farms.
4. Consumer debt adjustments.

The Bankruptcy Act also contains provisions regarding municipal bankruptcies, which are not covered in this chapter.

Liquidations

A liquidation proceeding, traditionally called **straight bankruptcy,** is brought under Chapter 7 of the Bankruptcy Act. The debtor must disclose all of the property he owns and surrender this bankruptcy estate to the **bankruptcy trustee.** The trustee separates out certain property that the debtor is permitted to keep and then administers, liquidates, and distributes the remainder of the bankrupt debtor's estate. There is a mechanism for determining the relative rights of the creditors, for recovering any preferential payments made to creditors, and for disallowing any preferential liens obtained by creditors. If the bankrupt person has been honest in his business transactions and in the bankruptcy proceedings, he is usually given a **discharge** (relieved) of his debts.

Reorganizations

Chapter 11 of the Bankruptcy Act provides a proceeding whereby a debtor engaged in business can work out a plan to solve its financial problems under the supervision of a federal court. A reorganization plan is essentially a contract between a debtor and its creditors. The proceeding is intended for debtors, particularly businesses, whose financial problems may be solvable if they are given some time and guidance and if they are relieved of some pressure from creditors.

Family Farms

Historically, farmers have been accorded special attention in the Bankruptcy Code. Chapter 12 of the Bankruptcy Act provides a special proceeding whereby a debtor involved in a family farming operation can develop a plan to work out his financial difficulties. Generally, the debtor remains in possession of the farm and continues to operate it while the plan is developed and implemented.

Consumer Debt Adjustments

Under Chapter 13 of the Bankruptcy Act, individuals with regular incomes who are in financial difficulty can develop plans under court supervision to satisfy their creditors. Chapter 13 permits compositions (reductions) of debts and/or extensions of time to pay debts out of the debtor's future earnings.

The Bankruptcy Courts

Bankruptcy cases and proceedings are filed in federal district courts. The district courts have the authority to refer the cases and proceedings to bankruptcy judges, who are considered to be units of the district court. If a dispute falls within what is known as a **core proceeding,** the bankruptcy judge can hear and determine the controversy. Core proceedings include a broad list of matters related to the administration of a bankruptcy estate. However, if a dispute is not a core proceeding, but rather involves a state law claim, then the bankruptcy judge can only hear the case and prepare draft findings and conclusions for review by the district court judge.

Certain proceedings affecting interstate commerce have to be heard by the district court judge if any party requests that this be done. Moreover, even the district courts are precluded from deciding certain state law claims that could not normally be brought in federal court, even if those claims are related to the bankruptcy matter. Bankruptcy judges are appointed by the president for terms of 14 years.

CHAPTER 7:
LIQUIDATION PROCEEDINGS

Petitions

All bankruptcy proceedings, including liquidation proceedings, are begun by the filing of a petition. The petition may be either a **voluntary petition** filed by the debtor or an **involuntary petition** filed by a creditor or creditors of the debtor. A voluntary petition in bankruptcy may be filed by an individual, a partnership, or a corporation. However, municipal, railroad, insurance, and banking corporations and savings or building and loan associations are not permitted to file for straight bankruptcy proceedings. A person filing a voluntary petition need not be insolvent that is, her debts need not be greater than her assets. However, the person must be able to allege that she has debts. The primary purpose for filing a voluntary petition is to obtain a discharge from some or all of the debts.

Involuntary Petitions

An involuntary petition is a petition filed by creditors of a debtor. By filing it, they seek to have the debtor declared bankrupt and his assets distributed to the creditors. Involuntary petitions may be filed against many debtors. However, involuntary petitions in straight bankruptcy cannot be filed against (1) farmers; (2) ranchers; (3) nonprofit organizations; (4) municipal, railroad, insurance, and banking corporations; (5) credit unions; and (6) savings or building and loan associations. If a debtor has 12 or more creditors, an involuntary petition to declare him bankrupt must be signed by at least 3 creditors. If there are fewer than 12 creditors, then an involuntary petition can be filed by a single creditor. The creditor or creditors must have valid claims against the debtor exceeding the value of any security they hold by $5,000 or more. To be forced into involuntary bankruptcy, the debtor must be unable to pay his debts as they become due—or have had a custodian for his property appointed within the previous four months.

If an involuntary petition is filed against a debtor engaged in business, the debtor may be permitted to continue to operate the business. However, the court may appoint an **interim trustee** if this is necessary to preserve the bankruptcy estate or to prevent loss of the estate. A creditor who suspects that a debtor may dismantle her business or dispose of its assets at less than fair value may apply to the court for protection.

Automatic Stay Provisions

The filing of a bankruptcy petition operates as an **automatic stay,** holding in abeyance various forms of creditor action against a debtor or her property. These actions include: (1) beginning or continuing judicial proceedings against the debtor; (2) actions to obtain possession of the debtor's property; (3) actions to create, perfect, or enforce a lien against the debtor's property; and (4) setoff of indebtedness owed to the debtor before commencement of the bankruptcy proceeding. A court may give a creditor relief from the stay if the creditor can show that the stay does not give her "adequate protection" and jeopardizes her interest in certain property. The relief to the creditor might take the form of periodic cash payments or the granting of a replacement lien or an additional lien on property.

The case that follows, *In Re Ionosphere Clubs, Inc.,* is an example of creditors trying to proceed independent of a bankruptcy court and having their efforts blocked.

IN RE IONOSPHERE CLUBS, INC.

111 B.R. 423 (Bankr. S.D. N.Y. 1990)

On March 4, 1989, the International Association of Machinists and Aerospace Workers, AFL–CIO (IAM) initiated a strike against Eastern Air Lines, Inc. Thereafter, both the Airline Pilots Association (ALPA) and the Transport Workers Union of America (TWU) initiated a sympathy strike. As a result, on March 9, 1989, Eastern and its affiliate, Ionosphere Clubs, Inc., each filed a voluntary petition for relief under Chapter 11. Since the bankruptcy filing, Eastern and Ionosphere continued to operate their businesses as debtors in possession.

During the strike, Eastern hired new pilots as permanent replacements for the striking pilots. On November 22, 1989, the ALPA notified Eastern that the sympathy strike had been concluded and that the approximately 2,000 striking pilots were willing to return to work. Eastern was not willing to displace the replacement pilots to make room for the returning strikers.

In February 1990, Morteson Rolleston and 17 formerly striking pilots filed a class action lawsuit in federal district court in Atlanta, claiming, among other things, that Eastern had failed to fund its pilot pension plan and to pay interest on certain pension benefits that had already been paid. The lawsuit sought to freeze the assets of Eastern until amounts allegedly due to certain benefit plans were paid. Eastern sought an injunction from the bankruptcy court enjoining the Rolleston lawsuit as a violation of the automatic stay provisions of the Bankruptcy Act.

Lifland, Chief Judge.   Section 362(a)(3) of the Code provides in pertinent part as follows:

(a) . . . a petition filed under . . . this title . . . operates as a stay, applicable to all entities, of—

(1) the commencement or continuation . . . of a judicial, administrative or other proceeding against the debtor that was or could have been commenced before the commencement of the case under this title, or to recover a claim against the debtor that arose before the commencement of the case under this title;

* * * * *

(3) an act to obtain possession of the property of the estate or of property from the estate or to exercise control over property of the estate;

* * * * *

(6) any act to collect, assess or recover a claim against the debtor that arose before the commencement of the case under this title.

It is beyond dispute that the Rolleston Plaintiffs seek to exercise control of at least $281 million of the cash assets of Eastern's estate by seeking to secure a court order "freezing" Eastern's assets and directing Eastern to pay this amount to the pilot pension plans. Additionally, the Rolleston Plaintiffs appear to request a temporary restraining order that would prohibit distributions under a reorganization plan, because "if the assets are distributed to creditors, it will be impossible for Plaintiffs to recover those assets." This direct attempt to secure preferred status for a discrete group of creditors runs directly counter to the distribution and oversight scheme established by the Code.

The Rolleston Plaintiffs also allege that the funds they seek to recover from Eastern on behalf of the pension plans "are not Eastern's assets but . . . are assets of the [Rolleston] Plaintiffs." It would appear that the Rolleston Plaintiffs are merely asserting unliquidated, contingent pre-petition claims against the Eastern estate and have no specific interest (other than the interest that all of Eastern's creditors have in property of the estate) in the property which they are attempting to gain control over.

Any attempt to "freeze" Eastern's assets and obtain an order requiring Eastern to transfer cash from its estate to the pilot pension plans is a direct and blatant attempt to assert control over the assets of the estate for the benefit of the Rolleston Plaintiffs. Such a distribution will reduce the amount to be paid to creditors and have an adverse effect on the feasibility of any plan of reorganization. Additionally, the Rolleston lawsuit interferes with this court's jurisdiction over essential core matters in the Eastern case, including claims issues and confirmation of a plan of reorganization.

Judgment in favor of Eastern enjoining the Rolleston lawsuit.

Order of Relief

Once a bankruptcy petition has been filed, the first step is a court determination that relief should be ordered. If a voluntary petition is filed by the debtor, or if the debtor does not contest an involuntary petition, this step is automatic. If the debtor contests an involuntary petition, then a trial is held on the question of whether the court should order relief. The court orders relief only (1) if the debtor is generally not paying his debts as they become due, or (2) if within four months of the filing of the petition a custodian was appointed or took possession of the debtor's property. The court also appoints an interim trustee pending election of a trustee by the creditors.

Meeting of Creditors and Election of Trustee

The bankrupt person is required to file a list of his assets, liabilities, and creditors and a statement of his financial affairs. Then, the court calls a meeting of the creditors. The creditors may elect a creditors' committee and a trustee who, if approved by the judge, takes over administration of the bankrupt's estate. The trustee represents the creditors in handling the estate. At the meeting, the creditors have a chance to ask the debtor questions about his assets, liabilities, and financial difficulties. These questions commonly focus on whether the debtor has concealed or improperly disposed of assets. See Figure 1.

Duties of the Trustee

The trustee takes possession of the debtor's property and has it appraised. The debtor must also turn over her records to the trustee. For a time, the trustee may operate the debtor's business. The trustee sets aside the items of property that a debtor is permitted to keep under state exemption statutes or federal law.

The trustee examines the claims filed by various creditors and objects to those that are improper in any way. The trustee separates the unsecured property from the secured and otherwise exempt property. He also sells the bankrupt's nonexempt property as soon as possible, consistent with the best interest of the creditors.

The trustee is required to keep an accurate account of all the property and money he receives and to promptly deposit moneys into the estate's accounts. At the final meeting of the creditors, the trustee presents a detailed statement of the administration of the bankruptcy estate.

Exemptions

Even in a liquidation proceeding, the bankrupt is generally not required to give up all of his property; he is permitted to **exempt** certain items of property. Under the new Bankruptcy Act, the debtor may choose to keep certain items or property either exempted by state law, or exempt under federal law—unless state law specifically forbids use of the federal exemptions. However, any such property concealed or fraudulently transferred by the debtor may not be retained.

The debtor must elect to use *either* the set of exemptions provided by the state or the set provided by the federal bankruptcy law; she may not pick and choose between them. A husband and wife involved in bankruptcy proceedings must both elect either the federal or the state exemptions; where they cannot agree, the federal exemptions are deemed elected.

The **exemptions** permit the bankrupt person to retain a minimum amount of the assets considered necessary to life and to his ability to continue to earn a living. They are part of the fresh start philosophy that is one of the purposes of the Bankruptcy Act. The general effect of the federal exemptions is to make a minimum exemption available to debtors in all states. States that wish to be more generous to debtors can provide more liberal exemptions.

The specific items that are exempt under state statutes vary from state to state. Some states provide fairly liberal exemptions and are considered "debtors' havens." Items that are commonly made exempt from sale to pay debts owed creditors include the family Bible, tools or books of the trade, life insurance policies; health aids, such as wheelchairs and hearing aids; personal and household goods, and jewelry, furniture, and motor vehicles worth up to a certain amount.

Eleven categories of property are exempt under the federal exemptions, which the debtor may elect in lieu of the state exemptions. The federal exemptions include:

1. The debtor's interest (not to exceed $7,500 in value) in real or personal property that the debtor or a dependent of the debtor uses as a residence.

2. The debtor's interest (not to exceed $1,200 in value) in one motor vehicle.

3. The debtor's interest (not to exceed $200 in value for any particular item) up to a total of $4,000 in household furnishings, household goods, wearing apparel, appliances, books, animals, crops, or musical instruments that are held primarily for

FIGURE 1   Order and Notice of Chapter 7 Bankruptcy Filing

Order and Notice of Chapter 7 Bankruptcy Filing

B16A United States Bankruptcy Court for the District of Maryland	ORDER AND NOTICE OF CHAPTER 7 BANKRUPTCY FILING, MEETING OF CREDITORS, AND FIXING OF DATES (Individual or Joint Debtor No Asset Case)

A. GENERAL INFORMATION		
Name of Debtor John B. Jones D/B/A THE BATH SHOP	**Address of Debtor** 195 MAIN STREET ANNAPOLIS MD, 21401	
	Date Filed 01/24/92	**Case Number** 90–60300–SD	**Soc. Sec. Nos./Tax ID Nos.** 050–30–4701
Addressee: WICKER PRODUCTS, INC. 2000 SMITH PIKE ALMA, MI 48030	**Address of the Clerk of the Bankruptcy Court** United States Bankruptcy Court 101 W. Lombard Street Baltimore, Maryland 21201	
Name and Address of Attorney for Debtor MARC A. BURNS 215 WATER STREET, BALTIMORE MD 21202	**Name and Address of Trustee** BRUCE A. SMITH 136 S. CHARLES STREET, BALTIMORE MD 21201	

B. DATE, TIME AND LOCATION OF MEETING OF CREDITORS

February 28, 1992, 09:15 A.M., U.S. Trustee, Fallon Federal Bldg., Rm. G–13, 31 Hopkins Plaza, Baltimore, MD 21201

C. DISCHARGE OF DEBTS

Deadline to File a Complaint Objecting to the Discharge of the Debtor or Dischargeability of a Debt: April 30, 1992

D. BANKRUPTCY INFORMATION

THERE APPEAR TO BE NO ASSETS AT THIS TIME FROM WHICH PAYMENT MAY BE MADE TO CREDITORS. DO NOT FILE A PROOF OF CLAIM UNTIL YOU RECEIVE NOTICE TO DO SO.

FILING OF A BANKRUPTCY CASE. A bankruptcy petition has been filed in this court for the person or persons named above as the debtor, and an order for relief has been entered. You will not receive notice of all documents filed in this case. All documents which are filed with the court, including lists of the debtor's property and debts, are available for inspection at the office of the clerk of the bankruptcy court.

CREDITORS MAY NOT TAKE CERTAIN ACTIONS. Anyone to whom the debtor owes money or property is a creditor. Under the bankruptcy law, the debtor is granted certain protection against creditors. Common examples of prohibited actions are contacting the debtor to demand repayment, taking action against the debtor to collect money owed to creditors or to take property of the debtor, except as specifically permitted by the bankruptcy law, and starting or continuing foreclosure actions, repossessions, or wage deductions. If unauthorized actions are taken by a creditor against a debtor, the court may punish that creditor. A creditor who is considering taking action against the debtor or the property of the debtor should review 11 U.S.C. § 362 and may wish to seek legal advice. The staff of the clerk's office is not permitted to give legal advice to anyone.

MEETING OF CREDITORS. The debtor (both husband and wife in a joint case) shall appear at the meeting of creditors at the date and place set forth above in box 'B' for the purpose of being examined under oath. ATTENDANCE BY CREDITORS AT THE MEETING IS WELCOMED, BUT NOT REQUIRED. At the meeting the creditors may elect a trustee as permitted by law, elect a committee of creditors, examine the debtor, and transact such other business as may properly come before the meeting. The meeting may be continued or adjourned from time to time without further written notice to the creditors.

LIQUIDATION OF THE DEBTOR'S PROPERTY. A trustee has been appointed in this case to collect the debtor's property, if any, and turn it into money. At this time, however, it appears from the schedules of the debtor that there are no assets from which any dividend can be paid to creditors. If at a later date it appears that there are assets from which a dividend may be paid, creditors will be notified and given an opportunity to file claims.

EXEMPT PROPERTY. Under state and federal law, the debtor is permitted to keep certain money or property as exempt. If a creditor believes that an exemption of money or property is not authorized by law, the creditor may file an objection. Any objection must be filed no later than 30 days after the conclusion of the meeting of creditors.

DISCHARGE OF DEBTS. The debtor is seeking a discharge of debts. A discharge means that certain debts are made unenforceable. Creditors whose claims against the debtor are discharged may never take action to collect the discharged debts. If a creditor believes the debtor should not receive a discharge under 11 U.S.C. § 727 or a specific debt should not be discharged under 11 U.S.C. § 523(c) for some valid reason specified in the bankruptcy law, the creditor must take action to challenge the discharge. The deadline for challenging a discharge is set forth above in box 'C.' Creditors considering taking such action may wish to seek legal advice.

DO NOT FILE A PROOF OF CLAIM UNLESS YOU RECEIVE A COURT NOTICE TO DO SO

For the Court:	
January 31, 1992	Michael Kostishak
Date	Clerk of the Bankruptcy Court

the personal, family, or household use of the debtor or a dependent of the debtor.

4. The debtor's aggregate interest (not to exceed $500 in value) in jewelry held primarily for the personal, family, or household use of the debtor or a dependent of the debtor.

5. $400 in value of any other property of the debtor's choosing, plus up to $3,750 of any unused homestead exemption.

6. The debtor's aggregate interest (not to exceed $750 in value) in any implements, professional books, or tools of the trade.

7. Life insurance contracts.

8. Interest up to $4,000 in specified kinds of dividends or interest in certain kinds of life insurance policies.

9. Professionally prescribed health aids.

10. Social security, disability, alimony, and other benefits reasonably necessary for the support of the debtor or his dependents.

11. The debtor's right to receive certain insurance and liability payments.

The term *value* means "fair market value as of the date of the filing of the petition." In determining the debtor's interest in property, the amount of any liens against the property must be deducted.

Avoidance of Liens

The debtor is also permitted to **void** certain liens against exempt properties that impair her exemptions. Liens that can be voided on this basis are judicial liens or nonpossessory, nonpurchase money security interests in: (1) household furnishings, household goods, wearing apparel, appliances, books, animals, crops, musical instruments, or jewelry that are held primarily for the personal, family, or household use of the debtor or a dependent of the debtor; (2) implements, professional books, or tools of the trade of the debtor or a dependent of the debtor; and (3) professionally prescribed health aids for the debtor or a dependent of the debtor. Debtors are also permitted to **redeem** exempt personal property from secured creditors by paying them the value of the collateral. Then, the creditor is an unsecured creditor as to any remaining debt owed by the debtor.

The case that follows, *In Re Moore*, illustrates the considerations a court might take into account in determining whether liens on particular items can be avoided.

IN RE MOORE

110 B.R. 53 (Bankr. N.D. Ala. 1988)[1]

In September 1987, Joseph and Justine Moore filed a voluntary Chapter 7 petition. In the petition, the Moores claimed as exempt all of their household goods and furnishings as well as certain guns. Listed as a secured creditor was ITT Financial Services (ITT), which held a nonpurchase money security interest in household goods. In July 1987, the Moores had refinanced a loan with ITT. As security for the loan, ITT insisted on, and was granted, a security interest in the Moores's personal property, which consisted of household furnishings, appliances, and musical instruments.

On November 30, 1987, the Moores filed a motion to avoid ITT's security interest in the household goods they were claiming as exempt. Bankruptcy Code section 522(f)(2) authorizes avoidance of nonpossessory, nonpurchase money security interests in "household goods." ITT objected to the motion on the grounds it sought avoidance of liens as to items of property that did not qualify as household goods. Specifically, ITT objected to the avoidance of its lien as to a .243 caliber rifle, a .308 caliber rifle, a 12-gauge shotgun, a Stihl chainsaw, a Kodak movie camera, a Kodak movie projector, and a 10-speed bicycle. ITT did not object to the motion as it affected its

---

[1]Printed as Appendix to In Re Gonshorowski, 110 B.R. 51 (Bankr. N.D. Ala. 1990).

lien on: (1) a television set, (2) stereo equipment, (3) musical instruments, (4) home workshop tools, and (5) garden equipment.

Wright, Chief Judge.   While numerous courts have addressed the question of what constitutes "household goods" under the Bankruptcy Act, there appears to be little uniformity in the manner in which the question has been answered. Some courts have decreed that section 522(f)(2)(A) should be construed strictly while other courts have adopted a more liberal view of the scope of lien avoidance.

Individuals who favor defining household in the narrowest of terms have relied heavily on guidelines published by the Federal Trade Commission (FTC). The FTC defines household goods as "clothing, furniture, appliances, one radio and one television, linens, china, crockery, kitchenware, and personal effects (including wedding rings) of the consumer and his or her dependents, provided that the following are not included within the scope of the term 'household goods': (1) works of art; (2) electronic entertainment equipment (except one television and one radio); (3) items acquired as antiques; and (4) jewelry (except wedding rings)."

Judges have however generally refused to adopt the FTC definition. As stated in the case of *In Re Boyer*, "it does not follow that if an item does not fall within the FTC definition of household goods, that it is not household goods for purpose of lien avoidance under the Bankruptcy Code." The FTC's definition, after all, was not promulgated simply for use in a bankruptcy context, but reflects a cost-benefit analysis of credit practice involving all consumer debtors. In *Boyer*, the court went on to hold that "household goods include more than those items that are indispensable to the bare existence of a debtor and his family. Items which, while not being luxuries, are convenient or useful to a reasonable existence must also be included."

The theme running throughout most of the cases which favor a broader definition of household goods is the belief that Congress intended to allow debtors to begin again without requiring them to give up each and every item of property they owned.

In order for debtors to have any meaningful chance at a fresh start bankruptcy courts must be willing to show some flexibility in deciding questions which arise under section 522(f)(2)(A). Thus this Court declines to adopt the FTC definition and instead adopts a rebuttable presumption that items used by debtors or their dependents in or around their residence are household goods. Since the presumption is a rebuttable one, the Court also adopts the following list of factors which it will consider in a case in which a lien avoidance question arises.

1. Whether the item in question is included within those items defined as household goods under the FTC definition;
2. The number of other like or similar items owned by the debtor;
3. The ages, sex and number of the debtor's dependents;
4. The standard of living to which the debtor and his family have become accustomed viewed in light of his annual income;
5. The standard of living of members of the debtor's neighborhood;
6. The use to which the item is put (i.e. recreational, personal or business);
7. Whether the item is one for which a certificate of title is issued;
8. Whether the items are luxury goods.

In applying the above cited factors to this case, the Court is of the opinion that the Moores's motion to avoid ITT's lien on the .243 caliber rifle, the .308 caliber, and the 12-gauge shotgun is due to be denied. The Court is presented with a more difficult decision as it relates to the Kodak movie camera, the Kodak projector, the Stihl chainsaw, and the 10-speed bicycle. While the camera, projector and bike are undisputedly recreational vehicles, the Court is not prepared to hold that recreational items are automatically excluded from being treated as household goods. Surely, there can be recreation in the home. The appropriate test is whether the items are (1) used in or around the debtor's home, (2) whether the goods are luxury goods, (3) whether the items are used for personal enjoyment as opposed to being used for the production of income, and (4) whether ownership of the goods would be considered outrageous in light of the community's standard of living. Based on these considerations, the Court is of the opinion that the Kodak camera, the Kodak projector, and the bike should be classified as household goods under the facts of this case. In addition, the Court holds that the Stihl chainsaw is an item of machinery used for the purpose of maintenance or upkeep of the homeplace and as such should be treated as a household good.

Judgment for ITT denying the motion as to avoidance of its lien on the guns, but otherwise granting the Moores's motion.

Preferential Payments

A major purpose of the Bankruptcy Act is to assure equal treatment for the creditors of an insolvent debtor. The act also prevents an insolvent debtor from distributing her assets to a few favored creditors to the detriment of the other creditors.

The trustee has the right to recover for the benefit of the bankruptcy estate all **preferential payments** in excess of $600 made by the bankrupt person.[2] A preferential payment is a payment made by an insolvent debtor within 90 days of the filing of the bankruptcy petition. Such a payment enables that creditor to obtain a greater percentage of a preexisting debt than other similar creditors of the debtor. It is irrelevant whether the creditor knew that the debtor was insolvent.

For example, Fredericks has $1,000 in cash and no other assets. He owes $650 to his friend Roberts, $1,500 to a credit union, and $2,000 to a finance company. If Fredericks pays $650 to Roberts and then files for bankruptcy, he has made a preferential payment to Roberts. Roberts has had his debt paid in full, whereas only $350 is left to satisfy the $3,500 owed to the credit union and finance company. They stand to recover only 10 cents on each dollar that Fredericks owes them. The trustee has the right to get the $650 back from Roberts.

If the favored creditor is an insider—a relative of an individual debtor or an officer, director, or related party of a company—then a preferential payment made up to one year prior to the filing of the petition can be recovered.

Preferential Liens

Preferential liens are treated in a similar manner. A creditor might try to obtain an advantage over other creditors by obtaining a lien on the debtor's property to secure an existing debt. The creditor might seek to get the debtor's consent to a lien or to obtain a lien by legal process. Such liens are considered *preferential* and are invalid if they are obtained on property of an insolvent debtor within 90 days of the filing of a bankruptcy petition and if their purpose is to secure a preexisting debt. A preferential lien obtained by an insider within one year of the bankruptcy can be avoided.

The provisions of the Bankruptcy Act that negate preferential payments and liens do not prevent a debtor from engaging in current business transactions. For example, George Grocer is insolvent. He is permitted to purchase and pay for new inventory, such as produce or meat, without the payment being considered preferential. His assets have not been reduced. He has simply traded money for goods to be sold in his business. Similarly, he could buy a new display counter and give the seller a security interest in the counter until he has paid for it. This is not a preferential lien. The seller of the counter has not gained an unfair advantage over other creditors, and Grocer's assets have not been reduced by the transaction. The unfair advantage comes where an existing creditor tries to take a lien or obtain a payment of more than his share of the debtor's assets. Then, the creditor has obtained a preference over other creditors, which is disallowed.

The act also permits payments of accounts in the ordinary course of business. Such payments are not considered preferential.

---

[2]In the case of an individual debtor whose debts are primarily consumer debts, the trustee is not entitled to avoid preferences unless the aggregate value of the property is $600 or more.

Fraudulent Transfers

If a debtor transfers property or incurs an obligation with *intent to hinder, delay, or defraud creditors,* the transfer is *voidable* by the trustee. Transfers of property for *less than reasonable value* are similarly voidable. Suppose Kasper is in financial difficulty. She "sells" her $5,000 car to her mother for $100 so that her creditors cannot claim it. Kasper did not receive fair consideration for this transfer. The transfer could be declared void by a trustee if it was made within a year before the filing of a bankruptcy petition against Kasper. The provisions of law concerning **fraudulent transfers** are designed to prevent a debtor from concealing or disposing of his property in fraud of creditors. Such transfers may also subject the debtor to criminal penalties and prevent discharge of the debtor's unpaid liabilities.

The *In Re Beckman* case, which follows, illustrates the attempt of some debtors in anticipation of bankruptcy to put some of their assets beyond the reach of their creditors and the response of the trustee who was able to avoid the transfers as fraudulent.

IN RE BECKMAN

104 B.R. 866 (Bankr. S.D. Ohio 1989)

In September 1985, Richard and Nancy Beckman believed they collectively owned assets in excess of $3 million and had a joint net worth in excess of $1.5 million. However, after consulting an attorney and having their assets appraised, it became apparent during October of 1985 that they had a negative net worth, that they were insolvent, and that bankruptcy was inevitable.

In December, the Beckmans each signed applications to Bankers National Life Insurance Company to purchase $100,000 worth of additional life insurance. At the time, Richard Beckman already had $300,000 in term life insurance, $100,000 in accidental life insurance, $10,000 in whole life, and $14,000 in credit life insurance. On January 11, 1986, Richard Beckman delivered $15,000 in cash to Bankers Life as the initial premium on the two policies ($10,000 on his policy and $5,000 on her policy). The source of the funds was fees earned in his dentistry practice during the preceding October through December. The beneficiaries on all of the insurance policies (except the credit life policy) were either the Beckmans or their children.

On January 9, 1986, the Beckmans signed a Chapter 7 bankruptcy petition, and it was filed on January 14, 1986. The trustee sought to avoid the purchase of insurance from Bankers Life as a fraud on creditors.

Cole, Bankruptcy Judge.   The Beckmans argue that it was perfectly proper and, hence, not fraudulent, to convert non-exempt cash to exempt property—the life insurance policies—on the eve of bankruptcy. Further, according to the Beckmans, the insurance purchase was made merely to "provide for each other and their children in the event that one or both of them died." For these reasons, the Beckmans submit that because the insurance purchase was not fraudulent under either federal or state law, the transfer of $15,000 is not avoidable.

The Trustee maintains the insurance purchase was undertaken with actual intent to hinder, delay and defraud the creditors of the estate, thereby rendering the transaction avoidable pursuant to Bankruptcy Code section 548(a)(1). This section states:

(a) The trustee may avoid any transfer of an interest of the debtor in property or any obligation incurred by the debtor that was made or incurred on or within one year before the date of the filing of the petition, if the debtor voluntarily or involuntarily

(1) made such transfer or incurred such obligation with actual intent to hinder, delay or defraud any entity to which the debtor was or became, on or after the date that such transfer was made or such obligation was incurred, indebted;

The issue for decision is whether the Beckmans's eve-of-bankruptcy conversion of non-exempt cash into exempt life insurance policies constitutes fraudulent conduct or merely prudent pre-bankruptcy planning.

Considerable debate in the case law has been engendered by pre-bankruptcy engineering—i.e., the practice of converting non-exempt property into exempt property in contemplation of filing a bankruptcy case. The general rule which has emerged from the decisional law is that mere conversion of property from non-exempt to exempt status on the eve of bankruptcy does not establish fraud. However, if extrinsic evidence of intent to defraud creditors is adduced, courts have: (1) disallowed the debtor's exemption claim and (2) held that the pre-bankruptcy transactions constitute avoidable fraudulent transfers.

Hence, the Court must determine here whether the Trustee has shown the existence of extrinsic evidence of fraud. Among the circumstances which courts focus upon in determining a debtor's intent in purchasing exempt life insurance on the eve of bankruptcy are the following:

1. Whether there was fair consideration paid for the life insurance policy;
2. Whether the debtor was solvent or insolvent as a result of the transfer or whether he was insolvent at the time of the transfer;
3. The amount of the policy;
4. Whether the debtor intended, in good faith, to provide by moderate premiums some protection to those to whom he had a duty to support;
5. The length of time between the purchase of a life insurance policy and the filing of the bankruptcy;
6. The amount of non-exempt property which the debtor had after purchasing the life insurance policy; and
7. The debtor's failure to produce available evidence and to testify with significant preciseness as to the pertinent details of his activities shortly before filing the bankruptcy petition.

Utilizing the foregoing factors as a guide, the Court concludes that in carrying out the insurance purchase the Beckmans intended to defraud their creditors. The factors delineated in paragraphs (2), (5) and (6) of the above list are clearly present. Debtors converted all of their remaining non-exempt property (p6) two days before their bankruptcy petition was filed (p5) and while they were admittedly insolvent (p2).

The amount of insurance purchased by the Beckmans (p3) likewise evinces a fraudulent purpose on their part. Notwithstanding the substantial amount of life insurance they had, the Beckmans consummated the purchase of additional insurance a mere three days prior to their bankruptcy filing. The Beckmans maintain the additional coverage was necessary for the protection of their family. But, having considered the record as a whole, the Court concludes that this testimony is not credible. To purchase an additional $200,000 in life insurance on the eve of bankruptcy and pre-pay the premiums thereon so that the cash surrender value of the the policies would be obtainable by the Beckmans upon the termination of their bankruptcy proceeding goes far beyond "providing in good faith by moderate premiums some protection to those to whom they had a duty to support."

Perhaps the most telling indicator of the Beckmans fraudulent intent is their attempted concealment or, at best, obfuscation of the insurance purchase in their bankruptcy schedule and the accompanying schedules.

Judgment in favor of Trustee avoiding the insurance purchase as made in fraud of creditors.

Claims

If creditors wish to participate in the estate of a bankrupt debtor, they must file a **proof of claim** in the estate within a certain time—usually six months—after the first meeting of creditors. Only unsecured creditors are required to file proofs of claims. However, a secured creditor whose secured claim exceeds the value of the collateral is an unsecured creditor to the extent of the deficiency. That creditor must file a proof of claim to support the recovery of the deficiency.

Allowable Claims

The fact that a proof of claim is filed does not assure that a creditor can participate in the distribution of the assets of the bankruptcy estate. The claim must also be allowed. If the trustee has a valid defense to the claim, he can use the defense to disallow or reduce it. For example, if the claim is based on goods sold to the debtor and the seller breached a warranty, the trustee can assert the breach as a defense. All of the defenses available to the bankrupt person are available to the trustee.

Secured Claims

The trustee must also determine whether a creditor has a lien or secured interest to secure an allowable claim. If the debtor's property is subject to a secured claim of a creditor, that creditor has first claim to it. The property is available to satisfy claims of other creditors only to the extent that its value exceeds the amount of the debt secured.

Priority Claims

The Bankruptcy Act declares certain claims to have **priority** over other claims. The six classes of priority claims are:

1. Expenses and fees incurred in administering the bankruptcy estate.

2. Unsecured claims in involuntary cases that arise in the ordinary course of the debtor's business after the filing of the petition but before the appointment of a trustee or the order of relief.

3. Unsecured claims of up to $2,000 per individual for employees' wages earned within 90 days before the petition was filed.

4. Contributions to employee benefit plans up to $2,000 per person (moreover, the claim for wages plus pension contribution is limited to $2,000 per person).

5. Claims of up to $900 each by individuals for deposits made on goods or services for personal use that were not delivered or provided.

6. Certain taxes owed to governmental units.

Distribution of the Debtor's Estate

The priority claims are paid *after* secured creditors realize on their collateral but *before* other unsecured creditors are paid. Payments are made to the six priority classes, in order, to the extent there are funds available. Each class must be paid in full before the next class is entitled to receive anything. To the extent there are insufficient funds to satisfy all the creditors within a class, each class member receives a pro rata share of his claim.

Unsecured creditors include: (1) those creditors who had not taken any collateral to secure the debt owed to them; (2) secured creditors to the extent their debt was not satisfied by the collateral they held; and (3) priority claimholders to the extent their claims exceed the limits set for priority claims.

Unsecured creditors, to the extent any funds are available for them, share in proportion to their claims. Unsecured creditors frequently receive little or nothing on their claims. Secured claims, trustee's fees, and other priority claims often consume a large part of the bankruptcy estate.

Special rules are set out in the Bankruptcy Act for distribution of the property of a bankrupt stockbroker or commodities broker.

CONCEPT REVIEW

DISTRIBUTION OF A DEBTOR'S ESTATE (Chapter 7)

Secured creditors proceed directly against the collateral. If debt is fully satisified, they have no further interest; if debt is only partially satisified, they are treated as general creditors for the balance.

Debtor's Estate Is Liquidated and Distributed

Priority Creditors (six classes)

1. Costs and expenses of administration.
2. If involuntary proceeding, expenses incurred in the ordinary course of business after petition filed but before appointment of trustee.
3. Claims for wages, salaries, and commissions earned within 90 days of petition; limited to $2,000 per person.
4. Contributions to employee benefit plans arising out of services performed within 180 days of petition; limit of $2,000 (including claims for wages, salaries, and commissions) per person.
5. Claims of individuals, up to $900 per person, for deposits made on consumer goods or services that were not received.
6. Government claims for certain taxes.

Distribution is made to the six classes of priority claims in order. Each class must be fully paid before the next class receives anything. If funds available are not sufficient to satisify everyone in a class, then each member of the class receives same proportion of claim.

General Creditors

1. General unsecured creditors.
2. Secured creditors for the portion of their debt that was not satisified by collateral.
3. Priority creditors for amounts beyond priority limits.

If funds remaining are not sufficient to satisify all general creditors, then they each receive the same proportion of their claims.

Debtor

Debtor receives any remaining funds.

DISCHARGE IN BANKRUPTCY

Discharge

A bankrupt person who has not been guilty of certain dishonest acts and has fulfilled his duties as a bankrupt is entitled to a **discharge in bankruptcy.** A discharge relieves the bankrupt person of further responsibility for dischargeable debts and gives him a fresh start. A corporation is not eligible for a discharge in bankruptcy. A bankrupt person may file a written waiver of his right to a discharge. An individual may not be granted a discharge if she obtained one within the previous six years.

Objections to Discharge

After the bankrupt has paid all of the required fees, the court gives creditors and others a chance to file objections to the discharge of the bankrupt. Objections may be filed by the trustee, a creditor, or the U.S. attorney. If objections are filed, the court holds a hearing to listen to them. At the hearing, the court must determine whether the bankrupt person has committed any act that is a bar to discharge. If the bankrupt has not committed such an act, the court grants the discharge. If the bankrupt has committed an act that is a bar to discharge, the discharge is denied. The discharge is also denied if the bankrupt fails to appear at the hearing on objections or if he refused earlier to submit to the questioning of the creditors.

Acts that Bar Discharge

Discharges in bankruptcy are intended for honest debtors. Therefore, these acts bar a debtor from being discharged: (1) the unjustified falsifying, concealing, or destroying of records; (2) making false statements, presenting false claims, or withholding recorded information relating to the debtor's property or financial affairs; (3) transferring, removing, or concealing property in order to hinder, delay, or defraud creditors; (4) failing to account satisfactorily for any loss or deficiency of assets; and (5) failing to obey court orders or to answer questions approved by the court.

Nondischargeable Debts

Certain debts are not affected by the discharge of a bankrupt debtor. The Bankruptcy Act provides that a discharge in bankruptcy releases a debtor from all provable debts except those that:

1. Are due as a tax or fine to the United States or any state or local unit of government.
2. Result from liabilities for obtaining money by false pretenses or false representations.
3. Are due for willful or malicious injury to a person or his property.
4. Are due for alimony or child support.
5. Were created by the debtor's larceny or embezzlement or by the debtor's fraud while acting in a fiduciary capacity.
6. Are certain kinds of educational loans that became due within five years prior to the filing of the petition.
7. Were not scheduled in time for proof and allowance because the creditor holding the debt did not have notification of the proceeding even though the debtor was aware that he owed money to that creditor.

The case that follows, *In Re Hott*, involves a denial of discharge of a debt on the grounds that the debtor obtained a loan using a materially false financial statement.

IN RE HOTT

99 B.R. 664 (Bankr. W.D. Pa. 1989)

David Hott was a college graduate with a degree in business administration who was employed as an insurance agent. He and his wife graduated from college in 1986. At the time he graduated, Hott had outstanding student loans of $14,500 for which he was given a grace period before he had to repay them.

Hott became unemployed. Bills began to accumulate and a number of outstanding bills were near the credit limits on his accounts. About that time, he received a promotional brochure by mail from Signal Consumer Discount Company, offering the opportunity to borrow several thousand dollars. The Hotts decided that it appeared to be an attractive vehicle for them to use to consolidate their debts. Hott went to the Signal office and filled out a credit application. He did not list the student loan as a current debt. He later claimed that someone in the office told him he didn't have to list it if he owned an automobile, but there was significant doubt about this claim. Had he listed it, he would not have met the debt/income ratio required by Signal and it would not have made the loan. As it was, Signal agreed to make the loan on the condition that Hott pay off a car debt in order to reduce his debt/income ratio and Hott agreed to do so. On March 30, 1987, Signal loaned the Hotts $3,458.01.

On June 24, 1988, the Hotts filed for bankruptcy. Signal objected to the discharge of the balance remaining on its loan on the grounds it had been obtained through the use of a materially false financial statement.

Markovitz, Bankruptcy Judge.   Section 523(a)(2)(B) a discharge under section 72 . . . does not discharge an individual debtor from any debt—

(2) for money . . . to the extent obtained by—
(B) use of a statement in writing—
(i) that is materially false;
(ii) respecting the debtor's financial condition;
(iii) on which the creditor to whom the debtor is liable for such money . . . reasonably relied; and
(iv) that the debtor caused to be made with intent to deceive. . . .

The parties agree that Hott did in fact obtain money as a result of his submission to Signal of a written statement of his financial condition. It appears that Hott does not contest Signal's reliance on the statement and it is clear that Signal's loss was proximately caused by Hott's financial statement. It is not clear if Hott concedes that the omission of the student loan caused the statement to be materially false. The major contested issue is whether Hott intentionally deceived Signal as to his true financial status in order to obtain the funds.

Material falsity has been defined as "an important or substantial untruth." It includes any omission, concealment or understatement of the Hotts' material liabilities. By omitting his single largest debt, a debt which by itself is as great as the remainder of his debt in combination, Hott created a material falsity in his financial statement.

Hott asserts that he fully intended to list his student loan debt on the application. He claims that said debt was in fact listed on the payment schedule his wife had prepared for him to take to Signal's office. That paper has admittedly long since been destroyed. Hott claims to have discussed the placement of the student loan with one of Signal's employees. Hott provided a physical description of the alleged employee. Signal's manager advised that the office had only three employees including himself. None of the three people even vaguely matched Hott's description.

Hott claims that the employee told him not to worry about the debt, so he did not. Given the size of the student loan in relation to the reminder of his debt, Hott's attitude certainly qualified as indifference and/or reckless disregard for accuracy.

We additionally reiterate Hott's education and qualifications in relation to his claim of innocence. Hott has a Bachelor's Degree in Business. He admits to having a knowledge of the concept called debt/income ratio and its purpose. Hott would easily have been able to determine that inclusion of his student loan on his application would cause his debt/income ratio to skyrocket. Hott asserts that he never stopped to perform any of the calculations. Hott may not assume the position of an ostrich with his head in the sand and ignore facts which were readily available.

This court finds that Hott's position lacks credibility and that Signal's witness was fully credible. We find at the very least Hott recklessly omitted the existence of his student loan when completing the credit application submitted for Signal's approval. Therefore, the debt must be found to be nondischargeable.

Judgment in favor of Signal.

The 1984 amendments established several additional grounds for nondischargeability relating to debts incurred in contemplation of bankruptcy. Congress was concerned about debtors who ran up large expenditures on credit cards shortly before filing for bankruptcy relief. Cash advances in excess of $1,000 obtained by use of a credit card and a revolving line of credit at a credit union obtained within 20 days of filing a bankruptcy petition are presumed to be nondischargeable. Similarly, a debtor's purchase of more than $500 in *luxury goods or services* on credit from a single creditor within 40 days of filing a petition is presumed to be nondischargeable.

There is also an exception from dischargeability for debts reflected in a judgment arising out of a debtor's operation of a motor vehicle while legally intoxicated.

All of these nondischargeable debts are provable debts. The creditor who owns these claims can participate in the distribution of the bankrupt's estate. However, the creditor has an additional advantage: His right to recover the unpaid balance is not cut off by the bankrupt's discharge. All other provable debts are dischargeable; that is, the right to recover them is cut off by the bankrupt's discharge.

Reaffirmation Agreements

Sometimes, creditors put pressure on debtors to reaffirm, or to agree to pay, debts that have been discharged in bankruptcy. When the 1978 amendments to the Bankruptcy Act were under consideration, some individuals urged Congress to prohibit such agreements. They argued that reaffirmation agreements were inconsistent with the fresh start philosophy of the Bankruptcy Act.

Congress did not agree to a total prohibition; instead, it set up a rather elaborate procedure for a creditor to go through to get a debt reaffirmed. Essentially, the creditor must do so before the discharge is granted, and the court must approve the reaffirmation. The debtor has 60 days after he agrees to a reaffirmation to rescind it. Court approval is not required for the reaffirmation of loans secured by real estate.

A debtor may voluntarily pay any dischargeable obligation without entering into a reaffirmation agreement.

Dismissal for Substantial Abuse

As it considered the 1984 amendments to the Bankruptcy Act, Congress was concerned that too many individuals with an ability to pay their debts over time pursuant to a Chapter 13 plan were filing petitions to obtain Chapter 7 discharges of liability. The consumer finance industry urged Congress to preclude Chapter 7 petitions where a debtor had the prospect of future disposable income to satisfy more than 50 percent of his prepetition unsecured debts. Although Congress rejected this approach, it did authorize Bankruptcy Courts to dismiss cases that they determined were a **substantial abuse** of the bankruptcy process. This provision appears to cover situations where a debtor has acted in bad faith or where she has the present or future ability to pay a significant portion of her current debts.

The case that follows, *In Re Newsom*, illustrates a situation where the court found the filing of a Chapter 7 petition by debtors with the ability to eventually pay off much of the unsecured debt they had accumulated to be a "substantial abuse" of the bankruptcy process.

IN RE NEWSOM

69 B.R. 801 (Bankr. D. N.D. 1987)

John and Christine Newsom were noncommissioned officers in the U.S. Air Force who each earned $1,408 net a month. In October 1986, they filed a voluntary petition in bankruptcy under Chapter 7. At the time, they had three secured debts totaling $21,956, $21,820 of which stemmed from the purchase of a 1986 Ford Bronco and a 1985 Pontiac Trans Am. They proposed to surrender the Bronco and a secured television set to the trustee, leaving $10,000 owing on the Pontiac as the only secured debt. Their unsecured debts totaled $20,911: $6,611 from bank card use, $12,764 from retail credit, and $1,350 from credit union loans. Of the unsecured debt, $11,563 was incurred in 1986.

The Newsoms filed an income and expense schedule showing that their monthly expenses totaled $2,232, including $100 per month for recreation and $150 for cigarettes and "walk around money." This left a surplus of $276 per month. The Bankruptcy Court, on its own motion, issued an order to the Newsoms to show why their petition should not be dismissed pursuant to the substantial abuse provision of the Bankruptcy Code.

Hill, Bankruptcy Judge.   Section 707(b) of the Bankruptcy Code, providing for the dismissal of Chapter 7 cases, provides as follows:

(b) After notice and a hearing, the court on its own motion or on a motion by the United States Trustee but not at the request or suggestion of any party in interest, may dismiss a case filed by an individual debtor under this chapter whose debts are primarily consumer debts if it finds that the granting of relief would be a substantial abuse of the provisions of this chapter. There shall be a presumption in favor of granting the relief requested by the debtor.

This section was enacted as part of the consumer credit amendments to the Bankruptcy Act in 1984 as a means of combating what Congress viewed as an abuse of Chapter 7 by consumer debtors who had the ability to pay.

From the developing case law, this court has adopted the following as criteria against which the facts of a particular case ought to be judged in determining whether substantial abuse exists sufficient to mandate dismissal under section 707(b):

1. Whether the debtors have a likelihood of sufficient future income to fund a Chapter 13 plan which would pay a substantial portion of the secured claims;

2. Whether the debtors' petition was filed as a consequence of illness, disability, unemployment or some other calamity;

3. Whether the schedules suggest the debtors incurred cash advances and consumer purchases in an excess of their ability to repay them;

4. Whether the debtors' proposed family budget is excessive or extravagant;

5. Whether the debtors' statement of income and expenses is misrepresentative of their true financial condition.

The Newsoms' unsecured obligations are comprised exclusively of consumer debt. Their schedule of unsecured debt is highly suggestive of individuals who, already aware of their financial limitations and already faced with financial difficulties, went ahead and rang up at least $11,500 of consumer debt in 1986—an amount equal to thirty percent of their combined annual net income and which was incurred when they already had unsecured obligations of over $9,000. Even worse, they apparently purchased a second vehicle during this time period. Such action can only be regarded by the court as a completely irresponsible use of credit for non-essential items.

The Newsoms' proposed family budget seems extravagant insofar as they profess to need $250 for entertainment and recreation, including $150 for cigarettes and "walk around money." The court finds this aspect of the budget as unacceptable. It appears that the Newsoms are making no effort to tighten their belts or maintain a conservative life style. With a combined annual net income of nearly $34,000 and no dependents, the Newsoms are far better off than many and ought to be able to live quite comfortably while at the same time making an effort to pay back at least a portion of their unsecured creditors.

The ability to pay back a substantial portion of unsecured debt does not require an ability to pay back one hundred percent. All that is required is that the payback be significant and that there be a likelihood of sufficient future income to maintain such a payback. In the present case, assuming future income and expenses remain stable, the Newsoms would at a minimum, be able to contribute $276 per month or $3,312 per year toward a repayment plan. Over a three-year period, they would have contributed $9,936 resulting in a repayment of forty-seven percent of their unsecured claims. Contributions over a five-year period would result in an eighty-percent payback. None of these figures can be regarded as insignificant as far as creditors are concerned and strongly suggest that a meaningful payback could be accomplished. An even greater payback could be accomplished by honing the Newsoms' entertainment budget to a more realistic level. At any rate, this court believes that the Newsoms have the financial means at hand and will continue to have the means to fund a Chapter 13 plan which would retire a substantial portion of the unsecured claims.

Newsoms' petition for Chapter 7 relief dismissed.

CHAPTER 11: REORGANIZATIONS

Reorganization Proceeding

Sometimes, creditors benefit more from the continuation of a bankrupt debtor's business than from the liquidation of the debtor's property. Chapter 11 of the Bankruptcy Act provides a proceeding whereby, under the supervision of the Bankruptcy Court, the debtor's financial affairs can be reorganized rather than liquidated. Chapter 11 proceedings are available to individuals and to virtually all business enterprises, including individual proprietorships, partnerships, and corporations (except banks, savings and loan associations, insurance companies, commodities brokers, and stockbrokers).

Petitions for reorganization proceedings can be filed voluntarily by the debtor or involuntarily by its creditors. Once a petition for a reorganization proceeding is filed and relief is ordered, the court usually appoints (1) a committee of creditors holding unsecured claims, (2) a committee of equity security holders (shareholders), and (3) a trustee. The trustee may be given the responsibility for running the debtor's business. He is also usually responsible for developing a plan for handling the various claims of creditors and the various interests of persons such as shareholders.

The reorganization plan is essentially a contract between a debtor and its creditors. This contract may involve recapitalizing a debtor corporation and/or giving creditors some equity, or shares, in the corporation in exchange for part or all of the debt owed to them. The plan must (1) divide the creditors into classes; (2) set forth how each creditor will be satisfied; (3) state which claims, or classes of claims, are impaired or adversely affected by the plan; and (4) provide the same treatment to each creditor in a particular class, unless the creditors in that class consent to different treatment.

The plan is then submitted to the creditors for approval. Approval generally requires that creditors holding two thirds in amount and one half in number of each class of claims impaired by the plan must accept it. Once approved, the plan goes before the court for confirmation. If the plan is confirmed, the debtor is responsible for carrying it out.

The case that follows, *Official Committee of Equity Security Holders v. Mabey*, shows that until a plan is confirmed, the bankruptcy court has no authority to distribute a portion of the bankruptcy assets to a portion of the unsecured creditors.

OFFICIAL COMMITTEE OF EQUITY SECURITY HOLDERS v. MABEY

832 F.2d 299 (4th Cir. 1987)

The A. H. Robins Company is a publicly held company that filed a voluntary petition for relief under Chapter 11 of the Bankruptcy Code. Robins sought refuge in Chapter 11 because of a multitude of civil actions filed against it by women who alleged they were injured by use of the Dalkon Shield intrauterine device that it manufactured and sold as a birth control device. Approximately 325,000 notices of claim against Robins were received by the Bankruptcy Court.

In 1985, the court appointed the Official Committee of Equity Security Holders to represent the interest of Robins's public shareholders. In April 1987, Robins filed a proposed plan of reorganization but no action was taken on the proposed plan because of a merger proposal submitted by Rorer Group, Inc. Under this plan, Dalkon Shield claimants would be compensated out of a $1.75 billion fund, all other creditors would be paid in full, and Robins's stockholders would receive stock of the merged corporation. However, at the time of other critical activity in the bankruptcy proceeding, no revised plan incorporating the merger proposal had been filed or approved.

Earlier, in August of 1986, the court had appointed Ralph Mabey as an examiner to evaluate and suggest proposed elements of a plan of reorganization. On Mabey's suggestion, a proposed order was put before the district court supervising the proceeding that would require Robins to establish a $15 million emergency treatment fund "for the purpose of assisting in providing tubal reconstructive surgery or in-vitro fertilization to eligible Dalkon Shield claimants." The purpose of the emergency fund was to assist those claimants who asserted that they had become infertile as a consequence of their use of the product. A program was proposed for administering the fund and for making the medical decisions required.

On May 21, 1987, the district court ordered that the emergency treatment fund be created, and the action was challenged by the committee representing the equity security holders.

Chapman, Circuit Judge.   The May 21, 1987, order of the district court approving the Emergency Treatment Fund makes no mention of its authority to establish such a fund prior to the allowance of the claims of the women who would benefit from the fund, and prior to the confirmation of a plan of reorganization of Robins. In its order denying the Equity Committee's Motion for a Stay Pending Appeal of the May 21 order, the district court relied on the "expansive equity power" of the court to justify its action.

While one may understand and sympathize with the district court's concern for the Dalkon Shield claimants who may desire reconstructive surgery or in-vitro fertilization, the creation of the Emergency Treatment Fund at this stage of the Chapter 11 bankruptcy proceedings violates the clear language and intent of the Bankruptcy Code, and such action may not be justified as an exercise of the court's equitable powers.

The Bankruptcy Code does not permit a distribution to unsecured creditors in a Chapter 11 proceeding except under and pursuant to a plan of reorganization that has been properly presented and approved. Sections 1122–1129 of the Bankruptcy Code set forth the required contents of the reorganization plan, the classification of claims, the requirements of disclosure of the contents of the plan, the method for accepting the plan, the hearing required on confirmation of the plan, and the requirements for confirmation. The clear language of these statutes does not authorize the payment in part or full, or the advance of monies to or for the benefit of unsecured claimants prior to the approval of the plan of reorganization. The creation of the Emergency Treatment Fund has no authority to support it in the Bankruptcy Code and violates the clear policy of Chapter 11 reorganizations by allowing piecemeal pre-confirmation payments to certain unsecured creditors. Such action also violates Bankruptcy Rule 3021 which allows distribution to creditors only after the allowance of claims and the confirmation of a plan.

Judgment reversed in favor of Official Committee of Equity Security Holders.

Use of Chapter 11

During the 1980s, attempts by a number of corporations to seek refuge in Chapter 11 as a means of escaping problems they were facing received considerable public attention. Some of the most visible cases involved efforts to obtain some protection against massive product liability claims and judgments for damages for breach of contract, and to escape from collective bargaining agreements. Thus, for example, Johns-Manville Corporation filed under Chapter 11 because of the claims against it arising out of its production and sale of asbestos years earlier, while A. H. Robins Company, as illustrated in the preceding case, was concerned about a surfeit of claims arising out of its sale of the Dalkon Shield, an intrauterine birth control device. And, in 1987, Texaco, Inc., faced with a $10.3 billion judgment in favor of Pennzoil in a breach of contract action, filed a petition for reorganizational relief under Chapter 11. Companies such as LTV and Allegheny Industries sought changes in retirement and pension plans, and other companies such as Eastern Airlines sought refuge in Chapter 11 while embroiled in labor disputes.

As the 1990s begin, a number of companies that were the subject of highly leveraged buyouts (LBOs) financed with so-called junk bonds, including a number of retailers, have resorted to Chapter 11 to seek restructuring and relief from their creditors. Similarly, companies such as Pan Am that were hurt by the economic slowdown and the increase in fuel prices filed Chapter 11 petitions.

Collective Bargaining Agreements

Collective bargaining contracts pose special problems. Prior to the 1984 amendments, there was concern that some companies would use Chapter 11 reorganizations as a vehicle to avoid executed collective bargaining agreements. The concern was heightened by the Supreme Court's 1984 decision in *NLRB v. Bildisco and Bildisco*. In that case, the Supreme Court held that a reorganizing debtor did not have to engage in collective bargaining before modifying or rejecting portions of a collective bargaining agreement and that such unilateral alterations by a debtor did not violate the National Labor Relations Act.

Congress then acted to try to prevent the misuse of bankruptcy proceedings for collective bargaining purposes. The act's 1984 amendments adopt a rigorous multistep process that must be complied with in determining whether a labor contract can be rejected or modified as part of a reorganization. Among other things that must be done before a debtor or trustee can seek to avoid a collective bargaining agreement are the submission of a proposal to the employees' representative that details the "necessary" modifications to the collective bargaining agreement and assures that "all creditors, the debtor and all affected parties are fairly treated." Then, before the bankruptcy court can authorize a rejection of the original collective bargaining agreement, it must review the proposal and find that (1) the employees' representative refused to accept it without good cause, and (2) the balance of equities clearly favors the rejection of the original collective bargaining agreement.

The case, *In Re Royal Composing Room, Inc.*, shows the scrutiny that the court gives the action of a debtor seeking to avoid a collective bargaining agreement.

In Re Royal Composing Room, Inc.

78 B.R. 671 (S.D. N.Y. 1987)

Royal Composing Room, Inc., is an advertising typography company, and one of the last unionized shops in an industry that was subjected to considerable stress as computer technology replaced the linotype machine. Royal was a party to a collective bargaining agreement with Typographical Union No. 6. Royal was a profitable company until 1982, when its gross revenues declined by $2 million; over the next four years, it sustained operating losses. Confronted with these difficulties, in 1983 Royal began to cut expenses by sharply cutting the compensation of its principal executives, freezing the salaries of salesmen and middle management foremen, eliminating company automobiles, and moving to a smaller location to save rent. At the start of 1986, Royal lost its largest customer, Doyle Dane Bernbach, Inc., and sought to convince the union, which theretofore had not made any sacrifices or concessions, to forgo a 3 percent wage increase agreed to earlier. When the union refused, Royal filed a petition for reorganization under Chapter 11 and sought to reject its collective bargaining agreement.

Under section 1113(b) of the Bankruptcy Code, before it could reject the collective bargaining agreement, Royal was required to make a proposal to the union "which provides for those necessary modifications in the employees' benefits and protections that are necessary to permit the reorganization of the debtor and assures that all creditors, the debtor and all of the affected parties are treated fairly and equally." Royal held a meeting with officals of the union and offered a proposal that included a reduction of benefits, changes in work rules, the elimination of the scheduled wage increase, and the elimination of the union's right to arbitration as the way to change the contract. The union rejected the proposal and did not negotiate. After a trial before the bankruptcy judge, Royal's motion to reject the existing collective bargaining contract was granted. The union then appealed to the District Court.

Keenan, District Judge.   Local 6 raises two arguments on appeal: (1) the Bankruptcy Court did not apply the proper definition of "necessary" under section 1113, and (2) Royal's proposal did not treat all affected parties fairly and equitably. Both positions are unavailing.

The Second Circuit has indicated that the term "necessary" contained in section 1113 does not mean "essential" or "bare minimum." It has ruled that "the necessary requirement places on the debtor the burden of proving that its proposal is made in good faith, and that it contains necessary, but not absolutely minimal, changes that will enable the debtor to complete the reorganization process successfully."

Applying the standard of necessity endorsed by the Second Circuit, Bankruptcy Judge Abram found that Royal had, "established that it had in good faith attempted to negotiate for necessary changes but had been unsuccessful because of the union's unwillingness to engage in serious discussions." The record supports this finding. Local 6 was unresponsive and dilatory in the face of management's financial condition and resulting proposal. Likewise, Judge Abram was correct in her analysis of Royal's proposal. She found that Royal had cut nonunion management and executive salaries, eliminated trade association memberships, and even reused old doorknobs. During this time, union labor costs were the only expenses not cut.

The correctness of Judge Abram's legal conclusion is bolstered by the Second Circuit's statement in Carey Transportation that courts "must consider whether rejection of a collective bargaining agreement would increase the likelihood of successful reorganization." This court cannot envision Royal being able to successfully reorganize absent at least enforcement of its proposal under section 1113. Rejection clearly increases the likelihood of successful reorganization.

Local 6 further asserts that Royal did not satisfy the statutory requirement that under the proposal "all creditors, the debtor and all affected parties are treated fairly and equitably." Judge Abram correctly found that Royal "had spread the burden of financial sacrifice." As noted earlier, Royal cut costs in many ways, including a decrease in executive compensation, the rescinding of raises and freezing of salaries of salesmen and middle level management, the elimination of company cars, and the moving of its premises to smaller quarters. The union's wages were neither frozen nor cut. The Second Circuit observed that a debtor need not show that managers and nonunion employees have their benefits cut to the degree union benefits are cut. In this case, the union's benefits were the last to be cut, and it certainly was not the only constituency in Royal to feel the financial pinch. Royal's proposal satisfied the statute's requirement of fairness and equity.

Judgment of the Bankruptcy Court rejecting the collective bargaining agreement affirmed.

CHAPTER 12: FAMILY FARMS

Relief for Family Farmers

Historically, farmers have been accorded special treatment in the Bankruptcy Code. In the 1978 act, as in earlier versions, small farmers were exempted from involuntary proceedings. Thus, a small farmer who filed a voluntary Chapter 11 or 13 petition could not have the proceeding converted into a Chapter 7 liquidation over his objection so long as he complied with the act's requirements in a timely fashion. Additional protection was also accorded through the provision allowing states to opt out of the federal exemption scheme and to provide their own exemptions. A number of states used this flexibility to provide generous exemptions for farmers so they would be able to keep their tools and implements.

Despite these provisions, the serious stress on the agricultural sector in the mid-1980s led Congress in 1986 to further amend the Bankruptcy Act by adding a new Chapter 12 targeted to the financial problems of the family farm. During the 1970s and 1980s, farmland prices appreciated and many farmers borrowed heavily to expand their productive capacity, creating a large debt load in the agricultural sector. When land values subsequently dropped and excess production in the world kept farm product prices low, many farmers faced extreme financial difficulty.

Chapter 12 is modeled after Chapter 13, which is discussed next. It is available only for family farmers with regular income. To qualify, a farmer and spouse must have not less than 80 percent of their total noncontingent, liquidated debts arising out of their farming operations. The aggregate debt must be less than $1.5 million and at least 50 percent of an individual's or couple's income during the year preceding the filing of the petition must have come from the farming operation. A corporation or partnership can also qualify, provided that more than 50 percent of the stock or equity is held by one family or its relatives and they conduct the farming operation. Again, 80 percent of the debt must arise from the farming operation; the aggregate debt ceiling is $1.5 million.

The debtor is usually permitted to remain in possession to operate the farm. Although the debtor in possession has many of the rights of a Chapter 11 trustee, a trustee is appointed under Chapter 12 and the debtor is subject to his supervision. The trustee is permitted to sell unnecessary assets, including farmland and equipment, without the consent of secured creditors and be-

fore a plan is approved. However, the secured creditor's interest attaches to the proceeds of the sale.

The debtor is required to file a plan within 90 days of the filing of the Chapter 12 petition—although the bankruptcy court has the discretion to extend the time. A hearing is held on the proposed plan, and it can be confirmed over the objection of creditors. The debtor may release to any secured party the collateral that secures the claim to obtain confirmation without the acceptance by that creditor.

Unsecured creditors are required to receive at least liquidation value under the Chapter 12 plan. If an unsecured creditor or the trustee objects to the plan, the court may still confirm the plan despite the objection so long as it calls for full payment of the unsecured creditor's claim or it provides that the debtor's disposable income for the duration of the plan is applied to making payments on it. A debtor who fulfills his plan, or is excused from full performance because of subsequent hardship, is entitled to a discharge.

CHAPTER 13: CONSUMER DEBT ADJUSTMENTS

Relief for Individuals

Chapter 13 of the Bankruptcy Act, entitled Adjustments of Debts for Individuals, gives individuals who do not want to be declared bankrupt an opportunity to pay their debts in installments under the protection of a federal court. Under Chapter 13, the debtor has this opportunity free of such problems as garnishments and attachments of her property by creditors. Only individuals with regular incomes (including sole proprietors of businesses) who owe individually (or with their spouse) liquidated, unsecured debts of less than $100,000 and secured debts of less than $350,000 are eligible to file under Chapter 13. Under the pre-1978 Bankruptcy Act, Chapter 13 proceedings were known as "wage earner plans." The 1978 amendments expanded the coverage of these proceedings.

Procedure

Chapter 13 proceedings are initiated only by the voluntary petition of a debtor filed in the Bankruptcy Court. Creditors of the debtor may not file an involuntary petition for a Chapter 13 proceeding. The debtor in the petition states that he is insolvent or unable to pay his debts as they mature and that he desires to effect a composition or an extension, or both, out of future earnings or income. A **composition of debts** is an arrangement whereby the amount the person owes is reduced, whereas an **extension** provides the person a longer period of time in which to pay his debts. Commonly, the debtor files at the same time a list of his creditors as well as a list of his assets, liabilities, and executory contracts.

Following the filing of the petition, the court calls a meeting of creditors, at which time proofs of claims are received and allowed or disallowed. The debtor is examined, and she submits a plan of payment. The plan is submitted to the secured creditors for acceptance. If they accept the plan and if the court is satisfied that the plan is proposed in good faith, meets the legal requirements, and is in the interest of the creditors, the court approves the plan. The court then appoints a trustee to carry out the plan. The plan must provide for payments over three years or less, unless the court approves a longer period of up to five years.

No plan may be approved if the trustee or an unsecured creditor objects, unless the plan provides for the objecting creditor to be paid the present value of what he is owed or provides for the debtor to commit all of his projected disposable income for a three-year period to pay his creditors.

Under the 1984 amendments, a Chapter 13 debtor must begin making the installment payments proposed in her plan within 30 days after the plan is filed. The interim payments must continue to be made until the plan is confirmed or denied. If the plan is denied, the money, less any administrative expenses, is returned to the debtor by the trustee. The interim payments give the trustee an opportunity to observe the debtor's performance and thus to be in a better position to make a recommendation about whether the plan should be approved.

Once approved, a plan may be subsequently modified on petition of a debtor or a creditor where there is a material change in the debtor's circumstances.

Suppose Curtis Brown has a monthly take-home pay of $1,000 and a few assets. He owes $1,500 to the credit union, borrowed for the purchase of furniture; he is supposed to repay the credit union $75 per month. He owes $1,800 to the finance company on the purchase of a used car; he is supposed to repay the company $90 a month. He has also run up charges of $1,200 on a MasterCard account, primarily for emergency repairs to his car; he must pay $60 per month to MasterCard. His rent is $350 per month, and food and other living expenses run him another $425 per month. Curtis was laid off from his job for a month and fell behind on his payments to his creditors. He then filed a Chapter 13 petition. In his plan, he might, for example, offer to repay the credit union $50 a month, the finance company $60 a month, and MasterCard $40 a month—with the payments spread over three years rather than the shorter time for which they are currently scheduled.

The *In Re Doersam* case, which follows, illustrates the scrutiny a bankruptcy judge may give a proposed plan.

IN RE DOERSAM

849 F.2d 237 (6th Cir. 1988)

Winifred Doersam was the borrower on three student loans made to her by First Federal Savings and Loan and guaranteed by the state of Ohio Student Loan Commission (OSLC) totaling $10,000 to finance her graduate education at the University of Dayton. Doersam also signed as the cosigner for a $5,000 student loan for her daughter, also made by First Federal and guaranteed by OSLC. With the use of the loans, she was able to obtain a position as a systems analyst with NCR Corporation, which required her to obtain a master's degree in order to retain her position at an annual salary of $24,000.

Approximately six weeks before her graduation, and before the first payment on her student loans was due, Doersam filed a petition and plan under Chapter 13. In her plan, she proposed to pay $375 a month to her unsecured creditors over a 36-month period. Doersam's total unsecured debt was $18,418, 81 percent of which was comprised of the outstanding student loans. Her schedules provided for payment of rent of $300 per month and food of $400 per month. Her listed dependents included her 23-year-old daughter and her 1-year-old granddaughter. At the time, her daughter was employed in the Ohio Work Program, a program designed to help welfare recipients, for which she was paid a small salary.

The OLSC objected to the plan proposed by Doersam on the grounds that it was filed in bad faith.

Keith, Circuit Judge.   The bankruptcy court chose not to deal with the question of bad faith, but did find that there was no hardship situation which prevented Doersam from satisfying the student loan debt. On appeal, the district court held that Doersam's plan was filed in bad faith.

In evaluating good faith in specific situations, we find helpful, as did the district court, the factors enumerated in *In Re Kitchens:*

1. The amount of debtor's income from all sources;
2. The living expenses of the debtor and his dependents;
3. The amount of attorney's fees;
4. The probable or expected duration of the debtor's Chapter 13 plan;
5. The motivations of the debtor and his sincerity in seeking relief under the provisions of Chapter 13;
6. The debtor's degree of effort;
7. The debtor's ability to earn and the likelihood of fluctuation in his earnings;
8. Special circumstances such as inordinate medical expenses;
9. The frequency with which the debtor has sought relief under the Bankruptcy Act;
10. The circumstances under which the debtor has contracted his debts and his demonstrated bona fides, or lack of same, in dealing with his creditors; and
11. The burden which the plan's administration would place on the trustee.

The fact that all or part of the debt consists of educational loans presents special problems. Ordinarily, such loans are not dischargeable under Chapter 7. The mere fact a debtor attempts to discharge a debt that would be nondischargeable under Chapter 7 is not sufficient in itself to warrant a finding that the plan was not proposed in good faith. However, whether the debt would be nondischargeable under Chapter 7 is a factor which is relevant to the determination of good faith. Moreover, the debt which the debtor seeks to discharge is also germane to the question of good faith. Here, the repayment structure of educational loans is of particular relevance.

Unlike most commercial loans which are granted only upon a showing of creditworthiness and ability to make repayments, most student loans, on the other hand, are granted only upon a debtor establishing need. Unlike most loans, guaranteed student loans do not require a borrower to commence repayment until the borrower has completed his or her education. It is therefore most questionable when a debtor accepts a student loan and then, prior to maturity, attempts to extinguish the debt in bankruptcy without ever making an attempt to repay it. It stretches credulity to say that the debtor has made an honest effort to pay these debts as required by 11 U.S.C. Section 1325(a)(3).

Based on the foregoing considerations, the district court correctly found that Doersam's plan had not been proposed in good faith. The bulk of Doersam's unsecured indebtedness consists of student loans which would not have been dischargeable under Chapter 7. Doersam made absolutely no effort to repay these loans despite their long-term character, and despite the fact that they were instrumental in her securing a position paying approximately $24,000 per year. Indeed, her student loans had not yet become due at the time she submitted her plan. Moreover, as both the bankruptcy court and the district court noted, the listing of a working daughter and a minor grandchild for whom Doersam is not legally responsible, and the budgeting of $400.00 per month for food based on those questionable listings, are further grounds for finding that the plan was not filed in good faith.

Judgment of district court affirmed.

Discharge

When the debtor has completed his performance of the plan, the court issues an order that discharges him from the debts covered by the plan. The debtor may also be discharged even though he did not complete his payments within the three years if the court is satisfied that the failure is due to circumstances for which the debtor cannot justly be held accountable. An active Chapter 13 proceeding stays, or holds in abeyance, any straight bankruptcy proceedings and any actions by creditors to collect consumer debts. However, if the Chapter 13 proceeding is dismissed (for example, because the debtor fails to file an acceptable plan or defaults on an accepted plan), straight bankruptcy proceedings may begin.

Advantages of Chapter 13

A debtor may choose to file under Chapter 13 to avoid the stigma of bankruptcy or to retain more of his property than is exempt from bankruptcy under state law. Chapter 13 can provide some financial discipline to a debtor as well as an opportunity to get his financial affairs back in good shape. It also gives him relief from the pressures of individual creditors so long as he makes the payments called for by the plan. The debtor's creditors may benefit by recovering a greater percentage of the debt owed to them than would be obtainable in straight bankruptcy.

CONCEPT REVIEW

COMPARISON OF MAJOR FORMS OF BANKRUPTCY PROCEEDINGS

Purpose	Chapter 7 Liquidation	Chapter 11 Reorganization	Chapter 12 Adjustments of Debts	Chapter 13 Adjustments of Debts
Eligible Debtors	Individuals, partnerships, and corporations *except* municipal corporations, railroads, insurance companies, banks, and savings and loan associations. Farmers and ranchers are eligible only if they petition voluntarily.	Generally same as Chapter 7 *except* a railroad may be a debtor, and a stockbroker and commodity broker may *not* be a debtor under Chapter 11.	Family farmer with regular income, at least 50 percent of which comes from farming, and less than $1.5 million in debts, at least 80 percent of which is farm related.	Individual with regular income with liquidated unsecured debts less than $100,000 and secured debts of less than $350,000.
Initiation of Proceeding	Petition by debtor (voluntary). Petition by creditors (involuntary).	Petition by debtor (voluntary). Petition by creditors (involuntary).	Petition by debtor.	Petition by debtor.

Purpose	Chapter 7 Liquidation	Chapter 11 Reorganization	Chapter 12 Adjustments of Debts	Chapter 13 Adjustments of Debts
Basic Procedure	1. Appointment of trustee. 2. Debtor retains exempt property. 3. Nonexempt property is sold and proceeds distributed based on priority of claims. 4. Dischargeable debts are terminated.	1. Appointment of trustee and committees of creditors and equity security holders. 2. Debtor submits reorganization plan. 3. If plan is approved and implemented, debts are discharged.	1. Trustee is appointed but debtor usually remains in possession of farm. 2. Debtor submits a plan in which unsecured creditors must receive at least liquidation value. 3. If plan is approved and fullfilled, debtor is entitled to a discharge.	1. Debtor indicates in petition that he is seeking a composition of debts or an extension. 2. If plan is approved after submitted to creditors, then trustee is appointed. 3. If plan is approved and fulfilled, debts covered by plan are discharged.
Advantages	After liquidation and distribution of assets, most or all of debts may be discharged and debtor gets a fresh start.	Debtor remains in business and debts are liquidated through implementation of approved reorganization plan.	Debtor generally remains in possession and has opportunity to work out of financial difficulty over period of time (usually three years) through implementation of approved plan.	Debtor has opportunity to work out of financial difficulty over period of time (usually three years) through implementation of approved plan.

ETHICAL AND PUBLIC POLICY CONCERNS

1. If a person receives a discharge of debts in bankruptcy, should the person feel an ethical obligation to reaffirm or to repay the debts that were discharged?

2. Is it ethical for a person facing the prospect of seeking relief under the bankruptcy laws to try to convert nonexempt property into exempt property on the eve of the filing of his petition? Does the relative economic condition of the debtor have any bearing on your response to this question?

3. As you have learned in this chapter, during the past decade corporations have filed petitions under Chapter 11 in order to deal with a variety of problems, including the threat of massive product liability claims and the desire of the company to get out of labor contracts. Is it ethical for a company to use Chapter 11 to try to get out of, or to modify, labor contracts or pension agreements that it now deems unfavorable to its interests? Is it ethical for a company to seek the shelter of Chapter 11 when faced with claims for product liability? Is the decision of the appeals court in *Official Committee of Equity Security Holders v. Mabey* to disallow the proposed emergency treatment fund good public policy?

4. As was discussed in this chapter, the federal bankruptcy law makes special provision for small farmers and some states are particularly generous in the exemptions they make available to farmers. Is this special treatment of farmers justifiable as sound and fair public policy?

SUMMARY

The Bankruptcy Act is a federal law providing an organized procedure for dealing with insolvent debtors under the supervision of a federal court. The act protects the rights of both creditors and debtors and also gives the debtor an opportunity to have most, if not all, of his debts discharged so that he will have a fresh start.

A liquidation proceeding under Chapter 7 can be initiated either by a voluntary petition of the debtor or by an involuntary petition filed by his creditors. After a determination that a debtor is entitled to relief, a meeting of creditors is held and a trustee in bankruptcy is elected or appointed. The trustee takes possession of all the assets of the bankrupt, collects all claims, sets aside the bankrupt's exemptions, liquidates the assets, and distributes the proceeds among the creditors.

A creditor wishing to participate in the bankrupt's estate must usually file a proof of claim in the estate within six months of the first meeting of creditors. Certain debts are given priority by the provisions of the Bankruptcy Act. Any payment made to a creditor by an insolvent debtor within three months of the filing of a bankruptcy petition, which enables the creditor to realize a greater percentage of his claim than is realized by other creditors of the same class, is a preferential payment. It may be recovered for the bankruptcy estate by the trustee. A preferential lien given by an insolvent debtor to secure a preexisting debt within three months of the filing of a bankruptcy petition is voidable by the trustee. Any transfer made or obligation incurred without consideration within one year before the filing of a bankruptcy petition is void as to creditors.

A bankrupt is granted a discharge unless she has been guilty of certain dishonest acts or has failed to fulfill her duties as a bankrupt. Corporations are not eligible to have their debts discharged, and an individual may not be granted a discharge if she has had one in the past six years. The grounds for denying a bankrupt's discharge are set out in the Bankruptcy Act. Certain kinds of debts are not dischargeable.

Under Chapter 11, business debtors can enter into reorganization proceedings under the supervision of the Bankruptcy Court to reorganize their financial affairs. A plan, which is essentially a contract between the debtor and the creditors, sets out how the various claims of the creditors will be met over a period of time.

Chapter 12, which was added to the Bankruptcy Code in 1986, makes a special provision for family farmers to work out their financial difficulties over a period of time under the protection of the court.

Plans for individual debtors under Chapter 13 give them voluntary opportunities to effect a composition or an extension of their debts under the protection of a court and free of certain action by their creditors.

PROBLEM CASES

1. Lois Perry filed a voluntary petition pursuant to Chapter 7 of the Bankruptcy Act. Among the items of personal clothing that Perry listed as exempt from her creditors was a mink coat with a value of approximately $2,500. The trustee objected to the claimed exemption, contending that the mink coat was not necessary clothing. The state of Virginia provides an exemption in bankruptcy for "all necessary wearing apparel of the debtor and his family." While limits were placed on the value of certain other kinds of property that could be retained under the exemption (such as a clothes dryer not to exceed $150 in value), no such limitation was specified as to wearing apparel. Should the mink coat be exempt?

2. On June 29, 1979, Gary Johnson filed a Chapter 13 bankruptcy petition. Acting on the advice of his lawyer shortly before filing the petition, Johnson sold an interest in real estate and used the proceeds to buy a life insurance policy with a face value of $31,460 and a cash value of $12,118. His wife was named as the beneficiary. Johnson claimed that the policy was exempt under South Dakota law, which provides for an exemption of up to $20,000 for the proceeds of a life insurance policy payable directly to the insured, his surviving spouse, or his family. A creditor objected to the exemption but made no showing of fraudulent intent on Johnson's part. Should the exemption be allowed?

3. On October 19, 1976, Wallace Tuttle, an attorney, and Peninsula Roofing entered into a retainer agreement for the performance of legal services at a stipulated hourly rate. In 1978 and 1979, Peninsula became delinquent in its payments for attorney's fees. The delinquencies reflected overall corporate financial problems that resulted in the permanent closing of Peninsula on July 25, 1979. On August 6, 1979, Peninsula received a check for $3,250 representing an account receivable due it. Peninsula turned the check over to Tuttle, who deposited it to his trust account, credited $1,946.96 against the past-due account, and created a trust fund from which payments for current services and disbursements would be made. On October 18, 1979, an involuntary petition was filed against Peninsula. The bankruptcy trustee sought to require Tuttle to return the $3,250 to him as a preferential payment. Should Tuttle be required to return the money he received?

4. On September 17, 1979, a jury rendered its verdict in favor of Chrysler Credit Corporation in the amount of $86,704 against Joseph Newman. Several days later, he assigned promissory notes due to him from the New Rochelle Manufacturing Corporation to his father-in-law, Andrew Charla. The notes were worth $93,337 at the time, but his father-in-law paid him only $54,500. On September 28, 1979, Newman formed a corporation known as J.E.S. Equities, Inc. Newman's children were the sole officers and stockholders. On November 15, Newman transferred $40,000 in cash to the corporation in return for a promissory note from it. The note called for no payment of principal or interest until November 1982, at which time the note was to be paid off with interest at 7 percent over a period of nearly 37 years at the rate of $100 per month. On November 24, an involuntary petition in bankruptcy under Chapter 7 was filed against Newman. The trustee in bankruptcy then brought an action to recover the transfers of assets to Charla and J.E.S. Equities. Should the conveyances made by Newman to Andrew Charla and J.E.S. Equities, Inc., be avoided as fraudulent transfers?

5. Augustine Calvo was the president and one-third owner of a Florida corporation that did business as Marine Mart. It was in the business of selling new and used boats, motors, and other products associated with recreational boating. Marine Mart borrowed money from Bombardier Credit in order to finance its inventory of boats. The security agreement between Marine Mart and Bombardier was personally guaranteed by Calvo. At the time, Calvo supplied a personal financial statement in which he listed $8,500 in promissory notes receivable and a 52-foot sailboat valued at $75,000 to $85,000 as part of assets of $291,800 and a net worth of $107,506. Marine Mart defaulted on its agreement with Bombardier and it sought to hold Calvo liable for $170,000 pursuant to his personal guarantee. Calvo then filed a petition for relief under Chapter 7. In his schedule of assets and liabilities, Calvo included his 52-foot sailboat, the same boat he had earlier included in his personal financial statement, and claimed it as part of his exemptions. In his bankruptcy filing, he swore under oath that it had little or no value. A boat appraiser valued it at $4,500 and established that it was in essentially the same condition as it had been in when Calvo had valued it at $75,000–85,000. It also turned out that he did not have $8,500 in promissory notes receivable but had based his earlier assertion on loans made 10 years earlier for which he had no written promise of repayment. Bombardier objected to the discharge in bankruptcy of Calvo's obligation to it on the grounds that Calvo had submitted a materially false statement to it with intent to deceive it and that it had relied on the statement. Should the court grant a discharge of Calvo's debt to Bombardier?

6. Paul George Conrad filed a voluntary petition in bankruptcy in October 1979, listing $37,354 in liabilities and $25 in assets. Conrad's obligations consisted of a loan executed in connection with a business venture, the Double Dip Ice Cream Company;

signature loans; revolving credit card accounts; and a student loan of $4,125.79 owed to the U.S. Department of Health, Education, and Welfare. Conrad had used the GI Bill of Rights to study at five different colleges and had also obtained three federally guaranteed long-term, low-interest student loans. After receiving his bachelor's degree, he had been employed as a teacher. He was terminated as a full-time teacher in April 1979; since that time, he had been on call as a substitute teacher, for which he was paid $33 each day he taught. He had not sought other full-time employment. He lived at home with his 75-year-old mother. He did not have a car of his own and used his mother's van. Several months after filing for bankruptcy, Conrad obtained a $5,000 loan, with his mother as a guarantor on the note. He used the proceeds only to make the monthly payments on the note. Section 523(a) of the Bankruptcy Code provides that a bankruptcy discharge will not extend:

(8) to a governmental unit, or a nonprofit institution of higher education, for an educational loan, unless . . . (B) excepting such debt from discharge under this paragraph will impose an undue hardship on the debtor.

Conrad sought to have his educational loan discharged and based his claim of hardship on two asserted facts: (1) that he had to support and provide for his elderly mother and (2) that he was unable to obtain employment because of his physical appearance (described by the court as "corpulent"). Is Conrad's student loan dischargeable in bankruptcy?

7. On December 19, 1986, Brian Scholz was involved in an automobile collision with a person insured by The Travelers Insurance Company. At the time, Scholz was cited for, and plead no contest to, a criminal charge of driving under the influence of alcohol arising out of the accident. Travelers paid its insured $4,303.68 and was subrogated to the rights of its insured against Scholz. Subsequently, Travelers filed a civil action against Scholz to recover the amount it had paid, and a default judgment was entered against Scholz. Eleven months later, Scholz sought relief from the bankruptcy court by filing a voluntary petition under Chapter 7. One of the questions in the bankruptcy proceeding was whether the debt owing to Travelers was nondischargeable. Is the debt dischargeable?

8. Bryant filed a Chapter 7 petition on January 7, 1984. On March 8, she filed an application to reaffirm an indebtedness owed to General Motors Acceptance Corporation (GMAC) on her 1980 Cadillac automobile. Bryant was not married, and she supported two teenage daughters. She was not currently employed, and she collected $771 a month in unemployment benefits and $150 a month in rental income from her mother. Her monthly house payments were $259. The present value of the Cadillac was $9,175; she owed $7,956.37 on it, and her monthly payments were $345.93. Bryant indicated that she wanted to keep the vehicle because it was reliable. GMAC admitted that Bryant had been, and continued to be, current in her payments. GMAC said that the car was in no danger of being repossessed but that, absent reaffirmation, it might decide to repossess it. Should the court grant Bryant's application to reaffirm her indebtedness to GMAC?

9. Roy Satterwhite filed a Chapter 13 petition. In his petition, Satterwhite listed his monthly take-home pay as $1,458 and his monthly expenses as $2,072.24, leaving a negative balance of $614.24. He claimed that all of his assets were exempt. He listed no secured debts and five unsecured debts totaling over $16,450. The largest of these debts was for a judgment against Satterwhite in the amount of $15,749.30 plus interest that stemmed from an action for assault brought against him by A. R. Regan. Under his Chapter 13 plan, Satterwhite proposed to make a one-time payment of $1 to each creditor. Approval of the plan would have resulted in a payout to unsecured creditors of substantially less than 1 percent on their claims, which was more than they would have received under a liquidation distribution. The bankruptcy trustee objected to confirmation of the plan. Should the court approve the Chapter 13 plan that provides only for a $1 payment to each creditor?

10. On December 8, 1981, Thomas Thompson filed a petition under Chapter 13 to pay his debts through a wage earner plan. After the notice to creditors, Ford Motor Credit Company, a secured creditor to which Thompson was indebted for payments on a 1980 Ford, filed a proof of claim and rejected the plan. The plan was confirmed over Ford's objections. It provided for payments to Ford of $22.90 a week, equivalent to the same rate and adding up to the same total as in the original sales contract, and enjoined Ford from foreclosing on the automobile. In 1982, Thompson was injured at work and able to work only part time. He then fell behind in his payments to Ford, even though he was regularly submitting his disability checks to the trustee. Ford then filed a petition to reclaim the car, alleging that Thompson had failed to make the payments due on the car. Should Ford be permitted to have the plan disregarded so that it can foreclose its security interest on the car?

COMMERCIAL PAPER

CHAPTER 23

NEGOTIABLE INSTRUMENTS

INTRODUCTION

As commerce and trade developed, people moved beyond exclusive reliance on barter to the use of money and then to the use, as well, of substitutes for money. The term *commercial paper* encòmpasses such substitutes in common usage today as checks, promissory notes, and certificates of deposit.

History discloses that every civilization that engaged to an appreciable extent in commerce used some form of commercial paper. Probably the oldest commercial paper used in the carrying on of trade is the promissory note. Archaeologists found a promissory note made payable to bearer that dated from about 2100 B.C. The merchants of Europe used commercial paper, which under the law merchant was negotiable, in the 13th and 14th centuries. Commercial paper does not appear to have been used in England until about A.D. 1600.

This chapter and the three following chapters outline and discuss the body of law that governs commercial paper. Of particular interest are those kinds of commercial paper having the attribute of negotiability—that is, they can generally be readily transferred, and accepted, as a substitute for money. This chapter discusses the nature and benefits of negotiable instruments and then outlines the requirements an instrument must meet to qualify as a negotiable instrument. Subsequent chapters discuss transfer and negotiation of instruments, the rights and liabilities of parties to negotiable instruments, and the rules applicable to checks.

NATURE OF NEGOTIABLE INSTRUMENTS

When a person buys a television set and gives the merchant a check drawn on his checking account, that person is using a form of negotiable commercial paper. Similarly, a person who goes to a bank or a credit union to borrow money might sign a promissory note agreeing to pay the money back in 90 days. Again, a form of negotiable commercial paper is being used.

Commercial paper is basically a *contract for the payment of money.* Commonly used as a substitute for money, it can also be used as a means of extending credit. When a television set is bought by giving the merchant a check, the check is a substitute for money. If a credit union gives a borrower money now in exchange for the borrower's promise to repay it later on certain terms, the promissory note signed by the borrower is a means of extending credit as well as a substitute for money.

Uniform Commercial Code

The law of commercial paper is covered in Article 3 (Commercial Paper) and Article 4 (Bank Deposits and Collections) of the Uniform Commercial Code. Other negotiable documents such as investment securities and documents of title are treated in other sections of the Code. Essentially, the Code makes no drastic changes in the basic rules governing the use of commercial paper that have been recognized for centuries, but it has adopted modern terminology and has coordinated, clarified, and simplified the law.

Commercial Paper

The two basic types of commercial paper are *promises to pay* money and *orders to pay* money. **Promissory notes** and **certificates of deposit** issued by banks are promises to pay someone money. **Drafts** and **checks** are orders to another person to pay money to a third person. A check is an order directed to a bank to pay money from a person's account to a third person.

Negotiability

Commercial paper that is **negotiable** or a **negotiable instrument** is a special kind of commercial paper. Commercial paper is negotiable, passes readily through our financial system, and is accepted in place of money. It has many advantages.

For example, Searle, the owner of a clothing store in New York, contracts with Amado, a swimsuit manufacturer in Los Angeles, for $10,000 worth of swimsuits. If negotiable instruments did not exist, Searle would have to send or carry $10,000 across the country, which would be both inconvenient and risky. If the money were stolen along the way, Searle would lose the $10,000 unless he could locate the thief. By using a check in which

Searle orders his bank to pay $10,000 from his account to Amado, or to someone designated by Amado, Searle makes the payment in a far more convenient manner. He has sent only a single piece of paper to Amado. If the check is properly prepared and sent, sending the check is less risky than sending money. Even if the check is stolen along the way, Searle's bank may not pay it to anyone but Amado or someone authorized by Amado. And because the check gives Amado the right to either collect the $10,000 or transfer the right to collect it to someone else, the check is a practical substitute for cash to Amado as well as Searle.

In this chapter and in the three following chapters, we discuss the requirements necessary for a contract to qualify as a negotiable instrument. We also explain the features that not only distinguish a negotiable instrument from a contract but also have led to the widespread use of negotiable instruments as a substitute for money.

KINDS OF COMMERCIAL PAPER

Promissory Notes

The **promissory note** is the simplest form of commercial paper; it is simply a *promise to pay money*. A promissory note is a two-party instrument in which one person (known as the **maker**) makes an unconditional promise in writing to pay another person (the **payee**), or a person specified by that person, a sum of money either on demand or at some particular time in the future.

The promissory note, shown in Figures 1 and 2, is a credit instrument; it is used in a wide variety of transac-

---

FIGURE 1   A Promissory Note

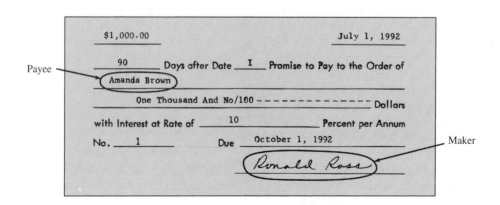

tions in which credit is extended. For example, if a person purchases an automobile on credit, the dealer probably has the person sign a promissory note for the unpaid balance of the purchase price. Similarly, if a person borrows money to purchase a house, the lender who makes the loan and takes a mortgage on the house has the person sign a promissory note for the amount due on the loan. The note probably states that it is secured by a

---

FIGURE 2   A Promissory Note (consumer loan note)

The National
**BANK OF
WASHINGTON**

CONSUMER LOAN NOTE

Date __November 21,__ , 19 _92_

The words I and me mean all borrowers who signed this note. The word bank means The National Bank of Washington.

Promise to Pay

Payee →

__30__ months from today, I promise to pay to the order of The National Bank of Washington
Seventy-Eight Hundred Seventy Five and
no/100 -----------------dollars ($ 7,875.00).

Responsibility

Although this note may be signed below by more than one person. I understand that we are each as individuals responsible for paying back the full amount.

Breakdown of Loan

This is what I will pay:

Amount of loan	1.$	6,800.00
Credit Life Insurance (optional)	2.$	100.00
Other (describe)	3.$	-0-
Amount Financed (Add 1 and 2 and 3)	4.$	6,900
FINANCE CHARGE	5.$	975.00
Total of Payments (Add 4 and 5)	$	7,875.00
ANNUAL PERCENTAGE RATE	10.5	%

Repayment

This is how I will repay:
I will repay the amount of this note in __30__ equal uninterrupted monthly installments of $ 262.50 each on the __1st__ day of each month starting on the __1st__ day of __December__ , 19 _92_ and ending on __May 1,__ , 19 _95_ .

Prepayment

I have the right to prepay the whole outstanding amount of this note at any time. If I do, or if this loan is refinanced—that is, replaced by a new note—you will refund the unearned finance charge, figured by the rule of 78—a commonly used formula for figuring rebates on installment loans.

Late Charge

Any installment not paid within ten days of its due date shall be subject to a late charge of 5% of the payment, not to exceed $5.00 for any such late installment.

Security

To protect The National Bank of Washington, I give what is known as a security interest in my auto and/or other: (Describe) __Ford Thunderbird__

__# Serial #115117-12-__ .

See the security agreement.

Credit Life Insurance

Credit life insurance is not required to obtain this loan. The bank need not provide it and I do not need to buy it unless I sign immediately below. The cost of credit life insurance is $____100.00 for the term of the loan.

Signed: _A. J. Smith_

Date: __November 21, 1992__

Default

If for any reason I fail to make any payment on time. I shall be in default. The bank can then demand immediate payment of the entire remaining unpaid balance of this loan, without giving anyone further notice. If I have not paid the full amount of the loan when the final payment is due, the bank will charge me interest on the unpaid balance at six percent (6%) per year.

Right of Offset

If this loan becomes past due, the bank will have the right to pay this loan from any deposit or security I have at this bank without telling me ahead of time. Even if the bank gives me an extension of time to pay this loan, I still must repay the entire loan.

Collection Fees

If this note is placed with an attorney for collection, then I agree to pay an attorney's fee of fifteen percent (15%) of the unpaid balance. This fee will be added to the unpaid balance of the loan.

Co-borrowers

If I am signing this note as a co-borrower. I agree to be equally responsible with the borrower for this loan. The bank does not have to notify me that this note has not been paid. The bank can change the terms of payment and release any security without notifying or releasing me from responsibility for this loan.

Copy Received

I received a completely filled in copy of this note. If I have signed for Credit Life Insurance. I received a copy of the Credit Life Insurance certificate.

Borrower: _A. J. Smith_   → Maker
A. J. Smith
3412 Brookdale, S. W. Washington D.C.
Address

Co-borrower: _Andrea H. Smith_   → Comaker
Andrea H. Smith
3412 Brookdale, S. W., Washington D. C.
Address

Co-borrower:_____

_____
Address

CONSUMER CREDIT HOTLINE: If you have any questions, please call us immediately at (202) 624-3450.
NBW 437 (Rev. 11-78)   1-Bank's copy 2-File copy 3-Customer's copy

mortgage. The terms of payment on the note should correspond with the terms of the sales contract for the purchase of the car or the house.

Certificates of Deposit

The **certificate of deposit** given by a bank or a savings and loan association when a deposit of money is made is a form of commercial paper and a type of note. Similiar to the promissory note, the certificate of deposit is a *promise to pay money*. When a bank issues a certificate of deposit (CD), as shown in Figure 3, it acknowledges receipt of a specific sum of money. The bank also agrees to pay the owner of the certificate the sum of money plus a stated rate of interest at some time in the future.

Many banks no longer issue certificates of deposit in paper form. Rather, the bank maintains an electronic deposit (CD) and provides the customer with a statement indicating the amount of principal held on a CD basis and the terms of the CD, such as the maturity and interest rate. Thus in these instances, the certificate of deposit is not in negotiable instrument form.

Drafts

A **draft** is a form of commercial paper that involves an *order to pay money* rather than a promise to pay money. The most common example of a draft is a check. A draft has three parties to it: one person (known as the **drawer**) orders a second person (the **drawee**) to pay a certain sum of money to a third person (the **payee**).

Drafts other than checks are used in a variety of commercial transactions. If Brown owes Ames money, Ames may draw a draft for the amount of the debt, naming Brown as drawee and herself or her bank as payee, and send the draft to Brown's bank for presentment and collection.

In freight shipments in which the terms are "cash on delivery," it is a common practice for the seller to ship the goods to the buyer on an "order bill of lading" consigned to himself at the place of delivery. The seller then indorses the bill of lading and attaches a draft naming the buyer as drawee. He then sends the bill of lading and the draft through banking channels to the buyer's bank. The draft is presented to the bank for payment, and when payment is made, the bill of lading is delivered to the buyer. Through this commercial transaction, the buyer gets the goods and the seller gets his money.

When credit is extended, the same procedure is followed, but a time draft—a draft payable at some future time—is used. See Figure 4. In such a transaction, the buyer "accepts" the draft instead of paying it. To accept the draft, he writes his name across its face, thereby obligating himself to pay the amount of the draft when due.

Checks

A **check** is a *draft* on which the *drawee is always a bank* and that is *payable on demand*. Checks are the most widely used form of commercial paper. The issuer of a check is ordering the bank at which he maintains an account to pay a specified person, or someone designated by that person, a certain sum of money from the account. For example, Elizabeth Brown has a checking account at the National Bank of Washington. She goes to Sears Roebuck & Co. and agrees to buy a washing machine priced at $459.95. If she writes a check to pay for it, she is the drawer of the check, the National Bank of Washington is the drawee, and Sears is the payee. By

---

FIGURE 3   A Certificate of Deposit

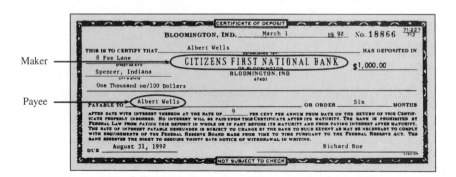

writing the check, Elizabeth is ordering her bank to pay $459.95 from her account to Sears or to Sears's order, that is, to whomever Sears asks the bank to pay the money. See Figure 5.

BENEFITS OF NEGOTIABLE INSTRUMENTS

Rights of an Assignee of a Contract

As we noted in the Rights of Third Parties chapter, which discussed the assignment of contracts, the assignee of a contract can obtain no greater rights than the

assignor had at the time of the assignment. For example, Frank Farmer and Neam's Market enter into a contract providing that Farmer will sell Neam's a dozen crates of fresh eggs a week for a year and that Neam's will pay Farmer $4,000 at the end of the year. If at the end of the year Farmer assigns to Bill Sanders his rights under the contract—including the right to collect the money from Neam's—then Sanders has whatever rights Farmer had at that time. If Farmer has delivered all the eggs to Neam's as he promised, then Farmer would be entitled to $4,000 and Sanders would obtain that right from him. However, if Farmer has not delivered all the eggs that he had promised to deliver, or if the eggs he delivered were not fresh, then Neam's might have

FIGURE 4   A Draft

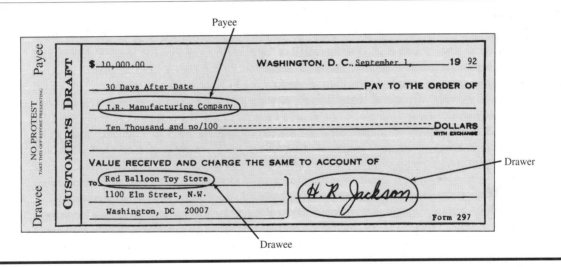

FIGURE 5   A Check

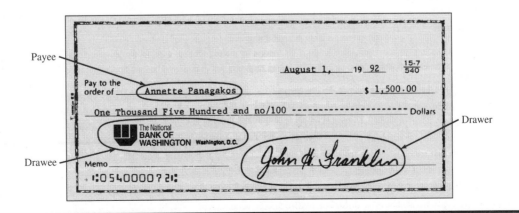

a valid defense or reason to refuse to pay the full $4,000. In that case, Sanders would have only what rights Farmer had and would also be subject to the defense Neam's has against full payment.

Taking an assignment of a contract involves assuming certain risks. The assignee (Sanders) may not be aware of the nature and extent of any defenses that the party liable on the contract (Neam's) might have against the assignor (Farmer). An assignee who does not know for sure what rights he is getting, or which risks he is assuming, may be reluctant to take an assignment of the contract.

Rights of a Holder of a Negotiable Instrument

The object of commercial paper (a contract for the payment of money) is to have it accepted readily as a substitute for money. To accept it readily, a person must be able to take it free of many of the risks assumed by the assignee of a regular contract. Under the law of negotiable instruments, this is possible if two conditions are met: (1) the contract for the payment of money must be in the proper form to qualify as a **negotiable instrument;** and (2) the person who is acquiring the instrument must qualify as a **holder in due course.** Basically, a holder in due course is a person who has good title to the instrument, paid value for it, acquired it in good faith, and had no notice of any claims or defenses against it.

The next section of this chapter discusses the proper form for a negotiable instrument. The Negotiation and Holder in Due Course chapter outlines the requirements that a person must meet to qualify as a holder in due course.

A holder in due course of a negotiable instrument takes the instrument free of all *personal defenses and claims* to the instrument except *those that concern its validity*; these are known as *real* defenses. For example, a holder in due course of a note given in payment for goods does not have to worry if the buyer is claiming that the seller breached a warranty. However, if the maker of a note wrote it under duress, such as a threat of force, or was a minor, then even a holder in due course who acquires the note is subject to the real defenses of duress or lack of capacity. The person who holds the note could not obtain the payment from the maker but would have to recover from the person from whom he got the note.

The Federal Trade Commission (FTC) has adopted a regulation that alters the holder in due course situation. This regulation is designed to allow a consumer who gives a negotiable instrument to use any defenses against payment of the instrument against even a holder in due course. Similarly, some states have enacted the Uniform Consumer Credit Code (UCCC), which produces a similar result. The Negotiation and Holder in Due Course chapter discusses the rights of a holder in due course, as well as the FTC rule.

FORMAL REQUIREMENTS FOR NEGOTIABILITY

Basic Requirements

An instrument such as a check or a note must meet certain formal requirements to be a negotiable instrument. If the instrument does *not* meet these requirements, it is *nonnegotiable*; that is, it is treated as a simple contract and not as a negotiable instrument. A primary purpose for these formal requirements is to ensure the willingness of prospective purchasers of the instrument, particularly financial institutions such as banks, to accept the instrument as a substitute for money.

For an instrument to be negotiable, it must:

1. Be in *writing*.
2. Be *signed by the maker or drawer*.
3. Contain an *unconditional promise or order to pay a sum certain in money*.
4. Be *payable on demand or at a definite time*.
5. Be *payable to order or to bearer*.
6. *Not contain any other promise, order, obligation, or power unless* it is *authorized* by the Code [3–104].[1]

Importance of Form

Whether or not an instrument is drafted so that it satisfies these formal requirements is important for only one purpose, that is, for determining whether an instrument is negotiable or nonnegotiable. Negotiability should not be confused with validity or collectibility. If an instrument is *negotiable*, the *law of negotiable instruments* in the Code controls in determining the rights and liabilities of the parties to the instrument. If an instrument is *nonnegotiable*, the *general rules of contract law control*. The purpose of determining negotiability is to ascertain whether a possessor of the instrument can become a holder in due course.

---

[1]The numbers in brackets refer to the sections of the Uniform Commercial Code.

An instrument that fills all of the formal requirements is a negotiable instrument even though it is void, voidable, unenforceable, or uncollectible. Negotiability is a matter of form and nothing else. Suppose a person gives an instrument in payment of a gambling debt in a state that has a statute declaring that any instrument or promise given in payment of a gambling debt is null and void. The instrument is a negotiable instrument if it is negotiable in form even though it is absolutely void. Also, an instrument that is negotiable in form is a negotiable instrument even though it is signed by a minor. The instrument is voidable at the option of the minor, but it is negotiable.

IN WRITING AND SIGNED

Writing

To be negotiable, an instrument must be *in writing* and must be *signed by the creator of the instrument, known as the maker or the drawer*. An instrument that is handwritten, typed, or printed is considered to be in writing [1–201(46)]. The writing does not have to be on any particular material; all that is required is that the instrument be in writing. A person could draw a negotiable instrument in pencil on a piece of wrapping paper. It would be poor business practice to do so, but the instrument would meet the statutory requirement that it be in writing.

Signed

An instrument has been *signed* if the maker or drawer has put a name or other symbol on it with *the intention of validating it* [3–401(2)]. Normally, the maker or drawer signs an instrument by writing his name on it; however, this is not required. A person or company may authorize an agent to sign instruments for it. A typed or rubber-stamped signature is sufficient if it was put on the instrument to validate it. A person who cannot write her name might make an X and have it witnessed by someone else.

UNCONDITIONAL PROMISE OR ORDER

Requirement of a Promise or Order

If an instrument is promissory in nature, such as a note or a certificate of deposit, it must contain an *uncondi-*

tional promise to pay or else it cannot be negotiable. Merely acknowledging a debt is not sufficient. For example, indicating "I owe you $100," does not constitute a promise to pay. An IOU in this form is not a negotiable instrument.

If an instrument is an order to pay, such as a check or a draft, it must contain an *unconditional order*. A simple request to pay as a favor is not sufficient; however, a politely phrased demand can meet the requirement. The language "Pay to the order of" is commonly used on checks. This satisfies the requirement that the check contain an order to pay. The order is the word *pay*, not the word *order*. The word *order* has another function—that of making the instrument payable "to order or to bearer."

Promise or Order Must Be Unconditional

An instrument is not negotiable unless the promise or order is *unconditional*. For example, a note that provides, "I promise to pay to the order of Karl Adams $100 if he replaces the roof on my garage," is not negotiable because it is payable on a condition.

To be negotiable, an instrument must be written so that a person can tell from reading the instrument alone what the obligations of the parties are. If a note contains the statement, "Payment is subject to the terms of a mortgage dated November 20, 1992," it is not negotiable. To determine the rights of the parties on the note, another document—the mortgage—would have to be examined.

However, the negotiability of a note would not be affected if the note contained this statement: "This note is secured by a mortgage dated August 30, 1992." In this case, the rights and duties of the parties to the note are not affected by the mortgage. It would not be necessary to examine the mortgage document to determine the rights of the parties to the note. The parties need only examine the instrument.

The negotiability of an instrument is not affected by a statement of the consideration for which the instrument was given or by a statement of the transaction that gave rise to the instrument. For example, a negotiable instrument may contain a notation stating that it was given in payment of last month's rent or a statement that it was given in payment of the purchase price of goods. The statement does not affect the negotiability of the instrument. The effect of a notation in the lower left corner of a check following the printed word *memo* is discussed in the *Western Bank v. RaDEC Construction Co., Inc.* case, which follows.

WESTERN BANK v. RaDEC CONSTRUCTION CO., INC.

42 UCC Rep. 1340 (S.D. Sup. Ct. 1986)

RaDEC Construction Company was involved as a general contractor in the construction of a medical center in Huron, South Dakota. One of RaDEC's subcontractors on this job was Carpet Center. RaDEC became aware that Carpet Center's financial problems were making it difficult to furnish the necessary materials and labor for the medical center job. RaDEC's president, Clarence Hoesing, had a conversation with Carpet Center on December 13, 1982, in which he agreed to send a check for $8,743.52 to Carpet Center, provided that Carpet Center (1) furnish certain paid invoices for material delivered, (2) provide certain additional material, and (3) assure the installation of the material on December 14. Hoesing then made out a handwritten check to Carpet Center. In the lower left corner of the check following the printed word *memo*, Hoesing typed the phrase, "Payee must prove clear title to material." Hoesing considered the check to be conditioned on Carpet Center's performance of the three conditions. After the check was delivered on December 14, Carpet Center deposited the check in the Western Bank, which allowed it to make an immediate withdrawal of the money. Later that day, RaDEC learned that Carpet Center had not performed the three requirements and filed a stop payment order on the check.

Unable to recover the money from Carpet Center, which was insolvent, the bank brought suit against RaDEC, claiming to be a holder in due course of the check. The trial court held in favor of the bank and RaDEC appealed.

Hertzel, Justice.   The trial court held as a matter of law that the phrase typed in at the lower left hand corner of the check, "Payee must prove clear title to material," did not have the effect of making the check conditional and that the bank was a bona fide holder in due course.

Section 3–104(1) sets forth four elements necessary to constitute a negotiable instrument: (a) It must be signed by the maker; (b) contain an unconditional promise or order to pay a sum certain in money and no other promise, order, obligation or power given by the maker or drawer except as authorized by this chapter; (c) be payable on demand or at a definite time; and (d) be payable to order or to bearer.

In this case there is no dispute that elements (a), (c) and (d) have been fulfilled. RaDEC claims, however, that element (b) has not been met because the check was a "conditional instrument" and therefore subject to its defenses.

RaDEC relies heavily on our decision in *Bank of America v. Butterfield*. In that case, the draft in question stated: "Subject to approval of title, pay to the order of Vernon H. Butterfield and Laura E. Butterfield." It is important to note that the phrase "subject to approval of title," immediately precedes the standard phrase, "Pay to the order of." In affirming the trial court we said: "The promise to pay money contained in the draft in question is clearly not unconditional. The payment ordered is subject to approval of title. Consequently, it is not a negotiable instrument."

Negotiability is determined from the face of the instrument without reference to extrinsic facts. The conditional or unconditional character is to be determined by what is expressed in the instrument itself.

RaDEC claims that the check was not a negotiable instrument because of the condition written on its face. Moreover, RaDEC argues that the location of the conditional language in the place usually reserved for "memo" is of little consequence, since the language itself was sufficient to give the bank notice that RaDEC's obligation to pay was conditioned upon Carpet Center's having proved clear title to the material. The bank, on the other hand, argues that the instant factual situation can be distinguished from that of Bank of America because in that case the conditional language, i.e., "subject to approval of title," preceded the words "Pay to the order of."

We conclude that the phrase "payee must prove clear title to material" written where it was, did not make the check conditional thereby depriving the bank of its status as a holder in due course. It appears that the notation in the "memo" area of the check is nothing more than a self-serving declaration by RaDEC for its own benefit and recordkeeping and for informational purposes only. An otherwise unconditional instrument cannot be rendered conditional by such a device.

Judgment for Western Bank affirmed.

A check may contain a notation as to the account to be debited without making the check nonnegotiable. For example, a check could contain the notation, "payroll account" or "petty cash." Similarly, the account number that appears on personal checks does not make the instrument payable only out of a specific fund. On the other hand, if a check states that it is payable only out of a specific fund, the check is generally not negotiable. In this case, the check is conditioned on there being sufficient funds in the account. Thus, the check would not be unconditional and could not qualify as a negotiable instrument. This rule does not apply to instruments issued by a government or a governmental agency. It is permissible for the instruments of such bodies to contain a provision saying that the instruments are payable only out of a particular fund [3–105(1)(g)].

A conditional indorsement does not destroy the negotiability of an otherwise negotiable instrument. We discuss conditional indorsements in the Negotiation and Holder in Due Course chapter. Negotiability is determined at the time an instrument is written, and it is not affected by subsequent indorsements.

SUM CERTAIN IN MONEY

Sum Certain

The promise or order in an instrument must be to pay a sum certain in money. The sum is certain if a person can compute from the information in the instrument the amount that is required to discharge—or pay off—the instrument at any given time. The Code permits an instrument to state different rates of interest before or after default. It also allows provisions for a discount or an addition if the note is paid early or if it is paid late. The key element is that a person can compute the amount that is due on the instrument at any given time. Thus, a provision for interest at "current bank rates" would not satisfy the requirement for a "sum certain."

The following *Taylor v. Roeder* case discusses the negotiability of a note that provided for interest at "3 percent over the Chase Manhattan Prime to be adjusted monthly." The Virginia Supreme Court held that the note was not negotiable because the current interest rate could not be determined from the face of the note. A number of states, concluding that such notes are recognized by commercial practice, have now acted to make adjustable rate notes negotiable.

TAYLOR v. ROEDER

360 S.E.2d 191 (Va. Sup. Ct. 1987)

VMC Mortgage Company was a mortgage lender that in the conduct of its business borrowed money from investors, pledging as security the notes secured by deeds of trust obtained from its borrowers. Olde Towne Investment Corporation borrowed $18,000 from VMC, evidenced by a promissory note secured by a deed of trust on land. The note provided for interest at "three percent (3.00%) over Chase Manhattan Prime to be adjusted monthly."

Subsequently, Frederick Taylor entered into a contract to buy from Olde Towne the land secured by the deed of trust. After requesting the payoff figure from VMC, Taylor forwarded the money it claimed was due on the note to VMC. Taylor, however, never received the canceled note.

In the meantime, VMC had borrowed money from a pension fund for which Roeder was the trustee and had pledged the Olde Towne note as collateral. No notice was given to Olde Towne that the note had been transferred and VMC accepted payments on the note. VMC defaulted on its obligation to the pension fund for which the note was collateral and filed a petition in bankruptcy. When Roeder tried to foreclose on the property Taylor had purchased, he filed suit against Roeder to stop the foreclosure. A key question in the litigation was whether the note was negotiable. If it was, then the liability on it would have been extinguished only by paying it to the holder—Roeder. If the note was not negotiable, then the liability on the note was satisfied by paying it to VMC where there was no notice received by Olde Towne of the assignment of the right to payment to Roeder.

Russell, Justice.   The dispositive question in this case is whether a note providing for a variable rate of interest, not ascertainable from the face of the note, is a negotiable instrument. We conclude that it is not.

Section 3–104 provides, in pertinent part, that: "Any writing to be a negotiable instrument . . . must . . . contain an unconditional promise or order to pay a sum certain in money." The meaning of "sum certain" is clarified by Section 3–106. Official Comment 1, to that section, states in part:

It is sufficient [to establish negotiability] that at any time of payment the holder is able to determine the amount then payable from the instrument itself with any necessary computation. . . . The computation must be one which can be made from the instrument itself without reference to any outside source, and this section does not make negotiable a note payable with interest "at the current rate."

We conclude that the drafters of the Uniform Commercial Code adopted criteria of negotiability intended to exclude an instrument which requires reference to any source outside the instrument itself in order to ascertain the amount due, subject only to the exceptions provided for in the UCC. Roeder points out the Official Comment to Section 3–104 holds open the possibility that some new types of commercial paper may be made negotiable by statute or by judicial decision. Roeder urges us to create, by judicial decision, just such an exception in favor of variable-interest notes.

Taylor concedes that variable-interest loans have become a familiar device in the mortgage lending industry. Their popularity arose when lending institutions, committed to long-term loans at fixed rates of interest to their borrowers, were in turn required to borrow short-term funds at high rates during periods of rapid inflation. Variable rates protected lenders when rates rose and benefited borrowers when rates declined. They suffer, however, from the disadvantage that the amount required to satisfy the debt cannot be ascertained without reference to an extrinsic source—in this case the varying prime rate charged by the Chase Manhattan Bank. Although that rate may readily be ascertained from published sources, it cannot be found within the "four corners" of the note.

The UCC introduced a degree of clarity into the law of commercial transactions which permits it to be applied by laymen daily to countless transactions without resort to judicial interpretation. The relative predictability of results made possible by that clarity constitutes the overriding benefit arising from its adoption. In our view, that factor makes it imperative that when change is thought desirable, the change should be brought about by statutory amendment, not through litigation and judicial interpretation. Therefore, we decline Roeder's invitation to create an exception, by judicial interpretation, in favor of instruments providing for a variable rate of interest not ascertainable from the instrument itself.

Judgment for Taylor.

Compton, Justice, Dissenting.   Instruments providing that loan interest may be adjusted over the life of the loan routinely pass with increasing frequency in this state and many others as negotiable instruments. This court should recognize this custom and usage, as the commercial market has, and hold these instruments to be negotiable.

The commercial market requires a self-contained instrument for negotiability so that a stranger to the original transaction will be fully apprised of its terms and will not be disadvantaged by terms not ascertainable from the instrument itself. For example, interest payable at the "current rate" leaves a holder subject to claims that the current rate was established by one bank rather than another and would disadvantage a stranger to the original transaction.

The rate which is stated in the note in this case, however, does not similarly disadvantage a stranger to the original agreement. Anyone coming into possession could immediately ascertain the terms of the notes: interest payable at three percent above the prime rate established by the Chase Manhattan Bank of New York City. This is a third-party objective standard which is recognized as such by the commercial market. The rate can be determined by a telephone call to the bank or from published lists obtained upon request.

Sometimes, notes contain a clause that provides for the payment of collection fees or attorney's fees in the event of a default on the note. Even though this would make the amount due on default uncertain until the collection or attorney's fees were determined, such a clause does not make the note nonnegotiable [3–106]. The amount can be determined at some time, and business practice justifies the inclusion of such a clause in the instrument.

Payable in Money

The amount specified in the instrument must be payable in *money,* which is a medium of exchange authorized or adopted by a government as part of its currency [1–201(24)]. If the person obligated to pay off an instrument can do something other than pay money, the instrument is not negotiable. For example, if a note reads, "I promise to pay to the order of Sarah Smith, at my option, $40 or five bushels of apples, John Jones," the note is not negotiable.

PAYABLE ON DEMAND OR AT A DEFINITE TIME

To be negotiable, an instrument must be payable either *on demand* or *at a specified time in the future.* This is so that the time when the instrument is payable can be determined with some certainty. An instrument that is payable on the happening of some uncertain event is not negotiable [3–109(2)]. Thus, a note payable "when my son graduates from college" is not negotiable, even though the son does graduate subsequently.

Payable on Demand

An instrument may state that it is payable on demand. If no time for payment is stated in an instrument, the instrument is considered to be payable on demand [3–108]. For example, if the maker forgets to state when a note is payable, it is payable immediately at the request of the holder of the note. A check is considered to be payable on demand. However, a postdated check is treated as a draft and is not properly payable until the day it is dated. An instrument can be negotiable even though it is undated, postdated, or antedated [3–114].

Payable at a Definite Time

An instrument is payable at a definite time if: (1) it is payable on or before a stated date, such as "on July 1, 1992," or "on or before July 1, 1992"; (2) it is payable at a fixed time after a stated date, such as "30 days after date," provided that the instrument is dated; or (3) it is payable at a fixed time "after sight," which is in effect a provision that it will be paid at a fixed time after it is presented to the drawee for acceptance.

If an instrument that is payable "30 days after date" is not dated, then it is not payable at a fixed date and it is not negotiable; however, this defect may be cured if the holder of the instrument fills in the date before he negotiates it to someone else [3–115].

Under the Code, an instrument may contain a clause permitting the time for payment to be accelerated at the option of the maker. Similarly, an instrument may contain a clause allowing an extension of time at the option of the holder or allowing a maker or acceptor to extend payment to a further definite time. Or the due date of a note might be triggered by the happening of an event, such as the filing of a petition in bankruptcy against the maker. These clauses are allowed as long as the time for payment can be determined with certainty [3–109].

PAYMENT TO ORDER OR BEARER

To be negotiable, an instrument must be *payable to order* or *to bearer*. A check that provides, "Pay to the order of Sarah Smith" or "Pay to Sarah Smith or bearer" is negotiable; however, one that provides "Pay to Sarah Smith" is not. The words *to the order of* or *to bearer* show that the drawer of the check, or the maker of a note, intends to issue a negotiable instrument. The drawer or maker is not restricting payment of the instrument to just Sarah Smith but is willing to pay someone else designated by Sarah Smith. This is the essence of negotiability.

The original payee of a check or a note can transfer the right to receive payment to someone else. By making the instrument payable "to the order of" or "to bearer," the drawer or maker is giving the payee the chance to negotiate the instrument to another person and to cut off certain defenses that the drawer or maker may have against payment of the instrument.

A check that is payable to the order of a specific person is known as **order paper.** Order paper can be negotiated or transferred only by indorsement. A check that is payable to bearer is known as **bearer paper.** A check made payable "to the order of cash" is considered to be payable to bearer and is also known as bearer paper [3–111]. Bearer paper can be negotiated or transferred without indorsement.

An instrument can be made payable to two or more payees. For example, a check could be drawn payable "to the order of John Jones and Henry Smith." Then, both Jones and Smith have to be involved in negotiating it or enforcing its payment. An instrument can also be made payable to alternative persons, for example, "to the order of Susan Clark or Betsy Brown." In this case, either Clark or Brown could negotiate it or enforce its payment.

CONCEPT REVIEW

REQUIREMENTS FOR NEGOTIABILITY

Requirement	Basic Rules
Must Be in Writing	The instrument may be handwritten, typed, or printed.
Must Be Signed by the Maker or Drawer	1. Person signing must do so with intent of validating his or her obligation. 2. Signature can be affixed in a variety of ways: for example, by word, mark, or rubber stamp. 3. Signature can be provided by an authorized agent or representative.
Must Contain a Promise or Order to Pay	1. Promise must be more than acknowledgment of a debt. 2. Order requirement is met by the word *pay.*
The Promise or Order Must Be Unconditional	1. Entire obligation must be found in the instrument itself and not in another document or documents. 2. Payment cannot be conditioned on the occurrence of an event. 3. Payment may not be limited to funds in a particular account (except government checks).

Requirement	Basic Rules
Must Call for Payment of a Sum Certain	1. Must be able to compute from the face of the instrument the amount required to pay it off. 2. May contain a clause providing for payment of collection or attorney's fees.
Must Be Payable in Money	1. Obligation must be payable in a medium of exchange authorized or adopted by a government as part of its currency. 2. Maker or drawer cannot have the option to pay in something other than money.
Must Be Payable on Demand or at a Definite Time	1. Requirement is met if instrument says it is payable on demand or if no time for payment is stated (then it is payable on demand). 2. Requirement is met if it is payable on a stated date, at a fixed time after a stated date, or a fixed time "after sight." 3. Instrument may contain an acceleration clause or a clause allowing holder to extend the payment date.
Must Be Payable to Bearer or to Order	1. Bearer requirement is met if instrument is payable "to bearer" or "to cash." 2. Order requirement is met if instrument is payable "to the order of" a specified person or persons.
May Not Contain any Other Promise, Order, Obligation, or Power unless Authorized by the Code	Certain terms such as the place of payment or a confession of judgment clause may be included without destroying negotiability.

Special Terms

Additional Terms

Banks and other businesses sometimes use forms of commercial paper that have been drafted to meet their particular needs. These forms may include terms that do not affect the negotiability of an instrument. Thus, a note form may provide for a place of payment without affecting the instrument's negotiability. Similarly, insurance reimbursement checks frequently contain a clause on the back stating that the payee, by indorsing or cashing the check, acknowledges full payment of the claim. This clause does not affect the negotiability of the check [3–112(1)(f)].

A term authorizing the **confession of judgment** on the instrument when due does not affect the negotiability of the instrument [3–112(1)(d)]. A confession of judgment clause authorizes the creditor to go into court if the debtor defaults and, with the debtor's acquiescence, to have a judgment entered against the debtor.

However, such clauses are not permitted in some states; moreover, even where they are permitted, some courts have held that a note is rendered nonnegotiable by a clause that authorizes confession of judgment and a demand for payment *prior* to the due date of the note.

Ambiguous Terms

Occasionally, a person may write or receive a check on which the amount written in figures differs from the amount written in words. Or a note may have conflicting terms or an ambiguous term. Where a conflict or an ambiguous term exists, there are general rules of interpretation that are applied to resolve the conflict or ambiguity: Where words and figures conflict, the words control the figures, unless the words are ambiguous. Similarly, handwritten terms prevail over printed and typed terms, and typed terms prevail over printed terms [3–118]. The following *Yates v. Commercial Bank & Trust Co.* case involves a check on which there was a difference between the figures and the written words.

YATES v. COMMERCIAL BANK & TRUST CO.
36 UCC Rep. 205 (Fla. Dist. Ct. 1983)

Emmett McDonald, acting as the personal representative of the estate of Marion Cahill, wrote a check payable to himself, individually, on the estate checking account in the Commercial Bank & Trust Company. The instrument contained an obvious variance between the numbers and the written words that indicated the amount of the check. It said: "Pay to the order of Emmett E. McDonald $10075.00 Ten hundred seventy five . . . Dollars."

The bank paid the $10,075 sum stated by the numerals to McDonald, who absconded with the funds. Yates, the successor representative, sued the bank on behalf of the estate to recover the $9,000 difference between that amount and the $1,075 that was written out. The trial court dismissed the complaint, and Yates appealed.

Schwartz, Chief Judge.   It is clear that the complaint stated a cognizable claim against the bank. Section 3–118 provides: "The following rules apply to every instrument: . . . (3) Words control figures except that if the words are ambiguous figures control."

Under this provision of the UCC, it was clearly improper for the bank to have paid the larger sum stated in numbers, rather than the smaller one unambiguously stated by McDonald's words. It is, therefore, prima facie liable to the estate for the excess.

Judgment reversed in favor of Yates.

If a note provides for the payment of interest, but no interest rate is spelled out, then interest is payable at the judgment rate (the rate of interest imposed on court awards until they are paid by the losing party) at the place of payment.

ETHICAL AND PUBLIC POLICY CONCERNS

1. The *Taylor v. Roeder* case presents the policy dilemma of whether the Uniform Commercial Code should be amended to accommodate the adjustable rate note that is in common use. If you were a commissioner on uniform state laws, how would you assess the policy considerations involved in this question?

2. The Uniform Commercial Code currently provides that in the case of ambiguity or conflict between the words and figures on a negotiable instrument, the words control the figures. A number of banks argue that in an era of computers, they encode checks based on the amount stated in figures and that the Code should be changed to provide for the dominance of figures over

words. What policy considerations are involved in deciding whether or not to adopt the bank's position in the Code?

SUMMARY

Commercial paper is basically a contract for the payment of money. The two types of commercial paper are promises to pay money and orders to pay money. Notes and certificates of deposit issued by banks are promises to pay people sums of money. Drafts and checks are orders to other persons to pay sums of money to third persons.

Commercial paper that is negotiable can pass readily through our financial system and be accepted in place of money. This gives it a number of advantages over a simple contract. Normally, the assignee of a contract can obtain no greater rights than his assignor had. However, a transferee of a negotiable instrument who qualifies as a holder in due course can obtain greater rights than his assignor had.

To qualify as a negotiable instrument, an instrument must (1) be in writing, (2) be signed by the maker or drawer, (3) contain an unconditional promise or order to pay a sum certain in money, (4) be payable on demand or at a definite time, (5) be payable to order or to bearer, and (6) not contain any other promise or obligation unless it is authorized by the Code. Since negotiability is merely a matter of form, an instrument that meets the formal requirements can be negotiable even though it is void, voidable, unenforceable, or uncollectible. If an instrument is negotiable, the law of negotiable instruments as set out in the Code controls in determining the rights and liabilities of the parties to the instrument. If an instrument is nonnegotiable, the general rules of contract law control.

Printed forms for commercial paper may contain certain clauses for business reasons that do not affect the negotiability of the instruments. If there are ambiguous terms in a negotiable instrument, the general rule of interpretation is that handwritten terms control typewritten and printed terms and that typewritten terms control printed terms. If there is a conflict between words and figures, the words control unless they are ambiguous, in which case the figures control.

PROBLEM CASES

1. Is the following instrument a note, a check, or a draft? Why? If it is not a check, how would you have to change it to make it a check?

To: *Arthur Adams* January 1, 1992
TEN DAYS AFTER DATE PAY TO THE ORDER OF:
    Bernie Brown
THE SUM OF: Ten and no/100 DOLLARS
SIGNED: *Carl Clark*

2. Wiley, Tate & Irby, buyers and sellers of used cars, sold several autos to Houston Auto Sales. Houston wrote out the order for payment on the outside of several envelopes. He signed them and they were drawn on his bank, Peoples Bank & Trust Co., to be paid on the demand of Wiley, Tate & Irby. Can the envelopes qualify as negotiable instruments?

3. Is the following a negotiable instrument?

IOU, A. Gay, the sum of seventeen and 5/100 dollars for value received.

    John R. Rooke

4. Holly Hill Acres, Ltd., executed a promissory note and mortgage and delivered them to Rogers and Blythe. The note contained the following stipulation:

This note with interest is secured by a mortgage on real estate, of even date herewith, made by the maker hereof in favor of the said payee, and shall be construed and enforced according to the laws of the State of Florida. *The terms of said mortgage are by this reference made a part hereof.* (Emphasis added.)

Rogers and Blythe assigned the note to Charter Bank of Gainesville to secure payment of an obligation they owed to Charter Bank. When the Holly Hill note was not paid, Charter Bank brought suit to collect the note and foreclose the mortgage. As a defense, Holly Hill asserted that fraud on the part of Rogers and Blythe induced the sale giving rise to the note and mortgage. Charter Bank contended that it was a holder in due course of a negotiable instrument and thus not subject to the defense of fraud. Was the note a negotiable instrument?

5. An instrument, otherwise in negotiable form, contained the following provision: "This note is given in payment for merchandise and is to be liquidated by payments received on account of sale of such merchandise." Is this a negotiable instrument?

6. Nation-Wide Check Corporation sold money orders to drugstores. The money orders contained the words, "Payable to," followed by a blank. Can the money order qualify as a negotiable instrument?

7. A note, otherwise negotiable in form, payable five years after date, contained the provision, "due if ranch is sold or mortgaged." Is the note negotiable?

8. In 1964, S. Gentilotti wrote a check for $20,000 payable to the order of his son, Edward J. Gentilotti. He postdated the check to November 4, 1984, which would be his son's 20th birthday. The father also wrote on the check that it should be paid from his estate if he died prior to November 4, 1984. The father then gave the check to Edward's mother for safekeeping. On May 31, 1972, the father died. The check was then presented for payment, but the bank refused to pay it. The mother and the son then brought a lawsuit against the executor of the father's estate to require payment. The executor claimed that the check was not a valid negotiable instrument because it had been postdated. Can a check be a negotiable instrument if it is postdated 20 years?

9. Holliday made out a promissory note to Anderson, leaving the date of payment of the note blank. Anderson filled in the words "on demand" in the blank without Holliday's knowledge. Does this alter the rights or obligations of the parties?

10. Louis Canino signed the following instrument:

$27,000   March 11, 1980
LOUIS G. CANINO for value received, does promise to pay to the order of CARL MESS the sum *Two Hundred Twenty-five* . . . . Dollars at *Lakewood, Colorado*, said principal *on the first day of each and every month commencing on April 1, 1980*, with interest at the rate of 8 percent per annum.

/s / Louis G. Canino

When Mess sued Canino for nonpayment of the note, Canino argued that the words "Two Hundred Twenty-five Dollars" should control the figures "$27,000" and that he was obligated to pay only $225. Is this a valid argument?

CHAPTER 24

NEGOTIATION AND HOLDER
IN DUE COURSE

INTRODUCTION

The preceding chapter discussed the nature and benefits of negotiable instruments. It also outlined the requirements an instrument must meet to qualify as a negotiable instrument and be accepted as a substitute for money.

This chapter focuses on negotiation—the process by which rights to a negotiable instrument are passed from one person to another. Commonly, this involves an indorsement and delivery of the instrument. This chapter also develops the requirements that a transferee must meet to qualify as a holder in due course and thus attain special rights under negotiable instruments law. We discuss these rights, which put a holder in due course in an enhanced position compared to an assignee of a contract, in some detail.

NEGOTIATION

Nature of Negotiation

Negotiation is the transfer of an instrument in such a way that the person who receives it becomes a holder. A **holder** is a person who is in possession of an instrument that *(1) was issued to him, (2) has been indorsed to him*

or to his order, or (3) is payable to bearer [1–201(20)].[1] For example, when an employer gives an employee a paycheck payable to her order, she is the holder of the check because the check was issued to her. When she writes her name on the back of the check and cashes it at the grocery store, she has negotiated the check to the grocery store because the store is in possession of a check indorsed to it.

Formal Requirements for Negotiation

The formal requirements for negotiation are very simple. If an instrument is payable to the order of a specific payee, it is called **order paper** and it can be negotiated only by delivery of the instrument after indorsement by the payee [3–202(1)].

For example, if Rachel Stern's employer gives her a check payable "to the order of Rachel Stern," then Stern can negotiate the check by indorsing her name on the back of the check and giving it to the person to whom she wants to transfer it. The check is order paper, not merely because the word *order* appears on the check, but also because it names a specific payee, Rachel Stern.

---

[1]The numbers in brackets refer to the sections of the Uniform Commercial Code.

If an instrument is *payable to bearer or to cash*, it is called **bearer paper** and negotiating it is even simpler. A person given a check made payable "to the order of cash" can negotiate the check by giving it to the person to whom he wishes to transfer it. No indorsement is necessary to negotiate an instrument payable to bearer [3–202(1)]. However, the person who takes the instrument may ask for an indorsement for his protection. Indorsing the check signifies an agreement to be liable for its payment to that person if the drawee bank does not pay it when it is presented for payment. We discuss this liability in the next chapter.

Nature of Indorsement

An **indorsement** is made by adding the signature of the holder of the instrument to the instrument, usually on the back [3–202(2)]. The signature can be put there either by the holder or by someone who is authorized to sign on behalf of the holder. For example, a check payable to "H&H Meat Market" might be indorsed "H&H Meat Market by Jane Franklin, president" if Franklin is authorized to do this on behalf of the market.

If the back of an instrument is full of indorsements, further indorsements should be made on a paper attached firmly to the instrument. Such a paper is called an **allonge.**

Wrong or Misspelled Name

The indorser of an instrument should spell his name in the same way as it appears on the instrument. If the indorser's name is misspelled or wrong, then legally the indorsement can be made either in his name or in the name that is on the instrument. However, any person who pays the instrument or otherwise gives something of value for it may require the indorser to sign both names [3–203].

Suppose Joan Ash is issued a check payable to the order of "Joanne Ashe." She may indorse the check as either "Joan Ash" or "Joanne Ashe." However, if she takes the check to a bank to cash, the bank may require her to sign both "Joanne Ashe" and "Joan Ash."

Indorsements by a Depository Bank

When a customer deposits a check to his account with a bank and the customer forgets to indorse the check, the bank normally has the right to supply the customer's indorsement [4–205]. Instead of actually signing the

customer's name to the check as the indorsement, the bank may just stamp on it that it was deposited by the customer or credited to his account. The only time the bank does not have the right to put the customer's indorsement on a check that the customer has deposited is when the drafter of the check specifically requires the payee's signature. Insurance and government checks commonly require the payee's signature.

Transfer of Order Instrument

If an order instrument is transferred without indorsement, the instrument has not been negotiated and the transferee cannot qualify as a holder. For example, Sue Brown gives a check payable "to the order of Susan Brown" to her grocer in payment for her groceries. Unless Sue indorses the check, it has not been "negotiated" and the grocer could not qualify as a "holder" of the check.

The transferee has the right to the unqualified indorsement of the transferor. Should the transferor refuse to indorse the instrument with an unqualified indorsement, the transferee would be entitled to a court order ordering the transferor to so indorse the instrument. The negotiation takes effect only when the indorsement is made, and until that time there is no presumption that the transferee is the owner.

INDORSEMENTS

Effects of an Indorsement

There are two aspects to an indorsement. First, an indorsement is necessary to negotiate an instrument that is payable to the order of a specific payee. Thus, if a check is payable to the order of James Lee, Lee must indorse the check before it can be negotiated. The form of the indorsement that Lee uses also affects future attempts to negotiate the instrument. For example, if Lee indorses the check "Pay to Sarah Hill," Hill must indorse it before it can be negotiated further.

Second, an indorsement generally makes a person liable on the instrument. By indorsing an instrument, a person makes a contractual promise to pay the instrument if the person primarily liable on it (for example, the maker of a note) does not pay it. The next chapter, Liability of Parties, discusses the contractual liability of indorsers. This chapter discusses the effect of an indorsement on further negotiation of an instrument.

Kinds of Indorsements

The four basic indorsements are (1) special, (2) blank, (3) restrictive, and (4) qualified.

Special Indorsement A **special indorsement** contains the signature of the indorser along with words indicating to whom, or to whose order, the instrument is payable. For example, if a check drawn "Pay to the Order of Marcia Morse" is indorsed by Morse "Pay to the Order of Sam Smith, Marcia Morse" or "Pay to Sam Smith, Marcia Morse," it has been indorsed with a special indorsement. An instrument that is indorsed with a special indorsement remains or becomes order paper. It can be negotiated only with the indorsement of the person specified [3–204(1)]. In this example, Sam Smith must indorse the check before it can be negotiated to someone else. See Figure 1 for an example of a special indorsement.

Blank Indorsement If an indorser merely signs her name and does not specify to whom the instrument is payable, the instrument has been indorsed in **blank.** For example, if a check drawn "Pay to the Order of Natalie Owens" is indorsed "Natalie Owens," it has been indorsed in blank. See Figure 2 for an example of a blank indorsement. An instrument indorsed in blank is payable to the bearer; that is, the person in possession of it. This means that the check is bearer paper. As such, it can be negotiated by delivery alone and no further indorsement is necessary for negotiation [3–204(2)].

If Owens indorsed the check in blank and gave it to Karen Foley, Foley would have the right to convert the blank indorsement into a special indorsement [3–204(3)]. She could do this by writing the words "Pay to the Order of Karen Foley" above Owens's indorsement. Then, the check would have to be indorsed by Foley before it could be negotiated further.

Similarly, the payee of a bearer instrument can make the instrument an order instrument by a special indorsement. For example, Harold Fisher is the holder of a check made payable to "cash." If Fisher indorses the instrument on the back "Pay to Arlene Jones, Harold Fisher," it would be an order instrument and it would have to be indorsed by Arlene Jones before it could be negotiated further.

If a person takes a check indorsed in blank to a bank and presents it for payment or for collection, the bank normally asks the person to indorse the check. The check does not need an indorsement to be negotiated, because the check indorsed in blank can be negotiated merely by delivering it to the bank cashier. The bank asks for the indorsement because it wants to make the person liable on the check if it is not paid when the bank sends it to the drawee bank for payment. The Liability of Parties chapter discusses the liability of indorsers.

The *Walcott v. Manufacturers Hanover Trust* case, which follows, illustrates how an instrument indorsed in blank can be negotiated merely by delivery. As you read this case, consider what the payee should have done to protect his interest in the check.

FIGURE 1 A Special Indorsement

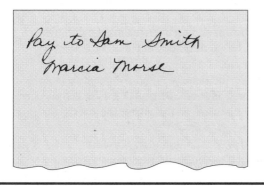

FIGURE 2 A Blank Indorsement

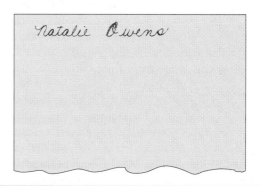

WALCOTT v. MANUFACTURERS HANOVER TRUST
507 N.Y.S.2d 961 (N.Y.C. Civ. Ct. 1986)

Kenneth Walcott was obligated to make monthly mortgage payments to Midatlantic Mortgage Company. He claimed that on November 1, 1985, he sent his October 19 paycheck in the amount of $359.05 along with a money order for $251.54 to Midatlantic as his November payment. He further claimed that he signed his name to the back of the check and placed his mortgage number and the Midatlantic mailing sticker on the back of the check. Then he put the checks in an envelope addressed to Midatlantic and put the envelope in a postal box.

In mid-November, he received a note that his November mortgage payment had not been received. When he inquired, he found that his check had been cashed by the Bilko Check Cashing Corporation on November 4 and deposited into the Bilko account at Manufacturers Hanover Trust. The money order was never cashed; payment was stopped on it and it was later replaced by a new money order. The check, as received by Manufacturers Hanover, contained Walcott's indorsement and the mortgage number 603052 but no sign of the sticker. Walcott claimed that an intervening thief must have stolen the check and cashed it at Bilko. He brought suit against Bilko and Manufacturers Hanover, claiming they had converted his interest in the check, which he intended to go to Midatlantic.

Harkavy, Judge. The issue presented to this court is whether Walcott's indorsement of his paycheck was such to be a special or restrictive indorsement, thus limiting the negotiation of the instrument or did it have the effect of creating a bearer instrument.

Uniform Commercial Code Section 3–204 (1) defines a special indorsement as being one that "specifies the person to whom or to whose order it makes the instrument payable. Any instrument specially indorsed becomes payable to the order of the special indorsee and may be further negotiated only by his indorsement."

Examination of the back of the check reveals that Walcott did not specify any particular indorsee. In order for the alleged attached sticker to have served that purpose it must have also complied with Section 3–202(2): "An indorsement must be written by or on behalf of the holder and on the instrument or a paper so firmly affixed thereto as to become a part thereof." The back of the check shows no sticker attached at all. Even if it had originally been affixed thereto, as Walcott claims, it obviously became detached easily, thus failing to meet the indorsement requirements under the UCC to constitute a special indorsement.

As to the numbers written underneath Walcott's signature, they do not have the effect of restricting Walcott's indorsement. Section 3–205 is very specific as to what constitutes a restrictive indorsement. The series of numbers representing Walcott's mortgage account was insufficient to restrict negotiation of Walcott's check.

Walcott's indorsement had the effect of converting the check into a bearer instrument. The series of numbers having no restrictive effect, Walcott indorsed the check in blank, or otherwise stated, he simply signed his name. A blank indorsement under Section 3–204(2) "specifies no particular indorsee and may consist of a mere signature." Additionally, "An instrument payable to order and indorsed in blank becomes payable to bearer and may be negotiated by delivery alone . . . " Consequently, since Walcott failed to limit his blank indorsement, the check was properly negotiated to Bilko and cashed by it.

Judgment for Manufacturers Hanover Bank and Bilko Check Cashing Corporation.

FIGURE 3   A Restrictive Indorsement

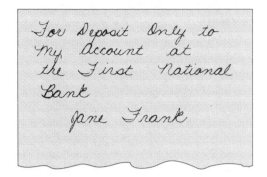

For Deposit Only to
my account at
the First National
Bank
Jane Frank

Restrictive Indorsement   A **restrictive** indorsement is one that specifies the purpose of the indorsement or the use to be made of the instrument. See Figure 3 for an example of a restrictive indorsement. Among the more common restrictive indorsements are:

1. Indorsements for deposit. For example, "For deposit only" or "For deposit only to my account at the First Trust Company."

2. Indorsements for collection, which are commonly put on by banks involved in the collection process. For example, "Pay to any bank, banker, or trust company" or "For collection only."

3. Indorsements indicating that the indorsement is for the benefit or use of someone other than the person to whom it is payable. For example, "Pay to Arthur Attorney in trust for Mark Minor."

4. Indorsements purporting to prohibit further negotiation. For example, "Pay to Carl Clark only."

5. Conditional indorsements, which indicate that they are effective only if a certain condition is satisfied. For example, "Pay to Bernard Builder only if he completes construction of my house by November 1, 1992."

A similar restriction by a maker or drawer would destroy the negotiability of the instrument; however, indorsers are permitted to so limit payment without affecting negotiability.

A restrictive indorsement does not prevent further negotiation of an instrument [3–206(1)]. However, the person who takes an instrument with a restrictive indorsement must pay or apply any money or other thing of value he gives for the instrument consistently with the indorsement.[2] Suppose a person takes a check payable to "Arthur Attorney in trust for Mark Minor." The money for the check should be put in Mark Minor's trust account. A person would not be justified in taking the check in exchange for a television set that he knew Attorney was acquiring for his own—rather than Minor's—use.

Similarly, suppose Clark indorses a check payable to his order "for deposit" and deposits it in a bank in which Clark has a commercial account. The bank then credits Clark's account with the amount of the check. The bank is a holder for value to the extent that it allows Clark to draw on the credit for the check because the bank has applied the value it gave for the instrument consistently with the indorsement. However, if the transferee of a restrictively indorsed instrument does not make payment in accordance with the restrictive indorsement, the transferee is liable to the indorser for any loss that results from the failure to comply with the indorsement.

In *AmSouth Bank, N.A. v. Reliable Janitorial Service, Inc.,* which follows, a depository bank was held responsible for following its customer's restrictive indorsement and required to credit the customer's account; the bank had improperly permitted the checks to be credited to another person's account.

---

[2]Except an intermediary bank, which, under § 3–206(2), is not affected by a restrictive indorsement of any person except its immediate transferor or the person presenting for payment.

AMSOUTH BANK, N.A. v. RELIABLE JANITORIAL SERVICE, INC.

548 So.2d 1365 (Ala. Sup. Ct. 1989)

Reliable Janitorial Service, Inc., maintained a bank account with AmSouth Bank. Rosa Pennington was employed by Reliable as a bookkeeper/office manager. She deposited checks made payable to Reliable but did not have authority to write checks on Reliable's account.

Beginning in January 1985, Pennington obtained counter deposit slips from AmSouth. She wrote on the deposit slips that the depositor was "Reliable Janitorial Services, Inc.," but in the space for the account number, Pennington wrote the account number for her own personal account with AmSouth. She stamped the checks that were made payable to "Reliable Janitorial Service, Inc.," with the indorsement "For Deposit Only. Reliable Carpet Cleaning, Inc." Over an 11-month period, Pennington was able to deposit 169 checks so indorsed. AmSouth credited the deposits to Pennington, not Reliable. Pennington spent all the funds that she diverted to her account. When Reliable discovered the fraud, it brought suit against AmSouth for conversion and sought to have its account credited with the improperly paid checks. The trial court granted summary judgment to Reliable, and AmSouth appealed.

Almon, Justice.   AmSouth's first issue is whether the trial court erred by granting summary judgment on Reliable's conversion claim. To examine this issue, we look to the statutes concerning restrictive indorsements and those concerning conversion. There is no dispute that Pennington stamped the checks whose funds she misdirected with the indorsement "For Deposit Only, Reliable Janitorial Service, Inc." or "For Deposit Only, Reliable Carpet Cleaning, Inc." Sections 3–205 and 3–206 address such indorsements. Section 3–205 provides:

§ 3–205. Restrictive indorsements.
   An indorsement is restrictive which either:
   (a) Is conditional; or
   (b) Purports to prohibit further transfer of the instrument; or
   (c) Includes the words "for collection," "pay any bank," or like terms signifying a purpose of deposit or collection; or
   (d) Otherwise states that it is for the benefit or use of the indorser or of another person.

Undeniably, the indorsements Pennington stamped on the checks were restrictive indorsements within the meaning of section 3–205(c).

Section 3–206 addresses the effect of such an indorsement, and pertinently, that section provides:

(3) Except for an intermediary bank, any transferee under an indorsement which is conditional or includes the words "for collection," "for deposit," "pay any bank," or like terms (subparagraphs (a) and (c) of section 3–205) *must* pay or apply any value given by him for or on the security of the instrument consistently with the indorsement. (Emphasis added.)

Thus, under the exact words of the statute, AmSouth *must* apply the value of Reliable's checks consistently with the indorsement, i.e., for deposit to Reliable's account.

Case remanded to trial court on other grounds.

Qualified Indorsement A **qualified indorsement** is one in which the indorser disclaims or limits his liability to make the instrument good if the drawer or maker defaults on the instrument. Words such as "without recourse" are used to qualify an indorsement; they can be used with a special, a blank, or a restrictive indorsement and thus make it a qualified special, a qualified blank, or a qualified restrictive indorsement. See Figure 4 for an example of a qualified indorsement. The use of a qualified indorsement does not change the negotiable nature of the instrument. The effect is to limit the contractual liability of the indorser. The chapter on Liability of Parties discusses this contractual liability in detail.

FIGURE 4   A Qualified Indorsement

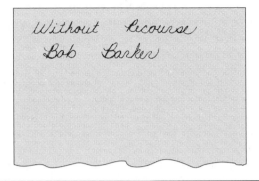

CONCEPT REVIEW

INDORSEMENTS

(Assume a check is payable "To The Order of Mark Smith.")

Type	Example	Consequences
Blank	Mark Smith	1. Satisfies the indorsement requirement for the negotiation of order paper. 2. The instrument becomes bearer paper and can be negotiated by delivery alone. 3. The indorser becomes contractually liable on the instrument. (See Liability of Parties chapter.)
Special	Pay to the Order of Joan Brown Mark Smith	1. Satisfies the indorsement requirement for the negotiation of order paper. 2. The instrument remains order paper and Joan Brown's indorsement is required for further negotiation. 3. The indorser becomes contractually liable on the instrument. (See Liability of Parties chapter.)
Restrictive	For deposit only to my account in First American Bank Mark Smith	1. Satisfies the indorsement requirement for the negotiation of order paper. 2. The person who pays value for the instrument is obligated to pay it consistent with the indorsement (i.e., to pay it into Mark Smith's account at First American Bank). 3. The indorser becomes contractually liable on the instrument. (See Liability of Parties chapter.)
Qualified	Mark Smith (without recourse)	1. Satisfies the indorsement requirement for negotiation of order paper. 2. Eliminates the indorser's contractual liability. (See Liability of Parties chapter.) 3. Modifies one of the transferor warranties made by the indorser. (See Liability of Parties chapter.)

Rescission of Indorsement

Negotiation is effective to transfer an instrument even if the negotiation is (1) made by a minor, a corporation exceeding its powers, or any other person without contractual capacity; (2) obtained by fraud, duress, or mistake of any kind; (3) part of an illegal transaction; or (4) made in breach of duty. A negotiation made under the preceding circumstances is subject to **rescission** before the instrument has been negotiated to a transferee who can qualify as a holder in due course [3–207]. The situation in such instances is analogous to a sale of goods where the sale has been induced by fraud or misrepresentation. In such a case, the seller may rescind the sale and recover the goods, provided that the seller acts before the goods are resold to a bona fide purchaser for value.

HOLDER IN DUE COURSE

A person who qualifies as a **holder in due course** of a negotiable instrument gets special rights. Normally, the transferee of an instrument—like the assignee of a contract—receives only those rights in the instrument that the transferor had in the instrument. But a holder in due course can obtain better rights than his transferor had. A holder in due course takes a negotiable instrument free of all **personal defenses** and claims to the instrument except for so-called **real defenses,** which go to the validity of the instrument. We develop the differences between personal and real defenses in more detail later in this chapter. The following example illustrates the advantage that a holder in due course of a negotiable instrument may have.

Carl Carpenter contracts with Helen Homeowner to build a garage for $10,500, payable on October 1, when the garage is expected to have been completed. Assume that Carpenter assigns his right to the $10,500 to First National Bank to obtain money for materials. If the bank tries to collect the money from Homeowner on October 1, but Carpenter has not finished building the garage, then Homeowner may assert the fact that the garage is not complete as a defense to paying the bank. As assignee of a simple contract, the bank has only those rights that its assignor, Carpenter, has and is subject to all of the claims and defenses that Homeowner has against Carpenter.

Now assume that instead of simply signing a contract with Homeowner, Carpenter had Homeowner give him a negotiable promissory note in the amount of $10,500

payable to the order of Carpenter on October 1. Carpenter then negotiated the note to the bank. If the bank qualifies as a holder in due course, it would be entitled to collect the $10,500 from Homeowner on October 1, even though she might have a personal defense against payment of the note in that Carpenter had not completed the work on the garage. Homeowner cannot assert that personal defense against a holder in due course. She would have to pay the note to the bank and then independently seek to recover from Carpenter for breach of their agreement. The bank's improved position is due to its status as a holder in due course of a negotiable instrument. If the instrument in question was not negotiable, or if the bank could not qualify as a holder in due course, then it would be in the same position as the assignee of a simple contract and would be subject to the personal defense.

We turn now to a discussion of the requirements that must be met for the possessor of a negotiable instrument to qualify as a holder in due course.

General Requirements

To become a holder in due course, a person who takes a negotiable instrument must be a *holder* and must take the instrument for *value*, in *good faith*, *without notice* that it is *overdue* or has been *dishonored*, and *without notice* of any *defense* against it or *claim* to it [3–302]. If a person who takes a negotiable instrument does not meet these requirements, he is not a holder in due course and is in the same position as an assignee of a contract.

Holder

To be a holder of a negotiable instrument, a person must have *possession* of an instrument that has *all of the necessary indorsements* and is *delivered* to him. For example, if Teresa Gonzales is given a check by her grandmother that is made payable "to the order of Teresa Gonzales," Teresa is a holder of the check because it is made out to her. If Teresa indorses the check "Pay to the order of Ames Grocery, Teresa Gonzales" and gives it to Ames Grocery in payment for some groceries, then Ames Grocery is the holder of the check. Ames Grocery is a holder because it is in possession of a check that is indorsed to its order and delivered to it. If Ames Grocery indorses the check "Ames Grocery" and deposits it in its account at First National Bank, the bank becomes the holder. The bank is in possession of an instrument that is indorsed in blank and has been delivered to it.

All indorsements on the instrument at the time it is payable to the order of a specified payee must be *authorized* indorsements. A *forged* indorsement is not an effective indorsement, and it prevents a person from becoming a holder. For example, the U.S. government mails to Robert Washington an income tax refund check payable to him. Tom Turner steals the check from Washington's mailbox, signs (indorses) "Robert Washington" on the back of the check, and cashes it at a shoe store. The shoe store cannot be a holder of the check, because a necessary indorsement has been forged. The check has to be indorsed by Robert Washington for there to be a valid chain of indorsements and for any subsequent possessor to be a holder. Turner's signature is not effective for this purpose, because Washington did not authorize Turner to sign Washington's name to the check.

The case which follows, *La Junta State Bank v. Travis*, illustrates that a party in possession of a check indorsed in blank is a holder of the instrument.

La Junta State Bank v. Travis

727 P.2d 48 (Colo. Sup. Ct. 1986)

On November 15, 1979, Katherine Warnock purchased a cashier's check in the amount of $53,541.93 payable to her order and drawn on the Pueblo Bank and Trust Company. At some time between November 15 and November 30, Warnock indorsed "Katherine Warnock" on the reverse side of the check, and Warnock's attorney, Jerry Quick, wrote the words "deposit only" under Warnock's indorsement. On November 30, Quick deposited the check into a trust account he maintained at the La Junta State Bank. Warnock did not maintain any type of account with La Junta State Bank. It collected the amount of the check from Pueblo Bank. Warnock died on November 10, 1981. Robert Travis, Warnock's personal representative, was unable to find a receipt in her personal papers for the sum of $53,541.93. On June 24, Travis demanded that the La Junta Bank repay that sum to Warnock's estate. At the time, no funds remained in Quick's trust account at the bank.

When the La Junta Bank refused the representative's demand, he brought suit against the bank claiming it had improperly paid the check by allowing it into any account other than one in Warnock's name. The trial court determined that Warnock had indorsed the check in blank and delivered it to Quick, that the check therefore became bearer paper upon Warnock's indorsement, and that the check was negotiable on delivery alone; it granted judgment to the bank. A divided court of appeals reversed in favor of the representative, holding that Quick's addition of the words "deposit only" below Warnock's signature created a restrictive indorsement and that because the bank failed to treat it as such, it was liable to the representative for the full amount of the check. The bank appealed.

Kirshbaum, Justice. It is undisputed that when Warnock indorsed the check in blank and delivered it to Quick, it was converted from order paper to bearer paper, negotiable by delivery alone until specially indorsed [3–204(2)]. The trial court also concluded that Quick's addition of "deposit only" below Warnock's signature did not convert Warnock's blank indorsement into a special indorsement.

Implicit in the trial court's conclusions is the assumption that Quick added the words "deposit only" to the check some time after Warnock's indorsement thereof. This implicit finding is supported by the stipulation of facts and the evidence disclosed by the record. Therefore, we also conclude that when Warnock indorsed the check in blank and delivered it to Quick, Quick became a holder of the instrument in bearer form with the right to transfer or negotiate it by delivery alone.

Warnock's representative argues that, assuming Quick was initially a holder of a check in bearer form, his act of affixing the words "deposit only" to the check deprived him of that status, destroyed the negotiability of the check, and converted Warnock's blank indorsement into a restrictive indorsement. This argument is untenable.

Quick, as holder of an instrument, was not authorized by any Code provision to conver this transferor's blank indorsement into a restrictive one (see section 3–204(3)—"The holder may convert a blank indorsement by writing over the signature of the indorser in blank any contract consistent with the character of the indorsement."). Furthermore, the representative incorrectly assumes that a blank indorsement and a restrictive indorsement create mutually exclusive methods for negotiation. As U.C.C. section 3–206 official comment 5 (1978) indicates, "indorsements 'for collection' or 'for deposit' may be either special or blank." A single indorsement, therefore, may be both in blank and restrictive. The nonrestrictive character of Warnock's indorsement was determined when she affixed her signature to the check. The fact that Quick was a holder of bearer paper does not end the inquiry into the propriety of the bank's conduct. Section 3–206(3) of Code requires a depositary bank, upon being presented with a negotiable instrument containing an indorsement which includes the words "for deposit" or like terms, to "pay or apply any value given by him for or on the security of the instrument consistently with the indorsement. . . ." This obligation affords protection to payees or indorsers who indorse items "for deposit" in the belief that such indorsement will guard against further negotiation of the instrument to a holder in due course by a finder or a thief.

In this case the bank, as a depository bank, received a check containing what appeared to be a restrictive indorsement by Katherine Warnock. The record does not reveal who actually delivered the check and deposit slip to the bank. Thus, at the moment it received the restrictively indorsed check, the bank appeared to owe a duty to Warnock to either comply with the directions of the indorsement or to inquire further concerning the transaction because of the simultaneous receipt of a deposit slip into an account other than Warnock's. However, because the check was bearer paper when Quick received it, he was free to direct its deposit in any manner he elected. Any inquiry by the bank would have revealed that, although the language inscribed on the instrument appeared to constitute a restrictive indorsement by Katherine Warnock, the words "deposit only" had been added by Quick on his own behalf; and the bank owed a duty to Quick on November 30, 1979, to honor his restrictive indorsement. Under the circumstances of the case, the bank owed no duty to Warnock and Warnock's representative is entitled to no damages.

Judgment for La Junta State Bank.

Value

To qualify as a holder in due course of an instrument, a person must give **value** for it. Value is different from simple consideration. Under the provisions of the Code, a holder takes an instrument for value if: (1) the agreed consideration has been performed—for example, if the instrument was given in exchange for a promise to deliver a refrigerator and the refrigerator has been delivered; (2) he acquires a security interest in, or a lien on, the instrument; (3) he takes the instrument in payment of, or as security for, an antecedent claim; (4) he gives a negotiable instrument for it; or (5) he makes an irrevoca-

ble commitment to a third person [3–303]. Thus, a person taking an instrument as a gift would not be able to qualify as a holder in due course.

A bank or any person who discounts an instrument in the regular course of trade has given value for it. Likewise, if a loan is made and an instrument is pledged as security for the repayment of the loan, the secured party has given value for the instrument to the extent of the amount of the loan. If Axe, who owes Bell a past-due debt, indorses and delivers to Bell, in payment of the debt or as security for its repayment, an instrument issued to Axe, Bell has given value for the instrument. If a bank allows its customer to draw against a check deposited for collection, it has given value to the extent of the credit drawn against.

The purchaser of a limited interest in an instrument can be a holder in due course only to the extent of the interest purchased [3–302(4)]. For example, Arthur Wells agrees to purchase a note payable to the order of Helda Parks. The note is for the sum of $5,000. Wells pays Parks $1,000 on the negotiation of the note to him and agrees to pay the balance of $4,000 in 10 days. Before making the $4,000 payment, Wells learns that James Dell, the maker of the note, has a valid defense to it. Wells can be a holder in due course for only $1,000.

A person who has given all of the value for an instrument that he agreed to give can be a holder in due course for the full amount of the instrument even if the amount is less than the face amount. For example, if Stu Hanks pays Linda Parish $975 for a $1,000 note, Hanks can be a holder in due course for the entire $1,000.

Good Faith

To qualify as a holder in due course of a negotiable instrument, a person must take it in **good faith,** which means that the person must obtain it honestly [1–201(19)]. If a person obtains a check by trickery or with knowledge that it has been stolen, the person has not obtained the check in good faith and cannot be a holder in due course. A person who pays too little for an instrument, perhaps because he suspects that something may be wrong with the way it was obtained, may have trouble in meeting the good faith test. The high discount itself suggests that the purchase was not in good faith. For example, because a finance company works closely with a door-to-door sales company engaging in shoddy practices, it is aware of past consumer complaints against the sales company. If the finance company buys consumers' notes from the sales company at a significant discount, it will not be able to meet the good faith test and qualify as a holder in due course of the notes.

The *Arcanum National Bank v. Hessler* case, which follows, illustrates the analysis a court goes through to ascertain whether good faith is present in a situation where the payee and a subsequent holder have had a close working relationship.

ARCANUM NATIONAL BANK v. HESSLER

69 Ohio St.2d 549 (Ohio Sup. Ct. 1982)

Kenneth Hessler was in the business of raising hogs for the John Smith Grain Company. John Smith Grain Company delivered hogs and feed to Hessler and required him to sign a promissory note payable to it to cover the cost of the hogs and feed. Without Hessler's knowledge or consent, John Smith Grain Company then sold the note to the Arcanum National Bank, which opened a commercial loan account in Hessler's name. When the hogs were sold by John Smith Grain Company, a portion of the proceeds was applied to satisfy Hessler's note held by the bank. Hessler received a flat fee and a share of the net profits on each hog sold.

On January 4, 1977, Hessler signed a promissory note for $16,800 payable to John Smith Grain Company for hogs delivered on that date. On the advice of an officer of John Smith Grain Company, Hessler also signed his wife's name, Carla Hessler, to the note, placing his initials, K. H., after her name. John Smith Grain Company, as payee, assigned the note to the Arcanum National Bank. The pigs delivered on January 4 had previously been mortgaged by John Smith Grain Company. Early in 1977, the mortgagee took the pigs from Hessler's farm because John Smith Grain Company was in serious financial difficulty. The company later went into receivership. As a result, no funds were available to pay the bank for Hessler's note.

The bank sued Kenneth and Carla Hessler to collect the face amount of the note. The Hesslers claimed that they had a defense of want of consideration and should not be liable to the bank on the note. The trial court and the court of appeals held that the bank was a holder in due course and that the defense of want of consideration could not be asserted against it. Hessler appealed.

Krupansky, Judge.   The sole issue in this case is whether the bank is a holder in due course who takes the note free from Hessler's defense of want of consideration.

Hessler contends the bank has not established holder in due course status because the bank took the instrument with notice of a defense against it. We agree.

The requirement that the purchaser take the instrument without notice of a claim or defense in order to qualify as a holder in due course is explained, under the heading of "Notice to Purchaser," at § 3–304, which provides in relevant part: "(A) The instrument is so incomplete, bears such visible evidence of forgery or alterations, or is otherwise so irregular as to call into question its validity, terms, or ownership or to create an ambiguity as to the party to pay."

Whether a transferee has taken an instrument with notice of a defense depends upon all the facts and circumstances of a particular situation and is generally a question of fact to be determined by the trier of fact.

Here the trial court, sitting as fact finder, weighed the evidence of the relationship between the bank and Hessler and reasoned: "The defect on the promissory note is that the signature of Carla Hessler was added by Kenneth Hessler and, since the Arcanum National Bank handled the Hesslers' personal finances, it should have noticed that there was a defect on the face of the instrument . . . The note also bears the initials 'K. H.,' indicating that Kenneth Hessler has signed Carla Hessler's name." Accordingly, the trial court specifically found "this 'irregularity' does call into question the validity of the note, the terms of the note, the ownership of the note or create an ambiguity as to the party who is to pay the note." Thus, the trial court, while specifically finding the bank took the note with notice of a defense, nonetheless erroneously held the bank qualified as a holder in due course.

Hessler also contends, in essence, the bank failed in its burden of proving holder in due course status because it failed to establish it took the note in good faith as required under 3–302(1)(b).

"Good faith" is defined as "honesty in fact in the conduct or transaction concerned." Under the "close connectedness" doctrine, which was established by the Supreme Court of New Jersey in *Unico v. Owen*, a transferee does not take an instrument in good faith when the transferee is so closely connected with the transferor that the transferee may be charged with knowledge of an infirmity in the underlying transaction. The rationale for the close connectedness doctrine was enunciated in *Unico* as follows:

In the field of negotiable instruments, good faith is a broad concept. The basic philosophy of the holder in due course status is to encourage free negotiability of commercial paper by removing certain anxieties of one who takes the paper as an innocent purchaser knowing no reason why the paper is not sound as its face would indicate. It would seem to follow, therefore, that the more the holder knows about the underlying transaction, and particularly the more he controls or participates or becomes involved in it, the less he fits the role of a good faith purchaser for value; the closer his relationship to the underlying agreement which is the source of the note, the less basis there is for giving him the tension-free rights considered necessary in a fast-moving, credit-extending world.

Soon after the decision in *Unico* was reached, the close connectedness doctrine was adopted by Ohio courts. *American Plan Corp. v. Woods* announced the following:

A transferee of a negotiable note does not take in "good faith" and is not a holder in due course of a note given in the sale of consumer goods where the transferee is a finance company involved with the seller of the goods, and which has a pervasive knowledge of factors relating to the terms of the sale.

According to White and Summers, noted authorities on the Uniform Commercial Code, the following five factors are indicative of a close connection between the transferee and transferor: (1) Drafting by the transferee of forms for the transferor; (2) approval or establishment or both of the transferor's procedures by the transferee (e.g., setting the interest rate, approval of a referral sales plan); (3) an independent check by the transferee on the credit of the debtor or some other direct contract between the transferee and the debtor; (4) heavy reliance by the transferor upon the transferee (e.g., transfer by the transferor of all or a substantial part of his paper to the transferee); and (5) common or connected ownership or management of the transferor and transferee.

An analysis of the above factors in relation to the facts of this case reveals an unusually close relationship between the bank (the transferee) and the John Smith Grain Company (the transferor-payee). The bank provided John Smith Grain Company with the forms used in the transaction and supplied the interest rate to be charged. At the time of the purchase of the first note, the bank ran an independent credit check on Hessler. There is evidence of a heavy reliance by John Smith Grain Company upon the bank insofar as it was customary for the grain company to transfer substantially all of its commercial paper to the bank. There was a common director of the bank and John Smith Grain Company.

The facts of this case clearly indicate such close connectedness between the bank and John Smith Grain Company as to impute knowledge by the bank of infirmities in the underlying transaction.

Judgment reversed in favor of Hessler.

Overdue and Dishonored

To qualify as a holder in due course, a person must take a negotiable instrument before it is overdue or has been dishonored. The reason for this is that obligations are generally performed when they are due. If a negotiable instrument is not paid when it is due, this is considered to put the person taking it on notice that there may be defenses to its payment.

Overdue Instruments   If a negotiable instrument due on a certain date is not paid by that date, then it is overdue at the beginning of the next day after the due date. For example, if a promissory note dated January 1 is payable "30 days after date," it is due on January 31. If it is not paid by January 31, it is overdue beginning on February 1.

If a negotiable instrument is payable on demand, a person must acquire it within a reasonable time after it was issued. A reasonable time for presenting a check for payment is presumed to be 30 days [3–304(3)(c)]. Thus, a person who acquires a check 60 days after the date it is dated is probably taking it after it is overdue.

In determining when a demand note is overdue, business practices and the facts of the particular case must be considered. In a farming community, the normal period for loans to farmers may be six months. A demand note might be outstanding for six or seven months before it is considered overdue. On the other hand, a demand note issued in an industrial city where the normal period of such loans is 30 to 60 days would be considered overdue in a much shorter period of time.

Dishonored Instruments

To be a holder in due course, a person must not only take a negotiable instrument before it is overdue but must also take it before it has been **dishonored.** A negotiable instrument has been dishonored when it has been *presented for payment* and payment has been *refused*.

For example, Susan Farley writes a check on her account at First National Bank that is payable "to the order of Sven Sorensen." Sorensen takes the check to First National Bank to cash it, but the bank refuses to pay it because Farley has insufficient funds in her account to cover it. The check has been dishonored. Sorensen then takes Farley's check to Harry's Hardware and uses it to pay for some paint. Harry's could not be a holder in due course of the check if Harry's is on notice that the check has been dishonored. It would have such notice if First National stamped the check "Payment Refused NSF" (not sufficient funds).

Similarly, suppose Carol Carson signs a 30-day note payable to Ace Appliance for $500 and gives the note to Ace as payment for a stereo set. When Ace asks Carson for payment, she refuses to pay because the stereo does not work properly. Ace then negotiates the note to First National Bank. If First National knows about Carson's refusal to pay, it cannot be a holder in due course.

Notice of Defenses

To qualify as a holder in due course, a person must also acquire a negotiable instrument without *notice* that there are any *defenses* or *adverse claims* to it. Notice of a possible defense might appear on the face of the instrument as it did in the *Arcanum National Bank* case, which appeared earlier, where a signature was accompanied by initials showing that it had been put there by someone other than the person whose name was signed. Similarly, in the *Key Bank of Southeastern New York, N.A. v. Strober Bros., Inc.* case, which follows, the notice was apparent on the face of the instrument.

KEY BANK OF SOUTHEASTERN NEW YORK, N.A. v. STROBER BROS., INC.

523 N.Y.S.2d 855 (N.Y. Sup. Ct., App. Div. 1988)

Eric Strober, the chairman of the board of Strober Bros., Inc., was approached by a business acquaintance, Sidney Pal, to make a short-term loan of $150,000 to a business venture operated by Pal. Pal indicated the loan would be collateralized by a negotiable certificate of deposit. Strober agreed to make the loan and made out a check for $150,000 drawn on the Strober Bros. account and made payable to the Tamara Trust, Pal's business venture. Pal urged the immediate delivery of the check to him and promised to deliver the negotiable certificate of deposit the next day. Strober agreed to deliver the check only on the condition that it be made nonnegotiable, that a stop order be placed on it, and that a trust agreement and the certificate of deposit be delivered by 4 o'clock the following day, at which point the stop order would be removed.

Strober struck out the words "the order of" on the check so that it read "pay to Tamara Trust" and placed a stop order on the check. Pal deposited the check in an account at the Key Bank and was allowed to draw out the funds in the account. When the check was sent to Strober's bank, payment was refused and it was returned marked "Payment Stopped." Pal never delivered a negotiable certificate of deposit.

Key Bank brought suit against Strober Bros. on the check seeking to hold Strober Bros. liable on the basis of its drawer's liability on the check. Key Bank claimed to be a holder in due course of the check who held it free of any defenses Strober Bros. might have against Pal and the Tamara Trust. The trial court granted summary judgment to Strober Bros. and Key Bank appealed.

Memorandum by the Court. The Supreme Court, Orange County, found that the check was nonnegotiable and that Key Bank was not a holder in due course. Upon determining that Strober Bros. had established its defense of a failure of a condition precedent to payment under the check, the court granted Strober Bros.'s motion for summary judgment.

We agree. The Key Bank has failed to demonstrate that it was a holder in due course of the check. The striking of the words "the order of" on the face of the check served to provide notice to the Key Bank that a claim or defense existed in favor of someone with an interest therein (see UCC section 3–304[1][a]). Therefore, Key Bank did not acquire the rights of a holder in due course under the requirements of UCC section 3–302. Since Key Bank was not a holder in due course of the instrument, it took the instrument subject to all claims and defenses against it (see UCC sections 3–305, 3–306).

Although UCC article 3 applies to non-negotiable checks such as the one at bar, it is specifically provided that there can be no holder in due course of such an instrument. Therefore, Key Bank must defend against the claims or defenses of Strober Bros.

Judgment for Strober Bros. affirmed.

Incomplete Paper A person cannot be a holder in due course of a check or other negotiable instrument if a *material term* is blank. If a person is given a check that has been signed, but the space where the amount of the check is to be written has been left blank, then he cannot be a holder in due course of that check. The fact that a material term is blank puts the person on notice that the drawer may have a defense to its payment. To be material, the omitted term must be one that affects the legal obligations of the parties to the negotiable instrument. Material terms include the amount of the instrument and the name of the payee. If a negotiable instrument is completed after it was signed but before it is acquired, the person who acquires it can qualify as a holder in due course if he had no knowledge about any unauthorized completion.

For example, Fred Young writes a check payable to the order of Slidell's Shoes and leaves the amount blank. He gives the check to his friend Alice Termon, asks her to pick up a pair of shoes for him at Slidell's, and tells her to fill in the amount of the purchase. If Termon gives the incomplete check to Slidell, it cannot be enforced as is. If Slidell fills in the check for $79.95, the cost of the shoes, the check could be enforced as completed because the completion was authorized.

However, if Slidell watched as Termon filled the blank in as $100 (and obtained the $20.05 difference in cash), Slidell could take the check as a holder in due course as long as he had no knowledge or notice that the completion was unauthorized. In addition, if Termon filled the amount in as $100 before she got to Slidell's, Slidell could be a holder in due course and enforce the check for $100. In each case, Young, who made the unauthorized completion possible, must bear the loss until he locates Termon.

Irregular Paper If there is something apparently wrong with a negotiable instrument, such as an obvious alteration in the amount, then it is considered to be **irregular paper.** A person who takes an irregular instrument is considered to be on notice of any possible

defenses to it. For example, Kevin Carlson writes a check for "one dollar" payable to Karen Held. Held inserts the word *hundred* in the amount, changes the figure "$1" to "$100," and gives the check to a druggist in exchange for a purchase of goods. If the alterations in the amount should be obvious to the druggist, perhaps because there are erasures, different handwritings, or different inks, then the druggist cannot be a holder in due course. The druggist would have taken irregular paper and would be considered to be on notice that there might be defenses to it. These defenses include Carlson's defense that he is liable for only $1 because that is the original amount of the check.

A person is put on notice if someone of his experience and training should, in the exercise of reasonable prudence, detect the irregularity. Any noticeable alteration makes an instrument irregular on its face, but a clever alteration does not. However, an alteration that might put a bank cashier on notice might not put on notice a person unaccustomed to handling negotiable instruments.

Voidable Paper A person cannot qualify as a holder in due course of a negotiable instrument if he is aware that the obligation of a party to it is *voidable*. Thus, if a person knows that a signature on the instrument was obtained by fraud, misrepresentation, or duress, he cannot be a holder in due course. If he knows that the instrument has already been paid, he cannot become a holder in due course. Of course, the best way for the person who is liable on an instrument to be protected after he pays it is to mark it "paid" or "canceled."

Negotiation by a Fiduciary A person may also be considered to be on notice of defenses if he is taking a negotiable instrument from a fiduciary such as a trustee. If a negotiable instrument is payable to a person as a trustee or an attorney for someone, then any attempt by that person to negotiate it on his own behalf or for his use (or benefit) puts the person on notice that the beneficiary of the trust may have a claim [3–304(2)].

For example, a check is drawn "Pay to the order of Anthony Adams, Trustee for Mary Minor." Adams takes the check to Ace Appliance Store, indorses his name to it, and uses it to purchase a television set for himself. Ace Appliance cannot be a holder in due course, because it should know that the negotiation of the check is in violation of the fiduciary duty Adams owes to Mary Minor. Ace should know this because Adams is negotiating the check for his own benefit, not Minor's. The following *Smith v. Olympic Bank* case illustrates this principle.

SMITH v. OLYMPIC BANK

693 P.2d 92 (Wash. Sup. Ct. 1985)

Charles Alcombrack was appointed guardian for his son Chad who was the beneficiary of his grandfather's life insurance policy. The insurance company issued a check for $30,588.39 made payable to "Charles Alcombrack, Guardian of the Estate of Chad Stephen Alcombrack a Minor." The attorney for the son's estate instructed the father to take the check, along with the guardianship papers, to the bank and open up a guardianship savings and checking account. Instead, the father took the check, without the guardianship papers, to the bank and opened personal savings and checking accounts in his own name. Despite the fact that the check was payable to Alcombrack as Guardian and that he indorsed the check as Guardian, the bank allowed him to place the entire amount in his newly opened personal accounts.

The father, and later his new wife, used all but $320.60 of the trust money for their own personal benefit. After the depletion of the son's estate, J. David Smith was appointed successor guardian. He obtained a judgment against the father and then brought suit against the bank, contending that it had converted the son's interest in the check. The trial court granted judgment in favor of the bank and Smith appealed.

Dore, Justice. Olympic Bank claims that it is a holder in due course (HIDC) and, as such, is not subject to the claims of Smith. In order to qualify as a HIDC, the bank must meet five requirements. It must be (1) a holder (2) of a negotiable instrument, (3) that took the instrument for value (4) in good faith and (5) without notice that it was overdue, dishonored, or of any defense or claim to it on the part of any person. We need not decide whether the bank met the first four conditions as we hold that the bank took the check with notice of an adverse claim to the instrument and, therefore, is not a holder in due course. Consequently, the bank is liable to the son's estate.

A purchaser has notice of an adverse claim when "he has knowledge that a fidicuary has negotiated the instrument in payment of or as security for his own debt or in any transaction for his own benefit or otherwise in breach of duty." Section 3–304(2). Thus the issue raised by this case is whether the bank had knowledge that the guardian was breaching his fiduciary duty when it allowed him to deposit a check, made payable to him in his guardianship capacity, into his personal accounts.

The bank knew it was dealing with guardianship funds. The check was payable to the father as guardian and not to him personally. The father indorsed it in his guardianship capacity. The bank received a call from the guardian's attorney inquiring about the fee charged for guardianship accounts, and a trust officer for the bank replied in a letter referring to the "Estate of Chad Alcombrack."

Reasonable commercial practices dictate that when the bank knew that the funds were deposited in a personal account instead of a guardianship account, it knew that the father was breaching his fiduciary duty. The funds lost the protection they would have received in a guardianship account. If the funds had been placed in a guardianship account, the bank would not have been permitted to accept a check drawn on the guardianship account, from the father in satisfaction of the father's unsecured personal loan in the amount of approximately $3,000. Nor could the father, or bank, have authorized his new wife to write checks against the guardianship account without court approval. A fiduciary has a duty to ensure that trust funds are protected. Here, the father breached his duty.

The policy reasons for holding a bank liable are compelling—especially in the situation presented in this case. The ward has no control of his own estate. He must rely on his guardian and on the bank for the safekeeping of his money. In order to protect the ward, the guardian and bank must be held to a high standard of care. For the guardian, this means that he must deposit guardian funds in a guardianship account. For the bank, it means that when it receives a check made payable to an individual as a guardian, it must make sure that the check is placed in a guardianship account. This will not place an undue burden on either banks or guardians and will have the beneficial effect of protecting the ward.

Judgment reversed in favor of son's guardian.

Payee as Holder in Due Course

A payee may be a holder in due course if he complies with all the requirements for a holder in due course [3–302(2)]. Ordinarily, a payee has notice or knowledge of defenses to the instrument and knows whether it is overdue or has been dishonored; consequently, he could not qualify as a holder in due course. For example, Drew draws a check on First Bank as drawee, payable to the order of Parks, but leaves the amount blank. Drew delivers the check to Axe, his agent, and instructs Axe to fill in $300 as the amount. Axe, however, fills in $500 as the amount, and Parks gives Axe $500 for the check. Axe then gives Drew $300 and absconds with the extra $200. In such a case, Parks, as payee, is a holder in due course of the check since he has taken it for value, in good faith, and without notice of defenses.

Similarly, assume that Jarvis owes Fields $200. Jarvis agrees to sell Kirk a used television set for $200 that Jarvis assures Kirk is in working condition. In fact, the set is broken. Jarvis asks Kirk to make her check for $200 payable to Fields and then delivers the check to Fields in payment of the debt. Fields, as the payee, can be a holder in due course of the check if she is not aware of the misrepresentation that Jarvis made to Kirk to obtain the check.

Shelter Provision

When an instrument is transferred, the transferee obtains those rights that the transferor had. This means that any person who can trace his title to an instrument back to a holder in due course receives the same rights of a holder in due course even if he cannot meet the requirements himself. This is known as the *shelter* provision of the Code. For example, Archer makes a note payable to Bryant. Bryant negotiates the note to Carlyle, who qualifies as a holder in due course. Carlyle then negotiates the note to Darby, who cannot qualify as a holder in due course, because she knows the note is overdue. Because Darby can trace her title back to a holder in due course (Carlyle), Darby has the rights of a holder in due course when she seeks payment of the note from Archer.

There is, however, a limitation on the shelter provision. A transferee who has himself been a party to any fraud or illegality affecting the instrument, or who as a prior holder has notice of a claim to or defense against the instrument, cannot improve his position by taking from a later holder in due course [3–201(1)]. For example, Archer, through fraudulent representations, induces Bryant to execute a negotiable note payable to Archer and then negotiates the instrument to Carlyle, who takes it as a holder in due course. If Archer thereafter takes the note for value from Carlyle, Archer cannot acquire Carlyle's rights as a holder in due course. Archer was a party to the fraud that induced the note, and the holder of an instrument cannot improve her position by negotiating the instrument and then reacquiring it.

CONCEPT REVIEW

REQUIREMENTS FOR HOLDER IN DUE COURSE STATUS

Requirement	Rule
1. Must be a *holder*.	A holder is a person who is in possession of an instrument "drawn, issued, or indorsed to him or his order or to bearer or in blank."
2. Must take for *value*.	A holder has given value: a. To the extent the agreed-on consideration has been paid or performed. b. To the extent a security interest or lien has been obtained. c. By payment of—or granting security for—an antecedent claim. d. By giving a negotiable instrument for it. e. By making an irrevocable commitment to a third person.
3. Must take in *good faith*.	Good faith means "honesty in fact."
4. Must take *without notice* that the instrument is *overdue*.	An instrument payable on a certain date is overdue at the beginning of the next day after the due date. An instrument that is payable on demand is overdue after a reasonable time after its date of issue. A reasonable time for presenting a check for payment is presumed to be 30 days.
5. Must take *without knowledge* that the instrument has been *dishonored*.	An instrument has been dishonored when it has been presented for payment and payment has been refused.
6. Must take *without knowledge* of a *claim or defense* against it.	A person who takes an instrument with a material term blank is on notice of possible claims or defenses. A person who takes irregular paper containing an obvious alteration is on notice of possible claims or defenses. A person who knows that an obligation or any part of the instrument is voidable is on notice of possible claims or defenses. A person who takes an instrument from a fiduciary is on notice of possible claims or defenses.

RIGHTS OF A HOLDER IN DUE COURSE

Importance of Being a Holder in Due Course

The Negotiable Instruments chapter showed that the advantage of negotiable instruments over other contracts is that they are accepted as substitutes for money. People are willing to accept negotiable instruments as substitutes for money because they can generally take them free of claims or defenses to payment between the original parties to the instruments. On the other hand, a person who takes an assignment of a simple contract receives only the same rights as the person had who assigned the contract.

A person who acquires a negotiable instrument must be concerned about two conditions in order to be free of claims or defenses between the original parties. First, the person who acquires the negotiable instrument must be a holder in due course. If not, he is subject to all of the claims or defenses to payment that any party to the instrument has. Second, the only claims or defenses that the holder in due course has to worry about are so-called **real defenses**—those that affect the validity of the instrument. For example, if the maker or drawer did not have legal capacity because she was a minor, the maker or drawer has a real defense. The holder in due course does not have to worry about so-called **personal defenses**.

Personal Defenses

The basic rule of negotiable instruments law is that a holder in due course of a negotiable instrument is not subject to any **personal,** or limited, **defenses** or claims that may exist between the original parties to the instrument [3–305]. Personal defenses include:

1. Lack or failure of consideration. For example, that a promissory note for $100 was given to someone without intent to make a gift and without receiving anything in return.

2. Breach of contract, including breach of warranty. For example, a check was given in payment for repairs to an automobile but the repair work was defective.

3. Fraud in the inducement of any underlying contract. For example, an art dealer sells a lithograph to Cheryl Crane, telling her that it is a Picasso, and takes Crane's check for $500 in payment. The art dealer knows that the lithograph is not a genuine Picasso but a forgery. Crane has been induced to make the purchase and give her check by the art dealer's fraudulent representation. Because of this fraud, Cheryl has a personal defense against having to honor her check to the art dealer.

4. Incapacity to the extent that state law makes the obligation voidable, as opposed to void. For example, where state law makes the contract of a person of limited mental capacity, but who has not been adjudicated incompetent, voidable, the person has a personal defense to payment.

5. Illegality that makes a contract voidable, as opposed to void. For example, where the payee of a check given for certain professional services was required to have a license from the state but did not have one.

6. Duress, to the extent it is not so severe as to make the obligation void but rather only voidable. For example, if an instrument was signed under a threat to prosecute the maker's son if it was not signed, the maker might have a personal defense.

7. Unauthorized completion or material alteration of the instrument. For example, the instrument was completed in an unauthorized manner, or a material alteration was made to it after it left the maker's or drawer's possession.

8. Nondelivery of the instrument. For example, that the person in possession of the instrument obtained it by theft or by finding it, rather than through an intentional delivery of the instrument to him.

The following example illustrates the limited extent to which a maker or drawer can use personal defenses as a reason for not paying a negotiable instrument that he signed: Trent Tucker bought a used truck from Honest Harry's, giving a 60-day promissory note for $2,750 in payment for the truck. Honest Harry's guaranteed the truck to be in good working condition, when in fact the truck had a cracked engine block. If Harry's tries to collect the $2,750 from Tucker, Tucker could claim breach of warranty as a reason for not paying Harry's the full $2,750 because Harry's is not a holder in due course. However, if Harry's negotiated the note to First National Bank and the bank was a holder in due course, the situation would be changed. If the bank tried to collect the $2,750 from Tucker, Tucker would have to pay the bank. Tucker's defense or claim of breach of warranty cannot be used as a reason for not paying a holder in due course. It is a personal defense and cannot be used against the bank, which qualifies as a holder in due course. Tucker must pay the bank the $2,750 and then pursue his breach of warranty claim against Honest Harry's.

The rule that a holder in due course takes a negotiable instrument free of any personal defenses or claims to it has been modified to some extent, particularly in relation to instruments given by consumers. We discuss these modifications in the next section of this chapter.

Real Defenses

Some claims and defenses to the payment of an instrument go to the *validity* of the instrument. These claims and defenses are known as **real,** or universal, **defenses.** They can be used as reasons against payment of a negotiable instrument to any holder, including a holder in due course (or a person who has the rights of a holder in due course) [3–305(2)]. Real defenses include:

1. Minority or infancy that under state law makes the instrument void or voidable. For example, if Mark Miller, age 17, signs a promissory note as maker, he can use his lack of capacity to contract as a defense against paying it even to a holder in due course.

2. Incapacity that under state law makes the instrument void. For example, if a person has been declared mentally incompetent by a court, then the person has a real defense if state law declares all contracts entered into by the person after the adjudication of incompetency to be void.

3. Duress that voids or nullifies the obligation of a party liable to pay the instrument. For example, if Carl

Hammond points a gun at his grandmother and forces her to execute a promissory note, the grandmother can use duress as a defense against paying it even to a holder in due course.

4. Illegality that under state law renders the obligation void. For example, in some states, checks and notes given in payment of gambling debts are void.

5. Fraud in the essence (or fraud in the factum). This occurs where a person signs a negotiable instrument without knowing or having a reasonable chance to realize that it is a negotiable instrument. For example, Amy Jones is an illiterate person who lives alone. She signs a document that is actually a promissory note, but she is told that it is a grant of permission for a television set to be left in her house on a trial basis. Jones has a real defense against payment on the note. She does not have to pay the note to even a holder in due course. Fraud in the essence is distinguished from fraud in the inducement, discussed earlier, which is only a personal defense.

6. Discharge of the party liable in bankruptcy proceedings. For example, if the maker of a promissory note had the debt discharged in a bankruptcy proceeding, she

is no longer liable on it and has a real defense against payment.

7. Forgery. For example, if a maker's signature has been put on the instrument without his authorization, the maker has a real defense against payment of the note.

8. Material alteration of a completed instrument. This is a complete defense against a nonholder in due course and a partial defense against a holder in due course. For example, a holder in due course can enforce a materially altered instrument against the maker or drawer according to its original tenor.

Real defenses can be asserted even against a holder in due course of a negotiable instrument, because it is more desirable to protect people who have *signed* negotiable instruments in these situations than it is to protect persons who have *taken* negotiable instruments in the ordinary course of business.

The case that follows, *Standard Finance Co., Ltd. v. Ellis*, illustrates the distinction between fraud in the inducement (a personal defense) and fraud in the essence (a real defense) and discusses the real defense of duress and the personal defense of failure of consideration.

STANDARD FINANCE CO., LTD. v. ELLIS

657 P.2d 1056 (Hawaii Ct. App. 1983)

On September 30, 1976, Betty Ellis and her then husband, W. G. Ellis, executed and delivered a promissory note for $2,800 payable to Standard Finance Company. Nothing was paid on the note, and on May 15, 1980, Standard Finance brought a collection action against Betty Ellis, who was divorced from W. G. The trial court awarded a judgment of $5,413.35 against Ellis. She appealed, claiming that she had defenses against payment of misrepresentation, duress, and failure of consideration.

Tanaka, Justice.   Betty Ellis indicates that "shortly before" W. G. Ellis executed the note, he gave her "constant assurance" that her "signature was a formality and that he alone was liable and that the debt would be repaid without any participation by her." Thereafter, Betty Ellis accompanied W. G. Ellis to Standard Finance's office and executed the note. Betty Ellis argues that W. G. Ellis's misrepresentation induced her to sign the note and since such misrepresentation dealt with its essential terms, her execution of the note was not a manifestation of her assent. Consequently, the note was void *ab initio* and unenforceable as to her.

The principles of law as to when misrepresentation prevents the formation of a contract and when it makes a contract voidable are set forth in *Restatement (Second) of Contracts*. Section 163 states:

§ 163. When a Misrepresentation Prevents Formation of a Contract.

If a misrepresentation as to the character or essential terms of a proposed contract induces conduct that appears to be a manifestation of assent by one who neither knows nor has reasonable opportunity to know of the character or essential terms of the proposed contract, his conduct is not effective as a manifestation of assent.

Comment a to § 163 provides in part as follows:

This Section involves an application of that principle where a misrepresentation goes to what is sometimes called the "factum" or the "execution" rather than merely the "inducement." If, because of a misrepresentation as to the character or essential terms of a proposed contract, a party does not know or have reasonable opportunity to know of its character or essential terms, then he neither knows nor has reason to know that the other party may infer from his conduct that he assents to that contract. In such a case there is no effective manifestation of assent and no contract at all.

Based on the facts in the record, we hold as a matter of law that the misrepresentation by W. G. Ellis was not a "fraud in the factum" or a "fraud in the execution" to render the note void at its inception.

A common illustration of "fraud in the factum" is that of the "maker who is tricked into signing a note in the belief that it is merely a receipt or some other document."

In the instant case, no representation was made to Betty Ellis that the note was anything other than a note. In fact, as indicated above, it is uncontradicted that Standard Finance's representative explained the "terms and conditions of the note" to Betty and W. G. Ellis prior to their execution of the note. Comment 7 to § 3–305 further states that the defense of "fraud in the factum" is that of "excusable ignorance of the contents of the writing signed" and the party claiming such fraud "must also have had no reasonable opportunity to obtain knowledge." *Page v. Krekey* and *First National Bank of Odessa v. Fazzari*, both cited by Betty Ellis, are examples in this category of "fraud in the factum." In *Page*, an intoxicated, illiterate defendant, who could not read or write, was induced to sign a guaranty on a false representation that it was an application for a license. In *Fazzari*, a defendant who was unable to read or write English was induced to sign a note upon the misrepresentation that it was a statement of wages earned.

The record in this case fails to show any fact constituting "excusable ignorance" of the contents of the paper signed or "no reasonable opportunity to obtain knowledge" on the part of Betty Ellis.

In her answers to interrogatories, Betty Ellis states that she was "forced" to sign the note under duress. "Physical beatings" and "psychological pressure" on her by Ellis for at least three years prior to signing the note constituted the duress. She argues that her execution of the note which was compelled by duress was not a manifestation of her assent. Thus, the note is void and unenforceable.

The law concerning duress resulting in void or voidable contracts is discussed in *Restatement (Second) of Contracts*. Section 174 reads:

§ 174. When Duress by Physical Compulsion Prevents Formation of a Contract.

If conduct that appears to be a manifestation of assent by a party who does not intend to engage in that conduct is physically compelled by duress, the conduct is not effective as a manifestation of assent.

Comment a to § 174 provides in part:

This Section involves an application of that principle to those relatively rare situations in which actual physical force has been used to compel a party to appear to assent to a contract. . . . The essence of this type of duress is that a party is compelled by physical force to do an act that he has no intention of doing.

We hold that as a matter of law the facts in the record do not constitute the type of duress which renders the note void under § 174. Such duress involves the use of actual physical force to compel a person to sign a document. It may include the example given in Comment 6 to § 3–305 of an "instrument signed at the point of a gun" being void.

Here, the only evidence of duress is "physical beatings" and "psychological pressure" by W. G. Ellis on Betty Ellis over a course of three years prior to her signing of the note. Without more, such evidence does not constitute duress resulting in the voiding of the note. From such evidence it cannot reasonably be inferred that the physical beatings by W. G. Ellis directly resulted in Betty Ellis signing the note in question.

Finally, Betty Ellis claims that the entire amount of the loan of $2,800 went to Ellis and she received no part of it. Thus, there was lack or failure of consideration and summary judgment was improper. We cannot agree.

Standard Finance's check for $2,800 was made payable to "W. G. Ellis and Betty Ellis." The reverse side of the check bears the indorsement of "Betty Ellis." This was sufficient evidence of consideration for the transaction involved.

However, Betty Ellis states that she "never got the money or the use of it" and "it all went to my ex-husband and this was understood by Standard Finance." This fact does not constitute lack or failure of consideration. It is fundamental that consideration received by a co-maker on a note from the payee is sufficient consideration to bind the other co-maker.

Judgment for Standard Finance affirmed.

Persons Not Holders in Due Course

As you have learned, negotiable commercial paper is basically a contract to pay money. If the holder of such paper is not a holder in due course, his rights are no greater than the rights of any promisee or assignee of a simple contract. Such a holder takes the paper subject to all valid claims on the part of any person and subject to all defenses of any party that would be available in an action on a simple contract [3–306].

CONCEPT REVIEW

DEFENSES AGAINST PAYMENT OF NEGOTIABLE INSTRUMENTS

Type of Defense	Examples
Personal (or Limited) Defense Valid against plain holders of instruments—but not against holders in due course or holders who have the rights of in due course holders through the shelter rule.	1. Lack or failure of consideration. 2. Breach of contract (including breach of warranty). 3. Fraud in the inducement. 4. Lack of capacity that makes the contract voidable (except minority). 5. Illegality that makes the contract voidable. 6. Duress that makes the contract voidable. 7. Unauthorized completion of an incomplete instrument, or material alteration of the instrument. 8. Nondelivery of the instrument.

Type of Defense	Examples
Real (or Universal) Defense Valid against all holders, including holders in due course and holders who have the rights of a holder in due course.	1. Minority that under state law makes the contract void or voidable. 2. Other lack of capacity that makes the contract void. 3. Duress that makes the contract void. 4. Illegality that makes the contract void. 5. Fraud in the essence (fraud in the factum). 6. Discharge in bankruptcy. 7. Forgery of the instrument. 8. Material alteration (partial defense).

CHANGES IN THE HOLDER IN DUE COURSE RULE

Consumer Disadvantages

The rule that a holder in due course of a negotiable instrument is not subject to personal defenses between the original parties to it makes negotiable instruments a readily accepted substitute for money. This rule can also result in serious disadvantages to consumers. Consumers sometimes buy goods or services on credit and give the seller a negotiable instrument such as a promissory note. They often do this without knowing the consequences of signing a negotiable instrument. If the goods or services are defective or not delivered, the consumer would like to withhold payment of the note until the seller corrects the problem or makes the delivery. Where the note is still held by the seller, the consumer can do this, because any defenses of breach of warranty or nonperformance are good against the seller.

However, the seller may have negotiated the note at a discount to a third party such as a bank. If the bank qualifies as a holder in due course, the consumer must pay the note in full to the bank. The consumer's personal defenses are not valid against a holder in due course. The consumer must pay the holder in due course and then try to get her money back from the seller. This may be difficult if the seller cannot be found or does not accept responsibility. The consumer would be in a much stronger position if she could just withhold payment, even against the bank, until the goods or services are delivered or the performance is corrected.

State Legislation

Some state legislatures and state courts have limited the holder in due course doctrine, particularly as it relates to consumers. In 1968, the National Conference of Commissioners on Uniform State Laws promulgated a Uniform Consumer Credit Code, and various consumer organizations have developed model consumer acts. The Uniform Consumer Credit Code, which has been adopted by a relatively small number of states, virtually eliminates negotiable paper in consumer credit sales by prohibiting the seller from taking a negotiable instrument other than a check as evidence of the obligation of the buyer. Some states now require that instruments evidencing consumer indebtedness must carry the legend "consumer paper" and must state that instruments carrying the legend are not negotiable. Other states have enacted comprehensive measures that effectively abolish the holder in due course doctrine. The law at the state level is far from uniform, and the position of a consumer who has signed a negotiable instrument varies from state to state. The trend, though, is clearly toward limiting the holder in due course doctrine as it adversely affects consumers in consumer transactions.

Federal Trade Commission Rules

The Federal Trade Commission (FTC) has promulgated a regulation designed to protect consumers against the operation of the holder in due course rule. The FTC rule applies to persons who sell to, or who finance sales to, consumers on credit and have consumers sign notes or installment sales contracts. The rule makes it an unfair trade practice for a seller, in the course of financing a consumer purchase of goods or services, to employ procedures that make the consumer's duty to pay independent of the seller's duty to fulfill his obligations.

The FTC regulation provides protection to the consumer in those situations where: (1) the buyer executes a sales contract that includes a promissory note; (2) the buyer signs an installment sales contract that includes a "waiver of defenses" clause; or (3) the seller arranges with a third-party lender for a direct loan to finance the buyer's purchase.

The FTC regulation deals with the first two situations by requiring that the following clause be included in bold type in any consumer credit contract to be signed by the consumer:

NOTICE: ANY HOLDER OF THIS CONSUMER CREDIT CONTRACT IS SUBJECT TO ALL CLAIMS AND DEFENSES WHICH THE DEBTOR COULD ASSERT AGAINST THE SELLER OF THE GOODS OR SERVICES OBTAINED PURSUANT HERETO OR WITH THE PROCEEDS HEREOF. RECOVERY HEREUNDER BY THE DEBTOR SHALL NOT EXCEED AMOUNTS PAID BY THE DEBTOR HEREUNDER.

Where the seller arranges for a direct loan to be made to finance a customer's purchase, the seller may not accept the proceeds of the loan unless the consumer credit contract between the buyer and the lender contains the following clause in bold type:

NOTICE: ANY HOLDER OF THIS CONSUMER CREDIT CONTRACT IS SUBJECT TO ALL CLAIMS AND DEFENSES WHICH THE DEBTOR COULD ASSERT AGAINST THE SELLER OF GOODS OR SERVICES OBTAINED WITH THE PROCEEDS HEREOF. RECOVERY HEREUNDER BY THE DEBTOR SHALL NOT EXCEED AMOUNTS PAID BY THE DEBTOR HEREUNDER.

The effect of the clause is to make a potential holder of the note or contract subject to all claims and defenses of the consumer. If the clause is not put in a note or contract where it is required, the consumer does not gain any rights that he would not otherwise have under state law. Thus, if the clause is omitted from the note or contract, the subsequent holder might qualify as a holder in due course. However, the FTC does have the right to seek a fine of as much as $10,000 for each violation against the seller, that is, each note or contract that fails to contain the required clause. The following *de la Fuente* case illustrates a situation where the clause required by the FTC was included in a note and served to preserve the makers' rights against a subsequent holder of the note.

The court decisions, new state laws, and the FTC regulations modifying the holder in due course doctrine are an effort to balance the societal interests (1) in protecting the consumer and (2) in assuring the availability of credit along with the marketability of commercial paper.

DE LA FUENTE v. HOME SAVINGS ASSOCIATION

38 UCC Rep. 196 (Tex. Ct. App. 1984)

Pedro and Paula de la Fuente were visited by a representative of Aluminum Industries, Inc., who was seeking to sell them aluminum siding for their home. They agreed to purchase the siding and signed a number of documents, including a retail installment contract and a promissory note for $9,138.24. The contract granted Aluminum Industries, Inc., a first lien on the de la Fuentes's residence; this was in violation of the Texas Civil Code, which prohibited such provisions. The promissory note contained a notice in bold type as required by the Federal Trade Commission. It read in part:

NOTICE: ANY HOLDER OF THIS CONSUMER CREDIT CONTRACT IS SUBJECT TO ALL CLAIMS AND DEFENSES WHICH THE DEBTOR COULD ASSERT AGAINST THE SELLER OF GOODS OR SERVICES OBTAINED PURSUANT HERETO OR WITH THE PROCEEDS THEREOF.

Aluminum Industries assigned the promissory note and first lien to Home Savings Association. Aluminum Industries subsequently went out of business. Home Savings brought suit against the de la Fuentes to collect the balance due on the note. The trial court held that Home Savings was a holder in due course and that the de la Fuentes could not assert any defenses against it that they had against Aluminum Industries. They appealed.

Kennedy, Judge.   We disagree that Home Savings was entitled to the protection of a holder in due course of a negotiable instrument because the holder in due course doctrine has been abolished in consumer credit transactions by FTC regulations, and this FTC Rule, subjecting the holder of the notice to the claims and defenses of the debtor, is in direct conflict with the doctrine of the holder in due course. The federal courts have stated, without so holding, that the effect of this FTC Rule is to abolish the holder in due course doctrine in consumer transactions.

The FTC, in its Statement of Basis and Purpose, specifically named the holder in due course doctrine as the evil addressed by its Holder in Due Course Rule. "A consumer's duty to pay for goods and services must not be separated from a seller's duty to perform as promised." The FTC intended the Rule to compel creditors to either absorb the costs of the seller misconduct or return the contracts to the sellers. The FTC "reached a determination that it constitutes an unfair and deceptive practice to use contractual boiler plate to separate a buyer's duty to pay from a seller's duty to perform." The effect of this Rule is to "give the courts the authority to examine the equities in an underlying sale, and it will prevent sellers from foreclosing judicial review of their conduct. Sellers and creditors will be responsible for seller misconduct." It was clearly the intention of the FTC Rule to have the holder of the paper bear the losses occasioned by the actions of the seller; therefore, the benefits of the holder in due course doctrine under § 3–302 are not available when the notice required by the FTC is placed on a consumer credit contract.

Judgment reversed in favor of the de la Fuentes.

ETHICAL AND PUBLIC POLICY CONCERNS

1. Suppose you have taken a promissory note from a customer in payment of some repair work you did on her house. You have some reason to believe that she is not pleased with the quality of the work you performed. Would it be ethical for you to try to sell the promissory note to a third person in order to make it more difficult for your customer to assert a claim of failure of consideration or breach of warranty against you? If you did try to sell the note, what ethical considerations are involved as to whether you should advise a prospective purchaser of the potential defenses against payment of the note even if you are not asked about them?

2. If you are in the business of buying commercial paper—such as consumer notes—from businesses such as home improvement companies, how much of an ethical obligation, if any, do you have to look into the sales practices and performance records of the companies to whom the consumers have made the notes payable? For example, would you have a concern about buying notes

from a home improvement company that has a record of using high-pressure sales tactics and having shoddy workmanship?

3. Suppose you have given a check in payment of a gambling debt in a state that makes such obligations void. Are there any ethical considerations involved as to whether you should assert the real defense of illegality against payment of the check to a holder in due course?

SUMMARY

Negotiation is the transfer of an instrument in such a way that the person who receives it becomes a holder. A holder is a person who is in possession of an instrument that was issued to him, that has been indorsed to him or to his order, or that is payable to bearer. An instrument payable to a specific payee is called *order paper*; it can be negotiated by delivery after indorsement by the payee. An instrument payable to bearer or to cash is called *bearer paper*; it can be negotiated simply by delivering it to the person to whom its possessor wishes to transfer it.

The holder of an instrument makes an indorsement by signing his name on the instrument or on a paper firmly affixed to it. When an instrument is transferred, the transferee acquires all of the rights that his transferor had in the instrument. The transferee for value of an unindorsed order instrument has the right, unless otherwise agreed, to have the unqualified indorsement of his transferor.

The four basic indorsements are (1) special, (2) blank, (3) restrictive, and (4) qualified. The first three have an effect on the negotiation of the instrument; the last affects the liability of the indorser who qualifies her indorsement.

To qualify as a holder in due course, the holder must take the instrument for value, in good faith, and without notice that it is overdue or has been dishonored or of any defense against or claim to it on the part of any other person. A payee may be a holder in due course. One who purchases a limited interest in an instrument can be a holder in due course only to the extent of the interest purchased.

A holder in due course of negotiable commercial paper takes free from the personal defenses existing between the parties but takes subject to the real defenses that generally go to the validity of the instrument. These include: minority and other incapacities available as a defense to a simple contract; duress or illegality of the transaction, which renders the obligation a nullity; fraud in the essence; and discharge in bankruptcy proceedings. A holder who is not a holder in due course takes negotiable commercial paper subject to all of the defenses that would be available to a promisor on a simple contract to pay money.

The holder in due course doctrine as it relates to negotiable instruments signed by consumers has been abolished or modified by new state laws and court decisions. In addition, a regulation promulgated by the Federal Trade Commission renders the doctrine inapplicable in certain consumer credit transactions.

PROBLEM CASES

1. Stone & Webster drew three checks in the total amount of $64,755.44 payable to the order of Westinghouse Electric Corporation. An employee of Stone & Webster obtained possession of the checks, forged West-

inghouse's indorsement to them, and cashed them at the First National Bank & Trust Company, and put the proceeds to his own use. The first two checks were indorsed in typewriting, "For Deposit Only: Westinghouse Electric Corporation By: Mr. O. D. Costine, Treasury Representative," followed by the ink signature "O. D. Costine." The third check was indorsed in typewriting, "Westinghouse Electric Corporation by: [Sgd.] O. D. Costine, Treasury Representative." Were the checks negotiated to the bank?

2. Louis Agaliotis took out a policy of insurance on his son, Robert. Louis paid all of the premiums on the policy, and under the terms of the policy he was entitled to any refunds on the premiums. The insurance company sent a refund check for $1,852 to Louis. By mistake, the check was made payable to "Robert L. Agaliotis." Louis indorsed the check "Robert L. Agaliotis" and cashed it. Robert then sued Louis to get the $1,852. Was Louis entitled to sign his son's name to the check and to keep the money when he cashed it?

3. A bank cashed the checks of its customer, Dental Supply, Inc., when they were presented to the bank by an employee of Dental Supply named Wilson. The checks were indorsed in blank with a rubber stamp of Dental Supply. Wilson had been stealing the checks by taking cash rather than depositing them to Dental Supply's account. What could Dental Supply have done to avoid this situation?

4. Raye Walker was a bookkeeper for O.K. Moving & Storage Company. She opened a checking account in her name at Elgin National Bank. She then took checks that were made payable to O.K. Moving & Storage, indorsed them "For Deposit Only, O.K. Moving & Storage Co., 80 Carson Drive, N.E., Fort Walton, Florida," and deposited them in her individual account at Elgin National Bank. In a period of one year, she deposited, and Elgin Bank accepted for deposit to her account, checks totaling $19,356.01. When O.K. Moving & Storage discovered this, it sued Elgin Bank for $19,356.01 for conversion of its checks. Should Elgin Bank have permitted the checks restrictively indorsed "For Deposit Only" to a corporation's account to be deposited to an individual account?

5. Reggie Bluiett worked at the Silver Slipper Gambling Hall and Saloon. She received her weekly paycheck made out to her from the Silver Slipper. She indorsed the check in blank and left it on her dresser at home. Fred Watkins broke into Bluiett's house and stole the check. Watkins took the check to the local auto store, where he bought two tires at a cost of $71.21. He obtained the balance of the check in cash. Could the auto store qualify as a holder in due course?

6. Horton wrote a check for $20,000 to Axe who in turn indorsed it to Halbert. In return, Halbert advanced $8,000 in cash to Axe and promised to cancel a $12,000 debt owed him by Axe. The check, when presented by Halbert to the bank, was not paid due to insufficient funds. Halbert thus never regarded the debt as canceled. To what extent can Halbert be a holder in due course of the check?

7. Kamensky gave a note for $19,000 to his brother. The sum of $1,000 was payable on February 15, 1985, and a like amount was payable on the 15th day of each month for the next 19 months. On January 17, 1987, after the note was past due, Kamensky's brother indorsed it over to Srochi, who knew it was past due. Srochi brought an action on the note for payment, and Kamensky sought to interpose personal defenses. Can they be asserted against Srochi?

8. Two smooth-talking salesmen for Rich Plan of New Orleans called on Leona and George Henne at their home. They sold the Hennes a home food plan. One of the salesmen suggested that the Hennes sign a blank promissory note. The Hennes refused. The salesman then wrote in ink "$100" as the amount and "4" as the number of installments in which the note was to be paid, and the Hennes signed the note. Several days later, the Hennes received a payment book from Nationwide Acceptance. The payment book showed that a total of $843.38 was due, payable in 36 monthly installments. Rich Plan had erased the "$100" and "4" on the note and typed in the figures "$843.38" and "36." The erasures were cleverly done but were visible to the naked eye. Rich Plan then negotiated the Hennes's note to Nationwide Acceptance. The Hennes refused to pay the note. Nationwide claimed that it was a holder in due course and was entitled to receive payment. Was Nationwide Acceptance a holder in due course?

9. Factor Cab Corporation issued a series of notes payable "to the order of Donald E. Richel as attorney for Francisco Silvestry." Twenty-one of the notes were indorsed by Richel and sold to Maber, Inc. In purchasing the notes, Maber made its check payable to Richel in his individual name, without qualification or restriction, in the amount of $5,796.24. In addition, it discharged by payment Richel's personal indebtedness to a bank in the amount of $3,903.75. Richel indorsed the notes as an individual and not in his fiduciary capacity. Can Maber be a holder in due course of the notes?

10. Panlick, the owner of an apartment building, entered into a written contract with Bucci, a paving contractor, whereby Bucci was to install asphalt paving on the parking lot of the building. When Bucci finished the job, Panlick gave Bucci a check for $6,500 and a promissory note for $7,593 with interest at 10 percent due six months from its date. When the note came due, Panlick refused to pay it. Bucci brought suit to collect the note, and Panlick claimed there had been a failure of consideration because the asphalt was defectively installed. Can Panlick assert this defense against Bucci?

11. Ralph Herrmann wrote a check for $10,000 payable to Ormsby House, a hotel-casino in Carson City, Nevada, and exchanged it for three counter checks he had written earlier that evening to acquire gaming chips. Ormsby House was unable to collect the proceeds from the check because Herrmann had insufficient funds in his account. The debt evidenced by the check was assigned to Sea Air Support, Inc., d/b/a Automated Accounts Associates, for collection. Sea Air was also unsuccessful in its attempts to collect and filed a lawsuit against Herrmann to recover on the dishonored check. Nevada law provides that all instruments drawn for the purpose of reimbursing or repaying any money knowingly lent or advanced for gaming are "utterly void, frustrate, and of none effect." Is Herrmann liable to Sea Air to make good the check?

12. Nickerson signed a promissory note marked "consumer note" to cover the cost of having his house covered with aluminum siding. The note was negotiated to a finance company, which claimed to be a holder in due course of the note. When the finance company tried to collect the note from Nickerson, he tried to defend against payment on the grounds that the aluminum siding was defective. A Massachussetts statute requires any note for the retail sale of consumer goods to be labeled "consumer note" and makes it nonnegotiable. Can Nickerson use the defense of breach of warranty against the finance company even if it is a holder in due course? *Yes*

CHAPTER 25

LIABILITY OF PARTIES

INTRODUCTION

Thus far in this Commercial Paper section, the focus has been on the nature of, and requirements for, negotiable instruments as well as the rights that a party to an instrument can obtain and how to obtain them. There is another important aspect to negotiable instruments; namely, how a person becomes liable on a negotiable instrument and the nature of the liability incurred.

When a person signs a promissory note, he expects to be liable for paying the note on the day it is due. Similarly, when a person signs a check and mails it off to pay a bill, he expects that it will be paid by the drawee bank out of his checking account and that if there are not sufficient funds in his account to cover it, he will have to make it good out of other funds he has. The liability of the maker of a note and of the drawer of a check is commonly understood.

However, a person can become liable on a negotiable instrument in other ways. A person who indorses a paycheck is assuming liability on it; and a bank that cashes a check with a forged indorsement on it is liable for conversion of the check. This chapter and the following chapter discuss the liabilities of the various parties to a negotiable instrument. These two chapters also cover what happens when an instrument is not paid when it is supposed to be paid. For example, a check may not be paid if there are insufficient funds in the drawer's

account or if the check has been forged. In addition, this chapter discusses the ways in which liability on an instrument can be discharged.

LIABILITY IN GENERAL

Liability may be based on the fact that a person has signed a negotiable instrument or has authorized someone else to sign it. In that case, the liability depends on the capacity in which the person has signed the instrument. Liability can also be based on (1) certain warranties that are made when an instrument is transferred or presented for payment, (2) negligence, (3) improper payment, or (4) conversion.

CONTRACTUAL LIABILITY

When a person signs a negotiable instrument, whether as maker, drawer, or indorser, or in some other capacity, he generally becomes *contractually liable* on the instrument. This contractual liability depends on the *capacity* in which the person signed the instrument. The terms of the contract of the parties to a negotiable instrument are not written out on the instrument; these terms are supplied by Article 3 of the Uniform Commercial Code, which deals with Commercial Paper. The terms of the contract are provided by law and are as much a part of the instrument as if they were written on it.

Primary and Secondary Liability

A party to a negotiable instrument may be either *primarily liable* or *secondarily liable* for payment of it. A person who is primarily liable has agreed to pay the negotiable instrument. For example, the maker of a promissory note is the person who is primarily liable on the note. A person who is secondarily liable is like a guarantor on a contract and is required to pay the negotiable instrument only if a person who is primarily liable defaults on that obligation. The Introduction to Credit and Secured Transactions chapter discusses guarantors.

Contract of a Maker

The maker of a promissory note is primarily liable for payment of it. The maker has made an unconditional promise to pay a sum certain and is responsible for making good on that promise. The *contract of the maker* is to *pay the negotiable instrument according to its terms at the time he signs it* [3–143].[1] If the material terms of the note are not complete when the maker signs it, then the maker's contract is that he will pay the note as it is completed, provided that the terms filled in are as authorized.

Contract of a Drawee

At the time a check or other draft is written, *no party is primarily liable on it*. Usually, a check is paid by the drawee bank when it is presented for payment and no

---

[1]The numbers in brackets refer to the sections of the Uniform Commercial Code.

person becomes primarily liable. However, the drawee bank may be asked by the drawer or by a holder of the check to **certify** the check. The drawee bank certifies the check by signing its name to the check and thereby accepting liability as drawee. The drawee bank debits, or takes the money out of, the drawer's account and holds the money to pay the check. If the drawee bank certifies the check, it becomes primarily, or absolutely, liable for paying the check as it reads at the time it is certified [3–413].

A drawee has no liability on a check or other draft unless it certifies or accepts the check; that is, agrees to be liable on it. However, a drawee bank that refuses to pay a check when it is presented for payment may be liable to the drawer for wrongfully refusing payment, if the drawer had sufficient funds in his checking account to cover it. The next chapter discusses this liability of a drawee bank.

Contract of a Drawer

The *drawer's contract* is that *if the check (or draft) is dishonored* and *if the drawer is given notice of the dishonor, he will pay the amount of the check (or draft) to the holder or to any indorser who takes it back* [3–413(2)]. For example, Janis draws a check on her account at First National Bank payable to the order of Collbert. If First National does not pay the check when Collbert presents it for payment, then Janis is liable to Collbert on the basis of her drawer's contractual liability.

Because a drawer's liability on a draft or check is secondary, she may *disclaim* this liability by drawing it *without recourse* [3–413(2)].

The case that follows, *First American Bank of Virginia v. Litchfield Company of South Carolina, Inc.*, illustrates circumstances under which a drawer might be held liable on its drawer's contractual liability.

FIRST AMERICAN BANK OF VIRGINIA v. LITCHFIELD COMPANY OF SOUTH CAROLINA, INC.
353 S.E.2d 143 (S.C. Ct. App. 1987)

On February 9, 1983, Litchfield Company drew a check payable to Jensen Farley Pictures, Inc., in the amount of $13,711.11, on its account with Bankers Trust of South Carolina. Litchfield sent the check to Jensen Farley, which negotiated the check on September 16 to First American Bank of Virginia with whom it had a checking account. First American gave Jensen Farley immediate credit on the check and forwarded it to Bankers Trust for payment. Unknown to First American, Litchfield had given Bankers Trust an oral stop payment order on the check. On September 19, Jensen Farley withdrew most of the balance in its First American account; it subsequently filed for bankruptcy. On September 21, Bankers Trust returned the Litchfield check to First American marked "payment stopped." First American then brought suit against Litchfield claiming that as drawer of the check, it was liable to First American, a holder in due course of the check. The trial court awarded First American Bank judgment for $9,369.37 (representing the amount it had been unable to recover from Jensen Farley), and Litchfield appealed.

Bell, Judge.   The drawer of a check engages that upon dishonor he will pay the amount of the draft to a holder in due course. Section 3–413(2). The drawer has the right to stop payment, but remains liable on the instrument to a holder in due course. Section 4–403 and comment 8; section 3–413(2). Since Litchfield has conceded First American was a holder in due course, Litchfield remains liable on the instrument unless it can establish a valid defense or set off.

Litchfield argues that its liability was discharged by First American's failure to give timely notice the check had been dishonored. This defense is unavailing for two reasons.

First, failure to give notice of dishonor discharges a drawer only to the extent he is deprived of funds maintained with the drawee bank to cover the check because the drawee bank became insolvent during the delay. Sections 3–501(2)(b) and 3–502(1)(b). A drawer is not otherwise discharged. In this case, Litchfield was not deprived of any funds in its account with Bankers Trust nor did Bankers Trust become insolvent during the delay.

Second, notice of dishonor is excused when the party to be charged has himself countermanded payment. Section 3–511(2)(b). Since Litchfield ordered payment stopped, it was not entitled to notice of dishonor.

Litchfield argues strenuously that it is unfair to apply section 3–511(2)(b) to the drawer of a check who has no means of knowing whether the check has been negotiated to a holder. This reasoning misses the mark. The maker of an outstanding negotiable instrument is presumed to know the instrument is subject to transfer to a holder in due course. The drawer is often without actual knowledge that his check has been negotiated, but that ignorance in no way diminishes the rights of a holder in due course. To hold otherwise would, as a practical matter, destroy the negotiability of a check.

Judgment for First American affirmed.

Contract of an Indorser

A person who indorses a negotiable instrument is usually secondarily liable. Unless the indorsement is qualified, the *indorser agrees* that *if the instrument is not paid when presented for payment, then the indorser will make it good to the holder or to any later indorser who had to pay it* [3–414]. The indorser can avoid this liability only by putting a qualified indorsement, such as "without recourse," on the instrument when he indorses it.

Indorsers are liable to each other in the chronological order in which they indorse, from the last indorser back to the first. For example, Mark Maker gives a promissory note to Paul Payee. Payee indorses it and negotiates it to Fred First, who indorses it and negotiates it to Shirley Second. If Maker does not pay the note when Second takes it to him for payment, then Second can require First to pay it to her. First is secondarily liable on the basis of his indorsement. First, in turn, can require Payee to pay him because Payee also became secondarily liable when he indorsed it. Then, Payee is left to try to collect the note from Maker. Second also could have skipped over First and gone directly against Payee on his indorsement. First has no liability to Payee, however, because First indorsed after Payee indorsed the note.

Contract of an Accommodation Party

An **accommodation party** is a person who signs a negotiable instrument for the purpose of lending his credit to another party to the instrument. For example, a bank might be reluctant to lend money to and take a note from Payee because of his shaky financial condition. However, the bank may be willing to lend money to Payee if he signs the note and has a relative or a friend also sign the note as an accommodation maker.

The contractual liability of an accommodation party depends on the capacity in which the party signs the instrument [3–415]. If Payee has his brother Sam sign a note as an accommodation maker, then Sam has the same contractual liability as a maker. Sam is primarily liable on the note. The bank may ask Sam to pay the note before asking Payee to pay. However, if Sam pays the note to the bank, he has the right to recover his payment from Payee—the person on whose behalf he signed.

Similarly, if a person signs a check as an accommodation indorser, his contractual liability is that of an indorser. If the accommodation indorser has to make good on that liability, he can collect in turn from the person on whose behalf he signed.

Signing an Instrument

No person is contractually liable on a negotiable instrument unless his authorized signature appears on the instrument. A **signature** can be any name, word, or mark used in place of a written signature [3–401]. A negotiable instrument can be signed either by a person or by an authorized agent. As discussed earlier, the capacity in which a person signs an instrument affects his liability on the instrument.

In determining the capacity in which a person has signed a negotiable instrument, the position of the signature is important. If a person signs a check in the lower right corner, the presumption is that he signed it as the drawer. If a person signs a promissory note in the lower right corner, the presumption is that she signed it as the maker. If the drawee named in a draft signs across the face of the instrument, it is a clear indication that he has accepted the draft; however, his signature on any part of the instrument, front or back, will be held to be an acceptance in the absence of credible evidence of an intent to sign in some other capacity. A signature on the back of an instrument is presumed to be an indorsement [3–402].

Signature by an Authorized Agent

A negotiable instrument can be signed by an authorized agent [3–403(1)]. If Sandra Smith authorized her attorney to sign checks as her agent, then she is liable on any checks properly signed by the attorney as her agent. All negotiable instruments signed by corporations have to be signed by an agent of the corporation who is authorized to sign negotiable instruments.

If an agent or a representative signs a negotiable instrument on behalf of someone else, the agent should clearly indicate that he is signing as the representative of someone else. For example, Kim Darby, the president of Swimwear, Inc., is authorized to sign negotiable instruments for the company. If Swimwear borrows money from the bank and is given a 90-day promissory note to sign, Darby should sign it either "Swimwear, Inc. by Kim Darby, President" or "Kim Darby, President, for Swimwear, Inc." Similarly, if Arthur Anderson, an attorney, is authorized to sign checks for Clara Carson, he should sign them "Clara Carson by Arthur Anderson, Agent." Otherwise, he risks being personally liable on them.

The agents or representatives who sign negotiable instruments are *personally liable* if they do not indicate that they are signing in a representative capacity and if they do not state the name of the person on whose behalf they are signing [3–403(2)]. Thus, if Kim Darby signed the promissory note merely "Kim Darby," she would be personally liable on the note. To protect herself and to ensure that the corporation is liable, Darby should sign the name of the company and her title or office as well as her signature. In the *Schwartz v. Disneyland Vista Records* case, which follows, the president of a company was held personally liable on some notes he signed for the corporation because he failed to indicate that he was signing in a representative capacity.

SCHWARTZ v. DISNEYLAND VISTA RECORDS

383 So.2d 1117 (Fla. Ct. App. 1980)

American Music Industries, Inc., and Disneyland Vista Records had ongoing business dealings during 1975 and 1976. As of May 21, 1976, American owed Disneyland over $93,000. As evidence of that indebtedness, American issued 10 promissory notes, payable to Disneyland and signed by Irv Schwartz, the president of American Music. The notes contained no reference to American Music Industries, Inc., nor was there any indication that Schwartz signed in a representative capacity.

American paid four of the notes, then defaulted on the rest. Disneyland brought suit against Schwartz to recover on the remaining six promissory notes. Schwartz claimed that the notes had been prepared by Disneyland; that they did not correctly reflect the intent of the parties, because they did not name American as the maker; and that he signed the notes individually by mistake. The trial court ruled in favor of Disneyland, and Schwartz appealed.

Downey, Judge.   Summary judgment against Schwartz was proper because his claim is controlled by § 3–403(2):

(2) An authorized representative who signs his own name to an instrument:
(a) Is personally obligated if the instrument neither names the person represented nor shows that the representative signed in a representative capacity;
(b) Except as otherwise established between the immediate parties, is personally obligated if the instrument names the person represented but does not show that the representative signed in a representative capacity.

The notes in question are payable to Disneyland and signed by Irv Schwartz. There is no indication that they are obligations of the corporation, American Music Industries, Inc., or that Irv Schwartz signed them in a representative capacity. Thus, under Section (2)(a), above, Irv Schwartz is liable on these notes as a matter of law.

The main thrust of Schwartz's defense is that he should be allowed to use parol evidence to show the parties intended the notes to be corporate obligations and that Schwartz's signing individually was a mistake. However, the evidence is not admissible to "disestablish" obligations such as the notes here involved. Paraphrased, the example used in the comment indicates the results that various signatures have upon the individual liability of an agent. If American Music Industries, Inc., is a principal and Irv Schwartz is its agent, a note might bear the following signatures affixed by the agent:

(a) American Music Industries, Inc.;

(b) Irv Schwartz;

(c) American Music Industries, Inc., by Irv Schwartz, agent;

(d) Irv Schwartz, agent;

(e) American Music Industries, Inc., Irv Schwartz.

A signature in form (a) does not bind Irv Schwartz if authorized. A signature as in (b) personally obligates Irv Schwartz, and parol evidence is inadmissible under § 3–403(2)(a) to disestablish his obligation. The unambiguous way to make clear that Irv Schwartz is signing in his representative capacity without personal liability is to sign as in (c).

Judgment for Disneyland affirmed.

An authorized representative might sign a negotiable instrument in his own name in a way that clearly indicates he has signed in a representative capacity, but he might fail to name the person represented. In this case, *parol evidence* is admissible, between the immediate parties to the instrument, to prove that they intended the principal to be liable and not the party who signed in the representative capacity. For example, a negotiable instrument is signed "Axe, agent" and retained by the payee, who then sues Axe on the instrument. Parol evidence would be admitted in a lawsuit to prove that the payee knew that Axe was acting as agent for Parks, his principal, and that the parties intended Parks to be bound rather than Axe. If this instrument had been negotiated to a holder in due course, however, Axe would be personally liable on the instrument and would be unable to use parol evidence to disprove his liability [3–403(2)].

Some state courts, albeit a minority, have declined to hold corporate officers personally liable on corporate checks they signed without indicating they were signing in a representative capacity. Typically, these courts have found that because the checks in question were imprinted with the corporation's name, the circumstances disclosed that the individuals signed as representatives. In the following *Valley National Bank v. Cook* case, the court followed the minority rule.

If a negotiable instrument is signed in the name of an organization and the name of the organization is preceded or followed by the name and office of an authorized individual, the organization and not the officer who signed the instrument in a representative capacity is bound [3–403(3)].

VALLEY NATIONAL BANK v. COOK
36 UCC Rep. 578 (Ariz. Ct. App. 1983)

J. M. Cook, then treasurer of Arizona Auto Auction, signed three corporate checks totaling $9,795 payable to Central Motors Company, which deposited them in its corporate account at Valley National Bank. Cook did not indicate on the check that she was signing as a representative of Arizona Auto Auction. When Valley National Bank sent the checks to the drawee bank, payment was refused because a stop payment order had been put on them. Valley National Bank charged back the checks to the account of Central Motors, but it was unable to recover the money from Central Motors.

Valley National Bank then brought suit against Arizona Auto Auction and J. M. Cook. The trial court held that the bank was a holder in due course, that Arizona Auto Auction was liable to the bank, and that J. M. Cook was not personally liable on the checks. The bank appealed the portion of the decision in favor of Cook.

Corcoran, Presiding Judge. The issue raised in this appeal is whether an individual who signs a check without indicating her representative capacity is personally liable on the obligation evidenced by the check when the check has the name of the corporate principal printed on it. We adopt the minority rule and hold that the individual is not personally liable.

The question of whether Cook signed in her individual or representative capacity is governed by § 3–403 of the Uniform Commercial Code as adopted in this state. It provides:

A. A signature may be made by an agent or other representative, and his authority to make it may be established as in other cases of representation. No particular form of appointment is necessary to establish such authority.

B. An authorized representative who signs his own name to an instrument:

    1. Is personally obligated if the instrument neither names the person represented nor shows that the representative signed in a representative capacity;

    2. Except as otherwise established between the immediate parties, is personally obligated if the instrument names the person represented but does not show that the representative signed in a representative capacity, or if the instrument does not name the person represented but does show that the representative signed in a representative capacity.

C. Except as otherwise established, the name of an organization preceded or followed by the name and office of an authorized individual is a signature made in a representative capacity.

The Bank argues that this section conclusively establishes Cook's personal liability on the checks. We do not agree. Admittedly, the checks fail to specifically show the office held by Cook. However, we do not find that this fact conclusively establishes liability since § 3–403(B)(2) imposes personal liability on an agent who signs his or her own name to an instrument only "if the instrument does not show that the representative signed in a representative capacity." Thus, we must look to the entire instrument for evidence of the capacity of the signer.

The checks are boldly imprinted at the top "Arizona Auto Auction, Inc.," and also "Arizona Auto Auction, Inc." is imprinted above the signature line appearing at the lower right-hand corner. Under the imprinted name of Arizona Auto Auction appears the signature of Cook without any designation of office or capacity on each of the checks before us. Cook did not indorse the checks on the back. The record does not reflect that Cook made any personal guaranty of these checks or any other corporate obligation. The Superior Court of Pennsylvania was confronted with a similar situation in *Pollin v. Mindy Mfg. Co., Inc.* There the court denied recovery by a third-party indorsee against one who affixed his signature to a payroll check directly beneath the printed corporate name without indicating his representative capacity. In *Pollin* the checks were boldly imprinted at the top with the corporate name, address, and appropriate check number. The printed name of the drawee bank appeared in the lower left-hand corner of the instrument, and the corporate name was imprinted in the lower right-hand corner. Directly beneath the corporate name were two blank lines. The officer had signed the top line without any designation of office or capacity. Pointing out that the Code imposes liability on the individual only when the instrument controverts any showing of representative capacity, the court considered the instrument in its entirety. The court in *Pollin* held that disclosure on the face of the instrument that the checks were payable from a special payroll account of the corporation over which the officer had no control as an individual negated any contention that the officer intended to make the instrument his own order to pay money to the payee.

In this case the checks clearly show the name of the corporation in two places and the money was payable from the account of Arizona Auto Auction, Inc., over which Cook as an individual had no control. Considering the instruments as a whole, we conclude under these circumstances that they sufficiently disclose that Cook signed them in a representative and not an individual capacity.

Judgment for Cook affirmed.

Unauthorized Signature

If a person's name is signed to a negotiable instrument without that person's authorization or approval, the person is not bound by the signature. For example, if Tom Thorne steals Ben Brown's checkbook and signs Brown's name to a check, Brown is not liable on the check because Thorne was not authorized to sign Brown's name. Thorne is liable on the check, however, because he did sign it, even though he did not sign it in his own name. Thorne's forgery of Brown's signature operates as Thorne's signature [3–404].

CONTRACTUAL LIABILITY IN OPERATION

To bring the contractual liability of the various parties to a negotiable instrument into play, it is generally necessary that the instrument be *presented for payment*. In addition, to hold the parties that are secondarily liable on the instrument to their contractual liability, it is generally necessary that the instrument be *presented for payment* and *dishonored*.

Presentment of a Note

The maker of a note is primarily liable to pay it when it is due. Normally, the holder takes the note to the maker at the time it is due and asks the maker to pay it. Sometimes, the maker sends the payment to the holder at the due date. The party to whom **presentment** is made may, without dishonoring the instrument, require the exhibition of the instrument, reasonable identification of the person making presentment, and evidence of his authority to make it if he is making it for another person [3–505]. If the maker pays the note, he is entitled to have the note marked "paid" or "canceled" or to have it returned so that it can be destroyed.

If the maker does not pay a note when it is presented at its due date, the note has been **dishonored** [3–507(1)]. If the note is dishonored, the holder can seek payment from any persons who indorsed the note before the holder took it. The basis for going after the indorsers is that they are secondarily liable on it. To hold the indorsers to their contractual liability, the holder must give notice of the dishonor. The notice can be either written or oral [3–508].

For example, Susan Strong borrows $100 from Jack Jones and gives him a promissory note for $100 at 9 percent annual interest payable in 90 days. Jones indorses the note "Pay to the order of Ralph Smith" and negotiates the note to Ralph Smith. At the end of the 90 days, Smith takes the note to Strong and presents it for payment. If Strong pays Smith the $100 and accrued interest, she can have Smith mark it "paid" and give it back to her. If Strong does not pay the note to Smith when he presents it for payment, then the note has been dishonored. Smith should give notice of the dishonor to Jones and advise him that he intends to hold Jones secondarily liable on his indorsement. Smith is entitled to collect payment of the note from Jones. Jones, after making the note good to Smith, can try to collect the note from Strong on the ground that she defaulted on the contract she made as maker of the note. Of course, Smith could also sue Strong on the basis of her maker's liability.

Presentment of a Check or a Draft

A check or draft should be presented to the drawee. The presentment can be either for payment or for acceptance (certification) of the check or draft. *No one is primarily liable on a check or draft*, and the *drawee is not liable on a check or draft unless it accepts (certifies) it*. An acceptance of a draft is the drawee's signed commitment to honor the draft as presented. The acceptance must be written on the draft, and it may consist of the drawee's signature alone [3–410].

A drawer who writes a check is issuing an order to the drawee to pay a certain amount out of the drawer's account to the payee (or to someone authorized by the payee). This order is not an assignment of the funds in the drawer's account [3–409]. The drawee bank does not have an obligation to the payee to pay the check unless it has certified the check. However, the drawee bank usually does have a contractual obligation to the drawer to pay any properly payable checks for which funds are available in the drawer's account.

For example, Janet Payne has $100 in a checking account at First National Bank and writes a check for $10 drawn on First National and payable to Ralph Smith. The writing of the check is the issuance of an order by Payne to First National to pay $10 from her account to Smith or to whomever Smith requests it to be paid. First National owes no obligation to Smith to pay the $10 unless it has certified the check. However, if Smith presents the check for payment and First National refuses to pay it even though there are sufficient funds in Payne's account, then First National is liable to Payne for breaching its contractual obligation to her to pay items properly payable from existing funds in her account. The Checks and Documents of Title chapter discusses the liability of a bank for wrongful dishonor of checks in more detail.

If the drawee bank does not pay or certify a check when it is properly presented for payment or acceptance (certification), the check has been **dishonored** [3–507]. The holder of the check can then proceed against either the drawer of the check or any indorsers on their secondary liability. To do so, the holder must give them **notice** of the dishonor [3–508].

Suppose Matthews draws a check for $100 on her account at a bank payable to the order of Williams. Williams indorses the check "Pay to the order of Clark, Williams" and negotiates it to Clark. When Clark takes the check to the bank, it refuses to pay the check because there are insufficient funds in Matthews's account to cover the check. The check has been presented and dishonored. Clark has two options: He can proceed against Williams on Williams's secondary liability as an indorser because by putting an unqualified indorsement on the check, Williams contracted to make the check good if it was not honored by the drawee. Or he can proceed against Matthews on Matthews's drawer's contractual liability because in drawing the check, Matthews promised to make it good to any holder if it was dishonored and he was given notice. Because Clark dealt with Williams, Clark is probably more likely to return the check to Williams for payment. Williams then has to go against Matthews on Matthews's contractual liability as drawer.

Time of Presentment

If an instrument is payable at a definite time, it should be presented for payment on the due date. In the case of a demand instrument, a reasonable time for presentment for acceptance or payment is determined by the nature of the instrument, by trade or bank usage, and by the facts of the particular case. In a farming community, for example, a reasonable time to present a promissory note that is payable on demand may be six months or within a short time after the crops are sold, because it is expected that the payment can be made from the proceeds of the crops.

A reasonable time to present a check to hold the drawer liable is presumed to be 30 days [3–503]. Delay in presentment may be excused where, for example, the party is without notice that the instrument is due, or where the delay is caused by circumstances beyond his control and he operates with reasonable diligence [3–511].

Effect of Unexcused Delay in Presentment

If presentment of a negotiable instrument is delayed beyond the time it is due, and if there is no valid excuse for the delay, then the indorsers are *discharged from liability* on the instrument. Under certain circumstances, a drawer or maker can also be discharged of liability if the bank in which the funds to pay the note or draft were deposited becomes insolvent during the delay [3–502(1)].

To be able to hold an indorser of a check liable, the check should be presented for payment within seven days after the indorser signed it. If the holder of the check waits longer than that without a valid excuse, the indorsers are relieved of their secondary liability and the holder's only recourse is against the drawer. The holder must give the indorsers timely notice of any dishonor.

WARRANTY LIABILITY

Whether or not a person signs a negotiable instrument, a person who transfers such an instrument or presents it for payment may incur liability on the basis of certain implied warranties. These warranties are (1) **transferor's warranties,** which are made by persons who *transfer* negotiable instruments; and (2) **presentment warranties,** which are made by persons who *present* negotiable instruments *for payment or acceptance (certification).*

Transferor's Warranties

A *person who transfers a negotiable instrument* to someone else and receives something of value in exchange makes five *warranties* to his transferee. The warranties are:

1. The person has *good title* to the instrument or is *authorized* to *obtain payment* by someone who has good title.

2. *All signatures* on the instrument are *genuine or authorized.*

3. The instrument has *not been materially altered.*

4. *No party* to the instrument has a *valid defense* against the person who is transferring it.

5. The person transferring the instrument has *no knowledge of any insolvency proceedings* against the maker, drawer, or acceptor [3–417(2)].

If the transfer is by indorsement, the warranties are made to any subsequent holder who takes the instrument in good faith.

Although contractual liability often furnishes a sufficient basis for suing a transferor when the party pri-marily liable does not pay, warranties are still important. First, they apply even when the transferor did not in-dorse. Second, unlike contractual liability, they do not depend on presentment, dishonor, and notice, but may be utilized before presentment has been made or after the time for giving notice has expired. Third, it may be easier to return the instrument to a transferor on the ground of breach of warranty than to prove one's status as a holder in due course against a maker or drawer.

CONCEPT REVIEW

TRANSFEROR'S WARRANTIES

The five transferor's warranties are:
1. The person transferring the instrument has *good title* or is authorized to obtain payment by someone who has good title.
2. All *signatures* are *genuine* or *authorized*.
3. The instrument has *not* been *materially altered*.
4. No *party* to the instrument has a *valid defense* against the person transferring it.
5. The person transferring it has *no knowledge* of any insolvency proceedings against the maker, drawer, or acceptor.

Who	What Warranties	To Whom
Nonindorsing Transferor	Makes all five transferor's warranties	To his immediate transferee only
Indorsing Transferor	Makes all five transferor's warranties	To all subsequent holders
Qualified Indorsing Transferor	Makes all five transferor's warranties, except the fourth one becomes, "The transferor has *no knowledge* of a valid defense against him."	To all subsequent holders

---

Rule of Finality of Payment

A person who presents a negotiable instrument for pay-ment or a check to be certified makes a different set of warranties. Normally, the person to whom a negotiable instrument is presented for payment does not pay it un-less he either is obligated to do so or is entitled to credit or payment from someone else if he does pay. For exam-ple, a drawee bank does not normally pay a check unless there are funds in the drawer's account. And it should know whether the signature on the check is that of its customer—the drawer of the check. If a drawee bank pays the check to a holder in due course, it cannot later get the money back from the holder in due course if it discovers that there are insufficient funds in the drawer's account. Payment is usually *final* in favor of a holder in due course or a person who in good faith changed his position in reliance on the payment [3–418] unless one of the three presentment warranties is broken.

Presentment Warranties

The three *warranties* that are made by a *person who is presenting an instrument for payment* are:

1. The presenter has *good title* to the instrument or is *authorized to obtain payment* by someone who has good title.
2. The presenter has *no knowledge that the signature of the maker or drawer is unauthorized*.
3. The instrument has *not been materially altered* [3–417(1)].

A holder in due course who presents a note to a maker does not warrant that the signature of the maker is valid or that the note has not been materially altered. The maker should recognize whether the signature on the note is her signature and whether the note has been altered. Similarly, a holder in due course does not warrant to the drawer of a check that the drawer's signature is valid or that the check has not been materially altered, because the drawer should recognize his signature and whether the check has been altered.

The *Garnac Grain Co. v. Boatmen's Bank & Trust Co. of Kansas City* case, which follows, illustrates the operation of presentment and transferor's warranties.

GARNAC GRAIN CO., INC. v. BOATMEN'S BANK & TRUST CO. OF KANSAS CITY
694 F. Supp 1389 (W.D. Mo. 1988)

Katherine Millison was employed by the Garnac Grain Company as a bookkeeper. She developed a scheme to embezzle money from Garnac whereby she would take home fully executed and valid checks payable to freight vendors and type "or L. R. Millison" (her husband's name) under the named payee with her manual typewriter. She would then indorse the check "L. R. Millison" on the back and deposit the check in a joint account she and her husband maintained at the State Bank of Oskaloosa. The altered checks were then forwarded through the Federal Reserve System (through First National Bank of Kansas City), presented for payment to the drawee bank, Boatmen's Bank & Trust Company of Kansas City, and paid. Millison would then intercept the monthly bank statements from Boatmen's Bank & Trust, remove the altered checks, and obliterate the "or L. R. Millison" on the face of the checks and the indorsement on the back.

The scheme was discovered and Millison was convicted of embezzlement. Garnac brought suit against Boatmen's Bank & Trust, alleging that the altered checks were wrongfully paid. It settled with Garnac and then brought suit against the State Bank of Oskaloosa, contending that it breached the UCC transfer warranties when it forwarded the altered checks for payment.

Hunter, Senior District Judge.   Boatmen's and First National contend that Oskaloosa is liable for the amount of their settlement with Garnac because it breached the UCC transfer warranties it made to them when it sent the checks altered by Millison to First National for payment by Boatmen's. Specifically it alleges that Oskaloosa breached the good title, material alterations, and genuine signature warranties.

Section 4–207 provides in pertinent part:

(1) Each customer or collecting bank who obtains payment or acceptance of an item and each prior customer and collecting bank warrants to the payor bank or other payor who in good faith pays or accepts the item that

   (a) he has good title to the item or is authorized to obtain payment or acceptance on behalf of one who has a good title; and

   (b) he has no knowledge that the signature of the maker or drawer is unauthorized . . . ; and

   (c) the item has not been materially altered . . .

(2) Each customer and collecting bank who transfers an item and receives a settlement or other consideration for it warrants to his transferee and to any subsequent collecting bank who takes the item in good faith that

   (a) he has a good title to the item or is authorized to obtain payment or acceptance on behalf of one who has a good title and the transfer is otherwise rightful; and

   (b) all signatures are genuine and authorized; and

   (c) the item has not been materially altered; . . .

Under this system, a payor bank in possession of a check containing, for example, a material alteration has the choice of bringing a warranty claim against the bank that transferred the check to it, or any other intermediate collecting bank or the depositary bank. If the payor bank brings the action against a bank other than the depositary bank, that bank can bring a claim against its transferor bank or any other previous collecting bank. As between the banks involved in the collection process, the liability for a materially altered check falls on the depositary bank. This is in accord with the loss allocation framework of Articles 3 and 4 of the U.C.C. which generally places the loss of a forged or altered item on the person or bank who dealt with the wrongdoer if the wrongdoer cannot be found or is judgment proof. Since there is no knowledge or notice requirement with respect to the material alteration warranties, the question of whether or not a party breached these warranties is simply a question of whether or not the checks were materially altered.

There seems to be no serious dispute among the parties but that the alterations made by Millison were material. Each check was drawn on Garnac's account at Boatmen's, was properly made out to barge freight vendors, and was properly signed by authorized representatives of Garnac. Millison altered the checks by typing "or L. R. Millison" underneath the payee's name. The court finds that, as a matter of law, an alteration which adds an alternative payee is a material alteration as that term is used in the U.C.C. *See* section 3–407. Thus, both Oskaloosa and First National breached their 3–207(1) warranties of no material alteration to Boatmen's; Oskaloosa breached its 4–207(2) warranty of no material alterations.

There is also no question that Oskaloosa breached its warranty of good title. Without the indorsement of the intended payees on the checks (i.e., the barge freight vendors) Oskaloosa could not obtain good title to the checks. The only indorsement on the back of the checks was "L. R. Millison." Neither Millison nor her husband was authorized to indorse the checks on behalf of the barge freight vendors shown as payees on the altered checks. Since Oskaloosa did not have good title when it transferred the checks to First National, it breached its section 4–207(1)(a) warranty to Boatmen's and its 4–207(2)(a) warranty to First National.

Summary judgment in favor of Boatmen's on its claims that the State Bank of Oskaloosa breached its warranties of good title and no material alterations.

Note: The court found that there were issues of material fact as to whether Garnac had exercised reasonable care and promptness in examining its bank statement to discover unauthorized signatures and alterations *and* whether Boatmen's had exercised ordinary care in paying the checks in question.

Operation of Warranties

Following are some examples that show how the transferor's and presentment warranties shift the liability back to a wrongdoer or to the person who dealt immediately with a wrongdoer and thus was in the best position to avert the wrongdoing.

Arthur makes a promissory note for $100 payable to the order of Betts. Carlson steals the note from Betts, indorses her name on the back, and gives it to Davidson in exchange for a television set. Davidson negotiates the note for value to Earle, who presents the note to Arthur for payment. Assume that Arthur refuses to pay the note because he has been advised by Betts that it has been stolen. Earle can then proceed to recover the face amount of the note from Davidson on the grounds that as a transferor Davidson has warranted that he had good title to the note and that all signatures were genuine. Davidson, in turn, can proceed against Carlson on the same basis—if he can find Carlson. If he cannot, then Davidson must bear the loss caused by Carlson's wrongdoing. Davidson was in the best position to ascertain whether Carlson was the owner of the note and whether the indorsement of Betts was genuine. Of course, even though Arthur does not have to pay the note to Earle, Arthur remains liable for his underlying obligation to Betts.

Anderson draws a check for $10 on her checking account at First Bank payable to the order of Brown. Brown cleverly raises the check to $110, indorses it, and negotiates it to Carroll. Carroll then presents the check for payment to First Bank, which pays her $110 and charges Anderson's account for $110. Anderson then asks the bank to recredit her account for the altered check, and it does so. The bank can proceed against Carroll for breach of the presentment warranty that the instrument had not been materially altered, which she implied to the bank when she presented the check for payment. Carroll in turn can proceed against Brown for breach of her transferor's warranty that the check had not been materially altered—if she can find her.

Bates steals Albers's checkbook and forges Albers's signature to a check for $100 payable to "cash," which he uses to buy $100 worth of groceries from a grocer. The grocer presents the check to Albers's bank, which pays the amount of the check to the grocer and charges Albers's account. Albers then demands that the bank recredit his account. The bank can recover against the grocer only if the grocer knew that Albers's signature had been forged. Otherwise, the bank must look for Bates. The bank had the responsibility to recognize the true signature of its drawer, Albers, and not to pay the check that contained an unauthorized signature. The bank, however, may be able to resist recrediting Albers's account if it can show he was negligent. The next section of this chapter discusses negligence.

OTHER LIABILITY RULES

Normally, a check that has a forged indorsement of the payee may not be charged to the drawer's checking account. Similarly, a maker does not have to pay a note to the person who currently possesses the note if the payee's signature has been forged. If a check or note has been materially altered—for example, by raising the amount—the drawer or maker is usually liable only for the instrument as it was originally written.

Negligence

A person can be so negligent in writing or signing a negotiable instrument that he in effect invites an alteration or an unauthorized signature on it. If a person has been negligent, he is not able to use the alteration or lack of authorization as a reason for not paying a holder in due course. A person is also not able to use the alteration or lack of authorization to claim that a payment was improperly made by a bank if the bank paid the item in good faith and in accordance with reasonable commercial standards [3–406].

For example, Diane Drawer makes out a check for $1 in such a way that someone could easily alter it to read $101. The check is so altered and is negotiated to Katherine Smith, who can qualify as a holder in due course. Smith can collect $101 from Drawer. Drawer cannot claim alteration as a defense to paying it, because of her negligence in making the alteration possible. Drawer then has to find the person who "raised" her check and try to collect the $100 from him.

The following case, *J. Gordon Neely Enterprises, Inc. v. National Bank of Huntsville*, illustrates the consequences to a drawer who is negligent in the way he draws a check.

J. GORDON NEELY ENTERPRISES, INC. v. NATIONAL BANK OF HUNTSVILLE

403 So.2d 887 (Ala. Sup. Ct. 1981)

Mr. and Mrs. Gordon Neely hired Louise Bradshaw as the bookkeeper for a Midas Muffler shop they owned and operated as a corporation, J. Gordon Neely Enterprises, Inc. (Neely). Bradshaw's duties included preparing company checks for Mrs. Neely's signature and reconciling the checking account when the bank statement and canceled checks were received each month. Bradshaw prepared several checks that were made payable to herself and contained a large space to the left of the amount written on the designated line. When the checks were signed by Mrs. Neely, she was aware of the large gaps. Subsequently, Bradshaw altered the checks by adding a digit or two to the left of the original amount and then cashed them at American National Bank, the drawee bank. Several months later, the Neelys hired a new accountant, who discovered the altered checks.

Neely brought suit against American National Bank to have its account recredited for the altered checks. The trial court held that the bank was not liable to Neely, and Neely appealed.

Adams, Justice.   Neely alleges that American is liable for paying out on altered instruments. Both parties rely upon Code section 3–406, stating:

> Any person who by his negligence substantially contributes to a material alteration of the instrument or to the making of an unauthorized signature is precluded from asserting the alteration or lack of authority against a holder in due course or against a drawee or other payor who pays the instrument in good faith and in accordance with the reasonable commercial standards of the drawee's or payor's business.

Neely argues that American National did not pay the instruments according to commercially reasonable standards because the checks allegedly bore visible marks of alteration. American National contends that Neely is precluded from asserting the material alterations as a basis for liability because Neely's negligence substantially contributed to the alterations by leaving large spaces to the left of the amount designation, and by entrusting the same employee with writing the checks and reconciling the bank statements without the protection of internal corporate controls.

We must first resolve whether American National acted in a commercially reasonable manner, because unless the bank acted reasonably, it cannot assert the defense that Neely's negligence substantially contributed to the alterations. American National produced expert witnesses testifying that although some of the words and numbers on the amount designation lines were slightly misaligned, and although a few checks visibly contained liquid erasure, the bank did not violate reasonable commercial standards when it paid out on these particular checks to Bradshaw. It was stated that the decision of whether to pay a particular check that may have appeared to be somewhat irregular on its face was based on a judgment call under the particular circumstances of that check. Based upon the judgment call surrounding the decision to pay each check, and after examining the checks exhibited, the trial court concluded that American National had acted in a commerically reasonable fashion under the circumstances.

We must next determine whether Neely, by its negligence, substantially contributed to the facilitation of the alterations. The Uniform Commercial Code does not define the negligence which will support the defense of section 3–406, and instructs that it is an issue strictly left to the factfinder. The official comment does advise, however, that "negligence usually has been found where spaces are left in the body of the instrument in which words or figures may be inserted." It is undisputed that Mrs. Neely signed the checks fully aware of the large gaps in front of the amount.

Similarly, two other examples of negligence are supported by the record: no inquiry was made into Bradshaw's veracity, although it was rumored that previously she had been in trouble with embezzlement in Tennessee; and Neely failed to maintain internal controls so that the employee writing the checks was not also the principal person reconciling the bank statements.

Based upon a thorough and sifting review of the record, we conclude that the accumulation of Mrs. Neely's negligent conduct set in motion an unfortunate chain of events which proximately culminated in the alterations, thus establishing Neely's substantial contribution.

Therefore, because American National acted in a commercially reasonable manner and Neely's negligence substantially contributed to the material alteration resulting in the bank's payment to Bradshaw, Neely cannot recover from American National.

Judgment for American National affirmed.

Impostor Rule

The Code establishes special rules for negotiable instruments made payable to *impostors* and *fictitious persons*. An **impostor** is a *person who poses as someone else and convinces a drawer to make a check payable to the person being impersonated.* When this happens, the Code makes any indorsement in the name of the impersonated person effective [3–405 (1)(a)]. For example, suppose that Arthur steals Paulsen's automobile. Arthur finds the certificate of title in the automobile and then, representing himself as Paulsen, sells the automobile to Berger Used Car Company. The car company draws its check payable to Paulsen for the agreed purchase price of the automobile and delivers the check to Arthur. Any person can negotiate the check by indorsing it in the name of Paulsen.

The rationale for the impostor rule is to put the responsibility for determining the true identity of the payee on the drawer of a check. The drawer is in a better position to do this than some later holder of the check who may be entirely innocent. The impostor rule allows that later holder to have good title to the check by making the payee's signature valid even though it is a forgery. It forces the drawer to go after the wrongdoer who tricked him into signing the check.

Fictitious Payee Rule

A **fictitious payee** commonly arises in the following situation: A dishonest employee draws checks payable to someone who does not exist, to a person who does not do business with his employer, or to a real person who does business with the employer but to whom the dishonest employee does not intend to send the check. If the employee has the authority to do so, he may sign the check himself. If he does not have such authority, he presents the check to his employer for signature and represents that the employer owes money to the person to whom the check is made payable. The dishonest employee then takes the check, indorses it in the name of the payee, presents it for payment, and pockets the money. The employee may be in a position to cover up the wrongdoing by intercepting the canceled checks and/or juggling the company's books.

The Code allows any indorsement in the name of the fictitious payee to be effective as the payee's indorsement [3–405(1)(b) and (c)]. For example, Anderson, who is employed by Moore Corporation as an accountant in charge of accounts payable, prepares a false invoice naming Parks, Inc., a supplier of Moore Corporation, as having supplied Moore Corporation with goods, and draws a check payable to Parks, Inc., for the amount of the invoice. Anderson then presents the check to Temple, treasurer of Moore Corporation, together with other checks with invoices attached, all of which Temple signs and returns to Anderson for mailing. Anderson then withdraws the check payable to Parks, Inc. Anyone, including Anderson, can negotiate the check by indorsing it in the name of Parks, Inc.

The rationale for the fictitious payee rule is similar to that for the impostor rule. If someone has a dishonest employee or agent who is responsible for the forgery of some checks, the immediate loss of those checks should rest on the employer of the wrongdoer rather than on some other innocent party. In turn, the employer must locate the unfaithful employee or agent and try to recover from him.

The *City of Phoenix v. Great Western Bank & Trust* case, which follows, illustrates the operation of the fictitious payee rule. As you read the case, determine what the city should have done to prevent the loss it suffered.

CITY OF PHOENIX v. GREAT WESTERN BANK & TRUST

42 UCC Rep. 1364 (Ariz. Ct. App. 1985)

Gary Hann opened a checking account at the Tucson branch of Great Western Bank & Trust in the name of Duncan Industries with a cash deposit of $200. He told the bank that Duncan Industries was a sole proprietorship involved in investments. Hann listed the mailing address of the business as a post office box and designated himself as the authorized signature on the account. Hann's confederate, Jay Maisel, worked for the City of Phoenix in a government-funded program to assist ex-convicts. Maisel had served nine years in prison for theft. City officials were aware of his background and initially placed him in a nonsensitive position. However, Maisel was promoted to a position in which he was responsible for preparing the documentation to pay the city's vendors. Six months after his promotion, Maisel prepared two claims packages for one vendor, Duncan Industries, causing the City to issue duplicate checks to the order of Duncan Industries, each in the amount of $514,320.40. The legitimate check was mailed to the vendor in Chicago; the fraudulent check was mailed to Hann in Tucson.

Hann deposited the check in the Duncan Industries account he had established where it was subject to a four-day hold. Once the hold expired, Hann withdrew over $441,000 from the account, much of it in cashier's checks made payable to coin, stamp, diamond, or bullion dealers. The city, on its own behalf and as assignee of the rights of the drawee bank, brought suit against the Great Western Bank to recover the amount of the check taken for deposit by it, contending, among other things, that the check contained a forged payee's indorsement. The trial court ruled in favor of the bank and the city appealed.

Corcoran, Judge. Section 3–405 provides an exception to the general rule that forged indorsements are ineffective to pass title or to authorize a drawee to pay. Under section 4–401, a drawer can usually require the drawee bank to recredit the drawer account when the drawee pays a check on which a necessary indorsement is forged. The drawee bank can then shift the loss to previous indorsers on the ground of breach of warranty. The loss under the general rule will ultimately rest with the person who forged the instrument or the bank which took the instrument from the forger.

Section 3–405(1)(c), often referred to as the "fictitious payee rule," provides in pertinent part:

A. An indorsement by any person in the name of a named payee is effective if: . . .

    3. An agent or employee of the maker or drawer has supplied him with the name of the payee intending the latter to have no such interest.

The exception places the loss from the activities of a faithless employee upon the employer rather than on the drawee bank. The loss is shifted by making the indorsement "effective" although it is unauthorized. Since the indorsement is "effective," the instrument passes as though there had been no forgery and as between a collecting bank and the drawer of the check, the loss must fall on the drawer employer. The rule, as applied, also eliminates any liability of a collecting bank for breach of warranty of the genuineness of the signatures because a signature that is "effective" is to be regarded as "genuine" for the purpose of warranty liability. Thus, in this case, the City, as assignee of its drawee bank, has no recourse against Great Western Bank based on the warranties contained in sections 3–417 and 4–207 owed by Great Western Bank to the drawee.

The basis of the fictitious payee rule is explained in section 3–405, Official Comment 4: The principle followed is that the loss should fall upon the employer as a risk of his business enterprise rather than upon the subsequent holder or drawee. The reasons are that the employer is normally in a better position to prevent such forgeries by reasonable care in the selection or supervision of his employees, or, if he is not, is at least in a better position to cover the loss by fidelity insurance: and that the cost of such insurance is properly an expense of his business rather than of the business of the holder or drawee.

The factual circumstances for application of the fictitious payee rule are met in this case. Maisel, an "employee" of the drawer, the City of Phoenix, supplied the City, as to the duplicate check, with the name of a "payee," Duncan Industries, with the intent of creating no interest in Duncan Industries.

Judgment for Great Western Bank affirmed.

Conversion

Conversion of an instrument is an *unauthorized assumption and exercise of ownership* over it. A negotiable instrument can be converted in a number of ways. For example, it might be presented for payment or acceptance, and the person to whom it is presented might refuse to pay, refuse to accept, or refuse to return it. An instrument is also converted if a person pays an instrument on a forged indorsement [3–419]. Thus, if a check that contains a forged indorsement is paid by a bank, the bank has converted the check by wrongfully paying it.

The bank then becomes liable for the face amount of the check to the person whose indorsement was forged [3–419].

For example, Arthur Able draws a check for $50 on his account at First Bank, payable to the order of Bernard Barker. Carol Collins steals the check, forges Barker's indorsement on it, and cashes it at First Bank. First Bank has converted Barker's property, because it had no right to pay the check without Barker's valid indorsement. First Bank must pay Barker $50, and then it can try to locate Collins to get the $50 back from her.

KELLY v. CENTRAL BANK & TRUST CO. OF DENVER

794 P.2d 1037 (Colo. Ct. App. 1990)

A number of investors, including Kelly, invested in a Cayman Islands entity, Tradecom, Ltd., a business involved in precious metals arbitrage. Their investments, in the form of cashier's checks, were payable to Tradecom and delivered to Arvey Down, Tradecom's agent. Down indorsed the checks and deposited them at the Central Bank & Trust Company of Denver into a checking account.

Most of the 934 checks worth $11,227,473 were indorsed:

Tradecom Limited
For deposit only
072 575

Other checks, totaling $576,850, were indorsed:

For deposit only
072 575

This included one check for $57,000, which apparently was deposited without indorsement and was indorsed by Central Bank's officer:

For deposit only
072 575
Tradecom by
Mark E. Thompson
Commercial Loan officer

The referenced account, No. 072 575, was not that of Tradecom (which had no accounts at Central Bank) but rather was that of Equity Trading Corporation, a company owned and managed by Down, also purportedly an agent of Tradecom.

The investors subsequently lost most of their investments in Tradecom and they sued Central Bank for, among other things, conversion. They alleged that neither Down nor Equity Trading was an agent of Tradecom and that the check indorsements were unauthorized and ineffective; that over the course of 13 months, the bank negligently or recklessly permitted Down to divert the checks payable to Tradecom into Equity Trading's checking acoount; and that Central Bank did not follow reasonable commercial standards. Central bank moved for summary judgment and in support of its motion submitted an executed power of attorney that indicated Down had the authority to indorse checks on behalf of Tradecom. The trial court awarded summary judgment to the Central Bank and the investors appealed.

Tursi, Judge.   Because there was no triable issue of fact concerning Down's agency and authority to indorse and deposit the cashier's checks, and because proof of a forged or unauthorized indorsement is a necessary predicate to Central Bank's liability, the investors could not prevail as to the 11 million dollars of checks that contained an indorsement which included the "Tradecom Limited" name. Consequently, with respect to the checks indorsed with Tradecom's name, we conclude that the trial court properly granted summary judgment for Central Bank.

The trial court erred, however, in granting Central Bank summary judgment on the $57,000 check indorsed by Central Bank's commercial loan officer. In order for Central Bank to have become a holder under this indorsement, and thus have obtained title, Central Bank would have had to have been authorized to provide Tradecom's indorsement under section 4–205(1). This, however, was impossible since Tradecom was not Central Bank's "customer." Consequently, this indorsement is unauthorized as a matter of law, and summary judgment should not have been ordered for Central Bank on this check.

The investors also contend that the trial court erred in granting summary judgment for Central Bank on the remaining $519,850 of cashier's checks lacking any signature and merely indorsed "For deposit only 072 575." We agree.

Under section 3–419(1)(c), a check is converted when it is paid on a forged indorsement. In this context, a collecting or paying bank "pays" a check when it credits its customer's account with the proceeds of a check collected from the drawee bank. If such a payment occurs on a check with no indorsement or a missing indorsement, it is the legal equivalent of payment on a forged indorsement.

The term "indorsement" is generally understood to mean the indorser's writing of his or her signature on the instrument or the affixing of the indorser's name or some designation identifying the indorser on the instrument. A check simply inscribed "For deposit only" to an account other than payee's account and without the payee's signature is not an effective "indorsement."

If the instrument is order paper and the depository bank does not, or cannot, supply the missing indorsement of its customer, the absence of the indorsement can be fatal to negotiation and transfer of title. One such situation is when the depository bank's customer and the payee are not the same person. In this case, the depository bank is unauthorized to, and cannot, supply the missing indorsement of the payee since the payee is not the bank's "customer" under section 4–205. In this situation, the depository bank does not become a holder of the checks and does not obtain good title to them. Payment of such proceeds to its depositor subjects the depository bank to liability for conversion.

In this case it was undisputed that Down, or someone in his employ, deposited $519,850 worth of cashier's checks at Central Bank bearing the simple inscription "For Deposit only 072 575." These checks, which bore no signature indorsement of the payee, Tradecom, or anyone else, were paid and credited to account 072 575. This was not an account of Tradecom, which was not a customer of Central Bank. Under these circumstances, Central Bank was not a holder of these checks by negotiation. It obtained no title to these checks. It is, consequently, subject to conversion liability under section 3–419(1)(c) for making payment on the equivalent of a forged indorsement.

Judgment for Central Bank reversed in part.

DISCHARGE OF NEGOTIABLE INSTRUMENTS

Discharge of Liability

Generally, all parties to a negotiable instrument are *discharged* or relieved from liability when the person who is primarily liable on it pays the amount in full to a holder of the instrument. Any person is discharged of his liability to the extent that the person pays the holder of the instrument [3–603]. For example, Anderson makes a note for $475 payable to the order of Bruce. Bruce indorses the note "Pay to the order of Carroll, Bruce" and negotiates it to Carroll. Carroll takes the note to Anderson, presents it for payment, and is paid $475 by Anderson. The payment to Carroll discharges Bruce's secondary liability as indorser and Anderson's primary liability as maker.

A person is not discharged of liability if he pays someone who acquired the instrument by theft or from someone who had stolen it [3–603(1)(a)]. Also, if a negotiable instrument has been restrictively indorsed, the person who pays must comply with the restrictive indorsement to be discharged [3–603(1)(b)]. For example, Arthur makes a note of $100 payable to the order of Bryan. Bryan indorses the note "Pay to the order of my account no. 16154 at First Bank, Bryan." Bryan then gives the note to his employee, Clark, to take to the bank. Clark takes the note to Arthur, who pays Clark the $100. Clark then runs off with the money. Arthur is not discharged of his primary liability on the note because he did not make his payment consistent with the restrictive indorsement. To be discharged, Arthur has to pay the $100 into Bryan's account at First Bank.

Discharge by Cancellation

The holder of a negotiable instrument may discharge the liability of the parties to the instrument by canceling it. If the holder mutilates or destroys a negotiable instrument with the intent that it no longer evidences an obligation to pay money, it has been canceled [3–605]. For example, a grandfather lends $1,000 to his grandson for college expenses. The grandson gives his grandfather a promissory note for $1,000. If the grandfather later tears up the note with the intent that the grandson no longer owes him $1,000, the note has been canceled.

An accidental destruction or mutilation of a negotiable instrument is not a cancellation and does not discharge the parties to it. If an instrument is lost, accidentally mutilated, or destroyed, the holder can still enforce it. In such a case, the holder must prove that the instrument existed and that she was its holder when it was lost, mutilated, or destroyed.

Discharge by Alteration

Generally, a *fraudulent and material change* in a negotiable instrument discharges any party whose contract is changed [3–407(2)]. An alteration of an instrument is material if it changes the contract of any of the parties to the instrument. For example, if the amount due on a note is raised from $10 to $10,000, the contract of the maker has been changed. The maker promised to pay $10, but after the change has been made, he would be promising to pay much more. A change that does not affect the contract of one of the parties, such as dotting an *i* or correcting the grammar, is not material.

Assume that Anderson signs a promissory note for $100 payable to Bond. Bond indorses the note "Pay to the order of Connolly, Bond" and negotiates it to Connolly. Connolly changes the $100 to read $100,000. Connolly's change is unauthorized, fraudulent, and material. As a result, Anderson is discharged from her primary liability as maker of the note and Bond is discharged from her secondary liability as indorser. Neither of them has to pay Connolly. The contracts of both Anderson and Bond were changed because the amount for which they agreed to be liable was altered.

There are exceptions to the general rule that a fraudulent and material alteration discharges parties whose contracts are changed. First, if in the preceding example Anderson was so negligent in writing the note that it could easily be altered, he cannot claim the alteration against a holder in due course of the note. Assume that Connolly indorsed the note "Connolly" and negotiated it to Davis, who qualifies as a holder in due course. If Davis was not aware of the alteration and it was not obvious, she could collect the $100,000 from Anderson. Anderson's only recourse would be to track down Connolly to try to get the difference between $100 and $100,000.

Second, a holder in due course who takes an instrument after it has been altered can enforce it for the original amount. When an incomplete instrument is completed after it leaves the drawer's or maker's hands, a holder in due course can enforce it as completed. For example, Swanson draws a check payable to Frank's Nursery, leaving the amount blank. He gives it to his gardener with instructions to purchase some fertilizer at

Frank's and to fill in the purchase price of the fertilizer when it is known. The gardener fills in the check for $100 and gives it to Frank's in exchange for the fertilizer ($7.25) and the difference in cash ($92.75). The gardener then leaves town with the cash. If Frank's had no knowledge of the unauthorized completion, it could enforce the check for $100 against Swanson.

Discharge by Impairment of Recourse

If a party to an instrument has posted collateral to secure his performance and a holder surrenders the collateral without the consent of the parties who would benefit from the collateral, such parties are discharged [3–606].

ETHICAL AND PUBLIC POLICY CONCERNS

1. Problem case 2 involves a situation where a sole shareholder of a corporation, Frederick J. Dowie, signed a corporate check without indicating he was signing in a representative capacity. If the state in which the activity took place follows the minority rule as set out in *Valley National Bank v. Cook*, should Dowie feel obligated by ethical considerations to personally make the check good?

2. Suppose you have taken a promissory note for $1,000 as payment for some carpentry work you did for a friend. You have some reason to believe that the maker is having some financial difficulty and may not be able to pay the note off when it is due. You discuss the possible sale of the note to an elderly neighbor as an investment and she agrees to buy it. Would it be ethical for you to indorse the note with a qualified indorsement ("without recourse")?

3. Problem case 11 involves a situation where a creditor made a mistake and returned a note marked "canceled" to the maker without collecting all of the interest due on it. Suppose that in that case, the maker/borrower realized that Crown Financial had made an error in not including in the subsequent note the interest due on the original note. Should the maker/borrower feel compelled by ethical considerations to pay the interest, even if not legally required to do so?

SUMMARY

Liability on a negotiable instrument may be based on (1) contract, (2) breach of warranty, (3) negligence,

(4) improper payment, or (5) conversion. When a person signs a negotiable instrument, he generally becomes contractually liable on it. The terms of the contract of parties to a negotiable instrument are not written out on the instrument; they are supplied by Article 3 of the Code. Parties may be either primarily or secondarily liable. Makers of notes and acceptors of drafts and checks are primarily liable, while drawers of checks and drafts and indorsers of notes, checks, and drafts are secondarily liable. An accommodation party is liable in the capacity in which he signed the instrument.

Under the Code, a person cannot be held contractually liable on a negotiable instrument unless his signature appears on the instrument. A person may use any name or symbol as his signature. A person who signs in a representative capacity should make it clear that she is signing as an agent, so that the principal rather than the agent will be liable.

Presentment for payment is necessary to hold parties liable on an instrument. Failure to present the instrument in a timely fashion discharges the indorsers from their contractual liability to make the instrument good. An instrument has been dishonored when it has been duly presented and acceptance or payment cannot be obtained within the prescribed time. When an instrument has been dishonored and required notices have been timely given, the holder has a right of recourse against the drawers and prior indorsers.

The transferor of an instrument warrants to his transferee that he has good title, that the signatures are genuine or authorized, that the instrument has not been materially altered, that no defenses of any party are good against him (if he qualifies his warranty, he warrants that he has no knowledge of defenses to the instrument), and that he has no knowledge of any insolvency proceedings against the maker, acceptor, or drawer of the instrument.

Any person who obtains payment or acceptance of an instrument warrants to a person who in good faith accepts or pays the instrument that she has good title to the instrument or is authorized to act for a person who has good title and that the instrument has not been materially altered. A holder in due course acting in good faith does not warrant to a maker or drawer the genuineness of the maker's or drawer's signature or that the instrument has not been altered.

A person who is negligent in writing or signing a negotiable instrument may be precluded from asserting an unauthorized signature or alteration as a reason for not paying a holder in due course. If a negotiable instrument is made payable to an impostor or a fictitious payee, any signature in the name of the payee is effective as an indorsement. A person who converts an instrument—that is, exercises unauthorized ownership over it—may be held liable to the real owner.

Liability of a party on an instrument may be discharged by payment, cancellation, material alteration, or impairment of recourse.

PROBLEM CASES

1. Janota's signature appeared under the name of a corporation on a note acknowledging a $1,000 debt. No wording appeared other than Janota's name and the corporate name. The holder of the note sues Janota on the note. What will Janota argue, and what will the result be?

2. Frederick Dowie was the president and sole stockholder of Fred Dowie Enterprises, Inc., a catering company. He obtained the opportunity to operate the concession stands at the Living History Farms during the pope's visit to Des Moines, Iowa. With high expectations, Dowie ordered 325,000 hot dog buns from Colonial Baking Company. Before the buns were delivered, he presented to Colonial Baking a postdated check in the amount of $28,640. The check showed the name of the corporation and its address in the upper left-hand corner. The signature on the check read "Frederick J. Dowie," and there were no other words of explanation. Unfortunately, only 300 buns were sold. Following a dispute over the ownership and responsibility for the remaining buns, Dowie stopped payment on the check. Colonial Baking then sued Dowie in his personal capacity as signer of the check. Is Dowie personally liable for the check?

3. Phoenix Steel's board of directors adopted a resolution authorizing the Wilmington Bank to honor checks drawn on Phoenix's payroll account that bore facsimile signatures of designated officers. The resolution provided that the bank would be fully protected in acting on such authority. An employee of Phoenix later dishonestly and improperly affixed a facsimile signature of an officer to several blank payroll checks, and the bank unknowingly honored them. In an action by Phoenix against the bank for the alleged wrongful payment of the checks, will Phoenix prevail?

4. Wilson was presented with a check payable to Jones and Brown and drawn on Merchant's Bank. The check was indorsed by Brown alone. Wilson accepted the check, indorsed it, and submitted it to Merchant's Bank for payment. Merchant's Bank paid Wilson. Does Merchant's Bank or Wilson bear the liability if Jones seeks payment on the check?

5. First National Bank certified Smith's check in the amount of $29. After certification, Smith altered the check so that it read $2,900. He presented the check to a merchant in payment for goods. The merchant then submitted the check to the bank for payment. The bank refused, saying that it had only certified the instrument for $29. Can the merchant recover the $2,900 from the bank?

6. A check was drawn on First National Bank and made payable to Howard. It came into the possession of Carson, who forged Howard's indorsement and cashed it at Merchant's Bank. Merchant's Bank then indorsed it and collected from First National. Assuming that Carson is nowhere to be found, who bears the ultimate liability?

7. Doris Strahl was the payee on a $3,000 check drawn on Pacific First Federal Savings and Loan (drawee) by Puget Sound National Bank (drawer). Peter Miller, the owner of a service station, replaced the engine in a motor home owned by Strahl. His charge for the new engine was $2,500. Strahl gave him the $3,000 check without indorsing it, and he gave her $500 change. On March 22, 1979, Miller deposited the check in his business account at Southwestern Bank, which sent it for payment to Puget Sound National Bank. Puget Sound returned the check to Southwestern Bank on May 17, 1979, on the ground that the absence of an indorsement by the payee, Doris Strahl, constituted a breach by Southwestern Bank of the presentment warranty of good title. Southwestern in turn charged back Miller's account. Since Miller had written checks on his account in the interim, the charge-back resulted in his account being overdrawn. Miller brought suit against Southwestern Bank challenging the charge-back. Does Miller have a valid legal basis for challenging the charge-back?

8. On August 3, 1961, J. P. Leonard made out a check for $600, signed it as drawer, and indorsed his signature on the back of the check. He did not date the check, nor did he fill in the payee's name. Leonard claimed that he gave the check to a man named Santo, to whom he owed $600, and that he indorsed the check on the back so that Santo could cash it "at the track." When the check was returned to Leonard by the National Bank of West Virginia after it had charged the check to his account, "Thrity" [sic] had been written in front of "Six hundred," the name Martin Mattson had been entered as payee, and the indorsement of Martin Mattson appeared on the back of the check above Leonard's signature. Leonard then sued National Bank to have his account recredited for $3,600. Should Leonard be entitled to have his account recredited?

9. Mrs. Johnson mailed a loan application to First National Bank in her husband's name and without his knowledge. Having dealt with her husband before, the bank approved the application and mailed a check in the amount requested to Mr. Johnson. Mrs. Johnson then indorsed the check in her husband's name and cashed it at Merchant's Bank. Merchant's Bank indorsed the check and presented it for payment. First National, having discovered the deception, refused to pay. Is First National liable on the check?

10. Clarice Rich was employed by the New York City Board of Education as a clerk. It was her duty to prepare requisitions for checks to be issued by the board, to prepare the checks, to have them signed by the authorized personnel, and to send the checks to the recipients. In some instances, however, she retained them. Also, on a number of occasions, she prepared duplicate requisitions and checks, which, when signed, she likewise retained. She then forged the indorsement of the named payees on the checks she had retained and cashed the checks at Chemical Bank, where the Board of Education maintained its account. After the board discovered the forgeries, it demanded that Chemical Bank credit its account for the amount of the forged checks. Is Chemical Bank required to credit the board's account as requested? *No*

11. Charles Peterson, a farmer and rancher, was indebted to Crown Financial Corporation on a $4,450,000 promissory note that was due on December 29, 1972. Shortly before the note was due, Crown sent Peterson a statement of interest due on the note ($499,658.850). Petersen paid the interest and executed a new note in the amount of $4,450,000 that was to mature in December 1975. The old note was then marked "canceled" and returned to Peterson. In 1975, Crown billed Peterson for $363,800 in interest that had been due on the first note but apparently not included in the statement. Peterson claimed that the interest had been forgiven and that he was not obligated to pay it. Was Peterson still obligated to pay interest on the note that had been returned to him marked "canceled"?

12. David Bluffestone lent money to Gary, Bert, and Lee Abrahams in connection with a car wash business that they operated together. When David died, his son-in-law, Alan Gilenko, came to help David's wife, Pearl, straighten out her financial affairs. He found a promissory note for $5,000 payable on demand signed by Gary, Bert, and Lee Abrahams among David's possessions. At the time, the note did not have any provision for monthly payments or for attorney's fees. Gilenko added provisions for monthly payments and attorney's fees to the note. Bert and Lee Abrahams then resigned the note with knowledge of the alterations. Gary did not sign the note again after the alterations had been made and did not have knowledge of them. When the Abrahams did not pay off the note, Pearl Bluffestone brought an action against Gary, Bert, and Lee to collect on the promissory note payable to her deceased husband. Gary Abrahams contended that he was not liable on the $5,000 note, because it had been materially altered without his consent or knowledge. Is the note enforceable against Gary Abrahams?

CHAPTER 26

CHECKS AND DOCUMENTS OF TITLE

INTRODUCTION

For most people, a checking account provides the majority of their contact with negotiable instruments. This chapter focuses on the relationship between the drawer with a checking account and the drawee bank. It addresses such common questions as: What happens if a bank refuses to pay a check even though the depositor has sufficient funds in her account? Does the bank have the right to create an overdraft in a depositor's account by paying an otherwise properly payable check? What are the depositor's rights and the bank's obligation if the depositor stops payment on a check? What is the difference between a certified check and a cashier's check? What are the depositor's responsibilities when she receives her monthly statement and canceled checks? The second half of the chapter discusses the Code rules that apply to negotiable documents of title such as warehouse receipts and bills of lading.

THE DRAWER-DRAWEE RELATIONSHIP

There are always two sources that govern the relationship between the depositor and the drawee bank: the deposit agreement and Articles 3 and 4 of the Code. Article 4, which governs Bank Deposits and Collec-tions, allows the depositor and drawee bank (which Article 4 calls the "payor bank") to vary Article 4's provisions with a few important exceptions. The deposit agreement cannot disclaim the bank's responsibility for its own lack of good faith or failure to exercise ordinary care or limit the measure of damages prescribed in Article 4 for such lack or failure [4–103(1)].[1]

The deposit agreement establishes many important relationships between the depositor and payor/drawee bank, one of which is their relationship as creditor and debtor, respectively. Thus, when a person deposits money in an account at the bank, he no longer is considered the owner of the money. Instead, he is a *creditor* of the bank to the extent of his deposits and the bank becomes his *debtor*. When the depositor deposits a check to a checking account, the bank also becomes his *agent* for collection of the check. The bank as the person's agent owes a *duty* to him to follow his *reasonable instructions* concerning payment of checks and other items from his account and a *duty of ordinary care* in collecting checks and other items deposited to the account.

---

[1]The numbers in brackets refer to the sections of the Uniform Commercial Code.

Bank's Duty to Pay

When a bank receives a properly drawn and payable check on a person's account and there are sufficient funds to cover the check, the bank is under a *duty* to pay it. If the person has sufficient funds in the account and the bank refuses to pay, or dishonors, the check, the bank is liable for the damages proximately caused by its wrongful dishonor. If the bank can show that it rejected the check by mistake, then the depositor can hold the bank liable only for any actual damages that the despositor can show that he suffered. These damages can include both direct and consequential damages [4–402]. Direct damages include charges imposed by retailers for returned checks; consequential damages include injury to the depositor's credit rating that results from the dishonor.

For example, Donald Dodson writes a check for $1,500 to Ames Auto Sales in payment for a used car. At the time that Ames Auto presents the check for payment at Dodson's bank, First National Bank, Dodson has $1,800 in his account. However, a teller mistakenly refuses to pay the check and stamps it NSF (not sufficient funds). Ames Auto then goes to the local prosecutor and signs a complaint against Dodson for writing a bad check. As a result, Dodson is arrested. Dodson can recover from First National the damages that he sustained because his check was wrongfully dishonored, including the damages involved in his arrest, such as his attorney's fees.

In the case that follows, *Buckley v. Trenton Savings Fund Society*, the bank is potentially liable for consequential damages sustained by the drawer if it cannot show that it dishonored checks by mistake.

BUCKLEY v. TRENTON SAVINGS FUND SOCIETY

524 A.2d 886 (N.J. Super. Ct. 1987)

Buckley maintained a checking account at the Trenton Savings Fund Society. In 1981, he separated from his wife, Linda, and entered into a consent agreement with her in which he agreed to pay her $150 per week for food and support for herself and their children. On January 13, 1984, Buckley wrote a check for $150 and gave it to his wife. The next Saturday, she presented it for payment at one of Trenton Savings' branches but payment was refused even though Buckley had $900 in the account at the time. The following Monday, she took it to another branch where payment was again refused. The bank told Linda that it would not cash the check for her because Linda did not have an account at the bank. Subsequently, the bank agreed to cash checks for Linda, but on March 4, 1984, the bank again refused to pay one of Buckley's checks that she presented for payment. Linda was known to the bank because it held a mortgage on the home that she and Buckley jointly owned.

Shortly after Trenton Bank's failure to cash the two checks, Buckley received an irate call from Linda. He also received calls from his parents, his sister, and his best friend inquiring as to why he was not making the support payments. In addition, his children inquired "why daddy wouldn't give them food money." Buckley incurred severe emotional distress over the matter. He brought suit against Trenton Savings for wrongful dishonor and sought compensatory damages, as well as punitive damages, for the mental anguish he sustained. The trial court entered judgment for Buckley based on a jury verdict for $25,000, and the bank appealed.

Stern, Judge.   The bank contends that the jury should not have been permitted to award damages for emotional distress under the facts of this case.

A bank's liability for wrongful dishonor of a customer's check is defined in section 4–402 of the Uniform Commercial Code:

A payor bank is liable to its customer for damages proximately caused by the wrongful dishonor of an item. When the dishonor occurs through mistake, liability is limited to actual damages proved. If so proximately caused and proved, damages may include damages for an arrest or prosecution of the customer or other consequential damages. Whether any consequential damages are proximately caused by the wrongful dishonor is a question of fact to be determined in each case.

The UCC does not indicate the theory or basis for a bank's liability for wrongful dishonor. As explained in the UCC official comment to section 4–402, "The liability of the drawee for dishonor has sometimes been stated as one for breach of contract, sometimes as for negligence or other breach of a tort duty, and sometimes as for defamation. The drafters of the UCC did not intend to exclude the possibility of mental distress damages upon a wrongful dishonor by a bank. Since section 4–402 is silent on any restriction of damages when the dishonor is grounded on an action other than mistake, it implies that these damages are not precluded by the Code. Thus, out-of-state courts interpreting section 4–402 have concluded that mental suffering is compensable under this section.

The Legislature adopted section 4–402 as promulgated in the Uniform Commercial Code without substantive change. The section expressly limits recovery for "actual damages" when the dishonor results from "mistake" but otherwise expressly permits recovery of "consequential damages" proximately caused. As *White and Summer* explains:

When wrongful dishonors occur not "through mistake" but willfully, the court may impose damages greater than "actual damages."

* * * * *

Might one argue that "actual damages" excludes recovery for mental distress? We think not. In the first place, the drafters went to great efforts to assure that customers can recover for arrest and prosecution. It is inconsistent to allow recovery for embarrassment and mental distress deriving from arrest and prosecution and to deny similar recovery in other cases. Moreover, cases under the predecessor to 4–402, the American Association Statute, held that "actual damages" includes damages for mental distress. Thus we believe . . . that the Code drafter intended to allow recovery for mental distress and other intangible injury.

In this case the judge's instructions failed to delineate the distinction between mistake and intentional mistake and an intentional breach or wilful, wanton or reckless conduct. As a result, the matter must be remanded for a new trial and for a determination of damages based on appropriate instructions.

We preclude an award of punitive damages. Punitive damages are not generally recoverable for breach of contract, at least when the breach of contract does not also constitute a tort for which punitive damages are recoverable.

Reversed and remanded for new trial.

Bank's Right to Charge to Customer's Account

The drawee bank has the right to charge any *properly payable check* to the account of the customer or drawer. The bank has this right even though payment of the check creates an overdraft in the account [4–401]. If an account is overdrawn, the customer owes the bank the amount of the overdraft and the bank may take that amount out of the next deposit that the customer makes or from another account that the depositor maintains with the bank. Alternatively, the bank might seek to collect the amount directly from the customer. The *Pulaski State Bank v. Kalbe* case, which follows, illustrates this situation.

PULASKI STATE BANK v. KALBE

364 N.W.2d 162 (Wis. Ct. App. 1985)

Louise Kalbe signed a check drawn on her account at the Pulaski State Bank; later, that check was lost or stolen. The check was drafted for $7,260 payable to cash. The bank paid the check, which created an overdraft of $6,542.12 in Kalbe's account. The bank brought a lawsuit against Kalbe to recover the overdraft. The trial court awarded judgment to the bank and Kalbe appealed.

Dean, Judge.   The bank could properly pay the check even though it created an overdraft. Section 4–401 unambiguously states that a bank may charge a customer's account for an item otherwise properly payable even though the charge creates an overdraft. The bank's payment of an overdraft is treated as a loan to the depositor, which may be recovered.

Kalbe argues that checks creating unusually large overdrafts are not properly payable. She relies on the definition of properly payable that "includes the availability of funds for payment at the time of decision to pay or dishonor." Section 4–104(1)(i). Section 4–104(1)(i), however, is a source of bank discretion and does not limit the bank's power to pay overdrafts. The statute gives banks the option of dishonoring checks when sufficient funds are not available. The bank may consider the check to be not properly payable and refuse to pay without risk for wrongful dishonor. This does not prevent the bank from alternatively paying the overdraft check and, if it is otherwise properly payable, charging the customer's account. Section 4–401(1) places no limit on the size of the overdraft or the bank's reason for payment. Construing the statutes together, "otherwise properly payable" refers to those requirements other than availability of funds.

It is undisputed that in all other respects, the check was properly payable. Kalbe does not argue that the bank honored an altered check or a check bearing a forged or unauthorized maker's signature. The check was therefore properly payable and Kalbe's liability is complete. The check creating the overdraft carried Kalbe's implied promise to reimburse the bank.

Judgment for bank affirmed.

The bank does not owe a duty to its customer to pay any checks out of the account that are more than six months old. Such checks are called *stale checks*. However, the bank may in good faith pay a check that is more than six months old and charge it to the drawer-depositor's account [4–404].

If the bank in good faith pays a check drawn by the drawer-depositor but subsequently altered, it may charge the customer's account with the amount of the check as originally drawn. Also, if an incomplete check of a customer gets into circulation, is completed, and presented to the drawee bank for payment, and the bank pays the check, the bank can charge the amount as completed to the customer's account even though it knows that the check has been completed, unless it has notice that the completion was improper [4–401(2)]. The respective rights, obligations, and liabilities of drawee banks and their drawer-customers concerning forged and altered checks are discussed in more detail later in this chapter.

Article 4 recognizes that the bank's right or duty to pay a check or to charge the depositor's account for the check (including exercising its right to set off an amount due to it by the depositor) may be terminated, suspended, or modified by the depositor's order to stop payment (which is discussed in the next section of this chapter) or by events external to the relationship between the depositor and the bank. These external events include the filing of a bankruptcy petition by the depositor or by the depositor's creditors, and the garnishment of the account by a creditor of the depositor. The bank must receive the stop-payment order from its depositor or the notice of the bankruptcy filing or garnishment before the bank has certified the check, paid it in cash, settled with another bank for the amount of the item without a right to revoke the settlement, completed the process necessary to its decision to pay the check, or otherwise become accountable for the amount of the check under Article 4 [4–303]. These restrictions on the bank's right or duty to pay are discussed in later sections of this chapter.

Stop-Payment Order

A **stop-payment order** is a request made by the drawer of a check to the drawee bank instructing it not to pay or certify the check. As the drawer's agent in the payment of checks, the drawee bank must follow the reasonable orders of the drawer about payments made on the drawer's behalf. To be effective, a stop-payment order must be received in time to give the drawee bank a *reasonable opportunity to act* on it. This means that the stop-payment order must be given to the bank before it has paid or certified the check. The stop-payment order also must come soon enough to give the bank time to instruct its tellers and other employees that they should not pay or certify the check [4–403(1)]. The stop-payment order also must describe the check with sufficient detail for the bank's employees to recognize it as the check corresponding to the stop-payment order.

An *oral stop-payment order* can be given to the bank, but it is valid for only 14 days unless it is confirmed in writing during that time. A *written stop-payment order* is valid for six months and can be extended for an additional six months by giving the bank instructions in writing to continue the order [4–403(2)]. See Figure 1.

Sometimes the information given the bank by the customer concerning the check on which payment is to be stopped is incorrect. For example, there may be an error in the payee's name, the amount of the check, or the number of the check. The question then arises whether the customer has accorded the bank a reasonable opportunity to act on his request. The following *FJS Electronics v. Fidelity Bank* case involves such a problem.

FIGURE 1 Stop-Payment Order

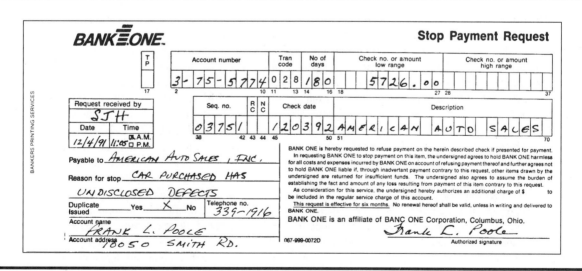

FJS ELECTRONICS, INC. v. FIDELITY BANK

28 UCC Rep. 1462 (Pa. Ct. C.P. 1980)

On February 27, 1976, Multi-Tek issued check number 896 in the face amount of $1,844.98, drawn on Multi-Tek's account at Fidelity and made payable to Multilayer Computer Circuits. However, on March 9, 1976, Frank J. Suttill, Multi-Tek's president, telephoned Fidelity and placed a stop-payment order on the check. The order was received and simultaneously recorded by Roanna M. Sanders, Fidelity's employee. This recordation contained the following information: the name of the account, the account number, the check number, the date of the check, the date and hour the stop-payment order was received, and the amount of the check as $1,844.48. This recordation was essentially correct in all respects, except for the amount of the check—there being a 50-cent difference between the face amount ($1,844.98) and the amount listed in the stop-payment order ($1,844.48).

Subsequently, a confirmation notice bearing the date "03/ 76" was mailed by Fidelity to Multi-Tek. It contained, among other things, the following information:

PAYEE: MULTILAYER COMPUTER CIRCUITS
AMOUNT: $1,844.48
CK. NO.: 896
DATE: 02/27/76

The instructions in this confirmation notice concluded with: PLEASE ENSURE AMOUNT IS CORRECT. This confirmation notice was signed by Suttill and returned to Fidelity.

Fidelity's computer was programmed to pull checks only if all of the digits on the stop-payment order agreed with those on the check. As a result, check number 896 was honored by Fidelity and charged to Multi-Tek's account. Multi-Tek then brought suit against Fidelity to recover $1,844.98 because the check was paid over the stop-payment order.

Marutani, Judge.   The Uniform Commercial Code, § 4–403(1), provides in pertinent part that: "A customer may by order to his bank stop payment of any item payable for his account but the order must be received at such time and in such manner as to afford the bank a reasonable opportunity to act on it prior to any action by the bank with respect to the item."

In this case, there is no question that the transmittal of the stop-payment order was made timely; this leaves for resolution only whether such order was given "in such *manner* as to afford the bank a reasonable opportunity to act on it": UCC § 4–403(1); emphasis added. While the parties "may by agreement determine the standards by which [the bank's] responsibility is to be measured if such standards are not manifestly unreasonable," at the same time "no agreement can disclaim a bank's responsibility for its failure to exercise ordinary care": UCC § 4–103(1).

The decisional law constituting § 4–403(1) appears to vary. Thus, in a recent decision of a trial court wherein the customer identified the check correctly as to the payee, the check number, and the date of issuance, but erred by 10 cents as to the amount of the check—$1,804.00 instead of the correct amount of $1,804.10—it was held that "the check was described with sufficient particularity and accuracy so that the bank should have known to give effect to the stop-payment order." However, where the customer provided the correct amount of the check but erred as to the date and name of the payee—one-day error in date, "Walter Morris Buick" instead of the correct name "Frank Morris Buick"—the Alabama Supreme Court held such to be insufficient notice.

In this case, as the parties by the stipulation agreed, "the Bank did not tell Mr. Suttill, nor did he request, information as to the procedure whereby the computer pulls checks on which stop payments have been issued." Under such circumstances, where the customer (Mr. Suttill) was called upon by the bank (Fidelity) to provide numerous data relating to the check in question, but the bank failed to emphasize to him that all such information may well be ineffective unless the amount of the check were absolutely accurate, we are constrained to be guided by the official comment to § 4–403 under "Purposes," which reads:

2. The position taken by this section is that stopping payment is a service which depositors expect and are entitled to receive from banks notwithstanding its difficulty, inconvenience and expense. The inevitable occasional losses through failure to stop should be borne by the banks as a cost of the business of banking.

Judgment for Multi-Tek.

Bank's Liability for Payment after Stop-Payment Order

While a stop-payment order is in effect, the drawee bank is liable to the drawer of a check that it pays for any loss that the drawer suffers by reason of such payment. However, the drawer has the burden of establishing the fact and amount of the loss. To show a loss, the drawer must establish that the drawee bank paid a person against whom the drawer had a valid defense to payment. To the extent that the drawer has such a defense, he has suffered a loss due to the drawee's failure to honor the stop-payment order.

For example, Brown buys what is represented to be a new car from Foster Ford and gives Foster Ford his check for $12,280 drawn on First Bank. Brown then discovers that the car is in fact a used demonstrator model and calls First Bank, ordering it to stop payment on the check. If Foster Ford presents the check for payment the following day and First Bank pays the check despite the stop-payment order, Brown can require the bank to recredit his account. (The depositor-drawer bases her claim to recredit on the fact that the bank did not follow her final instruction—the instruction not to pay the check.) Brown had a valid defense of misrepresentation that he could have asserted against Foster Ford if it had sued him on the check. Foster Ford would have been required to sue on the check or on Brown's contractual obligation to pay for the car.

Assume, instead, that Foster Ford negotiated the check to Smith and that Smith qualified as a holder in due course. Then, if the bank paid the check to Smith over the stop-payment order, Brown would not be able to have his account recredited, because Brown would not be able to show that he sustained any loss. If the bank had refused to pay the check, so that Smith came against

Brown on his drawer's liability, Brown's personal defense of misrepresentation of the prior use of the car could not be used as a reason for not paying Smith. Brown's only recourse would be to go directly against Foster Ford on his misrepresentation claim.

The bank may ask the customer to sign a form in which the bank tries to disclaim or limit its liability for the stop-payment order. As explained at the beginning of this chapter, the bank is not permitted to disclaim its responsibility for its failure to act in good faith or to exercise ordinary care in paying a check over a stop-payment order [4–103].

If a bank pays a check after it has been given a stop-payment order, it acquires all the rights of the person to whom it makes payment, including rights arising from the transaction on which the check was based [4–407]. In the previous example involving Brown and Foster Ford, assume that Brown was able to have his account recredited because First Bank had paid the check to Foster Ford over his stop-payment order. Then, the bank would have any rights that Brown had against Foster Ford for the misrepresentation.

If a person stops payment on a check and the bank honors the stop-payment order, the person may still be liable to the holder of the check. Suppose Peters writes a check for $450 to Ace Auto Repair in payment for repairs to her automobile. While driving the car home, she concludes that the car was not properly repaired. She calls her bank and stops payment on the check. Ace Auto negotiated the check to Sam's Auto Parts, which took the check as a holder in due course. When Sam's takes the check to Peters's bank, payment is refused because of the stop-payment order. Sam's then comes after Peters on her drawer's liability. All Peters has is a personal defense against payment, which is not good against

FIGURE 2   Certified Check

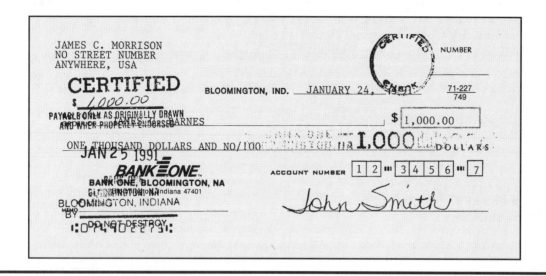

---

a holder in due course. So, Peters must pay Sam's the $450 and pursue her claim separately against Ace. If Ace were still the holder of the check, however, the situation would be different. Peters's personal defense concerning the faulty work could be used against Ace to reduce or possibly cancel her obligation to pay the check.

Certified Check

Normally, a drawee bank is not obligated to certify a check. When a drawee bank does *certify* a check, it substitutes its undertaking to pay the check and, as Article 3 provides, becomes *primarily liable for payment* of the check. At the time a check is certified, the bank usually debits the customer's account for the amount of the certified check and shifts the money to a special account at the bank. It also adds its signature to the check to show that it has accepted primary liability for paying it. The bank's signature is an essential part of the certification; the bank's signature must appear on the check [3–410(1)]. If the holder of a check chooses to have it certified, rather than seeking to have it paid at that time, the holder has made a conscious decision to look to the certifying bank for payment and is no longer relying on the drawer or the indorsers to pay it. See Figure 2 for an example of a certified check.

If a check is certified by the drawee bank at the request of the drawer, the drawer remains secondarily liable on the check. However, if the drawee bank certifies a check at the request of a holder of the check, then the drawer and any persons who have already indorsed the check are discharged of their liability on the check [3–411(1)].

Cashier's Check

A **cashier's check** differs from a **certified check.** A check on which a bank is both the drawer and the drawee is a cashier's check. The bank is primarily liable on the cashier's check. The question of whether a bank may refuse to honor a cashier's check has been the subject of considerable litigation. Some states consider the cashier's check to be a substitute for cash and do not allow banks to honor stop-payment requests against cashier's checks or to refuse to pay them. In other states, an issuing bank may raise appropriate defenses and may refuse to pay a cashier's check held by a party to the check with whom it has dealt. See Figure 3 for an example of a cashier's check. A **teller's check** is similar to a cashier's check in that it is a check on which one bank is the drawer and another bank is the drawee.

FIGURE 3 Cashier's Check

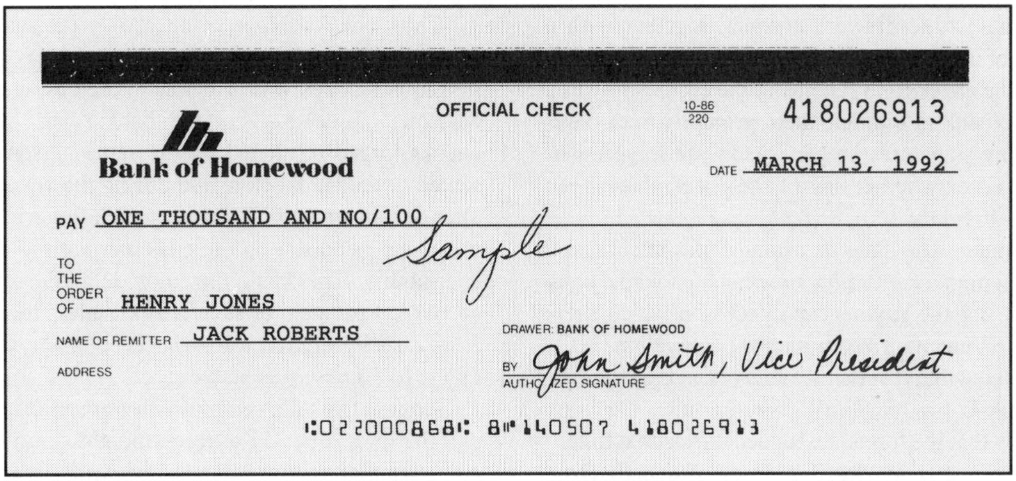

Death or Incompetence of Customer

Under the general principles of agency law, the death or incompetence of the principal terminates the agent's authority to act for the principal. However, slightly different rules apply to the authority of a bank to pay checks out of the account of a deceased or incompetent person. The bank has the right to pay the checks of an incompetent person until it has notice that a court has determined the person is incompetent. Once the bank learns of this fact, it loses its authority to pay that person's checks—because the depositor is not competent to issue instructions to pay.

Similarly, a bank has the right to pay the checks of a deceased customer until it has notice of the customer's death. Even if a bank knows of a customer's death, for a period of 10 days after the customer's death, it can pay checks written by the customer prior to his death. However, the deceased person's heirs or other persons claiming an interest in the account can order the bank to stop payment [4–405].

FORGED AND ALTERED CHECKS

Bank's Right to Charge Account

A check that bears a forged signature of the drawer or payee is generally not properly payable from the cus-tomer's account because the bank is not following the instructions of the depositor precisely as he gave them. The bank is expected to be familiar with the authorized signature of its depositor. If it pays such a check, Article 4 will treat the transaction as one in which the bank paid out its own funds, rather than the depositor's funds.

Similarly, a check that was altered after the drawer made it out—for example, by increasing the amount of the check—generally is not properly payable from the customer's account. However, as noted earlier, if the drawer is *negligent* and contributes to the forgery or alteration, he may be barred from claiming it as the reason that a particular check should not be charged to his account.

For example, Barton makes a check for $1 in a way that makes it possible for someone to easily alter it to read $101, and it is so altered. If the drawee bank pays the check to a holder in good faith, it can charge the $101 to Barton's account if Barton's negligence contributed to the alteration. Similarly, if a company uses a mechanical checkwriter to write checks, it must use reasonable care to see that unauthorized persons do not have access to blank checks and to the checkwriter.

If the alteration is obvious, the bank should note that fact and refuse to pay the check when it is presented for payment. Occasionally, the alteration is so skillful that the bank cannot detect it. In that case, the bank is allowed to charge to the account the amount for which the check was originally written.

Customer's Duty to Report Forgeries and Alterations

Commonly, the bank will return the checks it has charged against the drawer's account, together with a statement of account, to the customer once a month. On receiving the checks and statement, the customer owes a duty to the bank to examine them promptly to discover whether any signatures on the checks are forgeries or unauthorized or whether any of the checks have been altered [4–406(1)].

A customer who fails to examine the checks and statement within a *reasonable time* cannot hold the bank responsible for the payment of checks on which there are forgeries, unauthorized signings, or alterations if the bank can show that it suffered a loss because of the customer's failure [4–406(2)(a)]. For example, the bank might show that the forger absconded during that time.

A different rule applies if a series of unauthorized drawer's signatures or alterations are made by the same wrongdoer. The customer generally cannot hold the bank responsible for paying any such checks if the bank can show (1) that it paid the check in good faith, (2) that it paid after the first check that had been signed on behalf of the drawer or altered without the drawer's authority was available to the customer for a reasonable period not exceeding 14 calendar days, and (3) before the bank received notification from the customer of any such unauthorized signature or alteration [4–406(2)(b)]. Unless the customer has notified the bank about the forgeries or alterations, then any subsequent forgeries or alterations by the same wrongdoer are the responsibility of the customer unless she can establish a lack of ordinary care on the part of the drawee bank [4–406(3)]. A lack of ordinary care includes, for example, payment of a check on which the drawer's signature bears no resemblance to the depositor's signature on the deposit agreement, or of a check on which the alterations were very obvious.

Thus, checks forged or altered by the same person and presented to the bank more than 14 days after the first forged check was available to the customer are the customer's problem—not the bank's. The amount of checks forged or altered by the same person and presented to the bank before and during the 14-day period after the statement first revealing such forgeries or alterations has been sent to the customer are the bank's responsibility. The bank may not debit the customer's account in payment of such checks unless the bank can show that it suffered a loss because of the customer's failure to exercise reasonable care.

Suppose that Allen employs Farnum as an accountant and that over a period of three months, Farnum forges Allen's signature to 10 checks and cashes them. One of the forged checks is included in the checks returned to Allen at the end of the first month. Within 14 calendar days after the return of these checks, Farnum forges two more checks and cashes them. Allen does not examine the returned checks until three months after the checks that included the first forged check were returned to her. The bank would be responsible for the first forged check and for the two checks forged and cashed within the 14-day period after it sent the first statement and the canceled checks (unless the bank proves that it suffered a loss because of the customer's failure to examine the checks and notify it more promptly). It would not be liable for the seven forged checks cashed after the expiration of the 14-day period.

The case that follows, *Rhode Island Hospital Trust National Bank v. Zapata*, illustrates how the UCC applies to a series of a forgeries.

RHODE ISLAND HOSPITAL TRUST NATIONAL BANK v. ZAPATA CORP.
6 UCC Rep.2d 1 (1st Cir. 1988)

In early 1985, an employee of the Zapata Corporation stole some blank checks from the company. She wrote a large number of forged checks, almost all in amounts of $150 to $800 each, on Zapata's account at Rhode Island Hospital Trust National Bank. The bank, from March through July 1985, received and paid them. Bank statements that the bank regularly sent Zapata first began to reflect the forged checks in early 1985. Zapata failed to examine its statements closely until July 1985, when it found the forgeries. It immediately notified the bank, which then stopped clearing the checks. The bank had already processed and paid checks containing forged drawer's signatures totaling $109,247.16. Zapata then brought suit against the bank to have its account recredited for the checks. The district court held that the bank was liable to reimburse Zapata for the checks that it paid before April 25, 1985 (two weeks after Zapata received the first statement containing the forged checks), but held in favor of the bank as to the remaining checks. Zapata appealed.

Breyer, Circuit Judge.   The issue that this appeal presents is whether Zapata Corporation has shown that the system used by Rhode Island Hospital Trust National Bank for detecting forged checks—a system used by a majority of American banks—lacks the "ordinary care" that a bank must exercise under the Uniform Commercial Code section 4–406(3). The question arises out of the following district court determinations, all of which are adequately supported by the record and by Rhode Island law.

3. The Bank will (and legally must) reimburse Zapata in respect to all checks it cleared before April 25 (or for at least two weeks after Zapata received the statement that reflected the forgeries). See sections 3–401(1), 4–406(2).

4. In respect to checks cleared on and after April 25, the Bank need not reimburse Zapata because Zapata failed to "exercise reasonable care and promptness to examine the [bank] statements." Section 4–406(1).

The question before us is whether this last-mentioned conclusion is correct or whether Zapata can recover for the post–April 24 checks on the theory that, even if it was negligent, so was the Bank.

To understand this question, one must examine UCC section 4–406. Ordinarily a bank must reimburse an innocent customer for forgeries that it honors, section 3–401(1), but section 4–406 makes an important exception to the liability rule. The exception operates in respect to a series of forged checks, and it applies once a customer has had a chance to catch the forgeries by examining his bank statements and notifying the bank but has failed to do so.

The statute, in relevant part, reads as follows:

(1) *When a bank sends to its customer a statement of account* accompanied by items paid in good faith in support of the debit entries or holds the statement and items pursuant to a request or instructions of its customer or otherwise in a reasonable manner makes the statement and items available to the customer, *the customer must exercise reasonable care and promptness to examine the statement* and items *to discover his unauthorized signature* or any alteration on an item *and must notify the bank promptly* after discovery thereof.

(2) *If the bank establishes that the customer failed* with respect to an item *to comply with* the duties imposed on the customer by *subsection (1) the customer is precluded from asserting against the bank*

(a) *His unauthorized signature* or any alteration on the item if the bank also establishes that it suffered a loss by reason of such failure; *and*

(b) *An unauthorized signature or alteration by the same wrongdoer on any other item paid in good faith by the bank after the first item and statement was available to the customer for a reasonable period not exceeding fourteen (14) calendar days* and before the bank receives notification from the customer of any such unauthorized signature or alteration.

Section 4–406(1)–(2) (emphasis added).

The statute goes on to specify an important exception. It says:

(3) The preclusion under subsection (2) does not apply if the customer establishes lack of ordinary care on the part of the bank in paying the item(s).

Section 4–406(3). Zapata's specific claim on this appeal is that it falls within this "exception to the exception"—that the bank's treatment of the post–April 24 checks lacked "ordinary care."

The statute places the burden of proof on Zapata. It says that strict bank liability terminates fourteen days after the customer receives the bank's statement unless "the *customer establishes* lack of ordinary care."

The record convinces us that Zapata failed to carry its burden of establishing "lack of ordinary care" on the part of the Bank. First the Bank described its ordinary practices as follows: The Bank examines all signatures on checks for more than $1,000. It examines signatures on checks between $100 and $1,000 (those at issue here) if it has reason to suspect a problem, e.g. if a customer has warned it of a possible forgery or if the check was drawn on an account with insufficient funds. It examines the signatures of a randomly chosen one percent of all other checks between $100 and $1,000. But it does not examine the signatures on other checks between $100 and $1,000. Through expert testimony, the Bank also established that most other banks in the nation follow this practice and that banking industry experts recommend it. Indeed, the Bank's practices are conservative in this regard, as most banks set $2,500 or more, not $1,000, as the limit beneath which they will not examine each signature. This testimony made out a prima facie case of "ordinary care."

Second, both bank and industry experts pointed out that this industry practice, in general and in the particular case of the Bank, saved considerable expense, compared with the Bank's pre-1981 practice of examining each check by hand. To be specific, the change saved the Bank about $125,000 annually.

Third, both a Bank official and an industry expert testified that changing from an "individual signature examination" system to the new "bulk-filing" system led to *no* significant increase in the number of forgeries that were detected. Under the Bank's prior "individual signature examination" some forgeries still slipped through.

Fourth, even if one assumes, contrary to this uncontradicted evidence, that the new system meant *some* increase in the number of undetetected forged checks, Zapata still could not prevail, for it presented *no* evidence tending to show any such increased loss unreasonable in light of the costs that the new practice would save.

Judgment for Rhode Island Hospital Trust National Bank affirmed.

CONCEPT REVIEW

LIABILITY FOR MULTIPLE FORGERIES OR ALTERATIONS BY THE SAME PERSON

Date First Statement Disclosing an Altered or Forged Check Is Available to Customer	Date 14 Days Later	Date Customer Gives Notice of Alteration or Forgery
Customer is not liable for forged/altered checks paid during this period unless bank suffers a loss from customer's unreasonable delay in notifying bank of forgery or alteration.	Customer is liable for forged or altered checks paid during this period unless customer gives bank notice of forgery or alteration within a reasonable time after date the first statement containing a forged or altered check was available to customer.	Customer is not liable for forged or altered checks paid during this period.

In any event, a customer must discover and report to the bank any forgery of his signature or any alteration within one year from the time the checks are made available to him. If the customer does not do so, he cannot require the bank to recredit his account for such checks. Similarly, a customer has three years from the time his checks are made available to discover and report any unauthorized indorsement. The depositor's failure to discover and report these irregularities within the one- or three-year periods specified costs him the right to recredit the amount of the checks [4–406(4)].

CHECK COLLECTION AND FUNDS AVAILABILITY

Check Collection

As the Negotiable Instruments chapter describes, checks and other drafts collected through the banking system usually have at least three parties—the drawer, the drawee bank, and the payee. If the payee deposits the check at the same bank as the drawee bank, the latter will take a series of steps necessary to reflect the deposit as a credit to the payee's account and to decide whether to pay the check from the drawer's account. In connection with its handling of the deposit for the payee's benefit, it will make one ledger entry showing the deposit as a credit to the payee's account. In connection with its decision to pay, it will perform several steps commonly referred to as the *process of posting* [4–109]. These steps need not be taken in any particular order, but they customarily include comparing the drawer's signature on the check with that on the deposit agreement, determining whether there are sufficient funds to pay, debiting the drawer's account for the amount of the check, and placing the check into a folder for later return to the drawer (to satisfy its obligations under the "bank statement" rule [4–406(1)]).

If the payee deposits the check at a bank other than the drawee bank, the depositary bank, acting as the agent of the payee, will make the ledger entry showing the deposit as a credit to the payee's account. The next step of the collection process depends on where the depositary bank is located. If the drawee and depositary banks are in the same town or county, the depositary bank will indorse the check and deliver ("present") it to the drawee bank for payment. It may deliver it by courier or through a local association of banks known as a "clearing house" [4–104(1)(d)]. The drawee-payor bank must settle for the check before midnight of the banking day of its receipt of the check, which means that it must give the depositary bank funds or a credit equal to the amount of the check. Once it settles for the check, the drawee-payor bank has until midnight of the banking day after the banking day of receipt to pay the check or to return the check or send notice of dishonor. This deadline for the drawee-payor bank's action on the check is known as the bank's "midnight deadline" [4–104(1)(h)]. The drawee-payor bank's failure to settle by midnight of the banking day of receipt, or its failure to pay or return the check, or send notice of dishonor, results in the drawee-payor bank becoming "accountable" for the amount of the check, which means it must pay the amount of the check [4–302(a)].

If the drawee and depositary banks are located in different counties, or in different states, the depositary bank will use an additional commercial bank, and one or more of the regional Federal Reserve Banks, in the collection of the check. In these cases, the depositary bank will send the check on to the drawee-payor bank through these "collecting banks." Each bank in the sequence must use ordinary care in presenting the check or sending it for presentment, and in sending notice of dishonor or returning the check after learning that the check has not been paid [4–202(1)]. The depositary and collecting banks have until their respective midnight deadlines—or, in some cases, a further reasonable time—to take the action required of them in the sequence of collection steps.

If the drawee-payor bank dishonors the check prior to its midnight deadline or shortly after the midnight deadline under circumstances specified in "Regulation CC" of the Federal Reserve (described in the next section of this chapter), it will send the check back to the depositary bank. Until September 1, 1988, the drawee-payor bank customarily sent the dishonored check back to the collecting bank from which it received the check, and the collecting bank sent it back to the bank from which it had received it, and through any other bank that handled the check in the "forward collection" process until the check again reached the depositary bank. The provisions of Article 4 still describe this sequence of the "return collection" process, although Regulation CC imposes new reponsibilities on the payor bank and on any other returning bank. Each bank in the return sequence adjusts its accounts to reflect the return and has until its midnight deadline to send the check on to the bank from which it originally had received the check. After September 1, 1988 (or in states that previously had adopted "direct return" (4–212(2)), the drawee-payor bank may return the check *directly* to the depositary bank—skipping all of the collecting banks and the delay represented by the midnight deadlines that each bank otherwise would have had.

Direct return also increases the likelihood that the depositary bank will know whether the check has been dishonored by the day on which Regulation CC requires the depositary bank to allow the payee to write checks or otherwise make withdrawals against the deposit. The next section of this chapter discusses this aspect of Regulation CC in more detail.

On receipt of the dishonored check, the depositary bank will return the check or otherwise notify the payee (its depositor) of the dishonor and will debit or charge back her account for the check it did not collect [4–212]. The depositary bank may charge back the deposit even if it previously had allowed the payee-depositor to withdraw against the credit given for the deposit.

When the depositor receives the notice of dishonor and returned check, it will take one of several steps depending on whether it received the check directly from the drawer, or took it by indorsement from another person. If the depositor was not the original payee of the check, it usually will prefer to return the check—giving notice of dishonor unless already given by the drawee bank or another collecting bank—to the person who negotiated the check to her, the prior indorser. Recall that indorsers agree that they will take up the check following dishonor and notice of dishonor [3–414(1)].

If the depositor received the check directly from the drawer, for example as payee, the depositor normally will demand payment from the drawer. Recall that the drawer has a contractual obligation to pay the check upon dishonor and notice of dishonor [3–413(2)]; alternatively, the payee may seek to enforce the underlying obligation for which the drawer originally issued the check, such as the purchase of groceries or an automobile.

Funds Availability

When a bank takes a check for deposit to a customer's account, it typically places a hold on the funds represented by the deposited check because it runs a number of risks in allowing a customer to withdraw deposits that have not been finally collected from the drawee bank. The risks that the check may be returned include: (1) there may be insufficient funds in the drawer's account or the account may have been closed; (2) the check may contain a forged drawer's or indorser's signature, or there may have been a material alteration of the check; (3) the possibility that the drawer is kiting checks or playing two accounts off against each other; or (4) a stop-payment order may have been placed against the check. These are real concerns to a depositary bank, and it has a significant interest in protecting itself against these possibilities.

Until recently, the risks run by a depositary bank were complicated by a very slow process used by drawee-payor banks in returning a dishonored check or notifying the bank of the dishonor. Moreover, depositary banks do not get direct notice from drawee-payor banks when they pay checks. Accordingly, banks often restricted the depositor's use of the deposit by placing relatively long holds on checks deposited with them for collection; these sometimes ran 15 to 20 days for items drawn on other than local banks.

The extensive use of holds, and a growing public sentiment that they were excessive and often unfair, led to the passage by Congress in 1987 of the *Expedited Funds Availability Act*. In the act, Congress set out mandatory schedules limiting check holds and specifying when funds are to be made available to customers by depositary institutions. The act also delegated to the Federal Reserve Board the authority to speed up the check processing system. The regulations adopted by the Board to speed up check processing supersede the provisions of Article 4 of the UCC (Bank Deposits and Collections) in a number of respects but will not be covered in this text.

The key elements of the mandatory funds availability schedules, which are set out in Federal Reserve Board Regulation CC and which are effective September 1, 1990, are:

1. Local checks (those drawn on banks in the same Federal Reserve check region as the depositary bank) must be made available for the depositor to draw against by the second business day following deposit.

2. Nonlocal checks (those drawn on banks located in the United States but outside the Federal Reserve check processing region in which the depositary bank is located) must be made available by the fifth business day following deposit.

3. Certain items must be made available by the next day after the day of deposit. These include:

a. Cash deposits where the deposit is banked in person to an employee of the depositary bank (i.e., not at an ATM).

b. Electronic payments.

c. Checks drawn on the U.S. Treasury.

d. U.S. Postal Service money orders.

e. Checks drawn on a Federal Reserve Bank or Federal Home Loan Bank.

f. Checks drawn by a state or a unit of local government (under certain conditions).

g. Cashier's, certified, or teller's checks.

h. Checks drawn on the depositary bank.

i. The lesser of $100 or the aggregate deposit on any one banking day.

4. If the next-day items are not deposited in person with an employee of the depositary institution but rather are deposited in an ATM machine or by mail, then the deposit does not have to be made available for withdrawal until the second business day after deposit.

5. Generally, the depositary bank must begin accruing interest to a depositor's interest-bearing account from the day it receives credit for cash and check deposits to an interest-bearing account.

Figure 4 shows graphically how the funds availability schedule works.

There are six major exceptions to the mandatory availability schedules set out above that are designed to safeguard depositary banks against higher risk situations. The exceptions are:

1. *The new account exception*. The depositary bank may suspend the availability rules for new accounts and can limit the next-day and second-day availability to the first $5,000 deposited.

2. *The large deposit exception*. The hold periods can be extended to the extent the aggregate deposit on any banking day exceeds $5,000.

3. *The redeposited check exception*. The hold period can be extended where a check has been returned one or more times.

4. *The repeated overdraft exception*. A longer hold period may be required for deposits to accounts that have been overdrawn repeatedly.

5. *The reasonable cause exception*. The scheduled availability may be extended where the bank has reasonable cause to believe the check is uncollectible.

6. *The emergency conditions exception*. The scheduled availability may be extended under certain emergency conditions such as a communications interruption or a computer failure.

Banks are required to disclose their funds availability policy to all of their customers; they may provide different policies to different classes or categories of customers.

ELECTRONIC BANKING

With the development of computer technology, many banks are encouraging their customers to transfer funds electronically by using computers rather than paper drafts and checks. A bank customer may use a specially coded card at terminals provided by the bank to make deposits to an account, to transfer money from one checking or savings account to another, to pay bills, or   to withdraw cash from an account.

These new forms of transferring money have raised questions about the legal rules that apply to them, and the questions are only beginning to be resolved. In at least one court decision, *State of Illinois v. Continental Illinois National Bank*, which follows, the court held that a customer's withdrawal from a checking account by using a bank card at an electronic terminal should be treated in the same way as cashing a check.

FIGURE 4   Funds Availablility Schedules (availability of different types of checks deposited the same day)

Monday (Day 0)	Tuesday (Day 1)	Wednesday (Day 2)	Thursday (Day 3)	Friday (Day 4)	Monday (Day 5)	Tuesday (Day 6)	Wednesday (Day 7)	Thursday (Day 8)

Local

- $1,000 (Deposit, Monday)
- 1. $100 (Check Writing, Tuesday)
- 2. $900 (Check Writing, Wednesday)
- 1. $100 (Cash Withdrawal, Tuesday)
- 4. $400 (Cash Withdrawal, Wednesday)
- 5. $500 (Cash Withdrawal, Thursday)

Nonlocal

- $1,000 (Deposit, Monday)
- 1. $100 (Check Writing, Tuesday)
- 3. $900 (Check Writing, Tuesday Day 6)
- 1. $100 (Cash Withdrawal, Tuesday)
- 4. $400 (Cash Withdrawal, Tuesday Day 6)
- 5. $500 (Cash Withdrawal, Wednesday Day 7)

1. The first $100 of a day's deposit must be made available for either cash withdrawal or check-writing purposes at the start of the next business day § 229.10(c)(1)(vii).

2. Local checks must be made available for check-writing purposes by the second business day following deposit § 229.12(b).

3. Nonlocal checks must be made available for check-writing purposes by the fifth business day following deposit § 229.12(c).

4. $400 of the deposit must be made available for cash withdrawal no later than 5:00 P.M. on the day specified in the schedule. This is in addition to the $100 that must be made available on the business day following deposit § 229.12(d).

5. The remainder of the deposit must be made available for cash withdrawal at the start of business the following day § 229.12(d).

● Deposit   ▲ Check Writing   ▮ Cash Withdrawals

Source: Chart Provided by Federal Reserve (53 Federal Register 19375, May 27, 1988).

STATE OF ILLINOIS v. CONTINENTAL ILLINOIS NATIONAL BANK

536 F.2d 176 (7th Cir. 1976)

Continental Illinois National Bank operated several so-called Customer Bank Communication Terminals (CBCTs). These unstaffed terminals were connected directly with the main office computer of Continental Illinois. Customers of the bank inserted a specially coded card into the terminal, entered an identification number, and then pressed keys on the transaction keyboard to indicate the type and amounts of their transactions. The customer might:

1. Withdraw cash (in the amount of $25 or any multiple thereof, up to $100) from a savings, checking, or credit card account.

2. Deposit checks or currency in a checking or savings account. At the time of the transaction, the customer's receipt from the CBCT indicated the amount and date of the deposit. Until the deposit was received and verified at the main banking premises, it was not credited to his account and he could not draw on it.

3. Transfer funds between accounts: checking to savings, credit card to checking, or savings to checking.

4. Make payments on Continental Illinois installment loans or credit card charges.

When a transaction was completed, the customer received a receipt, and if she had withdrawn cash from her account, she received packets containing the cash. A copy of the receipt was retained in the machine, and the transaction was later verified by bank employees.

The Illinois banking commissioner brought an action against Continental Illinois to obtain a declaratory judgment that the unstaffed computer terminals that permitted customers using bank cards to withdraw cash, make deposits, transfer funds, or make payments constituted "branch banks." The U.S. district court held that the terminals amounted to branch banking, but it rejected the commissioner's contention that use of the machines to withdraw money from a customer's account constituted the "cashing of a check." The court of appeals reversed on this question, holding that this did constitute the cashing of a check.

Per Curiam.   The district court here based its conclusion on the functions of CBCT as to the withdrawing of cash and the payment of installments on loans upon the provisions of the Uniform Commercial Code (UCC), in particular § 3-104(2), which declares a check to be a negotiable instrument drawn on a bank and payable on demand; a writing signed by the maker or drawer and containing an unconditional promise or order to pay a sum certain in money; with negotiability being the essential characteristic of a check. From this the district court concluded that a card inserted into the CBCT machine to secure money was not the cashing of a check within the meaning of the UCC or in the common understanding of check cashing. We cannot agree. This is exalting form over substance. The check is merely the means used by the bank to attain the desired objective, i.e., the payment of money to its customer. The card serves the same purpose as the check. It is an order on the bank. Any order to pay which is properly executed by a customer, whether it be check, card, or electronic device, must be recognized as a routine banking function when used as here. The relationship between the bank and its customer is the same. Indeed, the trial court here recognized this when it characterized a CBCT withdrawal as the "functional equivalent" of a written check. And Continental Bank gives the card transaction the same significance:

The EFTS (Electronic Funds Transfer Systems) at issue in the present case are *extensions* of the principle of immediate access to customer accounts *in a manner dispensing with underlying paper such as checks. (Emphasis added.)*

Moreover, although the UCC defines a check as negotiable instrument, it also provides, § 3–104(3):

As used in other Articles of this Act, and as the context may require, the term "check" may refer to instruments which are not negotiable within this Article as well as instruments which are so negotiable.

Just as a transfer of funds by cable or telegraph is in law a check, despite the nonnegotiability of the cable, the card here for the purpose of withdrawing cash is a check. What must be remembered is that the foundation of the relationship between the bank and its customer is the former's agreement to pay out the customer's money according to the latter's order. There are many ways in which an order may be given, and one way of late is by computer record. And the Ninth Circuit accepts the same concept that computer impulses constitute sufficient writing to meet the order test.

Judgment for Continental Illinois.

Electronic Funds Transfer Act

The consumer who used electronic funds transfer systems (EFTs), the so-called cash machines or electronic tellers, in the early years often experienced problems in identifying and resolving mechanical errors resulting from malfunctioning EFTs. In response to these problems, Congress passed the Electronic Funds Transfer Act in 1978 to provide "a basic framework, establishing the rights, liabilities, and responsibilities of participants in electronic funds transfer systems" and especially to provide "individual consumer rights."[2]

The four basic EFT systems are automated teller machines, point-of-sale terminals, which allow consumers to use their EFT cards like checks; preauthorized payments, such as automatic paycheck deposits or mortgage or utility payments; and telephone transfers between accounts or to pay specific bills by phone.

Similar to the Truth in Lending Act and the Fair Credit Billing Act (FCBA) discussed in the Federal Trade Commission Act and Consumer Protection Laws chapter, the EFT Act requires disclosure of the terms and conditions of electronic fund transfers at the time the consumer contracts for the EFT service. Among the nine disclosures required are the following: the consumer's liability for unauthorized electronic fund transfers (those resulting from loss or theft), the nature of the

EFT services under the consumer's account, any pertinent dollar or frequency limitations, any charges for the right to make EFTs, the consumer's right to stop payment of a preauthorized transfer, the financial institution's liability to the consumer for failure to make or stop payments, and the consumer's right to receive documentation of transfers both at the point or time of transfer and periodically. The act also requires 21 days' notice prior to the effective date of any change in the terms or conditions of the consumer's account that pertains to the required disclosures.

The EFT Act does differ from the Fair Credit Billing Act in a number of important respects. For example, under the EFT Act, the operators of EFT systems are given a maximum of 10 working days to investigate errors or provisionally recredit the consumer's account, whereas issuers of credit cards are given a maximum of 90 days under the FCBA. The liability of the consumer is different if an EFT card is lost or stolen than it is if a credit card is lost or stolen. Another important difference is that financial institutions cannot send consumers EFT cards that they did not request unless the cards are not valid for use; an unsolicited EFT card can be validated only at the consumer's request and only after the institution verifies that the consumer is the person whose name is on the card.

The case that follows, *Ognibene v. Citibank, N.A.*, illustrates the application of the EFT Act's provisions that limit a customer's liability for the unauthorized use of his card.

---

[2]Title 20 of the Financial Institutions Regulatory and Interest Rate Control Act of 1978, 15 U.S.C. § 1693 et seq.

OGNIBENE v. CITIBANK, N.A.

446 N.Y.S.2d 845 (N.Y.C. Civ. Ct. 1981)

On August 16, 1981, Frederick Ognibene went to the ATM area at a Citibank branch and activated one of the machines with his Citibank card, pressed in his personal identification code, and withdrew $20. When he approached the machine a person was using the customer service telephone located between two ATM machines and appeared to be telling customer service that one of the machines was malfunctioning. As Ognibene was making his withdrawal, the person said into the telephone, "I'll see if his card works in my machine." He then asked Ognibene if he could use his card to see if the other machine was working. Ognibene handed his card to him and saw him insert it into the adjoining machine at least two times while saying into the telephone, "Yes, it seems to be working." When Ognibene received his Citibank statement, it showed that two withdrawals of $200 each from his account were made at 5:42 P.M. and 5:43 P.M., respectively, on August 16. His own $20 withdrawal was made at 5:41 P.M. At the time Ognibene was unaware that any withdrawals from his account were being made from the adjoining machine. Ognibene sought to have his account recredited for $400, claiming that the withdrawals had been unauthorized. Citibank had been aware for some time of a scam being perpetrated against its customers by persons who observed the customer inserting his personal identification number into an ATM and then obtaining access to the customer's ATM card in the same manner as Ognibene's card was obtained. After learning about the scam, Citibank posted signs in ATM areas containing a red circle approximately 2 ½ inches in diameter in which was written "Do Not Let Your Citicard Be Used For Any Transaction But Your Own."

Thorpe, Judge.   The basic rights, liabilities and responsibilities of the banks which offer electronic money transfer services and the consumers who use them have been established by the federal legislation called the Electronic Funds Transfers Act (EFT). The EFT Act places various limits on a consumer's liability for electronic fund transfers from his account if they are "unauthorized." Insofar as is relevant here, a transfer is "unauthorized" if (1) it is initiated by a person other than the consumer and without actual authority to initiate such transfer, (2) the consumer receives no benefit from it, and (3) the consumer did not furnish such person "with the card, code or other means of access" to his account.

In an action involving a consumer's liability for an electronic fund transfer, such as the one at bar, the burden of going forward to show an "unauthorized" transfer from his account is on the consumer. The EFT Act places on the bank, however, the burden of proof for any consumer liability for the transfer. To establish full liability on the part of the consumer, the bank must prove that the transfer was authorized. To be entitled to even the limited liability imposed by the statute on the consumer, the bank must prove that certain conditions of consumer liability, set forth in 15 U.S.C.A. 1693g(a) have been met and that certain disclosures mandated by 15 U.S.C.A. 1693c(a)(1) and (2) have been met.

Ognibene met his burden of going forward. He did not initiate the withdrawals in question, did not authorize the person in the ATM area to make them, and did not benefit from them.

However, Citibank's position is, in essence, that although Ognibene was duped, the bank's burden of proof on the issue of authorization has been met by Ognibene's testimony that he permitted his card to be used in the adjoining machine by the other person. The court does not agree.

The EFT Act requires that the consumer have furnished to a person initiating the transfer the "code, card, or other means of access" to his account to be eligible for the limitations on liability afforded by the Act when transfers are "unauthorized." The evidence establishes that in order to obtain access to an account via an automatic teller machine both the card and the personal identification code must be used. Thus, by merely giving his card to the person initiating the transfer, a consumer does not furnish the "means of access" to his account. To do so, he would have to furnish the personal identification code as well.

The court finds that Ognibene did not furnish his personal identification code to the person initiating the $400.00 transfer within the meaning of the EFT Act. There is no evidence that he deliberately or even negligently did so. On the contrary, the unauthorized person was able to obtain the code because of Citibank's own negligence. Since the bank had knowledge of the scam and its operation details (including the central role of the customer service telephone), it was negligent in failing to provide Ognibene with information sufficient to alert him to the danger when he found himself in the position of potential victim. Although in June, 1981, after the scam came to Citibank's attention, it posted signs in its ATM areas containing a red circle approximately 2 ½ inches in diameter in which is written "Do Not Let Your Citicard Be Used For Any Transaction But Your Own," the court finds that this printed admonition is not a sufficient security measure since it fails to state the reason why one should not. Since a customer of Citibank's electronic fund transfer service must employ both the card and the personal identification code in order to withdraw money from his account, the danger of loaning the card briefly for the purpose of checking the functioning of an adjoining automated teller machine would not be immediately apparent to one who has not divulged his personal identification number and who is unaware that it has been revealed merely by virtue of his own transaction with the machine.

Judgment for Ognibene for $400.

DOCUMENTS OF TITLE

Introduction

Storing or shipping goods, giving a **warehouse receipt** or **bill of lading** representing the goods, and transferring such a receipt or bill of lading as representing the goods are practices of ancient origin. The warehouseman or the common carrier is a bailee of the goods who contracts to store or transport the goods and to deliver them to the owner or to act otherwise in accordance with the lawful directions of the owner. The warehouse receipt or the bill of lading may be either negotiable or nonnegotiable. To be *negotiable*, a warehouse receipt, bill of lading, or other document of title *must provide that the goods are to be delivered to the bearer or to the order of a named person* [7–104(1)]. The primary differences between the law of negotiable instruments and the law of negotiable documents of title are based on the differences between the obligation to pay money and the obligation to deliver specific goods.

The *Bishop v. Allied Van Lines, Inc.* case, which follows, illustrates the responsibility a warehouseman has to deliver the goods only as directed by the owner.

BISHOP v. ALLIED VAN LINES, INC.
399 N.E.2d 698 (Ill. Ct. App. 1980)

Estelle Smiley and her husband, R. V. Smiley, entered into an agreement with Allied Van Lines for the transfer and storage of household goods and were given a bill of lading. Afterward, the Smileys began divorce proceedings. Estelle Smiley then notified the agent for Allied not to deliver the household goods to either her or her husband without further instructions from her. The goods were delivered to R. V. Smiley after the notice had been given.

Estelle died, and Bishop, the executor of her estate, brought an action against Allied Van Lines, Inc., to recover damages for misdelivery of goods. The trial court dismissed the case for failure to state a cause of action, and Bishop appealed.

Craven, Judge.   The trial judge stated that a bailee is required to deliver the goods to a person entitled under the document upon payment of the bailee's lien. Person entitled under the document is defined in § 7–403 of the Code, subparagraph (4), as a holder in the case of a negotiable document or the person to whom delivery is to be made by the terms of or pursuant to written instructions under a nonnegotiable document. The bill of lading in question is conspicuously and expressly noted as nonnegotiable. Section 7–404 provides that a bailee in good faith and using reasonable commercial standards who delivers or otherwise disposes of the goods according to the terms of the document of title is not liable.

The Comments under that section state that delivery in the case of a nonnegotiable document is to the one to whom delivery is to be made under its terms or pursuant to written instructions under it. Such instructions would be a delivery order [§ 7–102(1)(d)]. Delivery order is a written order to deliver goods directed to a warehouseman, carrier, or other person who in the ordinary course of business issues warehouse receipts or bills of lading. No delivery orders were given at any time. Therefore, the person entitled under the document here, this being a nonnegotiable document, must be the person to whom delivery is made by the terms of the nonnegotiable document.

Ordinarily in a bill of lading where no delivery orders are given, there is a blank space for the consignee and his or her address. Section 7–102(1)(b) defines "consignee" as the person named in a bill to whom or to whose order the bill promises delivery. The bill of lading in this case is no different. There is a blank space for a consignee, delivery address, city, and state. Also, there is a blank space at the bottom of the nonnegotiable bill of lading where the consignee is supposed to sign. The bill of lading in question had only blank spaces for this information. In other words, there was neither a consignee named nor any address given, nor was there a signature of any consignee. There was, then, no consignee at all, nor were any delivery orders given. The bill of lading, issued by Allied Van Lines, states that the shipper was Mr. and Mrs. R. V. Smiley, signed by R. V. Smiley.

[The estate of] Mrs. Smiley alleges in the complaint that she was the owner of the stored property and she was named as a joint shipper in the bill of lading. Mrs. R. V. Smiley would, then, be a joint bailor. A bailment is merely the delivery of goods for some purpose upon a contract, express or implied, and after the purpose has been fulfilled the goods are to be redelivered to the bailor, or otherwise dealt with according to his directions, or kept until reclaimed. Joint delivery by Mrs. Smiley and her then husband carries with it a presumption of joint title and a concession of a joint right of action.

Section 7–404 states that a bailee who in good faith, including observance of reasonable commercial standards, has received goods and delivered or disposed of them according to the terms of the document is not liable. Here it is alleged that the bailee had knowledge of an adverse claim between the bailors. On these pleadings, we hold that it cannot be said that the bailee acted in good faith. It cannot be said that the bailee observed reasonable commercial standards when the bailee delivered the bailed goods with knowledge of adverse claims between the bailors. Indeed, § 7–603 excuses the bailee from delivery until he had a reasonable time to ascertain the validity of adverse claims.

Judgment reversed in favor of the Estelle Smiley estate.

Warehouse Receipts

A warehouse receipt, to be valid, need not be in any particular form, but if it does not embody within its written or printed form each of the following, the warehouseman is liable for damages caused by the omission to a person injured as a result of it: (a) the location of the warehouse where the goods are stored; (b) the date of issue; (c) the consecutive number of the receipt; (d) whether the goods are to be delivered to the bearer or to the order of a named person;[3] (e) the rate of storage and handling charges; (f) a description of the goods or of the packages containing them; (g) the signature of the warehouseman or his agent; (h) whether the warehouseman is the owner of the goods, solely, jointly, or in common with others; and (i) a statement of the amount of the advances made and of the liabilities incurred for which the warehouseman claims a lien or security interest. Other terms may be inserted [7–202].

A warehouseman is liable to a purchaser for value in good faith of a warehouse receipt for nonreceipt or misdescription of goods. The receipt may conspicuously qualify the description by a statement such as "contents, condition, and quantity unknown" [7–203].

Because a warehouseman is a bailee of the goods, he owes to the holder of the warehouse receipt the duties of a mutual benefit bailee and must exercise reasonable care [7–204]. The Personal Property and Bailments chapter discusses the duties of a bailee in detail. The warehouseman may terminate the relation by notification where, for example, the goods are about to deteriorate or where they constitute a threat to other goods in the warehouse [7–206]. Unless the warehouse receipt provides otherwise, the warehouseman must keep separate the goods covered by each receipt; however, different lots of fungible goods such as grain may be mingled [7–207].

---

[3]Where goods are stored under a field warehouse arrangement, a statement of that fact is sufficient on a nonnegotiable receipt.

A warehouseman has a lien against the bailor on the goods covered by his receipt for his storage and other charges incurred in handling the goods [7–209]. The Code sets out a detailed procedure for enforcing this lien [7–210].

Bills of Lading

In many respects, the rights and liabilities of the parties to a negotiable bill of lading are the same as the rights and liabilities of the parties to a negotiable warehouse receipt. The contract of the issuer of a bill of lading is to transport goods, whereas the contract of the issuer of a warehouse receipt is to store goods. Like the issuer of a warehouse receipt, the issuer of a bill of lading is liable for nonreceipt or misdescription of the goods, but he may protect himself from liability where he does not know the contents of packages by marking the bill of lading "contents or condition of packages unknown" or similar language. Such terms are ineffective when the goods are loaded by an issuer who is a common carrier unless the goods are concealed by packages [7–301].

Duty of Care

A carrier who issues a bill of lading, or a warehouse operator who issues a warehouse receipt, must exercise the same degree of care in relation to the goods as a reasonably careful person would exercise under similar circumstances. Liability for damages not caused by the negligence of the carrier may be imposed on him by a special law or rule of law. Under tariff rules, a common carrier may limit her liability to a shipper's declaration of value, provided that the rates are dependent on value [7–309]. In the case that follows, *Calvin Klein Ltd. v. Trylon Trucking Corp.*, a court enforced a $50 per shipment limitation that had been part of a long series of shipping contracts where the customer had the opportunity to declare a higher value and failed to do so.

CALVIN KLEIN LTD. v. TRYLON TRUCKING CORP.

892 F.2d 191 (2d Cir. 1989)

Trylon Trucking Corporation is a New Jersey trucking firm that engaged in the business of transporting goods from New York City's airports for delivery to its customers' facilities. For three years prior to 1986, Calvin Klein, a New York clothing company, used the services of Trylon involving hundreds of shipments. Calvin Klein, through its customs broker, would contact Trylon to pick up the shipment from the airport for delivery to Calvin Klein's facility. After completing the delivery carriage, Trylon would forward to Calvin Klein an invoice, which contained a limitation of liability provision as follows:

In consideration of the rate charged, the shipper agrees that the carrier shall not be liable for more than $50.00 on any shipment accepted for delivery to one consignee unless a greater value is declared, in writing, upon receipt at time of shipment and charge for such greater value paid, or agreed to be paid, by the shipper.

A shipment of 2,833 blouses from Hong Kong arrived at John F. Kennedy International Airport for Calvin Klein on March 27, 1986. Calvin Klein arranged for Trylon to pick up the shipment and deliver it to Calvin Klein's New Jersey warehouse. On April 2, Trylon dispatched its driver, J. Jefferson, to pick up this shipment. Jefferson signed a receipt for the shipment from Calvin Klein's broker. Later, on April 2, the parties discovered that Jefferson had stolen Trylon's truck and its shipment. The shipment was never recovered.

Calvin Klein sent a claim letter to Trylon for the full value of the lost blouses. When it did not receive a response from Trylon, Calvin Klein filed suit against Trylon, seeking to recover $150,000, the alleged value of the blouses. In the pleadings before the court, the parties agreed that Trylon was liable to Calvin Klein for the loss of the shipment and that it had been grossly negligent in the hiring and supervision of Jefferson. They also agreed that "the terms and conditions of Trylon's carriage were that liability for loss or damage to cargo is limited to $50 in accordance with the provision in Trylon's invoice forms." Calvin Klein conceded that it was aware of the limitation of liability and that it did not declare a value on the blouses at the time of shipment.

Trylon contended that its liability was limited to $50 in accordance with the provision in its invoice forms. Calvin Klein argued that the limitation clause was not enforceable for two reasons: (1) no agreement existed between it and Trylon as to the limitation of liability; and (2) even if an agreement existed, public policy would prevent its enforcement because of Trylon's gross negligence. The district court held that Calvin Klein had not assented to the limitation clause for this shipment and awarded damages to Calvin Klein of $101,542.62. Trylon appealed.

Miner, Circuit Judge.   A common carrier is strictly liable for the loss of goods in its custody. Where the loss is not due to excepted causes [that is, act of God or public enemy, inherent nature of goods, or shipper's fault], it is immaterial whether the carrier was negligent or not. Even in the case of loss from theft by third parties, liability may be imposed upon a negligent common carrier.

A shipper and a common carrier may contract to limit the carrier's liability in cases of loss to an amount agreed to by the parties, so long as the language of the limitation is clear, the shipper is aware of the terms of the limitation, and the shipper can change the terms by indicating the true value of the goods being shipped. Section 7–309(2). Such a limitation agreement is generally valid and enforceable despite carrier negligence. The limitation of liability provision involved here clearly provides that, at the time of delivery, the shipper may increase the limitation by written notice of the value of the goods to be delivered and by payment of a commensurately higher fee.

The parties stipulated to the fact that the $50 limitation of liability was a term and condition of carriage and that Calvin Klein was aware of that limitation. This stipulated fact removes the first issue, namely whether an agreement existed as to a liability limitation between the parties. Calvin Klein's argument that it never previously acknowledged this limitation by accepting only $50 in settlement of a larger loss does not alter this explicit stipulation. The district court erred in not accepting the limitation of liability as stipulated.

The remaining issue concerns the enforceability of the limitation clause in the light of Trylon's conceded gross negligence.

Since carriers are strictly liable for loss of shipments in their custody and are insurers of those goods, the degree of carrier negligence is immaterial. The common carrier must exercise reasonable care in relation to the shipment in its custody. Section 7–309(2). Carriers can contract with their shipping customers on the amount of liability each party will bear for the loss of a shipment, regardless of the amount of carrier negligence. Unlike a merchant acquiring a burglar alarm, the shipper can calculate the specific amount of its potential damages in advance, declare the value of the shipment based on that calculation, can pay a commensurately higher rate to carry the goods, in effect buying additional insurance from the common carrier.

In this case Calvin Klein and Trylon were business entities with an on-going commercial relationship involving numerous carriages of Calvin Klein goods by Trylon. Where such entities deal with each other in a commercial setting, and no special relationship exists between the parties, clear limitations between them will be enforced. Here, each carriage was under the same terms and conditions as the last, including a limitation of Trylon's liability. This is not a case in which the shipper was dealing with the common carrier for the first time or contracting under new or changed conditions. Calvin Klein was aware of the terms and was free to adjust the limitation upon a written declaration of the value of a given shipment, but failed to do so with the shipment at issue here. Since Calvin Klein failed to adjust the limitation, the limitation applies here, and no public policy that dictates otherwise can be identified.

Calvin Klein also argues that the limitation is so low as to be void. The amount is immaterial because Calvin Klein had the opportunity to negotiate the amount of coverage by declaring the value of the shipment. Commercial entities can easily negotiate the degree of risk each party will bear and which party will bear the cost of insurance. Calvin Klein had the opportunity to declare a higher value and we find all of its arguments relating to the unreasonableness of the limitation to be without merit.

District court judgment reversed with instructions to enter judgment for Calvin Klein for $50.

Negotiation of Document of Title

A negotiable document of title and a negotiable instrument are negotiated in substantially the same manner. If the document of title provides for the delivery of the goods to bearer, it may be negotiated by delivery. If it provides for delivery of the goods to the order of a named person, it must be indorsed by that person and delivered. If an order document of title is indorsed in blank, it may be negotiated by delivery unless it bears a special indorsement following the blank indorsement, in which event it must be indorsed by the special indorsee and delivered [7–501].

A person taking a negotiable document of title takes as a bona fide holder if she takes in good faith and in the regular course of business. The bona fide holder of a negotiable document of title has substantially the same advantages over a holder who is not a bona fide holder or over a holder of a nonnegotiable document of title as does a holder in due course of a negotiable instrument over a holder who is not a holder in due course or over a holder of a nonnegotiable instrument.

Rights Acquired by Negotiation

A person who acquires a negotiable document of title by due negotiation acquires (1) title to the document, (2) title to the goods, (3) the right to the goods delivered to the bailee after the issuance of the document, and (4) the direct obligation of the issuer to hold or deliver the goods according to the terms of the document [7–502(1)].

Under the broad general principle that a person cannot transfer title to goods he does not own, a thief—or the owner of goods subject to a perfected security interest—cannot, by warehousing or shipping the goods on a negotiable document of title and then negotiating the document of title, transfer to the purchaser of the document of title a better title than he has [7–503].

Warranties of Transferor of Document of Title

The transferor of a negotiable document of title warrants to his immediate transferee, in addition to any warranty of goods, only that the document is genuine, that he has no knowledge of any facts that would impair its validity or worth, and that his negotiation or transfer is rightful and fully effective with respect to the title to the document and the goods it represents [7–507].

ETHICAL AND PUBLIC POLICY CONCERNS

1. Suppose you take your car to a garage to have it repainted. When you go to pick it up, you are not happy with the quality of the work, but the garage owner refuses to release the car to you unless you pay him in full for the work. You give him a check in the amount requested, and on the way home stop at your bank and request that the bank stop payment on the check you have just written, an action you decided to take when you were writing out the check. Have you acted ethically?

2. Some banks take the position that because they process checks with the use of computers, a customer seeking to stop payment on a check must provide them with the amount of the check with every digit correct in order for the bank to be able to stop payment. What policy considerations are involved in deciding whether the bank's position should establish the minimum information required for a bank to have a "reasonable opportunity" to respond to the customer's request?

3. Suppose that you own and operate a warehouse. A local liquor store owner occasionally uses your facilities to store shipments of wine from France until he has room for the wine in his store. You are aware that from time to time your warehouse employees "borrow" a bottle from the crates of wine being stored in your warehouse. After a number of crates with a total of four bottles missing are delivered to the liquor store, the store owner queries you about the missing bottles and you tell him that they must have been broken in transit to your warehouse. Have you acted ethically?

SUMMARY

The relationship between a bank and a customer having a commercial account on which checks may be drawn is

that of debtor and creditor and principal and agent. In drawing a check, the customer authorizes the bank to honor the check. The bank is under an obligation to pay all properly drawn checks, provided that the funds in the account are sufficient to cover the checks. A bank may pay a check even if doing so creates an overdraft. A bank does not owe a duty to pay stale checks—those over six months old—but it may do so in good faith.

The customer has the right to order the bank to stop payment on a check that has not been certified, and if the order to stop payment is received by the bank at such a time and in such form as to give it a reasonable opportunity to do so, the bank owes a duty to refuse payment on the check. If the bank pays a check in disregard of a valid stop-payment order, it is liable to the drawer for any direct and consequential damages.

A bank is not obligated to certify a check, but on certification the bank becomes primarily liable on the check and, if the check has been certified at the request of the holder, the drawer and all prior indorsers are discharged. A bank may pay checks drawn during a customer's lifetime or while the customer is competent and for a period of 10 days after the customer's death or until the bank learns of an adjudication of incompetence.

Checks that have forged drawer's or payee's signatures and checks that have been materially altered are generally not properly chargeable to a customer's account. However, if the drawer is negligent and contributes to the forgery or alteration, she may be barred from claiming it as the reason that a particular item should not be charged to her account.

A customer owes a duty to report to the bank, within a reasonable time after a statement of account and canceled checks have been made available, any unauthorized signatures and alterations. Forged drawer's signatures and alterations must in any event be reported within one year, and unauthorized indorsements within three years, or the drawer cannot require that his account be recredited.

When a bank takes a check for deposit to a customer's account, it typically places a hold on the funds in the account represented by the deposited check because it runs a number of risks in allowing a customer to withdraw deposits that have not been finally collected from the drawee bank. The extensive use of holds, and a growing public sentiment that they were excessive and often unfair, led to the passage by Congress in 1987 of the Expedited Funds Availability Act. In the act, Congress set out mandatory schedules limiting check holds and specifying when funds are to be made available to customers by depositary institutions.

Increasingly, banks are encouraging their customers to transfer funds electronically and automated teller machines are now commonplace. The Electronic Funds Transfer Act, enacted by Congress in 1978, establishes the rights, liabilities, and reponsibilities of the participants in electronic funds transfer systems.

The warehouseman or common carrier is a bailee of goods, and he contracts to store or transport them. The warehouse receipt or bill of lading may be either negotiable or nonnegotiable. If the warehouse receipt issued by the warehouseman omits in its written or printed terms the information required under the provisions of the Code, the warehouseman is liable to a purchaser in good faith of a warehouse receipt for failure to describe the goods or for their misdescription. He owes to the holder of a warehouse receipt the duties of a mutual benefit bailee. The common carrier's liability on a negotiable bill of lading is the same in most respects as that of the issuer of a negotiable warehouse receipt. His liability may be increased by special law or rule.

The rules of law governing the negotiation of a negotiable document of title are the same in most respects as the rules of law governing the negotiation of negotiable commercial paper. In general, a holder by due negotiation of a negotiable document of title gets good title to the document and the goods and the contractual rights against the bailee. However, a thief or an owner of goods subject to a valid security interest cannot, by warehousing or shipping the goods on a negotiable document of title and negotiating it, pass to the transferee greater rights in the goods than she has. A holder who transfers a negotiable document of title warrants to his immediate transferee that the document is genuine, that he has no knowledge of any facts that would impair its validity or worth, and that his transfer is rightful and fully effective.

PROBLEM CASES

1. J. E. B. Stewart received a check in the amount of $185.48 in payment of a fee from a client. Stewart presented the check, properly indorsed, to the Citizen's & Southern Bank. The bank refused to cash the check even though there were sufficient funds in the drawer's account. Stewart then sued the bank for actual damages of $185.48 and for punitive damages of $50,000 for its failure to cash a valid check drawn against a solvent account in the bank. Does Stewart have a good cause of action against the bank?

2. Fitting wrote a check for $800 and gave it to the payee. She then had second thoughts about the check. She contacted the bank at which she had her checking account about the possibility of stopping payment on the check. A bank employee told her she could not file a stop-payment order until the bank opened the next morning. The next morning Fitting did not file a stop-payment order. Instead, she withdrew money from her account so that less than $800 remained in it. She believed the bank would not pay the $800 check if there were not sufficient funds in the account to cover it. However, the bank paid the check and created an overdraft in Fitting's account. The bank then sued Fitting to recover the amount of the overdraft. Can the bank pay Fitting's check even if doing so creates an overdraft in her checking account?

3. On July 2, 1982, Staff Services Associates issued a check drawn on Midlantic National Bank payable to Lynn A. Gross for the sum of $4,117.12. On July 7, 1982, John Tracy, the president of Staff Services, executed a stop-payment order to Midlantic and incorrectly wrote the amount of the check as $4,117.72, an error of one digit. At the time, Tracy saw the statement at the bottom of the stop-payment order, which read:

IMPORTANT: The information on this Stop Payment Order must be correct, including the exact amount of the check to the penny, or the Bank will not be able to stop payment and this Stop Payment Order will be void.

As a result of the incorrect information provided by Tracy, the wrong amount was programmed in Midlantic's computer. When the check was presented for payment, it was paid, and the bank charged it to Staff Service's account. Staff Services then brought suit against Midlantic for wrongful payment of the check in violation of the stop-payment order. Was Midlantic justified in paying the check over the stop-payment order because of the one-digit error in the stop-payment order?

4. John Doe had a checking account at Highland National Bank in New York. Two days after John Doe died in Florida, but before Highland National knew of his death, John's sister appeared at the bank. She had a check signed by John Doe, but with the amount and the payee's name left blank. She told the bank her brother wanted to close his account. She asked how much was in the account, filled the check in for that amount, and made the check payable to herself. The bank checked her identification and verified the signature of John Doe. Then it paid the check to the sister. The executor of John Doe's estate later sued Highland National to recover the amount of money that was in John's account on the day that he died. The executor claimed that the bank had no authority to pay checks from John Doe's account after his death. Is the executor correct? *No*

5. Winkie, Inc., maintained a checking account at the Heritage Bank of Whitefish Bay. Although several persons were authorized to sign Winkie checks, W. J. Winkie, Jr., the company's president, was the only person who ever signed checks drawn on the Winkie account. Doris Britton, a secretarial employee of Winkie, recorded invoices for supplies and services rendered to the company and presented the invoices and checks drawn on the account in payment of the invoices to W. J. Winkie, Jr., for review of the invoices and execution of the checks. In the years 1965 to 1973, Britton forged the signature of W. J. Winkie, Jr., to hundreds of checks totaling $148,171.30 drawn on the Winkie, Inc., account. In addition to forging the signature of W. J. Winkie, Jr., Britton forged the indorsements of the payee on many of the checks. None of the payees of the checks supplied the services or materials to Winkie, Inc., for which the forged checks were payment. Winkie, Inc., neither intended payment nor received benefit of any kind by reason of the issuance of the checks. Britton directly or indirectly received all the proceeds of the forged checks. In 1973, after approximately eight years of repeated forgeries, W. J. Winkie, Jr., discovered a forged check and immediately notified the bank. During the eight-year period, W. J. Winkie, Jr., did not personally examine the Winkie checks or reconcile the bank statements of the account. Another Winkie, Inc., employee, not alleged to be involved in the systematic forgeries, was assigned those duties. Winkie, Inc., utilized the services of a certified public accountant, but those services did not expressly include bank statement reconciliation or an audit. Thus, the bank account examination and reconciliation were left to a single, unsupervised Winkie employee. Winkie brought an action against the Heritage Bank to have its account recredited for the checks that had been forged by the Winkie employee and paid by the bank. Should the Heritage Bank be required to recredit the Winkie account for the amount of the checks that contained forged drawer's and payee's signatures? *No, Negligence 3 year Statute of Limitations*

6. Jensen opened a checking account at the Essexbank on January 7, 1981, with a deposit of $7,500 to facilitate payment of bills from the sale of his business. Although he signed a bank form in which he designated himself as the sole signatory of the account, he directed the bank to send all bank statements and bank checks to his attorney. From time to time, he would request his attorney to send him blank checks for his use. A check for $5,000 was drawn on Jensen's account on April 17, 1981, and a check for $500 was drawn on the account on July 1, 1981. Both checks were payable to the order of his attorney; neither had been signed by Jensen but someone else had signed his name. In August 1981, Jensen tried to cash a check drawn on the account and was told the account was overdrawn. He tried without success to reach his attorney to obtain copies of his statements. In 1982, Jensen's attorney was disbarred from the practice of law. On July 9, 1983, Jensen notified the Essexbank that his signature had been forged on the $5,000 and $500 checks. He sought to have his account recredited for $5,500. Is the Essexbank required to recredit his account for the amount of the checks containing a forged drawer's signature? *No*

7. In 1982, Hirsch Food Company began storing cases of its pickles in a warehouse owned by Overmyer Company. Later that year, Overmyer began shutting down its warehouse operation and reduced its staff to one man who came to the warehouse only when Hirsch Company desired to remove some pickles. In 1983, when the last of the pickles were removed, 900 cases were missing. Where does the liability for the missing pickles lie? On what does it depend?

8. Griswold and Bateman Warehouse Company stored 337 cases of Chivas Regal Scotch Whiskey for Joseph H. Reinfeld, Inc., in its bonded warehouse. The warehouse receipt issued to Reinfeld limited Griswold and Bateman's liability for negligence to 250 times the monthly storage rate, a total of $1,925. When Reinfeld sent its truck to pick up the whiskey, 40 cases were missing. Reinfeld then brought suit seeking the wholesale market value of the whiskey, $6,417.60. Reinfeld presented evidence of the delivery of the whiskey, the demand for its return, and the failure of Griswold and Bateman to return it. Reinfeld claimed that the burden was on Griswold and Bateman to explain the disappearance of the whiskey. Griswold and Bateman admitted that it had been negligent, but sought to limit its liability to $1,925. Is Griswold and Bateman's liability limited to $1,925?

9. Everlens Mitchell entered into a written contract with All American Van & Storage to transport and store her household goods. She was to pay the storage charges on a monthly basis. As security, she granted All American a warehouseman's lien. All American had the right to sell the property if the charges remained unpaid for three months and if, in the opinion of the company, such action was necessary to protect the accrued charges. Mitchell fell eight months behind on her payments. On October 20, 1985, she received notice that if the unpaid charges, totaling $804.30, were not paid by October 31, her goods would be sold on November 7. Mitchell advised All American that she had a claim pending with the Social Security Administration and would soon receive a large sum of money. This was confirmed to All American by several government officials. However, All American sold Mitchell's property on November 7 for $925.50. At the end of the month, Mitchell received a $5,500 disability payment. She sued All American for improperly selling her goods. The trial court awarded judgment to All American. Should the decision be reversed on appeal?

10. On October 15, Young delivered 207 bags of rice to Atteberry's warehouse and received a nonnegotiable receipt. Young then transferred the receipt to Brock for a valuable consideration, and Brock notified Atteberry of the transfer on November 3. Prior to November 3, however, Young had procured a negotiable receipt for the rice along with some other rice he had deposited with Atteberry. Now Brock presents his nonnegotiable receipt to Atteberry and demands delivery of the rice. Atteberry contends that no rice is being held at the warehouse on Brock's account. Who is correct?

PART VI

AGENCY LAW

CHAPTER 27

The Agency Relationship

CHAPTER 28

Third-Party Relations of the Principal and the Agent

THE AGENCY RELATIONSHIP

INTRODUCTION

The Significance of Agency Law

In this text you encounter situations where businesses are legally bound by the actions of their employees or other representatives. For example, corporations frequently are liable on contracts their employees make or for torts those employees commit. We tend to take such liability for granted, but it is not immediately obvious why we should do so. A corporation is an artificial legal person distinct from the officers, employees, and other representatives who contract on its behalf and who may commit torts while performing their duties. Similarly, a sole proprietor is distinct from the people he may employ. How can corporations, sole proprietors, and other business actors be bound on contracts they did not make or for torts they did not commit? The reason is the law of **agency.**

Agency is a two-party relationship in which one party (the **agent**) is authorized to act on behalf of, and under the control of, the other party (the **principal**). Simple examples of the agency relation include hiring a salesperson to sell goods, retaining an attorney, and engaging a real estate broker to sell a house. Agency law's most important social function is to stimulate business and commercial activity. It does so by allowing people and businesses to increase the number of transactions that they can complete within a given time. Without agency, business and commercial life would proceed at a slow pace. A sole proprietor's ability to engage in trade would be limited by the need to make each of her purchase or sales contracts in person. As artificial persons, corporations can act *only* through their agents.

Topic Coverage and Organization

Agency law can be divided into two rough categories. The first involves the legal rules that control relations *between the principal and the agent*—including the rules governing formation of the agency relation, the duties the principal and the agent owe each other, and the ways that an agency can be terminated. Such topics and the principal's and the agent's liability on contracts made by the agent and for torts committed by the agent are this chapter's main concerns. The next chapter discusses the principal's and the agent's relations with *third parties*.

CREATION OF AN AGENCY AND RELATED MATTERS

Formation

An agency is created by the manifested agreement of two persons that one person (the agent) shall act for the benefit of the other (the principal) under the principal's direction.[1] As the term *manifested* suggests, the test for the existence of an agency is *objective*. If the parties' behavior and the surrounding facts and circumstances indicate an agreement that one person is to act for the benefit and under the control of another, courts hold that the relationship exists. If the facts establish an agency, it is immaterial whether either party knows of the agency's existence or subjectively desires that it exist. In fact, the agency relationship may be present even where the parties have expressly stated that they do not intend to create it, or intend to create some other legal relationship instead.

Often, parties create an agency by a written contract (sometimes called a *power of attorney*). But an agency contract may be oral unless state law provides otherwise.[2] Some states, for example, require written evidence of contracts to pay an agent a commission for the sale of real estate. More importantly, the agency relation need not be contractual at all. Thus, consideration is not necessary to form an agency. As the following *Warren v. United States* case illustrates, courts sometimes imply an agency from the parties' behavior and the surrounding circumstances without discussing the need for a contract or for consideration.

Capacity

A principal or agent who lacks the necessary mental capacity at the time the agency is formed ordinarily can release himself from the agency at his option. Examples include those who are minors or who are insane when the agency is created. Of course, incapacity may occur or exist at other times as well; at various points in this and the next chapter, we discuss its effect in such cases.

As you have seen, business organizations such as corporations can and must appoint agents. In a partnership, each partner normally acts as the agent of the partnership in transacting partnership business, and partnerships can appoint nonpartner agents as well.[3] In addition, corporations, partnerships, and other business organizations themselves can act as agents.

Nondelegable Obligations

Certain duties or acts cannot be delegated by a principal to an agent. This means that the principal must perform such duties or acts personally. For example, making statements under oath, voting in public elections, and the signing of a will cannot be delegated to an agent. The same is true for service contracts in which the principal's personal performance is crucial. Examples include certain contracts by lawyers, doctors, artists, and entertainers.

---

[1]Sometimes it is said that an agency may also be created by ratification, estoppel, or operation of law. Usually, however, ratification and estoppel are regarded as ways of binding the principal to an agent's actions, not as ways of forming an agency in the first place. Ratification is discussed in the following chapter, and estoppel resembles the concept of apparent authority discussed later in this chapter and in the next. It is uncommon for an agency to be created by operation of law. An example might be a state statute designating the state's secretary of state as an out-of-state motorist's "agent" for purposes of receiving a summons and a complaint in a lawsuit against the motorist.

[2]Usually, the state law in question is the state's statute of frauds. On the statute of frauds, see the Writing chapter. Also, it is sometimes said that if the contract the agent is to form must be in writing, the agency agreement likewise must be written. However, it is doubtful whether this "equal dignity rule" enjoys widespread acceptance.

[3]See the Operation of Partnership and Related Forms chapter for a discussion of how agency law operates in the partnership context.

WARREN v. UNITED STATES

613 F.2d 591 (5th Cir. 1980)

Bobby and Modell Warren were cotton growers. For two years, they took their cotton crops to certain cotton gins that ginned and baled the cotton. Then, after being instructed to do so by the Warrens, the gins obtained bids for the cotton from prospective buyers and the Warrens told the gins which bids to accept. The gins sold the cotton to the designated buyers, collecting the proceeds. At the Warrens' instruction, the gins deferred payment of the proceeds to the Warrens until the year after the one in which each sale was made.

The Warrens did not report the proceeds as taxable income for the year when the gins received the proceeds, instead including the proceeds in the return for the following year. After an IRS audit, the Warrens were compelled to treat the proceeds as taxable income for the year when the proceeds were received, and to pay accordingly. The Warrens eventually won a refund action in federal district court. The government appealed. Its position was that: (1) the gins were agents of the Warrens; and (2) because of the established rule that receipt of proceeds by an agent is receipt by the principal, the proceeds were taxable income for the year in which they were received by the gins.

Johnson, Circuit Judge.   The relationship between the Warrens and the gins for the purpose of selling the cotton was indisputably that of principal and agent. The Warrens instructed the gins to solicit bids, the Warrens decided whether to accept the highest price offered, and the Warrens determined whether or not to instruct the gins to hold the proceeds from the sale until the following year. The gins' role in the sale of the cotton was to adhere to the Warrens' instructions. The Warrens were the owners of the cotton held for sale; the Warrens were in complete control of its disposition.

This case is distinguishable from those cases where it was recognized that proceeds from the sale of a crop by a farmer, pursuant to a bona fide arm's-length contract between the buyer and seller calling for payment in the taxable year following delivery, are includable in gross income for the taxable year in which payment is received. In the case at bar the bona fide arm's-length agreement was not between the buyer and seller but rather between the seller and his agent. The income was received by the Warrens' agents in the year of the sale. The fact that the Warrens restricted their access to the sales proceeds does not change the tax status of the money received.

Judgment reversed in favor of the government.

AGENCY CONCEPTS, DEFINITIONS, AND TYPES

In its development, agency law has come to include various concepts, definitions, and distinctions. As you will see in this chapter and the next chapter, these matters often determine the rights, duties, and liabilities of the principal, the agent, and third parties. In addition, they sometimes are important outside agency law. Because these basic topics are so crucial in so many different contexts, we outline them together here.

Authority

As you have seen, agency law allows principals to multiply their dealings by employing agents to represent them. Presumably, however, a principal should not be liable for *any* deal that his agent concludes. Thus, agency law generally allows the agent to bind the principal only when the agent has **authority** to do so.

The *Restatement (Second) of Agency* defines authority as the agent's ability to affect the principal's legal relations with third parties.[4] Authority comes in two general forms: **actual authority** and **apparent authority.** Each is based on the principal's manifested consent that the agent may act for and bind the principal. For actual authority this consent is communicated to the *agent*, while for apparent authority it is communicated to the *third party.*

The two kinds of actual authority are **express authority** and **implied authority.** Express authority is created by the principal's actual *words* (whether written or oral). Thus, an agent has express authority to bind a principal only when the principal has made a fairly precise statement to that effect. Often, however, it is impractical or impossible for a principal to specify the agent's authority fully and exactly. To avoid unnecessary

---

[4]See *Restatement (Second) of Agency* sections 7–8 (1959).

restrictions on an agent's ability to represent her principal, therefore, agency law also gives agents *implied authority* to bind their principals. In general, an agent has implied authority to do whatever it is reasonable to assume that the principal wanted him to do, given the principal's express statements and the surrounding circumstances. Courts seeking to determine an agent's implied authority typically examine matters such as the principal's express statements, the nature of the agency, the acts reasonably necessary to carry on the agency business, and the acts customarily done when conducting that business.

Sometimes, an agent who lacks express or implied authority may still *appear* to have such authority, and third parties may reasonably rely on this appearance of authority. To protect the third party in such situations, agency law allows agents to bind the principal on the basis of their *apparent authority.* Apparent authority arises when the principal's behavior causes a third party to form a reasonable belief that the agent is authorized to act for the principal. Note that apparent authority is based on what the *principal* communicates to the third party; this may occur either directly or through the agent. Thus, a principal might clothe an agent with apparent authority by making direct statements to the third party, telling the agent to do so, or allowing the agent to behave in a way that creates an appearance of authority. Communications to the agent generally are irrelevant unless they become known to the third party or affect the agent's behavior. Also, agents cannot give themselves apparent authority, and apparent authority does not exist where the agent creates an appearance of authority without the principal's consent. Finally, note that the third party must *reasonably* believe that the agent has authority. Trade customs and business practices can help courts determine whether there was reason to believe that the agent had authority.

Authority is important in a number of legal contexts, and we discuss its specific applications in those contexts. As you will see in the next chapter, for example, a principal's liability on contracts made by his agent usually depends on the agent's authority to make the contract in question. Moreover, a proper grant of authority is needed to create the relation of *subagency* described below. As discussed later in the chapter, the agent's authority also helps determine when the principal has a duty to reimburse or indemnify the agent. Finally, the concept of authority also assumes importance in various situations outside agency law. To take just one example, the chapter on the FTC Act and other consumer protection laws discusses how the federal Truth in Lending Act limits a credit card holder's liability for unauthorized use of the card to $50. The act does so by effectively defining unauthorized use as use by someone who lacks express, implied, or apparent authority to use the card.

General and Special Agents

Although it may be falling out of favor with the courts, the blurred distinction between general and special agents still has some importance in agency law. A **general agent** is an agent *continuously* employed to conduct a series of transactions, while a **special agent** is an agent employed to conduct a single transaction or a small, simple group of transactions. Thus, a continuously employed general manager, construction project supervisor, or purchasing agent normally is a general agent; and a person employed to buy or sell a few objects on a one-shot basis usually is a special agent. In addition to being employed on a continuous basis, general agents often serve for longer periods, perform more acts, and deal with more parties than do special agents.

Gratuitous Agents

Earlier, you saw that consideration is not necessary for the creation of an agency. An agent who receives no compensation for his services is called a **gratuitous agent.** Gratuitous agents have the same power to bind their principals as do paid agents with the same authority. As discussed later in this chapter, however, the fact that the agent is gratuitous sometimes lowers the duties the principal and the agent owe each other, and also may increase the parties' ability to terminate the agency without incurring liability.

Subagents

A **subagent** basically is the agent of an agent. More precisely, a subagent is a person appointed by an agent to perform functions that the agent has undertaken to perform for his principal. For a subagency to exist, the agent must have the authority to make the subagent *his agent* for conducting the principal's business. If you retain an accounting firm as your agent, for example, the accountant actually handling your affairs is the firm's agent and your subagent. Sometimes, however, a party appointed by an agent is not a subagent because the appointing agent only had authority to appoint agents *for the principal*. For instance, sales agents appointed by a corporation's sales manager probably are agents of the corporation, not agents of the sales manager.

When an agent appoints a true subagent, the agent becomes a principal with respect to the subagent, his agent. Thus, the legal relations between agent and subagent closely parallel the legal relations between principal and agent. But the subagent is also the *original principal's* agent. Here, though, the normal rules governing principals and agents do not always apply. We occasionally refer to such situations in the pages ahead.

Employees and Independent Contractors

Many important legal questions hinge on a distinction between two relationships that overlap with the principal-agent relationship. These are an employer's (or master's) relationship with his **employee** (or servant), and a principal's relationship with an **independent contractor.** No sharp line separates these two relationships; the *VIP Tours* case that follows lists the factors often considered in making such determinations. By far the most important of these factors is the principal's *right to control the physical details of the work.* Employees typically are subject to such control. Independent contractors, on the other hand, generally contract with the principal to produce some result, and determine for themselves how that result will be accomplished.

Although many employees perform physical labor or are paid on an hourly basis, corporate officers also usually qualify as employees. Professionals such as brokers, accountants, and attorneys often are independent con-

tractors, although they may sometimes be employees. Consider the difference between a corporation represented by an attorney engaged in her own practice and a corporation that maintains a staff of salaried in-house attorneys. Franchisees, finally, usually are independent contractors.

When are employees and independent contractors agents? Although there is little consensus on this question, the *Restatement* position is clear, and we follow it in this text. According to the *Restatement*, employees are *always* agents, while independent contractors *may or may not* be agents.[5] An independent contractor qualifies as an agent when the basic tests for the existence of an agency—most importantly, sufficient control by the principal—are met. Figure 1 sketches the *Restatement's* position on the relationships among agents, employees, and independent contractors. In the *Warren* case, for example, the cotton gins probably were agent-independent contractors, while the cotton buyers discussed at the end of the opinion probably were nonagent-independent contractors.

As you will see in the next chapter, the employee-independent contractor distinction often is crucial in determining the principal's liability for an agent's torts. The distinction also can be important in defining the coverage of some of the employment regulations discussed in the Employment Law chapter. Unemployment compensation (the subject of *VIP Tours*) and workers' compensation are two clear examples.

---

[5]*Restatement (Second) of Agency* sections 2, 14N, 25, and the Introductory Note following section 218 (1959).

FIGURE 1   Agents, Employees, and Independent Contractors as the *Restatement* Sees Them

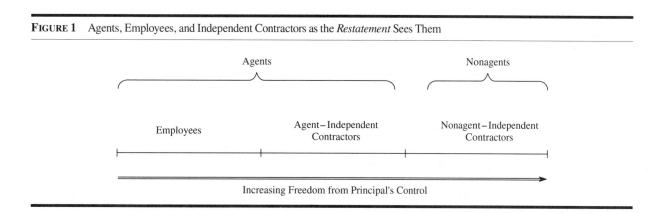

VIP TOURS, INC. v. FLORIDA

449 So. 2d 1307 (Fla. Ct. App. 1984)

VIP Tours, Inc., arranged tours of central Florida's attractions for visitors to the area. Cynthia Hoogland conducted 29 such tours for VIP between July 1980 and March 1981. Both Hoogland and VIP considered Hoogland an independent contractor. She worked for VIP only when it needed her services, and could reject particular assignments. She was also free to work for other tour services, and did so.

Once Hoogland accepted a job from VIP, she was told where to report and was given instructions about the job. She was also required to use a VIP-furnished vehicle and to wear a uniform with the VIP logo when conducting tours. Aside from ensuring that she departed on time, however, VIP did not tell her how long to stay or what kind of tour to conduct at each tourist attraction. Finally, Hoogland was paid on a per tour basis.

Hoogland later filed a claim for unemployment compensation benefits with the Florida Division of Labor and Employment Security. The division concluded that she was entitled to these benefits because she was VIP Tours' employee. VIP appealed the division's order to an intermediate appellate court.

Upchurch, Judge.   The [Florida] Supreme Court has approved the test set out in *Restatement (Second) of Agency* section 220 for determining whether one is an employee or an independent contractor:

In determining whether one acting for another is a servant or an independent contractor, the following matters of fact, among others, are considered:

  (a) the extent of control which, by the agreement, the master may exercise over the details of the work;
  (b) whether or not the one employed is engaged in a distinct occupation or business;
  (c) the kind of occupation, with reference to whether, in the locality, the work is usually done under the direction of the employer or by a specialist without supervision;
  (d) the skill required in the particular occupation;
  (e) whether the employer or the workman supplies the instrumentalities, tools, and the place of work for the person doing the work;
  (f) the length of time for which the person is employed;
  (g) the method of payment, whether by the time or by the job;
  (h) whether or not the work is part of the regular business of the employer;
  (i) whether or not the parties believe that they are creating the relationship of master and servant; and
  (j) whether the principal is or is not in business.

It has been said repeatedly that of all the factors, the right of control as to the mode of doing the work is the principal consideration.

VIP had no right of control over the tour guides other than to require them to show up at a particular place at a particular time wearing the VIP uniform and to travel in VIP transportation. These latter two factors appear to have been designed to facilitate identification of the guide and control insurance liability. VIP had little interest in the details of the guides' work, as is illustrated by the fact that the guides controlled the number of hours spent at a particular attraction and the nature of the tour at each exhibit. In addition, the guides were free to contract with other tour companies, as Hoogland did, and could accept or reject any assignment, factors further indicating a lack of control by VIP. Other factors set out in the *Restatement* also point toward independent contractor status here. The tour guides were engaged in a distinct occupation. They worked and were paid on a per-job basis. Both VIP and Hoogland considered the guides to be independent contractors.

Division order reversed.

DUTIES OF AGENT TO PRINCIPAL

Introduction

An agency normally is created by contract. Where this is so, the agent must perform according to the terms of the agreement and normal contract rules regarding interpretation, performance, and remedies apply. Also, regardless of whether the relationship is contractual, agency law establishes certain *fiduciary duties* owed by the agent to the principal. These duties exist because agency is a relationship of trust and confidence. They supplement the duties created by an agency contract. Often, however, the parties may eliminate or modify the fiduciary duties by agreement if they so desire.

Except for certain specific situations noted later, a *gratuitous agent* has the same fiduciary duties as a paid agent. But this is true only so long as a gratuitous agent continues to act as an agent. In other words, a gratuitous agent is not obligated to perform as promised, he normally can terminate the agency without incurring liability, and his fiduciary duties cease once the agency ends. However, a gratuitous agent *is* liable for his failure to perform as promised when his promise causes the principal to rely upon him to undertake certain acts, the principal thus refrains from performing those acts herself, and the principal suffers losses as a result. For example, suppose that the principal refrains from making a bid at an auction because her agent has gratuitously promised to make the bid for her, the agent attends the auction but fails to make the bid, and the bid would have been successful had it been made.

A *subagent* owes the agent (his principal) all the normal duties that agents owe their principals. A subagent who is aware of the original principal's existence also owes that principal all the usual duties agents owe their principals, except for those duties arising solely from the original principal's contract with the agent. Finally, the agent who appointed the subagent generally is responsible to the original principal for a subagent's conduct, and usually must compensate the principal when the principal is harmed by that conduct.

Agent's Duty of Loyalty

Because agency is a relationship of trust and confidence, an agent has a *duty of loyalty* to his principal. Thus, an agent must subordinate personal concerns by: (1) avoiding conflicts of interest with the principal, and (2) not disclosing confidential information received from the principal.

Conflicts of Interest An agent whose interests conflict with the principal's interests may not be able to represent his principal effectively. When conducting the principal's business, therefore, an agent generally is forbidden to *deal with himself*. For example, an agent authorized to sell property cannot sell that property to himself. This rule often includes an agent's transactions with his relatives or business associates, or with business organizations in which he has an interest. However, an agent may enter into such transactions if the principal consents to his doing so. For this consent to be effective, the agent must disclose all of the relevant facts to the principal before dealing with the principal on his own behalf.

Unless the principal agrees otherwise, an agent also is forbidden to *compete with the principal* regarding the agency business so long as he remains an agent. Thus, an agent employed to purchase specific property may not buy it himself if the principal still desires it. Moreover, an agent may not solicit the principal's customers for a planned competing business while still employed by the principal.

Finally, an agent who is authorized to make a certain transaction cannot *act on behalf of the other party* to the transaction unless the principal knowingly consents to this. Thus, one ordinarily cannot act as agent for both parties to a transaction without first disclosing the double role to, and obtaining the consent of, both principals. Here, the agent has a duty to disclose to each principal all of the factors reasonably affecting each principal's decision. Occasionally, though, an agent who acts as a middleman may serve both parties to a transaction without notifying either. For instance, an agent may simultaneously be employed as a "finder" by a firm seeking suitable businesses to acquire and a firm looking for prospective buyers, so long as neither principal expects the agent to advise it or negotiate for it.

Confidential Information Another facet of the agent's duty of loyalty is the obligation to ensure that the agency relation is one of *confidentiality*. Unless otherwise agreed, an agent has a duty not to *use* or *disclose* confidential information acquired through the agency. Confidential information means facts that are valuable to the principal because they are not widely known, or that would harm the principal's business if they became widely known. Examples include the principal's business plans, financial condition, contract bids, technolog-

ical discoveries, manufacturing methods, customer files, and other trade secrets.[6] However, an agent is free to reveal confidential information that the principal is committing or is about to commit a crime.

Unless there is an agreement to the contrary,[7] an agent is free to compete with her principal after termination of the agency. But as the following *ABKCO* case illustrates, the duty not to use or disclose confidential information still remains.[8] The former agent may, however, utilize general knowledge and skills acquired during the agency.

---

[6] Trade secrets law is discussed in the Intellectual Property, Competitive Torts, and Unfair Competition chapter.

[7] Covenants not to compete are discussed in the contracts chapter on Illegality.

[8] For a discussion of the patent and trade secrets problems that arise when an employee or a former employee tries to utilize ideas, discoveries, or inventions found or created during the course of her employment, see the Intellectual Property, Competitive Torts, and Unfair Competition chapter.

ABKCO MUSIC, INC. v. HARRISONGS MUSIC, LTD.

722 F.2d 988 (2d Cir. 1983)

In 1963, a song called "He's So Fine" was a huge hit in the United States and Great Britain. In February of 1971, Bright Tunes Music Corporation, the copyright holder of "He's So Fine," sued ex-Beatle George Harrison and Harrisongs, Music, Ltd., in federal district court. Bright Tunes claimed that the Harrison composition "My Sweet Lord" infringed its copyright to "He's So Fine." At this time, Harrison's business affairs were handled by ABKCO Music, Inc., and Allen B. Klein, its president. Shortly after the suit began, Klein unsuccessfully tried to settle it by having ABKCO purchase Bright Tunes.

Shortly thereafter, Bright Tunes went into receivership, and it did not resume the suit until 1973. At this time, coincidentally, ABKCO's management contract with Harrison expired. In late 1975 and early 1976, however, Klein continued his efforts to have ABKCO purchase Bright Tunes. As part of these efforts, he gave Bright Tunes three schedules summarizing Harrison's royalty income from "My Sweet Lord," information he possessed because of his previous service to Harrison. Throughout the 1973–76 period, Harrison's attorneys had been trying to settle the copyright infringement suit with Bright Tunes. Because Klein's activities not only gave Bright Tunes information about the economic potential of its suit but also gave it an economic alternative to settling with Harrison, Klein may have impeded Harrison's efforts to settle.

When the copyright infringement suit finally came to trial in 1976, the court found that Harrison had infringed Bright Tunes' copyright. The issue of damages was scheduled for trial at a later date and this trial was delayed for some time. In 1978, ABKCO purchased the "He's So Fine" copyright and all rights to the infringement suit from Bright Tunes. This made ABKCO the plaintiff in the 1979 trial for damages on the infringement suit. At trial, Harrison counterclaimed for damages resulting from Klein's and ABKCO's alleged breaches of the duty of loyalty. Finding a breach of duty, the district judge issued a complex order reducing ABKCO's recovery. ABKCO appealed.

Pierce, Circuit Judge.   The relationship between Harrison and ABKCO prior to termination of the management agreement in 1973 was that of principal and agent. An agent has a duty not to use confidential knowledge acquired in his employment in competition with his principal. This duty exists as well after the employment as during its continuance. On the other hand, use of information based on general business knowledge is not covered by the rule, and the former agent is permitted to compete with his former principal in reliance on such publicly available information. The principal issue before us, then, is whether Klein (hence, ABKCO) improperly used confidential information, gained as Harrison's former agent, in negotiating for the purchase of Bright Tunes' stock in 1975–76.

One aspect of this inquiry concerns the nature of the schedules of "My Sweet Lord" earnings which Klein furnished to Bright Tunes in connection with the 1975–76 negotiations. It appears that at least some of [this] information was confidential. The evidence is not at all convincing that the information was publicly available.

Another aspect of the breach of duty issue concerns the timing and nature of Klein's entry into the negotiation picture and the manner in which he became a plaintiff in this action. We find this case analogous to those where an employee, with the use of information acquired through his former employment, completes for his own benefit a transaction originally undertaken on the former employer's behalf. Klein had commenced a purchase transaction with Bright Tunes in 1971 on behalf of Harrison, which he pursued on his own account after termination of his fiduciary relationship with Harrison. Klein pursued the later discussions armed with the intimate knowledge not only of Harrison's business affairs, but of the value of this lawsuit. Taking all of these circumstances together, we agree that Klein's conduct during the period 1975–78 did not meet the standard required of him as a former fiduciary.

ABKCO also contends that even if there was a breach of duty, such breach should not limit its recovery for copyright infringement because its conduct did not cause the Bright Tunes/Harrison settlement negotiations to fail. ABKCO urges, in essence, that a breach of duty by an agent, to be actionable, must have been the proximate cause of injury to the principal. We do not accept ABKCO's proffered causation standard. An action for breach of duty is a prophylactic rule intended to remove all incentive to breach—not simply to compensate for damages in the event of a breach.

District court decision in favor of Harrison on the breach of duty issue affirmed.

Agent's Duty to Obey Instructions

Because an agent acts under the principal's control and for the principal's benefit, she has a duty to *obey all reasonable instructions* given by the principal for carrying out the agency business. For the reasons suggested earlier, however, a gratuitous agent need not obey his principal's order to continue to act as an agent. Also, agents generally have no duty to obey orders to behave *illegally or unethically.* Thus, a sales agent need not follow directions to misrepresent the quality of the principal's goods and professionals such as attorneys and accountants are not obligated to obey directions that conflict with accepted ethical rules governing their professions.

Agent's Duty to Act with Care and Skill

A paid agent must possess and exercise the degree of *care and skill* that is standard in the locality for the kind of work that the agent is employed to perform. A gratuitous agent need only exercise the degree of care and skill required of nonagents who perform similar gratuitous undertakings for others. Paid agents who represent that they possess a higher-than-customary level of skill may be held to a correspondingly higher standard of performance. Similarly, an agent's duty may change if the principal and the agent agree that the agent must possess and exercise a greater- or lesser-than-customary degree of care and skill.

Agent's Duty to Notify the Principal

An agent has a duty to promptly communicate to the principal matters within his knowledge that are reasonably relevant to the agency business and that he knows or should know are of concern to the principal. As the following *Levin* case suggests, this *duty to notify* sometimes is treated as one facet of the duty to act with care and skill. The basis for the duty to notify is the principal's obvious interest in being informed of matters that are important to the agency business.

However, there is no duty to notify where the agent receives information that is privileged or confidential. For example, an attorney may acquire confidential information from a client and thus be obligated not to disclose it to a second client. If the attorney cannot properly represent the second client without revealing this information, he should refuse to represent that client.

LEVIN v. KASMIR WORLD TRAVEL, INC.

540 N.Y.S.2d 639 (N.Y. Civ. Ct. 1989)

In July of 1987, Marsha Levin bought her daughter a round-trip plane ticket from New York City to Paris from Kasmir World Travel, Inc. Upon arriving in Paris, Mrs. Levin's daughter was denied entry and was placed on the next return flight to the United States because she did not have a visa. The apparent reason for the visa requirement was the French government's effort to deal with terrorist activities directed at Americans abroad. Neither Mrs. Levin nor her daughter was aware of the requirement; indeed, a few years earlier Mrs. Levin had traveled to France without being required to present a visa.

Levin sued Kasmir for failing to notify her about the visa requirement. Kasmir moved to dismiss her complaint.

Saxe, Judge. The duty of a travel agent has been held to include such responsibilities as verifying or confirming reservations. In general terms, travel agents are required to have the degree of skill and knowledge requisite to the calling; to exercise good faith and reasonable skill, care, and diligence; and to possess reasonable knowledge of the types of carriers, lines, and accommodations that they select for their principals, and all significant attendant matters. Beyond the duty to confirm travel reservations, travel agents should be expected to provide information which is necessary and of importance to the traveler.

I conclude that Kasmir had a duty to notify the traveler about the need for a visa before entering France. This view is in accord with the expanding role of the travel agent to provide all relevant and necessary information to the consumer who reasonably relies on the agent's expertise. Here, it was reasonable to expect Kasmir to alert its [principal] to important changes in the visa requirements of foreign nations. It was also reasonable for Mrs. Levin to rely on Kasmir to supply this information. After all, the travel agency was clearly in a position to assemble and disseminate this basic and significant type of travel information.

I am aware of Kasmir's contention that its relationship to the claimant was merely that of a ticketing agent, and that consequently duties beyond the actual sale of the ticket could not implicate such an agent. [But] information concerning entry or visa requirements into foreign lands is so basic to the purchase or sale of the ticket that the seller must be obliged to furnish it to all affected consumers.

Kasmir's motion to dismiss denied.

Agent's Duties to Account

The agent's duties of loyalty and care require that the agent give the principal any money or property received in the course of the agency business. This obviously includes profits resulting from the agent's breach of the duty of loyalty, or other duties. It also includes incidental benefits received through the agency business. Examples include bribes, kickbacks, and gifts from third parties with whom the agent deals on the principal's behalf. However, the parties may agree that the agent can retain certain benefits received during the agency. Courts often conclude that such an agreement exists when it is customary for agents to retain tips from customers, or to accept entertainment provided by third parties with whom the agent does business.

Another type of *duty to account* concerns agents whose business involves collections, receipts, or expenditures. Here, the agent must keep accurate records and accounts of all transactions, and disclose these to the principal once the principal makes a reasonable demand for them. Also, an agent who obtains or holds property for the principal usually may not commingle that property with her own property. For example, an agent ordinarily cannot deposit the principal's funds in her own name or in her own bank account.

Remedies of the Principal

A principal has a wide choice of claims and remedies when her agent breaches a duty. The following examples are not an exhaustive list. If the agency relation was created by contract, the agent's wrongdoing may be a breach of that contract. If so, the principal should get the various kinds of contract damages where appropriate. Also, a principal may obtain injunctive relief where, for example, an agent discloses or threatens to disclose confidential information, or misappropriates or threatens to misappropriate the principal's property. In addition, a principal may rescind contracts entered into by an agent who has represented two principals without the knowl-

edge of one or both, has dealt with himself, or has failed to disclose relevant facts to his principal. Agents who retain money or property due the principal (including bribes or gifts), or who profit from the breach of duty, also may be liable for the amount of their unjust enrichment.

Tort claims also are possible when the agent has misbehaved. A principal may recover for losses caused by his agent's negligent failure to follow instructions, to notify, or to perform with appropriate skill and care. The tort of conversion is available where an agent has unjustifiably retained, stolen, transferred, destroyed, failed to separate, or otherwise misappropriated the principal's property.

DUTIES OF PRINCIPAL TO AGENT

Introduction

If an agency is formed by contract, the contract should set out the duties the principal owes the agent. In addition, the law implies certain duties from the existence of an agency relationship, however formed. The most important such duties are the principal's obligations to *compensate* the agent, to *reimburse* the agent for money spent in the principal's service, and to *indemnify* the agent for losses suffered in conducting the principal's business.[9] These duties generally can be eliminated or modified by agreement between the parties. Although there obviously is no duty to compensate a gratuitous agent, the principal still owes such an agent the other two duties absent an agreement to the contrary.

---

[9] A principal also may have other duties, including the duties to: provide the agent with an opportunity for service, not interfere with the agent's work, keep accounts, act in a manner not harmful to the agent's reputation or self-esteem, and (in the case of employees) maintain a safe workplace. The last duty has been greatly affected, if not superseded, by workers' compensation systems and the Occupational Safety and Health Act, which are discussed in the Employment Law chapter.

An agent's duties to a subagent are the same as a principal's duties to an agent. Absent an agreement to the contrary, however, the original principal has no contractual liability to a subagent. For example, such a principal normally is not obligated to compensate a subagent. But a principal is required to reimburse and indemnify subagents as he would agents generally.

Duty to Compensate Agent

Where the agency contract states the agent's compensation, disputes about that compensation are settled by applying the rules of contract interpretation. In other cases, the relationship of the parties and the surrounding circumstances determine whether and in what amount the agent is to be compensated. Absent a contract provision on compensation, for example, a principal generally is not required to pay for undertakings that she did not request, services to which she did not consent, and tasks that typically are undertaken without pay. Also, a principal usually is not obliged to compensate an agent who has materially breached the agency contract or has committed a serious breach of a fiduciary duty. Where compensation is due but its amount is not expressly stated, the amount is the market price or the customary price for the agent's services, or, if neither is available, their reasonable value.

Sometimes an agent's compensation is contingent on the accomplishment of a specific result. For instance, a plaintiff's attorney may be retained on a contingent fee basis (being paid a certain percentage of the recovery if the suit succeeds or is settled), or a real estate broker may be entitled to a fee only if a suitable buyer is found. In such cases, the agent is not entitled to compensation unless he achieves the result within the time stated or, if no time is stated, within a reasonable time. This is true regardless of how much effort or money the agent expends. However, the principal must cooperate with the agent in achieving the result and must not do anything to frustrate the agent's efforts. Otherwise, the agent is entitled to compensation despite the failure to perform as specified.

Duties of Reimbursement and Indemnity

If, while acting on the principal's behalf, an agent makes expenditures that were expressly or impliedly authorized by the principal, the agent is entitled to *reimbursement* for those expenditures absent an agreement to the contrary. Unless otherwise agreed, for example, an agent requested to make overnight trips as part of his agency duties can recover reasonable transportation and hotel expenses.

A principal's duty of reimbursement overlaps with her duty of *indemnity*. Agency law implies a promise by the principal to indemnify an agent for losses that result from the agent's authorized activities. These include authorized payments made on the principal's behalf and payments on contracts on which the agent was authorized to become liable. A principal may also be required to indemnify an agent if the agent's authorized acts constitute a breach of contract or a tort for which the agent is required to pay damages to a third party.

So long as the principal did not benefit from such behavior, however, he is *not* required to indemnify an agent for losses resulting (1) from unauthorized acts or (2) solely from the agent's negligence or other fault. Even where the principal directed the agent to commit a tortious act, moreover, there is no duty to indemnify if the agent knew that the act was tortious. But the principal must indemnify the agent for tort damages resulting from authorized conduct that the agent did not believe was tortious. For example, if a principal directs his agent to repossess goods located on another's property and the agent, believing her acts legal, becomes liable for conversion or trespass, the principal must indemnify the agent for the damages the agent pays.

Remedies of the Agent

An agent's claim for breach of the duties just discussed often is contractual, and normal contract remedies—except specific performance—are available. In some cases, the principal's failure to pay, indemnify, or reimburse the agent enables the agent to acquire a lien on property or funds of the principal that are in the agent's possession. This usually allows the agent to hold the property or funds until the principal's obligation has been paid. Also, an agent whose principal violates the duties to pay, indemnify, or reimburse can refuse to render further services to the principal.

Of course, an agent's *own* breach of duty—especially the duties of loyalty and obedience—may defeat his claim against the principal. Where the breach is not serious enough to give the principal a complete defense, the principal may still set off losses caused by the breach against the agent's recovery.

FIGURE 2   The Duties the Principal and the Agent Owe
Each Other

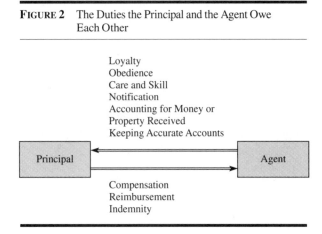

Loyalty
Obedience
Care and Skill
Notification
Accounting for Money or
Property Received
Keeping Accurate Accounts

Principal ⟷ Agent

Compensation
Reimbursement
Indemnity

TERMINATION OF THE AGENCY RELATIONSHIP

Agencies terminate in many ways.[10] These fall under two general headings: (1) termination by acts of the parties, and (2) termination by operation of law.

Termination by Acts of the Parties

The parties can control the termination of their agency through either the provisions they put in the agency agreement or their actions after concluding the agreement. Such *terminations by acts of the parties* occur in various ways.

1. An agency terminates at a time or upon the happening of an event *stated in the agreement.* If no such time or event is stipulated, the agency terminates after a *reasonable time.*

2. An agency created to accomplish a specified result terminates when *the specified result has been accomplished.* For example, if the only objective of an agency is to sell certain property, the agency terminates when the property is sold.

3. An agency may be terminated at any time by *mutual agreement of the parties.*

---

[10]The rules stated below generally apply to the termination of a subagent's authority as well. In general, a subagency terminates when relations between either the principal and the agent or the agent and the subagent are terminated in any of the ways to be described.

4. Finally, an agency can terminate at the *option of either party.* This is called *revocation* when done by the principal and *renunciation* when done by the agent. Generally, revocation or renunciation occurs when either party manifests to the other that he does not wish the agency to continue. Conduct inconsistent with the agency's continuance can constitute such a manifestation. For example, an agent may learn that his principal has hired another agent to perform the same job.

A party can revoke or renounce even if this violates the agency agreement. However, although either party has the *power* to terminate in such cases, there is no *right* to do so. This means that where one party terminates in violation of the agreement, she is not bound to perform any further but she may be liable for damages to the other party. As noted earlier, however, a gratuitous agency normally is terminable by either party without liability. Also, the terminating party is not liable where the revocation or renunciation is justified by the other party's serious breach of a fiduciary duty.

These principles are illustrated by the traditional termination rules governing agents who are paid *employees.* If the employment contract is for a *definite time period* and either party terminates before the period ends, the terminating party normally is liable to the other for breach of contract. Under the doctrine of **employment at will,** however, an employment contract for an *indefinite term* is not breached when either party terminates the employment. In such cases, both parties can end the employment at any time and for any reason without incurring contract liability. Nonetheless, terminated employees normally can recover for work actually done. Over the past 20 years, the courts of most states have recognized certain exceptions to the employment at will doctrine. These exceptions, which generally aim to protect employees against *wrongful discharge,* are discussed in detail in the Employment Law chapter.

Termination by Operation of Law

Numerous other events may terminate an agency. For the most part, these events do not involve the parties' willful choices. Instead, they normally involve situations where it is reasonable to believe that the principal would not wish the agent to act further, or where accomplishment of the agency objectives has become impossible or illegal. Although courts may recognize exceptions in certain cases, an agency relationship usually is terminated by:

1. *The death of the principal.* This is normally true even where the agent has no notice of the principal's death.

2. *The death of the agent.*

3. *The principal's permanent loss of capacity.* This is a *permanent* loss of capacity occurring *after* creation of the agency. The usual cause is the principal's insanity. Like the principal's death, the principal's permanent incapacity ends the agency even without notice to the agent. A brief period of insanity, on the other hand, may only cause a temporary suspension of the agency relation for the time that the principal is insane.

4. *The agent's loss of capacity to perform the agency business.* The scope of this basis for termination is unclear. As you will see in the next chapter, an agent who becomes insane or otherwise incapacitated after the agency is formed still can bind the principal to contracts with third parties. Thus, it probably makes little sense to treat the agency relationship as terminated in such cases. As a result, termination under this heading may be limited to such situations as the loss of a license needed to perform agency duties (for example, a license needed to sell certain goods).

5. *Changes in the value of the agency property or subject matter* (for example, a significant decline in the value of land to be sold by an agent).

6. *Changes in business conditions* (for example, a markedly lower supply and a greatly increased price for goods to be purchased by an agent).

7. *The loss or destruction of the agency property or subject matter or the termination of the principal's interest therein* (for example, a situation in which a house to be sold by a real estate broker burns down or is taken by a mortgage holder to satisfy a debt owed by the principal).

8. *Changes in the law that make the agency business illegal* (for example, a situation in which drugs to be sold by an agent are banned by the government).

9. *The bankruptcy of the principal*—as to transactions that the agent should realize are no longer desired by the principal. Consider, for example, the likely effect of the principal's bankruptcy on an agency to purchase antiques for the principal's home, as opposed to its likely effect on an agency to purchase necessities of life for the principal.

10. *The bankruptcy of the agent*—where the agent's financial condition affects his ability to serve the principal. This could occur where the agent is employed to purchase goods on his own credit for the principal.

11. *Impossibility of performance by the agent.* This covers a wide range of circumstances, some of which fall within the categories just stated. The *Restatement*, for example, includes within its definition of impossibility: (a) the destruction of the agency subject matter, (b) the termination of the principal's interest in the agency subject matter (as, for example, by the principal's bankruptcy), and (c) changes in the law or in other circumstances that make it impossible for the agent to accomplish the aims of the agency.[11]

12. *A serious breach of the agent's duty of loyalty.*

13. *The outbreak of war*—where this leads the agent to the reasonable belief that his services are no longer desired. One example might be the outbreak of war between the principal's country and the agent's country.

Termination of Agency Powers Given as Security

An agency power given as security for a duty owed by the principal, sometimes called an *agency coupled with an interest*, is an exception to some of the termination rules just discussed. Here, the agent has an interest in the subject matter of the agency that is distinct from the principal's interest and that is not exercised for the principal's benefit. This interest exists to benefit the agent or a third person by securing performance of an obligation owed by the principal. A common example is a secured loan agreement authorizing a lender (the agent) to sell property used as security if the debtor (the principal) defaults. For example, suppose that Allen lends Peters $100,000 and Peters gives Allen a lien or security interest on Peters's land to secure the loan. Such an agreement typically would authorize Allen to act as Peters's "agent" to sell the land if Peters fails to repay the loan.

Because the power given the "agent" in such cases is not for the principal's benefit, it is sometimes said that an agency coupled with an interest is not truly an agency. In any event, courts distinguish it from situations where the agent only has an interest in being compensated from the profits or proceeds of property held for the principal's benefit. For example, if an agent is promised a commission for selling the principal's property, the relationship is not an agency coupled with an interest. In this case, the power exercised by the agent (selling the principal's property) benefits the principal.

---

[11] *Restatement (Second) of Agency* section 124 (1959).

The main significance of the agency coupled with an interest is that the principal cannot revoke it. Also, it is not terminated by either the principal's or the agent's loss of capacity. In addition, the death of the agent does not terminate this relationship; the death of the principal does so only when the obligation owed by the principal ends with the principal's death. However, unless an agency coupled with an interest is held for the benefit of a third party, the agent can voluntarily surrender it. Of course, an agency coupled with an interest terminates when the principal performs her obligation as promised.

Effect of Termination on Agent's Authority

Sometimes agents continue to act on their principals' behalf even though the agency has ended. Do such ex-agents still have authority to bind their former principals? As Figure 3 states, once an agency has been terminated by any of the means just described, the agent's *express* authority and *implied* authority end along with the agency.

Third parties who are unaware of the termination, however, still may reasonably believe that the ex-agent has authority. To protect such parties when they rely on such a reasonable appearance of authority, an agent's *apparent authority* often persists after termination. This means that a former agent may be able to bind the principal under his apparent authority even though the agency has ended. But as Figure 3 also states, there are three important exceptions to this generalization. Apparent authority ends and an ex-agent cannot bind the principal where the termination was caused by: (1) the *principal's death*, (2) the *principal's loss of capacity*, or (3) *impossibility*.[12] Note from the previous discussion

---

[12]*Restatement (Second) of Agency* section 124A, comment a; and section 133 (1959). Subject to certain exceptions, moreover, section 132 of the *Restatement* says that the apparent authority of a *special agent* terminates along with termination of the agency.

that certain other bases for termination by operation of law may fit within the broad category of impossibility and also end the agent's apparent authority.

Notice to Third Parties   It follows from the nature of apparent authority that such authority ends when the third party receives appropriate *notice* of the termination. In general, any facts known to the third party that reasonably indicate the agency's termination constitute suitable notice. Some bases for termination by operation of law (for example, changed business conditions) may provide such notice.

To protect themselves against unwanted liability, however, prudent principals may want to notify third parties themselves. The type of notification required for this purpose varies with the third party in question.

1. *Third parties who have previously dealt with the agent or who have begun to deal with the agent.* Here, the principal must give *actual notification*. This can be accomplished by: (1) a direct personal statement to the third party; or (2) a writing delivered to the third party personally, to his place of business, or to some other place reasonably believed to be appropriate.

2. *All other third parties.* Usually, these are parties who are aware of the agency but did no business with the agent. For such parties, *constructive notification* is all that is required. This normally can be accomplished by advertising the agency's termination in a newspaper of general circulation in the place where the agency business regularly was carried on. Where no suitable publication exists, notification by other means reasonably likely to inform third parties of the termination —for example, posting a notice in public places— may suffice.

FIGURE 3   Termination of an Agent's Authority after Termination of the Agency

Type of Termination	Actual Authority	Apparent Authority
By Acts of the Parties	Ceases	Persists unless appropriate notice or notification to third party
By Operation of Law	Ceases	Ceases if termination by principal's death or loss of capacity, or by impossibility; persists in other cases unless appropriate notice or notification to third party

ETHICAL AND PUBLIC POLICY CONCERNS

1. Take another look at the doctrine of employment at will discussed in the section on termination of an agency. By now, the doctrine has various exceptions, which are discussed in the Employment Law chapter. In cases where the doctrine still applies, it allows employers to discharge employees for *any* reason, no matter how arbitrary, without suffering liability. Put more bluntly, it means that *you* might be fired from some future job for some arbitrary reason, even if your work performance was excellent. What can justify such a seemingly harsh rule?

2. Under one of the agent's duties to account, an agent might be required to return to the principal gifts from third parties with whom the agent deals on the principal's behalf. Where the gift is a genuine token of appreciation, the principal may be getting a windfall. What can justify this result?

3. A well-known ethical theory called *utilitarianism* generally asserts that the moral worth of actions should be judged by *their tendency to promote net aggregate satisfaction*. Some people regard the maximization of social wealth as a reasonable measuring rod for net aggregate satisfaction. Under a wealth-maximization criterion, does the rule forbidding an ex-agent from using or disclosing confidential information make sense? How might the rule promote wealth maximization? How might it hinder wealth maximization? In attempting to answer this question, you might consult the introduction to the section on trade secrets in the Intellectual Property, Competitive Torts, and Unfair Competition chapter.

What other ethical considerations might justify the rule against the disclosure of confidential information by an ex-agent? Are they utilitarian in the sense defined above?

SUMMARY

Because the agency relationship enables individuals and businesses to multiply their transactions, it is vital to a commercial economy. Courts hold that an agency exists if the facts indicate an agreement that one person will act for the benefit and under the control of another. However, certain duties cannot be delegated to an agent. Although the agency relationship is based on mutual consent, it need not be contractual. Thus, consideration is not essential and only rarely is a writing needed. The incapacity of either the principal or the agent at the time an agency is formed enables that party to avoid the agency at his option.

Agency law contains a number of basic definitions and concepts. An agent's *authority* is his ability to affect the principal's legal relations with third parties. Authority may be *express* (based on the principal's actual words), *implied* (created by operation of law from those words and the surrounding circumstances), or *apparent* (based on the third party's reasonable belief that the agent has authority). Agents may be classed as *general agents* (those authorized to perform a series of transactions involving continuity of service) or *special agents* (those authorized to conduct a few transactions or a single transaction not involving continuity of service). A *gratuitous agent* is an agent who receives no compensation or other consideration for his services. A *subagent* is an agent appointed to conduct the principal's business by an agent with authority to make the appointment. Parties who act for the principal, finally, may be classed as *employees* or *independent contractors*. The most important factor affecting the classification is the principal's right to control the physical details of the work.

Because the agency relationship is for the principal's benefit, agency law imposes a number of duties on the *agent*. These supplement the duties expressly created by an agency agreement. The agent's duties are: (1) loyalty to the principal; (2) obedience to the principal's reasonable, lawful, and ethical instructions; (3) care and skill in performing agency duties; (4) notification of matters affecting the principal's interest in the agency business; (5) the return of profits and other things of value received in the course of the agency business; and (6) an accounting of the agency's financial operations.

The agency relation also imposes certain duties on the *principal*. The most important such duties are: (1) to compensate the agent, (2) to reimburse the agent for expenditures connected with the agency business, and (3) to indemnify the agent for losses suffered in the course of the agency business.

An agency can be terminated by the acts of the parties or by operation of law. Termination by *acts of the parties* includes: (1) the occurrence of an event or the passage of a time period stated in the agency agreement, (2) the passage of a reasonable time (if no termination date has been set by agreement), (3) accomplishment of the results for which the agency was established, (4) mutual agreement of the parties, (5) the principal's revocation, and (6) the agent's renunciation. Termination *by operation of law* includes: (1) the death of the principal, (2) the death of the agent, (3) the principal's permanent loss of capacity, (4) the agent's loss of capacity to perform the agency business, (5) changes in the value of the agency property or subject matter, (6) changes in business conditions, (7) loss or destruction of the agency property or termination of the principal's interest therein, (8) changes in the law that make the agency business illegal, (9) the principal's or the agent's bankruptcy (in certain cases), (10) impossibility of performance (which includes various other grounds for termination by operation of law), (11) a serious breach of the agent's duty of loyalty, and (12) the outbreak of war (in certain cases). An agency coupled with an interest, however, cannot be terminated by the principal's revocation, the principal's or the agent's incapacity, the agent's death, or (sometimes) the principal's death.

Termination of the agency also terminates the agent's *express* and *implied* authority. Except where the termination is by the principal's death, the principal's loss of capacity, or impossibility, however, the agent's *apparent authority* continues until the third party receives proper *notice* of the termination. The type of notice required varies depending on the third party's previous dealings with the agent.

PROBLEM CASES

1. Joan Marie Ottensmeyer was a contestant for the title of Miss Hawaii–USA 1974. The pageant was run by Richard You as a franchisee of Miss Universe, Inc. After finishing as first runner-up, Ottensmeyer sued Miss Universe, Inc., arguing that as its agent, You had prevented her from winning a title to which she was rightfully entitled and from obtaining the benefits thereof. The franchise agreement between Miss Universe and You contained language explicitly stating that You was not Miss Universe's agent. By itself, is this language sufficient to prevent the formation of an agency relationship between Miss Universe and You?

2. Melabs of California manufactured a portable electric telephone that was designed to fit inside an attache case and to operate on the same airwaves as fixed telephone installations in vehicles. Melabs and Marlin American Corporation entered into a contract giving Marlin the right to distribute the phone. The contract gave Marlin the exclusive right to establish a sales and marketing program and to develop all brochures, sales

aids, forms, advertising materials, and other marketing aids. On the other hand, it gave Melabs the right to approve all contract forms. It also established that uniform terms, conditions, and prices would be offered to the ultimate distributors of the phones. In addition, it transferred ownership of subsequent distributorships established by Marlin to Melabs in the event that Marlin went bankrupt. Finally, there was evidence that, in practice, Melabs exercised approval rights over the use of its trademark in advertising matters. On these facts, did Melabs possess sufficient control over Marlin to create an agency relationship between Melabs and Marlin?

3. Betty Jones established VISA and MasterCard accounts with a bank, and had credit cards for each account issued to herself and her husband in each of their names. In November of 1977, Jones informed the bank that she would no longer honor charges made by her husband on the two accounts. The bank immediately revoked both accounts and requested the return of the two cards. Jones, however, did not return the cards until March 9, 1978. During the interim, Jones's husband apparently had run up $2,685.70 in purchases on the cards. Jones refused to pay this amount, arguing that the federal Truth in Lending Act limits a cardholder's liability for unauthorized use of the card to $50. The provision in question basically defines unauthorized use as use without express, implied, or apparent authority. Was Jones's liability limited to $50?

4. New World Fashions, Inc., a firm in the business of assisting persons interested in entering the retail clothing business, employed Abbott Lieberman as a sales representative. While working for New World, Lieberman told one potential client that he would soon go into business himself in competition with New World and that he could offer her either New World's services or his own. Later, he contracted to set up a retail store for this person, a service that New World would otherwise have provided. There was nothing to indicate that New World knew about Lieberman's dealings with this potential client, or that it acquiesced in these dealings. Did Lieberman breach his duty of loyalty to New World?

5. Mark and Roberta Murray purchased a single-family home. Some time after they moved in, cracks appeared at various places in the house, and the Murrays eventually discovered that its foundation was defective. They sued the real estate broker who had represented them in the purchase, arguing that he breached his duty of care and skill by failing to conduct a reasonable investigation of the house. Did their broker owe the Murrays such a duty? Assume that the *seller's* broker had a duty to make such an inspection and to disclose to the purchaser all facts materially affecting the value or desirability of the house.

6. In February of 1989, Thomas Fix arranged for a Florida vacation package for himself and his sister with Travel Help, a travel agency. The travel agent selected an Eastern Airlines package that included Eastern vouchers for a rental car, Howard Johnson's Fountain Park, and Sea World. Aware of the labor and other problems Eastern was experiencing at that time, Fix's sister contacted the agent several times requesting that all the arrangements be made with another airline. The agent assured her that the flights could be changed and that the vouchers would be honored. After Eastern went into bankruptcy on March 9, 1989, the agent arranged for Fix and his sister to be transported to Florida on a different airline. After they arrived, however, the providers of the voucher bookings refused to honor Eastern's vouchers. Did the agent breach a duty to Fix (and his sister)? If so, which duty? You can assume that the travel agent was acting for both Fix and his sister, and that the communications to the agent by Fix's sister were communications to an agent by his principal.

7. Southeastern Agri-Systems, Inc., was an agent for Otto Niederer. James Stanford was Agri-Systems' president and sole employee. Niederer instructed Stanford to accept payment for the sale of some equipment owned by Niederer, to deduct his commission from the payment, and to wire the remainder to Niederer. Instead, Stanford diverted the funds to his own purposes and refused to pay Niederer the amount due. When sued individually for breach of the agent's duty to obey, Stanford argued that Niederer had employed Agri-Systems as its agent, that he was merely an employee of Agri-Systems, and that he thus owed no duty to Niederer. Is Stanford correct?

8. Stanley Mazur owned an Oldsmobile Cutlass and a small Subaru pickup truck. He asked his insurance agent, Ken Curtis, to arrange "full coverage" on the truck similar to the coverage on his Cutlass. Although the policy on the Cutlass included personal injury protection, Curtis negligently failed to include such protection in the policy he obtained for the Subaru. Later, Mazur suffered personal injury from an accident in which he was involved while driving the Subaru. Because the policy did not cover such injury, he was unable to recover for it from the insurer, the Selected Risks Insurance Company.

Mazur recovered against Curtis for Curtis's failure to procure the requested coverage. Curtis then sued to have Selected indemnify him for this loss. Is Selected required to indemnify Curtis? Why or why not? You can assume that Curtis was acting as an agent for Selected as well as for Mazur.

9. Ella Kelly died in January of 1982. She left the bulk of her estate to charity and to her niece and executrix, Mary McDonald. Kelly's grandchildren then undertook a lengthy legal challenge to the will, a challenge to which McDonald was effectively the opposing party. In January of 1986, the grandchildren made a demand of $50,000 on McDonald through her attorney, Malcolm McNeil. By this time, McDonald was hospitalized with a serious illness, and McNeil was communicating with her through her husband even though he had broad authority to settle the dispute. After McNeil made a $40,000 counteroffer, the grandchildren agreed in principle to this figure. Not wishing to settle the case without written authority from McDonald, McNeil then got the grandchildren to agree to a $40,000 settlement that was conditioned on his obtaining such authority. Before McNeil could obtain written authority from McDonald, however, she died on January 22, 1986. Nonetheless, McNeil went ahead and settled the case for $40,000 on January 30, 1986. Still later, the grandchildren petitioned the court to set aside the settlement.

Did McNeil have actual authority to settle on January 30, 1986? Did he have apparent authority to settle on that date? In each case, why or why not?

THIRD-PARTY RELATIONS OF THE PRINCIPAL AND THE AGENT

INTRODUCTION

As you saw in the previous chapter, the agency relation allows people to multiply their dealings with third parties, thereby stimulating business activity. But an agent's interactions with such parties create legal problems that agency law must resolve if it is to perform its functions effectively and fairly.

Agency law stimulates business activity by enabling principals to contract through their agents. Thus, rules for determining the principal's and the agent's liability on contracts completed by the agent are crucial to the successful functioning of the agency relation. Principals need some ability to predict and control their liability on contracts made by their agents. Also, third parties need some assurance that such contracts really bind the principal. In addition, both agents and third parties have an interest in knowing when the *agent* is bound on these contracts. The first half of this chapter discusses the principal's and the agent's contract liability.

Also, agents may harm third parties in various ways while acting on the principal's behalf. Normally, this makes the agent liable to the injured party in tort. Sometimes, moreover, a *principal* is liable for his agent's torts. For obvious monetary reasons, the rules for determining the principal's and the agent's tort liability are of great concern to principals, their agents, and third parties. Thus, we examine these subjects in the second half of this chapter. The chapter concludes with a brief treatment of the principal's and the agent's criminal liability.

CONTRACT LIABILITY OF THE PRINCIPAL

A principal's liability for contracts completed by his agent depends mainly on whether the agent had *express, implied, or apparent authority* to make the contract in question.[1] Occasionally, however, a principal's contract liability may be affected by other factors. The principal's incapacity, for example, may enable him to avoid a contract made by an agent. Even where the agent lacked authority to contract, moreover, a principal may bind herself by later *ratifying* the contract.

Express Authority

As previously discussed, **express authority** is created by a principal's *words* to his agent, whether written or oral. Thus, an agent has express authority to bind the principal to a particular contract if the principal

---

[1]In this connection, recall from the previous chapter that termination of the agency may or may not end the agent's authority.

has clearly told the agent that she could make that contract on the principal's behalf. For example, suppose that Payne instructs his agent, Andrews, to contract to sell a specific antique chair for $400 or more. If Andrews contracts to sell the chair to Tucker for $425, Payne is liable to Tucker on the basis of Andrews's express authority. However, Andrews would not have express authority to sell the chair for $375, or to sell a different chair.

Implied Authority

If express authority were the only way that agents could bind their principals, agency law's ability to stimulate business activity would be limited. In many cases, it is difficult or impossible for a principal to specify his agent's authority completely and precisely. Thus, an agent also can bind his principal on the basis of the agent's **implied authority.** As the *Adams* case later in this chapter states, implied authority is determined by inference from the circumstances, nature, and purposes of the agency. Courts attempting to determine an agent's implied authority often ask what the agent could reasonably assume that the principal wanted him to do in light of all the factors known or reasonably known to the agent. In making this determination, courts consider the principal's express statements to the agent, the nature of the agency business, the relations between principal and agent, and other relevant facts and circumstances.

A principal's express statements to her agent are an important source of implied authority. Implied authority, that is, often derives from a grant of express authority. For example, an agency expressly set up to conduct a certain business ordinarily gives the agent implied authority to make those contracts that are reasonably necessary for conducting the business or that are customarily made in conducting that business. Implied authority, however, cannot conflict with the principal's express statements. Thus, there is no implied authority to contract where a principal has limited her agent's authority by express statement or clear implication and the contract would conflict with that limitation.

On occasion, implied authority may exist even where there is no relevant grant of express authority. Here, courts generally derive implied authority from the nature of the agency business, the relations between principal and agent, customs in the trade, and other facts and circumstances. For example, there may be implied authority to make a certain contract if the agent has made similar past contracts with the principal's knowledge and without his objection.

Specific Examples of Implied Authority   The courts have created several general rules or presumptions for determining the implied authority of certain agents in certain situations. For example:

1. As just noted, an agent hired to *manage a business* normally has implied authority to make those contracts that are reasonably necessary for conducting the business or that are customary in the business. These include contracts for obtaining equipment and supplies, making repairs, employing employees, and selling goods or services. However, a manager generally has no power to borrow money or issue negotiable instruments in the principal's name unless the principal is a banking or financial concern regularly performing such activities.

2. An agent given *full control over real property* has implied authority to contract for repairs and insurance, and may rent the property for certain periods if this is customary. But such an agent may not sell the property or allow any third-party liens or other interests to be taken on it.

3. Agents appointed to *sell the principal's goods* may have implied authority to make customary warranties on those goods and to bind the principal to such warranties. In states that still recognize the distinction, the *general agent* described in the previous chapter is more likely to have such authority than the *special agent* described in that chapter.

Apparent Authority

Sometimes a principal's actions create a reasonable appearance of authority in an agent who may or may not have actual authority. In such cases, the principal may be bound to the agent's contracts on the basis of the agent's **apparent authority.** Apparent authority to contract arises when the principal's acts cause a third party to reasonably believe that the agent is authorized to deal on the principal's behalf. It is based on what the *principal* communicates to the *third party*, either directly or through the agent. Communications to the agent are irrelevant except as they become known to the third party or affect the agent's behavior. Also, agents cannot give themselves apparent authority without the principal's consent.

Examples of Apparent Authority   Principals can give their agents apparent authority through the statements they make, or tell their agents to make, to third parties; and through the actions they knowingly allow their agents to take. In all such cases, the principal's acts must cause the third party to form a reasonable belief that authority exists. As the *Adams* case suggests, background factors such as trade customs and established business practices often play a role in determining the reasonableness of the third party's belief. For instance, if a principal appoints his agent to a position such as general manager that customarily involves the power to make certain kinds of contracts, the agent normally has apparent authority to make those contracts. Here, the principal's behavior in appointing the agent to the position, as reasonably interpreted in light of business customs, creates apparent authority in the agent. This is true even if the principal expressly told the agent not to make such contracts, so long as this limitation remains unknown to the third party. Because agents cannot give themselves apparent authority, however, there would be no such authority if the agent falsely told third parties that he had been promoted to general manager without the principal's knowledge or permission.

Established business customs can help create apparent authority in other ways as well. For example, an agent often can bind his principal to forbidden promises that customarily accompany contracts the agent actually is authorized to complete, if the third party is unaware that the promises were forbidden. In states that continue to recognize the distinction, general agents are much more likely to have this kind of apparent authority than are special agents. Suppose that Perry employs Arthur as general sales agent for his manufacturing business. Certain warranties customarily accompany the products Perry sells, and agents like Arthur ordinarily are empowered to give these warranties. But Perry tells Arthur not to make any such warranties to buyers, thus cutting off Arthur's express and implied authority. Despite Perry's orders, however, Arthur makes the usual warranties in a sale to Thomas, who is familiar with customs in the trade. If Thomas did not know about the limitation on Arthur's authority, Perry is bound by Arthur's warranties.

Finally, apparent authority sometimes is found where the principal has, to the knowledge of a third person, permitted the agent to make contracts that the agent was expressly forbidden to make. Suppose Potter has told Abram, the manager of his business, to hire loaders for his trucks for no more than one day at a time. No one else knows about this limitation on Abram's actual authority. With Potter's knowledge and without his objection, however, Abram frequently has employed loaders by the week. Then Abram agrees to employ Trapp as a loader for a week. If Trapp knew about the earlier employment

by the week, Potter would be bound to the one-week employment contract on the basis of Abram's apparent authority.

Effect of Agent's Notification and Knowledge

In a few situations, the general agency rules regarding *notification* and *knowledge* can affect the principal's contract liability. If a third party gives proper notification to an agent having actual or apparent authority to receive it, the principal is bound as if the notification had been given directly to him. For example, where a contract between Phillips and Thomas made by Phillips's agent Anderson contains a clause allowing Thomas to cancel if she notifies Phillips, she can cancel by notifying Anderson if Anderson has actual or apparent authority to receive the notification. Similarly, notification to a third party by an agent with the necessary authority is considered notification by the principal.

In certain circumstances, an agent's knowledge of certain facts is imputed to the principal. This means that the principal's rights and liabilities are what they would have been if the principal had known what the agent knew. Generally, the agent's knowledge is imputed to the principal when it is relevant to activities that the agent is authorized to undertake, or when the agent is under a duty to disclose the knowledge to the principal. Suppose that Ames contracts with Timmons on Pike's behalf, knowing that Timmons is completely mistaken about a matter material to the contract. Even though Pike knew nothing about Timmons's unilateral mistake, Timmons probably can avoid his contract with Pike.[2]

Incapacity of Principal or Agent

As discussed in the last chapter, a principal who lacks capacity at the time the agency is formed usually may avoid the agency, and a principal's permanent loss of capacity after the agency's formation terminates the agency. Where the agency continues to exist, however, is a principal of limited mental capacity such as a minor or an insane person bound on contracts made by the agent? Subject to the exceptions discussed in the contracts chapter on Capacity to Contract, such contracts are voidable at the principal's option. These contracts normally would be voidable if made by the principal himself, and it is difficult to see why acting through an agent should increase the principal's capacity.

---

[2]On unilateral mistake in contract law, see the Reality of Consent chapter.

Like the principal, an agent can avoid the agency agreement if she lacks capacity at the time it is formed. Where the agency survives, however, the agent's incapacity usually does *not* affect the contract liability of a principal who has capacity. Just as an agent cannot increase the principal's capacity, neither can she diminish it. However, sometimes the principal may escape liability where an agent's incapacity is so extreme that the agent cannot receive or convey ideas, or cannot follow the principal's instructions.

Ratification

Ratification is a process whereby a principal binds himself to an unauthorized act done by an agent or by a person purporting to act as an agent. Ratification relates back to the time when the act was performed. For contracts, its effect is to bind the principal as if the agent had possessed authority at the time the contract was made.

Conduct Amounting to Ratification For ratification to occur, the principal's words or other behavior must indicate an intent to treat the agent's unauthorized act as authorized. Ratification can be express or implied. An *express ratification* occurs when the principal communicates his intent to ratify by written or oral words to that effect. *Implied ratification* arises when the principal's behavior evidences an intent to ratify. Part performance of the agent's contract by a principal or a principal's acceptance of benefits under the contract may work an implied ratification. In some cases, even a principal's silence, acquiescence, or failure to repudiate the transaction may constitute ratification. This can occur in cases where the principal would be expected to object if he did not consent to the contract, the principal's silence leads the third party to believe that he does so consent, and the principal is aware of all the relevant facts.

Additional Requirements Even if a principal's behavior indicates an intent to ratify, other requirements must be met before ratification occurs. These requirements have been variously stated; the following list is typical.

1. The act ratified must be one that would have been *valid* at the time it was performed. For example, an agent's illegal contract cannot be made binding by the principal's subsequent ratification. However, a contract that was voidable when made due to the principal's incapacity may be ratified by a principal who has later attained or regained capacity.

2. The principal must have been *in existence* at the time the agent acted. However, as discussed in the Organization, Financial Structure, and Dissolution of Corporations chapter, corporations may bind themselves to their promoters' preincorporation contracts by adopting such contracts.

3. At the time the act to be ratified occurred, the agent must have indicated to the third party that she was acting for *a* principal, and not for herself. But the agent need not have disclosed the principal's identity.

4. The principal must be *legally competent* at the time of ratification. For instance, an insane principal cannot ratify.

5. The principal must have *knowledge* of all the material facts regarding the prior act or contract at the time it is ratified. Here, the agent's knowledge is not imputed to the principal. In the *Adams* case that follows, the principal did not ratify because it lacked sufficient knowledge.

6. The principal must ratify the *entire* act or contract. He cannot ratify the beneficial parts of a contract and reject those that are detrimental.

7. In ratifying, the principal must use the *same formalities* that are required to give the agent authority to execute the transaction. As the preceding chapter related, few formalities normally are needed to give an agent authority. But where the original agency contract requires a writing, ratification likewise must be written.

Intervening Events Certain events occurring after an agent's contract but before the principal's ratification may cut off the principal's power to ratify. These include:

1. The third party's *withdrawal* from the contract.
2. The third party's *death or loss of capacity.*
3. The principal's *failure to ratify within a reasonable time.* Of course, this assumes that the principal's silence did not already work a ratification.
4. *Changed circumstances.* Here, the power to ratify is especially likely to end where the change in circumstances places a greater burden on the third party than that party assumed when the contract was made.

In the following *Adams* case, a principal escaped liability because its agent lacked express, implied, or apparent authority, and because the principal did not ratify.

ADAMS v. LOUISIANA COCA-COLA BOTTLING CO.

531 So. 2d 501 (La. Ct. App. 1988)

Rosia Adams, an employee at a Jefferson Parish School Board warehouse, was injured when she slipped on a wet floor at the warehouse. The floor was wet because it had been mopped to clean a spill from a malfunctioning Coca-Cola vending machine leased to the school board by the Louisiana Coca-Cola Bottling Company (Coca-Cola). A warehouse inventory clerk had signed the lease on behalf of the school board.

Adams sued Coca-Cola for her injuries. Coca-Cola then filed a third-party action against the school board, alleging that under the terms of the lease, the school board was required to indemnify and insure Coca-Cola against injuries to employees like Adams. After trial, Adams obtained a jury verdict against Coca-Cola, and the trial judge dismissed Coca-Cola's claim against the school board. Coca-Cola then appealed the trial judge's decision dismissing its claim against the school board.

Ciaccio, Judge.   The question is whether the school board is obligated under the lease. The clerk who signed the lease did not have express authority to do so. Whether he had implied authority, the other component of actual authority, is determined by inference from the circumstances, purposes, and nature of the agency itself. An agent is invested with the implied authority to do all of those things necessary or incidental to the accomplishment of the purpose of the agency. Coca-Cola argues that the clerk was empowered with general authority to operate the warehouse. Such a mandate confers only a power of administration. The proof does not establish any particular circumstances, purposes, or nature of the agency beyond receiving and inventorying goods delivered to the warehouse. We do not find therein any implied authority to agree to indemnify and insure the lessor of a vending machine placed on the premises.

For apparent authority to apply, the principal must first act to manifest the agent's authority to [a] third party. Second, the third party must rely reasonably on the manifested authority of the agent. In support of its argument for the clerk's apparent authority to execute this lease on behalf of the board, Coca-Cola relies on the following facts. The clerk has worked for the school board for twenty years. During this time he has always handled soft drink vending machines on the premises. Either he or another school board employee initially contacted Coca-Cola to have a machine installed at the warehouse. The school board's representative admitted that employees all over the school board system were signing similar leases. He also admitted that some of the seven thousand school board employees have previously bound the school board without formal authorization.

There is no indication that the school board acted to manifest authority for the clerk to execute this lease. There is no evidence that the school board knew of the lease, much less its provisions. The board's role was passive; it apparently paid no attention to the vending machines on its premises. We do not find that this passiveness manifested authority in its employees to agree to indemnify and insure the lessor of these machines.

Further, we find unreasonable any reliance by Coca-Cola upon any perception of authority in the clerk. Coca-Cola did not inquire into the nature and extent of the clerk's authority. And agreeing to indemnify and insure Coca-Cola as lessor requires greater authority than one would reasonably perceive to be vested in an inventory clerk.

Coca-Cola finally argues that the school board ratified the lease by permitting the machine to remain at the warehouse, permitting another machine to be placed there, and [later] permitting over one hundred other machines to be placed at various other school board locations under similar lease conditions. There is no indication that the school board was aware that the machines were being leased, that the leases were being executed in its name, or that the leases contained onerous provisions that the board indemnify and insure Coca-Cola as lessor. We do not find the board's permitting the presence of the machine(s) to be a ratification of the lease provisions confected by Coca-Cola.

Judgment in favor of the school board on Coca-Cola's third-party claim affirmed.

Contracts Made by Subagents

The rules discussed in this section generally apply to contracts made by subagents. If an agent has authorized his subagent to make a certain contract and this authorization is within the authority granted the agent by his principal, the principal is bound to the subagent's contract. Suppose that Peters employs the Ajax Company to sell certain personal property while she is out of the country, with the understanding that one of Ajax's agents will handle the sale from start to finish. If Ajax authorizes its agent Sampson (Peters's subagent) to contract to sell the property and Sampson does so, Peters is bound to the contract.

Because the relationship between agent and subagent closely resembles the relationship between principal and agent, a subagent acting within the authority conferred by her principal (the agent) can bind the agent in contract. Finally, although it is difficult to find definitive statements on the subject, both the principal and the agent probably can ratify the contracts of subagents.

CONTRACT LIABILITY OF THE AGENT

Introduction

An *agent's* liability on contracts he makes for a principal usually depends on a different set of factors than those determining the principal's liability.[3] The most important of these variables is the *nature of the principal.* Thus, this section first examines the liability of agents who contract for several distinct kinds of principals. Then it discusses two ways that an agent can be bound

---

[3]The rules stated here generally should govern the contract liability of subagents as well as agents. See *Restatement (Second) of Agency* § 361 (1959).

after contracting for almost any type of principal: by expressly agreeing to be liable, or by contracting without the necessary authority.

Disclosed Principal

A principal is *disclosed* if a third party knows or has reason to know two things: (1) that the agent is acting for a principal, and (2) the principal's identity. Unless he agrees to be bound, an agent who represents a disclosed principal is *not liable* on authorized contracts made for such a principal. Suppose that Adkins, a sales agent for Parker, calls on Thompson and presents a business card clearly identifying her as Parker's agent. If Adkins contracts to sell Parker's goods to Thompson with authority to do so, Parker is bound on the contract. Adkins, however, is not bound because Parker is a disclosed principal. This rule usually is consistent with the third party's intentions. Here, Thompson probably intended to contract only with Parker.

Partially Disclosed Principal

A principal is *partially disclosed* if the third party: (1) knows or has reason to know that the agent is acting for *a* principal, but (2) does *not* know or have reason to know the principal's identity. This can occur where an agent simply neglects to disclose his principal's identity. Also, a principal may direct that her agent keep her identity secret to preserve her bargaining position or for other reasons.

Among the factors affecting anyone's decision to contract are the integrity, reliability, and creditworthiness of the other party to the contract. Where the principal is partially disclosed, the third party ordinarily cannot make a judgment on these matters. As a result, he usually is depending on the agent's reliability to some degree. For this reason, and to give the third party additional legal protection, an agent generally is liable on contracts made for a partially disclosed principal unless the parties agree otherwise.

Undisclosed Principal

A principal is *undisclosed* where a third party lacks knowledge or reason to know *both* the principal's existence and the principal's identity. Such situations can arise where a principal judges that he will get a better deal if his existence and identity remain secret. As the following *Jensen* case reveals, a principal also may remain undisclosed because the agent simply neglected to make adequate disclosure.

Like a third party who deals with an agent for a partially disclosed principal, a third party who deals with an agent for an undisclosed principal cannot assess the principal's reliability, integrity, and creditworthiness. Indeed, here the third party reasonably believes that the *agent* is the other party to the contract. For these reasons, an agent is liable on contracts made for an undisclosed principal.

JENSEN v. ALASKA VALUATION SERVICE, INC.

688 P.2d 161 (Alaska Sup. Ct. 1984)

Arthur Jensen was president of Arthur Jensen, Inc., an Alaska corporation engaged in the housing construction business. Alaska Valuation Service, Inc. (AVS) conducted appraisals for Jensen from the early 1970s until 1979. AVS's president, Alfred Ferrara, later claimed that throughout most of this period, he was unaware that Jensen was doing business as a corporation. Ferrara also testified that almost all the builders with whom AVS contracted were sole proprietorships. However, during the period in question, Jensen had always paid AVS with checks bearing the Arthur Jensen, Inc., name.

On July 19, 1979, Jensen telephoned Ferrara to order appraisals on five homes. Ferrara recorded the order as being for "Art Jensen," and invoices for the appraisals were later sent to "Art Jensen, Jensen Builders." AVS appraised the five homes as requested, but Jensen never paid AVS its $823 fee. In 1980, Arthur Jensen, Inc., went into bankruptcy. AVS later sued Jensen personally for the $823 in small claims court. It was successful there and on subsequent appeals. Jensen finally appealed to the Alaska Supreme Court.

Compton, Justice. Although officers of a corporation will not ordinarily be held personally liable for contracts they make as agents of the corporation, they must disclose their agency and the existence of the corporation before they will be absolved from liability. An agent who makes a contract for an undisclosed or partially disclosed principal will be liable as a party to the contract. Thus, Jensen can avoid liability only if his use of corporate checks disclosed the existence of Arthur Jensen, Inc. and Jensen's intention to contract on its behalf.

The question before us, then, is whether Jensen's continuing use of corporate checks gave AVS reason to know about the existence of Arthur Jensen, Inc. Courts in a number of jurisdictions have considered similar questions and have reached varying conclusions. The holdings have fallen into three categories: (1) that use of corporate checks is sufficient, as a matter of law, to provide notice; (2) that it is insufficient as a matter of law; and (3) that the question is one of fact which must be decided by the court.

We conclude that the third category of holdings is best supported by case law and by reason. It is neither possible nor desirable to announce a rigid rule of law identifying specific facts that constitute "full disclosure." An agent's use of corporate checks is one factor for consideration, but it is not necessarily determinative. The reasonableness of a third party's failure to deduce the existence of a corporate principal from its agent's use of corporate checks varies from case to case. In [one case], for example, where all meetings took place in the agent's house, and the transaction involved the printing of four issues of a new magazine, a court could reasonably conclude that the third party had insufficient notice of the corporation's existence. In [another case], where the transaction took place entirely in the corporation's offices, the corporation was a coal distributor, and $170,000 changed hands, the existence of the corporation was much more evident from the circumstances surrounding the use of corporate checks.

Since we have determined that the small claims court's finding that Jensen did not sufficiently disclose his agency is one of fact, we will not disturb it unless it is clearly erroneous. At trial, AVS's president testified that most builders he dealt with were not incorporated, and that he had done business with Jensen for many years without being aware that he represented a corporation. In light of this testimony we cannot say that the trial court clearly erred.

Judgment for AVS affirmed.

Nonexistent Principal

An agent who purports to act for a *legally nonexistent* principal such as an unincorporated association is personally liable. This is true even where the third party is aware that the principal is nonexistent.[4] However, this liability can be avoided if the parties so agree.

Principal Lacking Capacity

As stated earlier, a principal who lacks contractual capacity due to insanity or infancy can avoid contracts made by his agent. In this case, the *agent* also escapes liability unless: (1) she misrepresents the capacity of her principal, or (2) she has reason to believe that the third party is unaware of the principal's incapacity and she fails to disclose this. Also, unless the parties agree otherwise, an agent is liable on contracts made for a *wholly incompetent* principal such as a person who has been adjudicated insane.

Liability of Agent by Agreement

An agent may bind himself on contracts he makes for a principal by *expressly agreeing* that he is liable. This

generally is true regardless of the principal's nature. An agent may render himself liable by: (1) making the contract in his own name rather than in the principal's name, (2) joining the principal as an obligor on the contract, or (3) acting as surety or guarantor for the principal.

Problems of contract interpretation can arise when it is claimed that an agent has expressly promised to be bound. In general, the two most important factors affecting the agent's liability are the wording of the contract and the way the agent has signed it. If you are an agent wishing to avoid liability, you should be careful that *you* make no express promises in the body of the agreement, and that the agreement clearly names *the principal* as the only party to be bound. In addition, you should use a signature form that clearly identifies the principal and indicates your representative capacity—for example, "Parker, by Adkins," or "Adkins, for Parker." Simply adding the word "agent" when signing your name ("Adkins, Agent") or signing without any indication of your status ("Adkins") could subject you to liability. Sometimes, as in the following *Wired Music* case, the body of the agreement suggests one result and the signature form another. Here, and generally, oral evidence or other extrinsic evidence of the parties' understanding may help resolve the uncertainty.[5]

---

[4]For a closely analogous situation, see the Organization, Financial Structure, and Dissolution of Corporations chapter's discussion of a promoter's liability on contracts made for a corporation before it comes into existence.

[5]However, the introduction of such evidence may be blocked by the parol evidence rule. See the contracts chapter entitled Writing.

WIRED MUSIC, INC. v. GREAT RIVER STEAMBOAT CO.

554 S.W.2d 466 (Mo. Ct. App. 1977)

A sales representative of Wired Music, Inc., sold Frank Pierson, president of the Great River Steamboat Company, a five-year Muzak Program Service for a riverboat and restaurant owned by Great River. Pierson signed a form contract drafted by Wired Music in the following manner:

By /s/ Frank C. Pierson, Pres.
_____

Title

The Great River Steamboat Co.
~~Port of St. Louis Investments, Inc.~~
_____

For the Corporation

In signing, Pierson crossed out "Port of St. Louis Investments, Inc.," which had been incorrectly listed as the name of the corporation, and inserted the proper name. The contract included the following clause arguably making Pierson a surety or guarantor for Great River: "The individual signing this agreement for the subscriber guarantees that all of the above provisions shall be complied with."

Great River made approximately four payments under the contract and then ceased to pay. Wired Music brought an action for contract damages against Pierson personally. The trial court ruled in Pierson's favor, and Wired Music appealed.

Gunn, Judge.　The general rule regarding liability incurred by an individual who signs an instrument on behalf of another party is: where the principal is disclosed and the capacity in which the individual signs is evident, e.g., president, secretary, agent, the liability is the principal's and not that of the individual signing for the principal. Of course, where the circumstances surrounding the transaction disclose a mutual intention to impose personal responsibility on the individual executing the agreement, the individual may be personally liable even though the form of the signature is that of the agent.

The determinative issue here is whether, in view of the form of the signature to the agreement, the language of the so-called guaranty clause is sufficient to manifest a clear and explicit intent by Pierson to assume a personal guaranty contract. We hold that standing alone it does not. The contract language imposing a personal obligation is inconsistent with the form of execution, which positively limited Pierson's participation to his official corporate capacity and not as an individual. Such inconsistency creates at least a latent ambiguity which permits the admission of parol evidence to explain the true intent of the parties.

Pierson has stressed that he neglected to read the contract prior to its signing. The law is settled that one who signs a contract is presumed to have known its contents and accepted its terms. Thus, Pierson's failure to examine the terms of the instrument would afford no defense to the corporation regarding its obligations under the contract, as his signature was sufficient to bind the corporation. Such neglect is a relevant circumstance, however, in ascertaining Pierson's intent to assume personal liability, as his personal signature appeared nowhere on the instrument. Without knowledge of the guaranty clause he could not have possessed the requisite intent to assume obligations under it. The record is destitute of any indication that Pierson was ever made aware of potential personal liability under the guaranty clause, and he steadfastly denied any such knowledge. Wired Music drafted the contract, and its agents procured Pierson's corporate signature without explanation of or bargaining over its terms. Under these circumstances we find that there was an absence of the meeting of the minds as to the nature and the extent of the personal obligations imposed, essential to the formation of a binding guaranty.

Judgment for Pierson affirmed.

Agent's Liability on Unauthorized Contracts

Regardless of whether he would otherwise be bound, an agent also may become liable to a third party if he *lacked authority* to make the contract in question. Here, the principal is not bound, and it arguably is unfair to leave the third party without any recovery. Thus, an agent generally is bound on the theory that he has made an implied warranty of his authority to contract.[6]

To illustrate, suppose that Allen is a traveling salesman for Prine, a seller of furs. Allen has actual authority to receive offers for the sale of Prine's furs, but not to make contracts of sale, which must be approved by Prine himself. Prine has long followed this practice, and it is customary in the markets where his agents work. Representing himself as Prine's agent but saying nothing about his authority, Allen contracts to sell Prine's furs to Thatcher on Prine's behalf. Thatcher, who should have known better, honestly believes that Allen has authority to contract to sell Prine's furs. Prine is not liable on Allen's contract because Allen lacked actual or apparent authority to bind him. But Allen is liable to Thatcher for breaching his implied warranty of authority.

However, an agent is *not* liable for making an unauthorized contract if:

1. The third party *actually knows* that the agent lacks authority. In such situations, of course, the principal is not liable either. However, note from the above example that an agent still is liable where the third party had *reason to know* that authority was lacking but honestly failed to realize this.
2. The principal subsequently *ratifies* the contract. Here, the principal is bound and the agent is discharged. Because ratification relates back to the time the contract was made, the relation of

the parties is the same as if the agent had possessed authority in the first place.

3. The agent adequately *notifies* the third party that he does not warrant his authority to contract.

CONTRACT SUITS AGAINST PRINCIPAL AND AGENT

Figure 1 sketches the most important situations where the principal, the agent, or both are liable as a result of the agent's contracts. As it suggests, a third party usually has *someone* to sue if neither the principal nor the agent performs on the agent's contract.

Absent ratification, of course, a principal is not liable on contracts made by an agent who lacked authority to contract. Here, though, the agent usually is bound under an implied warranty of authority. In addition, the agent is bound on the contract where the principal was partially disclosed, undisclosed, or legally nonexistent.[7] Authorized contracts for a disclosed principal do not bind an agent unless he has agreed to be liable. But here, the agent's actual or apparent authority binds the principal.

As Figure 1 further illustrates, in certain situations both the principal and the agent are liable on a contract made by the agent. This can occur where an agent with appropriate authority contracts on behalf of a partially disclosed or undisclosed principal. Also, an agent can bind himself by express agreement in situations where the principal also is bound. In such cases, which party is ultimately responsible to the third person? The complicated rules governing this question vary from situation to situation. Due to their complexity and variety, they are beyond the scope of this text. Sometimes, however, the principal or the agent is discharged once the third

---

[6]Also, an agent who intentionally misrepresents his authority may be liable to the third party in tort. In addition, some states may allow tort liability for negligent misrepresentations. Where the third party has a tort suit, he may often elect to recover damages or rescind the contract.

[7]Note, however, that it is impossible for an agent for an undisclosed principal to have apparent authority. Apparent authority exists when the principal's communications to the third party cause that party to reasonably believe that the agent has authority to contract for another. How can this occur when the principal is undisclosed?

FIGURE 1   Contract Liability of Principal and Agent:
The Major Possibilities

	Agent's Authority		
Principal	**Actual**	**Apparent**	**None**
Disclosed	P liable; A not liable unless agreement	P liable; A not liable unless agreement	P not liable; A usually liable
Partially Disclosed	P liable; A liable	P liable; A liable	P not liable; A liable
Undisclosed	P liable; A liable	Impossible	P not liable; A liable

---

party obtains or satisfies a judgment against the other. As discussed in the previous chapter, though, a principal sometimes is required to indemnify an agent who is contractually liable to a third party.

TORT LIABILITY OF THE PRINCIPAL

Introduction

A principal's liability for her agent's torts is a many-faceted subject.[8] First, under the doctrine of **respondeat superior**, an employer is liable for an employee's torts if those torts are committed within the scope of the employee's employment. Second, if the principal herself was at fault, she may be *directly* liable for an agent's tort. Third, although principals generally are not liable for torts committed by *independent contractors*, such liability does exist in a few cases. Continuing our discussion of the principal's tort liability is a separate subject that straddles tort and contract: a principal's liability for the agent's *misrepresentations*. We discuss each of these subjects in turn, before examining a principal's liability for torts committed by subagents.

Respondeat Superior Liability

Under the doctrine of **respondeat superior** (let the master answer), a principal who is an *employer* is liable for torts committed by agents who are *employees* and who commit the tort while acting within the *scope of their*

employment. This doctrine applies to an employee's negligence, recklessness, or intentional torts. The *VIP Tours* case in the last chapter outlined the main factors courts consider when determining whether an agent is an employee.[9] Recall that the most important of these factors is a principal's right to control the physical details of an agent's work.

Respondeat superior is a rule of *imputed* or *vicarious* liability because it bases an employer's liability on his relationship with the employee rather than his own fault. This imputation of liability to the employer reflects the following beliefs: (1) that the economic burdens of employee torts can best be borne by employers; (2) that employers often can protect themselves against such burdens by self-insuring or purchasing insurance; and (3) that the resulting costs frequently can be passed on to consumers, thus "socializing" the economic risk posed by employee torts. *Respondeat superior* also gives employers an incentive to ensure that their employees avoid tortious behavior. Because they typically control the physical details of the work, employers are fairly well positioned to reduce employee torts.

Scope of Employment   *Respondeat superior*'s scope of-employment requirement has been formulated in many ways and is notoriously flexible and ambiguous. In the past, for example, some courts considering this question asked whether the employee was on a "frolic" of his own, or merely made a "detour" from his assigned activity. According to the *Restatement*, an employee's conduct is within the scope of his employment if it meets each of the following four tests:[10]

1. *It was of the* **kind** *that the employee was employed to perform.* To meet this test, an employee's conduct need only be of the same general nature as work expressly authorized, or be incidental to its performance. For instance, the following *Gatzke* case treats on-the-job smoking as an act incidental to an employee's authorized work. But an employee hired only to care for his employer's horses probably is not within the scope of employment if he paints the employer's house without the employer's authorization.

---

[8]In addition to the various forms of tort liability discussed below, a principal can also *ratify* an agent's torts.

[9]Also, recall that this text follows the *Restatement (Second) of Agency* by treating *all* employees as agents (and their employers as principals). Independent contractors, on the other hand, may or may not be agents.

[10]*Restatement (Second) of Agency* § 228(1) (1959). This section adds that if an employee intentionally uses force on another, this must have been "not unexpectable" by the employer to be within the scope of employment.

Even criminal conduct occasionally may be within the scope of employment. Here, the test seems to be whether the employer could reasonably anticipate the criminal behavior in question. Thus, a delivery driver who exceeds the speed limit while on a rush job probably is covered, but a driver who shoots another driver after a traffic altercation almost certainly is not.

2. *It occurred substantially within the* **time** *period authorized by the employer.* This is the time during which an employer has the right to control the details of an employee's work. Ordinarily, it is simply the employee's assigned time of work. Beyond this, there is an extra period of time during which the employment may continue. For instance, a security guard whose regular quitting time is 5:00 probably meets the time test if he unjustifiably injures an intruder at 5:15. Doing the same thing three hours later, however, would put the guard outside the scope of employment.

3. *It occurred substantially within the* **location** *authorized by the employer.* This is the location authorized by the employer or a location not unreasonably distant from it. Determining whether the employee's conduct met this third test is generally a question of degree. For example, a saleswoman told to limit her activities to New York City probably would satisfy the location requirement while pursuing the employer's business in suburbs just outside the city limits, but not while pursuing the same business in Philadelphia. Generally, the smaller the authorized area of activity, the smaller the departure from that area needed to put the employee outside the scope of employment. For example, consider the different physical distance limitations that should apply to a factory worker and a traveling salesperson.

4. *It was motivated* **at least in part** *by the* **purpose** *of serving the employer.* This test is met where the employee's conduct was motivated *to any appreciable extent* by the desire to serve the employer. Thus, an employee's tort may be within the scope of employment even if the motives for committing it were partly personal. For example, suppose than a delivery employee is behind schedule and for that reason has an accident while speeding to make a delivery in his employer's truck. The employee would be within the scope of employment even if another reason for his speeding was to impress a friend who was riding with him.

To repeat, the *Restatement* requires that an employee's tort meet *all four* of these tests to be within the scope of employment. This is exactly what happened in the *Edgewater Motels, Inc. v. Gatzke* case that follows.

EDGEWATER MOTELS, INC. v. GATZKE

277 N.W.2d 11 (Minn. Sup. Ct. 1979)

A. J. Gatzke, a district manager for the Walgreen Company, spent several weeks in Duluth, Minnesota, supervising the opening of a new Walgreen restaurant there. He remained at the restaurant approximately 17 hours a day, and he was on call 24 hours a day to handle problems arising in other Walgreen restaurants in the district. While in Duluth, he lived at the Edgewater Motel at Walgreen's expense. After some heavy drinking late one night, Gatzke returned to his motel room and spent some time at a desk filling out an expense account required by his employer. Gatzke was a heavy smoker, and he testified that he probably smoked a cigarette while completing the expense account. Shortly after Gatzke went to bed, a fire broke out in his motel room. Gatzke escaped, but fire damage to the motel totaled over $330,000. An expert witness testified that the fire was caused by a burning cigarette or a match and that it started in or near a wastebasket located beside the desk at which Gatzke worked.

Edgewater sued Walgreen for Gatzke's negligence. The jury found for Edgewater, in the process concluding that Gatzke acted within the scope of his employment when he filled out the form and disposed of the cigarette. The trial court, however, granted Walgreen's motion for judgment notwithstanding the verdict. Edgewater appealed. The question for the appellate court was whether the trial judge erred in setting aside the jury's finding that Gatzke's negligent conduct occurred within the scope of his employment.

Scott, Justice. Gatzke's negligent smoking of a cigarette was a direct cause of the damages sustained by Edgewater. The question is whether the facts reasonably support the imposition of vicarious liability on Walgreen's for the conceded negligent act of its employee.

For an employer to be held vicariously liable for an employee's negligent conduct, the employee's wrongful act must be committed within the scope of his employment. To support [such] a finding, it must be shown that his conduct was, to some degree, in furtherance of the interests of his employer. This principle is recognized by *Restatement (Second) of Agency* section 235, which states: "An act of a servant is not within the scope of employment if it is done with no intention to perform it as part of or incident to a service on account of which he is employed." Other factors to be considered in the scope of employment determination are whether the conduct is of the kind that the employee is authorized to perform and whether the act occurs substantially within authorized time and space restrictions.

The initial question is whether an employee's smoking of a cigarette can constitute conduct within his scope of employment. The courts which have considered the question have not agreed on its resolution. A number of courts have ruled that the act of smoking, even when done simultaneously with work-related activity, is not within the employee's scope of employment because it is a matter personal to the employee which is not done in furtherance of the employer's interest. Other courts have reasoned that the smoking of a cigarette, if done while engaged in the business of the employer, is within an employee's scope of employment because it is a minor deviation from the employee's work-related activities, and thus merely incidental to employment. We agree with this analysis and hold that an employer can be vicariously liable for an employee's negligent smoking of a cigarette if he was otherwise acting in the scope of his employment at the time of the negligent act.

Thus, we must next determine whether Gatzke was otherwise in the scope of his employment at the time of his negligent act. Even assuming that Gatzke was outside the scope of his employment while he was at the bar, Gatzke resumed his employment activities after he returned to his motel room and filled out his expense account. The expense account was completed so that Gatzke could be reimbursed by Walgreen's for his work-related expenses. In this sense, Gatzke is performing an act for his own personal benefit. However, the completion of the expense account also furthers the employer's business in that it provides detailed documentation of business expenses so that they are properly deductible for tax purposes. In this light, the filling out of the expense form can be viewed as serving a dual purpose: that of furthering Gatzke's personal interests and promoting his employer's business purposes. Accordingly, the completion of the expense account is an act done in furtherance of the employer's business purposes.

Additionally, the record indicates that Gatzke was an executive type of employee who had no set working hours. He considered himself a 24-hour-a-day man; his room at the Edgewater Motel was his "office away from home." It [is] therefore reasonable to determine that the filling out of his expense account was done within authorized time and space limits of his employment.

Judgment reversed in favor of Edgewater.

Direct Liability

As the following *J. v. Victory Tabernacle Baptist Church* case should make clear, a principal's **direct liability** for an agent's torts differs greatly from *respondeat superior* liability. Here, the principal's liability is direct rather than imputed because the principal *himself* is at fault. There is no scope-of-employment requirement in direct liability cases, and the agent need not be an employee. Of course, a principal might incur both direct liability and *respondeat superior* liability in cases where, due to the principal's fault, an employee commits a tort within the scope of her employment.

A principal is directly liable to third parties for an agent's tortious conduct if the principal *directs* that conduct and *intends* that it occur. In such cases, the *agent's* behavior might be intentional, reckless, or negligent. For instance, if Petty tells his agent Able to beat up Tabler and Able does so, Petty is directly liable to Tabler. Petty also would be liable for harm to third parties that results from his intentionally telling Able to do construction work in a negligent, substandard fashion.

The typical direct liability case, however, involves harm caused by the principal's *negligence* regarding the agent. In such cases, the normal negligence rules dis-cussed in the Negligence and Strict Liability chapter usually apply. Examples of direct liability for negligence include: (1) giving the agent improper or unclear instructions; (2) failing to make and enforce appropriate regulations to govern the agent's conduct; (3) hiring an unsuitable agent; (4) failing to discharge an unsuitable agent; (5) furnishing an agent with improper tools, instruments, or materials; and (6) carelessly supervising an agent. The complaint in the following *Victory Tabernacle* case alleged negligent hiring and negligent supervision, plus the defendant's negligent failure to warn.

J. v. VICTORY TABERNACLE BAPTIST CHURCH

372 S.E.2d 391 (Va. Sup. Ct. 1988)

A woman sued the Victory Tabernacle Baptist Church, alleging that due to its negligence, her 10-year-old daughter had been repeatedly raped and sexually assaulted by a church employee. The plaintiff's complaint claimed that when the church hired the employee, it knew or should have known that he had recently been convicted of aggravated sexual assault on a young girl, that he was on probation for this offense, and that a condition of his probation was that he not be involved with children. Despite all this, the complaint continued, the employee's duties allowed him freely to come into contact with children, including the plaintiff's daughter, and he was given keys enabling him to lock and unlock all the church's doors.

The complaint's three counts alleged negligent hiring, negligent supervision, and failure to warn the victim's parents of the employee's past criminal and sexual history. The church filed a demurrer to the entire complaint, and the trial court sustained the demurrer. The plaintiff appealed this decision, and the case reached the Virginia Supreme Court.

Thomas, Justice.   We decide only whether the allegations of negligent hiring state a cause of action in Virginia. This is so because the plaintiff failed to submit any authority concerning negligent supervision and failure to warn. Consequently, those issues have been abandoned.

Victory Baptist argues that the trial court properly sustained the demurrer on the question of negligent hiring because plaintiff failed to allege that the harm to the victim was caused by negligence on the part of the employee. According to this argument, the negligent hiring cause of action requires that the negligently hired individual negligently injured the plaintiff. We disagree. The very thing that allegedly should have been foreseen in this case is that the employee would commit a violent act upon a child. To say that a negligently hired employee who acts willfully or criminally thus relieves his employer of liability for negligent hiring when willful or criminal conduct is precisely what the employer should have foreseen would rob the tort of vitality.

Victory Baptist also argues that the [plaintiff's] allegations do not establish a sufficient nexus among the employer's breach of duty, the employee's conduct, and the employee's employment. In oral argument, counsel explained that there were no allegations that the employee was engaged in the church's business when the child was injured—no allegation, for example, that the employee was on duty for the church at the time the girl was raped. Counsel then made clear that what he was complaining about was that there were no allegations to bring the employee's conduct within the scope of his employment.

This argument demonstrates that Victory Baptist is confusing the doctrine of *respondeat superior* with the tort of negligent hiring. This distinction was succinctly stated in a recent law review article:

> Under *respondeat superior*, an employer is vicariously liable for an employee's tortious acts committed within the scope of employment. In contrast, negligent hiring is a doctrine of primary liability; the employer is principally liable for negligently placing an unfit person in an employment situation involving an unreasonable risk of harm to others. Negligent hiring, therefore, enables plaintiffs to recover in situations where *respondeat superior*'s scope of employment limitation previously protected employers from liability.

Thus, Victory Baptist's contention is misplaced.

In our opinion, the [complaint] was fully sufficient to state a claim of negligent hiring, and thus it was error for the trial court to sustain the demurrer on that issue. The trial court's disposition of [the other two negligence] counts will be affirmed.

Judgment for the church affirmed in part and reversed in part. Case remanded for trial consistent with the Supreme Court's opinion.

Liability for Torts of Independent Contractors

Generally, a principal is *not* liable for torts committed by *independent contractors*. As compared with employees, independent contractors are more likely to have the size and resources to insure against tort liability and to pass on the resulting costs themselves. In at least some cases, therefore, the risk still can be socialized if the independent contractor is held responsible. Because the principal does not control the manner in which an independent contractor's work is performed, moreover, he has less ability to prevent a contractor's torts than an employer has to prevent an employee's torts. Thus, imposing liability on principals for the torts of independent contractors may be relatively ineffective in reducing the contractor's tortious behavior.

However, the general rule that principals are not liable for torts committed by independent contractors has exceptions. For example:

1. A principal can be *directly* liable for tortious behavior connected with the retention of an independent contractor. One example is the negligent hiring of a dangerously incompetent independent contractor.

2. A principal is liable for harm resulting from the independent contractor's failure to perform a *nondelegable duty*. A nondelegable duty is a duty whose proper performance is considered so important to the community that a principal cannot avoid liability by contracting it away to another party. Examples include a carrier's duty to transport its passengers safely, a municipality's duty to keep its streets in repair, a railroad's duty to maintain safe crossings, and a landlord's duties to make repairs and to use care in doing so. Thus, a landlord who retains an independent contractor to repair the stairs in an apartment building is liable for injuries caused by the contractor's failure to repair the stairs properly.

3. A principal is liable for an independent contractor's negligent failure to take the special precautions needed to conduct certain *highly dangerous* or *inherently dangerous* activities.[11] Examples of such activities include excavations in publicly traveled areas, the clearing of land by fire, the construction of a dam, and the demolition of a building. For example, a contractor engaged in demolishing a building presumably has duties to warn pedestrians and to keep them at a safe distance. If injury results from the independent contractor's failure to meet these duties, the principal is liable.

Liability for Agent's Misrepresentations

A principal's liability for misrepresentations made by agents to third parties involves both contract and tort principles.[12] A principal is *directly* liable for misrepresentations made by her agent during authorized

---

[11]The range of activities considered "highly dangerous" or "inherently dangerous" is probably greater than the range of activities considered "ultrahazardous" or "abnormally dangerous" for strict liability purposes. On the latter activities, see the Negligence and Strict Liability chapter.

[12]On fraud and misrepresentation in the tort and contract contexts, see the Intentional Torts chapter and the Reality of Consent chapter.

transactions if she *intended* that the agent make the misrepresentations. In some states, a principal also may be directly liable if she *negligently* allows the agent to make misrepresentations.

Even where a principal is not directly at fault, she may be liable for an agent's misrepresentations if the agent had *actual or apparent authority to make true statements on the subject*. Suppose that an agent to sell farmland falsely states that a stream on the land has never flooded the property when in fact it does so almost every year, and that this statement induces a third party to buy the land. The principal is directly liable if she intended that the agent make this false statement. Even if the principal is personally blameless, she is liable if the agent had actual or apparent authority to make true statements about the spring.

If the agent intended to make the misrepresentation, or if the principal intended that the agent make it, the third party can recover in tort for the losses that result. In some states, a third party also may recover in tort for misrepresentations resulting from the principal's or the agent's negligence. In either case, the third party can elect to rescind the transaction instead of pursuing a tort suit.

Exculpatory Clauses Both honest and dishonest principals may attempt to avoid liability for an agent's misrepresentations by including an exculpatory clause in contracts that the agent makes with third parties. Such clauses typically state that the agent only has authority to make the representations contained in the contract and that only those representations bind the principal. Exculpatory clauses do not protect a principal who intends or expects that an agent will make false statements. Otherwise, though, they insulate the principal from *tort* liability if the agent misrepresents. But the third party still may *rescind* the transaction, because it would be unjust to let the principal benefit from the transaction while disclaiming responsibility for it.

Torts of Subagents

The *Restatement* declares that the rules governing a principal's liability for an agent's torts generally control a principal's liability for the torts of *subagents*.[13] Thus, a principal might be directly liable for a subagent's tort where, for example, he orders the subagent to commit the tort. However, because an employer-employee relationship between principal and subagent is unlikely, a principal usually is not subject to *respondeat superior* liability for a subagent's torts. Occasionally, though, courts have found principals liable for their subagents' misrepresentations.

---

[13]*Restatement (Second) of Agency* § 255 (1959).

CONCEPT REVIEW

AN OUTLINE OF THE PRINCIPAL'S TORT LIABILITY

Respondeat Superior	1. Agent must be an employee, *and* 2. Employee must act within scope of employment while committing tort
Direct Liability	1. Principal intends and directs agent's intentional tort, recklessness, or negligence, *or* 2. Principal is negligent regarding agent
Torts of Independent Contractors	1. Principal generally is *not* liable 2. Exceptions for direct liability, highly dangerous activities, and nondelegable duties
Misrepresentation	1. Direct liability 2. Vicarious liability where agent had authority to make true statements on the subject of the misrepresentation 3. An exculpatory clause may eliminate the principal's tort liability, but the third party still can rescind
Torts of Subagents	The preceding rules govern the principal's liability, but their application varies

TORT LIABILITY OF THE AGENT

The rules stated in the previous section generally govern the liability of *agents* for torts committed by subagents whom they have appointed.[14] In addition, agents usually are liable for their *own* torts. The fact that an agent has acted at the principal's command normally does not absolve the agent from liability. As you might guess, however, there are certain exceptions to this generalization.

1. An agent can escape liability if she was *exercising a privilege of the principal.* Suppose that Tingle grants Parkham a valid right-of-way to transport his farm products over a private road crossing Tingle's land. If so, Parkham's agent, Adams, would not be liable in trespass for driving across Tingle's land to transport farm products if she did so at Parkam's command. However, an agent must not exceed the scope of the privilege and must act for the purpose for which the privilege was given. Thus, Adams would not be protected if she took her Jeep on a midnight joyride across Tingle's land. Also, the privilege given the agent must be delegable in the first place. If Tingle had given the easement to Parkham exclusively, Adams would not be privileged to drive across Tingle's land.

2. A principal who is *privileged to take certain actions in defense of his person or property* often may authorize an agent to do the same. In such cases, the agent escapes liability if the principal could have done so. For example, a properly authorized agent may use force to protect the life or property of his principal if the principal could have done the same.

3. An agent who makes *misrepresentations* while conducting the principal's business is not liable in tort unless he either *knew or had reason to know* of their falsity. Suppose Parker authorizes Arnold to sell his house, falsely telling Arnold that the house is fully insulated. Arnold does not know that the statement is false, and could not discover its falsity through an ordinary, reasonable inspection. If Arnold tells Thomas that the house is fully insulated and Thomas relies on this statement in purchasing the house, Parker is directly liable to Thomas, but Arnold is not liable.

4. An agent is not liable for injuries to third persons caused by defective tools or instrumentalities furnished by the principal unless the agent had actual knowledge or reason to know of the defect.

---

[14]*Restatement (Second) of Agency* § 362 (1959).

TORT SUITS AGAINST PRINCIPAL AND AGENT

In many cases, both principal and agent are liable for an agent's torts. Here, the principal and the agent are *jointly and severally* liable. This means that a third party may join the principal and the agent in one suit and get a judgment against each, or may sue either or both individually and get a judgment against either or both. However, the third party is entitled to only one satisfaction for his claim. Once the third party actually collects in full from either the principal or the agent, no further recovery is possible.

In some cases, therefore, either the principal or the agent has to satisfy the judgment alone despite the other party's liability. Here, the other party sometimes is required to *indemnify* the party who has satisfied the judgment. As discussed in the previous chapter, for example, there are situations where a principal may be required to indemnify an agent for tort liability the agent incurs. On the other hand, some torts committed by agents may involve the breach of a duty agents owe their principals, and a principal may be able to recover from an agent on this basis.

CRIMINAL LIABILITY

As a general proposition, principals are not liable for crimes committed by their agents or employees unless they directed, approved, or participated in the crime. Also, agents usually are liable for their own crimes, and their status as agents or the fact that they acted at the principal's direction has no effect on their criminal liability. Various state and federal criminal statutes, however, create exceptions to these generalizations. Perhaps more importantly, different criminal liability rules may apply where the principal is a corporation or other business entity. The Crimes chapter and the Management of Corporations chapter discuss the criminal liability of corporations, their directors, and their officers. The Operation of Partnership and Related Forms chapter examines the criminal liability of partnerships and their partners.

1. As you have seen, one of the justifications for *respondeat superior* is that employers are in a relatively good position to absorb liability for employee torts, to insure against such liability, and to pass on the resulting costs. What are the advantages and disadvantages of applying this reasoning to make principals liable for all torts committed by *independent contractors* within the scope of their employment?

2. If the purposes underlying *respondeat superior* are sound ones, why limit the doctrine to employee torts committed within the scope of employment? In other words, why not make employers liable for *all* torts committed by their employees?

3. As you have seen, agents who make unauthorized contracts are not liable if the principal later ratifies the contract. The official justification for this rule is that, because ratification relates back to the time the unauthorized contract was made, the relations of the parties are the same as if the agent had originally had authority. However, there is another, much more down-to-earth, justification for this rule. What is it?

SUMMARY

A principal is liable on a contract made by his agent if the agent had *express, implied, or apparent authority* to make that contract. Even if the agent's contract was unauthorized, a principal may be bound to the contract by *ratifying* it. A principal who lacks capacity at the time of the contract may avoid it, but an agent's incapacity usually does not affect the liability of a principal who has capacity. Finally, a subagent with appropriate authority can bind the principal and the agent in contract.

An agent's contract liability usually depends on a different set of factors. Generally, an agent who contracts for a *disclosed principal* is not liable on contracts made for such a principal. However, an agent who contracts for a *partially disclosed* or an *undisclosed* principal typically is bound to the contract. Also, agents normally are liable on contracts they make on behalf of *legally nonexistent* principals. Moreover, agents may bind themselves to a contract by expressly so agreeing. And an agent who acts in excess of her authority may be liable to the third party under an implied warranty of authority, or for misrepresentation.

A principal's liability for his agent's torts comes in several forms. A principal is *vicariously* liable for the torts of an agent when the agent is an *employee* who has committed the tort within the *scope of his employment*. To be within the scope of employment, the employee's conduct usually must: (1) be of the kind that he was employed to perform, (2) occur substantially within the time limits of the employment, (3) occur substantially within the space limits of the employment, and (4) be motivated at least in part by the purpose of serving the employer. A principal is *directly* liable when he commands or authorizes the agent to engage in tortious behavior, or is negligent in hiring, retraining, instructing, directing, or equipping an agent. Subject to certain exceptions, a principal is not liable for the torts of *independent contractors*. Finally, a principal may be directly liable for her agent's *misrepresentations*, and also is liable for such misrepresentations when the agent had authority to make true statements on the subject of the misrepresentation. A principal who puts an *exculpatory clause* in contracts his agent makes with third parties, however, often escapes tort liability, although the third party usually may rescind the contract.

Agents generally are liable for their own torts, and, with a few exceptions, the fact that they acted for a principal does not relieve them of liability. Likewise, agents generally are liable for their own crimes. A principal usually is not liable for crimes committed by an agent unless he directed, approved, or participated in their commission. Under various statutes and the laws of corporations and partnership, however, different criminal liability rules sometimes obtain.

PROBLEM CASES

1. The Capital Dredge and Dock Corporation, a construction contractor, sued the city of Detroit for damages associated with certain construction work it had been performing for the city. One of the city's defenses was that Capital had released the city from liability on some of Capital's present claims during earlier, related litigation between Capital and the city. The releases were part of a settlement document signed by Capital Dredge's attorney, Alteri. Capital Dredge had held Alteri out as having authority to represent it in the relevant litigation, and this included authority to negotiate a settlement. However, unknown to the city, Capital Dredge also had specifically told Alteri not to compromise some of the claims he later actually settled. Under these circumstances, could Alteri have had implied authority to settle the claims in question? Could he have had apparent authority to do so?

2. Roma Funk, who co-owned a piece of land along with her seven brothers and sisters, contracted to sell the land to her neighbors. It was unclear whether Funk had authority to sell the land on behalf of her siblings. For certain, there was no writing giving her such authority. Funk's siblings eventually backed out of the deal, and the buyers sued for specific performance. They argued that Funk's siblings had ratified her contract by failing to come forward and repudiate it. Can a contract ever be ratified in this way? Regardless of your answer to this question, there is a dispositive reason why Funk's siblings could not have ratified this particular contract. What is it? Assume that in this state an agent who executes an agreement conveying an interest in land on behalf of his principal must be authorized in writing.

3. A certain law firm represented a man named Helric in a dispute over mining claims. The settlement reached in Helric's case permitted Helric to restake the disputed claims. The law firm assisted in having the claims restaked by retaining Free to do the job for Helric. When the firm first contacted Free, the partner in charge of the case told Free that the firm was representing Helric. Later correspondence between the firm and Free clearly stated that Helric was the owner of the claims Free was to restake. Free completed the job, and later sued the law firm for the amount due him. Is the firm liable to Free on the contract it made for Helric?

4. Seascape Restaurants, Inc., operated a restaurant called the Magic Moment. Jeff Rosenberg was one-third owner and president of Seascape. Van D. Costas, the president of Van D. Costas, Inc., contracted to construct a "magical entrance" to the Magic Moment. Jeff Rosenberg signed the contract on a line under which appeared the words "Jeff Rosenberg, the Magic Moment." The contract did not refer to Seascape, and Costas knew nothing of Seascape's existence. After a dispute over performance of the contract, Costas sued Rosenberg for breach of contract. Is Rosenberg personally liable to Costas?

5. Dale F. Everett did business as the Dale F. Everett Company, Inc. (the Company). He also formed a retail business known as The Clubhouse, which had no legal status aside from its registration as a trade name for the Company. Everett contracted with James Smith for $8,424 of advertising time. Everett signed his contract

with Smith as follows: "THE CLUBHOUSE, Client, By Dale F. Everett." Smith later sent billing statements for the ads to "The Clubhouse, Inc." Everett never paid Smith the $8,424, and Smith sued Everett personally. Is Everett personally liable on the contract with Smith?

6. Twelve individuals agreed to sponsor and promote a group of Little League baseball teams called the Golden Spike Little League. The league was a loosely formed voluntary association without any legal identity. The 12 individuals arranged with Smith & Edwards to furnish the needed uniforms and equipment, signed for them, picked them up, and distributed them to the teams. No one ever paid Smith & Edwards the $3,900 bill for the uniforms and equipment. Smith & Edwards sued the 12 individuals in their personal capacities for the amount due. If they defend by saying that they acted as agents for a disclosed principal (the league), will the defense be successful? Why or why not?

7. Redford had been a backhoe operator for five years. Although he had worked for other sign companies, he had spent 90 percent of his time during the past three years working for Tube Art Display, Inc. Redford generally dug holes exactly as directed by the sign company employing him. He did, however, pay his own business taxes, and he did not participate in any of the fringe benefits available to Tube Art employees.

Tube Art obtained a permit to install a sign in the parking lot of a combination commercial and apartment building. Telling Redford how to proceed, Tube Art's service manager laid out the exact location of a 4 x 4 feet square on the asphalt surface with yellow paint and directed that the hole be six feet deep. After Redford began the job, he struck a small natural gas pipeline with the backhoe. He examined the pipe, and, finding no indication of a leak or break, concluded that the line was not in use and left the worksite. Later, an explosion and fire occurred in the building serviced by the line. As a result, a business owned by Massey was destroyed. Massey sued Tube Art for Redford's negligence under the doctrine of *respondeat superior*. Will Massey recover? You can assume that Redford was negligent.

8. John Hondzinski delivered newspapers in his own car for a newspaper called the *News Herald*. Under the contract between Hondzinski and the *News Herald*, Hondzinski was obligated to pick up and promptly deliver newspapers provided by the *News Herald*, but the means and the routes for doing so were within Hondzinski's control. While in the process of making deliveries for the *News Herald* one day, Hondzinski negligently allowed his car to collide with a car driven by Peter Janice. Janice sued the *News Herald* for Hondzinski's negligence. Can Janice recover against the *News Herald* under the doctrine of *respondeat superior?* Why or why not?

9. Kathy Kendall ordered some food at a Whataburger, Inc. restaurant. After becoming dissatisfied with the food or her service, she voiced her displeasure to Isaac Ervin, a young Whataburger employee working behind the service counter. In response, Ervin threw a metal french fry basket containing hot grease into her face. Kendall sued Whataburger for her resulting injuries. Under the four *Restatement* tests discussed in the text, was Ervin's action within the scope of his employment, thus making Whataburger liable under the doctrine of *respondeat superior?* Under what other theory might Kendall possibly recover against Whataburger? In answering the *first* question, assume that Whataburger had no reason to suspect that Ervin was capable of doing what he did. In answering the *second* question, leave this possibility open.

10. Susie Mae Woodson's husband was killed as the result of a cave-in at a construction site where he was laying sewer pipe in a trench dug by an independent contractor of Davidson & Jones, Inc. (D&J). The trench in which Mr. Woodson was working had not been braced or shored to prevent a cave-in, and this was a violation of federal occupational safety regulations. Mrs. Woodson sued D&J for the independent contractor's negligence. Will she recover? Assume that D&J was not in any way *directly* liable regarding the independent contractor.

11. Letbetter purchased merchandise from a salesperson representing United Laboratories. The contract of sale expressly provided that no representations of the salesperson would be binding upon the seller unless they were written into the order. The salesperson made representations about the suitability of the materials for certain uses, but the representations were not included in the sales orders. The materials were not suitable for the purposes represented. Is United Laboratories liable in tort for the salesperson's representations? Assume that United Laboratories did not intend that the salesperson make the representations and that it had no reason to think that they would be made.

PART VII

PARTNERSHIP LAW

CHAPTER 29

Introduction to Forms of Business and Formation of Partnerships

INTRODUCTION TO FORMS OF BUSINESS AND FORMATION OF PARTNERSHIPS

INTRODUCTION

In this chapter, you begin your study of business organizations. In the next eight chapters, you will study seven forms of business, including the four most important ones:

1. Sole proprietorship.
2. Partnership (sometimes called general partnership).
3. Limited partnership.
4. Corporation.

Early in this chapter, you will preview the basic characteristics of these most important forms of business and learn how to select an appropriate form for your business venture. Following that introduction, you will begin your in-depth study of partnerships, learning their characteristics and the formalities for their creation. You will study the operation of partnerships and their dissolution, limited partnerships, and corporations in the chapters that follow.

CHOOSING A FORM OF BUSINESS

One of the most important decisions made by a person beginning a business is choosing a **form of business.**

This decision is important because, among other reasons, the business owner's liability and control of the business vary greatly among the many forms of business. In addition, some business forms offer significant tax advantages to their owners.

Although other forms of business exist, usually a person starting a business will wish to organize the business as a sole proprietorship, partnership, limited partnership, or corporation.

Sole Proprietorship

A **sole proprietorship** has only one owner. The sole proprietorship is merely an extension of its owner: a *sole proprietor* owns his own business, and no one else owns any part of it.

As the only owner, the sole proprietor has the right to make all the management decisions of the business. In addition, all the profits of the business are his. In return for his complete managerial control and sole claim to profits, he assumes great liability: he is *personally liable* for all the obligations of the business. All the debts of the business, including debts on contracts signed only in the name of the business, are his debts. If the assets of the business are insufficient to pay the claims of its creditors, the creditors may require the sole proprietor to pay the claims using his individual, nonbusiness assets, such as money from his bank account and the proceeds from the sale of his house. A sole proprietor may lose everything if his business becomes insolvent. Hence, the sole proprietorship is a risky form of business for its owner.

In light of this risk, you may ask why any person would organize a business as a sole proprietorship. There are two reasons. First, the sole proprietorship is formed very easily and inexpensively. No formalities are necessary. Second, few people consider the business-form decision. They merely begin their businesses. Thus, by default, a person going into business by herself automatically creates a sole proprietorship when she fails to choose another business form. These two reasons explain why the sole proprietorship is the most common form of business in the United States.

Because the sole proprietorship is merely an extension of its owner, it has no life apart from its owner. Therefore, while the business of a sole proprietorship may be freely sold to someone else, legally the sole proprietorship as a form of business cannot be transferred to another person. The buyer of the business must create his own form of business to conduct the business.

A sole proprietorship is not a legal entity. It cannot sue or be sued. Instead, creditors must sue the owner. The sole proprietor, in his own name, must sue those who harm the business.

A sole proprietor may hire employees for the business, but they are employees of the sole proprietor. Under the law of agency, the sole proprietor is responsible for her employees' authorized contracts and for the torts they commit in the course of their employment. Also, a sole proprietorship is not an income tax-paying entity for federal income tax purposes. All of the income of a sole proprietorship is income to its owner and must be reported on the sole proprietor's individual federal income tax return. Likewise, any business losses are deductible without limit on the sole proprietor's individual tax return. This loss-deduction advantage explains why some wealthier taxpayers use the sole proprietorship for selected business investments—when losses are expected in the early years of the business, yet the risk of liability is low. Such an investor may form a sole proprietorship and hire a professional manager to operate the business.

Many sole proprietorships have trade names. For example, Caryl Stanley may operate her bagel shop under the name Caryl's Bagel Shop. Caryl would be required to file the trade name under a state statute requiring the registration of fictitious business names. If she were sued by a creditor, the creditor would address his complaint to "Caryl Stanley, doing business as Caryl's Bagel Shop."

Partnership

A **partnership** has two or more owners, called *partners*. The partners have the right to make all the management decisions for the business. In addition, all the profits of the business are shared by the partners.

In return for their complete managerial control and sole claim to profits, the partners assume personal liability for all the obligations of the business. All the debts of the business, including debts on authorized contracts signed only by one partner or by a partnership employee, are the debts of all the partners. Likewise, partners are liable for the torts committed in the course of business by their partners or by partnership employees. If the assets of the business are insufficient to pay the claims of its creditors, the creditors may require one or more of the partners to pay the claims using their individual, nonbusiness assets. Thus, a partner may have to pay more than his share of partnership liabilities. Hence, the partnership is a riskier form of business for its partners than is the sole proprietorship.

Like the sole proprietorship, the partnership is not a tax-paying entity for federal income tax purposes. All of the income of the partnership is income to its partners and must be reported on the individual partner's federal income tax return, even if the partnership did not distribute any profits to the partners. Likewise, any business losses are deductible without limit on the partner's individual tax return. This loss-deduction privilege gives the partnership an advantage over the limited partnership and corporation, which limit the owner's ability to deduct business losses.

The partnership has no life apart from its owners. When a partner dies or otherwise leaves the business, the partnership is dissolved. Therefore, while the business of a partnership may be freely sold to someone else by agreement of the partners, legally the partnership as a form of business cannot be transferred to another person.

Why would persons organize a business as a partnership? As with the sole proprietorship, formation of a partnership requires no formalities. Also, many partnerships are formed by default. A partnership is created automatically when persons own a business together without selecting another form. Also, the deductibility of partnership losses on individual tax returns is an attractive feature.

Limited Partnership

A **limited partnership** has one or more general partners and one or more limited partners. General partners have rights and liabilities similar to partners in a partnership. They manage the business of the limited partnership and have unlimited liability for the obligations of the limited partnership. Thus, a general partner may have to pay more than his share of a limited partnership's liabilities. Typically, however, the only general partner is a corporation, thereby protecting the human managers from unlimited liability.

Because the limited partnership is not a tax-paying entity for federal income tax purposes, general partners report their shares of the limited partnership's income and losses on their individual federal income tax returns. For general partners, losses of the business are deductible without limit.

Limited partners have no liability for the obligations of the limited partnership once they have paid their capital contributions to the limited partnership. Limited partners have no right to manage the business and may lose their limited liability for the business's obligations if they do manage the business.

A limited partner must pay federal income tax on his share of the profits of the business, but he may deduct his share of losses only to the extent of his investment in the business. In addition, a limited partner, as a passive investor, usually may use the losses only to offset income from other passive investments. The loss-deduction privilege gives the limited partnership an advantage over the corporation, but its limitation is a disadvantage compared to the partnership.

A limited partnership may have a life apart from its owners. When a limited partner dies or otherwise leaves the business, the limited partnership is not dissolved. When a general partner dies or withdraws, however, the limited partnership is dissolved absent a contrary agreement.

A general or limited partner's interest in a limited partnership may not be transferred to another person, absent a contrary agreement by the partners. Although in the late 1980s there was an attempt by some so-called **master limited partnerships** to create free transferability of limited partners' interests, the Internal Revenue Service snuffed out the effort by classifying such limited partnerships as associations, which are taxed like

corporations, thus eliminating the ability of limited partners to deduct business losses on their individual federal income tax returns.

Unlike a sole proprietorship or partnership, a limited partnership may be created only by complying with a state statute permitting limited partnerships. Thus, no limited partnership may be created by default.

There are three main reasons why persons organize a business as a limited partnership. First, by using a corporate general partner, no human will have unlimited liability for the debts of the business. Second, losses of the business are deductible on individual owner's federal income tax returns. Third, because investors may contribute capital to the business and avoid unlimited liability and the obligation to manage the business, the limited partnership has the ability to attract large amounts of capital, much more than the sole proprietorship, which has only one owner, or the partnership, whose partners' fear of unlimited liability restricts the size of the business. Hence, for a business needing millions of dollars of capital and expecting to lose money in its early years, the limited partnership is a particularly good form of business.

Corporation

A **corporation** is owned by shareholders who elect a board of directors to manage the business. The board of directors often selects officers to run the day-to-day affairs of the business. Consequently, ownership and management of a corporation may be completely separate: no shareholder has the right to manage, and no officer or director needs to be a shareholder.

Like limited partners, shareholders have limited liability for the obligations of the corporation, even if a shareholder is elected as a director or selected as an officer. Directors and officers have no liability for the contracts they or the corporation's employees negotiate in the name of the corporation. The managers have no liability for corporate torts committed by corporate managers or employees other than themselves. Therefore, shareholders, officers, and directors have limited liability for the obligations of the business.

The usual corporation is a tax-paying entity for federal income tax purposes. The corporation pays taxes on its profits. Shareholders do not report their shares of corporation profits on their individual federal income tax returns. Instead, only when the corporation distributes its profits to the shareholders in the form of dividends or the shareholders sell their investments at a profit do the shareholders report income on their individual returns. This creates a *double-tax* possibility, as profits are taxed once at the corporation level and again at the shareholder level when dividends are paid.

Also, shareholders do not deduct corporate losses on their individual returns. They may, however, deduct their investment losses after they have sold their shares of the corporation.

There is one important exception to these corporate tax rules. The shareholders may elect to have the corporation and its shareholders taxed under Subchapter S of the Internal Revenue Code. By electing **S Corporation** status, the corporation and its shareholders are taxed nearly entirely like a partnership: income and losses of the business are reported on the shareholders' individual federal income tax returns. A corporation electing S Corporation status may have no more than 35 shareholders. Many of the shareholders of the typical S Corporation are involved in the management of the business.

A corporation has a life separate from its owners and its managers. When a shareholder or manager dies or otherwise leaves the business, the corporation is not dissolved. A shareholder may sell his shares of the corporation to other persons without limitation, absent a contrary agreement. The purchaser becomes a shareholder with all the rights of the selling shareholder. Like a limited partnership, a corporation may be created only by complying with a state statute permitting incorporation.

There are several reasons why persons organize a business as a corporation. First, no human has unlimited liability for the debts of the business. As a result, businesses in the riskiest industries—such as manufacturing—incorporate. Second, because investors may contribute capital to the business, avoid unlimited liability, escape the obligation to manage the business, and easily liquidate their investments by selling their shares, the corporation has the ability to attract large amounts of capital, even more than the limited partnership, whose partnership interests are not as freely transferable. Thus, the corporation has the capacity to raise the largest amount of capital.

The S Corporation has an additional advantage: losses of the business are deductible on individual federal income tax returns. However, because the S Corporation is limited to 35 shareholders, its ability to raise capital is severely limited. Also, while legally permitted to sell their shares, shareholders may be unable to find many investors willing to buy their shares and be re-stricted from selling the shares pursuant to an agreement between the shareholders. See Figure 1 (next page) for a summary of business forms characteristics.

Franchising

Franchising is an agreement by which a **franchisee** has the right to sell goods or services under a marketing plan prescribed in substantial part by a **franchisor.** Thus, when a franchisee purchases a franchise, the franchisee buys a *business opportunity,* which the franchisee may choose to operate as any form of business. For example, if you obtain a McDonald's restaurant franchise for the south side of Minneapolis, you will probably choose to operate the business as a corporation.

Franchising has advantages for both the franchisee and the franchisor. The franchisee receives the franchisor's assistance in setting up the business and training employees. In addition, the franchisee may benefit from the franchisor's national advertising and strong trademark and goodwill. For example, a McDonald's franchisee obtains instant visibility and credibility from displaying the McDonald's golden arches. In return for this assistance, the franchisee usually pays a substantial purchase price plus a fee based on income, sales, or the purchase price of specified supplies. For example, an ice cream restaurant franchise may pay its franchisor 15 percent of the price it pays for its ice cream mix. The fee is collected for the franchisor by an authorized supplier of the mix.

The franchisor also benefits. Instead of making a high investment in several business locations, the franchisor shifts most of the investment risk to the franchisees. Yet the franchisor receives income from the franchisees' operation of their businesses. And while the franchisor's profits are tied to the franchisee's success, the franchisees typically have a sizable investment in the franchises and have a strong incentive to succeed. Also, the franchisor can adopt standards to ensure it selects high-quality franchisees with superior financial strength. Using franchising allows a franchisor to exploit its trademark and goodwill, yet also protect itself by requiring franchisees to adopt uniform image and marketing practices.

Nature of Franchisor/Franchisee Relationship Because a franchisor may exercise some control over parts of a franchisee's business, there is a risk that the franchisor may be liable for the torts and contracts of the franchisee. Most franchising agreements provide that

FIGURE 1   General Characteristics of Forms of Business

	Sole Proprietorship	Partnership	Limited Partnership	Corporation	S Corporation
Formation	When one person conducts business without forming a corporation	By agreement of owners *or* by default when two or more owners conduct business together without forming a limited partnership or a corporation	By agreement of owners; must comply with limited partnership statute	By agreement of owners; must comply with corporation statute	By agreement of owners; must comply with corporation statute; must elect S Corporation status under Subchapter S of Internal Revenue Code
Duration	Terminates on death or withdrawal of sole proprietor	Dissolves on death or withdrawal of general partner	Dissolves on death or withdrawal of general partner	Unaffected by death or withdrawal of shareholder	Unaffected by death or withdrawal of shareholder
Management	By sole proprietor	By partners	By general partners	By board of directors	By board of directors
Owner Liability	Unlimited	Unlimited	Unlimited for general partners; limited to capital contribution for limited partners	Limited to capital contribution	Limited to capital contribution
Transferability of Owners' Interest	None	None	None, unless partners agree otherwise	Freely transferable	Freely transferable unless shareholders agree otherwise
Federal Income Taxation	Only sole proprietor taxed	Only partners taxed	Only partners taxed	Corporation taxed; shareholders taxed on dividends (double tax)	Only shareholders taxed

the franchisee is not an agent or partner of the franchisor. Some courts refuse to accept this characterization of the relationship, especially when the degree and type of control by the franchisor suggest an agency relationship.

Today, most franchisors are careful not to assume such control. Nonetheless, when a franchisor has the right to control a specified portion of the franchisee's conduct, a court may hold the franchisor liable for torts or contracts arising from the controlled conduct. For example, when a franchisor has the right to control a franchisee's prices, the franchisee may be responsible for any resulting antitrust violation resulting from the franchisee's pricing decisions.

Franchisee Protection   In response to abuses by franchisors, the courts, the Federal Trade Commission, and the states have created rules that protect franchisees. The typical franchising agreement gives a franchisor wide latitude to terminate a franchisee. Some courts have invalidated such termination power or required that terminations be made in good faith. In 1979, the Federal Trade Commission issued a franchise disclosure rule and guidelines requiring franchisors to disclose their financial fees and charges, the franchisees' obligations to purchase supplies, and territorial restrictions on the franchisees. In addition, most of the states require disclosure and termination protection for franchisees.

PARTNERSHIPS

History of Partnerships

The basic concept of partnership is as ancient as the history of collective human activity. Partnerships were known in ancient Babylonia, ancient Greece, and the Roman Empire. Hammurabi's Code, dating from 2300 B.C., regulated partnerships, and the definition of a partnership in the 6th-century Justinian Code of the Roman Empire does not differ materially from that in our laws today. The partnership was likewise known in Asian countries, including China. During the Middle Ages, much trade between nations was carried on by partnerships.

By the close of the 17th century, the partnership was recognized in the English common law. When the United States became an independent nation and adopted the English common law in 1776, the English law of partnerships became a part of American law. In the early part of the 19th century, the partnership became the most important form of association in the United States.

Modern American Partnership Law

Today, the American common law of partnership has been largely replaced by statutory law. Every state has a statute on partnership law. The Uniform Partnership Act (UPA) of 1914 has been adopted in 49 states (Louisiana is the exception) and the District of Columbia. The UPA is a model partnership statute that is the product of the National Conference of Commissioners on Uniform State Laws, a group of practicing lawyers, judges, and law professors. The aims of the UPA are to codify partnership law in one document, to make that law more nearly consistent with itself, and to attain uniformity throughout the country. Because of its nearly total adoption in the United States, the UPA is the framework of your study of partnerships. It is reproduced in an appendix to this book.

Entity and Aggregate Theories

Studying the list of partnership characteristics in Figure 2, you may perceive that in some respects the partnership is treated as an **entity,** that is, as a person separate and distinct from its partners. In other respects, the partnership is viewed as an **aggregate** of the partners, with no life or powers apart from them. The UPA recognizes the partnership primarily as an aggregate of the partners. In a few situations, however, the UPA confers entity status on a partnership, such as by permitting ownership of property in the firm name. In addition, the UPA gives creditors of the firm priority in partnership assets over creditors of the individual partners. It also permits the firm to continue its business in situations in which the aggregate theory would suggest immediate dissolution and liquidation.

CREATION OF PARTNERSHIP

Introduction

One of the most important issues in partnership law is whether two people who have associated in an enterprise have created a partnership. If they are partners, then the law of partnership applies to their disputes with each other and with persons with whom they have dealt.

No Formalities for Creation of Partnership

No formalities are necessary to create a partnership. Two persons may become partners in accordance with a written partnership contract (articles of partnership), they may agree orally to be partners, or they may become partners merely by arranging their affairs as if they were partners. If partners conduct business under a trade name, they must file the name with the secretary of state in compliance with state statutes requiring the registration of fictitious business names.

Articles of Partnership

When people decide to become partners, they should employ a lawyer to prepare a written partnership agreement. Although such **articles of partnership** are not required to form a partnership, they are highly desirable for the same reasons that written contracts are generally preferred. In addition, the statute of frauds requires a writing for a partnership having a term exceeding one year.

When there is no written partnership agreement, a dispute may arise over whether persons who are associated in some enterprise are partners. For example, someone may assert that she is a partner and, therefore, claim a share of the value of a successful enterprise. More frequently, an unpaid creditor may seek to hold a person liable for a debt incurred by another person in the same enterprise. To determine whether there is a partnership in the absence of an express agreement, the courts use the definition of partnership in the UPA.

FIGURE 2   Principal Characteristics of Partnerships under the UPA

1. A partnership may be created with no formalities. Two or more people merely need to agree to own and conduct a business together in order to create a partnership (aggregate theory).

2. Partners have unlimited liability for the obligations of the business (aggregate theory). However, a partner's personal creditors have first priority to that partner's assets, while partnership creditors have first priority to partnership assets (entity theory).

3. Each partner, merely by being an owner of the business, has a right to manage the business of the partnership (aggregate theory). He is an agent of the partnership and may make the partnership liable for contracts, torts, and crimes (entity theory). Because partners are liable for all obligations of the partnership, in effect each partner is an agent of the other partners. Each partner may hire agents, and every partner is liable for the agents' authorized contracts and for torts that the agents commit in the course of their employments (aggregate theory).

4. A partnership is not an employer of the partners, for most purposes. As a result, for example, a partner who leaves a partnership is not entitled to unemployment benefits (aggregate theory).

5. Partners are fiduciaries of the partnership. They must act in the best interests of the partnership, not in their individual best interests (entity theory).

6. The profits or losses of the business are shared by the partners, who report their shares of the profits or losses on their individual federal income tax returns, because the partnership does not pay federal income taxes (aggregate theory). Nonetheless, a partnership does keep its own financial records and must file an information return with the Internal Revenue Service (entity theory).*

7. A partnership may own property in its own name (entity theory).

8. A partnership may not sue or be sued in its own name. The partners must sue or be sued (aggregate theory).

9. A partner may not sue her partners. Her sole remedy is to seek an accounting between the partners (aggregate theory).

10. A partner's ownership interest in a partnership is not freely transferable A purchaser of a partner's interest does not become a partner, but is entitled to receive only the partner's share of the partnership's profits (aggregate theory).

11. Generally, a partnership has no life apart from its owners. If a partner dies, the partnership dissolves and may be terminated (aggregate theory). Under certain circumstances, however, the partnership may continue after the death of a partner (entity theory).

*The federal income tax return filed by a partnership is merely an information return in which the partnership indicates its gross income and deductions and the names and addresses of its partners (I.R.C. Sec. 6031). The information return allows the Internal Revenue Service to determine whether the partners accurately report partnership income on their individual returns.

UPA Definition of Partnership

UPA Section 6 defines a partnership as an "association of two or more persons to carry on as co-owners a business for profit." There are four distinct elements to the UPA definition:

1. An association of two or more persons.

2. Carrying on a business.

3. As co-owners of the business.

4. For profit.

If the definition is satisfied, then the courts will treat those involved as partners. A relationship may meet the UPA definition of partnership even when a person does not believe he is a partner, and occasionally, even if the parties agree that they are not partners.

Association of Two or More Persons

As an association, a partnership is a *voluntary and consensual relationship*. It cannot be imposed on a person; a person must agree expressly or impliedly to have a person associate with her. For example, a partner cannot force her partners to accept her daughter into the partnership.

No person can be a partner with herself: a partnership must have *at least two partners*. Nonetheless, a person may be a partner with his spouse.

Who Is a Person?   Not everyone or everything may be a partner. UPA Section 2 defines a person as an individual, partnership, corporation, or other association. A limited partnership may be a partner. Most states do not permit a trust to be a partner, but they allow the trustee of the trust to be a partner for the benefit of the trust.

Carrying On a Business

Any trade, occupation, or profession may qualify as a business. Carrying on a business usually requires a *series of transactions* conducted over a period of time. For example, a group of farmers that buys supplies in quantity to get lower prices is not carrying on a business, but only part of one. If the group buys harvesting equipment with which it intends to harvest crops for others for a fee for many years, it is carrying on a business.

Co-Ownership

Partners must *co-own the business* in which they associate. There is no requirement that the capital contributions or the assets of the business be co-owned.

Also, by itself, co-ownership of assets does not establish a partnership. For example, two persons who own a building as joint tenants are not necessarily partners. To be partners, they must co-own a business.

The two most important factors in establishing co-ownership of the business are the *sharing of profits* and the *sharing of management* of the business.

Sharing Profits   UPA Section 7(4) declares that the receipt by a person of a share of the profits of a business is *prima facie* evidence that she is a partner in the business. This means that persons sharing profits are partners, unless other evidence exists to disprove they are partners. The rationale for this rule is that a person would not be sharing the profits of a business unless she were a co-owner. This rule brings under partnership law many persons who fail to realize that they are partners. For example, two college students who purchase college basketball tickets, resell them, and split the profits are partners.

Sharing the gross revenues of a business does not create a presumption of partnership. The profits, not the gross receipts, must be shared. For example, brokers who split a commission on a sale of land are not partners.

Section 7(4) provides that *no* presumption of partnership may be made when a share of profits is received:

1. By a creditor as payment on a debt.
2. By an employee as wages.[1]
3. By a landlord as rent.[2]

---

[1] See, e.g., *Montana Bank of Red Lodge v. Lightfield*, 771 P.2d 571 (Mont. Sup. Ct. 1989); *Associated Reforestation Contractors, Inc. v. State*, 650 P.2d 1068 (Ore. Ct. App. 1982).

[2] See, e.g., *Chariton Feed and Grain, Inc. v. Harder*, 369 N.W.2d 777 (Iowa Sup. Ct. 1985).

4. By a widow, widower, or representative of a deceased partner for the value of that partner's share of the partnership.
5. By a creditor as interest on a loan.
6. As consideration to the transferor of a business or other property for his sale of the goodwill of the business or other property.

These exceptions reflect the normal expectations of the parties that no partnership exists in such situations.[3]

Sharing Management   Sharing management of a business is evidence tending to prove the existence of a partnership.[4] However, by itself, participation in management is not conclusive proof of the existence of a partnership. For example, a creditor may be granted considerable control in a business, such as a veto power over partnership decisions and the right of consultation, without becoming a partner. Also, a sole proprietor may hire someone to manage his business, yet the manager will not be a partner of the sole proprietor.

Although either sharing profits or sharing management is not, by itself, *conclusive* proof of a partnership, sharing both profits and management strongly implies the existence of a partnership.

Even if the parties claim that they share profits for one of the six reasons listed in UPA Section 7(4), the sharing of management may overcome the presumption that they are not partners. When the parties arrange their affairs in a manner that otherwise establishes an *objective intent* to create a partnership, the courts find that a partnership exists. For example, when a nonmanagerial employee initially shares profits as a form of employment compensation, the employee is not a partner of his employer. But when the employer and employee modify their relationship by having the employee exercise managerial control of the business, a partnership may exist. Nonetheless, when the employer and employee have agreed that the employee is a *managerial employee*, the managerial employee is not a partner of the employer, despite the employee's sharing profits and management.

Other persons sharing profits and control of a business may or may not be partners. For example, an owner of farmland and a farmer agree that the farmer will farm the land and that the owner and the farmer will share the

---

[3] *Peed v. Peed*, 325 S.E.2d 275 (N.C. Ct. App. 1985).

[4] *McCrary v. Butler*, 540 So.2d 736 (Ala. Sup. Ct. 1989).

FIGURE 3 Important Consequences of Being a Partner

FIGURE 3 Important Consequences of Being a Partner

1. You share ownership of the business. For example, you want to bring an employee into your business, which is worth $250,000. If you and the employee conduct your affairs like partners, your employee will own half of your business.
2. You share the profits of the business.
3. You share management of the business. Your partner must be allowed to participate in management decisions.
4. Your partner is your agent. You are liable for your partner's torts and contracts made in the ordinary course of business.
5. You owe fiduciary duties to your partnership and your partner, such as the duties to devote full time to the business, not to compete with the business, not to self-deal, and not to disclose confidential matters.

profits of the business. This is not a partnership, but merely a convenient way of paying rent to the owner for the value of the land to the farmer. Suppose, however, the owner and the farmer share not only the profits from the operation of the farm but also jointly determine which crops are to be planted or when livestock is to be sold. Courts often treat such an owner and a farmer as partners.

Creditors, however, occupy a privileged position. Many cases have permitted creditors to share profits and to exercise considerable control over a business without becoming partners. Creditor control is often justified on the grounds that it is merely reasonable protection for the creditor's risk.

For Profit

The owners of an enterprise must *intend to make a profit* to create a partnership. If the enterprise suffered losses, yet the owners intended to make a profit, a partnership may result. When an endeavor is carried on by several people for charitable or other nonprofit objectives, it is not a partnership. For example, Alex and Geri operate a restaurant booth at a county fair each year to raise money for a Boy Scout troop. Their relationship is not a partnership, but merely an association. (Nonetheless, like partners, they may be individually liable for the debts of the enterprise.)

Intent

Frequently, courts say that there must be *intent* to form a partnership. This rule is more correctly stated as follows: *the parties must intend to create a relationship that the*

law recognizes as a partnership. A partnership may exist even if the parties entered it inadvertently, without considering whether they had created a partnership. A written agreement to the effect that the parties do not intend to form a partnership is not conclusive if their *actions* provide evidence of their intent to form a relationship that meets the UPA partnership test. Intent is determined by the words and acts of the parties, interpreted in light of the circumstances.

There are several important consequences of being a partner. See Figure 3 for a summary of the most important consequences.

CREATION OF JOINT VENTURES AND MINING PARTNERSHIPS

Joint Ventures

Courts frequently distinguish **joint ventures** from partnerships. A joint venture may be found when a court is reluctant to call an arrangement a partnership because the purpose of the arrangement is not to establish an ongoing business involving many transactions; instead, it is limited to a single project. For example, an agreement to buy and resell for profit a particular piece of real estate, perhaps after development, is likely to be viewed as a joint venture rather than a partnership. In all other respects, joint ventures are created just as partnerships are created. The joint venturers may have a formal written agreement. In its absence, a court applies UPA Sections 6 and 7—modified so as not to require the carrying on of a business—to determine whether a joint venture has been created.

The legal implications of the distinction between a partnership and a joint venture are not entirely clear. Generally, partnership law applies to joint ventures. For example, all of the participants in a joint venture are personally liable for its debts, and joint venturers owe each other the fiduciary duties imposed on partners. Joint ventures are treated as partnerships for federal income tax purposes. The most significant difference between joint venturers and partners is that joint venturers are usually held to have *less implied and apparent authority* than partners, due to the limited scope of the enterprise.

The following cases illustrate the application of partnership law to the question of whether a joint venture has been created. In the first case, *Dority v. Driesel*, the court emphasized the importance of sharing profits and management.

DORITY v. DRIESEL

706 P.2d 995 (Ore. Ct. App. 1985)

Daon Corporation developed a housing subdivision near Portland, Oregon. It did not build any houses itself, but only improved the homesites for resale. To promote the sales of homesites, Daon created a marketing scheme, named Showcase of Homes, that involved Portland area builders. The builders, including Raymond Driesel, purchased homesites from Daon and built custom homes on the homesites. Daon advertised the Showcase of Homes, decorated and furnished model homes, and provided a landscaping plan to the builders. Both Driesel and Daon benefited from the Showcase program. Driesel benefited from Daon's advertising and the chance to show his home, leading to future home-building jobs. Daon benefited from having homes constructed in the subdivision, proving to prospective homesite buyers the feasibility and desirability of buying a homesite from Daon, leading to further homesite sales.

Theo Dority purchased the home built by Driesel. All negotiations and documents for the sale were between Dority, Driesel, and Driesel's real estate broker; Daon was not represented. Prior to the sale, Dority noticed obvious defects in the home. Driesel promised to correct the defects, but he failed to do so. Dority demanded that both Daon and Driesel correct the defects. When the defects were not remedied, Dority hired another contractor to make the corrections for $20,000. Dority sued Daon and Driesel for $20,000. The trial court found that a joint venture existed between Daon and Driesel; therefore, under the law of partnership, Daon was held liable to Dority for $20,000. Daon appealed to the Oregon Court of Appeals.

Gillette, Presiding Judge.   Simply stated, a joint venture is a partnership for a single transaction, and partnership law controls joint ventures. The essential test in determining the existence of partnership is whether the parties intended to establish such a relationship. However, the substance of legal intent rather than the actual intent may be controlling. Partnership status may be inferred from the conduct of the parties in relation to themselves and to third parties. The main earmarks of a partnership are the right of a party to share the profits and losses and the right to exert some control over the business.

Both Daon and Driesel denied any intention of creating a joint venture relationship when entering into the showcase project. In addition, the profits anticipated by Daon and Driesel to be derived from the Showcase were not to be shared jointly. Rather, each was hoping to enjoy a distinct form of gain independent of that of the other. Indeed, either one might profit from the Showcase while the other failed to receive any benefit at all. The fact that they acted in concert to achieve some economic objective, while relevant to the inquiry, is not enough to create a joint venture.

Also, any potential loss from the Showcase joint effort would also be unique to each party. Daon might fail to sell more lots, or Driesel might fail to obtain any future construction jobs, but the loss would not necessarily be a shared one.

Judgment reversed in favor of Daon.

In the following case, *In Re O. W. Limited Partnership*, a written agreement provided that the parties would share gross revenues. However, because the parties actually shared profits in their performance of the agreement, their relationship met the definition of partnership.

IN RE O.W. LIMITED PARTNERSHIP

668 P.2d 56 (Ha. Ct. App. 1983)

OWLP, a Hawaii limited partnership, owned the Outrigger West Hotel. In 1974, OWLP and Hawaii Hotels Operating Company (HHOC) agreed that OWLP and HHOC would jointly operate the hotel and share its revenues, allocating 73 percent to OWLP and 27 percent to HHOC. The agreement provided that revenues would be collected from the hotel and allocated daily according to the percentages above.

For the years 1974 through 1977, OWLP paid Hawaii's general excise taxes only on the gross hotel room revenues allocated to OWLP. The Hawaii Director of Taxes claimed that OWLP's gross revenues should have included the amount of revenues allocated to HHOC, unless OWLP and HHOC were partners. The Director of Taxes claimed that HHOC merely provided services to OWLP and that, therefore, OWLP and HHOC were not partners. Consequently, the Director of Taxes, assessed OWLP for additional taxes of $194,754. OWLP appealed the assessment to the tax appeal court, which ruled that OWLP and HHOC were partners or joint venturers. The Director of Taxes appealed.

Tanaka, Judge. A joint venture is a mutual undertaking by two or more persons to carry out a single business enterprise for profit. A joint venture is closely akin to a partnership and the rules governing the creation and existence of partnerships are applicable to joint ventures.

The Director concedes that the revenue-sharing agreement provides for a joint operation by the parties. However, the Director argues that the agreement does not contemplate a partnership in that it does not deal with a sharing of profits and losses, but only in sharing gross receipts.

It is true that the sharing of gross receipts is not even prima facie evidence of a partnership. However, the evidence indicates that from 1974 to 1977, the allocation percentages were changed six times to permit each party to recover out-of-pocket expenses and to provide ultimately a return of 98 percent of the net income to OWLP and of 2 percent of the net income to HHOC. Thus, any amount recovered by each party according to the predetermined percentage in excess of its expenses would be its profit. Losses were shared pro rata like the profits.

The agreement was a minimum document to outline the joint venture's operations in case something happened to the people running it. Although the form selected by OWLP and HHOC did not precisely fit into the mold of partnership or joint venture, the substance of their business transactions was that of joint venture. The operation was and continued to be a joint venture.

Judgment for OWLP affirmed.

Mining Partnerships

Although similar to an ordinary partnership or a joint venture, a mining partnership is recognized as a distinct relationship in a number of states. Persons who cooperate in the working of either a mine or an oil or gas well are treated as mining partners if there is (1) *joint ownership* of a mineral interest, (2) *joint operation* of the property, and (3) *sharing* of profits and losses. Joint operation requires more than merely financing the development of a mineral interest, but it does not require active physical participation in operations; it may be proved by furnishing labor, supplies, services, or advice. The delegation of sole operating responsibility to one of the participants does not bar treatment as a mining partnership.

PARTNERSHIP BY ESTOPPEL

Introduction

Two persons may not be partners, yet in the eyes of a third person, they may *appear* to be partners. If the third person deals with one of the apparent partners, he may be harmed and seek to recover damages from both of the apparent partners. The question, then, is whether the third person may collect damages from both of the apparent partners.

For example, Johnson thinks that Sanders, a wealthy person, is a partner of Dean, a poor person. Johnson decides to do business with Dean on the grounds that if Dean does not perform as agreed, he can recover damages from Sanders. If Johnson is wrong and Sanders is not Dean's partner, Johnson ordinarily has no recourse against Sanders. UPA Section 7(1) states that "persons who are not partners as to each other are not partners as to third persons." However, if Johnson can prove that Sanders led him to believe that she and Dean were partners, he may sue Sanders for Dean's failure to perform as agreed. This is an application of the doctrine of **partnership by estoppel.**

Partnership by estoppel is similar to two concepts that you have already studied: promissory estoppel[5] and apparent authority of agents.[6] It is based on a person's substantial, detrimental reliance on another person's representations.

---

[5] See the Introduction to Contracts chapter and the Consideration chapter.

[6] See the Third-Party Relations of the Principal and the Agent chapter.

Elements

UPA Section 16 defines partnership by estoppel. Essentially, Section 16 states that to recover against a party as if she were a partner, a person must prove that:

1. The party held herself out or consented to being held out as a partner of another person.
2. The person dealt with the party's purported partner in justifiable reliance on the holding out.
3. The person was injured as a result.

Holding Out Few problems arise in determining whether a person holds himself out as a partner. For example, he might refer to himself as another person's partner. Or he might appear frequently in the office of a purported partner and confer with him. Perhaps he and another person share office space, have one door to an office with both of their names on it, have one telephone number, and share a secretary who answers the phone giving the names of both persons.

More difficult is determining when a person *consents* to being held out as another's partner. Mere knowledge that one is being held out as a partner is *not* consent. But a person's silence in response to a statement that the person is another's partner is consent. For example, suppose Chavez tells Eaton that Gold is a partner in Barb Birt's new retail shoe business. In fact, Gold is not Birt's partner. Later, Gold learns of the conversation between Chavez and Eaton. Gold does not have to seek out Chavez and Eaton to tell them that he is not Birt's partner in order to avoid being held liable as a partner for Birt's business debts. Had Chavez made the statement to Eaton in Gold's presence, however, Gold must deny the partnership relation, or he will be held liable for Eaton's subsequent reliance on Gold's silence.

Reasonable Reliance and Injury A partner by estoppel is *not* liable to everyone who deals with the purported partnership. He is liable only to those persons who reasonably rely on the holding out and suffer injury thereby. This means that partnership by estoppel, like any estoppel concept, is determined on a case-by-case basis.

A person unaware of the holding out cannot prove partnership by estoppel.[7] For example, James tells Samuels that she is Timm's partner, but she does not tell this

---

[7] *Zehner v. MFA Ins.* Co., 451 N.E.2d 65 (Ind. Ct. App. 1983).

to Carlson. Samuels can prove partnership by estoppel, but Carlson cannot. If Samuels tells Carlson what James told him, then Carlson can prove partnership by estoppel.

A third person's reliance on the appearance of a partnership must be reasonable. When a person has information that would prevent a reasonable person from relying on the holding out, no partnership by estoppel may result. For example, Lindall knows that Frank and Stanton are employer and employee. Frank calls Stanton "my partner" in the presence of Stanton and Lindall. Frank and Stanton are not partners by estoppel. Because Lindall knows that Frank and Stanton are employer and employee, she may not rely on Frank's calling Stanton "my partner."

The injury suffered by the third person must be the result of his reliance. If the third person would have done business with another person whether or not that person was a partner of someone held out as a partner, there is no injury as a result of reliance. Hence, there is no partnership by estoppel.

Effect of Partnership by Estoppel

Once partnership by estoppel has been proved, the person who held himself out or who consented to being held out is liable as though he were a partner. He is liable on contracts entered into by third persons on their belief that he was a partner. He is liable for torts committed during the course of relationships entered by third persons who believed he was a partner.

Not a Partner in Fact Although two parties are partners by estoppel to a person who knows of the holding out and who justifiably relies on it to his injury, the partners by estoppel are *not* partners in fact and do not share the profits, management, or value of the business of the purported partnership. Partnership by estoppel is merely a device to allow creditors to sue parties who mislead them into believing that a partnership exists.

In the following case, *Volkman v. DP Associates*, the appearance of partnership led the court to a finding of partnership by estoppel.

VOLKMAN v. DP ASSOCIATES

268 S.E.2d 265 (N.C. Ct. App. 1980)

Alvin and Carol Volkman decided to build a house. They contacted David McNamee for construction advice. McNamee informed the Volkmans that he was doing business with Phillip Carroll. Subsequently, the Volkmans received a letter from McNamee on DP Associates stationery. They assumed that the DP was derived from the first names of McNamee and Carroll: David and Phillip. Prior to the signing of the contract, McNamee introduced Carroll to Mr. Volkman at the DP Associates office, where Carroll said, "I hope we'll be working together." Carroll stated that McNamee would be the person at DP Associates primarily doing business with the Volkmans, but indicated that he also would be available for consultation.

The Volkmans reviewed the written contract in the DP Associates office with McNamee. McNamee suggested that they use a form to identify DP Associates as acting as a general contractor. He then left the room saying, "I will ask Phil." When he returned, he said that they would use the form.

After the contract was signed but before construction of the house began, Mr. Volkman visited the office of DP Associates. He again saw and spoke with Carroll, who said to him, "I am happy that we will be working with you." During construction, Mr. Volkman visited the office of DP Associates several times and saw Carroll there. During one visit, he expressed to Carroll his concern about construction delays, but Carroll told him not to worry, because McNamee would take care of it.

When DP Associates failed to perform the contract, the Volkmans sued DP Associates, McNamee, and Carroll. Carroll argued that he could not be liable to the Volkmans because he and McNamee were not partners. The trial court agreed and refused to let the jury decide the case. The Volkmans appealed to the North Carolina Court of Appeals.

Vaughn, Judge.   If the Volkmans are unable to prove a partnership in fact, they may be able to show that Carroll should be held as a partner by estoppel or under the agency theory of apparent authority.

Liability by estoppel may result either from Carroll's representation of himself as a partner "by words spoken or written" or "by conduct" or Carroll's "consent" to such a representation by another. The Volkmans indicated they may be able to show that Carroll by his oral statements to them and conduct in their presence and by his consent to the representations of McNamee to the Volkmans, some of which were in the presence of Carroll, represented himself as a partner and should be estopped to deny such association. They may be able to show further they relied upon these representations not knowing them to be false and that based upon the representations of Carroll and McNamee, the Volkmans changed their position and were thereby damaged.

In addition to an estoppel theory of liability, Carroll may be liable under apparent authority, a theory of agency law applicable to partnerships. There is virtually no difference between estoppel and apparent authority. Both depend on reliance by a third person on a communication from the principal. Despite the title, "Partner by Estoppel," the form of liability is more akin to that of apparent authority than to estoppel.

If this view is taken, the liability of the person seeking to deny partner status is not based on estoppel to deny agency or authority but on the objective theory of contract law, *i.e.,* a person should be bound by his words and conduct. Thus, when Carroll told Mr. Volkman, "I am happy that we will be working with you," and conducted himself as he did in the DP Associates office in the presence of Mr. Volkman, the jury may find that Carroll was indicating a willingness to be bound by the statements and acts of McNamee, that Carroll held himself out as a partner of McNamee in DP Associates, that McNamee had apparent authority to act for Carroll, and that the Volkmans reasonably relied upon this holding out. If so, Carroll is bound as if he directly dealt with the Volkmans.

Judgment reversed in favor of the Volkmans. Remanded to the trial court for jury trial.

PARTNERSHIP CAPITAL, PARTNERSHIP PROPERTY, AND PARTNERS' PROPERTY RIGHTS

Partnership Capital

When a partnership is formed, partners contribute cash or other property to the partnership. The partners' contribution is called **partnership capital.** To supplement beginning capital, other property may be contributed to the partnership as needed, such as by the partners permitting the partnership to retain some of its profits. Partnership capital is the equity of the business.

Loans made by partners to a partnership are not partnership capital, but instead are liabilities of the business. Partners who make loans to a partnership are both owners and creditors.

Partnership Property

The partnership may own all or only a part of the property it uses. For example, it may own the business and perhaps a small amount of working capital in the form of cash or a checking account, yet own no other assets. All other tangible and intangible property used by the partnership may be individually or jointly owned by one or more of the partners or rented by the partnership from third parties. A determination of what is partnership property becomes essential when the partnership is dissolved and the assets are being distributed and when creditors of either the partnership or one of the partners is seeking assets to satisfy a debt.

UPA Rule Section 8 of the UPA provides that (1) all property originally brought into the partnership or subsequently acquired by purchase or otherwise, on account of the partnership, is partnership property, and (2) unless the contrary intention appears, property acquired with partnership funds is partnership property.

Intent The *intent* of the partners controls. It is best to have a written record of the partners' intent as to ownership of all property used by the partnership, such as in the articles of partnership. Other writings—such as accounting records—show the partnership assets; assets appearing in the partnership's books are presumed to belong to the partnership. Also, the partnership's paying rent on property provides strong evidence that the property belongs to the partner receiving the rent.

Source of Purchase Funds The presumption is very strong that property purchased with partnership funds and used in the partnership is partnership property.[8] No such presumption is accorded to a partner who purchases property with her own funds and then allows the partnership to use the property; other factors besides the partner's funding the purchase determine who owns the property.

Title to Partnership Property If title is taken in the partnership name, it is presumed that the property is partnership property. However, the presumption is not as strong that real property held in the name of a partner is individual property.[9] Other indicia may prove that property held in a partner's name belongs to the partnership.

---

[8]*McCrary v. Butler*, 540 So.2d 736 (Ala. Sup. Ct. 1989).
[9]Id.

Other Indicia The partnership's payment of property taxes or insurance premiums, the maintainance, repair, and improvement of property by the partnership, and the deduction of these expenses on the partnership income tax return are indications of the intent of the partners that property belongs to the partnership, despite title being held in the name of a partner.

Generally, the partnership's mere use of the property creates no presumption that it is partnership property. Nonetheless, it is presumed that money used by a partnership as working capital is partnership property in the absence of clear evidence that it was intended to be merely a loan.

Example A tax accountant discovers that a partnership is using a building to which a partner, Jacob Smith, holds title. The partnership pays rent monthly to Smith, but the partnership pays for all maintenance and repairs on the building. The accountant wants to know whether the partnership or Smith should be paying real property taxes on the building. Smith is the owner and should be paying taxes on it because his partners' intent to allow Smith to retain ownership is evidenced by the partnership paying rent to Smith.

Suppose, however, that the partnership pays no rent to Smith, the partnership maintains and repairs the building, and the partnership pays real property taxes on the building, but the title is in Smith's name. The property belongs to the partnership, because all the objective criteria of ownership point toward partnership ownership. Therefore, when the partnership is liquidated, the building will be sold along with other partnership assets, and the proceeds of its sale will be distributed to partnership creditors and to all of the partners, not merely to Smith.

In the following case, the court held that a truck trailer held in the partnership's name was partnership property.

IN RE FULTON

43 B.R.273 (M.D.Tenn. 1984)

Padgett Carroll and Walter Fulton operated as a partnership a trucking business under the name of C & F Trucking. Carroll contributed a semi truck, which Fulton drove for the business. Carroll used $4,600 of his personal funds to purchase a used 42-foot trailer for C & F Trucking. The seller's invoice listed C & F Trucking as the purchaser of the trailer. The trailer's certificate of title listed C & F Trucking as the owner.

Fulton's personal financial problems forced him to file for bankruptcy. Fulton claimed ownership of the trailer among his assets. Carroll claimed that the trailer was his individual asset.

Paine, Bankruptcy Judge. In determining whether property is partnership property or property owned by an individual, the court must focus primarily on the intentions of the partners at the time the property was acquired. Such intention of the partners must be determined from their apparent intention at the time the property was acquired and the conduct of the partners toward the property after the purchase.

Viewing evidence surrounding the purpose and use of the property, Tennessee courts have held that when property is titled in the name of the partnership, the party asserting that the property is not partnership property has the burden of proof.

The evidence establishes that the trailer is partnership property. Both a sales invoice and a certificate of title list the owner of the trailer as C & F Trucking. The trailer was purchased by Carroll for use in the C & F Trucking business and Fulton actually used the trailer in the business.

The claims of individual ownership asserted by both Fulton and Carroll lack substance. The property was indeed partnership property.

Judgment for Carroll.

Partners' Property Rights

Under UPA Section 24, a partner has three property rights:

1. Her rights in specific partnership property.
2. Her partnership interest.
3. Her right to participate in the management of the business.

The first two rights are discussed here. The management right is discussed in the Operation of Partnership and Related Forms chapter.

Rights in Partnership Property

According to UPA Section 25, partnership property is owned by partners as **tenants in partnership.** This means that the partners as a group own partnership property as a whole; the partners as individuals do not own proportionate interests in separate items of partnership property.

As a tenant in partnership, each partner has the right to possess partnership property for partnership purposes. A partner has no individual right to use or possess partnership property for her own purposes, such as paying a personal debt, unless she has the consent of the other partners. Likewise, a partner's personal creditor may not make a claim against partnership assets.

On the death of a partner, his rights in partnership property pass to the surviving partners. This is called the **right of survivorship.**

The nature of a partner's rights in partnership property is explored in the following case, *State v. Birch.*

STATE v. BIRCH
675 P.2d 246 (Wash. Ct. App. 1984)

Richard DeLong and Ken Birch formed a partnership to build houses. They agreed that all sales proceeds would be deposited in a partnership bank checking account and that both of them must sign all checks. For two years, Birch and DeLong signed all checks, but then DeLong agreed that Birch could sign partnership checks by himself. Six years later, DeLong discovered that Birch paid some of his personal expenses with partnership checks. DeLong reported his discovery to the Prosecuting Attorney for the State of Washington, who prosecuted Birch for the crime of embezzlement. Embezzlement was defined in the Washington statute as exerting unauthorized control over the property of another. The trial judge ruled that a partner could not embezzle partnership funds because the partner would not be exerting unauthorized control over the property of another. The Prosecuting Attorney appealed to the Washington Court of Appeals.

Munson, Chief Judge. In *State v. Eberhart (1919)*, the Supreme Court of Washington held that a partner cannot be prosecuted for use of partnership property because the theft statute requires the theft be of property of another. The title to partnership property cannot be in another because each partner is the ultimate owner of an undivided interest in all the partnership property, and none of such property can be said, with reference to any partner, to be the property of another.

Under both the common law and the Uniform Partnership Act, partnerships are treated both as aggregates of individuals and entities distinct from the people involved in the partnership. The common law indicated that each partner's interest in the property of a partnership was as a joint tenant. This is an aggregate theory because it does not recognize the partnership as a separate entity.

Although the Uniform Partnership Act speaks of the partnership as a separate entity, the issue is whether the title to property is in another. The title is not in another; the UPA retains the aggregate approach under which partners own partnership property as joint tenants.

The Prosecuting Attorney contends that the UPA imposes limitations upon partners' use of partnership property. Section 25 of the UPA states:

(1) A partner is a co-owner with his partners of specific partnership property holding as a tenant in partnership.

(2) The incidents of this tenancy are such that:

(a) A partner . . . has an equal right with his partners to possess specific partnership property for partnership purposes; but he has no right to possess such property for any other purpose without the consent of his partners.

Under the UPA, each partner's right in specific partnership property is subordinated to partnership use of the property for partnership purposes.

The Prosecuting Attorney correctly contends that the UPA Section 25 modifies the definition of property of another as it relates to partnership property. However, a statute relating to larceny by a partner was repealed by the Legislature in 1909. The statute construed in *Eberhart* remains substantially the same today. The Legislature is presumed to be aware of both *Eberhart* and the adoption of the UPA. The Legislature had the opportunity to make theft of partnership funds a crime. It did not do so.

Judgment for Birch affirmed.

Partnership Interest

As a co-owner of a partnership, a partner has an ownership interest in the partnership. A partner's ownership interest is called a **partnership interest** and is part of his personal property. Although a partner may not give his personal creditors any interest in separate items of partnership property, Section 27 of the UPA permits a partner to assign his partnership interest to a creditor. And although a partner's personal creditors may not obtain an execution of judgment against separate items of partnership property, a creditor may obtain execution against a partner's partnership interest by obtaining a charging order against that interest.

Assignment

The **assignment of a partnership interest** is a voluntary act of a partner. It entitles the assignee to receive the assigning partner's share of the partnership's profits, but it does not give the assignee the right to inspect the partnership's books and records or to manage the partnership.

A partner's assignment of his partnership interest does not dissolve the partnership; the assigning partner remains a partner. An assignee for value, including a creditor, may ask a court to dissolve a partnership at will.[10] Dissolution may be followed by liquidation of the partnership's assets and result in the creditor being paid from the proceeds of the sale of the partnership's assets.

The nonassigning partners may not exclude the assigning partner from the partnership. They may, however, rightfully dissolve the partnership by their *unanimous* agreement, even if the term or objective of the partnership has not been met.

Charging Order

Under UPA Section 28, a partner's personal creditor with a judgment against the partner may ask a court to issue a **charging order**; that is, an order charging the partner's partnership interest with payment of the unsatisfied amount of the judgment. Unlike assignment, a charging order is obtained without the partner's consent. As with assignment, however, the partner remains a partner, and the creditor is entitled to receive only the partner's share of the profits. If the profits are insufficient to pay the debt, the creditor may ask the court to order foreclosure and to sell the partner's interest to satisfy the charging order.

Neither the issuance of a charging order nor the purchase of a partnership interest at a foreclosure sale causes a dissolution. But the purchaser of a partnership interest, like the assignee for value, may ask a court to dissolve a partnership at will. Under UPA Section 28, the other partners may eliminate this potential threat to the continuation of the partnership by *redeeming* the charging order. The other partners redeem a charging order by paying the creditor the amount due on the judgment against the partner. If the other partners so choose, however, they may dissolve the partnership by their

unanimous agreement, just as nonassigning partners may do.

Joint Venturers

Transfers of interests in joint ventures are treated in the same way as transfers of partnership interests.

Mining Partners

A mining partner's interest is *freely transferable*. The transferee becomes a partner with all the rights of ownership and management, and the transferor loses all of his partnership rights. The other mining partners cannot object to the transfer, and their consent to a transfer is not required.

ETHICAL AND PUBLIC POLICY CONCERNS

1. A person who carefully considers which business form to use for his one-person business can achieve nearly any combination of results desirable to him. For example, by incorporating and electing S Corporation status, a person can limit his personal liability, deduct business losses on his individual federal income tax return, yet control the business by electing himself to the board of directors. Why should a careful planner obtain such advantages, while a person who merely begins his business has unlimited liability as a sole proprietor? Is the business of the careful planner more valuable to our society than the business of the person who does not choose a business form?

2. Why should all the partners in a partnership be individually liable for all the obligations of the partnership, while shareholders and managers of a corporation have no liability beyond their capital contributions? Is the corporate form of business or the business conducted by corporations more important to society than the partnership form or the business conducted by partnerships? Would benefits that businesses provide to society be reduced if limited liability were not extended to shareholders and managers of corporations?

3. What are the ethical underpinnings of partnership by estoppel? Why should a person be held liable for the business debts of another person when he does not benefit from the business? Could the person who relied on the appearance of partnership have protected himself by making inquiries? Should he be required to make such inquiries?

---

[10] A partnership at will is a partnership with no term, which may rightfully be dissolved by any partner at any time.

SUMMARY

The choice of business form is an important decision, for it affects the liability and taxation of the owners. The sole proprietorship imposes unlimited liability on its owner, and any income or loss of the business is income or loss of the owner. The partnership is like the sole proprietorship for liability and taxation purposes, but it has two or more partners. General partners of a limited partnership are treated like partners in an ordinary partnership, but limited partners have limited liability and limited ability to deduct business losses on their individual federal income tax returns. A corporation's shareholders enjoy limited liability, but there is a risk of double taxation, unless the shareholders elect S Corporation status.

Franchising provides significant advantages for both franchisees and franchisors. Franchisees may receive a virtual turnkey operation, while franchisors receive substantial income with small investment risk. Franchisors who control the activities of franchisees may have liability for the franchisees' torts and contracts. In addition, recent laws protect franchisees from franchisors' fraudulent disclosures and abusive terminations of franchising agreements.

The Uniform Partnership Act contains most of the law affecting partnerships. In some respects, the UPA treats the partnership as an entity separate from its members, but in other respects it adopts the aggregate theory.

No formalities are required to create a partnership. It is a voluntary association of two or more persons to carry on as co-owners a business for profit. Any person with legal capacity may become a partner, including partnerships and corporations. An association to conduct a single transaction is not a partnership but a joint venture, to which much of partnership law applies.

One who receives a share of the profits of a business is viewed as a partner unless it can be shown that the sharing was for certain specified purposes. The co-ownership requirement applies to the business; it is not necessary that all partners co-own the property used in the business. Generally, sharing the profits and the management of a business is sufficient evidence of the existence of a partnership.

People who hold themselves out or who permit others to hold them out as partners will be held liable as partners to persons who rely on these holdings out, under the doctrine of partnership by estoppel.

Whether property used by a partnership is partnership property is fundamentally a question of determining the intent of the parties. A written agreement is the best evidence, but title in the partnership's name and use of partnership funds to make the purchase are also important.

Each partner has the right to use partnership property for partnership purposes. The property is owned by the partners as tenants in partnership. A partner may not use partnership assets to pay his personal creditors, and a partner's personal creditor may not satisfy his claim against partnership property. A partner may assign his partnership interest to creditors, who then receive the assigning partner's share of the profits. Creditors may obtain charging orders against the interest of a partner; these orders entitle them to the debtor's share of the profits.

PROBLEM CASES

1. Gail Neild and Charles Wolfe were lovers who moved into an apartment in New York City. Only Charles signed the lease, but they agreed that Charles would pay two thirds of the rent and Gail would pay one third. Charles paid for all of the furnishings in the apartment. When their relationship deteriorated, Charles refused to let Gail into the apartment, and she found another place to live. Six months later, the landlord notified the tenants that the building would be converted to a cooperative. The conversion offered each tenant the opportunity to purchase his apartment at a bargain price below the fair market value of the apartment. Charles purchased the apartment he and Gail occupied. Gail sued Charles, seeking one third of the difference between Charles's purchase price of the apartment and its fair market value on the grounds that she and Charles had formed a partnership or joint venture, giving her a one-third interest in the apartment. Was there a partnership or joint venture?

2. Rusty Holler made an agreement with P & M Cattle Company, a partnership owned by Bill Poage and L. W. Maxfield, pursuant to which Rusty would pasture P & M's cattle on Rusty's land. The agreement provided that the cattle would be sold at a time agreeable to all the parties. Also, it provided that Rusty would receive 50 percent of the net proceeds from the sale of the cattle after deducting the cost of the cattle, freight charges, salt costs, and Rusty's $300 monthly salary. When the cattle were sold at a loss, P & M argued that Rusty was a partner or joint venturer with P & M and must undertake his share of the loss. Was P & M correct?

3. Vearle Edwards owned and operated Edwards IGA grocery. Vearle advertised his grocery in the South Sioux City Star, but failed to pay for the advertising. When Vearle filed for bankruptcy, the Star sued Vearle's wife, Ila. The Star's managing editor believed that the grocery was a family-owned business, but he said that he spoke very few times with Ila about advertising since "she was not around." At one time, Ila had done some bookkeeping at the store, but for the last seven years she had no dealings with the grocery. She at no time dealt directly with any suppliers, made any management decisions, ordered any food or supplies, supervised any employees, or placed any advertisements. She contributed no resources to the store. She did not share in the profits or losses of the store, except as the wife of Vearle. Is Ila obligated to pay for the advertising in the Star?

4. Dr. Woodward and Dr. Kaplan were the only shareholders and medical doctors in a professional corporation, Neurological Consultants, P.C. Dr. Woodward performed a spinal tap on Eugene Gibson. When the spinal tap was unsuccessful, he called Dr. Kaplan, who also performed unsuccessful taps. When requesting consent for the spinal taps from Gibson's wife, Dr. Woodward referred to Dr. Kaplan as "his partner." Subsequently, Gibson suffered permanent nerve damage from Dr. Kaplan's negligently performed spinal taps. Gibson sued Dr. Woodward claiming that Dr. Woodward was Dr. Kaplan's partner by estoppel. Was Dr. Woodward liable for Dr. Kaplan's negligence?

5. Coy Stephens did business as Audio Works. When he needed a bank loan for the business, Coy and his father, Vastine Stephens, executed a document stating that they were partners in the business and that Coy had the authority to sign for the business in all respects. In fact, Coy and Vastine were not partners, but they executed the document solely to induce a bank to loan the necessary funds to Coy. Relying on the document, Angelina National Bank loaned $33,000 to Audio Works. Angelina would not have loaned the money to Audio Works had it not believed that Vastine was Coy's partner. When Coy failed to repay the loan, Angelina sued Vastine. Was Vastine liable to Angelina?

6. Joe Johnson, a logging contractor, hired Steve Olsen to log timber. Johnson advanced money to Olsen, totaling over $8,000 by July 1979. That same month, Bill Slusser worked for Olsen for three days. Johnson asked Olsen who was the stranger working with him, and he replied that it was his future father-in-law and that "they would probably go partners." Johnson paid Olsen and Slusser separately for their work. Slusser did not work again until late October, when he began to work full time. By that time, Johnson had advanced Olsen almost $10,000. In 1980, Olsen stopped working for Johnson. Olsen still had not repaid the $10,000 of advances. Slusser continued to work until Johnson refused to pay him for his work because Olsen had not repaid the $10,000 advance. Although Olsen and Slusser were not partners when the advances were made, Johnson argued that they were partners by estoppel and that, therefore, Slusser is obligated to repay the $10,000. Is Johnson correct?

7. Barry Wilen owned a one-third interest in Bay Country Investments, a partnership. During the term of Barry's marriage to Loveta Wilen, Bay Country sold real property for $126,500. The partnership reinvested the proceeds in other real property. Subsequently, Loveta and Barry had marital problems. During a divorce proceeding, Loveta claimed that she was entitled to receive half of Barry's one-third share of the $126,500 proceeds. Was she correct?

8. Claude Gauldin and Joe Corn formed a partnership to raise cattle and hogs on land owned by Corn. Partnership funds were used to build two buildings on the land for use by the partnership. Gauldin and Corn did not discuss who owned the buildings. Gauldin knew when the buildings were constructed that they would be permanent improvements to the land and would become part of it. The partnership paid no rent for the land, and there was no agreement to consider the use of the land as a contribution by Corn. The taxes on the land were paid by Corn, as was the cost of upkeep. When Corn left the partnership, Gauldin claimed that the buildings were partnership assets and that he was entitled to half of their fair market value. Was Gauldin correct?

CORPORATIONS

CHAPTER 30

MANAGEMENT OF CORPORATIONS

INTRODUCTION

Although shareholders own a corporation, they traditionally have possessed no right to manage the business of the corporation. Instead, shareholders elect individuals to a **board of directors,** to which management is entrusted. Often, the board delegates much of its management responsibilities to officers.

In publicly held corporations, shareholders have no power or right to interfere with the legitimate managerial discretion of the board or the officers. In close corporations, however, some courts have granted shareholders some management authority. Modern close corporation statutes have gone so far as to grant the shareholders of a close corporation the option of dispensing with a board of directors and managing the corporation as if it were a partnership.

This chapter explains the legal aspects of the board's and officers' management of the corporation. While the board and officers have management authority, they do not possess unlimited management discretion. Their management of the corporation must be consistent with the objectives and powers of the corporation, and they owe duties to the corporation to manage it prudently and in the best interests of the corporation and the shareholders as a whole. In addition, under tort and criminal law, management owes duties to the persons with whom it deals on behalf of the corporation.

CORPORATE OBJECTIVES AND POWERS

Profit Objective

Management of a corporation must be *consistent with the objectives* of business corporations as stated by the courts and the legislatures. The traditional objective of the business corporation has been to *enhance corporate profits and shareholder gain*. According to this objective, the managers of a corporation must seek the accomplishment of the profit objective to the exclusion of all inconsistent goals. Other interests such as employee and customer welfare must be subordinated to the interest of corporate profits. Interests other than profit maximization may be considered, provided that they do not hinder the ultimate profit objective.

Other Objectives

Nonetheless, some courts have permitted corporations to take *socially responsible actions* that were *beyond the profit-maximization requirement*.[1] In addition, every state recognizes corporate powers that are not economically inspired.[2] For example, corporations may make

---

[1]Mangrum, "In Search of a Paradigm of Corporate Social Responsibility," 17 *Creighton L. Rev.* 21, 55–65 (1983).

[2]Id. at 66.

contributions to colleges, political campaigns, child abuse prevention centers, literary associations, and employee benefit plans, regardless of economic benefit to the corporations. Also, every state expressly recognizes the right of shareholders to choose freely the extent to which profit maximization captures all of their interests and all of their sense of responsibility.[3]

Presently management can freely choose to act socially responsible, even if there exists no likelihood of resulting profits. At the same time the corporation may choose to be strictly profit oriented.[4]

In the following case, the court held that the board acted improperly by failing to act to maximize shareholder profit.

---

[3]Id. at 68.

[4]Id. at 65.

REVLON, INC. v. MACANDREWS & FORBES HOLDINGS, INC.

506 A.2d 173 (Del. Sup. Ct. 1986)

In 1985, Pantry Pride, Inc., informed Revlon, Inc., of its intent to acquire Revlon. Pantry Pride planned to "bust up" Revlon after the acquisition by selling its various lines of businesses individually. Revlon's board of directors rejected Pantry Pride's plan. Nonetheless, Pantry Pride made a hostile takeover bid for Revlon's shares at $47.50 per share.

In response to Pantry Pride's bid, Revlon's board sought to reduce the number of shares Pantry Pride could acquire by repurchasing some of it shares in exchange for new Senior Notes. The contract with the new Senior Noteholders protected the noteholders with covenants limiting Revlon's ability to incur more debt, sell assets, or pay dividends. The covenants, however, could be waived by the board's independent directors.

When this defense failed to deter Pantry Pride, the board recognized that a takeover was inevitable. Consequently, the board agreed to a friendly acquisition by Forstmann Little & Co. for $56 per share. Realizing the inevitability of a bust-up, Revlon's board agreed to break up its assets by selling its cosmetic division; Forstmann planned to sell two other divisions after the purchase.

In addition, Revlon's independent directors agreed to waive the Senior Note covenants. As a result, the value of the Senior Notes dropped 12 percent. Angry Senior Noteholders threatened to sue Revlon's directors. Concerned about their personal liability to the Senior Noteholders, the Revlon directors amended their agreement with Forstmann. Forstmann increased its offer to $57.25 per share and agreed to support the value of the Senior Notes. In return, Revlon gave Forstmann a lock-up option, promising to sell two valuable divisions to Forstmann at nearly $200 million below their market value if Pantry Pride was successful in taking over Revlon.

Pantry Pride sued Revlon to invalidate the lock-up option as beyond the objectives of the corporation. The trial court enjoined Revlon's directors from making concessions to Forstmann. Revlon appealed to the Supreme Court of Delaware.

Moore, Justice.   The lock-up with Forstmann had as its emphasis shoring up the market value of the Senior Notes. The directors made support of the Senior Notes an integral part of the company's dealings with Forstmann, even though their primary responsibility at this stage was to the shareholders.

The original threat posed by Pantry Pride—the break-up of the company—had become a reality that even the directors embraced. Selective dealing to fend off a hostile bidder was no longer a proper objective. Instead, obtaining the highest price for the benefit of the shareholders should have been the central theme guiding director action.

The Revlon board argued that it acted in good faith in protecting the Senior Noteholders because Delaware law permits consideration of other corporate constituencies. Although such considerations may be permissible, there are fundamental limitations upon that prerogative. A board may have regard for various constituencies, provided there are rationally related benefits accruing to the shareholders. However, such concern for non-shareholder interests is inappropriate when an auction among active bidders is in progress, and the object no longer is to protect or maintain the corporate enterprise but to sell it to the highest bidder.

Revlon also contended that it had contractual obligations to the Senior Noteholders. However, any such duties are limited to the principle that one may not interfere with contractual relationships by improper actions. Here the rights of the Senior Noteholders were fixed by agreement, and there is nothing to suggest that any of those terms were violated. The Senior Notes covenants specifically contemplated a waiver.

In granting an asset option lock-up to Forstmann, the directors allowed considerations other than the maximization of shareholder profit to affect their judgment to the ultimate detriment of shareholders. No such defensive measure can be sustained.

Judgment for Pantry Pride affirmed.

Corporate Constituency Statutes

The decision in the *Revlon* case prodded most of the states to enact **corporate constituency statutes,** which broaden the legal objectives of corporations. Such statutes permit or require directors to take into account the interests of constituencies other than shareholders. These statutes direct the board to act in the best interests of the corporation, not just the interests of the shareholders, and to maximize corporate profits *over the long term.* The new laws recognize that a corporation is a collection of interests working together for the purpose of producing goods and services at a profit, and that the goal of corporate profit maximization over the long term is not necessarily the same as the goal of stock price maximization over the short term. For an example of the new statutes, see the excerpt from the Indiana statute in Figure 1.

Corporate Powers

The actions of management are limited not only by the objectives of business corporations but also by the *powers* granted to business corporations. Such limitations may appear in the state statute, the articles of incorporation, and the bylaws.

State Statutes The primary source of a corporation's powers is the corporation statute of the state in which it is incorporated. Some state corporation statutes ex-

FIGURE 1 Indiana Code 23-1-35-1

(d) A director may, in considering the best interests of a corporation, consider the effects of any action on shareholders, employees, suppliers, and customers of the corporation, and the communities in which offices or other facilities of the corporation are located, and any other factors the director considers pertinent.

(f) [D]irectors are not required to consider the effects of a proposed corporate action on any particular corporate constituent group or interest as a dominant or controlling factor.

pressly specify the powers of corporations. These powers include making gifts for charitable and educational purposes, lending money to corporate officers and directors, and purchasing and disposing of the corporation's shares. Other state corporation statutes limit the powers of corporations, such as prohibiting the acquisition of agricultural land by corporations.

Modern statutes attempt to authorize corporations to engage in *any* activity. Model Business Corporation Act (MBCA) Section 3.02 contains an extensive list of corporate powers, but the preamble to that list makes it clear that a corporation has the power to do *anything that an individual may do.*

Articles of Incorporation Most corporation statutes require a corporation to state its purpose in its articles of incorporation. The purpose is usually phrased in broad terms, even if the corporation has been formed with only one type of business in mind. For example, a corporation formed to mine gold may have a purpose clause stating that it has been formed "to mine gold and to engage in any other lawful business." Such a corporation would not be limited by its articles of incorporation. Most corporations have purpose clauses stating that they may engage in any lawful business.

Under the MBCA, the inclusion of a purpose clause in the articles is optional. Also, any corporation incorporated under the MBCA has the purpose of engaging in any lawful business, unless the articles state a narrower purpose. Hence, under the MBCA, a corporation with no purpose clause in its articles may engage in any lawful business, thereby being able to do what any individual may do.

Nonetheless, the promoters or the shareholders may desire to use the statement of purpose as a self-imposed limitation. In such instances, the purpose clause states the express powers of the corporation and becomes a promise of the corporation to its shareholders that it will confine its business to those express powers and the powers that may be implied therefrom.

The *Ultra Vires* Doctrine Historically, an act of a corporation beyond its powers was a nullity, as it was *ultra vires*, which is Latin for *beyond the powers*. Therefore, any act not permitted by the corporation statute or by the corporation's articles of incorporation was void due to lack of capacity.

This lack of capacity or power of the corporation was a *defense to a contract* assertable either by the corporation or by the other party that dealt with the corporation. Often, *ultra vires* was merely a convenient justification for reneging on an agreement that was no longer considered desirable. This misuse of the doctrine has led to its near abandonment.

Today, the *ultra vires* doctrine is of small importance for two reasons. First, the MBCA and other modern business corporation statutes grant corporations broad powers, and nearly all drafters of articles of incorporation use broad purpose clauses, thereby preventing any *ultra vires* problem. Second, the MBCA and most other statutes do not permit a corporation or the other party to an agreement to avoid an obligation on the ground that the corporate action is *ultra vires*.

Under MBCA Section 3.04, *ultra vires* may be asserted by only three types of persons: (1) by a shareholder seeking to enjoin a corporation from executing a proposed action that is *ultra vires*, (2) by

the corporation suing its management for damages caused by exceeding the corporation's powers, and (3) by the state's attorney general, who may have the power to enjoin an *ultra vires* act or to dissolve a corporation that exceeds its powers.

THE BOARD OF DIRECTORS

Introduction

Traditionally, the board of directors has had the power and the duty to manage the corporation. Yet in a large publicly held corporation, it is impossible for the board to manage the corporation on a day-to-day basis, since many of the directors are high-level executives in other corporations and devote most of their time to their other business interests. Therefore, MBCA Section 8.01 permits a corporation to be managed *under the direction of* the board of directors. Consequently, the board of directors delegates major responsibility for management to committees of the board such as an executive committee, to individual board members such as the chairman of the board, and to the officers of the corporation, especially the chief executive officer (CEO). In theory, the board supervises the actions of its committees, the chairman, and the officers to ensure that the board's policies are being carried out and that the delegatees are managing the corporation prudently. Figure 2 lists the results of a survey of directors concerning their primary responsibilities.

FIGURE 2 Primary Responsibilities of Directors

	Percent*
1. Assure integrity of corporation's operations	60%
2. Counsel top management	58
3. Assure strategic plan for the future	55
4. Monitor performance of the CEO	47
5. Assure management succession	43
6. Serve the public interest	15
7. Monitor financial reporting	9

*Percent of directors surveyed citing each responsibility.
Source: Survey of directors, published by Arthur Young Executive Resource Consultants in *The New Director: Changing Views of the Board's Role* (1989).

Board Powers under Corporation Statutes

By statute, the board of directors may take several corporate actions *by itself*, that is, without obtaining shareholder approval of the action. These powers include not only the board's general power to manage or direct the corporation, but also the power to issue shares of stock and to set the price of shares. Among its other powers, the board may repurchase shares, declare dividends, adopt and amend bylaws, elect and remove officers, and fill vacancies on the board.

Some corporate actions require *board initiative*. That is, board approval is necessary to *propose such actions to the shareholders* who then must approve the action. Board initiative is required for important changes in the corporation, such as amendment of the articles of incorporation; merger of the corporation; the sale of all or substantially all of the corporation's assets; and voluntary dissolution.

Committees of the Board

Most publicly held corporations have committees of the board of directors. These committees, which have fewer members than the board has, can more efficiently handle management decisions and exercise board powers than can a large board. Only directors may serve on board committees.

Although many board powers may be delegated to committees of the board, some decisions are so important that corporation statutes require their *approval by the board as a whole*. Under MBCA Section 8.25(e), the powers that may not be delegated concern important corporate actions such as declaring dividends, filling vacancies on the board or its committees, adopting and amending bylaws, approving issuances of shares, and approving repurchases of the corporation's shares.

Executive Committee   The most common board committee is the executive committee. It is usually given authority to act for the board on most matters when the board is not in session. Generally, it consists of the inside directors and perhaps one or two outside directors who can attend a meeting on short notice.[5] Historically, the executive committee has been the most important com-

mittee of the board. Today, its importance has diminished. It is likely to be used only for routine matters.

Other Committees   Other common board committees include audit, nominating, compensation, and shareholder litigation committees. The membership of these committees usually includes only outside directors in order to eliminate potential conflicts of interests that may exist if inside directors were to make decisions affecting their personal interests.

Audit committees recommend independent public accountants and supervise the public accountants' audit of the corporate financial records. The Securities and Exchange Commission (SEC) strongly encourages all publicly held firms to have audit committees comprising independent directors.

Nominating committees choose management's slate of directors that is to be submitted to shareholders at the annual election of directors. Nominating committees also often plan generally for management succession. The SEC encourages corporations to form nominating committees that wholly or largely comprise outside directors.

Compensation committees review and approve the salaries, bonuses, stock options, and other benefits of high-level corporate executives. Although compensation committees usually comprise directors who have no affiliation with the executives or directors whose compensation is being approved, compensation committees may also set the compensation of their members. Outside directors of most large publicly held firms are compensated by an annual retainer fee plus an attendance fee for each board or committee meeting attended. Figure 3 lists the nine corporations that pay the highest director's fees.

---

[5]The term *inside director* is applied to one who is an officer of a corporation or its affiliated corporation and devotes substantially full time to it. The term is also often applied to controlling shareholders who are not officers and to former officers. *Outside directors* have no such affiliations with the corporation.

FIGURE 3   Highest Average Total Director Compensation for 1988

ITT	$86,400
Sears	63,200
General Motors	58,917
Ford	57,750
Coastal	57,600
Dow Chemical	57,000
USX	55,833
Citicorp	53,759
RJR Nabisco	53,750

Source: Spencer Stuart.

A shareholder litigation committee is given the task of determining whether a corporation should sue someone who has allegedly harmed the corporation. Usually, the committee of disinterested directors is formed when a shareholder asks the board of directors to cause the corporation to sue some or all of the directors for mismanaging the corporation. The use of shareholder litigation committees is discussed more fully in the Shareholders' Rights and Liabilities chapter.

Powers, Rights, and Liabilities of Directors as Individuals

A director is not an agent of the corporation *merely* by being a director. The directors may manage the corporation only when they act as a board, unless the board of directors grants agency powers to the directors individually.

A director has the *right to inspect* corporate books and records that contain corporate information essential to the director's performance of her duties. The director's right of inspection is denied when the director has an interest adverse to the corporation, as in the case of a director who plans to sell a corporation's trade secrets to a competitor.

Normally, a director does not have any personal liability for the contracts and torts of the corporation.

ELECTION AND REMOVAL OF DIRECTORS

Qualifications of Directors

MBCA Section 8.02 states no qualifications for directors. Generally, any individual may serve as a director of a corporation. A director need not even be a shareholder. Nonetheless, a corporation is permitted to specify qualifications for directors in the articles of incorporation.

Number of Directors

A board of directors may not act unless it has the number of directors required by the state corporation law. MBCA Section 8.03 and several state corporation statutes require a minimum of one director, recognizing that in close corporations with a single shareholder-manager, additional board members are superfluous. Several statutes, including the New York statute, require at least three directors, unless there are fewer than three shareholders, in which case the corporation may have no fewer directors than it has shareholders.

A corporation may have more than the minimum number of directors required by the corporation statute. The articles of incorporation or bylaws will state the number of directors of the corporation. Most large publicly held corporations have boards with more than 10 members. For example, General Motors has 25, IBM has 24, and ITT has 13.

Election of Directors

Directors are elected by the shareholders at the annual shareholder meeting. Usually, each shareholder is permitted to vote for as many nominees as there are directors to be elected. The shareholder may cast as many votes for each nominee as he has shares. The top vote-getters among the nominees are elected as directors. This voting process, called **straight voting,** permits a holder of more than 50 percent of the shares of a corporation to dominate the corporation by electing a board of directors that will manage the corporation as he wants it to be managed.

Class Voting and Cumulative Voting   To avoid domination by a large shareholder, among other reasons, some corporations allow class voting or cumulative voting. **Class voting** may give certain classes of shareholders the right to elect a specified number of directors. **Cumulative voting** permits shareholders to multiply the number of their shares by the number of directors to be elected and to cast the resulting total of votes for one or more directors. As a result, cumulative voting may permit minority shareholders to obtain representation on the board of directors. Class voting, cumulative voting, and other shareholder voting rights are discussed in detail in the Shareholders' Rights and Liabilities chapter.

The Proxy Solicitation Process

Most individual investors purchase corporate shares in the public market to increase their wealth, not to elect or to influence the directors of corporations. Nearly all institutional investors—such as pension funds, mutual funds, and bank trust departments—have the same profit motive. Generally, they are passive investors with little interest in exercising their shareholder right to elect directors by attending shareholder meetings.

Once public ownership of the corporation's shares exceeds 50 percent, the corporation cannot conduct any business at its shareholder meetings unless some of the shares of these passive investors are voted. This is because the corporation will have a shareholder *quorum* requirement, which may require that 50 percent or more of the shares be voted for a shareholder vote to be valid. Since passive investors rarely attend shareholder meetings, the management of the corporation must solicit **proxies,**[6] if it wishes to have a valid shareholder vote. Shareholders who will not attend a shareholder meeting must be asked to appoint someone else to vote their shares for them. This is done by furnishing each such shareholder with a proxy to sign. The proxy designates a person who may vote the shares for the shareholder.

Management Solicitation of Proxies To ensure its *perpetuation in office* and the *approval of other matters* submitted for a shareholder vote, the corporation's management solicits proxies from shareholders for directors' elections and other important matters on which shareholders vote, such as mergers. The management designates an officer, a director, or some other person to vote the proxies received. The person who is designated to vote for the shareholder is also called a *proxy.* Typically, the chief executive officer (CEO) of the corporation, the president, or the chairman of the board of directors names the person who serves as the proxy.

Usually, the proxies are merely signed and returned by the public shareholders, including the institutional shareholders. Passive investors follow the **Wall Street rule:** either support management or sell the shares. As a result, management almost always receives enough votes from its proxy solicitation to ensure the reelection of directors and the approval of other matters submitted to the shareholders, even when other parties solicit proxies in opposition to management.

Effect on Corporate Governance Management's solicitation of proxies produces a result that is quite different from the theory of corporate management that directors serve as representatives of the shareholders. The CEO usually nominates directors of his choice, and they are almost always elected. The directors appoint officers chosen by the CEO. The CEO's nominees for director are not unduly critical of his programs or of his methods for carrying them out. This is particularly true if a large proportion of the directors are officers of the company and thus are more likely to be dominated by the CEO.

In such situations, the CEO, not the shareholders, selects the directors, and the CEO, not the board of directors, manages the corporation. Furthermore, the board of directors does not even function effectively as a representative of the shareholders in supervising and evaluating the CEO and the other officers of the corporation. The board members and the other officers, who are generally chosen by the CEO, are, in effect, subordinates of the CEO, even though, as is true in most publicly held corporations, the CEO is not a major shareholder of the corporation.

Improving Corporate Governance Proposals for improving corporate governance in public-issue corporations seek to develop a board that is capable of functioning independently of the CEO by changing the composition or the operation of the board of directors.

Independent Directors Some corporate governance critics propose that a federal agency such as the Securities and Exchange Commission appoint one or more directors to serve as watchdogs of the public interest. Other critics would require that shareholders elect at least a majority of directors without prior ties to the corporation, thus excluding shareholders, suppliers, and customers from the board. The New York Stock Exchange requires a minimum of two directors independent of management for its listed companies.

Codetermination Under codetermination, employee representatives constitute one third or more of the board. The corporation has two boards: a *supervisory board,* on which the employee representatives sit with the shareholder representatives, and a *managing board,* composed solely of corporate officers. Codetermination developed in post–World War II Germany, and it has spread through several countries of the European Economic Community. Recently, several American corporations, of which Chrysler is the best known, have put one or more *labor union representatives* on their boards.

Director Nominations Other proposals recommend changing the method by which directors are nominated for election. One proposal would encourage shareholders to make nominations for directors. Supporters of this proposal argue that in addition to reducing the influence of the CEO, it would also broaden the range of backgrounds represented on the board. The SEC recommends that publicly held corporations establish a nominating committee composed of outside directors. This proposal has broad support, and many publicly held corporations have already adopted it.

Board Staff The American Law Institute's Corporate Governance Project recommends that nonmanage-

---

[6]A proxy is usually a preprinted data processing form (computer card) with spaces for voting on matters submitted for a shareholder vote. See the Securities Regulation chapter for a discussion of the proxy requirements of the U.S. Securities and Exchange Commission.

ment directors be empowered to hire, at the corporation's expense, lawyers, accountants, and other experts to advise them on extraordinary problems arising in the exercise of their oversight function. By not relying on the CEO's staff, the board should be better able to exercise independent judgment.

Specialist Directors Ralph Nader and his associates propose that each board member be assigned to, if not especially chosen for, a special area of oversight responsibility, such as employee welfare, consumer protection, and environmental protection. Assignment of specific responsibilities to board committees would make the board of directors better informed and permit it to function more effectively.

Impact of Corporate Governance Proposals Mostly due to SEC and public pressures for changes in corporate governance, current boards of directors operate significantly differently from the boards of the 1960s and the early 1970s. Boards supervise officers more closely. More directors are outside rather than inside directors. Boards meet more frequently, and more important, they have working committees that assume specific responsibilities. In addition, today's directors *perceive* themselves as being more nearly independent of the CEO. As a consequence, they *are* more nearly independent of the CEO. See Figure 4.

Figure 4 Influence of Board on Key Management Decisions

	Strong*	Moderate*	None or Unknown*
Compensation of top management	71%	27%	2%
Mergers and acquisitions	62	33	5
Capital expenditures	32	60	8
Selection of senior executives	22	64	14
Long-range planning	21	70	9

*Percentage of directors surveyed citing the board's influence as strong, moderate, none, or unknown.

Source: Arthur Young Executive Resource Consultants survey of directors published in *The New Director: Changing Views of the Board's Role (1989).*

Term of Office

Directors usually hold office for only one year, but they may have longer terms. MBCA Section 8.06 permits *staggered terms* for directors. A corporation having a board of nine or more members may establish either two or three approximately equal classes of directors, with only one class of directors coming up for election at each annual shareholders' meeting. If there are two classes of directors, the directors serve two-year terms; if there are three classes, they serve three-year terms.

The original purpose of staggered terms was to permit continuity of management. Today, staggered terms are frequently used to make it difficult to remove existing directors. Someone who wants to replace management must mount successful proxy solicitation fights several years in a row. Staggered terms also frustrate the ability of minority shareholders to use cumulative voting to elect their representatives to the board of directors.

Vacancies on the Board

MBCA Section 8.10 permits the directors to fill vacancies on the board. A majority vote of the remaining directors is sufficient to select persons to serve out unexpired terms, even though the remaining directors are less than a quorum.[7]

Removal of Directors

Modern corporation statutes permit shareholders to remove directors *with or without cause*, unless the articles provide that directors may be removed only for cause. The rationale for the modern rule is that the shareholders should have the power to judge the fitness of directors at any time.

Most corporations have provisions in their articles authorizing the shareholders to remove directors *only for cause*. Cause for removal would include mismanagement or conflicts of interest. Before removal for cause, the director must be given notice and an opportunity for a hearing.

If a director has been elected by a class of shareholders or through cumulative voting, different rules apply.

---

[7]A quorum of directors is usually a majority of directors. Quorum requirements are discussed later in this chapter.

A director elected by a separate class of shareholders may be removed only by that class of shareholders, thereby protecting the voting rights of the class. A director elected by cumulative voting may not be removed if the votes cast against her removal would have been sufficient to elect her to the board, thereby protecting the voting rights of minority shareholders.

In the following case, a director—a minority shareholder—would not have been removed as a director had there been cumulative voting of shares.

LEHMAN v. PIONTKOWSKI

460 N.Y.S.2d 817 (N.Y. App. Div. 1983)

Jacob Lehman and Shlomo Piontkowski were surgeons who practiced together in a professional corporation. They were the directors and only shareholders, Lehman owning six shares and Piontkowski owning four shares. Each was an employee of the corporation. Piontkowski's employment contract granted to the board of directors of the corporation the power to terminate his employment for "personal misconduct of such a material nature as to be professionally detrimental to the corporation."

From 1977 to 1979, Lehman and Piontkowski disagreed on the distribution of the corporation's income. Dissatisfied with his share of the income, Piontkowski canceled surgery, informed his patients that he was on vacation, and planned to open his own office nearby.

Acting as president of the corporation, Lehman sent Piontkowski a letter stating that Piontkowski's actions violated his employment contract. As president, Lehman stated that he deemed these actions to be personal misconduct so material as to be professionally detrimental to the corporation.

At a special shareholder meeting, Lehman proposed that Piontkowski be removed as a director and voted his six shares to oust Piontkowski. Piontkowski did not vote his four shares. Lehman then nominated himself as sole director, voted his shares to elect himself sole director, and adjourned the shareholder meeting. Lehman then called the special directors' meeting to order and, as the sole director, dismissed Piontkowski as an employee.

Afterward, Lehman and the corporation sued Piontkowski, seeking to recover damages of $500,000 for Piontkowski's breach of contract by opening a competing medical practice. Piontkowski argued that his expulsion from the corporation was illegal and that therefore the corporation was not entitled to enforce the contract. The trial court denied Piontkowski's motion for summary judgment, and Piontkowski appealed.

Memorandum by the Court.   Piontkowski's expulsion as director and the termination of his employment were improper.

By letter, Piontkowski was informed that Lehman, as president, deemed Piontkowski's actions to be personal misconduct that was so material as to be professionally detrimental to the corporation. This opinion was not that of the board of directors, as was required by the employment contract, but rather was that of Lehman individually and as president of the corporation. The board had not formally met to make a determination that Piontkowski had committed detrimental misconduct as a material breach of the contract. Therefore, the letter was of no legal effect.

At the special shareholder meeting, Lehman's first order of business was to vote his majority of the shares to dismiss Piontkowski as a director. Such an act was of no effect in the present matter. The New York Business Corporation Law provides that "the number of directors . . . shall not be less than three, except that where all the shares of a corporation are owned . . . by less than three shareholders, the number of directors may be less than three but not less than the number of shareholders."

Here there were two shareholders at the commencement of the special shareholder meeting. Piontkowski's expulsion as a director and the election of Lehman as the sole director were therefore improper. The removal of Piontkowski as a director left the corporation with only one director and without a validly constituted board of directors. The New York statute prohibits such an occurrence. The subsequent act of an illegally constituted one-man board of directors in terminating Piontkowski's employment was invalid.

As Piontkowski's unilateral expulsion from the corporation was illegal, the corporation is not entitled to enforce Piontkowski's employment contract.

Judgment reversed in favor of Piontkowski.

DIRECTORS' MEETINGS

Traditionally, directors could act only when they were properly convened as a board. They could not vote by proxy or informally, as by telephone. This rule was based on a belief in the value of consultation and collective judgment.

Today, the corporation laws of a majority of the states and MBCA Section 8.21 specifically permit action by the directors without a meeting if all of the directors consent in writing to the action taken. Such authorization is useful for dealing with routine matters or for formally approving an action based on an earlier policy decision made after full discussion. Close corporations are more likely to take advantage of this method of action than are large public corporations that hold monthly meetings of the board.

MBCA Section 8.20 permits a board to meet by telephone or television hookup. This section permits a meeting of directors who may otherwise be unable to convene. The only requirement is that the directors be able to hear one another simultaneously.

Directors are entitled to reasonable notice of all *special* meetings, but not of regularly scheduled meetings. Most of the corporation statutes require that the notice for a special meeting state the purpose of the meeting, but the MBCA does not. A director's attendance at a meeting *waives* any required notice, unless at the beginning of the meeting the director objects to the lack of notice.

For the directors to act, a *quorum* of the directors must be present. The quorum requirement ensures that the decision of the board will represent the views of a substantial portion of the directors. MBCA Section 8.24 provides that a quorum shall be a *majority* of the number of directors, unless the articles or bylaws states a number that is no fewer than one third of the number of directors.

Each director has *one vote*. If a quorum is present, a vote of a majority of the directors present is an act of the board, unless the articles or the bylaws require the vote of a greater number of directors. Such *supermajority voting provisions* are common in close corporations but not in publicly held corporations. The use of supermajority voting provisions by close corporations is covered later in this chapter.

OFFICERS OF THE CORPORATION

Appointment of Officers

The board of directors has the authority to appoint the officers of the corporation. Most of the corporation statutes provide that the officers of a corporation shall be the *president*, one or more *vice presidents*, a *secretary*, and a *treasurer*. Some of the statutes permit fewer than four officers, and most allow more than four. Usually, any two or more offices may be held by the same person, except for the offices of president and secretary. Since some corporate documents must be signed by both the president and the secretary, the prohibition against having one person hold both offices provides a measure of safety by ensuring that no single individual can execute such documents.

MBCA Section 8.40 grants the corporation unusual flexibility in determining the number of its officers. The section requires only that there be an officer performing the duties normally granted to a corporate secretary. Under the MBCA, one person may hold several offices, including the offices of president and secretary.

Authority of Officers

The officers are agents of the corporation. As agents, officers have *express authority* conferred on them by the bylaws or the board of directors. In addition, officers have *implied authority* to do the things that are reasonably necessary to accomplish their express duties. Also, officers have *apparent authority* when the corporation leads third parties to believe reasonably that the officers have authority to act for the corporation. Like any principal, the corporation may *ratify* the unauthorized acts of its officers. This may be done expressly by a resolution of the board of directors or impliedly by the board's acceptance of the benefits of the officer's acts.

Inherent Authority The most perplexing issue with regard to the authority of officers is whether an officer has *inherent authority* merely by virtue of the title of his office. Courts have held that certain *official titles confer authority* on officers, but such powers are much more restricted than you might expect.

Traditionally, a *president* possesses no power to bind the corporation by virtue of the office. Instead, she serves merely as the presiding officer at shareholder meetings and directors' meetings. Fewer problems arise in assessing the authority of a president with an additional title such as *general manager* or *chief executive officer*. Titles of this kind give the officer broad implied authority to make contracts and to do other acts in the ordinary business of the corporation.

A *vice president* has no authority by virtue of that office. An executive who is vice president of a specified department, however, such as a vice president of marketing, will have the authority to transact the normal corporate business falling within the function of the department.

The *secretary* usually keeps the minutes of directors' and shareholder meetings, maintains other corporate records, retains custody of the corporate seal, and certifies corporate records as being authentic. The secretary has no authority to make contracts for the corporation by virtue of that office. Nonetheless, the corporation is bound by documents certified by the secretary. For example, a corporation is bound by a board resolution certified by the secretary stating the president's authority to contract for the corporation even if the resolution was not properly adopted by the board.

The *treasurer* has custody of the corporation's funds. He is the proper officer to receive payments to the corporation and to disburse corporate funds for authorized purposes. The treasurer binds the corporation by his receipts, checks, and indorsements, but he does not by virtue of that office alone have authority to borrow money, to issue negotiable instruments, or to make other contracts on behalf of the corporation.

Officer Liability Like any agent, a corporate officer ordinarily has *no liability on contracts* that she makes on behalf of her principal, the corporation. To avoid personal liability on corporate contracts, an officer should make clear that she signs for the corporation and not in her individual capacity. However, an officer who acts within her apparent authority, but beyond her actual authority, will be liable to the corporation for resulting losses for *exceeding her actual authority*.

Employees of the corporation who are not officers may also be empowered to act as agents for the corporation. The usual rules of agency apply to their relationships with the corporation and with third parties.

Termination of Officers Officers serve the corporation at the pleasure of the board of directors, which may remove an officer at any time with or without cause. An officer who has been removed without cause has no recourse against the corporation, unless the removal violates an employment contract between the officer and the corporation.

MANAGING CLOSE CORPORATIONS

Many of the management formalities that you have studied in this chapter are appropriate for publicly held corporations, yet inappropriate for close corporations. Close corporations tend to be more loosely managed than public corporations. For example, they may have few board meetings. Frequently, each shareholder wants to be involved in management of the close corporation, or if he is not involved in management, he wants to protect his interests by placing *restrictions on the managerial discretion* of those who do manage the corporation.

Initially, courts struggled with the management problems of close corporations, attempting to solve those problems by applying traditional corporation law, which was designed with the publicly held corporation in mind. In recent years, however, courts and legislatures have adopted rules that respond to the special management problems of close corporations. These rules are designed to *reduce management formalities* and to *prevent the domination of minority shareholders*.

Reducing Management Formalities

Modern close corporation statutes permit close corporations to dispense with most, if not all, management formalities. Section 10 of the Statutory Close Corporation Supplement to the MBCA permits a close corporation to *dispense with a board of directors* and to be *managed by the shareholders*. California General Corporation Law Section 300 permits the close corporation to be managed *as if it were a partnership*.

Preventing Domination

A minority shareholder of a close corporation may be dominated by the shareholders who control the board of directors. These shareholders may dominate by dismissing the dominated shareholder as an employee or by paying her a lower salary than is paid to the dominating shareholder-employees. To prevent such domination, close corporation shareholders have resorted to two devices: *supermajority voting requirements* for board actions and *restrictions on the managerial discretion* of the board of directors.

Supermajority Director Voting   Any corporation may require that board action be possible only with the approval of more than a majority of the directors, such as three fourths or unanimous approval. Supermajority voting requirements are uncommon in publicly held corporations, but their ability to protect valuable interests of minority shareholders makes their use in close corporations almost mandatory. A supermajority vote is often required to terminate the employment contract of an employee-shareholder, to reduce the level of dividends, and to change the corporation's line of business. Supermajority votes are rarely required for ordinary business matters, such as deciding with which suppliers the corporation should deal.

Restrictions on Board Discretion   Traditionally, shareholders could not restrict the managerial discretion of directors. This rule recognized the traditional roles of the board as manager and of the shareholders as passive owners. Modern close corporation statutes permit shareholders to intrude into the sanctity of the boardroom. In Section 11, the Statutory Close Corporation Supplement grants the shareholders *unlimited* power to restrict the discretion of the board of directors. For example, the shareholders may agree that the directors may not fire or reduce the salaries of employee-shareholders and may not lower or eliminate dividends. And, as was stated above, close corporation statutes even permit the shareholders to dispense with a board of directors altogether and to manage the close corporation as if it were a partnership.

DIRECTORS' AND OFFICERS' DUTIES TO THE CORPORATION

Introduction

Directors and officers are in positions of trust and therefore owe *fiduciary duties* to the corporation. These duties are similar to the duties that an agent owes his principal. They are the duties to act within the authority of the position and within the objectives and powers of the corporation, to act with due care in conducting the affairs of the corporation, and to act with loyalty to the corporation.

Acting within Authority

Like any agent, an officer or director has a duty to act *within the authority* conferred on her by the articles of incorporation, the bylaws, and the board of directors. As discussed above in the section on corporate objectives, ordinarily the directors and officers must manage the corporation in the best interests of the corporation. In addition, as discussed in the section on the *ultra vires* doctrine, the directors and officers must act within the scope of the powers of the corporation. An officer or a director may be liable to the corporation if it is damaged by an act exceeding that person's or the corporation's authority.

Duty of Care

Directors and officers are liable for losses to the corporation resulting from their lack of *care or diligence*. MBCA Sections 8.30 and 8.42 are typical of modern statutes, which expressly state the standard of care that

(a) A director shall discharge his duties as a director, including his duties as a member of a committee:

(1) in good faith;

(2) with the care an ordinarily prudent person in a like position would exercise under similar circumstances; and

(3) in a manner he reasonably believes to be in the best interests of the corporation.

(b) The articles of incorporation may set forth:

(4) a provision eliminating or limiting the liability of a director to the corporation or its shareholders for money damages for any action taken or any failure to take any action, as a director, except liability for

(A) the amount of financial benefit received by a director to which he is not entitled;

(B) an intentional infliction of harm on the corporation or the shareholders;

(C) a violation of Section 8.33 [illegal payment of dividends]; or

(D) an intentional violation of criminal law.

must be exercised by directors and officers. Section 8.30 appears in Figure 5.

Prudent Person Standard Managers need merely meet the standard of the ordinarily prudent *person* in the same circumstances, a standard focusing on the basic manager attributes of common sense, practical wisdom, and informed judgment. The duty of care does *not* hold directors and officers to the standard of a prudent businessperson, a person of some undefined level of business skill. A director's or officer's performance is evaluated at the time of the decision, thereby preventing the application of hindsight in judging her performance.

Good Faith and Reasonable Belief The MBCA duty of care test requires that a director or officer make a *reasonable investigation* and *honestly believe* that her decision is in the best interests of the corporation. For example, the board of directors decides to purchase an existing manufacturing business for $15 million without inquiring into the value of the business or examining its past financial performance. Although the directors may believe that they made a prudent decision, they have no reasonable basis for that belief. Therefore, if the plant is worth only $5 million, the directors will be liable to the corporation for its damages—$10 million—for breaching the duty of care.

Recent Changes In response to insurance companies' increasing unwillingness to insure directors and officers for breaches of their duty of care (and the resulting exodus of outside directors from corporate boards of directors), many state legislatures changed the wording of the duty of care, typically imposing liability only for willful or wanton misconduct or for gross negligence. While seemingly changing the duty of care, most of the changes are largely window dressing and nonsubstan-

tive, since courts—applying the business judgment rule—have imposed liability only for grossly negligent decisions. The business judgment rule is discussed in detail in the next section.

Changes in some statutes, however, are more substantial. For example, Ohio protects directors from monetary liability except when clear and convincing evidence demonstrates the directors' deliberate intent to injure the corporation or the directors' reckless disregard for its welfare. Delaware corporation law and MBCA Section 2.02(b)(4) allow corporations to amend their articles to reduce or eliminate directors' liability for monetary damages for breaches of the duty of care. Figure 6 contains the MBCA provision.

The Business Judgment Rule

Absent bad faith, fraud, or breach of fiduciary duty, the judgment of the board of directors is conclusive. This is the **business judgment rule.** When directors and officers have complied with the business judgment rule, they are protected from liability to the corporation for their unwise decisions. The business judgment rule precludes the courts from substituting their business judgment for that of the corporation's managers. The business judgment rule recognizes that the directors and officers—not the shareholders and the courts—are best able to make business judgments and should not ordinarily be vulnerable to second-guessing. Shareholders and the courts are ill-equipped to make better business decisions than those made by the officers and directors of a corporation, who have more business experience and are more familiar with the needs, strengths, and limitations of the corporation.

Purpose of Business Judgment Rule

The business judgment rule is designed to encourage persons to become corporate managers and to encourage them to make difficult business decisions. Boards of directors and officers continually make decisions involving the balancing of risks and benefits to the corporation. With the advantage of hindsight, some of these decisions may appear unwise. Such a result, however, should not by itself provide the basis for imposing personal liability on directors and officers.

Elements of the Business Judgment Rule

Three requirements must be met for the business judgment rule to protect a manager from liability:

1. The manager must make an informed decision.
2. The manager may have no conflicts of interest.
3. The manager must have a rational basis for his decision.

Managers must make an *informed decision*. They must take the steps necessary to become informed about the relevant facts before making a decision. These steps may include merely listening to a proposal, reviewing written materials, or making inquiries. Managers may rely on information collected and presented by other persons. In essence, the informed-decision component means that managers should do their homework if they want the protection of the business judgment rule.

Managers must be *free from conflicts of interest*. The managers may not benefit personally—other than as shareholders—when they transact on behalf of the corporation.

Managers must have a *rational basis* for believing that the decision is in the best interests of the corporation. This is the most difficult element to understand, for it seemingly contradicts the most fundamental aspect of the business judgment rule, namely, that the courts may not judge the correctness, wisdom, or reasonableness of the managers' decision.

Based on courts' statements of the business judgment rule, it appears that the rational basis element requires only that the managers' decision have a *logical connection to the facts* revealed by a reasonable investigation or that the decision *not be manifestly unreasonable*. Some courts have held that the directors' wrongdoing must amount to *gross negligence* for the directors to lose the protection of the business judgment rule.

When Business Judgment Rule Is Inapplicable

If the business judgment rule *does not apply* because one or more of its elements are missing, a court may *substitute its judgment* for that of the managers. If the court finds that the managers made an unwise decision that harmed the corporation, it may impose liability on the managers and order them to pay damages to the corporation. In addition, the court may award equitable relief, such as an injunction or rescission of the wrongful action.

Nonetheless, courts rarely refuse to apply the business judgment rule. As a result, the rule has been criticized frequently as providing too much protection for the managers of corporations. In one famous case, the court applied the business judgment rule to protect a 1965 decision made by the board of directors of the Chicago Cubs not to install lights and not to hold night baseball games at Wrigley Field.[8] Yet the business judgment rule is so flexible that it protected the decision of the Cubs' board of directors to install lights in 1988. The *Van Gorkom* case, noted in Figure 7, is one of the few cases that have held directors liable for failing to comply with the business judgment rule.

---

[8]*Shlensky v. Wrigley*, 237 N.E.2d 776 (Ill. Ct. App. 1968).

FIGURE 7   Note on *Smith v. Van Gorkom**

In *Smith v. Van Gorkom* (also referred to as the *Trans Union* case), the Supreme Court of Delaware seemingly limited the scope of protection of the business judgment rule. In that case, the court found that the business judgment rule did not apply to the board's approval of an acquisition of the corporation for $55 per share. The board approved the acquisition after only two hours' consideration. The board received no documentation to support the adequacy of the $55 price. Instead, it relied entirely on a 20-minute *oral* report of the chairman of the board. No written summary of the acquisition was presented to the board. The directors failed to obtain an investment banker's report, prepared after careful consideration, that the acquisition price was fair.

*488 A.2d 858 (Del. Sup. Ct. 1985).

FIGURE 7   *(concluded)*

In addition, the court held that the mere fact that the acquisition price exceeded the market price by $17 per share did not legitimize the board's decision. The board had frequently made statements prior to the acquisition that the market had undervalued the shares, yet the board took no steps to determine the intrinsic value of the shares. Consequently, the court found that at a minimum, the directors had been grossly negligent.

Van Gorkom has been heralded as restricting the application of the business judgment rule and imposing higher standards on directors. It is the only case in which the directors have been held personally liable for damages for selling the company at a large cash premium over market price. On the other hand, *Van Gorkom* has been described as "surely one of the worst decisions in the history of corporate law."[†] The increased unwillingness of insurance companies to insure directors and officers for breaches of the duty of care is in part due to the *Van Gorkom* decision. The decision is also at least partly responsible for recent state legislation limiting the liability of directors for violating the duty of care.

†Fischel, *The Business Judgment Rule and the Trans Union Case*, 40 Bus. Law. 1437, 1455 (1985).

Opposition to Acquisition of Control of a Corporation

In the last 25 years, many outsiders have attempted to acquire control of publicly held corporations. Typically, these outsiders (called **raiders**) will make a **tender offer** for the shares of a corporation (called the **target**). A tender offer is an offer to the shareholders to buy their shares at a price above the current market price. The raider hopes to acquire a majority of the shares, which will give it control of the target corporation.[9]

Most tender offers are opposed by the target corporation's management. The defenses to tender offers are many and varied, and they carry interesting names, such as the Pac-Man defense, the white knight, greenmail, the poison pill, and the lock-up option. See Figure 8 for definitions of these defenses.

When takeover defenses are successful, shareholders of the target may lose the opportunity to sell their shares at a price up to twice the market price of the shares prior to the announcement of the hostile bid. Frequently, the loss of this opportunity upsets shareholders, who then decide to sue the directors who have opposed the tender offer. Shareholders contend that the directors have opposed the tender offer only to preserve their corporate positions. Shareholders also argue that the target corporation's interests would have been better served if the tender offer had succeeded.

Generally, courts have refused to find directors liable for opposing a tender offer because the business judgment rule applies to a board's decision to oppose a tender offer, provided the board made an informed decision, had no conflicts of interest, and had a rational basis for its decision to oppose the tender offer. Many courts have held that directors are able to separate their interest in remaining directors from the best interests of the corporation. Therefore, a conflict of interest does not arise automatically when directors oppose a tender offer.

Nonetheless, the business judgment rule will not apply when the directors make a decision to oppose the tender offer before they have carefully studied it. In addition, if the directors' actions indicate that they opposed the tender offer in order to preserve their jobs, they will be liable to the corporation.

Recent court decisions have seemingly modified the business judgment rule as it is applied in the tender offer context. For example, a May 1985 decision of the Delaware Supreme Court, *Unocal Corp. v. Mesa Petroleum Co.*,[10] upheld the application of the business judgment rule to a board's decision to block a hostile tender offer by making a tender offer for its own shares that excluded the raider.[11] But in so ruling, the court held that the board does not have "unbridled discretion to defeat any perceived threat by any Draconian means available," but may use those defense tactics that are *reasonable* compared to the takeover threat. The board may consider a variety of concerns, including the "inadequacy of the price offered, nature and timing of the offer, questions of illegality, the

---

[9]Tender offer regulation is covered in the Securities Regulation chapter.

[10]493 A.2d 946 (Del. Sup. Ct. 1985).

[11]Discriminatory tender offers are now illegal pursuant to Securities Act Rule 13e-4. The rules regarding tender offers are addressed in the Securities Regulation chapter.

FIGURE 8 Tender Offer Defenses

<table>
<tr>
<td>

Pac-Man

The target corporation turns the tables on the tender offeror or raider (which often is another publicly held corporation) by making a tender offer for the raider's shares. As a result, two tender offerors are trying to buy each other's shares. This is similar to the Pac-Man video game, in which Pac-Man and his enemies chase each other.

</td>
<td>

Lock-Up Option

Used in conjunction with a white knight to ensure the success of the white knight's bid. The target and the white knight agree that the white knight will buy a highly valuable asset of the target at a very attractive price for the white knight (usually a below-market price) if the raider succeeds in taking over the target. For example, in the *Revlon* case, Revlon gave a lock-up option to Forstmann to reduce the amount of profit that Pantry Pride would make had it completed its takeover of Revlon.

</td>
</tr>
<tr>
<td>

Greenmail

The target's repurchase of its shares from the raider at a substantial profit to the raider, upon the condition that the raider sign a standstill agreement in which it promises not to buy additional shares of the target for a stated period of time.

</td>
<td rowspan="2">

Poison Pill

Also called a shareholders' rights plan. There are many types, but the typical poison pill involves the target's issuance of a new class of preferred shares to its common shareholders. The preferred shares have rights (share options) attached to them. These rights allow the target's shareholders to purchase shares of the raider or shares of the target at less than fair market value. The poison pill deters hostile takeover attempts by threatening the raider and its shareholders with severe dilutions in the value of the shares they hold.

</td>
</tr>
<tr>
<td>

White Knight

A friendly tender offeror whom management prefers over the original tender offeror–called a black knight. The white knight rescues the corporation from the black knight (the raider) by offering more money for the corporation's shares. In the *Revlon* case that appeared earlier in the chapter, Forstmann was a white knight for Revlon.

</td>
</tr>
</table>

impact on 'constituencies' other than shareholders (i.e., creditors, customers, employees, and perhaps even the community generally), the risk of nonconsummation, and the quality of securities being offered in the exchange."[12]

In *Unocal*, the threat was a two-tier, highly coercive tender offer. In the typical two-tier offer, the raider first offers cash for a majority of the shares. After acquiring a majority of the shares, the offeror initiates the second tier, in which the remaining shareholders are forced to sell their shares for a package of securities less attractive than the first tier. Because shareholders fear that they will be forced to take the less attractive second-tier securities if they fail to tender during the first tier, shareholders—including those who oppose the offer—are coerced in to tendering during the first tier. *Unocal* and later cases specifically authorize the use of defenses to defeat a coercive two-tier tender offer.

Since its decision in *Unocal*, the Supreme Court of Delaware has applied this modified business judgment rule to validate a poison pill tender offer defense tactic in *Moran v. Household Int'l, Inc.*[13] and to invalidate a lock-up option tender offer defense in the *Revlon* case, which appears earlier in this chapter. These cases confirmed the *Unocal* holding that the board of directors must show that:

1. It had reasonable grounds to believe that a danger to corporate policy and effectiveness was posed by the takeover attempt.

2. It acted primarily to protect the corporation and its shareholders from that danger.

3. The defense tactic was reasonable in relation to the threat posed to the corporation.

Such a standard appeared to impose a higher standard on directors than the rational basis requirement of

---

[12]493 A.2d at 955.

[13]500 A.2d 346 (Del. Sup. Ct. 1985).

the business judgment rule, which historically has been interpreted to require only that a decision of a board not be manifestly unreasonable. In addition, the *Revlon* case required the board to establish an auction market for the company and to sell it to the highest bidder when the directors have abandoned the long-term business objectives of the company by embracing a bust-up of the company.

In 1990, in the following case, the Supreme Court of Delaware expanded board discretion in fighting hostile takeovers, holding that a board may oppose a hostile takeover provided the board had a *pre-existing, deliberately conceived corporate plan* justifying its opposition. The existence of such a plan enabled Time's board to meet the rational-basis element of the business judgment rule.

PARAMOUNT COMMUNICATIONS, INC. v. TIME, INC.
571 A.2d 1140 (Del. Sup. Ct. 1989)

Since 1983, Time, Inc., had considered expanding its business beyond publishing magazines and books, owning Home Box Office and Cinemax, and operating television stations. In 1988, Time's board approved in principle a strategic plan for Time's acquisition of an entertainment company. The board gave management permission to negotiate a merger with Warner Communications, Inc. The board's consensus was that a merger of Time and Warner was feasible, but only if Time controlled the resulting corporation, preserving the editorial integrity of Time's magazines. The board concluded that Warner was the superior candidate because Warner could make movies and TV shows for HBO, Warner had an international distribution system, Warner was a giant in the music business, Time and Warner would control half of New York City's cable TV system, and the Time network could promote Warner's movies.

Negotiations with Warner broke down when Warner refused to agree to Time dominating the combined companies. Time continued to seek expansion, but informal discussions with other companies terminated when it was suggested the other companies purchase Time or control the resulting board. In January 1989, Warner and Time resumed negotiations, and on March 4, 1989, agreed to a combination by which Warner shareholders would own 62 percent of the resulting corporation, to be named Time-Warner. To retain the editorial integrity of Time, the merger agreement provided for a board committee dominated by Time representatives.

On June 7, 1989, Paramount Communications, Inc., announced a cash tender offer for all of Time's shares at $175 per share. (The day before, Time shares traded at $126 per share.) Time's financial advisers informed the outside directors that Time's auction value was materially higher than $175 per share. The board concluded that Paramount's $175 offer was inadequate. Also, the board viewed the Paramount offer as a threat to Time's control of its own destiny and retention of the Time editorial policy; the board found that a combination with Warner offered greater potential for Time.

In addition, concerned that shareholders would not comprehend the long-term benefits of the merger with Warner, on June 16, 1989, Time's board recast its acquisition with Warner into a two-tier acquisition, in which it would make a tender offer to buy 51 percent of Warner's shares for cash immediately and later buy the remaining 49 percent for cash and securities. The tender offer would eliminate the need for Time to obtain shareholder approval of the transaction.

On June 23, 1989, Paramount raised its offer to $200 per Time share. Three days later, Time's board rejected the offer as a threat to Time's survival and its editorial integrity; the board viewed the Warner acquisition as offering greater long-term value for the shareholders. Time shareholders and Paramount then sued Time and its board to enjoin Time's acquisition of Warner. The trial court held for Time. Paramount and Time shareholders appealed to the Supreme Court of Delaware.

Horsey, Justice.   Our decision does not require us to pass on the wisdom of the board's decision. That is not a court's task. Our task is simply to determine whether there is sufficient evidence to support the initial Time-Warner agreement as the product of a proper exercise of business judgment.

We have purposely detailed the evidence of the Time board's deliberative approach, beginning in 1983–84, to expand itself. Time's decision in 1988 to combine with Warner was made only after what could be fairly characterized as an exhaustive appraisal of Time's future as a corporation. Time's board was convinced that Warner would provide the best fit for Time to achieve its strategic objectives. The record attests to the zealousness of Time's executives, fully supported by their directors, in seeing to the preservation of Time's perceived editorial integrity in journalism. The Time board's decision to expand the business of the company through its March 4 merger with Warner was entitled to the protection of the business judgment rule.

The revised June 16 agreement was defense-motivated and designed to avoid the potentially disruptive effect that Paramount's offer would have had on consummation of the proposed merger were it put to a shareholder vote. Thus, we decline to apply the traditional business judgment rule to the revised transaction and instead analyze the Time board's June 16 decision under *Unocal*.

In *Unocal*, we held that before the business judgment rule is applied to a board's adoption of a defensive measure, the burden will lie with the board to prove (a) reasonable grounds for believing that a danger to corporate policy and effectiveness existed; and (b) that the defensive measure adopted was reasonable in relation to the threat posed.

Paramount argues a hostile tender offer can pose only two types of threats: the threat of coercion that results from a two-tier offer promising unequal treatment for nontendering shareholders; and the threat of inadequate value from an all-shares, all-cash offer at a price below what a target board in good faith deems to be the present value of its shares.

Paramount would have us hold that only if the value of Paramount's offer were determined to be clearly inferior to the value created by management's plan to merge with Warner could the offer be viewed—objectively—as a threat.

Paramount's position represents a fundamental misconception of our standard of review under *Unocal* principally because it would involve the court in substituting its judgment as to what is a "better" deal for that of a corporation's board of directors. The usefulness of *Unocal* as an analytical tool is precisely its flexibility in the face of a variety of fact scenarios. Thus, directors may consider, when evaluating the threat posed by a takeover bid, the inadequacy of the price offered, nature and timing of the offer, questions of illegality, the impact on constituencies other than shareholders, the risk of nonconsummation, and the quality of securities being offered in the exchange.

The Time board reasonably determined that inadequate value was not the only threat that Paramount's all-cash, all-shares offer could present. Time's board concluded that Paramount's offer posed other threats. One concern was that Time shareholders might elect to tender into Paramount's cash offer in ignorance or a mistaken belief of the strategic benefit which a business combination with Warner might produce.

Paramount also contends that Time's board had not duly investigated Paramount's offer. We find that Time explored the available entertainment companies, including Paramount, before determining that Warner provided the best strategic "fit." In addition, Time's board rejected Paramount's offer because Paramount did not serve Time's objectives or meet Time's needs. Time's board was adequately informed of the potential benefits of a transaction with Paramount. Time's failure to negotiate cannot be fairly found to have been uninformed. The evidence supporting this finding is materially enhanced by the fact that twelve of Time's sixteen board members were outside independent directors.

We turn to the second part of the *Unocal* analysis. The obvious requisite to determining the reasonableness of a defensive action is a clear identification of the nature of the threat. This requires an evaluation of the importance of the corporate objective threatened; alternative methods of protecting that objective; impacts of the defensive action, and other relevant factors.

The fiduciary duty to manage a corporate enterprise includes the selection of a time frame for achievement of corporate goals. Directors are not obliged to abandon a deliberately conceived corporate plan for a short-term shareholder profit unless there is clearly no basis to sustain the corporate strategy. Time's responsive action to Paramount's tender offer was not aimed at "cramming down" on its shareholders a management-sponsored alternative, but rather had as its goal the carrying forward of a pre-existing transaction in an altered form. Thus, the response was reasonably related to the threat. The revised agreement did not preclude Paramount from making an offer for the combined Time-Warner company or from changing the conditions of its offer so as not to make the offer dependent upon the nullification of the Time-Warner agreement. Thus, the response was proportionate.

Judgment for Time affirmed.

Shareholder Derivative Suits A special application of the business judgment rule is made in the context of directors terminating a derivative suit by a shareholder of a corporation. Such a use of the business judgment rule is discussed in the shareholders' rights portion of the Shareholders' Rights and Liabilities chapter.

Duties of Loyalty

Directors and officers owe a duty of *utmost loyalty and fidelity* to the corporation. Judge Benjamin Cardozo stated this duty of trust. He declared that a director:

owes loyalty and allegiance to the corporation—a loyalty that is undivided and an allegiance that is influenced by no consideration other than the welfare of the corporation. Any adverse interest of a director will be subjected to a scrutiny rigid and uncompromising. He may not profit at the expense of his corporation and in conflict with its rights; he may not for personal gain divert unto himself the opportunities which in equity and fairness belong to his corporation.[14]

Directors and officers owe the corporation the same duties of loyalty that agents owe their principals, though many of these duties have special names in corporation law. The most important of these duties of loyalty are the duties not to *self-deal*, not to *usurp a corporate oppor-*

tunity, not to *oppress minority shareholders*, and not to *trade on inside information*.

Self-Dealing with the Corporation

When a director or officer *self-deals* with his corporation, the director or officer has a **conflict of interest** and may prefer his own interests over those of the corporation. The director's or officer's interest may be *direct*, such as his interest in selling his land to the corporation, or it may be *indirect*, such as his interest in having another business of which he is an owner, director, or officer supply goods to the corporation. When a director has a conflict of interest, the director's transaction with the corporation may be voided or rescinded.

Intrinsic Fairness Standard Under MBCA Section 8.31, a self-dealing transaction will not be voided merely on the grounds of a director's conflict of interest when any one of the following is true:

1. The transaction has been approved by a majority of informed, disinterested directors,
2. The transaction has been approved by a majority of the shares held by informed, disinterested shareholders, or
3. The transaction is fair to the corporation.

Nonetheless, even when disinterested directors' or shareholders' approval has been obtained, courts will

---

[14]*Meinhard v. Salmon*, 164 N.E.2d 545, 546 (N.Y. Ct. App. 1928).

void a conflict-of-interest transaction that is unfair to the corporation. This is true even when the approval of the disinterested directors is accorded deference under the business judgment rule. Therefore, every corporate transaction in which a director has a conflict of interest must be fair to the corporation. If the transaction is fair, the self-dealing (interested) director is excused from liability to the corporation.[15]

A transaction is fair if reasonable persons in an *arm's-length bargain* would have bound the corporation to it. This standard is often called the **intrinsic fairness standard.**

Effect of Board or Shareholder Approval

The function of disinterested director or disinterested shareholder approval of a conflict-of-interest transaction is merely to shift the burden of proving unfairness. Under the MBCA, the burden of proving fairness lies initially on the interested director. The burden of proof shifts to the corporation that is suing the officer or director for self-dealing if the transaction was approved by the board of directors or the shareholders. Nonetheless, when disinterested directors approve a self-dealing transaction, substantial deference is given to the decision in accordance with the business judgment rule, especially when the disinterested directors compose a majority of the board.

Effect of Unanimous Shareholder Approval

Generally, *unanimous* approval of a self-dealing transaction by informed shareholders *conclusively* releases an interested director or officer from liability for self-dealing even if the transaction is unfair to the corporation. The rationale for this rule is that fully informed shareholders should know what is best for themselves and their corporation.

Loans to Directors

Under early corporation law, *loans* by the corporation *to directors or officers* were illegal, on the grounds that such loans might result in the looting of corporate assets. Modern corporation statutes, like MBCA 8.32, allow loans to directors only after certain procedures have been followed. Either the shareholders must approve the loan, or the directors, after finding that the loan benefits the corporation, must approve it.

---

[15]The MBCA conflict-of- interest rules do not apply to officers. Instead, general agency rules apply to an officer having a conflict of interest.

Parent-Subsidiary Transactions Self-dealing is a concern when a parent corporation *dominates* a subsidiary corporation. Often, the subsidiary's directors will be directors or officers of the parent also. When persons with dual directorships approve transactions between the parent and the subsidiary, the opportunity for *overreaching* arises. There may be *no arm's-length bargaining* between the two corporations. Hence, such transactions must meet the *intrinsic fairness* test.

Usurpation of a Corporate Opportunity

Directors and officers may steal not only assets of their corporations (such as computer hardware and software) but also *opportunities* that their corporations could have exploited. Both types of theft are equally wrongful. As fiduciaries, directors and officers are liable to their corporation for **usurping corporate opportunities.**

The opportunity must come to the director or officer *in her corporate capacity.* Clearly, opportunities received at the corporate offices are received by the manager in her corporate capacity. In addition, courts hold that CEOs and other high-level officers are nearly always acting in their corporate capacities, even when they are away from their corporate offices.

The opportunity must have a *relation or connection* to an *existing or prospective* corporate activity. Some courts apply the *line of business test*, considering how closely related the opportunity is to the lines of business in which the corporation is engaged. Other courts use the *interest or expectancy test*, requiring the opportunity to relate to property in which the corporation has an existing interest or in which it has an expectancy growing out of an existing right.

The corporation must be able *financially* to take advantage of the opportunity. Managers are required to make a good faith effort to obtain external financing for the corporation, but they are not required to use their personal funds to enable the corporation to take advantage of the opportunity.

A director or officer is free to exploit an opportunity that has been rejected by the corporation. Generally, an informed, disinterested majority of the directors may reject an opportunity unless rejection by the board is manifestly unreasonable. Informed, disinterested shareholders may also reject an opportunity.

In the following case, the court found that an opportunity to become the manufacturer of Pepsi-Cola syrup was usurped by the president of a corporation that manufactured beverage syrups and operated soda fountains.

GUTH v. LOFT, INC.

5 A.2d 503 (Del. Sup. Ct. 1939)

Loft, Inc., manufactured and sold candies, syrups, and beverages and operated 115 retail candy and soda fountain stores. Loft sold Coca-Cola at all of its stores, but it did not manufacture Coca-Cola syrup. Instead, it purchased its 30,000-gallon annual requirement of syrup and mixed it with carbonated water at its various soda fountains.

In May 1931, Charles Guth, the president and general manager of Loft, became dissatisfied with the price of Coca-Cola syrup and suggested to Loft's vice president that Loft buy Pepsi-Cola syrup from National Pepsi-Cola Company, the owner of the secret formula and trademark for Pepsi-Cola. The vice president said he was investigating the purchase of Pepsi syrup.

Before being employed by Loft, Guth had been asked by the controlling shareholder of National Pepsi, Megargel, to acquire the assets of National Pepsi. Guth refused at that time. However, a few months after Guth had suggested that Loft purchase Pepsi syrup, Megargel again contacted Guth about buying National Pepsi's secret formula and trademark for only $10,000. This time, Guth agreed to the purchase, and Guth and Megargel organized a new corporation, Pepsi-Cola Company, to acquire the Pepsi-Cola secret formula and trademark from National Pepsi. Eventually, Guth and his family's corporation owned a majority of the shares of Pepsi-Cola Company.

Very little of Megargel's or Guth's funds were used to develop the business of Pepsi-Cola. Instead, without the knowledge or consent of Loft's board of directors, Guth used Loft's working capital, its credit, its plant and equipment, and its executives and employees to produce Pepsi-Cola syrup. In addition, Guth's domination of Loft's board of directors ensured that Loft would become Pepsi-Cola's chief customer.

By 1935, the value of Pepsi-Cola's business was several million dollars. Loft sued Guth, asking the court to order Guth to transfer to Loft his shares of Pepsi-Cola Company and to pay Loft the dividends he had received from Pepsi-Cola Company. The trial court found that Guth had usurped a corporate opportunity and ordered Guth to transfer the shares and to pay Loft the dividends. Guth appealed.

Layton, Chief Justice. Public policy demands of a corporate officer or director the most scrupulous observance of his duty to refrain from doing anything that would deprive the corporation of profit or advantage. The rule that requires an undivided and unselfish loyalty to the corporation demands that there shall be no conflict between duty and self-interest.

The real issue is whether the opportunity to secure a very substantial stock interest in a corporation to be formed for the purpose of exploiting a cola beverage on a wholesale scale was so closely associated with the existing business activities of Loft, and so essential thereto, as to bring the transaction within that class of cases where the acquisition of the property would throw the corporate officer purchasing it into competition with his company.

Guth suggests a doubt whether Loft would have been able to finance the project. The answer to this suggestion is two-fold. Loft's net asset position was amply sufficient to finance the enterprise, and its plant, equipment, executives, personnel and facilities were adequate. The second answer is that Loft's resources were found to be sufficient, for Guth made use of no other resources to any important extent.

Guth asserts that Loft's primary business was the manufacturing and selling of candy in its own chain of retail stores, and that it never had the idea of turning a subsidiary product into a highly advertised, nation-wide specialty. It is contended that the Pepsi-Cola opportunity was not in the line of Loft's activities, which essentially were of a retail nature.

Loft, however, had many wholesale activities. Its wholesale business in 1931 amounted to over $800,000. It was a large company by any standard, with assets exceeding $9 million, excluding goodwill. It had an enormous plant. It paid enormous rentals. Guth, himself, said that Loft's success depended upon the fullest utilization of its large plant facilities. Moreover, it was a manufacturer of syrups and, with the exception of cola syrup, it supplied its own extensive needs. Guth, president of Loft, was an able and experienced man in that field. Loft, then, through its own personnel, possessed the technical knowledge, the practical business experience, and the resources necessary for the development of the Pepsi-Cola enterprise. Conceding that the essential of an opportunity is reasonably within the scope of a corporation's activities, latitude should be allowed for development and expansion. To deny this would be to deny the history of industrial development.

We cannot agree that Loft had no concern or expectancy in the opportunity. Loft had a practical and essential concern with respect to some cola syrup with an established formula and trademark. A cola beverage has come to be a business necessity for soft drink establishments; and it was essential to the success of Loft to serve at its soda fountains an acceptable five-cent cola drink in order to attract into its stores the great multitude of people who have formed the habit of drinking cola beverages.

When Guth determined to discontinue the sale of Coca-Cola in the Loft stores, it became, by his own act, a matter of urgent necessity for Loft to acquire a constant supply of some satisfactory cola syrup, secure against probable attack, as a replacement; and when the Pepsi-Cola opportunity presented itself, Guth having already considered the availability of the syrup, it became impressed with a Loft interest and expectancy arising out of the circumstances and the urgent and practical need created by him as the directing head of Loft.

The fiduciary relation demands something more than the morals of the marketplace. Guth did not offer the Pepsi-Cola opportunity to Loft, but captured it for himself. He invested little or no money of his own in the venture, but commandeered for his own benefit and advantage the money, resources, and facilities of his corporation and the services of his officials. He thrust upon Loft the hazard, while he reaped the benefit. In such a manner he acquired for himself 91 percent of the capital stock of Pepsi-Cola, now worth many millions. A genius in his line he may be, but the law makes no distinction between the wrongdoing genius and the one less endowed.

Judgment for Loft affirmed.

Oppression of Minority Shareholders

Directors and officers owe a duty to manage a corporation in the best interests of the corporation and the shareholders as a whole. When, however, a group of shareholders has been isolated for beneficial treatment to the detriment of another isolated group of shareholders, the disadvantaged group may complain of **oppression.**

For example, oppression may occur when directors of a close corporation who are also the majority shareholders pay themselves high salaries yet refuse to pay dividends or to hire minority shareholders as employees of the corporation. Since there is no market for the shares of a close corporation (apart from selling to the other shareholders), these oppressed minority shareholders have investments that provide them no return. They receive no dividends or salaries, and they can sell their shares only to the other shareholders, who are usually unwilling to pay the true value of the shares.

Generally, courts treat oppression of minority shareholders the same way courts treat director self-dealing: The transaction must be intrinsically fair to the corporation and the minority shareholders.

Freeze-Outs   Since the late 1960s, a special form of oppression, the **freeze-out,** has proliferated. A freeze-out is usually accomplished by merging a corporation with a newly formed corporation under terms by which the minority shareholders do not receive shares of the new corporation, but instead receive only cash or other securities. The minority shareholders are thereby *frozen out as shareholders*.

Going private is a special term for a freeze-out of shareholders of *publicly owned corporations*. Some public corporations discover that the burdens of public ownership—such as the periodic disclosure requirements of the SEC—exceed the benefits of being public. Many of these publicly owned companies choose to freeze out their minority shareholders to avoid such burdens. Often, going private transactions appear abusive because the corporation goes public at a high price and goes private at a much lower price.

In 1977, the Supreme Court of Delaware, in *Singer v. Magnavox*,[16] adopted a *fairness* test and a *business purpose* test for freeze-outs. The court held that the use of corporate power *solely* to eliminate the minority shareholders violated the directors' fiduciary duty to the minority shareholders. Later in 1977, the same court, in *Tanzer v. Int'l Gen. Indus., Inc.*,[17] held that the interest of a majority shareholder could provide the proper business purpose justifying a freeze-out of minority shareholders.

In 1983, in *Weinberger v. UOP*,[18] the Delaware Supreme Court abandoned the business purpose test as un-

---

[16]380 A.2d 969 (Del. Sup. Ct. 1977).

[17]379 A.2d 1121 (Del. Sup. Ct. 1977).

[18]457 A.2d 701 (Del. Sup. Ct. 1983).

workable. The court held that a freeze-out between a parent corporation and a subsidiary that was dominated by the parent had to meet only the intrinsic fairness test applied to self-dealing transactions. The court held that in the freeze-out context, total fairness had two basic aspects: *fair dealing* and *fair price*. Fair dealing requires disclosing material information to directors and shareholders and providing an opportunity for negotiation. A determination of fair value requires the consideration of all *the factors relevant to the value* of the shares, except speculative projections.

Most states apply the total fairness test to freeze-outs. Some states apply the business purpose test as well. Other states place no restrictions on freeze-outs provided a shareholder has a **right of appraisal**, which is discussed in the Shareholders' Rights and Liabilities chapter. SEC Rules 13e-3 and 13e-4 under the Securities Exchange Act of 1934 require a *publicly held* company to make a statement on the fairness of its proposed going private transaction and to discuss in detail the material facts on which the statement is based.

In the next case, the court required that a freeze-out of minority shareholders of the New England Patriots football team meet both the business purpose and intrinsic fairness tests. The court held that freezing out the minority shareholders merely to allow the corporation to repay the majority shareholder's personal debts was not a proper business purpose.

COGGINS V. NEW ENGLAND PATRIOTS FOOTBALL CLUB, INC.

492 N.E.2d 1112 (Mass. Sup. Jud. Ct. 1986)

In 1959, the New England Patriots Football Club, Inc. (Old Patriots), was formed with one class of voting shares and one class of nonvoting shares. Each of the original 10 voting shareholders, including William H. Sullivan, purchased 10,000 voting shares for $2.50 per share. The 120,000 nonvoting shares were sold for $5 per share to the general public in order to generate loyalty to the Patriots football team. In 1974, Sullivan was ousted as president of Old Patriots. In November 1975, Sullivan succeeded in regaining control of Old Patriots by purchasing all 100,000 voting shares for $102 per share. He again became a director and president of Old Patriots.

To finance his purchase of the voting shares, Sullivan borrowed $5,350,000 from two banks. The banks insisted that Sullivan reorganize Old Patriots so that its income could be used to repay the loans made to Sullivan and its assets used to secure the loans. To make the use of Old Patriots' income and assets legal, it was necessary to freeze out the nonvoting shareholders. In November 1976, Sullivan organized a new corporation called the New Patriots Football Club, Inc. (New Patriots). Sullivan was the sole shareholder of New Patriots. In December 1976, the shareholders of Old Patriots approved a merger of Old Patriots and New Patriots. Under the terms of the merger, Old Patriots went out of business, New Patriots assumed the business of Old Patriots, Sullivan became the only owner of New Patriots, and the nonvoting shareholders of Old Patriots received $15 for each share they owned.

David A. Coggins, a Patriots fan from the time of their formation and owner of 10 Old Patriots nonvoting shares, objected to the merger and refused to accept the $15 per share payment for his shares. Coggins sued Sullivan and Old Patriots to obtain rescission of the merger. The trial judge found the merger to be illegal and ordered the payment of damages to Coggins and all other Old Patriots shareholders who voted against the merger and had not accepted the $15 per share merger payment. Sullivan and Old Patriots appealed to the Massachusetts Supreme Judicial Court.

Liacos, Justice. When the director's duty of loyalty to the corporation is in conflict with his self-interest, the court will vigorously scrutinize the situation. The dangers of self-dealing and abuse of fiduciary duty are greatest in freeze-out situations like the Patriots merger, when a controlling shareholder and corporate director chooses to eliminate public ownership. Because the danger of abuse of fiduciary duty is especially great in a freeze-out merger, the court must be satisfied that the freeze-out was for the advancement of a legitimate corporate purpose. If satisfied that elimination of public ownership is in furtherance of a business purpose, the court should then proceed to determine if the transaction was fair by examining the totality of the circumstances. Consequently, Sullivan and Old Patriots bear the burden of proving, first, that the merger was for a legitimate business purpose, and second, that, considering the totality of circumstances, it was fair to the minority.

Sullivan and Old Patriots have failed to demonstrate that the merger served any valid corporate objective unrelated to the personal interests of Sullivan, the majority shareholder. The sole reason for the merger was to effectuate a restructuring of Old Patriots that would enable the repayment of the personal indebtedness incurred by Sullivan. Under the approach we set forth above, there is no need to consider further the elements of fairness of a transaction that is not related to a valid corporate purpose.

Judgment for Coggins affirmed as modified.

Trading on Inside Information

Officers and directors have *confidential access* to nonpublic information about the corporation. Sometimes, directors and officers purchase their corporation's securities with knowledge of inside information. Often, disclosure of previously nonpublic, **inside information** affects the value of the corporation's securities. Therefore, directors and officers may make a profit when the prices of the securities increase after the inside information has been disclosed publicly. Shareholders of the corporation claim that they have been harmed by such activity, either because the directors and officers misused confidential in-

formation that should have been used only for corporate purposes or because the directors and officers had an unfair informational advantage over the shareholders.

In this century, there has been a judicial trend toward finding a duty of directors and officers to disclose information that they have received confidentially from inside the corporation *before they buy or sell* the corporation's securities. As will be discussed fully in the Securities Regulation chapter, the illegality of insider trading is already federal law under the Securities Exchange Act; however, it remains only a minority rule under state corporation law.

Disclosure of Merger Negotiations

Sometimes, a shareholder will sell her shares, only to discover a few days later that at the time she sold her shares, her corporation was engaged in merger negotiations. Often those merger negotiations result in a merger agreement providing that a shareholder will be able to sell her shares at a price in excess of the previous market price. Not surprisingly, the shareholder who has already sold her shares at a lower price is upset that she has not been informed of the merger negotiations. Consequently, she sues the directors for failing to disclose the negotiations, arguing that had she known, she would have waited to sell her shares.

State corporation law has not imposed liability on the directors merely for failing to disclose secret merger negotiations. However, federal securities law—especially Securities Exchange Act Rule 10b-5—imposes disclosure duties on directors and officers. Among the most important of these duties is the obligation to disclose material corporate information, an obligation that is discussed in *Levinson v. Basic, Inc.,* which appears in the Securities Regulation chapter. The Supreme Court of the United States suggested that a corporation need not disclose secret merger negotiations that are material to a shareholder's investment decision absent special circumstances, such as when news of merger negotiations has leaked from the company into the market.[19] The Court hinted also that a board statement that "no corporate developments exist" when secret merger negotiations are ongoing imposes liability on the directors for making false statements.[20] The Court suggested, however, that silence or a response of "no comment" would not result in liability when the corporation has a business purpose to maintain the secrecy of merger negotiations.[21] The securities laws and their effect on the duties of directors, officers, and others who are considered insiders are discussed in detail in the Securities Regulation chapter.

Director's Right to Dissent

A director who *assents* to an action of the board of directors may be held liable for the board's exceeding its authority or its failing to meet its duty of due care or loyalty. A director who *attends a board meeting* is deemed to have assented to any action taken at the meeting, *unless he dissents.*

Under MBCA Section 8.24(d), to register his dissent to a board action, and thereby to protect himself from liability, the director must *not vote in favor* of the action and must *make his position clear* to the other board members. His position is made clear either by requesting that his dissent appear in the minutes or by giving written notice of his dissent to the chairman of the board at the meeting or to the secretary immediately after the meeting. These procedures ensure that the dissenting director will attempt to dissuade the board from approving an imprudent action.

Generally, directors are not liable for failing to attend meetings. However, a director is liable for *continually failing* to attend meetings, with the result that the director is unable to prevent the board from harming the corporation by its self-dealing.

CORPORATE AND MANAGEMENT LIABILITY FOR TORTS AND CRIMES

When directors, officers, and other employees of the corporation commit torts and crimes while conducting corporate affairs, the issue arises concerning who has liability. Should the individuals committing the torts and crimes be held liable, the corporation, or both?

Liability of the Corporation

Although courts struggled for many years to find a theory making a corporation liable for its agents' torts and crimes, today special statutes and the law of agency provide bases for imposing liability on corporations.

Torts For torts, the vicarious liability rule of *respondeat superior* applies to corporations. The only issue is whether an employee acted within the scope of her employment, which encompasses not only acts the employee is authorized to commit, but may also include acts that the employee is expressly instructed to avoid.

Crimes The traditional view was that a corporation could not be guilty of a crime, because criminal guilt required intent and a corporation, not having a mind, could form no intent. In addition, a corporation had

---

[19]485 U.S. 224, 234 n. 17 (U.S. Sup. Ct. 1988).

[20]Id. at 235 and n. 20.

[21]Id. at 234 n. 17.

nobody that could be imprisoned.[22] In essence, courts refused to find corporate criminal liability for violations of statutes that set standards for persons by holding that a corporation was not a person for purposes of criminal liability.

Today, few courts have difficulty holding corporations liable for crimes. Modern criminal statutes either expressly provide that corporations may commit crimes or define the term *person* to include corporations.[23] In addition, some criminal statutes designed to protect the public welfare do not require intent as an element of some crimes, thereby removing the grounds used by early courts to justify relieving corporations of criminal liability.

Courts are especially likely to impose criminal liability on a corporation when the criminal act is requested, authorized, or performed by:

1. The board of directors.
2. An officer.
3. Another person having responsibility for formulating company policy.
4. A high-level administrator having supervisory responsibility over the subject matter of the offense and acting within the scope of his employment.

---

[22]*State v. Summers,* 692 S.W.2d 439 (Tenn. Ct. Crim. App. 1985) (since corporations cannot be incarcerated, it would seem necessary that fines be substantial for corporations to feel any sting from the punishment).

[23]*People v. General Dynamics Land Systems,* 438 N.E.2d 359 (Mich. Ct. App. 1989).

In addition, courts hold a corporation liable for crimes of its agent or employee committed within the scope of his authority, even if a higher corporate official has no knowledge of the act and has not ratified it.[24]

Directors' and Officers' Liability

A person is always *liable for his own torts and crimes*, even when committed on behalf of his principal. Every person in our society is expected to exercise independent judgment, not merely follow orders. Therefore, directors and officers are personally liable when they commit torts or crimes during the performance of their corporate duties.

A director or officer is usually not liable for the *torts* of employees of the corporation, since the corporation, not the director or the officer, is the principal. He will be liable, however, if he *authorizes* the tort or *participates* in its commission.

A director or officer has *criminal* liability if she *requests, authorizes, conspires,* or *aids and abets* the commission of a crime by an employee.

In the next case, *United States v. Cattle King Packing Co., Inc.,* the court considered the criminal liability of a corporation and its officers.

---

[24]*CGM Contractors v. Environmental Services, Inc.,* 383 S.E.2d 861 (W. Va. Sup. Ct. 1989).

UNITED STATES v. CATTLE KING PACKING CO., INC.

793 F.2d 232 (10th Cir. 1986)

On June 1, 1981, Butch Stanko started a meatpacking plant in Adams County, Colorado, under the name of Cattle King Packing Company, Inc. Stanko was an officer and shareholder of Cattle King. Gary Waderich was a general sales manager primarily responsible for commercial sales of meat food products and for the daily operation of Cattle King. Stanko set company policies and practices to circumvent the Federal Meat Inspection Act (FMIA), which policies and practices he instructed Waderich and other employees to follow. When Stanko returned to his home in Scottsbluff, Nebraska, he monitored operations by phone and visits to the plant to make certain that the policies and practices that he had established were being followed.

Among the violations of the Federal Meat Inspection Act were the following:

1. Stanko gave a Cattle King employee directions on how, when the government inspector was not around, to mix inedible scrap with edible meat and thereby increase the poundage of the meat.

2. When a shipment of meat was rejected by a grocer and returned to Cattle King, Waderich instructed an employee to rebox the meat and resell it, without government inspection. (The FMIA required all returned meat to be government inspected.) When a government veterinarian came on the reboxing scene and demanded to know what was going on, Waderich denied he knew of the reboxing. Later, Waderich told another employee, "Well, we tried, but we got caught."

3. Cattle King employees dated meat the date it was shipped rather than the date it was produced as required by the FMIA.

4. Spoiled meat rejected by a buyer and returned to Cattle King was in bags that were puffy with gas caused by the spoilage. On instructions by Waderich, an employee reworked the meat by poking the bags to release the gas, and the meat was reshipped to the same buyer.

The U.S. Attorney General prosecuted Waderich, Stanko, and Cattle King for criminal violations of the FMIA. The jury convicted them, and all three defendants appealed.

McWilliams, Circuit Judge.   There is little doubt that Cattle King's operation violated federal meat inspection law at about every turn. Cattle King employees adulterated the meat, misdated the meat, and evaded federal inspection when rejected meat was returned to the plant. Cattle King employees also reworked the returned meat and resold it. Because this activity directly involved Gary Waderich, his challenge of the sufficiency of the evidence must clearly fail.

Stanko would make much of the fact that he returned to Scottsbluff, Nebraska in February 1982, and points out that all of the crimes occurred after that date. He would have us believe that he was somehow insulated from transactions occurring in Colorado when he was in Nebraska. This is an overly simplistic view of the matter. The fact that Stanko was in Scottsbluff does not absolve him of the criminal acts, for example of Waderich, which were committed pursuant to instructions from Stanko himself.

As a variation on his "I-was-in-Scottsbluff" defense, Stanko charges that the trial court's reliance on *United States v. Park* (1975) was error. The rationale of the Supreme Court's decision in *Park* is based upon this premise: Companies that engage in the food business, and the people who manage them, have an affirmative duty to insure that the food they sell to the public is safe. Accordingly, a corporate officer, who is in a "responsible relationship" to some activity within a company that violates federal food laws, can be held criminally responsible even though that officer did not personally engage in that activity. The trial court gave the jury the opportunity to decide whether Butch Stanko was responsible for Cattle King's violations of federal meat inspection laws. The jury found that he was.

In any event, this is not an instance where Stanko was in Scottsbluff, Nebraska, *not* knowing what his employees were doing in Colorado. Rather, Stanko set in motion the very acts which were carried out, pursuant to his direction, by his employees. Scottsbluff is not a shield for Stanko.

The trial court instructed the jury that Cattle King could be found guilty only if one of its agents committed the crimes, and the other three elements were met:

1. The agent was acting within the scope of his or her employment.

2. The agent was authorized to do the act.

3. The agent was motivated, at least in part, to benefit the corporation.

Gary Waderich, an officer of Cattle King, was personally responsible for the commission of all the crimes. Given Waderich's position within Cattle King, there is no doubt that elements 1 and 2 are met. As for element 3, there is also no doubt that Cattle King benefited by the commission of these crimes. The principal effect of all the crimes committed was that Cattle King reaped great economic rewards. Selling meat which should be condemned, misdating boxes so that meat could be stockpiled and thus produced more cheaply, all directly benefited Cattle King economically. There is, therefore, sufficient evidence that Cattle King, as a company, is also guilty of all the crimes.

Judgment convicting Waderich, Stanko, and Cattle King affirmed.

INSURANCE AND INDEMNIFICATION

The extensive potential liability of directors deters many persons from becoming directors. They fear that their liability for their actions as directors may far exceed their fees as directors. To encourage persons to become directors, corporations *indemnify* them for their outlays associated with defending lawsuits brought against them and paying judgments and settlement amounts. In addition, or as an alternative, corporations purchase *insurance* that will make such payments for the directors. Indemnification and insurance are provided for officers also.

Indemnification of Directors

Today, all of the corporation statutes limit the ability of corporations to indemnify directors in order to preserve the deterrence function of tort and criminal law. For example, directors may not be indemnified if they personally benefited from a decision for which they were held liable. In addition, the corporation may indemnify directors only in regard to a legal proceeding in which the director is a party because he was a director of the corporation. If a director is sued because he is alleged to have harmed someone when he was not acting as a director, the corporation may not indemnify the director.

Mandatory Indemnification   Under MBCA Section 8.52, a director is entitled to *mandatory indemnification* of her reasonable litigation expenses when she is sued and *wins completely* (is *wholly successful*). The greatest part of such expenses is attorney's fees. Because indemnification is mandatory in this context, when the corporation refuses to indemnify a director who has won completely, she may ask a court to order the corporation to indemnify her.

Voluntary Indemnification   Under MBCA Section 8.51, a director who loses a lawsuit *may* be indemnified by the corporation. This is called *voluntary indemnification,* because the corporation may choose to indemnify the director, but is not required to do so.

The corporation must establish that the director acted in *good faith* and reasonably believed that she acted in the *best interests* of the corporation. When a director seeks indemnification for a *criminal* fine, the corporation must establish a third requirement: that the director had no reasonable cause to believe that her conduct was unlawful. Finally, any voluntary indemnification must be approved by someone independent of the director receiving indemnification: a disinterested board of directors, disinterested shareholders, or independent legal counsel. Voluntary indemnification may cover not only the director's reasonable expenses but also fines and damages that the director has been ordered to pay.

A corporation may not elect to indemnify a director who was held *liable to the corporation* or who was found to have received a *personal benefit*. Such a rule tends to prevent indemnification of directors who have wronged the corporation by failing to exercise due care or by breaching a fiduciary duty. However, if the director paid an amount to the corporation as part of a *settlement*, the director may be indemnified for his reasonable expenses, but not for the amount that he paid to the corporation. The purpose of these rules is to avoid the circularity of having the director pay damages to the corporation and then having the corporation indemnify the director for the same amount of money.

Court-Ordered Indemnification   A court may order a corporation to indemnify a director if it determines that the director meets the standard for *mandatory* indemnification or if the director is *fairly and reasonably* entitled to indemnification in view of all the relevant circumstances.

Advances A director may not be able to afford to make payments to her lawyer prior to the end of a lawsuit. More important, a lawyer may refuse to defend a director who cannot pay legal fees. Therefore, MBCA Section 8.53 permits a corporation to make advances to a director to allow the director to afford a lawyer.

Indemnification of Nondirectors

Under the MBCA, officers and employees who are not directors are entitled to the same mandatory indemnification rights as directors. The corporation may, however, expand nondirectors' indemnification rights beyond the limits imposed on directors' indemnification rights.

Insurance

The MBCA does not limit the ability of a corporation to purchase insurance on behalf of its directors, officers, and employees. Insurance companies, however, are unwilling to insure all risks. In addition, some risks are *legally uninsurable as against public policy.* Therefore, liability for misconduct such as self-dealing, usurpation, and securities fraud is uninsurable.

ETHICAL AND PUBLIC POLICY CONCERNS

1. Do you agree that the primary objective of a corporation should be to maximize profits for its shareholders? What other objectives should a corporation have in addition to or instead of maximizing profits? Should the board of directors engage in an activity that maximizes profits but harms the community in which the corporation is located? Is it possible for a board to maximize profits and to be socially responsible to the community in which the corporation is located?

2. Should corporation law absolutely prevent CEO domination of a corporation or merely allow shareholders to restrict CEO power if shareholders choose? Why do shareholders invest in a corporation in which the CEO dominates the corporation? Why don't shareholders elect directors who control the CEO?

3. Should corporation law allow a board of directors great discretion in fighting hostile takeovers of a corporation? Is your answer affected by whether the raider is able to manage the corporation better than current management? Is your answer affected by whether the raider intends to move the operations of the target to another community? What other factors might affect your view

of the law we have concerning takeover defenses? Suppose the raider plans to break up the corporation and to sell the divisible parts of the corporation's business to other corporations. Is board opposition to such a hostile bid more justifiable? Does society benefit from such a bust-up takeover?

SUMMARY

The objectives and powers of a corporation are determined by the state corporation statute, the articles of incorporation, and the bylaws. Corporate actions beyond the powers of the corporation are *ultra vires.* Modern statutes do not permit the corporation and the other party to a contract to use *ultra vires* as a defense. Shareholders may sue to enjoin an *ultra vires* act.

A corporation is managed under the direction of its board of directors. The board delegates many of its duties to committees of the board and to officers, but some board functions may not be delegated. Generally, directors may take action only at a properly convened meeting, yet many statutes permit action without a meeting if all of the directors consent in writing.

The directors are elected by the shareholders and may be removed by them. Some states require a minimum of three directors; the MBCA requires only one. In publicly held corporations, the proxy solicitation process frequently permits the chief executive officer to cause the election of his nominees and to dominate the board of directors. Recently, board members have assumed more independence. Directors normally hold office until the next annual meeting, but most of the corporation statutes also permit staggered terms.

Numerous proposals for changing the composition and functions of the board have been made. Audit, nominating, and compensation committees, when composed entirely or predominantly of outside directors, tend to strengthen the independence of the board.

Officers are agents of the corporation, and like all agents, they have express, implied, and apparent authority. Some officers, such as the treasurer, also have inherent authority, which arises from the titles of the offices they hold.

Special rules apply to the management of close corporations. Modern statutes permit a close corporation to dispense with a board of directors and to be managed like a partnership. Restrictions on the management discretion of the directors are permitted in close corporations.

Directors and officers must act within their authority and within the powers given to the corporation. They also have the duty to act with due care. Their duty of loyalty requires them to act in the best interests of the corporation as a whole. Most management actions are protected from judicial scrutiny by the business judgment rule.

The general agency rules concerning torts apply to corporations. Corporations may also be found guilty of crimes, including those requiring intent, if the offenses are authorized or performed by policymaking managers or high-level administrators acting within the scope and in the course of their employments.

Corporations are permitted to purchase insurance policies that will pay for a director's or officer's legal costs and judgments. Within constraints, a corporation may also indemnify a director or an officer.

PROBLEM CASES

1. A ballot in the San Francisco city election included Proposition T, which would prohibit the construction of any building more than 72 feet high unless plans for the proposed building were approved in advance by the voters. PG&E's management concluded that the proposition would raise its property taxes by an estimated $380,000 in the first year and by as much as $1,135,000 per year in 10 years and that the proposition would also require redesigning and obtaining additional land for an already planned electric power substation. Consequently, the executive committee approved a $10,000 political contribution to a group opposing Proposition T. Neither PG&E's articles of incorporation nor the laws of California expressly permitted PG&E to make political donations. Is the contribution *ultra vires?*

2. Concerned Citizens of the CVEC, Inc., is a nonprofit Alabama corporation. The Alabama Business Corporation Act provides that a director may be removed with or without cause. The bylaws of Concerned Citizens provides that a director may be removed only for cause. The members of concerned citizens wish to remove a director, J. P. Mitchell. Mitchell argues that the members must have cause to remove him. Is Mitchell correct?

3. Lillian Pritchard was a director of Pritchard & Baird Corporation, a business founded by her husband. After the death of her husband, her sons took control of the corporation. For two years, they looted the assets of the corporation through theft and improper payments. The corporation's financial statements revealed the improper payments to the sons, but Mrs. Pritchard did not read the financial statements. She did not know what her sons were doing to the corporation or that what they were doing was unlawful. When Mrs. Pritchard was sued for failing to protect the assets of the corporation, she argued that she was a figurehead director, a simple housewife who served as a director as an accommodation to her husband and sons. Was Mrs. Pritchard held liable?

4. The Chicago National League Ball Club, Inc. (Chicago Cubs), operated Wrigley Field, the Cubs' homepark. Through the 1965 baseball season, the Cubs were the only major league baseball team that played no home games at night because Wrigley Field had no lights for nighttime baseball. Philip K. Wrigley, director and president of the corporation, refused to install lights because of his personal opinion that baseball was a daytime sport and that installing lights and scheduling night baseball games would result in the deterioration of the surrounding neighborhood. The other directors assented to this policy. From 1961 to 1965, the Cubs suffered losses from their baseball operations. The Chicago White Sox, whose weekday games were generally played at night, drew many more fans than did the Cubs. A shareholder sued the board of directors to force them to install lights at Wrigley Field and to schedule night games. What did the court rule?

5. The management of MacMillan Corporation recognized that it would not be able to prevent a takeover of the corporation. Therefore, management convinced the directors to authorize an auction of the company. Only two bidders emerged: Kohlberg Kravis Roberts & Co. (KKR) and Robert Maxwell. Management preferred KKR, and took steps to ensure than KKR would win the auction. Only hours before the deadline for bids, MacMillan's chairman and CEO tipped KKR that Maxwell's bid was lower than KKR's. Two hours before the deadline, MacMillan's auctioneer understood that Maxwell would top any KKR bid, yet allowed Maxwell to believe that he had made the higher bid. The board granted KKR a lock-up option of MacMillan's crown jewels— its most valuable assets. Has MacMillan's board acted properly?

6. Sinclair Oil Corporation (Sinclair), an oil explorer, producer, and marketer, owned about 97 percent of the shares of Sinclair Venezuelan Oil Company (Sinven). Nearly all of Sinven's directors were officers, directors, or employees of corporations owned by Sinclair. In 1961, Sinclair created Sinclair International Oil Company (International), a wholly owned subsidiary used for the purpose of coordinating all of Sinclair's foreign operations. Sinclair caused Sinven to make a contract with International that obligated Sinven to sell all of its crude oil and refined oil products to International. Sinclair caused International to breach this contract by allowing it to delay payments and to fail to comply with minimum purchase requirements under the contract. Francis Levien, a shareholder of Sinven, sued Sinclair on behalf of Sinven, alleging that Sinclair breached a fiduciary duty to Sinven. Is Levien correct?

7. Arthur Modell owned 53 percent of the shares of the Cleveland Browns Football Company, Inc. (the Browns), a Delaware corporation. Robert Gries owned 43 percent of the shares. The directors of the Browns were Modell, Modell's wife, Gries, James Bailey, James Berick, Richard Cole, and Nate Wallack. Modell also owned 80 percent of the shares and was a director of Cleveland Stadium Corporation (CSC), which leased Cleveland Municipal Stadium from the city of Cleveland. Gries, Bailey, Berick, Cole, and Wallack were the other shareholders and directors of CSC. Modell proposed that the Browns purchase all the shares of CSC for $6 million. Gries believed the price to be inflated. The purchase was approved by the Browns' directors by a vote of 4 to 1, with Gries being the sole dissenter and the Modells not voting. Gries filed a shareholder suit challenging the action. He claimed that the intrinsic fairness standard should apply to the transaction. The Browns argued that the business judgment rule should apply. Who is correct?

8. Bryant, Phelps, and May were the majority shareholders, officers, and directors of Greene Group, a company that operated a greyhound racing track in Greene County, Alabama. When a new greyhound racing track was proposed in Macon County, Alabama, Bryant, Phelps, and May, on their own behalf, contracted with the owners of the new track for Bryant, Phelps, and May to operate the new track. The owners of the new track did not want Greene Group to be involved in the operation of the new track because of the bickering between the majority and minority shareholders of Greene Group. The owners of the new track specifically requested that Bryant, Phelps, and May alone operate the new track. In the process of obtaining the contract to operate the new track, the three men used some property belonging to the Greene Group, including architectural plans and confidential marketing studies, and Greene Group employees and their expertise. Have Bryant, Phelps, and May done anything wrong?

9. Edwin Walhof and his family owned all the shares of Micom Holding Company, a corporation that owned 93 percent of Micom Corporation, a Minnesota corporation. To make Micom Corporation a closely held corporation owned only by the Walhof family, Micom Corporation merged into Micom Holding Company pursuant to the merger requirements of the Minnesota Corporation Law. Under the terms of the merger, Micom Holding Company, as the surviving corporation, carried on the prior business of Micom Corporation; the minority shareholders of Micom Corporation received $10 cash per share. James Sifferle, one of the minority shareholders of Micom Corporation, refused to accept the $10 per share and sued to set aside the merger. Was Sifferle successful?

10. A school bus was returning children to their homes in Livingston County, Kentucky. Phillip Kirkham, age 10, and his sister, Windy Kirkham, age 6, left the bus and attempted to cross the highway when a truck came on the scene. The truck was owned by Fortner LP Gas Company, Inc. The driver of the truck saw the bus, geared down, applied the brakes, but failed to stop the truck. The truck struck both children, injuring Phillip and killing Windy instantly. A subsequent inspection of the truck revealed grossly defective brakes. The Commonwealth of Kentucky prosecuted the corporation for manslaughter in the second degree for causing Windy's death. The corporation claimed that it could not commit the crime of manslaughter. Was it correct?

11. Shareholders collectively owning 80 percent of the shares of the Bank of New Mexico Holding Company made a shareholder's buy-sell agreement. Those shareholders included directors of the corporation. One of the agreeing shareholders sued the other shareholders, including the directors, to obtain a determination of the price of the shares under the agreement. The corporation reimbursed the legal expenses of the directors who, as shareholders, were defendants in the litigation. Did the corporation act properly in indemnifying the directors?

CHAPTER 31

SECURITIES REGULATION

INTRODUCTION

Background

Modern securities regulation arose from the rubble of the great stock market crash of October 1929. After the crash, Congress studied its causes and discovered several common problems in securities transactions, the most important ones being:

1. Investors lacked the necessary information to make intelligent decisions whether to buy, sell, or hold securities.
2. Disreputable sellers of securities made outlandish claims about the expected performance of securities and sold securities in nonexistent companies.

Faced with these perceived problems, Congress chose to require securities sellers to **disclose** the information that investors need to make intelligent investment decisions. Congress found that investors are able to make intelligent investment decisions if they are given sufficient information about the company whose securities they are to buy. This **disclosure scheme** assumes that investors need assistance from government in acquiring information but that they need no help in evaluating information.

To implement its disclosure scheme, in the early 1930s Congress passed two major statutes, which re-

main essentially unchanged and are the hub of federal securities regulation in the United States today. These two statutes, the **Securities Act of 1933** and the **Securities Exchange Act of 1934**, have three basic purposes:

1. To require the disclosure of meaningful information about a security and its issuer to allow investors to make intelligent investment decisions.[1]
2. To impose liability on those persons who make inadequate and erroneous disclosures of information.
3. To require the registration of issuers, insiders, professional sellers of securities, securities exchanges, and other self-regulatory securities organizations.

The most important of these purposes is the first. The crux of the securities acts is to impose on issuers of securities, other sellers of securities, and selected buyers of securities the affirmative duty to disclose important

---

[1] An issuer of a security is the person in whom the security represents an ownership interest or of whom the security represents an obligation. For example, GM is the issuer of its common stock, which represents an ownership interest in GM. Also, GM is the issuer of its debentures, which represent debt obligations of GM.

information, even if they are not asked by investors to make the disclosures. This is a dramatic departure from the law of contracts and torts that was applied to securities transactions before 1933.

By requiring disclosure, Congress hoped to restore investor confidence in the securities markets. Congress wanted to bolster investor confidence in the honesty of the stock market and thus encourage more investors to invest in securities. Building investor confidence would increase capital formation and, it was hoped, help the American economy emerge from the Great Depression of the 1930s.

Securities Act of 1933

The Securities Act of 1933 (1933 Act) is concerned primarily with **public distributions** of securities. That is, the 1933 Act regulates the sale of securities while they are passing from the hands of the issuer into the hands of public investors. An issuer selling securities publicly must make necessary disclosures at the time the issuer sells the securities to the public. The 1933 Act is chiefly a **one-time disclosure** statute. Although some of the 1933 Act's liability provisions cover all fraudulent sales of securities, the mandatory disclosure provisions apply only during a public distribution of securities by the issuer and those assisting the issuer.

Securities Exchange Act of 1934

By contrast, the mandatory disclosure provisions of the Securities Exchange Act of 1934 (1934 Act) require **periodic disclosures** by issuers of securities. An issuer with publicly traded equity securities must report annually and quarterly to its shareholders. Any material information about the issuer must be disclosed as the issuer obtains it, unless the issuer has a valid business purpose for withholding disclosure.

Integrated Disclosure

Since the information required in the 1933 and 1934 acts' disclosure documents is duplicative in many respects, the SEC has taken steps to reduce the disclosure burdens of public issuers subject to the disclosure requirements of both acts. As a result, an issuer already making periodic disclosures of information under the 1934 Act may substantially reduce its 1933 Act disclosure burden by using 1934 Act documents when making an issuance under the 1933 Act. For example, the 1933

Act's Regulation D—which is discussed later in this chapter—permits an issuer to use the 1934 Act 10-K annual report to meet its disclosure obligations under Regulation D.

Securities and Exchange Commission

The Securities and Exchange Commission (SEC) was created by the 1934 Act. Its responsibility is to administer the 1933 and 1934 acts and other securities statutes. Like other federal administrative agencies, the SEC has legislative, executive, and judicial functions. Its legislative branch promulgates rules and regulations; its executive branch brings enforcement actions against alleged violators of the securities statutes and their rules and regulations; its judicial branch decides whether a person has violated the securities laws. For more information on the functions of administrative agencies like the SEC, see the Administrative Agencies chapter.

SEC Actions

The SEC is empowered to investigate violations of the 1933 and 1934 acts and to hold hearings to determine whether these acts have been violated. Such hearings are held before an administrative law judge, who is an employee of the SEC. The administrative law judge (ALJ) is a finder of both fact and law. Decisions of the ALJ are reviewed by the commissioners of the SEC. Decisions of the commissioners are appealed to the U.S. courts of appeals.

Most SEC actions are not litigated. Instead, the SEC issues consent orders, by which the defendant promises not to violate the securities laws in the future but does not admit to having violated them in the past.

In 1990, the SEC was granted new powers to impose civil penalties (fines) up to $500,000 and to issue **cease and desist orders**. A cease and desist order directs a defendant to stop violating the securities laws and to desist from future violations. Nonetheless, the SEC does not have the power to issue injunctions; only courts may issue injunctions. The 1933 Act and the 1934 Act empower the SEC only to ask federal district courts for injunctions against persons who have violated or are about to violate either Act. The SEC may also ask the courts to grant ancillary relief, a remedy in addition to an injunction. Ancillary relief may include, for example, the disgorgement of profits that a defendant has made in a fraudulent sale or in an illegal insider trading transaction.

CONCEPT REVIEW

THE SECURITIES AND EXCHANGE COMMISSION

Members of the Commission	□ Five commissioners □ Appointed by the president of the United States with the advice and consent of the Senate □ Serve five-year terms □ No more than three commissioners may be members of the same political party
Statutes Administered by the SEC	□ Securities Act of 1933; primarily regulates the sale of securities by issuers to public investors □ Securities Exchange Act of 1934; primarily regulates the trading of securities after issuers have sold the securities to the public □ Trust Indenture Act of 1939; requires the use of a trust indenture for debt securities issued under the 1933 Act □ Investment Company Act of 1940; regulates the operation of mutual funds and the marketing of their securities □ Investment Advisers Act of 1940; regulates all types of investment advisers, including those who provide individualized advice and those who publish investment newsletters □ Bankruptcy Reform Act of 1978; the SEC serves as an adviser to the bankruptcy courts in corporate reorganization proceedings in which there is a substantial public interest
Divisions and Offices of the SEC	□ Division of Enforcement □ Division of Market Regulation □ Division of Corporate Finance □ Division of Investment Management □ The General Counsel □ Office of Economic Analysis □ Office of Chief Accountant □ Office of EDGAR Management (Electronic Data Gathering, Analysis, and Retrieval System) □ Office of Opinion and Review □ Office of Administrative Law Judges □ Office of Consumer Affairs and Information Services □ Office of International Affairs □ Office of Applications and Report Services
Powers of the SEC	□ Investigate violations of the securities laws □ Subpoena witnesses with evidence relevant to its investigations □ Compel the production of books and records relevant to its investigations □ Promulgate rules and regulations □ Order and conduct administrative hearings □ Adjudicate civil liability for violations of the securities laws □ Issue cease and desist orders □ Impose monetary penalties on a defendant □ Issue consent orders in which the defendant promises not to violate the securities laws in the future □ Suspend brokers and accountants from practicing before the SEC □ Suspend the sale of securities
Powers the SEC Does *Not* Have	□ Bring criminal actions against violators of the securities laws; but the SEC may refer a criminal matter to the U.S. Department of Justice (attorney general), which brings criminal actions □ Issue injunctions; but the SEC may ask a court to issue an injunction; the SEC may also ask a court to award ancillary relief, which may include disgorgement of profits made in a transaction violating the securities laws

WHAT IS A SECURITY?

The first issue in securities regulation is the definition of a security. If a transaction involves no security, then the law of securities regulation does not apply. The 1933 Act defines the term *security* broadly:

Unless the context otherwise requires the term "security" means any note, stock, bond, debenture, evidence of indebtedness, certificate of interest of participation in any profit-sharing agreement, . . . preorganization certificate or subscription, . . . investment contract, voting trust certificate, . . . fractional undivided interest in oil, gas, or mineral rights, . . . or, in general, any interest or instrument commonly known as a "security."

The 1934 Act definition of security is similar, but excludes notes and drafts that mature not more than nine months from the date of issuance.

Investment Contract

While typical securities like common shares, preferred shares, bonds, and debentures are defined as securities, the definition of a security also includes many contracts that the general public may believe are not securities. This is because the term **investment contract** is broadly defined by the courts. The Supreme Court's three-part test for an investment contract, called the *Howey* test, has been the guiding beacon in the area for the past 45 years.[2] The *Howey* test states that an investment contract is an investment of money in a common enterprise with an expectation of profits solely from the efforts of others.

1. An investment of money. The purchaser must have an investment motive, not a consumption motive (as with a golfer purchasing a membership in a country club) or a commercial motive (as with a bank lending money to a corporate creditor).

2. A common enterprise. The fortunes of the investors must be similarly affected by the efforts of the investment promoters or managers.

3. An expectation of profits from the efforts of others. The undeniably significant efforts that determine the success or failure of the venture must be those of the investment promoters or managers, not those of the investors.[3]

Examples In the *Howey* case, the sales of plots in an orange grove along with a management contract were held to be sales of securities. The purchasers had investment motives (they did not consume the oranges produced by the trees). They were similarly affected by the efforts of the sellers who grew and sold the oranges for all investors. The sellers, not the buyers, did all of the work needed to make the plots profitable.

In other cases, sales of limited partnership interests, Scotch whisky receipts, and restaurant franchises have been held to constitute investment contracts and, therefore, securities. In the following case, *Long v. Shultz Cattle Co., Inc.,* the court applied the *Howey* test to cattle feeding consulting agreements.

---

[2] *SEC v. W. J. Howey Co.,* 328 U.S. 293 (U.S. Sup. Ct. 1946).

[3] *SEC v. Glenn W. Turner Enterprises, Inc.,* 474 F.2d 476, 482 (9th Cir.), cert. denied, 414 U.S. 821 (1973).

LONG v. SHULTZ CATTLE CO., INC.

881 F.2d 129 (5th Cir. 1989)

Jim Long, Jerome Atchley, and Jon and Linda Coleman invested in a cattle-feeding program offered by Shultz Cattle Company, Inc. (SCCI). They first intended to be limited partners in SCCI's cattle-feeding limited partnership, but when SCCI failed to obtain regulatory approval of the sale of limited partnership interests, they switched to SCCI's individual feeding program, under which investors would purchase and raise their own cattle. However, each investor was required to sign a consulting agreement by which SCCI agreed to provide advice regarding the purchase, feeding, and sale of the investor's cattle. SCCI received only a flat-rate consulting fee of $20 per head of cattle for these services and received no share of the investors' profits.

To receive tax benefits from the investment, the tax laws required investors to participate actively in farming. Therefore, SCCI required each investor to represent that "he will exert substantial and significant control over, and will, exercising independent judgment, make all principal and significant management decisions concerning his cattle feeding operations."

Investors could limit any real risk of loss of investment by hedging their cattle: By buying or selling commodities futures they could lock in a price and minimize their potential losses. SCCI arranged for hedging transactions to be conducted through financial institutions, feedyards, and a brokerage firm of which SCCI was a branch office.

Long, Atchley, and the Colemans' cattle were fed, along with those of many other SCCI clients, in a feedyard in which the cattle were commingled. The cattle were tagged by pen number and not by individual investor. Each investor therefore owned a percentage of the total pounds of cattle in the pen. If any cattle died, the loss was not attributed to a single investor, but was distributed pro rata among the investors.

During the first year, Long, Atchley, and the Colemans hedged all their cattle and lost half of the money they had invested. In the second year, they decided to hedge only half of their 1,450 head of cattle. When beef prices declined drastically, they lost over $100,000. They sued SCCI for selling unregistered securities. The jury found that the consulting agreements were not investment contracts or otherwise securities. Long, Atchley, and the Colemans appealed.

King, Circuit Judge.   In *S.E.C. v. W. J. Howey Co.* (1946), the Supreme Court held that to determine whether a scheme is an investment contract, the test is whether the scheme involves (1) an investment of money (2) in a common enterprise (3) with profits to come solely from the efforts of others. The parties do not dispute that the first prong of the *Howey* test is satisfied in this case. Only the latter two elements—whether the cattle-feeding scheme was a common enterprise and whether the investors expected profits solely from the efforts of others—are contested. Because the controversy centers primarily on the third prong, we will discuss that issue first.

To ensure that the securities laws are not easily circumvented by agreements requiring a "modicum of effort" by investors, the word "solely" in the third prong of the *Howey* test has not been construed literally. The critical inquiry is instead whether the efforts made by those other than the investor are the undeniably significant ones, those essential managerial efforts which affect the failure or success of the enterprise. Even where an investor formally possesses substantial powers, the third prong of the *Howey* test may be met if the investor demonstrates that he is so inexperienced and unknowledgeable in the field of business at issue that he is incapable of intelligently exercising the rights he formally possesses.

Long, Atchley, and the Colemans had a substantial degree of theoretical control over their investments. They could, theoretically, move their cattle to a different feedyard, decide what to feed them, provide their own veterinary care, or seek buyers on their own. Moreover, the investors were *required* to authorize every management decision involving their cattle. However, at each juncture, the investors relied solely on the advice of SCCI: they followed SCCI's recommendations regarding the purchase of cattle, the choice of a feedyard, the choice of financial institution to provide financing, the choice of commodities brokers, the decision when to sell, and the decision to whom to sell.

Long, Atchley, and the Colemans, who lived in places far removed from their cattle, lacked the experience necessary to care for, feed, and market their cattle. SCCI relies on the theory that the cattle-feeding business does not require a great deal of specialized knowledge but rather depends upon a finite number of macroeconomic or big picture decisions. There is one crucial flaw in SCCI's theory: its clients acquire *from* SCCI all of the knowledge necessary to "actively manage" their "individual" cattle-feeding businesses. SCCI contends, in other words, that investors may become knowledgeable through the educative efforts of the promoters. We do not believe that the securities laws may be avoided so easily.

SCCI hopes to avoid the securities laws by simply attaching the label "consulting agreement" to a package of services which otherwise would clearly be an investment contract. The label "consulting agreement" cannot bear the meaning SCCI has given it. Indeed, SCCI's "individual" cattle-feeding program differs only in form from its limited partnerships. Although clients in the individual program technically were required to make their own decisions, SCCI performed for them—*at a higher cost*—all the services it performed for the limited partners in the other program.

Although Long, Atchley, and the Colemans's decision to hedge only half of their cattle was "undeniably significant" in terms of the risks to which the investors were exposed, it does not alter the essential character of the SCCI scheme. An investor may authorize the assumption of particular risks that would create the possibility of greater profits or losses but still depend on a third party for all of the essential managerial efforts without which the risk could not pay off. The fact that Long, Atchley, and the Colemans chose the riskier course cannot, by itself, transform the essential nature of the underlying contract any more than the fact that an individual investor chooses to buy high-risk junk bonds rather than low-risk AAA bonds causes one bond and not the other to be a security.

We conclude that the third prong of the *Howey* test was established as a matter of law. The jury's verdict would nevertheless stand if the evidence could support the conclusion that the second prong of the *Howey* test—the existence of a common enterprise—was not met. The Third, Sixth, and Seventh Circuits hold that a showing of "horizontal commonality"—a pooling of investors—is necessary to meet the common enterprise requirement. Under this standard, investors' fortunes must be tied to one another in order to constitute a common enterprise.

This court, together with the Ninth and Eleventh Circuits, has explicitly rejected the view that horizontal commonality is a prerequisite to establishing a common enterprise and has focused instead on the "vertical commonality" between the investors and the promoter. The critical factor is not the similitude or coincidence of investor input, but rather the uniformity of impact of the promoter's decisions.

While our standard requires interdependence between the investors and the promoter, it does not define that interdependence narrowly in terms of shared profits and losses. Rather, the necessary interdependence may be demonstrated by the investors' collective reliance on the promoter's expertise even where the promoter receives only a flat fee or commission rather than a share in the profits of the venture.

We recognize that under our standard the second and third prongs of the *Howey* test may in some cases overlap and that our standard has been criticized for that reason. We are not convinced that it would be desirable to adopt a rigid requirement that profits and losses be shared on a *pro rata* basis among investors, or that the promoter's fortunes correlate directly to the profits and losses of investors.

Here, all of SCCI's clients were dependent on SCCI's expertise to manage their investments. Moreover, SCCI's fortunes clearly were interwoven with those of their clients. SCCI received substantial "consulting fees" from its clients in exchange for its services in constructing and administering effective tax shelters through the cattle-feeding business. Through the inexorable force of the market, SCCI's success would correspond to that of its clients.

Judgment reversed in favor of Long, Atchley, and the Colemans.

Economic Realities Test

In recent years, the courts have used the *Howey* test to hold that some contracts with typical security names are not securities. Using an economic realities test, the courts point out that some of these contracts possess few of the typical characteristics of a security. For example, in *United Housing Foundation, Inc. v. Forman*,[4] the Supreme Court held that although tenants in a cooperative apartment building purchased contracts labeled as stock, the contracts were not securities. The "stock" possessed few of the typical characteristics of stock and the economic realities of the transaction bore few similarities to those of the typical stock sale: The stock gave tenants no dividend rights or voting rights in proportion to the number of shares owned, it was not negotiable, and it could not appreciate in value. More important, tenants bought the stock not for the purpose of investment but to acquire suitable living space.

However, the Supreme Court has made it clear that when investors are misled to believe that the securities laws apply because a seller sold a contract bearing both the name of a typical security and significant characteristics of that security, the securities laws do apply to the sale of the security.[5] The application of this doctrine led, in 1985, to the Supreme Court's rejection of the sale-of-business doctrine, which had held that the sale of 100 percent of the shares of a corporation to a single purchaser who would manage the corporation was not a security.[6] The rationale for the sale-of-business doctrine was that the purchaser failed to meet element 3 of the *Howey* test because he expected to make a profit from his own efforts in managing the business. Today, when a business sale is effected by the sale of stock, the transaction is covered by the securities acts if the stock possesses the characteristics of stock.

Family Resemblance Test

In 1990, the Supreme Court further extended this rationale in *Reves v. Ernst & Young*,[7] adopting the **family resemblance test** to determine whether promissory notes were securities. The Supreme Court held that it is inappropriate to apply the *Howey* test to notes. Instead, applying the family resemblance test, the Court held that notes are presumed to be securities unless they bear a "strong family resemblance" to a type of note that is not a security. Types of notes that are not securities include consumer notes, mortgage notes, short-term notes secured by a lien on a small business, short-term notes secured by accounts receivable, and notes evidencing loans by commercial banks for current operations.

In addition, the Court listed four factors relevant to a determination of whether a note is a security. The four factors are:

1. The motivations that would prompt a reasonable buyer and seller to enter into the transaction. For example, when the seller's purpose is to raise money for the general use of the business and the buyer is primarily interested in the profit the note is expected to generate, the note is likely to be a security.

2. The plan of distribution of the note to determine whether there was common trading for speculation or investment.

3. The reasonable expectations of the investing public concerning whether the notes are securities.

4. Whether some factor, such as the existence of another regulatory scheme, reduces the risk of the notes, thereby rendering application of the securities statutes unnecessary.

SECURITIES ACT OF 1933

Introduction

The 1933 Act has two principal regulatory components: (1) registration provisions and (2) antifraud provisions. The registration requirements of the 1933 Act are designed to give investors the information they need to make intelligent decisions whether to purchase securities when an issuer sells its securities to the public. The issuer of the securities is required to file a **registration statement** with the Securities and Exchange Commission and to make a **prospectus** available to prospective purchasers. The various antifraud provisions in the 1933 Act impose liability on sellers of securities for misstating or omitting facts of material significance to investors.

---

[4] *United Housing Foundation, Inc. v. Forman*, 421 U.S. 837 (U.S. Sup. Ct. 1975).

[5] *Id.*

[6] *Landreth Timber Co. v. Landreth*, 471 U.S. 681 (U.S. Sup. Ct. 1985). *Accord, Gould v. Ruefenacht*, 471 U.S. 701 (U.S. Sup. Ct. 1985) (privately negotiated sale of 50 percent of shares of corporation is a sale of securities).

[7] 110 S.Ct. 945 (U.S. Sup. Ct. 1990).

Registration of Securities under the 1933 Act

The 1933 Act usually requires the issuer of securities to register the securities with the SEC prior to the issuer's offer or sale of the securities.

Registration Statement   Historical and current data about the issuer and its business, full details about the securities to be offered, and the use of the proceeds of the issuance, among other information, must be included in a **registration statement** prepared by the issuer of the securities. Generally, the registration statement must include audited balance sheets as of the end of each of the two most recent fiscal years, in addition to audited income statements and audited statements of changes in financial position for each of the last three fiscal years. The issuer must file the registration statement with the SEC.

The registration statement must be signed by the issuer, its chief executive officer, its chief financial officer, its chief accounting officer, and at least a majority of its board of directors. Signing a registration statement is an important event, for it makes a person potentially liable for errors in the statement.

The registration statement becomes **effective** after it has been reviewed by the SEC. The SEC reviews only whether a registration statement is complete and whether it contains *per se fraudulent* statements. Examples of per se fraudulent statements are statements that tout the securities ("These are the best securities you can buy") and forecasts that are not reasonably based (a start-up company promising a 35 percent annual return on investment on its common stock).

The 1933 Act provides that the registration statement becomes effective on the 20th day after its filing. However, the SEC may advance the date or it may require an amendment that will restart the 20-day period; because the SEC usually requires an amendment, the effective date is usually later than 20 days after the original filing date.

Prospectus   The prospectus is the basic selling document of an offering registered under the 1933 Act. Most of the information in the registration statement must be included in the prospectus. It must be furnished to every purchaser of the registered security prior to or concurrently with the delivery of the security to the purchaser. The prospectus enables an investor to base his investment decision on all of the relevant data concerning the issuer, not merely on the favorable information that the issuer may be inclined to disclose voluntarily.

Section 5: Timing, Manner, and Content of Offers and Sales

The 1933 Act restricts the issuer's ability to communicate with prospective purchasers of the securities. Section 5 of the 1933 Act states the basic rules regarding the timing, manner, and content of offers and sales. It creates three important periods of time in the life of a security offering: (1) the pre-filing period, (2) the waiting period, and (3) the post-effective period.

The Pre-filing Period

Prior to the filing of the registration statement (the **pre-filing period**), the issuer and any other person may **not offer or sell** the securities to be registered. A prospective issuer, its directors and officers, and its underwriters must avoid publicity about the issuer and the prospective issuance of securities during the prefiling period. Press releases, advertisements, speeches, and press conferences may be deemed offers if their intent or effect is to *condition the market* to receive the securities.

SEC Rule 135 permits the issuer to publish a notice about a prospective offering during the pre-filing period. The notice may contain only the name of the issuer and a basic description of the securities and the offering. It may not name the underwriters or state the price at which the securities will be offered.[8]

The Waiting Period

The **waiting period** is the time between the filing date and the effective date of the registration statement, when the issuer is waiting for the SEC to declare the registration statement effective. During the waiting period, Section 5 permits the securities to be **offered but not sold.** However, not all kinds of offers are permitted. Face-to-face oral offers (including personal phone calls) are allowed during the waiting period. However, written offers may be made only by a statutory prospectus, usually a **preliminary prospectus** that often omits the price of the securities. (A final prospectus will be available after the registration statement becomes effective. It will contain the price of the securities.)

---

[8] In this context, underwriters are professional sellers of securities whom the issuer hires to assist the issuer's sale of the securities to the public. The definition of underwriter in this context should not be confused with the broader definition of underwriter in the Rule 144 context discussed later in this chapter.

FIGURE 1 Example of Tombstone Ad

This announcement is neither an offer to sell nor a solicitation of an offer to buy any of these Securities.
The offer is made only by the Prospectus.

April 27, 1990

2,250,000 Shares

Common Stock

Price $8 Per Share

Copies of the Prospectus may be obtained in any State from only such of the
undersigned as may legally offer these Securities in compliance with
the securities laws of such State.

Robertson, Stephens & Company

Bateman Eichler, Hill Richards
Incorporated

Donaldson, Lufkin & Jenrette
Securities Corporation

Hambrecht & Quist
Incorporated

Merrill Lynch Capital Markets

Prudential–Bache Capital Funding

Blunt Ellis & Loewi
Incorporated

Crowell, Weedon & Co.

Gordon, Haskett Capital Corporation

Interstate/Johnson Lane
Corporation

Needham & Company, Inc.

Ragen MacKenzie
Incorporated

Seidler Amdec Securities Inc.

Sutro & Co.
Incorporated

Tucker Anthony
Incorporated

Wedbush Morgan Securities

Wessels, Arnold & Henderson

As during the pre-filing period, general publicity during the waiting period may be construed as an illegal offer because it conditions the market to receive the securities. One type of general advertisement, called the **tombstone ad** (see Figure 1), is permitted during the waiting period and thereafter. The tombstone ad, which appears in financial publications, is permitted by SEC Rule 134, which allows disclosure of the same informa-tion as is allowed by Rule 135 plus the general business of the issuer, the price of the securities, and the names of the underwriters who are helping the issuer to sell the securities. In addition, Rule 134 requires the tombstone ad to state that it is not an offer.

The waiting period is an important part of the regulatory scheme of the 1933 Act. It provides an investor with adequate time (at least 20 days) to judge the wisdom of buying the security during a period when he cannot be pressured to buy it. Not even a contract to buy the security may be made during the waiting period.

The Post-effective Period

After the effective date (the date on which the SEC declares the registration effective), Section 5 permits the security not only to be offered but also to be sold, provided that the buyer has received a **final prospectus** (a preliminary prospectus is not acceptable for this purpose). Written offers not previously allowed are permitted during the post-effective period, if each offeree has received a final prospectus.

CONCEPT REVIEW

COMMUNICATIONS WITH INVESTORS BY OR ON BEHALF OF ISSUER PERMITTED BY SECTION 5 DURING A 1933 ACT REGISTRATION

Type of Communication	Pre-filing Period	Filing Date of Registration Statement / Waiting Period	Effective Date of Registration Statement / Post-effective Period
Annual Reports, Press Releases, and Quarterly Reports	Yes; unless designed to assist the placement of securities or arouse interest in a prospective sale of securities	Yes; unless designed to assist the placement of securities or arouse interest in a prospective sale of securities	Yes; without restriction if used contemporaneously with or after delivery of final prospectus
Notice of Proposed Offering (Rule 135)	Yes	Yes	Yes
Tombstone Ad (Rule 134)	No	Yes	Yes
Offer by Preliminary Prospectus	No	Yes	No
Offer by Final Prospectus	No	No	Yes
Oral-Face-to-Face Offers (including telephone calls)	No	Yes	Yes
Oral Offers at Sales Meeting	No	Yes, if each investor has an opportunity to ask unlimited questions	Yes, if each investor has an opportunity to ask unlimited questions, or if each investor has received a final prospectus
Offer by Free-Writing	No	No	Yes, contemporaneously with or after delivery of final prospectus
Sale	No	No	Yes, contemporaneously with or after delivery of final prospectus

EXEMPTIONS FROM THE REGISTRATION REQUIREMENTS OF THE 1933 ACT

Complying with the registration requirements of the 1933 Act is a burdensome, time-consuming, and expensive process. Planning and executing an issuer's first public offering may consume six months and cost in excess of $1 million. Consequently, some issuers prefer to avoid registration when they sell securities. Fortunately for them, several exemptions from registration are available to issuers.

There are two types of exemptions from the registration requirements of the 1933 Act: securities exemptions and transaction exemptions.

Exempt Securities

Exempt securities never need to be registered, regardless of who sells the securities, how they are sold, or to whom they are sold. The following are the most important securities exemptions.[9]

1. *Securities issued or guaranteed by any government in the United States and its territories.* For example, municipal bonds (issued by city governments) are exempt securities. A debenture issued by a corporation and guaranteed by the federal government is also exempt.

2. A *note or draft that has a maturity date not more than nine months after its date of issuance.* For example, commercial paper issued by General Motors Corporation and due in three months is exempt. The reasons for the exemption are that such commercial paper is used primarily in lending transactions, not investment transactions, and that the lender and the borrower have nearly equal bargaining power. The lender should be able to protect itself without the benefit of a securities registration.

3. A *security issued by a nonprofit religious, charitable, educational, benevolent, or fraternal organization.* For example, bonds issued by a nonprofit university

or by a nonprofit church would be exempt from registration under the 1933 Act.

4. *Securities issued by banks and by savings and loan associations.* The issuance of these securities is subject to regulation by other administrative agencies.

5. *Securities issued by railroads and trucking companies regulated by the Interstate Commerce Commission.* The ICC regulates the issuance of such securities.

6. *An insurance policy or an annuity contract.* For example, a life insurance contract is exempt from 1933 Act registration. Such contracts are regulated by the various state insurance departments.

Not Antifraud Exemptions

Although the types of securities listed above are exempt from the registration provisions of the 1933 Act, they are not exempt from the antifraud provisions of the act. Therefore, any fraud committed in the course of selling such securities can be attacked by the SEC and by the persons who were defrauded.

Transaction Exemptions

The most important 1933 Act exemptions are the transaction exemptions. If a security is sold pursuant to a transaction exemption, that sale is exempt. Subsequent sales, however, are not automatically exempt. Future sales must be made pursuant to a registration or another exemption.

As with the securities exemptions, the transaction exemptions are exemptions from the registration provisions only. The antifraud provisions of the 1933 Act apply equally to exempted and nonexempted transactions.

Transaction Exemptions for Issuers

The most important transaction exemptions are those available to issuers of securities. These exemptions are the intrastate offering exemption, the private offering exemption, and the small offering exemptions.

Intrastate Offering Exemption

Under section 3(a)(11), an offering of securities solely to investors in one state by an issuer resident and doing business in that state is exempt from the 1933 Act's registration requirements. The reason for the exemption is that there is little federal government interest in

---

[9] Excluded from the list of securities exemptions are the intrastate offering and small offering exemptions. Although the 1933 Act denotes them (except for the section 4(6) exemption) as securities exemptions, they are in practice transaction exemptions. An exempt security is exempt from registration forever. But when securities originally sold pursuant to an intrastate or small offering exemption are resold at a later date, the subsequent sales may have to be registered. The exemption of the earlier offering does not exempt a future offering. The SEC treats these two exemptions as transaction exemptions. Consequently, this chapter also treats them as transaction exemptions.

an offering that occurs in only one state. Although the offering may be exempt from SEC regulation, state securities law may require a registration.[10] The expectation is that state securities regulation will adequately protect investors.

---

[10] State securities law is covered at the end of this chapter.

The SEC has defined the intrastate offering exemption more precisely in Rule 147. An issuer must have 80 percent of its gross revenues and 80 percent of its assets in the state and use 80 percent of the proceeds of the offering in the state. Resale of the securities is limited to persons within the state for nine months.

Rule 147, however, is not an exclusive rule. In the following case, the court applied only the standard in Securities Act section 3(a)(11).

BUSCH v. CARPENTER

827 F.2d 653 (10th Cir. 1987)

Sonic Petroleum, Inc., was incorporated in Utah for the purpose of acquiring, extracting, and marketing natural resources such as oil, gas, and coal. Its corporate office, books, and records were in Utah. During October and November 1980, Sonic publicly offered and sold 25 million shares entirely to residents of Utah. The proceeds were $500,000. Sonic did not file a Securities Act registration statement with the SEC, instead relying on the exemption from registration for intrastate offerings. At the time of the offering, Sonic had not undertaken any business activities in Utah or anywhere else.

Craig Carpenter, Sonic's president, negotiated Sonic's acquisition of an Illinois drilling corporation owned by William Mason. On May 25, 1981, Sonic issued a controlling block of its shares to Mason in exchange for Mason's corporation. Shortly thereafter, Sonic deposited in Illinois $350,000 of the proceeds from the sale of shares to Utah residents. At about the same time, Mason and Carpenter helped create a public market for Sonic shares. As a result, Paul and Linda Busch, who were California residents, purchased Sonic shares from Utah residents who had purchased shares in October and November 1980. When the shares' value dropped, the Busches sued Carpenter for selling unregistered securities. The trial court held that Sonic sold the shares pursuant to the intrastate offering exemption and, therefore, did not need to register the shares. The Busches appealed.

Seymour, Circuit Judge. Section 5 of the Securities Act of 1933 prohibits the offer or sale of any security unless a proper registration statement has first been filed with the SEC. However, Congress also recognized that the protections of the 1933 Act were not essential for those securities that could be supervised effectively by the states. Section 3(a)(11) therefore exempts from the Act's registration requirements

Any security which is part of an issue offered and sold only to persons resident within a single State or Territory, where the issuer of such security is a person resident and doing business within or, if a corporation, incorporated by and doing business within, such State or Territory.

In order to fall within the intrastate exemption, initial sales to state residents must be bona fide. The intrastate exemption becomes unavailable whenever sales or purchases by a subsequent purchaser circumvent the federal securities laws. The SEC has consistently maintained that a distribution of securities must have actually come to rest in the hands of the resident investors—persons purchasing for investment intent and not for purpose of resale.

The Busches contend that Sonic had the burden to prove that the original buyers bought with investment intent. We reject this argument. The intrastate offering exemption requires that the issue be "offered and sold only to persons resident within a single state." In face of Sonic's undisputed showing that all of the original buyers were Utah residents, the Busches were therefore required to produce evidence that the stock had not come to rest but had been sold to people who intended to resell it out of state. The interstate purchases of freely trading shares several months after the completion of the intrastate offering do not, without more, impugn the investment intent of the original buyers.

The Busches alternatively contend that Sonic was not entitled to the intrastate exemption because the corporate issuer was not doing business in Utah as required by section 3(a)(11). There is no dispute that the newly formed company, not yet operational, maintained its offices, books, and records in Salt Lake City. The decisive issue concerns whether Sonic's failure to invest a portion of the proceeds from its initial public offering in Utah could defeat the intrastate exemption.

An issuer cannot claim the exemption simply by opening an office in a particular state. Conducting substantially all income-producing operations elsewhere defeats the exemption, as do the plans of recently organized companies to invest the net proceeds of initial public offerings only in other states.

Here Sonic never did more than maintain its office, books, and records in Utah. This was not sufficient to make a showing of compliance with the intrastate offering exemption. Sonic transferred essentially all of its assets to Illinois and made no prior efforts whatever at locating investment opportunities within Utah. Sonic may have been intending all along to invest its assets outside the state. A newly formed company may not claim the exemption while planning covertly to invest the proceeds of a local offering in other states.

Judgment reversed in favor of the Busches; remanded for trial.

Private Offering Exemption

Section 4(2) of the 1933 Act provides that the registration requirements of the 1933 Act "shall not apply to transactions by an issuer not involving any public offering." The rationale for the private offering exemption is that the purchasers in a private placement of securities do not need the registration protections of the 1933 Act. Such purchasers can protect themselves because they are wealthy or because they are sophisticated in investment matters and have access to the information that they need to make intelligent investment decisions.

Courts have struggled to define the private offering exemption, leading to a great deal of subjectivity in court decisions. To create greater objectivity—and also greater certainty for issuers—the SEC adopted Rule 506. Although an issuers may exempt a private offering under either the courts' interpretation of section 4(2) or Rule 506, the SEC tends to treat Rule 506 as the exclusive way to obtain the exemption.

Rule 506   Under Rule 506, which is part of Securities Act Regulation D,[11] the issuer must reasonably believe that each purchaser is either (a) an accredited investor or (b) an unaccredited investor who "has such knowledge and experience in financial and business matters that he is capable of evaluating the merits and risks of the prospective investment." Accredited investors include institutional investors (such as banks and mutual funds), wealthy investors, and high-level insiders of the issuer (such as executive officers, directors, and partners).

An issuer may sell to no more than 35 unaccredited purchasers who have sufficient investment knowledge and experience, but it may sell to an unlimited number

---

[11] SEC Regulation D was promulgated in 1982 to make the private offering and small offering exemptions more easily available for small issuers. The purpose of Regulation D is to promote capital formation for small issuers. Regulation D includes the small offering exemption Rules 504 and 505, which are discussed later in this chapter in addition to Rule 506.

of accredited purchasers, regardless of their investment sophistication.

Each purchaser must be given or have access to the information she needs to make an informed investment decision. For an issuer required to make periodic disclosure under the 1934 Act, purchasers must receive information in a form required by the 1934 Act, such as a 10-K or annual report.[12] For an issuer that is not a 1934 Act reporting company, the issuer must provide much of the same information required in a registered offering. If the amount of the issuance is $2 million or less, only one

year's balance sheet need be audited. If the amount issued is $7.5 million or less, only one year's financial statements need be audited. If the amount issued exceeds $7.5 million, financial statements must be audited as required in a registration statement. In any offering of any amount under Rule 506, when auditing would involve unreasonable effort or expense, only an audited balance sheet is needed. However, whenever a limited partnership issuer finds that auditing involves unreasonable effort or expense, the limited partnership may use financial statements prepared by an independent accountant in conformance with the requirements of federal tax law. Figure 2 summarizes the disclosure requirements of Regulation D.

---

[12] Issuers required to disclose under the 1934 Act and the disclosure requirements of the 1934 Act are covered later in this chapter.

FIGURE 2   Disclosure under Regulation D

Type of Issuer \ Size of Offering	$2 Million or Less	More Than $2 Million But Not More Than $7.5 Million	More Than $7.5 Million	Any Amount When Auditing Involves Unreasonable Effort or Expense
Issuer Required to Disclose under 1934 Act	Same nonaccounting information as disclosed under the 1934 Act. The following financial statements must be audited: Balance sheet for last 2 years. Income statement for last 3 years. Statement of changes in financial position for last 3 years.			
Issuer Not Required to Disclose under 1934 Act	Same nonaccounting information as required for 1933 Act registration statement.			
Non-1934 Act Issuer Is Not a Limited Partnership	Only balance sheet for last year must be audited.	Balance sheet, income statement, and statement of changes in financial position for last year must be audited.	The following financial statements must be audited: Balance sheet for 2 years. Income statement for 3 years. Statement of changes in financial position for 3 years.	Only balance sheet for last year must be audited.
Non-1934 Act Issuer Is a Limited Partnership				Issuer may use financial statements prepared for tax purposes.

Rule 506 prohibits the issuer from making any general public selling effort. This prevents the issuer from using the radio, newspapers, and television. In addition, the issuer must take reasonable steps to ensure that the purchasers do not resell the securities in a manner that makes the issuance a public distribution rather than a private one. Usually, an **investment letter** is used to provide this information. In such a letter, the investor states that she is purchasing the securities for investment and not for resale within two years.

In the following case, *Mark v. FSC Securities Corp.*, the issuer failed to prove it was entitled to a private offering exemption under section 4(2) or Rule 506.

MARK v. FSC SECURITIES CORP.

870 F.2d 331 (6th Cir. 1989)

FSC Securities Corp., a securities brokerage, sold limited partnership interests in Malaga Arabian Limited Partnership to James Mark and his wife. A total of 28 investors purchased limited partnership interests in Malaga. All investors were asked to execute subscription documents, including a suitability letter in which the purchaser stated his income level, that he had an opportunity to obtain relevant information, and that he had sufficient knowledge and experience in business affairs to evaluate the risks of the investment.

When the value of the limited partnership interests fell, the Marks sued FSC to rescind their purchase on the grounds that FSC sold unregistered securities in violation of the Securities Act of 1933. The jury held that the offering was exempt as an offering not involving a public offering. The Marks appealed.

Simpson, Judge.   Section 4(2) of the Securities Act exempts from registration with the SEC "transactions by an issuer not involving any public offering." There are no hard and fast rules for determining whether a securities offering is exempt from registration under the general language of section 4(2). However, several factors are significant: (a) the number of offerees; (b) the manner of the offering; (c) the number of units offered; (d) the relationship of the offerees to each other and to the issuer; and (e) the size of the offering.

Based on consideration of those factors, only one conclusion is, in this case, reasonable: The Malaga limited-partnership offering was not exempt under section 4(2). FSC offered no evidence as to the actual *number* of offerees, let alone their individual characteristics. Moreover, numerous broker-dealers undertook to sell interests in the Malaga offering, somewhere between ten and twenty. As for the number of units offered, the copy numbers on the Marks' "Receipt for Private Placement Offering Memorandum" were 135, 274, and 477, suggesting the broker-dealers distributed the offering memorandum for the Malaga offering to many more than the ultimate 28 purchasers.

These factors, taken together, indicate a wide-ranging sales effort and suggest a public, rather than a private, offering. Once such a wide-ranging distribution scheme is undertaken, evidence that each and every offeree had access to enough relevant information so as to make registration unnecessary is required to rebut the public offering inference. For example, if there is some special, close relationship between the offerees and issuer, then there may be access to the sort of information that registration would disclose. But in this case, there was no evidence that any of the offerees had any relationship to the issuer. Instead, the list of 28 purchasers shows they were a diverse, unrelated group who resided in many different communities in twelve different states. That the purchasers are so diverse suggests the offerees were likewise diverse and unrelated, militating against a private offering. Without evidence that *all* those offerees had information enabling them to fend for themselves, there is no section 4(2) exemption.

Even if FSC failed to prove an exemption under the subjective test of section 4(2), the "safe harbor" provision of Regulation D, Rule 506, deems certain transactions to be not involving any public offering within the meaning of section 4(2). However, FSC had to prove that certain objective tests were met. These conditions include the general conditions not in dispute here, and the following specific conditions:

(i) *Limitation on number of purchasers*. The issuer shall reasonably believe that there are no more than thirty-five purchasers of securities in any offering under this Section.

(ii) *Nature of purchasers*. The issuer shall reasonably believe immediately prior to making any sale that each purchaser who is not an accredited investor either alone or with his purchaser representative(s) has such knowledge and experience in financial and business matters that he is capable of evaluating the merits and risks of the propective investment.

In this case, we take the issuer to be the general partners of Malaga. FSC is required to offer evidence of the issuer's reasonable belief as to the nature of *each* purchaser. The only testimony at trial competent to establish the issuer's belief as to the nature of the purchasers was that of Laurence Leafer, a general partner in Malaga. By his own admission, he had no knowledge about any purchaser, much less any belief, reasonable or not, as to the purchasers' knowledge and experience in financial and business matters.

Q: What was done to determine if investors were, in fact, reasonably sophisticated?

A: Well, there were two things. Number one, we had investor suitability standards that had to be met. You had to have a certain income, be in a certain tax bracket, this kind of thing. Then in the subscription documents themselves, they, when they sign it, supposedly represented that they had received information necessary to make an informed investment decision, and that they were sophisticated. And if they were not, they relied on an offering representative who was.

Q: Did you review the subscription documents that came in for the Malaga offering?

A: No.

Q: So do you know whether all of the investors in the Malaga offering met the suitability and sophistication requirements?

A: I don't.

FSC also offered as evidence the Marks' executed subscription documents, as well as a set of documents in blank, to establish the procedure it followed in the Malaga sales offering. Although the Marks' executed documents may have been sufficient to establish the reasonableness of any belief the issuer may have had as to the Marks' particular qualifications, that does not satisfy Rule 506. The documents offered no evidence from which a jury could conclude the issuer reasonably believed *each* purchaser was suitable. Instead, all that was proved was the sale of 28 limited partnership interests, and the circumstances under which those sales were *intended* to have been made. The blank subscriptions documents simply do not amount to probative evidence, when it is the answers and information received *from* purchasers that determine whether the conditions of Rule 506 have been met.

Having concluded that the Malaga limited-partnership offering did not meet the registration exemption requirement of either section 4(2) or Rule 506 of Regulation D, we conclude that the Marks are entitled to the remedy of rescission.

Judgment reversed in favor of the Marks; remanded to the trial court.

Small Offering Exemptions

Sections 3(b) and 4(6) of the 1933 Act permit the SEC to exempt from registration any offering by an issuer not exceeding $5 million. Several SEC rules and regulations permit an issuer to sell small amounts of securities and avoid registration. The rationale for these exemptions is that the dollar amount of the securities or the number of purchasers is too small for the federal government to be concerned with registration. State securities law may require registration, however.

Rule 504 Rule 504 of Regulation D allows the issuer to sell up to $1 million of securities in a 12-month period and avoid registration. However, any amount of a securities offering under Rule 504 exceeding $500,000 must be registered under state securities law. For example, an issuer planning to sell $800,000 of securities under Rule 504 may sell $500,000 of securities without any federal or state registration, but $300,000 of the securities must be registered under state law.

As with Rule 506, no general selling efforts are permitted and resale is restricted. Rule 504 sets no limits on the number of offerees or purchasers. The purchasers need not be sophisticated in investment matters, and the issuer need disclose information only as required by state securities law.

Rule 505 Rule 505 of Regulation D allows the issuer to sell up to $5 million of securities in a 12-month period and, as with Rules 504 and 506, no general selling efforts are allowed and resale is restricted. There may be no more than 35 purchasers, but there is no limit on the

number of accredited investors. Rule 505 has the same disclosure requirements as Rule 506. As with Rule 504, the purchasers need not be sophisticated in investment matters.

Regulation A Regulation A permits an issuer to sell up to $1.5 million of securities in a one-year period. There is no limit on the number of purchasers, no purchaser sophistication requirement, and no resale restriction.

For offerings that exceed $100,000, Regulation A requires disclosure and regulates the manner and timing of offers and sales much as a registered offering is regulated. In fact, Regulation A is more nearly a low-level registration than an exemption from registration. The Regulation A disclosure document is the offering circular, which must be filed with the SEC. Financial statements in the offering circular must be audited if the issuer is a 1934 Act reporting company. There is a 10-day waiting period after the filing of the offering circular, during which no offers or sales may be made. Ten days after the filing date, oral offers are permitted, as are written offers accompanied or preceded by an offering circular. Sales are permitted after the waiting period.

Integration of Offerings

It might seem possible to avoid a registration by separating one offering into several smaller offerings and finding an exemption for each of the smaller offerings. Not surprisingly, the SEC has acted to stop such a circumvention of the registration provisions of the 1933 Act by requiring the integration of offerings that are essentially only one offering.

COMPARISON OF RULES 504, 505, AND 506 OF REGULATION D

	Issuers Covered	Amount Sold	Number of Purchasers	Must Purchasers Be Sophisticated?	Disclosure Required	General Solicitations Permitted	Resale Restricted	File Form D
Rule 504	Only nonpublic issuers	$1 million; but any amount exceeding $500,000 must be unregistered under state law	No limit	No	No	No	Yes	Yes
Rule 505	All	$5 million	35 unaccredited purchasers; unlimited number of accredited purchasers	No	Yes, unless sold to accredited purchasers only	No	Yes	Yes
Rule 506	All	No limit	35 unaccredited purchasers; unlimited number of accredited purchasers	Yes, unless accredited investors	Yes, unless sold to accredited purchasers only	No	Yes	Yes

Transaction Exemptions for Nonissuers

Although it is true that the registration provisions apply primarily to issuers and those who help issuers sell their securities publicly, the 1933 Act states that every person who sells a security is potentially subject to Section 5's restrictions on the timing of offers and sales. You must learn the most important rule of the 1933 Act: **Every transaction in securities must be registered with the SEC or be exempt from registration.**

This rule applies to every person, including the small investor who, through the New York Stock Exchange, sells securities that may have been registered by the issuer 15 years earlier. That small investor must either have the issuer register her sale of securities or find an exemption from registration that applies to her situation. Fortunately, most small investors who resell securities will have an exemption from the registration requirements of the 1933 Act. The transaction exemption ordinarily used by these resellers is Section 4(1) of the 1933

Act. It provides an exemption for "transactions by any person other than an issuer, underwriter, or dealer."

For example, if you buy GM common shares on the New York Stock Exchange, you may freely resell them without a registration. You are not an issuer (GM is). You are not a dealer (because you are not in the business of selling securities). And you are not an underwriter (because you are not helping GM distribute the shares to the public).

Application of this exemption when an investor sells shares that are already publicly traded is easy; however, it is more difficult to determine whether an investor can use this exemption when the investor sells **restricted securities.**

Sale of Restricted Securities

Restricted securities are securities issued pursuant to a private or small offering exemption, including

FIGURE 3   Securities and Transaction Exemptions from the Registration Requirements of the Securities Act of 1933

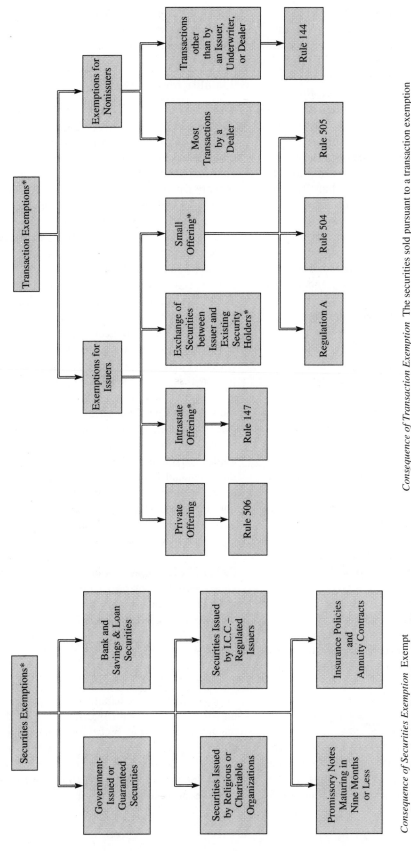

Consequence of Securities Exemption Exempt securities never need to be registered regardless of how, when, or to whom they are sold. The exemption attaches to the security and is available regardless of the type of transaction by which it is sold.

Consequence of Transaction Exemption The securities sold pursuant to a transaction exemption are exempt from registration only for that particular transaction. In effect, the transaction exemption is for the transaction, not the security. If the securities are resold, the securities must be registered, unless the securities are sold pursuant to another transaction exemption.

Note: These are exemptions from the *registration* provisions of the 1933 Act. The 1933 Act *antifraud* provisions apply to these transactions and these securities.

*The Securities Act of 1933 lists the small offering, intrastate offering, and exchange of securities between issuers and existing securities holders as **securities** exemptions, yet they are *in effect* **transaction** exemptions, because the exemptions apply only when the securities are sold in these types of transactions. The exemptions do not attach to the exemptions securities. If the securities are resold, the securities must be registered, unless the securities are sold pursuant to another transaction exemption.

Rules 504, 505, and 506. Restricted securities are supposed to be held by the purchaser for two years. If they are sold earlier, the investor may be deemed an underwriter.

For example, an investor buys 10,000 common shares issued by Arcom Corporation pursuant to a Rule 506 private offering exemption. One month later, the investor sells the securities to 40 other investors. The original investor is an *underwriter* because he has helped Arcom distribute the shares to the public. The original investor may not use the issuer's private offering exemption because it exempted only the issuer's sale to him. This example illustrates the importance of heeding the rule discussed earlier: every transaction in securities must be registered with the SEC or be exempt from registration.

SEC Rule 144   SEC Rule 144 allows purchasers of restricted securities to resell the securities and not be deemed underwriters. The resellers must hold the securities for at least two years. Investment information concerning the issuer of the securities must be publicly available. In any three-month period, the reseller may sell only a limited amount of securities: the greater of 1 percent of the outstanding securities or the average weekly volume of trading. And the reseller must file a notice (Form 144) with the SEC.

If a purchaser who is not an insider of the issuer has held the restricted securities for at least three years, Rule 144 permits her to sell unlimited amounts of the securities. In addition, investment information concerning the issuer need not be publicly available.

Figure 3 summarizes the 1933 Act exemptions from registration.

LIABILITY PROVISIONS OF THE 1933 ACT

Introduction

To deter fraud, deception, and manipulation and to provide remedies to the victims of such practices, Congress included a number of liability provisions in the Securities Act of 1933.

Liability for Improper Offers and Sales

Section 12(1) of the 1933 Act imposes liability on any person who violates the provisions of Section 5. As you learned above, Section 5 states when sales may be made and what types of offers may be made at what times during the registration process. Liability extends to any purchaser to whom an illegal offer or sale was made. The purchaser's remedy is rescission or damages.

Liability for Defective Registration Statements

Section 11 of the 1933 Act provides civil liabilities for damages when a 1933 Act registration statement on its effective date misstates or omits a material fact. A purchaser of securities issued pursuant to the defective registration statement may sue certain classes of persons that are listed in Section 11: the issuer, its chief executive officer, its chief accounting officer, its chief financial officer, the directors, other signers of the registration statement, the underwriter, and experts who contributed to the registration statement (such as auditors who certified the financial statements or lawyers who issued an opinion concerning the tax aspects of a limited partnership). The purchaser's remedy under Section 11 is for damages caused by the misstatement or omission.

Section 11 was a radical liability section when it was enacted, and it remains so today. It is radical for three reasons. First, reliance is usually not required; that is, the purchaser need not show that she relied on the misstatement or omission in the registration statement. In fact, the purchaser need not have read the registration statement or have seen it. Second, privity is not required; that is, the purchaser need not prove that she purchased the securities from the defendant. All she has to prove is that the defendant is in one of the classes of persons liable under Section 11. Third, the purchaser need not prove that the defendant negligently or intentionally misstated or omitted a material fact. Instead, the defendant has the burden of proving that he exercised due diligence.

Section 11 Defenses   A defendant can escape liability under Section 11 by proving that the purchaser knew of the misstatement or omission when she purchased the security. The defendant's other defense is the **due diligence defense.** It is the more important of the two defenses.

The Due Diligence Defense   Any defendant except the issuer may escape liability under Section 11 by proving that he acted with due diligence in determining the accuracy of the registration statement. The due diligence defense basically requires the defendant to prove that he was not negligent. The exact defense varies, however, according to the class of defendant and the portion of the registration statement that is defective. Most defendants must prove that after a *reasonable investigation* they had *reasonable grounds to believe and did believe* that the registration statement was true and contained no omission of material fact.

Experts need to prove due diligence only in respect to the parts that they have contributed. For example, independent auditors must prove due diligence in ascertaining the accuracy of financial statements they certify. Due diligence requires that an auditor at least comply with generally accepted auditing standards (GAAS).

Nonexperts (the directors, officers, partners, and underwriters) are liable for the entire registration statement. However, they generally have no duty of investigation in respect to the parts of the registration statement contributed by experts (*expertised portions*). The nonexperts need merely show that they had *no reason to believe and did not believe* that the expertised portions of the registration statement contained any misstatement or omission of material fact. For the *nonexpertised* portions of the registration statement, nonexperts must make a *reasonable investigation and reasonably believe* that those portions contain no misstatements or omissions of material fact.

Other Liability Provisions

Section 12(2) prohibits misstatements or omissions of material fact in any written or oral communication in connection with the offer or sale of any security (except government-issued or -guaranteed securities). Section 17(a) prohibits the use of any device or artifice to defraud, or the use of any untrue or misleading statement, in connection with the offer or sale of any security. Two of the subsections of Section 17(a) require that the defendant merely act negligently, while the third subsection requires proof of scienter. Scienter is the intent to deceive, manipulate, or defraud the purchaser. Some courts have held that scienter also includes recklessness. The Supreme Court has not decided whether a buyer has a private right of action for damages under Section 17(a), and the courts of appeals are split on the issue.

Jurisdictional Requirement

Since these liability sections are part of federal law, there must be some connection between the illegal activity and interstate commerce for liability to exist. Section 11 merely requires the filing of a registration statement with the SEC. Sections 12(1), 12(2), and 17(a) require the use of the mails or other instrumentality or means of interstate communication or transportation.

Criminal Liability

Section 24 of the 1933 Act provides for criminal liability for any person who willfully violates the Act or its rules and regulations. The maximum penalty is a $10,000 fine and five years' imprisonment. Criminal actions under the 1933 Act are brought by the attorney general of the United States, not by the SEC.

In the following case, the court construed the due diligence defense of Section 11.

ESCOTT v. BARCHRIS CONSTRUCTION CORP.

283 F. Supp. 643 (S.D.N.Y. 1968)

BarChris Construction Corporation was in the business of constructing bowling centers. With the introduction of automatic pinsetters in 1952, there was a rapid growth in the popularity of bowling, and BarChris's sales increased from $800,000 in 1956 to over $9 million in 1960. By 1960, it was building about 3 percent of the lanes constructed, while Brunswick Corporation and AMF were building 97 percent. BarChris contracted with its customers to construct and equip bowling alleys for them. Under the contracts, a customer was required to make a small down payment in cash. After the alleys were constructed, customers gave BarChris promissory notes for the balance of the purchase price. BarChris discounted the notes with a factor. The factor kept part of the face value of the notes as a reserve until the customer paid the notes. BarChris was obligated to repurchase the notes if the customer defaulted.

In 1960, BarChris offered its customers an alternative financing method in which BarChris sold the interior of a bowling alley to a factor, James Talcott, Inc. Talcott then leased the alley either to a BarChris customer (Type A financing) or to a BarChris subsidiary that then subleased to the customer (Type B financing). Under Type A financing, BarChris guaranteed 25 percent of the customer's obligation under the lease. With Type B financing, BarChris was liable for 100 percent of its subsidiaries' lease obligations. Under either financing method, BarChris made substantial expenditures before receiving payment from customers and, therefore, experienced a constant need of cash.

In early 1961, BarChris decided to issue debentures and to use part of the proceeds to help its cash position. In March 1961, BarChris filed with the SEC a registration statement covering the debentures. The statement became effective on May 16. The proceeds of the offering were received by BarChris on May 24, 1961. By that time, BarChris had difficulty collecting from some of its customers, and other customers were in arrears on their payments to the factors of the discounted notes. Due to overexpansion in the bowling alley industry, many BarChris customers failed. On October 29, 1962, BarChris filed a petition for bankruptcy. On November 1, it defaulted on the payment of interest on the debentures.

Escott and other purchasers of the debentures sued BarChris and its officers, directors, and auditors, among others, under Section 11 of the Securities Act of 1933. BarChris's registration statement contained material misstatements and omitted material facts. It misstated current assets by $609,689 (15.6 percent) in the 1960 balance sheet certified by its auditors, Peat, Marwick, Mitchell & Co. Sales for 1960 were overstated by $653,900 (7.7 percent) and earnings per share by 10 cents (15.4 percent). The registration statement understated BarChris's contingent liabilities by $618,853 (42.8 percent) as of April 30, 1961. It overstated gross profit for the first quarter of 1961 by $230,755 (92 percent), and sales for the first quarter of 1961 by $519,810 (32.1 percent). The March 31, 1961, backlog was overstated by $4,490,000 (186 percent). The 1961 figures were not audited by Peat, Marwick.

In addition, the registration statement reported that prior loans from officers had been repaid, but failed to disclose that officers had made new loans to BarChris totaling $386,615. BarChris had used $1,160,000 of the proceeds of the debentures to pay old debts, a use not disclosed in the registration statement. BarChris's potential liability of $1,350,000 to factors due to customer delinquencies on factored notes was not disclosed. The registration statement represented BarChris's contingent liability on Type B financings as 25 percent instead of 100 percent. It misrepresented the nature of BarChris's business by failing to disclose that BarChris was already engaged and was about to become more heavily engaged in the operation of bowling alleys, including one called Capitol Lanes, as a way of minimizing its losses from customer defaults.

Trilling, BarChris's controller, signed the registration statement. Auslander, a director, signed the registration statement. Peat, Marwick consented to being named as an expert in the registration statement. All three, therefore, would be liable to Escott unless they could meet the due diligence defense of Section 11.

McLean, District Judge.   The question is whether Trilling, Auslander, and Peat, Marwick have proved their due diligence defenses. The position of each defendant will be separately considered.

TRILLING

Trilling was BarChris's controller. He signed the registration statement in that capacity, although he was not a director. Trilling entered BarChris's employ in October 1960. He was Kircher's [BarChris's treasurer] subordinate. When Kircher asked him for information, he furnished it.

Trilling was not a member of the executive committee. He was a comparatively minor figure in BarChris. The description of BarChris's management in the prospectus does not mention him. He was not considered to be an executive officer.

Trilling may well have been unaware of several of the inaccuracies in the prospectus. But he must have known of some of them. As a financial officer, he was familiar with Bar Chris's finances and with its books of account. He knew that part of the cash on deposit on December 31, 1960, had been procured temporarily by Russo [BarChris's executive vice president] for window-dressing purposes. He knew that BarChris was operating Capitol Lanes in 1960. He should have known, although perhaps through carelessness he did not know at the time, that BarChris's contingent liability on Type B lease transactions was greater than the prospectus stated. In the light of these facts, I cannot find that Trilling believed the entire prospectus to be true.

But even if he did, he still did not establish his due diligence defenses. He did not prove that as to the parts of the prospectus expertised by Peat, Marwick he had no reasonable ground to believe that it was untrue. He also failed to prove, as to the parts of the prospectus not expertised by Peat, Marwick, that he made a reasonable investigation which afforded him a reasonable ground to believe that it was true. As far as appears, he made no investigation. He did what was asked of him and assumed that others would properly take care of supplying accurate data as to the other aspects of the company's business. This would have been well enough but for the fact that he signed the registration statement. As a signer, he could not avoid responsibility by leaving it up to others to make it accurate. Trilling did not sustain the burden of proving his due diligence defenses.

AUSLANDER

Auslander was an outside director, i.e., one who was not an officer of BarChris. He was chairman of the board of Valley Stream National Bank in Valley Stream, Long Island. In February 1961, Vitolo [BarChris's president] asked him to become a director of BarChris. In February and early March 1961, before accepting Vitolo's invitation, Auslander made some investigation of Bar-Chris. He obtained Dun & Bradstreet reports that contained sales and earnings figures for periods earlier than December 31, 1960. He caused inquiry to be made of certain of BarChris's banks and was advised that they regarded BarChris favorably. He was informed that inquiry of Talcott had also produced a favorable response.

On March 3, 1961, Auslander indicated his willingness to accept a place on the board. Shortly thereafter, on March 14, Kircher sent him a copy of BarChris's annual report for 1960. Auslander observed that BarChris's auditors were Peat, Marwick. They were also the auditors for the Valley Stream National Bank. He thought well of them.

Auslander was elected a director on April 17, 1961. The registration statement in its original form had already been filed, of course without his signature. On May 10, 1961, he signed a signature page for the first amendment to the registration statement which was filed on May 11, 1961. This was a separate sheet without any document attached. Auslander did not know that it was a signature page for a registration statement. He vaguely understood that it was something "for the SEC."

At the May 15 directors' meeting, however, Auslander did realize that what he was signing was a signature sheet to a registration statement. This was the first time that he had appreciated the fact. A copy of the registration statement in its earlier form as amended on May 11, 1961, was passed around at the meeting. Auslander glanced at it briefly. He did not read it thoroughly. At the May 15 meeting, Russo and Vitolo stated that everything was in order and that the prospectus was correct. Auslander believed this statement.

In considering Auslander's due diligence defenses, a distinction must be drawn between the expertised and nonexpertised portions of the prospectus. As to the former, Auslander knew that

Peat, Marwick had audited the 1960 figures. He believed them to be correct because he had confidence in Peat, Marwick. He had no reasonable ground to believe otherwise.

As to the nonexpertised portions, however, Auslander is in a different position. He seems to have been under the impression that Peat, Marwick was responsible for all the figures. This impression was not correct, as he would have realized if he had read the prospectus carefully. Auslander made no investigation of the accuracy of the prospectus. He relied on the assurance of Vitolo and Russo, and upon the information he had received in answer to his inquiries back in February and early March. These inquiries were general ones, in the nature of a credit check. The information which he received in answer to them was also general, without specific reference to the statements in the prospectus, which was not prepared until some time thereafter.

It is true that Auslander became a director on the eve of the financing. He had little opportunity to familiarize himself with the company's affairs. The question is whether, under such circumstances, Auslander did enough to establish his due diligence.

Section 11 imposes liability upon a director, no matter how new he is. He is presumed to know his responsibility when he becomes a director. He can escape liability only by using that reasonable care to investigate the facts that a prudent man would employ in the management of his own property. In my opinion, a prudent man would not act in an important matter without any knowledge of the relevant facts, in sole reliance upon general information which does not purport to cover the particular case. To say that such minimal conduct measures up to the statutory standard would, to all intents and purposes, absolve new directors from responsibility merely because they are new. This is not a sensible construction of Section 11, when one bears in mind its fundamental purpose of requiring full and truthful disclosure for the protection of investors.

Auslander has not established his due diligence defense with respect to the misstatements and omissions in those portions of the prospectus other than the audited 1960 figures.

PEAT, MARWICK

The part of the registration statement purporting to be made upon the authority of Peat, Marwick as an expert was the 1960 figures. But because the statute requires the court to determine Peat, Marwick's belief, and the grounds thereof, "at the time such part of the registration statement became effective," for the purposes of this affirmative defense, the matter must be viewed as of May 16, 1961, and the question is whether at that time Peat, Marwick, after reasonable investigation, had reasonable ground to believe and did believe that the 1960 figures were true and that no material fact had been omitted from the registration statement which should have been included in order to make the 1960 figures not misleading. In deciding this issue, the court must consider not only what Peat, Marwick did in its 1960 audit, but also what it did in its subsequent S–1 review. The proper scope of that review must also be determined.

THE 1960 AUDIT

Peat, Marwick's work was in general charge of a member of the firm, Cummings, and more immediately in charge of Peat, Marwick's manager, Logan. Most of the actual work was performed by a senior accountant, Berardi, who had junior assistants, one of whom was Kennedy.

Berardi was then about 30 years old. He was not yet a CPA. He had had no previous experience with the bowling industry. This was his first job as a senior accountant. He could hardly have been given a more difficult assignment.

It is unnecessary to recount everything that Berardi did in the course of the audit. We are concerned only with the evidence relating to what Berardi did or did not do with respect to those items which I have found to have been incorrectly reported in the 1960 figures in the prospectus. More narrowly, we are directly concerned only with such of those items as I have found to be material.

First and foremost is Berardi's failure to discover that Capitol Lanes had not been sold. This error affected both the sales figure and the liability side of the balance sheet. Fundamentally, the error stemmed from the fact that Berardi never realized that Heavenly Lanes and Capitol were two different names for the same alley. Berardi assumed that Heavenly was to be treated like any other completed job.

Berardi read the minutes of the board of directors meeting of November 22, 1960, which recited that "the Chairman recommended that the Corporation operate Capitol Lanes." Berardi knew from various BarChris records that Capitol Lanes, Inc., was paying rentals to Talcott. Also, a Peat, Marwick work paper bearing Kennedy's initials recorded that Capitol Lanes, Inc., held certain insurance policies.

Berardi testified that he inquired of Russo about Capitol Lanes and that Russo told him that Capitol Lanes, Inc., was going to operate an alley someday but as yet it had no alley. Berardi testified that he understood that the alley had not been built and that he believed that the rental payments were on vacant land.

I am not satisfied with this testimony. If Berardi did hold this belief, he should not have held it. The entries as to insurance and as to "operation of alley" should have alerted him to the fact that an alley existed. He should have made further inquiry on the subject. It is apparent that Berardi did not understand this transaction.

He never identified this mysterious Capitol with the Heavenly Lanes which he had included in his sales and profit figures. The vital question is whether he failed to make a reasonable investigation which, if he had made it, would have revealed the truth.

Certain accounting records of BarChris, which Berardi testified he did not see, would have put him on inquiry. One was a job cost ledger card for job no. 6036, the job number which Berardi put on his own sheet for Heavenly Lanes. This card read "Capitol Theatre (Heavenly)." In addition, two accounts receivable cards each showed both names on the same card, Capitol and Heavenly. Berardi testified that he looked at the accounts receivable records but that he did not see these particular cards. He testified that he did not look on the job cost ledger cards because he took the costs from another record, the costs register.

The burden of proof on this issue is on Peat, Marwick. Although the question is a rather close one, I find that Peat, Marwick has not sustained that burden. Peat, Marwick has not proved that Berardi made a reasonable investigation as far as Capitol Lanes was concerned and that his ignorance of the true facts was justified.

I turn now to the errors in the current assets. As to cash, Berardi properly obtained a confirmation from the bank as to BarChris's cash balance on December 31, 1960. He did not know that part of this balance had been temporarily increased by the deposit of reserves returned by Talcott to BarChris conditionally for a limited time. I do not believe that Berardi reasonably should have known this. It would not be reasonable to require Berardi to examine all of BarChris's correspondence files [which contained correspondence indicating that BarChris was to return the cash to Talcott] when he had no reason to suspect any irregularity.

THE S–1 REVIEW

The purpose of reviewing events subsequent to the date of a certified balance sheet (referred to as an S–1 review when made with reference to a registration statement) is to ascertain whether any material change has occurred in the company's financial position which should be disclosed in order to prevent the balance sheet figures from being misleading. The scope of such a review, under generally accepted auditing standards, is limited. It does not amount to a complete audit.

Berardi made the S–1 review in May 1961. He devoted a little over two days to it, a total of 20½ hours. He did not discover any of the errors or omissions pertaining to the state of affairs in 1961, all of which were material. The question is whether, despite his failure to find out anything, his investigation was reasonable within the meaning of the statute.

What Berardi did was to look at a consolidating trial balance as of March 31, 1961, which had been prepared by BarChris, compare it with the audited December 31, 1960 figures, discuss with Trilling certain unfavorable developments which the comparison disclosed, and read certain minutes. He did not examine any important financial records other than the trial balance.

In substance, Berardi asked questions, he got answers which he considered satisfactory, and he did nothing to verify them. Since he never read the prospectus, he was not even aware that there had ever been any problem about loans from officers. He made no inquiry of factors about delinquent notes in his S–1 review. Since he knew nothing about Kircher's notes of the executive committee meetings, he did not learn that the delinquency situation had grown worse. He was content with Trilling's assurance that no liability theretofore contingent had become direct. Apparently the only BarChris officer with whom Berardi communicated was Trilling. He could not recall making any inquiries of Russo, Vitolo, or Pugliese [a BarChris vice-president].

There had been a material change for the worse in BarChris's financial position. That change was sufficiently serious so that the failure to disclose it made the 1960 figures misleading. Berardi did not discover it. As far as results were concerned, his S–1 review was useless.

Accountants should not be held to a standard higher than that recognized in their profession. I do not do so here. Berardi's review did not come up to that standard. He did not take some of the steps which Peat, Marwick's written program prescribed. He did not spend an adequate amount of time on a task of this magnitude. Most important of all, he was too easily satisfied with glib answers to his inquiries.

This is not to say that he should have made a complete audit. But there were enough danger signals in the materials which he did examine to require some further investigation on his part. Generally accepted auditing standards require such further investigation under these circumstances. It is not always sufficient merely to ask questions.

Here again, the burden of proof is on Peat, Marwick. I find that burden has not been satisfied. I conclude that Peat, Marwick has not established its due diligence defense.

Judgment for Escott and the other purchasers.

SECURITIES EXCHANGE ACT OF 1934

Introduction

The Securities Exchange Act of 1934 is chiefly concerned with requiring the disclosure of material information to investors. Unlike the 1933 Act, which is primarily a one-time disclosure statute, the 1934 Act requires *periodic disclosure* by issuers with publicly held equity securities. In addition, the 1934 Act regulates insiders' transactions in securities, proxy solicitations, tender offers, brokers and dealers, and securities exchanges. The 1934 Act also has several sections prohibiting fraud and manipulation in securities transactions. The ultimate purpose of the 1934 Act is to keep investors fully informed to allow them to make intelligent investment decisions.

Registration of Securities under the 1934 Act

Under the 1934 Act, issuers must register *classes* of securities. This is different from the 1933 Act, which requires issuers to register *issuances* of securities. Under the 1933 Act, securities are registered only for the term of an issuance. Under the 1934 Act, registered classes of securities remain registered until the issuer takes steps to deregister the securities.

Issuers with securities registered under the 1934 Act become subject to certain further requirements that will be discussed later in this chapter, such as the rules pertaining to the solicitation of proxies and the filing of certain periodic reports. In addition, **insiders** of issuers with registered securities may be required to report their transactions in the shares of the company and may be subject to the recapture of profits they make on company shares.

Securities Covered   Two types of securities must be *registered* under the 1934 Act.

1. An issuer whose total assets exceed $5 million must register a class of equity securities with at least 500 shareholders, if the securities are traded in interstate commerce.
2. An issuer must register any security traded on a national security exchange, such as common shares traded on the American Stock Exchange.

The information required in the 1934 Act registration statement is similar to that required under the 1933 Act, except that offering information is omitted.

Termination of Registration   An issuer may avoid the expense and burden of complying with the periodic disclosure and other requirements of the 1934 Act if the issuer terminates its registration. A 1934 Act registration may be terminated if the issuer has fewer than 300 shareholders. In addition, such a registration may be terminated if the issuer has fewer than 500 shareholders of any class of equity securities and assets of no more than $5 million. However, an issuer with securities listed on a national securities exchange would not be able to terminate a registration of the listed securities.

Periodic Reports

To maintain a steady flow of material information to investors, the 1934 Act requires public issuers to *file periodic reports* with the SEC. Three types of issuers must file such reports:

1. An issuer with assets of more than $5 million and at least 500 holders of any class of equity securities traded in interstate commerce.
2. An issuer whose equity securities are traded on a national securities exchange.
3. An issuer who has made a registered offering under the 1933 Act.

The first two types of issuers—which are issuers that must also register securities under the 1934 Act—must file several periodic reports, including an annual report (Form 10-K) and a quarterly report (Form 10-Q). They must file a monthly report (Form 8-K) when material events occur. Comparable reports must also be sent to their shareholders. The third type of issuer—an issuer who must disclose only because it has made

a public offering under the 1933 Act—must file the same reports as the other issuers, except that it need not provide an annual report to its shareholders. Despite its significance as part of the federal securities disclosure system, the annual report to shareholders is not a part of the requirement to file periodic reports with the SEC, but rather is required by the proxy rules in connection with the annual shareholders' meeting. Since the proxy rules apply only to issuers with securities registered under the 1934 Act, the third type of issuer does not have to distribute an annual report to shareholders.

The *10-K* annual report must include audited financial statements plus current information about the conduct of the business, its management, and the status of its securities. The 10-K financial-statement auditing requirements are the same as for a 1933 Act registration statement: two years' audited balance sheets and three years' audited income statements and audited changes in financial position. The 10-K report is intended to update the information required in the 1934 Act registration statement.

The quarterly report, the *10-Q*, requires only a summarized, unaudited operating statement and unaudited figures on capitalization and shareholders' equity. The *8-K* monthly report must be filed within 10 days of the end of any month in which any specified event occurs, such as a change in the amount of securities, a default under the terms of an issue of securities, an acquisition or disposition of assets, a change in control of the company, a revaluation of assets, or "any materially important event."

Most securities issuers file paper reports with the SEC. Since September 1984, however, a few issuers have filed computerized reports, transmitting them by telephone or by sending computer tapes or disks to the SEC. These computerized filings are made with the SEC's Electronic Data Gathering, Analysis, and Retrieval system: EDGAR. The purpose of EDGAR is to ease the issuer's burden of filing reports and to facilitate access to filed reports.

Suspension of Duty to File Reports   An issuer's duty to file periodic reports is suspended if the issuer has fewer than 300 shareholders. In addition, a suspension occurs if the issuer has fewer than 500 shareholders of any class of equity securities and assets of no more than $5 million. However, an issuer with securities traded on a national securities exchange would remain obligated to file periodic reports.

Holdings and Trading by Insiders

Section 16(a) of the 1934 Act requires that statutory insiders individually file a statement disclosing their holdings of any class of the issuer's equity securities. A **statutory insider** is a person who falls into any of the following categories:

1. An *officer* of a corporation with equity securities registered under the 1934 Act.

2. A *director* of such a corporation.

3. An *owner of more than 10 percent* of a class of equity securities registered under the 1934 Act.

In addition, statutory insiders must report any transaction in such securities within 10 days following the end of the month in which the transaction occurs. They must also report purchases and sales made up to six months before and up to six months after becoming an officer, director, or a 10 percent holder.

Short-Swing Trading by Insiders   Section 16(b) of the 1934 Act provides that any profit made by a statutory insider is recoverable by the issuer if the profit resulted from the purchase and sale (or the sale and purchase) of any class of the issuer's equity securities within less than a six-month period. This provision was designed to stop speculative insider trading on the basis of information that "may have been obtained by such owner, director, or officer by reason of his relationship to the issuer." The application of the provision is without regard to intent to use or actual use of inside information. However, a few cases, such as the following, have held that sales made by a statutory insider without actual access to inside information do not violate Section 16(b).

C.R.A. REALTY CORP. v. CROTTY

878 F.2d 562 (2d Cir. 1989)

Joseph Crotty was a vice president of United Artists Communications, Inc. (UA), a corporation with equity securities registered under the Securities Exchange Act of 1934. Crotty was the head film buyer of UA's western division, supervising a staff of 30 people. He had virtually complete and autonomous control of film buying for the 351 UA theaters in the western United States, including negotiating and signing movie acquisition agreements, supervising movie distribution, and settling contracts after the movies had been shown. Consequently, Crotty knew how many contracts were being negotiated at any one time and the price UA was paying for the rental of each movie.

Crotty was required to consult with higher officers only if he wanted to exceed a certain limit on the amount of the cash advance paid to a distributor for a movie. This occurred no more than two or three times a year. The gross revenue from Crotty's division was about 35–36 percent of UA's gross revenue from movie exhibitions and around 15–18 percent of its total gross revenue.

During a six-month period, Crotty purchased 7,500 shares of UA and sold 3,500 shares, realizing a large profit. C.R.A. Reality Corp., a UA shareholder, sued Crotty on behalf of UA to recover Crotty's profit, on the grounds that Crotty's trading violated Section 16(b) of the 1934 Act. The trial court held that Crotty was not an officer for purposes of Section 16(b), and C.R.A. appealed.

Timbers, Circuit Judge.   Section 16(b) imposes a strict prophylactic rule with respect to insider, short-swing trading. Any corporate official within the statutory meaning of an officer who engages in short-swing trading automatically will be required to surrender any profit from the trading, without proof of actual abuse of insider information, and without proof of intent to profit on the basis of such information. This objective test was chosen by Congress because of the difficulty of proving whether a corporate insider actually abused confidential information to which he had access or purchased or sold an issuer's stock with the intention of profiting from such information.

In Securities Exchange Act Rule 3b-2, the SEC defined the term officer as including a vice-president of an issuer. C.R.A. asserts that, since Crotty is a vice-president of UA, this rule places him within the purview of Section 16(b). It is significant, however, that the SEC itself does not believe that this rule should be rigidly applied in determining who is an officer within the meaning of Section 16. For example, two SEC releases show that the SEC does not consider an employee's title as an officer to bring the employee automatically under Section 16.

Moreover, the trial court's holding is consistent with the law of this Circuit. In *Colby v. Klune* (1949), we held that a corporate employee who did not hold the title of a corporate officer nevertheless could be an officer within the meaning of Section 16(b) if he performed important executive duties of such character that he would be likely, in discharging these duties, to obtain confidential information about the company's affairs that would aid him if he engaged in personal market transactions. We believe that the reasoning of *Colby* applies here. It is an employee's duties and responsibilities—rather than his actual title—that determine whether he is an officer within the purview of Section 16(b).

The Supreme Court of the United States has emphasized that potential access to inside information is the key to finding liability, rather than rigid application of statutory designations. In *Kern County Land Co. v. Occidental Petroleum Corp.* (1973), the Court held that, even if a hostile bidder held 10 percent or more of the stock of a target company when it exchanged the issuer's stock for stock issued as part of a merger designed to fend off the bidder, the bidder didnot come within the ambit of Section 16(b), since its hostile status precluded it from having any inside information about the target issuer. These cases reflect an interpretation of Section 16(b) that best serves the congressional purpose of curbing short-swing speculation by corporate insiders.

All that is required by *Colby* is that the plaintiff establish that it is more likely than not that the employee's duties gave him access to inside information. A plaintiff need not show that the employee actually obtained inside information or used it to his advantage.

Viewing his responsibilities, Crotty had no access to inside information such as the financial or operational plans of UA. He was not a director of the company, never attended a directors' meeting, and never received any information from the Board of Directors that was not available to the general public.

The only information that Crotty had that arguably might be said to be inside information was concerning daily revenue receipts or film grosses from UA's movie exhibition. Entertainment Data, Inc., an independent contractor, collected the daily film grosses from the western division theaters and gave them to Crotty on an overnight basis. Entertainment Data, however, also gave daily film gross information to most of the major movie exhibitors and distributors in Los Angeles and San Francisco. This information also was distributed to daily trade publications. Accordingly, the film gross information was not inside information and gave Crotty no advantage over other investors.

Judgment for Crotty affirmed.

Proxy Solicitation Regulation

Introduction

Section 14 of the 1934 Act regulates the *solicitation of proxies*. In a public corporation, shareholders rarely attend and vote at shareholder meetings. Many shareholders are able to vote at shareholder meetings only by **proxy,** a document by which shareholders direct other persons to vote their shares. Just as investors need information to be able to make intelligent investment decisions, shareholders need information to make intelligent voting and proxy decisions.

Proxy Statement

SEC Regulation 14A requires any person soliciting proxies from holders of securities registered under the 1934 Act to furnish each holder with a **proxy statement** containing voting information. Usually, the only party soliciting proxies is the corporation's management, which is seeking proxies from common shareholders to enable it to reelect itself to the board of directors.

If the management of the corporation does not solicit proxies, it must nevertheless inform the shareholders of material information affecting matters that are to be put to a vote of the shareholders. This **information statement,** which contains about the same information as a proxy statement, must be sent to all shareholders that are entitled to vote at the meeting. The proxy statement or information statement must be filed with the SEC at least 10 days before it is mailed to the shareholders. If the proxy or information statement is issued in connection with an annual meeting of shareholders at which directors are to be elected, the shareholders must also receive a current annual report of the corporation.

The primary purpose of the SEC rules concerning information that must be included in the proxy or information statement is to permit shareholders to make informed decisions while voting for directors and considering any resolutions proposed by the management or shareholders. Information on each director nominee must include the candidate's principal occupation, his shareholdings in the corporation, his previous service as a director of the corporation, his material transactions with the corporation (such as goods or services pro-

vided), and his directorships in other corporations. The total remuneration of the five directors or officers who are highest paid, including bonuses, grants under stock option plans, fringe benefits, and other perquisites, must also be included in the proxy statement.

Proxies

The rules regarding the content of proxies ensure that the shareholder understands how his proxy will be voted. The proxy form must indicate in boldface type on whose behalf it is being solicited—for example, the corporation's management. Generally, the proxy must permit the shareholder to vote for or against the proposal or to abstain from voting on any resolutions on the meeting's agenda. The proxy form may ask for discretionary voting authority if the proxy indicates in bold print how the shares will be voted. For directors' elections, the shareholders must be provided with a means for withholding approval for each nominee.

False Statements

Rule 14a-9 prohibits misstatements or omissions of material fact in the course of a proxy solicitation. If a violation is proved, a court may enjoin the holding of the shareholders' meeting, void the proxies that were illegally obtained, or rescind the action taken at the shareholders' meeting. In the following case, the court held that management did not violate Rule 14a-9 by failing to disclose its motives for seeking amendment of the company's articles of incorporation.

LEWIS v. POTLATCH CORP.

716 F. Supp. 807 (S.D.N.Y. 1989)

Potlatch Corporation was in the forests products industry, an industry that had experienced a wave of takeovers in the 1980s. In 1985, the Potlatch board of directors approved a voting rights amendment to the articles of incorporation. The amendment granted four votes per share to current shareholders and other specified shareholders. New shareholders would have only one vote per share until they held the shares for four years. The effect of the amendment, if it were approved by shareholders, would be to deter and frustrate a hostile takeover of Potlatch. To obtain shareholder approval of the voting rights amendment, on October 22, 1985, the board issued a proxy statement in connection with its solicitation of proxies from the shareholders. The voting rights amendment was approved by shareholders on December 12, 1985.

Harry Lewis and other Potlatch shareholders sued the company under Section 14(a) of the 1934 Act, seeking to void the shareholders' approval of the voting rights amendment. Lewis claimed that the shareholders' votes were procured by fraud because the board's proxy statement was materially false and misleading.

Sprizzo, Judge.   A letter issued along with the proxy statement stated that the intent of the voting rights amendment was to give longterm shareholders a greater voice in the affairs of Potlatch. Lewis alleges that this statement was false because management's real purpose was entrenchment.

However, where all of the relevant facts which a reasonable shareholder would need to make a decision on a proposed corporate action are disclosed, the proxy material need not disclose management motive. In this case, the proxy statement fully described the proposed voting rights amendment and the effect it would have on stockholders. Indeed, it specifically disclosed that directors and officers of the company could have an increasingly higher percentage of the voting power of the company if the amendment were adopted. Moreover, it stated that "the Amendment could increase the likelihood that incumbent Directors and officers will retain their positions." Any shareholder voting for the proposal, therfore, was informed that passage of the amendment could concentrate control in hands of present management and that entrenchment of the present board could result.

The proxy statement disclosed that under current New York Stock Exchange rules, adoption of the voting rights amendment could lead to the delisting of Potlatch stock on the exchange, that the NYSE rules were being reviewed, and that "stockholders should assume that if [the] Amendment is adopted the Common Stock may not be permitted to continue to be listed on the NYSE." Lewis alleges that the proxy statement failed to disclose that the possible delisting of Potlatch stock on the NYSE was a disadvantage.

The disclosure here was clearly adequate. A proxy statement need not state what would be apparent to a reasonable shareholder. Moreover, a proxy statement need not characterize the obvious effect of disclosed information.

Judgment for Potlatch.

Proxy Contests

A shareholder may decide to solicit proxies in competition with management. Such a competition is called a **proxy contest,** and a solicitation of this kind is also subject to SEC rules. To facilitate proxy contests, the SEC requires the corporation either to furnish a shareholder list to shareholders who desire to wage a proxy contest or to mail the competing proxy material for them.

Shareholder Proposals

In a large public corporation, it is very expensive for a shareholder to solicit proxies in support of a proposal for corporate action that she will offer at a shareholders' meeting. Therefore, she usually asks the management to include her proposal in its proxy statement. SEC Rule 14a-8 covers proposals by shareholders.

Under Rule 14a-8, the corporation must include a shareholder's proposal in its proxy statement if, among other things, the shareholder owns at least 1 percent or $1,000 of the securities to be voted at the shareholders' meeting. A shareholder may submit only one proposal per meeting. The proposal and its supporting statement may not exceed 500 words.

Excludable Proposals   Under Rule 14a-8, a corporation's management may exclude many types of shareholder proposals from its proxy statement. For example, the following are excludable:

1. The proposal deals with the ordinary business operations of the corporation. Few well-drafted proposals are excluded on this basis. For example, TRW, Inc., was required to include in its proxy statement a proposal that it establish a shareholder advisory committee that would advise the board of directors on the interests of shareholders. However, Pacific Telesis Group was permitted on this ground to omit a proposal that the board consider adding an environmentalist director and designate a vice president for environmental matters for each subsidiary.

2. The proposal relates to operations that account for less than 5 percent of a corporation's total assets and is not otherwise significantly related to the company's business. For example, Harsco Corp. could not omit a proposal that it sell its 50 percent interest in a South African firm even though the investment was arguably economically insignificant—only 4.5 percent of net earnings, because the issues raised by the proposal were significantly related to Harsco's business.

3. A proposal that would require the issuer to violate a state or federal law. For example, one shareholder asked North American Bank to put a lesbian on the board of directors. The SEC staff advised North American Bank that the proposal was excludable because it may have required the corporation to violate antidiscrimination laws.

4. The proposal relates to a personal claim or grievance. A proposal that the corporation pay the shareholder $1 million for damages that she suffered from using one of the corporation's products would be excludable.

In addition, one part of Rule 14a-8 prevents a shareholder from submitting a proposal similar to recent proposals that have been overwhelmingly rejected by shareholders in recent years.

Liability Provisions of the 1934 Act

To prevent fraud, deception, or manipulation and to provide remedies to the victims of such practices, Congress included a number of liability provisions in the 1934 Act.

Manipulation of a Security's Price

Section 9 specifically prohibits a number of deceptive practices that may be used to cause security prices to rise or fall by stimulating market activity. The prohibited practices include simultaneous purchases and sales of securities (called wash sales).

Liability for False Statements in Filed Documents

Section 18 is the 1934 Act counterpart to Section 11 of the 1933 Act. Section 18 imposes liability on any person responsible for a false or misleading statement of material fact in any document filed with the SEC under the 1934 Act. (Filed documents include the 10-K report, 8-K report, and proxy statements, but not the 10-Q report.) Any person who relies on a false or misleading statement in such a filed document may sue for damages. As with Section 11, the purchaser need not prove that the defendant was negligent or acted with scienter. Instead, the defendant has a defense that he acted in good faith and had no knowledge that the statement was false or misleading. This defense is easier to meet than the Section 11 due diligence defense, requiring only that the defendant prove that he did not act with scienter.

Section 10(b) and Rule 10b-5

The most important liability section in the 1934 Act is Section 10(b), an extremely broad provision prohibiting the use of any manipulative or deceptive device in contravention of any rules that the SEC prescribes as "necessary or appropriate in the public interest or for the protection of investors." Rule 10b-5 was adopted by the SEC under Section 10(b). The rule states:

It shall be unlawful for any person, directly or indirectly, by use of any means or instrumentality of interstate commerce or of the mails, or of any facility of any national securities exchange,

(a) to employ any device, scheme, or artifice to defraud,
(b) to make any untrue statement of a material fact or to omit to state a material fact necessary in order to make the statements made, in the light of the circumstances under which they were made, not misleading, or
(c) to engage in any act, practice, or course of business which operates or would operate as a fraud or deceit upon any person,

in connection with the purchase or sale of any security.

Rule 10b-5 applies to all transactions in all securities. Securities need not be registered under the 1933 Act or the 1934 Act for Rule 10b-5 to apply.

Elements of a Rule 10b-5 Violation

The most important elements of a Rule 10b-5 violation are a misstatement or omission of material fact, scienter, and reliance. In addition, private persons suing under the rule must be purchasers or sellers.

Misstatement or Omission of Material Fact   The essence of fraud, deception, and manipulation is *falsity* or *nondisclosure when there is a duty to speak*. Liability for falsity occurs when a person *misstates* material facts. For example, if a manager of an unprofitable business induces shareholders to sell their stock to him by stating that the business will fail, although he knows that the business has become potentially profitable, he violates Rule 10b-5.

Liability for nondisclosure arises when a person *omits* material facts when he has a *duty to disclose*. For a person to be liable for an omission, there must be a duty of trust or confidence breached either by a nondisclosure or by the incomplete disclosure of information. For example, a securities broker is liable to his customer for not disclosing that he owns the shares that he recommends to the customer. As an agent of the customer, he owes a fiduciary duty to his customer to disclose his conflict of interest. In addition, a person is liable for omitting to tell all of the material facts after he has chosen to disclose some of them. His incomplete disclosure created the duty to disclose all of the material facts.

However, in *Santa Fe Industries, Inc. v. Green*,[13] the Supreme Court held that a mere breach of a fiduciary duty, such as mismanagement of the company by the directors, creates no Rule 10b-5 liability. In addition to a breach of a fiduciary duty, there must be deception or manipulation. Deception may be proved when the fiduciary duty breached is a duty of confidentiality or a duty of disclosure.

Materiality   The misstated or omitted fact must be material. In essence, material information is any information that is likely to have an impact on the price of a security in the market. In *TSC Industries, Inc. v. Northway*,[14] a Rule 14a-9 case, the Supreme Court stated:

An omitted fact is material if there is a substantial likelihood that a reasonable shareholder would consider it important to his decision. The standard contemplates a showing of a substantial likelihood that the omitted fact would have assumed actual significance in the deliberations of the reasonable shareholder. There must be a substantial likelihood that the disclosure of the omitted fact would have been viewed by the reasonable investor as having significantly altered the total mix of information made available.

It is generally believed that the *Northway* materiality standard applies to all of the liability sections of the securities acts. Such matters as proposed mergers, tender offers for the corporation's shares, plans to introduce an important new product, or indications of an abrupt change in the expectations of the company are examples of what would be considered material facts. The Supreme Court expressly adopted the *Northway* test for the Rule 10b-5 context.

In some situations, there is doubt whether an important event will occur. In the *Texas Gulf Sulphur* case,[15] the court held that materiality of the doubtful event can be determined by "a balancing of both the indicated probability that the event will occur and the anticipated magnitude of the event in light of the totality of the company activity." The Supreme Court has approved this definition of materiality.

Scienter   For fraud, deception, or manipulation to exist, the defendant must have acted with scienter. **Scienter** is an intent to deceive, manipulate, or defraud. The Supreme Court has not decided whether recklessness is sufficient for the scienter requirement, though many lower courts have held that reckless conduct violates Rule 10b-5. Mere negligence is *not* enough under Rule 10b-5.[16]

Other Elements   The Supreme Court has held that Rule 10b-5 requires that private plaintiffs seeking damages be *actual purchasers or sellers* of securities.[17] Persons who were deterred from purchasing securities by fraudulent statements may not recover lost profits under Rule 10b-5.

Under Rule 10b-5, private plaintiffs alleging misstatements must prove that they *relied* on the misstatement of material fact. The SEC as plaintiff need not prove reliance. For private plaintiffs, reliance is not usually required in omission cases; the investor need merely prove that the omitted fact was material.

---

[13] 430 U.S. 462 (U.S. Sup. Ct. 1977).
[14] 426 U.S. 438 (U.S. Sup. Ct. 1976).
[15]*SEC v. Texas Gulf Sulphur Co.*, 401 F.2d 833 (2d Cir. 1968).
[16]*Ernst & Ernst v. Hochfelder*, 425 U.S. 185 (1976).
[17]*Blue Chip Stamps v. Manor Drug Stores*, 421 U.S. 723 (1975).

In *Shores v. Sklar*,[18] the court held that an investor's reliance on the availability of the securities on the market satisfied the reliance requirement of Rule 10b-5 because the securities market had been defrauded as to the value of the securities. Due to the fraud on the securities market, this market reliance existed even though the sellers had never communicated with the purchaser. In *Levinson v. Basic, Inc.*,[19] the Supreme Court held that the fraud-on-the-market theory permits a court to presume an investor's reliance merely from the public availability of material misrepresentations. That presumption, however, is rebuttable, such as by evidence that an investor knew the market price was incorrect.

For Rule 10b-5 to apply, the wrongful action must be accomplished by the mails, with an instrumentality of interstate commerce, or on a national securities exchange. This element satisfies the federal jurisdiction requirement. Use of the mails or a telephone within one state has been held to meet this element.

Conduct Covered by Rule 10b-5

The scope of activities proscribed by Rule 10b-5 is not immediately obvious. While it is easy to understand that actual fraud and price manipulation are covered by the rule, two other areas are less easily mastered: the corporation's continuous disclosure obligation and insider trading.

Continuous Disclosure of Material Information

The purpose of the securities acts is to ensure that investors have the information they need in order to make intelligent investment decisions *at all times*. The periodic reporting requirements of the 1934 Act are designed to accomplish this result. If important developments arise between the disclosure dates of reports, however, investors will not have all of the information they need to make intelligent decisions unless the corporation discloses the material information immediately. Rule 10b-5, as interpreted in the *Texas Gulf Sulphur* case,[20] may be read to require a corporation to disclose material information immediately, unless the corporation has a valid business purpose for withholding disclosure. In addition, *Texas Gulf Sulphur* held that when the corporation does choose to disclose information or comment on information that it has no duty to disclose, it must do so accurately.

Until 1988, courts had disagreed on whether Rule 10b-5 requires disclosure of merger and other acquisition negotiations prior to an agreement in principle. In the close corporation context especially, courts have been willing to find materiality of preliminary acquisition negotiations. For example, in *Michaels v. Michaels*, the court held that a shareholder in a closely held company purchasing another shareholder's shares had a duty to disclose that acquisition negotiations were going to be initiated.[21]

In the following case, decided in 1988, the Supreme Court of the United States held that materiality of merger negotiations is to be determined on a case-by-case basis. The Court held that materiality depends on the probability that the transaction will be consummated and its significance to the issuer of the securities. In addition, the Court stated that a corporation that chooses to comment on acquisition negotiations must do so truthfully.

---

[18]647 F.2d 462 (5th Cir. 1982).
[19]485 U.S. 224 (U.S. Sup. Ct. 1988).

[20]401 F.2d 833 (2d Cir. 1968).
[21]767 F.2d 751 (2d Cir. 1984).

LEVINSON v. BASIC, INC.

485 U.S. 224 (U.S. Sup. Ct. 1988)

For over a decade, Combustion Engineering, Inc. (CEI) had been interested in acquiring Basic, Inc. When antitrust barriers to such an acquisition were eliminated in 1976, CEI's secret strategic plan listed the acquisition of Basic as an objective. Between September 1976 and October 1977, the managements of Basic and CEI privately discussed several times a possible acquisition of Basic by CEI. Throughout 1977 and 1978, despite the secrecy of merger negotiations, there were repeated instances of abnormal trading in Basic's shares on the New York Stock Exchange. On October 19 and 20, 1977, the trading volume in Basic's shares rose from an average of 7,000 shares per day to 29,000 shares. On October 21, 1977, Max Muller, the president of Basic, made a public announcement, reported in a major newspaper, that "the company knew no reason for the stock's activity and that no negotiations were under way with any company for a merger."

Secret contacts between Basic and CEI continued, however. On June 7, 1978, CEI offered $28 per share for Basic, which Basic rejected as too low. CEI stated it would make a better offer, but Muller told CEI to "hold off until we tell you," because Muller wanted to see an investment banker's valuation of Basic before evaluating any CEI offer. Muller and other Basic officials decided to ask CEI for its "best offer." On July 10, 1978, Muller and CEI agreed that CEI would make an informal offer to Basic. CEI advised Muller to make no public disclosures about the negotiations.

On July 14, 1978, the price of Basic shares rose more than 12 percent to $27 per share on trading of 18,200 shares. The New York Stock Exchange called Basic and asked it to explain the trading in its shares. Basic denied that any undisclosed merger or acquisition plans or any other significant corporate development existed. On September 24, 1978, the price of Basic shares rose more than 2 points to $30 per share on volume of 31,900 shares. The next day, the price rose almost 3 points to $33 per share on volume of 28,500 shares, even though the Dow Jones Industrial Average fell more than 3 points. Again the Exchange asked Basic whether there were any undisclosed acquisition plans or any other significant corporate developments. Basic flatly denied that there were any corporate developments and issued a press release that stated:

management is unaware of any present or pending corporate development that would result in the abnormally heavy trading activity and price fluctuation in company shares that have been experienced in the past few days.

Secret contacts between Basic and CEI continued. In early November, Basic sent a quarterly report to its shareholders in which it stated:

With regard to the stock market activity in the Company's shares we remain unaware of any present or pending developments that would account for the high volume of trading and price fluctuations in recent months.

On November 27, 1978, CEI secretly offered to buy Basic's outstanding shares for $35 per share. Basic rejected the offer. On December 14, 1978, CEI offered $46 per share. The next day, Friday, December 15, the price of Basic's shares soared. Again Basic answered the Exchange's inquiry with a denial of corporate developments. On Monday, December 18, 1978, Basic asked the Exchange to suspend trading in Basic shares, because it had been "approached" concerning a possible merger. The next day, Basic accepted CEI's offer. On the following day, December 19, Basic announced its acceptance of CEI's offer to buy Basic's outstanding shares for $46 per share.

Max Levinson and several other Basic shareholders sold their Basic shares between October 21, 1977 and December 15, 1978, at a price lower than CEI's offer. They claimed that Basic's statements denying that any merger discussions were occurring violated Section 10(b) and Rule 10b-5 of the Securities Exchange Act of 1934. The district court held that the statements were not material as a matter of law. Levinson appealed to the Sixth Circuit Court of Appeals, which held that although possessing no general duty to disclose the merger negotiations, Basic released statements that were so incomplete as to be misleading. Basic appealed to the Supreme Court.

Blackmun, Justice.   Underlying the adoption of extensive disclosure requirements of the 1934 Act was a legislative philosophy: There cannot be honest markets without honest publicity. Manipulation and dishonest practices of the market place thrive upon mystery and secrecy.

The Court previously has explicitly defined a standard of materiality under the securities laws, concluding in the proxy-solicitation context that "[a]n omitted fact is material if there is a substantial likelihood that a reasonable shareholder would consider it important in deciding how to vote." *TSC Industries, Inc. v. Northway, Inc.* (1976). Acknowledging that certain information concerning corporate developments could well be of "dubious significance," the Court was careful not to set too low a standard of materiality; it was concerned that a minimal standard might bring an overabundance of information within its reach, and lead management "simply to bury the shareholders in an avalanche of trivial information—a result that is hardly conducive to informed decisionmaking." It further explained that to fulfill the materiality requirement "there must be a substantial likelihood that the disclosure of the omitted fact would have been viewed by the reasonable investor as having significantly altered the 'total mix' of information made available." We now expressly adopt the *TSC Industries* standard of materiality for the Section 10(b) and Rule 10b-5 context.

The application of this materiality standard to preliminary merger discussions is not self-evident. Where the event is contingent or speculative in nature, it is difficult to ascertain whether the "reasonable investor" would have considered the omitted information significant at the time. Merger negotiations, because of the ever-present possibility that the contemplated transaction will not be effectuated, fall into this category.

Basic urges upon us the Third Circuit test for resolving this difficulty. Under this approach, preliminary merger discussions do not become material until "agreementin-principle" as to the price and structure of the transaction has been reached between the would-be merger partners. See *Greenfield v. Heublein, Inc.* (3d Cir. 1984). By definition, then, information concerning any negotiations not yet at the agreement-in-principle stage could be withheld or even misrepresented without a violation of Rule 10b-5.

Three rationales have been offered in support of the "agreement-in-principle" test. The first derives from the concern expressed in *TSC Industries* that an investor not be overwhelmed by excessively detailed and trivial information and focuses on the substantial risk that preliminary merger discussions may collapse: because such discussions are inherently tentative, disclosure of their existence itself could mislead investors and foster false optimism. The other two justifications for the agreement-in-principle standard are based on management concerns: because the requirement of "agreement-in-principle" limits the scope of disclosure obligations, it helps preserve the confidentiality of merger discussions where earlier disclosure might prejudice the negotiations; and the test also provides a usable, bright-line rule for determining when disclosure must be made.

None of these policy-based rationales, however, purports to explain why drawing the line at agreement-in-principle reflects the significance of the information upon the investor's decision. The first rationale "assumes that investors are nitwits, unable to appreciate—even when told— that mergers are risky propositions up until the closing." *Flamm v. Eberstadt* (7th Cir. 1987).

The second rationale, the importance of secrecy during the early stages of merger discussions, also seems irrelevant to an assessment whether their existence is significant to the trading decision of a reasonable investor. To avoid a "bidding war" over its target, an acquiring firm often will insist that negotiations remain confidential and at least one Court of Appeals has stated that "silence pending settlement of the price and structure of a deal is beneficial to most investors, most of the time." *Flamm v. Eberstadt.*

We need not ascertain, however, whether secrecy necessarily maximizes shareholder wealth— although we note that the proposition is at least disputed as a matter of theory and empirical research—for this case does not concern the timing of a disclosure; it concerns only its accuracy and completeness. We face here the narrow question whether information concerning the existence and status of preliminary merger discussions is significant to the reasonable investor's trading decision. Arguments based on the premise that some disclosure would be "premature" in a sense are more properly considered under the rubric of an issuer's duty to disclose. The "secrecy" rationale is simple inapposite to the definition of materiality.

The final justification offered in support of the agreement-in-principle test seems to be directed solely at the comfort of corporate managers. A bright-line rule indeed is easier to follow than a standard that requires the exercise of judgment in light of all the circumstances. But ease of application alone is not an excuse for ignoring the purposes of the securities acts and Congress' policy decisions.

We therefore find no valid justification for artificially excluding from the definition of materiality information concerning merger discussions, which would otherwise be considered significant to the trading decision of a reasonable investor, merely because agreement-in-principle as to price and structure has not yet been reached by the parties or their representatives.

Even before this Court's decision in *TSC Industries*, the Second Circuit had explained the role of the materiality requirement of Rule 10b-5, with respect to contingent or speculative information or events. Under such circumstances, materiality "will depend at any given time upon a balancing of both the indicated probability that the event will occur and the anticipated magnitude of the event in light of the totality of the company activity." *SEC v. Texas Gulf Sulphur Co.* (2d Cir. 1968).

The late Judge Friendly applied the *Texas Gulf Sulphur* probability/magnitude approach in the specific context of preliminary merger negotiations. He stated:

Since a merger in which it is bought out is the most important event that can occur in a small corporation's life, to wit, its death, we think that inside information, as regards a merger of this sort, can become material at an earlier stage than would be the case as regards lesser transactions—and this even though the mortality rate of mergers in such formative stages is doubtless high. *SEC v. Geon Industries, Inc.* (2d Cir. 1976).

We agree with that analysis.

Whether merger discussions in any particular case are material therefore depends on the facts. Generally, in order to assess the probability that the event will occur, a factfinder will need to look to indicia of interest in the transaction at the highest corporate levels. Board resolutions, instructions to investment bankers, and actual negotiations between principals or their intermediaries may serve as indicia of interest. To assess the magnitude of the transaction to the issuer of the securities allegedly manipulated, a factfinder will need to consider such facts as the size of the two corporate entities and of the potential premiums over market value. No particular event or factor short of closing the transaction need be either necessary or sufficient by itself to render merger discussions material.

As we clarify today, materiality depends on the significance the reasonable investor would place on the withheld or misrepresented information. Because the standard of materiality we have adopted differs from that used by both courts below, we remand the case for reconsideration.

We turn to the question of reliance and the fraud-on-the market theory. Succinctly put:

The fraud on the market theory is based on the hypothesis that, in an open and developed securities market, the price of a company's stock is determined by the available material information regarding the company and its business. . . . Misleading statements will therefore defraud purchasers of stock even if the purchasers do not directly rely on the misstatements. . . . The causal connection between the defendants' fraud and the plaintiffs' purchase of stock in such a case is no less significant than in a case of direct reliance on misrepresentations. *Peil v. Speiser* (3d Cir. 1986).

Our task is to consider whether it was proper for the courts below to apply a rebuttable presumption of reliance, supported in part by the fraud-on-the-market theory.

Reliance is an element of a Rule 10b-5 cause of action. Reliance provides the requisite causal connection between a defendant's misrepresentation and a plaintiff's injury. There is, however, more than one way to demonstrate the causal connection.

In face-to-face transactions, the inquiry into an investor's reliance upon information is into the subjective pricing of that information by that investor. With the presence of a market, the market is interposed between seller and buyer and, ideally, transmits information to the investor in the processed form of a market price.

Thus the market is performing a substantial part of the valuation process performed by the investor in a face-to-face transaction. The market is acting as the unpaid agent of the investor, informing him that given all the information available to it, the value of the stock is worth the market price. *In re LTV Securities Litigation* (N.D. Tex. 1980).

The presumption of reliance employed in this case supports the congressional policy embodied in the 1934 Act. In drafting that Act, Congress expressly relied on the premise that securities markets are affected by information, and enacted legislation to facilitate an investor's reliance on the integrity of those markets:

No investor, no speculator, can safely buy and sell securities upon the exchanges without having an intelligent basis for forming his judgment as to the value of the securities he buys or sells. The idea of a free and open public market is built upon the theory that competing judgments of buyers and sellers as to the fair price of a security bring about a situation where the market price reflects as nearly as possible a just price. Just as an artificial manipulation tends to upset the true function of an open market, so the hiding and secreting of important information obstructs the operation of the markets as indices of real value. H.R. Rep. No. 1383, 73 Cong., 2d Session 11 (1934).

The presumption is also supported by common sense and probability. Recent empirical studies have tended to confirm Congress' premise that the market price of shares traded on well-developed markets reflects all publicly available information, and hence, any material misrepresentations. Because most publicly available information is reflected in market price, an investor's reliance on any public material misrepresentations, therefore, may be presumed for purposes of a Rule 10b-5 action.

The Court of Appeals found that Basic "made public, material misrepresentations and Levinson sold Basic stock in an impersonal, efficient market. Thus Levinson and the other shareholders have established the threshold facts for proving their loss." The court acknowledged that Basic may rebut proof of the elements giving rise to the presumption, or show that the misrepresentation in fact did not lead to a distortion of price or that a shareholder traded or would have traded despite his knowing the statement was false.

Any showing that severs the link between the alleged misrepresentation and either the price received (or paid) by the plaintiff, or his decision to trade at a fair market price, will be sufficient to rebut the presumption of reliance.

Judgment vacated and remanded to the Court of Appeals.

In response to the *Basic* decision, in 1989 the SEC released guidelines to help public companies decide whether they must disclose merger negotiations. A company is not required to disclose merger negotiations if

1. The company did not make any prior disclosures about the merger negotiations,

2. Disclosure is not compelled by other SEC rules, and

3. Management determines that disclosure would jeopardize completion of the merger transaction.

Trading on Inside Information

Many interesting Rule 10b-5 cases involve securities trading by a corporate insider possessing nonpublic, corporate information. Some of these cases involve face-to-face transactions between an insider who has corporate information and another shareholder who does not possess similar information. In other cases, the buyer and seller have not met face-to-face. Instead, the transaction has been executed on a stock exchange. Even though the buyer and the seller never meet, trading on an exchange by a person in possession of confidential corporate information has been held to violate Rule 10b-5.

In **insider trading** cases, a person with nonpublic, confidential, inside information may not use that information when trading with a person who does not possess that information. He must either *disclose the information before trading or refrain from trading.* The difficult task in the insider trading area is determining when a person is subject to this *disclose-or-refrain rule.*

Insider Liability   In *United States v. Chiarella*,[22] the Supreme Court laid down the test for determining an insider's liability for trading on nonpublic, corporate information:

The duty to disclose arises when one party has information that the other party is entitled to know because of a fiduciary or similar relation of trust and confidence between them. A relationship of trust and confidence exists between the shareholders of a corporation and those insiders who have obtained confidential information by reason of their position with that corporation. This relationship gives rise to a duty to disclose because of the necessity of preventing a corporate insider from taking unfair advantage of the uninformed stockholders.

---

[22] 445 U.S. 222 (U.S. Sup. Ct. 1980).

Under this test, insiders include not only officers and directors of the corporation, but also anyone who is *entrusted with corporate information for a corporate purpose.* Insiders include outside consultants, lawyers, independent auditors, engineers, investment bankers, public relations advisers, news reporters, and personnel of government agencies who are given confidential corporate information for a corporate purpose.

Tippee Liability   **Tippees** are recipients of inside information (tips) from insiders. Tippees of insiders, such as relatives and friends of insiders, stockbrokers, and security analysts, are forbidden to trade on inside information and are subject to recovery of their profits if they do.

In the following case, the Supreme Court stated the applicability of Rule 10b-5 to tippees. The Court held that a tippee has liability if (1) an insider has breached a fiduciary duty of trust and confidence to the shareholders by disclosing to the tippee and (2) the tippee knows or should know of the insider's breach. In addition, the court held that an insider has not breached her fiduciary duty to the shareholders unless she has received a personal benefit by disclosing to the tippee.

SEC v. DIRKS

463 U.S. 646 (U.S. Sup. Ct. 1983)

On March 6, 1973, Raymond Dirks, a security analyst in a New York brokerage firm, received nonpublic information from Ronald Secrist, a former officer of Equity Funding of America, a seller of life insurance and mutual funds. Secrist alleged that the assets of Equity Funding were vastly overstated as the result of fraudulent corporate practices. He also stated that the SEC and state insurance departments had failed to act on similar charges of fraud made by Equity Funding employees. Secrist urged Dirks to verify the fraud and to disclose it publicly.

Dirks visited Equity Funding's headquarters in Los Angeles and interviewed several officers and employees of the corporation. The senior management denied any wrongdoing, but certain employees corroborated the charges of fraud. Dirks openly discussed the information he had obtained with a number of his clients and investors. Some of these persons sold their holdings of Equity Funding securities.

Dirks urged a *Wall Street Journal* reporter to write a story on the fraud allegations. The reporter, fearing libel, declined to write the story.

During the two-week period in which Dirks investigated the fraud and spread the word of Secrist's charges, the price of Equity Funding stock fell from $26 per share to less than $15 per share. The New York Stock Exchange halted trading in Equity Funding stock on March 27. On that date, Dirks voluntarily presented his information on the fraud to the SEC. Only then did the

SEC institute an action for fraud against Equity Funding. Shortly thereafter, California insurance authorities impounded Equity Funding's records and uncovered evidence of the fraud. On April 2, *The Wall Street Journal* published a front-page story based largely on information assembled by Dirks. Equity Funding immediately went into receivership.

The SEC brought an administrative proceeding against Dirks for violating Rule 10b-5 by passing along confidential inside information to his clients. The SEC found that he had violated Rule 10b-5, but it merely censured him, since he had played an important role in bringing the fraud to light. Dirks appealed to the Court of Appeals for the District of Columbia Circuit. The court of appeals affirmed the judgment. Dirks then appealed to the Supreme Court.

Powell, Justice.   In *U.S. v. Chiarella* (1980), we accepted the two elements set out in *In re Cady, Roberts* (1961) for establishing a Rule 10b-5 violation: (i) the existence of a relationship affording access to inside information intended to be available only for a corporate purpose, and (ii) the unfairness of allowing a corporate insider to take advantage of that information by trading without disclosure. The Court found that there is no general duty to disclose before trading on material nonpublic information, and held that a duty to disclose under Section 10(b) does not arise from the mere possession of nonpublic market information. Such a duty arises from the existence of a fiduciary relationship.

There can be no duty to disclose when the person who has traded on inside information was not the corporation's agent, was not a fiduciary, or was not a person in whom the sellers of the securities had placed their trust and confidence. Not to require such a fiduciary relationship would depart radically from the established doctrine that duty arises from a specific relationship between two parties and would amount to recognizing a general duty between all participants in market transactions to forgo actions based on material, nonpublic information.

This requirement of a specific relationship between the shareholders and the individual trading on inside information has created analytical difficulties for the SEC and courts in policing tippees who trade on inside information. Unlike insiders who have independent fiduciary duties to both the corporation and its shareholders, the typical tippee has no such relationship.[23] In view of this absence, it has been unclear how a tippee acquires the *Cady, Roberts* duty to refrain from trading on inside information.

We affirm today that a duty to disclose arises from the relationship between the parties and not merely from one's ability to acquire information because of his position in the market.

The conclusion that recipients of inside information do not invariably acquire a duty to disclose or abstain does not mean that such tippees always are free to trade on the information. Not only are insiders forbidden by their fiduciary relationship from personally using undisclosed corporate information to their advantage, but also they may not give such information to an outsider for the same improper purpose of exploiting the information for their personal gain. The transactions of those who knowingly participate with the fiduciary in such a breach are as forbidden as transactions on behalf on the trustee himself. A contrary rule would open up opportunities for devious dealings in the name of the others that the trustee could not conduct in his own. Thus, the tippee's duty to disclose or abstain is derivative from that of the insider's duty. As we noted in *Chiarella*,

---

[23] [Footnote 14 by the Court.] Under certain circumstances, such as where corporate information is revealed legitimately to an underwriter, accountant, lawyer, or consultant working for the corporation, these outsiders may become fiduciaries of the shareholders. The basis for recognizing this fiduciary duty is not simply that such persons acquired nonpublic corporate information, but rather that they have entered into a special confidential relationship in the conduct of the business of the enterprise and are given access to information solely for corporate purposes. When such a person breaches his fiduciary relationship, he may be treated more properly as a tipper than a tippee. For such a duty to be imposed, however, the corporation must expect the outsider to keep the disclosed nonpublic information confidential, and the relationship at least must imply such a duty.

the tippee's obligation has been viewed as arising from his role as a participant after the fact in the insider's breach of a fiduciary duty.

Thus, a tippee assumes a fiduciary duty to the shareholders of a corporation not to trade on material nonpublic information only when the insider has breached his fiduciary duty to the shareholders by disclosing the information to the tippee and the tippee knows or should know that there has been a breach.

In determining whether a tippee is under an obligation to disclose or abstain, it thus is necessary to determine whether the insider's tip constituted a breach of the insider's fiduciary duty. Whether disclosure is a breach of duty therefore depends in large part on the purpose of the disclosure. Thus, the test is whether the insider personally will benefit, directly or indirectly, from his disclosure. Absent some personal gain, there has been no breach of duty to stockholders. And absent a breach by the insider, there is no derivative breach.

This requires courts to focus on objective criteria, *i.e.*, whether the insider receives a direct or indirect personal benefit from the disclosure, such as a pecuniary gain or a reputational benefit that will translate into future earnings. For example, there may be a relationship between the insider and the recipient that suggests a *quid pro quo* from the latter, or an intention to benefit the particular recipient. The elements of fiduciary duty and exploitation of nonpublic information also exist when an insider makes a gift of confidential information to a relative or friend who trades. The tip and trade resemble trading by the insider himself followed by a gift of the profits to the recipient.

Under the inside-trading and tipping rules set forth above, we find that there was no violation by Dirks. Dirks was a stranger to Equity Funding, with no pre-existing fiduciary duty to its shareholders. He took no action, directly or indirectly, that induced the shareholders or officers of Equity Funding to repose trust or confidence in him. There was no expectation by Dirks' sources that he would keep their information in confidence. Nor did Dirks misappropriate or illegally obtain the information about Equity Funding. Unless the insiders breached their *Cady, Roberts* duty to shareholders in disclosing the nonpublic information to Dirks, he breached no duty when he passed it on to investors as well as to *The Wall Street Journal.*

It is clear that neither Secrist nor the other Equity Funding employees violated their *Cady, Roberts* duty to the corporation's shareholders by providing information to Dirks. Secrist intended to convey relevant information that management was unlawfully concealing, and he believed that persuading Dirks to investigate was the best way to disclose the fraud. The tippers received no monetary or personal benefit for revealing Equity Funding's secrets, nor was their purpose to make a gift of valuable information to Dirks. The tippers were motivated by a desire to expose the fraud. In the absence of a breach of duty to shareholders by the insiders, there was no derivative breach by Dirks. Dirks therefore could not have been a participant after the fact in an insider's breach of a fiduciary duty.

Judgment reversed in favor of Dirks.

Misappropriation of Nonpublic Information In *Chiarella* and *Dirks*, the Supreme Court held that liability for inside trading is premised on an insider's breach of a fiduciary duty owed to the shareholders of the corporation whose shares are traded. Some federal courts of appeals have held that a misappropriation of confidential information from someone other than the corporation whose shares are traded or a breach of a fiduciary duty owed to someone other than the shareholders of the corporation whose shares are traded can create Rule 10b-5 liability.

Relying on Justice Burger's dissent in *Chiarella*,[24] the Second Circuit held in *United States v. Newman*[25] that criminal liability might attach to a person who had breached a duty of confidentiality owed to his employer by misappropriating nonpublic information, even though no duty was owed to the shareholders of the corporation whose shares were purchased. In *Moss v. Morgan Stanley*,[26] a case with the same facts as *Newman*, the same court held that the shareholders could *not* bring a suit for damages against the person who breached a fiduciary duty to his employer but breached no duty owed to the shareholders of the corporation whose shares he traded. The court refused to expand the holding of *Newman* to create a duty of disclosure to the general public.

In 1987, the Supreme Court declined an opportunity to clarify its position concerning the misappropriation theory when the justices upheld the conviction of R. Foster Winans on mail fraud grounds, but could not agree whether he had violated Rule 10b-5.[27] Winans, the "Heard on the Street" columnist for *The Wall Street Journal*, had been charged with violating Rule 10b-5 because he had tipped his lover about which companies he planned to feature in upcoming columns. The justices' disagreement left standing the Second Circuit's holding that Winans's misappropriation of the *Journal*'s confidential information operated as a fraud or deceit.

Extent of Liability for Insider Trading   Section 20A of the 1934 Act allows persons who traded in the securities at about the same time as the insider or tippee to recover damages from the insider or tippee. However, as there may be several persons trading at about the same time, the insider or tippee's total liability cannot exceed the profit she has made or the loss she has avoided by trading on inside information.

This limitation, which merely requires disgorgement of profits, has been assailed as not adequately deterring insider trading, because the defendant may realize an enormous profit if her trading is not discovered, but lose nothing beyond her profits if it is. In response to this issue of liability, in 1984 Congress passed an amendment to the 1934 Act permitting the SEC to seek a civil penalty of three times the profit gained or the loss avoided by trading on inside information. This treble penalty is paid to the Treasury of the United States. The penalty applies only to SEC actions; it does not affect the amount of damages that may be recovered by private plaintiffs. The 1988 Insider Trading and Securities Fraud Enforcement Act amended the 1934 Act and granted the SEC power to award up to 10 percent of any triple-damage penalty as a bounty to informants who helped the SEC uncover insider trading.

Criminal Liability

Like the 1933 Act, the 1934 Act provides for liability for criminal violations of the Act. Section 32 provides for a fine of up to $2.5 million and imprisonment of up to five years for willful violations of the 1934 Act or the related SEC rules.

TENDER OFFER REGULATION

History

Until the early 1960s, the predominant procedure by which one corporation acquired another was the merger, a transaction requiring the cooperation of the acquired corporation's management. Since the 1960s, the **tender offer** has become an often used acquisition device. A tender offer is a public offer by a **bidder** to purchase a **subject company's** equity securities directly from its shareholders at a specified price for a fixed period of time. The offering price is usually well above the market price of the shares. Such offers are often made even though there is opposition from the subject company's management. Opposed offers are called hostile tender offers.[28]

---

[24]"There is some language in the Court's opinion to suggest that only 'a relationship between the defendant and the sellers . . . could give rise to a duty [to disclose].' The Court's holding, however, is much more limited, namely, that mere possession of material, nonpublic information is insufficient to create a duty to disclose or to refrain from trading. Accordingly, it is my understanding that the Court has not rejected the view that an absolute duty to disclose or refrain arises from the very act of misappropriating nonpublic information." 445 U.S. at 245, n. 4 (Burger, C. J., dissenting).

[25]664 F.2d 12 (2d Cir. 1981).

[26]719 F.2d 5 (2d Cir. 1983).

[27]*United States v. Carpenter,* 484 U.S. 19 (U.S. Sup. Ct.1987).

---

[28] Defenses to hostile tender offers are addressed in detail in the Management of Corporations chapter.

In 1968, the Williams Act amendments to the 1934 Act were passed to provide shareholders with more information on which to base their decision whether to sell their shares to a bidder. The aim of the amendments is to give the bidder and the subject company equal opportunities to present their cases to the shareholders. Strict disclosure and procedural requirements are established for both parties. The Williams Act applies only when the subject company's equity securities are registered under the 1934 Act.

Definition of Tender Offer

The Williams Act does not define a tender offer, but the courts have compiled a list of factors to determine whether a person has made a tender offer. The greater the number of people solicited and the lower their investment sophistication, the more likely it is that the bidder will be held to have made a tender offer. Also, the shorter the offering period, the more rigid the price, and the greater the publicity concerning the offer, the more likely it is that the purchase efforts of the bidder will be treated as a tender offer. Given these factors, a person who purchases shares directly from several shareholders risks having a court treat the purchases like a tender offer. The Williams Act clearly states, however, that there is no tender offer unless the bidder intends to become a holder of at least 5 percent of the subject company's shares.

Regulation of Tender Offers

A bidder making a tender offer must file a tender offer statement, Schedule 14D-1, with the SEC when the offer commences. The information in this schedule includes the terms of the offer (for example, the price), the background of the bidder, and the purpose of the tender offer (including whether the bidder intends to control the subject company).

SEC Rule 14e-1 requires the bidder to keep the tender offer open for at least 20 business days and prohibits any purchase of shares during that time. The purpose of this rule is to give shareholders adequate time to make informed decisions regarding whether to tender their shares. Rule 14d-7 permits tendering shareholders to withdraw their tendered shares during the entire term of the offer. These rules allow the highest bidder to buy the shares, as in an auction.

All tender offers, whether made by the issuer or by a third-party bidder, must be made to all holders of the targeted class of shares.[29] When a bidder increases the offering price during the term of the tender offer, all of the shareholders must be paid the higher price even if they tendered their shares at a lower price.[30] If more shares are tendered than the bidder offered to buy, the bidder must prorate its purchases among all of the shares tendered.[31] This proration rule is designed to foster careful shareholder decisions about whether to sell shares. Shareholders might rush to tender their shares if the bidder could accept shares on a first-come, first-served basis.

Subject Company's Response   The management of the subject company is required to inform the shareholders of its position on the tender offer, with its reasons, within 10 days after the offer has been made.[32] It must also provide the bidder with a list of the holders of the equity securities that the bidder seeks to acquire.

Private Acquisitions of Shares

The Williams Act regulates private acquisitions of shares differently from tender offers. When the bidder privately seeks a controlling block of the subject company's shares on a stock exchange or in face-to-face negotiations with only a few shareholders, no advance notice to the SEC or disclosure to shareholders is required. However, a person making a private acquisition is required to file a *Schedule 13D* with the SEC and to send a copy to the subject company within 10 days after he becomes a *holder of 5 percent* of its shares. A *Schedule 13G* (which requires less disclosure than a 13D) must be filed when a 5 percent holder has purchased no more than 2 percent of the shares within the past 12 months.

In the following case, the Belzbergs violated the 1934 Act by filing a Schedule 13D 12 days after the 10-day deadline.

---

[29] SEA Rule 14d-10(a)(1).
[30] SEA Rule 14d-10(a)(2).
[31] SEA Rule 14d-8.
[32] SEA Rule 14e-2.

SEC v. First City Financial Corp., Ltd.

890 F.2d 1215 (D.C. Cir. 1989)

First City Financial Corp., a Canadian company controlled by the Belzberg familty, was engaged in the business of investing in publicly held American corporations, often by hostile acquisition. Marc Belzberg identified Ashland Oil Company as a potential target and on February 11, 1986, secretly purchased 61,000 shares of Ashland stock for First City. By February 26, additional secret purchases of Ashland shares pushed First City's holdings to just over 4.9 percent of Ashland's stock. These last two purchases were effected for First City by Alan "Ace" Greenberg, the chief executive officer of Bear Stearns, a large Wall Street brokerage. On March 4, Belzberg called Greenberg and told him, "It wouldn't be a bad idea if you bought Ashland Oil here." Immediately after the phone call, Greenberg purchased 20,500 Ashland shares for about $44 per share. If purchased for First City, those shares would have increased First City's Ashland holdings above 5 percent. Greenberg believed he was buying the shares for First City under a put and call agreement, under which First City had the right to buy the shares from Bear Stearns and Bear Stearns had the right to require First City to buy the shares from it. Between March 4 and 14, Greenberg purchased an additional 330,700 shares. On March 17, First City and Bear Stearns signed a formal put and call agreement covering all the shares Greenberg purchased.

On March 25, First City announced publicly for the first time that it intended to make a tender offer for all of Ashland's shares. First City filed a Schedule 13D on March 26. First City's 13D stated its intent to make a tender offer for all of Ashland's shares at $60 per share. Almost immediately, the market price of Ashland's shares rose to $55. Ashland convinced the Kentucky legislature to pass legislation hampering First City's takeover, with the result that First City abandoned its takeover attempt. To eliminate First City as a shareholder, Ashland purchased First City's holdings for $51 per share.

The SEC brought an action against First City, claiming that Greenberg's March 4 purchase of Ashland shares triggered First City's obligation to file a Schedule 13D within 10 days. The SEC asked the district court to enjoin First City from violating section 13(d) and to order First City to disgorge the profit it made on shares purchased between March 14 and 25. The district court ordered an injuction and disgorgement of $2.7 million. First City appealed on the grounds that its intent and belief was that Greenberg bought the shares for Bear Stearns's account.

Silberman, Circuit Judge.   A shareholder must comply with the section 13(d) disclosure law if he beneficially owns 5 percent of a public company's equity securities. Under Securities Exchange Act Rule 13d-3(a), whenever a person possesses investment or voting power through any agreement or understanding, he enjoys beneficial ownership. Rule 13d-3 is crafted broadly enough to sweep within its purview informal, oral arrangements that confer upon a person voting or investment power. A put and call agreement, even if informal, constitutes beneficial ownership to the investor of the stock subject to the agreement.

The case turns on the question whether the put and call agreement between First City and Bear Stearns was entered into on March 4 or not until March 17. We think the SEC presented a powerful case that Belzberg did intend to enter into a put-call agreement with Greenberg on March 4 and therefore purposely sought to circumvent section 13(d)'s disclosure requirements.

First, on February 26, Belzberg asked Greenberg to buy directly approximately 53,000 shares of Ashland *for First City*. It certainly seems more than a little strange that after having directed Bear Stearns to buy for First City's account, Belzberg, only a week later, would call Greenberg only to suggest that Bear Stearns buy Ashland stock for itself.

Perhaps the most important piece of circumstantial evidence tending to show that Belzberg had asked Greenberg on March 4 to buy stock for First City under a put-call agreement is the price First City paid Bear Stearns for the stock. The price was $450,000 below market on March 17, but reflected the market price on the dates that Bear Stearns purchased the stock.

At the threshold of Belzberg's version of the events is his claim that on March 4 he had "recommended" to Greenberg that Bear Stearns buy Ashland stock for Bear Stearns's own account, because *if* it subsequently turned out that First City wished to acquire Ashland, the takeover would be more easily accomplished if Ashland stock were held by arbitrageurs (short-term speculators more inclined to cash in on a quick profit) rather than remain in what First City refers to as forgotten safe deposit boxes. This explanation is unconvincing. Although it may well be true that *after* a tender offer is launched the acquiring company would wish as much stock as possible to be gathered by arbitrageurs, who typically buy for the very purpose of tendering, we had not previously heard the theory that it would be helpful for arbitrageurs to start their buying *before* the acquiring company publicly signals its intention.

During the period before it unveiled its takeover plan, First City took pains to keep its interest in Ashland secret. The very last thing Belzberg would do in light of those efforts would be to tout Ashland to a prospective speculator as a good investment. Indeed, if his purpose was to induce arbitrageurs to buy Ashland, he presumably would have contacted more than just Bear Stearns; he would have openly disclosed his interest to all of Wall Street.

Moving on to other elements in Belzberg's story, we are struck by his reaction to the $450,000 discount off the market price that Greenberg offered him on March 17 if there had been no put-call agreement on March 4. Belzberg said he was not surprised by the price since he thought Bear Stearns was acting like "Santa Claus" by offering "a bit of a break" to gain more First City business. Bit of a break indeed! And unsolicited at that. We thought that Wall Street Santa Clauses were confined to the sidewalk during Christmas time. Greenberg testified that if he gave clients a half million dollar break on stock for which Bear Stearns bore the market risk, he would "go broke within a week." Greenberg added, quite convincingly we might add, that he "does not run that risk for anybody."

We conclude that the district court's finding that First City deliberately violated section 13(d) should be affirmed.

The district court directed disgorgement of profits. This presents an issue of first impression—whether federal courts have the authority to employ that remedy with respect to section 13(d) violations and whether it is appropriate in this sort of case.

Disgorgement is an equitable remedy designed to deprive a wrongdoer of his unjust enrichment and to deter others from violating the securities laws. Disgorgement is rather routinely ordered for insider trading violations despite a lack of specific authorizations for that remedy under the securities laws. We see no relevant distinction between disgorgement of inside trading profits and disgorgement of section 13(d) violation profits.

There remains the question of how the court measures those illegal profits. First City vigorously disputes the $2.7 million figure that the district court arrived at by calculating all of the profits First City realized on the 890,000 shares First City purchased between March 14 and 25. This disgorgment figure is predicated on the assumption that had First City made its section 13(d) disclosure on March 14, at the end of the statutory 10-day period, the stock it purchased during the March 14–25 period would have been purchased in a quite different and presumably more expensive market. That market would have been affected by the disclosure that the Belzbergs had taken a greater than 5 percent stake in Ashland and would soon propose a tender offer.

First City asserts that the hypothetical market the district court accepted was simplistic and quite unrealistic. It did not take into account other variables—besides the section 13(d) disclosure—which caused the price of the stock to rise. If exact information were obtainable at negligible cost, we would not hesitate to impose upon the government a strict burden to produce data to measure the precise amount of the ill-gotten gains. Despite sophisticated econometric modeling, predicting stock market responses to alternative variables is at best speculative. Rules for calculating disgorgement must recognize that separating legal from illegal profits exactly may at times be a near-impossible task. Accordingly, disgorgement need only be a reasonable approximation of profits causally connected to the violation. The line between restitution and penalty is unfortunately blurred, but the risk of uncertainty should fall on the wrongdoer whose illegal conduct created that uncertainty.

We uphold the permanent injuction and disgorgement orders.

Judgment for the SEC affirmed.

State Regulation of Tender Offers

Statutes that apply to tender offers have been enacted by about two thirds of the states. Until the mid-1980s, many state statutes were held unconstitutional as being preempted by the Williams Act or as violating the Commerce Clause of the U.S. Constitution.[33] In recent years, however, state statutes like Indiana's control share law, which is highly protective of subject companies, have been held constitutional by the Supreme Court of the United States.[34] The Indiana statute gives shareholders other than the bidder the right to determine whether the shares acquired by the bidder may be voted in directors' elections and other matters. The statute, which essentially gives a subject company the power to require shareholder approval of a hostile tender offer, has been copied by several states.

Other states, like Delaware, have adopted business-combination moratorium statutes. These statutes delay the effectuation of a merger of the corporation with a shareholder owning a large percentage of shares (such as 15 percent), unless the board of director's approval is obtained. Because the typical large shareholder in a public company is a bidder who has made a tender offer, these state statutes primarily affect the ability of a bidder to effectuate a merger after a tender offer, and therefore, may have the effect of deterring hostile acquisitions.

THE FOREIGN CORRUPT PRACTICES ACT

Background

The Foreign Corrupt Practices Act (FCPA) was passed by Congress in 1977 as an amendment to the Securities Exchange Act of 1934. Its passage followed discoveries that more than 400 American corporations had given bribes or made other improper or questionable payments in connection with business abroad and within the United States. Many of these payments were bribes to high-level officials of foreign governments for the purpose of obtaining contracts for the sale of goods or services. Officers of the companies that had made the payments, even when admitting that the payments were bribes, argued that such payments were customary and necessary in business transactions in many countries. This argument was pressed forcefully with regard to *facilitating payments.* Such payments were said to be essential to get lower-level government officials in a number of countries to perform their nondiscretionary or ministerial tasks, such as preparing or approving necessary import or export documents.

In a significant number of cases, bribes had been accounted for as commission payments, as normal transactions with foreign subsidiaries, or as payments for services rendered by professionals or other firms, or had in other ways been made to appear as normal business expenses. These bribes were then illegally deducted as normal business expenses in income tax returns filed with the Internal Revenue Service.

The FCPA makes it a crime for any American firm—whether or not it has securities registered under the 1934 Act—to offer, promise, or make payments or gifts of anything of value to foreign officials and certain others. The FCPA also establishes recordkeeping and internal control requirements for firms subject to the periodic disclosure provisions of the Securities Exchange Act of 1934.

The Payments Prohibition

Payments are prohibited if the person making the payment knows or should know that some or all of it will be

---

[33] For example, *Edgar v. MITE Corp.,* 457 U.S. 624 (U.S. Sup. Ct. 1982).

[34] *CTS Corp. v. Dynamics Corp.,* 481 U.S. 69 (1987).

used for the purpose of influencing a governmental decision. An offer to make a prohibited payment or a promise to do so is a violation even if the offer is not accepted or the promise is not carried out. The FCPA prohibits offers or payments to foreign political parties and candidates for office as well as offers and payments to government officials. Payments of kickbacks to foreign businesses and their officials are not prohibited unless it is known or should be known that these payments will be passed on to government officials or other illegal recipients.

Facilitating or grease payments are not prohibited by the FCPA. Payments are not illegal so long as the recipient has no discretion in carrying out a governmental function. For example, suppose a corporation applies for a radio license in Italy and makes a payment to the government official who issues the licenses. If the official grants licenses to every applicant and the payment merely speeds up the processing of the application, the FCPA is not violated. On the other hand, if only a few applicants are granted licenses and the payment is made to ensure that the corporation will obtain a license, the payment is illegal.

Substantial penalties for violations may be imposed. A company may be fined up to $2 million. Directors, officers, employees, or agents participating in violations are liable for fines of up to $100,000 and prison terms of up to five years.

Recordkeeping and Internal Controls Requirements

The FCPA added Section 13(b)(2) to the 1934 Act. It imposes recordkeeping and internal controls requirements on firms that are subject to the 1934 Act. The purpose of such controls is to prevent unauthorized payments and transactions and unauthorized access to company assets that may result in illegal payments.

The new section requires the making and keeping of records and accounts "which, in reasonable detail, accurately, and fairly reflect the transactions and dispositions of the assets of the issuer" of securities. It also requires the establishment and maintenance of a system of internal accounting controls. This system must provide "reasonable assurances" that the firm's transactions are executed in accordance with management's authorization and that the firm's assets are used or disposed of only as authorized by management. In addition, the recording of transactions must permit the preparation of financial statements that conform to generally accepted accounting principles. Furthermore, at reasonable intervals,

management must see that the records are compared with the actual assets available, and if they do not agree, it must determine the reason for the discrepancy.

These requirements apply not only to transactions and records relating to business with foreign governments or conducted in foreign countries but also to purely domestic business activities. The payment of a bribe is not essential to a violation of this part of the act. No specific penalties are provided; the general penalties of the 1934 Act apply.

STATE SECURITIES LEGISLATION

Purpose and History

State securities laws are frequently referred to as **blue-sky laws,** since the early state securities statutes were designed to protect investors from promoters and security salespersons who would "sell building lots in the blue sky." The first state to enact a securities law was Kansas, in 1911. All of the states now have such legislation.

Uniform Securities Act

The National Conference of Commissioners on Uniform State Laws has adopted the Uniform Securities Act of 1956. The act contains antifraud provisions, requires the registration of securities, and demands broker-dealer registration. About two thirds of the states have adopted the act, but many states have made significant changes in it.

Securities Fraud

All of the state securities statutes provide penalties for fraudulent sales and permit the issuance of injunctions to protect investors from additional or anticipated fraudulent acts. Most of the statutes grant broad power to investigate fraud to some state official—usually the attorney general or his appointee as securities administrator. All of the statutes provide criminal penalties for selling fraudulent securities and conducting fraudulent transactions.

Registration of Securities

Most of the state securities statutes adopt the philosophy of the 1933 Act that informed investors can make intelligent investment decisions. The states with such statutes have a registration scheme much like the 1933 Act, with required disclosures for public offerings and exemptions from registration for small and private offerings. Other states reject the contention that investors with full information can make intelligent investment decisions. The securities statutes in these states have a *merit registration* requirement, giving a securities administrator power to deny registration on the merits of the security and its issuer. Only securities that are not unduly risky and promise an adequate return to investors may receive administrator approval.

All state statutes have a limited number of exemptions from registration. Most statutes have private offering exemptions that are similar to Securities Act Rule 506 of Regulation D. In addition, a person may avoid the registration requirements of state securities laws by not offering or selling securities. However, as illustrated by the *Capital General* case, which follows, state courts broadly define the term *sale* in order to prevent abusive attempts to circumvent the registration requirements.

Registration by Coordination The Uniform Securities Act permits an issuer to register its securities by coordination. Instead of filing a registration statement under the Securities Act of 1933 and a different one as required by state law, registration by coordination allows an issuer to file the 1933 Act registration statement with the state securities administrator. Registration by coordination decreases an issuer's expense of complying with state law when making an interstate offering of its securities.

CAPITAL GENERAL CORP. v. UTAH DEPARTMENT OF BUSINESS REGULATION, SECURITIES DIVISION
777 P. 2d 494 (Utah Ct. App. 1989)

On January 7, 1986, Amenity, Inc., was incorporated with capitalization of 100 million shares. On January 8, 1986, 1 million shares of Amenity, Inc., stock were issued to Capital General Corporation (CGC), a financial consulting firm, for $2,000. CGC distributed a total of 90,000 of those shares to approximately 900 of its clients, business associates, and other contacts to create and maintain goodwill among its clients and contacts. CGC did not receive any monetary or other direct financial consideration from those receiving the stock.

Amenity, Inc., had no actual business function at this time and its sole asset was the $2,000 CGC had paid for the 1 million shares. Through CGC efforts, Amenity, Inc., was acquired by another company, which paid CGC $25,000 for its efforts.

On June 5, 1986, the Utah Securities Division sought to suspend trading in Amenity, Inc., stock on the grounds that CGC distributed the Amenity, Inc., stock in violation of the Utah Securities Act.

A hearing was held before an administrative law judge, who held that the Act's registration requirements did not apply to CGC's distribution of the Amenity, Inc., stock. The Securities Division obtained a hearing by the Utah Securities Advisory Board. The Board concluded that CGC's distribution of the 90,000 shares was covered by the Act. The Board issued an order of suspension. CGC filed a petition in the district court seeking reversal of the Board's order. The district court affirmed the Board's decision, and CGC appealed.

Orme, Judge. The Utah Securities Act provides, "It is unlawful for any person to *offer or sell* any security in this state unless it is registered . . . or the security or transaction is exempted." Thus, we must determine if CGC's disposition of the 90,000 shares was an "offer or sale" of Amenity, Inc., securities.

The Act provides that an "offer or sale" includes the "disposition of . . . a security for value." Value is gained by the creation of a public market. Such value includes: 1) an enhanced ability to borrow; 2) an enhanced ability to raise equity; 3) the availability of a method of valuing assets; 4) an enhanced liquidity of assets; and 5) the prestige associated with publicly held companies.

The Board's determination that CGC's disposition of the Amenity, Inc. stock was "for value" is reasonable and rational. By "giving away" 90,000 shares (or 9 percent of its total holdings), CGC essentially transformed Amenity, Inc., into a publicly held company, ripe for acquisition, in which it held most of the stock. "Value" can include enhanced abilities to borrow, raise capital, and other general benefits associated with publicly held companies, all of which CGC received through the disposition. These economic benefits render the disposition "for value" even though those benefits flowed indirectly from the marketplace rather than directly from the transferees.

CGC additionally argues the disposition was a "good faith gift" under the Act. CGC bears the burden to prove its entitlement to the "good faith gift" exception to the definition of "offer or sale." CGC fails to meet this burden. CGC's veiled but fairly obvious purpose was to advance its own economic objectives rather than to make a gift for reasons of simple generosity.

CGC's actual purpose in making the distribution included an intent to convert a private company into a public company without registration. The effect of this transformation, in addition to circumventing the Act's registration requirements, was to greatly enhance the value of the significant block of Amenity, Inc.'s outstanding stock which CGC continued to hold. CGC similarly converted at least thirty other private companies into public companies using the same method employed here. At least three of these companies were then acquired by other companies, resulting in substantial profits for CGC.

Judgment for the Securities Division affirmed.

ETHICAL AND PUBLIC POLICY CONCERNS

1. Should the federal and state governments require disclosure by issuers of securities? Are investors able to protect themselves by insisting that issuers provide relevant information prior to the investors' purchasing securities from issuers? How can current securities owners ensure that they will continue to receive relevant investment information?

2. Who are the primary beneficiaries of the securities laws; that is, who primarily buys and sells securities? Nearly all securities are owned by persons whose wealth places them in the top 10 percent of the population. Is securities regulation merely welfare for the wealthy? Does anyone else benefit from securities regulation? Does the benefit to those persons justify the costs of securities regulation?

3. Should insider trading be illegal? Is insider trading unfair? To whom is it unfair? What are the social and economic costs of insider trading? What are the social and economic benefits of insider trading? Does insider trading improve the efficiency of the securities markets? Should shareholders be given the power to authorize insiders to trade on inside information? Why might shareholders want insiders to trade on inside information?

4. Should the payments prohibition part of the Foreign Corrupt Practices Act be repealed? What is unethical about an American corporation making bribes to foreign government officials and political parties? What benefits does the United States receive from the making of such payments? What detriments does the United States suffer from the making of such payments? Does the analysis change if bribery is a standard way of business life in a foreign country?

SUMMARY

The federal securities acts passed in 1933 and 1934 require that investors be given accurate and adequate information concerning securities. They also prohibit fraudulent, deceptive, and manipulative practices. A security is broadly defined to include any investment in a common enterprise with an expectation of profits from the efforts of others.

The Securities Act of 1933 requires issuers of securities to file a registration statement with the SEC. There are two categories of exemptions from this requirement: securities exemptions, such as government-guaranteed securities; and transaction exemptions, such as the small offering exemptions, the private offering exemption, and the intrastate offering exemption.

The most important liability provision of the 1933 Act is Section 11, which imposes liability on certain defendants for material defects in the registration statement, unless they can prove their due diligence defenses.

Issuers register classes of securities under the 1934 Act, rather than issuances of securities. Companies of a certain size must register, whether or not their securities are traded on a stock exchange. The 1934 Act also imposes periodic reporting requirements on issuers and regulates proxy solicitations.

Directors, officers, and 10 percent holders of registered shares must file reports of their shareholdings and transactions in the shares of an issuer with securities registered under the 1934 Act. Insiders' profits from transactions in the issuer's shares may be recovered by the corporation.

The most often used liability provision of the 1934 Act is Section 10(b), under which SEC Rule 10b-5 has been issued. The rule has been used extensively to impose liabilities for failure to provide an investor with adequate information, for deceptive practices, and for insider trading.

The 1934 Act regulates tender offers, requiring bidders to disclose material information concerning the acquisition. SEC rules give shareholders procedural protections to allow them to make careful, intelligent decisions.

The Foreign Corrupt Practices Act was passed in 1977. It prohibits payments or gifts to officials and political parties in foreign governments. Grease payments, however, are not prohibited. The FCPA also requires all issuers of registered securities to maintain accurate accounting records.

All of the states have enacted blue-sky laws in order to protect investors. Some of these laws are quite similar in approach to the federal securities statutes. Others give a state administrator authority to bar the sale of unduly risky securities.

PROBLEM CASES

1. In 1980, Continental Minerals Corporation (CMC), a gold-mining company, devised a means of raising capital by selling its gold in the form of coins. Purchasers could buy 12 one-ounce coins either by paying for each coin separately 30 days in advance of delivery or by prepaying for the entire set of coins. If purchasers prepaid for the entire set, the price was $375 per coin, about 48 percent below the prevailing market price for gold. CMC promised to begin delivery on November 15, 1980, and to deliver an additional coin every two months. To provide purchasers protection against a decrease in the price of gold below $375 per ounce, CMC promised to pay purchasers the difference between the prepayment price and the world price of gold on the delivery date. CMC informed the purchasers that "the gold offered for future delivery has not yet been extracted. Obviously, if sufficient quantities of gold were being mined currently, these would be sold at world market prices and not offered at substantial discount." Subsequently, CMC failed to make any deliveries of gold coins. CMC had spent all $3.5 million it received from the sale of coins. The SEC sued 24 salesmen of CMC gold coins on the grounds that they had sold unregistered securities in violation of Section 5 of the Securities Act. Were any securities involved in the sale of the gold coins?

2. Attempting to reach as wide an audience as possible, a mutual fund company inserts prospectuses for the issuance of its shares in local newspapers and magazines. In subsequent editions of the newspapers and issues of the magazines, the company distributes additional sales materials. Is the company violating the requirements of Section 5 of the Securities Act of 1933?

3. King's College is a private college organized under the not-for-profit corporation law of New York. The Internal Revenue Service has issued King's College an exemption from federal income taxation. The college proposes to sell $500,000 of bonds to raise funds for equipment purchases and other capital improvements. The college will sell the bonds in the minimum amount of $500 and will offer them to no more than 1,000 individuals. Only individuals having shown a prior interest in King's College will be solicited. Is the bond offering exempt from the registration requirements of the 1933 Act?

4. Western-Realco Limited Partnership sold $800,000 of its limited partnership interests through the services of securities brokers. Western-Realco did not supervise the brokers and was unaware of whether the brokers solicited their clients in a newsletter or to the public in general. Will Western-Realco be able to use the private offering exemption or Rule 504 to avoid a 1933 Act registration?

5. Capital Sunbelt Securities, Inc. (Sunbelt) and Phoenix Financial Corp. were two brokerages that sold limited partnership interests in Capital: Maple Leaf Estates, Ltd. (Capital) and Maple Leaf Estates, Ltd. (Maple Leaf). Capital was to purchase a mobile home park that would be operated by Maple Leaf. Sunbelt and Phoenix kept logs reflecting the persons to whom they distributed copies of the limited offering circulars for Capital and Maple Leaf. Ninety-six persons received copies of the Capital offering circular and 34 received the Maple Leaf circular. The circulars contained the same information as a 1933 Act registration statement. In addition, Capital and Maple Leaf promised to make available any additional information requested by investors. All offerees had a prior relationship with Phoenix or Sunbelt, and there were no seminars or meetings attended by the general public. There was no advertising, and each offering circular was addressed to a specific person. All investors were required to state that they were acquiring the limited partnership interests for investment. Proceeds of the offerings were $2,677,000 for Capital and $950,000 for Maple Leaf. Phoenix offered to sell Capital limited partnership interests to 228 persons and sold to 33 investors, 16 of which had a net worth in excess of $1 million. There were 187 offerees of the Maple Leaf limited partnership interests and 13 purchasers, 9 of whom had a net worth over $1 million. At the conclusion of the offerings, no Form D was filed with the SEC. Were the offerings exempt from registration under Section 4(2) or Rule 506 of the Securities Act?

6. Commonwealth Edison Co. registered 3 million common shares with the SEC and sold the shares for about $28 per share. The price of the purchasers' stock dropped to $21 when the Atomic Safety and Licensing Board denied ComEd's application to license one of its reactors. It was the first and only time the Board had denied a license application. ComEd assumed that the license would be granted; therefore its registration statement failed to disclose the pendency of the license application. Did ComEd violate Section 11 of the Securities Act?

7. Two limited partnerships created a partnership for the purpose of attempting a takeover of Goodyear Tire and Rubber Co. One limited partnership acquired 8.17 percent and the other 2.37 percent of Goodyear's shares. Although combined the two limited partnerships owned

11.5 percent of the shares, their partnership held no Goodyear shares for its own account. The limited partnerships sold their Goodyear shares at a profit in fewer than six months after the purchases. Have the limited partnerships violated Section 16(b) of the 1934 Act?

8. J. C. Harrelson, the president and chief shareholder of Alabama Supply and Equipment Company (ASECo), and Clarence Hamilton conspired to defraud investors. They induced Frisco City, Alabama, to create the Industrial Development Board of Frisco City to issue tax-exempt bonds to investors. The Board offered and sold bonds pursuant to an offering circular, which misstated or omitted several material facts, due to misrepresentations made by Harrelson and Hamilton. The Board used the proceeds of the bond issuance to build a manufacturing plant for ASECo. After the ASECo plant was constructed, ASECo ceased all operations and defaulted on its rental payments to the Board, causing the value of the bonds to drop precipitously. The building was sold in an attempt to pay the principal on the bonds. After the sale of the industrial facility, the bondholders received only $373.33 for each $1,000 bond. Clarence Bishop had purchased four of the bonds for $4,096. He never saw the offering circular or knew that one existed. He bought the bonds solely on his broker's oral representations that they were a good investment and that others in the community had purchased them. Can Bishop sue Harrelson and Hamilton under Rule 10b-5 even though he failed to read or even to seek to read the offering circular?

9. James Jordan was a shareholder of Duff & Phelps, Inc., a closely held corporation, and one of its employees in its Chicago office. The transferability of his shares was restricted, such that if he terminated his employment with Duff & Phelps, he was required to resell his shares to the corporation. Between May and August 1983, Duff & Phelps and Security Pacific Corporation negotiated a merger of the two corporations. The negotiators reached an agreement, but it was vetoed by a high official within Security Pacific on August 11, 1983. During this same time, Jordan was looking for a new job. On November 16, 1983, Jordan told Duff & Phelps that he was going to resign effective at the end of the year in order to accept a job in Houston. Jordan did not ask about any potential merger and Duff & Phelps did not volunteer any information, even though two days earlier its board of directors had decided to seek offers to acquire the company. In December 1983, Duff & Phelps and Security Pacific had serious merger discussions after the high official who vetoed the deal on August 11 changed his mind. On December 30, 1983, Jordan delivered his shares to Duff & Phelps and received a check for $23,225. On January 6, 1984, Duff & Phelps and Security Pacific reached an agreement in principle to merge. The agreement was announced on January 10, at which point Jordan realized that he would have received at least $452,000 for his shares had he not resigned from Duff & Phelps. Does Jordan have any recourse against Duff & Phelps under Rule 10b-5?

10. In May 1983, Phil Gutter read a report in *The Wall Street Journal* that listed certain corporate bonds as trading with interest. Relying on the report, Gutter purchased $36,000 of the bonds. In reality, the bonds were trading without interest. When *The Wall Street Journal* corrected its error, the price of the bonds fell, resulting in Gutter suffering a loss of $1,692. Is *The Wall Street Journal* liable to Gutter for his loss under Rule 10b-5?

11. When he was the Oklahoma Sooner football coach, Barry Switzer attended a track meet, where he met and spoke with friends and acquaintances, including G. Platt, a director of Phoenix Corporation and chief executive officer of Texas International Company (TIC), a business that sponsored Switzer's coach's television show. TIC owned more than 50 percent of Phoenix's shares. Switzer moved around the bleachers at the track meet in order to talk to various people. After speaking with Platt and his wife Linda for the last of five times, Switzer lay down to sunbathe on a row of bleachers behind the Platts. G. Platt, unaware that Switzer was behind him, carelessly spoke too loud while talking with his wife about his desire to sell or liquidate Phoenix. He also talked about several companies making bids to buy Phoenix. Switzer also overheard that an announcement of a possible liquidation of Phoenix might be made within a week. Switzer used the information he obtained in deciding to purchase Phoenix shares. Did Switzer trade illegally on inside information?

12. Edper, Inc., identified Brascan, Inc., as a potential takeover target. On behalf of Edper, a securities broker contacted 40 institutional investors and 12 substantial individual holders of Brascan shares who were his clients. The broker told the investors that Edper was interested in buying 3 to 4 million shares. Eventually, Edper bought 6.3 million shares—nearly 25 percent of Brascan's outstanding shares—from these investors at a price that the broker and each individual investor agreed upon. Did Edper make a tender offer for Brascan's shares that required it to file a Schedule 14D-1 prior to the making the offers to the investors?

PART IX

SPECIAL TOPICS

CHAPTER 32

Estates and Trusts

ESTATES AND TRUSTS

INTRODUCTION

One of the basic features of the ownership of property is the right to dispose of the property during life and at death. You have already learned about the ways in which property is transferred during the owner's life. The owner's death is another major event for the transfer of property.

Most people want to be able to choose who will get their property when they die. There are a variety of ways in which a person may control the ultimate disposition of his property. He may take title to the property in a form of joint ownership that gives his co-owner a right of survivorship. He may create a trust and transfer property to it to be used for the benefit of a spouse, child, elderly parent, or other beneficiary. He may execute a will in which he directs that his real and personal property be distributed to persons named in the will.

If, however, a person makes no provision for the disposition of his property at his death, his property will be distributed to his heirs as defined by state law. This chapter focuses on the transfer of property at death and on the use of trusts for the transfer and management of property, both during life and at death.

ESTATE PLANNING

A person's **estate** is all of the property owned by that person. **Estate planning** is the popular name for the complicated process of planning for the transfer of a person's estate in later life and at death. Estate planning also concerns planning for the possibility of prolonged illness or disability. An attorney who is creating an estate plan will take an inventory of the client's assets, learn client's objectives, and draft the instruments necessary to carry out the plan. This plan is normally guided by the desire to reduce the amount of tax liability and to provide for the orderly disposition of the estate.

WILLS

Right of Disposition by Will

The right to control the disposition of property at death has not always existed. In the English feudal system, the king owned all land. The lords and knights had only the right to use land for their lifetime. A landholder's rights in land terminated upon his death, and no rights descended to his heirs. In 1215, the king granted the nobility the right to pass their interest in the land they held to their heirs. Later, that right was extended to all property owners. In the United States, each state has enacted statutes that establish the requirements for a valid will, including the formalities that must be met to pass property by will.

Nature of a Will

A **will** is a document executed with specific legal formalities by a **testator** (person making a will) that contains his instructions about the way his property will be disposed of at his death. A will can dispose only of property belonging to the testator at the time of his death. Furthermore, wills do not control property that goes to others through other planning devices (such as life insurance policies) or by operation of law (such as by right of survivorship). For example, property held in joint tenancy or tenancy by the entirety is not controlled by a will, because the property passes automatically to the surviving cotenant by right of survivorship. In addition, life insurance proceeds are controlled by the insured's designation of beneficiaries, not by any provision of a will. (Because joint tenancy and life insurance are ways of directing the disposition of property, they are sometimes referred to as "will substitutes.")

Common Will Terminology

Some legal terms commonly used in wills include the following:

1. *Bequest.* A **bequest** (also called **legacy**) is a gift of personal property or money. For example, a will might provide for a bequest of a family heirloom to the testator's daughter. Since a will can direct only property that is owned by the testator at the time of his death, a specific bequest of property that the testator has disposed of before his death is ineffective. This is called **ademption.** For example, Samuel's will states that Warren is to receive Samuel's collection of antique guns. If the guns are destroyed before Warren's death, however, the bequest is ineffective because of ademption.

2. *Devise.* A **devise** is a gift of real property. For example, the testator might devise his family farm to his grandson.

3. *Residuary.* The **residuary** is the balance of the estate that is left after specific devises and bequests are made by the will. After providing for the disposition of specific personal and real property, a testator might provide that the residuary of his estate is to go to his spouse or be divided among his descendants.

4. *Issue.* A person's **issue** are his lineal descendants (children, grandchildren, great-grandchildren, and so forth). This category of persons includes adopted children.

5. *Per capita.* This term and the next one, *per stirpes,* are used to describe the way in which a group of persons are to share a gift. **Per capita** means that each of that group of persons will share equally. For example, Grandfather dies, leaving a will that provides that the residuary of his estate is to go to his issue or descendants *per capita.* Grandfather had two children, Mary and Bill. Mary has two children, John and James. Bill has one child, Margaret. Mary and Bill die before Grandfather (in legal terms, *predecease* him), but all three of Grandfather's grandchildren are living at the time of his death. In this case, John, James, and Margaret would each take one-third of the residuary of Grandfather's estate.

6. *Per stirpes.* When a gift is given to the testator's issue or descendants **per stirpes** (also called **by right of representation**), each surviving descendant divides the share that his or her parent would have taken if the parent had survived. In the preceding example, if Grandfather's will had stated that the residuary of his estate was to go to his issue or descendants *per stirpes,* Margaret would take one half and John and James would take one quarter each (that is, they would divide the share that would have gone to their mother). Figure 1 illustrates the difference between *per capita* and *per stirpes.*

Testamentary Capacity

The capacity to make a valid will is called **testamentary capacity.** To have testamentary capacity, a person must be *of sound mind* and *of legal age,* which is 18 in most states. A person does not have to be in perfect mental health to have testamentary capacity. Because people often delay executing wills until they are weak and in ill health, the standard for mental capacity to make a will is fairly low. To be of "sound mind," a person need only be sufficiently rational to be capable of understanding the nature and character of his property, of realizing that he is making a will, and of knowing the persons who

FIGURE 1   Comparison of Per Capita and Per Stirpes

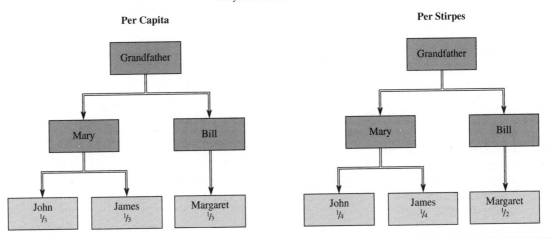

Note: Grandfather, Mary and Bill are deceased.
Mary and Bill both died before Grandfather.

would normally be the beneficiaries of his affection. A person could move in and out of periods of lucidity and still have testamentary capacity if he executed his will during a lucid period.

Lack of testamentary capacity is a common ground upon which wills are challenged by persons who were excluded from a will. Fraud and undue influence are also common grounds for challenging the validity of a will.[1] The *Prigge* case, which follows, is a good example of a will contest based on lack of testamentary capacity and undue influence.

---

[1] Fraud and undue influence are discussed in detail in the Reality of Consent chapter.

IN THE MATTER OF ESTATE OF PRIGGE

352 N.W.2d 443 (Minn. Ct. App. 1984)

John Prigge died in 1982, survived by two sisters, Marian and Jean; one brother, Louis; and some nephews and nieces. John had never married and had been a farmer all his life. In 1980, he sold his farm and moved in with his sister Marian. While John was living with her, Marian, at John's request, prepared a handwritten document expressing his testamentary intent. John took the document to a lawyer, who prepared a will based on the contents of the document. John executed the will in 1981. In the will, John devised his entire estate to Marian and her six children in equal shares and specifically excluded Louis and Jean. John died in 1982. Louis and Jean contested the will on grounds of lack of testamentary capacity and undue influence. The trial court found that the will was valid. Louis and Jean appealed.

Nierengarten, Judge.   Louis and Jean initially contend that John did not possess the capacity to make a will. A testator will be found to have testamentary capacity if, when making the will, he understands the nature, situation, and extent of his property and the claims of others on his bounty or his remembrance, and he is able to hold these things in his mind long enough to form a rational judgment concerning them. Less mental capacity is required to make a will than to conduct regular business affairs.

It is undisputed that John was a man of average or below average intelligence who sometimes needed direction. His mother would have to balance his checkbook and take care of his bookwork. He had to be constantly reminded to do things around the house. He failed to do his tax returns in 1978 and 1979 and did not keep good track of his bills. Following the death of his mother and uncle, who helped him farm, the family operation declined in quality. These are the characteristics that Louis and Jean claim evidenced John's lack of testamentary capacity.

To rebut this, the attorney who drafted John's will testified that John was of sound mind, had testamentary capacity, knew the natural heirs of his bounty, knew the extent of his property, and was under no restraint when he made his will. The attorney also testified that John did not appear to have any doubts as to what he wanted in his will and had no difficulty arriving at the decisions on the various questions asked of him. There was additional testimony that John had, over the years, signed many documents, such as security agreements, mortgages, and contracts, without anyone's aid. In 1980, John held an auction in which he sold most of his farming equipment. The sale required execution of an auction sale agreement with the Lake City Bank. The Vice-President of the bank testified he had no doubt that John had the ability to understand the agreement. A first cousin of John testified that John mentioned to her he had made out a will and that "some of them aren't going to like it." The circumstances here are not so unusual as to disturb the trial court's findings of testamentary capacity.

Louis and Jean also argue that John was unduly influenced and susceptible to suggestion. To show undue influence, the evidence must show not only that the influence was exerted, but that it was so dominant and controlling of the testator's mind that he ceased to act of his own free volition and became a mere puppet of the wielder of that influence. Among the factors important as bearing upon undue influence are the opportunity to exercise it, active participation in the preparation of the will by the party exercising it, a confidential relationship between the person making the will and the party exercising the influence, disinheritance of those whom the decedent probably would have remembered in his will, singularity of the provisions of the will, and the exercise of influence or persuasion to induce him to make the will.

Louis and Jean's undue influence claim centers around the handwritten will drafted by John's sister, Marian, while he lived with her. That act, in itself, creates a situation where close scrutiny of possible undue influence is required. Where the beneficiary sustains confidential relations and drafts the will, or controls its drafting, a presumption of undue influence arises or an inference to that effect may be drawn.

John requested Marian to write down what he wanted in his will and to make sure the spelling of the names was correct. But it didn't end there. John then took the draft into an attorney's office where he received advice and assistance. As the attorney testified, John knew what he wanted and what he was doing. The relationship between John and his brothers and sisters negated undue influence. Whereas Marian and her husband had helped John on many occasions for at least eight years before he sold the family farm, John had an estranged relationship with Louis and Jean and had not associated with them except on a very limited basis. The record supports a finding of no undue influence.

Judgment upholding the validity of the will affirmed.

Execution of a Will

Unless a will is executed with the formalities required by state law, it is *void*. The courts are strict in interpreting statutes concerning the execution of wills. If a will is declared void, the property of the deceased person will be distributed according to the provisions of state laws that will be discussed later.

The formalities required for a valid will differ from state to state. For that reason, an individual should consult the laws of his state before making a will. If he should move to another state after having executed a will, he should consult a lawyer in his new state to determine whether a new will needs to be executed. All states require that a will be *in writing*. State law also requires that formal wills be *witnessed*, generally by two or three *disinterested* witnesses (persons who do not stand to inherit any property under the will), and that it be *signed* by the testator or by someone else at the testator's direction. Most states also require that the testator *publish* the will, that is, declare or indicate at the time of signing that the instrument is his will. Another formality required by most states is that the testator sign the will in the presence and the sight of the witnesses and that the witnesses sign in the presence and the sight of each other. As a general rule, an **attestation clause,** which states the formalities that have been followed in the execution of the will, is written following the testator's signature. These detailed formalities are designed to prevent fraud.

In some situations, a lawyer might arrange to have the execution of a will *videotaped* to provide evidence relating to the testator's capacity and the use of proper formalities. (Note that the will is executed in the normal way; the videotape merely records the execution of the will.) Some state probate codes specifically provide that videotapes of the executions of wills are admissible into evidence.

Informal Wills

Some states recognize certain types of wills that are not executed with these formalities. These are:

1. *Nuncupative wills*. A **nuncupative** will is an oral will. Such wills are recognized as valid in some states, but only under limited circumstances and to a limited extent. In a number of states, for example, nuncupative wills are valid only when made by soldiers in military service and sailors at sea, and even then they will be effective only to dispose of personal property that was in the actual possession of the person at the time the oral will was made. Other states place low dollar limits on the amount of property that can be passed by a nuncupative will.

2. *Holographic wills*. **Holographic wills** are wills that are written and signed in the testator's handwriting. They are recognized in about half of the states, even though they are not executed with the formalities usually required of valid wills. For a holographic will to be valid in the states that recognize them, it must evidence testamentary intent and must actually be *handwritten* by the testator. A typed holographic will would be invalid. Some states require that the holographic will be *entirely* handwritten, and some also require that the will be dated.

Construction of Wills

Even in carefully drafted wills, questions sometimes arise as to the meaning or legal effect of a term or provision. Disputes about the meaning of the will are even more likely to occur in wills drafted by the testator himself, such as holographic wills. To interpret a will, a court will examine the entire instrument in an attempt to determine the testator's intent. The following case, *Haag v. Stickley,* provides a good example of the methods and principles courts use to interpret wills.

HAAG v. STICKLEY

389 S.E.2d 691 (Va. 1990)

Kenneth Haag owned Front Royal Supply Company. Charles Smoot had worked for Haag as the manager of the Front Royal store for a number of years. John Stickley was the manager of the company's Winchester store but had not worked for Haag as long as Smoot had. Wayne Blye was assistant manager of the Winchester store and had worked for the company for a lesser amount of time than had Stickley. Melvin Printz was also an employee of Haag's, but was fired in 1984–85.

On January 20, 1983, Haag executed a holographic will. The will contained a specific bequest of stock to his employees who were still with Front Royal at the time of his death. It stated as follows:

In October of 1985, Haag executed a holographic codicil. This codicil provided that "In case Chs. Smoot is deceased or any other receipient [sic] their stare [sic] will go back in the estate." Haag died in 1986. His will was admitted to probate, and his former wife, Helen, was named executor. At the time of Haag's death, he owned 689 shares of Front Royal stock, the value of which was at least $254,000. A dispute arose between Mrs. Haag, as executor, and Stickley and Blye about whether they were entitled to any shares. Mrs. Haag maintained that the will should be interpreted to give 500 shares of stock to Smoot, and none to Stickley and Blye, with the remaining 189 shares going into the residuary of the estate. Stickley and Blye filed this action asking the court to construe and interpret the will in order to determine their rights to the shares of stock. The court determined that Smoot should get the first 500 shares, and the remaining 189 shares should be divided equally between Stickley and Blye, with the odd share going to the person with longer service. Mrs. Haag appealed.

Compton, Justice. In construing a will, the testator's intention controls, unless contrary to an established rule of law. The whole will must be examined to determine the testator's intention and effect should be given to all parts of the document, as far as possible. Even though the language of the will may be obscure or uncertain, the testator's intention will prevail, if it can be ascertained.

Moreover, when the words of the will are capable of two different constructions, that should be adopted which is most consistent with the intention of the testator as ascertained by other provisions in the will; and when the intention of the testator is incorrectly expressed, the court will effectuate it by supplying the proper words.

It is true that in ascertaining the testator's intent we examine the words used in light of the circumstances surrounding the testator at the time of the will's execution. However, we cannot ignore subsequent changes to the will as we consider that intent. A will is an ambulatory instrument, not intended or allowed to take effect until the death of the maker. It may be changed during life as often as the mind and purposes of the testator change.

Against the background of the foregoing principles, we cannot say that the chancellor misinterpreted or misconstrued the testamentary documents. Insofar as the bequest of company stock is concerned, the testator's plan clearly appears from the will and from the circumstances prevailing at the time the will was drawn. The testator wished to reward company employees for their past and continued service by leaving all his stock in the company to such of those employees who were living and still working for the company at the time of his death.

Thus, he bequeathed "my shares of the stock" in the company, intending to give all the shares he owned. The quantity "500 shares" follows Smoot's name. No quantity is shown after Stickley's or Blye's names. Mrs. Haag contends the bequest is incomplete because it contains what she has labeled "blanks" or omissions. We perceive no blanks or omissions. Rather, we view the terms to state individual bequests.

Where a bequest is to several individuals, whatever may be their relationship to each other, equality is the rule, unless the testator has established a different one. Therefore, we conclude from the language and arrangement of the words that the testator intended to make a gift of all of his shares to three persons with one receiving 500 shares and the other two receiving the balance, which they divide equally, the longer in service to the company receiving the odd share.

The testator's intent is further indicated by the manner in which he made corrections on the holograph. He struck through the name of Melvin Printz, probably after Printz had been fired in 1984–85. He initialled the deletion writing "no" before "shares." This demonstrates the testator's method of deleting a beneficiary and canceling a bequest. He made other deletions in other portions of the will and codicil and initialled them also. In contrast, the names of Stickley and Blye remained in the will without being initialled but separately joined to the words "shares" by dashes or connecting lines, not blanks. The lines are undulating and not straight as a blank line usually appears. It cannot be successfully argued that these lines serve to negate the bequest to Stickley or Blye. There are at least two plausible reasons why the testator did not specify the number of shares allocated to Stickley or Blye. First, the testator was probably uncertain whether both would remain company employees until his death. Second, the testator was uncertain about the number of shares of company stock he would own when he died. For these reasons, the testator probably concluded that the exact number of shares passing to these two employees could be more accurately determined after his death.

For these reasons, we find no error in the decision of the trial court.

Judgment for Stickley and Blye affirmed.

Limitations on Disposition by Will

A person who takes property by will takes it subject to all outstanding claims against the property. For example, if real property is subject to a mortgage or other lien, the beneficiary who takes the property gets it subject to the mortgage or lien. In addition, the rights of the testator's creditors are superior to the rights of beneficiaries under his will. Thus, if the testator was insolvent (his debts exceeded his assets), persons named as beneficiaries do not receive any property by virtue of the will.

Under the laws of most states, the surviving spouse of the testator has statutory rights in property owned solely by the testator that cannot be defeated by a contrary will provision. This means that a husband cannot effectively disinherit his wife, and vice versa. Even if the will provides for the surviving spouse, he or she can elect to take the share of the decedent's estate that would be provided by state law rather than the amount specified in the will. As a general rule, a surviving spouse is given the right to use the family home for a stated period as well as a portion of the deceased spouse's estate. At common law, a widow had the right to a life estate in one third of the lands owned by her husband during their marriage. This was known as a widow's **dower right.** A similar right for a widower was known as **curtesy.** A number of states have changed the right by statute to give a surviving spouse a one-third interest in fee simple in the real and personal property owned by the deceased spouse at the time of his or her death. Naturally, a testator can leave his spouse more than this if he desires. In community property states, each spouse has a one-half interest in community property that cannot be defeated by a contrary will provision. (Note that the surviving spouse will obtain *full* ownership of any property owned by the testator and the surviving spouse as joint tenants or tenants by the entirety.)

Children of the testator who were born or adopted after the will was executed are called **pretermitted** children. There is a presumption that the testator intended to provide for such a child, unless there is evidence to the contrary. State law gives pretermitted children the right to a share of the testator's estate. For example, under the Uniform Probate Code, which is law in 15 states, a pretermitted child has the right to receive the share he would have received under the state intestacy statute unless it appears that the omission of this child was intentional, the testator gave substantially all of his estate to the child's other parent, or the testator provided for the child outside of the will.[2]

Revocation of Wills

One important feature of a will is that it is *revocable* until the moment of the testator's death. For this reason, a will confers *no present interest* in the testator's property.

A person is free to revoke a prior will and, if she wishes, to make a new will. Wills can be revoked in a variety of ways. Physical destruction and mutilation done with intent to revoke a will constitute revocation, as do other acts such as crossing out the will or creating a writing that expressly cancels the will. In addition, a will is revoked if the testator later executes a valid will that expressly revokes the earlier will. A later will that does not *expressly* revoke an earlier will operates to revoke only those portions of the earlier will that are inconsistent with the later will. In some states, a will is presumed to have been revoked if it cannot be located after the testator's death, although this presumption can be rebutted with contrary evidence.

Wills can also be revoked by operation of law without any act on the part of the testator signifying revocation. State statutes provide that certain changes in relationships operate as revocations of a will. In some states, marriage will operate to revoke a will that was made when the testator was single. Similarly, a divorce may revoke provisions in a will made during marriage that leave property to the divorced spouse. Under the laws of some states, the birth of a child after the execution of a will may operate as a partial revocation of the will.

Codicils

A **codicil** is an amendment of a will. If a person wants to change a provision of a will without making an entirely new will, she may amend the will by executing a codicil. One may *not* amend a will by merely striking out objectionable provisions and inserting new provisions. The same formalities are required for the creation of a valid codicil as for the creation of a valid will.

---

[2]*Uniform Probate Code* section 2–302.

FIGURE 2 A Living Will

DECLARATION made this 31st day of December, 1987.

I, JOHN SMITH, being at least eighteen (18) years old and of sound mind, willfully and voluntarily make known my desires that my dying shall not be artificially prolonged under the circumstances set forth below, and I declare: If at any time I have an incurable injury, disease, or illness certified in writing to be a terminal condition by my attending physician, and my attending physician has determined that my death will occur within a short period of time, the use of life-prolonging procedures would serve only to artificially prolong the dying process, I direct that such procedures be withheld or withdrawn, and that I be permitted to die naturally with only the provisions of appropriate nutrition and hydration and the administration of medication and the performance of any medical procedure necessary to provide me with comfort, care, or to alleviate pain.

In the absence of my ability to give directions regarding the use of life-prolonging procedures, it is my intention that this declaration be honored by my family and physician as the final expression of my legal right to refuse medical or surgical treatment and accept the consequence of the refusal.

I UNDERSTAND THE FULL IMPORT OF THIS DECLARATION.

Signed: _____

JOHN SMITH

PLANNING FOR DISABILITY

Living Wills

Advances in medical technology now permit a person to be kept alive by artificial means, even in many cases in which there is no hope of the person being able to function without life support. Many people are opposed to their lives being prolonged with no chance of recovery. In response to these concerns, most states have enacted legislation allowing individuals to execute **living wills.** Living wills are documents in which a person states his intention to forego certain life-prolonging medical procedures. The execution of a living will is often part of the process of planning a person's estate. The effect of a valid living will is to serve as an expression of the person's beliefs regarding life support systems.

If the attending physician is opposed to a living will, it is up to that physician to transfer the patient's care. In some states, living wills are to be given to the physician and are to be placed with the patient's medical records. Because living wills are created by statute, it is important that all terms and conditions of the statute be followed. Figure 2 shows an example of a living will, which is contained in Indiana's living will statute.[3]

The importance of living wills and durable powers of attorney (which are discussed in the next section) was underscored in the recent Supreme Court case of *Cruzan v. Director, Missouri Department of Health. Cruzan,* which follows, holds that it is constitutionally permissible for a state to refuse to permit the guardians of an incompetent person to terminate life support without clear and convincing evidence that the incompetent person would consent to such termination.

---

[3]Indiana Code 16–8–11–12.

CRUZAN V. DIRECTOR, MISSOURI DEPARTMENT OF HEALTH

110 S. Ct. 2841 (U.S. S. Ct. 1990)

On the night of January 11, 1983, 25-year-old Nancy Cruzan lost control of her car while driving down Elm Road in Jasper County, Missouri. The vehicle overturned, and Cruzan was discovered lying face down in a ditch without detectable respiratory or cardiac function. Paramedics were able to restore her breathing and heartbeat at the accident site, and she was transported to a hospital. There she was diagnosed as having sustained probable cerebral contusions compounded by significant anoxia (lack of oxygen). She remained in a coma for three weeks and then progressed to an unconscious state in which she was able to orally ingest some nutrition. To ease feeding and further her recovery, surgeons implanted a gastrostomy feeding and hydration tube. She then lay in a Missouri state hospital in what is commonly referred to as a persistent vegetative state.

After it became apparent that Cruzan had virtually no chance of regaining her mental faculties, her parents (also her legal guardians) asked hospital employees to terminate the artificial nutrition and hydration procedures, which would cause her death. The employees refused to do so without court approval. The parents then sought authorization from the state trial court for termination. Cruzan had not executed a living will, but a former roommate of Cruzan's testified that Cruzan had told her that if she were sick or injured she would not wish to continue her life unless she could live at least halfway normally. The trial court granted authorization to terminate nutrition and hydration, holding that a person in Cruzan's position had a fundamental constitutional right to refuse or direct the withdrawal of "death prolonging procedures." It also found that Cruzan's conversation with her roommate indicated that she would not want to continue with life support. The Supreme Court of Missouri reversed on the ground that no one can assume the choice regarding termination of medical treatment for an incompetent person in the absence of the formalities required under the Living Will Statute or clear and convincing evidence, which evidence it found to be lacking in this case. The U.S. Supreme Court then granted certiorari to consider whether the U.S. Constitution would require the hospital to withdraw life-sustaining treatment from Cruzan under these circumstances.

Rehnquist, Chief Justice.   Petitioners insist that the forced administration of life-sustaining medical treatment, and even of artificially-delivered food and water essential to life, would implicate a competent person's liberty interest. For purposes of this case, we assume that the United States Constitution would grant a competent person a constitutionally protected right to refuse life-saving hydration and nutrition.

Petitioners go on to assert that an incompetent person should possess the same right in this respect as is possessed by a competent person. The difficulty with petitioners' claim is that an incompetent person is not able to make an informed and voluntary choice to exercise a hypothetical right to refuse treatment or any other right. Such a "right" must be exercised for her, if at all, by some sort of surrogate. Here, Missouri has in effect recognized that under certain circumstances a surrogate may act for the patient in electing to have hydration and nutrition withdrawn in such a way as to cause death, but it has established a procedural safeguard to assure that the action of the surrogate conforms as best it may to the wishes expressed by the patient while competent. Missouri requires that evidence of the incompetent's wishes as to the withdrawal of treatment be proved by clear and convincing evidence. The question, then, is whether the United States Constitution forbids the establishment of this procedural requirement by the State. We hold that it does not. The choice between life and death is a deeply personal decision of obvious and overwhelming finality. We believe Missouri may legitimately seek to safeguard the personal element of this choice through the imposition of heightened evidentiary requirements. It cannot be disputed that the Due Process Clause protects an interest in life as well as an interest in refusing life-sustaining medical treatment. Not all incompetent patients will have loved ones available to serve as surrogate decisionmakers. And even where family members are present, there will, of course, be some unfortunate situations in which family members will not act to protect a patient. A State is entitled to guard against potential abuses in such situations. Similarly, a State is entitled to consider that a judicial proceeding to make a determination regarding an incompetent's wishes may very well not be an adversarial one, with the added guarantee of accurate factfinding that the adversary process brings with it. Finally, we think a State may properly decline to make judgments about the "quality" of life that a particular individual may enjoy, and simply assert an unqualified interest in the preservation of human life to be weighed against the constitutionally protected interests of the individual.

It is also worth noting that most, if not all, States simply forbid oral testimony entirely in determining the wishes of parties in transactions which, while important, simply do not have the consequences that a decision to terminate a person's life does. In most states, the parol evidence rule prevents the variations of the terms of a written contract by oral testimony. The statute of frauds makes unenforceable oral contracts to leave property by will, and statutes regulating the making of wills universally require that those instruments be in writing. There is no doubt that [these statutes] on occasion frustrate effectuation of the intent of a particular decedent just as Missouri's requirement of proof in this case may have frustrated the effectuation of the not-fully-expressed desires of Nancy Cruzan. But the Constitution does not require general rules to work faultlessly; no general rule can.

In sum, we conclude that a State may apply a clear and convincing evidence standard in proceedings where a guardian seeks to discontinue nutrition and hydration of a person diagnosed to be in a persistent vegetative state. The Supreme Court of Missouri held that the testimony adduced at trial did not amount to clear and convincing proof of the patient's desire to have hydration and nutrition withdrawn. We cannot say that the Supreme Court of Missouri committed constitutional error in reaching the conclusion that it did.

Judgment for the Missouri Department of Health affirmed.

Durable Power of Attorney

Another concern that people have as they plan for the future is that an accident or illness would deprive them of the ability to take care of themselves. One technique used to plan for this possibility is the execution of a document that gives another person the legal authority to act on one's behalf in the case of mental or physical incapacity. This document is called a **durable power of attorney.**

A *power of attorney* is an express statement in which one person (the **principal**) gives another person (the **attorney in fact**) the authority to do an act or series of acts on his behalf. For example, Andrews enters into a contract to sell his house to Willis, but he must be out of state on the date of the real estate closing. He gives Paulsen a power of attorney to attend the closing and execute the deed on his behalf. Ordinary powers of attorney terminate upon the principal's incapacity. By contrast, the *durable power of attorney* is not affected if the principal becomes incompetent.

A durable power of attorney permits a person to give someone else extremely broad powers to make decisions and enter transactions such as those involving real and personal property, bank accounts, and health care, and to specify that those powers will not terminate upon incapacity. The durable power of attorney is an extremely important planning device. For example, a durable power of attorney executed by an elderly parent to an adult child at a time in which the parent is competent would permit the child to take care of matters such as investments, property, bank accounts, and hospital admission. Without the durable power of attorney, the child would be forced to apply to a court for a guardianship, which is a more expensive, and often a less efficient manner in which to handle personal and business affairs.

Durable Power of Attorney for Health Care   A growing number of states have enacted statutes specifically providing for **durable powers of attorney for health care** (sometimes called **health care representatives**). This is a type of durable power of attorney in which the principal specifically gives the attorney in fact the authority to make certain health care decisions for him if the principal should become incompetent. Depending on state law and the instructions given by the principal to the attorney in fact, this could include decisions such as consenting or withholding consent to surgery, admitting the principal to a nursing home, and possibly withdrawing or prolonging life support. Note that the durable power of attorney becomes relevant only in the event that the principal becomes incompetent. So long as the principal is competent, he retains the ability to make his own health care decisions. This power of attorney is also revocable at the will of the principal. The precise requirements for creation of the durable power of attorney differ from state to state, but all states require a written and signed document executed with specified formalities, such as witnessing by disinterested witnesses. Figure 3 provides an example of a durable power of attorney for health care which is contained in the District of Columbia's statute.[4]

INTESTACY

If a person dies without making a will, or if he makes a will that is declared invalid, he is said to have died **intestate.** When that occurs, his property will be distributed to the persons designated as the intestate's heirs under the appropriate state's **intestacy** or **intestate succession** statute. The intestate's real property will be distributed according to the intestacy statute of the state in which the property is located. His personal property will be distributed according to the intestacy statute of the state in which he was **domiciled** at the time of his death. A domicile is a person's permanent home. A person can have only one domicile at a time. Determina-

tions of a person's domicile turn on facts that tend to show that person's intent to make a specific state his permanent home.

Characteristics of Intestacy Statutes

The provisions of intestacy statutes are not uniform. Their purpose, however, is to distribute property in a way that reflects the *presumed intent* of the deceased, that is, to distribute it to the persons most closely related to him. In general, such statutes first provide for the distribution of most or all of a person's estate to his surviving spouse, children, or grandchildren. If no such survivors exist, the statutes typically provide for the distribution of the estate to parents, siblings, or nieces and nephews. If no relatives at this level are living, the property may be distributed to surviving grandparents, uncles, aunts, or cousins. Generally, persons with the same degree of relationship to the deceased person take equal shares. If the deceased had no surviving relatives, the property **escheats** (goes) to the state.

Figure 4 depicts a typical distribution scheme of an intestacy statute.

Special Rules

Under intestacy statutes, a person must have a relationship to the deceased person through blood or marriage in order to inherit any part of his property. State law includes adopted children within the definition of "children," and treats adopted children in the same way as it treats biological children. (An adopted child would inherit from his adoptive parents, not from his biological parents.) Half brothers and half sisters are usually treated in the same way as brothers and sisters related by whole blood. An illegitimate child may inherit from his mother, but as a general rule, illegitimate children do not inherit from their fathers unless paternity has been either acknowledged or established in a legal proceeding.

A person must be alive at the time the decedent dies to claim a share of the decedent's estate. An exception may be made for pretermitted children or other descendants who are born *after* the decedent's death. If a person who is entitled to a share of the decedent's estate survives the decedent but dies before receiving his share, his share in the decedent's estate becomes part of his own estate.

Murder Disqualification   Many states provide that a person who is convicted of the homicide (murder or

---

[4]D.C. Code section 21–2207 (1990).

FIGURE 3   Example of a Durable Power of Attorney for Health Care

---

INFORMATION ABOUT THIS DOCUMENT:

THIS IS AN IMPORTANT LEGAL DOCUMENT. BEFORE SIGNING THIS DOCUMENT, IT IS VITAL FOR YOU TO KNOW AND UNDERSTAND THESE FACTS:

THIS DOCUMENT GIVES THE PERSON YOU NAME AS YOUR ATTORNEY IN FACT THE POWER TO MAKE HEALTH-CARE DECISIONS FOR YOU IF YOU CANNOT MAKE THE DECISIONS FOR YOURSELF.

AFTER YOU HAVE SIGNED THIS DOCUMENT, YOU HAVE THE RIGHT TO MAKE HEALTH-CARE DECISIONS FOR YOURSELF IF YOU ARE MENTALLY COMPETENT TO DO SO. IN ADDITION AFTER YOU HAVE SIGNED THIS DOCUMENT, NO TREATMENT MAY BE GIVEN TO YOU OR STOPPED OVER YOUR OBJECTION IF YOU ARE MENTALLY COMPETENT TO MAKE THAT DECISION.

YOU MAY STATE IN THIS DOCUMENT ANY TYPE OF TREATMENT THAT YOU DO NOT DESIRE AND ANY THAT YOU WANT TO MAKE SURE YOU RECEIVE.

YOU HAVE THE RIGHT TO TAKE AWAY THE AUTHORITY OF YOUR ATTORNEY IN FACT, UNLESS YOU HAVE BEEN ADJUDICATED INCOMPETENT, BY NOTIFYING YOUR ATTORNEY IN FACT OR HEALTH-CARE PROVIDER EITHER ORALLY OR IN WRITING. SHOULD YOU REVOKE THE AUTHORITY OF YOUR ATTORNEY IN FACT, IT IS ADVISABLE TO REVOKE IN WRITING AND TO PLACE COPIES OF THE REVOCATION WHEREVER THIS DOCUMENT IS LOCATED.

IF THERE IS ANYTHING IN THIS DOCUMENT THAT YOU DO NOT UNDERSTAND, YOU SHOULD ASK A SOCIAL WORKER, LAWYER, OR OTHER PERSON TO EXPLAIN IT TO YOU.

YOU SHOULD KEEP A COPY OF THIS DOCUMENT AFTER YOU HAVE SIGNED IT. GIVE A COPY TO THE PERSON YOU NAME AS YOUR ATTORNEY IN FACT. IF YOU ARE IN A HEALTH-CARE FACILITY, A COPY OF THIS DOCUMENT SHOULD BE INCLUDED IN YOUR MEDICAL RECORD.

POWER OF ATTORNEY FOR HEALTH CARE

I, John Jones, hereby appoint Carla Woods* as my attorney in fact to make health-care decisions for me if I become unable to make my own health-care decisions. This gives my attorney in fact the power to grant, refuse, or withdraw consent on my behalf for any health-care service, treatment or procedure. My attorney in fact also has the authority to talk to health-care personnel, get information and sign forms necessary to carry out these decisions.

If the person named as my attorney is not available or is unable to act as my attorney in fact, I appoint the following persons to serve in the order listed below: 1) Timothy Jones;* 2) Fred Jones.*

With this document, I intend to create a power of attorney for health care, which shall take effect if I become incapable of making my own health-care decisions and shall continue during incapacity.

My attorney in fact shall make health-care decisions as I direct below or as I make known to my attorney in fact in some other way.

(a) STATEMENT OF DIRECTIVES CONCERNING LIFE-PROLONGING CARE, TREATMENT, SERVICES, AND PROCEDURES:

(b) SPECIAL PROVISIONS AND LIMITATIONS:

BY MY SIGNATURE I INDICATE THAT I UNDERSTAND THE PURPOSE AND EFFECT OF THIS DOCUMENT.

"I sign my name to this form on ___December 20, 1991___ at ___2:00 p.m.___ "

___John Jones___
Signature*

FIGURE 3   *(concluded)*

WITNESSES

I declare that the person who signed or acknowledged this document is personally known to me, that the person signed or acknowledged this durable power of attorney for health care in my presence, and that the person appears to be of sound mind and under no duress, fraud, or undue influence. I am not the person appointed as the attorney in fact by this document, nor am I the health-care provider of the principal or an employee of the health-care provider of the principal.

First Witness
Signature:*   *Matilda Webb*

Second Witness
Signature:*   *Howard Rabb*

(At least one of the witnesses listed above shall also sign the following declaration.)

I further declare that I am not related to the principal by blood, marriage, or adoption, and to the best of my knowledge, I am not entitled to any part of the estate of the principal under a currently existing will or by operation of law.

Signature: *Matilda Webb*

Signature: *Howard Rabb*

*The suggested form calls for the addresses and telephone numbers of the principal, attorney-in-fact, as well as the addresses of the witnesses.

FIGURE 4   The Distribution Scheme under a Typical Intestacy Statute

Person Dying Intestate Is Survived by	Result
1. Spouse* and child or issue of a deceased child	Spouse $\frac{1}{2}$, Child $\frac{1}{2}$
2. Spouse and parent(s) but no issue	Spouse $\frac{3}{4}$, Parent $\frac{1}{4}$
3. Spouse but no parent or issue	All of the estate to spouse
4. Issue but no spouse	Estate is divided among issue
5. Parent(s), brothers, sisters, and/or issue of deceased brothers and sisters but no spouse or issue	Estate is divided among parent(s), brothers, sisters, and issue of deceased brothers and sisters
6. Issue of brothers and sisters but no spouse, issue, parents, brothers, and sisters	Estate is divided among issue of deceased brothers and sisters
7. Grandparents, but no spouse, issue, parents, brothers, sisters, or issue of deceased brothers and sisters	All of the estate goes to grandparents
8. None of the above	Estate goes to the state

*Note, however, second and subsequent spouses who had no children by the decedent may be assigned a smaller share.

manslaughter) of another person may not inherit any of the victim's property. Similarly, a person usually cannot share in the proceeds of life insurance on the life of a person he has murdered.

Simultaneous Death   A statute known as the Uniform Simultaneous Death Act provides that where two persons who would inherit from each other (such as husband and wife) die under circumstances that make it difficult or impossible to determine who died first, each person's property is to be distributed as though he or she survived. This means, for example, that the husband's property will go to his relatives and the wife's property to her relatives.

ADMINISTRATION OF ESTATES

When a person dies, an orderly procedure is needed to collect his property, settle his debts, and distribute any remaining property to those who will inherit it under his will or by intestate succession. This process occurs under the supervision of a probate court and is known as the **administration process** or the **probate process.** Summary (simple) procedures are sometimes available when an estate is relatively small—for example, when it has assets of less than $7,500.

The Probate Estate

The probate process operates only on the decedent's property that is considered to be part of his **probate estate.** The probate estate is that property belonging to the decedent at the time of his death other than property held in joint ownership with right of survivorship, proceeds of insurance policies payable to a trust or a third party, property held in a revocable trust during the decedent's lifetime in which a third party is the beneficiary, or retirement benefits, such as pensions, payable to a third party. Assets that pass by operation of law and assets that are transferred by other devices such as trusts or life insurance policies do not pass through probate.

Note that the decedent's probate estate and his *taxable estate* for purposes of federal estate tax are two different concepts. The taxable estate includes all property owned or controlled by the decedent at the time of his death. For example, if a person purchased a $1,000,000 life insurance policy made payable to his spouse or children, the policy would be included in his taxable estate, but not in his probate estate.

Determining the Existence of a Will

The first step in the probate process is to determine whether the deceased left a will. This may require a search of the deceased person's personal papers and safe-deposit box. If a will is found, it must be *proved* to be admitted to probate. This involves the testimony of the persons who witnessed the will, if they are still alive. If the witnesses are no longer alive, the signatures of the witnesses and the testator will have to be established in some other way. In many states, a will may be proved by an affidavit (declaration under oath) sworn to and signed by the testator and the witnesses at the time the will was executed. This is called a **self-proving affidavit.** If a will is located and proved, it will be admitted to probate and govern many of the decisions that must be made in the administration of the estate.

Selecting a Personal Representative

Another early step in the administration of an estate is the selection of a **personal representative** to administer the estate. If the deceased left a will, it is likely that he designated his personal representative in the will. The personal representative under a will is also known as the **executor.** Almost anyone could serve as an executor. The testator may have chosen, for example, his spouse, a grown child, a close friend, an attorney, or the trust department of a bank.

If the decedent died intestate, or if the personal representative named in a will is unable to serve, the probate court will name a personal representative to administer the estate. In the case of an intestate estate, the personal representative is called an **administrator.** A preference is usually accorded to a surviving spouse, child, or other close relative. If no relative is available and qualified to serve, a creditor, bank, or other person may be appointed by the court.

Most states require that the personal representative *post a bond* in an amount in excess of the estimated value of the estate to ensure that her duties will be properly and faithfully performed. A person making a will often directs that his executor may serve without posting a bond, and this exemption may be accepted by the court.

Responsibilities of the Personal Representative

The personal representative has a number of important tasks in the administration of the estate. She must see that an inventory is taken of the estate's assets and that the assets are appraised. Notice must then be given to creditors or potential claimants against the estate so that they can file and prove their claims within a specified time, normally five months. As a general rule, the surviving spouse of the deceased person is entitled to be paid an allowance during the time the estate is being settled. This allowance has priority over other debts of the estate. The personal representative must see that any properly payable funeral or burial expenses are paid and that the creditors' claims are satisfied.

Both the federal and state governments impose estate or inheritance taxes on estates of a certain size. The personal representative is responsible for filing estate tax returns. The federal tax is a tax on the deceased's estate, with provisions for deducting items such as debts, expenses of administration, and charitable gifts. In addition, an amount equal to the amount left to the surviving spouse may be deducted from the gross estate before the tax is computed. State inheritance taxes are imposed on the person who receives a gift or statutory share from an estate. It is common, however, for wills to provide that the estate will pay all taxes, including inheritance taxes, so that the beneficiaries will not have to do so. The personal representative must also make provisions for filing an income tax return and for paying any income tax due for the partial year prior to the decedent's death.

When the debts, expenses, and taxes have been taken care of, the remaining assets of the estate are distributed to the decedent's heirs (if there was no will) or to the beneficiaries of the decedent's will. Special rules apply when the estate is too small to satisfy all of the bequests made in a will or when some or all of the designated beneficiaries are no longer living.

When the personal representative has completed all of these duties, the probate court will close the estate and discharge the personal representative.

TRUSTS

Nature of a Trust

A **trust** is a legal relationship in which a person who has legal title to property has the duty to hold it for the use or benefit of another person. The person benefited by a trust is considered to have **equitable title** to the property, because it is being maintained for his benefit. This means that he is the real owner even though the trustee has the legal title in his or her name. A trust can be created in a number of ways. An owner of property may *declare* that he is holding certain property in trust. For example, a mother might state that she is holding 100 shares of General Motors stock in trust for her daughter. A trust may also arise *by operation of law*. For example, when a lawyer representing a client injured in an automobile accident receives a settlement payment from an insurance company, the lawyer holds the settlement payment as trustee for the client. Most commonly, however, trusts are created through *express instruments* whereby an owner of property transfers title to the property to a trustee who is to hold, manage, and invest the property for the benefit of either the original owner or a third person. For example, Long transfers certain stock to First Trust Bank with instructions to pay the income to his daughter during her lifetime and to distribute the stock to her children after her death.

Trust Terminology

A person who creates a trust is known as a **settlor** or **trustor.** The person who holds the property for the benefit of another person is called the **trustee.** The person for whose benefit the property is held in trust is the **beneficiary.** Figure 5 illustrates the relationship between these parties. A single person may occupy more than one of these positions; however, if there is only one beneficiary, he cannot be the sole trustee. The property held in trust is called the **corpus** or **res.** A distinction is made between the property in trust, which is the principal, and the income that is produced by the principal.

A trust that is established and effective during the settlor's lifetime is known as an ***inter vivos* trust.** A trust can also be established in a person's will. Such trusts take effect only at the death of the settlor. They are called **testamentary trusts.**

Why People Create Trusts

Bennett owns a portfolio of valuable stock. She has two young children and an elderly father for whom she would like to provide. Why might it be advantageous to Bennett to transfer the stock to a trust for the benefit of the members of her family?

First, there may be income tax or estate tax advantages in doing so, depending on the type of trust she establishes and the provisions of that trust. The tax implications of a trust are very complicated. A person who is interested in setting up a trust to obtain tax advantages should seek the advice of a competent attorney experi-

FIGURE 5   A Trust

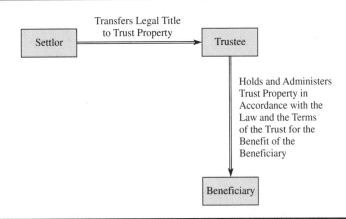

enced in estate planning. In addition, the trust property can be used for the benefit of others and may even pass to others after the settlor's death without the necessity of having a will. Many people prefer to pass their property by trust rather than by will because trusts afford more privacy: unlike a probated will, they do not become an item of public record. Trusts also afford greater opportunity for postgift management than do outright gifts and bequests. If Bennett wants her children to enjoy the income of the trust property during their young adulthood without distributing unfettered ownership of the property to them before she considers them able to manage it properly, she can accomplish this through a trust provision. A trust can prevent the property from being squandered or spent too quickly. Trusts can be set up so that a beneficiary's interest cannot be reached by his creditors in many situations. Such trusts, called **spendthrift trusts,** will be discussed later.

Placing property in trust can operate to increase the amount of property held for the beneficiaries if the trustee makes good investment decisions. Another important consideration is that a trust can be used to provide for the needs of disabled beneficiaries who are not capable of managing funds.

Creation of Express Trusts

There are five basic requirements for the creation of a valid express trust, although special and somewhat less restrictive rules govern the establishment of charitable trusts. The requirements for forming an express trust are:

1. *Capacity.* The settlor must have had the *legal capacity* to convey the property to the trust. This means that the settlor must have had the capacity needed to make a valid contract if the trust is an *inter vivos* trust or the capacity to make a will if the trust is a testamentary trust. For example, a trust would fail under this requirement if at the time the trust was created, the settlor had not attained the age required by state law for the creation of valid wills and contracts (age 18 in most states).

2. *Intent and formalities.* The settlor must *intend* to create a trust at the present time. To impose enforceable duties on the trustee, the settlor must meet certain formalities. Under the laws of most states, for example, the trustee must accept the trust by signing the trust instrument. In the case of a trust of land, the trust must be in writing so as to meet the statute of frauds. If the trust is a testamentary trust, it must satisfy the formal requirements for wills.

3. *Conveyance of specific property.* The settlor must convey *specific property* to the trust. The property conveyed must be property that the settlor has the *right to convey.*

4. *Proper purpose.* The trust must be created for a *proper purpose.* It cannot be created for a reason that is contrary to public policy, such as the commission of a crime.

5. *Identity of the beneficiaries.* The *beneficiaries* of the trust must be described clearly enough so that their identities can be ascertained. Sometimes, beneficiaries may be members of a specific class, such as "my children."

Charitable Trusts

A distinction is made between private trusts and trusts created for charitable purposes. In a private trust, property is devoted to the benefit of specific persons, whereas in a charitable trust, property is devoted to a charitable organization or to some other purposes beneficial to society. While some of the rules governing private and charitable trusts are the same, a number of these rules are different. For example, when a private trust is created, the beneficiary must be known at the time or ascertainable within a certain time (established by a legal rule known as the **rule against perpetuities**). However, a charitable trust is valid even though no definitely ascertainable beneficiary is named and even though it is to continue for an indefinite or unlimited period.

The Doctrine of Cy Pres   A doctrine known as **cy pres** is applicable to charitable trusts when property is given in trust to be applied to a particular charitable purpose that becomes impossible, impracticable, or illegal to carry out. Under the doctrine of *cy pres,* the trust will not fail if the settlor indicated a general intention to devote the property to charitable purposes. If the settlor has not specifically provided for a substitute beneficiary, the court will direct the application of the property to some charitable purpose that falls within the settlor's general charitable intention.

Totten Trusts

A **Totten trust** is a deposit of money in a bank or other financial institution in the name of the depositor *as trustee* for a named beneficiary. For example, Bliss deposits money in First Bank in trust for his daughter, Bessie. The Totten trust creates a revocable living trust. At Bliss's death, if he has not revoked this trust, the money in the account will belong to Bessie.

Powers and Duties of the Trustee

In most express trusts, the settlor names a specific person to act as trustee. If the settlor does not name a trustee, the court will appoint one. Similarly, a court will replace a trustee who resigns, is incompetent, or refuses to act.

The trust codes of most states contain provisions giving trustees broad management powers over trust property. These provisions can be limited or expanded by express provisions in the trust instrument. The trustee must use a *reasonable degree of skill, judgment, and care* in the exercise of his duties unless he holds himself out as having a greater degree of skill, in which case he will be held to a higher standard. He *may not commingle* the property he holds in trust with his own property or with that of another trust.

A trustee owes a *duty of loyalty* (fiduciary duty) to the beneficiaries. This means that he must administer the trust for the benefit of the beneficiaries and avoid any conflict between his personal interests and the interest of the trust. For example, a trustee cannot do business with a trust that he administers without express permission in the trust agreement. He must not prefer one beneficiary's interest to another's, and he must account to the beneficiaries for all transactions. Unless the trust agreement provides otherwise, the trustee must make the trust productive. He may not delegate the performance of discretionary duties (such as the duty to select investments) to another, but he may delegate the performance of ministerial duties (such as the preparation of statements of account).

A trust may give the trustee discretion as to the amount of principal or income paid to a beneficiary. In such a case, the beneficiary cannot require the trustee to exercise his discretion in the manner desired by the beneficiary.

Allocating between Principal and Income   One of the duties of the trustee is to distribute the principal and income of the trust in accordance with the terms of the trust instrument. Suppose Wheeler's will created a testamentary trust that provided that his wife was to receive the income from the trust for life and, at her death, the trust property was to be distributed to his children. During the duration of the trust, the trust earns profits, such as interest or rents, and has expenses, such as taxes or repairs. How should the trustee allocate these items as between Wheeler's surviving spouse, who is an **income beneficiary,** and his children, who are **remaindermen?**

The terms of the trust and state law bind the trustee in making this determination. As a general rule, ordinary profits received from the investment of trust property are allocated to income. For example, interest on trust property or rents earned from leasing real property held in trust would be allocated to income. Ordinary expenses such as insurance premiums, the cost of ordinary maintenance and repairs of trust property, and property taxes, would be chargeable to income. The principal of the trust includes the trust property itself and any extraordinary receipts, such as proceeds or gains derived from the sale of trust property. Extraordinary expenses—for example, the cost of long-term permanent improvements to real property or expenses relating to the sale of property—would ordinarily be charged against principal.

Spendthrift Trusts

Generally, the beneficiary of a trust may voluntarily assign his rights to the principal or income of the trust to another person. In addition, any distributions to the beneficiary are subject to the claims of his creditors. Sometimes, however, trusts contain provisions known as spendthrift clauses, which restrict the voluntary or involuntary transfer of a beneficiary's interest. Such clauses are generally enforced, and they preclude assignees or creditors from compelling a trustee to recognize their claims to the trust. The enforceability of such clauses is subject to four exceptions, however:

1. A person cannot put his own property beyond the claims of his own creditors. Thus, a spendthrift clause is not effective in a trust when the settlor makes himself a beneficiary.

2. Divorced spouses and minor children of the beneficiary can compel payment for alimony and child support.

3. Creditors of the beneficiary who have furnished necessaries can compel payment.

4. Once the trustee distributes property to a beneficiary, it can be subject to valid claims of others.

The *Tidrow v. Director, Missouri State Division of Family Service* case, which follows, presents an example of the use of spendthrift trusts.

TIDROW v. DIRECTOR, MISSOURI STATE DIVISION OF FAMILY SERVICE
688 S.W.2d 9 (Mo. Ct. App. 1985)

Bruce Tidrow, age 34, has been severely mentally retarded since birth. Bruce was cared for at home until his mother became critically ill. When Bruce's mother died, his father applied for future residential services for him, which at that time cost $1,234 per month. Mr. Tidrow was aware that funds were generally available for financial assistance of residential-type programs and that Bruce would have to be institutionalized as long as he lived. A week after making this application, Mr. Tidrow executed a will, leaving the bulk of his estate in a discretionary, spendthrift trust for the benefit of Bruce, and secondarily for the benefit of his other son, Kim, with the remainder to go to Kim outright upon Bruce's death. The assets of the trust, valued at approximately $175,000, consisted mainly of a residence and proceeds of life insurance policies.

Mr. Tidrow died in July 1981, and Bruce was placed in a residential program. Medical assistance to pay the cost of this residential care was applied for. State law prohibits assistance payments to anyone who is the owner or beneficial owner of cash or securities in the amount of $1,000 or more or any kind of property of a value in excess of $20,500. The Division of Family Services imputed the $175,000 trust assets to Bruce and denied his application on the ground that he had "resources in excess of the maximum allowed," and was thus financially unqualified for public assistance. Bruce appealed to the Circuit Court, which affirmed the decision of the Division of Family Services. Bruce appealed.

Stephan, Judge. The trust here in question is a true spendthrift trust in that it expressly provides that no beneficiary may alienate his interest therein and that no creditor of a beneficiary may reach such interest in satisfaction of any claim against a beneficiary.

Similarly, the trust is wholly discretionary in that it authorizes but does not require the trustee to pay from interest or principal any amount the trustee deems necessary, in its discretion, to provide for Bruce's "reasonable comfort" during his life. The trustee is also authorized to pay to Bruce's younger brother, Kim, such amounts as may be warranted by his needs.

The Director concedes that if Mr. Tidrow were living, his net worth would not disqualify his adult retarded son from receiving the medical assistance benefits here in issue. From the instrument involved here, it is abundantly clear that Bruce's father intended that payments from the trust for Bruce were to supplement, rather than supplant the benefits to which Bruce would otherwise be entitled. Earl Tidrow was aware that Bruce's age and good physical health augured a long life expectancy for him, that Bruce will need custodial care for as long as he lives, and that the cost of such care was increasing. In view of such facts, it would not comport with common sense to have created a gift of total support which would be wholly dissipated in a matter of a few years. On the contrary, the repeated references in the trust to Bruce's "lifetime" as well as the provision that, upon Bruce's death, the remaining assets would be paid to Kim or his descendants argue forcefully for the conclusion that settlor's intent was that the trust would continue throughout Bruce's life and that it would be supplementary to support received from the State. A contrary conclusion would totally frustrate the settlor's intent that his other son Kim would, at least ultimately, derive benefits from the settlor's estate.

Although the trust authorizes and contemplates the bestowal of benefits upon Bruce, it does not mandate payments. Thus, at any given time, Bruce may or may not have in his possession anything received from the trust and nothing had been received at the time this application for benefits was made. The Director's determination that the total assets of the trust are presently available to Bruce is in conflict with the clear intent that the trust would last for the duration of Bruce's life and beyond.

Judgment reversed in favor of Bruce.

Termination and Modification of a Trust

Normally, a settlor cannot revoke or modify a trust unless he reserves the power to do so at the time he establishes the trust. However, a trust may be modified or terminated with the consent of the settlor and all of the beneficiaries. When the settlor is dead or otherwise unable to consent, a trust can be modified or terminated by consent of all the persons with a beneficial interest, but only when this would not frustrate a material purpose of the trust. Because trusts are under the supervisory jurisdiction of a court, the court can permit a deviation from the terms of a trust when unanticipated changes in circumstances threaten accomplishment of the settlor's purpose.

Implied and Constructive Trusts

Under exceptional circumstances in which the creation of a trust is necessary to effectuate a settlor's intent or avoid unjust enrichment, the law *implies* or imposes a trust even though no express trust exists or an express trust exists but has failed. One trust of this type is a **resulting trust,** which arises when there has been an incomplete disposition of trust property. For example, if Hess transferred property to Wickes as trustee to provide for the needs of Hess's grandfather and the grandfather died before the trust funds were exhausted, Wickes will be deemed to hold the property in a resulting trust for Hess or Hess's heirs. Similarly, if Hess had transferred the property to Wickes as trustee and the trust had failed because Hess did not meet one of the requirements of a valid trust, Wickes would not be permitted to keep the trust property as his own. A resulting trust would be implied.

A **constructive trust** is a trust created by operation of law to avoid fraud, injustice, or unjust enrichment. This type of trust imposes on the constructive trustee a duty to convey property he holds to another person on the ground that the constructive trustee would be unjustly enriched if he were allowed to retain it. For example, when a person procures the transfer of property by means of fraud or duress, he becomes a constructive trustee and is under an obligation to return the property to its original owner.

ETHICAL AND PUBLIC POLICY CONCERNS

1. What should a state legislature take into account when adopting a living will statute or a durable power of attorney for health care statute?

2. Why should the law require so much formality to create a valid will? Would it be preferable for the law to lift some of the formalities surrounding wills and allow people to make valid wills orally, by informal letters, or by videotapes or audio recordings?

3. What is the ethical basis of a constructive trust?

SUMMARY

A person may dispose of his property by will if he has testamentary capacity and executes a will in compliance with the formalities required by state statute. State statutes normally require that the will be in writing, that it be witnessed by a specified number of disinterested persons, and that it be published and signed by the testator in the presence of witnesses. A will procured by fraud or undue influence will not be accepted as a valid will. Property that passes to another by operation of law or by a contract such as a life insurance contract is not controlled by the provisions of a will. Surviving spouses have statutory rights to receive a share of the estate of their deceased spouses. A will transfers no interest in property until the death of the testator. The testator can revoke the will at any time before his death. In addition, wills can be revoked by operation of law, such as by the divorce or marriage of the testator after the will has been executed.

As part of the estate planning process, a person may want to plan for the possibility of disability. Most states permit a person to execute a living will, in which he can state his intention to forego life-prolonging medical treatment if there is no chance that he will recover from an illness or accident. A durable power of attorney permits a person to appoint another to make decisions and enter transactions on his behalf if he becomes incapacitated. Some states permit the principal to appoint a special durable power of attorney for health care to give or withhold consent to medical treatment on his behalf if he should become incompetent.

The property of a person who dies intestate (without leaving a valid will) will be distributed to the persons who are his heirs under state intestacy laws, or laws of intestate succession. Real property will descend according to the laws of the state in which the intestate had his permanent home or domicile.

Estates are administered under the supervision of a probate court. If a will exists, the testator may have named a personal representative called an executor to administer his estate. The personal representative for an intestate estate is called an administrator. If there is no will or the named executor cannot serve, the court will select a personal representative. The personal representative has a number of important duties, including the duty to prepare estate and income tax returns. The steps in the administration of an estate include taking an inventory of the assets, having them appraised, determining the creditors and the persons to whom the estate is to be distributed, paying all proper debts, taxes, and expenses, and distributing the remainder to those who are entitled to it.

A trust arises when one person who has legal rights to certain property also has the duty to hold it for the use or benefit of another person. *Inter vivos* trusts are those that are established during the lifetime of the person who created the trust (the settlor). Testamentary trusts are those that are created in a will and take effect at death. Trusts may be expressly created, or they may arise by implication or the operation of law. Totten trusts are created when the depositor opens a bank account *as a trustee* for some other person. They create revocable living trusts. If not revoked at the trustee's death, the beneficiary will receive the money in the account.

Generally, the beneficiary of a trust has the right to assign the principal or interest in his share of the trust and his rights are subject to the claims of his creditors, unless the trust is a spendthrift trust. Normally, the creator of a trust may not revoke or modify the trust unless he reserves the right to do so at the time he establishes it; however, there are some exceptions. The trustee owes a duty to use reasonable skill, judgment, and care in the exercise of his duties. He also owes the beneficiaries a duty of loyalty.

PROBLEM CASES

1. Cunningham died in 1983, leaving a writing that purported to be his will. The writing was on a preprinted will form in which the first and last part of the will were printed and the rest of the will was handwritten by Cunningham. The first paragraph reads: "In the name of God, Amen. I," which is printed, followed by the handwriting: "Thomas John Cunningham—Social Security number 55–24–3083," which in turn is followed by printing: "being of sound mind, memory and understanding, do make and publish this my Last Will and Testament, in the manner following, that is to say: . . ." This is followed by the body of the will in Cunningham's handwriting, which gives instructions concerning the donation of bodily remains, specific bequests, and the distribution of the remainder of his estate. A printed clause appears after the body of the will, and immediately below this clause is a printed line upon which a testator normally signs his name, at the end of which is printed "Seal." Cunningham did not sign his name on this line; instead, the line contains the signature of a Notary Public of New Jersey, together with his notarial seal impressed over the printed word "Seal." Two people, a realtor (who was also the notary) and the realtor's secretary, witnessed the writing. Cunningham came to the realtor's office with the proposed will fully completed except for the witnesses' signatures. The writing was offered for probate as a will. Is the will valid?

2. In January of 1980, Borsch, age 80, wrote a will dividing his property among several friends and his niece. Borsch had a close friend, Herbert, who had been his friend for 25 years. Borsch saw Herbert and his wife on a daily basis and they frequently ate meals together. Borsch consulted Herbert on all of his business and personal matters. In 1981, Borsch showed Herbert the will that he had previously written. Herbert advised Borsch that it "won't stand up for 30 seconds," and suggested seeing an attorney. In March of 1981, Herbert helped Borsch prepare an inventory of his holdings and accompanied Borsch to an attorney's office. Although Herbert did not sit in on the conferences, he gave the attorneys a small notebook containing a listing of Borsch's properties and a list of the particular percentages allotted to various individuals. In March of 1981, Borsch executed another will leaving virtually all of his property to the Herberts. In July of 1981, Herbert noticed some clerical errors in this will and took Borsch back to the attorney's office for the execution of a new will correcting these errors. Borsch died in November of 1981, leaving no surviving spouse, siblings, or children. The nearest relatives at the time of his death were his niece and nephew. The July 1981 will was offered for probate, and the niece and nephew contested the will on the ground of undue influence. Will they be successful?

3. Roy and Icie Johnson established two revocable *inter vivos* trusts in 1966. The trust provided that upon Roy and Icie's deaths, income from the trusts was to be paid in equal shares to their two sons, James and Robert, for life. Upon the death of the survivor of the sons, the trust was to be *divided equally between all of my grandchildren, per stirpes.* James had two daughters, Barbara and Elizabeth. Robert had four children, David, Rosalyn, Catherine, and Elizabeth. James and Robert disclaimed their interest in the trust in 1979, and a dispute arose about how the trust should be distributed to the grandchildren. The trustee filed an action seeking instructions on how the trusts should be distributed. What should the court hold?

4. Natalie Elson was killed in an automobile accident at the age of 27. She had lived almost all of her life in Illinois, where she pursued a strong interest in horsemanship. After graduating from college in Illinois and receiving further training in horsemanship, she decided to move to Pennsylvania to study dressage. She hoped to compete in the 1984 Olympics as a rider. She told several friends that she intended to return to Illinois after a year. Her stepmother found an unmailed letter that Natalie had written to her sister shortly before her death, stating that she had "moved to Pennsylvania!" When Natalie left for Pennsylvania, she took her horse and a carload of her belongings with her. She left some items in storage in Illinois, and she left her jewelry in a safe-deposit box in Illinois. Upon arriving in Pennsylvania, she opened new bank accounts in Delaware (she lived near the Delaware border) and also established a safe-deposit box there. She retained her Illinois driver's license. Had Natalie changed her domicile to Pennsylvania?

5. Damme died leaving a valid will, which was admitted to probate. Prior to Damme's death, he owned substantial properties, consisting mostly of land, securities, and crops in storage. A large amount of the land, which was located in five states, was held by Damme in joint tenancy with right of survivorship with his brothers, William and Theodore. In his will, Damme gave his widow a life estate in all of his property. He then distributed the remainder of his estate as follows: he gave all real and personal property he owned in Kansas and all real property other than his Texas property to William and Theodore. He then specified that "[a] like amount in value . . ." should be divided half to his brothers-in-law, Percy and Duane, and half to his five nieces. A dispute arose about whether the property that passed to William and Theodore as joint tenants with right of survivorship should be included in the calculation of "like amount in value" for purposes of determining the amount of the bequest to Percy, Duane, and the five nieces. Should the properties held in joint tenancy be included in the calculation of "like amount in value?"

6. Bauert and Lightfoot operated a business partnership. Each took out a policy of life insurance in the amount of $200,000 and named the other as beneficiary. The premiums on the insurance were paid from the partnership bank account. The two men orally agreed that if either of them died, the survivor would use the life insurance proceeds to pay any partnership indebtedness and would pay the remaining proceeds to the widow and heirs of the deceased partner. Bauert died. At the time, the partnership owed a debt of $48,000 to First National Bank. Lightfoot assigned the proceeds of the insurance policy to the bank to partially cover a debt of $400,000 that he personally owed to the bank. Bauert's widow then brought an action against the bank, claiming that she was entitled to the insurance proceeds that exceeded the $48,000 debt. Should the court impose a constructive trust for the benefit of Mrs. Bauert?

7. Hotarek's parents were divorced when he was two. For about 13 years after that, Hotarek's mother, Benson, had no contact with him, did not provide financial support to him, and did not display interest in her son. In 1986, at the age of 15, Hotarek was killed in an automobile accident. After his death, his estate settled a claim against the other driver for $20,000 and was awarded uninsured motorist's benefits in the amount of $525,000. These proceeds made up Hotarek's estate. Following Hotarek's death, Benson could not be located.

Once she was located, the probate court ordered half of Hotarek's estate distributed to her in accordance with Connecticut's intestacy statute. It provides that if a person dies intestate leaving no spouse or children, the residue of the estate shall be distributed equally to the decedent's parent or parents. Hotarek's father objected to the distribution to Benson on the ground that she had abandoned her minor child during his life and should not be entitled to share in his estate after his death. Is Benson entitled to share in her intestate son's estate?

8. Weir was a lifelong bachelor. Shortly after World War II, he met Holmstead, a widow who was about his age. They were close friends until Weir died in 1971. Although they had separate apartments, they traveled together, ate their meals together, and were constant companions. In 1956, Weir executed a will that left a life estate to Holmstead and the remainder to his brother, or, if his brother was dead, to his brother's children. In 1965, Weir's brother died. In 1966, Weir executed a new will that left $10,000 each to his niece and nephew and the remainder of his estate to Holmstead. When Weir died, his niece, Margaret, challenged the 1966 will. She claimed that Weir did not have testamentary capacity and that he had been unduly influenced by Holmstead. Margaret said that Weir dressed conservatively, was occasionally forgetful, was sometimes untidy (he left his socks on the floor), and had some strange habits such as picking dust up from the floor and inspecting it. Was Weir's 1966 will invalid on the grounds of lack of capacity and undue influence?

THE CONSTITUTION OF THE UNITED STATES

PREAMBLE

We the People of the United States, in Order to form a more perfect Union, establish Justice, insure domestic Tranquility, provide for the common defence, promote the general Welfare, and secure the Blessings of Liberty to ourselves and our Posterity, do ordain and establish this Constitution for the United States of America.

ARTICLE I

Section 1.   All legislative Powers herein granted shall be vested in a Congress of the United States, which shall consist of a Senate and House of Representatives.

Section 2.   [1] The House of Representatives shall be composed of Members chosen every second Year by the People of the several States, and the Electors in each State shall have the qualifications requisite for Electors of the most numerous Branch of the State Legislature.

[2] No Person shall be a Representative who shall not have attained to the Age of twenty five Years, and been seven Years a citizen of the United States, and who shall not, when elected, be an Inhabitant of that State in which he shall be chosen.

[3] Representatives and direct Taxes shall be apportioned among the several States which may be included within this Union, according to their respective Numbers, which shall be determined by adding to the whole Number of free Persons, including those bound to service for a Term of Years, and excluding Indians not taxed, three fifths of all other Persons. The actual Enumeration shall be made within three Years after the first meeting of the Congress of the United States, and within every subsequent Term of ten Years, in such Manner as they shall by Law direct. The Number of Representatives shall not exceed one for every thirty Thousand, but each state shall have at Least one Representative; and until such enumeration shall be made, the State of New Hampshire shall be entitled to chuse three, Massachusetts eight, Rhode Island and Providence Plantations one, Connecticut five, New York six, New Jersey four, Pennsylvania eight, Delaware one, Maryland six, Virginia ten, North Carolina five, South Carolina five, and Georgia three.

[4] When vacancies happen in the Representation from any State, the Executive authority thereof shall issue Writs of Election to fill such Vacancies.

[5] The House of Representatives shall chuse their Speaker and other Officers; and shall have the sole Power of Impeachment.

Section 3.   [1] The Senate of the United States shall be composed of two Senators from each State, chosen by the Legislature thereof, for six Years; and each Senator shall have one Vote.

[2] Immediately after they shall be assembled in Consequence of the first Election, they shall be divided as equally as may be into three Classes. The Seats of the Senators of the first Class shall be vacated at the Expiration of the second Year, of the second Class at the Expiration of the fourth Year, and of the third Class at the Expiration of the sixth Year, so that one third may be chosen every second Year; and if Vacancies happen by Resignation, or otherwise, during the Recess of the Legislature of any State, the Executive thereof may make temporary

Appointments until the next Meeting of the Legislature, which shall then fill such Vacancies.

[3] No Person shall be a Senator who shall not have attained to the Age of thirty Years, and been nine Years a Citizen of the United States, and who shall not when elected, be an Inhabitant of that State for which he shall be chosen.

[4] The Vice President of the United States shall be President of the Senate, but shall have no Vote, unless they be equally divided.

[5] The Senate shall chuse their other Officers, and also a President pro tempore, in the Absence of the Vice President, or when he shall exercise the Office of President of the United States.

[6] The Senate shall have the sole Power to try all Impeachments. When sitting for that Purpose, they shall be on Oath of Affirmation. When the President of the United States is tried, the Chief Justice shall preside: And no Person shall be convicted without the Concurrence of two thirds of the Members present.

[7] Judgment in Cases of Impeachment shall not extend further than to removal from Office, and disqualification to hold and enjoy any Office of honor, Trust, or Profit under the United States: but the Party convicted shall nevertheless be liable and subject to Indictment, Trial, Judgment, and Punishment, according to Law.

Section 4. [1] The Times, Places and Manner of holding election for Senators and Representatives, shall be prescribed in each State by the Legislature thereof; but the Congress may at any time by Law make or alter such Regulations, except as to the Places of chusing Senators.

[2] The Congress shall assemble at least once in every Year, and such Meeting shall be on the first Monday in December, unless they shall by Law appoint a different Day.

Section 5. [1] Each House shall be the Judge of the Elections, Returns, and Qualifications of its own Members, and a Majority of each shall constitute a Quorum to do Business; but a smaller Number may adjourn from day to day, and may be authorized to compel the Attendance of absent Members, in such Manner, and under such Penalties as each House may provide.

[2] Each House may determine the Rules of its Proceedings, punish its Members for disorderly Behaviour, and with the Concurrence of two thirds, expel a Member.

[3] Each House shall keep a Journal of its Proceedings, and from time to time publish the same, excepting such Parts as may in their Judgment require Secrecy; and the Yeas and Nays of the Members of either House on any question shall, at the Desire of one fifth of those Present, be entered on the Journal.

[4] Neither House, during the Session of Congress, shall, without the consent of the other, adjourn for more than three days, nor to any other Place than that in which the two Houses shall be sitting.

Section 6. [1] The Senators and Representatives shall receive a Compensation for their Services, to be ascertained by Law, and paid out of the Treasury of the United States. They shall in all Cases, except Treason, Felony and Breach of the Peace, be privileged from Arrest during their Attendance at the Session of their respective Houses, and in going to and returning from the same; and for any Speech or Debate in either House, they shall not be questioned in any other Place.

[2] No Senator or Representative shall, during the time for which he was elected, be appointed to any civil Office under the Authority of the United States, which shall have been created, or the Emoluments whereof shall have been increased during such time; and no Person holding any Office under the United States, shall be a Member of either House during his Continuance in Office.

Section 7. [1] All Bills for raising Revenue shall originate in the House of Representatives; but the Senate may propose or concur with Amendments as on other Bills.

[2] Every Bill which shall have passed the House of Representatives and the Senate, shall, before it become a Law, be presented to the President of the United States; If he approve he shall sign it, but if not he shall return it, with his Objections to that House in which it shall have originated, who shall enter the Objections at large on their Journal, and proceed to reconsider it. If after such Reconsideration two thirds of that House shall agree to pass the Bill, it shall be sent together with the Objections, to the other House, by which it shall likewise be reconsidered, and if approved by two thirds of that House, it shall become a Law. But in all such Cases the Votes of both Houses shall be determined by Yeas and Nays, and the Names of the Persons voting for and against the Bill shall be entered on the Journal of each House respectively. If any Bill shall not be returned by the President within ten Days (Sundays excepted) after it shall have been presented to him, the Same shall be a Law, in like Manner as if he had signed it, unless the Congress by their Adjournment prevent its return in which Case it shall not be a Law.

[3] Every Order, Resolution, or Vote, to Which the Concurrence of the Senate and House of Representatives may be necessary (except on a question of Adjournment) shall be presented to the President of the United States; and before the Same shall take Effect, shall be approved by him, or being disapproved by him, shall be repassed by two thirds of the Senate and House of Representatives, according to the Rules and Limitations prescribed in the Case of a Bill.

Section 8. [1] The Congress shall have Power To lay and collect Taxes, Duties, Imposts and Excises, to pay the Debts and provide for the common Defence and general Welfare of the United States; but all Duties, Imposts and Excises shall be uniform throughout the United States;

[2] To borrow money on the credit of the United States;

[3] To regulate Commerce with foreign Nations, and among the several States, and with the Indian Tribes;

[4] To establish an uniform Rule of Naturalization, and uniform Laws on the subject of Bankruptcies throughout the United States;

[5] To coin Money, regulate the Value thereof, and of foreign Coin, and fix the Standard of Weights and Measures;

[6] To Provide for the Punishment of counterfeiting the Securities and current Coin of the United States;

[7] To Establish Post Offices and Post Roads;

[8] To promote the Progress of Science and useful Arts, by securing for limited Times to Authors and Inventors the exclusive Right to their respective Writings and Discoveries;

[9] To constitute Tribunals inferior to the supreme Court;

[10] To define and punish Piracies and Felonies committed on the high Seas, and Offences against the Law of Nations;

[11] To declare War, grant Letters of Marque and Reprisal, and make Rules concerning Captures on Land and Water;

[12] To raise and support Armies, but no Appropriation of Money to that Use shall be for a longer term than two Years;

[13] To provide and maintain a Navy;

[14] To make Rules for the Government and Regulation of the land and naval Forces;

[15] To provide for calling forth the Militia to execute the Laws of the Union, suppress Insurrections and repel Invasions;

[16] To provide for organizing, arming, and disciplining, the Militia, and for governing such Part of them as may be employed in the Service of the United States, reserving to the States respectively, the Appointment of the Officers, and the Authority of training the Militia according to the discipline prescribed by Congress;

[17] To exercise exclusive Legislation in all Cases whatsoever, over such District (not exceeding ten Miles square) as may, by Cession of particular States, and the Acceptance of Congress, become the Seat of the Government of the United States, and to exercise like Authority over all Places purchased by the Consent of the Legislature of the State in which the Same shall be, for the Erection of Forts, Magazines, Arsenals, dock-Yards, and other needful Buildings;—And

[18] To make all Laws which shall be necessary and proper for carrying into Execution the foregoing Powers, and all other Powers vested by this Constitution in the Government of the United States, or in any Department or Officer Thereof.

Section 9.   [1] The Migration or Importation of Such Persons as any of the States now existing shall think proper to admit, shall not be prohibited by the Congress prior to the Year one thousand eight hundred and eight, but a Tax or duty may be imposed on such Importation, not exceeding ten dollars for each Person.

[2] The Privilege of the Writ of Habeas Corpus shall not be suspended, unless when in Cases of Rebellion or Invasion, the public Safety may require it.

[3] No Bill of Attainder or ex post facto Law shall be passed.

[4] No Capitation, or other direct, Tax shall be laid, unless in Proportion to the Census or Enumeration herein before directed to be taken.

[5] No Tax or Duty shall be laid on Articles exported from any State.

[6] No Preference shall be given by any Regulation of Commerce or Revenue to the Ports of one State over those of another: nor shall Vessels bound to, or from, one State be obliged to enter, clear, or pay Duties in another.

[7] No money shall be drawn from the Treasury, but in consequence of Appropriations made by Law; and a regular Statement and Account of the Receipts and Expenditures of all public Money shall be published from time to time.

[8] No Title of Nobility shall be granted by the United States: And No Person holding any Office of Profit or Trust under them, shall, without the consent of the Congress, accept of any present, Emolument, Office, or Title, of any kind whatever, from any King, Prince, or foreign State.

Section 10.   [1] No State shall enter into any Treaty, Alliance, or Confederation; grant Letters of Marque and Reprisal; coin Money; emit Bills of Credit; make any Thing but gold and silver Coin a Tender in Payment of Debts; pass any Bill of Attainder, ex post facto Law, or Law impairing the Obligation of Contracts, or grant any Title of Nobility.

[2] No State shall, without the consent of the Congress, lay any Imposts or Duties on Imports or Exports, except what may be absolutely necessary for executing its inspection Laws: and the net Produce of all Duties and Imposts, laid by any State on Imports or Exports, shall be for the Use of the Treasury of the United States; and all such Laws shall be subject to the Revision and Control of the Congress.

[3] No State shall, without the consent of the Congress, lay any Duty of Tonnage, keep Troops, or Ships of War in time of Peace, enter into any Agree-ment or compact with another State, or with a foreign Power or engage in War, unless actually invaded, or in such imminent Danger as will not admit of delay.

Article II

Section 1.   [1] The executive Power shall be vested in a President of the United States of America. He shall hold his Office during the term of four Years, and together with the Vice President, chosen for the same Term, be elected, as follows:

[2] Each State shall appoint, in such Manner as the Legislature thereof may direct, a Number of Electors, equal to the whole Number of Senators and Representatives to which the State may be entitled in the Congress; but no Senator or Representative, or Person holding an Office of Trust or Profit under the United States, shall be appointed an Elector.

[3] The Electors shall meet in their respective States, and vote by Ballot for two Persons, of whom one at least shall not be an Inhabitant of the same State with themselves. And they shall make a List of all the Persons voted for, and of the Number of Votes for each; which List they shall sign and certify, and transmit sealed to the Seat of the Government of the United States, directed to the President of the Senate. The President of the Senate shall, in the Presence of the Senate and House of Representatives, open all the Certificates, and

the Votes shall then be counted. The Person having the greatest Number of Votes shall be the President, if such Number be a Majority of the whole Number of Electors appointed; and if there be more than one who have such Majority, and have an equal Number of Votes, then the House of Representatives shall immediately chuse by Ballot one of them for President; and if no Person have a Majority, then from the five highest on the List the said House shall in like Manner chuse the President. But in chusing the President, the Votes shall be taken by States, the Representation from each State having one Vote; a quorum for this Purpose shall consist of a Member or Members from two thirds of the States, and a Majority of all the States shall be necessary to a Choice. In every Case, after the Choice of the President, the Person having the greater number of Votes of the Electors shall be the Vice President. But if there should remain two or more who have equal Votes, the Senate shall chuse from them by Ballot the Vice President.

[4] The Congress may determine the Time of chusing the Electors, and the Day on which they shall give their Votes; which Day shall be the same throughout the United States.

[5] No person except a natural born citizen, or a citizen of the United States, at the time of the Adoption of this Constitution, shall be eligible to the Office of President; neither shall any Person be eligible to that Office who shall not have attained to the Age of thirty-five Years, and been fourteen Years a Resident within the United States.

[6] In case of the removal of the President from Office, or of his Death, Resignation or Inability to discharge the Powers and Duties of the said Office, the Same shall devolve on the Vice President, and the Congress may by Law provide for the Case of Removal, Death, Resignation or Inability, both of the President and Vice President, declaring what Officer shall then act as President, and such Officer shall act accordingly, until the Disability be removed, or a President shall be elected.

[7] The President shall, at stated Times, receive for his Services, a Compensation, which shall neither be increased nor diminished during the Period for which he shall have been elected, and he shall not receive within that Period any other Emolument from the United States, or any of them.

[8] Before he enter on the Execution of his Office, he shall take the following Oath or Affirmation: "I do solemnly swear (or affirm) that I will faithfully execute the Office of President of the United States, and will to the best of my Ability, preserve, protect and defend the Constitution of the United States."

Section 2.   [1] The President shall be Commander in Chief of the Army and Navy of the United States, and of the militia of the several States, when called into the actual Service of the United States; he may require the Opinion, in writing, of the principal Officer in each of the Executive departments, upon any Subject relating to the duties of their respective Offices, and he shall have Power to grant Reprieves and Pardons for Offenses against the United States, except in Cases of Impeachment.

[2] He shall have Power, by and with the Advice and Consent of the Senate to make Treaties, provided two thirds of the Senators present concur; and he shall nominate, and by and with the Advice and Consent of the Senate, shall appoint Ambassadors, other public Ministers and Consuls, Judges of the supreme Court, and all other Officers of the United States, whose Appointments are not herein otherwise provided for, and which shall be established by Law; but the Congress may by Law vest the Appointment of such inferior Officers, as they think proper, in the Heads of Departments.

[3] The President shall have Power to fill up all Vacancies that may happen during the Recess of the Senate, by granting Commissions which shall expire at the End of their next Session.

Section 3.   He shall from time to time give to the Congress Information of the State of the Union, and recommend to their Consideration such Measures as he shall judge necessary and expedient; he may, on extraordinary Occasions, convene both Houses, or either of them, and in Case of Disagreement between them, with Respect to the Time of Adjournment, he may adjourn them to such Time as he shall think proper; he shall receive Ambassadors and other public Ministers; he shall take Care that the Laws be faithfully executed, and shall Commission all the Officers of the United States.

Section 4.   The President, Vice President and all civil Officers of the United States, shall be removed from Office on Impeachment for, and Conviction of, Treason, Bribery, or other high Crimes and Misdemeanors.

Article III

Section 1.   The judicial Power of the United States, shall be vested in one supreme Court, and in such inferior Courts as the Congress may from time to time ordain and establish. The Judges, both of the supreme and inferior Courts, shall hold their Offices during good Behaviour, and shall, at stated Times, receive for their Services a Compensation, which shall not be diminished during their Continuance in Office,

Section 2.   [1] The judicial Power shall extend to all Cases, in Law and Equity, arising under this Constitution, the Laws of the United States, and Treaties made or which shall be made, under their Authority;—to all Cases affecting Ambassadors, other public Ministers and Consuls;—to all Cases of admiralty and maritime Jurisdiction;—to Controversies to which the United States shall be a Party;—to Controversies between two or more States;—between a State and Citizens of another State;—between Citizens of different States;—between Citizens of the same State claiming Lands under the Grants of different States, and between a State, or the Citizens thereof, and foreign States, Citizens or Subjects.

[2] In all Cases affecting Ambassadors, other public Ministers and Consuls, and those in which a State shall be a Party, the supreme Court shall have original Jurisdiction. In all the other Cases before mentioned, the supreme Court shall have

appellate Jurisdiction, both as to Law and Fact, with such Exceptions, and under such Regulations as the Congress shall make.

[3] The trial of all Crimes, except in Cases of Impeachment, shall be by Jury; and such Trial shall be held in the State where the said Crimes shall have been committed; but when not committed within any State, the Trial shall be at such Place or Places as the Congress may by Law have directed.

Section 3. [1] Treason against the United States, shall consist only in levying War against them, or, in adhering to their Enemies, giving them Aid and Comfort. No Person shall be convicted of Treason unless on the Testimony of two Witnesses to the same overt Act, or on Confession in open Court.

[2] The Congress shall have Power to declare the Punishment of Treason, but no Attainder of Treason shall work Corruption of Blood, or Forfeiture except during the Life of the Person attainted.

ARTICLE IV

Section 1. Full Faith and Credit shall be given in each State to the Public Acts, Records, and judicial Proceedings of every other State. And the Congress may by general Laws prescribe the Manner in which such Acts, Records and Proceedings shall be proved, and the Effect thereof.

Section 2. [1] The Citizens of each State shall be entitled to all Privileges and Immunities of Citizens in the several States.

[2] A Person charged in any State with Treason, Felony, or other Crime, who shall flee from Justice, and be found in another State, shall on demand of the executive Authority of the State from which he fled, be delivered up, to be removed to the State having Jurisdiction of the Crime.

[3] No Person held to Service or Labour in one State, under the Laws thereof, escaping into another, shall, in Consequence of any Law or Regulation therein, be discharged from such Service or Labour, but shall be delivered up on Claim of the Party to whom such Service or Labour may be due.

Section 3. [1] New States may be admitted by the Congress into this Union; but no new State shall be formed or erected within the Jurisdiction of any other State; nor any State be formed by the Junction of two or more States, or Parts of States, without the Consent of the Legislatures of the States concerned as well as of the Congress.

[2] The Congress shall have Power to dispose of and make all needful Rules and Regulations respecting the Territory or other Property belonging to the United States; and nothing in this Constitution shall be so construed as to Prejudice any Claims of the United States, or of any particular State.

Section 4. The United States shall guarantee to every State in this Union a Republican Form of Government, and shall protect each of them against Invasion; and on Application of the Legislature, or of the Executive (when the Legislature cannot be convened) against domestic Violence.

ARTICLE V

The Congress, whenever two thirds of both Houses shall deem it necessary, shall propose Amendments to this Constitution, or, on the Application of the Legislatures of two thirds of the several States, shall call a convention for proposing Amendments, which in either case, shall be valid to all Intents and Purposes, as part of this Constitution, when ratified by the Legislatures of three fourths of the several States, or by Conventions in three fourths thereof, as the one or the other Mode of Ratification may be proposed by the Congress; Provided that no Amendment which may be made prior to the Year One thousand eight hundred and eight shall in any Manner affect the first and fourth clauses in the Ninth Section of the first Article; and that no State, without its Consent, shall be deprived of its equal Suffrage in the Senate.

ARTICLE VI

[1] All Debts contracted and Engagements entered into, before the Adoption of this Constitution, shall be as valid against the United States under this Constitution, as under the Confederation.

[2] This Constitution, and the Laws of the United States which shall be made in Pursuance thereof; and all Treaties made, or which shall be made, under the Authority of the United States, shall be the supreme Law of the Land; and the Judges in every State shall be bound thereby, any Thing in the Constitution or Laws of any State to the Contrary notwithstanding.

[3] The Senators and Representatives before mentioned, and the Members of the several State Legislatures, and all executive and judicial Officers, both of the United States and of the several States, shall be bound by Oath or Affirmation, to support this Constitution; but no religious Test shall ever be required as a Qualification to any Office or public Trust under the United States.

ARTICLE VII

The Ratification of the Conventions of nine States shall be sufficient for the Establishment of this Constitution between the States so ratifying the Same.

AMENDMENTS

Articles in addition to, and amendment of, the Constitution of the United States of America, proposed by Congress, and ratified by the Legislatures of the several States pursuant to the Fifth Article of the original Constitution.

Amendment I [1791]

Congress shall make no law respecting an establishment of religion, or prohibiting the free exercise thereof; or abridging the freedom of speech, or of the press, or of the right of the people peaceably to assemble, and to petition the Government for a redress of grievances.

Amendment II [1791]

A well regulated Militia, being necessary to the security of a free State, the right of the people to keep and bear Arms, shall not be infringed.

Amendment III [1791]

No Soldier shall, in time of peace be quartered in any house, without the consent of the Owner, or in time of war, but in a manner to be prescribed by law.

Amendment IV [1791]

The right of the people to be secure in their persons, houses, papers, and effects, against unreasonable searches and seizures, shall not be violated, and no Warrants shall issue, but upon probable cause, supported by Oath or affirmation, and particularly describing the place to be searched, and the persons or things to be seized.

Amendment V [1791]

No person shall be held to answer for a capital, or otherwise infamous crime, unless on a presentment or indictment of a Grand Jury, except in cases arising in the land or naval forces, or in the Militia, when in actual service in time of War or public danger; nor shall any person be subject for the same offence to be twice put in jeopardy of life or limb; nor shall be compelled in any criminal case to be a witness against himself, nor be deprived of life, liberty, or property, without due process of law; nor shall private property be taken for public use, without just compensation.

Amendment VI [1791]

In all criminal prosecutions, the accused shall enjoy the right to a speedy and public trial, by an impartial jury of the State and district wherein the crime shall have been committed, which district shall have been previously ascertained by law, and to be informed of the nature and cause of the accusation; to be confronted with the witnesses against him; to have compulsory process for obtaining witnesses in his favor, and to have the Assistance of Counsel for his defence.

Amendment VII [1791]

In Suits at common law, where the value in controversy shall exceed twenty dollars, the right of trial by jury shall be preserved, and no fact tried by jury, shall be otherwise re-examined in any Court of the United States, than according to the rules of common law.

Amendment VIII [1791]

Excessive bail shall not be required, nor excessive fines imposed, nor cruel and unusual punishments inflicted.

Amendment IX [1791]

The enumeration in the Constitution, of certain rights, shall not be construed to deny or disparage others retained by the people.

Amendment X [1791]

The powers not delegated to the United States by the Constitution, nor prohibited by it to the States, are reserved to the States respectively, or to the people.

Amendment XI [1798]

The Judicial power of the United States shall not be construed to extend to any suit in law or equity, commenced or prosecuted against one of the United States by Citizens of another State, or by Citizens or Subjects of any Foreign State.

Amendment XII [1804]

The Electors shall meet in their respective states and vote by ballot for President and Vice-President, one of whom, at least, shall not be an inhabitant of the same state with themselves; they shall name in their ballots the person voted for as President, and in distinct ballots the person voted for as Vice-President, and they shall make distinct lists of all persons voted for as President, and of all persons voted for as Vice-President, and of the number of votes for each, which lists they shall sign and certify, and transmit sealed to the seat of the government of the United States, directed to the President of the Senate;— The President of the Senate shall, in the presence of the Senate and House of Representatives, open all the certificates and the votes shall then be counted;—The person having the greatest number of votes for President, shall be the President, if such number be a majority of the whole number of Electors appointed; and if no person have such majority, then from the persons having the highest numbers not exceeding three on the list of those voted for as President, the House of Representatives shall choose immediately, by ballot, the President. But in choosing the President, the votes shall be taken by states, the representation from each state having one vote; a quorum for this purpose shall consist of a member or members from two-thirds of the states, and a majority of all the states shall be necessary to a choice. And if the House of Representatives shall not choose a President whenever the right of choice shall devolve upon them before the fourth day of March next following, then the Vice-President shall act as President, as in the case of the death or other constitutional disability of the President.—The person having the greatest number of votes as Vice-President, shall be the Vice-President, if such number be a majority of the whole number of Electors appointed, and if no person have a majority, then from the two highest numbers on the list, the Senate shall choose the Vice-President; a quorum for the purpose shall consist of two-thirds of the whole number of Senators, and a majority of the whole number shall be necessary to a choice. But no person constitutionally ineligible to the office of President shall be eligible to that of Vice-President of the United States.

Amendment XIII [1865]

Section 1.   Neither slavery nor involuntary servitude, except as punishment for crime whereof the party shall have been duly convicted, shall exist within the United States, or any place subject to their jurisdiction.

Section 2.   Congress shall have power to enforce this article by appropriate legislation.

Amendment XIV [1868]

Section 1.   All persons born or naturalized in the United States, and subject to the jurisdiction thereof, are citizens of the United States and of the State wherein they reside. No State shall make or enforce any law which shall abridge the privileges or immunities of citizens of the United States; nor shall any State deprive any person of life, liberty, or property, without due process of law; nor deny to any person within its jurisdiction the equal protection of the laws.

Section   2.   Representatives   shall   be   apportioned among the several States according to their respective numbers, counting the whole number of persons in each State, excluding Indians not taxed. But when the right to vote at any election for the choice of electors for President and Vice President of the United States, Representatives in Congress, the Executive and Judicial officers of a State, or the members of the Legislature thereof, is denied to any of the male inhabitants of such State, being twenty-one years of age, and citizens of the United States, or in any way abridged, except for participation in rebellion, or other crime, the basis of representation therein shall be reduced in the proportion which the number of such male citizens shall bear to the whole number of male citizens twenty-one years of age in such State.

Section 3.   No person shall be a Senator or Representative in Congress, or elector of President and Vice President, or hold

any office, civil or military, under the United States, or under any State, who having previously taken an oath, as a member of Congress, or as an officer of the United States, or as a member of any State legislature, or as an executive or judicial officer of any State, to support the Constitution of the United States, shall have engaged in insurrection or rebellion against the same, or given aid or comfort to the enemies thereof. But Congress may by a vote of two-thirds of each House, remove such disability.

Section 4.   The validity of the public debt of the United States, authorized by law, including debts incurred for payment of pensions and bounties for services in suppressing insurrection or rebellion, shall not be questioned. But neither the United States nor any State shall assume or pay any debt or obligation incurred in aid of insurrection or rebellion against the United States, or any claim for the loss or emancipation of any slave; but all such debts, obligations and claims shall be held illegal and void.

Section 5.   The Congress shall have power to enforce, by appropriate legislation, the provisions of this article.

Amendment XV [1870]

Section 1.   The right of citizens of the United States to vote shall not be denied or abridged by the United States or by any State on account of race, color, or previous condition of servitude.

Section 2.   The Congress shall have power to enforce this article by appropriate legislation.

Amendment XVI [1913]

The Congress shall have power to lay and collect taxes on incomes, from whatever source derived, without apportionment among the several States, and without regard to any census or enumeration.

Amendment XVII [1913]

[1] The Senate of the United States shall be composed of two Senators from each State, elected by the people thereof, for six years; and each Senator shall have one vote. The electors in each State shall have the qualifications requisite for electors of the most numerous branch of the State legislatures.

[2] When vacancies happen in the representation of any State in the Senate, the executive authority of such State shall issue writs of election to fill such vacancies: *Provided,* That the legislature of any State may empower the executive thereof to make temporary appointments until the people fill the vacancies by election as the legislature may direct.

[3] The amendment shall not be so construed as to affect the election or term of any Senator chosen before it becomes valid as part of the Constitution.

Amendment XVIII [1919]

Section 1. After one year from the ratification of this article the manufacture, sale, or transportation of intoxicating liquors within, the importation thereof into, or the exportation thereof from the United States and all territory subject to the jurisdiction thereof for beverage purposes is hereby prohibited.

Section 2. The Congress and the several States shall have concurrent power to enforce this article by appropriate legislation.

Section 3. This article shall be inoperative unless it shall have been ratified as an amendment to the Constitution by the legislatures of the several States, as provided in the Constitution, within seven years from the date of the submission hereof to the States by the Congress.

Amendment XIX [1920]

[1] The right of citizens of the United States to vote shall not be denied or abridged by the United States or by any State on account of sex.

[2] Congress shall have power to enforce this article by appropriate legislation.

Amendment XX [1933]

Section 1. The terms of the President and Vice President shall end at noon on the 20th day of January, and the terms of Senators and Representatives at noon on the 3d day of January, of the years in which such terms would have ended if this article had not been ratified; and the terms of their successors shall then begin.

Section 2. The Congress shall assemble at least once in every year, and such meeting shall begin at noon on the 3d day of January, unless they shall by law appoint a different day.

Section 3. If, at the time fixed for the beginning of the term of the President, the President elect shall have died, the Vice President elect shall become President. If the President shall not have been chosen before the time fixed for the beginning of his term, or if the President elect shall have failed to qualify, then the Vice President elect shall act as President until a President shall have qualified; and the Congress may by law provide for the case wherein neither a President elect nor a Vice President elect shall have qualified, declaring who shall then act as President, or the manner in which one who is to act shall be selected, and such person shall act accordingly until a President or Vice President shall have qualified.

Section 4. The Congress may by law provide for the case of the death of any of the persons from whom the House of Representatives may choose a President whenever the right of choice shall have devolved upon them, and for the case of the death of any of the persons from whom the Senate may choose a Vice President whenever the right of choice shall have devolved upon them.

Section 5. Sections 1 and 2 shall take effect on the 15th day of October following the ratification of this article.

Section 6. This article shall be inoperative unless it shall have been ratified as an amendment to the Constitution by the legislatures of three-fourths of the several States within seven years from the date of its submission.

Amendment XXI [1933]

Section 1. The eighteenth article of amendment to the Constitution of the United States is hereby repealed.

Section 2. The transportation or importation into any State, Territory, or possession of the United States for delivery or use therein of intoxicating liquors, in violation of the laws thereof, is hereby prohibited.

Section 3. This article shall be inoperative unless it shall have been ratified as an amendment to the Constitution by conventions in the several States, as provided in the Constitution, within seven years from the date of the submission hereof to the States by the Congress.

Amendment XXII [1951]

Section 1. No person shall be elected to the office of the President more than twice, and no person who has held the office of President, or acted as President for more than two years of a term to which some other person was elected President shall be elected to the office of President more than once. But this Article shall not apply to any person holding the office of President when this Article was proposed by the Congress, and shall not prevent any person who may be holding the office of President, or acting as President, during the term within which this Article becomes operative from holding the office of President or acting as President during the remainder of such term.

Section 2. This article shall be inoperative unless it shall have been ratified as an amendment to the Constitution by the legislatures of three-fourths of the several States within seven years from the date of its submission to the States by the Congress.

Amendment XXIII [1961]

Section 1. The District constituting the seat of Government of the United States shall appoint in such manner as the Congress may direct:

A number of electors of President and Vice President equal to the whole number of Senators and Representatives in Congress to which the District would be entitled if it were a State, but in no event more than the least populous state; they shall be in addition to those appointed by the states, but they shall be considered, for the purposes of the election of President and Vice President, to be electors appointed by a state; and they shall meet in the District and perform such duties as provided by the twelfth article of amendment.

Section 2.   The Congress shall have power to enforce this article by appropriate legislation.

Amendment XXIV [1964]

Section 1.   The right of citizens of the United States to vote in any primary or other election for President or Vice President, for electors for President or Vice President, or for Senator or Representative in Congress, shall not be denied or abridged by the United States, or any State by reason of failure to pay any poll tax or other tax.

Section 2.   The Congress shall have power to enforce this article by appropriate legislation.

Amendment XXV [1967]

Section 1.   In case of the removal of the President from office or of his death or resignation, the Vice President shall become President.

Section 2.   Whenever there is a vacancy in the office of the Vice President, the President shall nominate a Vice President who shall take office upon confirmation by a majority vote of both Houses of Congress.

Section 3.   Whenever the President transmits to the President pro tempore of the Senate and the Speaker of the House of Representatives his written declaration that he is unable to discharge the powers and duties of his office, and until he transmits to them a written declaration to the contrary, such powers and duties shall be discharged by the Vice President as Acting President.

Section 4.   Whenever the Vice President and a majority of either the principal officers of the executive departments or of such other body as Congress may by law provide, transmit to the President pro tempore of the Senate and the Speaker of the House of Representatives their written declaration that the President is unable to discharge the powers and duties of his office, the Vice President shall immediately assume the powers of the office as Acting President.

Thereafter, when the President transmits to the President pro tempore of the Senate and the Speaker of the House of Representatives his written declaration that no inability exists, he shall resume the powers and duties of his office unless the Vice President and a majority of either the principal officers of the executive department or of such other body as Congress may by law provide, transmit within four days to the President pro tempore of the Senate and the Speaker of the House of Representatives their written declaration that the President is unable to discharge the powers and duties of his office. Thereupon Congress shall decide the issue, assembling within forty-eight hours for that purpose if not in session. If the Congress, within twenty-one days after receipt of the latter written declaration, or, if Congress is not in session, within twenty-one days after Congress is required to assemble, determines by two-thirds vote of both Houses that the President is unable to discharge the powers and duties of his office, the Vice President shall continue to discharge the same as Acting President; otherwise, the President shall resume the powers and duties of his office.

Amendment XXVI [1971]

Section 1.   The right of citizens of the United States, who are eighteen years of age or older, to vote shall not be denied or abridged by the United States or by any State on account of age.

Section 2.   The Congress shall have power to enforce this article by appropriate legislation.

INDEX